DATE DUE

			PRINTED IN U.S.A.

Literature Criticism from 1400 to 1800

Guide to Gale Literary Criticism Series

When you need to review criticism of literary works, these are the Gale series to use:

If the author's death date is:	You should turn to:
After Dec. 31, 1959 (or author is still living)	***Contemporary Literary Criticism*** for example: Jorge Luis Borges, Anthony Burgess, William Faulkner, Mary Gordon, Ernest Hemingway, Iris Murdoch
1900 through 1959	***Twentieth-Century Literary Criticism*** for example: Willa Cather, F. Scott Fitzgerald, Henry James, Mark Twain, Virginia Woolf
1800 through 1899	***Nineteenth-Century Literature Criticism*** for example: Fedor Dostoevski, Nathaniel Hawthorne, George Sand, William Wordsworth
1400 through 1799	***Literature Criticism From 1400 to 1800*** (excluding Shakespeare) for example: Anne Bradstreet, Daniel Defoe, Alexander Pope, François Rabelais, Jonathan Swift, Phillis Wheatley
	Shakespearean Criticism Shakespeare's plays and poetry
Antiquity through 1399	***Classical and Medieval Literature Criticism*** for example: Dante, Homer, Plato, Sophocles, Vergil, the Beowulf Poet

Gale also publishes related criticism series:

Children's Literature Review

This series covers authors of all eras who have written for the preschool through high school audience.

Short Story Criticism

This series covers the major short fiction writers of all nationalities and periods of literary history.

Poetry Criticism

This series covers poets of all nationalities and periods of literary history.

Drama Criticism

This series covers dramatists of all nationalities and periods of literary history.

ISSN 0740-2880

Volume 19

Literature Criticism from 1400 to 1800

Excerpts from Criticism of the Works
of Fifteenth-, Sixteenth-, Seventeenth-, and
Eighteenth-Century Novelists, Poets, Playwrights,
Philosophers, and Other Creative Writers,
from the First Published Critical Appraisals
to Current Evaluations

James E. Person, Jr.
Editor

Tina N. Grant
Joann Prosyniuk
Mark Swartz
Associate Editors

 Gale Research Inc. · DETROIT · LONDON

STAFF

James E. Person, Jr., *Editor*

O. Krstovic, Joann Prosyniuk, Mark Swartz, *Associate Editors*

John P. Daniel, David J. Engelman, Christine Haydinger, Andrew M. Kalasky, Elisabeth Morrison, Debra A. Wells, Allyson J. Wylie, *Assistant Editors*

Jeanne A. Gough, *Permissions and Production Manager*

Linda M. Pugliese, *Production Supervisor*
Paul Lewon, Maureen A. Puhl, Camille Robinson, Jennifer VanSickle, *Editorial Associates*
Donna Craft, Brandy C. Johnson, Sheila Walencewicz, *Editorial Assistants*

Victoria B. Cariappa, *Research Manager*

Maureen Richards, *Research Supervisor*
Mary Beth McElmeel, Tamara C. Nott, *Editorial Associates*
Daniel J. Jankowski, Julie K. Karmazin, Julie A. Synkonis, *Editorial Assistants*

Sandra C. Davis, *Text Permissions Supervisor*
Maria L. Franklin, Josephine M. Keene, Denise Singleton, Kimberly F. Smilay, *Permissions Associates*
Michele M. Lonoconus, Shelly Rakoczy, Shalice Shah, *Permissions Assistants*

Margaret A. Chamberlain, *Permissions Supervisor (Pictures)*
Pamela A. Hayes, *Permissions Associate*
Amy Lynn Emrich, Karla A. Kulkis, Nancy M. Rattenbury, Keith Reed, *Permissions Assistants*

Mary Beth Trimper, *Production Manager*
Mary Winterhalter, *External Production Assistant*

Arthur Chartow, *Art Director*
C. J. Jonik, *Keyliner*

Contents

Preface vii

Acknowledgments xi

Preface

Literature Criticism from 1400 to 1800 (LC) presents criticism of world authors of the fifteenth through eighteenth centuries. The literature of this period reflects a turbulent time of radical change that saw the rise of drama equal in stature to that of classical Greece, the birth of the novel and personal essay forms, the emergence of newspapers and periodicals, and major achievements in poetry and philosophy. Much of modern literature reflects the influence of these centuries. Thus the literature treated in *LC* provides insight into the universal nature of human experience, as well as into the life and thought of the past.

Scope of the Series

LC is designed to serve as an introduction to authors of the fifteenth through eighteenth centuries and to the most significant interpretations of these authors' works. The great poets, dramatists, novelists, essayists, and philosophers of this period are considered classics in every secondary school and college or university curriculum. Because criticism of this literature spans nearly six hundred years, an overwhelming amount of critical material confronts the student. *LC* therefore organizes and reprints the most noteworthy published criticism of authors of these centuries. Readers should note that there is a separate Gale reference series devoted to Shakespearean studies. For though belonging properly to the period covered in *LC,* William Shakespeare has inspired such a tremendous and ever-growing corpus of secondary material that the editors have deemed it best to give his works extensive coverage in a separate series, *Shakespearean Criticism.*

Each author entry in *LC* attempts to present a historical survey of critical response to the author's works. Early criticism is offered to indicate initial responses, later selections document any rise or decline in literary reputations, and retrospective analyses provide students with modern views. The size of each author entry is intended to reflect the author's critical reception in English or foreign criticism in translation. Articles and books that have not been translated into English are therefore excluded. Every attempt has been made to identify and include the seminal essays on each author's work and to include recent commentary providing modern perspectives.

The need for *LC* among students and teachers of literature was suggested by the proven usefulness of Gale's *Contemporary Literary Criticism (CLC), Twentieth-Century Literary Criticism (TCLC),* and *Nineteenth-Century Literature Criticism (NCLC),* which excerpt criticism of works by nineteenth- and twentieth-century authors. Because of the different time periods covered, there is no duplication of authors or critical material in any of these literary criticism series. An author may appear more than once in the series because of the great quantity of critical material available and because of the aesthetic demands of the series's *thematic organization.*

Thematic Approach

Beginning with Volume 12, roughly half the authors in each volume of *LC* are organized in a thematic scheme. Such themes include literary movements, literary reaction to political and historical events, significant eras in literary history, and the literature of cultures often overlooked by English-speaking readers. The present volume, for example, focuses upon the legend of Robin Hood. Future volumes of *LC* will devote substantial space to the English Metaphysical poets and authors of the Spanish Golden Age, among many others. The rest of each volume will be devoted to criticism of the works of authors not aligned with the selected thematic authors and chosen from a variety of nationalities.

Organization of the Book

Each entry consists of the following elements: author or thematic heading, introduction, list of principal works (in author entries only), annotated works of criticism (each followed by a bibliographical citation), and a bibliography of further reading. Also, most author entries contain author portraits and other illustrations.

- The **author heading** consists of the author's full name, followed by birth and death dates. If an author wrote consistently under a pseudonym, the pseudonym is used in the author heading, with the real name given in parentheses on the first line of the biographical and critical introduction. Also located here are any name variations under which an author wrote, including transliterated forms for authors whose native languages use nonroman alphabets. Uncertain birth or death dates are indicated by question marks. The **thematic heading** simply states the subject of the entry.

- The **biographical and critical introduction** contains background information designed to introduce the reader to an author and to critical discussion of his or her work. Parenthetical material following many of the introductions provides references to biographical and critical reference series published by Gale in which additional material about the author may be found. The **thematic introduction** briefly defines the subject of the entry and provides social and historical background important to understanding the criticism.

- Most *LC* author entries include **portraits** of the author. Many entries also contain illustrations of materials pertinent to an author's career, including author holographs, title pages, letters, or representations of important people, places, and events in an author's life.

- The **list of principal works** is chronological by date of first book publication and identifies the genre of each work. In the case of foreign authors whose works have been translated into English, the title and date of the first English-language edition are given in brackets beneath the foreign-language listing. Unless otherwise indicated, dramas are dated by first performance, not first publication.

- **Criticism** is arranged chronologically in each author entry to provide a useful perspective on changes in critical evaluation over the years. For the purpose of easy identification, the critic's name and the composition or publication date of the critical work are given at the beginning of each piece of criticism. Unsigned criticism is preceded by the title of the source in which it appeared. All titles by the author featured in the critical entry are printed in boldface type. Publication information (such as publisher names and book prices) and parenthetical numerical references (such as footnotes or page and line references to specific editions of works) have been deleted at the editors' discretion to provide smoother reading of the text.

- Critical essays are prefaced by **annotations** as an additional aid to students using *LC*. These explanatory notes may provide several types of useful information, including: the reputation of a critic, the importance of a work of criticism, the commentator's individual approach to literary criticism, the intent of the criticism, and the growth of critical controversy or changes in critical trends regarding an author's work. In some cases, these notes cross-reference the work of critics within the entry who agree or disagree with each other.

- A complete **bibliographical citation** of the original essay or book follows each piece of criticism.

- An annotated bibliography of **further reading** appears at the end of each entry and suggests resources for additional study of authors and themes. It also includes essays for which the editors could not obtain reprint rights.

Cumulative Indexes

Each volume of *LC* includes a cumulative **author index** listing all the authors that have appeared in *Contemporary Literary Criticism, Twentieth-Century Literary Criticism, Nineteenth-Century Literature Criticism, Literature Criticism from 1400 to 1800,* and *Classical and Medieval Literature Criticism,* along with cross-references to the Gale series *Short Story Criticism, Poetry Criticism, Children's Literature Review, Authors in the News, Contemporary Authors, Contemporary Authors Autobiography Series, Contemporary Authors Bibliographical Series, Dictionary of Literary Biography, Concise Dictionary of Literary Biography, Something about the Author, Something about the Author Autobiography Series,* and *Yesterday's Authors of Books for Children.* Readers will welcome this cumulative author index as a useful tool for locating an author within the various series. The index, which includes authors' birth and death dates, is particularly valuable for those authors who are identified with a certain period but whose death dates cause them to be placed in another, or for those authors whose careers span two periods. For example, F. Scott Fitzgerald is found in *TCLC,* yet a writer often associated with him, Ernest Hemingway, is found in *CLC.*

Beginning with Volume 12, *LC* includes a cumulative **topic index** that lists all literary themes and topics treated in *LC, NCLC* Topics volumes, *TCLC* Topics volumes, and the *CLC* Yearbook. Each volume of *LC* also includes a cumulative **nationality index** in which authors' names are arranged alphabetically under their respective nationalities and followed by the numbers of the volumes in which they appear.

Each volume of *LC* also includes a cumulative **title index,** an alphabetical listing of the literary works discussed in the series since its inception. Each title listing includes the corresponding volume and page numbers where criticism may be located. Foreign-language titles that have been translated are followed by the titles of the translations—for example, *El ingenioso hidalgo Don Quixote de la Mancha (Don Quixote)*. Page numbers following these translated titles refer to all pages on which any form of the titles, either foreign-language or translated, appear. Titles of novels, dramas, nonfiction books, and poetry, short story, or essay collections are printed in italics, while individual poems, short stories, and essays are printed in roman type within quotation marks.

A Note to the Reader

When writing papers, students who quote directly from any volume in the Literary Criticism Series may use the following general forms to footnote reprinted criticism. The first example pertains to material drawn from periodicals, the second to material reprinted from books.

T. S. Eliot, "John Donne," *The Nation and the Athenaeum,* 33 (9 June 1923), 321-32; excerpted and reprinted in *Literature Criticism from 1400 to 1800,* Vol. 10, ed. James E. Person, Jr. (Detroit: Gale Research, 1989), pp. 28-9.

Clara G. Stillman, *Samuel Butler: A Mid-Victorian Modern* (Viking Press, 1932); excerpted and reprinted in *Twentieth-Century Literary Criticism,* Vol. 33, ed. Paula Kepos (Detroit: Gale Research, 1989), pp. 43-5.

Suggestions Are Welcome

In response to various suggestions, several features have been added to *LC* since the series began, including a nationality index, a Literary Criticism Series topic index, thematic entries, a descriptive table of contents, and more extensive illustrations.

Readers who wish to suggest new features, themes, or authors to appear in future volumes, or who have other suggestions, are cordially invited to write to the editor.

ACKNOWLEDGMENTS

The editors wish to thank the copyright holders of the excerpted criticism included in this volume, the permissions managers of many book and magazine publishing companies for assisting us in securing reprint rights, and Anthony Bogucki for assistance with copyright research. We are also grateful to the staffs of the Detroit Public Library, the Library of Congress, the University of Detroit Library, Wayne State University Purdy/Kresge Library Complex, and the University of Michigan Libraries for making their resources available to us. Following is a list of the copyright holders who have granted us permission to reprint material in this volume of *LC*. Every effort has been made to trace copyright, but if omissions have been made, please let us know.

COPYRIGHTED EXCERPTS IN *LC*, VOLUME 19, WERE REPRINTED FROM THE FOLLOWING PERIODICALS:

COPYRIGHTED EXCERPTS IN *LC*, VOLUME 19, WERE REPRINTED FROM THE FOLLOWING BOOKS:

Guillén de Castro

1569-1631

(Full name Guillén de Castro y Belvís) Spanish dramatist.

An important dramatist of Spain's Golden Age, a period of intense literary and cultural growth, Castro is best remembered for his plays *Las mocedades del Cid,* parts I and II. These works were based on the ballad tradition celebrating the heroic deeds of the Cid, the honorary name given to the eleventh-century Spanish hero Rodrigo (Ruy) Díaz de Vivar. Like his friend Lope de Vega, the most prominent dramatist of the Golden Age, Castro skillfully transformed material from Spanish folk literature and popular ballads into verse dramas exploring cultural beliefs about honor and heroism.

Castro was born to an aristocratic family in Valencia. Between 1591 and 1594, he was active in the Academia de los Nocturnos, a literary society to which he contributed poems and prose compositions. Castro married Marquesa Girón de Rebolleda in 1595—the same year Lope, exiled from Madrid after being accused of libel, moved to Valencia. Castro and Lope apparently became friends, dedicating some of their collections of plays to each other and to each other's families. Already established as one of Spain's preeminent dramatists when he met Castro, Lope exerted a strong influence on Castro's development as a playwright. Lope's writings helped define the genre of *comedia,* the verse drama characterized by a disregard for the Aristotelian unities, the matching of a character's patterns of speech to his or her social status, and the juxtaposition of humorous and serious situations; Castro's dramas share these attributes with Lope's body of work.

Sometime after 1602 Castro moved to Italy, where he served as governor of Scigliano from 1607 until 1609, when he returned to Spain; it is likely that his wife died during his stay in Italy. He continued to be active in various literary societies in Valencia and later in Madrid, where he was reunited with Lope and became acquainted with other prominent dramatists, including Tirso de Molina and Calderón de la Barca. In 1618, Juan Téllez Girón became his patron and granted him a parcel of land. Castro was accused of paying an assassin to kill a nobleman in 1624, but the charges were never substantiated. He remarried in 1626 and died five years later.

A chief concern of Castro's dramas is the exploration of what constitutes dignified behavior and finding a paradigm of *"el perfecto caballero,"* or "the perfect knight," a phrase which became the title of one his plays. According to the complex Spanish code of honor observed during Castro's day, a man must preserve his reputation and the reputations of the female members of his household above all else, and any physical attack or verbal insult must be swiftly avenged. The plot of a *comedia* frequently centered around a conflict between an individual's honor and the cultural belief in the divine right of monarchs. In these plays, the king commits an offense, and the hero must de-

cide whether the offense is great enough to warrant the murder of the king. Castro addresses this issue in one of his earliest *comedias, El amor constante.* The play is about a love affair between Nísida and Celauro, the brother of the King of Hungary. Because the king desires Nísida, he imprisons Celauro for fifteen years. When Celauro's sentence is completed, the king banishes him; nevertheless, Celauro vows to return with an army that will conquer the king. In the melodramatic climax—a typical device in Castro's works—Celauro's army is defeated and he is killed, Nísida takes poison to avoid marrying the king, and the long-lost son of Celauro and Nísida kills the king and assumes power. Castro returned to the theme of the unjust king in many of his plays, including *El Conde Alarcos, El nacimiento de Montesinos, El perfecto caballero,* and *Las mocedades del Cid II.* All these works exhibit sympathy for victims of tyranny, an aspect of Castro's works that some critics cite as the reason for his popularity.

Castro often turned to Spain's ballad tradition for the plots and characters in his plays. *El Conde Alarcos* and *El nacimiento de Montesinos* are both adaptations of long ballads. The Cid, revered as a national hero for his leadership in the reconquest of northern Spain from the occupying Moors, was the most famous of the ballad heroes, and Castro was the first writer to dramatize his adventures. In *Las mocedades del Cid I,* which scholars believe to have been written after part II, Castro chronicles the love affair between the Cid and Jimena, the daughter of Count Lozano, as well as a battle with the Moors in Castile and a pilgrimage to Santiago. All of the action and large parts of the dialogue are borrowed from ballad sources familiar to Castro's audience, but the dramatist introduced a more pious and submissive conception of the legendary hero to better reflect contemporary heroic ideals. The French dramatist Pierre Corneille adapted *Las mocedades del Cid I* for his *Le Cid* (1637), a play that is widely recognized as a masterpiece of French Classical drama. Obligated by the dictates of Aristotelian drama which require a play to have only one setting, Corneille presented a sparer version of *Las mocedades del Cid I.* However, he retained crucial structural elements from Castro's play, and some critics view the French author's role as no more than that of translator. *Las mocedades del Cid II,* also referred to as *Las hazañas del Cid,* focuses on the siege of Zamora and the death of King Sancho of Castile at the hands of Bellido Delfos. Critics find this play less successful than part I, largely owing to the fact that the Cid is treated as a minor character. In addition to ballads, Castro also drew upon the first book of Miguel de Cervantes's famous novel *Don Quixote* (1605). Castro's *Don Quixote de la Mancha* adapts chapters 23-6, narrating the story of the love intrigues involving Cardenio, Lucinda, Fernando, and Dorotea, and his *El curioso impertinente* dramatizes chapters

33-5, centering on the friendship between Anselmo and Lotario.

Although he was a popular and respected figure during his age, Castro never achieved the renown of such luminaries of the Golden Age of Spanish drama as Lope de Vega, Tirso de Molina, or Calderón de la Barca. He is best remembered as the author of the source of Corneille's *Le Cid;* in his *Introduction to Spanish Literature* (1925), George Tyler Northup expressed the opinion of many literary historians when he wrote, "Castro, if unable to produce a masterpiece, at least inspired one." Commentators in the second half of the twentieth century, however, have shown a renewed appreciation of Castro, exploring his contribution to the development of the *comedia* genre and studying his dramas as a means of understanding the complexities of the Spanish code of honor.

PRINCIPAL WORKS

El caballero bobo (drama) 1595?-1605?
La humildad soberbia (drama) 1595?-1605?
Los mal casados de Valencia (drama) 1595?-1604?
El nacimiento de Montesinos (drama) 1595?-1602?
El amor constante (drama) 1596?-99?
El desengaño dichoso (drama) 1599?
El conde Alarcos (drama) 1600?-02
El conde de Irlos (drama) 1605?-10?
El curioso impertinente (drama) 1605-08?
Don Quixote de la Mancha (drama) 1605-08?
Progne y Filomena (drama) 1608?-12?
La verdad averguada (drama) 1608?-12
La fuerza de la costumbre (drama) 1610?-20?
Las mocedades del Cid II (drama) 1610?-18?; also referred to as *Hazañas del Cid*
El perfecto caballero (drama) 1610?-15?
Las mocedades del Cid I (drama) 1612?-18?
El Narciso en us opinión (drama) 1612?-15?
Dido y Eneas (drama) 1613?-16?
La fuerza de la sangre (drama) 1613-14
Cuánto se estima el honor (drama) 1615?-24
Los enemigos hermanos (drama) 1615?-20?
La piedad en la justicia (drama) 1615?-20?; also referred to as *La justicia en la piedad*
El mejor esposo (drama) 1617-20?
Engañarse engañando (drama) 1620?-24
El pretender con pobreza (drama) 1620?-24
La tragedia por los celos (drama) 1622
El vicio en los extremos (drama) 1623?

George Ticknor (essay date 1849)

[*Ticknor was an American educator and historian best known for his three-volume* History of Spanish Literature *(1849). In the following excerpt from that work, Ticknor provides a brief summary of Castro's literary career.*]

Very few of [Guillen de Castro's] works have been pub-lished, except his plays. Of these we have twenty-seven or twenty-eight, printed between 1614 and 1625. They belong decidedly to the school of Lope, between whom and Guillen de Castro there was a friendship, which can be traced back, by the Dedication of one of Lope's plays and by several passages in his miscellaneous works, to the period of Lope's exile to Valencia; while, on the side of Guillen de Castro, a similar testimony is borne to the same kindly regard by a volume of his own plays addressed to Marcela, Lope's favourite daughter.

The marks of Guillen de Castro's personal condition, and of the age in which he lived and wrote, are no less distinct in his dramas than the marks of his poetical allegiance. His **Mismatches in Valencia** seems as if its story might have been constructed out of facts within the poet's own knowledge. It is a series of love intrigues, like those in Lope's plays, and ends with the dissolution of two marriages by the influence of a lady, who, disguised as a page, lives in the same house with her lover and his wife, but whose machinations are at last exposed, and she herself driven to the usual resort of entering a convent. His **Don Quixote,** on the other hand, is taken from the First Part of Cervantes's romance, then as fresh as any Valencian tale. The loves of Dorothea and Fernando, and the madness of Cardenio, form the materials for its principal plot; and the *dénouement* is the transportation of the knight, in a cage, to his own house, by the curate and barber, just as he is carried home by them in the romance;—parts of the story being slightly altered to give it a more dramatic turn, though the language of the original fiction is often retained, and the obligations to it are fully recognized. Both of these dramas are written chiefly in the old *redondillas,* with a careful versification; but there is little poetical invention in either of them, and the first act of the **Mismatches in Valencia** is disfigured by a game of wits, fashionable, no doubt, in society at the time, but one that gives occasion, in the play, to nothing but a series of poor tricks and puns.

Very unlike them, though no less characteristic of the times, is his **Mercy and Justice;** the shocking story of a prince of Hungary condemned to death by his father for the most atrocious crimes, but rescued from punishment by the multitude, because his loyalty has survived the wreck of all his other principles, and led him to refuse the throne offered to him by rebellion. It is written in a greater variety of measures than either of the dramas just mentioned, and shows more freedom of style and movement; relying chiefly for success on the story, and on that sense of loyalty which, though originally a great virtue in the relations of the Spanish kings and their people, was now become so exaggerated, that it was undermining much of what was most valuable in the national character.

Santa Bárbara, or the Mountain Miracle and Heaven's Martyr, belongs, again, to another division of the popular drama as settled by Lope de Vega. It is one of those plays where human and Divine love, in tones too much resembling each other, are exhibited in their strongest light, and, like the rest of its class, was no doubt a result of the severe legislation in relation to the theatre at that period, and of the influence of the clergy on which that legislation was founded. The scene is laid in Nicomedia, in the third century, when it was still a crime to profess Christianity; and the story is that of Saint Barbara, according to the legend that represents her to have been a contemporary of Origen, who, in fact, appears on the stage as one of the principal personages. At the opening of the drama, the heroine declares that she is already, in her heart, attached to the new sect; and at the end, she is its triumphant martyr, carrying with her, in a public profession of its faith, not only her lover, but all the leading men of her native city.

One of the scenes of this play is particularly in the spirit and faith of the age when it was written; and was afterwards imitated by Calderon in his *Wonder-working Magician.* The lady is represented as confined by her father in a tower, where, in solitude, she gives herself up to Christian meditations. Suddenly the arch-enemy of the human race presents himself before her, in the dress of a fashionable Spanish gallant. He gives an account of his adventures in a fanciful allegory, but does not so effectually conceal the truth that she fails to suspect who he is. In the mean time her father and her lover enter. To her father the mysterious gallant is quite invisible, but he is plainly seen by the lover, whose jealousy is thus excited to the highest degree; and the first act ends with the confusion and reproaches which such a state of things necessarily brings on, and with the persuasion of the father that the lover may be fit for a mad-house, but would make a very poor husband for his gentle daughter.

The most important of the plays of Guillen de Castro are two which he wrote on the subject of Rodrigo the Cid,— *Las Mocedades del Cid,* The Youth, or Youthful Adventures, of the Cid;—both founded on the old ballads of the country, which, as we know from Santos, as well as in other ways, continued long after the time of Castro to be sung in the streets. The first of these two dramas embraces the earlier portion of the hero's life. It opens with a solemn scene of his arming as a knight, and with the insult immediately afterwards offered to his aged father at the royal council-board; and then goes on with the trial of the spirit and courage of Rodrigo, and the death of the proud Count Lozano, who had outraged the venerable old man by a blow on the cheek;—all according to the traditions in the old chronicles.

Now, however, comes the dramatic part of the action, which was so happily invented by Guillen de Castro. Ximena, the daughter of Count Lozano, is represented in the drama as already attached to the young knight; and a contest, therefore, arises between her sense of what she owes to the memory of her father and what she may yield to her own affection; a contest that continues through the whole of the play, and constitutes its chief interest. She comes, indeed, at once to the king, full of a passionate grief, that struggles with success, for a moment, against the dictates of her heart, and claims the punishment of her lover according to the ancient laws of the realm. He escapes, however, in consequence of the prodigious victories he gains over the Moors, who, at the moment when these events occurred, were assaulting the city. Subsequently, by the contrivance of false news of the Cid's death, a confession of her love is extorted from her; and at last her full consent

to marry him is obtained, partly by Divine intimations, and partly by the natural progress of her admiration and attachment during a series of exploits achieved in her honour and in defence of her king and country.

This drama of Guillen de Castro has become better known throughout Europe than any other of his works; not only because it is the best of them all, but because Corneille, who was his contemporary, made it the basis of his own brilliant tragedy of *The Cid;* a drama which did more than any other to determine for two centuries the character of the theatre all over the continent of Europe. But though Corneille—not unmindful of the angry discussions carried on about the unities, under the influence of Cardinal Richelieu—has made alterations in the action of his play, which are fortunate and judicious, still he has relied, for its main interest, on that contest between the duties and the affections of the heroine which was first imagined by Guillen de Castro.

Nor has he shown in this exhibition more spirit or power than his Spanish predecessor. Indeed, sometimes he has fallen into considerable errors, which are wholly his own. By compressing the time of the action within twenty-four hours, instead of suffering it to extend through many months, as it does in the original, he is guilty of the absurdity of overcoming Ximena's natural feelings in relation to the person who had killed her father, while her father's dead body is still before her eyes. By changing the scene of the quarrel, which in Guillen occurs in presence of the king, he has made it less grave and natural. By a mistake in chronology, he establishes the Spanish court at Seville two centuries before that city was wrested from the Moors. And by a general straitening of the action within the conventional limits which were then beginning to bind down the French stage, he has, it is true, avoided the extravagance of introducing, as Guillen does, so incongruous an episode out of the old ballads as the miracle of Saint Lazarus; but he has hindered the free and easy movement of the incidents, and diminished their general effect.

Guillen, on the contrary, by taking the traditions of his country just as he found them, instantly conciliated the good-will of his audience, and at the same time imparted the freshness of the old ballad spirit to his action, and gave to it throughout a strong national air and colouring. Thus, the scene in the royal council, where the father of the Cid is struck by the haughty Count Lozano, several of the scenes between the Cid and Ximena, and several between both of them and the king, are managed with great dramatic skill and a genuine poetical fervour.

The following passage, where the Cid's father is waiting for him in the evening twilight at the place appointed for their meeting after the duel, is as characteristic, if not as striking, as any in the drama, and is superior to the corresponding passage in the French play, which occurs in the fifth and sixth scenes of the third act.

> The timid ewe bleats not so mournfully,
> Its shepherd lost, nor cries the angry lion
> With such a fierceness for its stolen young,
> As I for Roderic.—My son! my son!
> Each shade I pass, amid the closing night,
> Seems still to wear thy form and mock my arms!

O, why, why comes he not?—I gave the sign,—
I marked the spot,—and yet he is not here!
Has he neglected? Can he disobey?
It may not be! A thousand terrors seize me.
Perhaps some injury or accident
Has made him turn aside his hastening step;—
Perhaps he may be slain, or hurt, or seized.
The very thought freezes my breaking heart.
O holy Heaven, how many ways for fear
Can grief find out!—But hark! What do I hear?
Is it his footstep? Can it be? O, no!
I am not worthy such a happiness!
'T is but the echo of my grief I hear.—
But hark again! Methinks there comes a gallop
On the flinty stones. He springs from off his
    steed!
Is there such happiness vouchsafed to me?
Is it my son?

The Cid. My father?

The Father. May I truly
Trust myself, my child? O, am I, am I, then,
Once more within thine arms? Then let me thus
Compose myself, that I may honour thee
As greatly as thou hast deserved. But why
Hast thou delayed? And yet, since thou art here,
Why should I weary thee with questioning?—
O, bravely hast thou borne thyself, my son;
Hast bravely stood the proof; hast vindicated
    well
Mine ancient name and strength; and well hast
    paid
The debt of life which thou receivedst from me.
Come near to me, my son. Touch the white hairs
Whose honour thou hast saved from infamy,
And kiss, in love, the cheek whose stain thy
    valour
Hath in blood washed out.—My son! my son!
The pride within my soul is humbled now,
And bows before the power that has preserved
From shame the race so many kings have owned
And honoured.

The Second Part, which gives the adventures of the siege of Zamora, the assassination of King Sancho beneath its walls, and the defiance and duels that were the consequence, is not equal in merit to the First Part. Portions of it, such as some of the circumstances attending the death of the king, are quite incapable of dramatic representation, so gross and revolting are they; but even here, as well as in the more fortunate passages, Guillen has faithfully followed the popular belief concerning the heroic age he represents, just as it had come down to him, and has thus given to his scenes a life and reality that could hardly have been given by anything else.

Indeed, it is a great charm of this drama, that the popular traditions everywhere break through so picturesquely, imparting to it their peculiar tone and character. Thus, the insult offered to old Laynez in the council; the complaints of Ximena to the king on the death of her father, and the conduct of the Cid to herself; the story of the Leper; the base treason of Bellido Dolfos; the reproaches of Queen Urraca from the walls of the beleaguered city, and the defiance and duels that follow,—all are taken from the old ballads; often in their very words, and generally in their fresh spirit and with their picture-like details. The effect

must have been great on a Castilian audience, always sensible to the power of the old popular poetry, and always stirred as with a battle-cry when the achievements of their earlier national heroes were recalled to them.

In his other dramas we find traces of the same principles and the same habits of theatrical composition that we have seen in those we have already noticed. The ***Impertinent Curiosity*** is taken from the tale which Cervantes originally printed in the First Part of his *Don Quixote*. The ***Count Alarcos,*** and the ***Count d' Irlos,*** are founded on the fine old ballads that bear these names. And the ***Wonders of Babylon*** is a religious play, in which the story of Susanna and the Elders fills a space somewhat too large, and in which King Nebuchadnezzar is introduced eating grass, like the beasts of the field. But everywhere there is shown a desire to satisfy the demands of the national taste; and everywhere it is plain Guillen is a follower of Lope de Vega, and is distinguished from his rivals more by the sweetness of his versification than by any more prominent or original attribute. (pp. 263-72)

> *George Ticknor, "The Drama of Lope's School," in his* History of Spanish Literature, *Vol. II, 1849. Reprint by Frederick Ungar Publishing Co., 1965, pp. 256-85.*

Sturgis E. Leavitt   (essay date 1927)

[*In the following essay, Leavitt discusses the workings of fate in* Las mocedades del Cid II, *arguing that King Sancho could have taken measures to avoid his death as predicted by the soothsayer in* Las mocedades del Cid I.]

Critics who have interested themselves in the Second Part of Guillén de Castro's ***Mocedades del Cid,*** or, as it is more commonly called, the ***Hazañas del Cid,*** have almost unanimously praised his masterly use of the ballads, his attainment of local color, and the effectiveness of the thrilling combat between Diego Ordóñez and the sons of Arias Gonzalo. Other good qualities less frequently mentioned are the characterization of the Cid, the scenes in Toledo, and the poetical language of the play.

English and American critics, however, have not been overgenerous in their praise of the work, and of these Lord Holland is the most severe. "There are few passages . . . . which rise above mediocrity. It excites little interest and abounds in improbable and unconnected events . . . ." [*Some Account of the Lives and Writings of Lope Félix de Vega Carpio and Guillén de Castro,* 1817]. Reading further to discover the reason for Lord Holland's unfavorable attitude, we find that the circumstances attending the assassination of King Sancho struck him as very indelicate and shocked him exceedingly. Nothing in the play, apparently, can atone for such lack of decorum. Ticknor is of the same opinion with regard to the death of Sancho, but he has words of praise for the popular traditions which "break through so constantly" and add a "great charm" to the play.

A few other writers mention the episode of the death of King Sancho, but have only scattered words of commendation for particular incidents. [A.] Gassier states that the *"apparition shakesperienne du roi Fernand . . . fait une forte belle scène."* Menéndez Pidal in his work on the Infantes de Lara speaks of the *"emoción extraña"* which must have seized all the audience when the voice of Arias Gonzalo was heard warning Sancho against the traitor, Bellido de Olfos. [L. de] Viel Castel mentions the miracle of the apparition which saves Zamora, and, in speaking of Bellido, states that he is

> animé de toute l'exaltation d'un patriotisme sombre et sincère, . . . il semble que une fatalité plane sur lui, qu'elle l'entraîne a accomplir l'arrêt de la Providence, qu'à cet effet, elle jette dans son âme lâche et perfide quelques étincelles d'un entousiasme sincère, d'un patriotisme ardent quoique dépravé; c'est bien là la terrible et mysterieuse puissance du fanatisme politique.

Finally, [A.] Schaeffer, taking up the idea expressed by Bellido as he hurls the javelin at the defenseless Sancho,

> Cielo, cielo soberano,
>
> . . . . .
>
> Esforzad mi corazón,
> pues castigáis con mi mano.

briefly states that Bellido is the tool of avenging justice and fate.

An extended examination of the events preceding the death of King Sancho will show, perhaps, that this episode is worthy of further comment. The first link in the peculiar chain of circumstances which led to the murder of Sancho is found, not in the *Hazañas* but in the *Mocedades del Cid.* It will be recalled that in that play Sancho, following his quarrel with the fencing master, mentions a vague statement by the soothsayers that he will be killed by an *"arma arrojadiza"* and the cause will be *"cosa muy propincua suya."* At this point Guillén de Castro makes it very clear that even though such a prophecy has been made it will not necessarily be fulfilled, since astrology is not to be believed, though its predictions should be feared. In other words, if Sancho is warned and acts aright, the terrible and mysterious blow may be averted.

At the beginning of the *Hazañas,* Sancho's father has died, leaving the kingdom to be divided between the children, Urraca receiving the city of Zamora. Fernando, who has had reason to fear Sancho's rapacity, has given his son warning that a curse will fall upon him if he attempts to disobey his father's will. Sancho, as we know, does this very thing, imprisoning one brother and forcing the other to flee to Toledo. Here it is that the Cid reminds Sancho (and incidentally the audience) of the curse of Fernando. But this warning, even coming from one so important as the Cid, is to no avail, and Sancho proceeds to attack Zamora. At this stage in the action divine justice takes a hand and begins to carry out the prophecy. It must be kept in mind, however, that Guillén de Castro has informed us that the prophecy is not necessarily certain of fulfilment. It seems to be the author's purpose to show that a change of heart on the part of Sancho would have saved him just as surely as did his unchecked ambition bring about his ruin. It is to be noted that Castro again and again repeats

that the cause of Zamora is just and that Heaven is on the side of Urraca.

In besieging Zamora Sancho is only too successful, but at the moment when he has victory almost within his grasp Urraca calls upon him to fear the vengeance of his father. To this Sancho replies:

> ¿Tu padre llamas? ¡Para hacerme guerra
> baje del cielo, o salga de la tierra!

In answer to these impious words the ghost of Fernando appears, armed with a bloody javelin, and this apparition, visible only to Sancho, warns him to desist, saying that the weapon before him will be the instrument of his death. Sancho is greatly affected by the strange vision and orders a retreat. At this very moment, though he does not realize it, divine retribution is setting in motion the wheels that will grind him to dust if he does not heed the supernatural admonition. It has chosen for its agent a wretched individual, Bellido de Olfos, and has kindled in his heart a courage and a desire absolutely unknown to him before. With this God-given impulse Bellido hints to Urraca a way to free Zamora and, fired by divine madness, he dares to defy no less a warrior than Arias Gonzalo. The resulting quarrel gives to Bellido's escape to the enemy an appearance of truth.

At the moment when Bellido is in danger of death at the hands of Arias, Sancho is in a state of uncertainty, consulting Diego Ordóñez about continuing the siege. If Sancho is considering abandonment of the attack because disobedience to his father weighs upon his conscience, then a retreat is proper, says Diego Ordóñez, but if it is only through fear of a fantastic vision, then he should go on. Sancho's lust for power is too strong for him and he decides to resume the siege. Here again he openly defies fate by saying if he is threatened with a javelin he too will arm himself with one. This defiance finds an immediate answer in the appearance of Bellido who has been miraculously saved from the wrath of Arias. Had Sancho decided differently, Fate no longer needing Bellido, he would have perished at the hands of Arias and his men. The instrument of vengeance and the agent to execute retribution have now been brought together.

As the traitor is about to reveal the weakness of Zamora, a strange occurrence interrupts. The hand of Heaven is giving Sancho another chance to repent as Arias calls down from the walls of Zamora to beware of Bellido. The words of the staunch old warrior have the ring of the utmost sincerity and the king stands bewildered. His words,

> ¿Qué es esto, Bellido?

betray his indecision and the divine courage of Bellido leaves him, since the cause for it (Sancho's intention to disobey his father) is now absent. He is therefore an ordinary mortal, and afraid.

> Ay, cielo,
> De congoja estoy temblando.

And when the Cid supports Arias, Bellido fairly grovels on the ground. But Sancho is unpersuaded by Arias and Rodrigo, both of whom he had every reason to believe, and he decides to listen to Bellido. This act, prompted by the king's desire for power, restores the traitor's courage and he who had trembled a moment before now defies even the Cid. Rodrigo is banished but warns Sancho that Heaven punishes ungrateful kings.

A few moments later Sancho's momentary decision about trusting himself alone with Bellido again leaves the way open for repentance. But Sancho's desires are too strong for him and the opportunity is lost. (It may be remarked in passing that the extreme improbability of the king's venturing out of the camp alone with Bellido finds an explanation if we admit that Sancho is blinded by passion and led by the hand of fate.) Another possibility of salvation occurs when the Cid, returning from exile at the king's request, passes near the strangely assorted pair. Even this remote chance of change of heart on the part of Sancho dispels Bellido's courage again:

> Tiembla la tierra que piso.

This fear is only momentary, however, for the king turns toward Zamora. Shortly after this, Bellido apparently has his opportunity when he stands behind the king with a dagger drawn ready to stab him in the back. But Heaven is still giving Sancho time to change his mind. A mysterious something stays Bellido's hand. The king's hour has not yet come and the prophecy has mentioned an "*arma arrojadiza*" and not a dagger.

Finally, Bellido, owing to circumstances familiar to all of us, comes into possession of the javelin and the king is defenseless. Comment on the influence of fate in bringing this about seems unnecessary. Even at this late hour Heaven grants Sancho a moment for repentance since we see Bellido seized with a cold terror, which restrains him when he has his arm actually drawn back to hurl the javelin. Sancho fails to repent and the weapon is driven home, Bellido exclaiming that Heaven punishes by his hand. All that is left now is for the king to acknowledge that his death is just and that neither Bellido nor the city of Zamora is responsible:

> Causa es de causas quien la causa ha sido.
> Fuí hijo inobediente, estuve ciego,
> y el cielo me castiga, . . .

And Bellido, having accomplished the will of Heaven, loses his divine frenzy and again becomes a cringing human being to whom is eventually meted out punishment in accordance with the standards of mortals who do not comprehend the hidden and terrible ways of Providence.

If we review the series of steps by which Sancho moved forward toward his doom, we shall see that numerous chances to escape the prophecy are presented to him and, as he disregards these opportunities, the dangers surrounding him increase. After the appearance of his father's ghost, Sancho is in the midst of his men and far from any real peril; at the time of the warning of Arias he is with his soldiers but the instrument of punishment is at hand and likewise the agent of vengeance; after the Cid's warning he is alone with Bellido but still in his own camp; the next time he is alone with Bellido outside the camp, but soldiers are within hailing distance; finally, the king and Bellido are absolutely alone and all that stands between

Sancho and death is the decree of Fate that Sancho shall die by an "*arma arrojadiza.*"

It seems clear that the exaltation of Bellido is not, as Viel Castel suggests, "*un patriotisme sombre et sincère*" but the mysterious thrill of an agent divinely chosen for vengeance. This frenzy, dependent as it is upon the attitude of the king, does not always sustain the traitor. Whenever the king even remotely considers withdrawing from the siege, the spirit animating Bellido departs and he finds himself in a very desperate situation. In these moments he becomes his real and cowardly self, appreciating fully the danger he is in and reacting to it in a very natural manner. At other times he is not a free agent and, driven on by something he does not understand, he becomes a superman in courage. As the javelin is driven home the mission of Bellido is revealed to him, though he does not mention this fact later when he tries to defend his crime to the incensed inhabitants of Zamora.

It may be argued that if divine vengeance is using Bellido as an agent, this mysterious force is guilty of persuading the king to do wrong. Is Bellido, for example, tempting the king when he says he can reveal to him a way to take Zamora? Is this the case, too, when Bellido again mentions the fact that there is a postern gate which never is closed and threatens to leave the king and go over to the Moors if Sancho does not believe him? Cases like these, however, either precede or follow some suggestion to the contrary and what is really happening is that Providence, or Divine Justice, is bringing the scales into a fine balance susceptible to the slightest touch. Sancho's most secret thoughts are of vital importance, and upon his decision depends his life. (pp. 141-46)

> *Sturgis E. Leavitt, "Divine Justice in the 'Hazañas Del Cid'," in* Hispania, *Vol. XII, No. 2, March, 1927, pp. 141-46.*

L. L. Barrett   (essay date 1937)

[*Barrett is an American educator, translator, and critic. In the following essay, he examines the use of omens in Castro's dramas, noting that the "dramatist's originality . . . lies in the extraordinary degree of realism with which he presents* omina."]

Nineteen of Guillén de Castro's plays contain omens or some metaphorical use of the word "*agüero.*" Since many of these latter instances are of no dramatic value, this discussion will be limited to those portents which, in the words of E. Juliá Martínez, "*constituyen recursos escénicos.*"

There is nothing startlingly new in the types of omens used by Castro. We find the usual ones derived from birds and their actions, the howling of dogs, unusual weather phenomena, the breaking of mirrors, the causeless fall of precious stones from ring-settings, the spilling of wine and oil, the sight of bloody weapons, weeping, and the like. Nearly all these incidents have parallels in the drama of Lope de Vega and other playwrights of the time. However, certain types are conspicuous by their omission: for example, Castro never mentions a raven or crow, birds of omen since ancient days, and he never terms a stumble definitely ominous, despite the numerous cases of such accidents in his theater.

The opening scene of **Progne y Filomena** presents a dialogue between Filomena and Teosindo in which the lady weeps at the prospect of her lover's departure in the near future. Teosindo vainly tries to reassure her, protesting the constancy of his love and the needlessness of her tears. Hence his remark: ". . . *el llorar sin ocasión más es agüero que llanto.* " During the scene the roar of cannon is heard, saluting the arrival of Tereo, who is to marry Progne. A few moments later, after Teosindo's exit, Progne stumbles in with blood on her face. She tells her sister that, drowsy from her early rising to meet Tereo, she dozed at her dressing-table with a mirror in her hand. She dreamed there that her heart was cut from her breast and given to Tereo, who ate it greedily. Shocked in her dream, she was startled awake by the salvo of cannon already mentioned, and in her dazed condition she fell against the mirror, which broke, cutting her face with a sliver of the glass. Filomena attempts to soothe her with an *al revés* interpretation of the dream, but she admits aside that these *"agüeros mortales"* are significant. Certainly they prophesy correctly coming misfortunes.

A sequence of supernatural devices builds up to the tragedy in **El amor constante.** Nísida tells Celauro that her love for him can end only with death, and at the word she swoons. Recovering, she explains that as she spoke that fatal word she saw what she calls *"una muerte."* Celauro is unwillingly impressed by the omen. In Act II, Celauro, waiting one night for Nísida, mentions *omina* in his monologue: he speaks of the horrors of the night, the howling of a dog, and other omens, unspecified. *"Con ellos he tropezado,"* he adds. Then Nísida appears, as perturbed as her love, and, being pressed for the reason, she admits that she is upset by the breaking of her mirror and the inexplicable fall of the stone from her ring; she had touched neither article. Celauro remarks, *aparte,* on the coincidence of her omens with his, and offers to exchange rings with her. His attempt to calm Nísida fails when the stone starts from his ring as she puts it on her finger. The catastrophe prophesied by these events is Nísida's poisoning by the King and Celauro's consequent madness and death.

In contrast to these highly unfavorable portents, **La tragedia por los celos** offers two good omens—the only favorable ones in Castro's drama. Young Prince Fernando, brought up as a peasant by Galíndez in ignorance of the boy's royal birth, is sent by his supposed father to fetch some oil. The old man threatens punishment if Fernando spills the oil as he had previously spilled the wine when sent on a similar errand. The lad replies that he will be careful with the oil, because, while spilled wine is a good omen, it is unlucky to waste *aceite.* However, returning from the errand, Fernando does overturn the oil in his effort to conceal his menial task from visitors. Twitted with the act by Galíndez, Fernando's retort is prompt: *"Derramado aposta, no es agüero."* The visitors mentioned have come to reveal the boy's identity; so the omens are good, as Fernando claims.

Offsetting this momentary lapse into the use of good

omens, Castro resumes his usual line with several very evil presages in the same act (the third) of this play. The piece concerns the illicit love of Alfonso V of Aragon for Margarita, a lady at court. The King, to distract his mind from his worries over the Queen's natural hatred of Margarita, goes hunting, but the pleasure of the chase cannot relieve his pessimistic view of the future: everything reminds him of the hopeless situation. He sees, high in the air above him, an eagle bearing off a dove in its beak, and, with a mind predisposed to reading ill omens in anything, the King considers the eagle and dove symbolic of the Queen and Margarita, respectively. He fires at the eagle in an effort to frighten it into releasing its prey; at that moment his face and costume are spattered with drops of blood from the dove's wounds. An instant later the dead bird falls at his feet. Struck by the ominous incident, Alfonso immediately dispatches Diego to Valencia to see that all is well with Margarita. Very soon thereafter the King hears a shepherd singing the tragic balled, *"¿Dónde vas, el caballero . . . ?"* and the song intensifies his foreboding. The scene shifts now to the royal palace, where Margarita, unable to sleep, appears in disarray, her hair disheveled, and relates fateful presages of misfortune that have beset her since the preceding day: the stone dropped from her ring without having been touched, the mirror broke as she saw *"una muerte"* in it; and the howling of a dog and the hooting of an owl have destroyed her rest. She knows that she will never see the King or their son again. At this point the Queen enters, and, with bitter reproaches and insults, stabs the ill-fated woman to death.

A more unusual omen occurs in **Dido y Eneas,** Act II, when Dido consults the portrait of her late husband, Siqueo, for guidance: she loves Eneas, yet she fears the anger of heaven if she yields to her emotions. The picture seems to turn its face away and threaten her with its hand; then it vanishes, to be replaced by the picture of a bloody sword. Temporarily a prey to foreboding, Dido nevertheless listens, half-fearful, half-eager, to Eneas when he later leads delicately up to a declaration of his love. A terrific storm breaks into the scene; it is a sign of supernatural displeasure, disregarded by Eneas because it affords him an opportunity to carry Dido in his arms to shelter. Shortly afterward, Dido is startled by Siqueo's ghostly voice, calling to her to flee. She departs, and in her absence Eneas sees horrible visions in the air, the sun turns greenish-black, and fountains run red. The specter of Anquises appears in warning to his son, vanishing as Dido returns to say that the storm was apparently concentrated on them, disturbing no one elsewhere. Eneas feels a cooling of his ardor! Still later (Act III) Dido relates to her sister Ana certain portents assailing her: in the oppressive darkness of the night dogs howled, birds shrieked, the holy water turned bloody and brackish as she offered it in propitiatory sacrifice, and she saw Siqueo again in a dream. Her suicide follows soon, and the sword she uses, belonging to Eneas, is the bloody weapon represented in the picture mentioned already.

Another omen involving an eagle opens the play **Los enemigos hermanos.** The Infanta rushes onstage, her comb in her hand and her hair streaming loose; she cries hysterically for aid. The King and the brothers Otón and Ceslau hurry to her. She tells them that she went to sleep beside a fountain, after veiling her head against the sun. Hardly had she closed her eyes when an eagle swooped down and snatched away the veil, tearing out a lock of hair and lacerating the scalp. She demands that someone free her from this omen, a term which the King approves. Specifically, they fear that the incident means the Infanta's loss of the kingdom.. The King offers a huge reward for the return of the *volante,* symbolic of the royal crown. It is this offer that sets in motion the intrigues that follow. Otón, aided by Briseida who actually kills the eagle, is the successful man; he turns out to be the rightful heir to the throne and marries Briseida, while the Infanta and Ceslau must be content with a mere dukedom.

Other omens are of less importance in Castro's drama, and may be briefly summarized here. Few of these portents occur onstage. For instance, there is the Duke's description, in *El caballero bobo,* of the fearsome weather portents accompanying the birth of the Infanta, leading to an astrologer's prediction of dire calamities unless certain precautions were taken. There is, in *Las mocedades del Cid, primera comedia,* the bloody javelin. This is discussed in an article by Professor Leavitt ["Divine Justice in the *Hazañas del Cid,*" Hispania, XII, March 1927]. There are also numerous hyperbolic uses of the term *"agüero"* without great significance, all of which cases may be omitted here.

In all instances of *omina* used by Castro, the author prepares the way for their presentation by creating, in the lines of the personages concerned, an atmosphere of melancholy, of gloom or of fear. When the omen finally occurs, then, the characters involved are the more deeply impressed by it. In the broader view, omens themselves contribute to an atmosphere of fatality in the play as a whole. Most of them are warnings, but some appear too close to the catastrophe to be successful warnings: they allow no time for the personage to alter his course and thus avert disaster. Seldom do they motivate action; but important exceptions are Eneas (*Dido y Eneas),* some of the characters in *Los enemigos hermanos,* and to some extent Sancho (*Mocedades del Cid*). Omens chiefly aid in building up an atmosphere of fatality, and forewarn personages of future misfortune. Still, most of these qualities are common to omens in general, not peculiar to Castro's portents.

The Valencia dramatist's originality in using this type of the supernatural lies in the extraordinary degree of realism with which he presents *omina.* Note, for example, in *Progne y Filomena* how naturally one incident leads to the next, how neatly the whole series works out to predict calamity lying in wait for the sisters, especially Progne. She arises earlier than usual, and with sleep still dragging at her eyes, falls into a doze as she bedecks herself for her betrothal. The shock of the cannon's roar, coming as if in climax to her evil dream, causes her to break the mirror and cut her cheek. Each step is perfectly logical, granted the initial incident in the series.

In *El amor constante* the only dramatic omen is the fall of the stone from Celauro's ring as Nísida slips it on her finger, but how appositely it comes! The sequence in *La tragedia por los celos* is even more impressive. Just after

Alfonso sees the birds, drops of blood from the wounded dove splash his face and collar as the eagle passes over. He fires, and an instant later—just long enough for a bird to fall from a height—the dove falls dead at his feet, released by the startled eagle. Less dramatic because merely narrated, Margarita's omens nevertheless intensify the effect by their close proximity to the scene of the birds and the *arfil.* It is easy to draw here a direct analogy to that modern movie device, the "cut-back," and thus understand Margarita's scene as taking place at the moment the King sees the birds—fateful portents in different locales but pointing to the same catastrophe. Assuming this "cut-back," the shepherd's ballad would follow Margarita's death, and so announce it to the King as an accomplished fact with greater truth. Such an interpretation seems reasonable; it would not be the only analogy between Castro's dramas and the cinema.

In so far as omens are concerned, then, Guillén de Castro frequently succeeds in dovetailing his effects so extraordinarily neatly that they seem almost *too* pat, with unusually vivid touches of realism. If some of these plays are not "four-star" dramas, it may be that, in popular parlance, Castro "could not see the woods for the trees," the trees being the details and the woods the play as a whole. (pp. 73-8)

> *L. L. Barrett, "The Omen in Guillén de Castro's Drama," in Hispania, Vol. XXII, No. 1, February, 1937, pp. 73-8.*

William C. McCrary   (essay date 1967)

[*In the following essay, McCrary outlines the traditional elements of the Cid legend as presented in ballads and in the* Crónica rimada del Cid *and analyzes how Castro modified the tradition in his* Las mocedades del Cid I *and II to make the Cid fit the heroic archetype.*]

The Valencian dramatist Guillén de Castro published the *Moçedades* and *Hazañas del Cid* in the *Primera Parte* of 1618. From that date until the present, surprisingly little critical attention has been dedicated to the first of these dramas despite its universal appeal. Far too often editors of the play and historians of Spanish literature have contented themselves with a few passing remarks about Castro's position in the Valencian theater, Corneille's adaptation, and the *romance* tradition from which Castro drew his inspiration. The present essay is an attempt to examine what the dramatist took from the earlier legends, what he added and modified, and how he organized his materials according to a specific design, in an effort to appraise the art—the *poesis*—of the play. The following study is divided into two parts: the first will discuss the Cid's profile as it was delineated in the ballads and the *Crónica rimada* prior to Castro, and the second will be devoted to the accommodation of this heritage in the drama.

In the Introduction to his edition of Castro's masterpiece, E. Merimée states: "La source principale, & je dirais volontiers la source unique, à laquelle a puisé l'auteur des *Moçedades* & des *Hazañas del Cid,* c'est le *Romancero.*" It should be remembered, however, that the ballads themselves represent fragmented compositions deriving from a common fund of legends. The *materia de las mocedades* is posterior to the time of Alfonso X: the *Primera crónica* contains no reference to the Cid's early exploits. The bulk of Alfonso's remarks about Rodrigo begin in the section devoted to the reign of Sancho II and extend through that of Alfonso VI. The early fourteenth-century *Crónica de los Reyes de Castilla* together with the *Crónica de 1344* embody prosifications of a lost *Gesta de las moçedades de Rodrigo*. The *Crónica rimada del Cid* was composed in the late fourteenth or early fifteenth century and is the only extant composition in verse older than the sixteenth century to treat of the *mocedades*. Since this poem and the *romances* share common themes, it will be well to provide a résumé of those sections of it that are pertinent to Castro's drama. It should not be inferred that the *Crónica rimada* was one of Castro's sources. The purpose of the following condensation is to demonstrate the order of events as they are expressed in the *Crónica*. Since the same sequence is found in the *Crónica de 1344* and in Mariana's *Historia de España*, it is not unwarrantable to presume that the plot of the *Crónica rimada* reflects those of earlier versions of the Cid's *mocedades*. This disposition of events remained more or less intact throughout the fifteenth and sixteenth centuries and provided a general pattern for Castro's ordering of the independent *cuadros* which the ballads preserved.

The Kingdom is at peace when Count Gómez de Gormaz invades the lands of Diego Laínez, attacks the latter's shepherds, and seizes some cattle (vv. 293-295). In reprisal, Laínez and his men ride into the Count's territory, burn several fields, capture the vassals and "lavanderas" working there, and make off with all the livestock they can find. Later, the serfs and washerwomen are returned. Within nine days, Rodrigo, a mere lad of twelve years, meets and kills the Count (vv. 296-326). Ximena and her sisters then appear before Diego to beg him to release their brothers who were also taken prisoner. Rodrigo urges his father to honor the request since the women had taken no part in their father's transgressions and are in need of their brothers for protection. Ximena journeys subsequently to Zamora to claim damages before the King (Fernando el Magno) against Rodrigo for the murder of her father. The Monarch replies that he dares not offend the Castilians lest they rebel against him in his hour of need. Ximena, understanding the King's plight, requests that she be married to Rodrigo, a solution that pleases the Sovereign (vv. 427-381). Fernando summons Diego and his son, both of whom go to Zamora accompanied by three hundred armed men because Rodrigo suspects the invitation to be an ambush. Ximena is presented, the King announces the marriage, and Rodrigo, somewhat displeased by the sudden turn of events, swears that he will not live with the maiden until he has won five battles (vv. 382-448). The remainder of the *Crónica* recounts the *cinco lides campales,* ending with the journey to France of Fernando and Rodrigo to confront the Pope. The second of the five battles involves two episodes of special interest to this study: the Aragonese claim to Calahorra and the encounter with Saint Lazarus disguised as a leper. In the third *lid* the young paladin defeats the five Moorish kings. Such are the pertinent sections of the *Crónica rimada.*

Rodrigo's character as depicted therein deserves some comment. First, he does not entirely identify himself with Fernando as a loyal vassal until the third battle. In the first, he explicitly denies his fealty to the King: "maguera non so tu vasallo . . . " (v. 485). Second, the Cid of the *Crónica* is somewhat impulsive, proud, and for a while, at least, suspicious of Fernando. There is no emotional rapport between Rodrigo and Ximena: once he agrees to marry her she disappears from the narrative. Love, then, is not a motive in this early version.

The ballads and the *Crónica,* as it survives in the Paris manuscript, probably contain the essentials of the material concerning the *mocedades, scil.,* the combat with Gormaz, Ximena's *demandas,* the battle with the five Moslem kings, the leper incident, and the Calahorra dispute with the victory over Martín González. These episodes are the basic actions on which Castro has rested his dramatic artifice. Rodrigo's knighting, Diego's test of his sons, the Cid's preparation for the engagement with the Count, Fernando's decision to partition the realm, and Urraca's jealousy of Ximena are drawn from the ballads and are not found in the *Crónica.* Neither the *romances* nor the *Crónica* have anything to say about the character of Sancho during his father's reign. Castro has also omitted much of the ballad material, most of which is a further elaboration of the core of motifs set forth above.

Interestingly, the play begins with an investiture ceremony, a ritual that elevates the worthy man to a position of national responsibility. The entire conception of Castro's drama can be seen here. The stage is trisected into three planes or fields recessed into space. In the center stands the young Rodrigo, farther back is the venerable old Sovereign (the middle plane), flanked on either side by the royal onlookers. The aggregate of characters serves to frame the altar of Santiago, the patron Saint of Spain. The eye is led from the charismatic youth (the present generation), to the aged King (the past), back to the altar representing the eternal and mystically patronized Kingdom. Time is contained in spatial dispositions. Rodrigo is, in effect, the centerpiece, the focal point of a ceremony that conjoins individual destiny to national history. No better beginning could be imagined for a play which is to dramatize the emergence of a new leader.

Immediately we are taken from a public scene into the private chambers of government. A quarrel breaks out between Rodrigo's father and the Count concerning the appointment of an *ayo* for the prince; the King's choice is Laínez. Loçano takes exception, objecting that don Diego is "con el peso de los años/ caduco ya . . . (vv. 187-188)." The fierce disagreement is highly ironic since, in their behavior, both men prove to be morally unworthy of the responsibility to educate the future King of Castile. It is here, in the royal privy council, that Castro first directs the spectator's attention toward the latent *sparagmos* in the Kingdom which momentarily erupts at the highest level of authority. The Monarch is incapable of controlling the wrath of his most trusted and wisest advisers: indeed, his dialogue is limited to short and futile expostulations interspersed between the volley of insults exchanged by the *privados.* Fernando and Diego are depicted, according to the stage directions at the beginning of the play, as *an-cianos* "los dos de barba blanca [y éste] decrépito," which fact demonstrates, perhaps sadly, the truth of the Count's allegations.

Fernando's inability to impose his rule effectively is worked into the grain of the dramatic action from the opening moments to the last. Apart from the initial *re-yerta,* it is seen again in Ximena's three appearances to demand justice. On each occasion he simply postpones any real solution to the legal problem, first by exiling Rodrigo, then by allowing the plaintiff to set her own terms for trial. In Act III, when the King proclaims his intention to partition the Kingdom, Arias remarks: "Si bien lo adviertes, Señor,/ mal prevalece una casa/ cuyas fuerças, reparti-das,/ es tan cierto el quedar flacas (vv. 1273-76)." Sancho, on hearing of the arrangement, duplicates the quarrel scene of Act I: Fernando is no more able to cope with his son's fierce temperament here (vv. 2790-2890) than he was to reconcile Loçano and Diego. The tragedy is, of course, that Arias and Diego are correct in their appraisals.

Diego's *caducidad* is stated in two ways. First, he places the affront above his duty to the state, albeit he has cause for satisfaction of some order. In this regard Laínez and the Count are of a similar persuasion. The latter refuses to subordinate his personal image to the need for unity in the nation. To Peransules's entreaty to apologize, the proud nobleman retorts: "¿Perderme? No,/ que los hom-bres como yo/ tienen mucho que perder,/ y ha de perderse Castilla/ antes que yo (vv. 619-622)." As Gormaz would sacrifice Castile itself on the altar of personal honor, so Diego would risk his son's life against a mighty warrior to restore his own dignity and public image. Nowhere, however, is Diego's old age more poignantly expressed than in his long soliloquy (vv. 359-429). Yielding to rage and self-indulgence, he foolishly attempts to wield Mudar-ra's ancient and apparently massive battle sword only to discover the bitter truth: "Bien me puedo aventurar;/ mas ¡ay cielo! engaño es,/ que qualquier tajo o revés/ me lleva tras sí la espada,/ bien en mi mano apretada,/ y mal segura en mis pies (vv. 392-397)."

The schism in the government is further reflected by an even more ominous family rupture involving Sancho and Urraca. In the opening ceremony the dramatist allowed his audience to catch a glimpse of the high-strung, impetu-ous character of the *Infante.* After Fernando has invested Rodrigo with the sword, Sancho fancifully transfers its symbolic power to himself: "Y si Dios me da lugar/ de ceñilla . . . verá el mundo que me fundo/ en ganalle; y si le gano,/ verán mi valor profundo,/ sustentando en cada mano/ un polo de los del mundo (vv. 105-111)." His defi-ant words echo those of Loçano spoken shortly before and thus serve to reverberate the growing turbulence in the af-fairs of the royal house. In the midst of Fernando's woes, Sancho's instability is again released in a moment of mel-ancholic clairvoyance clearly presaging even greater tur-moil for the Kingdom when he foretells his own death by an "arma arrojadiza . . . y será cosa muy propinqua mía/ la causa (vv. 1539-43)." Urraca's untimely arrival with the bloody javelin in her hand sends the overwrought Prince into an attack of paranoia (vv. 1605-12). Sancho's virtual

promise in Act III (vv. 2790-2890) to precipitate civil war if the realm is partitioned refers back to his tormented vi-sion in Act II. These interstitial scenes establish the causes, psychological and legal, of the holocaustic *sparag-mos* in which the nascent hero is to play such an important role. Is it any wonder that the queen mother, ". . . huyen-do/ de entre la confusa grita,/ donde unos toman vengan-ça/ quando otros piden justicia . . . (vv. 1313-16)," retires to the serenity of the country?

Rigidity, impotence, the righteous but irresponsible anger of an old man, and the budding anxieties of a paranoid heir to the throne bond together in an atmosphere of inter-nal pressure to form the epicenter of a spiritual convulsion that is to hurl Castilian-Leonese Christendom into civil war. They represent, in the life of the hero, the many-headed hydra, the enemy that menaces dismemberment from within, over which the youthful *Campeador* must somehow prevail and because of which he must begin his journey into the heroic condition. With the death of Lo-çano Rodrigo has cut off one of the heads of the monster, but others grow in its place immediately.

However much the loss of the Count excises a moral unde-sirable from the land, his demise, nonetheless, creates a state of exposure to external hostility. Loçano was a very powerful man, both politically and militarily. His judg-ment was the most respected in the government, his "lança" and "braço," the terror of foreign foes (vv. 505-509, 553), and with his "mil amigos asturianos (vv. 548-549)" he commanded powerful forces. The Moorish infi-dels are quick to exploit Fernando's military inadequacy. In Act II, Diego informs us that the Moslem host has raid-ed Burgos, Nágera, Logroño, and Bilforado, all Christian cities in the north (vv. 1260-71). Paradoxically, the only man capable of any effective resistance to this menace from without is in exile because of the debility from with-in. The same ironic turnabout occurs in Act III when the Aragonese giant appears as his monarch's champion in the dispute over Calahorra. Laínez asks Fernando if there is no worthy Castilian knight to uphold the national honor, to which the King replies sadly: "Días ha que en mi coro-na/ miran mi respuesta en duda,/ y no hay un hombre que acuda a ofrecerme su persona (vv. 2419-22)." Diego's ob-servation, "¡Ah, Castilla! ¿a qué has llegado? (v. 2427)" epitomizes the crisis in the Kingdom.

Counterposed to the disorder and instability of the world in which they move stand Ximena and Rodrigo, both vic-tims of the breakdown of justice. The gradual transforma-tion of Rodrigo from a private individual into a redeemer figure is accomplished in a series of incidents which devel-op the hero's character by illuminating his virtues. The metamorphosis begins when he disciplines his personal feelings for Ximena to defend Diego's outraged honor: that is to say, that he willingly subordinates self-interest to a more comprehensive moral posture involving his fam-ily. The comparison of Rodrigo's resolve in Act I with Fernando's impotence, Loçano's arrogance, and Diego's myopic rage majestically aggrandizes the profile of the youth and diminishes correspondingly the stature of his elders. The same loyalty that impels him to defend his fa-ther's house is recapitulated in the defense of his Sovereign against the Moors and the Aragonese. The constancy of his love for Ximena is brilliantly indicated when he takes his leave of Urraca. Had he responded to her near declaration of love (vv. 1385-91), he might have spared himself the rigors and dangers of exile. He elects, however, to depart with a simple avowal of his great attachment to the homeland (vv. 1411-14). Both constancy and compassion are fused when the hero visits the grieving Ximena to offer his life for having slain her father (vv. 1116-54).

But it is the scene with the *gafo* that reveals the source of Rodrigo's moral integrity. His reaction to Lazarus bespeaks the charity and humility that inform the character of the Christian hero. That he attains Christian perfection is attested by the miraculous visitation of Saint Lazarus. During the knighting in Act I, Rodrigo remarks to the Princess, who concludes the ceremony: "Al cielo me has levantado (v. 77)." The mystical investiture of this ritual is completed in Act III when Lazarus literally blows the breath of God into the hero's breast. Rodrigo's is a triumph of charity and humility over pride and anger. This is the boon he brings back to his people from exile.

The deployment of the second investiture is highly revealing. To grasp fully its impact on the drama it may be well to review briefly the orchestration of the plot. In each act there is a major combat (Loçano, Moors, Martín González). Alternating in sequence with the battles are Ximena's audiences, which accentuate the suspension of justice in the present, and those interstitial scenes—dramatic *vislumbres*—which prefigure the future antagonism between Sancho and his sister. The action mode shifts, then, regularly from internal to external dangers. It is out of these disturbances in the moral and political order that the hero is brought forth. The leper incident is, in effect, a "nativity scene" which heralds the birth of the national hero of Spain. Once Lázaro has invested Rodrigo with providential sympathy the action returns again to the royal court. The King and his council are seen discussing the gravity of the Aragonese claim to Calahorra when Martín González arrives to ask for a Castilian response. It is appropriate that this champion should be a giant, because at this point, just after the nativity, Rodrigo has emerged as a moral giant, one of the anointed of God, the elected man on whose shoulders will rest the future honor of Castile, as it does in the Calahorra dispute. Fernando's total dependence on Rodrigo is proclaimed when he says: "En ti confío,/ Rodrigo; el imperio mío es tuyo (vv. 2548-50)." In one of those rare *coups de théâtre* the now invincible *Campeador* smites the last head of the threatening hydra, gains the maiden's hand as a consequence, and thereby restores justice and moral integrity to his homeland. Fernando's confidence was not in vain.

From the foregoing analysis it should be clear that Castro has introduced several major modifications in the *mocedades* material. The first has to do with the cause of the hostility between Loçano and Diego Laínez. None of the *romances* provides an explanation. The motive which Castro has devised clearly involves the two men in high affairs of state. The second, and by far the most significant, is the young hero's exile which is, at first, self-imposed. Having offered his life to Ximena (vv. 1106-08), he resolves to re-

deem himself by serving in the defense against the marauding Moors as his father advises (vv. 1278-80). That his departure is, however, in essence, an exile is made clear when Ximena appears before the King for the second time to seek justice. Fernando, hard pressed to hand down a decision, remarks: "Pero por hazeros gusto/ *buelva a salir desterrado,/* y huyendo de mi rigor/ exercite el de sus braços . . . (vv. 1785-88, italics mine)." The third alteration represents a re-ordering of the marriage to Ximena and the Cid's departure. In the *Crónica* and the ballads the forthcoming *bodas* are proclaimed, after which the hero leaves of his own volition. Ximena, in some of the *romances,* asks to be married as indemnity for her father's loss; in others Fernando proposes this solution. In neither case does Rodrigo take any part in the decision. Castro, on the other hand, inverts the concatenation of events in such a way that the reconciliation between the two young people occurs at the end of the play after the Cid's exploits. The dramatist has, then, explained the reason for the *reyerta,* introduced a banishment because of this clash, and thus subordinated the marriage to the *destierro* and all it implies in the play.

Castro himself supplies the key to the understanding of his rather striking interpretation of the *mocedades* tradition. In Act III, Rodrigo is compared to Atlas, on whose shoulders the heavens were supported, and to David, who smote the giant Goliath and thus saved Israel from the wrath of the Philistines (vv. 2415-18). The image of Rodrigo as Castro defines it in the **Moçedades** represents an accommodation of the medieval legends to the universal hero myth of which David, in particular, is an example. In recent years a number of investigators have turned their attentions to the myth of the hero. Otto Rank, Carl Jung, Lord Raglan (Fitzroy Richard Somerset), Joseph Campbell, Mary Esther Harding, Alfred Neumann, and Arnold Toynbee have all made significant contributions to this fascinating area.

The hero archetype can be succinctly described as follows: a) he is often of royal lineage, although sometimes illegitimate; b) the circumstances attending his birth may involve unusual manifestations in nature; c) during childhood or youth he is separated from his people; d) in his late youth or early manhood he enters into a round of adventures, overcomes a hostile and menacing enemy or series of enemies; e) because of this victory or victories he returns with a magic elixir or some other redemptive symbol without which his people would perish; f) marries a princess or high-born lady (if the enemy is human, the bride may be either the antagonist's wife [Oedipus] or daughter [Pelops]); g) after which he becomes king or exercises a similar function; h) later he may lose favor with the gods or his people, be driven from the land, and i) subsequently die a mysterious death, or the circumstances surrounding his demise may be bizarre. Not infrequently the hero's life, especially during the time of adventure and trials, invites a divine or miraculous intervention through which he gains his most crucial victory.

Before proceeding to a detailed comparison of Castro's interpretation of the *mocedades* within the design of this monomyth (the term belongs to Campbell), it should be noted that the *traditiones Roderici Didaci* divide themselves into three cycles: those having to do with the early period, those which make up the *Cerco de Zamora,* and those out of which the *Poema* was formed. In the second cycle there is an exile, which Castro preserves in his **Hazañas,** and, of course, the entire *Poema* records the deeds of the *Campeador* in his banishment. Only the *mocedades* period lacks an exile, and, as we have seen, Castro's introduction of an expatriation is his principal innovation. It is because of the Cid's involvement throughout his career with a *destierro* that Castro has inserted an exile into the early period.

The first six stages of the hero's development are pertinent to the **Moçedades.** Castro has, however, altered the normal order in the sequence for reasons to be discussed later. The third and fourth categories (c and d) relate to the childhood and early youth. Rodrigo's separation from his people is achieved through the exile. Banishment, according to Covarrubias, is imposed on those deemed to be "perniciosa a la república (*Tesoro,* s. v. *desterrar*)." If the penalty is just it follows that the state will improve its well-being by expelling the harmful and potentially injurious element. On the other hand, if the expulsion is unjust, the absence of the banished individual diminishes the moral integrity of the land from which he is cast out. It was demonstrated in the foregoing discussion that Rodrigo's absence creates a two-headed monster expressed in the play as internal and external dangers. His exile was engendered by the weaknesses of age and vested interest, and in turn begets even greater debilitation in the land. The need for Rodrigo's strength is made painfully manifest in his absence. Castro's hero, then, is a symptom rather than a cause of disorder. He is the standard of strength and constancy by which all that is infirm and unstable in the state may be measured. Paradoxically, his expulsion subjects the Kingdom to the perils of exposure more than it threatens him. Castro has established, therefore, a cause and effect nexus between phases (c) [separation] and (d) [round of adventures]: it is because of the expulsion that the hero meets and overcomes the ogre.

The alteration in the usual pattern of the monomyth has to do with the first two stations of the hero's passion: his lineage and birth. The development of Rodrigo's virtues is achieved through his exile. And it is during his sojourn that the pariah leper appears before the outcast knight to herald the birth of the Castilian hero. Castro has shaped the action of his play in such a way, then, that the spectator is invited to infer that the young man's comportment in exile brings about the visitation. The announcement of the hero's glorious future by Lazarus assures the audience that Rodrigo will prevail over all the enemies of Castile. But the real significance of the leper's communication (vv. 2331-52) concerns Ruy Diaz himself, for *it is here that he becomes conscious* of his mission and destiny in the world (vv. 2309-23). The metamorphosis from *mozo* to *campeador* is realized at this moment. Rodrigo emerges from this nativity invested with a new moral nobility which towers above the inherited royalty of Fernando, Loçano, Sancho, and Urraca. The rationale of the modification from abcd to cdba (exile, adventures, birth, lineage) is inherent in the concept of *mocedades* which is, after all, a formative peri-

od—an *epistasis*—during which the hero must develop those qualities of character uniquely appropriate to his future deeds. In brief, Rodrigo proves his mettle, and his reward is the infusion of divine grace that signals the birth of a national redeemer.

Stages (e) [magic elixir] and (f) [marriage to the princess] likewise are merged in Castro's art to form a cause and effect sequence. Rodrigo triumphs over impotence (Fernando, Laínez), self-centered wrath (Laínez), egocentric arrogance (Loçano), and foreign arrogance (Moors, Martín González). He brings back to his crisis-laden homeland constancy, love, compassion, charity, humility, loyalty, and divine sympathy. It is precisely because of this synthesis of virtue in the hero that he rescues the maiden from the bondage of compromised honor and the embrace of an unwanted spouse simultaneously. His redemption of Ximena's integrity, therefore, restores justice to the state. Thus the ultimate result of Rodrigo's expatriation and exploits introduces a new distributive justice into the body of his ancient nation that has become so paralyzed by the excesses of retributive justice. Campbell's remarks on the return of the hero are appropriate:

> The effect of the successful adventure of the hero is the unlocking and release again of the flow of life into the body of the world. The miracle of the flow may be represented in physical terms as a circulation of food substance, dynamically as a streaming of energy, or spiritually as a manifestation of grace. Such varieties of image alternate easily, representing three degrees of condensation of the one life force . . . Grace, food substance, energy: these pour into the living world, and wherever they fail, life decomposes into death. [*The Hero with a Thousand Faces,* 1961]

For all of its apparent episodic complexion, the unity of **Las moçedades del Cid** rests on a carefully articulated infra-structure of causal premises: because of the exile the hero is forced into a round of trials and adventures that eventually engender the providentially elected redeemer who then returns vitality and moral fortitude to the infirm order which brought about his expulsion to begin with. The master event to which all the others are subordinated is the exile: it is this innovation that co-ordinates the independent action and plot nuclei of the *romances* and confers an internal cohesion on them. By introducing these subtle yet profound adjustments, Castro has realized an extraordinarily graceful accommodation of the *mocedades* legends to the catholic blueprint of the hero. (pp. 89-102)

> *William C. McCrary, "Guillén de Castro and the 'Moçedades' of Rodrigo: A Study of Tradition and Innovation,"* in Romance Studies in Memory of Edward Billings Ham, *Hayward, 1967, pp. 89-102.*

James Crapotta   (essay date 1984)

[*In the following excerpt from his full-length study of Castro, Crapotta discusses the dramatist's handling of the complexities that result when Christian law and the King's law are in opposition. The critic points out that "there exists a tension between a social code that relates personal honor to submission to the king and a moral code that is outraged when the king's actions are manifestly unjust."*]

The problem of the abuse of power by the unjust or tyrannical monarch stands out as an important dramatic motif in the theater of the Valencian dramatist Guillén de Castro y Bellvis. It is the central theme of what may well be Castro's first dramatic effort, *El amor constante,* and recurs in at least four other plays, the last of which were written some fifteen to twenty years later, that is, close to the date of composition of his most famous play, *Las mocedades del Cid.* Castro's preoccupation with royal injustice and his repeated portrayal of the king as the source of social disorder contrast sharply with the glorification of monarchy found in the *comedias* of Lope de Vega. The Valencian's personal view of royal power was decisively shaped not by Lope, whose prestige had not yet peaked at the time Castro began writing his works, but by the neo-Senecan tragedy, cultivated in Valencia by Cristóbal de Virués, and by the natural law philosophy of sixteenth-century Spanish theorists. These influences are most strongly manifest in the open condemnation of the tyrannical king found in . . . *El amor constante* and *El Conde Alarcos.* . . . *El nacimiento de Montesinos, El perfecto caballero* and *Las hazañas del Cid* . . . seem to draw closer to Lope's works in their apparent respect for kingly authority. However, Castro never fully abandoned his earlier, more critical orientation, and what appears to be a celebration of the principle of absolute loyalty to the king is actually an ambivalent, and even ironic, undercutting of the values and solutions of the Lopean *comedia.*

At the center of Castro's dramatic cosmos is the conflict between arbitrary power (and the social codes that support that power) and natural and Christian law. Stated in other terms, there exists a tension between a social code that relates personal honor to submission to the king and a moral code that is outraged when the king's actions are manifestly unjust. Whereas the former code demands that the king be obeyed, the latter recognizes that the monarch may not always merit the respect due his office. In the presentation and resolution of this conflict Castro gives far more validity than is usually found in the *comedia* to the principles and claims of Christian morality and natural law. Indeed, in all five of these plays he not only condemns the unjust king but also portrays defiance of royal authority as a morally licit, although a socially and personally problematic, means towards the restoration of order. In the cases of *El amor constante* and *El perfecto caballero* this defiance is carried out to the point of regicide, and in *Las hazañas del Cid,* an assassination traditionally considered an act of treason, Bellido Dolfos's murder of King Sancho, is reinterpreted as an act of divine justice. The presence of such works in a genre usually characterized by the celebration of the subject's unquestioning reverence for the monarch, even when the conduct of the latter proves to be morally questionable, is a phenomenon that has received scant attention. (pp. 11-12)

In general . . . there has been no critical consensus as to Castro's treatment of the problem of royal injustice. Critics have tended to overlook the dramatic integrity of the works by stressing individual statements or scenes taken out of their dramatic context. The results have been a series of diametrically opposed interpretations. For some, Castro supports a doctrine of defiance, while for others he rejects that doctrine. Similarly, his *comedias* are regarded either as original and revolutionary or as merely conforming to Lope's dramatic formula.

To a certain extent the plays themselves invite these contradictory readings. If these works seem to support both submission and resistance it is because Castro repeatedly plays off opposite stances of loyalty and defiance in such a way as to make the audience feel that each holds a just claim. Within each of these structurally-related plays the playwright presents a society of loyal subjects forced, in spite of itself, to acknowledge the monarch's betrayal of his own kingdom and to come to terms with those who seek to rescue that kingdom by active resistance. While largely sympathetic to those who would remain loyal to their king, Castro suggests in these plays that loyalty must, at times, be put aside and that defiance, and even regicide, are morally defensible under certain circumstances.

Castro's highly personal vision of these issues can be placed in its proper perspective only if it is seen as, in part, emerging from a dramatic tradition that predates the triumph of the Lopean *comedia.* The pre-Lope orientation of Guillén de Castro's early theater has been noted by a number of scholars, although most of their observations have been of a very generalized nature. (pp. 16-17)

. . . . .

Guillén de Castro repeatedly portrays kings as the source of social and moral disorder, and his plays implicitly call into question the legitimacy of a social code that places personal honor and submission to the king above reason, morality and the welfare of the Christian state. The result is not an unambiguous celebration of the honor code but a heightened awareness of its moral shortcomings. In the most profound sense—that is, in the system of values that he espouses—Castro cannot be said to be a mere follower of Lope de Vega. From the very outset of his career, Castro reveals a personal vision of kingship and honor that he never abandons, not even when Lope's popularity is at its zenith. When Castro adopts elements of Lope's dramatic system in his later plays, he treats them in a highly problematic and ambiguous fashion.

Throughout his introductory study to Castro's theater Eduardo Juliá Martínez has shown how many characteristics of Castro's "first period" works can be attributed to an imitation of the works of Virués: scenes of cruelty and bloodshed, a certain bombastic rhetoric, scenes of madness, settings in the fantastic kingdom of Hungary, names such as Lotario and Celauro, the character of the vengeful and cruel woman, to mention just a few details. But Virués serves as an inspiration to Castro for more than just the external elements mentioned by Juliá. The whole underlying structure of Castro's plays of unjust power takes its point of departure from the older dramatist, with its emphasis on a trilogy of characters: the unjust king, the male subject caught in a conflictive situation precipitated by an act of royal injustice, and a deliverer/avenger.

Castro's unjust king is a direct literary descendant of Virués' tyrant: a monarch who places his own will over his kingly duties and who exploits his position of power to achieve personal satisfaction. He expects unquestioning submission to his mandates, destroying all those who stand in the way of his gratification. What Castro adds in certain instances to Virués' stock figure is an inner consciousness of his own evil, an awareness of the human weakness that makes him a slave to his emotions. In *El amor constante* the King watches himself descend into a Hell-like state until he finally wishes for his own death; the King of *El nacimiento de Montesinos* realizes the wrong he is committing but finds himself overpowered by love and unable to control himself; in the later *Hazañas del Cid* King Sancho knowingly deafens himself to Heaven's warning in order to satisfy his political ambition. In these three cases this inner awareness adds a tragic dimension to the coldblooded tyrant of the earlier dramatist.

Castro's plays of unjust power are above all studies of individual subjects and of the way they attempt to come to terms with tyranny. As we trace the development of Castro's conception of the central protagonist, a loyal subject unjustly treated by his monarch, we can detect the ways in which Lope's theater merges with the early pattern of *El amor constante.* In Virués' tragedies those subject to the tyrant, whether the faceless masses of the *Atila* or the more individualized Menón of *La gran Semíramis,* emerge not as positive heroes, but as victims of royal power. The case of Menón is of particular importance, for here Virués begins to explore, however superficially, the interior reactions of a loyal subject betrayed by his king. Though King Nino's self-serving exploitation of his position of authority sends Menón's personal fortune plummeting, it is Menón's inner sense of helplessness and impotence that leads to a deeper psychological defeat. Guillén de Castro takes this spiritually defeated character as the model for the central figure of Celauro of *El amor constante* and of Count Alarcos. Both of these protagonists define themselves as subjects loyal to their king when they are suddenly confronted with demands they find both unjust and immoral: Celauro, like Menón, is to cede his beloved to a king already married, and Alarcos is to kill his wife to avenge the supposedly offended honor of the king. Each takes an openly defiant stand against the king but upon experiencing the king's power as greater than his own each undergoes a process of spiritual disintegration. Celauro's inability to justify in his own mind the moral legitimacy of his revolt leads to vacillation, a guilty conscience and a madness that culminates in his death. Alarcos' opposition to the King's violation of Christian law is silenced by the latter's threat to kill the Count's entire family; forced to carry out an act against his conscience, Alarcos, too, goes mad.

However, beginning with *El nacimiento de Montesinos* Castro gives evidence of moving towards Lope in his portrayal of this central protagonist. Both Grimaltos of that play and Miguel Centellas of *El perfecto caballero* believe submission to the king to be an absolute obligation and re-

main faithful to that principle even when faced with unjust, and even immoral, orders from their sovereign. Like Rodrigo of *Las mocedades del Cid,* the internal conflict between duty and human emotion is resolved with the decision to follow the socially honorable course of action. In making this choice, these characters, in contrast to Celauro and Alarcos, remain spiritually and psychologically whole in the face of crisis. Yet, as Castro ironically suggests, this unquestioning submission gives free rein to tyranny. Finally, *Las hazañas del Cid* brings together the opposing personalities of Rodrigo and Diego Ordóñez. The latter's unwillingness to question his king's actions and his unswerving devotion to King Sancho, even after the monarch's death, lead to continued disorder and further political disunity. Rodrigo, on the other hand, tempers his loyalty with moral questioning. Although Rodrigo cannot rescue Castile from inner strife, his awareness of a higher ethical law singles him out as a moral exemplar.

The resolution of the problem of tyranny in these plays also initially takes its point of departure from Virués. In both *Atila furioso* and *La gran Semíramis* the king meets his death at the hands of an individual who can no longer tolerate the existence of a morally perverse ruler. Such characters, while they act on behalf of moral law, can themselves offer no hope for a restoration of order. Flaminia, herself a woman as immoral as Atila until the point of her conversion, dies along with her victim as a punishment for her sinful life, and Ninias gives signs of beginning a new reign of vice similar to that of his mother. In his earlier plays Guillén de Castro transforms this character into a mythical saviour figure who embodies the spirit of natural and Christian law and in whose action Castro dramatizes the moral superiority of those laws to the arbitrary will of the king. In *El amor constante, El Conde Alarcos* and *El nacimiento de Montesinos* this figure is the young son of the protagonist. Born and raised in the woods, he lives by the laws of nature and judges the king's actions against those laws. Unlike his father, his instinctive ability to judge good from evil allows him to take action effectively against the king when he sees a moral wrong without feeling restrained by respect for the king's social position. It is through his positive intervention, carried out with the absolute conviction of its righteousness, that order is restored to the kingdom. In these works the promise of a new moral order is assured when the young hero is proclaimed the new ruler.

This positive young hero undergoes transformation into a much more problematic and ambivalent character in our later two plays. In *El perfecto caballero* Castro sets against the submissive Miguel Centellas the more emotionally explosive character of Ludovico who, in a moment of rage, kills the usurping tyrant so honored by Miguel. In so doing, Ludovico ironically carries out the mandate of natural law and is hailed as the new king. And in *Las hazañas del Cid* Castro creates a new dramatic tension by setting against the traditional interpretation of Bellido Dolfos as a traitor the startling idea that he acts as an instrument of Divine Justice.

Influenced by the ideological currents of the late sixteenth century, Castro brings a new political dimension to the pattern set by his predecessor. At the heart of [*El amor constante, El conde Alarcos, El nacimiento de Montesinos,* and *Las mocedades del Cid: comedia segunda*] stands the conflict between two opposing views of royal power: the position espoused by natural law theorists that natural and Christian laws stand above the will of the king, and that espoused by the absolutists that the king's will is law. The conflict between resistance and obedience existed not only between these two diverse ideological poles but also within the writings of the proponents of natural law. While these doctrinal works supported disobedience, armed resistance and even regicide, they tempered their position with cautionary warnings that there must exist sound proof that the king is a tyrant before any move against him may be deemed licit, and with the seemingly contradictory affirmation that the state must suffer the tyrant in cases where the public welfare might be endangered by an act of opposition. For these thinkers defiance was a morally problematical issue, a difficult decision of conscience.

Castro's works mirror the complexity of this controversial issue. If in all five plays opposition to the king is seen as justified and sanctioned by the tenets of natural and divine laws, those characters whom we have identified as the "loyal male subject" cannot fully reconcile this point of view with what they feel to be the honorable (i.e. loyal) behavior demanded of a perfect subject. While Castro ultimately sides with the proponents of natural law and Christian morality his chief concern as a dramatist is to explore the vital conflicts that arise both within and among individual subjects when the king turns against his own kingdom. And while Castro looks to the doctrine of natural law to bring these works to a positive conclusion, the works themselves, filled as they are with ambivalencies towards both "imperfect" emotional characters (Celauro, Alarcos, Roldán, Ludovico, Bellido Dolfos) and "perfectos caballeros" (Grimaltos, Miguel Centellas, Diego Ordóñez), must be seen as morally problematic dramas of opposing tensions rather than as vehicles of political propaganda. (pp. 179-82)

James Crapotta, in his Kingship and Tyranny in the Theater of Guillen de Castro, *Tamesis Books Limited, 1984, 188 p.*

FURTHER READING

Bruerton, Courtney. "The Chronology of the *Comedias* of Guillén de Castro." *Hispanic Review* XII, No. 2 (April 1944): 89-151.
   Determines the order of Castro's dramas based on patterns of versification.

La Du, Robert R. "A Rejoinder to: 'Matrimony in the Theatre of Guillén de Castro'." *Bulletin of the Comediantes* XI, No. 2 (Fall 1959): 10-16.
   Disputes the findings of John G. Weiger (see below), ob-

jecting to the rigidity of his conditions for a happy marriage as depicted in Castro's dramas.

Lauer, A. Robert. "The Use and Abuse of History in the Spanish Theater of the Golden Age: The Regicide of Sancho II as Treated by Juan de la Cueva, Guillén de Castro, and Lope de Vega." *Hispanic Review* 56, No. 1 (Winter 1988): 17-37.
   Depicts Castro's portrayal of Sancho in *Las Mocedades del Cid* as a hybrid of the styles of Cristóbal de Virués and of Lope de Vega.

Matulka, Barbara. "The Courtly Cid Theme in the 'Primaleón'." *The Romanic Review* XXV, No. 4 (October-December 1934): 298-313.
   Credits the popular romance "Primaleón," and not Castro's *Las mocedades del Cid,* with reinventing the legendary Cid figure as a gallant courtier.

Northup, George Tyler. "Lope de Vega and His Dramatic School." In his *An Introduction to Spanish Literature,* pp. 264-90. Chicago: University of Chicago Press, 1925.
   Includes the judgment: "Castro, if unable to produce a masterpiece, at least inspired one."

Weiger, John G. "Matrimony in the Theatre of Guillén de Castro." *Bulletin of the Comediantes* X, No. 2 (Fall 1958): 1-3.
   Examines the theme of matrimony in Castro's plays "as an integral part of his theater."

———. "Forced Marriage in Castro's Theatre." *Bulletin of the Comediantes* XV, No. 1 (Fall 1963): 1-4.
   Focuses on scenes in Castro's plays in which a character consents to marriage out of fear rather than love.

———. "Initial and Extended Speech in the Theater of Guillén de Castro." In *Studies in Honor of Gerald E. Wade,* edited by Sylvia Bowman, et al, pp. 217-27. Madrid, Spain: Studia Humanitatis, 1979.
   Examination of the length of opening speeches in Castro's dramas.

Wilson, William E. "A Note on Fifteen Plays Attributed to Guillén de Castro." *Modern Language Quarterly* 8, No. 4 (December 1947): 393-400.
   Investigates patterns of verb form and morphology as a means of testing the authorship of dramas attributed to Castro.

———. "The Orthoëpy of Certain Words in the Plays of Guillén de Castro." *Hispanic Review* XXI, No. 2 (April 1953): 146-50.
   Investigates the frequencies of dieresis and dipththong as a means of testing the authorship of dramas attributed to Castro.

———. "Two Recurring Themes in Castro's Plays." *Bulletin of the Comediantes* IX, No. 2 (Fall 1957): 25-7.
   Notes the recurrence of the theme of the marriage of King don Pedro el Católico of Aragon and doña María la Santa, and that of "an attack by a few ruffians upon a lone individual, generally a woman."

———. *Guillén de Castro.* New York: Twayne Publishers, 1973, 166 p.
   General critical biography, including chapters on "Guillén de Castro and the Spanish Code of Honor," "Castro's Technique," and "Castro's Influence."

Chin p'ing mei

c. 1573-1606

(Also known as *Jin p'ing mei*) Chinese novel.

Considered one of four novelistic masterpieces of the Ming dynasty (1368-1644), *Chin p'ing mei* is praised by many scholars as the first artistically and thematically modern Chinese novel. It incorporates traditional and popular literature in an original narrative marked by coherence and realism, breaking with the tradition of works comprising heroic or melodramatic episodes tenuously linked by narrative. In rendering the daily life of members of Hsi-men Ch'ing's household—including controversial depictions of their sexual exploits—the novel presents realistic characters that contrast with the faultless heroes and simplistic female characters of earlier Chinese fiction. C. T. Hsia observed: "*Chin p'ing mei* certainly is a milestone in the development of Chinese fiction: it has departed from history and legend to treat a world of its own creation, peopled by life-size men and women in their actual bourgeois surroundings divested of heroism and grandeur."

The title *Chin p'ing mei,* meaning literally "Plum in a Golden Vase," is generally agreed to have derived from three female characters in the novel whose names—P'an *Chin*-lien, Li *P'ing*-erh, P'ang Ch'un-*mei*—translate as Golden Lotus, Vase, and Plum Blossom. Though the original manuscript is presumed lost, analysis of histories, diaries, and personal correspondences has led many scholars to agree that the date of the completed text falls within the Wan-li period (1573-1620), very likely no later than 1606. The most widely read and earliest extant edition of the novel was published in 1617 or shortly thereafter, and is attributed in a preface to Hsiao-hsiao sheng, which means "The Scoffing Scholar." A number of the variant extant editions subsequently published during the seventeenth century were each signed with a different name. One theory suggests that the work is a product of the oral storytelling tradition and thus was composed by many people over the course of several generations, while another maintains that *Chin p'ing mei* was published anonymously by a lone author who did not want to be held publicly accountable for the pornographic nature of the novel. The essential unity of the narrative—despite its length—has most often been interpreted as an indication of a single author, and numerous candidates have been suggested. The most famous explanation is that one Wang Shih-chen conceived the novel as a scathing satire on the private life of the unscrupulous politician Yen Shih-fan, a conspirator against Wang's father. According to this legend, the paper of the edition presented to Yen was tainted with a deadly poison that entered his skin as he turned the pages.

Written in the tradition of the *chang-hui* novel—a novel form comprised of 100 chapters—the work was published in editions divided into either ten standard printing units, called *chüan,* of ten chapters each or twenty *chüan* of five

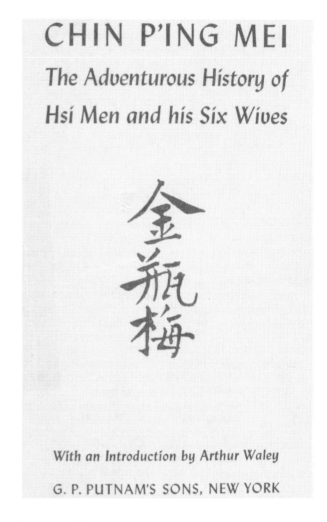

chapters each. Every ten chapters in *Chin p'ing mei* delineates a significant subplot or episode that is punctuated near the midpoint by heightened activity. The first and last twenty chapters of the novel, respectively, describe the assembling and scattering of the protagonists, and function as the introduction and conclusion to the main plot—which closes with the death of the central male protagonist. The order manifested in the narrative is emphasized by the extensive use of devices such as metaphor, allusion, and repetition. The author often recalls events elsewhere in the novel by employing similar phrases, images, characters, or plot constructions, thereby emphasizing particular themes and relationships. The narrative also incorporates seventeenth-century stories, historical anecdotes, drama, and songs, which are sometimes presented as the declamation of a character or woven into the dialogue, plot, or description. P. D. Hanan considered the novel "a veritable storehouse of copied works, an anthology of popular literature." The most evident appropriation involves an epic novel of the fourteenth century, *Shui hu chuan* (*The Water Margin*), from which an episode was borrowed as the point of departure for *Chin p'ing mei.*

The events of *Chin p'ing mei* are set in the Sung empire during the years 1112 through 1127, a period that ended with the loss of the Sung capital in K'ai-feng in North China to the nomadic Juchen tribes. Hsi-men Ch'ing aspires to political, economic, and sexual power through bribes, ingratiation with corrupt state officials, and the acquisition of property, numerous wives, and dowries. The novel documents his rise to power, the attendant business dealings and lavish parties, and the eventual demise of his estate. Within Hsi-men's household, his wives also vie for power and struggle for status within a patriarchal society. Wu Yüeh-niang is Hsi-men's legitimate first wife and, as custom dictates, deserves the most respect. However, Li P'ing-erh, the low-ranking last wife, gains preeminence by her conjugal devotion and by bearing Hsi-men's first son. P'an Chin-lien, who is the fifth wife and regarded by some critics as the novel's main character, also garners Hsi-men's favor. She satisfies his aberrant and frequent sexual demands—for instance, bestowing her maid P'ang Ch'un-mei as a gift to him—and cunningly manipulates the relationships in the household, including arranging the murder of Li P'ing-erh's child. Hsi-men eventually dies of sexual dissipation, an event that coincides with the birth of his second and only remaining son. Upon Hsi-men's death, minions plunder the estate, and the wives are left to fend for themselves. As the novel concludes, the first wife, Wu Yüeh-niang, remains at home, but the other wives either remarry, become prostitutes, or die. The last chapter reveals that Hsi-men has been reincarnated as his remaining son and consecrated to life in a monastery. In effect, the Hsi-men lineage comes to an end.

Chin p'ing mei did not enjoy a wide readership at first, circulating only in a literary coterie early in the seventeenth century. Though the novel subsequently became popular, little commentary on the work appeared until the mid- and late-seventeenth century because of the nascent state of Chinese literary criticism at that time. Furthermore, the Edict of 1687 outlawed improper novels, and the perception of the forbidden *Chin p'ing mei* as a licentious novel inhibited scholarly analysis of its contents. Nevertheless, in 1695 Chang Chu-p'o lauded the skill of the author in a seminal commentary on the novel that is acknowledged by many critics to be perhaps the most perceptive and thorough early discussion of a work of Chinese literature. In 1725 a clause was added to the Manchu dynasty code that imposed stricter penalties, such as official demotion, banishment, or lashes, for the publication, sale, or ownership of obscene literature. This law remained in effect until the fall of the Manchu dynasty in 1912, necessitating that the book be sold surreptitiously. Variously interpreted as a celebration of the irrational and passionate side of human nature or as an account of sexual perversion, frustration, and yearning, the work was largely dismissed as pornography or simply an erotic novel with no literary merit.

Since the 1960s, critics have tended to deemphasize the role of the sexual element of *Chin p'ing mei,* focusing in- stead on the novel's artistic accomplishment and its political and philosophical themes. Parallels have been drawn between the Hsi-men family and twelfth-century state politics, noting, for example, that the power struggle of the six wives and the mismanagement and downfall of the Hsi-men estate are analogous to the corruption of the six ministers in the Chinese emperor's court and the loss of the northern province to the Juchens. Scholars have also highlighted Hsi-men's dishonest interactions with public officials and other leaders, with some reading this as an indication that the author intended the novel as a subtle indictment of government during his own time rather than as a commentary on politics during the twelfth-century Sung dynasty. Other commentators have asserted that the novel was written primarily from a Neo-Confucian perspective which upholds such Confucian concerns as the observance of rules of propriety and morality, and the attainment of a well-ordered society through properly administered government. According to this assessment, the death of Hsi-men, the break-up of the household, and the want of progeny are punishments for such Confucian transgressions as decadence, the breach of law in business dealings, the violation of filial piety through incest and adultery, and the inversion of social hierarchy that results when preeminence is granted women other than the first wife. This interpretation conflates the issues of governance and moral law. According to Katherine Carlitz: "The central maxim [of *Chin p'ing mei*] is that the power of example can strengthen or corrupt the whole state, and hence that good or bad government rests ultimately on the self-cultivation of the individual, and, most importantly, of the ruler." Thus, high officials determine morality through the example of their actions and are indirectly responsible for the values of Hsi-men; he, in turn, is accountable for the social ills of his clan.

Chin p'ing mei is also valued for the commentary on everyday life in late seventeenth-century China that the author incorporated into a twelfth-century setting. As Andrew Plaks maintained, "Many readers have been impressed by the degree of detail with which the author constructs his physical setting, to the point at which the novel can serve as a source for the study of Ming urban planning, architecture, and interior design." The novel is replete with details concerning popular songs, finance, religious rituals, and the lives of government officials. At the same time, some critics have claimed that the realism of *Chin p'ing mei* is dispelled by the use of contradictory facts and inconsistent descriptions, resulting in a haphazard narrative effect. Additionally, some commentators have found the extraneous entertainment included in the work to be encumbering and often melodramatic or frivolous. Such efforts at technical innovation, Hsia maintained, compromise the quality of *Chin p'ing mei*: "In view of the author's inveterate passion for quoting songs and adapting stories . . . , he appears to us as a perverse writer who apparently prizes his ingenuity as much as, if not more than, his creativity." Nevertheless, most critics consider the work an early exemplar of the modern Chinese novel that features an authentic portrayal of society and realistic characterizations. According to Hanan, "The reason why we find the *Chin p'ing mei* so 'modern,' so 'realistic,' is precisely that it reminds us of the kind of novel with which we are most familiar, the novel which is in some way concerned with social change, and which presents us with 'a cross-section of society'."

PRINCIPAL WORK

Chin p'ing mei (novel) 1617?
  [*Chin p'ing mei: The Adventurous History of Hsi Men and His Six Wives,* 1939; also published as *The Golden Lotus: A Translation from the Chinese Original of the Novel "Chin p'ing mei."* 4 vols., 1939]

*Translated into English from a German abridged edition.

Chang Chu-p'o   (essay date 1695)

[*Chang was a Chinese poet and critic. The following excerpt is from his essay "How to Read the* Chin p'ing mei,*" written in Chinese in 1695; it includes the translator's annotations and bracketed Chinese phrases offered for comparison. In this influential early commentary on the novel, Chang enumerates aspects of the work, such as characterization, technique, and plot, that demonstrate the ingenuity and expertise of the anonymous author.*]

1. The author has invented [*p'i-k'ung chuan-ch'u*] the three characters [whose names make up the title], P'an *Chin*-lien, Li *P'ing*-erh, and Ch'un-*mei*. Notice how he brings them together into one place and then disperses them again. In the first half [*ch'ien pan-pu*] of his work the focus is on P'an Chin-lien and Li P'ing-erh, but in the second half [*hou pan-pu*] it is on Ch'un-mei. In the first half Hsi-men Ch'ing manages, by hook and by crook, to obtain for himself the gold [*Chin*-lien] and the vase [*P'ing*-erh] that had belonged to other men; but in the second half the plum blossom [Ch'un-*mei*] which was his to begin with falls easily into the hands of another man.

2. The action begins in the Yü-huang miao [Temple of the Jade Emperor] and ends in the Yung-fu ssu [Temple of Eternal Felicity], and both these temples are introduced in the first chapter. These two are places of pivotal importance [*kuan-chien ch'u*] in the book.

3. First Wu Shen-hsien [Wu the Immortal] surveys Hsi-men Ch'ing's household at its height, then Huang Chen-jen [His Holiness Huang] sustains it somewhat in its decline, and finally Master P'u-ching purges the sins of the main characters. The way in which these episodes are correlated [*chao-ying*] is highly significant.

4. Wu Shen-hsien's mirrorlike forecast of the fates of the members of Hsi-men Ch'ing's household is a kind of summation [*chieh-shu*], but Ch'en Ching-chi is conspicuously absent. P'an Chin-lien is not present when her fellow ladies lightheartedly have their fortunes told by means of the tortoise, but she makes good the deficiency by what she says when she comes on the scene immediately afterward, so she is not really left out. It is only Hsi-men Ch'ing

and Ch'un-mei who are not included here, but Li P'ing-erh's two appearances in Hsi-men Ch'ing's dreams supply the missing data for him. It is not until Ch'en Ching-chi is physiognomized by Yeh T'ou-t'o [Yeh the Ascetic], however, that his final fortune is foretold.

5. Before introducing P'an Chin-lien, the author introduces Li P'ing-erh. Only after Hsi-men Ch'ing takes P'an Chin-lien into his household does the author introduce Ch'un-mei. However, before Hsi-men Ch'ing takes P'an Chin-lien into his household, he first marries Meng Yü-lou. Again, before Hsi-men Ch'ing takes Li P'ing-erh into his household, the author introduces Ch'en Ching-chi. The skill with which these elements of the plot are dovetailed [*ch'uan-ch'a*] cannot be described in words. But the way in which the author goes on to weave in [*chia-hsieh*] the stories of Sung Hui-lien, Wang Liu-erh, Pen the Fourth's wife, Ju-i, and the rest only demonstrates once again that he has mastered the creative skills of Heaven [*t'ien-kung*] itself.

6. Those who really know how to read the **Chin P'ing Mei** appreciate the second half [*hsia pan-pu*], yet it is also only those who really know how to read it who prefer the first half [*shang pan-pu*]. You can only understand this after having fully savored scenes, of which there are too many to enumerate, such as those where the play about Han Hsiang-tzu's quest for his uncle, Han Yü, is performed and where the song "Alas! Life Is like a Dream" is called for during the celebrations that mark the birth of Kuan-ko and Hsi-men Ch'ing's appointment to office.

7. The **Chin P'ing Mei** exhibits certain regular structural devices ["*pan-ting ta chang-fa*"]. For example, whenever P'an Chin-lien gets angry about something, the author arranges to have Meng Yü-lou at her side. This is done without any variation each time and is a seasoned stylistic technique [*chang-fa lao-ch'u*]. Another example is the way that every time Hsi-men Ch'ing is about to go out drinking at someone else's place, some guest or official turns up for a visit and he has to delay his departure in order to entertain him. This is a major structural device [*chang-fa*] used in the chapters after the birth of Kuan-ko and Hsi-men Ch'ing's appointment to office.

8. Each of the hundred chapters of the **Chin P'ing Mei** is constructed by means of the structural device of juxtaposing two episodes [*liang-tui chang-fa*], so that there are two hundred episodes in all. However, there are some chapters in which the transition [*kuo-chieh*] between the two episodes is effected by means of a single expression, while there are others in which the two episodes are mortised [*kuo-hsia*] by a hidden tenon [*sun*]. For example, Chao Yüan-t'an's tiger performs this function in chapter 1.

There are some chapters in which the two episodes are further subdivided, the author narrating the first half of the first episode, shifting to the first half of the second, then going back to finish off the first, and only then going on to complete the second episode. There are some chapters in which the two episodes are completely intermingled [*san-wu ts'o-tsung*], and there are some in which the treatment of other matters is inserted into the narration of the two main episodes. In short, the two episodes form the framework [*t'iao-kan*] of each chapter. If you savor carefully the way in which they are handled from one chapter to another, you will know what I mean.

9. It is true that two episodes are juxtaposed [*tso-tui*] in every chapter of the **Chin P'ing Mei,** but there are also cases of episodes in different chapters that parallel each other at a distance [*yao-tui*]. Examples of this include the parallel episodes [*tui*] of P'an Chin-lien playing the *p'i-p'a* and Li P'ing-erh playing elephant chess and the paired episodes [*tui*] of the hiding of the wine pot and the theft of the gold bracelet. I could go on, but there are too many to enumerate fully.

10. In the first half [*ch'ien-pan*] of the book, the motif of "cold" [*leng*] is repeated so effectively that one can hardly bear to read on, whereas in the second half [*hou-pan*] the motif of "heat" [*je*] recurs but is not readily apparent to the reader. In the first half the motif of "cold" occurs where the greatest "heat" is being described. If you savor these passages you will know what I mean. The way that the motif of "heat" occurs in the second half can be seen in the description of Meng Yü-lou's visit to Hsi-men Ch'ing's grave where the author provides an elaborate description of the beauties of spring on the Ch'ing-ming Festival.

11. In this book there are examples of the most dubious and unimportant characters who nevertheless play significant roles, such as Han Ai-chieh. Innumerable women appear in the work, but why does the author choose to end it with the example of Han Ai-chieh's integrity? He has a profound reason for doing so. Han Ai-chieh's mother, Wang Liu-erh, becomes a prostitute, and Han Ai-chieh herself, after her return from the Eastern Capital, also engages in this profession, but as soon as she becomes interested in Ch'en Ching-chi, she remains faithful to him until death. If we compare this with the way in which Li P'ing-erh and Ch'un-mei treat their husbands, Hua Tzu-hsü and Chou Hsiu, it certainly puts them to shame. If we compare P'an Chin-lien's conduct after meeting Hsi-men Ch'ing with that of Han Ai-chieh after meeting Ch'en Ching-chi, we see that she is unfaithful first with Ch'in-t'ung, later on with Ch'en Ching-chi, and finally even with Wang Ch'ao, so that she is not even the equal of a repentant prostitute. Thus the author concludes [*chieh*] his book with Han Ai-chieh in order to put to shame the other female characters and to emphasize the contrast between a repentant prostitute who can preserve her integrity and those who not only fail to correct their faults while living in luxury but, abandoning all integrity and shame, go unrepentant to their deaths.

12. In reading the **Chin P'ing Mei** we must pay attention to the significant features of the spatial setting [*ta chien-chia ch'u*]. These include the location of P'an Ch'in-lien and Ch'un-mei in one place and Li P'ing-erh in another and the placing of all three of them in the single larger setting of the front garden. The fact that P'an Chin-lien and Ch'un-mei are placed together accentuates the isolation of Li P'ing-erh. The fact that P'an Chin-lien and Li P'ing-erh live close to each other in the garden allows their jealousy to flourish, while the fact that Wu Yüeh-niang lives far re-

moved from them gives Ch'en Ching-chi his chance to get at P'an Chin-lien.

13. In reading the **Chin P'ing Mei** we must pay attention to the points at which one element in the narrative is used to lead into another [*ju-sun ch'u*]. For example, the theme of slaying a tiger is introduced [*ch'a-ju*] amid the joking in the Yü-huang miao. The fact that Hua Tzu-hsü is Hsi-men Ch'ing's next-door neighbor is introduced when he is proposed for membership in the brotherhood. In chapter 8, when P'an Chin-lien is suffering from the heat, during her tirade at Tai-an the information that Hsi-men Ch'ing has taken Meng Yü-lou into his household is introduced. Li Kuei-chieh is brought out [*ch'a ch'u*] when Hsi-men Ch'ing asks Ying Po-chüeh where he has been the last few days. Ch'en Ching-chi's establishment of intimacy with P'an Chin-lien is introduced on the occasion of the completion of the summer-house. Wang Liu-erh's submission to Hsi-men Ch'ing's demands is introduced as a result of Chai Ch'ien's request for a concubine. Li P'ing-erh's pregnancy is introduced in the course of her bout with Hsi-men Ch'ing in the Fei-ts'ui hsüan [Kingfisher Pavilion]. The origin of Li P'ing-erh's illness is introduced with the trial of the Indian monk's medicine. The monk P'u-ching is introduced into the story as a result of the events in the Pi-hsia kung [Temple of the Goddess of the Iridescent Clouds]. Li Kung-pi is introduced on the occasion of the visit to Hsi-men Ch'ing's grave, and the first indication that there is anything going on between Tai-an and Hsiao-yü is introduced when he is sent home for the fur coats. Such examples of the author's ability to accomplish his aims without leaving a trace are innumerable. This is due to the skill with which he employs indirect [*ch'ü-pi*] and unexpected [*ni-pi*] techniques to tell his story. He is not willing to start a new narrative thread [*t'ou-hsü*] from scratch or to use direct [*chih-pi*] or straightforward [*shun-pi*] techniques to tell his story. There is no end to the separate narrative threads in this book, and if each of them were started from scratch, one could not even count them. When I take up my brush I also try to use indirect and unexpected techniques but, unlike the author, I am unable to be indirect [*ch'ü*] without leaving traces or to be unexpected [*ni*] without tipping my hand. This is what makes his book so marvelous.

14. There are many episodes in the **Chin P'ing Mei** in which the clandestine activities of some of the characters are disclosed [*p'o-chan*] to others. For example, Hsi-men Ch'ing's sexual intercourse with P'an Chin-lien during the funeral service for her husband is overheard by the monks outside the window; P'an Chin-lien's affair with Ch'in-t'ung is discovered by Sun Hsüeh-o, and the even more incriminating perfume sachet that P'an Chin-lien has given him is also found on Ch'in-t'ung's person; P'an Chin-lien discovers Hsi-men Ch'ing's secret assignations with Li P'ing-erh over the garden wall and stumbles upon Sung Hui-lien's affair with Hsi-men Ch'ing; Li P'ing-erh's remarks in the Fei-ts'ui hsüan are overheard by P'an Chin-lien, but her own antics in the grape arbor are witnessed by T'ieh-kun; no sooner does Hsi-men Ch'ing accept the bribe of stolen goods from Miao Ch'ing than he incurs the wrath of the regional inspector; no sooner does Wu Yüeh-niang implore the aid of the magistrate in her suit against

Ch'en Ching-chi than P'ing-an gives false testimony against her in the court of Wu Tien-en; immediately after P'an Chin-lien's affair with Ch'en Ching-chi is first consummated, Hsi-men Ch'ing actually touches the evidence without realizing it, and when Hsi-men Ch'ing burns moxa on Wang Liu-erh's pudendum, Hu Hsiu is an unseen witness to the scene. Examples of this kind are too many to enumerate. In general, the author uses this risky technique [hsien-pi] in order to show the predicaments to which human emotions can lead. But even more remarkable is the way in which he enables the characters whose clandestine activities are disclosed to cover their tracks with plausible alibis so that he does not have to waste his energy on tedious explanations. This is why his technique is so miraculous [hua-pi].

15. There are instances in the **Chin P'ing Mei** in which the author seems to have deliberately created episodes or characters that appear from nowhere and disappear for no apparent reason [wu-wei]. Shu-t'ung is an example. Who knows how much planning went into the author's creation of this single character? It goes without saying that he serves the purpose of depicting Hsi-men Ch'ing's depravity and polymorphous promiscuity, but it is not so apparent that the author has created Shu-t'ung in order to prepare the ground for the departure of another character from Hsi-men Ch'ing's household. What is the explanation for this? Li P'ing-erh and Wu Yüeh-niang start out estranged but end up on intimate terms. P'an Chin-lien and Wu Yüeh-niang start out on intimate terms but end up estranged. Although the rift between them develops over the expulsion of Lai Chao and the banishment of Lai Wang, it need never have been as serious as it becomes when P'an Chin-lien throws her tantrum. This tantrum is precipitated by Yü-hsiao's willingness to repeat every word of Wu Yüeh-niang's private conversation to P'an Chin-lien. Why should Yü-hsiao tell her everything? Because she has accepted her three conditions. Why does she accept these three conditions? Because P'an Chin-lien discovers her affair with Shu-t'ung. The author does not want to have to account for the affair between Yü-hsiao and Shu-t'ung from scratch at this point in the narrative, so he describes the hiding of the wine pot and the ill will it engenders at an earlier point. But the reason why the author goes to such pains [yao-yao hsieh lai] is because he needs P'an Chin-lien to have her tantrum. Why is this? The [tantrum] episode is needed to account for the fact that when P'an Chin-lien has to depart from the household, Wu Yüeh-niang abandons her to her fate without the slightest regret and P'an Chin-lien's downfall is complete. How can anyone say that there is a single example of irrelevant [wu-wei] writing in the **Chin P'ing Mei?**

16. In the **Chin P'ing Mei** the author devotes serious attention to the description [cheng-ching hsieh] of six women, and of these he really concentrates on only four, that is, Wu Yüeh-niang, Meng Yü-lou, P'an Chin-lien, and Li P'ing-erh. But he describes Wu Yüeh-niang only because of the requirements of the plot [ta-kang] and uses different techniques to depict Meng Yü-lou because she is a person of superior gifts who resents her unjust neglect. Thus he describes Wu Yüeh-niang only because he has to and is unwilling to describe Meng Yü-lou the way he does his

other characters. Neither one of them is given full treatment [cheng hsieh]. The full treatment is reserved for Li P'ing-erh and P'an Chin-lien. But again, he describes Li P'ing-erh by what he does not say about her, which is to say, he describes her while keeping his focus [hsieh-ch'u] elsewhere. This is because the focus of his description is always on P'an Chin-lien. Because he always concentrates [tan-hsieh] on P'an Chin-lien, it is no wonder that she emerges as the most vicious of all his characters. Such, indeed, is the awesome power of the writer's brush.

17. There are two characters in the **Chin P'ing Mei** to whom the author devotes special attention and whose final fates are also noteworthy: Ch'un-mei and Tai-an. While she is still only one of the maidservants, the author indicates in numerous passages that Ch'un-mei possesses a sense of self-esteem and ambition that sets her apart from the others. While he is still only one among the many manservants, Tai-an is described by the author in passage after passage as being adept at pleasing people in everything he does. Why does the author insist on having Ch'un-mei become a lady of rank and Tai-an a man of wealth and position at the end of the book? In order that his novel on the theme of "heat and cold" [yen-liang] should illustrate the reversal of fortunes [fan-an]. Notice how the other characters can only see that the Ch'un-mei before them is merely a maidservant—they have no idea that later she will become a lady of rank. Notice how they only see that the Tai-an before them is merely a manservant—they have no idea that later he will become a man of wealth and position. When their status changes, not only do others look upon Ch'un-mei and Tai-an in a new light and pay court to them, even Wu Yüeh-niang has to look on them differently, treating Ch'un-mei as her social superior and placing herself under Tai-an's protection after the decline of the Hsi-men family. Of what utility then is judging people according to transitory social status [yen-liang]? The author's acupuncture [chen-pien] uses satiric barbs instead of regular needles. In order to make the later reversal of their fortunes plausible, the author must first demonstrate the special qualities of Ch'un-mei and Tai-an.

18. What need does the author have for the characters Li Chiao-erh and Sun Hsüeh-o? He uses Li Chiao-erh to imply that even before Hsi-men Ch'ing meets P'an Chin-lien or Li P'ing-erh he is already a dissolute wastrel who is capable of any crime. In his treatment of P'an Chin-lien and Li P'ing-erh, he describes certain of Hsi-men Ch'ing's crimes in full [shih-hsieh], whereas in his treatment of Li Chiao-erh he describes others of Hsi-men Ch'ing's crimes by implication [hsü-hsieh]. If the crimes that are actually described are as bad as they are, those that are not portrayed leave us free to wonder how many other indescribable crimes he has committed in the past. How deep is the author's hatred of Hsi-men Ch'ing!

As for Sun Hsüeh-o, why should the author devote the space he does to this person of humble origins whose status is only that of a maidservant who has been seduced by her master? This is an example of the author's Bodhisattva-like compassion. How could the retribution [pao] due a character as vicious as Hsi-men Ch'ing be complete without his wife's becoming a prostitute? But since the author has already decided to handle Wu Yüeh-niang in a different way, he certainly could never bring himself to reduce her to this. Meng Yü-lou is an innocent victim of Hsi-men Ch'ing's depravity, so the author could scarcely endure to expose her to any additional suffering for the sake of punishing Hsi-men Ch'ing. Li Chiao-erh is a prostitute to begin with. Li P'ing-erh is destined to play a role in Hsi-men Ch'ing's retribution while he is still alive. As for P'an Chin-lien, not only does she have a nemesis of her own, but even if she were to become a prostitute, it would not harm Hsi-men Ch'ing and might even be beneficial to P'an Chin-lien, who would probably be nothing loath. How could this be called retribution? Thus the author describes Sun Hsüeh-o as being reduced to prostitution in order to accentuate the retribution visited upon Hsi-men Ch'ing and at the same time unobtrusively to bring to a conclusion [*an-chieh*] the case of Sung Hui-lien. As for the subsequent incidents involving Chang Sheng and Ch'en Ching-chi, they are merely dictated by the exigencies of the plot [*ch'ing yin wen sheng*] and represent an expedient tidying up [*sui-shou shou-shih*] of loose ends. Otherwise how could Sun Hsüeh-o's life as a prostitute be brought to a conclusion [*chieh-kuo*]?

19. Li Chiao-erh represents the role of money [*ts'ai*] in the realm of sex [*se*] This is apparent from the fact that she takes charge of the household accounts and that she lines her pockets before leaving the household. Wang Liu-erh represents the role of sex in the realm of money. When she meets with Hsi-men Ch'ing she is always talking about business deals, getting maidservants and houses, fixing up things for Miao Ch'ing, and so forth, all of which profitable subjects are broached by way of sex.

20. The author needs Sung Hui-lien in his book in order to bring out as completely as possible the viciousness of P'an Chin-lien. This early trial of her powers against Sung Hui-lien foreshadows what she does later on out of jealousy of Li P'ing-erh. How can we see this? When Sung Hui-lien succeeds in attracting her master's attentions, it is P'an Chin-lien who first becomes aware of it, just as it is she who first catches sight of Ying-ch'un pretending to call the cat as a signal for Hsi-men Ch'ing's assignation with Li P'ing-erh. How does P'an Chin-lien's willingness to send Ch'un-mei with a brazier to warm the grotto for Hsi-men Ch'ing and Sung Hui-lien differ from her urging Hsi-men Ch'ing to take Li P'ing-erh into his household and offering to share her quarters with her for the time being? How do her apparent willingness to forgive Sung Hui-lien when she kneels and throws herself upon her mercy and all the other tricks by which she keeps the upper hand over her differ from her pretending to be drunk when Li P'ing-erh first enters the household and saying to her, "Now we walk together on the same path"? How does her double-tongued troublemaking between Sun Hsüeh-o and Sung Hui-lien differ from her telling tales about Li P'ing-erh to Wu Yüeh-niang? To make a long story short, Lai Wang's narrow escape from death and the needless suicide of Sung Hui-lien are both P'an Chin-lien's doing. The author times this subplot to coincide with Li P'ing-erh's entry into the household for the express purpose of providing her with a warning, but she does not realize her danger and actually befriends P'an Chin-lien. How fitting that disaster should

not be long in overtaking her and that she should suffer the fate of which she has been so clearly forewarned [*hou-ch'e chung fu*]. This episode, which I interpret as an early trial of her powers, greatly accentuates P'an Chin-lien's viciousness, but the author has also created here a cautionary example [*yang-tzu*] for those who do not know how to keep danger at a distance. If you read this episode inattentively you may think that it describes nothing more than Hsi-men Ch'ing's having another affair with the wife of one of his servants. But Hsi-men Ch'ing is a man who kills husbands in order to take their wives and money, protects servants who have killed their master, and puts the law of the land up for sale, so the author scarcely needs to create [*chuan*] this episode merely to add another item to the roster of his crimes. The reader, however, is often deceived by the author.

21. Why does the author in the later part of his narrative depict the relationship between the wet nurse Ju-i and Hsi-men Ch'ing? This is also clearly directed against P'an Chin-lien, for it demonstrates that her successful elimination of Sung Hui-lien and Li P'ing-erh has been an exercise in futility. How can we see this? When Sung Hui-lien dies, P'an Chin-lien is delighted, but then Kuan-ko is born and Li P'ing-erh wins Hsi-men Ch'ing's favor. When Kuan-ko dies and Li P'ing-erh follows him to the grave, P'an Chin-lien is again delighted; but before she knows it, the fragrance of Ju-i's cosmetics attracts Hsi-men Ch'ing's attention by the very side of his dead favorite's spirit tablet. Every time P'an Chin-lien eliminates a rival another comes to take her place. No matter how good she may be at maintaining her lover's favor and gaining the upper hand, what can she do in the face of a situation like this but acknowledge the futility of her efforts and retire from the field? Thus the author's portrayal of Ju-i is really a means of getting at P'an Chin-lien and of expressing the indignation he feels on behalf of Sung Hui-lien and Li P'ing-erh.

22. But why does the author devote space to the various singing girls such as Li Kuei-chieh, Wu Yin-erh, and Cheng Ai-yüeh? They serve the purpose of demonstrating the insatiability, frivolity, and vulgarity of Hsi-men Ch'ing. Li Kuei-chieh and Wu Yin-erh are purposeful duplications [*t'e-fan*] of P'an Chin-lien and Li P'ing-erh, respectively, demonstrating that by taste and affinity the latter pair are indistinguishable from prostitutes and that though they may never have actually engaged in that trade, their wantonness and depravity are such that they not only show the same proclivities as prostitutes, but will go even further than they do. The author portrays Cheng Ai-yüeh in yet another way—as fragrant, smooth, and soft—in order to bring out the unrelieved boorishness of Hsi-men Ch'ing, who is depicted by contrast [*fan-ch'en*] as being incapable of fully appreciating even the refinements of a high-class whore.

23. Why has the author created Wang Liu-erh, Pen the Fourth's wife, and Lady Lin? These three characters are depicted in different ways and serve different purposes. The depiction of Wang Liu-erh is solely intended to illustrate the theme that money [*ts'ai*] commands sex [*se*]. If you observe the lengths to which she goes to ingratiate

An unhappy P'an Chin-lien with her first husband, a dwarf.

herself with Hsi-men Ch'ing when he is alive and the alacrity with which she absconds with his property as soon as he is dead, you will see that in the relationship between them, Hsi-men Ch'ing is using money to seek sex and Wang Liu-erh is using sex to seek money. Hsi-men Ch'ing's death follows upon a visit to Wang Liu-erh, so that in the end he finds both sex and money to be empty [*k'ung*]. When Wang Liu-erh subsequently meets Ho Kuan-jen, she ends up using sex to seek money just as before. Indeed, though sex can move people, it is no match for money which can be used anywhere for any purpose and is loved by everyone. Thus the author does not conclude [*chieh*] the story of Wang Liu-erh, who symbolizes the lust for money, until his last chapter.

The author has created Pen the Fourth's wife as a means of revealing Tai-an's character. He shows that Hsi-men Ch'ing, who seeks only to indulge his own insatiable desires, is unaware of the fact that the example he sets will be followed by his subordinates, who have already learned from him how underlings can take advantage of their masters. Thus, Tai-an's seduction of Hsiao-yü, which eventuates in his marriage to her, is foreshadowed [*fu-hsien*] in his relations with Pen the Fourth's wife. You may say that

Pen the Fourth's wife is used as a foil to depict [*p'ei-hsieh*] Wang Liu-erh, but this is a subsidiary function.

As for Lady Lin, she serves as a vehicle for expressing the incalculable resentment the author feels in his heart for P'an Chin-lien. Not only does he have her murdered and mutilated, but he is not satisfied until he has damned even the household in which she got her start in life and the persons who taught her to be what she is. How can we see this? P'an Chin-lien is sold as a child into the household of Imperial Commissioner Wang where she is taught to sing and dance. To argue that she is utterly devious and shameless from birth is not consonant with the doctrines that conscience is innate and that human nature is basically good. I am sure that she was not necessarily as dissolute as this at the age of three or four. During the time when she was a member of Imperial Commissioner Wang's establishment, if the male members of the household had shown respect for propriety and righteousness and the female members of the household had honored chastity and integrity so that obscene words and deeds were neither to be heard nor seen, then, even if she had been dissolute to begin with, she would have been transformed into a chaste girl. How is it that this imposing imperial commissioner neither pacifies distant peoples in the name of the Son of

Heaven nor proclaims the imperial majesty and virtue but, instead, when the ten-year-old daughter of a tailor enters his household, devotes his leisure time to teaching her how to paint her face with cosmetics and encourages her to put on airs? If he carries on like this with a lowly serving maid, the way he conducts himself with his legitimate wife can be imagined. How fitting that his son, Wang San-kuan, should be a good-for-nothing profligate and his own wife, Lady Lin, a dissolute adulteress. Who is there to blame but himself? But what the imperial commissioner teaches P'an Chin-lien results in incalculable harm to many people, from Wu Ta in the beginning to Hsi-men Ch'ing at the end. It is certainly fitting that the imperial commissioner's retribution [*huan-pao*] should come in the form of Lady Lin's adultery with Hsi-men Ch'ing. This is why I say the author has a profound hatred for P'an Chin-lien, a hatred that extends even to the household in which she got her start in life, and this is why he devotes attention to Lady Lin.

But Chang Ta-hu also contributes to P'an Chin-lien's corruption, so why does the author neglect him? The answer is that it is his nephew, Chang Erh-kuan, who takes over Hsi-men Ch'ing's official post after the latter's death, and it is he whom Ying Po-chüeh persuades to take Li Chiao-erh into his household. Clearly, he is another Hsi-men Ch'ing who will suffer a similar indescribable retribution for his own sins. In this novel, undescribed but implied incidents ["*pu cho pi-mo ch'u*"] occur without number. In the case of Chang Erh-kuan, the author has hidden another large book between the lines of his text [*wu-pi ch'u*]. This is an example of material implied but not directly written out on the page ["*pi pu tao erh i tao*"].

24. As for the depiction of Wu Yüeh-niang in the ***Chin P'ing Mei,*** people all say that Hsi-men Ch'ing is lucky to have such a wife. They do not understand that the author describes Wu Yüeh-niang's crimes in such a subtle way [*yin-pi*] that people do not realize what he is up to. How can we see this? A husband is the person whom a wife looks up to and depends upon for the remainder of her life. If her husband spent large sums of money on concubines in order to secure a male heir and Wu Yüeh-niang raised no objections, this would truly be an ideal marriage and she would be an exemplary wife. But Hsi-men Ch'ing murders husbands in order to steal their wives, which is the conduct of a gangster. Now, when a husband engages in the conduct of a gangster and his wife does not tearfully remonstrate with him but instead neither expresses approval nor disapproval, treats him as a stranger whose welfare is no concern of hers, and regards her compliance as a virtue, can such an attitude withstand scrutiny? As for her relationship with Ch'en Ching-chi, the author goes out of his way to emphasize Wu Yüeh-niang's responsibility for bringing the fox into the chicken coop, an act of indescribable folly. When she finally gets wind of her son-in-law's adultery with P'an Chin-lien, she can think of nothing better to do than to keep the doors locked in the daytime. Afterward, when she drives Ch'en Ching-chi out of the household, sends his wife back to him, and agrees to sell Ch'un-mei to Chou Hsiu, she is merely adjusting her rudder to the wind without any convictions of her own. Moreover, her fondness for hearing Buddhist nuns recite

pious texts and her indiscriminate burning of incense are not proper activities for a wife to engage in. It follows from all this that the words "did not pay much attention to his studies" are the source of the complete ruination of both Hsi-men Ch'ing and Wu Yüeh-niang. How can we see this? If Hsi-men Ch'ing had adhered to the rules of propriety himself, he would have been able to mold his wife accordingly. But instead, merely because he pays no attention to his studies, Wu Yüeh-niang, who has the capacity for goodness, also ends up lacking any understanding of the dictates of propriety. Her everyday activities show no evidence of the protocol a wife should observe in her relations with her husband, but only a lot of superficial gestures in that direction. Wu Yüeh-niang is described as a woman with good intentions who is ignorant of propriety. But good intentions alone are not enough, for ignorance of propriety can lead to incalculable harm. If Wu Yüeh-niang is ultimately responsible for Ch'en Ching-chi's evil deeds, how much worse might things have been if she were not even well intentioned? However, although it is Wu Yüeh-niang who makes Ch'en Ching-chi's crimes possible, it is Hsi-men Ch'ing who must bear responsibility for having failed to set a proper example for his wife.

25. In the art of writing there is a mode of description characterized by the incremental repetition ["*chia i-pei hsieh-fa*"] [of a motif]. This book excels at this type of incremental description [*chia-pei hsieh*]. For example, after describing Hsi-men Ch'ing's "heat" [*je*] the author goes on to describe that of the two censors, Ts'ai and Sung, then that of Grand Marshal Huang, then that of Grand Preceptor Ts'ai, and finally the "heat" of the imperial court itself. This is the incremental repetition [*chia i-pei*] of [the motif of] "heat." After describing Hsi-men Ch'ing's "cold" [*leng*] the author goes on to describe Ch'en Ching-chi in the Beggars' Rest, Grand Preceptor Ts'ai's exile, and finally the captivity of the emperors Hui-tsung and Ch'in-tsung. This is incremental repetition of [the motif of] "cold." In brief, the incremental repetition of [the motif of] "heat" is used especially to show the way that "heat" of the sort Hsi-men Ch'ing attains is no rare thing, but Hsi-men Ch'ing knows nothing but to rely on his wealth to commit crimes. The incremental repetition of [the motif of] "cold" is used precisely to show that "cold" of the sort Hsi-men Ch'ing experiences knows no limit, but this is a point that Hsi-men Ch'ing himself fails to see.

26. The author insists upon describing Wu Yüeh-niang as a pious Buddhist. Does the reader understand the reason for this? In his opening remarks the author enjoins us to purify our six senses, so we can anticipate that he will certainly conclude [*chieh*] his work by showing that the two words money [*ts'ai*] and sex [*se*] are empty [*k'ung*]. But only a monk will do to exemplify the conclusion [*chieh*] that everything is empty. Hsi-men Ch'ing is not the sort of person to repent before his dying day, and after his death who is there to play this role? Even if Wu Yüeh-niang, after her husband's death, were to disregard the family property and take the tonsure, what would that have to do with the author's use of Hsi-men Ch'ing to exemplify Buddhist doctrine? Thus the only thing is to have Hsi-men Ch'ing himself take the vows. But how is one to get around the fact that he is already dead? The author,

after some hesitation, arranges to have Hsiao-ko born at the very hour of Hsi-men Ch'ing's death, so that in the end he may repent and achieve deliverance. The author's mind is that of a Confucian sage, but he has taken the compassionate vow of a Bodhisattva in the hope that there should be no one in the world who conceals his faults to the end or fails to correct them. He hopes that even those who die unrepentant may be able to correct their faults in the life to come. What magnanimity and compassion the author shows for Hsi-men Ch'ing and how great are his efforts to admonish future generations! The author has this denouement [*ta chieh-shu*] in mind from the outset, but he does not want baldly to introduce Master P'u-ching all of a sudden at the end to spirit Hsiao-ko away without tying this into the rest of the narrative [*wu-t'ou wu-hsü*]. First, to do that would be to use a hackneyed narrative cliché [*hsün-ch'ang k'o-chiu*]. Second, the ending would then seem unconnected [*t'o-lo*] with the body of the text and would appear contrived [*hen-chi*]. Therefore he must depict the motif of Wu Yüeh-niang's Buddhist piety off and on throughout his narrative so that it appears and disappears like a snake in the grass or a [discontinuous] chalk line [*ts'ao-she hui-hsien*]. He especially describes Wu Yüeh-niang's pilgrimage to the Pi-hsia kung in order to lead up to the scene in the Hsüeh-chien tung [Snow Stream Cave], where he gives the reader a glimpse of P'u-ching. It is not until ten years later in the narrative that he brings them together again in the Yung-fu ssu, where all the major characters in the novel reappear in a phantasmagoria only to fade finally from sight, one after the other. Thus the biography [*chuan*] of each of the characters, all of whom are fated to suffer separation in this life and the next, is brought to a conclusion [*chieh*]. This is the grand finale [*ta chieh-shu*] in which the myriad threads [*ch'ien-chen wan-hsien*] of the author's narrative are all resolved and allowed to recede into the great void from whence they came.

Thus, in depicting Wu Yüeh-niang's Buddhist piety the author is certainly not merely describing in a general way the everyday practices of a lay believer for the benefit of pious village women. The marvelous quality of this book lies in the skill with which the arteries that connect widely separated elements of the plot [*ch'ien-li fu-mai*] are concealed. The author never resorts to facile writing [*i-an chih pi*] or the use of elements for which connections [*sun*] have not been prepared. That is why the **Ch'in P'ing Mei** surpasses all other books. (pp. 202-18)

36. The writers of novels never divulge their names, either because they have some axe to grind [*yü-i*] in their works or because they contain covert references to real people. Since the authors have decided to abide by the principle of only speaking well of others without dwelling on their faults ["*yin-e yang-shan chih pi*"] and conceal the real names of the people on whom their characters are modeled and since they choose not to divulge their own real names, why are men of later times so anxious to search for clues to the underlying reality and call every person by his right name? How petty such desires are! Moreover, hearsay in such matters is generally apocryphal and not to be taken seriously. To sum the matter up in a word: if the author had not had intense feelings he would never have written the book. If the persons whom he wished to describe duly make their appearance in his book, but the author, who had such intense feelings about them, could not bring himself to name them explicitly, it would be the height of inanity for us, who have no such intense feelings ourselves, to insist on identifying them. Therefore I shall ignore the theory that Hsi-men Ch'ing was intended to represent Yen Shih-fan [1513-1565], whose style was Tung-lou [Eastern Tower] and whose childhood name was Ch'ing-erh. As for the person who wrote this book, I shall simply refer to him as the author. Since he did not choose to attach his name to the book, why should I try to second-guess him? (p. 222)

The author achieves his effects with such supernatural skill ["*shen-kung kuei-fu chih pi*"] that the twists and turns [*ch'ü-che*] of the plot beguile the reader without permitting him to see where the golden needle has done its work ["*chin-chen chih i tu*"]. That is why I say that his mode of composition is purely that of Ssu-ma Ch'ien [*Lung-men wen-tzu*]. Whenever I concentrate my attention on this kind of writing, following its every twist and turn and exploring its structure [*ch'i-chin*], I feel just as though I were discovering the extraordinary sights of the five sacred mountains and the three islands of the immortals. I can never tire of pleasures such as these. (p. 230)

> *Chang Chu-p'o, "How to Read the 'Chin P'ing Mei'," translated by David T. Roy, in* How to Read the Chinese Novel *by Shuen-fu Lin and others, edited by David L. Rolston, Princeton University Press, 1990, pp. 202-43.*

P. D. Hanan   (essay date 1961)

[*Hanan is a New Zealand-born critic and educator in the field of Asian studies specializing in the study of Chinese traditional fiction and the influence of foreign literature on the modern Chinese writer. In the following essay, he discusses aspects of* Chin p'ing mei, *such as plot, characterization, authentic contemporary detail, and the work's focus on socioeconomic status, that contribute to its reputation as an artistically and thematically modern novel.*]

The **Chin P'ing Mei** is one of the great works of Chinese classical fiction—great in quality as well as in volume. It is also, I imagine, among the novels best-known to readers of English. There is more than one translation of it, and although even the fullest of these is not a translation of the most authentic kind of edition but of an inferior "sub-edited" version instead, there is no doubt that it will give the modern reader an approximate idea of what the original is like.

Few of the facts we usually require about a work of literature are known in the case of this novel. The question of the author's identity has defied the guesswork of over three centuries. It is only by a good deal of luck that the date has been established at all. It was written at some stage between the years 1582 and 1596, and the discovery is owed to a chance remark about a current scandal made by a character in the novel and to a chance reference in a poet's letter. Yet despite our lack of information about it, there has never been any doubt in any modern critic's mind that it represents a new departure in Chinese literature. It is only when we come to ask how it is different, and why it should be different, and just what kind of novel it is, that the answers so far given seem less than satisfactory.

It differs from earlier novels, of course, in one very clear way indeed—the manner in which it was written. Whereas the other novels are concerned with traditional story-cycles, and some at least are recensions of earlier written versions, the **Chin P'ing Mei** is to a large extent the product of one man's imagination. This is not by any means to say that it has no sources; on the contrary, it is a veritable storehouse of copied works, an anthology of popular literature at least as varied as any that has appeared until modern times. The point of difference is that it is less dependent upon its sources. The author chose to develop a single episode in an earlier novel, the great heroic novel of the fourteenth century, the *Shui hu chuan,* and the circumstances of his choice meant that there was no large body of traditional material to which he might have felt obliged to adhere. Hence he has taken from earlier and contemporary literature only those passages which suited his purpose, adapting them freely as he thought fit. Even the episode from the *Shui hu chuan* which forms the starting-point of the novel has largely changed its significance. The centre of interest is no longer the hero Wu Sung, but a secondary figure, P'an Chin-lien, and a minor figure, Hsi-men Ch'ing. Wu Sung is no more than a kind of *deus ex machina,* whose re-appearance is delayed until the novel is nearly over. And the other two characters, in so far as they are delineated at all precisely in the *Shui hu chuan,* are subtly altered in the later work.

Yet one has to admit that this obvious difference, important though it is for the history of literature, really tells us very little about the novel. It is not at all obvious, merely because it is the work of a single writer, why it should lack the characteristics of the earlier novels, such as their episodic arrangement and their larger-than-life characterization. And a glance at the host of imitators of the heroic and supernatural kinds of novel will quickly satisfy us that this need not be the case at all. The fact is that the circumstances of the novel's composition are really the consequences of something else altogether. We must suppose that the purpose or preoccupation which engrossed its author must have led him to dispense with the ways of the old kind of novel, and to evolve a new kind.

This preoccupation has usually been related to the author's attitude (described as one of "realism") or to his subject ("ordinary life," "a cross-section of society," and so forth). And each of these terms could be defined in such a way as to be descriptively true of the novel. It is doubtful, however, whether the word "realism" is worth the time it would take to define it, and so I will examine instead the group of qualities, mainly relating to plot, character, and background detail, which differentiate this novel from the earlier ones.

One striking difference between the **Chin P'ing Mei** and all earlier fiction is its total rejection of the traditional kinds of plot. It is an interesting indication of the strong,

if perhaps unconscious, sense of unity which the author possessed that those places in which an element of the melodramatic enters the novel have almost invariably been copied from other books. This applies to the long, rather circumlocutory account of Wu Sung's adventures which starts the novel and also to the trials and tribulations of Wu Yüeh-niang on her journey to Mt. T'ai in chapter 84. This adventure of Wu Sung is taken, as we have already noted, from an episode in the *Shui hu chuan;* the Yüeh-niang episode is compounded of passages derived from no less than four different parts of the same work. Another melodramatic incident—and another rupture of that unity with which the novel gradually impresses the reader—is provided by the murder of Miao T'ien-hsiu in chapter 47; yet this is copied almost entirely from a Ming crime story. Still another example is provided by the picaresque adventures of Hsi-men's son-in-law, Ch'en Ching-chi, in the last few chapters of the novel. Here, where the author seems unaccountably to relax his artistic grip, at least one of the adventures is derived from an earlier short story, and I suspect that it may not be the only one. In the body of the work, there is only one incident which, I suppose, could be regarded as in any way melodramatic, and that is the murder of the baby Kuan-ko by P'an Chin-lien, although this can hardly be said to rupture the novel's tacitly-imposed unity. And even here, after the murder has been described, the author finds it necessary to add a little note to the reader, comparing the deed to one perpetrated in ancient history, and in effect justifying himself.

What has happened is that a great shift of emphasis has taken place from incident (in the sense of melodramatic incident) to character, and so pronounced is this shift that it is hardly possible to talk of "plot" at all in connection with the **Chin P'ing Mei.** This leads one to ask whether, after all, the kind of characters portrayed in the novel may not be its main distinguishing feature. It is true that the majority of them are "lifesize," that is, that they seem to us a fairly naturalistic representation of actual types of people. By contrast, the heroes of the *Shui hu chuan* seem, most of them, just a little enhanced, just a little larger than life, rather like the heroes of those Icelandic sagas which stick closest to actual events, like Gunnar and Skarp-Hedin in *Njal's saga,* for example. But it is doubtful if this is a useful distinction to make. The secondary characters of the *Shui hu chuan,* as well as the characters of some of the early colloquial short stories—certain of them precede the **Chin P'ing Mei** by several centuries—are equally "lifesize," although they belong to a narrower range of types. Here there is certainly one genuine difference. Whereas the female characters of the *Shui hu chuan* are, roughly speaking, either hoydens or Amazons, and the heroines of the short stories are often either plaster saints or *femmes fatales,* in the **Chin P'ing Mei** we are at last confronted with women of a satisfying, indeed astonishing degree of complexity.

This interest in female character is a feature which is found elsewhere in late-Ming literature. To take merely one instance, there is a long-short story in Classical Chinese called *The Autobiography of a foolish woman (Ch'ih p'o tzu chuan)* which purports to be the sexual history of a woman from a precocious childhood to a disillusioned and rejected maturity. The story is surprising because of the sympathy it appeals to in the reader; the narrator is Moll Flanders [in *Moll Flanders*] rather than the Wife of Bath [in *The Canterbury Tales*], more sinned against than sinning. In this respect it reflects a characteristic temper of the later stories, which exhibit a leniency of moral judgment unknown to the early story-teller; characters quite often escape the direct consequences of their folly. The story is, of course, in the tradition of the erotic novel, and it may well be that it was the erotic novel, to which tradition the **Chin P'ing Mei** also belongs—although it transcends it by far, as *Hamlet* the revenge play—which was the first kind of fiction to portray women in any adequate manner. The other kind of literature which may have influenced this development is the popular song, which enjoyed a golden age in the sixteenth century. The genuine popular songs are a woman's literature, in that they are dramatic, and the "I" of the song is almost always a woman (naturally, since they were most often sung by singing-girls). This argument may seem somewhat far-fetched, but, in fact, the author of the **Chin P'ing Mei** has himself indicated its validity by employing the unique device of the dramatic use of song in his novel. (What this means, put briefly, is that when their feelings are deeply stirred, characters sometimes break into song, the actual popular songs of the period.)

The *Autobiography* claimed to be personal experience, and this is how the **Chin P'ing Mei** also appeared, to the eyes of at least one contemporary, the poet and diarist Yüan Chung-tao:

> In years gone by, there was a Captain Hsi-men in the capital, who engaged an old scholar from Shaohsing to serve in his household. The scholar had little to occupy his time, and so day by day he recorded the erotic and licentious things that went on there. In the figure of Hsi-men Ch'ing, he portrayed his master, and in the other figures, his master's various concubines.

Although this interpretation need not, of course, be taken seriously, it is true that there is a great deal of authentic, contemporary detail in the novel, detail of a kind which makes it plausible to assume that a good part of the work derives from personal experience rather than from traditional, collective experience. It is impossible here to go into all the cases in which the novel has been shown to represent the actual conditions of the time at which it was written. We have, in any case, already mentioned that the dating of the novel partly depends on a reference to a contemporary scandal—the squandering by the Emperor of certain funds. But there are two significant fields in which the novel, despite the fecundity of Ming literature on every conceivable topic, is especially detailed. In the history of the popular song, which is one of the most important new forms of the Ming dynasty, the **Chin P'ing Mei** is by far the most comprehensive source of reference. The other field is that of money and prices.

The subjects we have so far dealt with, plot, character, and authentic contemporary detail, all show features which the **Chin P'ing Mei** shares with other works of its time but which have not appeared in the earlier novel. Yet none of

them is satisfactory as anything more than a partial interpretation. Other features, such as the extreme naturalness of the language, which is functional rather than expressive, lacking, except in some of the erotic scenes, the heroic flights of the earlier novel, have similar disadvantages. An equally unsatisfactory interpretation is to regard it as an erotic novel; it is probable that the **Chin P'ing Mei** is in some way a response to the existence of an erotic tradition, and not a simple response by any means, but if the novel as a whole were to be regarded in this light, the greater part of it would be meaningless. There is a similar objection to describing it simply as a "novel of exposure." Exposure it certainly contains, and the extent of its satire of social conditions has usually been underestimated. All these explanations are true, but true only partially and descriptively. So are the explanations which refer to the subject of the novel ("it holds a mirror to society"). Indeed it is doubtful if a reference to a novel's subject—by which is meant the sphere of life it represents—ever holds true in an interpretative sense. It seems always at a tangent to what one feels to be the main issue.

There are two questions in which the **Chin P'ing Mei** is saturated: money and social status. It would be surprising if they did not form part of any reasonable interpretation of the novel. I have mentioned above that the work is a mass of detail about money and prices, and it is not possible to resume it all here. A few examples can perhaps be given, however. The first chapter in the novel which is substantially by the author, and not adapted from the *Shui hu chuan,* is chapter 7; it is devoted to Hsi-men's successful attempt to marry Meng Yü-lou, an attempt which he undertakes at least partly in order to secure her property, and which is very nearly foiled by her grasping relatives. The case is similar to the complicated negotiations about marrying Li P'ing-erh; again the transfer of wealth is an important factor, and is seen to be one. The connection between money and politics is also much stressed. By bribes, Hsi-men Ch'ing escapes the consequences of one murder and several other crimes; by bribes, in effect, he obtains an official post. There is also the matter of trade. When the story opens, Hsi-men runs a herbalist's shop in a provincial town. Gradually he extends his business to cover textiles, sending his buyers as far as Hangchow with large quantities of money. He is also a money-lender, making small loans as well as backing great contracting merchants to fill their quotas of commodities for the Imperial palaces. Money is in the very fabric of the story. It is made unambiguously clear how most things depend on it.

If there is one thing above all others in the book which is seen to depend on money, it is social status. Here again let us take Hsi-men as our example. As the book opens, he is a small-town merchant. He is barely literate; he has to puzzle over his correspondence. And during the whole course of the novel he remains barely literate. Yet he becomes the confidential friend, if not of the highest official in the country, then of the controller of that official's household. He entertains, and patronizes, two graduates fresh from the examinations in the capital. These men were the very *élite* of Chinese society—yet an unlettered ex-shopkeeper can afford to patronize them! This meeting with the two graduates, and the later meetings with them separately, are described in considerable detail, and we can surely suppose that they had a piquancy for the contemporary reader. The visits of the eunuchs in charge of the nearby tile factory no doubt serve a similar purpose. (Here, incidentally, is another authentic detail, for the contemporary reader could hardly fail to connect this tile factory with the great Imperial tileworks at Linch'ing.) These incidents must have allowed the reader to savour an interesting situation; from another point of view, they document Hsi-men's rise in social status. Such considerations are no doubt behind Hsi-men's hiring of a secretary to fit his station in life, and it is possible that they are also behind his indecorous affair with the aristocratic Lady Lin.

This view also illuminates other sections of the novel. Towards the end, there is a scene in which Wu Yüeh-niang and the other ladies are returning from a visit to Hsi-men's grave and stop to rest at a temple outside the town. When the abbot bustles a way to attend to some other lady, they realize she must be someone very grand indeed. She turns out in fact to be none other than Ch'un-mei, the maid who has been expelled from the household with ignomity on Yüeh-niang's express orders—she has made the fortunate leap from concubine to first wife of the army officer who is the temple's patron. Ch'un-mei can, of course, afford to be gracious. Surely this incident was guaranteed to send a shiver down the reader's back!

Whereas Hsi-men's struggle for social status takes place in the corrupt world of business and politics, that of his wife and concubines takes place inside his household. The women are rightly considered to be the centre of interest in the novel, and the author has indicated that this was his intention by naming the work after three of them. The fierce struggle among them for Hsi-men's favour is essentially a struggle for status; this will be obvious to any reader, and need not be dwelt on. But it would be easy to pass over the host of minor characters in whose tragedies the attempt to win or maintain status is the chief element. Such a one is Sung Hui-lien; her tragedy is told, in just a few chapters, with an objectivity worthy of de Maupassant. She is the pretty young wife of one of Hsi-men's buyers, and has the status of a servant in his household. When her husband is absent on a buying trip, she is seduced, needing little persuasion, by Hsi-men Ch'ing. Showered with his gifts, she takes the opportunity to rise a step in status. She ceases to do her kitchen-work, and instead consorts with Hsi-men's wife and concubines and is accepted by them almost on equal terms. She hopes that Hsi-men will give her husband some lucrative job which will keep him away from home. But when her husband returns, inevitably discovers the truth, and in a drunken rage threatens Hsi-men Ch'ing, the latter considers it more prudent to have him framed for a theft he did not commit, beaten, and sent away to another district. Hui-lien hangs herself, partly out of shame, for she lacks the ruthlessness essential for her kind of ambition, and partly out of mortification, for she realizes that, having failed to get her own way in this matter, she will also fail to get it in others.

Such bare accounts cannot give an adequate idea of the extent to which the novel is steeped in questions of status. In fact, almost every speech is given significance as a social act. Every detail of dress, furnishings and behaviour has significance as a symbol of social status. If, as we have said, the world of business and politics is the place where the struggle is really decided, then in conversation, in the confrontation of person by person, it is seen to be won or lost, and in the trappings of dress and property are to be observed its trophies of success. Naturally for the women the struggle is a little different; it is decided in domestic intrigue or in the bed-chamber. But its meaning is the same.

Viewed in the light of this preoccupation with money and status, many of the other distinctive features of the novel become comprehensible. Differences in status can only be appreciated in the minutest and most authentic detail. The field in which such differences show to best advantage is that of speech, and the dialogue of the *Chin P'ing Mei* is more natural, more expressive of minute shades of social significance, and more subtly differentiated than that of any Chinese novel before it, and of all but one after it. The detail of daily life, all the rich social texture of the work, would be pointless if it was not up-to-date and freshly observed. That is why it contains the authentic argot of different kinds of people—beggars and prostitutes among them. That is also the reason why the reader is kept constantly aware of the social background of all the various characters: Li P'ing-erh was a great man's concubine, Chin-lien an ordinary local girl, Ch'en Ching-chi the spoilt young son of rich parents living in the capital, and so forth. But more than this follows from the concern with status; the very form of the novel is also a consequence of it. The short-story form, or the episodic-novel form, the only ones in existence before the author wrote, were both too loose for his purpose, for only the tightly-meshed texture of the *Chin P'ing Mei* allows questions of status to be seen comparatively and competitively. And status is nothing if not competitive. (That is why the women's struggle inside the household remains firmly in our minds, while Hsi-men's rise in the world and all its manifestations, which are of considerable—though not equal—importance, become forgotten. We do not see enough of the competition he survives.) Finally, if we assume this preoccupation to be the author's, even the presence of the erotic scenes is partially explained. They are part of the detailed description of social confrontation, and they are the field in which the battle for status among the women is at its fiercest. Many of them also afford direct motivation for later events in the novel. (Yet one has to admit that this explanation hardly accounts for the relish with which they are described, or their occasional use of hyperbole.)

If one compares the *Chin P'ing Mei* with earlier literature, especially earlier novel literature, it is as if some new, pervading element of life had been discovered in a scientific sense for the first time. Among late-Ming works, on the other hand, although there is nothing to set beside the *Chin P'ing Mei,* there is often a thicker social texture than is found before. The author of the collection of stories named *Shih tien t'ou,* who in several ways departs further from the traditional form of the short story than do other writers, shows clearly that he is aware of the problems of adjustment which a beggar-girl must face if she is to make the Eliza Doolittle-like transformation to scholar's wife.

But none of the full-length novels which deal with city life at an unexalted social level can in any way be likened to the *Chin P'ing Mei; The Jealous Wife (T'su hu lu)*, for example, which might seem of a comparable kind—it deals in tiresome repetition with the efforts of a hen-pecked husband to obtain a concubine—has a far looser social texture. This illustrates quite clearly the inadequacy of interpreting the *Chin P'ing Mei's* distinctive quality as the sphere of life with which it deals. *The Jealous Wife,* bad novel though it is, equally deals with ordinary life; yet it is not concerned, like the *Chin P'ing Mei,* to fill up all the interstices of the social fabric.

Although the key questions with which the *Chin P'ing Mei* deals are those of money and status, the relationship between them is not an equal one. The central question is undoubtedly status, and money is merely one of the means, the most important one so far as this novel is concerned, in seeing that status is assured. The society, in short, which is depicted in the novel is one in which money is the most effective means of acquiring status, at any but the highest level. The reasons for Hsi-men's rise to power are all reducible in the end to money, and the same applies to other figures, less prominent in the novel, such as Miao Ch'ing. This suggests that there may be a relationship between social change as depicted in the novel and social change at the time the novel was written.

Of all the literary kinds, the novel—and especially the sort of novel to which the *Chin P'ing Mei* so pre-eminently belongs—is the one most likely to be concerned with social and cultural change. There is no doubt that in the sixteenth and seventeenth centuries particularly, there occurred a spectacular rise to wealth and influence by a class of merchants. A modern historian [Ping-ti Ho in his *Studies on the Population of China, 1368-1953*] writes as follows: "Whatever the institutional and ethical checks on the growth of capital, the late Ming period witnessed the rise of great merchants." This was no inconspicuous rise. People who lived through this time were aware of the change, and commented freely upon it. What is more to our purpose, it was also taken account of in imaginative literature. While it is true that one could adduce examples from among the short stories, perhaps the most interesting ones are provided by the songs. When men-of-letters turned to composing words for the tunes of the popular song, a thing they not infrequently did in the sixteenth century, they often departed from the usual theme of clandestine love, and produced a lively and pertinent commentary on the times in which they lived. Two such men were Chu Tsai-yü (born in 1536), a theorist of music, and Hsüeh Lun-tao, a retired army officer. The songs of the former show an almost obsessive interest in money, an interest made up both of contempt and an anguished regret. Hsüeh Lun-tao has a set of four songs describing a young salt-merchant in all his finery, riding on a white horse (like Hsi-men Ch'ing) and "hobnobbing with officials."

But the association of the parvenu Hsi-men Ch'ing with a contemporary social change, while easy enough to grant in a general way, is by no means all the significance which can be extracted from this point. For in a society in which there is a newly-emerging group of persons, social con-

tacts, social relationships, "manners" in the old sense not merely of that group but of all groups, become important. A rise in status for one group calls everybody's status into question. And if we can imagine the rise of Hsi-men Ch'ing, representing a contemporary social phenomenon, as being near to the heart of the author's conception, then the whole development of the work becomes, not obvious, but at least understandable.

Comparison between unrelated literatures is most often a blind alley, useful for orientating oneself, but not worth pursuing to any great distance. But I think that the novel, more particularly a certain kind of novel, for reasons given above, may be an exception. At any rate, the hypothesis sketched out in the previous few pages is under a heavy debt to Lionel Trilling's thesis of the novel's distinctive quality ["Manners, Morals, and the Novel," in his *The Liberal Imagination*]. Furthermore, I believe that the reason why we find the *Chin P'ing Mei* so "modern," so "realistic," is precisely that it reminds us of the kind of novel with which we are most familiar, the novel which is in some way concerned with social change, and which presents us with "a cross-section of society."

While the interpretation outlined above seems to me to be central to our understanding of the *Chin P'ing Mei,* it should be emphasized that what has been done in this exploratory essay is merely to suggest the kind of novel to which the *Chin P'ing Mei* belongs, the kind of novel, in fact, of which it is the quintessence. None of the novel's other themes has been touched upon. Nor has there been any attempt, except in a few chance comparisons, to place it in its context of Ming dynasty literature. (pp. 325-35)

> *P. D. Hanan, "A Landmark of the Chinese Novel," in* The Far East: China and Japan *by Joseph R. Levenson and others, edited by Douglas Grant and Millar Maclure, University of Toronto Press, 1961, pp. 325-35.*

C. T. Hsia   (essay date 1968)

[*A Chinese-born critic and educator, Hsia has written extensively on Chinese literature. In the following excerpt, he suggests that* Chin p'ing mei *is a work of moral realism, graphically and powerfully depicting the degeneracy that may result from a preoccupation with sexual pleasures.*]

When all the points that conspire to make [*Chin p'ing mei*] a work of haphazard realism and moral ambiguity are conceded, a strong case can nevertheless be made for its being a work of terrifying moral realism if one is able to concentrate on the major episodes involving the main characters—especially Hsi-men, Lotus, Vase, and Moon Lady—and to refuse to be distracted by all the intervening passages of satire and burlesque, of comic frivolity and didactic solemnity. Fortunately, nearly all the "romance" episodes come pell-mell after chapter 80 so that they hardly affect the "novel" within the novel [chapters 9-79 of the 100-chapter novel] that we shall be considering [here].

Golden Lotus is clearly the dominant character in that "novel." Except in her poetic moments, when she appears languid and dispirited, she is the most clear-headed and calculating character of the lot. She is born and reared a slave, and her savagery is the savagery of the slave, abject in her selfishness, cunning in her struggle for security and power, and ruthless toward her rivals and enemies. The plaything of an old roué and the victim of a travesty of marriage to a "seven-inch dwarf," she is definitely among the injured and insulted, and the modern tendency, among playwrights and novelists who have portrayed her career, is to sympathize with her, at least for her early attempt to achieve a kind of normal happiness with her brother-in-law Wu Sung. But in the novel there is little evidence that she feels romantic about him, certainly not after her beauty has caught the eye of Hsi-men Ch'ing. (In the end, of course, Wu Sung returns as her nemesis. But one cannot take Part III seriously: if she were consistent with her earlier character, she would have tried to avoid rather than have entered with apparent alacrity the trap he sets for her.) And there is little in her character that calls for pity. She herself is unpitiful, and [the maid], Plum Blossom, in defending her against her detractors, once praises her spirit of *cheng-ch'iang,* that is, her fierce determination to excel and beat the competition. She is pitiless in her murder of her first husband, as in her treatment of her stepdaughter, Ying-erh. When Hsi-men deliberately neglects her following their first fling together, she releases her fury by clawing Ying-erh's face until blood flows. This is a recurring situation: whenever she feels mistreated or sexually frustrated, she inflicts sadistic punishment on her own slave, whether she be the stepdaughter or the maid Chrysanthemum (Ch'iu-chü).

Her drama proper begins with her removal to the Hsi-men house. Upon being introduced to the other wives, she knows right away that none is her match in beauty. Nevertheless, to safeguard her position, she ingratiates herself with [Hsi-men's first wife] Moon Lady and assiduously cultivates the favor of her lord not only by eagerly complying with his sexual demands but by making him a present of her pretty maid, Plum Blossom. With his favor more or less assured, she further strengthens her position by forming an alliance with the good-natured Meng Yü-lou, and then she tests her power by picking a fight with the wife enjoying the least favor with their husband, Hsüeh-o. Hsi-men is prevailed upon to kick and beat the latter violently. His eagerness to please her reassures Lotus and emboldens her to adopt a more aggressive policy toward Moon Lady. In the future she will time and again incite her lord to punish her enemies and demand from him proofs of his love.

But Lotus is also a nymphomaniac. Early conditioned to the notion that a woman's duty is to please her man, she has long capitalized on her slavery to make her lot endurable: to regard herself indeed as a sex instrument, but not so much to please her partner as to gratify herself. Soon she finds Hsi-men's sexual attentions inadequate: though spending little time with the other wives, he is a man of vigor with a roving eye, and a habitué of the local brothels. During one of his prolonged absences, therefore, Lotus forms a liaison with a boy servant, Ch'in T'ung, to satisfy her sexual hunger, but in doing so she incautiously affords the other wives a chance to avenge themselves. Hsüeh-o

and Li Chiao-erh inform against her, and the enraged Hsi-men immediately orders his servants to give the boy "thirty terrible stripes till his flesh was torn and the blood ran down his legs," and then dismisses him from service. But Lotus herself receives much lighter punishment: she is stripped of her clothes and commanded to kneel before her master to be cross-examined. Since the boy has already been harshly punished for his undeniable crime, one might logically expect Hsi-men to exact a confession from her: if he so wishes, he could beat her to death without incurring any legal difficulty. During the interrogation he does lash her once, but then he "looked again at the kneeling woman, her flower-like body unclothed. She was uttering piteous sounds and weeping so touchingly. His anger flew to Java, and with it all but a fraction of his determination to punish her." Then he beckons Plum Blossom to come over. As he asks her to confirm Lotus' lying words, he keeps on fondling her. His undignified manner of holding court indicates that Lotus' nudity has aroused him (hence his need to fondle Plum Blossom) and he questions the latter so as to get out of a difficult situation without losing face. In this round of battle with her master, Lotus is exposed to public shame and she will be from then on much more on her guard when having trysts with Ching-chi. But the fact that Hsi-men does not have the heart to give her due punishment shows that she still enjoys the upper hand.

Then, to the further advantage of Lotus, Hsi-men becomes much more mellowed as the novel progresses. He still seeks sexual diversity, but more out of habit than out of an inner compulsion. His outbursts of anger become fewer as he becomes increasingly inured to his social and official routine. As a lover, he is now more intent on impressing women with his sexual prowess and giving them pleasure than on receiving pleasure himself. An occasional sadist, he is almost masochistically resigned to punishing himself with strenuous dissipation. In time he shows a more accommodating disposition which finds satisfaction in doing favors for others. His cruel treatment of Vase for her marriage to Dr. Chiang may be said to represent his last imperious act of domestic despotism. Upon installing her as his sixth wife, he absents himself from her chamber for the first three nights. Highly humiliated, she attempts suicide on the third night but, still in a punishing mood the next evening, he whips her and orders her to kneel before him in her nakedness. From then on, however, he finds so much contentment in her love and devotion that he cannot help being humanized under her influence. Vase's great love for Hsi-men is not something easily reconcilable with her cruelty to her first two husbands: this change in her character is primarily dictated by plot requirements so that she may serve as a complete foil to the aggressive and selfish Lotus. But, psychologically speaking, it is not entirely implausible that she should undergo this transformation because, as she repeatedly tells Hsi-men, with him she has finally found sexual fulfillment. He is able to satisfy her as no one else has been, and out of her supreme gratitude she becomes a concerned and affectionate wife.

For Lotus, Vase constitutes the greatest threat to her continuing enjoyment of her privileged position. Quite unlike Vase, she uses her sex primarily as a weapon in the battle

A gathering of Hsi-men Ch'ing's household.

for domination and measures her security by the frequency of her husband's visits. She tolerates his desire for sexual diversity only so long as the objects of his attention pose no threat to that security. In chapters 11-50, she has two rivals besides Vase, neither quite so serious. The first is the courtesan Cassia (Li Kuei-chieh), Li Chiao-erh's niece, who takes herself seriously because Hsi-men is her first, deflowering patron. She engages Lotus in a minor feud but, with so many other minor characters to attend to, the novelist soon loses interest in her and she drops out of the competition after chapter 12. The other rival is the pathetic and simple-minded Hui-lien, whom Lotus regards as more dangerous because there is the possibility of her becoming the seventh wife and therefore sharing Hsi-men's favors with her on a legal basis. And she cannot stand her bragging about her improved status as a mistress. When Hui-lien's husband grumbles about his cuckoldom, therefore, it is Lotus who incites Hsi-men to take harsh measures against him. He is first maltreated in prison and then banished to his home town, and the heartbroken Hui-lien commits suicide as a result. Lotus gloats over this triumph.

But Vase is much harder to dispose of. She is a rich lady well liked by everybody whereas Lotus herself is a low-born slave generally detested in the household. Moreover, the fair-skinned Vase is a beauty in her own right, and

once Lotus whitens her own body in an attempt to lure Hsi-men from his new love. But not only is he genuinely fond of Vase and grateful for her money; she soon becomes pregnant whereas, despite her practice of black magic, Lotus remains childless after her two miscarriages. Powerless to score any advantage over her rival, she is reduced to making jeering remarks about her pregnant condition in front of their husband. Hsi-men, however, immediately puts a stop to her impudence by inflicting upon her a mild form of sadism (in chapter 27, generally regarded by Chinese readers as the most obscene chapter in the whole book). The form of her punishment, however, still expresses his fondness for her in that it merely serves him as an excuse for further sexual experimentation. But insofar as Lotus is denied equal partnership in the game, she is being punished. She suffers a temporary setback.

After Vase has given birth to a boy, Lotus feels keenly her total eclipse. In her desperation, she tries to win her man back with proofs of sexual solicitude or to persuade the other wives to turn against her rival. When nothing comes of these efforts, she punishes her own slave, the maid Chrysanthemum, often without the slightest provocation, to give vent to her frustration. The most shocking instance occurs in chapter 58 where her torture of Chrysanthemum serves at once to spite Vase and to aggravate the condition of her sickly baby, Kuan-ko. That evening Lotus has stepped on dog dung and her new shoes are soiled. With a heavy stick she first beats the guilty dog, whose howling wakes up the child in the adjacent suite of rooms. But she continues beating it for a while even after Vase has sent her maid Welcome Spring over to ask her to desist. Next, Lotus berates Chrysanthemum for having kept the dog in her compound at this late hour and orders her to come forward to examine the shoes:

> Tricked, she bent her head to look at them. Golden Lotus struck her face several times with one of the shoes until her lips were cut. Chrysanthemum drew back and tried to stop the blood with her hand.
>
> "You slave, so you want to get away from me, eh?" Golden Lotus cursed her. Then to Plum Blossom: "Drag her here and have her kneel down before me. Then get the whip and strip all her clothes off her. I will give her thirty stripes if she takes them nicely. If she tries to dodge, I'll whip her all over."
>
> Plum Blossom pulled off Chrysanthemum's clothes. Golden Lotus bade her hold the girl's hands, and the blows fell upon her like raindrops. That slave girl shrieked like a pig being killed.
>
> Kuan-ko had only just closed his eyes and now he was startled by the noise. This time Vase bade Embroidered Spring come to Golden Lotus, saying, "My mistress asks the Fifth Lady please to forgive Chrysanthemum. She is afraid the noise will frighten the baby."
>
> A little earlier, old woman P'an [Lotus' mother, who was paying a visit] was lying on the brick-bed in the inner room when she first heard the screams of Chrysanthemum. She hurriedly got up and asked her daughter to stop, but Golden Lotus would not listen to her. Now that Vase had sent Embroidered Spring over, she again came forward and tried to snatch the whip from her daughter's hand, saying, *"Chieh-chieh,* please don't beat her any more and give the lady over there cause to complain that you are trying to frighten her baby. I don't mind your breaking a stick over a donkey, but we must not harm that precious sapling."
>
> Golden Lotus was already wild enough, but when she heard her mother's words she was so inflamed with anger that her face turned purple. She pushed her mother away and the old woman all but fell down. "Old fool," she said, "you go over there and sit. This doesn't concern you and why do you want to interfere? What's all this crap about a precious sapling and breaking a stick over a donkey? You are in league with everyone else to injure me."
>
> "You thief, you will surely die an untimely death," retorted the old woman. "When did I behave like a spy? I came here only to beg a little cold food. How could you push me around like that!"
>
> "If you put in a word for her again, see if I don't fix that old bitch over there," Golden Lotus warned. "And I can tell you this: nobody is going to stew me in a pot and eat me up."
>
> Hearing her daughter scolding her so, old woman P'an went to her room and whimpered. Golden Lotus lashed Chrysanthemum twenty or thirty more times. Then she beat her with a stick until her skin and flesh were torn. Before she let the girl go, she drove her sharp nails into her cheeks and scratched them all over.
>
> All this time Vase could only cover the baby's ears with her hands. Tears coursed down her cheeks. She was furious but there was nothing she could do.

By this scene Lotus has already decided on her course of revenge: to kill Vase's son and deprive her of her major source of advantage. Since the child is especially susceptible to fright, she now trains a cat to pounce on him. Long plagued by illness, he succumbs to the traumatic experience.

Confronted with Lotus' second major act of treachery (her first being her adultery with Ch'in T'ung), Hsi-men acts with surprising timidity. Though both Vase and Moon Lady have no reason to doubt that Lotus has deliberately trained the cat to scare the boy, Hsi-men makes no attempt to find out the truth when informed of his critical condition:

> Hsi-men Ch'ing flew into a furious rage. He went straight to Golden Lotus' room and, without a word, took the cat by the legs and dashed out its brains on the stone flags underneath the eaves. There was a thud. The cat's brain was scattered like ten thousand peach blossoms, and its teeth like broken jade. Verily,
>
> No longer would it catch mice in the world of men,
> As it returned to the world of shades as a feline fairy.
>
> When Golden Lotus saw her cat destroyed, she just sat on her bed and did not stir once. But no sooner had he crossed her doorsill than she muttered a curse, "Thief, someday you will die a robber's death. If you dragged me out of here and killed me, you would indeed be a hero. But what had the cat done to you that you should rush in like one gone crazy and hurl him to his death? When he goes to the court in hell and demands his life from you, I hope you will then be prepared. You thief and fickle scoundrel, you will come to no good end."

Recall how, in dealing with her earlier adultery, Hsi-men has at least gone through the motions of an interrogation; at this more dangerous manifestation of her malignity, he merely vents his wrath on the cat without even bothering to ask her any question. Though at the moment he may be too upset to punish her, still, he never returns to this task following the death of his son. We may blame the novelist for his failure to provide a major scene of confrontation, but his quiet handling of the present scene may imply that Hsi-men is now too much aware of Lotus' power over him to want to challenge it. She remains thoroughly insolent, acting the part of an injured woman whose beloved pet has been unaccountably destroyed. Hsi-men appears to beat a hasty retreat as Lotus' muttered curses trail after him.

The death of her son has also completely broken Vase's spirit. She no longer cares to keep up her struggle against Lotus and resigns herself to ill-health and death, leaving Hsi-men disconsolate and Lotus in a position to regain her dominance. But, in the short run, the removal of her rival has the effect of further alienating Hsi-men from Lotus not because he bears her any grudge but because, in the clutches of grief, he wants to keep vigil in Vase's bedchamber and does not feel the usual sexual stimulation. Then, one night, out of his gratitude to the nurse-maid Ju-i (Heart's Delight, in Egerton's translation), who has remained doggedly loyal to her dead mistress, he takes her to bed with him and lets nature reassert itself. Lotus is amused but not alarmed: she cannot dominate him unless he takes an active interest in women. While still grieving for Vase, Hsi-men now spends his nights with Ju-i; the affectionate courtesan Moon-beam (Cheng Ai-yüeh-erh), certainly the most charming girl in the whole book; and, of course, Lotus. Then he takes his trip to the capital.

Lotus' specialty as a sex partner takes the form of fellatio or, in Chinese euphemism, *p'in-hsiao* (tasting or playing the flute). The night before Hsi-men takes off for the capital, he and Lotus play that game, indicating his increasingly passive role even in bed. Upon his return, he spends his first night with Lotus, but he cannot fall asleep even after he has made love to her. Since Lotus also remains unsatisfied, she again suggests the game of *p'in-hsiao* to prove her utter devotion to him. At the risk of offending the reader, I must quote the ensuing important passage which happens to be one of the most disgusting scenes in the novel:

> The woman made that suggestion for no other reason than to tie Hsi-men's heart to her. Moreover, he had been away from her for half a month; during all that time she had been so starved of sex that she was aflame with lust. Now that he was again with her, she wished she could enter his belly and stay there for good. So for the whole night she relished the flute without once letting it leave her mouth. When finally Hsi-men wanted to get off the bed to urinate, the woman still would not release the flute. . . . (pp. 186-95)

For emphasis, the author concludes the scene with a didactic comment:

> Readers, concubines are always ready to lead their husbands on and bewitch them. To this end, they will go to any length of shamelessness and endure anything no matter how revolting. Such practices would be abhorrent to a real wife properly married to her husband.

This episode, which could have been thought up only by a perverted genius, marks a new stage of Hsi-men's dotage. Apparently under the impression that Lotus really cares for him, from then on he spends most of his nights with her, to the consternation of his other wives, and she in turn becomes far more demanding and censorious of his behavior. A tired debauchee now occasionally complaining of aches in the groin and limbs, he almost has to get Lotus' permission to stay with other women. One evening he tells her that he is going to stay with Ju-i:

> "Why don't you undress?" she asked.

> He hugged her and smiled apologetically. "I came especially to tell you I am going over there tonight. Please give me that bundle of love-instruments."

> "You convict," the woman scolded him. "So you think you can hoodwink me and get by with a nice excuse. If I had not been waiting at the side door, you would have gone there already. You think you would then have asked for my permission? This morning you promised that slut that you would sleep with her tonight and tell stories about me. That's why you didn't send a maid here, but asked her to bring the fur coat herself and kowtow to me. That slut, what does she take me for, trying to play tricks on me that way! When Vase was alive, you treated me like dirt. You think I won't get mad just because you are going to her old nest with some other birdie?"

> "Who said I promised her anything?" Hsi-men Ch'ing said, again putting on a smile. "If she hadn't come and kowtowed to you, you would have had just as much cause to curse her."

> The woman deliberated for a long while and then said, "I will let you go, but you shall not take along that bundle. The things will all be filthy after you are through with that slut. Since you are going to sleep with me tomorrow anyway, let them stay clean."

> "But I am so accustomed to them I don't know what to do without them."

> Hsi-men Ch'ing badgered her for a long time, and she finally threw the silver clasp at him. "Take this thing if you must have it," she said. Hsi-men Ch'ing put it into his sleeve as he said, "This is better than nothing." Then he eagerly stepped out.

> The woman called him back. "Come here. I am talking to you. I suppose you are going to sleep with her in the same bed the whole night through? If you do so, even the two maids there will feel ashamed. You'd better stay a little while and then let her sleep elsewhere."

> "Who said I shall sleep with her long?" Hsi-men said. He was leaving again.

> Again the woman called him back. "Come here," she said, "I order you. Why are you in such a hurry?"

> "What do you want now?" Hsi-men Ch'ing said.

> "You can sleep with her only because I let you, but I forbid you to talk a lot of nonsense about me. If you do, you'll encourage her to be brazen in front of us. If I find out you have done anything of the sort, I will bite off your thing the next time you come to my room."

"Oh, you funny little whore," Hsi-men Ch'ing said, "how can I put up with so many of your instructions?" Then he went straight to that other place.

One perceives a changed tone in their relationship: Hsi-men is now the furtive and apologetic husband and Lotus the righteous, commanding wife who has him at her beck and call with such rude commands as "I am talking to you" and "I order you."

The next evening Lotus counts on Hsi-men's presence in her bedroom. According to the calendar, it is an auspicious night for getting pregnant, and she has prepared a special medicine for that purpose. But Hsi-men, after a busy day with his colleagues, is being detained in Moon Lady's room where other ladies of the house and women guests are gathered for a party. Impatient, Lotus goes straight to Moon Lady's suite to call him:

> Seeing that Hsi-men Ch'ing showed no sign of leaving, she stepped forward and pulled aside the curtain, saying, "If you are not coming, I shall go. I haven't patience to wait for you any longer."
>
> Hsi-men Ch'ing said, "My child, you go first. I will come when I've finished my wine." Golden Lotus went away.

Even for Lotus, this is unheard-of impudence: to charge into Moon Lady's room uninvited and try to drag their common husband away from her in front of all her guests. Little wonder the hitherto uncomplaining Moon Lady is provoked to pour forth in a magnificent tirade the accumulated resentments of the other wives against Lotus:

> Then Moon Lady said, "I don't want you to go to her. And I have something more to tell you. It looks as if you two were wearing only one pair of pants. What kind of manners are these to barge in like that and force you to leave! That shameless slut! She thinks that she alone is your wife and the rest of us nobodies, and you are contemptible enough to go along with her. No wonder people are criticizing you behind your back. We are all your wives and you ought to treat us decently. You needn't advertise the fact that that one in the front court has got you body and soul. Since you came back from the Eastern Capital, you haven't spent a single night in the inner courts. Naturally people are annoyed. You should put fire into the cold stove before you begin on the hot one, and you have no right to allow one woman to monopolize you. So far as I am concerned, it doesn't matter because I don't care for games of this sort. But the others can't stand it. They don't say anything but, however good-natured they are, they must feel resentful. Third Sister Meng didn't eat a thing all the time we were at Brother Ying's place. She probably caught a chill in the stomach and has been feeling nauseated ever since. Mistress Ying gave her two cups of wine, but she couldn't keep it down. You should really go and see her."

Hsi-men stays that night with Meng Yü-lou. But, even though her plans for the night remain unfulfilled, Lotus has affronted Moon Lady not thoughtlessly but deliberate-

ly, to advertise her improved position that can stand the combined assault of the other wives. Chapter 75, from which the preceding three excerpts have been taken, details their belated desperate attempts to curb her power. But their efforts come to little: Lotus is brought to give perfunctory apologies to Moon Lady but she retains her absolute dominion over their common husband.

By now Lotus is openly carrying on with Ching-chi whenever Hsi-men is not around to watch her. Precisely because Hsi-men himself is approaching his end (he dies in chapter 79), he seems to have partially recovered his zest for sexual conquest. His new mistress is Madame Lin, a lewd woman of the higher class, but for the first time in his life he is itching after something virtuous and unobtainable: the young and attractive wife of his newly arrived colleague, Captain Ho. The night during the Lantern Festival when he is keeping his tryst with Wang VI, remembrance of the beautiful image of Mrs. Ho gives him a semblance of passion and he is literally exhausted. He falls into a dead sleep as soon as he returns to Lotus' bed in the small hours of the night. Lotus, wide awake with lust, finds him completely limp and incapable of sexual combat. In deep frustration, she finally wakes him up to ask where the aphrodisiac pills are, empties out the last four pills in the box, and takes one herself. Though well aware that the normal dosage per night is one pill (and Hsi-men has already taken that pill in readiness for his bout with Wang VI), Lotus has him swallow all three with a cup of strong white liquor so as to restore his virility even in his state of extreme fatigue. Soon the pills take effect. She then sits astride his inert body, applies some aphrodisiac ointment to harden the erection, and hungrily seeks deep penetration. She reaches orgasm twice, wetting in all five towels. But the somnolent Hsi-men cannot release himself even though his thoroughly congested glans is now assuming the color of raw liver. Scared, Lotus sucks it with her mouth until a large quantity of semen finally squirts out.

> At first it was semen, and then it turned into a fluid composed mainly of blood, and there was no more hope for him. Hsi-men had fainted away, with his stiff limbs outstretched. Frightened, the woman hurriedly placed a few red dates in his mouth. But blood had followed semen and, now that the blood supply had been exhausted, his penis kept on squirting nothing but cold air until the ejaculatory motion stopped.

The author immediately adds to this grim passage a didactic summary of Hsi-men's career as follows:

> Gentle reader, a man's supply of vitality is limited even though there are no bounds to his desire for sexual pleasure. It is also said that the addict to sexual pleasure has shallow spiritual capacities. Hsi-men Ch'ing had abandoned himself to lust, not realizing that when the oil in a lamp is exhausted its light will fail and that when the marrow in his bones goes dry a man will die.

But even a short-lived rake doesn't necessarily have to die a horrible death. The ghastly account of Hsi-men's collapse, while supporting the didactic passage, actually gives the impression of his murder by an unfeeling and insatiable nymphomaniac. In the next few days, while the best doctors are being summoned to succor him, Lotus still takes advantage of his peculiar condition ("His swollen scrotum was large and shiny like an eggplant") to get sexual satisfaction: "His penis was firm as iron and day and night it stayed erect. At night, Lotus, who should have known better, would still sit astride him and have intercourse with him. And during a single night he would faint away and then regain consciousness several times over."

The cumulative use of explicit pornography has finally yielded an unmistakable moral interest—in her triumphant posture over a moribund body to extract the last few pleasurable moments out of it and in her total contempt for the person of Hsi-men Ch'ing, Lotus is herself exposed as a loathsome creature of utter depravity. But, ultimately, Lotus' triumph proves her undoing. If Hsi-men is her instrument of pleasure, he is more importantly her source of power and security. Without his protection, she will be again a slave girl defenseless against the world. But in her insane pursuit of momentary pleasure, she becomes quite reckless of her future, and the ultimate pathos of her life is that all her cunning and cruel schemes for assuring herself a favored position in the Hsi-men household have been designed to secure a steady supply of sexual pleasure. She sees nothing beyond sex.

In reviewing the highlights of this self-contained novel about Lotus and Hsi-men, we have seen that their relationship is informed neither by the sentiment of love nor by what we would normally call sexual passion. As Westerners understand it, passion demands exclusiveness: though for obvious reasons Lotus wants to monopolize Hsi-men, she does not seriously expect from him complete loyalty, nor is she loyal to him though, confined to the house under the jealous surveillance of all the womenfolk, she has far less opportunity for promiscuity than her husband. She takes a passing fancy to a boy servant and later forms a liaison with a son-in-law, practically the only man in the household besides her master who is not of the servant class. For both sensualists, their bond is mainly physical: with all his variety of erotic adventures, Hsi-men still regards Lotus as the most satisfactory bedfellow, and Lotus, with her limited association with men, cannot expect a sexual partner of greater virility. On the elementary level, therefore, theirs is the biological drama of animal copulation. While man appears initially more aggressive and domineering than woman, he is her biological inferior and is inevitably beaten in the unequal combat. On that level Lotus appears as the queen bee or black widow spider except that, in her conscious contrivance for pleasure, her rapacity has ceased to be procreative.

Their relationship further shows the degeneracy of love in a polygamous and promiscuous society. When a man can buy as many concubines and slave girls and enjoy as many mistresses and prostitutes as his money and strength incline him to, he tends to regard each of his acquisitions as a thing rather than as a person. (It is of interest to note that in China pornographic stories began as reports of life in a royal or imperial harem.) A concubine can, of course, secure the love of her husband with her infinite solicitude, as Vase does in the novel, but normally when a woman is

regarded by her master as a thing, she, too, loses sight of her humanity. The apparent irony that the slave girl Lotus should turn out to be far more evil than the slave master Hsi-men is therefore understandable. As a man of wealth and position, he receives so much flattering attention from his wives and mistresses, his friends and hangers-on, that he can afford to be pleased with himself and to appear good-natured and generous. Though obsessed with sex, he has so many business interests and official duties to attend to that he turns to his women in the evenings as an agreeable break in his routine. Moreover, as a social conformist, he has to be pleasant and polite to the outside world and maintain a facade of good manners. Lotus, on the other hand, enjoys none of these social advantages. Isolated from the outside world and living in a household of constant squabbles, she doesn't have to be pleasant and watch her manners (in contrast, the courtesans, because it is their job to entertain their customers, appear much more vivacious and courteous than the wives of Hsi-men). She pursues no cultural interests (except her occasional singing) and has no visitors of her own (except her mother). All her thoughts are therefore directed to the one object that redeems her dull and mean existence—her enjoyment of sex—and her life is further brutalized as a consequence.

Katherine Anne Porter once wrote that *Lady Chatterley's Lover* describes a life that is nothing "but a long, dull grey, monotonous chain of days, lightened now and then by a sexual bout." If this description is somewhat unfair to Lawrence's novel, it could be applied to *Chin P'ing Mei* with far greater justice except that the chain of days in the Hsi-men household is not lightened but rendered more ponderous by the high frequency of sexual combat. Lotus is so dead earnest about sex that its enjoyment leaves no room for spontaneous and carefree fun. She is at nearly all times so grimly occupied that one is almost startled to find her in a rare moment of thoughtless merriment. In chapter 15, while on a visit to Vase's house during the Lantern Festival, Lotus stays upstairs to watch the street sights below:

> Golden Lotus, Meng Yü-lou, and two singing-girls continued to look out the window at the fair.
>
> Golden Lotus rolled up the sleeves of her white-silk outer jacket to show off the sleeves of her inner jacket which were embroidered all over with gold thread. She further displayed her ten fingers, all lustrous and daintily shaped like stalks of scallion. On them were six gold rings in the form of stirrups. Leaning half out of the window, she cracked melon seeds with her teeth and threw the shells at the people in the street. She laughed with Yü-lou all the time. Now and again she would point to something in the street and say excitedly, "Big sister, come and look at the pair of hydrangea-lanterns under the eaves of that house. They whirl back and forth and up and down so prettily." Then: "Second sister, come and look at the big fish-lantern hanging from the lantern-frame by the gate opposite our house. Dangling from that big fish are so many little fish, turtles, shrimps, and crabs. They move about in unison so gaily." Then she called Yü-

Hsi-men Ch'ing's garden.

lou, "Third sister, look over there at the grandma-lantern and grandpa-lantern."

Suddenly a gust of wind made a large hole in the
lower part of the grandma-lantern, and Golden
Lotus laughed unceasingly.

In this scene Lotus is still new in the Hsi-men household
and she flaunts her beauty without guile and retains the
natural grace of a child in her gleeful enjoyment of the
sights. The child in her rarely emerges after that. For
Lotus as for most other members of that household, it is
their willing forfeiture of innocence through their preoccupation with pleasure, security, or salvation that spells
the boredom and horror of their existence. (pp. 195-202)

> *C. T. Hsia, "Chin P'ing Mei," in his* The Clas-
> sic Chinese Novel: A Critical Introduction,
> *Columbia University Press, 1968, pp. 165-202.*

Katherine Carlitz   (essay date 1986)

[*Carlitz has written extensively on* Chin p'ing mei. *In
the following excerpt, she asserts that the primary intent
of the novel is to emphasize that neglecting the Confucian concept of self-cultivation results in social and political dissipation, as evinced in the novel's treatment of the
dissolute Hsi-men household and the corrupt last court
of the Sung dynasty.*]

The Chinese fiction that criticized the emperor was traditionally set in his inner court, the rooms he shared with
eunuchs and concubines, concealed from his subjects. The
emperor's sexual excesses might be given in lurid detail,
but he was still a being apart from the people, living in a
court that most of his subjects would never see. *Chin p'ing
mei,* by contrast, is set in a household at the middle of the
traditional social scale, a milieu familiar to the urban
dweller of comfortable means. Nevertheless, *Chin p'ing
mei* brings as strong an indictment against the government
of the day as any conventional satire on the emperor himself. By focusing on the Hsi-men family, who imitate their
superiors and in turn corrupt their servants, the author
calls up the weight of Confucian tradition. In this tradition, rulers are implicated when their subjects rebel; disarray among the people is an implicit sign of misgovernment
by the court. "Morals and customs are inextricably linked
to government," warned Ho Liang-chün in his *Cheng-su*
(On the Reform of Morals and Customs), turning his attention from drama and song to the degenerate customs
of his day. Ho tactfully excused the reigning emperor from
responsibility for the debacle, but warned in the next
breath that the decline in morals prefigured the imminent
end of another dynastic cycle. A variety of clues in the text
suggest that *Chin p'ing mei* was meant to convey the same
message. We will turn below to the image of the ruler in
popular literature and in *Chin p'ing mei,* but first let us examine the basic texts in which the ruler's traditional au-

thority and responsibilities are set forth. In fundamentally Confucian fashion, these texts link the fortunes of the state to individual sincerity and self-cultivation. And as we shall see, they provided the explicit categories for a great deal of the practical advice that was given to the emperor.

Confucian texts establish the link between family and state by defining essential social relations in terms of the family or extensions of the family. Filial piety trains the son for service to the emperor, fraternal loyalty is the basis for friendship, and so on. Foremost among these texts is the *Ta-hsüeh,* one of the Four Books of the Ming examination curriculum, and thus memorized by every aspirant to official success. The brief text of the *Ta-hsüeh* begins by stating the three goals of self-cultivation, and follows them with an eight-point program for the achievement of these goals. The *Ta-hsüeh* amplifies and systematizes concepts found in earlier and contemporary writings; it was not the only source of these ideas either at the time of its formulation in the Han or during the centuries in which it was central to Confucian education. But it is perfectly representative of those ideas, and its conciseness and wide currency in the intellectual world of the Ming make it appropriate for a discussion of the relation between state and household, as perceived by the author and audience of **Chin p'ing mei.** The central ideas of the *Ta-hsüeh* are contained in the following passages, with which the text begins:

> The way of the Great Learning consists in clearly exemplifying illustrious virtue, in loving the people, and in resting in the highest good.
>
> Only where one knows where one is to rest can one have a fixed purpose. Only with a fixed purpose can one achieve calmness of mind. Only with calmness of mind can one attain serene repose. Only in serene repose can one carry on careful deliberation. Only through careful deliberation can one have achievement. Things have their roots and branches; affairs have their beginning and end. He who knows what comes first and what comes last comes himself near the Way.
>
> The ancients who wished clearly to exemplify illustrious virtue throughout the world would first set up good government in their states. Wishing to govern well their states, they would first regulate their families. Wishing to regulate their families, they would first cultivate their persons. Wishing to cultivate their persons, they would first rectify their minds. Wishing to rectify their minds, they would first seek sincerity in their thoughts. Wishing for sincerity in their thoughts, they would first extend their knowledge. The extension of knowledge lay in the investigation of things. For only when things are investigated is knowledge extended; only when knowledge is extended are thoughts sincere; only when thoughts are sincere are minds rectified; only when minds are rectified are our persons cultivated; only when our persons are cultivated are our families regulated; only when families are regulated are states well-governed; and only when states are well-governed is there peace in the world.

The remainder of the text is an exegesis of this program,

with supporting quotations from earlier classics, and edifying examples from the lives of sage emperors. The text is quite clear on the responsibilities of rulership, as we can see from the following passage:

> If one family [that is to say, the family of the ruler] exemplifies humanity, humanity will abound in the whole country. If one family exemplifies courtesy, courtesy will abound in the whole country. On the other hand, if one man exemplifies greed and wickedness, rebellious disorder will arise in the whole country. Therein lies the secret. Hence the proverb: One word ruins an enterprise; one man determines the fate of an empire.

This was not meant to undercut the bureaucratic apparatus that already existed in the Han; on the contrary, one of the ways in which the ruler manifests his humanity is by choosing wise ministers. But the emperor is at the apex of this pyramid of influence. Thus in all periods when Confucianism dominated Chinese political discourse, the emperor's observance of appropriate rites, his choice of a mate and his veneration of his ancestors, were considered central to the success of his government.

Specific advice was therefore given to him on these topics. One splendid example, dating from the Sung, is the *Ta-hsüeh yen-i* (Extended Meaning of the Great Learning) of Chen Te-hsiu (1178-1235). Chen's commentary on the slender *Ta-hsüeh* fills several fat volumes with illustrations of virtue and cautionary tales of emperors who brought their states to collapse. A product of the Sung Neo-Confucian revival, the *Ta-hsüeh yen-i* spends far fewer pages on the actual government of the state than it does on the self-cultivation necessary to govern the state. It seems to have been assumed that a properly edified emperor would govern properly. Regulation of the family is the immediate precondition in the *Ta-hsüeh* for governing the state, and as such it concludes and dominates the second half of the *Ta-hsüeh yen-i.* Popular literature tells us how dangerous it is for the royal ladies to quarrel, or for the wrong sort of woman to be elevated above her palace colleagues. Here in the *Ta-hsüeh yen-i* we learn just who the wrong sort of woman is likely to be, and where the susceptibilities of an amorous but misguided emperor are likely to lead. The empress bears (or, at the very least, educates) the crown prince, and is in a position to admonish the emperor. The choice of a proper empress is thus "the great affair of the nation," the fundamental affair of state. Breeding tells: she must not be a singing-girl, like Empress Chao of Han Ch'eng-ti (r. 32-6 B.C.), who brought his family line to an end. (The text reminds us that the bad last rulers of the three legendary dynasties of antiquity also chose singing-girls as their consorts.) The example she sets makes her the mother of the empire. There must be no confusion in the hierarchy of empress, consorts, and concubines, and the emperor must at all costs avoid partiality to a favorite concubine or her son. His failure to do so would put the imperial succession in question, inviting faction and intrigue. (Numerous examples are given.) This is a specific (and central) instance of household disorder leading directly to calamity at the level of the state. The interdependence of household and state are further underscored by quotations from the *Li chi* (Records of Ritual) and standard commentaries in which an exact parallel is drawn between the "Six Palaces" of the Empresses, and the "Six Ministries" of the bureaucracy. In the Six Palaces, the emperor's three consorts, nine secondary wives, twenty-seven palace ladies, and eighty-one concubines constitute his "inner government," while in the Six Ministries, his three dukes, nine censors, twenty-seven *ta-fu*, and eighty-one *yüan-shih* constitute his "outer government." Though this perfect numerical parallel is the idealized description of antiquity, not corresponding to actual practice in either Han or Sung, it serves to emphasize the importance for the entire empire of regulating the "inner government," the royal family. (The eunuchs, another component of the "inner government," must also be properly restrained.) The *Ch'un-ch'iu* (Spring and Autumn Annals) is quoted to the effect that the three primary sources of social disorder are *ping-hou* (placing empresses and other palace ladies on the same footing), *p'i-ti* (ranking concubines with the legitimate first wife), and *liang-cheng* (the usurpation of the emperor's power by his ministers). Inner and outer government must be ruled by the same hierarchical principles.

In the Ming, a massive "supplement" to the *Ta-hsüeh yen-i* appeared, the *Ta-hsüeh yen-i pu* (Supplement to the Extended Meaning of the Great Learning) of Ch'iu Chün (1420-1495). More practical and less speculative than Chen Te-hsiu, Ch'iu Chün devoted his treatise to the last two points of the *Ta-hsüeh* program: governing the state and pacifying all under heaven. The *Ta-hsüeh yen-i*, drawing its models primarily from remote history, warns the emperor against any deviation from the ideal conduct and standards of the ancients. The *Ta-hsüeh yen-i pu*, by contrast, instructs the emperor on numerous practical matters, ranging from village rites and sacrificial customs to the conduct of the border defenses. But Ch'iu Chün begins his monumental treatise on the government of the state with a section on the regulation of the court, and that section begins with a subsection on putting the canonical familial relations in order.

The *Ta-hsüeh yen-i* was reprinted during the Ming, and it was also brought to the attention of Ming readers by Ch'iu Chün's preface, which discusses the earlier work. Ch'iu Chün's own treatise is extant in a Wan-li edition of 1605. These two explications demonstrate a habit of thought that will be central to our analysis of **Chin p'ing mei**, namely, that it apparently made sense in Sung and Ming China to ask how the program of the *Ta-hsüeh* would work in actual practice, and to illustrate it with examples. Moreover, one need not have been an educated reader of the classics to assimilate the central ideas of the *Ta-hsüeh*, as a glance at fiction and drama will show.

In 1967, farmers in Kiangsu province found among the artifacts in a well-preserved tomb a collection of *shuo-ch'ang tz'u-hua* (*chantefable*) tales published during the Ch'eng-hua era (1465-1478) of the Ming. The collection is a luxury edition, clearly printed and copiously illustrated. The tales are not the sort of literature we associate with scholars. With their limited and highly formulaic vocabulary, they are examples of the popular *chantefable* literature.

The tales were found buried in the grave of what is thought to have been a low-ranking official's wife, and we may conjecture that books of this sort were read by those of limited literacy in any household wealthy enough to buy books for recreation. For our purposes, the most interesting of these tales is *Shih-lang fu-ma chuan* (The Biography of Imperial Son-in-Law Shih.)

This tale is a fictional account of the fall of the Posterior T'ang dynasty (923-936). The Shih-lang of the title is Shih Ching-t'ang (892-942), first emperor of another short-lived dynasty, the Posterior Chin (936-947), during the period of disunion that followed the T'ang. The tale is cast in a conventional mold: Lu Wang (Li Ts'ung-k'o, 885-936), the "bad last emperor" of the Posterior T'ang, shows himself unfit to rule, and is supplanted by a leader of unquestionable moral authority, Shih Ching-t'ang. Lu Wang proves his unfitness to rule by the havoc he creates within his own family, preferring the upstart Empress, a former singing-girl, to his own sister the Princess. The Princess, moreover, is the wife of the valorous Shih-lang, on whom the border defenses depend.

In the incident that ultimately causes his downfall, Lu Wang sends the Princess to make a courtesy call on the Empress. The Empress refuses to acknowledge her presence for half a day. The two women quarrel over who is constrained by ritual to bow first. The quarrel ends in a shouting-match and fistfight, from which the maids extract their respective ladies. The Empress then gives Lu Wang a highly embroidered account of the incident, including the charge that his sister has insulted Lu Wang himself. Lu Wang imprisons the Princess, who says darkly that he is unfit to rule, if he would harm his own flesh and blood on the strength of tales brought by the upstart Empress. A virtuous minister makes the same complaint, and Lu Wang releases the Princess. By this time, however, she is bent on revenge, and she sends for Shih-lang, who besieges the imperial city, defeats the Empress's brother in single combat, has the Empress put to death, and establishes himself on the throne.

The state, it is clear, is only as secure as the familial tie between Shih-lang and the Emperor. Almost the entire tale is set within the Emperor's immediate family and court. The actors are bound to each other as ruler and minister, as husband and wife, or as siblings. The Emperor transgresses the loyalty due a virtuous member of his own family (it is clear that the upstart Empress does not merit his fidelity), and he loses his empire in consequence. As the Princess and Shih-lang say in separate, nearly identical speeches, governing a household is like governing a country; household and state are to be ruled in just the same fashion.

Moreover, it is clear from Shih-lang's and the Princess's speeches that misconduct on the Emperor's part is a sort of moral poison, which will inevitably infect the entire society. Both Shih-lang and the Princess warn that if the Emperor deviates a whit from proper conduct, the world will fall into disorder, and they themselves cannot be expected to behave in a moral fashion. His actions, the tale makes clear, have freed them to topple the throne, an action justifiable only when an emperor's conduct has already effectively corrupted society.

Shih-lang fu-ma chuan thus illustrates simply but forcefully the teaching that the family must be regulated before the state can be governed. Shih-lang and the Princess also remind us that the emperor sets a pattern for those below him. In *Shih-lang fu-ma chuan,* far removed from the examination curriculum or philosophical debate, these ideas are not scrutinized or developed. They function simply as accepted criteria for judgment, needing no justification. They function in similarly unexamined fashion in the tag-ends and doggerel verses found throughout Ming fiction and drama. In the play *Huan-tai chi* (The Return of the Belts), for example, a general sings that his banners and troops are arrayed for battle, and he is answered with shouts of

> Execute the rebels!
> Put the *kang-ch'ang* (canonical relations) in order!

In a Wan-li (1573-1620) edition of the anonymous *ch'uan-ch'i Yü-huan chi* (The Jade Ring), the passing observation of a military official links family to state in a similar fashion:

> My life has been spent in the administration of my household and the empire.

Both of these works are mentioned in **Chin p'ing mei,** and the novel is filled with hints that the author intended us to recall the conventional Confucian teachings on family and state, though the emperor himself makes only the briefest of appearances. The venal court that the novel portrays has clearly forfeited its mandate over what has become a society of merchants and prostitutes. Let us now examine the ways in which **Chin p'ing mei** holds the court responsible for this moral decline. We will see that the traditional Confucian chain of authority is a central theme of the book.

It must be noted, first, that the government of the mature Ming dynasty was structured in such a way as to insure Confucian criticism of its excesses. The emperor held unprecedented power in the Ming autocracy, but the bureaucratic functions of government were carried out by a class of Confucian scholars whose weight in the government was equally unprecedented. Early Ming emperors had turned to this group of Confucian scholars for practical rather than ideological reasons: they needed a pool of competent, literate officials, and the Confucian officials stood ready to hand. The nobles and military officials, alternate elites progressively displaced by the Confucian scholars, were simply less competent to administer a large peacetime empire. Early Ming emperors sought to mould the scholars' thinking by bringing them all to the bureaucracy through the examination system [which was a requirement for entry into the civil service], but this strategy inadvertently fostered a kind of class solidarity among Confucian scholars. Their sense of membership in a powerful group encouraged certain of them to draw on their tradition to criticize the government that had empowered them. The emperors excised the Mencian right to rebellion against unkingly rule from the standard examination

texts, but we have seen from the *Shih-lang fu-ma chuan* that they could not excise it from the popular consciousness. Thus they could not possibly excise it from the consciousness of well-educated, widely-read Confucian scholars. . . . [There are] reasons for thinking that **Chin p'ing mei** was probably written by someone of this class, so it is not surprising that we find the Confucian chain of influence emphasized in this novel, constituting an implied rebuke to the government of the day. The transgressions of Hsi-men Ch'ing and his family are never presented in such a way that individual punishment would cure the problem. They are always linked to the example set by superiors.

Chin p'ing mei is set almost entirely within a single household, and thus emphasizes the canonical relations of ruler, subject, and family in Confucian tradition. Never for a chapter are we away from their definition and violation. While Ming *hua-pen* tales were not uncommonly set within a single family, such a setting was unprecedented in the novel-length fiction of the Ming. The recognized classics of the genre were episodic; the world was seen in them through the eyes of the traveler, the soldier, the stopper-at-inns. Even in the *ch'uan-ch'i* dramas that explicitly celebrated the canonical relations, the typical plot involved the separation of the hero from his family, to undergo a series of trials before their eventual reunion. It seems reasonable to suppose that the author of **Chin p'ing mei** knew that he was creating a new sort of narrative structure, which could demonstrate more effectively than the *ch'uan-ch'i* of the day the force of the ruler's example. The head of the Hsi-men household becomes a minor official, and in his administration of justice he is self-interested and ruthless. These qualities he learns directly from his official superiors, with whom he is in contact throughout the narrative.

His fortunes are linked primarily to those of Ts'ai Ching (1046-1126), successively Secretary of the Board of Revenue and Senior Tutor to the Heir Apparent. Ts'ai falls from power shortly after Hsi-men Ch'ing's death. His fall demonstrates the insecurities of patronage, a lesson Hsi-men Ch'ing ought to have learned early in the novel from the fall of his kinsman Yang Chien, another of Sung Hui-tsung's ministers. (Hsi-men Ch'ing is related to Yang Chien through the marriage of his daughter). In Chapter 17, Yang Chien is impeached for inadequate military preparations; the same memorial goes on to cite the irregularities in the Hsi-men household and to demand punishment. The accusations against Yang Chien and Hsi-men Ch'ing are both placed in the context of dangers menacing the empire, which is likened to a body, ravaged from within and therefore unable to withstand invasions from without. Hsi-men Ch'ing has already obtained Ts'ai Ching's intercession in Chapter 10, to shield him from the consequences of murder. A similar appeal and gifts to Ts'ai Ching assure Hsi-men Ch'ing's safety after the fall of Yang Chien in Chapter 17, and by Chapter 25, Hsi-men Ch'ing's apparent power is such that the salt merchants in his region send gifts to him, to procure his intercession on their behalf with Ts'ai Ching. Hsi-men Ch'ing becomes the conduit for bribes in his own district, a miniature Ts'ai Ching. In Chapter 30, a midwife surnamed Ts'ai delivers

Li P'ing-erh's child, Hsi-men Ch'ing's first son Kuan-ko ("Official Elder Brother"), just as Ts'ai Ching "delivers" his first official post to Hsi-men Ch'ing in response to elaborate birthday gifts. The favoritism shown the son gives rise to the jealousy that will endanger the family line when the boy is murdered, just as the sins of the bureaucracy, for which the boy is named, bring down the empire at the close of the book.

We come to know certain of the corrupt officials quite well, as Hsi-men Ch'ing is repeatedly their host: Ts'ai Ching's adopted son Ts'ai Yün, given first prize in the civil service examination after the actual prizewinner is deposed through political intrigue; An Ch'en, the original prizewinner, who oversees the construction of Sung Hui-tsung's mausoleum, built with the proceeds of excessive taxation; and the eunuch chamberlains Liu and Hsüeh, incredulous at the folly of censors willing to endanger themselves by remonstrating with the emperor. Hsi-men Ch'ing extorts money from the brother of Chamberlain Liu, convicted of using imperial timber in the construction of a private dwelling; in the following chapter, he uses imperial tiles in the construction of his own elaborate mausoleum. In Chapter 49, the virtuous Censor Tseng links Hsi-men Ch'ing to Ts'ai Ching once again, as he criticizes both Hsi-men Ch'ing (for his pardon of the murderous servant Miao Ch'ing) and Ts'ai Ching (for his suggestions for governmental reorganization). The censor is cashiered for his pains, and severely disciplined, in the same manner as Hsi-men Ch'ing has unjustly flogged, jailed, or exiled various innocent characters who have come before him for judgment. Hsi-men Ch'ing himself visits the capital in Chapters 70 and 71, and is singled out for recognition by Chu Mien (d. 1126), another canonical "bad last minister" of the Sung emperor. His perfect conformity to the corrupt standards of the day is underscored in Chapters 65 and 66, when the same eminent Taoist offers a funeral service for Hsi-men Ch'ing's wife Li P'ing-erh, and conducts a sacrifice for the welfare of the court.

Events within the household mirror the pattern of corrupt intercession in the world outside, as we see from the constant juxtaposition of the two spheres. The memorial in Chapter 17, likening the empire to an unhealthy body, caps an account of the sexual, financial, and judicial irregularities attending Hsi-men Ch'ing's marriage to Li P'ing-erh. In Chapters 34 and 35, Ying Po-chüeh helps to settle a court-case by having the homosexual servant Shu-t'ung intercede with Hsi-men Ch'ing through Li P'ing-erh. Hsi-men Ch'ing's visit to the capital is followed in Chapter 72 by accounts of dreadful quarrels in his absence: the wives vie as savagely for access to him as do competing factions at court for access to the emperor. When the household and the border defenses weaken in the period after Hsi-men Ch'ing's death, Wu Yüeh-niang herself becomes sexually vulnerable. Her son-in-law Ch'en Ching-chi becomes suggestive and irreverent. She is the victim of an attempted rape at the temple where she fulfills vows made at the time of Hsi-men Ch'ing's death, and she relinquishes her son Hsiao-ko ("Filial Elder Brother") in the final chapter after a nightmare in which she is nearly raped by the boy's intended father-in-law.

Just as officials at court provide models for Hsi-men Ch'ing, so Hsi-men Ch'ing sets the tone for his household. His wife Yüeh-niang reminds him repeatedly that "When the ridgepole is crooked, the rafters run awry," but he is deaf to her warnings. The infractions that he punishes are often patterned on his own: in Chapter 22, for example, he begins a flirtation with the maid Sung Hui-lien, but the musician Li Ming is abused and expelled for allegedly attempting the same sort of seduction of P'an Chin-lien's maid Ch'un-mei. And in Chapter 76, the *hsiu-ts'ai* Tutor Wen is driven ignominiously from the household for engaging in the very homosexual acts that we have seen Hsi-men Ch'ing practice since he was given the servant Shu-t'ung in honor of his first official post. When Hsi-men Ch'ing seduces Sung Hui-lien, her husband Lai Wang lays the blame on P'an Chin-lien, whose dress and hairstyles Sung Hui-lien has been imitating. Lai Wang recalls that P'an Chin-lien entered the household by responding sexually to the master, and he fears that his own wife has now done the same. In the meantime he himself has imitated his master by committing adultery with the despised fourth wife Sun Hsüeh-o.

In Chapters 46 and 75, the Hsi-men ladies go out to pay calls, and in their absence the maidservants make similar visits of their own, with drinking, games, and entertainment. The status differences that the maids perceive among themselves are thrown into relief during these visits, recalling the constant quarrels between the wives, whose effective status within the household is based on wealth and degree of access to Hsi-men Ch'ing.

The book's last twenty chapters show the continuing force of Hsi-men Ch'ing's example after his death, as various lesser characters who had been associated with him attempt petty tyrannies of their own. His employee Han Tao-kuo makes off with the profits from his cloth trade; the servant Lai Pao rapes the maidservants he is delivering to Chai Ch'ien. Ch'en Ching-chi, the son-in-law to whom Hsi-men Ch'ing had once promised his power and his property, is murdered in Ch'un-mei's bed. He is Hsi-men Ch'ing's "son," and Ch'un-mei, given the pseudo-kinship relation of mistress to maid, is P'an Chin-lien's "daughter." (Ch'en Ching-chi is then mourned by Han Ai-chieh, the daughter of Hsi-men Ch'ing's mistress Wang Liu-erh.) Those at the bottom of this pyramid of influence and power finally turn against their masters. P'an Chin-lien's despised servant Ch'iu-chü bears the tales that lead to the expulsion of P'an Chin-lien and Ch'un-mei from the household. The second wife Li Chiao-erh foments a quarrel, returns to the brother where Hsi-men Ch'ing had originally found her, and marries a rival of his. Sun Hsüeh-o, who has for years been a maid of all work to the other wives, runs off with Lai Wang, taking with her a share of the household goods. (She is captured and sold as a servant to Ch'un-mei, now the wife of a military commander; so far are the original fortunes of mistresses and maids reversed.) It is the genius of this novel not to condemn these characters, but rather to make clear how it is that they have been driven to their actions. In the words of a proverb that occurs more than once in ***Chin p'ing mei,*** "When authority fails, servants will scorn their masters." Hsi-men Ch'ing's personal prestige masks the actual weakness of authority within his household, a weakness apparent as soon as he dies, when those who had been his servants rise to positions of influence and ignore or patronize his remaining family. (When Ch'un-mei, wealthy and pregnant, pays a visit in Chapter 96, we see the once elegant Hsi-men garden overgrown and in decay.)

The revolt of the oppressed in *Chin p'ing mei* can be read as a warning to the rulers of the day, and this warning becomes even clearer when we turn to suggestions in the text that Hsi-men Ch'ing is a miniature emperor himself. The events of the Chia-ching and Wan-li reign periods subtly color this tale, though no emperor actually speaks from its pages.

The treatment of the last Northern Sung court in *Chin p'ing mei* levels an implicit criticism at the government of the day. We know from fiction and drama that the court of Sung Hui-tsung (r.1100-1126) was a byword, in the late Ming, for misgovernment and abuse of power. The villains controlling the empire in *Chin p'ing mei* are the stock group of Sung Hui-tsung's evil ministers. The ruin of the empire in the novel results from the usual sins described in fiction and drama: the self-aggrandizement of corrupt officials, excessive taxation for unnecessary and capricious building projects, the muzzling of upright officials who speak the truth. This is the canonical list of sins ascribed to the degenerate last court of any dynasty. *Chin p'ing mei*, however, describes the Ming society of the author's day, as is clear from allusion to Ming administrative geography, Ming titles and insignia, and—most easily apparent—Yuan and Ming drama and song. Occasionally, historical Ming figures are mentioned in the book's quotations from "official" documents. This actual Ming setting has been understood since the novel's first appearance, and it associates the ruling dynasty with a particular "bad last court" of history and legend.

The structure of the Hsi-men household associates Hsi-men Ch'ing with this "bad last court." The parallels drawn in the *Li Chi* between wives and ministers, inner and outer government, have been noted above in the discussion of the *Ta-hsüeh yen-i*. There, the Six Palaces of the empresses and the Six Ministries of the officials are shown to be analogous to one another. In *Chin p'ing mei*, Hsi-men Ch'ing presides over a yamen, in which the *liu-fang* (six chambers) represent the Six Ministries at the local level. The pleasantry of a visiting nun in Chapter 21 reminds us of the numerical correspondence between the *liu-fang* and Hsi-men Ch'ing's six wives, as she tells a joke whose point is just this correspondence. Lest we forget the link between the *liu-fang* and the Six Ministries, the author has Ying Po-chüeh remind us in Chapter 31 that all officials, from the first to the ninth rank, are equally responsible to the throne. The analogy between virtuous wives and virtuous ministers is a staple of the classical tradition, and as we watch Hsi-men Ch'ing's six quarrelling wives we see a model for the factional strife that divided the Wan-li court. If the Hsi-men household is a miniature court (or indeed, a miniature empire, given the servants who are governed by Hsi-men Ch'ing and his wives), then Hsi-men Ch'ing is its emperor. He is a bad emperor in the classical mold: two of his wives (P'an Chin-lien and Li

Chiao-erh) have been trained as singing-girls; he is intemperate and devoted to sensual pleasure; and he neglects his legitimate first wife for a concubine. His open preference for P'an Chin-lien or Li P'ing-erh at different points in the novel makes it impossible for the first wife Wu Yüeh-niang to regulate her household. Most damaging is the favoritism shown Li P'ing-erh after she conceives Hsi-men Ch'ing's first son. *Chin p'ing mei* quotes from drama and song in such a way as to suggest that the resulting jealous quarrels are to be read as court drama.

On at least nine occasions, songs are sung for Hsi-men Ch'ing or his wives that either offer congratulations to the emperor or express gratitude for imperial favor. Most telling is the appearance of these "imperial" songs in Chapters 43 through 58, where they combine with allusions to drama to suggest that Hsi-men Ch'ing's son Kuan-ko be viewed as the "crown prince" of the household, and P'an Chin-lien's murder of him as the work of a jealous empress. At the time of Kuan-ko's birth, P'an Chin-lien refers sarcastically to the infant as a "crown prince," and it has been observed that snatches of dialogue from *Ju-i chün chuan* (The Lord of Perfect Satisfaction), a Ming classical tale of the T'ang empress Wu Tse-t'ien, are given to P'an Chin-lien in Chapter 27, the chapter in which she learns that Li P'ing-erh has conceived a child. In Chapter 31, visiting eunuchs call for a song, in the baby's honor, from the *tsa-chü Pao chuang-ho* (Carrying the Dressing-Case). They are reproved for choosing a song whose performance would be inauspicious, as the play is a tale of a crown prince menaced by a jealous empress. In Chapter 43, when Kuan-ko is betrothed to a neighbor's daughter, two songs of gratitude for imperial favor are sung. They follow the statement by a prominent visitor (a kinswoman to the consort of the Heir Apparent) that "even the emperor takes commoners as his concubines!" In Chapter 58, the chapter before P'an Chin-lien has her cat frighten the infant to death, she herself calls for the performance of such a song. The birth of a son to Li P'ing-erh is the event that motivates much of the action of the novel from Chapter 27 until her death in Chapter 62. The Taoist ceremonies associated with the baby and his mother recall the Taoist enthusiasm of the Chia-ching emperor, and the "succession problem" suggested by P'an Chin-lien's repeated questioning of the baby's legitimacy can be seen in its full significance when we recall the succession problem at the Wan-li court.

The Wan-li emperor refused for over a decade to designate as heir apparent his eldest son, borne to him by a maid in service to the empress. He did not, despite the urging of the court, designate the mother of his eldest son as his Imperial Consort. The honor went instead to Cheng Kuei-fei (ca.1568-1630), the palace lady who became his obvious favorite, and whose son he was suspected of wishing to choose as his heir. The emperor's conduct was denounced in handbills and anonymous manifestos on the streets of Peking. The succession problem thus was not a matter internal to the palace. It agitated the capital and was laid to rest only when Cheng Kuei-fei's son reached his majority and was sent to live on a distant princely estate. The controversy weakened the court by calling the emperor's moral authority into question. The emperor's refusal to designate an heir apparent was perceived as a violation of the prescribed hierarchy, resulting from his infatuation with a concubine. Historical accounts of the controversy adhere to the traditional categories of such works as the *Ta-hsüeh yen-i,* and we must recall that whatever causes modern historians uncover for the weakness of the Wan-li throne, the succession controversy was perceived by contemporaries as central to this weakness. This perception, in turn, shaped events: if accountability within the bureaucracy was predicated on the emperor's maintaining a certain hierarchical order, his authority and that of those who held their authority in his name would be eroded if he did not. The Wan-li controversy spanned the decades in which *Chin p'ing mei* was written, and the book, with its six quarrelling consorts and its crown prince, calls the whole affair forcibly to mind. (The singing-girl Cheng Ai-yüeh, whom Hsi-men Ch'ing patronizes, has the same surname as the Wan-li emperor's favorite, and Ch'en Ching-chi, who is Hsi-men Ch'ing's surrogate in the last twenty chapters of the novel, patronizes another singing-girl whose surname is changed from Feng to Cheng, for no other apparent reason than to emphasize the surname Cheng. And Hsi-men Ch'ing's first son will be reborn into a Cheng household!)

Other fiction of the age also took the emperor to task. But a comparison with *Sui Yang-ti yen-shih,* supposedly modeled on the Wan-li emperor's career, shows us the striking novelty of *Chin p'ing mei,* whose critique of the emperor is set outside the court altogether. By choosing to focus on the Hsi-men household, the author could simultaneously adumbrate the reigning emperor and show the effect of his conduct on his subjects. He does not do this by giving us a disguised catalogue of specific political abuses. He goes, instead, to the ideological root of these abuses: the violation of hierarchy and the refusal of the ruler to rule.

In the fictional stereotype of the bad last ruler, this abdication of responsibility is conventionally coupled with sexual excess. The author of *Chin p'ing mei* followed this pattern in his creation of Hsi-men Ch'ing, as we will see below. The sexual behavior described in the novel is thus part of the cautionary design of the work.

Chin p'ing mei has long been plagued by critics who either discount it as a work of pornography, or celebrate it as a bawdy classic that affirms the sexuality it describes. This second reading runs directly counter to the norms of late Ming society, and it cannot account for the intimate relation in *Chin p'ing mei* between sexual and official corruption. But this does not mean that sexual description is incidental to the narrative. The description of sexual activity serves to deepen the social critique inherent in the novel's juxtaposition of family and state, demonstrating the protagonists' compulsive expenditure of scarce resources, and their obstinate blindness to their own failings. We must not simply read these sexual descriptions with modern eyes, applauding what we may think they show us of "liberating" polymorphous perversity. (Such a reading is forced to ignore the narcissism and sadism that mark many of these sexual acts.) There is nothing liberating about the *consequences* of unregulated sexuality in *Chin p'ing mei.* Hsi-men Ch'ing's mistress Wang Liu-erh is the

most cooperative and inventive of his sexual partners, but this is exactly what exhausts him and costs him his life in Chapter 79. The notion of sexual excess had a set of conventional expectations attached to it by the late Ming, and we must allow these expectations to guide us if we are to fathom the design of the novel.

In the handbooks of sexual hygiene that circulated during the Ming, there is a notion of sexual economy, of getting and spending, that is fundamental both to the role of sex in *Chin p'ing mei* and to the role of women in the traditional characterization of the "bad last ruler." Women are, potentially, instruments of dangerous disorder, and they are also sexually enervating. In the Taoist lore that gave rise to these handbooks, men and women seek to capture each other's vital essence through sexual intercourse. A principal aim of sexual hygiene was to avoid "overspending" on the part of the male, who needed to nourish himself through sexual activity, rather than destroying himself. This notion of expenditure makes an equation between money and semen, physical resources and financial resources, a natural one. In *Chin p'ing mei* this equation is underscored by the prominence of both *yin* (licentiousness) and *yin* (silver), and by the central figure of Ts'ai Ching, whose name puns on the characters for money and semen. In the Hsi-men household we witness a prodigious financial and sexual overspending, whose significance is made clear to us at the midpoint of the narrative, the key chapters 49 through 51.

The officials, musicians, and menials who pass in and out of the Hsi-men household must all be entertained, paid, or fed for their services. (Hsi-men Ch'ing's sycophants are fed even when they render no service at all: in the period of physical debilitation that precedes his death, they eat up the food supposed to restore him to health.) The male employees' parties that follow most of the official receptions remind us of the sheer number of people whom the household must support. The expenditures to which the state is subject are listed for us in memorials or in passing references to the emperor's tomb, reminding us of the steady financial pressure on the imperial finances. In Chapters 47 through 49, the "spending" requirements of corrupt government show us how we are to view Hsi-men Ch'ing's sexual activity: in these three chapters, Hsi-men Ch'ing's mistress Wang Liu-erh uses her sexual tie to Hsi-men Ch'ing to procure his intercession on behalf of the murderous servant Miao Ch'ing. Her efforts, and Miao Ch'ing's payment to her, are interleaved paragraph by paragraph with an account of the lavish gifts Hsi-men Ch'ing must send to counter the impeachment that results from this intercession. At the end of Chapter 49, Hsi-men Ch'ing receives from a monk of mysterious origins the aphrodisiac whose final effect will be the "overspending" that causes his death. The memorial quoted at the beginning of Chapter 49 provides the context in which the gift of the aphrodisiac must be viewed. In this memorial, the same Censor Tseng who impeached Hsi-men Ch'ing in the previous chapter now turns his attention to the seven-point program suggested by Ts'ai Ching, a program that would alter the basis for imperial finance and civil-service recruitment. Tseng argues that the proposed plan would insure an excess of expenditures over revenues, causing the state to run dry. The reader is thus warned at the midpoint of the novel of the calamity that will overtake the state in the final chapters. Hsi-men Ch'ing is similarly warned by the mysterious monk to avoid excessive use of the aphrodisiac, a warning he disregards, just as Ts'ai Ching disregards the warning of Censor Tseng. Hsi-men Ch'ing's financial and physical spending continue in an upward spiral until Chapter 79, when his successive sexual encounters with Wang Liu-erh and P'an Chin-lien drain him completely and bring on his fatal illness.

The resources lost in this "overspending" are not simply physical money and semen. Rather, the book's constant juxtaposition of illicit sexuality and corrupt official dealings suggests that the loss of diversion of these entities connotes a moral exhaustion from which neither the person nor the state can recover. The defrocked Nun Hsüeh, attending Wu Yüeh-niang in Chapter 50, assures her of the efficacy of retribution, the certainty that men will reap what they sow. Appearing as it does at the midpoint of so highly symmetrical a novel as *Chin p'ing mei,* this conventional statement must be understood in its full significance for the narrative. The midpoint of *Chin p'ing mei* functions as a pivot on which the action turns, giving us the information we need to sense the probable outcome. Nun Hsüeh's statement about retribution functions similarly here, coupled as it is not only with the mysterious monk's gift of the aphrodisiac to Hsi-men Ch'ing, but also with the nun's parallel gift to Wu Yüeh-niang of the fertility potion that will enable her to conceive her son Hsiao-ko. As the two drugs—each the gift of a heretical practitioner—work in concert, Hsiao-ko is conceived in such a way as to undermine any suggestion that he is meant to fulfill the dictates of filial piety. Instead, the twenty chapters of his life in the novel show us simultaneously the extinction of the strife-ridden household and the loss to invaders of the empire's ancestral northern lands.

The notion of prostitution provides a central metaphor in *Chin p'ing mei* for the forces behind this disintegration. (This metaphor was a conventional one; the author of *Chin p'ing mei* developed but did not invent it.) The male figures of *Chin p'ing mei* all patronize singing-girls, who cannot, by definition, promise fidelity. These merchants and officials use expensive gifts to insinuate themselves into the powerful Hsi-men household, whose fidelity to them is insured only as long as material advantage results. Similarly, in Chapters 60 through 79, Hsi-men Ch'ing makes prodigal efforts to retain the favor of the minister Ts'ai Ching, virtually prostituting himself. This emphasis on actual or metaphorical prostitution is not redeemed in *Chin p'ing mei* by any suggestion of an alternative morality. There are no virtuous singing-girls in the novel, though they may be found in other works of Yuan and Ming literature. In *Chin p'ing mei,* the typical prostitutes are Li Kueh-chieh, who deceives her patron Hsi-men Ch'ing, and Li Chiao-erh, who returns to the brothel immediately upon Hsi-men Ch'ing's death. The singing-girls not only accept payment for their services; they themselves are the currency for the corrupt official dealings of their patrons. When Hsi-men Ch'ing provides the adopted son of Ts'ai Ching with the services of an elegant singing-girl in Chapter 49, his aim is to have Ts'ai's son intercede on behalf

of his proteges. The inconstancy of these women (a common theme even in the literature of the virtuous singing-girl, whose complaint is precisely that she is forced to be inconstant) functions in *Chin p'ing mei* to point up the disloyalty and inconstancy of the officials who patronize them.

The force of the novel's equation between household and state is used to deepen our sense of this inconstancy, as the Hsi-men wives are likened, in various ways, to the singing-girls who entertain them. Wu Yüeh-niang flies into querulous rage at the suggestion that she is no better than a madam; Hsi-men Ch'ing indulgently offers to pay P'an Chin-lien for certain sexual acts; P'an Chin-lien, acceding, demands a skirt "just like Li Kueh-chieh's." Wu Yüeh-niang observes in Chapter 74 that the intrigues of the entertainers' quarters cannot be worse than those in her own household. The "inner government" of the Hsi-men household is thus plagued by the same rivalries that beset the pleasure-houses. If the wives are prostitutes, however, the novel's underlying equation between wives and ministers, household and state, demonstrates to us that the ministers are prostitutes themselves. By the conclusion of the book, those who prostitute themselves have center stage: Ch'en Ching-chi, reduced to beggary, lives by his sexual favors in a Taoist temple, and he finds Wang Liu-erh and her daughter, who have fled the capital after the fall of Ts'ai Ching, also making their living by prostitution. The empire is falling about their ears, however, and Ch'en Ching-chi's manipulative sexual behavior is a wildly ineffectual attempt at the sort of control that P'an Chin-lien once *almost*—but never *quite*—exercised over Hsi-men Ch'ing. The ministers have similarly lost control of the state.

Sexual activity in *Chin p'ing mei* is primarily an instrument of punishment or of gain. Just as P'an Chin-lien is humiliated sexually for her attraction to the servant Ch'in-t'ung, so Li P'ing-erh is humiliated, upon her entry into the household, for her attraction to Doctor Chiang. In Chapter 27, in the novel's most notorious passage of extended sexual description, P'an Chin-lien is tormented by Hsi-men Ch'ing, to repay her for her jealousy of Li P'ing-erh. Hsi-men Ch'ing's own pleasure is depicted as narcissistic and vulgar: he frightens his sexual partners with the size of his penis (which makes intercourse painful for them), and in Chapter 59 he dismays the elegant singing-girl Cheng Ai-yüeh by the crudity of his demands. The women with whom he has intercourse demand badges of status from him: clothing, ornaments, money. Sexual acts are used to enforce a perverted hierarchy, as P'an Chin-lien, desperate for the tokens that would put her on a footing with the wealthier wives, is goaded into certain acts on the grounds that others have performed them. (The servant Ju-i is then urged to follow her example.) *Chin p'ing mei* shows us no sexual generosity that we can admire. There are no Molly Blooms [as in James Joyce's *Ulysses*], no Lady Chatterleys [as in D. H. Lawrence's *Lady Chatterley's Lover*]. The only appearance of generosity is in Hsi-men Ch'ing's relation to his sixth and favorite wife Li P'ing-erh. Even here, however, we must not be misled by the couple's obvious enjoyment of each other. In the jealousy she provokes and the disasters that ensue, Li P'ing-erh exactly fits the role of "favored concubine" in the traditional description of imperial decline. She has entered the Hsi-men household, as did P'an Chin-lien, after the virtual murder of her husband. Before his death she had already spirited a great deal of his family's wealth into Hsi-men Ch'ing's possession. In her generosity to the other wives she is oblivious to the jealousy excited by her riches. (The servants' comments make clear that she is heedless of the family's finances.) Hsi-men Ch'ing's genuine affection for Li P'ing-erh has moved many a reader, as has Li P'ing-erh's grief at the death of her son. Hsi-men Ch'ing's affection is expressed, however, as a damaging partiality that causes him to neglect his other wives. The sexuality depicted in *Chin p'ing mei* is destructive, and this is precisely why there are no extended passages describing Hsi-men Ch'ing's sexual relations with Wu Yüeh-niang or Meng Yü-lou: Meng Yü-lou does her best to remove herself from the patterns of destructive interaction within the household, and Wu Yüeh-niang is reserved for a fate whose cause is religious credulity rather than sexual excess.

The representation of sexuality in *Chin p'ing mei* is central to a system of false relationships, of which incest is the most serious. False claims abound in the novel, as when Hsi-men Ch'ing and Wu Yüeh-niang dress in official garments to which they are not entitled (much as the favored maids demand clothing to which they are not entitled), or when Hsi-men Ch'ing's crony Wu Tien-en advances himself by asserting that he is the brother of Wu Yüeh-niang. The mutual seduction of P'an Chin-lien and Ch'en Ching-chi, who is technically a generation beneath her, is incestuous, and Li Kuei-chieh establishes an incestuous relation to the family, when despite her position as an acknowledged sexual favorite of Hsi-men Ch'ing, she presents herself to Wu Yüeh-niang as an adopted daughter. (Hsi-men Ch'ing deepens this incestuous connection when he adopts Wang San-kuan, the young man with whom Li Kuei-chieh has deceived him.)

Given a traditional morality grounded in patriarchal, hierarchical, essentially familial ties, it is difficult to conceive that these incestuous relationships, these violations of hierarchy, were intended by their author as positive acts. There exist songs collected during the Ming which treat sex (even adulterous sex) in an entirely playful fashion, but the mood of these songs is far removed from that of *Chin p'ing mei.* The songs do not describe sexual coercion, nor do they call up the expectations traditionally aroused by evil empresses, favored concubines, or rulers who neglect their responsibilities. *Chin p'ing mei* does call up these expectations. In Chapter 51, P'an Chin-lien tells Hsi-men Ching that the drug he has acquired freezes her womb, making her entire body numb. Death, and not life, is the outcome of sexual excess in *Chin p'ing mei.*

The author of *Chin p'ing mei* thus depicts sexual attraction as a force of disorder, both a cause and a metaphor for the dangers that menace the state. Sexual activity sustains a system of corrupt and coercive relationships that the novel in its entirety will not allow us to admire. Certain readers of *Chin p'ing mei* have, however, sensed an inconsistency between the obvious corruption surround-

ing sexual activity in the novel, and the apparent relish with which that activity is sometimes described. But we need only look at a novel like Zola's *Nana,* in our own tradition, to see that the two attitudes are not necessarily inconsistent. The two novels are written from opposite points of view: in *Nana,* the aristocracy demonstrates by its corruption that it deserves to be supplanted as a governing class, whereas in *Chin p'ing mei,* society is called upon to return to the purity of its original hierarchical descriptions, to "rectify the names" and thus achieve stable and just government. Nevertheless the two novels exhibit remarkable similarities. In both, the corruption of the governing class is presented primarily through the metaphor of sexual corruption. In each, the collapse of the household in question is preceded by a compulsive overspending that drains the protagonists financially and sexually. Both contain the apparent message that women corrupt society, and a deeper message that the society in question has corrupted itself. The narrator of *Chin p'ing mei* reminds us that "Sex does not mislead men; men mislead themselves," and Nana wreaks her vengeance upon a ruling class that has "suffered a poison to ferment among the people." Both novels end in tumultuous rapidity, the suddenly heightened pace of the narrative helping to demonstrate the inevitability of retribution, the unmanageability of the consequences that the protagonists have brought upon themselves. In their concluding pages, both novels turn from individual drama to the larger drama of the state in decline.

Zola insures our belief in Nana's sexual attractiveness, and in the pleasure she brings to young Georges Hugon and the anxious, repressed Muffat. Looked at from our twentieth-century perspective, these both begin as liberating relationships for the men involved—and yet both men are destroyed by them. We cannot understand this destruction, however, unless we too experience the attraction the men feel, and so the sexual description central to the novel's depiction of corruption must at least begin by seeming attractive. We ourselves must then be made to feel surfeited by the increasing extravagance of the narrative. Zola brings on this sense of surfeit by piling one sexual episode upon another, and finally allowing us to participate, with poor Muffat, in the discovery of Nana and the aged, decrepit Chouard. The author of *Chin p'ing mei,* more subtly, communicates the illicit nature of *Chin p'ing mei's* sexual encounters by making us voyeurs: in clandestine company with P'an Chin-lien, Ying Po-chüeh, or various little boys, we watch these encounters through keyholes, we listen through walls. These other characters catch *us* in the act of watching Hsi-men Ch'ing and his various partners, thus exposing our own frailties, demonstrating that the reader has as great a need for self-cultivation as do any of the characters in the novel.

Sexual description in *Chin p'ing mei* is thus a means of probing the characters' self-awareness, on which true enlightenment depends. (pp. 28-52)

Katherine Carlitz, in her The Rhetoric of "Chin p'ing mei," *Indiana University Press, 1986, 239 p.*

Andrew H. Plaks   (essay date 1987)

[*In the following excerpt, Plaks argues that the author of* Chin p'ing mei *employed a deliberate structure—which served as a model for subsequent Ming novels—to emphasize particular themes, relationships, and patterns in the novel, such as a correlation between seasonal change and the rise and fall of the Hsi-men household.*]

[In examining the structure of **Chin P'ing Mei**], I will first draw attention to its invariable hundred-chapter length, with all the potential symmetries and numerological patterns implied by that number. As we shall see, this order of magnitude had become by the time of the composition of the **Chin P'ing Mei**—with some room for variation—a standard generic feature of the [Chinese] literati novel form. The division of the text into *hui*-units, however, should not be taken for granted, since modern scholarship has shown that the *chang-hui* format was only a later phenomenon in the development of Ming fiction, before which time fictional narratives had been divided into other types of single-episode units (e.g., *tse* and *kuan-mu*). The insistence on creating the patently false impression that such full-length texts are comprised of strings of independent *hui*-units from street-side storytelling is in itself not without significance for the aesthetics of the Chinese novel in general, and this is particularly striking in the case of the **Chin P'ing Mei,** for which we have no evidence of a prior tradition of oral story cycles or other forms of continuous narrative on the same theme.

Of greater importance for our understanding of the underlying structure of the novel, however, is its division into the standard printing units of the *chüan*. As far as I can tell, nearly every known printing of the two earliest recensions of the **Chin P'ing Mei** was divided into either ten *chüan* of ten *hui* chapters each, or twenty *chüan* of five *hui* chapters, like many of the earliest editions of *San-kuo yen-i, Shui-hu chuan,* and *Hsi-yu chi.* . . . This seemingly fortuitous bibliographical detail leads me to my first major point regarding the structural design of the novel, when we note that the narrative continuum of the text also breaks down into a fairly clear rhythm of ten-chapter units—punctuated by events of crucial importance to the structural outlines of the story, or of prophetic significance, in the ninth and tenth chapters of each "decade."

Let us take a moment to set forth in some detail the division of the text into these ten-chapter units. The first of these units is devoted to the expanded retelling of the *Shui-hu* episode of the liaison between Hsi-men Ch'ing and P'an Chin-lien, the murder of her husband Wu Ta, and Wu Sung's attempted revenge and banishment, concluding with P'an Chin-lien's acceptance into the Hsi-men household in chapter 9. This is followed immediately by another ten-chapter section covering the parallel story of Hsi-men Ch'ing's adulterous affair with Li P'ing-erh, the unpleasant demise of her two husbands in quick succession, and her own entry into Hsi-men Ch'ing's fold in chapter 19. Chapters 20 to 29 then develop the seeds of internal dissension within the outward prosperity of the Hsi-men household, culminating in the fortunetelling session in chapter 29 and in the double triumph of Kuan-ko's birth and Hsi-men's simultaneous ascension to official sta-

tus in chapter 30. The following ten chapters trace the increasingly dangerous behavior of servants and masters leading up to the discussions of karmic retribution in chapter 39. The ten chapters starting from chapter 40 develop the deepening enmity between P'an Chin-lien and Li P'ing-erh and the vulnerability of P'ing-erh's baby, as Hsi-men Ch'ing's fortunes spiral higher and his sexual powers receive a boost from the strange foreign monk who appears in chapter 49, followed by the repetition of images of sickness and intimations of impending tragedy that lead into the cruel events of chapter 59. From chapter 60 to 69 we witness the rapid waning of P'ing-erh, and her replacement first by Ju-i and then by Madame Lin, after which time the narrative enters a ten-chapter coda of feverish sexual activity resulting in Hsi-men Ch'ing's collapse in chapter 79.

Even after the narrative pace slows down and loses its centripetal focus with the death of the nuclear figure, we can still observe the manner in which the author maintains a rough ten-chapter rhythm, using chapters 80 to 90 or 91 to empty out the household and send all of the concubines off to their separate fates, then turning to a final section devoted primarily to the humbling of Ch'en Ching-chi, bringing us up to the closing scenes.

Once the reader's attention becomes attuned to the rhythm of these ten-chapter units of text, certain other related structural patterns also begin to emerge. On the one hand, within the space of each decade we can perceive a type of smaller internal patterns of oscillation on the level of narrative action. Thus, in the same way that I have identified the special function of the ninth and tenth chapters of each decade within this structural arrangement, we may also note the recurrence of peaks of excitement—gaiety, anger, or grief—placed in the fifth chapter of many sections, generally flanked by troughs of relative inactivity in the intervening periods. As many critics have pointed out, it is during these scenes of apparent inaction that some of the most meaningful developments in the narrative actually transpire.

On the other hand, these basic ten-chapter units are themselves linked in various combinations to yield broader structural divisions of the narrative. For example, we immediately observe the obvious point of articulation that separates the first eighty chapters of the book from the last twenty in terms of a number of literary variables, as well as the apparent symmetry between the opening and closing two decades (1-20 and 80-100), the action of both of which takes place primarily outside the Hsi-men compound. In the same way, the first twenty chapters, in which the household takes shape with the addition of three new wives, clearly balance the concluding twenty chapters, in which the same household breaks up with accelerating rapidity. In all of these schemes the ten-chapter units of the text may be understood as forming the basic building blocks of its overall structure.

The widespread critical observation that the last twenty chapters of the **Chin P'ing Mei** constitute a separate structural division brings us to another generic feature of the Ming-Ch'ing novel form. That is, we see here a good example of the tendency of these narratives to present the downfall and elimination of their central figures at a point only about two-thirds or three-fourths of the way through the text, followed by a lengthy final section in which the remaining actors who had gathered onstage during the early phases are steadily dispersed. In this light, it seems to be less than sheer coincidence that Hsi-men Ch'ing dies in chapter 79 of *Chin P'ing Mei,* almost precisely the same point at which Ts'ao Ts'ao falls in *San-kuo yen-i,* ushering in a chain of short-lived successors whose failings quickly bring his dynasty to ruin.

A similar instance of overall structural design in which the *Chin P'ing Mei* exemplifies the generic model of the Ming literati novel is its neat cleavage into two equal textual hemispheres. In a number of senses the celebrations in chapter 49 capped by Hsi-men Ch'ing's acquisition of a magic potency drug mark a great divide between the first half of the book, outlining his steady rise to economic, political, and sexual power, and the second, in which his very triumphs on all these fronts bring upon him an inexorable process of self-destruction. Chang Chu-p'o [in his essay "How to Read the *Chin P'ing Mei*"] refers to this fundamental structural division in a number of critical passages as a key to understanding the work, although at some point he uses the terms "first half" and "second half" more loosely to signify the rise and fall of Hsi-men Ch'ing's world. (pp. 72-6)

One more aspect of the structure of the *Chin P'ing Mei* that provides a retrospective model of the generic assumptions of the sixteenth-century Chinese novel may be seen in the special functions reserved for its opening and closing sections. For the purpose of my interpretive analysis, the fact that the novel starts with the expanded retelling of an episode from another novel, the *Shui-hu chuan,* is of interest not so much because it is a striking example of the novelist's adaptation of preexisting source materials, as because it demonstrates another major compositional principle: the prefixing of a structurally distinct prologue section to the main body of the work. This common feature of the Ming-Ch'ing novel evidently bears some genetic relation to the prologue section (*ju-hua*) in the colloquial short-story genre, which was being standardized in this same period, although here the common view that this is a direct reflection of the original demands of oral storytelling performance is no longer relevant. Instead, it is more useful to understand this to be a self-conscious literary device, one designed to fulfill the structural function of counterbalancing the formal conclusion, while also setting up a narrative model that alerts the reader to certain issues to be raised more seriously in the main body of the text.

The opening chapters of the *Chin P'ing Mei* are set effectively outside of the central world of the novel, that is, apart from the day-to-day flow of experience within and around the Hsi-men compound. But at the same time, they serve to set in motion the chain of events that leads up to (and later down from) the major events of the narrative, while also contriving to bring onstage nearly all of the main characters: Hsi-men Ch'ing and P'an Chin-lien at center stage, Li P'ing-erh and P'ang Ch'un-mei in the wings by oblique reference, and Meng Yü-lou in the interlude of chapter 7. Even more important to this discussion

is the fact that the borrowed "prologue" section takes advantage of the fairly straightforward tale it tells of adultery and revenge to implicate—with a greater sense of detachment precisely because it draws on familiar material—some of the more serious issues regarding sexual excess and the larger social order to be taken up in the text, before we are drawn into a more intimate, and hence less objective, view of the main protagonists.

In evaluating the structural significance of the opening of the novel, we must also take into account the prologue to the prologue—the initial disquisition that precedes the start of the narrative proper. Our judgment of this point depends, of course, on which of the two basic recensions we choose to work with. Regardless of whether one feels that the structural integrity of the book is enhanced or distorted by the inclusion of the section on the formation of the boon brotherhood in chapter 1 of the Ch'ung-chen edition (with its obvious parody on the opening scene of *San-kuo yen-i*), it is interesting that the initial verses and discussion of the problem of excessive emotional attachment (*ch'ing*) in the *Tz'u-hua* text is matched by the opening verses and discussion of what I have termed the "four vices of excess" (*ssu t'an*) in the other recension. As mentioned earlier, Wei Tzu-yün contends that the pages that, to use his figure of speech, "crown" the opening of the *Tz'u-hua* text represent a pointed reflection of the excesses of the bearer of the imperial crown in the Wan-li period, which had been so scathingly criticized not long before in Lo Yü-jen's shocking memorial. Thus the striking revision in the Ch'ung-ch'en edition, in his view, reveals a politically motivated softening of the blow. For the purposes of the present discussion, however, I will stress instead the fact that the openings of both of these recensions retain the same aesthetic function—that of breaking the narrative ice while explicitly raising some of the fundamental issues to be addressed in the book. . . . (pp. 76-7)

At the other Aristotelian extremity of the text, the use of the fulfillment of a preordained destiny—the reclaiming of Hsi-men Ch'ing's orphan-heir Hsiao-ko by the monk P'u-ching—as a device of closure is not ostensibly linked to any specific points in the prologue section. This has left many readers with a sense that the ending, like the beginning, is something tacked on gratuitously, that it leaves us up in the air. Indeed, Chang Chu-p'o seizes precisely on this point to argue that the evocation of a final sense of emptiness is exactly what the author has in mind, and that this, in turn, resonates with the note of vanity of vanities sounded in the opening pages. (p. 78)

[I] will simply add that what the conclusion accomplishes, over and above providing the final dispensation of Hsi-men's estate, is to use the deracination of this "filial son" and the final vision of Hsi-men Ch'ing in chains to close the bracket on the theme of filiality, and thus remind the reader that the issue of filial responsibility in its broadest sense forms a crucial nexus of meaning in the novel. Moreover, the inexorable convergence of the destiny of the household with the fate of the Sung empire in the concluding scenes also sets the final seal on the pattern of cross-reflection between the microcosm of the enclosed compound and the world at large, which accounts for yet another central framework of meaning in the book.

In reviewing some of the more obtrusive structural patterns in **Chin P'ing Mei** that contribute to the generic model of the sixteenth-century Chinese novel, I would also mention certain other spatial and temporal schemes of organization. As for the spatial outlines of the narrative, many readers have been impressed by the degree of detail with which the author constructs his physical setting, to the point at which the novel can serve as a source for the study of Ming urban planning, architecture, and interior design. Chang Chu-p'o, for example, pays particular attention in a number of discussions to the manner in which the positioning of the main characters within the compound sets up more complex relationships in the narrative. Other scholars have drawn attention beyond the household itself to the commercial streets, entertainment quarters, and local temples in Ch'ing-ho prefecture, or to the geographical routing of Hsi-men Ch'ing's several trips down the Grand Canal and over to Kaifeng. These various aspects of spatial setting take on what I would call structural significance in connection with the periodic contrast between the central mimetic world of the narrative: Hsi-men Ch'ing's compound with the pleasure garden at its heart, and the world beyond its walls. In fact, we can see in **Chin P'ing Mei** the same design later exploited in *Hung-lou meng*: an enclosed garden within a walled compound, leading outward through its immediate neighborhood to the surrounding city, on to the imperial capital, and thus by implication to the entire world scope.

The same degree of attention to significant detail is evident in the author's handling of the temporal coordinates of his narrative. Numerous modern critics have pointed to inconsistencies in this aspect of the text as proof of what they see as the structural weakness of the work. Chang Chu-p'o, on the other hand, defends the book against this charge, claiming that every example of apparent sloppiness in this area in fact indicates deliberate manipulation of detail in accordance with the author's grand design. This is also the assumption of Wei Tzu-yün, when he explains [in his *Wen-shih yü yen-pien*] one particularly troubling discrepancy in the internal dates of the story as a deliberate allusion to the one-month reign of the T'ai-ch'ang emperor.

Once again, the notion of slipshod design is easy to counter by calling attention to the author's controlling hand in certain other aspects of temporal organization. Chief among these is his masterful manipulation of the details of seasonal change that fill out the three or four years of calendar time spanned by the main body of the novel. The outline of the text is very noticeably constructed on a grid of recurring annual events: festivals and ritual observances, most typically the birthdays of the principal characters. With regard to the latter point, the attention to birthdays is practically unavoidable in a work of "domestic fiction" such as the **Chin P'ing Mei,** but the fact that the author's control in this area goes somewhat beyond mechanical plotting is indicated by the frequency with which these occasions are pointedly pegged to special moments in the seasonal cycle. For example, Wu Yüeh-

niang's birthday falls on the day of the Mid-Autumn Festival (the fifteenth day of the eighth lunar month), that of P'an Chin-lien during the New Year season (the ninth day of the first lunar month), P'ing-erh's on the Yüan-hsiao Festival (the fifteenth day of the first lunar month), Hsi-men Ch'ing's at the passing of summer (the twenty-eighth day of the seventh lunar month). The degree to which these birthdays coincide with one another further strengthens the impression of deliberate design.

As for the detailed descriptions of the observance of the seasonal festivals themselves, this too is in a sense a requisite of quotidian narrative; but the author again reveals his guiding hand through his rich interweaving of the traditional imagery of the festivals with the physical conditions of temperature and precipitation attendant upon the respective seasons, a dimension of far greater significance than may first appear. Since . . . this heightened sensitivity to seasonal plotting (and, in particular, the rich associations of the Mid-Autumn Festival and the New Year feasts, culminating in the carnival atmosphere of the Yüan-hsiao night) marks another common compositional focus of the Chinese novel in general, I will take some time here to consider this question in greater detail.

The degree to which the author's control over details of the seasonal round goes beyond the straightforward description of physical setting or sheer chronological sequencing of events—and reaches a point at which we may rightly speak of seasonality as a structural principle— becomes most evident when we consider the manner in which he constructs his scenes to highlight a sense of incessant alternation between heat and cold. The most notable examples of this include the sultry summer days in chapters 8, 27, and 82; the snowscapes and bitter cold in chapters 20-21, 70-71, and 81; and the brilliant spring garden scenes in chapters 25, 48, and 89. This in itself, again, might be regarded as simply part of the continuity of quotidian description at the heart of the art of the novel. But the artistry of the **Chin P'ing Mei** in this respect demonstrates the particular aesthetics of the Chinese novel in two important ways.

First, the descriptions of shifts in physical temperature in the text are designed in such a way as to bring them into alignment with other more abstract variables, also conceived in terms of "heat" and "cold." The fact that the story as a whole begins in a blithe spring and ends in a desolate autumn immediately alerts us to this sort of correspondence, and throughout the novel we often observe significant correlation between the seasonal moment and the alternation of scenes of heated excitement (*je-nao*) and cold loneliness (*ch'i-liang*). Similarly, we can trace a movement analogous to the seasonal cycle in the alternation of hot and cold periods in the vicissitudes of Hsi-men Ch'ing's fortunes. The terms *leng* and *je* and their counterparts virtually stud the text in poems, chapter titles, and narrative details, often going far beyond reference to temperature alone. And this sort of structural correspondence is rendered more complex and interesting by a second aesthetic sense, whereby, in keeping with traditional Chinese conceptual models, the representation of the ebb and flow of experience is based on patterns of the interpenetration of heat within cold and cold within heat.

With this extension of the meanings of heat and cold in mind, we can see this principle at work in the construction of many major scenes in the book. In the one arc of the seasonal cycle, many of the "hottest" scenes are deliberately set in the coldest months of the year, those same months that happen to contain the season of most intense merrymaking in the Chinese ritual calendar. This principle of composition may partially explain the special fascination for the Yüan-hsiao Festival in the eyes of the Ming-Ch'ing novelists. In the course of the ***Chin P'ing Mei,*** the annual cycle rolls around and stops on the Yüan-hsiao Festival four times, and each time the general gaiety and abandon, the blazing lights in the crackling air, give rise to events of special significance. Conversely, the author often chooses to dwell on the oppressive heat of the summer months precisely when he wishes to convey a certain chill with respect to the dangerous consequences of sensual excess, as for example in the notorious escapade in the Grape Arbor in chapter 27, or the ominous fulfillment of incestuous passion in chapter 82.

In such examples, the constant shifting between cold inspiring feverish activity and heat that leaves one cold yields a major overlay of irony that contributes substantially to the rich suggestiveness of the novel. A few more examples may help to demonstrate the extent to which the ironic manipulation of the hot-cold axis governs the use of many specific images and details of the text. One of these may be seen in the intimations of cold that dominate the treatment of the brief existence of Kuan-ko: his incessant shivering (*leng-chan*), the inordinate fear that he may catch a chill, and most pointedly, the furor over his contact with cold metal bangles in chapter 43—all of this set against the hottest phase of Hsi-men Ch'ing's career.

Another example even more explicitly linked to seasonal imagery materializes in the cold backdrop to the ten-chapter section that sees Hsi-men Ch'ing finally burn himself out. After a series of snowy days and frosty nights in chapters 67, 68, and 69, the trip to the capital in chapters 70 and 71 is pointedly set against the bone-chilling cold of the waning year. There, the author masterfully executes a series of scenes combining images of coldness, whiteness, and emptiness, which cut right through the splendor of the court and Hsi-men Ch'ing's own personal glory. Following this point, the cold images continue to pile up as Hsi-men's dizzying spiral of political and sexual advances reaches its climax, just as the festivities of the New Year season move into full swing. In chapter 77 the author once again pulls together imagery of snow, warm inner apartments, and escalating sexual fantasy in Hsi-men's visit to Cheng Ai-yüeh-erh, and this sets the stage for his stark end as he expends the last of his remaining vitality amidst a flurry of fireworks, lanterns, incense, and other images of fragile warmth, all set against the snowy cold whiteness of a late winter scene. Here, in the final flare of Hsi-men Ch'ing's dying embers, the reader is reminded of the ironic linkage of images of heat and cold with scenes of pointless sexuality that had been made repeatedly earlier in the narrative, especially during the first decade of the body of the

novel, chapters 20 to 29. The most obvious instance is the heated union in chapter 27, so conspicuously lacking in warmth for all its violent thrashing about, which is set after a cooling shower on a languorous summer day. Lest we miss the connection here between the seasonal setting and the purport of the scene, the author interjects a highly suggestive *tz'u* poem on the heat, and places the action of this white-hot episode in the Grape Arbor near a section of the garden known as the Snow Cave (*Hsüeh-tung*)—itself apparently located inside the Grotto of Sequestered Spring (*Ts'ang-ch'un wu*). The reader recalls that this is the same place where in chapter 23 the passionate embraces of Hsi-men Ch'ing and Sung Hui-lien were turned into a night of teeth-chattering cold; and later the same spot is used as the scene of many comparable conjunctions of cold and heat.

These are only a few examples of the complex use of heat and cold imagery in the construction of many major scenes in the novel. Through the exploitation of this device, the cycles of seasonal change that form the temporal warp of the narrative come to merge with the overall patterns of prosperity and decline, gathering and dispersion, that comprise its significant structure. This is the sense in which Chang Chu-p'o speaks of the work as a whole as "a book of heat and cold" (*yen-liang shu*). (pp. 78-84)

> *Andrew H. Plaks, " 'Chin P'ing Mei': Inversion of Self-Cultivation," in his* The Four Masterworks of the Ming Novel: Ssu ta ch'i-shu, *Princeton University Press, 1987, pp. 55-182.*

Ying-Ying Chien   (essay date 1988)

[*In the following excerpt, Chien offers a feminist interpretation of* Chin p'ing mei, *suggesting that the novel's central character is Chin-lien, who uses her beauty and sexuality to overcome the oppression and discrimination she suffers in a patriarchal society.*]

The ***Chin P'ing Mei*** (***CPM***), one of the six greatest classical Chinese novels, has long been neglected by scholars until the last twenty years. Due to its sensuous descriptions and erotic passages, ***CPM*** has been attacked as "yin-shu" (a pornographic book) or "hui-shu" (a dirty book) and has been censored and banned by the Chinese government. This notorious book has been, however, praised by some recent scholars as the first "modern" Chinese novel and a masterpiece of realism, with natural "life-size" characters and relatively complex and insightful female characters.

The history of the ***CPM*** scholarship can be divided in general into three stages: first, before 1960; second, the 1960's; third, from 1970 until the present. From the first to the third stage, while scholarly attention focuses primarily on the text, the form, and the structure of the novel, there has been an increasing interest in the characterization, especially that of females. Considering the ***CPM*** as the first important domestic novel in depicting the life of Chinese women, in the present study I offer a re-reading of the novel from a feminist perspective to re-evaluate some aspects of the novel, especially in the areas of the representation of women in literature and the problem of the sexes, and to offer a new interpretation of the *CPM.* (p. 607)

In the opening poem of the *CPM,* the ruination of two great historical heroes is told: Hsiang Yü and Liu Pang's ruins are attributed to the beauty of two women, Yü-chi and Ch'i-shih. Comparing man to iron and stone, while woman to the flower, the poem indicates that the power of the former will eventually be dissolved by the latter. As the narrator starts introducing the subject of *ch'ing* (love, passion) and *sê* (carnal love, lust) immediately after the poem, the idea that woman is dangerous and destructive as the primary source of man's passion and lust becomes evident. Essentially, woman is blamed here as the cause of man's disaster or misfortune.

The stereotype of the fatal woman, or the so-called "femme fatale" in the *CPM* is first suggested by Patrick Hanan [in "The Sources of the *Chin P'ing Mei,*" *Asia Major* 10, No. 1 (1963)]. According to him, by including the two historical characters and the story of their downfall at the hands of beautiful women in the opening poem of the novel, the author sets up a parallel between these women and Pan Chin-lian and thus reveals his intention of creating "a femme fatale heroine (Pan Chin-lian) of inordinate sexual appetite who ruins physically or financially all the men she captivates." Along the same lines, Te-wei Wang criticizes Pan Chin-lian as a "bad woman," or more specifically, the worst woman in the world of Chinese fiction. Although Wang disagrees with the western usage of the term "femme fatale," regarding Chin-lian as the reincarnation of evil, he names her a "huo-shui" (literally, the troubling water) from the traditional Chinese view point.

Indeed, for hundreds of years, the image of Chin-lian has aroused an immediate sense of dislike and shame in the mind of the reader and critic. For example, C. T. Hsia [in his *The Classical Chinese Novel,* 1968] calls her "an unfeeling and insatiable nymphomaniac," and "the queen bee or black widow spider" who would sacrifice man to gratify her own sexual desire. Both Katherine Carlitz and Mary Scott [in "Puns and Puzzles in the *Chin p'ing mei:* A Look at Chapter 27," *T'oung Pao* 67 (1981) and "The Image of the Garden in *Jin ping mei* and *Hongloumeng,*" *Chinese Literature: Essays, Articles, Reviews* 8, No. 1-2 (July 1986), respectively] compare her to the cutting west wind in autumn that symbolizes sterility and brings coldness and destruction. Shu-yu Sun adopts the Buddhist term *ch'ên* (anger), which is one of the three poisons at the root of *avidya* (*wu-ming,* evil), to criticize Chin-lian. Other Chinese critics have called her a sensualist, avenger, murderer, and used terms like evil, jealousy ruthlessness, etc. to summarize her nature.

To the feminists, however, the origins of the misogynous nature of the "femme fatale" or "huo-shui" stereotype in literature are due to the faulty assumptions about sex and gender differences. According to the traditional Freudian definition of feminity, feminine sexuality, and the idea of "penis envy," women are biologically inferior to men and are passively waiting to be fulfilled and defined by men. Women are, therefore, [according to Juliet Mitchell], degraded as "the lack," "the other," or "the second sex" in

a phallogocentristic society. In everyday life, they are dehumanized to men's possessions, like houses or jewelry; in the fictional world, they are not represented as what they really are and are perceived merely as objects. Due to men's desire and fear of women, women are trivialized into two opposing sterotypes in literature—the angel and the good wife vs. the demon and the bad woman (or femme fatale). Such a myth of the "eternal feminine" is used as one of the "moral technologies" to dominate our (especially women's) thinking and behavior in a patriarchal society.

In light of the sexually biased nature of the femme fatale or evil woman type, in the following section, I shall reevaluate the representation of Chin-lian in the *CPM* to question the traditional criticism of her as a bad woman on both the historical and literary levels.

From the historical view point, the *CPM* is a novel of social realism which depicts truthfully various aspects of the late Ming society. Patronized by the government, the neo-Confucianism represented by Chu-hsi had a strong impact on the politics, philosophy, and daily existence of the people. Not only the social but the family structure was built upon the patriarchal hierarchy of the neo-Confucian ideology. Consequently, men's status was higher than that of women and they also enjoyed more "rights." The common practices of polygamy, concubinage, slavery, prostitution, and footbinding reveal such sexual inequalities of that time.

Under the Confucian ideas of the "three obediences" and "four virtues," women were confined to the home and their duties were to serve and be submissive. With low social and legal status, they were viewed as *sex objects*—bearers of sons and helpers to the husbands—and they were denied access to the rites of ancestor worship and the inheritance of family properties. While any sexual transgressions on the women's part would result in humiliation, physical punishment, or divorce, men could enjoy the liberty of having more than one wife and were not penalized for extra-marital relationships.

Further, women were degraded into *commercial objects* readily sold or exchanged among men. In a society where only sons could earn money and continue the family line, daughters were unwelcome. As the "spilled water," a daughter, being married, "belonged to" the family of her husband. Among poor families, incidents of female infanticide were not unusual, and the selling of daughters as maids or slaves was also a common practice. Once having been sold to rich families, the poor women had no protection from society or their original family—they could be punished, tortured, or transferred.

In the *CPM,* the Hsi-men household is the microcosm of such a patriarchal society, and Chin-lian can be seen as the representative of the women sacrificed under this unjust system. Her experiences portray a woman subjected to adversities completely beyond her control and imposed on her by the patriarchal society. Born in a poor tailor's family as the sixth daugther, she is sold three times and transferred twice throughout her life. According to the novel, Chin-lian is first sold at age nine by her mother for finan-

Hsi-men Ch'ing possesses a bottled aphrodisiac.

cial reasons when her father dies. Thus the poor girl becomes a slave/maid to the rich Wang Chao-hsüan for six years. When Master Wang dies, she is sold again by her mother to the old Chang Ta-hu for twenty liang of silver. In short, before reaching sixteen years of age, Chin-lian has already been sold like a commodity twice by her own mother.

Having been bought as a monetary object in the first place, she is further exploited as a sex object by men. At the age of eighteen, the fully mature and beautiful Chin-lian is raped by her lascivious master. The result: she is beaten cruelly by her jealous mistress and then given away free (transferred for the first time) to a poor, ugly, dwarf as wife. Married to the cowardly Wu Ta against her will on the one hand, Chin-lian is used secretly by her old master as mistress on the other. Her bitterness and helplessness are subtly revealed through a sad song, in which Chin-lian laments that she has no freedom in choosing a husband to match her beauty and no control whatsoever over her ill fate.

Under such miserable circumstances, Chin-lian's feelings are suppressed and almost always denied since the day she was sold. In light of her great distress, Chin-lian's instinctive attraction toward her handsome, strong, and tall brother-in-law, Wu Sung, the hero who just killed a tiger, is more of a natural consequence of her young, unfulfilled love than a shameful deed of seduction. In addition, Chin-

lian's affair with Hsi-men Ch'ing results partly from her unrequited love toward Wu Sung and mostly from the trap set by Hsi-men Ch'ing and the bawd. Furthermore, Chin-lian's role in poisoning Wu Ta is forced upon her because of Hsi-men's lust for possessing Chin-lian and Mother Wang's greediness for money. Actually, Mother Wang is the one who conceives the murder consented to by Hsi-men and who carries out most of it step by step, while Chin-lian has no other choice but to follow instructions and become the scapegoat of the two evil powers.

The second transference of Chin-lian occurs when Hsi-men, the rich rogue, succeeds in taking her in as his fifth wife (or fourth concubine). Born low and poor, she is already inferior in the cruel and fierce competition among wives for their common husband's favor, not to mention that she never bears him any son. So when Hsi-men dies, Chin-lian is driven away to be sold at the order of Wu Yüeh-niang, the first wife. Eventually, she is sold (the third and last time) for 100 liang of silver by Mother Wang to Wu Sung, and killed mercilessly by him in the end.

Throughout her short life, Chin-lian is sold and transferred like merchandise in the market, used and exploited like a sex object by men. From childhood, she is subjected to humiliation, hatred, cruelty, disgrace, and betrayal, without any real love or caring. She is raped, tortured, threatened, despised, and eventually killed. In light of these conditions forced upon her, Chin-lian, rather than being a bad or fatal woman, is a poor victim whose miserable encounters in the novel create the picture of a degraded woman sacrificed by an unjust world of patriarchy.

The degradation of Chin-lian can be seen not only through reevaluation of the plot concerning her life but also through literary devices employed in the novel. To begin with, the novel is told through two points of view: first, a collective male consciousness represented by poems of patriarchal morality above the narrative; second, a male narrator who actually tells the story. Under such a double narrative device, the real Chin-lian is twice removed from the reader. In other words, the reader can only see the distorted picture of her representation through these biased perspectives. In addition to the element of point of view, the frequent use of animal imagery and sexual symbolism in relation to Chin-lian suggests the dehumanization of her character in the novel. The various animals associated with Chin-lian in the *CPM* can be divided in general into two types: the first type concerns her sexuality; the second, her nature.

In her sexual relationship with men, Chin-lian is often related to animal images. For example, in Chapter 4, she is presented as a snake when making love to Hsi-men; in Chapter 12, she is degraded to the position of a horse while being beaten ruthlessly by the enraged Hsi-men with a horsewhip. And in Chapter 19, she is likened to a butterfly when flirting with Chen Ching Chi in the flower garden. It is in the famous Chapter 27 that the drunken Chin-lian is humiliated as a dragon bound and hung with legs wide apart under the vine lattice by the sadistic Hsi-men. Indeed, as an imprisoned beauty (symbolized by the female dragon), Chin-lian can never escape the net of her society (symbolized by the entangled vine lattice) and the exploitation of men (symbolized by Hsi-men himself). Associated with a snail after the sexual assault of Hsi-men in the same chapter, she is further degraded to an insect in the dirt.

The second type of animal images in the novel reveals Chin-lian's animal-like nature. For example, in Chapter 52, she is compared to a black cat, and especially to "hsüeh-shih-tzû" (The Snowy-White-Lion), the white cat with a black line on its back, which was said to cause the death of Kuan-kê in Chin-lian's fierce competition with Li P'ing-êrh for Hsi-men's love. Compared to the rich and favoured P'ing-êrh, the poor and jealous Chin-lian is no more than the dog or the dog's dung which has stained Chin-lian's red shoes; while in the eyes of Yüeh-niang, Chin-lian is nothing but the transformation of a "nine-tailed fox spirit" which should be gotten rid of as soon as possible. Above all, Chin-lian is associated with the furious tiger in the beginning of the story. Here, the tiger not only reflects on Chin-lian's character but also foreshadows her death in Chapter 87 at the hand of Wu Sung. Although she is compared to a violent female tiger which kills many people, Chin-lian is nonetheless a prey at the mercy of the male hunter.

While the frequent association of Chin-lian with animals indicates her sexuality and animal-like nature, it also reminds us of the constant struggle between woman and man, nature and culture, individual will and social norm.

The subordination of the former to the latter is revealed through the trials of the degraded Chin-lian, a bare-footed animal in a hostile society full of traps and snares.

Chin-lian is not only degraded with animal imagery but also dehumanized to sex object in the *CPM.* The dehumanization and passivity of Chin-lian are best illustrated in Chapter 27, where she is seen as a "jou-hu" (a vase of flesh). Here, Hsi-men's act of "t'ou-hu" (aiming at the vase or throwing things into the vase) has sexual connotations. By using the plums (symbolized by *Li* P'ing-êrh and P'ang Ch'un-*mei*) to stimulate Chin-lian's "jou-hu" (her sexual organ), Hsi-men is actually enjoying a metaphorical sexual orgy. In fact, his near sadistic treatment by inserting a plum into her vagina and wild invasion of her sexual organ with the help of sexual aids almost kills her.

In addition to the symbol of a vase of flesh, Chin-lian is also associated with the small, bound feet, common among women of the time, through the association of her name. The term "chin-lian" or "san-tśun chin-lian" becomes not only the symbol of beauty and sexuality but also of inferiority and restriction. The smaller the feet are, the more sexually attractive the woman is and therefore more popular in the market. In the novel, Hsi-men is attracted to Chin-lian primarily by her small feet, and it is through the successful scheme of touching them under the table that Hsi-men reveals his desire of possessing her. Hsi-men also shows his admiration of Chin-lian's beauty through the act of putting a wine cup in her embroidered shoes and then drinking the wine as if from the shoes. Thus, diminished into a pair of three-inch deformed feet covered by beautiful shoes and leggings, which paradoxically are the center of women's attraction, Chin-lian becomes a mere sex object for Hsi-men's sexual desire and pleasure.

Chin-lian's name has sexual connotations through its literal meaning as well—a gilded lotus flower. Throughout the novel women are frequently referred to as "hua" (flower), which, among its various implications, has the sexual meaning of prostitute, vagina, or dissipation. Since the title of the *CPM* may be interpreted as "plums (flowers) in a golden vase," the novel may be seen as the life of women in the rich Hsi-men household. While the lotus can also be related to the female sexual organ, having all the sexual activities carried out in Hsi-men's glamorous and golden environment, Chin-lian, the golden lotus, is depicted as nothing but a sex object, from which the sexual joy of men, and especially that of Hsi-men, derives. As the life span of flowers in a golden vase is sure to be short, so is that of a lotus flower with gold covering.

To sum up, on the historical level, Chin-lian the woman is sacrificed by the discriminating customs of the patriarchal society; on the literary level, Chin-lian the character is degraded to animal associations and sex objects exploited by men. Far from being a bad or fatal woman as the traditional criticism claims, seen from a feminist view point, she is a mere victim.

From the traditional male perspective, the characterization of Pan Chin-lian is not only dehumanized as the stereotype of a bad or fatal woman but also trivialized as a marginal figure. Hsi-men Ch'ing is usually regarded as the "hero" the focus of the novel. Some critics have commented that **CPM** is a novel of the progress and decline of a rogue, or the adventure of a Chinese libertine. In contrast, the importance of the role of women, especially that of Chin-lian, is either distorted or neglected.

In fact, the very title of the **CPM,** which is named after three major female characters in the novel: Pan *Chin*-lian, Li *P'ing*-êrh, and P'ang Ch'un-*mei,* clearly indicates that it is a novel primarily about women. As the character of P'ing-êrh can be seen as a foil of Chin-lian and that of Ch'un-mei as a copy of her, these two heroines serve to enhance the character of Chin-lian in the novel.

Further, paralleling Hsi-men's struggle for wealth and status in the society, the fierce competition for position among wives of the Hsi-men household and the sexual battle for the power between men and women, especially between Hsi-men and Chin-lian, are the major concerns of the novel. Instead of remaining a helpless and passive victim in the patriarchal society, Chin-lian struggles to get power by subverting male domination paradoxically through the only means available to her—her sexuality. Although she sometimes victimizes other people in the process of power struggle, it is through her displacement of the traditional role of male and female, subject and object, master and slave, as well as husband and wife (however symbolic and temporary it may be) that from a feminist perspective Chin-lian is seen as holding the most central and significant position of the novel.

As the narrator several times comments that it is better not to be born a woman for all her woes and joys depend solely on man, the author's attitude toward Chin-lian and all the women of his time may be understanding and sympathetic. Dependent upon and at the mercy of male power, Chin-lian has been sold, transferred, raped, beaten, and humiliated. She does not, however, yield totally to such a situation of inferiority and powerlessness. Instead of passively accepting the miserable fate imposed upon her from without, within the limit of her confinement Chin-lian strives to survive and even to get what she wants with ambition and utmost will, sometimes at the expense of others.

Sold to be a maid in the Wang Chao-hsüan family, Chin-lian is trained to use cosmetics and employ pretentious manners to please men and to attract their attention. Being witty and quick to adapt, the innocent Chin-lian soon equips herself for more mature adventures. It is from her experience with Master Chang that the potential power of Chin-lian's beauty and sex is gradually revealed. Although Chin-lian herself is a victim in this relationship as analyzed previously, her sexual potency is nonetheless one of the indirect causes of her master's sudden death.

If Chang's death is seen as just punishment for the rapist, Chin-lian can not be completely guiltless for Wu Ta-lang's murder. Regarding her marriage to the "three-inch dwarf with rough-tree skin," both Chin-lian and the narrator lament her ill fate. Without any freedom of choice, Chin-lian, likened to gold and the phoenix, is given away free to a loathsome match likened to copper and the crow. To such a deformed and cowardly husband, it is only natural

that the beautiful and lonely Chin-lian will yearn for a better match. Though she did not intend to kill Wu Ta in the first place, under the forces of Hsi-men and Mother Wang on the one hand and the prospects of a better husband and environment on the other, Chin-lian eventually yields to the evil plan of poisoning her husband. From then on, she becomes not only an adulteress but also a murderer and sinks gradually into the dark side of the world.

Although Chin-lian is "freed" from her forced marriage by sacrificing Wu Ta, she is trapped into an even more fierce competition between women for their common husband in the Hsi-men household. To procure economic security, social status, and physical pleasure, Chin-lian is degraded to a "private possession" of Hsi-men, now the owner of her body. Since Hsi-men marries not only for pleasure but also for money—the dowry from the bride's family—poor Chin-lian from the lower class is in an unfavorable position when she becomes the fifth wife of Hsi-men Ch'ing. She has to struggle with bare hands both with other wives at home and with women outside the house for the attention and favor of Hsi-men, their common interest. As an aggressive and strong-willed woman, Chin-lian determines to do whatever she can to excel in the cruel competition for survival and position.

The practical and calculating Chin-lian employs different strategies to deal with her competitors as soon as she steps in Hsi-men's household. For her own benefit, she pretends to befriend the first and fourth wife. As the only legal wife in a traditional Chinese family, Wu Yüeh-niang has the highest status and absolute power among women at home. Though ordinary in appearance, she is a lady from a moderately rich family. Since Yüeh-niang is secure in position and finance, Chin-lian tries to flatter her to win her approval. Mên Yü-lou, the fourth wife, is a graceful, rich, and kind woman. She is the only wife of Hsi-men who treats Chin-lian as equal and calls her "sister" sincerely throughout the novel. As such a pleasant and unaggressive woman is far from a threat to her position, Chin-lian considers her more an ally than an enemy.

To the second and third wives who are as poor and low as she is, however, the sharp-tongued Chin-lian would use provocative or aggravating words to undercut them. Regarding Li Chiao-êrh who was originally a prostitute, Chin-lian attacks her as a "yin-fu" (debauched woman) in front of Yüeh-niang. As to Sun Hsüeh-ê who was a maid and now a cook, Chin-lian mocks her as a "nu-tśai" (slave maid) and talks Hsi-men into beating her severely just for small trifles (such as not having prepared breakfast on time).

As the sixth wife on Hsi-men, Li P'ing-êrh is Chin-lian's chief competitor at home. In contrast to Chin-lian, P'ing-êrh is not only rich and generous but also tender and submissive. As the widow of the son of a wealthy and powerful eunuch, she brings enormous wealth and treasure to Hsi-men and generously gives money, jewelry, and valuable gifts away which result in Hsi-men's good luck in business and her popularity at home. Though similar to Chin-lian, P'ing-êrh is an adultress who hurries her husband to death in order to marry Hsi-men, she is nevertheless tamed by Hsi-men and becomes a fully-devoted wife.

In addition to her wealth and submissiveness, P'ing-êrh gives birth to a son, Kuan-kê (Official Brother), the first son to the Hsi-men family whose name suggests Hsi-men's ambition in politics and foreshadows his first official job immediately after Kuan-kê's birth. Thus, P'ing-êrh doubles the luck she brings and strengthens her position at home. This is threatening to other wives and especially to Chin-lian whose position is only one step above her.

Since P'ing-êrh and Kuan-kê attract Hsi-men's complete attention, Chin-lian is gradually neglected. This sudden change of Hsi-men's attitude prompts Chin-lian's jealousy and hatred. To win back Hsi-men's favor and to secure her position, Chin-lian schemes to get rid of the child. She succeeds in scaring Kuan-kê to death by creating different kinds of shrieking noise to disturb the physically weak child and by creating chances for the cats to frighten the poor sick child. If Chin-lian is the direct cause of Kuan-kê's death, she may also be the indirect cause of P'ing-êrh's death. Mocked and irritated by Chin-lian behind her back, the defenseless P'ing-êrh gradually withdraws to silence and melancholy. The loss of her child and sorrows inside revive the former disease of incessant bleeding, and she eventually dies.

In the process of securing her power and position, Chin-lian victimizes men, women, and even innocent children. In a sense, her practicality, jealousy, hatred, and ruthlessness are due to the unjust marital system in which woman is exploited as either sexual or monetary object and her basic needs are slighted. Under such circumstances, Chin-lian has no other choice but to fight for her own security and benefit, sometimes at the cruel expense of others. From a victim to victimizer, the metamorphosis of Chin-lian exemplifies the evolution of a passive, helpless woman to an active, powerful one.

Although Chin-lian harms other people in her power struggle in the Hsi-men household, her major goal is to control Hsi-men himself, his body and mind. Victimized by her inferior sexual identity, economic status, and social class, Chin-lian becomes the sex object, playmate, and private possession of Hsi-men. With strong will and skillful maneuvering, however, Chin-lian gradually turns the tables: by employing her physical beauty and sexual potency as an instrument and weapon, she eventually dominates Hsi-men and completely victimizes him in the end.

As a woman endowed with natural charm since childhood, Chin-lian soon learns how to artificially make herself beautiful and attractive for men. In a male-oriented society, this is certainly one effective way for a maid to rise from her miserable situation. Both Master Chang and Hsi-men Ch'ing are attracted by her appearance. After marrying Hsi-men and being placed in competition with other beautiful women, Chin-lian works harder to adorn herself: she tries different hair styles, wears shining clothes, puts on gold jewelry, and manages to get new red shoes. All her devices are prompted not only by her sense of vanity but also by her intention to catch Hsi-men's attention. To cover her relatively dark skin, she puts white power mixed with jasmine fragrance all over her body to compete with P'ing-êrh's fair skin and to allure Hsi-men. To excite Hsi-men's lust, the witty Chin-lian dresses up in the disguise

of a cute maid. With naughty behavior and heavy make-up, Chin-lian wins Hsi-men over for a night and the promise of more new clothes.

Although the concealment of identity and the excitement of changing physical appearances sometimes help Chin-lian to catch Hsi-men's wandering heart, it is through her sexuality and her willingness to engage in Hsi-men's lascivious sexual activities that Chin-lian gradually controls his body. As the very symbol of female sexuality, Chin-lian does whatever necessary to please Hsi-men and to satisfy his sexual desire. Paradoxically, it is through passivity and obedience that Chin-lian gets what she wants from Hsi-men. For example, she yields to Hsi-men's request for the sexual position of "hou-ting-hua" after Hsi-men promises to buy her a new yellow silk skirt. She also practices the act of "p'in-hsiao" with Hsi-men to please him, and even humiliates herself by swallowing Hsi-men's urine afterwards to win back his heart and body.

Only after degrading herself to a passive vase for the joy of Hsi-men does Chin-lian start gaining the upper hand in their relationship. Before the death of P'ing-êrh, she is more passive and reserved; after she is sure of Hsi-men's favor again, however, Chin-lian becomes aggressive and demanding in fulfilling her own physical desire. For example, she begins practicing the position of "tao-chiao-chü" for her own sexual pleasure. Furthermore, she willfully replaces the "yin-tó-tzŭ" used by Hsi-men for stimulation with a long piece of white silk cloth, complaining that the former is not ideal for her. In contrast to the image of a profligate named "the leader of wife-beating and womanizing" in the past, Hsi-men is now seen passively led by Chin-lian. If he had received pleasure by exploiting women's bodies in the past, Hsi-men is now trapped by his over-indulgence in sex symbolized by the white silver cloth made by Chin-lian, which shall bind him and bring him to destruction.

Chin-lian not only becomes demanding in her sexual relationship with Hsi-men; she wants to monopolize him. She beats the wet nurse Ju-yi-êrh, who almost replaces P'ing-êrh's position for Hsi-men, and she further controls Hsi-men's action toward other wives. Eventually, Hsi-men even has to ask her permission for staying over-night in other women's rooms. Assured of Hsi-men's favor, Chin-lian starts arguing and fighting deliberately with the first wife in public. Hereafter, Hsi-men is fully controlled by Chin-lian, whose ever increasing power and position at home are reflected in Yüeh-niang's dream in which her large red coat, a symbol of authority and power, is grabbed away by the ambitious Chin-lian.

While Chin-lian's power and desire are increasing on the one hand, Hsi-men's mind and body are deteriorating on the other. In the famous Chapter 79, Hsi-men finally collapses on Chin-lian's bed. To satisfy her sexual desire, Chin-lian first tries to stimulate Hsi-men's penis by mouth. Then she gives three aphrodisiac pills to the drunken and exhausted Hsi-men with strong wine, despite the fact that one is the maximum dose. Further, she uses the white silk rope and applies ointment to the head of Hsi-men's bulging penis for her own excitation. While the voluptuous Chin-lian greedily enjoys herself, Hsi-men's swollen and erect penis, however, will not release itself . . .

> Finally a large quantity of semen squirts out. At first it was semen, and then it turned into a fluid composed mainly of blood, and there was no hope for him. Xi-men [Hsi-men] had fainted away, with his stiff limbs outstretched. . . . blood had followed semen and, now that the blood supply had exhausted, his penis kept on squirting nothing but cold air until the ejaculatory motion stopped.

As a sharp contrast to Chapter 27, in which Chin-lian is tortured by Hsi-men and almost passes away, here the tormentor is tormented: Hsi-men is now used as a sex object by Chin-lian, whose preoccupation with dominion and sexual pleasure leads to Hsi-men's downfall. Even until the end of Hsi-men's life, Chin-lian still utilizes his iron-like "chên-ping" to get pleasure:

> At night, Jin-lian [Chin-lian] who should have known better, would still sit astride him and have intercourse with him. And during a single night he would faint away and then regain consciousness several times over.

If Chin-lian has been used by Hsi-men as a sex object and viewed as a horse before, ironically, it is Hsi-men who is now likened to a male horse mounted by Chin-lian for her satisfaction. The non-human identity of the degraded Hsi-men is epitomized in his erect penis, which is literally exhausted by Chin-lian until the last minute. By reversing the traditional male-female role and power structure through the subtle manipulation of sexuality, Chin-lian the victim succeeds in transforming into a victimizer and in controlling Hsi-men totally. The victimizer of women is victimized by a woman—the death of Hsi-men on Chin-lian's bed bespeaks Chin-lian's symbolic victory over Hsi-men in particular and over the patriarchal system in general.

In her struggle for wealth, power, and pleasure, Chin-lian metamorphosizes from a victim to a victimizer of not only other women but also men, especially Hsi-men, who is the master and provider of all her desires. As the death of Hsi-men symbolizes Chin-lian's ultimate triumph over Hsi-men's mind and body, paradoxically it also leads to Chin-lian's own downfall. Though critics claim that Chin-lian is cold and heartless, it is in fact her emotions, along with the persecution of the male power, that bring about her death.

Like a double of Hsi-men, Chin-lian is ambitious, aggressive, and ruthless. Yet, unlike Hsi-men who has many opportunities to get in touch with the outside world, to travel, and to enjoy sexual relationships with the opposite sex, Chin-lian has none of these rights and advantages reserved for men. Not only is she confined to the house but she has to endure the pain and loneliness in time of Hsi-men's negligence and absence. Without proper outlets, all of Chin-lian's energy and talent is devoted to one goal—the possession of her husband's heart and body. Nonetheless, Chin-lian is not without genuine feelings and emotions. It is the prejudice against women in the society, along with the intense competition among wives in the family, and the pres-

sure of the dull, monotonous daily life imposed on women that gradually wears away Chin-lian's natural, spontaneous, and tender self.

In the beginning of the novel, Chin-lian tries to express her emotions with musical instruments and singing in time of distress and loneliness: she would play the *p'i-p'a* and sing songs to herself. As Hanan aptly points out, the dramatic use of songs in the novel is "the most remarkable technical innovation" revealing the psychological insight of the character's feelings. Chin-lian's singing on different occasions subtly express her hidden anguish and yearnings. For example, in the first chapter, Chin-lian laments her ill match with Wu Ta and her desperate loneliness by singing to herself alone in the tune of "Shan-p'o-yang." On another occasion, Chin-lian expresses her mixed feeling of romantic love and jealous doubt toward Hsi-men by playing the *p'i-p'a* and singing in the tune of "Mien-ta-hsü" alone at night. Through the lyrics of her song, Chin-lian is presented as a woman capable of sensitive and delicate feelings. In Chapter 38, the lonely Chin-lian plays the *p'i-p'a* awaiting Hsi-men's visit on a snowy windy night. Mistaking the noise from the tin roof for Hsi-men's knocking at her door, the disappointed Chin-lian sings two sad songs and scolds Hsi-men for being a "fu-hsin-tsei." Realizing later that Hsi-men is actually having wine with P'ing-êrh in the next room, the heart-broken Chin-lian cannot but shed tears for the first time in the novel and sings a sorrowful song to herself. With the lyric "My heart aches. I cannot comfort it. Sorrow and misery consume me utterly . . . ," we are presented the picture of a desolate, melancholic Chin-lian, a slighted concubine whose long-suppressed feelings and pathetic situation deserve our understanding and sympathy.

Chin-lian is not only talented in playing musical instruments and singing, but she also knows how to read and write. While Hsi-men is depicted as an illiterate, Chin-lian is educated: she knows how to play chess, write good calligraphy, and create poems of her own. When lonely or desperately in love, Chin-lian would write poems or letters to express her feelings. Yet her romantic tendency and individual passion are not fully understood by Hsi-men, whose communication with her is solely based on physical contact and lust.

It is in her relationship with Chen Ching-chi that Chin-lian fulfills her romantic love. As a counterpart to Hsi-men, Chen Ching-chi is handsome, attractive, and playful. In addition, he is given the power to manage the money and property of the entire household as Hsi-men's son-in-law. Further, he is young and romantic. Despite the fact that their relationship is highlighted by the sexual orgy with Ch'un-mei in Chapter 83, Chin-lian and Ching-chi's love affair is more romantic than that of Chin-lian and Hsi-men for the former are constantly expressing their feelings and yearnings for each other through poems and letters and even through sentimental gifts such as hair and a fan.

As a concubine and private possession of Hsi-men, Chin-lian is not allowed to have any extra-marital relationship, however romantic or passionate it may be, not to mention that it would be near incestuous. The discovery of such a relationship by Yüeh-niang thus provides a good chance for getting rid of her enemies—first, she sells Ch'un-mei for 50 liang of silver; then, she asks Mother Wang to take Chin-lian away for sale which eventually leads to her death in the hands of Wu Sung.

The death of Chin-lian is inevitable for the society will not allow such a daring and aggressive woman who has attempted to express herself and has threatened the patriarchal power and the domestic hierarchy to get away unpunished. It is worth noting that the two women directly related to Chin-lian's death are instruments used by the patriarchal society: Yüeh-niang, who sells Chin-lian like merchandise to maintain her own status and domestic order, is the symbol of male power; Mother Wang, who transfers Chin-lian like a sex object to men for financial profits, is a bawd and a womanizer of her fellow sisters. While Wu Sung, who carries out his furious revenge not through justice but through deception and violence, is the very symbol of patriarchal vengeance. Pretending that he is in love with Chin-lian and would like to marry her, Wu Sung deceives the once shrewd Chin-lian and purchases her from Mother Wang. Chin-lian's sentimental attraction toward Wu Sung blinds her sharp eyes in the crucial moment for she is most vulnerable when her feelings appear.

In Chapter 87, Wu Sung mercilessly kills Chin-lian. The brutal scene of Chin-lian's death reminds us of the tiger killed by him in the opening chapter:

> Wu Song [Wu Sung] took a handful of dust from the incense-burner and threw it into her mouth so that she could not make any more noise. He tugged at her hair and threw her down upon the ground. . . . Wu Song [Wu Sung] thought it possible that she might try to run away, and kicked her in the ribs. Then he stamped upon her arms with both his feet. . . . he tore her arms apart, and thrust the knife deep into her soft white bosom. One Slash, and there was a bleeding hole in her breast. Blood gushed forth. . . . [Wu Sung] took the knife in his teeth, tore open her breast with both hands, and dragged her heart and entrails from her body. . . . The blood streamed from them. . . . Then, with a single stroke, he cut off her head. . . . The blood flowed over the floor.

Transforming from a victim to a victimizer, Chin-lian fails to be a real victor. Rather than representing poetic justice of an evil woman as most critics assert, her bloody death and the disintegration of her butchered body become a silent protest against the injustice and violence imposed by a male-centered society upon a woman struggling for expression and power.

From a feminist perspective, Pan Chin-lian can be seen as the focus and central figure of the novel. The Hsi-men household and its garden serve as the stage for her rise and fall; all the major male and female characters serve either to echo or contrast with her personality. She is the one who carries all the life force in the story. Even her male counterpart, Hsi-men Ch'ing, is not as dynamic, energetic, and overwhelming a character as Chin-lian.

As a central figure, Chin-lian can be seen as complex rath-er than just being the stereotype of a fatal woman. On the one hand, she is a victim of the social norms, economic structure, and marriage system of her time. She is used as a sex object and commodity; her tender, romantic feelings are all but smothered. On the other hand, she is a victimizer in her struggle for money, pleasure, and power. Possessing utmost will and perseverance, she is shown as strong, ambitious, licentious, and sometimes ruthless.

Although from the traditional male perspective, ambition and aggressiveness are positive attributes for the 16th-century Chinese men like Hsi-men Ch'ing, they are signs of evil and destructiveness for the Chinese women like Pan Chin-lian. As the ideas of "san-kang wu-ch'ang" and "t'ien-li jen-yü" are pushed to their limit by the neo-Confucianists in the Ming dynasty, the destiny of any woman who rebels against her position at home and in society is shame and death. While traditional critics interpret Chin-lian's death as an indictment of Chin-lian herself, I suggest that in light of feminist critique her death, instead, is an indictment of her society. Far from being the author's device to punish a bad woman and thereby warn the reader, her tragic downfall and resulting conspicuous silence hint at his sympathy toward P'an Chin-lian—a woman who by attempting to transcend the inferior role and the domestic boundaries assigned to her, is eventually sacrificed at the hands of a brutal chauvinistic society. (pp. 609-24)

> *Ying-Ying Chien, "Sexuality and Power: A Feminist Reading of 'Chin P'ing Mei',"* in Tamkang Review, *Vol. XIX, Nos. 1-4, Autumn, 1988, pp. 607-29.*

FURTHER READING

Bishop, John L. "A Colloquial Short Story in the Novel *Chin p'ing mei.*" *Harvard Journal of Asiatic Studies* 17, Nos. 3-4 (December 1954): 394-402.

> Asserts that an episode in *Chin p'ing mei* was borrowed from a short story contained in the collection *Ku-chin hsiao-shuo.* Bishop concludes: "If we were to feel that the artistic stature of *Chin p'ing mei* was lessened by such a discovery, we would also be forced to lower our esteem for such works as *The Canterbury Tales* and many of Shakespeare's plays on the same grounds."

Carlitz, Katherine. "The Conclusion of the *Jin ping mei.*" *Ming Studies* No. 10 (Spring 1980): 23-9.

> Rejects the assumption that chapter 100 of *Chin p'ing mei* is informed by Buddhist teachings that would encourage a positive, redemptive interpretation of the novel's close: "The real intent of this chapter, I feel, is to emphasize the need for a traditional Confucian sort of self-cultivation, and to stress the parallel dangers to household and empire that arise when this self-cultivation is neglected."

——. "Puns and Puzzles in the *Chin p'ing mei:* A Look at

Chapter 27." *T'oung Pao Revue Internationale De Sinologie* LXVII, Nos. 3-5 (1981): 216-39.

Finds that the events, images, and allusions in chapter 27 of the earliest extant edition of *Chin p'ing mei* belie an ostensible celebration of aberrant sexual practices, emphasizing "the danger of giving oneself over to luxury and extravagance."

———. "Codes and Correspondences in *Jin Ping Mei.*" *Chinese Literature: Essays, Articles, Reviews* 8, Nos. 1-2 (July 1986): 7-18.

Argues that *Chin p'ing mei*'s apparently optimistic conclusion, in which the protagonists are reincarnated, is undermined by metaphors and structural and linguistic patterns within the text.

Chaoyang Liao. "Three Readings in the *Jinpingmei cihua.*" *Chinese Literature: Essays, Articles, Reviews* 6, No. 1-2 (July 1984): 77-99.

Maintains that the plurality of narrative voices in *Chin p'ing mei* comprise an "extremely problematic existential world."

Chi Ch'iu-lang. " 'Fair Needs Foul': Moral Ambiguity in *Chin p'ing mei.*" *Tamkang Review* XIII, No. 1 (Fall 1982): 71-86.

Defends *Chin p'ing mei* against charges of pornography, claiming that through its moral ambiguity and its portrayal of diverse experiences the novel conveys life as eclectic and complex.

Egerton, Clement. Introduction to *"The Golden Lotus": A Translation from the Chinese Original, of the Novel "Chin P'ing Mei,"* vol. I, translated by Clement Egerton, pp. vii-x. London: Routledge & Kegan Paul, 1972.

States that *Chin p'ing mei* is not only a source of psychological and cultural material but also a masterpiece of the novel form, as evidenced by its "power of conveying the essential with the utmost economy in the use of literary devices."

Hanan, P. D. "The Text of the *Chin p'ing mei.*" *Asia Major: A British Journal of Far Eastern Studies* IX, No. 1 (1962): 1-57.

Discusses the authenticity and early history of the various texts and manuscripts of *Chin p'ing mei.*

———. "Sources of the *Chin p'ing mei.*" *Asia Major: A British Journal of Far Eastern Studies* X, No. 1 (1963): 23-67.

Enumerates "those works which have been copied into the *Chin p'ing mei* in sufficient amounts for us to identify them," including a novel, short stories, histories, dramas, and popular songs. Hanan asserts that *Chin p'ing mei* is "remarkable in patently accepting so many diverse influences; the implication for us is that we should regard it as transcending earlier patterns, rather than conforming to them."

Lévy, André. "Perspectives on the *Jin ping mei*: Comments and Reminiscences of a Participant in the *Jin ping mei* Conference." *Chinese Literature: Essays, Articles, Reviews* 8, Nos. 1-2 (July 1986): 1-6.

Reflects on scholarly papers on *Chin p'ing mei* presented at a May 1983 conference at Indiana University.

Plaks, Andrew H. "The Chongzen Commentary on the *Jin ping mei*: Gems amidst the Dross." *Chinese Literature: Essays, Articles, Reviews* 8, Nos. 1-2 (July 1986): 19-30.

Examines a critical commentary, attributed to the late Ming literary figure Li Zhi, on the Chongzen-period edition of the *Chin p'ing mei.* Plaks notes that "the early date of the commentary . . . affords it a very special significance, since it gives a unique glimpse into what the *Jin ping mei* means to readers that had not yet witnessed in their own lives the collapse of the Ming world-order analogically prophesied [in the novel] in the fall of the Sung house."

Roy, David T. "Chang Chu-p'o's Commentary on the *Chin p'ing mei.*" In *Chinese Narrative: Critical and Theoretical Essays,* edited by Andrew H. Plaks, pp. 115-23. Princeton, N.J.: Princeton University Press, 1977.

Observes that the critical analysis written sometime between 1666 and 1684 by Chang Chu-p'o on the *Chin p'ing mei* "is the most illuminating critical analysis in depth of any Chinese novel with which I am familiar in any language."

Scott, Mary. "The Image of the Garden in *Jin ping mei* and *Hongloumeng.*" *Chinese Literature: Essays, Articles, Reviews* 8, Nos. 1-2 (July 1986): 83-94.

Claims that the dominant image in *Chin p'ing mei* is the garden, asserting that in Hsi-men Ch'ing's garden "people act on the basis of their desires (*qing*), and are only minimally constrained by the ordained social hierarchies." Scott notes that the ruin and abandonment of the garden suggests that "if it is not to destroy the structure of society, *qing* must be channeled into socially sanctioned relationships."

Waley, Arthur. Introduction to *Chin p'ing mei: The Adventurous History of Hsi Men and His Six Wives,* translated by Bernard Miall, pp. ix-xxiv. New York: G. P. Putnam's Sons, 1940.

Notes that according to a popular legend concerning the history of *Chin p'ing mei,* the novel is a tribute to filial piety and a pitiless satire of an unscrupulous politician. Waley also discusses the censorship of the novel and proposes the writer Hsü Wei (1520-1593) as the most likely candidate for authorship of the work.

William Langland

1330?-1400?

English poet.

Generally considered the greatest of the Middle English dream poets, Langland is the author of the medieval allegory *Piers Plowman.* He has been classified as a poet, a mystic, and a social reformer, and likened to a medieval William Blake. His *Piers Plowman,* which he revised over the course of thirty years, survives in three separate versions (the A, B, and C texts) each grouped according to the state of its revision. In its longest form, the C-text, the story of Will the dreamer's search for the key to salvation, extends to over 7,000 lines. Critics agree that the poem vividly presents medieval social and theological problems in all their complexity, but they also attest to the difficulty of understanding Langland's commentary. As Robert Worth Frank, Jr. writes: "*Piers Plowman* enjoys a dubious distinction. Few will question its importance as a literary and social document in medieval English literature, but fewer still are certain of its meaning."

Almost no information on Langland's life is available. Researchers have been able to reconstruct aspects of his biography from hints in *Piers Plowman* itself, believing the poem the most reliable source for such data. Some have suggested the poet's name to be Robert and his surname to be De Langlonde or Langley, but most have agreed with Walter W. Skeat's conclusion that it was William Langland. The poet was probably born in the West Midlands of England, either in Cleobury Mortimer, Shropshire, about eight miles from the Malvern Hills (the setting for a large portion of his poem) or in Herefordshire, between Colwall and Ledbury, just north of the Malvern Hills. Several other manuscripts also contain references to Langland, one calling him the son of a nobleman named Stacey (Eustace) de Rokayle. Scholars surmise that Langland was educated in the Benedictine priory of the Great Malvern in Worcestershire, but that the death of his father and a close friend left him with no benefactor. Unable to complete his education, he was forced to abandon his training as a priest and take only minor orders. Langland probably earned meager wages as a cleric, possibly performing offices of the dead in London, where he lived in Cornhill with his wife Kitte and his daughter Callote. The first manuscript of *Piers Plowman* appeared in approximately 1362, and literary historians estimate that Langland spent between fifteen and thirty-three years revising and refining his work. Nothing is known of the rest of his life.

Piers Plowman is unique among fourteenth-century Christian allegories because, while other poems take place in symbolic or otherworldly realms, Langland's work is set in the real world of medieval England. Will, the narrator of the work, whom many critics believe to be a thinly-veiled representative of the poet himself, opens the poem's prologue as he begins a stroll in the Malvern Hills of England on a May morning. When he pauses to rest, he falls asleep and experiences a vision in which "a faire felde ful of folke" from all levels of medieval life proceed about their daily business, in a land bordered by the Tower of Truth to the east and the Dale of Death to the west. The first major section of the poem, the *Visio,* begins as the dreamer meets Lady Holy Church. When he questions her on how to recognize Falsehood, Holy Church answers by showing him Lady Meed, a complex satirical personification of *cupiditas,* or covetousness, the desire for earthly wealth. Lady Meed and Falsehood are to be wed, but Theology protests the match. The group appears before the king, who refuses to allow the union, permitting Meed to marry only Conscience, one of his knights. Conscience refuses to cooperate, however, without the counsel of Reason, who, when summoned, opposes their marriage. Meed is banished and the king proposes that Reason serve as his Chancellor and Conscience as his Justice. The dreamer's next vision is also set in the "felde ful of folke," where he observes Reason advising a crowd to repent and to seek Truth. The Seven Deadly Sins then come forward; Pride, Lechery, Envy, Wrath, Avarice, Sloth, and Gluttony each confess their sins and are absolved. The "folke" then take the advice of Reason, beginning their search for Truth. It is here that Piers Plowman makes his first appearance in the poem and offers to guide the crowd to their destination, informing them, however, that he must first plow his half-acre of land. Some of the people begin to help him, but the pilgrimage never takes place. Instead, Truth sends Piers a pardon saying that those who do well will be saved, and those who do not will be damned. When a priest claims that the message is not a pardon at all, Piers proceeds to tear it up, leaving his farm work to begin a life of prayer and penance in search of Do-Well, a quality representing the first step in a three-step process to attaining Christian perfection.

The second major section of the poem, the *Vita of Do-Well, Do-Better, and Do-Best* consists of Will's quest for these three qualities. Though scholars debate their significance, they generally agree that the terms correspond to the Active, Contemplative, and Mixed lives of Christianity: Do-Well represents the good works associated with the life of a layman; Do-Better the religious reflection associated with the life of a priest; and Do-Best a combination of the two, associated with the life of a bishop. In the *Vita of Do-Well,* Will consults several allegorical figures for answers in his search for Do-Well. He eventually meets Haukyn, or Active Man, whose coat is covered with stains representing the Seven Deadly Sins. When Patience informs Haukyn of his Christian duty, he repents his sins and wakes the dreamer, ending the first section of the *Vita.* In the *Vita of Do-Better,* Piers appears again, this time as the guardian of the Tree of Charity. Will then observes the passion of Christ, a vision of Christ jousting in the armor of Piers Plowman, the Harrowing of Hell, and the Resurrection. The *Vita of Do-Best* portrays Piers as Christ's vicar on Earth. When Conscience learns that the Antichrist is preparing to attack them, Piers builds a fortress for humanity called the House of Unity, but when the attack comes the Christians are unprepared. In the wake of the destruction, Conscience vows to become a pilgrim in search of Piers Plowman, who has once again disappeared from the vision. With this, the dreamer awakes and the poem ends.

The poem must have been popular with its early readers, for an estimated fifty-one surviving manuscripts (seventeen A-texts, fifteen B-texts, and nineteen C-texts) of *Piers Plowman* are extant, dating from the fourteenth and fifteenth centuries. Scholars agree on approximate dates of composition for each group based on internal references to historical events. The A-text, written around 1362, contains 2,572 lines and twelve passus, or "steps," while the B-text, written fifteen years later, expands the poem by another 4,670 lines and adds eight new passus. The C-text, which enlarges the B-text by 115 lines and three passus, has posed especially difficult problems for scholars attempting to date the work, and estimates of its date of composition range from 1377 to 1395. The first printed edition of the poem was Robert Crowley's 1550 version of the B-text. No new edition of *Piers Plowman* appeared for over 200 years following this publication, until T. D. Whitaker offered the first edition of the C-text in 1813. Walter W. Skeat's 1886 parallel edition of the three texts included the first publication of the A-text, and many scholars have since hailed his work as an essential tool for studying Langland.

While these early editions of *Piers Plowman* led scholars to question textual issues, they also opened debate on the validity of attributing the poem to Langland. From Elizabethan times to the early nineteenth century, Langland was accepted as the undisputed author of *Piers Plowman,* but in 1865 Thomas Wright proposed that the work was actually the work of two poets. The controversy continued into the twentieth century when, in 1908, J. M. Manly led a group of scholars who claimed that *Piers Plowman* was actually the work of five separate authors. Critics continued to debate the point even after the appearance of A. H. Bright's 1928 study *New Light on Piers Plowman,* which concludes that the poem was definitely the work of one author, William Langland. Recently, scholars have come to accept Langland as the sole author of the poem and the controversy has generally disappeared as a critical issue. Another contested point in Langland studies has been the attribution of the medieval poem *Richard the Redeless* to Langland. Though Skeat included it in his 1886 edition of *Piers Plowman,* twentieth-century researchers have concluded that the poem is probably the work of another author. In 1983, A. G. Rigg and Charlotte Brewer published a new version of *Piers Plowman,* the Z-text, "a copy of a version written *before* the A-text"; their findings have sparked scholarly speculation, but have not yet gained widespread acceptance. Although Skeat's edition is still considered a standard text of the poem, George Kane's editions of the A- and B-text are also considered noteworthy modern versions of the poem.

Piers Plowman is written in the alliterative long line associated with medieval homiletic and didactic writings. In most lines of the poem, three main stresses are held together by the sound of initial accented syllables, creating a flowing rhythm: "In a somer seson when soft was the sonne . . .". Langland's style, described as colloquial and often prosaic, is unlike that of the other poets of the Middle English Alliterative Revival, but critics acknowledge that his particular blend of satire and allegory does follow in the tradition of Guillaume de Lorris and Jean de Meung's *Roman de la Rose*. Commentators have praised Langland for effectively infusing *Piers Plowman* with his anger at corrupt church practices. His broad, dark satire portrays large crowds at work cheating, robbing, and tricking each other, and his combination of disdain and humor strengthens the ironic depiction of dishonest church officials. The overall structure of *Piers Plowman* also differs from the highly stylized and symbolic organization of other works of its age: passus are frequently begun and ended haphazardly, with no apparent logical connections. Some scholars view the poem's seeming lack of organization as a fault; others have remarked that Langland's unique use of dream poem conventions lends a modern feel to the poem. Unlike most medieval dream poems, in which the dream itself is generally presented as a copy of the actual world, Langland's treatment of Will's dream is characterized by an indifference to traditional chronological order, distortion of reality, and highly ambiguous renderings of many of the characters, particularly Piers Plowman. "It has been argued that Piers represents mankind, the Church, the Pope, St. Peter, Christ in His humanity and other allied subjects," Rosemary Woolf observes, adding that "the figure of Piers has in fact the peculiar force of something which is only half understood. This kind of romantic uncertainty, however, was quite alien to the earlier Middle Ages." Scholars have noted ambiguousness not only in the representation of certain characters in the poem but in the very meaning of *Piers Plowman:* Langland's irony seems to continually shift focus and resist logic, making it difficult to arrive at an all-encompassing interpretation of the allegory. Whether *Piers Plowman* reflects the confused ramblings of a medieval theologian, an early surrealistic treatment of dreams, or something entirely different is still being debated. Meanwhile, critics continue to appreciate Langland's varied approaches to the theme of the religious quest. As Elizabeth Salter has observed, the poem is at once "a satirical commentary on the mediaeval scene," "a subtly performed exercise in religious allegory," and "a deepening analysis and correction of sin."

Although *Piers Plowman* was widely read in its day, no new editions of the poem appeared from 1550 to 1813. In the latter part of the sixteenth century, Langland came to be seen as a radical social reformer, a follower of John Wycliffe, and a forerunner of the Protestant Reformation noted for his criticism of the medieval Catholic Church. Langland was rediscovered in the mid-nineteenth century, with most literary historians recognizing him as a representative medieval English poet. Modern scholars have come to view him not as a precursor to the Reformation, but as "the most Catholic of English poets," as Christopher Dawson has called him; Langland was intolerant of such medieval church corruptions as papal wealth and the abuse of indulgences, and he earnestly advocated the merit of good works and voluntary poverty. In discussing *Piers Plowman* in terms of its literary value, some twentieth-century scholars have concluded that Langland's writing is choppy and disorganized. C. S. Lewis wrote: "He lacks the variety of Chaucer, and Chaucer's fine sense of language: he is confused and monotonous, and hardly makes his poetry into a poem." But other Langland scholars such as Henry W. Wells and Nevill Coghill have uncovered an intricate underlying structure in *Piers Plowman,* especially in the *Vita* itself, as well as in the relationship between the *Vita* and the *Visio.* Langland's poem still challenges critics to explore a range of topics concerning its structure and significance, including the difficulty of assigning the poem to any one genre, the ambiguity of Langland's language and its effect on the allegory, and the theory that, in ending on a note of despair, the poem is meant to reflect the general social upheaval of the late fourteenth century.

Piers Plowman has continued to intrigue readers for centuries, partly because of its complexity and the sheer difficulty of pinning down its precise meaning. As Barbara Nolan has observed, the poem represents an irreversible shift in perspective "from the sureness of a soul *in aveo* to the linear uncertainties of a spirit *in medias res,* desperately dreaming of finality." While understanding God's will for humanity and achieving ultimate salvation may appear almost unattainable in *Piers Plowman,* the poet portrays the pursuit of these desires as a lifelong search—one in which, as Nolan writes, "Piers (and Langland) war against human failure and boldly point the way on a journey to an ultimate historical moment beyond the chaos of the contemporary world."

PRINCIPAL WORKS

*The Vision of Pierce Plowman [edited by Robert Crowley] (poetry) 1550
†Visio Willi de Petro Plouhman [edited by Thomas Dunham Whitaker] (poetry) 1813
The Vision of William concerning Piers the Plowman in Three Parallel Texts together with Richard the Redeless [edited by W. W. Skeat] (poetry) 1866
‡The Vision of Piers Plowman Newly Rendered into Modern English [translated by H. W. Wells] (prose) 1935
#Piers the Ploughman [translated by J. F. Goodridge] (prose) 1959; revised edition 1966
Piers Plowman: The A Version. Will's Visions of Piers Plowman and Do-Well [edited by George Kane] (poetry) 1960; revised edition, 1988
Piers Plowman: The B Version. Will's Visions of Piers Plowman, Do-Well, Do-Better, and Do-Best [edited by George Kane and E. Talbot Donaldson] (poetry) 1975; revised edition 1988
Piers Plowman: The Z Text [edited by A. G. Rigg and Charlotte Brewer] (poetry) 1983

*An edition of the B-text, written in approximately 1377.

†An edition of the C-text, written sometime between 1377 and 1395.

‡A translation based on a conflation of the A-, B-, and C-texts.

A translation based on the B-text.

Robert Crowley   (essay date 1550)

[*In the following prefatory note, "The Printer to the Reader," appended to the first published edition of* Piers Plowman *(1550), Crowley discusses the authorship, date, and versification of Langland's poem and compares its religious tone to the works of John Wycliffe.*]

Beynge desyerous to knowe the name of the Autoure of this most worthy worke (gentle reader) and the tyme of the writynge of the same: I did not onely gather togyther suche aunciente copies as I could come by, but also consult such mē as I knew to be more exercised in the studie of antiquities, then I my selfe haue ben. And by some of them I haue learned that the Autour was named Roberte langelande, a Shropshere man borne in Cleybirie, about viii. myles from Maluerne hilles.

For the time when it was written: it chaunced me to se an auncient copye, in the later ende whereof was noted, that the same copye was written in the yere of oure Lorde .M.iiii.C. and nyne, which was before thys presente yere, an hundred & xli. yeres. And in the seconde side of the .lx-viii. leafe of thys printed copye, I finde mētion of a dere yere, that was in the yere of oure Lorde, M.iii. hundred and .L. Iohn Chichester than beynge mayre of London. So that this I may be bold to reporte, that it was fyrste made and wrytten after the yeare of our lord .M.iii.C.L. and before the yere .M,iiiiC, and .ix which meane spase was .lix yeres. We may iustly cōiect therfore yt it was firste written about two hundred yeres paste, in the tyme of Kynge Edwarde the thyrde. In whose tyme it pleased God to open the eyes of many to se hys truth, geuing them boldenes of herte, to open their mouthes and crye oute agaynste the worckes of darckenes, as did Iohn wicklefe, who also in those dayes translated the holye Bible into the Englishe tonge, and this writer who in reportynge certaine visions and dreames, that he fayned him selfe to haue dreamed: doeth moste christianlye enstruct the weake, and sharply rebuke the obstinate blynde. There is no maner of vice, that reigneth in anye estate of men, whiche this wryter hath not godly, learnedlye, and wittilye, rebuked. He wrote altogyther in miter; but not after ye maner of our rimers that write nowe adayes (for his verses ende not alike) but the nature of hys miter is, to haue thre wordes at the leaste in euery verse whiche beginne with some one letter. As for ensample, the firste two verses of the boke renne vpon .s. as thus.

In a somer season whan sette was the Sunne,
I shope me into shrobbes, as I a shepe were.

The next runneth vpon .H. as thus.

> In habite as an Hermite vnholy of werckes. &c.

This thinge noted, the miter shal be very pleasaunt to read. The Englishe is according to the time it was written in, and the sence somewhat darcke, but not so harde, but that it may be vnderstande of suche as will not sticke to breake the shell of the nutte for the kernelles sake.

As for that is written in the .xxxvi. leafe of thys boke concernynge a dearth thē to come: is spokē by the knoweledge of astronomie as may wel be gathered bi that he saith, Saturne sente him to tell And that whiche foloweth and geueth it the face of a prophecye: is lyke to be a thinge added of some other man than the fyrste autour. For diuerse copies haue it diuerslye. For where the copie that I folowe hath thus.

> And when you se the sunne amisse, & two
> monkes heades
> And a mayde haue the maistrye, and multiplie
> by eyght.

Some other haue

> Three shyppes and a shefe, wyth an eight fo-
> lowynge
> Shall brynge bale and battell, on both halfe the
> mone.

Nowe for that whiche is written in the .l, leafe, cōcerning the suppression of Abbaies: the scripture there alledged, declareth it to be gathered of the iuste iudgment of god, whoe wyll not suffer abomination to raigne vnpunished.

> Loke not vpon this boke therfore, to talke of wonders
> paste or to
> come, but to amende thyne owne misse, which thou
> shalt fynd here
> moste charitably rebuked. The spirite of god gyue
> the grace to walke in the waye of truthe,
> to Gods glory, & thyne owne
> soules healthe.
> So be it.

> (pp. lxxiii-lxxv)

Robert Crowley, in an excerpt in The Vision of William concerning Piers the Plowman in Three Parallel Texts, Vol. II *by William Langland, edited by Walter W. Skeat, Oxford University Press, London, 1924, pp. lxxiii-lxxv.*

E. Cooper   (essay date 1737)

[*An English critic and dramatist, Cooper was the principal compiler of* The Muses Library, *an important early study of English poets. In the following excerpt from that work she calls Langland "the first of the* English Poets." *Although she notes that* Piers Plowman *appears fragmented, with "every Vision seeming a distinct Rhapsody, and not carrying on either one single Action, or a Series of many," Cooper praises the forcefulness of the moral lesson the poem imparts.*]

The Author of the Satire, intitled, **The Vision of Piers the Plowman** . . . may be truly call'd the first of the *English* Poets. [John] *Selden,* in his Notes on *Draiton's Poly-Olbion,* quotes him with Honour; but he is not so much as mention'd either by [Edward] *Philips* or [Gerrard] *Winstanly,* though, in my Judgment, no Writer, except *Chaucer,* and *Spencer,* for many Ages, had more of real Inspiration. I must own I can't read his Work, without lamenting the Unhappiness of a fluctuating Language, that buries even Genius it self in its Ruins: 'Tis raising Edifices of Sand, that every Breath of Time defaces; and, if the Form remains, the Beauty is lost. This is the Case of the Piece before us; 'Tis a Work of great Length, and Labour; of the Allegorick-kind; animated with a rich Imagination, pointed with great Variety of just Satire, and dignify'd with many excellent Lessons of Morality and Virtue: And, to say all in a Word, if I may presume to say so much, *Chaucer* seems to have this Model in his Eye; and, in his *Pardoners Prologue,* particularly, has a Feature or two nearly resembling the Speech and Character of *Sloth* hereafter quoted.

I am not ignorant that the Author of the Art of *English Poesy,* mention'd in the Preface, ranks him, in Point of Time, after *Chaucer;* but as he is not so much as acquainted with his Name, there is little Reason to depend on his Authority. Besides, 'tis notorious *Langland* copies his Characters, and Manners from the Age he lived in, and we find him, in one Passage, seating *Reason* between the King and his Son: In another, *Conscience* reproaches *Mede* with causing the Death of the King's Father, which exactly tallies with the Fall of *Edward* II. And, in a Third, *Mede* speaks of the Siege of *Calais,* as a recent Fact, and upbraids *Conscience* as the only Impediment to the Conquest of *France;* which, says she, if I had govern'd, could have been easily effected. From which Historical References, I make no Scruple to place him in the Reign of *Edward* III. or that of *Richard* II. his Successor. To this may be added; That the worst Writer, after *Chaucer,* had some regard to Measure, and never neglected Rhymes: Whereas

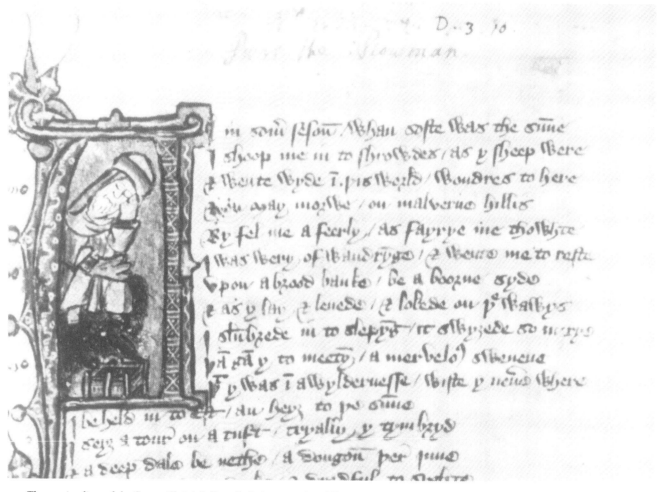

The opening lines of the Corpus Christi College, Oxford manuscript of Piers Plowman, *whose illuminated initial depicts the sleeping dreamer.*

this is greatly defective in both; seldom affording a perfect Verse, and using a Dialect hardly intelligible. But of this enough! This work is divided into *Twenty* Parts; the Arguments of which are wrote with uncommon Spirit; and several Passages in it deserve to be immortal; But, as to the Conduct of the whole, I must confess it does not appear to me of a Piece; every Vision seeming a distinct Rhapsody, and not carrying on either one single Action, or a Series of many. But we ought rather to wonder at its Beauties, than cavil at its Defects; and, if the Poetical Design is broken, the Moral is entire; which is, uniformly, the Advancement of Piety, and Reformation of the *Roman* Clergy. (pp. 7-9)

> *E. Cooper, in an excerpt in* The Muses Library, *Vol. I.,* J. Wilcox, 1737, pp. 7-9.

Thomas Dunham Whitaker   (essay date 1813)

[*In the following excerpt from his introduction to his* Visio Willi de Petro Plouhman *(1813), the first edition of the C-text, Whitaker calls Langland "an observer and a reflector of no common power," praising him for his "acute moral sense" and "keen sarcastic humor."*]

During the reign of Edward the Third, one of the most splendid, but not the most refined in our annals, yet equally removed from both these extremes, arose in this country two poets, the writings of one of whom contributed to enlarge the minds, and of the other to improve the moral feelings of their contemporaries in a degree unfelt since the æras of the great Roman satirists. The first of these [Chaucer], a man of the world and a courtier, at once informed and delighted the higher orders by his original and lively portraits of human nature in every rank, and almost under every modification, while he prevented or perverted the proper effect of satire by the most licentious and obscene exhibitions. The latter [Langland], an obscure country priest, much addicted to solitary contemplation, but at the same time a keen and severe observer of human nature; well read in the scriptures and schoolmen, and intimately acquainted with the old language and poetry of his country, in an uncouth dialect and rugged metre, by his sarcastic and ironical vein of wit, his knowledge of low life, his solemnity on some occasions, his gaiety on others, his striking personifications, dark allusions, and rapid transitions, has contrived to support and animate an allegory (the most insipid for the most part and tedious of all vehicles of instruction) through a bulky volume. By what inducement he was led to prefer this vehicle, it is not difficult to conjecture. From his subordinate station in the church, this free reprover of the higher ranks was exposed to all the severities of ecclesiastical discipline: and from the aristocratical temper of the times he was liable to be crushed by the civil power. Everything, therefore, of a personal nature was in common prudence to be avoided. The great were not then accustomed, as a licentious press has since disciplined them, to endure the freedoms of reprehension:—authority was, even when abused, sacred; and rank, when united with vice, was enabled to keep its partner in countenance. Above all, the great ecclesiastics were as vindictive as they were corrupt: and hence the satirist was compelled to shelter himself under the distant generalities of personification.

But, unfortunately, by this means, whatever he gained in personal security, he lost in the point and distinctness of his satire. Mere personifications of virtues and vices, however skilfully and powerfully touched, are capable of few strokes: the quality is simple, but different individuals, who partake of it in a degree however preeminent, combine and modify it in such an infinite variety of ways, with other subordinate traits and features of character, that while the abstract property is one and the same, in its actual existence, as part of the moral nature of man, it is capable in skilful hands of infinite diversities of representation. It is indeed far from being necessary that the characters be real, but, for the purposes of satirical painting, they must be *persons*.

From this uniformity of appearance in his abstract qualities the author has been betrayed, by the necessity of combination in some way or other, into the fault of mixing his personifications with each other; as, *ex. gr.* avarice and fraud, qualities which, though nearly akin, have no necessary co-existence; and, for the same reason, wherever he deviates into personality, as in the coarse but striking scene of "Glutton's" Debauch, where the characters, though imaginary, are persons, not personifications, he paints with all the truth and distinctness of a Dutch master. . . . .

Wherever born or bred, and by whatever name distinguished, the author of these Visions was an observer and a reflector of no common powers. I can conceive him (like his own visionary William) to have been sometimes occupied in contemplative wanderings on the Malvern Hills, and dozing away a summer's noon among the bushes, while his waking thoughts were distorted into all the misshapen forms created by a dreaming fancy. Sometimes I can descry him taking his staff, and roaming far and wide in search of manners and characters; mingling with men of every accessible rank, and storing his memory with hints for future use. I next pursue him to his study, sedate and thoughtful, yet wildly inventive, digesting the first rude drafts of his Visions, and in successive transcriptions, as judgment matured, or invention declined, or as his observations were more extended, expanding or contracting, improving and sometimes perhaps debasing his original text. The time of our author's death, and the place of his interment, are equally unknown, with almost every circumstance relating to him. His contemporaries, Chaucer

and Gower, repose beneath magnificent tombs, but Langland (if such were really his name) has no other monument than that which, having framed for himself, he left to posterity to appropriate. . . . .

The Reformers of the sixteenth century claimed as their own the Author of these Visions; but surely on no good grounds. That he believed and taught almost all the fundamental doctrines of Christianity has no tendency to prove him a Wickliffite or Lollard. The best and soundest members of the church of Rome have done the same. It is not defects but redundancies which we impute to them. Of the predestinarian principles afterwards professed by Wickliff, Langland seems to think with disapprobation; and when his visionary hero speaks of himself as belonging to the Lolleres, he evidently means, not the religious party distinguished by a similar name, but, in the usual strain of his irony, a company of idle wanderers. Yet in the midst of darkness and spiritual slavery, his acute and penetrating understanding enabled him to discover the multiplied superstitions of the public service, the licentious abuse of pilgrimages, the immoral tendencies of indulgences, the bad effects upon the living of expiatory services for the dead, the inordinate wealth of the papacy, and the usurpations of the mendicant orders, both on the rights of the diocesans and of the parochial clergy. These abuses Langland, with many other good men who could endure to remain in the communion of the church of Rome, saw and deplored; but though he finally conducted his pilgrim out of the particular communion of Rome into the universal church, he permitted him to carry along with him too many remnants of his old faith, such as satisfaction for sin to be made by the sinner, together with the merit of works, and especially of voluntary poverty; but, above all, the worship of the cross; incumbrances with which the Lollards of his own, or the Protestants of a later age, would not willingly have received him as a proselyte.

Neither was he an enemy to monastic institutions themselves: on the contrary, he appears to have sighed for the quiet and contemplative life of the cloister, could it have been restored to its primitive purity and order.

On the nature and origin of civil society, as on most other subjects, he thought for himself; and, at a period when mankind had scarcely begun to speculate on such subjects at all, he boldly traced the source of kingly power to the will of the people, and considered government as instituted for the benefit of the governed. Indeed a strong democratic tendency may be discovered in many passages of his work. . . . .

Crowley's editions of the Visions are printed from a MS. of late date and little authority, in which the division of the passus is extremely confused, and the whole distribution of the work perplexed. Still, it must be confessed, that, with the advantage of better MSS., the investigation of the general plan of these Visions is not without its difficulties. The work is altogether the most obscure in the English language, both with respect to phraseology, to the immediate connection of the author's ideas, and to the leading divisions of the subject. . . . .

All these varieties [of text], however, bear marks, not of

the same spirit and genius only, but of the same peculiar and original manner, so that it is scarcely to be conceived that they are interpolations of successive transcribers. Whatever be the cause, however, it may confidently be affirmed, that the text of no ancient work whatever contains so many various readings, or differs so widely from itself.

To account for this phenomenon, however, in the penury, or rather in the absence of original information relating to the author, we are at liberty to suppose that the first edition of his work appeared when he was a young man, and that he lived and continued in the habit of transcribing to extreme old age. But a man of *his* genius would not submit to the drudgery of mere transcription; his invention and judgment would always be at work; new abuses, and therefore new objects of satire, would emerge from time to time: and as a new language began to be spoken, he might, though unwillingly, be induced to adopt its modernisms, in order to make his work intelligible to a second or third generation of readers. In this last respect, however, it is not improbable that his transcribers might use some freedoms; for while we deny them invention to add, we may at least allow them skill to translate. . . . .

The writer of these Visions had the first, though perhaps not the most splendid, qualification of a moral poet, an acute moral sense, with a vehement indignation against the abuses of public and the vices of private life; to this was added a keen sarcastic humour, and a faculty of depicting the manners of low life with an exactness and felicity, which have never been surpassed, but by the great satirist of the present day. His conscience appears to have held the torch to his understanding, rather than the reverse. He judges of actions by feelings, more than by induction. His casuistry is sometimes miserably perplexed, and his illustrations very unhappy. The first of these defects is to be ascribed to his acquaintance with the schoolmen, the second to his ignorance of classical antiquity; in his views of morality an understanding naturally perspicuous was clouded by the one, while in his powers of adorning a subject, a taste perhaps naturally coarse was left wholly unpolished by the other. He often sinks into imbecility, and not unfrequently spins out his thread of allegory into mere tenuity. But, on other occasions, when aroused by the subject, he has a wildness of imagination, which might have deserved to be illustrated by the pencil of Fuseli, and a sublimity (more especially when inspired by the great mysteries of revelation) which has not been surpassed by Cowper.

He had a smattering of French, but no Italian. I have endeavoured in vain to discover in these Visions any imitations of Dante, whose *Inferno* and *Purgatorio,* in some respects, resemble them. But the boldness of those works, which the familiarity of the Italians with the vices of their Popes rendered tolerable, and even popular, beyond the Alps, would have appalled the courage of a tramontane satirist, and shocked the feelings of his readers, in the fourteenth century.

To the author of these Visions has been ascribed by some Protestant writers an higher inspiration than that of the muse, and his famous prediction of the fall of the religious houses has invested him with the more sacred character

of a prophet . . . . There is just enough in this celebrated prediction, compared with its supposed fulfilment, to excite a momentary surprise.

The erudition of Langland, if such were really the author's name, besides his Saxon literature, consisted in a very familiar knowledge of the *Vulgate,* and the schoolmen: the first of which he appears to quote from memory, as he frequently deviates from the letter of that version. . . . . . His citations from the schoolmen I am unable to trace. (pp. xl-xlv)

> *Thomas Dunham Whitaker, "Criticisms on the Poem: Dr. Whitaker,"* in The Vision of William concerning Piers the Plowman in Three Parallel Texts, *by William Langland, edited by Walter W. Skeat, revised edition, Oxford University Press, London, 1924, pp. xxxix-xlv.*

Thomas Wright   (essay date 1842)

[*In the following excerpt from his introduction to his 1842 edition of the B-text, Wright calls* Piers Plowman *"peculiarly a national work," claiming that Langland tended to "debase the great" in support of the common people of England.*]

[*Piers Ploughman*] was given to the world under a name which could not fail to draw the attention of the people. Amid the oppressive injustice of the great and the vices of their idle retainers, the corruptions of the clergy, and the dishonesty which too frequently characterised the dealings of merchants and traders, the simple unsophisticated heart of the ploughman is held forth as the dwelling of virtue and truth. It was the ploughman, and not the pope with his proud hierarchy, who represented on earth the Saviour who had descended into this world as the son of the carpenter, who had lived a life of humility, who had wandered on foot or ridden on an ass. "While God wandered on earth," says one of the political songs of the beginning of the fourteenth century, "what was the reason that he would not ride?" The answer expresses the whole force of the popular sentiment of the age: "because he would not have a retinue of greedy attendants by his side, in the shape of grooms and servants, to insult and oppress the peasantry." (p. xi)

[It] will be seen that the Latin poems attributed to Walter Mapes, and the *Collection of Political Songs,* form an introduction to the **Vision of Piers Ploughman.** It seems clear that the writer was well acquainted with the former, and that he not unfrequently imitates them. The Poem on the Evil Times of Edward II. already alluded to (in the *Political Songs*) contains within a small compass all his chief points of accusation against the different orders of society. But a new mode of composition had been brought into fashion since the appearance of the famous *Roman de la Rose,* and the author makes his attacks less directly, under an allegorical clothing. The condition of society is revealed to the writer in a dream, as in the singular poem just mentioned, and as in the still older satire, the *Apocalypsis Goliæ;* but in **Piers Ploughman** the allegory follows no systematic plot, it is rather a succession of pictures in which the allegorical painting sometimes disappears altogether, than a whole like the *Roman de la Rose,* and it is on that account less tedious to the modern reader, while the vigorous descriptions, the picturesque ideas, and numerous other beauties of different kinds, cause us to lose sight of the general defects of this class of writings. (pp. xiii-xiv)

The writer of **Piers Ploughman** was neither a sower of sedition, nor one who would be characterized by his contemporaries as a heretic. The doctrines inculcated throughout the book are so far from democratic, that he constantly preaches the Christian doctrine of obedience to rulers. Yet its tendency to debase the great, and to raise the commons in public consideration, must have rendered it popular among the latter: and, although no single important doctrine of the popish religion is attacked, yet the unsparing manner in which the vices and corruptions of the church are laid open, must have helped in no small degree the cause of the Reformation. Of the ancient popularity of **Piers Ploughman** we have a proof in the great number of copies which still exist, most of them written in the latter part of the fourteenth century; and the circumstance that the manuscripts are seldom executed in a superior style of writing, and scarcely ever ornamented with painted initial letters, may perhaps be taken as a proof that they were not written for the higher classes of society. From the time when it was published, the name of **Piers Ploughman** became a favourite among the popular reformers. (pp. xxii-xxiii)

The **Poem of Piers Ploughman** is peculiarly a national work. It is the most remarkable monument of the public spirit of our forefathers in the middle, or, as they are often termed, dark ages. It is a pure specimen of the English language at a period when it had sustained few of the corruptions which have disfigured it since we have had writers of "Grammars;" and in it we may study with advantage many of the difficulties of the language which these writers have misunderstood. (pp. xxvii-xxviii)

> *Thomas Wright, in an introduction to* The Vision and Creed of Piers Ploughman *by William Langland, edited by Thomas Wright, revised edition, John Russell Smith, 1856, pp. v-xl.*

Thomas R. Lounsbury   (essay date 1875)

[*Lounsbury was an American scholar noted for his pioneering work in literary history. In the excerpt below, he underscores the importance of* Piers Plowman *"as a picture of the social and political condition of the times," and suggests that the poem has suffered critical neglect because of its "tiresome" allegory and obscure Middle English phraseology.*]

As a picture of the social and political condition of the times, [**Piers Plowman**] is almost without a rival; and in this point of view it deserves far more attention than it has hitherto received. If about the life of the author little is known, there is no such uncertainty attaching to his character. His personality is prominent on every page of his production. The Puritans, as a sect, were not in existence.

But there has never been a period when the Puritan element has not been a conspicuous factor in English character, and a conspicuous agency in English history; and in his seriousness, his earnestness, his lofty conception of personal righteousness, his aversion not simply to sin but to anything which might possibly lead to sin, and not unfrequently in his intolerance, Langland is a Puritan of the Puritans. The very term *sad man*—the serious or grave man—by which, in one or two places, he calls the righteous man, is of itself suggestive. This state of mind, while it sharpened his insight and added bitterness and point to his invective, gave without doubt an unnecessarily gloomy coloring to his views of things; but, fortunately for our knowledge, it had the effect of leading him to strengthen his statements by describing minutely the things themselves. There was no class in the community which was not to a greater or less extent taken in hand by this worker for reform, in whom patriotism in the highest sense of the word was intensified by profound moral convictions and burning zeal for religion, pure and undefiled. It was, to be sure, against the clergy that the fiercest of his denunciations were levelled. The avarice and ambition of the secular priests; the simony which had turned the house of God into a den of thieves; the greed and gluttony of the monks; the idleness and dissoluteness of the mendicant friars: all these were attacked with a violence, the effect of which was not lessened by the fact, made manifest in many places, that the poet still clung to the old faith, or at least had not put himself in opposition to it. But though he devoted his chief denunciation to the clergy, he did not confine himself to them; and in reading his invective, it certainly affords some gratification to feel that if there is no good thing that is new, there is no bad thing that is not old. No sharper attack can be found in the whole poem than where Langland arraigns the dishonest practices which prevailed among the tradesmen of the time, the adulteration of liquors, the stretching of cloth so as to make ten or twelve yards amount to thirteen, the use of fraudulent weights and measures; and, it may be added, there is nothing which he says of the corruptions current about him, whether existing on a grand or a petty scale, in which he is not more than borne out by the accounts which his contemporary, Gower, gives in his *Vox Clamantis.* In these days, when "the fierce light" which the press causes to beat upon every form of fraud often leads us to fear that our own century surpasses all others in evildoing, it must be confessed that it is somewhat encouraging to find on trustworthy testimony that we are far from having the monopoly of the sin that is going; that, indeed, in corrupt practices, for which we have been disposed to claim for ourselves the merit of originality in the absence of any other kind of merit, we are nothing but humble imitators of past ages. It is no unreasonable inference that among the lost arts of ancient times may be included many kinds of fraudulent procedure which the rascality of modern times has not yet succeeded in reviving.

Indeed, the **Vision of Piers Plowman** is in its general effect a melancholy book. It is a work such as might have been expected to be produced by a man of great abilities, of lofty ideas of personal integrity and piety, of earnest love to his country, who, however, had so turned his thoughts to the consideration of those forces in society which tended to bring it to ruin, that he had nearly lost sight of the recuperative forces which were in active operation upon the other side. The state of mind caused by such warped views of the social problems which are ever working their own solution about us, is common enough in every age: but in that age, owing to peculiar circumstances, it had become more general than in most. There was a wide-spread feeling that not only was the world wickeder than it had ever been, but that the day of its destruction was at hand. From the point of view of that time the sentiment was not altogether unwarrantable: for there had been much to sober and sadden men's minds. For a large part of the century the curse of God had fallen upon western Europe in its heaviest form. Long-continued wars had desolated many of its fairest portions, had rendered recuperative industry impossible, had sent to early graves the most vigorous of the population. The frightful license of camps had largely demoralized society. Upon the heels of the desolation and woe thus wrought followed a still heavier calamity. What the sword had spared the plague came to devour. Three times did that terrible pestilence, immortalized by Boccaccio, sweep through Europe and slay its tens of thousands, where war had slain its thousands. Under such circumstances it is no wonder, to men keenly sensitive to the evils crowding in on every side, with pictures of woe and death ever before their eyes, that every unusual event should seem the direct warning of the Almighty to a sinful world or a direct judgment upon it; that to them the mystic visions of the Apocalypse should become the most vivid of realities. The opening of the seven seals had been begun, the last age of the Church was drawing nigh. This feeling, which is found in Gower, which is conspicuously manifest in the writings of Wycliffe and his followers, from which Chaucer alone seems to be thoroughly free, shows itself to some extent in Langland; and at the time when the second of his versions appeared, the changes through which England had passed, and the condition in which he saw it, only strengthened the melancholy forebodings to which he had given utterance fifteen years before. The reign of Edward III, which had opened so gloriously, had ended in disaster and gloom. The king, worn out physically and mentally, had lingered along to an old age, in the character of which there was nothing to excite respect, nothing indeed to preserve from the severest censure, save the irresponsibility that springs from irrationality. The Black Prince, the hope and pride of the people, had died in his prime. The government was alternately in the hands of warring factions, whose members may have been actuated by a desire to save their country, but who were certainly determined that it should be saved in their own particular way and by nobody but themselves. At this crisis a boy of eleven years old mounted the throne. Then it was that Langland, with the words of the wisest of Israel's monarchs in his mouth, "Woe to thee, O land, when thy king is a child," took up again the poem once completed, and drew in detail that picture of the social, political, and religious condition of the times, which in vividness and fullness is surpassed by no other work accessible to the student of English history. The events of war and peace, the rise and fall of parties, the particulars of battles or of treaties, can always be found recorded in chronicles and State papers; but he who wishes to learn how the England

of the latter half of the fourteenth century thought and felt, how it lived and moved, can find what he desires to know best, and perhaps only, in the writings of Langland, Gower, and Chaucer.

Yet it must be said that it is only in the first half of the poem that this particular kind of importance attaches to the work. The latter part is to a great extent taken up with religious dissertations and discussions, which doubtless had a living interest to the men of that day. But controversy on theological topics has in modern times so shifted its ground, that much of the long-drawn allegory contained in the poem is apt to grow wearisome to a generation which does not need to be told that holy living is more essential to salvation than a pilgrimage to the Holy Land. True, from the very design of the work, questions connected with religion were given the chief place; but in the former half, the half which was first composed, they are much more largely intermingled with references to the social and political condition of the times. Indeed, one could not easily be discussed without more or less of allusion to the other. The number of manuscripts still existing show conclusively how great must have been the popularity of the poem; and this popularity is of itself a sufficient proof of the extent to which religious questions had become the common subjects of thought and discourse during the latter half of the fourteenth century. In particular, Langland makes perfectly clear a point which the writings of his greater contemporary, Chaucer, often suggest. In that age, the reaction against the Roman Catholic faith in some cases resulted, as it has so often since, not in leading men to have a reformed faith, but in leading them to have no faith at all. This was especially true among the higher classes. They passed not from Popery to Protestantism, but from Popery to infidelity. No close student of Chaucer can fail to notice the tone of skepticism that pervades his writings; the cautiously-conveyed contempt for ecclesiastical threatenings; the half-drawn inferences from or satirical allusions to dogmas then deeply cherished; the half-hinted avowal of disbelief as to any knowledge of the future state, in such lines as these:

> His spiryt chaungede hous, and wente ther,
> As I cam nevere, I can nat tellen wher.
> Therfore I stynte, I nam no dyvynistre;
> Of soules fynde I not in this registre,
> Ne mene list thilke opynyouns to telle
> Of hem, though that thei writen wher they dwel-
> le.

If this be observable in the writings of a man upon whose mind all questions connected with life and destiny rested lightly, much more must it have been true of many who, while not sharing in the doctrines of Wycliffe, shared yet in his disgust at the abuses which were perpetrated and the absurdities which were taught in the name of religion. Naturally, the same dark questions, which have always perplexed the minds of men, were lifted into prominence. Here what can only be inferred from Chaucer is directly stated by Langland. He declares with great bitterness that noblemen, sitting at their tables, discuss religious topics just as if they were clergymen, asking why the serpent was permitted to deceive our first parents, what justice there was in making men now living perish for Adam's sin, and by this sort of talk leading those who listened into disbelief. In another passage he says it was a custom of some to discuss religious topics at meal times, and in particular to speak contemptuously of the doctrine of the Trinity. It does not follow, from such passages, that the reaction in the direction here indicated had been great: it is clear that it amounted to enough to excite the indignation and alarm of men of fervent faith.

It may be thought strange that a work so striking and so invaluable, not merely to the man of letters but to the historian, should have fallen into so much neglect. But after all, the causes of this are not far to seek. They exist partly in the nature of the poet's views, partly in the nature of the methods by which he gave them utterance. In morbid feeling, no matter how powerfully expressed, there is never any vital element of perpetuity. But besides this, there are in the poem certain defects which impair its value as a work of art. It is not a single vision, but a series of visions, and these, though in some measure bound together by the unity of a common interest, are in most respects entirely independent of one another. Moreover, it is an allegory; and though allegory was a most popular species of composition to our forefathers, it is to modern ears inexpressibly tiresome. Not all the wealth of imagery and sweetness of versification found in the *Fairy Queen* have been able to save Spenser's great work from being so tedious to the large majority of even cultivated men, that few ever succeed in reading it through. And in the ***Vision of Piers Plowman*** the allegory is not simply the form in which the poem as a whole is cast, but is frequently carried out into particulars, the details of which almost border on the grotesque. A striking illustration of this can be found in Passus xix (Text B; Passus xxii, Text C), in which Grace, or the Holy Spirit, constitutes Piers his plowman, and furnishes him with an outfit, of which the following verses describe a part:

> Grace gave Piers a teme foure gret oxen;
> That on was Luke, a large beste and a lowe-
>   chered,
> And marke, and mathew the thrydde myghty
>   bestes bothe,
> And joigned to hem one Johan most gentil of
>   alle,
> The prys nete of Piers plow passyng alle other.
> And Grace gave Pieres of his goodnesse, foure
>   stottis,
> Al that his oxen eryed they to harwe after.
> On highte Austyne and Ambrose another,
> Gregori the grete clerke and Jerome the gode;
> Thise foure, the feithe to teche folweth Pieres
>   teme,
> And harwed in an handwhile al holy scripture,
> With two harwes that thei hadde and olde and
>   a newe.
>   *Id est, vetus testamentum et novum.*

But, after all, the chief hindrance to its popularity, even in the most restricted sense of that word, lies in the language itself. It seems to us that Mr. [Walter W.] Skeat underrates the obscurity of the phraseology, and that on this point his own familiarity with the poem has had the tendency to warp his judgment. Certain it is that the ancient alliterative verse had peculiar difficulties in its very nature.

The necessity always existed of finding a number of words beginning with the same letter; it was often an unavoidable consequence that to accomplish this, the writer was obliged to resort to expressions little known. The frequent appearance of terms used only once, twice, or three times in all, is one of the most formidable obstacles to the thorough comprehension of Anglo-Saxon poetry; and we are confident that it will turn out a far harder task to the ordinary student to master Langland's vocabulary than that of his contemporary, Chaucer. Certainly the very prevalent impression, that a far greater number of words of Romantic origin is proportionally employed by the latter is very wide of the truth; though this is an impression for which scholars of some repute are themselves responsible. Mr. Wright, in his introduction to the Harleian manuscript of the *Canterbury Tales,* took occasion to contrast the two poets in this respect, and asserted that Langland, as more particularly representing the feelings of the people, had fewer French words than Chaucer. How any one could have come to such a conclusion after having edited the leading works of both authors, is very strange; that is, if anything which a careless man says or does can be considered strange. The incorrectness of the statement is apparent on even the slightest examination. In fact, Langland introduced or rather employed foreign words with an indifference, not to say recklessness, which must have made life a burden to the purists of that time, if any such there were. Lines like these can be found on almost every page:

> And that is the profession appertly that appen-
>   deth for Knyghtes.

> And portatyf and persant as the poynt of a nedle.

> In marchandise is no mede I may it wel avowe;
> It is a permutacioun apertly a penyworth for an
>   othre.

But not to speak of passages like these, this poet of the common people, as he is called, actually terms a daughter a *file,* a cave a *spelonke,* a feast a *maungerie,* and uses many other words which are not only never heard in our period, but have never been common in any period of English speech. (pp. 278-84)

> *Thomas R. Lounsbury, "Langland's Vision of Piers Plowman," in* The New Englander, *Vol. XXXIV, No. II, April, 1875, pp. 274-85.*

J. J. Jusserand   (essay date 1894)

[*Jusserand was the French Ambassador to the United States from 1903 to 1924 and a noted historian—the only non-American ever to head the American Historical Society. In addition, he was the recipient of the first Pulitzer Prize for history for his* With Americans of Past and Present Days *(1916). In the following excerpt, he explores Langland's style, language, and artistic purpose, claiming that the poet formed his thoughts into "proverbs and proverbial sayings" to make his message accessible to "the poor and lowly."*]

All Langland's art and all his teaching can be summed up in one word: sincerity. He speaks, as he thinks, impetuously, recking little of the consequences of his words either for himself or for others; they flow in a burning stream, and could no more be checked than the lava of Vesuvius. At moments the crater seems extinguished, and the rumblings of the tempest subside to a murmur. But storm and calm are both beyond human control; Langland's violence and gentleness depend on internal forces over which he has no power; a sort of dual personality exists in him; he is the victim, not the master, of his thought; and his thought is so completely a separate entity, with wishes opposed to his desires, that it appears to him in the solitude of Malvern; and the melody of lines heard not long ago [in Alfred de Musset's "La Nuit de Décembre"], recurs to our memory:

> Je marchais un jour à pas lents
> Dans un bois, sur une bruyère;
>
> Au pied d'un arbre vint s'asseoir
> Un jeune homme vêtu de noir
> Qui me ressemblait comme un frère. . . .
>
> Partout où, sans cesse altéré
> De la soif d'un monde ignoré,
> J'ai suivi l'ombre de mes songes;
> Partout où, sans avoir vécu,
> J'ai revu ce que j'avais vu,
> La face humaine et ses mensonges. . . .
>
> Partout où j'ai voulu dormir . . .
> Sur ma route est venu s'asseoir
> Un malheureux vêtu de noir
> Qui me ressemblait comme un frère.

Filled with a similar feeling, the wandering dreamer had met, five hundred years before, in a "wilde wildernesse and bi a wode-syde," a "moche man," who looked "lyke to himself"—qui lui ressemblait comme un frère—who knew him, and called him by his real name:

> And thus I went wide-where walkynge myne one (alone),
> By a wilde wildernesse and bi a wode-syde . . .
> And under a lynde uppon a launde lened I a stounde. . . .
> A moche man, as me thoughte and lyke to my-selve
> Come and called me by my kynde name.
> "What artow," quod I tho (then) "that thow my name knowest?"
> "That thow wost wel," quod he "and no wyghte bettere."
> "Wote I what thow art?" "Thought," seyde he thanne,
> I have suwed (followed) the this sevene yere sey thou me no rather (sooner)?"

"Thought" reigns supreme, and does with Langland what he chooses. Langland is unconscious of what he is led to: his visions are for him real ones; he tells them as they rise before him; he is scarcely aware that he invents; he stares at the sight and wonders as much as we do; he can change nothing; his personages are beyond his reach. There is therefore nothing prepared, artistically arranged, or skilfully contrived, in his poem. The deliberate hand of the man of the craft is nowhere to be seen. He obtains artistic effects, but without seeking for them; he never selects or co-ordinates. He is suddenly led, and leads us, from one

subject to another, without any better transition than an "and thanne" or a "with that." And "thanne" we are carried a hundred miles away, among entirely different beings, and frequently we hear no more of the first ones. Or sometimes even, the first re-appear, but they are no longer the same; Piers Plowman personifies now the honest man of the people, now the Pope, now Christ. Dowel, Dobet and Dobest have two or three different meanings. The art of transitions . . . is as much dispensed with in his poem as at the opera: a whistle of the scene-shifter, an "and thanne" of the poet—the palace of heaven fades away, and we find ourselves in a smoky tavern in Cornhill.

Clouds pass over the sky, and sometimes sweep by the earth; their thickness varies, they take every shape: now they are soft, indolent mists, lingering in mountain hollows, that will rise towards noon, laden with the scent of flowering lindens; now they are storm-clouds, threatening destruction and rolling with thunder; night comes on, and suddenly the blackness is rent by so glaring a light, that the plain assumes for an instant the hues of mid-day; then the darkness falls again, deeper than before.

The poet moves among realities and abstractions, and sometimes the first dissolve in fogs, while the second condense into human beings, tangible and solid. On the Malvern hills, the mists are so fine, it is impossible to say: here they begin and here they end; it is the same in the Visions.

In the world of ethics, as among the realities of actual life, Langland excels in summing up in one sudden memorable flash the whole doctrine contained in the nebulous sermons of his abstract preachers. He then attains to the highest degree of eloquence, without striving after it. In another writer, the thing would have been premeditated, and the result of his skill and cunning; here the effect is as unexpected for the author as for the reader. He so little pretends to such felicities of speech, that he never leaves us on the grand impressions thus produced; he utilises them, he is careful to make the best of the occasion; it seems as if he had conjured the lightning from the clouds unawares, and he thinks it his duty to turn it to use. The flash had unveiled the uppermost summits of the realm of thought, and there will remain in our hands a flickering rushlight that will, at most, help us upstairs.

Piers Plowman comes back from Rome, where he too has gone on a pilgrimage. When those who take such journeys return home, they have a bagful of indulgences and holy relics; some are destined for their friends, there are enough for everybody; pleasant gifts and souvenirs, scraps of heaven are brought back from Rome. Piers, have you not brought back indulgences? Why take so much trouble if you come home empty-handed? Piers, show us your pardons; the mere sight of them will do us good; share with us these marvellous wares:

> "Pers," quod a prest tho "thi pardon must I reden,
> For I wol construe uch a clause and knowen hit in Englisch."
> And Pers at his preyere the pardon unfoldeth,
> And I bi-hynden hem bothe bi-heold al the bulle.
> In two lines hit lay and not a lettre more,

> And was i-written riht thus in witnesse of treu-
>   the:
>   *Et qui bona egerunt ibunt in vitam eternam;*
>   *Qui vero mala, in ignem eternum.*
> "Peter," quod the preost tho "I con no pardoun
>   fynde . . ."

"Those who do well shall go into everlasting life." These few words, that are like a flash of light, unassailable words, drawn from the purest doctrine, sum up all Langland's theories on life, and all the sermons of his preachers. Indulgences are condemned; more than that, they are condemned by preterition, without being so much as named, and, with them, all that was then the great evil of the soul: the love of "Fals-Semblant," of easy redemption, of bargains and transactions (pay, and I absolve thee), and the belief in a paradise that can be won by proxy.

To these words, whose weight will be felt, if we remember the importance religion then had in life, succeeds a practical discussion between Piers and the priest, that Langland would surely have left unwritten, had his mind been in the slightest degree preoccupied by artistic aims. He inserted it in his first text, and repeated it in his second. Late in life it seems to have occurred to him that the poem would be improved by the suppression of those lines; they disappear accordingly in text C; but they are cut off so clumsily that a visible gap is left behind; now that they have been suppressed, they are wanted:

> The preest *thus* and Perkyn of the pardon jan-
>   gled.

"Thus" is left to stand out there as a sign-post, to remind us that here was, in former times, a practicable road, leading to somewhere: the reverse of what a born artist would have done.

Langland follows no rule, no literary guide, no precedent. He has passed his life in dreaming and observing; he has followed his thoughts with the attention of a psychologist, and he has observed around him all that lives and moves, from crowned kings to birds on the trees and worms on the ground. He tells what he has seen and nothing else; his sole guide is the light that shines over the tower where "Truth" is imprisoned.

This light serves him in the material as well as the moral world; it illumines the road during a mystic journey through the Ten Commandments, one of those numerous Pilgrim-Progresses incessantly re-begun in the poem; and it also clears the darkness of the London lanes, where, under the pent-roof of their shops, the merchants make Gyle, disguised as an apprentice, sell their adulterated wares; it brightens the hovel in Cornhill where the poet lodges his emaciated body; it throws its rays on the scared faces of sinners for whom the hour of punishment has rung. We have here a whole gallery of portraits, which stand out in an extraordinary manner, people whose every attitude betray the ruling vice, personified abstractions as living as the characters of La Bruyère; and in truth, this canto of the poem contains nothing but a description of the "Caractères et Mœurs de ce Siècle," the "siècle" of Edward III.

The courtier, vain and boastful, laughs aloud at his sligh-test sallies, for untaught people must know he is wittier and wiser than another. He is proud of his fine clothes and of his superb oaths ("meny bolde othes"), of his person and of his grace on foot, on horseback, and even in bed. He has seen marvels and performed wonders. Ask this man here, or that lady there; they will tell you what I did, what I endured, what I saw, what I sometime possessed, what I know, "and what kyn ich kam of !"

The envious man, who lives alone, "lyke a luther dogge," is wrinkled as a leek that has lain long in the sun:

> And as a leke hadde yleyen longe in the sonne,
> So loked he with lene chekes.

He dwells among the burghers of London, in the City, where the struggle for riches and for the pleasures of life was already keen.

The old debauchee denies himself nothing:

> As wel fastyngdaies as Frydaies and heye-feste
>   evenes,
> As luf (leaf) in lente as oute of lente alle tymes
>   liche . . .
> Til we myghte no more: thanne hadde we murye
>   tales
> Of . . . paramours.

All his life long, he had a taste for the very *risqué* fabliaux and tales in vogue at that time, "murye tales," "sotilede songes," "lecherous tales," and had "lykynge to lauhe" at such stories. Now that he is "old and hor," this is his last pleasure, and he continues "lykynge tales of paramours." But he will forsake the same and all carnal delights; and forswear wine and "drynke bote with the douke" (the ducks).

The Miser, whose cheeks hang down like a leathern purse ("as a letherene pors lollid hus chekus"), has much to tell concerning the manner in which fortunes are made at the great fairs of Weyhill and Winchester, whose fame was European; or in the back shops of the City, or on the markets of Bruges. He has learnt usury from Jews and Lombards, and lends money at high interest to all lords and knights who offer good securities. Poor men, sometimes, must needs borrow:

> "Hastow pite on pore men that mote nedes
>   borwe?"
> "I have as moche pite of pore men as pedlere
>   hath of cattes,
> That wolde kille hem, yf he cacche hem myghte
>   for coveitise of here skynnes."

But here is Gloton going to shrive himself, and trudging along to church. It is Friday, and he is fasting; he passes before the door of Betone (Beatrice) the "brew-wif," who gives him good-day and asks where he is going:

> "To holy churche," quath he "for to hure masse;
> And sitthen sitte and be yshriven and synwe
>   namore."
> "Ich have good ale, godsyb Gloton, wolt thow
>   assaye?"
> "What havest thow," quath he "eny hote
>   spices?"
> "Ich have piper and pionys and a pound of gar-
>   lik,

> A ferthyng-worth of fynkelsede for fastinge-
>   daies."
> Thenne goth Gloton yn and grete othes after.

There sat on the bench Cecil the laundress, with Wat the gamekeeper and his wife, both drunk; Tim the tinker and two of his knaves, Hick the hackneyman, Hugh the needler, Clarice of Cocklane (a street of ill-fame), the clerk of the church, Sir Piers of Priedieu (a priest), and Peronelle of Flanders, a hayward, a hermit, the hangman of Tyburn, Dawe the dykeman, and a dozen idlers, porters, cutpurses, teeth-drawers, rebec-players, rat-catchers, streetsweepers, rope-makers, in addition to Rose the "disshere," Godfrey the garlicmonger, Griffin the Welshman, and "heps" of others: all settled there since early morn, and ready to welcome Gloton.

An immense tavern, as we see. Langland has the eyes of "Ymagynatyf"; his tavern holds all the men and women he has met at the ale-house during his whole life; just as his plain of Malvern was wide enough to contain all mankind. Under the smoky rafters, along the blackened tables, to the noise of tankards and cups, sit the drinkers, made thirsty by words and by pæony seeds; they drink and drink again; shouts of laughter, blows, cries of "let go the coppe!" resound "til evensong rang." Screams, oaths, odours rise, all of them "trop horribles," as the Commons would have said. Escape who can! but every one cannot. Gloton, set with difficulty on his legs, is unable to stand. A staff is brought him, and he staggers along, taking one step sideways, and one backwards, as a trained dog, "lyke a glemannes bycche." At last he reaches the door of his house; but his eyes are dim, he stumbles on the threshold and falls to earth; Clement, the cobbler, catches him up by the waist and tries to lay him on his knees. . . . Let us hastily leave the group. . . . With all the trouble in the world, his wife and his daughter bear him to bed, and this "excesse" is followed by complete rest; he sleeps Saturday and Sunday till sunset; he wakes pale and thirsty, and his first words are: "Who holds the bowl?"

We see that Langland does not always keep company with mere abstractions. Many other personages might be singled out from his gallery of portraits, but these specimens will doubtless suffice to give an idea of the realistic vigour with which he painted and put on the stage the "Caractères et mœurs" of that far-off century.

The poet's language is, if one may use the expression, like himself, absolutely sincere. Chaucer, with his great literary experience and good sense, wished that words were used which were in closest relation to things:

> The wordes must be cosyn to the dede.

Thanks to Langland's passionate sincerity, the same close relationship is established between his thoughts and his words. His thoughts are suited to his feelings, and his words to his thoughts. He is sincere in all things; he seeks neither to deceive nor dazzle; he never wishes to screen a weak thought by a forcible expression. The many quotations given above have already allowed the reader to perceive this; and examples might be multiplied without number. While, in the mystic parts of his Visions, Langland uses a superabundance of fluid and abstract terms,

that look like morning mists and float along with his thoughts, his style becomes suddenly sharp, nervous, sinewy, when he comes back to earth and moves in the world of realities. Let some sudden emotion fill his soul, and he will rise again, not in the mist this time, but in the rays of the sun; he will soar aloft, and we shall wonder at the grandeur of his eloquence. Some of his simplest expressions are real *trouvailles;* he penetrates into the innermost recesses of our hearts, and then goes on his way, and leaves us pondering and thoughtful, filled with awe. What two-hours sermon is worth this simple line: Christ became man,

> And baptised and bishoped (confirmed) with the
>   blode of his herte.

Some of his apostrophes, not a few of his rough but energetic sketches, recall the more perfect examples of the poetic art of a later date; more than once uncouth Langland reminds us of noble Milton [Sonnet xviii]:

> Avenge, o God, thy slaughtered saints! . . .
>
> . . . Pore peple, thi prisoners lorde, in the put
>   of myschief,
> Conforte tho creatures that moche care suffren
> Thorw derth, thorw drouth alle her dayes here,
> Wo in wynter tymes for wantyng of clothes,
> And in somer tyme selde soupen to the fulle;
> Conforte thi careful Cryste, in thi ryche! (king-
>   dom)

If he wants floating words to follow close upon his mystic thoughts, he uses realistic terms, noisy, ill-favoured expressions, when clouds have dispersed, and he sits at table with Gloton. Whatever be his subject, he will forge a word, or distort a meaning, or cram into an idiom more meaning than grammar, custom, or dictionary allow, rather than leave a gap between word and thought; both must be fused together and made one. To give us an impression of the splendid tall-roofed hostels which merchants built for themselves in London with their ill-gotten gains, Langland does not stop in the street to make a sketch and description, but merely says in one word: if they had been honest, they would not "timber" so high. Saracens and Jews ought to be taught; the root of our faith is in them; they had "a lippe of owre byleve." Many of his short sayings, burning with enthusiasm, take hold of the reader's mind and will not be easily forgotten. Some of his sketches are doubtless scarcely visible now on the paper; still, when once seen, they live in the memory. The picture in three words representing Piers as being Truth's "pilgryme atte plow" is as grand and simple as a drawing by Miller, and the three words might indeed have served as a motto for both.

His vocabulary of words is the normal vocabulary of the period, the same nearly as Chaucer's. The poet of the *Canterbury Tales* has been often reproached with having used his all-powerful influence to obtain rights of citizenship in England for French words. But the accusation does not stand good. Chaucer wrote in the language of his time, such as it was; he never tried to alter it, or to make it more French; he was very far from the pedantry of which examples have been seen in several countries at a more recent date; attempts to latinise the French tongue, at the Renaissance; or to make English more Saxon, in our day. Langland's works may serve as a proof of this. He did not write for the court, and was in no way concerned with the fashions and elegances of his time. However, the admixture of French words is not less considerable in his poem than in the works of his illustrious contemporary. The visionary spoke, without the slightest affectation, the language used by everybody; but everybody's language was permeated as was the genius itself of the new-formed race, with French elements.

His poem offers a combination of several dialects. Forms are found in his Visions, derived from a variety of regions in England, and this may be taken as pointing to sojourns made by the poet in other places besides Malvern and London. Northern, western, southern forms meet in the poem, and, in many cases, the discrepancy must needs be attributed to the author himself, not to copyists. One dialect, however, predominates, that is, the Midland dialect; Chaucer used the East Midland, which is nearly the same, and was destined to prevail and become the English language.

An increase in the use of western words and forms has been noticed in the last or C version of the text: we must see in this a proof of Langland having probably returned to the Malvern region, during the last years of his life.

Langland did not accept any of the metres used by Chaucer; he preferred to remain in closer contact with the Germanic past of his kin, and stuck to alliteration. The main ornament of French verse, namely rhyme, had been vulgarised in England, owing to the Norman conquest; Chaucer wrote in rhyming lines, though he found their rules difficult. The scarcity of rhymes in the English language was for him a source of trouble, "a grete penaunce," and he envied the facilities afforded by the French tongue:

> And eke to me hit is a grete penaunce,
> Syth ryme in Englissh hath such skarseté,
> To folowe worde by worde the curiosité
> Of Graunsoun, floure of hem that make in Fr-
> aunce.
> ["Complaynt of Mars and Venus"]

Chaucer, however, wavered not in his allegiance to the prosody of "Fraunce," which had become, by this time, the prosody of the greatest number in England too. He did not like alliteration, and sneered at it:

> I can not geste, run, ram, ruf, by letter.
> ["Prologe of the Persone"]

Alliteration was the main ornament of the verses composed by the Germanic, and Scandinavian, and Anglo-Saxon poets. It consisted in the use of a certain number of accented syllables beginning with the same letter. This metre had survived the Conquest, but in a more or less broken state; many poets used it clumsily, mingling the rules of the two prosodies. So did, for example, Layamon, whose *Brut* offers, at the beginning of the XIIIth century, a strange mixture of rhyme and alliteration. Some authors, however, had a greater respect for the older system, and wrote, according to fixed rules, poems, the fame of which has survived. Among them stand foremost, in the XIVth century, *Sir Gawayne and the Green Knight,* and, above all, the **Visions** of Langland.

Langland wrote in long lines, divided into half-lines by a pause, usually marked by a particular sign in manuscripts (and by a raised full stop in printed editions). Each line contains strong, that is strongly accented, syllables, in fixed or nearly fixed number, and weak, that is unaccented or slightly accented, syllables, in varying number. The rules according to which these elements are combined in Langland's verse have been summed up as follows by Mr. Skeat [in his Oxford edition]:

> Each half-line contains two or more strong syllables, two being the original and normal number. More than two are often found in the first half-line, but less frequently in the second.
>
> The initial-letters which are common to two or more of these strong syllables being called the *rhyme-letters,* each line should have two rhyme-letters in the first and one in the second half. The two former are called *sub-letters,* the latter *chief-letter.*
>
> The chief-letter should begin the former of the two strong syllables in the second half-line. If the line contain only two rhyme-letters, it is because one of the sub-letters is dispensed with.
>
> If the chief-letter be a consonant, the sub-letters should be the same consonant, or a consonant expressing the same sound. If a vowel, it is sufficient that the sub-letters be also vowels; they need not be the same, and in practice are generally different. If the chief-letter be a combination of consonants, such as *sp, ch, str,* and the like, the sub-letters frequently present the same combination, although the recurrence of the first letter only would be sufficient.

These rules are not very difficult, and it must be added, besides, that the poet handles them in a way which renders them even more easy. Sometimes he allows himself to begin a weak syllable with a rhyme-letter; at other places he uses two rhyme-letters in the second half-line, and one only in the first. Take, for example, the first four lines of the poem:

> In a *s*ómer *s*éson whan *s*óft was the *s*ónnë
> I *sh*ópe me in *shr*oúdes as I a *sh*épe wérë,
> In *h*ábite as an *h*éremite un*h*óly of wórkës
> *W*ent *w*ýde in this *w*órld *w*óndres to hére.

Two only among those four lines are absolutely regular; the first has four rhyme-letters instead of three; the fourth is similarly constructed, and, besides, the first of the rhyme-letters begins a weak syllable.

The alliterative prosody, of which Langland's **Visions** are the most important specimen in England, survived till the XVIth century. The taste for the tinklings and tollings of such verses was deep-rooted in the race; and recurring sounds were long used, without rules, and merely for the sake of the noise; they are to be found in most unexpected places. There had been examples of them even in the Latin hexameters of English poets of the XIIth century; they abound in Joseph of Exeter [in his "De bello trojano," book iii]:

> Audit et audet
> Dux falli: fatisque favet cum fata recuset.

. . . . .

> Ardet et audet
> Promissorque ingens, facilis præsagia prædæ
> Ducit amor.
>
> . . . . .
> Postquam Helenes Paridi patuit præsentia,
>   classem
> Deserit.

In this shape, it may be said that alliteration never died out; it came down to our times, and there is frequent use of it in Byron [in "Corsair"]:

> Our bay
> Receives that prow which proudly spurns the
>   spray.
> How gloriously her gallant course she goes!
> Her white wings flying—never from her foes.
>
> . . . . .
> Or fallen too low to fear a further fall.
>
> . . . . .
> Of flight from foes with whom I could not cope.

Langland's erudition is such as might be expected from one who described himself as anxious to know, but "loth for to stodie." He has visibly read much, but hastily and without method; he has read at random, and never taken the trouble to classify and ticket what he remembered. Except when it is a question of the Scriptures, which were for him the subject of constant meditations, he quotes at random; his Scriptural quotations even are not always quite accurate. He thinks he remembers this or that author has said something in support of a favourite theory of his; he therefore names the author, and refers us, without chapter or verse, to Ovid, Aristotle and Plato; and it would be very bad luck indeed, if one or the other, in some work or other, had not said, in some manner, something to the purpose. Most of his references are mere guesses. At a certain place, to feel perfectly secure of not standing alone and unsupported, he appeals to "Porfirie and Plato, Aristotile, Ovidius, . . . Tullius, Tholomeus," and "elevene hundred" more; a very long roll of authorities, as we see.

If the quotations from the Bible and the works of the Fathers are not always accurate, the superabundance of them, and the ease with which they recur under his pen, are proof sufficient of his having been impregnated, as it were, with religious literature. His mistakes even are, in a sense, an additional proof, as they show that he does not open his books to find out appropriate passages; he quotes from memory; his memory, however, is not absolutely trustworthy; and Ymagynatyf, as usual, plays him some very bad turns.

Besides the ancients and the Bible, Langland shows a knowledge of a good many more recent authors. He is familiar with French ballads and romances, with English and Latin works, with Robin Hood and Guy of Warwick, the Seven Sleepers, the Golden Legend. He represents his London workmen singing French songs: "Dieu vous save, Dame Emme." He knows the "Goliardeys . . . glotoun of wordes" and the satirical poems of which they were the heroes. He has read Rutebeuf's "Voie de Paradis," the "Pélerinages" of Deguileville, the "Roman de la Rose";

and more or less conscious reminiscences of those poems are afloat in his memory.

Langland addresses men of good will, whatever be their rank or avocations; he writes for the mass of the people rather than for the small group of the exalted ones. Sincere and upright, he wants to be understood; he is never purposely obscure; his aim is never to please or astonish or dazzle connoisseurs; he seeks, simply, means to direct rays of light to obscure corners usually left in darkness. Thus he is original and worthy the attention of artists, because he is so intensely honest, not by reason of his cleverness. All his Latin quotations are translated into English, for he never loses sight of the untaught part of his audience:

> "I can nought construe al this," quod Haukyn
> "ye moste kenne me this on Englisch."
>
> . . . . .
> To Englisch-men this is to mene. . . .
>
> . . . . .
> If lewed men wist what this Latyn meneth. . . .

And he turns "this Latyn" into English. All the better, he thinks, if he is read by the learned and the wealthy; but he means, before all, to be accessible to the poor and lowly, to "lewede men." He therefore shapes his thoughts into the form that will better appeal to this sort of men; proverbs and proverbial sayings abound in his works; most numerous, too, are practical counsels for everyday life, given in the half serious, half humorous tone which the wisdom of nations usually affects.

A catechism of memorable sayings, and a collection of curious mottoes, might easily be made out of his *Visions.* Let Common Sense "be wardeyne, yowre welthe to kepe." "Mesure is medcyne." Faith without deeds is "as ded as a dore-tre." Chastity without charity "is as lewed as a laumpe that no lighte is inne." "The Comune ys the kynges tresour." Trust in God and in his mercy; wicked deeds

> Fareth as a fonk (spark) of fuyr that ful a-myde
> Temese (Thames).

I tell you, rich, it cannot possibly be, that you should

> Have hevene in yowre here-beyng and hevene
>   her-after.
>
> . . . . .
> Selden moseth (becomes mossy) the marbelston
>   that men ofte treden.

Some of the people Langland produces on his stage are "as wroth as the wynd—as comune as the cartwey—as hende (courteous) as hounde is in kychyne," &c.

Langland is a true Englishman, as truly English as Chaucer; even more so. One important characteristic is wanting in Chaucer: he is not insular; there is an admixture of French and Italian ideas in his mind; at bottom, no doubt, he is mainly English, but still, there is something of a cosmopolitan tinge about him. Continental "makers" acknowledged him as a brother; "Fraunces Petrark, the laureat poet," told him, it seems, when they met near "Padowe," the tale of patient Grisilde; Des Champs praised him for having "planté le rosier" on British ground. Not so with Langland, who is nothing if not insular; he may even be said to be the typical insular; and one of the first on record. He is not a brother poet for continental poets; he will not be praised by Des Champs. Other countries are nothing to him but with reference to his own. His views accord very well with this most important period in the history of England, when the nation, growing conscious of its own individuality, becomes decidedly averse to over-extension, does not want the Pyrenees for its frontier, nor a French town for its capital; but seeks, on the contrary, whatever its leaders and kings may aspire to, to gather itself up, to concentrate its forces, to become a strong, well-defined, powerful body, and cease to be a large and loose invertebrate thing. Only when this gathering up shall have been successfully accomplished, will the nation lend itself readily to a policy of expansion. This second phase was not to be seen by Langland, for it took place only in Elizabeth's reign. The Hundred Years war was a royal, not a national, war; the movement for expansion did not assume a national character before the XVIth century. English *kings* fought against France; the English *nation* peopled the shores of America. Our visionary thoroughly belongs to his day and country; he is afraid lest England should be drawn into a policy of adventures; he wants peace with France; he rejoices, as we have seen, when he hears that Edward has consented

> To leve that lordschupe for a luitel selver.

This is, according to Langland, one of the best things Edward did; he followed in this the advice of Conscience. When the question is of peace, Langland is always ready to cry with the Commons: "Oïl! oïl!" Yes, yes. He wants the nation to spend its energies at home, and not to be disturbed from this noblest of tasks, the improvement of the machinery of the State, and the establishment of a more perfect balance of power between King and Parliament.

This equilibrium was to be, and Langland longed for it. Constitutional ideas had not, in the whole field of English literature, during the XIVth century, a better representative than Langland; it may almost be said that they had no other. We have noticed how closely he identified himself with the Commons of England, wanting what they wanted, hating what they hated. There is almost no remonstrance in the Rolls of Parliament that is not to be found also in the *Visions.* The same reforms are advocated, the same abuses denounced. The Commons are, like the poet, intensely insular; but, insular as they show themselves to be, they offer a most happy combination of the Norman and Saxon genius. They have sometimes the boundless audacities of mystic dreamers, whom nothing stops, because they build in the air. But this same impossible dream, doomed, it would seem, to vanish like smoke, this dream is appropriated, transformed, made useful and practical, by the Norman Mind that is on the watch in the "chambre depeinte" at Westminster; and the shadow becomes reality. Thus has worked for centuries, to the great profit of the nation, the dual genius inherited from remote ancestors. The Saxon dreams his dream and sings his song; the Norman listens and says: Why not? be it so! To pass from the absolute monarchy of the early Plantagenets, to a limited monarchy in which the main source of power will be vested in the Commons: what an exorbitant dream,

fit only for the wanderer resting his limbs by the shade of the Malvern linden trees! A few generations come and go, and fancy becomes truth; the thing is there, realised, and the poet goes to Westminster, and states in his verses that there it is. It took other nations four hundred years more to reach the same goal.

Another important characteristic increased the hold of Langland over his contemporaries and the men who came after; namely, his unconquerable aversion for all that is mere appearance and show, self-interested imposture; for all that is antagonistic to conscience, abnegation, sincerity. Such is the great and fundamental indignation that is in him; all the others are derived from this one. For, while his mind was impressed with the idea of the seriousness of life, he happened to live when the mediæval period was drawing to its close; and, as usually happens towards the end of epochs, people no longer took in earnest any of the faiths and feelings which had supplied foregoing generations with their strength and motive power. He saw with his own eyes knights prepare for war as if it were a hunt; learned men consider the mysteries of religion as fit subjects to exercise one's mind in after-dinner discussions; the chief guardians of the flock busy themselves with their "owelles" only to shear, not to feed, them. Meed was everywhere triumphant; her misdeeds had been vainly denounced; her reign had come; under the features of Alice Perrers she was now the paramour of the king!

At all such, men and things, Langland thunders anathema. Lack of sincerity, all the shapes and sorts of "faux semblants," fill him with inextinguishable hatred. In shams and "faux semblants," he sees the true source of good and evil, the touchstone of right and wrong, the main difference between the worthy and the unworthy. He constantly recurs to the subject by means of his preachings, epigrams, portraits, caricatures; he manages to bring forward anew, to magnify and multiply, his precepts and his curses, so as to increase our impression of the danger and number of the adherents to "Fals-Semblant." By such means, he hopes, we shall at last hate those whom he hates. Endlessly therefore, in time and out of time, among the mists, across the streets, under the porches of the church, to the drowsy chant of his orations, to the whistle of his satires, ever and ever again, he conjures up before our eyes the hideous grinning face of "Fals-Semblant" the insincere. Fals-Semblant is never named by name; he assumes all names and shapes; he is the king who reigns contrary to conscience, the knight perverted by Lady Meed, the heartless man of law, the merchant without honesty, the friar, the pardoner, the hermit, who conceal under the garment of saints, hearts that will rank them with the accursed ones. Fals-Semblant is the pope who sells benefices, the histrion, the tumbler, the juggler, the adept of the vagrant race, who goes about telling tales and helping his listeners to forget the seriousness of life. From the unworthy pope, down to the lying juggler, all these men are the same man. Deceit stands before us; God's vengeance be upon him! Whenever and wherever Langland detects Fals-Semblant, he loses control over himself; anger blinds him; it seems as if he were confronted by Antichrist.

No need to say whether he is then master of his words and

able to measure them. With him, in such cases, no *nuances* or extenuations are admissible; you are with or against Fals-Semblant; there is no middle way; a compromise is a treason; and is there anything worse than a traitor? And thus he is led to sum up his judgment in such lines as this:

> He is worse than Judas that giveth a japer silver.

If we allege that there may be some shade of exaggeration in such a sentence, he will shrug his shoulders. The doubt is not possible, he thinks, and his plain statement is self-evident.

No compromise! Travel through life without bending; go forward in a straight line between the high walls of duty. Perform your own obligations; do not perform the obligations of others. To do over-zealously your duty, to take upon you the duty of others, would trouble the State; you approach, in so doing, the borderland of Imposture. The knight will fight for his country, and must not lose his time in fasting and in scourging himself. A fasting knight is a bad knight.

Many joys are allowed. They are included, as a bed of flowers, between the high walls of duty; love flowers even grow there, to be plucked, under the blue sky. But take care not to be tempted by that wonderful female Proteus, Lady Meed, the great corruptress. She disappears and re-appears, and she too assumes all shapes; she is everywhere at the same time; it seems as if the asp of Eden had become the immense reptile that circles the earth. Meed is the more dangerous because she is at times legitimate reward, and at times odious bribery; and as she always comes with her same bewitching, beautiful face, it is sometimes difficult to know which Meed stands near, beckoning us. Langland therefore uses all the means in his power to put the faithful adherents of the Plowman on their guard. Were Meed ever bribery, the danger would be immensely lessened; but she is often Compromise; and with Compromise heads become giddy; the abyss opens wide and near. Piers Plowman undertakes to do duty as a guide; a salary would be both welcome and legitimate; but he refuses, fearing Lady Meed.

All the aversions of Langland are fused into this one; and a grand and splendid thing it is to contemplate the out-bursts of such a fiery hatred against the most trifling exten-uations of truth. He does not spare himself; his want of ab-negation draws from him bitter tears. Kneeling on the stone flags, he cries mercy to his other self that tortures him; his long frame is shaken by sobs.

This hatred is immense; but stands alone in the heart of the poet; to all the rest he is comparatively merciful. It is a strange but certain fact that, with all his indignation, he is at bottom an optimist. His mind, no doubt, is traversed by melancholy thoughts, as was the mind of the Saxon an-cestor; the idea of death and the charnel-house weights upon him:

> For in charnel atte chirche cherles ben yvel to
>   knowe,
> Or a knighte fram a knave there knowe this in
>   thin herte.

Such were the Saxon anxieties, and such was also the pe-culiar sadness which, pervading the works of Villon, has secured for him a place apart in the literature of old France. He, too, thought of the charnel-house and stared at the skulls thrown together there [in his "Le grand testa-ment"]:

> Et ycelles qui s'inclinaient
> Une contre autres en leurs vies,
> Desquelles les unes régnaient
> Des autres craintes et servies,
> Là les vois toutes assouvies
> Ensemble, en un tas, pêle-mêle. . . .

But, in truth, when the gusts of the tempest have ceased,—and no violent tempest lasts very long,—Langland shows himself an optimist. Death even appears to him sometimes with a sweet face, death,

> The which unknitteth al kare and comsynge is
>   of reste.

He does not believe that humanity is doomed to total and final perdition. He does not despair of future, not even of present times. Men will perhaps be converted, and become better, and act better. They are not so wicked, and their organisation so monstrous, that society must be upset and rebuilt again. Actual arrangements must be improved, not destroyed. He leaves untouched, ecclesiastical hierarchy, dogma, the division of classes; but, above all, he shudders at the mere idea that any damage might be sustained by that holy and peerless institution, that palladium of liberty and progress: the Parliament and Commons of England.

He goes about, preaching disinterestedness, abnegation, austere virtues; but there is often, at the same time, kind-ness in his voice; comfort is derived from the very sound of his words. A feeling of sympathy for the suffering ones warms the whole work; he is visibly one with them; his sternest precepts are softened by the tone in which they are delivered. There is something pathetic, and tragic also, in his having to acknowledge that there is no cure for many evils, and that, for the present, resignation only can soothe the pain. With a throbbing heart he shows the un-happy and the lowly, who will die before having seen the better days that are to come, the only talisman that may help them: a scroll with the words, "Thy will be done!":

> But I loked what lyflode (means of life) it was
>   that Pacience so preysed,
> And thanne was it a pece of the *pater noster*
>   "Fiat voluntastua."

Piers the Plowman is the ideal of the poet; but Langland is not blind to the possible merits of the rich and the pow-erful. Charity sometimes lives among them, as among the poor:

> For I have seyne hym in sylke and somme tyme
>   in russet.

He is a strict adherent to dogmas, and to the traditional teaching of the Church; but the idea of so many Saracens and Jews, doomed wholesale to everlasting pain, is repel-lent to him; he can scarcely accept it; he hopes they will be all converted and "turne in-to the trewe feithe"; for "Cryste cleped us alle . . . Sarasenes and scismatikes . . . and Jewes."

The truth is, that there was a tender heart under the rough and rugged exterior of the impassioned, indignant, suffering poet. Much of what has been pointed out before leads to such a conclusion; and if an additional proof were wanted, it would be found in the motto adopted by him, which shows, better than all the rest, what were his aims in life: *Disce, Doce, Dilige.* In these words will be found the true interpretation of Dowel, Dobet, and Dobest: Learn, Teach, Love:

> Thus taughte me ones
> A lemman that I loved Love was hir name.

What is then to be learnt above all things in this life?

> "Conseille me, Kynde (nature)," quod I "what
>   crafte is best to lerne?"
> "Lerne to love," quod Kynde "and leve of alle
>   othre."

(pp. 153-85)

J. J. Jusserand, "The Art and Aim of Langland," in his "Piers Plowman": A Contribution to the History of English Mysticism, *revised edition, T. Fisher Unwin, 1894, pp. 153-85.*

W. J. Courthope   (essay date 1895)

[*Courthope was an English educator, poet, literary critic, and biographer whose most notable work is his six-volume* History of English Poetry *(1895-1910). In the following excerpt from the first volume of that work, he provides a summary of* Piers Plowman *concentrating on the first eight passus, which he calls "by far the most interesting and artistic part of the* Vision.*"*]

[No one who has studied Langland's **Piers Plowman**] in itself can doubt that he was a man of profound religious conviction; that, by force of character and intellect, he was qualified to form a right judgment of man and society; that experience had acquainted him with the minutest details of the life which he described; and that—making allowance for the archaic vehicle of expression he adopted—he possessed all the genius, insight, and literary skill necessary to present his poetical conceptions in an artistic form.

Like Dante and John de Meung, Langland made the framework of his poem the Vision which, since the model afforded by Boethius, had been accepted as a conventional form of art. But, for no very apparent reason, he conducts his action through a succession of dreams, and at different epochs he greatly altered and extended the design with which he originally started. The first draft of the poem was made in 1361, and his conception, evidently the result of a deep sense of the disorders of the time, is mainly ethical and practical in its scope. It sets forth (1) the actual evils which ruin man and society; (2) the means of reformation; (3) the true theory of life. In 1377, the last year of Edward's reign, when the king was plainly sinking into his grave, and serious troubles were anticipated in consequence both of the tender age of the heir apparent, and the predominance of John of Gaunt, the poet revised his work. Preserving the substance of what he had originally written, he made many important additions, and so greatly ex-

panded the last portion, relating to the true theory of life, that the length of the poem was more than doubled. Finally, in the last years of Richard II. he produced another revised edition, with fresh passages of an autobiographical nature, and with retrenchments and transpositions of the original matter, which showed his critical capacity to be as great as his powers of invention. By far the most interesting and artistic part of the *Vision* is the first eight Passus or Fyttes, and I therefore propose to give the reader a somewhat full account of their contents, noticing more briefly the Vita of Do-Wel, Do-Bet, Do-Best, in which, for various reasons, the poetical success is less conspicuous.

The poem opens with a description of the visionary wandering in the Malvern Hills, where he falls asleep and dreams a marvellous dream. He thought he was in a wilderness, to the eastward of which he beheld a tower on a hill, and beneath this a deep and doleful dungeon. Between them was a fair field full of folk, each and all engaged in some line of action, of which the peculiarity was, that, in almost every case, it had diverged from its true purpose. Some indeed were industriously employed in ploughing and sowing, but only that their idle companions might waste the fruits of their labours. There were a few harmless minstrels, bent on making an honest livelihood, but most of this profession resembled the ribald storytellers, whose loose tales in earlier times had provoked the indignation of Robert of Brunne and the author of *Cursor Mundi.* Pilgrims and palmers were journeying to the shrine of St. James of Compostella, that they might have the privilege of lying for the rest of their lives. Here and there a pious hermit was dwelling quietly in his retreat, but others were roaming about the country with companions by no means in keeping with the garb of sanctity. Friars of all the four orders were interpreting the text of Scripture in a sense agreeable to the low desires of their audience. A pardoner was proclaiming his commission from the Pope to give absolution, at a proper price, for breach of vows and fasts, and was sharing with the parish priest the money which should have gone to the poor. Bishops were devoting their energies to the secular work of the State instead of to the service of religion. The rule of the Church was given over to the cardinals at the Papal court, rather than to those to whom St. Peter had left it, the Cardinal Virtues. Then the dreamer beheld a king, led by knighthood, and acclaimed by the voice of the commons, who appointed ploughmen to provide the sustenance of the realm, while the rulers took thought for law and order. A lunatic kneeled before the king, praying that he might govern well; and then, as if at a coronation, Conscience (or, as it is in some versions, an angel) proclaimed with a loud voice, but in the Latin tongue, so that the unlearned might not dispute on the matter, a number of maxims on good government; while the commons replied in Latin verse, which few of them could construe: "Precepta regis sunt nobis vincula legis." Thereupon it seemed to the dreamer that all the human figures disappeared from his vision, and a rout of rats and small mice rushed upon the scene, deliberating on the measures to be taken with the cat. A rat proposed that their enemy should be killed, but a mouse, "striding sternly forth," pointed out that, even if the cat were killed, another would come in its place. "I have heard my father say," continued the mouse, that where the cat is a kitten, wretched is the court, and as the book of Ecclesiastes says, "Væ terræ ubi puer rex est." Better is a little loss than a long sorrow for most of us, though we get rid of a tyrant, for we mice should destroy many men's malt, and you rabble of rats would rend men's clothes, if there were no cat of the court to leap upon you; for if you rats had your will you could not rule yourselves. For my part I say that I see so much evil to come, that, by my counsel, neither cat nor kitten shall be harmed, and I will never pay my share of the collar.

After this apologue, so vividly illustrative alike of the political situation and the character of the poet, and so prophetic of the approaching calamities of the kingdom, the dreamer resumes the vision of humanity, and closes his prologue with a view of the avarice of the lawyers, and the idleness and ill-living of the labouring classes.

Having exhibited his *dramatis personæ,* the dreamer proceeds to explain the meaning of his vision. A lovely lady descends from a castle, and shows him that the tower he had seen was Truth, the abode of God the Father. God gives all men enough, and the only three things really needful for them are clothes, meat, and drink. We are not to follow the instincts of the flesh, for that is under the influence of a lying spirit, but are to obey the rule of reason and common sense. The lady further shows him that the dungeon in the deep dale was the Castle of Care, the dwelling of the Father of Falsehood, who hinders Love and deceives all that trust in treasure. Then the dreamer asks the lady's name. "I," said she, "am Holy Church, who held thee at thy baptism, and taught thee thy creed, and thou gavest me pledges to do my bidding, and love me loyally while thy life endureth." The dreamer begs that she will teach him, not how to get treasure, but how to save his soul. Holy Church replies that Truth is the best of treasures, and to follow Truth should be the aim of kings and knights, rather than to conform strictly to those outward rules of fasting and the like, which the ordinary oath of knighthood requires. Christ knighted Cherubim and Seraphim to know the truth and obey it; Lucifer and his angels fell through disobedience and are condemned to hell; but they who obey Truth and God's law may certainly hope for heaven. Still the dreamer urges that he has no natural knowledge of Truth; but Holy Church replies with severity that he should know it through conscience; that Truth is to love God better than himself, and to do no deadly sin. Truth tells us that Love is the medicine of Heaven, and that to love and pity the poor, and to comfort the sad, is the best way to heaven.

To complete his knowledge the dreamer prays his teacher to give him skill to know the false, whereupon she bids him turn his eyes to the left. He does so, and beholds a woman splendidly arrayed in rich garments and precious stones, and on his asking Holy Church her name, "That," she replied, "is Mede (Bribery) the maiden, my enemy. My Father is Almighty God, and every merciful man is my lord and husband. But Mede is to be married to-morrow to one False Fickle-tongue, and then you may see the whole crew that belong to that lordship." After which Holy Church leaves the dreamer, and the action of the allegory begins with the marriage, which is a satire of the

most vivid kind on the corruptions of the civil and ecclesiastical courts. Every rank and condition of men connected with these courts is brought under the lash. The two chief offenders are Simony and Civil, representing civil and ecclesiastical corruption; but besides these there are bidden to the wedding the Sizours or Jurymen; the Summoners who cited offenders to appear in the Consistory Court; the Beadles who impanelled the juries; the For-goers and Victuallers, who were charged with the execution of the hateful privilege of Purveyance. The first to bring Mede from her bower is Favel the flatterer, a broker of the class which in those days was employed in arranging treaties of marriage; and when the parties are ready, Liar produces a charter, whereby the various goods and possessions of Mede are granted to Falsehood. At the sight of these monstrous proceedings Theology waxes wroth, insisting that Mede ought to be married to Truth, and that before the marriage is consummated the parties must proceed to Westminster, to see whether the law will permit it. Simony and Civil assent to the proposal, but Favel prepares the way with florins, which he takes care to distribute to the scribes. Then follows a passage of remarkable humour and power, which seems to condense into a few lines all the

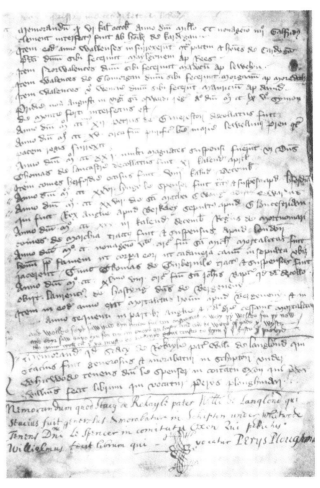

An ascription from the C-text manuscript of Piers Plowman *in Trinity College, Dublin, naming Stacy de Rokayle as the father of Langland.*

complaints of the injustice of the times scattered through the political songs of the preceding reigns:—

> Ac thanne cared thei for caplus to kairen hem thider,
> And Favel sette forth thanne folus ynowe,
> And sette Mede upon a schyreve shodde al newe,
> And Fals sat on a sisoure that softlich trotted,
> And Favel on a flaterere fetislich atired.
> Tho haued notaries none annoyed thei were,
> For Symonye and Cyuile shulde on hire fete gange.
> Ac thanne swore Symonye and Cyuile bothe,
> That sompnoures shulde be sadled and serue hem uchone
> And lat apparaille this prouisores in palfreis wyse;—
> "Sire Symony hymseluen shal sitte upon here bakkes.
> Denes and suddenes draw yow togideres,
> Erchdekenes and officiales and alle yowre Registreres,
> Lat sadel hem with siluer owre synne to suffre;
> As auoutrye and deuorses and derne usurye,
> To bere bischopes about abrode in visitynge.
> Paulynes pryues for pleyntes in the consistorie
> Shall serue my-self that Cyuile is nempned;
> And cartisadel the commissarie owre carte shal he lede,
> And fecchen us vytailles at *fornicatores*.
> And maketh of lyer a long carte to lede alle these othere,
> As Freres and faitoures that on here fete rennen."
> And thus Fals and Fauel fareth forth togideres,
> And Mede in the myddes and alle thise men after.

Soothness (Truth), however, marks the company on the road, and without saying anything pushes on and enables Conscience to give the king warning of their approach. The king, enraged at the news, declares that if he could catch Falsehood and Favel he would hang them both. Dread, hearing his exclamation at the door, conveys a friendly warning to Falsehood and his followers, who scatter in confusion. Guile is sheltered by tradesmen, and Liar, after being forced for a long time to lurk in by-lanes, is taken in, washed, clothed, and entertained by Pardoners, and afterwards by Friars.

Mede, who has thus been left alone, is brought before the king in his chamber at Westminster, and the latter expresses his intention of forgiving her if she conforms to his wishes. The justices and clerks go to wait upon her with many offers of assistance, and on promising to glaze a window in the monastery, she is duly absolved of her sins by a confessor in the garb of a friar. She is then courteously asked by the king whether she is prepared to amend her ways and to wed Conscience, one of his knights. As she declares her willingness to do so, Conscience is called by the king, and asked whether he will take her to wife. He flatly refuses, and sets forth Mede's whole manner of life; how she releases the guilty, throws the just into prison, and hangs the innocent; how she gets absolution when she pleases; how, as the *provisors* show, she is privy with the Pope; how she lets priests live in concubinage, corrupts the judges, and makes it difficult for the poor to get justice, in

consequence of the law's delays. Mede, being called upon for her defence against these charges, makes, it must be admitted, an extremely able speech. Beginning with an invective against Conscience, whom she accuses of cowardice in persuading the king to the Treaty of Bretigny, she goes on to show how necessary the intervention of Mede is in all the relations of life, between master and servant, king and subject, priest and people, buyer and seller; indeed, so powerful is her argument, that she persuades the king she is well worthy to rule. Conscience, however, has not studied logic in the schools for nothing, and proves himself quite a match for Mede, whose fallacies he exposes point by point. There are, he shows, two kinds of Mede, one the just reward for service, the other the price of misdoing. What labourers receive is not Mede, but wages; in merchandise there is no Mede, but exchange; priests no doubt must be maintained, but those who take money for masses look for their Mede in this world. (pp. 208-15)

Mede has now no argument left but misquotation of Scripture. Solomon, says she, declares in the Book of Wisdom that they that give gifts win the victory and obtain honour—*Honorem adquirit qui munera dat.* But Conscience, whose memory is as good as his logic, at once reminds her that she has left out the last part of the text—*Animam autem aufert accipientium:* "He that giveth a gift shall have honour, but the soul of them that receive it is bound thereby."

Although Conscience would seem to have fairly worsted Mede in argument, yet the king is still apparently unconvinced. He bids the parties be reconciled. Conscience, who represents the right disposition of the heart, rather than Philosophy, declines to submit unless Reason assents, whereupon the king commands him to fetch this councillor to court. Reason, when summoned by Conscience, bids his man Cato saddle his horse Suffer-till-I-see-my-time, on which he sets out for court with his friend. On the way they observe riding behind them two men of law, Garyn (Wary) Wisdom, a character resembling Bunyan's Worldly-Wiseman, and Witty or Policy, who are riding posthaste to the king, lest Reason should get an advantage over them. Arrived at court Reason is graciously received by the king, who places him between himself and his son, and a scene follows which is evidently intended to paint the actual corruptions of justice, as the preceding Passus had been devoted to the exposure of the unjust motives which sway men's hearts. Peace comes into court and presents a bill, one of those petitions by which the commons, in the infancy of Parliament, were accustomed to obtain remedies for grievances. The bill is put forth against Wrong, and illustrates the evils caused by the privilege of Purveyance—

> "Both my gees and my grys his gadelynges feccheth;
> I dar nought for fere of hym fyghte ne chyde.
> He borwed of me Bayard he broughte hym home neuere,
> Ne no ferthyng ther-fore for naughte I couthe plede.
> He meyneteneth his men to morther myne hewen,

> Forestalleth my feyres and fighteth in my chepy-
> nge;
> And breketh up my bernes dore and bereth
> aweye my whete,
> And taketh me but a taile for ten quarters of
> otes."

Wrong, alarmed at this accusation, secures the services of Wary Wisdom and Witty, who take Mede with them, but the king orders Wrong to be put into irons, and refuses to listen to the two men of law when they suggest that the accused should be bailed. Peace, the petitioner, is then pressed by Mede to be content with money compensation, and would have consented, had not the king shown himself inexorable. Reason's interest being asked for on behalf of the prisoner—

> "Rede me noughte," quod Resoun, "no reuthe
> to have,
> Till lordes and ladies lovien alle treuthe,
> And haten al harlotrye to heren it or to mouthen
> it;
> Tyl Pernelle's purfil be put in here hucche;
> And children's cherissyng be chastyng with
> yerdes;
> And harlotes holynesse be holden for an hyne;
> Till clerken coueitise be to clothe the pore and
> to fede,
> And religious romares *recordare* in here clois-
> teres,
> As Seynt Benet hem bad Bernarde and Fr-
> aunceys;
> And tyl prechoures prechyng be preved on hem-
> seluen;
> Tyl the kynges conseille be the comune profyte;
> Tyl Bisschopes' Baiardes ben beggares cham-
> bres,
> Here haukes and her houndes helpe to pore Reli-
> gious," etc.

Until this reformation is accomplished, says Reason, there should be no pity, and no wrong in this world should go unpunished, or be atoned for by gifts. At this Wary Wisdom winked at Mede,

> And seide, "Madame, I am yowre man what so
> my mouth jangleth
> I falle in floreines," quod that freke "an faile spe-
> che ofte."

All good men, however, thought that Reason was right, and the king, being of the same opinion, rebuked his lawyers, declaring that all injustice should be punished. Conscience doubts that it will be hard to govern thus; but Reason, on the contrary, declares it will be easy, if the king be obedient to his rules, and Conscience be of the council.

> "And I graunt," quod the kynge "goddes for-
> bode it faile,
> Als long as owre lyf lasteth lyue we togideres."

Here ends that part of the *Vision* which is more particularly directed to the exposure of the corruptions of the State: what follows has reference to the sins of individuals. When the king and his knights, after the trial of Mede, went to the church to hear matins, the dreamer woke, but he soon fell asleep again, and imagined himself to be listening to the sermon of Reason, already alluded to, in which the preacher pointed to the manifest judgments of God sent upon the nation, and exhorted all men everywhere to repent. Moved by his eloquence, the Seven Deadly Sins come to confession, and are described one by one in passages of extraordinary dramatic power, revealing to the fullest extent the poet's gifts of imagination, observation, and judgment. Pride and Lechery are very roughly sketched; but in the confession of Envy, Wrath, Avarice, Gluttony, and Sloth, these passions exhibit their effects, in rapid transformation, on every rank and condition of men,—mostly of the lower classes,—with whom the writer is best acquainted. Thus Envy confesses that he would sooner see his neighbour Gybbe have mischance than get a pound of Essex cheese, and that he had hired Backbiting as a broker to depreciate his fellow-tradesman's wares. Wrath has lived at one time as gardener, and at another as scullion, in a convent, and has set the whole society by the ears. Avarice has mastered all the tricks of every trade, from the time when he learned the art of lying and false weights at Weyhill and Winchester fairs, down to the time when he began to lend to lords and ladies, and to acquire manors, through his debtors being in arrear with their payment. He knows how to clip coin, and how to lend it in exchange for valuable pledges; and his wife Rose the regrater (retail dealer) is well skilled to give under-payment for the weight of cloth she buys, and to adulterate poor people's drink. Glutton, on his way to confession, is tempted into the public-house, where he drinks, in company with Cis the shoemaker's wife, Wat the Warrener, Tim the tinker, Hick the ostler, and other choice spirits, to such an extent that he has to be put to bed by his wife, and needs all Saturday and Sunday to sleep off the effects of his debauch.

As each sin comes to the close of his confession, Repentance rebukes and admonishes him, and informs him what he must do to obtain mercy and absolution. Then Hope seizes a horn and blows it with *Beati quorum remissœ sunt iniquitates,* and a vast crowd of penitents throng together, hoping to find Truth. Meeting one in pilgrim's dress, they ask if he has ever heard tell of a saint named Truth; but though he has been to Sinai, and to Bethlehem, and Babylon, he can tell them nothing of that shrine. Suddenly a ploughman puts forth his head—

> "I knowe him as kyndely as clerk doth his bokes;
> Conscience and kynde witt kenned me to his
> place,
> And deden me suren hym sikerly to serue hym
> for euere,
> Both to sowe and to sette the while I swynke
> mighte.
> I have ben his folwar al this fifty wyntre;
> Both ysowen his sede and sued his bestes,
> With-inne and with-outen wayted his profyt.
> I dyke and I delue I do that treuthe hoteth;
> Some tyme I sowe and some tyme I thresche,
> In tailours crafte and tynkares craft what treu-
> the can devyse,
> I weue and I wynde and do what treuthe hoteth.
> For thoughe I seye it my-self I serue hym to
> paye;
> I haue myn huire of hym wel and otherwhiles
> more;
> He is the prestest payer that pore men knoweth;

He ne withalt non hewe his hyre that he ne hath
  it at euen.
He is as low as a lombe and louelich of speche,
And if ye wilneth to wite where that he dwelleth,
I shal wisse yow wetterly the weye to his place."

All the pilgrims press round the ploughman, whose name
is Piers, proffering him money, which he refuses; he gives
them, however, very minute instructions how to find the
road to the wicket gate leading into Paradise, which, says
he, is kept by seven sisters, Abstinence, Humility, Charity,
Chastity, Patience, Peace, and Bounty, in other words the
Seven Christian Virtues, the exact opposites of the Seven
Deadly Sins. Some of the pilgrims, especially a cut-purse
and an ape-ward, declare that they can have no kindred
there; but Piers reminds them that Mercy (the Virgin
Mary) dwells there also, through whom they may get
grace.

Having thus given his view of the corruptions of the State,
of the sins of men, and of the cure for both kinds of evils,
the poet proceeds to consider the duties of the various constituent portions of society. The pilgrims declare that they
shall never find their way without a guide; whereupon
Piers professes his readiness to lead them as soon as he has
ploughed his half acre. Meantime all are to occupy themselves with some useful business: ladies are to sew chasubles and to comfort the needy and naked; the knight is to
preserve Church and State from the disorders caused by
wicked men; the rest are to help Piers in his ploughing,
and as their reward are promised the right of gleaning in
harvest time. Piers then makes his will in preparation for
his journey, and sets all his labourers to work. Now, however, great difficulties begin. At nine o'clock in the morning Piers, leaving his plough, goes out to see what his
workmen are doing, and finds some in the ale-house drinking and singing, while others are feigning infirmity in
order to avoid the necessity of labour. "I will soon find
out," says Piers, "whether you are telling the truth: Truth
shall teach you to drive his team." Anchorites and hermits
shall have only one meal a day; and the run-about recluse
shall have nothing. An idle Frenchman insolently refuses
to do his bidding, and Piers appeals for protection to the
knight, whose courteous intervention being of no avail, the
ploughman summons Hunger to his assistance. Hunger
seized on the rebel, and so buffeted him that he looked like
a lantern for ever after; while the other idlers, dismayed
at his fate, all rushed to do their work. Piers is filled with
compassion for their distress, but fears that they will fall
again into evil ways when Hunger has once departed. He
therefore asks his terrible ally for advice before the latter
departs, and Hunger counsels him to feed "bold, big beggars" with horse-bread and beans, while the really poor
and afflicted are to be assisted, in view of the text, "Bear
ye one another's burdens." In answer to Piers' question
whether men can be compelled to work, Hunger refers to
Genesis iii. 19, and to other passages of Holy Writ.

Kynde witt wolde that eche a wyght wroughte
Or in dykinge or in deluinge or trauaillynge in
  preyeres,
Contemplatyf lyf or actyf lyf Crist wolde men
  wroughte.
The Sauter seyth in the psaalme of *beati omnes*

The freke that fedyth hymself with his feythful
  laboure
He is blessed by the boke in body and in soule.

Asked whether he can recommend any physic for the remedy of Piers and his servants, Hunger replies that they
overfeed themselves, and that they should not eat till they
are hungry. Piers having thanked him for his counsel,
Hunger refuses to depart till he has dined; and the ploughman, professing that he can give him neither geese nor
pigs, brings him cheese, curds, cream, oatcake, and bean
bread, with parsley, leeks and cabbages, while the poorer
classes contribute peascods, beans, and cherries. When
Hunger still demanded more they sought to poison him
with young onions and peas, but after a good harvest they
fed him with the best; beggars would touch only the finest
bread; labourers dined daily on fresh fish and flesh.

And but if he be heighlich huyred ellis wil he
  chyde,
And that he was workman wroughte waille the
  tyme,
Ayeines Cato's conseille comseth he to jangle
Paupertatis onus pacienter ferre memento.
He greueth hym ayeines God and gruccheth ay-
  eines resoun,
And thanne curseth he the kynge and al his con-
  seille after,
Such lawes to loke laboreres to greve.
Ac whiles hunger was her maister there wolde
  none of hem chyde,
Ne stryue ayeines his statut so sternelich he
  loked.

The poet in conclusion solemnly warns the working classes of the divine judgment coming upon them if they refuse
to labour. Every line of this part of the poem is a vivid illustration of social life at the time of the Black Death and
the great famines, of the habits of the villeins, and of the
feelings of the people with regard to the Statute of Labourers.

Truth, hearing of the pilgrimage, sends Piers, and all who
help him, a pardon. By this document kings and knights,
who have done their duty in maintaining religion and
order, are allowed to pass lightly through purgatory. Bishops who have observed both the laws, that is their duty to
God and their neighbour, shall be placed with the apostles. Merchants, however, will not have plenary pardon,
because they do not keep the holy days of the Church, and
swear falsely for gain; they had better trade fairly, aid hos-
pitals, repair bridges, give marriage portions to brides,
help the poor, and put scholars to school. On hearing the
terms of their pardon the merchants wept for joy; but the
lawyers were more severely treated, because they took
bribes. Honest and humble-minded labourers had the
same pardon as Piers, but not the feigning beggar, the false
hermit, or any of the "loller" classes. A priest asks to look
at the pardon: it is all contained in two lines:—

Et qui bona egerunt ibunt in vitam eternam,
Qui vero mala in ignem eternum.—(St. Matt.
  XXV. 46.)

The priest says this is no pardon, and a dispute ensues between him and Piers, the noise of which awakes the
dreamer, who finds himself mealless and moneyless on

Malvern Hills. Reflecting on his dream, he cannot say how much weight should be attached to it, for Cato thinks lightly of dreams; nevertheless he often meditates on the dispute between Piers and the priest, and is of opinion that Do-Well is better than indulgences. He believes the Pope has power to grant pardon; but trusting to masses is very unsafe; and mayors and judges who break the ten commandments will find that pardons and provincial letters, purchased from the Pope, will avail them little hereafter.

Finally the poet concludes:—

> For-thi I conseille alle cristene to crye God
>   mercy,
> And Marie his moder be owre mene betwene,
> Thet God gyue us grace here ar we gone hennes,
> Suche werkes to werche while we ben here,
> That after owre deth-day Do-well reherce
> At the day of dome we did as he highte.

Up to this point all has been perfectly clear, consistent, and intelligible, because the poet has been working according to a settled plan. The allegory relates to the moral life of men, and it is represented in a definite scheme of poetical action. But having reached his ethical conclusion, it seems to have occurred to Langland that he must found his system of morals on a metaphysical basis, and he accordingly embarked on a new poem which he called *Vita de Do-Well, Do-Bet, Do-Best.* To analyse this sequel in detail would be foreign to the design of our [essay], especially as the poet himself seems to have often wandered aimlessly in the mazes of his thought. It will be seen, however, that his work falls naturally into three divisions, in the first of which he appears to be defining for his readers what is the true theory of moral action. The visionary falls in with Thought and Wit, and learns from them that Do-Well dwells in a castle called Caro (the Flesh), together with the Lady Anima (the Soul), the Constable Inwit (Conscience), and his five sons (the Senses). But no use is made of this allegory in the action, which is almost entirely occupied with long interviews between William and such personages as Study, Clergy, and Scripture, with whom he holds much dispute, without however being far advanced towards the discovery of Do-Well. He has also a vision of Fortune, Nature, and Reason, which lets us see the influence exercised on the poet's thought by the *Romance of the Rose.* Imagination afterwards appears to him and rebukes him for his impatience; while, finally, in company with Conscience and Patience, he falls in with one Activa Vita or Haukyn, the Active Man, whose coat—the only one in his possession—is covered with stains symbolical of the seven deadly sins. Haukyn, being duly instructed in his duties by Patience, repents, and bewails his sins; the noise wakes the dreamer and puts an end to this part of the vision.

The *Vita de Do-Bet* sets forth the spiritual life of the soul. The object of the dreamer is to discover the nature of Charity. He meets with Faith in the person of Abraham and Spes (Hope), who are in quest of Piers the Plowman, now become identical with Charity or Christ. A wounded man is discovered in the way; Faith and Hope pass by him; but the good Samaritan, or Piers Plowman, or Charity, binds up his wounds, leaving him to be attended at an inn called *Lex Christi.* Then follows a description of the joust-

ing of Jesus, and his triumph over Death and Hell, the allegory being based on the text of the *Gospel of Nicodemus;* and with the news of Piers' victory, announced by the ringing of the Easter Bells, the dreamer is awakened and the second part of the *Vision* ends.

In the *Vita de Do-Best* the Saviour has departed from the earth, and henceforth Piers the Plowman typifies the life of the Christian Church. Christ's place is supplied by Grace, who makes Piers his ploughman, providing for his labour four oxen (the four Gospels), four "stottes" (bullocks or horses, the Four Evangelists), and four seeds (the cardinal virtues). Piers builds the House of Unity, but it is attacked by Pride, and in the concluding Passus of the poem Antichrist becomes master of the world. Conscience advises the world to come into the House of Unity; and Nature, hearing the address of Conscience, lets loose Disease upon mankind. Many perish. Eld bears Death's banner: Death strikes into the dust Popes and Kings: Eld attacks the poet himself: Death draws nigh to him: he cries to Nature, who advises him to take refuge in Unity; but, coming thither, he finds it besieged by seven giants (the Deadly Sins) and Antichrist. Flattery (a friar) treacherously gains admission into the castle, and Conscience declares that he will become a pilgrim and go forth to seek Piers Plowman. "And then," says the poet, "he cried aloud for Grace, and I awoke." Thus the poem concludes in gloom and defeat. (pp. 216-26)

> *W. J. Courthope, "Langland," in his* A History of English Poetry, Vol. I, *Macmillan and Co., 1895, 200-46.*

Walter W. Skeat   (essay date 1923)

[*Skeat was an English philologist and critic who edited authoritative texts of the works of Chaucer and of* Piers Plowman *(1886). In the following excerpt, he contrasts Chaucer's satirical humor with Langland's earnest tone. He also points to two "curious" aspects of the poem: the evolution of Piers Plowman's character from the "small farmer" of the A-text to his identification with God in the B-text, and the work's detailed description of London life in Langland's day.*]

Just as Christian is not the author of Bunyan's *Pilgrim's Progress,* but only the subject of it, so Piers the Plowman is not the author of the *Vision,* but the subject of it; he is the personage seen in a dream, not the dreamer himself. Neither does the Book describe one continuous dream, but a succession of several; in some of which Piers is neither seen nor mentioned. Yet the whole poem is named from him, because he is the most remarkable figure in the group of allegorical personages who pass successively before the dreamer's sleeping sight. He is of more importance than either Lady Holy-church, Lady Meed, Falsehood, Conscience, Reason, Hunger, or the impersonations of the Seven Deadly Sins; for he is the type of a truly honest man. (pp. vii-viii)

Strictly speaking, only a *part* of the poem was *at first* named after Piers. The true title of the latter portion was originally *Visio ejusdem de Do-wel, Do-bet, et Do-best,* or the *Vision of the Same [William] concerning Do-well, Do-*

better, and Do-best; but the two portions were subsequently treated as constituting one long Book, and the name *Liber de Petro Plowman* was conferred upon the whole. (p. viii)

The usual date assigned to [*Piers Plowman*], 1362, is very misleading; for all depends upon which form of the poem is in question. It was in hand and subject to variation during twenty or thirty years, the date 1362 expressing merely the time of its commencement. Hence William was, in fact, absolutely contemporaneous with Chaucer, and cannot fairly be said to have preceded him. A comparison between these two great writers is very instructive; it is soon perceived that each is, in a great measure, the supplement of the other, notwithstanding the sentiments which they have in common. Chaucer describes the rich more fully than the poor, and shows us the holiday-making, cheerful, genial phase of English life; but William pictures the homely poor in their ill-fed, hard-working condition, battling against hunger, famine, injustice, oppression, and all the stern realities and hardships that tried them as gold is tried in the fire. Chaucer's satire often raises a good-humoured laugh; but William's is that of a man who is constrained to speak out all the bitter truth, and it is as earnest as is the cry of an injured man who appeals to Heaven for vengeance. Each, in his own way, is equally admirable, and worthy to be honoured by all who prize highly the English character and our own land. The extreme earnestness of our author and the obvious truthfulness and blunt honesty of his character are in themselves attractive, and lend a value to all he utters, even when he is evolving a theory or wanders away into abstract questions of theological speculation. It is in such a poem as his that we get a real insight into the inner every-day life of the people, their dress, their diet, their wages, their strikes, and all the minor details which picture to us what manner of men they were.

One very curious variation occurs in the character of Piers the Plowman himself. In the A-text, he is merely the highest type of the honest small farmer, whose practical justice and Christianity are so approved of by truth (who is the same with God the Father), that he is entrusted with a bull of pardon of more value than even the Pope's. But towards the conclusion of the B-text, the poet strikes a higher note, and makes him the type of the human nature in its highest form of excellence, the human flesh within whom dwelt the divine soul of Christ our Saviour. By a sort of parody upon the text in I Cor. x. 4, he asserts that *Petrus est Christus,* that Piers is Christ, and he likens the Saviour to a champion who fights in Piers' armour, that is to say, in human flesh—*humana natura.* When the fact is once fully perceived that, in a part of the poem, Piers is actually identified with our Lord and Saviour, the notion of imagining him to have been *an old English author* stands revealed in all its complete and irreverent absurdity.

The reader should beware also of being much influenced by the mention of the Malvern Hills. The name of William of Malvern has been proposed for the poet, in order to meet the objection that his surname is not certainly known. In my opinion, such a name is hardly a fit one, as likely to add to the numerous misconceptions already current concerning him. One great merit of the poem is, that it chiefly exhibits London life and London opinions, which are surely of more interest to us than those of Worcestershire. He does but mention Malvern three times, and those three passages may be found within the compass of the first eight Passus of Text A. But how numerous are his allusions to London! He not only speaks of it several times, but he frequently mentions the law courts of Westminster; he was familiar with Cornhill, East Cheap, Cock Lane in Smithfield, Shoreditch, Garlickhithe, Stratford, Tyburn, and Southwark, all of which he mentions in an off-hand manner. He mentions no river but the Thames, which is with him simply synonymous with river; for in one passage he speaks of two men thrown into the Thames, and in another he says that rich men are wont to give presents to the rich, which is as superfluous as if one should fill a tun with water from a fresh river, and then pour it into the Thames to render it fuller. To remember the London origin of a large portion of the poem is the true key to the right understanding of it. (pp. xxvii-xxix)

> *Walter W. Skeat, in an introduction to* The Vision of William concerning Piers the Plowman *by William Langland, edited by Walter W. Skeat, revised edition, Oxford at the Clarendon Press, 1923, pp. vii-xlv.*

Henry W. Wells   (essay date 1929)

[*Wells was an American educator and critic whose writings include a translation of* The Vision of Piers Plowman *(1959) into modern English. In the following excerpt, he considers the relationship between the three subsections of the* Visio *and the* Vita *of Piers Plowman, noting their individual themes and structures.*]

The relation of the *Visio* and the *Vita* has never been carefully stated and often has been, at least from my own point of view, ill understood. The *Visio* is a study of the life of the laity both as it is and as it should be. We have in this part of the poem that which the common communicant ought to know, and nothing more. We have no abstruse theological or philosophical problems, no allegory of learning, no account of the saintly life and no thorough and detailed analysis of the functioning of the Church as the coördinating principle in society. On the other hand, we have such social satire and such an account of man's religious duties as the humblest medieval reader might be expected to understand. If he follows the road here traced by the poet, he is considered to be sure of salvation. With the *Vita* the theme is changed. We have an account of the world as seen by the thinker who has passed through the medieval disciplines of learning, asceticism and priestly responsibility. He has known the intellectual life, the mystic and the active life, and so fulfilled the more arduous duties which heaven imposes upon its specially chosen warriors. In this part of the poem the satire falls not upon delinquencies in secular duties, but upon faults peculiar to persons dedicated to the life of scholarship and religious practice: upon those who, like the gluttonous Doctor, the feigning Hermit and the over-indulgent Confessor, betray learning, devotion and the institution of the Church. This part of the poem deals with ideals superfluous to and improper in a layman, but to which God's select soldiers must conform if they are to remain loyal and in turn win their salvation.

To a certain point the two Lives agree. This is why the author of the so-called A-Text continued his poem beyond the *Visio.* The *Vita* begins humbly. It gives an account of the life of man from his birth to his intellectual and spiritual maturity. It contains passages dealing successively with the creation of the world, the birth and care of children, marriage and the preliminary disciplines of study. The chief figures encountered in the allegory are Will, the name symbolically given to the Christian Pilgrim at birth, Thought, who meets him in his earliest years, Wit, his first teacher, and Study, who gives him elementary training and who introduces him to Scripture and to Clergy, who is with Scripture. But in the A-Text the pilgrim learns little from Scripture and nothing from Clergy, who will have nothing to do with him. The word Clergy the poet here uses, of course, as virtually synonymous with learning. In short, the A-Text breaks off just where the education of the more enterprising layman would be expected to conclude. Born with will, early endowed with thought and wit, acquainted with elementary learning, he represents the foundation upon which, after all, even the greatest seer and the deepest thinker of the Church must build.

We may now see why the A-Text was circulated so widely. It contained what the common man needed to know and no more. If the A-Text had ended with the *Visio,* it would have instructed the layman in all his primary duties to God and man, but it would not have shown him concretely his place in society and his relation to the Clergy and the Religious. Thus the section of the *Vita* included in the A-Text formed a part of that Manuscript Version as circulated among the people. I have no opinion as to whether the author soon after writing the A-Text died, or continued his poem and encouraged reproductions of the A-Text even after the B-Text had been finished. I observe, however, that the A-Text ends at a point which, if unsatisfactory from an æsthetic standpoint, is entirely satisfactory from a doctrinal standpoint. The *Vita* repeats certain elements of the *Visio.* The man of religion must be born, possess will, thought and wit, and know his A.B.C. just as a common communicant. His salvation comes from the same source. Piers the Plowman saves one no less than the other. Each must to some degree Do Well. Each must know and seriously consider the Creed and Paternoster and follow the road of the Ten Commandments. Each requires the same sacraments. Thus in each section we have allusions to baptism and burial and elaborate passages dealing with penance and the Mass. These repetitions may or may not, I take it, be viewed as inartistic, but are clearly necessary to the subject in hand. The poem in its design may be thought of as one of those great canvasses which Veronese and Tintoretto delighted to paint in which a pillar divides the picture into two finely balanced scenes of approximately equal magnitude, although one is slightly more significant than the other. (pp. 124-26)

While the *Vita* is clearly stated to be divided into three parts, it is commonly observed that the *Visio* is also divided into three parts. Closely following upon the first vision of the Field of Folk and of Holy Church, which is clearly introductory, we have the Story of Lady Meed, the Confession and Absolution of the Sins at Church, and the two concluding Passus dealing with Piers and his servants and concluding with the story of the Pardon. I shall later examine the character of the transitions in greater detail. For the present, however, I am concerned only with observing those parallels which I believe to be deliberate between the three parts of the *Visio* and the three parts of the *Vita.* (pp. 126-27)

The first main part of the *Visio,* namely the Story of Lady Meed, deals with the problem of secular government and nearly at its conclusion introduces us to a figure named Reason, who decides for the king the quarrel between Meed and Conscience. Reason thus becomes the central figure in this section of the poem. The first part of the *Vita,* or the *Vita de Do-Well,* deals with problems of theology. Again Reason proves the culminating figure, since all the preceding allegorical types in the *Vita de Do-Well* lead up to it, and after its appearance we enter the long transition to the *Vita de Do-Bet.* The chief problem in the Story of Lady Meed is man's well-being in this world. The chief problem debated in the *Vita de Do-Well* is man's eternal well-being. One section deals with the active life of secular affairs, the other, with the active life of industrious theological study. The Story of the Confession and Absolution of the Sins deals obviously with the more personal, intimate and inner life. It concludes with an allegory of the Mass, the sacrament which restores man to the Grace of his Creator. The *Vita de Do-Bet* deals with the life of solitude and contemplation (of this I shall have more to say later), and concludes with the bells that ring in Easter and which summon the dreamer to the sacrament. The Story of Piers in the *Visio* deals with the theme of honest work and its reward, which is pardon and salvation. Here for the first time we meet the image of the plow, in this case simply the plow of the farmer. In outward appearance at least even Piers himself is no more than an overseer or even a participant in these physical labors. He exacts honest labor and receives no easy indulgences in his pardon. In the *Vita de Do-Best* we have an allegory of the entire community envisaged as *Unitas* laboring at its myriad tasks under the guidance of the Church. Here Piers and his plow once more appear, but Piers is now indubitably Christ, his plow the word of God, man the harvest and the barn the heaven of divine rest. This imagery has, to be sure, been hinted in the *Vita de Do-Bet,* but here is first objectified. Piers' wicked servants, the unscrupulous priests and friars, grant easy indulgences. In the *Visio* we have seen the promise of salvation for the honest worker. The individual may be saved. In the *Vita* we have the picture of society retrogressing rather than progressing. Individuals, as notably an honest priest, may still be saved. But the community goes from bad to worse. We should, I think, regard as deliberate both these comparisons and these contrasts between the six major sections of the poem. In each case the lines seem to me to have been too sharply drawn to be accidental. I believe that the author or authors deliberately repeated the major elements in the design.

The *Vita* is obviously the more complex part of the poem,

as it is also the longer part. It has, however, been the less discussed. I shall glance comparatively briefly at the outstanding features in the construction of the *Visio.* I consider that they show a point of view by no means haphazard or confused. For each of the major images presented there can, I think, be given convincing reasons as to why it is pertinent to the theme of the poem as a whole and as to why it occupies the position which it actually holds in the work.

We are introduced to the Field of Folk because the poet begins his teaching not with revelation nor with religion but with nature. So he begins later in his *Vita de Do-Well* and at the conclusion of that section of the poem assures us that even Saracens in substance know the first Person of the Trinity. Moreover *Piers Plowman,* unlike the poems by Dante and Milton, contains no scene in heaven. Once only and for the space of but three hundred lines the scene sinks to the deep dungeon and dark from which Christ rescues our forefathers in darkness. With the exception of the Harrowing of Hell the poet avoids all scenes that belong to another life than that of this world. In short, the scene of *Piers Plowman* is precisely the opposite of that of Dante's poem. The Italian poet deals only with life beyond the grave, the English poet only with life upon this side of the grave. The whole poem deals in this sense with the Field of Folk. Its author or authors contrived most vividly and forcefully to state an initial proposition. The work remains in this respect at least remarkably true to its premises. Even from an aesthetic standpoint it holds faithful to this field and to this earth. Its varied imagery always breathes earth-odors.

Holy Church, the figure who next appears, begins her instructions with homely and materialistic observations. She too acknowledges first of all the animal nature of man. Three things she tells the dreamer are necessary, food, drink, and clothing. From this characteristic teaching she elevates her discussion till at the last she states the doctrine of the Redemption and its moral of charity. But she always fulfills the function of a Prologue. She never tells the dreamer more than any child might be expected to know. She reads him, as it were, his catechism, stating simply those ideas upon which the whole of the Christian System rests: the doctrine of free will, of the depravity of the body, of obedience to God, of charity and of grace.

In her last words Holy Church warns the pilgrim of evil and bids him be wary of distributing blame. She disappears, after serving not only as a Prologue but as a link to the first part of the story proper, the allegory of Lady Meed. The Greek mind would of course have left the problem of the state to the last, as the highest and most important of all problems. The medieval poet, however, true to premises already contained in his poem, regards religion and the Church as the supreme guide in life, and treats the state as an initial problem to be faced before proceeding to far graver problems. Thus the political life vividly introduces us to sin. Man's error lies not in false political theory but in his personal weakness. Sin becomes the vital issue. Thus we are logically led to the second chief division of the *Visio,* the Story of the Confession and Absolution of the Sins.

If it should be urged against my view of the distinct functions of the *Visio* and the *Vita* that of the six or seven characters representing the sins (for the number differs in the different texts) one of the characters is a priest, I should reply that in embodying sloth in human form the poet followed a well-tried tradition in making Sloth a priest. It should be noted that the faults ascribed to this idler include many omissions and commissions not in the least peculiar to his profession. He is the eternal truant from duty. His truancy, not his duty, concerns the poet here. Sloth cannot be said to represent the short-comings of the Clergy as such. A further objection might be raised in that the C-Text of the *Visio* and this only contains a passage of some length on the sins of monks and friars. The lines occur in the sermon of Reason, which introduces the Story of the Sins and links it with the preceding Story of Lady Meed, wherein Reason is also a character. Reason's sermon is obviously intended to enumerate the outstanding sins of all orders of society. That in two texts the clergy and the religious receive slight notice and in the third no more than a moderate proportion of attention, seems to me on the whole to support rather than to damage my position. The clergy appear almost forgotten in many long passages. In the lines dealing with Hunger we hear of the friars only as laborers in the common fields, driven by famine to desert their normal course of life. We should of course remember that the *Visio* reflects life as the layman sees it, not merely as he lives it. Although not a participant in their peculiar problems, he both observes the clergy and the learned and recognizes the great influence which they exercise upon him.

The confession of the Sinners is followed by their absolution and by the quest of society for a better life. This leads us to the third section of the *Visio.* The extremely popular appeal of the *Visio* as a whole is powerfully enhanced by the allegory in the Passus dealing with Famine. Although in this section of the poem the activities of the higher orders of society are noted, as that of knights and ladies, we hear most of the common laborers and especially of their unwillingness to do honest work in the plowfields. The opening of the last Passus of the *Visio* gives a list of all classes, in which the clergy are but hastily mentioned, while detailed attention is accorded to merchants, lawyers and, once more, to laborers. Laymen pretending to be priests are condemned.

We should observe caution in our interpretation of Piers' pardon. It states that all who do well shall be saved and that all who do evil shall be damned. Later the author gives his own view as somewhat more moderate, for he grants that the Pope and the prayers of the Church have some power to save souls, although to trust in such aids is not so safe as to do well. Piers' pardon is simply *Do-Well* as applied in particular to the laity. The clergy and the religious must also *Do-Well,* and in a more exacting degree. By "doing" and by "working" medieval authors do not of course mean merely temporal actions. Thus Hilton's treatise *On Daily Work* deals in large part with prayer and meditation. Piers never of course fancied that a Christian could forsake faith, devotion and the sacraments and by mere bodily works go to heaven. He meant that a man must be saved primarily upon his own merits and by

God's grace, and not by the aid of indulgences. It is not from the nature of this pardon but from the character of the *Visio* as a whole that we may safely regard the *Visio* as addressed primarily to the laity. Piers' pardon, even in the *Visio,* applies to all mankind. That a priest scorns it, however, helps us to perceive its applicability to the people. The *Visio* ends with the pardon because with the need for a pardon it begins. Man is shown in a transient state. He may, on dying, go either to the deep dungeon or to the fair tower. The first prayer which the pilgrim passionately addresses to Holy Church consists in the one vital question for every devout medieval man. The question is simply, how may I save my soul? We may conclude then that so far as the larger contours of form are concerned the *Visio* is a well arranged poem. Like the typical dream allegory, it appears even wildly discordant upon the surface. But when the meanings of the symbols are considered, we become aware of the presence of no inconsiderable design.

The *Visio* introduces us not only to the name of *Do-Well* but to the need for the *Vita* as a whole. In his last speeches Piers in the *Visio* states that he will change his course of life: instead of being so busy about his physical welfare, he will do as the apostles did and turn chiefly to the cultivation of his soul. This forewarns us of the change which we are about to encounter in the Second Part of the poem. And here we are faced with our gravest problems, to which, however, answers may be given I think with even more assurance than in the case of the *Visio. . . .* (pp. 128-32)

Let us review a few of the outstanding features of the *Vita de Do-Well, Do-Bet* and *Do-Best.* This part of the poem represents the search of an imaginary pilgrim for three "lives" or "virtues" or, as we should be more likely to say in the language of present-day psychology, three states. The pilgrim meets many characters, the chief of whom are in the order in which he meets them, Thought, Wit, Study, Scripture, Clergy, Nature, Patience, Hawkin the Active Man and Piers Plowman. From most of these characters the pilgrim inquires who are Do-Well, Do-Bet and Do-Best, and from no two of them does he receive quite the same answer. Had they agreed, he might possibly have given up the quest. Wit tells him that Do-Well is to labor honestly, while Clergy tells him that Do-Well is principally to be loyal to the Faith. Clearly each character has something to contribute to the pilgrim's growing knowledge of his life's journey. Each represents a progressive stage in his education. The different answers show not that the poet himself is confused (the poet knew, I think, his answer from the beginning) but that his pilgrim is groping his way, as do all men toward a solution of life's difficulties. He quarrels with all his teachers, makes mistakes, falls by the way, because of his peculiar temperament profits more from some teachers than from others and ultimately reaches the knowledge which he desires, only to find that in forgetting himself and taking upon him the burden of society he has borne Christ's cross. For the individual Christian may be saved, but society as a whole is not destined to achieve harmony on earth. The kingdom of Piers the Plowman is not of this world.

The three stages of life are always described as three

grades of holiness. About the last grade we have from the first the greatest agreement. Again and again it is allegorized in the image of the bishop who guards his flock. To rule others is to Do Best. To rule one's self is to Do Well. Do-Bet is described as an advanced state of charity and humility. But the states are clearly and consistently presented in themselves, that is, in the three several parts of the poem; and we need not be over-puzzled by what the first persons whom the pilgrim meets say about them. We may I think say confidently on the basis of the entire character of the Passus dealing with Do-Well that this state is one of self-culture through knowledge. All the chief figures whom the pilgrim meets until very near the end of this section of the poem are evidently stages in his scholastic training. If he lapses for a time to follow Desire of the Eyes and Lust of the Flesh, he in time returns. Even his detour with Nature is at least a part of his academic life. The Life of Do-Bet begins with a long passage in praise of faithful hermits and in behalf of a true priesthood, introducing us to the three Christian or Contemplative Virtues, Faith, Hope and Charity, here named Abraham, Spes and Piers Plowman. This part of the poem is centered in the biblical narrative. Its chief images are not, as elsewhere, of the poet's own invention, but are drawn from the synoptic Gospels and from the Apocrypha. The *Vita de Do-Best* narrates the history of the Church from its beginning in the Resurrection, through the period of its primitive purity to its present state of degeneration. The story is told primarily not from the individual but from the social point of view. It is the story of *Unitas,* of Piers' family. It deals in particular with the government, or misgovernment, of this family, and hence with the responsibility of those who rule the Church, the confessors and prelates. It tells of the Christian Society that, although protected by the Holy Spirit and sustained by the bread of the sacrament, is subject to ceaseless incursions from its enemies, led by Satan. The Four Active or Cardinal Virtues, Justice, Prudence, Fortitude and Temperance, are discussed at considerable length. Allusions of a clearly secondary importance, however, are still made to the pilgrim, who is now old and hoar, but has not as yet attained true happiness on earth. The Field of Folk cannot give such happiness. Salvation is not of this world. Here the poem ends.

Once in the course of his journey the Pilgrim expresses surprise to learn that there are three states of life instead of two. He had always supposed that the two stages were the active life and the contemplative life. But he finds himself unmistakably in a world ordered in patterns of three. His teacher at this point gives just such an ambiguous answer as a good teacher always gives when he knows that it is best for his pupil to find the answer in his own experience. . . . (pp. 132-34)

There is still a further organizing factor to be noted in the instance of the poem. St. Augustine had advanced what has come to be known as the "psychological trinity." *Piers Plowman* does not follow Augustine's thought but presents a somewhat similar conception. The poet several times quotes the familiar text which declares man to be fashioned in God's image. He evidently considered that, since God is a Trinity, man must in some sense also be a trinity. Each of the three Parts of the *Vita* begins with allusions to the interrelation of the three parts of the Trinity and each is clearly dedicated to a special Person of the Trinity. At the conclusion of the *Vita de Do-Well* we are told that even the Saracens believe in God the Father. It is this Person of the Trinity who clearly presides over the Life of Do-Well. Christ as Piers the Plowman is the central theme of the *Vita de Do-Bet.* In this part of the poem the life of Christ, his crucifixion and the harrowing of hell supply the chief narrative elements. The *Vita de Do-Best* is no less clearly dedicated to the Holy Spirit, since it narrates at considerable length the descent of the Spirit at Pentecost, the Gifts of the Spirit and the rule of the Spirit within the Church, protecting it from even greater inroads than have as yet been made by the armies of Anti-Christ. Such is the spiritual trinity of man according to *Piers Plowman,* a thought of no inconsiderable importance in the organization of the work.

It would be manifestly impossible in the brief space of this paper to discuss any large number of details in the *Vita* which indicate the organizing genius of its author or authors. I should prefer to allow my statements relative to the major plan of the poem to stand out for the time being conspicuously, rather than to run the risk of smothering these primary outlines under a mass of detail, however interesting that detail might be to careful students of the poem. A few observations of lesser importance may however detain us.

In the first place it will not of course be assumed that because the Life of Do-Best is dedicated to God the Holy Spirit and the Life of Do-Well to God the Father that the poet had fallen into the heresy of holding the Third greater than the First Person of the Trinity. The poem and the states are of course cumulative. The poet learns early in his career that the Life of Do-Best for example presumes that of Do-Bet. And it not only presumes this preceding life, but includes it. This the imagery of the poem makes clear. Piers the Plowman is still active in the Life of Do-Best. But to know Piers the Plowman it becomes necessary to meet him in the Life of Do-Bet. Man never loses his need for learning or contemplation. He does not outgrow these powers but by them and by their constant use attains a third power, namely, the ability and the right to rule other men. It is better to know two persons of the Trinity than to know one, and better to know three Persons than to know two. Indeed none can truly be known without a knowledge of all.

The first third of the *Vita de Do-Well,* that is, the part contained in the A-Text, is naturally the easiest and most straightforward. We should never here be seriously in doubt of the reasonable sequence of the thought. As first episode we have the meeting of the pilgrim with the two friars. The friars give him no satisfactory answer to his questions. The poet probably means to satirize the friars, who in reply to a serious question give merely an entertaining story. In any event, the incident teaches the pilgrim the need of searching for Truth deeply and the vanity of relying upon persons. He learns at once that no glib phrases can solve his problem. He must labor himself. He cannot, as the illiterate poor, merely believe what he hears without long pondering upon it. He must use his own wit

and go through the arduous disciplines of thought, study, learning, reason, humility and contemplation.

Having brushed specious explanations aside, the pilgrim is prepared to begin his quest in earnest, and to consider man from the cradle to beyond the grave. He first hears from Wit, who is of course Mother Wit or the primitive natural reason, of the creation of the world and of the soul, of the vital principle, or *anima,* and of the rational nature of man, or Inwit. This Inwit, we are told, is the greatest of gifts after the grace of God. By an exercise of Inwit the pilgrim is of course to advance on the road to knowledge. But Inwit does not exist in drunkards, imbeciles and children. Therefore men should avoid excessive drink and care for helpless children and imbeciles. The theme of child-care leads naturally to the subject of marriage. The pilgrim has now reached a stage in his progress when a new teacher is required. He goes therefore to Dame Study, who begins with a long satirical address against the abuse of study and learning by the unfit. Study says that she has taught Scripture the rudiments of learning, and in due time turns over the youthful adventurer to his new master. He has now passed through trivium and quadrivium and may commence his theological studies. These studies however begin badly. The pilgrim is recalcitrant, and quotes Augustine to the effect that many a poor man enters the palace of heaven with no other help than good works and a paternoster. Naturally Scripture and Clergy (learning) will have nothing to do with such a perverse pupil. Here the A-Text ends.

The B- and C-Texts relate how the pilgrim, after trying the joys of a worldly life, returns at length to his old teachers, Scripture and Clergy. But he returns by no means wholly cured of his bad manners, and shortly after some reckless words (in the C-Text they are assigned to Recklessness, but this is merely a name which the pilgrim assumes during a reckless stage in his career) he goes off with Nature. This teacher however can give him no knowledge which aids the solution of the supreme problem, that of salvation. He now meets one Imaginatif who recalls to him all the points in the previous debates, and carefully sets him right as to the advantage of learning, the necessity of a priesthood, the danger of overemphasizing the virtues of poverty and the vanity of merely natural reason. Much rectified in heart, he now enters the house of Theological Reason, accompanied by Patience and by Conscience. Conscience is of course also a character in the *Visio.*

Here occurs some fine satire on false Doctors of Divinity, with their gross habits and really superficial learning. The pilgrim sees however that the best learning has its limitations. Learning is not enough. It is necessary also to lead the life of penance, devotion and contemplation. The figure of Activa Vita appears and confesses himself unworthy and a sinner. He must purge himself by meditation. The poet passes therefore to an account of the contemplative life, which begins in the despising of earthly goods and in the love of meekness and poverty. His new teacher informs him both wherein the true life of devotion consists and how basely the clergy and the religious have in the fourteenth century betrayed their duty towards that life. Thus we are introduced to the *Vita de Do-Bet.*

The Life of Do-Well is in fact the only part of the second half of the poem difficult to follow. This is because throughout his Life the pilgrim engages in many arguments with his teachers, showing all the restlessness of a disputatious nature. We easily infer from it how lively and contentious medieval schools of philosophy and theology as a rule became. The scholar's obstinacy accounts for the vitality of this section of the poem and totally precludes the insipidity into which an allegory of the life of learning is only too likely to fall. The relatively straightforward arguments of the *Vita de Do-Bet,* depicting the Christian or Contemplative Virtues, and of the *Vita de Do-Best,* depicting the reception which the four Active or Moral Virtues meet with at the hands of the Christian world, scarcely need further comment than that which they have already received in preceding paragraphs. (pp. 135-38)

I have attempted in this paper to show the poem to be a really finely built structure, the nave for the people, the choir for the clergy, yet, like many a church in the Middle Ages, so crowded with tombs, rood-screens, chantries and side altars, that the total effect is a most curious blending of order and confusion. On the whole I am chiefly impressed by the order of the work, and this has I feel certain been the aspect of the poem the more slighted by its critics. However, I should not wish to deny that *Piers Plowman* is rough in certain elements of construction as well as in language. Nor do I regard the departures from logical precision to be invariably artistic defects. (p. 140)

Henry W. Wells, "The Construction of 'Piers Plowman'," in PMLA, *Vol. XLIV, No. 1, March, 1929, pp. 123-40.*

Howard William Troyer   (essay date 1932)

[*In the following excerpt from an essay originally published in* PMLA *in 1932, Troyer analyzes the significance of the character of Piers Plowman in Langland's poem, concluding that he is "a multifold symbol" representing alternately "man the race," "an individual man," and "the great God-man," or Jesus Christ.*]

For the sake of clarity we may divide our study of that part of the poem relating to Piers into (a) those passus or visions where Piers appears as an actual character, and (b) those passus or visions in which reference is made to Piers, but in which he does not actually appear as a character.

Piers assumes the rôle of a character in four of the visions. We may group these passages as the episode of the pilgrimage to Truth, the episode of Hunger, the episode of the pardons, the brief episode in the C-text of Piers at the dinner of the Friar, the vision of the Tree of Charity, and the episode of Pentecost. In each case a character called Piers is present and assumes an active rôle in the vision.

(a) The pilgrimage episode, chronologically the first, is as strategic as any for our purpose. The incident itself relates simply. After the opening passus concerning the field-of-folk, the trial of Lady Mede, and the confession of the seven deadly sins,

A thousand of men tho thrungen togyderes;
Criede vpward to Cryst and to his clene moder

To haue grace to go with hem Treuthe to seke.

Because they had no guide, they blindly "blustreden forth as bestes ouer bankes and hilles" until they met a pilgrim who though he had many "signes of Synay and shelle of Galice" knew nothing at all of the great Saint Treuthe. Then one a plowman swore by St. Peter and "put forth his hed." He knew Treuthe for Treuthe was his master who paid him promptly for his faithful services. The pilgrims proffer him a reward if he will guide them to the dwelling place of Treuthe, but he rejects it angrily, for Treuthe would love him less if he took hire. Then he sets them the way. It runs through Meekness into Conscience, through the Ten Commandment country of "berghes and brakes" to the court of Truth, whose walls are of Wit and whose mote is of Mercy. The castle is buttressed by Bileve-so and roofed with Love. Grace is the gate-keeper and Amende-you lifts the Wicket, but Mercy is the maid, who has might over all.

A cutpurse objects that he has no kin there, and an apeward likewise; a pardoner sends for his brevets and his bull, and a common woman joins his company.

The significance of the story is less simple however than the mere tale, and the conventional interpretation of Piers as a simple plowman, pointing the way out to the author's fourteenth-century world, is almost at once inadequate. The thousand of men thronging together and crying to God may represent fourteenth-century England, but they also represent the human race. The plowman who "put forth his hed" is also a Nazarene carpenter, who also came from among men to show men the way to God. He too, was a plowman, though of the heart of man, and a perfect laborer whose will was submission to the will of the Father. He it was who gave himself willingly and without hope of gain to show men the way to God; he who came to fulfil the Old Law and lead men to God through the mercy of the New. If in simple aspect the story is that of a loyal plowman teaching his fellows the way to truth, the deeper significance of the incident lies in the moral teaching of the great plowman who gave himself unselfishly and without reward, and in the divine revelation of the mission of the Son of God among men. Which is to say as far as our interpretation of the symbol goes, that the rôle of Piers here in its very inception is more than that of a mere plowman. It is a symbol of multifold aspect revealing multifold truth.

There is at least one other aspect of Piers in this pilgrimage episode that merits attention in our consideration. His commission to both "sowe and to sette the while he might swynke" is reminiscent of God's words to Adam, and Piers in the immediate lines is less a plowman or Christ than he is the race. He "dykes" and "delves," he plants and harvests, he is a tailor, a tinker, and a weaver. All of these aspects we have noticed are important. We shall find them repeated throughout the poem.

The next passus, which has for its central interest the episode with Hunger, is somewhat more complicated in story. We have not yet finished with the idea of a pilgrimage, though it is a new kind of pilgrimage that now concerns us, for the word pilgrim as well as Piers is a symbol for many truths. Before it was a pilgrimage of man in search of God, now it is the pilgrimage of men in this life between the deep dale and high tower. Before Piers and his followers may see God, they have a half-acre to plow. To facilitate matters Piers sets them to work, each according to his station. With the knights he makes a covenant to supply them with sustenance in return for protection for himself and the church. When he becomes old and the pilgrimage of death (still another aspect of the pilgrimage symbol) awaits him, he writes his bequest. With the idea of death and the final pilgrimage, we have, however, gotten ahead of the story, so we return to the time when Piers and his followers are at work. At high prime Piers leaves the plow to supervise the work of others. Unfortunately he finds many wasters and gluttons who eat, but who do not produce. His rebuke to them ends in a quarrel, and when the Knight proves himself incapable of performing his part of the convenant he has with Piers, the latter perforce "houped after Hunger" and famine results. Only an old loaf of pea-bread saved Wastour from death and the insolent Britoner "loked like a lanterne al his life after." But Hunger drives men to work and then there is food enough. Piers learns two important principles from Hunger, and then he with the help of his neighbors feeds him and succeeds in putting him to sleep, only to find, of course, that once Hunger has been put to sleep, there are wasters and gluttons anew.

The rôle of Piers needs to be indicated in some detail. The predominating one is certainly the one already indicated in the earlier episode, that of man on his pilgrimage of life. It is Piers and his fellows who have the half-acre to plow ere they turn home in old age to the final pilgrimage to heaven. It is out of the experience of the race that the task of each has been assigned according to his station. It is man who is married to Worche-whan-tyme-is, whose daughter is Do-rizte-so-or-thy-dame-shall-the-beat, whose son is Suffre-thi-souerrynes-to-hauen-their-wille-deme-them-nouzte-for-if-thow-doste-thow- shalt- it- dere-abugge. It must have been man himself who when the gluttons and wasters lived upon the fat of the land "houped after Hunger," as it was man who after the famine with its lesson of moderation and its dictum of charity for the infirm, but only "horse-bread" and beans for the idle, had learned a little, and could say sometime later,

> I shall cessen of my sowyng and swynk nouȝt so harde,
> Ne about my bely-ioye so bisi be namore!

And it is man who has perennially found that when food is plentiful and Hunger put to sleep, the idlers and wasters return ever again.

If, however, the predominating aspect of Piers is the race, the rôle of Piers narrows somewhat at times. It is more properly the function of the state to set "each man in his manere" and to covenant with the Knights to keep the church and commons from wastours and wicked men and the fields from foxes and boars in exchange for their livelihood off the land. Or did the fourteenth-century Englishman feel the social and political status as ancient and ordered as society itself? It is in the function of an overseer or Lord of a manor that Piers lets the plow stand to over-

see the work of others, to reprove the idle and those who feign infirmity, but to feed the poor and needy.

> And yf thow be of power Peers, ich the rede,
> Alle that greden at they gate for godes loue, after fode,
> Parte with hem of thy payn of potage other of souel,
> Lene hem som of thy loof thauh thou the lasse chewe.
> And thauh lyers and lacchedrawers and lolleres knocke,
> Let hem abyde tyl the bord be drawe ac bere hem none cromes,
> Til alle thyn nedy neihebores haue none ymaked.

It is too, in the function of a baron or king that Piers after the famine is over realizes anew that it was the "defaute of her food" that put this folk "at my will" and ponders how he might "amaistrien hem and make hem to worche."

There are too, several places in the episode where the Piers rôle definitely suggests being that of Christ. The Piers of the passage beginning

> And I shal apparaille me, (quod Perkyn) in pilgrimes wise,
> And wende with ȝow I wil til we fynde Treuthe

is more than the laborer, he is also the Son of God who became man to lead man to God. It is he to whom Truth told once that "Iake the iogeloure, Ionet of the stues, Danyel the dysplayer, Denote the Bawde, Frere the faytoure and folke of his ordre" were blotted out of the book of life, a statement that becomes the precedent for refusing them material sustenance unless they reform their ways. Likewise the overseer who at high prime leaves the plow

> To oversen hem hym-self and who-so bet wroughte,
> He shulde be huyred ther-after whan hervesttyme come

represents the Christ, who shall come at the last day to judge the quick and the dead. And the lines

> And I am his olde hyne and highte hym to warne
> Which thei were in this worlde his werkemen appeyred

are certainly suggestive of the pope or church.

We have then in this single episode at least six varying aspects of the Piers rôle, i.e., the race, individual man at death writing his bequest, an overseer on a manor ordering his laborers, the head of a state governing society, the church with her spiritual charge, and Christ the great pilgrim leading man to God. It would be perhaps impossible to indicate all of the truths the symbol of Piers yields in this episode in all its variants. One may note, however, to suggest only the most obvious of them, such material truths in Piers as the allegorical figure for the race, as the classes of society, the division of labor, the relation of industry to production, of moderation to health, such moral truths in Piers as representative of man in the functions of society as the care for the sick and the infirm, the support of the church, the maintenance of justice, the commendation of honest neighborliness, and such divine truths in Piers as Christ, as the incarnation, the stewardship of the church, the final judgment of man, and the equality in heaven.

The next episode is the one dealing with pardons. In simple outline Piers, still tilling his half-acre, is sent a pardon by Truth for "hym, and for his heires for euermore after." Included in it are all "kings and knightes that kepen holy-cherche, and ryztfullych in reumes reulen the peple" and "bisshopes yblessed if thei ben as thei shulden," and

> Alle lybbing laboreres that lyuen with hondes,
> That trewlich taken and trewlich wynnen,
> And lyuen in loue and in lawe for her lowe her-
>   tis,
> Haueth the same absolucion that sent was to
>   Peres.

Merchants are not in the bull, but they have a gloss in the margin and some letters under seal. Men of law, especially those pleading for reward have no pardon, and beggars and "lolleres" unless honestly in need "beth nouzte in the bulle." There is great rejoicing among all included and the merchants praise Piers for purchasing this bull. Then a bit later a priest, in a dramatic moment, reduces the pardon to its first principle of

> Dowel, and haue wel and god shal haue thi
>   sowle,
> And do yuel, and haue yuel hope thow non other
> But after thi ded-day the deuel shal haue thi
>   sowle!

And Piers in the A and B version of the episode for "pure tene" pulls the pardon in two.

The significance of Piers is here less complicated than in the preceding episode. In simple aspect Piers is a laborer who is the recipient of a bull from the pope. He is more than that, however; Piers is also man, who while tilling his half-acre, was sent a pardon from God in the form of his son. And when the merchants praise him for purchasing the pardon, he is not only the laborer but also Christ, who gave his life for man. The incident of the tearing of the pardon is in simple aspect probably nothing more than the portrayal of a contemporary incident. Many a poor plowman in the indulgence traffic of the middle ages must have been imposed upon by unscrupulous pardoners, who preyed upon their gullible market with unwarranted eloquence as they went about vending their forged drafts on the heavenly exchequer. Many a poor plowman when informed of the imposition, must in chagrin have torn his pardon in two. On the other hand it is quite within the spirit of the poem and the general method of the author to suppose the inclusion of the incident because the author saw in it a deeper truth he meant to convey. Theologically men held a pardon from God in the atonement of Christ, but as the years went on men came more and more to rely on that pardon and less and less on the merits of their own deeds until they indeed believed themselves saved by it irrespective of their conduct. Though they were liars, bribetakers, wasters, and gluttons, they rejoiced with the faithful kings, knights, and bishops, until they in their own deception of themselves had destroyed any probability of receiving the grace which Christ's atonement had provided for them. And the plowman tearing his pardon was perhaps to be symbolic of how utterly futile the author felt

men had made the atonement by their own lives, a view certainly not out of harmony with the note of despair on which the poem itself ends later on. Whether or not such an extreme interpretation is justified, it is apparent that the episode, as those preceding it, is one of multifold aspect. In addition to the moral lesson of the abuse of pardons, there is the revelation of the divine redemption of man in the pardon of Christ.

There are three distinct appearances of Piers as a character in the portion of the poem known as the *Vita.* The first, peculiar to the C-text, is on the occasion when Conscience and Clergy take the dreamer to dine with a friar. As they are sitting down to meat, a minstrel at the gate, one Patience, joins them, and is seated opposite the dreamer at a side table. When the conversation afer dinner has turned to the quest of Dowel, Dobet, and Dobest, Piers Plowman himself suddenly appears in the midst of the assembly. He urges the power of love and patience in words with a Sinaic ring, and then mysteriously disappears.

> And whanne he hadde worded thus wiste no
>   man after,
> Where Peers Plouhman by-cam so prieliche he
>   wente.

The relation between Patience and Piers is not quite clear from the context. In the B-text it is Patience who plays the rôle allotted here to Piers, and there is, at least, a suggestion that the two rôles are identical. At any rate in this incident so strongly remindful of the road to Emmaus both Patience and Piers obviously represent Christ. The incident as a whole is too brief and indefinite to add very much to our understanding of the Piers symbol. Perhaps the most interesting feature about it is this merging of the figures of Patience and Piers, which is only another illustration of the general method of the author.

The second appearance of Piers as a character in the *Vita* is in the vision of the Tree of Charity. Though there is a divergence in the C- and B-texts in the identity of the guide, the vision is otherwise essentially the same. The dreamer beholds the Tree of Charity or the Tree of True Love planted in the heart of man. The tree is sustained and upheld by the triple prop of the Trinity and produces the fruit of chastity. While the dreamer is still gazing, the image shifts into one of the Tree of Life, whose fruit is the patriarchs and prophets of the Old Testament. When the Tree is shaken, the patriarchs and prophets fall into the hands of the Devil, who carries them off to the "Lymbo inferni" from which they are rescued later by the *Filius.* In the B-text we are told that Piers Plowman is the guide showing the vision to the dreamer. It is he who rocks the Tree of Life when the patriarchs and the prophets fall into the hands of the Devil and he who cudgels the latter for his trouble.

The character of Piers as guide is an intricate one. It carries us back to the rôles he appeared in, in the *Visio;* Piers is our guide in multifold aspect. First of all it is the Piers-Christ who is our guide to the Father. It is, however, in men that the Tree of Charity or True Love grows, as it is in Piers as man that Christ the great Tree of Charity became incarnate. Hence it is man that shows to us the divine, for it was in his own form that man once had the opportunity to see God. It is of Piers as the race that one may speak of the patriarchs and prophets of old as having been "Piers fruit the Plowman."

The incident in the B-text of Piers rocking the Tree of Life and then a minute later cudgeling the Devil for seizing the fruit thus shaken down, is an interesting version of the Eve and Mary relationship in medieval literature, and adds directly to our understanding of the Piers symbol. The meaning is obvious. As Adam the first man, brought death to mankind, so Jesus another man, brought deliverance from death. Both Adam and Christ are here represented by the symbol of Piers; that is to say, Piers is both Adam and Christ, for he is man. Since this point is quite pertinent to our entire discussion, it will not be out of the way to quote an exact parallel from the medieval *Stanzaic Life of Christ.*

> by mon came deth to al his kynde,
> and dede schul rise withouten wer
> thurgh him bodely, as I finde. . . .

The final actual appearance of Piers in the poem which we shall need to consider is the pentecostal episode. After the resurrection, Conscience tells the dreamer how Christ taught Dobest and gave to Piers power

> To bynde and to unbynde bothe here and elles-
>   where,
> And assoille men of alle synes saue of dettes one.

A little later the dreamer sees the *spiritus paraclitus* [Holy Spirit (Paraclete)] descend on Piers and his fellows in the "lykeness of a lightning." Grace bestows upon them the gifts of the faithful life in all its callings. Piers is created the "procurator and reve" of the physical church; he is given a team of "foure gret oxen" to plow the hearts of men, "foure stottis" to harrow after, four virtues to plant there, a house against the harvest, the "holicherche on Englische," and a cart "hyzte Christendome to carye Pieres sheues." Piers goes to the plow, and "Pruyde it aspyde, and gadered hym a grete oest" to overthrow Piers. Conscience counsels all Christian people to come into Unity and hold themselves safe, and with it the final appearance of Piers as a character in the poem ends. The passage is quite obvious and the meaning throughout allows of less multifold interpretation than many. Piers is first of all St. Peter, and thereafter he is the pope who inherited his power, "the procurator and reve of the physical church."

This completes a rather hurried survey of those parts of the poem in which Piers appears as an actual character. It has shown, it seems to me, that quite in accord with the principles suggested in the earlier part of the paper, the central and prevailing representation of Piers is man the race, and that within the generic symbol the representation sometimes narrows to a simple laborer, to an overseer or lord, to a king, to Adam, to St. Peter, to the pope, and to Christ.

(b) We may next confine our attention to passages in the poem in which Piers is referred to either by the dreamer or by characters appearing in the dream. In this case our interest will be to see whether or not the references to him corroborate in general such rôles as we have found him assume when he appeared in the poem. If this is true, it would seem to be an additional warrant for our interpretation.

There are no references to Piers in the *Visio* save those in the incidents where he himself appears, and the reference there is, of course, to the rôle he has assumed in its immediate context. In the *Vita* our first reference to him comes in the C-text in an incident already referred to. When the dreamer is dining with the friar in company with Conscience and Clergy, there is a stranger at the gate asking for charity.

> Pacience as a poure thyng cam and preide mete
>   for charite,
> Ylike to Peers Plouhman as he a palmere were.

Our question is, of course, who is the Piers Plowman to whom Patience is "ylike"? There are two rôles of Piers to which there is an obvious likeness. Patience was a palmer who wandered the continent of Europe; we have seen Piers as man, a pilgrim in this world between the deep dale and high tower. Patience came in poverty and humility, Piers as Christ had come likewise.

Our next reference to Piers comes again in the C-text, when Conscience having forsaken the company of the friar and his books for the companionship of Patience, they meet one Activa-vita who is, as he says, an apprentice to Piers Plowman. Again if we take only the more obvious suggestions of Activa-vita, we find the master of the apprentice one of multifold aspect. Activa-vita too, is a minstrel, type of the wanderer, and thus an apprentice to Piers as man on his pilgrimage. However he is also a wafer-seller, type of the food-provider, and thus an apprentice to Piers Plowman the laborer. Finally he comes "all peuple to comfortye" and is a provider of wafers for the sacrament, and so an apprentice to the Piers as Christ, who had given his body.

An interesting reference is the one in B Passus XV (C. XVIII) where after a long discussion of abstractions, Anima finally tells the dreamer, who desires to know charity, that without the help of Piers Plowman his person can never be seen. Which is to say, had there been no incarnation all men would have been lost and should not see God. The B-text then goes on to quote *Petrus, id est, Christus.* This quotation was taken by Skeat as the key for the interpretation of the Piers symbol in the *Vita,* but, though it is obviously correct here, the applicability of the quotation to Piers at this point is no warrant for restricting the rôle elsewhere to this one aspect of the symbol.

There are a number of references to Piers by Conscience in the post-pentecostal passage of B Passus XIX (C. XXII). Some of them refer to Piers the Christ and some of them to Piers the pope. Conscience counsels all Christians to pray for peace in the barn of Piers Plowman, which is, of course, the church of Christ. Then he bids men come and receive the sacrament.

> Here is bred yblessed and goddes body ther-
>   vnder.
> Grace thorw goddes worde gaue Pieres power,
> And myztes to maken it and men to ete it
>   after. . .

Here Piers is the pope and those to whom his power is delegated. However, only three lines later Conscience again refers to the Piers-Christ in his invitation to all those "that hadde ypayed to Pieres pardoun the Plowman, *redde quod debes*" [pay back what you owe].

One of the most interesting of all references to Piers comes in the abrupt tirade of the "lewd vicar" against the pope's cardinals, who make the country the worse for their sojourn in it. In an apocalyptical passage he asks that they hold themselves at Avignon or Rome, that Conscience stay at the king's court, that Grace be the guide for all clerks, and that the Piers-Christ with "his newe plow and eke with his olde" be emperor of all the world. Then he concludes with a direct admonition for the pope.

> Inparfyt is that pope that al peple shulde helpe,
> And sendeth hem that sleeth suche as he shulde saue;
> And wel worth Piers the Plowman that pursueth god in doynge,
> *Qui pluit super iustos et iniustos at ones,*
> [Who sends rain at the same time on the just and on the unjust,]
> And sent the sonne to saue a cursed mannes tilthe,
> As bryghte as to the best man and to the beste woman.
> Righte so Piers the Plowman peyneth hym to tulye
> As wel for a wastour and wenches of the stuwes,
> As for hym-self and his seruauntz saue he is firste yserued;
> And trauailleth and tulyeth for a tretour also sore
> As for a trewe tydy man al tymes ylyke.

There is again in these references an interesting merging of the rôles within the Piers symbol. The first Piers the Plowman, cautioned in his conduct to follow God, whose rain falls on the just and unjust alike and whose son was sent to save the wicked as well as the good, is obviously the Piers-pope, as is clear from the preceding context. The second Piers who is set up as an example is a multifold figure. He is the Piers who is the perfect laborer and provides food for the wasters and traitors as well as for himself. He is the Piers who is the faithful priest administering the sacrament, after "he is firste yserued." And more than either he is also the Piers who is Christ, giving himself for all without respect to person.

There is one more reference to Piers that merits attention. In that strange last passus the author depicts once more the fourteenth-century field-of-folk. Only now he depicts it not in terms of bishops and kings, commoners and knights, feigning friars and unlearned priests, but as the forces of evil arrayed against the forces of good. Holy Church and Anti-Christ, Conscience and Covetousness, Contrition and Pride, Kynde Wit and Elde, Life and Death are in the struggle, and the picture the dreamer leaves with us is quite as despairing as the one at the end of the *Visio.* Here, deserted on all sides by his confederates, who have been put to sleep by the "phisick" of the friar, Conscience vows a new pilgrimage to seek Piers the Plowman. Not in fourteenth-century England had the quest for Christ-like men been completed. Morally, the

world was still needing commoners and laborers, lords and kings, bishops and popes who could destroy pride and restore friars to sincerity. And the world was still awaiting the divine fulfilment of the promise of the great Piers Plowman, whom they contemplated coming in clouds of glory to receive his faithful.

There are several factors worthy of note concerning these references to Piers the Plowman. First, the references to him no more confine his figure to one rôle than do his appearances in the poem. Second, if we assume for the reference the interpretation obvious from the context, we find Piers referred to in practically every rôle in which we had previously seen him appear. And finally we may note that there is the same merging of rôles and the same shifting from one rôle to another as there is in the passages where he actually appears.

After our analysis of the author's usage of the symbol throughout the poem we may revert to the question, who is Piers the Plowman? The examination has shown, it seems to me, that Piers is a multifold symbol. He is allegorically man the race. He is sometimes an individual man, who is in his integrity a picture of moral perfection in the functions of society which the race has developed. And he is also the great God-man, the highest achievement of the race in the figure of its own redeemer.

This interpretation has a significance for us in the title of the poem itself. It is apparent from the manuscripts that the poem early, if not from the very first, became known by the title, **Visio Willelmi de Petro le Plowman,** which was taken by Skeat to apply particularly to the **Visio,** and less particularly to the **Vita,** which was entitled **Vita de Dowel, Dobet, Dobest, Secundum Wit et Resoun.** Skeat goes on to point out the slight ambiguity, as he calls it, since the author had in his earlier text already three separate visions, and suggests that the author later called his poem after his favorite character, **Liber de Petro Plowman.** In Skeat's own interpretation of the Piers symbol the appropriateness of such a title is less apparent. If Piers is no more in the **Visio** than a plowman and no less in the **Vita** than Christ, the rôle is after all limited to minor portions of the poem. If one considers the poem as a whole, in only four out of the twenty passus does Piers become an active figure, and in only nine out of the twenty does he receive any reference at all. It is as we see the organic unity of the Piers symbol uniting all of its variants, that we see the significance of the title **Visio Willelmi de Petro le Plowman,** for which the symbol standing for man, for humanity, the work becomes entitled for what it is—a vision concerning man in this life, in his attainment of economic and political well-being, and in his attainment of salvation and a free access to heaven, through the medium of the Son of God who became man to save men. In this sense the poem is truly a vision concerning Piers the Plowman. (pp. 162-73)

Howard William Troyer, "Who is Piers Plowman?" in Style and Symbolism in "Piers Plowman": A Modern Critical Anthology, *edited by Robert J. Blanch, The University of Tennessee Press, 1969, pp. 156-73.*

Nevill K. Coghill   (essay date 1933)

[*Coghill was a scholar of Middle English who completed a modern translation of* Piers Plowman *in his* Visions from Piers Plowman *(1949), and an edition of Chaucer's* The Canterbury Tales *(1951). In the excerpt below, he discusses the portrayal of Piers Plowman as "the allegorical symbol for three cumulative ways of life" in the B-text. Once it is understood that Piers represents the lives of Do-well, Do-bet, and Do-best, Coghill claims, "the poem becomes harmonious and consistent, declaring itself logically, as well as psychologically, a unity."*]

The allegory of Piers . . . [in ***Piers Plowman***] is simply this, that he successively embodies the ideas of Dowel, Dobet, and Dobest. These are the three stages recognized by [W. W.] Skeat and [J. J.] Jusserand, but interpreted in accordance with the design of the poem. Piers is therefore *not a man at all,* neither an individual nor an aggregate; he is the allegorical symbol for *three cumulative ways of life.* These three ways of life are exhibited in him, made incarnate; and since it is open to all human beings to live any one of them, it need not surprise us that he appears to be 'a labourer, an overseer, a king, the pope, Adam, St. Peter, and Christ, sometimes individually, sometimes compositely' (to quote . . . from Mr. [H. W.] Troyer's article ["Who is Piers Plowman?" *PMLA* XLVII, No. 2]). For to be Piers is to do well or to do better or to do best, as this essay hopes to show; once this is recognized and applied to the visions as a whole, the poem becomes harmonious and consistent, declaring itself logically, as well as psychologically, a unity.

Two lines of argument will be followed in support of this interpretation.

1. To consider, in their order, each personal entry of Piers into the poem, together with the changes that seem to occur in his nature at those entries, and to show not only that the timing of his entries corresponds with the divisions of the poem (***Visio de Petro Plowman, Vita de Dowel, Vita de Dobet, Vita de Dobest***), but that the changes in his nature are equally relevant to those divisions.

2. To consider the three groups of abstract virtues which Langland laid down as appropriate to the three types of life respectively, and to show their exact correspondence to the moral qualities that are stressed in the nature of Piers step by step as it unfolds.

If these arguments can be substantiated they will be seen to lead from different premises to the same conclusion, namely that Langland intended the character of Piers to be the organ of his three abstractions, the Good Life, the Better and the Best; for such a correspondence could not happen accidentally inasmuch as Langland (as Dr. [H. W.] Wells has demonstrated ["The Construction of *Piers Plowman,*" *PMLA* XLIV, No. 1]) had special genius in the disposing of the larger architectural lines of his work; a man capable of such gigantic and comprehensive planning could not without absurdity be supposed ignorant of the movements of his own hero, of their dovetailing with the main divisions of his poem and of his hero's specific possession of the abstract virtues about which he had chosen to write.

Since the contentions here advanced unite the character of Piers with the structure of the poem as a whole, some account of that structure must first be given. . . . (pp. 111-12)

The poem is divided into four major sections usually designated as the ***Visio de Petro Plowman*** (Prol. to VII inclusive), ***Vita de Dowel*** (VIII to XV inclusive), the ***Vita de Dobet*** (XVI to XVIII inclusive) and the ***Vita de Dobest*** (XIX to the end). Of these sections the least obviously picturesque, and therefore the most generally neglected, is the second, the ***Vita de Dowel.*** Yet this ***Dowel*** expounds the basic doctrines of all Langland's thought, and for an understanding enjoyment of his poem it is the critical section, as will be presently shown.

The first section (the ***Visio de Petro Plowman***) is a study of human life in the Active World as it existed before Langland's eyes; it concerns itself particularly with the following problems (in brief analysis):

1. What, in this business of honest and dishonest money-making that seems to keep the Field of Folk on the move, is to be rendered to Cæsar, and what to God? (Prol., I.)

2. How is a corrupt administration to be set to rights? (II, III, IV.)

3. How is society in general to purify itself ? (V.)

4. The problem of Labour versus Famine and the twin problems of the Shirkers and the Impotent. (VI.)

5. Whether the solutions offered to these problems as they arise are pleasing to God, and if so, what is the meaning of Pardon, and what disciplines or virtues underlie these solutions? (VII.) *This sub-section may be regarded as the hinge upon which the poem turns towards an abstract consideration of Dowel, Dobet, and Dobest.*

All these problems are considered *sub specie æternitatis,* and are riders to the principal problem (which is the Grand Subject of the whole poem), namely, how is man to work out his Salvation? Thus far the first major section, which concerns the existing order of the Active Life in the World, as lived by all men, but particularly as lived by the Laity.

The second section, the ***Vita de Dowel,*** immediately following, holds the keys to all the others. This section, under the guise of a vague allegorical autobiography of the poet, considers (1) what abstract virtues should underlie the Active Life, and whether they can win Salvation; (and in the answers which this study suggests lie the full understanding of what has gone before in the ***Visio***); (2) the virtues that should underlie the Contemplative or Clerkly Life (i.e. the ***Vita de Dobet***); and (3) the virtues that should underlie the Pontifical Life or Life of Spiritual Authority, which is the Life of Dobest.

The whole of his great section (***Dowel***), and all these disquisitions are seasoned as well with Langland's mental autobiography as with a running commentary on the existing state of affairs (with particular reference to the Clergy and their shortcomings), and on problems germane to the central argument, such as the possibility of Salvation for pre-Christian 'clerks' (like Aristotle), or 'worthies' (like Trajan), and the general unreasonableness of man in the indulging of his instincts, contrasted with the notorious decency and sweet moderation of the lower creatures.

This section, then, expounds the true principles upon which to base human conduct if Salvation is to be attained, whether by living the 'lewed' life of Dowel, the 'clerkly' life of Dobet, or the 'episcopal' life of Dobest; thus it supplies the *moral argument* upon which the whole fabric of vision and allegory is based. Unless that argument be grasped it is almost impossible to understand what the poem as a whole is driving at; and because it has been neglected, Langland has no general fame other than as the author of discontented and disconnected satires, somewhat lively in their presentation, but defaced by a dreary intermingling of prolonged theologizings; matter enough for social historians and philologists, but no great matter for those who ask of a poet some largely imagined and harmonious unit of vision. And yet, in this precise respect, *Troilus and Criseyde* itself is not greater than **Piers Plowman.**

The third section (**Dobet**) is simply the embodiment of Langland's foregoing theories of the Clerkly Virtues, shown allegorically in a narrative; and the fourth section (**Dobest**) allegorically embodies the Life of Authority, and the need for it in a world beset by corruption from within the human heart, and menaced by the assault of Antichrist from without.

Of these four sections, as has been said, the second is a kind of abstract of the other three, or, if that is too inaccurate an expression, it has a more-than-narrative relationship to them; it is their exposition. Of the other three, the first is concerned with, or as if dedicated to, God the Father; the next (**Dobet**) with God the Son, and the last with God the Holy Ghost, proceeding from Them just as **Dobest** proceeds from **Dowel** and **Dobet:** as if God in creating the world was Active, in redeeming the world was Contemplative, and in sustaining the spiritual life of Christendom was Authoritative. This last is the anagogical aspect of the poem.

Into this structure, at certain premeditated points, irrupts the figure of Piers Plowman. Perhaps in no other work of equal scope does the Hero appear so seldom in person; but every appearance in this poem has a calculated significance.

Piers first 'put forth his hed' (V 544) when the secular world of Action had confessed its sins and was attempting satisfaction for them (the third part of a valid penance) by seeking St. Truth. This would seem a late entry for the hero; but if he be accepted as an emblem of Dowel, of the Active Unlettered Life as it should be, there is no earlier point at which he could have made his appearance; for a glance at the analysis of the first section (above) shows that the first three sub-sections are quite general, and deal with all the world, not omitting the Governing Class, and

as such are not amenable to the simple solution of 'Dowel', but ask the higher wisdom of Holy Church who offers advanced reflections on the purposes of human life under the hand of God; her teaching is quite beyond the province of Piers as Dowel, just as is the advice later given to the King. Up to this point, therefore, there is no mention of either Dowel or Piers. The Confession of the Seven Sins is again quite general; it is not even confined to the Laity (Wrath was a Regular), and it is prompted by the sermon of Reason, who proves that the pestilences were in consequence of sin (V 15) and for no other reason. Here again it would not have been becoming to the trend of the allegory for simple unlettered Dowel to usurp the position and authority of Reason in preaching repentance to the world. And therefore the figure of Piers is still withheld. Indeed he remains hidden until the more exalted and theoretic advice has failed. In their efforts to seek the Shrine of Truth the worldlings 'blustreden forth as bestes' (V 521), not knowing which way to turn. They had had *spiritual* advice from their Confessor, and were trying to follow it; what they lacked was *practical* advice; and this, as might be expected, the finical Palmer, all decked out and arrayed with the trophies of his pilgrimages, could not supply. For practical advice a practical man is needed and therefore, modestly, but with the assurance of one who speaks from fifty years' experience, Piers emerges as a leader, 'the type of ideal honest man', in short *Dowel.*

At first he offers them spiritual advice in practical form, a sort of map of the common road to Truth (i.e. to Honesty, Evenhandedness), a Mosaic *Carte du Tendre* (V 568 onwards); and in this there is nothing which the ordinary unlettered Christian was not supposed to know . . . the ten Commandments, the obligations of Penance and Amendment and Charity, etcetera. But even this is too abstruse for the for-wandered world:

> This were a wikked way but who-so hadde a
>   gyde
>   (VI I.)

So with a still more practical insight Piers sets them all to *work.* That had been his own solution to the problem of seeking Truth; that had been his own life;

> I dyke and I delue I do that Treuthe hoteth.
>   (V 552.)

that, in fact, was as much as, in his simplicity, he knew, or needed to know, in the Active Life of Dowel.

It should be noted that the problems of Famine and Unemployment, which in essence are no less general than those of Public Administration or Social Purification, were shelved by Langland until after the emergence of Piers. This is because Langland believed that Famine and Unemployment could be avoided if only the secular world would lead the simple, honest, hard-working Life of Dowel, each according to his station; whereas those other problems of the purposes of human endeavour in general, and the right practice of statecraft, were above the powers and pretensions of a simple farmer. They therefore come under the arbitration, not of Piers, but of Conscience or Reason or Holy Church.

The last and most vexed matter in this first epiphany of

Dowel under the form of Piers is that of the Pardon sent by Truth to his servant.

> Treuthe herde telle her-of and to Peres he sent,
> To taken his teme and tulyen the erthe,
> And purchaced hym a pardoun *a pena et a culpa*
> For hym, and for his heires for euermore after.
>
> (VII 1-4.)

The 'purchace' is of course the purchase on Calvary when 'god boughte vs alle' (VI 210), and is our Redemption. Now, that Redemption is believed, and has always been believed, *conditional;* it is for the Christian to avail himself of it by Faith and Works. It will be seen presently that the essence of Dowel, theoretically speaking, includes Faith and Works with no little emphasis. And this should be borne in mind in considering the enigmatic text of the Pardon sent by Truth. (This pardon, it may be noted, links up with that other pardon that is conditional upon *redde quod debes* in XIX 388; virtually they are the same in promise and condition.)

The condition in the pardon of VII is thus expressed:

> Al in two lynes it lay and nought a leef more,
> And was written right thus in witnesse of treu-
>   the;
>   *Et qui bona egerunt, ibunt in vitam eternam;*
>   *Qui vero mala, in ignem eternum.*
>
> (VII 110-113.)

This pardon lay in the hand of Piers the unlettered plough-man, simplest embodiment of Dowel, or *Bonum Agere;* there is an irony in that he could not even read it, did not know that it referred precisely and exclusively to himself. He had accepted it without examination upon pure Faith; he had not so much as unfolded it.

> 'Pieres,' quod a prest tho 'thi pardoun most I
>   rede,
> For I wil construe eche a clause and kenne it the
>   on Engliche.'
> And Pieres at his preyere the pardoun vnfoldeth.
>
> (VII 106-8.)

This trustful illiteracy of Piers, because it is entirely in character with the Life of Dowel, is the first of two important points that emerge from this episode of Truth's pardon. The second is the 'pure teen' (VII 116) for which Piers tore up the pardon when the priest (who could not recognize *Bonum Agere* in Piers any more than Piers did himself) explained to him that it was no pardon at all but the simple statement of an exactly proportionate requital; such a pardon as might be conceded by Mrs. Be-done-by-as-you-did.

Perhaps all readers have found this 'teen' obscure. Vexation or petulance seem scarcely appropriate impulses in a character such as that of Piers, whatever that character embodies; yet the action of pardon-tearing is somehow satisfactory to the reader psychologically; it is almost as if Piers had torn the priest up, and revenged us upon his sophistries. But I think a better explanation would be to think of 'teen' as disappointed mortification. *Piers believed the priest* (Dowel is humble and obedient to the Church); their later jangle does not concern the pardon but arises from his resentment of the gratuitous and insulting mock-

ery flung at him by the priest. Piers believed that the pardon (like so many others in the fourteenth century) was worthless, and so, in his disappointment, committed himself to the pure assurance of his Faith rather than to a piece of parchment; for as he tears it he repeats:

> *Si ambulavero in medio umbre mortis, non time-*
> *bo mala; quoniam tu mecum es.*

But there is mortification as well as disappointment; as if he thought that perhaps after all the simple Life of Action was of insufficient merit, in spite of his fifty years of following Truth. More could be demanded of him.

> 'I shal cessen of my sowyng,' quod Pieres 'and
>   swynk nought so harde,
> Ne about my bely-ioye so bisi be namore!
> Of preyers and of penaunce my plow shal ben
>   herafter,
> And wepen whan I shulde slepe though whete-
>   bred me faille.'
>
> (VII 117-120.)

These are the words immediately following in which Piers announces his conversion to the clerkly Life of Dobet; and for this reason *he does not return in person into the narrative* until Passus XVI, *'primus de Dobet'.*

It may well be asked: 'If Piers embodies Dowel, why does he drop out of the poem through all those long Passus that purport to deal with Dowel?' (VII-XV). I suggest in answer that in the first place the **Visio de Petro Plowman** (Prol.—VII) exhibits Dowel allegorically, whereas the **Vita de Dowel** exhibits it morally; in the case of Dowel alone the practice is discussed before the moral theory; (whereas in the case of Dobet and Dobest the theory is fully discussed in the preceding **Vita de Dowel,** and the practice of those Higher Lives is not shown until the sections that bear their name). Thus, since Piers has demonstrated how to handle the Active World, there is no need for him to reappear until he is wanted to demonstrate the handling of the Contemplative World. He makes three Grand Appearances, one for each kind of Life, and it would have confused the symmetry of the allegory to have brought him in redundantly as Dowel. Secondly the **Vita de Dowel,** as has been said, is really far wider in scope than the mere good Active Life, inasmuch as it includes disquisitions on the other Lives, and on other matters. It is, in so far as it concerns the Lives of Piers, purely theoretic or moral, whereas the Hero is *always* flesh and blood, a figure of the actual world, whether Active, Contemplative, or Authoritarian. Compare with the robustness of Piers those shadowy phantoms, Thought, Clergye, Imaginatyf, or even Haukyn; Piers is not a theory but a Life, and for so long as he represents Dowel, the perfection of Unletteredness, it would be inappropriate to introduce him into a realm of disputation such as is the section called the **Vita de Dowel.**

Piers, then, bursts into the poem at precisely the point where the practice and example of a simple honest man (Dowel) can benefit the Active World, and disappears, uttering a prophecy of his transformation into Dobet (VII 117-20) just at the moment when Langland retires into a realm of speculation, whither Piers as Dowel cannot follow him, and where the path of Dobet has not yet sufficiently been marked out for Piers as Dobet to be intelligible. Without that long hiatus in the narrative allegory of the poem, where Dowel, Dobet, and Dobest are theoretically evaluated, the changes in the meaning of Piers would indeed have been confusing; for imagine Passus VIII to XV omitted; what key would then remain to the triple gates of Langland's thought?

The correspondence that has been traced between Piers and the structural disposition of Dowel, exists also, and more obviously, in Dobet. No sooner does *Passus xvj et primus de Dobet* begin than Piers returns into the poem in person; and he returns a changed being; here is no more the simple, unlettered and incorruptible farmer, but a teacher who can expound the allegory of the Tree of Charity, with its Triune props (XVI 21-72), and, later, the Holy Trinity Itself (XVII 138-256); a healer and tender of the sick and afflicted (in the person of the Good Samaritan, XVII 48 onwards; identified with Piers in XVII 10); and a Jouster in whose armour Christ is to ride to His Passion (XVIII 21-25). The full importance of these rôles will be seen when the theoretical essences of Dowel, Dobet, and Dobest have been considered; what is here emphasized is that a strong change takes place in the character of Piers, and that *this change coincides with the Dobet division of the poem;* this correspondence, too, cannot be accidental.

From XVIII 25, there is no more mention of Piers until XIX 6. In these 412 lines are described the Passion of Christ and the Harrowing of Hell. Let us for the moment be cautions of any hasty identification of Christ with Piers; that they are in an important sense identified cannot be denied; but it would be truer to say of them that Jesus *lives* Piers (for Piers is a way of Life), than that Jesus *is* Piers or that Piers *is* Jesus. Indeed the plain truth is best stated by Langland himself when he says:

> This Iesus of his gentrice wole iuste in Piers armes,
> In his helme and in his haberioun *humana natura;*
> That Cryst be nought biknowe here for *consummatus deus,*
> In Piers paltok the Plowman this priker shal ryde;
>
> (XVIII 22-25.)

The reason for our caution is that Piers is primarily of *this* world (as, humanly speaking, are the Active, Contemplative, and Pontifical Lives). This explains why there is no mention of Piers in the long and splendid Harrowing of Hell; Christ had for a while borrowed the human garments of Piers, but yielded them up again (it may be understood) at death, at the line:

> 'Consummatum est,' quod Cryst and comsed forto swowe.
>
> (XVIII 57.)

Thereafter Christ clearly is recognized as Divine (though some still deny and scoff); Lucifer and Goblin know with Whom they have to deal.

> Some seyde that he was goddes sone that so faire deyde,
> *Vere filius dei erat iste, etc.*
> And somme saide he was a wicche . . .
>
> (XVIII 68-9.)

Piers does not return to the poem until after Hell has been harrowed: he returns in the opening lines of XIX, which is headed *Passus xixus; et explicit Dobet; et incipit Dobest.*

I do not know what importance to attach to this heading; it contains the suggestion that we are to expect a little Dobet (which will be concluded), and that the rest will begin Dobest. If this suggestion be accepted, it will be found to support the theory here advanced. What is most noticeable about this re-entry of Piers is its likeness to his re-entry at the beginning of the previous Passus. *No apparent change has taken place in the character of Piers.* If the passage already quoted (XVIII 22-25) be compared with the lines

> thise aren Pieres armes,
> His coloures and his cote-armure ac he that cometh so blody
> Is Cryst with his crosse conqueroure of Crystene
>
> (XIX 12-14.)

the similarity is obvious.

If this similarity be taken in conjunction with the hint given by the Passus-heading, it is not difficult to believe that we still have here to do with Piers as **Dobet;** and this interpretation of the allegory fits with the return of Christ to Galilee after His descent into Hell and *before* the sending-forth of the Disciples with loosing and binding power, which, for Langland, is one of the turning-points in Christian history. For Christ was still *humanly embodied,* as the episode of Doubting Thomas proves (XIX 161-176), and it was in the body of Piers, who had not yet become Dobest. '*Explicit Dobet*' might then properly be written after line 176 of XIX (the story of Doubting Thomas), which is immediately succeeded by these lines:

> And whan this dede was done Dobest he taughte,
> And ȝaf Pieres power and pardoun he graunted
> To alle manere men mercy and forghyfnes,
> Hym myghte men to assoille of alle manere synnes,
> In couenant that thei come and knowleche to paye,
> To Pieres pardon the Plowman *redde quod debes.*
>
> (XIX 177-82.)

Whether or not this explanation puts too much weight on the mere heading of a Passus, the final change in the significance of Piers does not come until this point. He is no longer identifiable in any sense with Christ, but is one to whom Christ *delegates power.* The power was won by Christ (as Langland explains in the mouth of Conscience, XIX 26-55) when he descended into and harrowed Hell, an action in which Piers, as we have seen, had no part. Christ, therefore, *as God,* has won a Victory, the fruits of which are entrusted to the New Piers. And in this way the New Piers becomes Dobest, the embodiment of the Life of Authority. This Authority is confirmed and upheld by the Holy Ghost at Pentecost (XIX 196), and is the sanction by which Piers is to build the House of *Unitas,* 'holicherche on Englisshe' (XIX 325).

The argument here offered has so far shown a correspondence between each change in the significance of Piers and the several transitions from Dowel to Dobet and Dobet to Dobest. It may be objected as follows: 'Why, if Piers is Dobest, the Life of Authority that should sustain the Church, does he appear to desert his trust, or at least to leave it in the hands of Conscience?' It is true that after XIX 331 Piers ceases to dominate the poem and Conscience assumes the rôle of Hero. Indeed Piers once more is lost . . . we are not told when or how he vanishes from the Barn of Holy Church which he has been at such pains to build; when he is most needed (at the onslaughts of the Deadly Sins under Pride, XIX 331, and of the Host of Anti-Christ, XX 52), he is nowhere to be found, and the poem ends with the quest for its Hero:

> 'Bi Cryste,' quod Conscience tho 'I wil bicome
>   a pilgryme, . . .
>   . . . To seke Piers the Plowman that Pryde may
>   destruye . . .
>   . . . . now Kynde me auenge,
> And sende me happe and hele til I haue Piers the
>   Plowman!'
> And sitthe he gradde after grace til I gan awake.
>   (XX 378 to end.)

I think this was intended as a melancholy comment on the world; an intimation that in Langland's opinion the proper exercise of Authority had vanished from the earth; and it is in keeping with his expressed estimate of Bishops and Cardinals. It may be noted that the difficulty of Piers' vanishing at this point is not overcome by supposing him to be the Pope or Man the Race. Neither of these had disappeared; indeed there were shortly to be two Popes at once; on the other hand the Babylonish Captivity at Avignon had been in full swing, at the time of the writing of the B Text, for nearly seventy years. Possibly Langland had this declension of the Life of Authority in mind. There are other possibilities also that suggest themselves glibly enough; such as that perhaps Langland had in mind a more general collapse of the Order of Christendom than that figured forth in the Papal Captivity, which he might have regarded as a symptom of his declining era rather than as its disease: or possibly Langland wished to stress the necessity of a renewed personal effort in all men, and therefore chose to portray them as fighting through the Dark Night of the Soul under Conscience only; or, like earlier prophets he may have had no wish to speak smooth things to an unruly people. Conjectures of this kind are always easy and often worthless; readers of Langland are more likely to experience surprise at the absence of topical allusion that can now be understood than the reverse. The matter of dating the texts illustrates this paucity of topical comment, this reserve of allusion that should caution us against rash assignment of historical interpretations, and inner readings of Langland's unexpressed sentiments about contemporary personages and events.

A correspondence between the personal entries of Piers and the architectural divisions, Dowel, Dobet, and Dobest, has been indicated, and a second line of argument remains, namely the discovery and tabulation of the Virtues assigned by Langland to those ways of life, and the fitting of them to Piers in the three stages of growth.

Before this new phase in the argument is attempted, a consideration of the supposed identity of Piers and Christ may be offered. What is here contended is that Piers and Christ are parallel exemplars of the same sets of ideas. That Christ lived Dowel, Dobet, and Dobest successively, Langland explicitly tells us (XIX 104-189); that Piers is a parallel embodiment of those lives is the thesis of this paper. I use the word parallel designedly, for by a curious but not unlawful play of ideas, the metaphor from Geometry fits the thesis with a pleasing exactness; for we are told of parallel straight lines that they meet at Infinity; and that is precisely where the characters of Piers and Jesus meet, and are one. They meet in the Infinity of Christ's Nature and in that of Dowel and Dobet:

> . . . Dowel and Dobet aren two infinites,
> Whiche infinites, with a feith fynden oute Dob-
>   est,
> Which shal saue mannes soule thus seith Piers
>   the Ploughman.
>   (XIII 127-9.)

These three ways of life, lived allegorically by Piers and historically by Christ, are inexhaustible. An infinite goodness in simplicity and even-handed Action; an infinite goodness in compassionate care for the ignorant and the sick and a readiness to suffer for others, learnt in Contemplation; and an infinite goodness in Command; each road leads to Salvation. Each way of life is to be understood *allegorically,* as bodied in Piers and as touching the proper relations between man and man; and each is in the same way to be understood *morally,* as having in the abstract certain basic essential or characteristic virtues; and each way is to be understood as touching everlasting things, analogically that is, namely the fulfilling of God's purposes in creating, redeeming and giving Grace to man.

I do not say that Langland was meticulously precise in his use of the Piers symbol; it would, for instance, be impossible, perhaps, to go through the poem substituting for every mention of Piers the words Dowel, Dobet, or Dobest; in the last-cited passage, for instance, it is not very clear in which capacity Piers is being quoted. We are told immediately before that 'one Pieres the Ploughman' has 'sette alle sciences at a soppe saue loue one', and this suggests Dowel, the first Piers. But to overwork the interpretation of an allegory that has so large and general a scope is the treason of pedantry. There is, however, one passage in the poem which seems to undo much of the argument so far advanced by this paper. It occurs in Passus XV, in the allocution of that strangely tongueless and toothless being *Anima.* Anima is defining Charity to the Dreamer in a passage of extraordinary poetic force. The passus in question is headed *Passus XVus: finit Dowel; et incipit Dobet,* and if this can be accepted as evidence, we are justified in supposing that somewhere within this passus is the turning-point away from the matter of Dowel and towards the matter of Dobet. I suggest that the turning-point comes at XV 144; for it is at this line that the nature of Charity comes up for discussion; now Faith, Hope, and Charity, under the forms of Abraham, Moses, and the Good Samaritan, are the subjects of Passus XVI and XVII, so that this turning-point passage can be considered as a *moral* explanation of or introduction to the Good Samaritan, who is an *allegorical* emblem of Charity; and this figure turns out later (XVIII 10 onwards) to be indistinguishable from Piers and Jesus, so that it is raised, and with it the whole discussion, to the *anagogical* plane of heavenly Truth.

If these three shadowings of meaning be allowed to drift like veils over the discourse of Anima, an understanding of it will arise that is not inconsistent with the interpretation of Piers as Dowel, Dobet, and Dobest; the passage in question is as follows: Langland is moved to exclaim at the lyrical account of the person of Charity given by Anima:

> 'By Cryst, I wolde that I knewe hym,' quod I 'no
> creature leuere!'
> 'With-outen helpe of Piers Plowman,' quod he
> 'his persone seestow neuere.'
> 'Where clerkes knowen hym,' quod I 'that kepen
> holykirke?'
> 'Clerkes haue no knowyng,' quod he 'but by
> werkes and bi wordes.'
> Ac Piers the Plowman parceyueth more depper
> What is the wille and wherfore that many
> wyghte suffreth,
>   *Et vidit deus cogitaciones eorum.*
> . . . For there ar beggeres and bidderes bede-
> men as it were,
> Loketh as lambren and semen lyf-holy,
> Ac it is more to haue her mete with such an esy
> manere,
> Than for penaunce and parfitnesse the pouerte
> that such taketh.
> There-fore by coloure ne by clergye knowe shal-
> tow hym neuere,
> Noyther thorw wordes ne werkes but thorw
> wille one.
> And that knoweth no clerke ne creature in erthe,
> But Piers the Plowman *Petrus, id est, Christus.*
>   (XV 189-206.)

It would seem clear from Langland's instant association of the name Piers the Plowman with Clerkes (for the force of the question in the third line of the above seems to be 'Then do the Clergy recognize true Charity in the hearts of men?'), that Piers as Dobet, allegory of the Clerkly Life, was intended (this would corroborate the *incipit Dobet* suggestion made above); and indeed I think it is for Dobet that Piers is here standing. But it is a Piers-Dobet on the anagogical plane; for *Anima* associates Piers not with 'clerkes' as the Dreamer does, but with God and Christ. What then is to be understood by this passage? The virtues of Dobet . . . are to teach, to heal and to suffer; these, on the heavenly or anagogical plane, as attributes of God would be just such as Christ manifested on earth in his contemplative character, when he 'did bet'; but the contemplations of God penetrate into the human heart, and can see if Charity exists there or not. Since, however, Christ was God uniquely incarnate, that knowledge of the inner human motive was also, for the first and last time, known upon earth, by Jesus during his ministry of Dobet, when he was living the second life of Piers. No Piers-life, *of itself,* can teach men to see into the true motives of their fellows; but the Piers-life raised to the Heavenly plane, as it was by Jesus, could bring that knowledge to earth in virtue of the Incarnation. This gives a new and I believe a true value to the phrase *Petrus, id est Christus* and saves the allegory from obscurity and even from wreck. Another

analogy from Euclid may clarify my contention; a chord cuts a circle at two points; if the chord be moved to a tangential position, there are still two points at which it cuts; but they are coincident. The chord of Dobet cuts the circle of life in Heaven and on Earth; and in Christ Heaven and Earth were united; the symbol Piers is filled by the reality Christ: symbol and reality coincide. (pp. 112-25)

> *Nevill K. Coghill, "The Character of Piers Plowman Considered from the B Text," in* Medium Aevum, *Vol. II, No. 2, June, 1933, pp. 108-35.*

Christopher Dawson (essay date 1934)

[*Dawson was an English educator and medievalist. In the following excerpt from an essay originally published in 1934, he claims that the goal of* Piers Plowman *is to bring religion to common humanity. Langland, Dawson adds, followed Christianity by way of "the muddy high-road of common life, and he found his guide and saviour in the common man, Piers Plowman."*]

It would be strange to write of medieval religion without some mention of one who is not only one of the greatest of English religious poets but also the most remarkable and the most authentic representative of the religious sentiment of the common people of medieval England.

And yet for some reason William Langland has never received the attention that he deserves. He is little read, and those who read him seldom realize his true greatness. It is a reproach to modern England that when every minor poet has been edited and re-edited to satiety, and when the classics of foreign literature are to be found on every bookstall, this great classic, which is one of the landmarks of English literature and English religion, should be inaccessible to the ordinary man except in abridged or incomplete forms and that the only standard work on the subject should have been written by a foreigner. And this reproach ought to be felt by Catholics before all others, since for them Langland's poem is a part of their special heritage. Here is the Catholic Englishman *par excellence,* at once the most English of Catholic poets and the most Catholic of English poets: a man in whom Catholic faith and national feeling are fused in a single flame. He saw Christ walking in English fields in the dress of an English labourer, and to understand his work is to know English religion in its most autochthonous and yet most Catholic form.

It is true that there is much in Langland that is likely to prove shocking to Catholics who know their Middle Ages only in a modern bowdlerized form. His England is not the idealized Catholic England of the apologist, nor the Merry England of the medievalist myth. It is a grim enough land where oppression and misgovernment are rife, and famine and pestilence are never far away. For Langland, with all his Christian idealism, is also a realist who does not shrink from describing in pitiless detail the corruptions of the Church, the wrongs of the poor and the vices of the rich. He belongs to his age—the fourteenth century—which, in spite of Boccaccio and Chaucer, was not a cheerful one, but which, none the less, was a time of immense spiritual vitality and of momentous consequences for the future of Western civilization.

The fourteenth century was an age of profound social and spiritual change: an age of ruin and rebirth, of apocalyptic fears and mystical hopes. It was the age of the Great Schism and the Black Death and the Hundred Years War, but it was also the age of Dante and Petrarch, of St. Catherine and St. Bridget, of Tauler and Suso and Ruysbroeck, an age of poets and mystics and saints. It saw the breakdown of the universal theocratic order of medieval Christendom and the rise of political nationalism and religious division, and at the same time it witnessed the passing of the old agrarian feudal society and the rise of capitalism and urban industrialism. Western Europe was stirred from end to end by a wave of social unrest which showed itself in revolutionary movements and bitter class warfare. At no other time in European history has the common people asserted itself more vigorously or found more remarkable leaders. It was the age of the Jacquerie and the Peasants' Revolt, of the wars of the Swiss peasants and the German towns against the princes, and the still more heroic struggle of the Flemish proletariat against their own ruling classes and the power of the French monarchy.

It was in the midst of this turmoil of change that the English people first attained maturity and self-consciousness. Three centuries earlier it had been submerged by a wave of foreign invasion, and the Norman conquest had made England for a time a province of continental culture. Its churchmen belonged to the international unity of Latin Christendom and its nobles to the hardly less international society of French chivalry. Latin was the language of learning, and French the language of society. English became the speech of peasants, the mark of the simple and the uneducated. As the first English chronicler, Robert of Gloucester, writes as late as the beginning of the fourteenth century: "If a man does not know French he is little esteemed, but low-born people hold still to English and their own tongue." The fourteenth century changed all that, and before its close English was not only the language of the people but was making its way into court and parliament, until in the last year of the century the first English-speaking king opened his first parliament in English words. Trevisa dates the change, at least in education, from the time of the Black Death, and no doubt the great pestilence and the great war with France mark a dividing line in the history of English culture. But the vital factor in the new development was not so much the decay of the artificial Norman-French culture as the spiritual rebirth of the national consciousness. The English genius found simultaneous expression in the work of Chaucer and Langland, the poet of the *Canterbury Tales* and the poet of **Piers Plowman.**

These two great voices of England expressed the two aspects of English character and English culture. Chaucer represents all that England had learnt from its three centuries of incorporation in continental culture. He is a courtier and a scholar who looks at the English scene with the humorous detachment of a man of the great world. He clothed the courtly tradition in an English dress and gave the common Englishman a right of entry into the cultivated society which had hitherto been the monopoly of clerks and knights.

This achievement is reflected in his style, which is so characteristically English and his own, and yet owes so much to the cultivation and imitation of French and Italian models. It is essentially classical in spirit, far more classical indeed than that of his French masters, such as Guillaume Machaut, since it is the result of a long process of experiment and elaborate artifice, which bears fruit not in the wooden rhetoric of Lydgate and Occleve or the empty grace of fifteenth-century French verse but in a simplicity and strength that make it not incomparable with that of the great Italian classics of the Trecento.

Nothing could be more different from this than the other great work of the new age, for it is as formless and as lacking in conscious literary artifice as any great work can be. It is a voice from another world—the submerged world of the common English—a voice that is by turns harsh and pitiful and comic, but always the authentic voice of the English people. Where Chaucer took the world as he found it, and found it good, the author of **Piers Plowman** judged the world and found it wanting. He represents the English view of life as it had been formed by nearly a thousand years of Christian faith, not the official view of the theologian and the scholar, but the spiritual vision of a prophet chosen among his fellows by his inspiration alone.

And this contrast is not simply a matter of temperament or class: it has its basis in a profound difference of cultural tradition. Chaucer belongs, as I have said, to the international tradition of the courtly culture, and already has his eyes open to the dawn of the Italian Renaissance, but Langland owes nothing to the courtly tradition with its gay rhymed measures and its cult of love and romance. He looks back to the forgotten Nordic world and to the grave Christian poetry of Saxon England. He uses the old alliterative accentual measure which was the native speech of English and Teutonic poetry and which now suddenly arose, as it were from the dead, as a sign of the renaissance of the English spirit. This return to the old alliterative metre was not peculiar to Langland—we find it also in the work of Huchtown of the *Awle Ryale* and of the poet of the *Pearl* and *Gawain.* But Langland inherited the spirit as well as the form of the old Northern poetry. He has the same attitude to life—that profound and gloomy meditation on the world and the fate of man that distinguishes the old Teutonic poetry from the light-hearted courtly literature that had its origin in Provence.

There is a striking example of this in Langland's vision of "The Mountain called Middelerde":

> And I bowed my body beholding all about,
> And saw the sun and the sea and the sand after,
> Where that birds and beasts wander with their
>   mates,
> Wild worms in the woods and wonderful fowls
> With flecked feathers of full many a colour.
> Man and his mate both might I see,
> Poverty and plenty peace and war,
> Bliss and bitter bale both saw I at once;
> And how that men took meed and mercy re-
>   fused.

In sooth I saw Reason ruling all beasts
Save man and his mate and thereof I wondered.

Poetry such as this stands entirely outside contemporary literary tradition. Nevertheless, it has its tradition which is that of the old Teutonic literature. It has far more in common with the melancholy of Anglo-Saxon elegiac poetry or with the oracular solemnity of *Muspili* than with the smooth technical dexterity of Machaut or Froissart. And it is characteristic of the Nordic strain in Langland's poetry that his Christian epic should end, like the *Volospa* and the epics of the heathen North, on a note of defeat and despair—with the vision of a final battle for a lost cause against the unloosed hosts of hell.

On the other hand, Langland's style has none of the stately and artificial rhetoric of ancient Teutonic poetry. His language is the everyday speech of his time—at least of the friars and the popular preachers. It is full of racy vernacular turns of expression, as well as of latinisms and gallicisms borrowed from the mixed language of lawyers and clerks. Moreover, he belongs to his own age—the century of Boccaccio and Chaucer—by his interest in the spectacle of human life and his keen eye for realistic detail. And this union of profound melancholy and vivid realism shows itself in all that he wrote and imparts an extremely personal character to his poetry. There are, I know, learned men who deny the traditional authorship and the unity of the poem, and would make it the work of a whole platoon of poets. But it would be little short of a miracle if a single age had produced a succession of poets, or even two of them, with the same general attitude to the social and spiritual problems of their age and the same highly individual blend of realism and mysticism. It is true that there are considerable differences between the successive versions of the poem that have been classified by Professor [Walter W.] Skeat as the A, B and C texts. But these are no greater than might be expected if the different versions reflect the changes of thirty years' experience; in fact, they seem to show a continuous development of thought and purpose which is entirely consistent with the author's character as he draws it himself. (pp. 239-45)

[Langland's] poem is not a work of art like the poems of Chaucer; it is the vessel into which the poet poured his doubts, his hopes, his criticism of life and his prophetic message. There is no other work of medieval literature, not even the *Testaments* of Villon, which has such a direct contact with life and which gives us such an insight into the heart of medieval humanity. It is true that though his style owes nothing to the medieval romance tradition, he borrowed from that tradition the external machinery of vision and allegory. All these cumbrous personifications of virtues and vices are the lay figures that had been the stock-in-trade of medieval didactic literature for centuries. And yet nowhere is the irrepressible originality and realism of the English poet more apparent. These abstractions are apt suddenly to become more personal and nearer to life than even the human characters of a great poet like Chaucer. As Blake showed, the classicism of the latter makes the Canterbury Pilgrims themselves universal human types, while Langland's realism transforms his allegorical abstractions into individual men and women. Gluttony goes into the alehouse and sits on the bench with

Watt the warner and his wife both,
Tim the tinker and twain of his prentices,
Hick the hackneyman and Hugh the needeler,
Clarice of Cockslane and the clerk of the church,
Dawe the diker and a dozen other;
A ribibor, a ratoner a raker of Chepe,
A roper, a retainer and Rose the disher,
Godfrey of Garlickhythe and Gryffin the Welsh,
And a heap of upholsterers.

And he drinks with the best of them as though he were an honest drunkard instead of a moral abstraction.

In the same way Sloth appears as a lazy priest who knows the rhymes of Robin Hood better than his *Paternoster,* and who

can find in a field or in a furrow a hare
Better than in *Beatus vir* or *Beati omnes*
Construe one clause well and ken it to my parishioners,

while Avarice is a merchant who recounts his rogueries with naïve relish and apologizes for himself as a plain man who knows no French but that of the far end of Norfolk.

All this is characteristic of Langland's strength and weakness. He has no control over his pen. He is hardly launched on his sermon before reality bursts in tumultuously and turns his moral allegory into a vivid portrayal of the vulgar humanity of a fourteenth-century English crowd.

Yet this realism is not always present. He is often content to leave his allegory on a plane of frigid abstraction, and there are occasions in which Langland surpasses the Puritans themselves in the grotesqueness of his nomenclature. He tells us of a croft called "Covet-not-men's-cattle-nor-wives-nor-none-of-their-servants-that-might-annoy-them", and the children of Piers Plowman have names that are longer and odder than those of the Barebones family. Nevertheless, at any moment the flame of pure poetry may blaze out and silence the creaking machinery of didactic allegorism, and the artificial vision of medieval literary tradition may pass into the spiritual vision of the seer. His art is more like that of the Hebrew prophets than that of the modern poet, since it is not literature but the utterance of the word that God has put into his mouth. It is the common speech, which human folly has spoiled, brought back to its true function. For speech, he says

is a shoot of grace,
And God's gleeman and a game of heaven.
Would never the faithful Father [that] his fiddle
were untempered,
Nor his gleeman a gadabout a goer to taverns.

The one poet with whom one may compare him is his greater predecessor, Dante, though they represent in many respects the opposite poles of fourteenth-century literature. For Dante, no less than Langland, conceived his task in a prophetic spirit and used the convention of the vision to convey his criticism of life and his religious ideal. Both of them felt that the world had gone astray, and themselves with it: both had an intense faith in the Catholic way and yet were profoundly dissatisfied with the state of the Church and convinced of the need for a drastic re-form. Both looked for a deliverer who should set priests and people on the right way. But Dante brought to his task all the wisdom of the schools and the art of a highly con-scious literary culture. His way was the highway of classi-cal tradition—the royal road of imperial Rome—and he found his guide in Virgil and his saviour in the Messianic Emperor, the *Messo di Dio,* who will slay the harlot and the giant with whom she sins.

Langland, on the other hand, had the scanty learning of a poor clerk, a knowledge of the liturgy and the Bible and the common faith of Christendom. His way was the muddy highroad of common life, and he found his guide and saviour in the common man, Piers Plowman, who is the type of Labour and Christian charity and at last of Christ Himself. (pp. 247-50)

> *Christopher Dawson, "The Vision of Piers Plowman," in his* Medieval Essays, *Sheed and Ward, 1953, pp. 239-71.*

Henry W. Wells   (essay date 1938)

[*In the following excerpt, Wells asserts that the lives of Do-well, Do-bet, and Do-best in the B- and C-texts of* Piers Plowman *represent not the vocational callings of layman, priest, and bishop, but the three mental states through which Christians were expected to pass.*]

Inviting the reader to exercise his own imagination with the aid of hints and cues rather than putting his meaning in prosaic terms, the meditative author of **Piers Plowman** takes one of the well-known roads of poetical composition. He stands with the poets who find it more to their liking to hint than to assert. On this account their work becomes relatively difficult to interpret. Time further adds to the obstacles implicit in their technique. Hence many of the controversies of scholars and the justification for what may at first glance seem a wasteful commentary. One can-not expect to leap suddenly to an understanding of so sub-tle and complex an allegory as **Piers Plowman.** Only through honest controversy and repeated effort is marked progress to be made.

The subject is complicated by discrepancies between the versions of the poem as preserved in the manuscripts. The facts in a broad way are so familiar as to call for only the briefest summary. The version commonly called the A Text consists of approximately twelve passus. The **B Text** contains considerable rewriting of the A text and nine long additional passus. The **C Text** is marked by further rewrit-ing and occasional expansions or omissions. Presumably the major lines of thought in B and C are much the same. But students of the A Text are obviously criticizing a work considerably different from either of the longer versions, the differences being in about equal proportion in style and thought. The B Text does not, I think, greatly alter the thought of the earlier so far as the two run parallel, but obviously contributes much that is new in its additional passus.

Since the present study is a commentary on the B and C

Texts, it is not primarily concerned with A Text or its crit-ics. (p. 339)

Langland was concerned with ideas which he expressed in the somewhat awkward terminology of the Life of Do Well, Do Bet, and Do Best. As his poem enters its most critical stage these terms in over a score of places are used and observations made as to their meaning. Numbering the passus as in the B Text, the first seven following the original glosses may be called the *Visio,* while the thirteen succeeding sections are described in turn as the *Life of Do Well* (VIII-XIV), the *Life of Do Bet* (XV-XVIII), and the *Life of Do Best* (XIX-XX). Thus in the simplest way pos-sible one sees how important in Langland's eyes these three categories become. The only question is what he meant by them.

There are several ways of attacking the problem. One is to seek in mediæval literature for a less cryptic and poeti-cal, a simpler and more prosaic statement of what appears to be the same idea, and so, if possible, to find the sources of Langland's view. Some such sources I believe are found in quotations which I advanced from the popular *Medita-tiones Vitæ Christi* and from [Saint Thomas] Aquinas. Briefly, the *Life of Do Well* thus appears as the first or lower stage of the active life, wherein a man by moral and intellectual discipline and simple faith learns to rule him-self wisely and to live honestly and humbly in his vocation. He who does well by satisfying these requirements and who essays nothing further will be saved. The *Life of Do Bet* becomes the contemplative life or the life of devotion. This too is a good and safe road for those strong enough to follow it. Finally the *Life of Do Best* presumes previous discipline in both the preceding lives, and consists in au-thority, as, for example, in episcopal authority. It is the second stage of the active life, based upon the theory that he who has already learned to rule himself will alone know how to rule others. It was sometimes termed the Mixed Life.

So far as I am aware no one has questioned my evidence that Langland actually held these conventional views ex-pressed in the *Meditationes.* The discussion of scholastic training and intellectual problems, of the active life as such and of the elements of Christian morality in VIII-XIV is evidence; so is the long discussion of asceticism in the prologue to the *Life of Do Bet* (XV) and the devotion-al character of this section of the poem. And the repeated statement that Do Best is the episcopal life and the empha-sis in passus XIX-XX upon the active virtues and the gov-ernment of Unitas, or The Church (with mention also of the State), make Langland's conventional intention abun-dantly clear. The relation of this tripartite system to the Trinity and a few other matters likewise contribute . . . to the poet's organizing ideas.

But the grave limitation of my previous presentation lies, I believe, in its disposition to make Langland almost whol-ly conventional. While he remains broadly typical of his age, his thought cannot be rightly understood merely through reference to ulterior sources. He has, in fact, used much more than other men's words. His peculiarly daring, imaginative, and penetrating mind turns the ideas of oth-ers gently but firmly to his own purposes. It is a most familiar error to overlook a poet's originality through attention to a limited range of source material. While Langland seems never to have been in the least heretical, the originality of his poem lies in the rearrangement of old ideas and images.

Mr. [Nevill K.] Coghill has stressed certain qualifying ideas in his study of the text ["The Character of Piers Plowman," *Medium Aevum,* II, June 1933]. He has distinguished sharply between two phases of the life of Do Well: the simple piety and honesty embodied in the figure of Piers as the honest laborer, and the moral and intellectual life in its advanced stages. His comments upon the **Life of Do Bet** have been especially illuminating. While Langland himself seldom if ever directly refers to this state as the life of contemplation, he frequently refers to it in terms that suggest the priestly life, a life of aggressive altruism and sacrifice to one's neighbors. Mr. Coghill cannot, of course, say that Do Well is the laity, Do Bet the priesthood, and Do Best the episcopacy—if for no other reason than that the intellectual life so clearly included under the heading of Do Well hardly corresponds with mediæval notions of the life of those out of holy orders. Nevertheless, Mr. Coghill points so strongly to the note of active, wholly altruistic service in his conception of Do Bet that one almost loses sight of the description of this state as the life of contemplation. He is particularly categorical in his interpretation of Do Best as the episcopal life.

The danger of this method of approach is that unchecked from other sources it becomes over-literal. The question is simply asked: what passages in Langland's poem make specific statements regarding the three terms. Now in the story of the poem a pilgrim is depicted as seeking for these three virtues. But the poem itself is divided into sections which are themselves designated as the states in question. Most of the specific statements within the poem regarding the virtues occur in the earlier and obviously more naïve sections of the **Life of Do Well.** It therefore becomes natural that very concrete and simple answers are commonly given. We may easily mistake a symbol for a reality or a part for the whole. The mediæval conception of simplification is always to give the more concrete statement at the expense of the more abstract, to represent God the Father, for example, with hands and feet, or in some other way to allegorize an idea by making it visible. Thus a manifestation of an idea in action is substituted for the more abstract but more direct and adequate expression. One must be on guard against all these pedagogical simplifications of poetic language, for, if pressed no further, they give us only a half truth, or even a palpable misrepresentation. Do Well, Do Bet, and Do Best are most fully expressed by Langland, not in aphorisms, but in the general conduct of the poem itself, and there they must chiefly be sought by the imaginative reader rather than in these incidental and literal statements of the author or even in parallels drawn to his literary sources. Useful as the citations and the sources may be, they can also be overused.

I am still persuaded that Do Well, Do Bet, and Do Best signify in Langland the two stages of the active life divided by the contemplative life; I am still persuaded of the force of all that Mr. Coghill has said regarding the moral or intellectual life, the priestly life and the episcopal life. But Langland's thought here goes further than anyone has shown.

Let us begin with the leading properties of his poetic mind. Keenly observant, deeply spiritual, profoundly social—these three I think characterize him best. No author has a sharper or more realistic eye for the outward features of the human scene; none a deeper penetration into the inner springs of the religious life; and finally, none a more powerful sense of the Christian commune as a living organism. His bright and child-like gregariousness plus his spirituality produce his crowning vision of society itself as the body of Christ. This is Langland's threefold vision, and its destined culmination. He is in turn a satirist, a dreamer, and a social prophet. From this psychological triplicity all parts and virtues, literary or spiritual, of his work proceed. Seldom has an author measured his accomplishment so perfectly in terms of his genius.

As I have previously noted, his poem falls into two major divisions, the **Visio** and the allegory of the three Lives. These two sections develop along strictly parallel lines. There are no guiding thoughts in the second Part which are not to be found in the corresponding sections of the first Part. The **Visio** begins with a pragmatic allegory of political and civil corruption (the story of Lady Mede); secondly, it proceeds to an account of the inner life, wherein sins are passionately confessed and absolution accompanies the Mass; and thirdly, the Christian community is depicted as one organism dedicated to one end through all its various pursuits, namely, the quest for Truth, or Well Doing, or the Salvation of Souls. The second and longer part of the poem faithfully preserves the essential outlines of its predecessor. Instead of treating the problems of practical politics and affairs, the first section now deals with the most pressing philosophical, ethical, and theological problems; the second section depicts the mysteries of the faith as represented in the Scriptures, implying a devotional attitude, and also concluding with a penitential attitude and the celebration of the Mass; finally, the third section deals primarily with *Unitas* or the corporate body of the Church, Christendom conceived here as a brotherhood and living society. Many lesser points of comparison which might be adduced would only serve in summary to obscure the profound unity of the design. The best initial guide to a study of Do Well, Do Bet, and Do Best is thus a study of the **Visio.** The three lives are the moral and intellectual life, the intuitive and devotional life, and the social or communal life. The first life affords the bare necessities for salvation. It includes faith, good works, and the hope of heaven. But to it may be added the more inward life of fervent worship, and the inwardness that also radiates outward until the individual realizes himself and all men as part of a brotherhood whose root is in God—namely, the vine of Christ.

It is an error to give too narrow an interpretation to any of these three views. Thus especially in his generous interpretation of the life of Do Well, rather, I think, than in his views of Do Bet and Do Best, is Mr. Coghill to be congratulated. For he has shown very clearly that the flexible conception of Do Well includes both the piety and virtue of the simple Christian, as symbolized in Piers Plowman's first appearance in Passus V, and the more intellectual interpretation obviously intended in Passus X-XIII. The humblest Christian, however, fails to obtain the spiritual stature and complexity requisite to experience either the fullest devotional ardors of Do Bet or the complete realization of the fellowship that is Do Best. While his faith is sound, his devotion is only incipient; while he is a good citizen, he has scarcely entered into a full realization of the meaning of the City of God. The humble Christian has indeed made very imperfect progress even in the higher spheres of the Life of Do Well. He has never debated the grave intellectual problems of the Church; and in recompense for this he has never suffered from theological doubts or from the dread of heresy.

Here it becomes necessary to turn to Father Dunning's observations regarding the *Vita* of the A Text. He points out [in his *"Piers Plowman": An Interpretation of the A-Text,* 1937] that the view of the three "lives" most often held in this passage is that of the Purgative, Illuminative, and Unitive states of the soul. "Dowel is to fear God, Dobet to suffer and to be chastised, and from both these arises Dobest." What Father Dunning fails to observe, as being outside the scope of his immediate inquiry, is that these states bear a striking relation to the Active, Contemplative, and Mixed states as described by Langland. The knowledge and fear of God is described by the poet as a part of the life of Do Well; the **Life of Do Bet** stresses not only contemplation but asceticism and the passion of Christ; while the life of Do Best is clearly the ideal or unitive life. In the B Text this general view is stressed in relation to the sacrament of penance. Contrition, Confession, and Satisfaction, for example, in the opening of passus XIV are said to be Do Well, Do Bet, and Do Best.

Father Dunning stresses the point that the dreamer in the A Text twice repudiates the explanation of the three lives offered him by his interlocutors as the Active, Contemplative and Mixed states of the soul. But this does not imply that the author of the A Text repudiated the theory or cast it aside finally in relation to Do Well, Do Bet and Do Best. The dreamer is always pictured as less enlightened than his spiritual teachers and as frequently fallible. Such is a convention of moral allegory. Similarly Dante objects to Virgil's advice upon their proposed journey through hell and heaven on the ground that he is neither Æneas nor Paul. But the poet of the Divine Comedy clearly intends his pilgrim to be in error here. To his own amazement he is about to be taken in the body to hell and heaven, as were Æneas and Paul before him. In short, Father Dunning's view of the *Vita* in the A Text confirms my general view of the B Text and by no means clashes with it. Particularly are we in agreement that the *Vita* in the A Text merely covers once more the main thesis of the *Visio,* leaving further development to the later section of the poem. But I am rather more sure than Father Dunning that the author of the B Text understood the A Text. I suspect that he understood it much better than we do. I even suspect he was the same man.

Caution must be observed in describing the Life of Do Bet as the Priestly Life, or that of Do Best as the Episcopal Life, lest we mistake the language of poetry for that of criticism. The question at once arises what Langland means by his classifications. Does he mean them to be stages in the social order, such as the laity, the clergy, and the episcopacy? Does he mean that only one of the lives can be led at a time? Is his poem simply chastisement administered to group after group of the social scale? Because a person has made but slight progress in the more advanced realms of the Christian life, does it follow that he has in no way participated in the Life of Do Bet or of Do Best? At times Mr. Coghill would seem to answer these questions in the affirmative, whereas I should answer them in the negative. I do not believe that the Life of Do Bet is literally the priestly life. Langland does not say categorically that it is. Yet I should not object to it being called the priestly life provided this is understood in a figurative sense. Priests, Langland naturally holds, should be above all superior to their parishioners in contemplation and devotion. Their inner life should be peculiarly astir. By virtue of this superior warmth and charity they will, ideally speaking, be led to a more active life; their prayers, Langland observes, will be of the greater efficacy. But the priesthood is rather a part of Do Bet than Do Bet of the priesthood. Contemplation, devotion, the life "withinforth" becomes a supreme reality. According to familiar Christian teaching all who are to be saved must in some degree participate in it. It is, as Langland says, a "state"; but not, I think, merely one of the estates of society. In short, it proves a state of the soul through which the Christian will a thousand times pass, however well he knows it or understands it. It is but one of the three districts of the city in which he lives. In the three passus forming the body of the **Life of Do Bet** (XVI-XVIII) little specifically is said of the priesthood. Moreover, I greatly doubt if the life of Christ, which is here depicted, is intended as an allegory of true priesthood. Rather priesthood would be an allegory of Christ. Such symbolism customarily proceeds not from the greater to the less, but from the less to the greater. Christ's life is here ardently presented as the object of devotion, and not as an intellectual allegory. Again, to describe Do Bet too narrowly even as the life of contemplation would violate Langland's intention. The inward life has many facets, some even pointing outwardly. From the sanctuaries of the contemplatives, according to mediæval belief, issue prayers of the sanctified, of the utmost service to the welfare not only of men's souls but of their bodies. Again, devotion leads to saintly acts of more than common charity which are in themselves neither the fruits of Do Well nor of Do Best. Repeatedly Langland describes Do Bet as a prodigal giver. He gives many things, first of all being prayers. Then he may preach and exhort men and women. In doing so he does not assume rule, infringe on the episcopal authority, or deal in the academic or merely factual matter pertaining to Do Well. Talking from the fullness of a heart fired with devotion, he speaks as an individual to the individual soul. The secret chambers of the heart produce a voice that is heard also by the private ear, though in the midst of multitudes. When Langland emphasizes the giving properties of Do Bet he thinks, I believe, generally of spiritual gifts. Yet more material charities may also in a secondary way be included. Contemplation, needing little, can spare much for his neighbors. Only the heart fired with devotion will experience the zeal for charity, whether to bestow the highest or the lowest things.

Especially one must guard against a too literal view of the phrase common in Langland and in his able critic, Mr. Coghill, that Do Best is the Episcopal Life. The phrase was originally written, I believe, metaphorically. What better symbol is there for the Christian Community as such than the man, or type of man, ultimately responsible for its integrity? "Do Best is a bishop"—but only with this figurative meaning. The entire texture of Langland's poem shows it to be no merely objective statement about society, nor can we think of its conclusion as becoming merely objective. Poems of the curious and inner fervor of Langland's are intimately personal. Although Langland has much to say regarding all orders of the clergy and the religious, he has much more to say on the salvation of every man and on his own salvation. There is the rub for him, his poem including but transcending a merely social or political satire. Thus he writes about Do Well, Do Bet, and Do Best not alone because these are constituent parts of society, but because they are parts of himself and of every man. In any case they are potentially the parts of each man. As Langland says in Passus IV, man is made in the image of the Trinity. The realization that the forces of which he writes are operating within himself is the best explanation for the peculiar poignancy of his style. He introduces himself as an old man (and surely the dreamer is no bishop) into passus XX. In short, his three states are psychological rather than sociological. It is chiefly because Mr. Coghill fails to make this clear to me that I have written the present paper.

Let us examine the **Life of Do Best** further. As Mr. Coghill very shrewdly states, this section begins not quite with the beginning of a Passus. Or in any case the Prologue to the **Life of Do Best** consists of Passus XIX, 1-176. The Life proper extends from here to the end of the poem. Now in this section very little is said of bishops, less indeed than in several other parts of the poem. Looking simply at what Langland writes we shall find that the interest actually centers upon *Unitas,* the symbol for the company of the faithful on earth, the true and loyal Church. All emphasis is throughout upon the idea of the brotherhood of Christendom. The poet, ever gregarious and socially minded, has here plucked the heart of the theme. No longer does he deal merely with the field of folk—the indiscriminate mass of mankind as it appears to the animal eye—but with the fraternity of Christians held together by faith and good works and by the grace and the sacrifice of Christ. The name *Unitas* proves an inspiration, for it perfectly expresses Langland's thought. He has put into the center of his canvas what deserves to stand there, enlarged on precisely what requires enlargement, leaving other matters for the periphery. Just as the Schools are the center of Do Well, and Christ is of Do Bet, so here *Unitas* proves the keystone of the final arch. In seeking a phrase to express Langland's meaning it would thus be much better to conclude that Do Best is *Unitas* than the Episcopal Life. If Do Best is ill and distraught, this only means that the Christian Commune has fallen far short of its perfection.

Do Best, we have often been told in earlier sections of the poem, is to command. But such is its most dramatic meaning. Actually to achieve unity in society it becomes equally important that there be both command and obedience to command. Whoever in any capacity acts consciously to aid *Unitas,* does best, whether it be the Pope himself who issues the command, or the most humble subject who piously obeys it.

A further means of understanding the **Life of Do Best** is to review the two steps leading up to it. As the poet and his sources repeatedly say, the states are accumulative. Intellectual and moral laws and religious faith are formulated and molded in the state of Do Well. The fires of charity are lighted in the furnaces of Do Bet. In these fires the vessels are created that acquire their fullest social significance only in the Life of Do Best. First comes law and reason; then emotion and devotion; and finally the consecration to a communal utility. Langland's poem, beginning with a lively but unregenerate picture of the commune, ends with a profound and spiritual picture of the same world transformed by religion. Because modern readers possess a better eye for picturesque realism than for social and religious visions, the opening lines regarding the field of folk have become much better known than the closing lines regarding *Unitas.* But this is not even the fault of Langland as an artist. The more serious view of the poem hangs upon the interpretation of its last few pages.

The poet is skillful in social satire and admirable in mysticism, but not wholly effectual along more strictly intellectual lines. Thus the racy realism of much of the **Visio** has rightly attracted many admirers, and at least a few critics have testified as to the profundity of religious emotion expressed, for example, in his passages in the **Visio** on the sins and on the Mass, and in the **Lives of Do Bet** and **Do Best.** The most disputed, the most perplexing, and apparently the least admired section is that on the intellectual and moral life, the section on Do Well. Even Langland himself may have broken down here, for he seems to have settled upon no entirely satisfactory form for his work. He apparently left it a fragment for many years, unable to continue the **Life of Do Well** to his liking. Do Well *secundum Wyt et Resoun* he finished, but neglected the evidence of his other allegorical figures, Scripture and Clergy. Artistically and in every way he becomes more surefooted and effective with the lives of Do Bet and Do Best. It deserves especially to be noted that while others have surpassed him in theologizing in verse, few have equalled him in powerful presentation of the inner life, and none quite rivalled him in a vivid, visionary realization of the Christian or social commune. It is with this keen awareness that men are members of one Catholic organism that his august poem concludes, and because his communal vision proves at once so darkly veiled in allegory and so darkly magnificent it deserves special study, and once grasped, a tenacious hold. Our conception of his poetic stature depends upon our understanding of these problems.

Finally, Langland's somewhat difficult allegory of the three states is illumined by his own frequent allusions to the Trinity. In my previous article on the subject I pointed out that each of the three divisions of the *Vita* begins with lines on the Trinity, turning special attention to the Person of the Trinity to whom the particular life is, so to speak, dedicated, but presuming the unity as well as the Trinity of God. Langland frequently states that man is made in the image of the Trinity. And clearly, just as the Persons of the Trinity are according to the doctrine of the Church inseparable, so the states of the soul are ultimately inseparable—each, even Do Well, implying the others. In addition to his anagogical, moral, and personal allegories Langland has a historical allegory also intimately associated with theology. **The Life of Do Well** deals especially with the heathen or pre-Christian world which believes in God but not in the Trinity. **The Life of Do Bet** is associated with the world during the lifetime of Jesus. **The Life of Do Best** is the subsequent dispensation of the Holy Spirit after the Ascension and both before and after the poet's own lifetime. Here Langland approximates though by no means follows the historical teaching of Joachim of Flora, who, unlike Langland, pressed his mystical views of the three periods of history so far as to impugn the unity of the Trinity and so to become questionable in his orthodoxy. Langland's psychological trinity is intended as a microcosm or an emanation of the divine.

The gist of this article is that Langland's three lives are not vocational callings but mental states; that they rise in a perfectly familiar ascending scale but remain nevertheless a ladder up and down which the true Christian was expected by the poet to pass at will. Some good but simple men would in his view have only a slender acquaintance with the last two "virtues." But they would have some acquaintance; and the fully developed soul on earth, whether bishop or no, would be richly endowed with all three. Such is, I believe, the key to most of the problems in the philosophical interpretation of *Piers Plowman.* (pp. 340-49)

Henry W. Wells, "The Philosophy of Piers Plowman," in PMLA, *Vol. LIII, No. 2, June, 1938, pp. 339-49.*

C. S. Lewis   (essay date 1938)

[*Lewis is considered one of the foremost authors on Christian and mythopoeic issues of the twentieth century. Indebted principally to George MacDonald, G. K. Chesterton, Charles Williams, and the writers of ancient Norse myths, he is regarded as a formidable logician and Christian polemicist, a perceptive literary critic, and—most highly—as a writer of fantasy literature. Lewis also held academic appointments at Oxford and Cambridge, where he was an acknowledged authority on medieval and Renaissance literature. A traditionalist in his approach to life and art, he opposed the movement in modern criticism toward biographical and psychological interpretation, preferring instead to practice and propound a theory of criticism that stresses the author's intent, not the reader's presuppositions and prejudices. In the following excerpt from the 1938 corrected reprint of his* Allegory of Love: A Study in Medieval Tradition, *Lewis maintains that the form Langland chose for* Piers Plowman, *that of moral allegory, is less extraordinary than the poet's sublime poetic imagination.*]

Scholars more interested in social history than in poetry have sometimes made [*Piers Plowman*] appear much less ordinary than it really is as regards its kind, and much less extraordinary as regards the genius of the poet. In fact, its only oddity is its excellence; in *Piers Plowman* we see an exceptional poet adorning a species of poetry which is hardly exceptional at all. He is writing a moral poem, such as Gower's *Miroir de l'homme* or Gower's Prologue to the *Confessio Amantis,* and throwing in, as any other medieval poet might have done, a good deal of satire on various 'estates'. His satire falls heaviest where we should expect it to fall—on idle beggars, hypocritical churchmen, and oppressors. Like Chaucer he reverences knighthood. Even as a moralist he has no unique or novel 'message' to deliver. As a cure for all our ills he can offer us only the old story—do-wel, do-bet, and do-best. His advice is as ancient, as 'conventional', if you will, as that of Socrates; not to mention names more august. It is doubtful whether any moralist of unquestioned greatness has ever attempted more (or less) than the defence of the universally acknowledged; for 'men more frequently require to be reminded than informed'. As a politician, Langland has nothing to propose except that all estates should do their duty. It is unnecessary, I presume, to state that his poem is not revolutionary, nor even democratic. It is not even 'popular' in any very obvious sense. A poem every way unsuitable for recitation cannot have been addressed to those who could not read; and any one who supposes that Langland had in view an audience very different from the audience of Gower and Chaucer may be advised to imagine the probable results of reading aloud in a tavern or on a village green such lines as the following:

> The whiles I quykke the corps, quod he, called
> am I *Anima;*
> And whan I wilne and wolde, *Animus* ich hatte;
> And for that I can and knowe, called am I *Mens;*
> And whan I make mone to God, *Memoria* is my
> name.

Or, if he prefers,

> Thus is relacion rect ryht as adiective and sub-
> stantif
> Acordeth in alle kyndes with his antecedent.

Langland is a learned poet. He writes for clerks and for clerkly minded gentlemen. The forty-five manuscripts, and the presence of quotation from Langland in Usk's *Testament of Love,* prove that he did not write in vain. It would have been strange if he had. He offered to his educated contemporaries fare of a kind which they well understood. His excellent satiric comedy, as displayed in the behaviour of the seven Deadly Sins belongs to a tradition as old as the *Ancren Riwle;* and his allegorical form and pious content were equally familiar.

What is truly exceptional about Langland is the kind, and the degree, of his poetic imagination. His comedy, however good, is not what is most characteristic about him. Sublimity—so rare in Gower, and rarer still in Chaucer—is frequent in *Piers Plowman.* The Harrowing of Hell, so often and so justly praised, is but one instance. There is not much medieval poetry that does not look pale if we set it beside such lines as these:

Kinde huyrde tho Conscience, and cam out of
   the planetes
And sente forth his foreyours, fevers and flux-
   es—
Ther was 'Harow!' and 'Help! Here cometh
   kynde,
With Deth that is dredful to undo us alle!'
The Lord that lyuede after lust, tho aloude
   criede
After Comfort, a knyght, to come and bere hus
   baner.
'Alarme, alarme!' quath that Lord, 'eche lyf
   kepe hus owene!'

In a quieter mood, the great vision wherein the poet beholds 'the sea, and the sun, and the sand after' and sees
'man and his make' among the other creatures, is equally
distinctive. There is in it a Lucretian largeness which, in
that age, no one but Langland attempts. It is far removed
from the common, and beautiful, descriptions of nature
which we find in medieval poetry—the merry morning
and the singing birds; it is almost equally far from the
sterner landscapes of *Gawain and the Greene Knight*. It belongs rather to what has been called the 'intellectual imagination'; the unity and vastness were attained by thought,
rather than by sense, but they end by being a true image
and no mere conception. This power of rendering imaginable what before was only intelligible is nowhere, I think,
not even in Dante, better exemplified than in Langland's
lines on the Incarnation. They are, so far as I know, perfectly accurate and clear in doctrine; and the result is as
concrete, as fully incarnate, as if the poet were writing
about apples or butter:

Love is the plonte of pees and most precious of
   vertues;
For hevene holde hit ne myghte so hevy hit
   semede,
Til hit hadde on erthe ghoten hym-selue.
Was never lef upon lynde lyghter ther-after,
As whanne hit hadde of the folde flesch and
   blode ytake.
Tho was it portatyf and pershaunt as the poynt
   of a nelde.

Doubtless such heights are rare in Langland, as they are
rare in poetry at all; but the man who attains them is a
very great poet. He is not, indeed, the greatest poet of his
century. He lacks the variety of Chaucer, and Chaucer's
fine sense of language: he is confused and monotonous,
and hardly makes his poetry into a poem. But he can do
some things which Chaucer cannot, and he can rival
Chaucer in Chaucer's special excellence of pathos. (pp.
158-61)

> *C. S. Lewis, "Chaucer," in his* The Allegory
> of Love: A Study in Medieval Tradition,
> *1936. Reprint by Oxford University Press,
> 1959, pp. 157-97.*

Greta Hort (essay date 1938)

[*In the following excerpt, Hort focuses on the search for
the elusive meaning of "the greatest of Middle English
dream poems," the B-text of* Piers Plowman. *She maintains that despite its complexity, the poem is shaped by*

*its theological content and Langland's answer to the
question "What shall I do in order to save my soul?"*]

In a somer seson whan soft was the sonne,
I shope me in shroudes as I a shepe were,
In habite as an heremite vnholy of workes,
Went wyde in þis world wondres to here.
Ac on a May mornynge on Maluerne hulles
Me byfel a ferly of fairy me thoughte;
I was wery forwandred and went me to reste
Vnder a brode banke bi a bornes side,
And as I lay and lened and loked in þe waters,
I slombred in a slepyng it sweyued so merye.

These are the opening lines of *Piers Plowman,* and they
are also *mutatis mutandis* the opening lines of many another medieval dream poem. They give the setting for the
story the poet is going to tell us in the approved medieval
way. Though the poet distinctly tells his audience that he
himself set out in search of marvels, and then happened
to fall asleep, no medieval listener would be misled by that
statement, for who ever heard of a poet who actually went
to sleep and dreamt his strange tales? No, the poet's falling
asleep was as much a device as his waking up and dozing
again, all within the dream and the dream-device; and
very well-known things they were to his hearers. But once
the poet had escaped into the topsy-turvydom of the land
of sleep, anything might happen, as the medieval listener
knew from long and varied experience of poets and their
ways. Their dreams might be a cloak for a song in praise
of love, for an elegy, for a didactic poem, for a utopia, or
simply for a good story. But dreams are puzzling things;
and we may find a certain fitness in the fact that *Piers
Plowman,* the greatest of Middle English dream poems,
shares the puzzling quality of dreams, and gives rise to
more questionings and doubts than any other Middle English poem. Not even five hundred years of literary criticism has as yet succeeded in determining the apparently
simple question of what is the main subject of this long
poem of 7150 lines; and scholars provide us with a bewildering mass of appellations for its author. Langland has
been called a prophet-poet, a preacher, a mystic, an ardent
social reformer, an introspective writer of autobiography,
a commentator on the Rolls of Parliament, a medieval
Carlyle, a medieval Blake, a medieval Tolstoy. (pp. 1-2)

[The] characters of the poem are William (the dreamer
himself), and the various persons he meets during his
wanderings in and out of dreamland. The most important
of these 'persons' are all allegorical figures, such as Holy
Church, Activa Vita, Anima, Clergy, Reason, Judgment,
Hope. The minor characters either belong to the same
kind of allegory as the major characters, or they represent
one of the many classes and types that make up society.

A consideration of the characters of *Piers Plowman* reveals at once one of the outstanding peculiarities of the
poem: on the one hand the ease with which concrete characters become allegorical, and on the other hand the vividness of the original allegorical characters. Thus the central
character, when first we meet him in the poem, is a
ploughman, and anything more enduring and solid than
the honest peasant with his homely name of Piers the
Plowman can hardly be imagined. But soon we find that
Piers the Plowman has become Holy Church, and when

Frontispiece to a manuscript of Piers Plowman *in the Library of Trinity College, Cambridge.*

we reach passus xix, we are left in little doubt that by Piers we are to understand Christ himself. The opposite process may be seen at work in the case of the Seven Deadly Sins: Gluttony is no abstract vice, but a big fellow, full of drink; Envy is Sir Hervy, with bleared eyes, greasy beard, a threadbare and torn coat. So vividly are these sins described that one scribe has even been tempted to draw their portraits in the margin of his manuscript; he has but followed the poet's description, and we recognize the figures immediately. Another feature of the allegory is the alternation of the allegorical personalities, as shown in what has been said about the figure of Piers the Plowman [G. R. Owst, *Literature and Pulpit in Medieval England*, 1933]. The peculiarities of the allegory do not, however, interfere with a straightforward reading of **Piers Plowman**; on the contrary, they stimulate the interest of a reader with no taste for the argument behind the allegory.

In an ordinary epic poem it is generally what the characters do that is of most importance for the story, but in **Piers Plowman** it is what the characters say that arouses our interest, and what they do is merely a part of the machinery for making them talk. Because **Piers Plowman** is a dream poem, the machinery is very simple: the poet wanders about, grows tired, falls asleep, dreams, and then sees someone coming to him in his dream. Or the dream-device

may be varied a little, and we have a dream within a dream. (pp. 2-4)

Students of **Piers Plowman** have from time to time debated, whether Langland left his poem unfinished or not. The summary of the poem certainly gives colour to the view that Langland at the end of the **B-text** did what he had done at the end of the A-text, and broke off his work at the crucial point. But if this were so, why should the B-text leave us with the curious feeling that it is both finished and unfinished? The explanation of the anomaly may perhaps be sought in the conclusion for which we wait in vain; for what is lacking is obviously a description of the dreamer's finding of Christ. And perhaps we may discover both that such a description is superfluous, and that the poet was wiser than we in not attempting to describe what in a sense he had already described. In this connection we may remember the paradox so well stated by the author of *The Cloud of Unknowing*: 'Forasmuch as thou willest it [that is the knowledge of God] and desirest it, so much hast thou of it, and no more and no less.' In this sense we may say that **Piers Plowman** is a finished poem, and that William is at the end of his journey, when his desire for God has killed his desire for all other things. But even this is not altogether a satisfactory explanation; it is too intellectual, too much a matter of reflection to be able to account for the feeling of finality given by the ending of **Piers**

Plowman. The peculiar nature of poetry baffles us here. It is just possible that the last line of *Piers Plowman* may contain more than a mere repetition of Langland's usual transition from one dream to another. As it stands in this last line, his usual phrase has a force which it has nowhere else:

> And sitthe he gradde after grace *til I gan awake.*

This may of course be a perfectly plain statement, meant to introduce a vision never written; or it may be that Langland wrote better than he knew, and then discovered that he had said all that there was to be said.

Let us now consider the contents of *Piers Plowman,* and the various questions that arise out of it. It is clear that the unifying and controlling force in the poem is given by its theological element; but that does not entitle us to call the poem a work of theology, if we confine the use of the word theology to learned treatises like the *Summae* or series like the Bampton Lectures. Langland's attitude to theology, we might say, resembled for instance Sir Henry Newbolt's attitude to history, as shown in his book *The New June.* But this comparison will have to be discarded, for an author of a historical novel may write his book with some other purpose than that of giving his readers historical insight; and consequently the comparison may make us lose sight of an essential aspect of *Piers Plowman.* It would on the other hand give an equally misleading impression of *Piers Plowman,* if we substituted the word religious for theological in our description of it. The distinction between religion and theology may be said to lie in the fact that religion deals with practice, theology deals with theory. A mass of books are published which are neither strictly theological nor strictly religious, but a blending of both. These books are written by more or less good theologians for the benefit of the general reader; they may be written in order to remove intellectual doubts, or to explain some doctrine that the reader may the more easily avail himself of its practical value. The ultimate end of these books will be practice (religion); their proximate end will be theory (theology). It is in this latter sense of the word that we can say that *Piers Plowman* is a theological poem, and it is in this sense I shall use the word theological. We may compare *Piers Plowman* on the one hand with a book like *Belief in God,* and find that Langland was a poet and not only a theologian and pastor like Bishop Gore; or we may compare it with the *Theologia Germanica,* and find that Langland was not only a religious man, but also a theologian, and no less so, because his heart prompted him to write in such a way as to be understood by those who had little theology.

Like other poems *Piers Plowman* has a recognizable form; we can unhesitatingly say that it is a dream poem, exactly in the same way as we can say that *Lycidas* is an elegy and *Paradise Lost* an epic. We can confidently state what medium the poet used for conveying what he saw, and expect other people to agree with us. But we must not forget that *Piers Plowman* is not only a writing in verse, not only 'a metrical piece of unusual charm and vivacity', but that it is poetry and not a variant of prose. In this connection it may not be wholly irrelevant to quote a passage from T.

S. Eliot's essay on *Hamlet and his Problems* [in *The Sacred Wood,* 1932]:

> *Qua* work of art, the work of art cannot be interpreted; there is nothing to interpret; we can only criticize it according to standards, in comparison to other works of art; and for 'interpretation' the chief task is the presentation of relevant historical facts which the reader is not assumed to know.

Among these historical facts, as far as *Piers Plowman* is concerned, are undoubtedly the social conditions and the institutions of its time, and the life led by the people among whom Langland lived, and of whom he was one himself; and readers of *Piers Plowman* must be grateful for the work done by the social historian. Those who avail themselves of the material thus put within their reach will know how it helps to bridge the gap of centuries and provides an answer to many a puzzled 'why'. But for all that the historical facts cannot tell us what the poem is.

Dr Owst, for instance, has put the readers of *Piers Plowman* under a heavy debt by showing how likely it is that the sermons Langland had read or heard were parts of the material that went to make up *Piers Plowman.* But when the same writer goes on to claim that *Piers Plowman* is 'a typical product of the preacher's art' and substantiates that claim by showing 'the kind of sources from which Langland drew the first great message of his *Vision*', then he forgets the importance of what he has seen himself:

> (The reader) will be able to recognize, emerging from its pages (i.e. the pages of Bromyard's sermon collection, the *Summa Predicantium*) here and there, very dimly, very tentatively, the familiar features of a literary hero. It is none other than our immortal PIERES THE PLOWMAN, he who *by a stroke of poetic genius* was one day himself to become the chosen prophet of the Gospel of Truth and Reconciliation.

Long ago Coleridge levelled a trenchant criticism against all theories which try to explain the higher and more developed in terms of the lower and less developed. It is the mistake of thinking that *Piers Plowman* is identical with that from which it has developed, which is responsible for the variety of descriptions given of the poem. If we keep steadily before our minds that *Piers Plowman* is a poem, and then begin to interpret it, we may be grateful to other readers for showing us sides and aspects of it, which we had not seen for ourselves, and thus we may avoid making an exclusive claim for our own reading of the poem.

The quotation given above from T. S. Eliot's essay on *Hamlet* appears to reduce all interpretation of poetry to the adducing of relevant historical facts. A simple enough task, we might say, were it not for the fact that it is not until we have interpreted the poem that we are able to say what facts are relevant. To say that *Piers Plowman* is a poem is to say that it embodies an experience which Langland had and to which he was forced to give expression—because he was a poet, necessity was laid upon him. The relevant facts will be the thoughts and circumstances that formed the starting-point for his experience. What the experience was in itself, we can only know by having a similar one; of what it was an experience, we may gather from his poem. However high the poem may soar, it had a foothold on this earth; to search for that, and to present it in the form in which we think it presented itself to Langland, is the task of an interpreter of ***Piers Plowman;*** it is only by attempting to think his thoughts after him that we can hope to be led to see what is embodied in his poem. Perhaps the work done by various scholars may send us back to ***Piers Plowman,*** not bewildered and baffled by the strife of opinion, but ready to see that Langland was a poet and a man who might rightly say, *homo sum, humani nihil a me alienum puto.* (pp. 14-18)

But what was Langland's aim in writing ***Piers Plowman?*** Had he any conscious aim at all? or did he merely write because he had to? The answer we give should be of the greatest importance for our view of the poem—at the very least it would indicate from what angle we ought to approach our subject. It would, moreover, tell us, what Langland intended by his work, and what he conceived it to be.

Now, we are fortunate enough to have Langland's own answer to our question. It occurs in the passage in which Imagination accuses the dreamer and says:

> 'And þow medlest þe with makynges and myghtest go sey þi sauter,
> And bidde for hem þat ghiueth þe bred; for þere ar bokes ynowe
> To telle men what dowel is dobet, and dobest bothe,
> And prechoures to preue what it is of many a peyre freres.'
> I seigh wel he sayde me soth and, somwhat me to excuse,
> Seide, 'catoun conforted his sone þat, clerke þough he were,
> To solacen hym sum tyme as I do when I make;
> *Interpone tuis interdum gaudia curis, etc.*
> And of holy men I herde,' quod I 'how þei otherwhile
> Pleyden, þe parfiter to be in many places.
> Ac if þere were any wight þat wolde me telle
> What were dowel and dobet and dobest atte laste,
> Wolde I neuere do werke but wende to holicherche,
> And þere bydde my bedes but whan ich eet or slepe.'

Can we take Langland's and Imagination's words out of their context, and say that Langland's aim in writing ***Piers Plowman*** was to tell men what Do-Well, Do-Bet, and Do-Best are? It might be worth while to look a little closer at the passage.

Imagination states what Langland is doing: he is busy writing a book, which will tell people what Do-Well, Do-Bet, and Do-Best are, while all the time he really ought to be doing something quite different. Langland, be it noted, does not attempt to refute this; but says something in order to excuse himself—it is a solace to him, is all he can say at first; and then a little later he adds that there is no one else who will do it, and therefore he must. What is the real meaning of this helpless answer which is no answer? First, we may say, that it stamps Langland as a poet,

at one with the artists and prophets who all down the ages have given similar replies to those who would foolishly set them about their work. But secondly, and this is what is of importance for the present discussion, it shows us that Langland himself regarded his poem as a theological work. An author may, of course, be wrong in judging of what kind of book he has actually written, and therefore we cannot on the strength of this passage say that ***Piers Plowman*** is a theological poem, the gap between intention and consequence forbids it; but the passage tells us plainly where we are to look for the relevant historical facts, and what subject it was which filled Langland's mind at the time of writing; and for that we could not have any better witness than Langland himself. If we find that the historical facts to which he refers us are relevant, then we may feel sure that Langland's description of his own work holds good about the accomplished fact no less than of the intention.

Langland's professed motive in writing ***Piers Plowman*** was then to set forth the good life that men might know what it was, and thus be brought to lead it. If we take him at his word, we are led to inquire what conception he had of the good life, and we find, not unnaturally, that he thought of it in the terms of his age. As set forth by Langland the good life appears exclusively as a means by which men are led to God; it is to be lived here on earth that one may enjoy God for ever in heaven. The hero of ***Piers Plowman*** asks what Do-Well, Do-Bet, and Do-Best are; but as the poem develops, we see that that question is only asked in order to get an answer to the further question: What shall I do in order to save my soul?

'Even he that leadeth an uncorrupt life and doeth the thing which is right', was David's answer. 'Thou knowest the commandments. . . . Go thy way, sell whatsoever thou hast, and give to the poor', was the interpretation given by Jesus. But the words of Jesus were clearly addressed to one individual person, and were not applicable to all. Medieval theologians saw that. But they saw too that because men have a common humanity, there must be an answer applicable to all men; and, being children of their age, they sought to systematize their answer; truth for them was one, and truth could be analysed into a system. David's answer was applicable to all men, but it led them on to ask: In what does an uncorrupt life consist? And only they know the answer who in trying to solve it have forgotten why they asked it. The beginning of the search may be the cry for salvation, but the end will only come through the cry for God. But each individual has to learn that for himself; the Church may tell him in what an uncorrupt life consists, it may tell him the way of salvation, but he has to recapitulate in himself the whole process that leads to the final answer.

When therefore Langland began to describe the way of salvation, he took a concrete instance, and tried to make it understandable by all, by showing how one man, William or the dreamer, had passed through it. His hero thus comes to be stripped of all individualizing features in his search for salvation: though the questions of poverty and riches, of virginity and marriage, of learning and ignorance, are discussed, William never asks whether he ought to embrace the monastic life or study in the schools. And though Langland tells us that William was tall and gaunt, that his work was to sing the Psalms and say the Offices for the Dead, that he had a wife and daughter, he never lets him think of these individualizing features in his search for salvation—the question is, what shall *a* man do to save his soul; and it is only what *a* man may do that is described, though it is the man William who seeks to do it. (pp. 18-22)

> Greta Hort, "What is 'Piers Plowman'?" in her Piers Plowman and Contemporary Religious Thought, *The Macmillan Company, 1938, pp. 1-27.*

Helen C. White   (essay date 1944)

[*White was an American educator and critic. In the following excerpt, she studies the "highly critical attitude of the author of* Piers the Plowman *to the church and society of his day." Langland used his work, White asserts, to denounce poverty, oppression by the wealthier classes, and corruption within the church.*]

Whether religion in general, and the Christian religion in particular is to be regarded as basically an instrument of social stimulation and disturbance, or as a means of social reconciliation and stabilization, is a question at least as old as Christianity. Probably, they are right who find in the very early days of the church evidence of the presence of both points of view. Later, it is quite easy to see in certain periods of church history the triumph of the stabilizers and in certain movements the protests of those who were not satisfied with that general attitude. But it would be a mistake to take one attitude as the tradition and the other as the innovation in the sixteenth century or any other century. For both have their place in the tradition.

We are today accustomed to think of regard for tradition and attention to tradition as in itself a characteristic of the conservative and the conformist. As a matter of fact, the reformer is often very much alive to the advantages of the appeal to tradition, and, if often far from comprehensive in his appropriations, nevertheless ready to turn to his use the help it affords. Indeed, he is often very generous in his readiness to make the most of a congenial suggestion and to carry it to conclusions that would have surprised the original author. This is especially true of a time like the sixteenth century in England when the solid regard for the tried and established maintained a firm hold in most men's consciences even when they were sensitive to the challenge of the up-to-date.

In fact, as Mr. [G. R.] Owst has so brilliantly shown in his *Literature and Pulpit in Medieval England,* the sixteenth-century social and religious reformer had at his disposal a singularly rich store of congenial criticism, by no means so systematically accessible to him as Mr. Owst has made it to us, but nonetheless immediately pervasive and effective as only a continuous and living tradition can be. True, as we shall see presently, the sixteenth-century reformer was, often enough, going to use this criticism for ends of which the earlier preachers and writers had hardly dreamed, for the destruction of institutions which they believed essential and only wanted to see reformed. That is the risk which the reformer always runs at the hands of the revolutionary in the history of all institutions. The important point for us is that the sixteenth-century reformers inherited a tradition of social-religious criticism from which they made their own selections, and which they carried on to their own ends, often, in all probability, not entirely aware of what they were doing. For they were not interested in history but in the solution of the problems of their own time; their obligations were not to scholarship but to the accomplishment of the contemporary purposes to which they had dedicated themselves.

Their task of appropriation was made easier by two facts. The first was that already alluded to above, namely, that convinced supporters of the established religious order had made criticisms of the way in which that order was functioning that left little to be desired by the revolutionary either in severity or in range of condemnation. The second was that side by side with the criticism of practice was a criticism of basic theory that at many points of illustration and application ran parallel to it, that, in fact, to a man primarily interested not in theory but in practice was hardly distinguishable from it, and that in many literary instances intermingled with the orthodox criticism of practice in a highly confusing manner. A good many examples could probably be found, but one is so striking that it may serve as a type for all. It is the transformation which the work of Langland underwent mainly through the influence of that of his great contemporary, John Wycliff.

The Vision of William concerning Piers the Plowman is a poem, of course, and not a work of original or systematic thought in the philosophical sense, but after the *Canterbury Tales* of Chaucer, it is probably the most comprehensive literary expression of medieval England. Since our interest is in the ideas expressed rather than in the poem for its own sake, there is no need of going into the problems of authorship. If it could be proved that the poem was the work of several authors, it would only heighten its representative character; it would certainly in no way detract from its importance as an expression of the tradition we are studying. To assume that it is the work of one man, Langland, is merely a convenience. For in spite of some differences of opinion on details, some differences of emphasis on various elements in the situation, and certain differences with regard to hope and expectation, it still remains true that the same approach to the basic problems of religion and society, the same scale of values, social and religious, the same basic purposes govern all three of the existing versions of the poem. In that sense, for all the very complicated textual problems involved, the work may be regarded as a unit, and will be so regarded here.

The highly critical attitude of the author of *Piers the Plowman* to the church and society of his day has been noted by every student of the work. But the character of his criticism has not always been fully appreciated. For that reason it is worthwhile to recapitulate its main lines. The central issue for Langland is the problem of poverty. On the negative side, that involves a failure of two of the basic requirements of the Christian life, justice and charity. On the positive, it involves an appreciation of the meaning of poverty for the social aspects of the Christian life. Poverty is the touchstone of the existing order in church and society; it is both the explanation of the problem of the world's wrong and the solution to it. Of course, this sounds paradoxical, but the paradox rests on a perfectly serious and quite viable interpretation of Christian theory, that, as we shall see presently, is by no means peculiar to Langland in his own time or later.

Langland is not, of course, writing a scientific treatise, or an objective criticism, or even a satire. What he is writing is a prophet's vision in which the light of the professions of a whole society is turned upon its performance with devastating results. But one thing should be noted here. It is that that light would be visible only to those who share the professions. To one who was indifferent to them there would be nothing to bother about. Of course it would be quite possible for one who did not share those aspirations to measure the profession and the performance and to point out the discrepancies dispassionately, cynically, or contemptuously. There is nothing of that in Langland. The discrepancy is for him a matter of outrage and of heart-break. The very bitterness of his criticism is understandable only in the light of his allegiance to the basic principles that his fellow Christians have violated. He has not only the radical idealism of the mystic who cannot rest content with the shows of things, but the thorough-going tenacity of the mystic whose very impatience with illusion has made him proof against disillusionment.

The very word "idealism" is in this context dangerously misleading. For there is a very practical side to the idealism of Langland as of so many mystics. To him the symbol and the reality are intimately bound up in a relation that gives the symbol, on the one hand, merely an intermediary validity and, on the other, a scope and significance of wider and more nearly final validity. It must be remembered, too, that he is not a philosopher, but an artist, that he is working, not through definition and analysis, but through the direct and immediate presentment of the data on which he is operating. The result is that the forefront of his work will be held not by the outlines of his analysis but by the fully-drawn figures of his illustrations. That is why his indictment of the world's wrong has so taken the eye of his readers that it is easier to remember the dramatic figures of the Plowman and of Mede than the ideas which they embody. That is why the wrath and the grief of the visionary are usually appreciated more fully than his faith.

There is no mistaking the grim intensity with which Langland beheld the particular forms which the world's immemorial wrong took in his day, nor the grim intensity with which he portrayed them. For instance, he concludes one of the most eloquent descriptions of the miseries of the poor in this wry world by saying that those who take such woe with patience have their penance and their purgatory on this earth, not only a lively comfort to the victims of such misfortune but also an equally lively comment on the intensity of the sufferings portrayed.

Langland had no doubt as to the human agencies responsible for such suffering. The root was the love of personal and material gain which Langland found the prime cause of the world's injustice. It is that which betrays all fealties to the seduction of Mede, or bribery. The terms in which Conscience repudiates the King's offer of Mede as a bride is one of the most vivid indictments on record of the swath which the love of wealth cuts in all human relations. She corrupts women and so marriage and the family; she corrupts the church from the pope down; she corrupts justice from the local officers, the sheriffs, up. She is the fitting bride for that Falsehood who is the father of the world's wrong. "The Worlde is a wykked wynde to hem that wolden treuthe," cried the dreamer to Piers.

As for the specific forms of the world's injustice, the indictment against the rich may be summed up in two words: oppression and waste. Langland's admonition to the friars to refuse gifts made out of the unjust exactions of landlords from their tenants and to bid the would-be pious to make proper restitution points to one of the commoner forms of injustice, involving, in his eyes, not only the perpetrator and the sufferer but the churchman who connives at injustice. In the same spirit, Langland asserts that if priests were perfect, they would not take either payment for religious services or gifts for their support from usurers. The notion of tainted money seems very deep-ingrained in his thought, and responsibility for the acceptance of a gift apparently extends to the way in which the resources for the gift were obtained. An analogous responsibility is enjoined upon mayors to see that when they grant the freedom of a craft to a man he be neither a usurer nor a huckster.

It is eminently characteristic of Langland that his attack upon the problem of the behavior of the church is soon revealed to be only the spearhead of his attack on all the social problems of the day. For instance, some of his sharpest invective is devoted to the cheating of merchants as described at length in the confession of Avarice. In that inclusive confession he does not hesitate to particularize with graphic detail of the devices of the clothmakers for stretching cloth.

For, unlike some of his successors, Langland was aware of small sinners as well as great. He saw the world's exploiters in the greedy nobles and the grasping landlords and the oppressive magistrates, but he saw, also, the small fry, the bandits of the village, as it were, the brewers and the bakers, the butchers and the cooks, who took their toll of the poor who must buy in small quantities, and he asked for them punishment on the appropriate scale, pillories and "pynynge-stoles."

But cheating and oppression are only one side of the injustice of the controlling order of society. The other is waste. Again, waste is not confined to one class. It is revealed in the luxury of the rich, but it is revealed, also, in the idleness of the poor, and the frivolity of the rascal. Worst of all is waste of time, clearly because waste of time is waste of opportunity to win immortal life. It is significant that when the knight offers his service, Piers enthusiastically undertakes to support him in order that he may keep holy church and himself from the wasters and the wicked men that destroy the world. For Piers works for them all, the wasting and the wicked.

The medieval character of Langland's whole approach to the social problem is of course apparent in this diagnosis of the ills of society in terms of the seven deadly sins. But the medieval character is also apparent in the remedy he suggests, essentially a spiritual one. "Love is leche of lyf." To do as the law requires is "dowel," but to love friend and foe is "dobet." Pious works are vain without kindness to one's fellow man. Chastity without charity is like an unlighted lamp. None is so poor or so wretched that he may not love his fellow and give kindness to all sorts of men.

But still more medieval is this inclusion of the poor in the prescription of the remedy for social ill. For Langland the poor are neither a cause nor an object. They have their faults, and he is as unsparing in his indictment of them as of the faults of the rich. He is as severe on the false beggar as on any other rogue. For he defrauds the needy as well as deceives the charitable. And even the large charity of Piers draws the line at a lot of rascals, some of whom, from the modern point of view, would not seem nearly so much of a threat to general society as others, a juggler, a prostitute, a dice-player, a bawd, a vagabond. But they waste the substance of society, contributing nothing but frivolity and corruption—such are the main lines of Langland's attack upon them.

This distinction between the worthy and the unworthy poor concerns more than the problems of relief for which it later became so important. Rather it is essential to something of more profound and intrinsic importance. That is Langland's insistence that the poor man should be worthy of his calling because that calling is so high. Poverty is kin to God himself and so to his saints. Clerks and learned men have God much in their mouths, but the humble have him in their hearts. Once, contemplating the physical sufferings of the poor on this hard earth, Langland prayed that Christ would send to those who had had such lack here in this world, summer and some sort of joy when they left it for another. But in general he thought the poor had better prospects than the rich. Turning to those of the latter group who were wont to invite minstrels to those feasts which they gave to other rich men, he advised them to invite rather the beggars who are God's minstrels, for their prayers would be comfort to them in the hour of their own dying.

Indeed, when it came to the comparative prospects of the rich and the poor, Langland had little doubt. It was not just that he who was an underling now on earth might have a worthier place in heaven, a possibility of which he vigorously reminded the landlord who was tempted to take gifts from the poor which they could not afford and to which he had no right. Rather it is that poverty is spared some of the temptations that afflict the rich. It was much in Langland's thought that the founder of Christianity himself had made some reflections on the savableness of the rich, reflections which Scripture, in a characteristically extreme form, put even more discouragingly. Certainly, as Patience pointed out, pride is not so likely to be found among the poor as the rich, nor is the perilous duty of judgment of other men. The poor man is not so apt to cheat his neighbors, nor is he furnished with the means to commit folly against sobriety, nor to corrupt himself with

dissipation. He is not worried for fear someone will take his possessions; not facing the temptation of treasure, he is more apt to speak the truth. He is a faithful worker who would not take more than is coming to him. Finally the life of a poor man is a blessed thing in itself in its freedom from care. No wonder, as Patience told Activa Vita, the rich dread death more than the poor, for they are in arrears to their maker. But the poor by right claim the joy of heaven from a just judge. So the dreamer hopes that it is for the best that some are rich and some poor. No wonder he concludes that a good plowman can be saved as soon as any. Indeed, in view of what Langland makes of the symbol of Piers it may be concluded that a good plowman will be saved sooner than most.

It should never be forgotten in considering all this social criticism of the clergy that it is the work of an intellectual, and though intellectuals are doubtless as disposed as any other group to defend the interests of their guild in their more aggressive moments, in their moments of discouragement, they are perhaps more alive than most groups to their generic shortcomings. For it is one of the penalties of the strain of the mind that it should lose confidence in its own operations. Probably this aspect of the ecclesiastical criticism of the time should be given more attention than it has hitherto received. Certainly, Langland is running true to form when he points out that no one is sooner taken from the true belief than the clerk. And still more so, when Liberum Arbitrium in a moving description of charity says that it is not to the clerks that the dreamer should go for the desired knowledge of charity but to Piers, for he sees deeper than the words and works out of which the knowledge of clerks is made. It is soon after that conclusion that the revelation is finally made, and it is known that it is Christ who is speaking in the Plowman.

With such a glorification of poverty itself it is hardly surprising that there is no call to revolt in Langland. Patience is what he enjoins upon the suffering. The basis of this prescription is, of course, the belief that one's station and fortune in life are appointed by the will of God:

> Loke thou grucche not on god thaugh he the
>   gheve luytel,
> Beo payed with thi porcion porore or ricchore.

But Langland's conception of patience has a positive side, quite in keeping with his whole respect for poverty, and this is made clear when he declares that "Poure pacient is parfitest lif of alle." And when this brief life is over,

> . . . al pore paciente is may claymen and asken
> After her endynge here hevene-riche blisse.

The responsibility of the church for the social evils of the day is probably the most persistent and the most famous of the themes of *Piers the Plowman.* The sharpness of Langland's arraignment of the friars is one of the sources of the dramatic interest of the work, hardly exceeded even by the colorful pictures of the seven deadly sins which inspire some of the best writing in the whole poem. There is the fuller satiric indictment like the advice of Covetyse-of-eyes to Recchelesnes:

> . . . 'have no conscience how thow come to
>   gode;

> Go confesse the to som frere and shewe hym thi
> synnes.
> For whiles Fortune is thi frende freres will the
> lovye.'

There is the swift thrust, all the more effective for its brevity, of that passage in which Langland says that once Charity was found in a friar's frock, but it was a long time ago in Saint Francis' time. And then there is the repeated and continued indictment of the easy penances of the friars, of their money-seeking, and their neglect of the poor. In all this one hears the voice of a widespread and sustained criticism of the mendicant orders.

But Langland's protest against the behavior of churchmen is not confined to the friars. He finds in the corruption and weakness of the clergy at large one of the great sources of social ill, just as he sees in devotion to the ideals which they preach the great hope of the restoration of the peoples of christendom and the hope of the conversion of the heathen.

Especially did he arraign the less satisfactory bishops of the time when he drew up his specifications for the ideal bishop:

> Bisshopes yblessed if thei ben as thei sholde,'
> Leel and ful of love and no lord dreden,
> Merciable to meek and mylde to the goode,
> And bytynge on badde men bote yf thei wolde
> amende,
> And dredeth nat for no deth to distruye, by here
> powere,
> Lecherie a-mong lordes and hure luther cus-
> tomes,
> And sitthen lyve as thei lereth men oure lord
> treuthe hem graunteth
> To be peeres to a-posteles alle puple to ruele,
> And deme with hem at domes day bothe quike
> and ded.

But it is significant that here as in the indictment of the friars, it is discrimination between the poor and the rich, the powerful and the weak, that is the basic object of the criticism. In the friars that discrimination led to the courting and the coddling of the rich to the neglect of the poor. In the bishops it led to severity to the humble and indulgence to the powerful, even submissiveness in matters in which the church should preserve its spiritual authority. In both the social basis of the criticism of the church is clear. This does not mean that Langland on occasion does not criticize the church of his day on other grounds. For instance, as in the passage above, he is very severe on those clerics who do not do their best to maintain high moral standards in their charges. But in general his criticisms of the church and of churchmen tend to gravitate to a social center.

For Langland, however critical, was a convinced and loyal member of his church, as were probably most of the critics of his day. The instruction of Wit is thoroughly representative of his creator's position:

> Bi counseil of Conscience a-cordynge with holy
> churche,
> Loke thou wisse thi wit and thi werkes aftur.

Or, to approach the problem from another angle, as good a test of orthodoxy as any is the treatment of the monastic ideal, an ideal the social significance of which was so soon to be lost among many of the critics of the church. Langland's attitude is revealed in the very fact that when Piers called the pilgrims to the journey to Truth, "on heihte Actif " began to find excuses like a Biblical wedding guest, but Contemplation immediately embraced the way which Piers held out:

> Quath Contemplaction, 'by Crist thauh ich care
> suffre,
> Famyn and defaute folwen ich wolle Peers.'

When Grace gave to each group of men the power to fulfill their function in the Christian community, the service of the monastic life was fully recognized:

> And some he lered to lyve in longynge to ben
> hennes,
> In poverte and in penaunce to preye for alle
> Crystene.

Above all, it was in the cloister or the school that Clergy found heaven on earth if it was to be anywhere found. In other words what Piers sought was the fulfilment of the religious professions of his day and not their rejection.

Much the same thing is true of his intentions in the sphere of secular life. The ideal society of which he dreams is not organized on a different plan from the one he knows. Rather it is made up of pretty much the existing classes and groups of his day. It is the spirit of the organization that is different. For it is a society in which all classes coöperate, each making its contribution to the whole. The lovely ladies with their long fingers are to make silken chasubles for the clergy, while the wives and widows of lesser rank spin wool and flax for the clothing of the poor and their own satisfaction. This allotment is made by the plowman himself who will sweat and sow for the support of all society. Peace and cooperation for the common good is the pattern, such a state as was in heaven until Lucifer decided that he was wiser and worthier than his master.

But there is in all this no thought of having all things common in the England of his day. That such a doctrine was preached by some of the friars seems clear, for the author represents Envye as sending the friars to school to learn how to preach to men out of Plato and prove their preaching by Seneca: "That alle thinges under hevene oughte to ben in comune." It is clear that Piers' creator regarded such a point of view as at once the fruit and the source of envy. It is clear, too, that Langland was quite aware of something that was to trouble later writers a good deal, the fact that the layman was often misled by an unwise curate.

Now this social-religious position was not something peculiar to Langland. Rather *The Vision of William concerning Piers the Plowman* expresses in a powerful way a central tradition of social criticism, for as Mr. Owst has so brilliantly pointed out, far from being unique, the tone of thought of *Piers the Plowman* is in perfect accord with that of the ordinary orthodox preachers of the period, "indeed a perfect echo in every respect of the Church's message to the world." Far from being an isolated or extraordinary phenomenon, *The Vision concerning Piers the*

Plowman was actually in the main stream of a tradition of moral and social denunciation pouring from the pulpit itself. And this tradition of thoroughly orthodox condemnation continued, with, of course, its tribute to the psychology of another age, through the next century, to find with the invention of printing even wider circulation and influence upon public opinion in still another century. (pp. 1-12)

> Helen C. White, "The Piers Plowman Tradition," in her Social Criticism in Popular Religious Literature of the Sixteenth Century, *The Macmillan Company, 1944, pp. 1-40.*

D. W. Robertson, Jr. and Bernard F. Huppé (essay date 1951)

[*Huppé was a noted American educator and medievalist whose writings include* Piers Ploughman and Scriptural Tradition, *written with D. W. Robertson. In the excerpt below from that study, the critics, focusing on the B-text, reveal how and why* "the basic structure of Piers Plowman *rests on contrasts which express in various ways the Medieval ideal and its corruption." It is through the character of Will and his reactions to these contrasts, the critics maintain, that the poem develops its structural coherence.*]

[To] understand *Piers Plowman* we must be prepared not only to see it in terms of the bitter controversy between the friars and the seculars or in the light of the tradition of Biblical commentary; we must understand its full human import, the permanent symbolic value of the search for Piers Plowman. If the thought of *Piers Plowman* is demonstrably clear, if the poem reveals intellectual integrity, and if it reflects a great tradition of Western civilization, it must reveal something of the human heart for all time.

The poem opens with a preliminary vision of the folk of the world, viewed in the perspective of eternity, wandering in the field of the earthly Church between the ditches of Babylon and the hill of Jerusalem. Pitifully few are approaching the tower on the hill. Implicit in the vision is the question of the Psalmist:

> Lord, who shall abide in thy tabernacle? who
>   shall dwell in thy holy hill?

Also implicit in the vision is the answer to this question, Christ's warning: "Few are chosen." The members of the ecclesiastical hierarchy for the most part seek the transitory satisfactions of the flesh, pretending to offices which they make no effort to fulfil. And the laymen have corrupted their institutions in the interests of self love. The words of Christ, "I am that bread of life," are lost in shouts of "Hot pies!"

In this picture of confusion lies the fundamental problem of the poem. When the fourteenth century poet looked around him he saw only the shadow of what once had been. The ideals that had motivated Innocent III in his attempt to bring the new theology of the sacraments to every remote parish, the feeling for a natural hierarchy under Divine Law that had inspired the Magna Charta, the pen-

etrating intellectual elaboration of the doctrine of charity developed in the thirteenth century universities, the operative piety exemplified by such kings as Alfred and St. Louis—all these were now only empty forms. Men walked in the shadows of the great cathedrals, and on some of them work continued, but the spirit which produced them was gone. Structures like the cathedral at Chartres would grow no more in a soil that had become spiritually sterile. The Prologue to *Piers Plowman* gives us a glimpse of this sterility. The poem itself analyzes its causes and describes in detail the ideals which must be reactivated if the Christian world is ever to go again on the greatest of all crusades, the pilgrimage to the heavenly Jerusalem.

To understand the poem in its relevance to ourselves, we must attempt to recapture some of the old enthusiasm for this goal. In many respects, the elaboration of Biblical teaching developed in the thirteenth century schools was history's most significant intellectual achievement. It was the result of centuries of continuous philosophical tradition supported by cumulative pastoral experience. Both the speculative tradition of the schools and the empirical tradition of the parishes were maintained by a single institution so that one could interact freely with and control the other. Philosophers might differ in detail, but in general they agreed on a hierarchy of values the elements of which could be grasped by even the most ignorant and at the same time could win the profound respect of the most cultivated. Medieval thinkers realized to the full that without some concept of value it is impossible to lend the events of everyday existence significance beyond animal satisfaction. To the poet it was of the utmost importance that the system of values which he found symbolized in Jerusalem be maintained, lest the vision fade away entirely from the sight of men. The fears of the poet were justified. What the poet was witnessing and attempting to counteract was the beginning of the great intellectual chaos which produced the Waste Land, a country which has become so much more terrifying than the poet's Field of Folk that the modern reader is apt to overlook as insignificant some of the poem's bitterest portrayals of evil. *Piers Plowman* is the epic of the dying Middle Ages.

The basic structure of *Piers Plowman* rests on contrasts which express in various ways the Medieval ideal and its corruption. The clarity of these contrasts is largely dependent upon an understanding of the application of the traditional levels of meaning. Each level has a symbolic context appropriate to it. The allegorical level, for example, is concerned with the church, and the basic classification of persons in the poem under Dowel, Dobet, and Dobest rests on the traditional division of persons in the church as active, contemplative, and prelatical. More exactly, Dowel, Dobet, and Dobest represent the ideals which persons in these states should follow. Actual persons either exemplify these ideals or their corruption. . . . One of the principal objects of the poem is to give the various states' inner content. For this reason, the tropological level, which indicates the inner moral qualities of individuals and their moral duties is of especial importance. A general scheme of the tropological level may be represented in terms of the three parts of the image of God in man; the memory, the intellect, and the will. Any individual in any of the three allegorical states ideally preserves the image in terms of faith, hope, and charity. . . . Although each status has as its end charity, the tropological duties of the members of the various external statuses vary. To illustrate the special duties of each status, the poet uses several symbols. For example, the relationship of the various statuses to the world is indicated progressively by the terms *conjugatos, viduatos, virgines.* Again, the person in the active status must learn, the contemplative must teach, and the prelate must practice the highest form of charity in self-sacrifice for his flock: *disce, doce, diligere.* The members of all three states must direct themselves toward charity. Anima explains charity in terms of three levels which suggest its functions in the three states (xv, 171-78). When it consists simply in desiring and receiving spiritual food, it symbolizes Dowel. When it includes this and acts of devotion accompanied by the function of teaching, it is Dobet. Finally, when it includes both of these and the apostolic act of washing away sin, it symbolizes Dobest. When they practice charity, the three states are related to the world in terms of ascending degrees of self denial; they are related to society in terms of ascending degrees of service. . . . (pp. 234-38)

Charity is the basis for perfection in any state, but charity was brought to man by Dobest in its highest form, Christ. Only through teaching of charity in the apostolic succession can it be continued on earth, so that the existence of Dowel and Dobet is dependent on the function of Dobest. Thus the person in the active state who wishes to attain the ideal of Dowel must be aided by Dobest. This fact is illustrated in Conscience's instruction of Hawkin, the active man who asks how he may cleanse his soiled robes of innocence. The cleansing may be accomplished through penance in all of its three parts: *contritio, confessio, satisfactio.* But each of the three parts may be considered a function of Dobest. Contrition, the waking of the mind from oblivion in faith, is encouraged by the priest through preaching and example. The searching of the conscience in oral confession, the casting out of ignorance in hope, is the function of the priest as teacher. Finally, the setting of penance and the granting of absolution, the direction of the will away from cupidity toward charity, is a function of the priest exercising his apostolic powers. In Christ all three states find their highest example. Dobest, in the imitation of Christ the Redeemer, teaches the imitation of Christ in the other two states.

When the mind is governed by cupidity rather than by charity, there is a progression of evil beginning with the sin against the Father in oblivion, continuing with the sin against the Son in ignorance, and culminating with the sin against the Holy Spirit and the triumph of cupidity over the will. These conditions may be considered as opposites of the ideals represented by Dowel, Dobet, and Dobest. They reveal increasing degrees of desire for worldly satisfaction and with relation to society increasing degrees of disservice to mankind. . . . (pp. 238-39)

On the anagogical level are revealed the ultimate sources of good and its corruption. The forces of good are symbolized by Holy Church, the bride of Jerusalem; those of evil are symbolized by Lady Meed, the Whore of Baby-

lon. . . . These levels form the ultimate frame of reference around which the others are constructed. For example, on the tropological level, the memory, the intellect, and the will are governed either by the Father, the Son, and the Holy Spirit respectively, or by the world, the Flesh, and the Devil. The tropological corruption of these levels produces the opposites of Dowel, Dobet, and Dobest. Dowel is characterized by obedience to the Father, Dobet by the removal of the sin against the Son, and Dobest by the maintenance of the Holy Spirit or charity.

The various spiritual levels are exemplified externally and particularly on the historical level with characters from the Bible and the modern Church. . . . The basic contrast lies between the true priesthood of God and the ministry of Antichrist. The patriarchs and prophets could not find salvation in the Old Law; only through the New Law of charity were they able to leave Hell. Similarly, Dowel and Dobet cannot be saved without Piers, who bears the tradition of the Redemption. The tragedy of the poem is that the human will seeking salvation cannot find Piers in the Church. The place of Piers has been usurped by the Friars under the guidance of Antichrist.

It is through the character Will that we see these contrasts operating on various levels. Will is many-sided because he has the flexibility of the faculty he represents which moves between the opposites of willfulness and charity. Because the poet has been successful as a poet, he has created in Will so appealingly human a character that through interest in him many have lost sight of the fact that Will is merely a device by means of which the poet may set off the actual against the ideal in the poem and so develop his major theme. For this purpose Will is portrayed at the beginning as one among the wolves in sheep's clothing. His clothes reflect the manner in which he has been misled. They improve as Will, serving as a hypothetical example, is brought nearer his ideal goal. The persons who mislead him typify the misleading forces of the actual world. But the forces which bring about his ultimate rise to a state of grace are not actual forces in the earthly Church; they are the forces which should operate there. Similarly, the pattern of Will's salvation is a pattern of what should be, not of what is. Thus Will is instructed first not by an actual priest but by the anagogical church itself who reveals her own nature to him and the nature and operation of her opposite, the Whore of Babylon. Actually, a successor to Piers Plowman should be the one who explains to the human will the ideal which the heavenly Jerusalem represents and the origin of its corruption on earth; the fact that Holy Church herself instructs Will is a negative intimation of the theme that Piers Plowman is absent from the church militant. Will's Vision of the struggle against Lady Meed carried on by the King who calls Reason and Conscience to his aid is only a vision of the possible, a suggestion as to the means by which the earthly community may be made to resemble its eternal counterpart. Will himself does not take part in the vision, and it is obvious that it is not a picture of anything the poet could see around him or reasonably predict in the near future. As a result of Reason's teaching, Repentance moves the will of the folk to weep, and they confess in a manner which prepares them for the guidance of Piers Plowman. The vision of the

Half Acre is an ideal vision of God's ministry, demonstrating the lesson of good works in the earthly church. Even in the episode of the Half Acre, which is an ideal vision, the salvation of the folk of the field is not shown to be assured. Indeed it becomes clear that confession without satisfaction through good works is unavailing. Though the commons assent to the rule of Reason through their confessions, they must implement their faith and hope through the works of charity. But humans are lazy and are repelled by the need to work; in the face of work many of those who had confessed prefer to sing "Trolli-lolli" in a ditch. Piers attempts to bring them back through spiritual hunger and the threat of eternal punishment, but these threats have only temporary effectiveness. Finally, salvation through pardon is suggested, but the pardon of Piers Plowman is an affirmation that faith, hope, and the labors of charity in the field are necessary, that the way of Piers is the right way. Positively, the pardon shows that only through the fulfilment of the obligation to the redemption is salvation possible. But the position of the earthly church is made apparent at once in the person of the Priest who neither recognizes nor understands his pardon. It is significant that in spite of Will's vision, his position at the end of it is exactly that of the Priest. The human will, although it naturally desires the good, unguided by Piers is incapable of understanding the basic contrast between Jerusalem and Babylon or the means by which the earthly church may be made to resemble its heavenly counterpart.

In the *Vitae,* which are concerned with the way Will may find the truth of Piers Plowman, there is a similar series of contrasts between the actual and the ideal. There is no steady progression toward salvation. Those episodes which are concerned with the exposition of the ideal move to the point at which it becomes clear that what is needed in the church militant is Piers Plowman. Thereupon the poet develops the unhappy conclusion that Piers is not present in the earthly church and the ideal is succeeded by a picture of the corrupt actuality. Although Will has seen Piers in the *Visio,* he does not in Dowel begin his search with instruction by a true priest. Instead he meets two friars. As a result of their ministrations, Will's thought is confused and misled so that he cannot properly act upon the possibilities of both good and evil presented by Wit, the speculative intellect. Although Will still desires the good, he proceeds to corrupt the teaching of the intellect, learns nothing through Study and Clergy, finally corrupts Scripture through his own willfulness, and falls into the sleep of the Land of Longing. Will's progressive descent from being simply misled by the friars to his abandonment of the true good typifies what the human will actually faces in the Church militant. Through God's providence he sees the evils of the friars who have comforted him in his evil life. Through his knowledge of evil he finds loyalty to the true church. With Loyalty, Scripture's teachings become effective and Will is able to profit by the vision of Nature and the teaching of Imagination. But Piers must direct the human will in its study of Scripture and in the understanding of the truth which makes conscience operative, so that the poet is here again concerned with the ideal pattern of the development of the human will. When Conscience comes to guide Will, he must, of course, guide him within the church. Again the poem turns to the actual church from the vision of the ideal to discover that the place of Piers has been usurped by the Master Friar. The result of this usurpation is shown to Will in the figure of Hawkin the active man. Hawkin cannot perform true penance without Piers. Although Conscience teaches him what true penance should be, he makes it clear that true penance without Piers Plowman is impossible. The *Vita de Dowel* ends on the same desperate note as does the *Visio.* Unless the prelatical status reflects Dobest, unless Piers Plowman is in the church, those in the active status face inevitable and tragic doom.

In the *Vita de Dobet* Will does find Piers Plowman, but he does not find him on earth. He learns through Anima what is wrong with the Church militant. When he asks her where he may find Piers, he is told that Piers guards the Tree of Charity. In other words, he may be seen only in a spiritual vision. Will's vision again pictures the ideal. In this episode, the high point in the poem, Will is shown in one supreme figure the ideals of Dowel, Dobet, and Dobest combined. Moreover, Will learns his relation in the image of God to the other faculties of the human mind. He learns that together the three faculties must live in charity. But when he hears the Easter bells tolling, he understands that he must worship God in the Church. Again the poem reaches the place at which it is necessary to look for Piers Plowman in the Church militant: the life of prayer and contemplation also needs Piers Plowman. But in the *Vita de Dobest* it is made perfectly clear that the force which is alone able to bring salvation is absent from the Church militant. Piers has been supplanted by a host of friars under the leadership of Antichrist. The only hope left for the human will is the collective force of the Christian Conscience insisting that in its priests the image of Piers be found. We remember that the evil of the friars had this much of good; it succeeded in awakening Will to Loyalty. The purpose of the poet was not simply to expose the evil of the friars; it was to arouse his readers to a realization of the immediacy of their danger in the hope that they would be stirred to action so that Piers might again walk on earth.

In the figure of Will we have seen one of the chief means by which the poet achieves coherence in *Piers Plowman.* In what Will does and in his reactions are developed the progressive contrasts which contribute materially to the structural integrity of the poem. In the *Visio* these contrasts are based on the most general of possible symbols for good and evil. In the *Vitae* they become particularized and progress in scope and significance until we reach the poet's crowning picture of the Redemption and his description of the historically progressive corruption of the church militant culminating in the vision of the perils in those late days which came through the friars. As the movement of the poem develops naturally from the needs of the human will represented by the dreamer, the structure of the poem may be shown to develop naturally out of the needs of the folk in the field as pictured in the Prologue. The Prologue contains, in fact, all of the major themes of the poem. It sets at once the basic contrast between true and false prelates, and suggests the discrepancy between the ideals of the three states and their actual counterparts. The Babylonian confusion of the Kingdom ruled by self-love implies by contrast the vision of Peace which appears immediately in Passus I in the figure of Holy Church descending from the mountain. It is this same Babylonian kingdom with which is contrasted the Kingdom governed by Reason and Conscience. The members of the Prologue's realm are those who mislead Will in the *Vitae*, and in the closing episode of the poem the poet explains in detail the source of the Babylonian confusion. Meanwhile, the positive ideas developed as ideals or as ideal patterns of conduct stem from the theme of Holy Church's sermon: *Deus caritas*.

There are certain images set in the Prologue, those of food and clothing for example, that are used to give coherence to the poem. The clothing of the plowmen is contrasted with that of the followers of pride as Holy Church's clothing is contrasted with that of Lady Meed. Will's clothing has progressive symbolic value, notably in the change from his early clothing to the "dear robes" of Passus XIX. The clothing of Hawkin is of central importance in Dowel. The clothing image is reflected in the armor of Piers in which Christ fights. Holy Church uses Lot's drunkenness in illustration of the misuse of temporal goods. Piers employes Hunger to frighten the wasters who seek to forget their spiritual hunger in the pleasures of the flesh. The feast placed before Patience and Will is sharply contrasted with the dainty worldly fare of the Master Friar, who must drink before he preaches. In the final passus Will is concerned with the problem of sustenance in the world. There are many other such images repeated and elaborated in Passus XIX. The Plant of Peace introduced by Holy Church becomes central in Anima's instruction of Will. The image of the tower set in the Prologue is reflected in Holy Church's sermon, in the instructions of Piers to the pilgrims, in Wit's discussion of the castle of Caro, and finally in the Barn of Christendom. These images and others are used so consistently and repeatedly that it is impossible to do more than supply a few illustrations here. Indeed, we may make the generalization that the structure of the poem is based largely on the repetition and contrast of symbols which are progressively elaborated and developed.

The development by symbolic repetition may sometimes be obscured by the fact that the connection between symbols is often made through an understood Scriptural nexus. Thus Piers' half-acre is closely related to the Barn of Christendom through the parable of the gathering of the harvest (Matt. 13, 24ff.). The tower of Truth, which is the end of man's search, is related to the Castle of Caro through the implied Biblical idea of man made in the image of God. The imagery when taken with the symbolic values it acquires from Biblical contexts serves as a means of poetic condensation in the maintenance of the major themes of the poem. Similarly, the Scriptural quotations when taken on the level of the *sentence* as developed in traditional exegesis furnish a key to wider vistas of meaning which relate the parts of the poem in much the same way that the parts of the Bible were related by the commentators. It would not be surprising if a reader ignorant of the fact that Piers Plowman represents the central tradition of Christ's ministry might be led to suppose that there was a lack of connection between the parts of the poem, each

of which is united to the other in an increasing emphasis on the tragic absence of the traditional figure from the Church. If the identification of Holy Church with the heavenly Jerusalem and of Lady Meed with the Whore of Babylon is not kept steadily before the mind's eye, it is possible to fail to see the relationship between the sermon of Holy Church and what follows. Altogether, when the poem is read on the level of the *sentence*, the development of its themes becomes clear and it is seen to progress logically and coherently to its conclusion.

Like any great work of art **Piers Plowman** has a quality which defies critical analysis. It is possible to repeat the testimony of others who have felt the varied powers of the poet from the ecstatic verse with which he describes the Redemption to the realistically powerful picture of Glutton in the tavern. It would be possible to add further testimonial to the way in which in individual passages we have been moved to wonder and delight, to the quietness of spirit which is the particular effect of the greatest poetry. But that has not been the service which we have hoped to render in this [discussion]. We have wished first to show that the charge that the poem as a whole is chaotic and formless is false. Then we have wished to show the greatness of the ideal presented in **Piers Plowman** and to demonstrate passage by passage the intellectual grandeur and clarity with which the great ideal is developed. It is true that the architecture of the poem is not so obvious to the modern reader as that of the *Divine Comedy*, but when the principles governing that architecture are known, it becomes clear that the English poem is no less perfect structurally than the Italian. Many of the most startling poetic effects of the poem are achieved through its deliberate Scriptural connotations. The picture of Holy Church descending from the mountain is striking in itself, but its Scriptural connotations make the picture more than merely striking, suggesting as they do the Transfiguration in the Gospel, the Bride of Christ in the Apocalypse, and Sion and Jerusalem throughout the Scriptures. If the *Divine Comedy* is an expression of the ideals of the thirteenth century, **Piers Plowman** is a projection of those ideals against the actuality of fourteenth century life. The English poem is representative of its turbulent and critical age and place, but it is also an expression of some of man's most cherished ideals. Society is still being misled by false leaders. Modern man, like Will, is still searching for leadership which will embody traditional belief with human compassion, which can reformulate and activate the principles of charity and bring the world a little nearer the Vision of Peace. In short, the heirs to the tradition of medieval England may add to the annals of their literature a work of epic scope with only one peer in any other medieval vernacular. (pp. 239-48)

> *D. W. Robertson, Jr. and Bernard F. Huppé,*
> *"Some Conclusions," in their* Piers Plowman
> and Scriptural Tradition, *Princeton University*
> *Press, 1951, pp. 234-48.*

E. M. W. Tillyard   (essay date 1954)

[*Tillyard was an English scholar of Renaissance literature and the author of widely respected studies of John*

Milton, William Shakespeare, and the epic genre. In the following excerpt, he examines Piers Plowman *as an epic poem, considering its ability to speak for all ranks of society, and discussing its chief religious themes "of salvation and of the earthly pilgrimage."*]

There is one epic quality which no one would deny Langland: that of speaking for a great body of people. It may well be that he was not personally a sociable man; but that did not prevent him speaking with the voice that thousands recognised as *their* voice. He may have been very much more pious than most of his readers; but that piety of which he may have had more was *their* piety. He had the keenest eye for the things around him; but the things he saw were what his fellows saw, however much more clearly he focussed them. Apparently he did not become a part of literature till after his death; he wrote not for a literary circle but for the people at large. And though he knew the customs that prevailed in sermon-writing, he did not share the polite notions of poetry-writing as an exercise of rhetoric. He wrote consciously to teach, unconsciously to ease his mind of its burden. The result was that the people at large read him widely, the polite writers of the age ignored him, and later ages grouped him with Chaucer, Gower, and Lydgate as the earliest English Classics. The fate of his poem was thus much like that of Bunyan's *Pilgrim's Progress* except that it was luckier in being born in an England unsevered by a great religious feud. But Langland, though as English as a man could be, speaks also for his age. His poem illustrates to perfection the violences and the extremes of sentiment which [Johan] Huizinga in his *Waning of the Middle Ages* [1927] has so convincingly demonstrated as typical of all western Europe. Or take a single point. There is a famous passage where Imaginative argues with the dreamer about the vanity of his spending his time verse-making when he could be saying his psalter:

> And thow medlest the with makynges and
>   myghtest go sey thi sauter
> And bidde for hem that yiveth the bred, for there
>   are bokes ynowe
> To tell men what dowel is, dobet and dobest
>   bothe,
> And prechoures to preve what it is.

['And meddle with writing poetry while you might say your psalter and pray for those who give you bread. For there are books enough telling men what Do-wel is, and Do-bet and Do-best too, and preachers to prove it.']

And Langland replies with the well-known plea that occasional recreation may fit a man for more serious things. Such a debate between the call of poetry and the call of religion is central to the whole age. Langland talking to Imaginative is like Petrarch talking to Augustine in his *Secretum.*

It is easy to pass from Langland's success in speaking for many men to the variety of his substance. And here again I believe him to fulfil any possible epic requirement. In some ways he is more varied, or presents sharper contrasts, than Chaucer himself. **Piers Plowman,** however much of England he puts into it, is in substance a religious poem. The books behind it are the Vulgate, some of the

Fathers, the proverbs of Cato, all the common property of western Europe. The allegory, the different layers of meaning, belong no more to London than to Paris, Warsaw, Bologna, or Fulda. But this common European material is put into the purely English alliterative metre which, going right behind the Norman Conquest, managed to survive in the west and north of the country. It is a vivid, a spicy contrast; and its successful creation resembles another masterly thing in literature, Henryson's successful bending and suppling of the strong obstinate northern dialect to the dulcet requirements of Cressid's lament in the *Testament of Cressid.* Not that we must think of the alliterative metre as something mean or unaristocratic. On the contrary, as R. W. Chambers [in his *Man's Unconquerable Mind,* 1939] points out, this metre was the vehicle of poems that delighted the gentry of England in the west and in the north. Its character is regional, not proletarian. The mention of the west, or rather West Midlands, of which Langland was native, suggests another contrast betokening variety. Though born in the district of Malvern and writing in the local alliterative metre, he spent most of his life in London and many of his descriptions are of the London scene. Chaucer wrote in the speech and prosody of the East Midlands and describes mainly what he found there; and though he may have been more European than Langland, he does not unite as Langland does the two great regions of the Severn and the Thames watersheds, regions which in the fourteenth century were more separated and individual than we now find easy to imagine.

It is not only regions of England that Langland brings together, but all ranks of society. It was what Chaucer did in the Prologue to the *Canterbury Tales,* but Langland includes more of the wreckage of society and he is didactic where Chaucer is, or at least appears, descriptive only. Langland does not hesitate to speak plainly about kings, as in the fable of the cat and the rats, and in his picture of the king seeking to wed Meed and Conscience. And he gives the sense of life in the highest places in two passages to which I have already referred: the attempted wedding of Meed to False and the sermon preached by Reason before the king, with Conscience holding his crosier. Lower in the social scale, but like Chaucer's monk within the gentry, is Religion pictured as a worldly cleric:

> Ac now is Religioun a ryder, a rowmer bi stretes,
> A leder of lovedayes and a londe-bygger,
> A priker on a palfrey from manere to manere,
> An heep of houndes at his ers as he a lorde were.
> And but if his knave knele that shall his cuppe
>   brynge,
> He loureth on hym and axeth hym: who taughte
>   hym curteisye?

['But now Religion is mounted and frequents the highroads; he takes the chair at arbitration-courts and buys land; he spurs from manor to manor on his palfrey, with a pack of hounds at his arse as if he were a lord. And if the servant who brings his drink fails to kneel to him, he glowers at him and asks: who taught him manners?']

There is abundance of low life. The most ebullient description, in the classic manner of the Low Countries, is that of Glutton's performance at the tavern and, afterwards, in the setting of the Seven Deadly Sins. His description of downright poverty has no fellow in English poetry, Blake's *London* in *Songs of Experience* coming nearest to it in spirit but lacking the detail. He speaks of the women in the cottages squeezed almost dry of money by paying the rent, scarcely able to provide pap enough to still the cries of their children, having to rise at night in winter to rock the cradle and to work,

> That reuthe is to rede othere in ryme shewe
> The wo of these women that wonyeth in cotes,
> And of meny other men that muche wo suffren
> Bothe a-fyngrede and a-furst, to turne the fayre
>   outwarde
> And beth abasshed for to begge.

['So that it is piteous either to read about, or to express in verse, the misery of these women who live in cottages, and that of many other folk who suffer much misery, both from hunger and thirst, so as to present a decent appearance and are too modest to beg.']

But most characteristic of all the passages in Langland about the different classes of society are those that treat them together. Langland was of gentle birth on his father's side and he was brought up in a part of the country which still maintained its antique feudal character. He was anything but a leveller and believed in a strictly hierarchical society, but he held the accompanying belief that ennobled the hierarchical theory: that no grade in the hierarchy, however lowly, was less necessary than any other to make up the whole. The great jig-saw puzzle of life was incomplete if the humblest piece was lacking. These passages are so important in illustrating not only Langland's range but his creed that I must mention several. In Reason's long discourse on Charity in B xv all sorts of men are included, while in these lines kings, clerics, knights, and poor men are deliberately approximated:

> Edmonde and Edwarde eyther were kinges
> And seyntes ysette fro Charite hem folwed.
> I have seyne Charity also singen and reden,
> Ryden, and rennen in ragged wedes.

['Edmund and Edward were both kings, and held saints, for Charity followed. I have also seen Charity sing and read, ride, and run in ragged clothing.']

In the first section of the poem Reason's speech to the whole people has a tremendous effect. The Seven Sins confess and are taken in hand by Repentance. In fact, we have a picture of a vast medieval revivalist meeting. The multitude on the wave of their enthusiasm set out on a pilgrimage to Truth. Only Piers Plowman can show them the way and he says he has first to 'plough his half-acre by the highway': in other words, there are first of all urgent practical reforms that must be put through. At this point a gentlewoman wearing a wimple asks what the women are to do meanwhile. Piers answers that some must sew sacks to contain the wheat, and, turning to the gentlewoman,

> And ye, lovely ladyes with youre longe fyngres,

> That ye han silke and sendal to sowe, whan tyme
>   is,
> Chesibles for chapelleynes cherches to honoure.

['And you, lovely ladies with your long fingers, see that you have silk and sendal to sew, as the time offers, chasubles for chaplains for the honouring of churches.']

And he tells the middle-class wives and widows to spin wool and flax and help clothe the naked. All classes of women must be active in plying their needles, but the materials they sew must suit their social degree. To illustrate the different degrees in Paradise Langland takes the act of dining in the hall of a gentleman's house.

> Right as sum man yeve me mete and sette me
>   amydde the flore,
> Ich have mete more than ynough ac nought so
>   moche worship
> As tho that seten atte syde table or with the sov-
>   ereignes of the halle,
> But sitte as a begger bordelees by myself on the
>   grounde.

['As if someone gave me food and seated me on the floor: I have more than enough food but not so much honour as those that sit at a side-table or as the principal guests in the hall; I sit as a beggar without a seat, apart, on the ground.']

Here, though the beggar has the lowliest place, he is part of the community of the hall and he has all the food he can eat. More explicit still is the attack on lords and ladies who do not eat in hall but in private.

> Elyng is the halle uche daye in the wyke
> There the lorde ne the lady liketh noughte to
>   sytte.
> Now hath uche riche a reule to eten by hymselve
> In a pryve parloure for pore mennes sake
> Or in a chambre with a chymneye and leve the
>   chief halle,
> That was made for meles men to eten inne;
> And all to spare to spille that spende shal anoth-
>   er.

['Unhappy is the hall, every day in the week if it happens, where neither lord nor lady pleases to sit. Now every rich man makes it a rule to eat alone in a private parlour, on account of the poor men (whom they wish to avoid), or in a room with a chimney, and forsake the great hall, which was made for men to eat their meals in; and all to avoid spending what another shall spend in his turn.']

The great hall is at once the preserver of rank and the means of uniting all classes of society; and the lord who eats apart breaks the social bond.

But if Langland showed great variety in picturing human society, this was not his main theme. His true reach is apparent only when we see this society in another and wider setting. Langland's pictures of the life around him and his hierarchical but organic conception of society are subordinated to larger religious motives. The religious theme of his poem is personal salvation, and the religious complexion is that of the unmitigated Christian doctrine of self-sacrifice and love as found in the Gospels and in the life of St Francis. Although Langland mentions and quotes St Paul and the four great Fathers and is perfectly orthodox dogmatically, and though he seeks God in the mirror of nature in the correct manner, it is the imitation of Christ that counts for most, and the law of Charity is greater than any formulated rule. Charity was found supremely in Christ,

> And in a freres frokke he was yfounde ones,
> Ac it is ferre agoo in Seynt Fraunceys tyme.

> ['And Charity was found once in a friar's habit,
> but that was long ago in St Francis time.']

The law of Charity is also powerfully vindicated in one of the most original passages in **Piers Plowman:** the consideration of the righteous heathen and their possible salvation. This consideration comes at the end of Passus x and in Passus xi and xii in the B-text, and it represents both a struggle in Langland's mind and a shift of position. Admitting that the doctors of the Church have consigned Aristotle to Hell, for all his wisdom and uprightness, while the dying thief and Mary Magdalen for all their unholy lives were saved, he passionately embraces the saying of Augustine that simpletons storm the sky, while we wise men are sunk in Hell, thus side-tracking the heathendom of Aristotle and accepting his damnation as belonging to the case, common to baptised and unbaptised alike, of mere learning without simple faith being insufficient for salvation. But Aristotle could not, for Langland, be permanently settled thus; and in the sequel the matter of the virtuous pagans comes up again. First, Trajan interposes, the virtuous pagan who was undoubtedly saved at the instance of Pope Gregory. Yet Langland will not have it that it was the Pope's prayers that brought salvation; Trajan's own love and loyalty were the cause. Finally, at the end of Passus xii Langland goes further (through the mouth of Imaginative) and seeks to extend Trajan's salvation to an indefinite number of virtuous heathen. To his earlier acceptance of Aristotle's damnation, now repented of, he retorts that we do not *know* whether he was saved or not: Scripture tells us nothing. But he hopes that God is good enough to save Aristotle and the other good heathen who have taught us so much. And he finds hope in there being two other ways of baptism than by water: namely by blood and by fire. And these, he would have us think, may extend to places beyond the reach of orthodox formulations. The whole discussion shows Langland right beyond the common thought of his day, and in so doing adds yet another element to his variety.

But most plainly of all the rule of Charity is shown in the culminating episodes of **Piers Plowman.** Passus xvi had described Faith through the person of Abraham. Passus xvii goes on to Hope in the person of Moses. But Charity is figured not by any Old Testament figure but by the Good Samaritan, who turns out to be Christ himself on his way to Jerusalem to put his charity to the supreme test on the cross and to its supreme fulfilment towards mankind in haling out Adam and Eve, the cause of his own passion, from Hell.

These culminating episodes, however important and solemn in content and pre-eminent poetically, are yet subordinated to the main theme of salvation through a pilgrim-

age. But before entering on that theme, I must point out that these episodes, together with a part of the next Passus (xix) do make up a heroic poem, a *Christiad.* (Earlier in this book I said that the shift of emphasis from one world to more than one had made heroic poetry impossible as the most serious type. I omitted to say that the one possible heroic poem in which a writer could feel full confidence was a *Christiad.* Langland by including his *Christiad* in his larger allegory gave his poem a weight that contributes to the epic effect.) One of Langland's habitual pieces of technique is to sow the seeds of a new motive well in advance; and he uses it in his treatment of Jesus. In Passus xvi, arising out of a reference to Adam and the forbidden fruit and the Devil's success in making his hoard of men in Hell, comes a short account of the life of Jesus ending with Good Friday, when for mankind's sake he 'jousted in Jerusalem' and on the cross won the battle against death and the Devil. The notion of Christ as the jousting Knight, striking though as old as the old English *Dream of the Rood,* anticipates a later episode. Then Langland drops this theme, to interpose other matter, before returning to it. He manipulates his return as follows. His ruling theme in this part of the poem has been different trinities, and he chooses another entry into the life of Christ, through the Pauline trinity of Faith, Hope, and Charity. After Faith and Hope have been described, a man on a mule, a Samaritan, on the way from Jericho to a tournament in Jerusalem, overtakes them. The Samaritan is Charity and as such has nothing to do with the heroic world of the tournament; but the seed has been sown in these two passages for the transformation of the Samaritan, who is Charity, into Jesus, who in Piers's armour, or the human body, will win his heroic victory. And the Passion is described in terms of a fight. When darkness descended and there was an earthquake, dead bodies rose and one said that Life and Death were in this darkness in a struggle, and that mankind will not know the issue till daybreak on Sunday. Thereafter Christ is the heroic conqueror. The gates of Hell cannot resist him; and, when, after the harrowing of Hell, the dreamer awakes and sleeps again, his first vision is of Christ in his armour, blood-smeared but the conqueror. And Conscience explains that Jesus, Knight and King, is now Christ, the Conqueror, the invading monarch who can free men held captive. So much for the incidental *Christiad.*

I come now to Langland's main theme, that of salvation and of the earthly pilgrimage, and I cannot maintain that it is strikingly obvious. On the contrary, we tend to forget it (if we have ever noticed it) for long stretches. Langland knew the plain motive of the pilgrim's progress well enough, for Piers Plowman himself at his first appearance sketches it out for the benefit of the great multitude, fresh from the exhortations of Reason and Repentance and anxious to set forth on their pilgrimage. But immediately after, Piers cut short this general pilgrimage with the assertion that he cannot act as guide till he has ploughed his half-acre; and it is never resumed. Langland, indeed, does not care for simple, sustained allegory. He prefers to push an allegory to a certain length, to achieve some kind of approximation and then suddenly to drop it and to substitute something which, though different, may yet end in working in the same direction. Thus though the multitude with their desire to find Truth through a pilgrimage fade away, their place is soon taken by the dreamer who 'roamed about all a summer season to seek Do-wel'. This kaleidoscopic use of allegory has something to do with the cast of Langland's mind. Jusserand perceived it when he used the metaphor of clouds [in his *L'Épopée Mystique de William Langland,* 1893], although he went wrong in implying through it a confusion of mind of which Langland was not in fact guilty:

> Par moments les nuages, les brouillards, les abstractions remplissent la scène; on est aveuglé, on étouffe; et tout à coup la nuée se déchire, le vent l'emporte, et nous voyons, nets comme si nous y étions, une rue de Londres au XIVe siècle.

Jusserand, who in this passage does admirable justice to Langland's realism, should have distanced his clouds and seen them not from within but as a pageant in the sky. That pageant presents definite shapes, but these keep moving and one melts into another. Though Langland had at times the keenest eye for things presented simply to the senses and could give them the solidest embodiment, at others he felt only their insubstantiality and that only the divine was firm. It is because of this sense of insubstantiality that it suits him to keep his allegory perpetually on the move, or to make Piers appear and disappear so suddenly.

But though there is no one overriding allegorical pilgrimage, the motive exists in three main forms as well as in details like Piers Plowman's sketch of the pilgrim's way, just referred to. There is the quest of the dreamer for salvation, there is the progress from Do-wel through Do-bet to Do-best, and there is the progress of Christ to the status of victorious king. By their combined force these themes do indeed make the pilgrimage the dominant concern of the poem. In his characteristic manner Langland inserts the notion of the dreamer's pilgrimage in an alien context and long before he develops it. When early in the poem he meets Holy Church the dreamer beseeches her to tell him how he may save his soul. After that he pursues his search for the means of salvation, questioning this and that allegorical figure with imperfect satisfaction. By the middle of the poem he is still in doubt. In Passus xi he questions not only the salvation of the virtuous heathen but his own:

> And in a were gan I wex and with myself to dispute
> Whether I were chosen or nought chosen.

> ['And I began to grow in doubt and to question myself whether I were chosen or not chosen.']

It may be perilous to seek an end to the dreamer's pilgrimage. Langland may well have dropped it before completion and passed on to the other two themes of progress. But he may have meant us to take great note of the passage in Passus xvii where the dreamer runs after the Good Samaritan (who has completed his deed of mercy and is riding to Jerusalem in company of Faith and Hope) and offers to serve him. The Good Samaritan accepts his offer and says he will prove a friend to him in need. And his certainty of salvation is proclaimed in the most wonderful and violent turn of the whole poem: his awakening from his vision of the Four Daughters of God dancing to celebrate

the harrowing of Hell, and calling to his family to kiss the cross:

> Tyl the daye dawed this damaiseles daunced
> That men rongen to the resurrexioun; and right with that I waked,
> And called Kit my wife and Kalote my daughter:
> 'Ariseth and reverenceth goddes resurrexioun,
> And crepeth to the crosse on knees and kisseth it for a juwel.
> For goddes blissed body it bar for owre bot,
> And it afereth the fende, for such is the myghte
> May no grysly gost glyde there it shadweth.'

> ['Till the day dawned these damsels danced, when men rang to celebrate the Resurrection; and straitway with that I waked, and called Kit my wife and Calote my daughter. "Get up and do reverence to God's resurrection and creep to the cross and kiss it as a precious thing. For it carried God's blessed body for our salvation, and it scares the Devil; for so strong is it that no frightful phantom may glide where it casts its shadow." ']

But though these words may ratify the dreamer's salvation, his own case, after he has been accepted as the Good Samaritan's servant, is in a way merged into the case of Christ's other servants. His, like theirs, depends on the issue of the 'jousting in Jerusalem'. And this brings us to another of the three main pilgrimages: that of Jesus from an embodiment of Charity to the Conqueror. Of it I have said enough earlier in this chapter, except of the reason why Langland chose to make the harrowing of Hell the central event of Christ's career and the climax of the whole poem. Deriving from the apocryphal Gospel of Nicodemus, the story of Christ's irruption into Hell between his burial and resurrection to hale out Adam and Eve from the Devil's clutches should never have been allowed to fall out of Christian mythology, for it brings the story of the Fall and the redemption back to the place where it began: in Adam and Eve. In Langland's day it ranked with the canonical stories and he might have used it for his climax for no more reason than that he was thrilled by it. But I think he chose it because it was the most concrete expression, in the whole Christian story, of human salvation. The cross expressed the struggle which made salvation possible, but it was a struggle in which ordinary humanity had no part. The harrowing of Hell presented the first example of human salvation itself. It was thus peculiarly fitted to catch up and bring to fulfilment the theme of human salvation that had been fitfully presented through the dreamer. It may be significant that at the end of the poem, when the pilgrimage motive recurs, it is Conscience not the dreamer who is the pilgrim. The dreamer, though never in this life released from the quest for personal salvation, now knows the conditions of its attainment. So Langland turns to the Christian commonwealth, that has been betrayed from within; and it is not just one man but a general figure, an allegory of Conscience, who leaves the home country of the commonwealth to find Piers Plowman where he may.

The progress of Do-wel through Do-bet to Do-best has been described well enough in other books to make long comment superfluous. *Do-wel* is the active life, the life of the good layman; *Do-bet* is the contemplative life, the life of the man of a religious order; *Do-best* is the life of the highest human responsibility made possible by the union of activity and contemplation, the life of the Bishop. It was common at one time to contrast this scale unfavourably with that of Dante, who in his Paradise places the great saints of contemplation highest of all and above the most virtuous rulers; and Langland was suspected of being after all the practical Englishman at bottom, prone to compromise. One of the most valuable aids to understanding **Piers Plowman** was the discovery by H. W. Wells [in *Publications of the Modern Language Association of America*, 1929] that Langland in placing the mixed life above the other two was following excellent medieval precedent, including that of Thomas Aquinas. R. W. Chambers pointed out that Langland's contemporary, Walter Hilton, was familiar with the notion. And after all, if we need more precedent, is there not Plato himself? In the myth of the cave in the *Republic* the exceptional men who have turned from the shadows and seen the fire that cast them on the wall of the cave return to instruct their fellows concerning their vision. Granted then that Langland's scale is not something merely personal or provincial, it can reinforce the general theme of life being a pilgrimage towards a definite goal.

Finally, before I leave the allegory, I must point out that Langland's method of allowing one allegorical significance to melt into another did not preclude his using the medieval convention of three or four layers of meaning. Exactly how far one can detect this use will never be decided; and to *try* to detect it is perilous in the extreme, because ingenuity will nearly always crown the trial with success and end by achieving absurdity. But those who know the poem best agree that these significances are to be found to some extent. Nevill Coghill believes that certain of the main themes can be schematised under the four senses or meanings. I refer the reader to his discussion and reproduce his scheme below. The italicised words refer to the four senses.

Literalis	*Allegoricus*	*Moralis*	*Anagogicus*
Piers the Farmer	Laity	Do-wel	God the Father
Piers the Teacher	Clergy	Do-bet	God the Son
Piers Barn-Builder	Episcopate	Do-best	God the Holy Ghost

So far I have said nothing of what Langland makes of the sum of the admirable details I have touched on. The epic ingredients are there for certain, but what of their organisation?

First, Langland had the courage to make the great choice of risking everything on one long poem and the staying power to keep at it for many years on end. He had the heroic cast of mind. But did his heroism extend beyond mere dogged aggregation of details to a total conception which moulded and modified those details till they became inseparable? Did he patch together predetermined items, or did the items remain fluid and susceptible of modification during the whole course of composition? The answer cannot be simple *yes* or *no;* it has to be much more complicated.

First, the reader who insists on reading with an eye to the whole and refuses to confine his interest to whatever detail he is now concerned with must admit that there is a great deal of repetition. This repeated material is mainly homiletic: the stuff of the medieval sermon. Those who know Langland best are apt to grow interested in him for reasons other than literary (which is legitimate enough) and to allow that interest to weaken their critical insight (which is quite another matter). They can be too tolerant of Langland's repetitions and irrelevant moralising. But at least one of the specialists, Nevill Coghill, recognised these shortcomings by the drastic cuts he made in his abbreviated translation for the modern reader [*Visions from Piers Plowman*]. The plain fact is that Langland was moralist and preacher as well as poet, and that certain topics, bribery and corruption, ecclesiastical sloth, the sufferings of the poor, and the virtues of poverty, roused him to such a reforming passion that he spoke of them out of season as well as in. Let me give a short and simple example first. The discourse of Imaginative in B xii is one of the most varied and beautiful things in the poem. In it occurs the passage about Nature's way with the animals ('He is the pyes patroun'), so certain and yet so obscure to human understanding: the passage I chose to illustrate Langland's power of sustaining his poetry. Immediately after the magpie and Adam and Eve and Nature's prompting of them through the instincts comes more about the peacock. And instead of driving home his point and using the peacock as another instance of Nature's prompting, Langland uses him as an allegorical invective against the evils of wealth, an invective which is both perfectly inept in the context and the substance of which we have heard a dozen times before. Even in the last passus, which on the whole is greatly to the point and where irrelevance is peculiarly disastrous, he inserts a separable and inorganic invective against degenerate friars. The effect of so much repetition is to destroy the illusion of art and temporarily to reduce the poem to a political pamphlet. When Langland dwells too insistently on the sufferings of the poor, I feel like the man who reviewed the *Lyrical Ballads* for the *Monthly Review*. Of Goody Blake he wrote, 'She should have been relieved out of the *two millions* annually allowed by the State to the poor of this country.'

Such homiletic accretions, however annoying, are not necessarily fatal. I am reminded of Langland's own fable of the man in the boat in a rough sea. He may reel and stumble, yet if he can somehow control the rudder he may make his journey. But there is one much more serious structural flaw: one which amounts to a prolonged abandonment of the rudder and the danger of complete disaster. The poem is divided into four sections: the Vision (Prologue and i-vii), Do-wel (viii-xiv), Do-bet (xv-xviii), and Do-best (xix and xx), all these numbers referring to the B-text. The transition from the Vision, which mainly concerns contemporary England, to Do-wel, which concerns the active life in general, occurs in Passus vii, where Piers, now busy with ploughing his half-acre, is granted a pardon for himself and his helpers. The meaning of this pardon, of its sudden challenging by the priest, and of Piers's destroying it, is much in dispute; but it is generally clear that the pardon does not reach far enough and that some more inclusive principles must be sought for. The dreamer is not satisfied and in the next passus sets out in search of Do-wel, Do-bet, and Do-best; and in that order. But such a pilgrimage is structurally shocking because most of the poem has already concerned Do-wel, the practical life. Langland thus sets out on a pilgrimage to a place where he has already arrived. Nor do I think it helps the structure to draw, as H. W. Wells does, a distinction between the two places. He holds that the Vision concerns one department of active life, secular government, while Do-wel concerns another department of it, church government and its theological side generally. Technically Wells may be right; but in actual fact the overlap of the two departments is such that in reading we fail to separate them. The Vision is full of clerical life, and both sections are full of a general life that eludes classification. How much on the same lines they run appears from the accounts of the Seven Deadly Sins which occur towards the end of both sections. In the Vision the Sins confess in response to Reason's sermon; in Do-bet they appear as the spots on the coat of Haukyn, the active man. But the treatment is identical. That is, in the B-text. In his final version Langland transferred the second set of descriptions and embodied them in the first set, thus betraying that he perceived the redundance. It may have been this same fear of redundance that prompted him to cut out Haukyn's repentance (the Seven Sins having repented in the Vision), to the great detriment of the poem.

But when the worst is said, *Piers Plowman* is after all nobly planned. Even if Langland repeats himself, he never quite loses sight of his goal, and the turning-points of the plot are usually magnificent. The appearances of Piers himself, of the priest who questions the pardon, and of Imaginative are thrilling in their suddenness, and force on us the sense of something most significant in the poem's progress. And we must not minimise Langland's power of enlightening us later about things that at first sight appear irrelevant. In Passus xi the remarks of Imaginative on Nature, splendid in themselves, come in abruptly. But in the end we see their point. He draws two lessons from the operations of Nature: one that unlike man Nature is ruled by Reason, the other that the operations of Nature are beyond man's ken. The dreamer then turns to Reason personified and asks why he treats man so ill. Reason retorts that such inquiries are futile and illustrate the very lack of reason to which man is prone. The dispositions of Nature are none of his business, but 'suffrance is a sovereign virtue'; and by suffrance is meant not mere subjection to pain but self-control and patience. Reason's rebuke, arising easily out of the context, touches the dreamer, who had shown himself impatient in his judgements, and when he awakes he now realises that 'to see much and suffer more is Do-wel'; and this marks a stage in his spiritual pilgrimage. When Do-wel gives way to Do-bet, the plotting becomes masterly, and there is much less irrelevant matter. The progression from Faith and Hope to Charity, who becomes the Good Samaritan, who becomes Jesus on his way to joust in Piers's armour in Jerusalem and, having won, to free Adam and Eve from Hell, is entirely convincing; technically a most brilliant contrivance. Not less masterly is the building of the barn (the foundation of the church) in the Do-best section. It catches up the imagery of the Plowman and the ploughing of the half-acre. It also

introduces, through the notion of the Bishop as the embodiment of Do-best, the practical life once more. And having done thus much, Langland with perfect propriety introduces echoes of the beginning of his poem to make it end, as it began, in the life of the present. Apart from some homiletic irrelevance, the last passus is perfectly plotted, and it ends, as in the circumstances of the time— the great schism and the many ecclesiastical abuses—it was bound to end, in sorrow but not despair. Though driven out of what should be his home, Conscience has yet the strength to set out on another pilgrimage to find Piers Plowman. It is the same end as that of *Paradise Lost* or of a typical Charlie Chaplin film, and there is no fault to be found with it.

In spite then of numerous small and one very large fault in plotting, *Piers Plowman* does yet emerge as the contrivance of no small mind. Curiously enough, the major work so far discussed most like it in point of plot is the *History* of Herodotus. What travel for its own sake was to Herodotus, the desire to denounce certain evils of the time was to Langland. Both proclivities diverted them from their main theme. Yet through all their truancies they never quite forget their goal, and they make recoveries of a magnificence that forces us to pardon most previous lapses.

I conclude, therefore, that *Piers Plowman* emerges as the undoubted, if imperfect, English epic of the Middle Ages. The only literary phenomenon that could at all match it would be a complete cycle of Miracle Plays, which might stand to its age a little as Shakespeare's History Plays do to the Elizabethan. But *Piers Plowman* contains more areas of the mind, and in any case I am not meddling with the drama.

Taking *Piers Plowman* as the medieval epic, we can see that to a large extent it set the pattern for all the subsequent English works (history and translations apart) that can claim the status of epic. It is of course not a case of direct influence. Langland worked out his own method for himself, and the others in reaching similar effects worked out *their* method without any debt to Langland. But this independence does not make the similarities less worthy of note; and they consist in all these authors' combining a public theme, whether political or religious, with the individual, tragic theme of personal salvation. In Langland the public theme is powerful at the opening, but it is never lost in the greater theme of personal salvation and it re-emerges at the end with the thought of the corruption of official Christianity. In the first two books of the *Faerie Queene* Spenser makes the theme of personal salvation the chief one, but the public theme is there too. In the fifth book there are the same themes but with the emphasis reversed. Sidney, too, combines public and private in *Arcadia,* the latter emerging with special plainness when Pamela and Philoclea are tested in prison. Milton does the same in *Paradise Lost,* though the actual references to contemporary public life may be a subordinate feature of the whole. Into the *Pilgrim's Progress* there enters the theme of the England Bunyan knew besides the more obvious one of personal salvation. Shakespeare's Histories, which I hold to express, as a sequence, something of the epic spirit, are rather different. Their theme is mainly public, and they had to be supplemented not from within themselves but by the Tragedies, for the expression of personal salvation or integrity.

In sum, however different in technique from these other books, *Piers Plowman* is their kin, and we shall understand each the better for dwelling on the kinship of them all. (pp. 157-71)

E. M. W. Tillyard, "Langland," in his The English Epic and Its Background, *Oxford University Press, 1954, pp. 151-71.*

Elizabeth Suddaby   (essay date 1955)

[*In the following essay, Suddaby explores several elements of Langland's style, including his use of alliterative meter and handling of concrete and specific details in his poetry. She also notes the poem's emphasis on "the love and mercy of God rather than on hell fire and the terror of judgement."*]

In spite of some welcome signs of a reaction from it, the tradition would still appear to flourish of considering *Piers Plowman* "as a document of major importance to the social historian, as a puzzling allegory, and as a vehicle of certain great theological and spiritual truths [J. Lawlor, "Piers Plowman—The Pardon Reconsidered," *MLR,* XLV (October, 1950)], but only exceptionally as a poem, a work which gives pleasure and which can be read and re-read with a sense of exhilaration and discovery. This preoccupation with the subject matter is understandable, since *Piers Plowman* presents many difficulties of interpretation; and it is of course true that much of its power lies in its central theme, as relevant today as it was to Langland's contemporaries. But there have been many other works written about the evils of the times and the problem of Salvation, which have now dropped out of sight. What sets *Piers Plowman* in that comparatively small group of poems which are still living works and not historical monuments is—as always—not so much its subject as the vantage point from which that subject is observed, and its vigorous and sensitive use of words, both of which are reflections of Langland's personality. It is, first, with certain aspects of the style, and secondly, with the poem's angle of observation that this article is concerned.

There is a short passage in Passus I which will serve as an introductory illustration of the style of *Piers Plowman.* It is not one of the great passages, but it is a fair example of the norm from which the great passages rise, and it illustrates some characteristic features of Langland's style. It is part of the preliminary statement of the theme of the poem, and deals with the all-importance of that charity without which we are as sounding brass or a tinkling cymbal:

> For though ye be trewe of yowre tonge and
> *trewliche wynne,* [*gain money honestly.*]
> And as chaste as a childe that in cherche wepeth,
> But if ye loven *lelliche* and *lene* the poure, [*faithfully: give to*]
> Such good as god yow sent godelich parteth,

> Ye ne have na more meryte in masse ne in
> houres,
> Than Malkyn of hire maydenhode that no man
> desireth.
>   For James the gentil jugged in his bokes,
> That faith with-oute the *faite* is righte no thinge
> worthi, [*deed*]
> And as ded as a dore-tre *but yif* the dedes
> folwe; . . . [*unless*]
> For-thi chastite with-oute charite *worth* cheyned
> in helle; [*shall be*]
> It is as *lewed* as a laumpe that no lighte is inne.
> [*useless*]
>   Many chapeleynes arne chaste *ac* charite is
> away; [*but*]
> Aren no men avarousere than *hij* whan thei ben
> avaunced; [*they*]
> Unkynde to her kyn and to alle cristene,
> Chewen here charite and chiden after more.
> Such chastite with-outen charite worth cheyned
> in helle!

(B.I.177 ff.)

The passage serves first of all as an example of the alliterative meter, progressing from its two springboards of fully stressed syllables in each half line, and bringing with it the simple sensuous pleasure of the consonantal repetition. The alliteration, moreover, serves to emphasize what is already emphatic; it reinforces the full stress and helps to give vigor to the line. If there were a common rhythm running through the line, or a fixed number of syllables this might seem an excess of emphasis. But in fact the number of syllables and the arrangement of the stressed and unstressed elements vary from half-line to half-line. The hammer-blows of stress and alliteration together do not normally fall in exactly the same place for two lines consecutively. And it is perhaps the combination of the double emphasis and the shifting pattern of where that emphasis falls that keeps the reader alert to the verse.

The alliterative meter is not, of course, always equally effective; this passage from Passus I, for example, contains too many end-stopped lines to be completely pleasing. But at its best, since the possible metrical patterns of the half-lines are all those of normal colloquial speech, the meter can be used in sustained passages without producing any sense of strain, or of an artificial order of words cutting across the grain of the sense. And besides giving an impression of ease and flexibility in the longer passages, it offers also the satisfaction of a clearly defined form in the individual lines, with the balance of the half-lines against each other and the alliteration spanning both. Part at least of the pleasure that alliterative poetry gives lies in the occurrence of those lines which, perfectly in keeping with their context, flash out with a miniature completeness of their own—"And ye, lovely ladyes with youre longe fyngres," or, from the passage under consideration—"And as chaste as a childe that in cherche wepeth."

This particular line is also an example of the way in which Langland obtains sharpness of outline by the narrowing of the focus from a general conception to a single selected detail. Here it narrows from a general conception of angel-infancy—"as chaste as a childe"—to that of a child at the one particular moment of baptism when its innocence is most complete. Further examples of this feature of his style occur in his rebuke to lords who give away their land to negligent monks:

> To religious, that have no reuthe though it reyne
> on here auteres!
>
> (B.X.313)

and in the line in which Langland, speaking of the realm of France, brings it directly before the eyes as a landscape with clouds brooding over it:

> That is the richest rewme that reyne over ho-
> veth!
>
> (B.III.207)

The other two similes in this passage from Passus I—"as ded as a dore-tre," "as lewed as a laumpe that no lighte is inne,"—are not particularly remarkable, and can be paralleled by many others throughout the poem—"as comune as a cartwey," "also wroth as the wynde," "as naked as a nedle," etc. The light they throw on the surrounding passage varies in intensity. What they all share, and in this their value chiefly lies, is the appearance of popular wisdom (like that embodied in proverbs) which they bring to the poem. However much the poem is concerned ultimately with spiritual things, it is always firmly rooted in the earth; and Langland, dealing with a subject of great importance and seriousness, chooses his illustrations with perfect freedom from where he will. It is this readiness to include any aspect of human experience which sets the poem on a broad and steady foundation, and which gives it that quality of toughness which makes for endurance. It also enables Langland to make his point as effectively as possible. There could hardly be a more stinging rebuke to self-righteous and coldhearted virtue than his comparison with the ill-favored slut who is chaste of necessity:

> Ye ne have na more meryte in masse ne in
> houres
> Than Malkyn of hire maydenhode that no man
> desireth.

The introduction of Malkin at this point also illustrates that outstanding characteristic of Langland's style—his use of the concrete and the specific. The most noticeable feature of his vocabulary is his constant preference for a word which carries with it some physical image or sensation. The child in his simile is not only in the church, it is *crying* in the church; the uncharitable priests do not merely not give alms, they themselves eat up what ought to be given:

> Unkynde to her kyn and to alle cristene
> Chewen her charite and chiden after more.

Similarly, in Passus III (where Lady Meed is speaking), it is the use of concrete vocabulary that conveys the psychological effect that the hope of gain produces in dispirited troops:

> There I *lafte* with my lorde his lyf for to save,
> [*stayed behind*]
> I made his men meri and *mornyng lette.* [*stop
> complaining*]
> I batered hem on the bakke and bolded here her-
> tis,

And *dede* hem hoppe for hope to have me at
wille. [*made*]

> (B.III.196ff.)

And there is a later example where the choice of concrete and somewhat crude vocabulary not only gives the passage vigor, but carries with it the overtones of Langland's contempt and loathing as well. He is talking about men who discuss theological problems frivolously, as an intellectual amusement, an alternative to ribald minstrelsy after dinner:

> Ac if thei carpen of Cryst this *clerkis* and this
> *lewed,* [*clergy: and layfolk*]
> Atte mete in her murthes whan mynstralles ben
> stille,
> Thanne telleth thei of the trinite a tale *other
> tweyne,* [*or two*]
> And bringen forth a *balled* resoun and taken
> Bernard to witnesse, [*trite*]
> And putten forth a presumpsioun to preve the
> sothe.
> Thus thei dryvele at her deyse the deite to
> knowe,
> And gnawen god with the gorge whan her gutte
> is fulle.
>
> (B.X.51 ff.)

But it is not simply the choice of individual words which produces the effect of hardness and precision. It is also the choice of specific examples to illustrate an abstract idea. When Langland wishes to express the commonplace that in death all men are equal, he does so with a rattle of bones:

> For in charnel atte chirche cherles ben yvel to
> knowe,
> Or a knighte fram a knave there knowe this in
> thin herte.
>
> (B.VI.50-51)

And when he is showing how the poor are protected from the worst effects of sin, since excesses in one direction are balanced by privations in another, he does so in these terms:

> And though his glotonye be to gode ale he goth
> to cold beddynge,
> [*uncovered: uncomfortably blanketed*]
> And his heved *un-heled un-esiliche i-wrye;*
> For whan he streyneth hym to streche the strawe
> is his schetes.
>
> (B.XIV.231 ff.)

The concreteness and selectiveness of Langland's style, his constant awareness of and power to communicate physical reality are strikingly illustrated in the well-known Passus V, the Vision of the Seven Deadly Sins. Among its outstanding passages are the presentation of turbulent humanity in the ale-house into which Gluttony is lured on his way to church; and the masterly suggestion (in Wrath's confession) of some really vicious gossip and backbiting among the ladies of the convent. Particularly is the passus remarkable for its power in suggesting the outward appearance of repellent-looking humanity—the outward appearance which reflects and symbolizes the inner corruption. Sometimes the repulsive figure is conjured up, with great concentration, in two lines:

Now awaketh Wratthe with two whyte eyen,
And nyvelynge with the nose and his nekke
    hangynge.

Sometimes the description is rather more elaborate:

And thanne cam Coveytise can I hym noughte
    descryve
So hungriliche and holwe sire Hervy hym loked.
He was bitelbrowed and *baberlipped* also, [*thick-
    lipped*]
With two blered eyghen as a blynde hagge;
And as a letheren purs lolled his chekes,
Wel *sydder* than his chyn thei *chiveled* for elde;
    [*lower: trembled*]
And as a bondman of his bacoun his berde was
    bidraveled.
With an hode on his hed a lousi hatte above,
And in a tauny tabarde of twelve wynter age,
Al totorne and *baudy* and ful of lys crepynge;
    [*dirty*]
But if that a lous couthe have *lopen* the bettre,
    [*leapt*]
She sholde noughte have walked on that *welche*
    so was it thredebare. [*cloth*]

Here, besides the selection of salient detail, the concrete vocabulary, the simple comparisons, there is at the end a culminating twist, when Langland, again utilizing prover-bial wit, suddenly presents his hearers with the image of one intrepid louse leaping perilously from thread to dis-tant thread while her less agile companions hold back de-feated—a good example of his occasional use of the gro-tesque image. (The wrestling match, declared to be impos-sible, between Avarice and Poverty (B.XIV.238) is anoth-er example.) *Piers Plowman* is frequently—perhaps too frequently—compared with a medieval church or cathe-dral, but the comparison is an apt one, even to the gar-goyles.

The personification of the Deadly Sins however is a subject which lends itself comparatively easily to striking presen-tation. The resources of Langland's style are tested far more severely and are most triumphantly successful when he is dealing with intractable subjects like divine love or divine omnipotence, or presenting the central incidents of Christianity—the Incarnation or the Crucifixion—so that, without distortion they come home to the hearer with all the freshness of something heard or fully apprehended for the first time. (Earlier in the same tradition, the poet of *The Dream of the Rood* displays a similar power.) And again it is by the selection of the concrete and specific that his effects are chiefly gained.

There is an example of this in the A version, where Lang-land suggests the splendor and omnipotence of God in these three lines:

The tour ther Treuthe is inne i-set is above the
    sonne,
He may do with the day-sterre what him deore
    lyketh;
Deth dar not do thing that he defendeth.
                                        (A.VI.82 ff.)

The effect is produced by the selection of three details only; height in the heavens—"i-set is above the sonne"; the negative point of the reduction of death to submissive-

ness; and the central unexpected choice of positive exam-ple of God's power, "he may do with the day-sterre what him deore lyketh"—he may do as he pleases with the morning star. It is probable that part of the appeal that this makes to the imagination lies in the biblical echoes it sets up in the mind, of that occasion, for example, "when the morning stars sang together, and all the sons of God shouted for joy"; or the promise in the Revelation of St. John, "and I will give him the morning star." Undoubted-ly a great part of the force of the poem as a whole is to be found in the immense weight and pressure behind it of Christian belief and tradition, and the tact with which Langland makes use of it; so that, for example, memories of the Gospel narrative give strength to his own highly se-lective visions of the Incarnation. One of these, which is part of Holy Church's dissertation on divine love (B.I.151) is a very well-known and much quoted passage; there also occur in a later Passus three much less familiar lines which present the same subject in an almost instantaneous flash of illumination. They occur in the section where Langland is answering his own doubts about the value of learning, and appear in the form of a prophecy:

For the heihe holigoste hevene shal to-cleve,
And love shal lepe out after in-to this lowe erthe,
And *clennesse* shal cacchen it and *clerkes* shul-
    len it fynde. [*purity: wise men*]
                                    (B.XII.141 ff.)

The extreme brevity, the active, almost violent signifi-cance of the verbs upon which most of the emphasis of the lines falls, gives the passage an air of joyous rapidity, pre-senting the Incarnation as a sort of divine game played with the whole universe for its playground. But in spite of the tremendous concentration all the essential details of the doctrine are there. The passage is complete in itself and wholly adequate to its theme.

We have been warned by E. Talbot Donaldson [in his *"Piers Plowman": The C-Text and Its Poet*] against admir-ing "the one-line gems" to the neglect of the broad signifi-cance of the poem which was certainly Langland's main concern. But it is arguable that the "one-line gems" and the comparatively short passages of the type I have been quoting—and they are frequent throughout the poem—are one of the chief means by which Langland pricks his readers on to a discovery of the broad significance. En-couragement is often necessary. In spite of all that has been written of the essential clarity and coherence of the theme of *Piers Plowman,* it is very often a clarity and co-herence apparent more in analysis than at the time of read-ing. And Langland's habit of arguing things out as he goes along often leads him to include matter which obscures rather than illuminates his meaning. Even in the short pas-sage quoted from Passus I the argument is confused by his introducing into the middle of a denunciation of virtue without charity, a reference to St. James and faith without works. Even in the finest section of the poem, the *Vita de Dobet,* the dramatic sweep of the poetry is sometimes checked by theological arguments incompletely assimilat-ed. Throughout the poem there are passages of consider-able tediousness, and at least superficial muddle. But saved by the vitality of the poetry when Langland is writ-ing at his best, it remains a living work, part of a living tradition, when the works of many of his contemporaries of perhaps equal moral earnestness and desire to reach the hearts of their readers, are corpses artificially preserved in University Schools of English Language and Literature.

It is not of course only in the brief passages that Langland's imaginative powers are seen at their brightest. He is capable too of passages of sustained beauty, like his vision of the middle earth and all the wonder of its living creatures (B.XI.318 ff.); or in particular, the section of the **Vita de Dobet,** which deals with the life of Christ. In spite of some weak passages already referred to, the section is distinguished by its handling of the material as a whole— the freedom of movement between allegory and gospel narrative, the recurring and unifying imagery of the joust at Jerusalem, which is how Langland visualizes the Crucifixion, and the skillful changes in mood and variations in speed throughout. The tide of the poetry ebbs and flows until its final triumphant sweep through the scene of the Crucifixion into that of the Harrowing of Hell, which is, poetically, the climax not only of the Vita de Dobet but of the whole poem as well. Much of the account of the Harrowing of Hell is in direct speech and highly dramatic, and what makes this part of the poem memorable is not so much the visual imagery, as the speech cadences, the sound of the voice crying out of the great light:

> Dukes of this dym place anon undo this yates,
> That Cryst may come in the kynges sone of he-
> vene.
>
> (B.XVIII.317-18)

or the speech, addressed to Lucifer, in which Christ claims the souls in hell as his right, a speech unequalled in its sustained eloquence, ranging between triumph and tenderness:

> Now bygynneth thi gyle ageyne the to tourne,
> And my grace to growe ay gretter and wyder.
> The bitternesse that thow hast *browe* brouke it
> thi-selven, [*brewed*]
> That art doctour of deth drynke that thow mad-
> est!
> For I, that am lorde of lyf love is my
> drynke,
> And for that drynke to-day I deyde upon erthe.
> I faughte so, *me threstes* yet for mannes soule
> sake; [*I thirst*]
> May no drynke me moiste ne my thruste slake,
> Tyl the *vendage* falle in the vale of Iosephath,
> [*vintage*]
> That I drynke righte ripe *must* "resureccio mort-
> uorum," [*new wine*]
> And thanne shal I come as a kynge crouned with
> angeles,
> And *han* out of helle alle mennes soules. [*take*]
> (B.XVIII.359 ff.)

It is in this section of the Harrowing of Hell too that there occur some of the best examples of that wider selectiveness and sound sense of values which, together with the concentrated strength and unexpectedness of his poetry, most distinguishes Langland and keeps **Piers Plowman** on the right side of that great barrier which in literature separates the living from the dead and the moribund. The use which Langland makes of Hell is as good an example as any of his power to distinguish between the permanent and the

perishable. For Hell is the setting for the climax of Langland's poem, as it is for many other pieces of medieval devotional and didactic literature from Anglo-Saxon times onwards. But whereas in most of these the emphasis is upon the torments of the damned, a playing upon a crude physical horror which has now lost its potency, Langland's hell is a hell radiant with light and love, the scene not of torment, but of release from torment, and its emotional and dramatic effect is as powerful as ever. And what is true of Passus XVIII is true of the whole poem. In form, in theme, and in detail, it is completely of its age. Many contemporary parallels could be found for its use of allegory, with its four levels of significance, for its threefold classification of the good life, for the chief theological problems discussed—even for details like the louse on Avarice's coat. The external features of the poem are thoroughly "medieval" and conventional. But the spirit informing them, and the sense of values they embody are neither "medieval" nor "modern," but ones valid in any period. Some knowledge of the period and of fourteenth-century English is necessary to get through the external crust which time has deposited on the poem. But once that is past **Piers Plowman** demands few further concessions. It is still possible to respond to it as Langland intended.

It is not that he was a particularly profound or original thinker, or that he is often found consciously rejecting contemporary opinion; his treatment of the problem of salvation for the righteous heathen is almost the only part where he appears to feel himself in a minority. What gives the poem its durable quality is his instinct for the placing of the emphasis, for selecting from the material available those parts which are of permanent value, and passing lightly over the rest.

There is a point of detail which illustrates this further. Langland, it is plain from his description of the Tree of Charity (B.XVI), shares the contemporary belief that the verse in the parable—"But other fell upon good ground and brought forth fruit, some an hundredfold, some sixtyfold, some thirtyfold"—was to be interpreted as referring to the degree of treasure in heaven which would be the reward of virginity, continent widowhood, and matrimony, in that order of merit. But when he has occasion to consider the question of marriage at all fully, he is not concerned with the comparative merits of matrimony and celibacy (with the bias heavily against marriage, as in that unpleasing little thirteenth-century tract *Hali Meithhad*). All his energies are expended on a denunciation of mercenary marriages, and a plea for marriages of affection:

> For no londes, but for love loke ye be wed-
> ded. . . .
>
> (B.IX.175)

It is this which is the basis of one of the most pleasing of his longer similes, in a passage where, after speaking of certain spiritual advantages to be found in unavoidable poverty, he goes on to speak of the much higher claims of voluntary poverty:

> Moche hardier may he axen that here myghte
> have his wille
> In londe and in lordship and likynge of bodye,

And for goddis love leveth al and lyveth as a beg-
gere;
And as a mayde for mannes love her moder for-
saketh,
Hir fader and alle her frendes and folweth hir
make,
Moche is suche a mayde to lovie of hym that
such one taketh,
More than a mayden is that is maried thorw
brokage,
As bi assent of sondry partyes and sylver to bote,
More for coveitise of good than kynde love of
bothe;—
So it fareth bi eche a persone that possessioun
forsaketh,
And put hym to be pacient and poverte weddeth,
The which is sybbe to god hym-self and so to his
seyntes.

(B.XIV.261 ff.)

In the main, however, Langland retains a lasting hold on the sympathies of his readers by his steady placing of the emphasis on the love and mercy of God rather than on hell fire and the terror of judgment; and on the importance of human kindness and neighborly love, rather than on an ideal of exaggerated asceticism. And in his conception of God at least, he was certainly writing against a strong contemporary bias, for

a curious agreement manifests itself among contemporary moralists of all classes with regard to
the fact that this "presumpcion and overhopy-
nge in the mercy of God" is one, if not actually
the most potent and deadly of current popular
heresies. Bromyard recognizes it as a characteristic subtlety of the devil's predication and of all
heretics after him: " *'Howsoever great thy sins
may be, greater is his mercy.'* And in this third
point he deceives many, nay rather well-nigh the
whole world. And therefore more preaching is
to be made against this deception of the devil's
and little or nothing of the mercy of God. Because, as against a hundred who attend preaching and sin in presuming overmuch upon the Divine mercy, there is not one who sins in desperation" [G. R. Owst, *Preaching in Medieval England,* 1926].

But Langland's God is the God of mercy, not the God of Wrath, as is exemplified most strikingly in Christ's speech during the Harrowing of Hell, but also throughout the poem in details like the speed with which, in the confession of the Seven Deadly Sins, Avarice's despair is countered with the very text that Bromyard denounces:

Have mercye in thi mynde and with thi mouth
biseche it,
For goddes mercye is more than alle hise other
werkes; . . .
And al the wikkednesse in this worlde that man
myghte worche or thynke,
Ne is no more to the mercye of god than in the
see a *glede.* [*glowing coal*]

(B.V.288 ff.)

This conception of God reflects back into Langland's treatment of human relationships, in which all the forces of his indignation and compassion come into play— indignation against those who by living selfishly and care-

lessly endanger the spiritual and physical well-being of others, compassion for those who suffer. It is a compassion all the more impressive for being so clear-sighted and without illusions. Langland knew, without its affecting his sympathy and sense of responsibility, that the poor were often greedy and lazy and that many of the beggars were frauds (e.g., B.VI.123 ff.). He saw, too, beyond the more spectacular forms of poverty to the hidden miseries of the respectable poor, struggling against odds to keep up appearances (C.X.71 ff.). And the range of his compassion is wide. For though his treatment of the classes with the money and the authority is chiefly remarkable for its satirical ferocity—the natural complement of his sympathy for their victims—there are also to be found in it examples of his anxiety for the spiritual welfare of the rich, and a desire not for retribution but for reform, for their own sakes as well for the sake of those they could help. The best single example of this is Passus XIV, a disquisition by Patience on Poverty, which at first reading seems to lack all the most impressive qualities of Langland's verse, but which on closer examination is seen to be alight with human kindness, unsentimental and unembittered. The strength of the passage lies largely in the effect of the Passus as a whole, but the following extract illustrates both Langland's moving representation of the miseries of the poor, unrelieved even by those seasonal pleasures the animals enjoy, and also his consciousness of the spiritual dangers of the rich, prevented by their wealth from detecting any danger signals:

For moche murthe is amonges riche as in mete
and clothynge,
And moche murthe in Maye is amonges wilde
bestes,
And so forth whil somer lasteth her solace du-
reth.
Ac beggeres aboute Midsomer bredlees thei
soupe,
And yit is wynter for hem worse for wete-shodde
thei gange,
A-fyrst sore and *afyngred* and foule yrebuked,
[*very thirsty and hungry*]
And arated of riche men that reuthe is to here.
Now, lorde, sende hem somer and some manere
Ioye,
Hevene after her *hennes-goynge* that here han
such defaute! [*death*]
For alle myghtest thow have made none mener
than other,
And *yliche* witty and wyse if the wel hadde
lyked. [*alike*]
And have reuthe on thise riche men that *rewarde*
noughte thi prisoneres; [*look after*]

Of the good that thow hem gyvest "ingrati" ben
manye;
Ac, god, of thi goodnesse gyve hem grace to
amende.
For may no derth *ben hem dere* drouth, ne weet,
[*be grievous to them*]
Ne noyther hete ne haille have thei here *hele,*
[*health*]
Of that thei wilne and wolde wanteth hem
nought here.
Ac pore peple, thi prisoneres lorde, in the
put of myschief, [*pit*]

Conforte tho creatures that moche care suffren
Thorw derth, thorw drouth alle her dayes here,
Wo in wynter tymes for wantyng of clothes,
And in somer tyme selde soupen to the fulle;
Comforte thi careful Cryst, in thi *ryche,* [king-
dom.]
For how thow confortest alle creatures clerkes
bereth witnesse. . . .

(B.XIV.157 ff.)

Even if such passages, where Langland is writing with
most passion and sincerity, lack, as they sometimes do, the
hard and epigrammatic originality of some of the other
parts of the poem, they make their own contribution to the
durability of *Piers Plowman.* For the things that mattered
most to Langland are the things that matter still; the standards by which he made his judgments are still valid. And
the simple philosophy which underlies the poem is strong
and sound enough to bear the weight of the massive structure of the allegory, and stand the test of years. Towards
the end of *Piers Plowman,* in the last Passus, when the
forces of Antichrist are arrayed against Christendom,
when old age has attacked Langland, the dreamer of the
poem, and death approaches, he calls out to Kynde (Nature) who advises him to betake himself into the House of
Unity, and learn some trade to practice until his summons
comes. Whereupon Langland asks what is the best trade
to learn:

"Conseille me, Kynde," quod I "what crafte is
best to lerne?"
"Lerne to love," quod Kynde "and leve of alle
othre."

(B.XX.206-207)

It is the final statement of what has been said or implied
many times before; and there are no lines which provide
a more adequate summing-up of the theme of the poem
and the spirit in which it is written. (pp. 91-103)

> *Elizabeth Suddaby, "The Poem 'Piers Plow-
> man'," in* The Journal of English and Ger-
> manic Philology, *Vol. LIV, No. 1, January,
> 1955, pp. 91-103.*

T. P. Dunning   (essay date 1956)

[*In the following excerpt from an essay originally published in 1956 in* The Review of English Studies, *Dunning examines the fourteenth-century connotations of
the active (Do-well), contemplative (Do-bet), and mixed
(Do-best) lives as portrayed in the B-text of Langland's*
Piers Plowman.]

It is now very generally agreed that the organizing factors
in the **B-text** of *Piers Plowman* are the concepts of the Active, Contemplative, and Mixed Lives as distinguished by
the medieval theologians and spiritual writers. There is,
however, no general agreement as to how these factors operate in determining the structure of the poem. Certain
questions still present themselves, of which the most insistent is concerned with the relationship between the two
main parts into which the poem is divided, the *Visio de
Petro Plowman* and the *Vita de Dowel, Dobet, et Dobest.*
If Dowel, Dobet, and Dobest represent the Active, Contemplative, and Mixed Lives, with what aspect—if any—

of the spiritual life of man is the *Visio* concerned? And in
what sense and to what extent do the three divisions of the
Vita represent the traditional divisions of the spiritual life?

I hope to show that a closer examination of the terms "Active," "Contemplative," and "Mixed" Lives in their fourteenth-century connotation will throw some further light
on these questions.

It is first useful to recall that Langland had a vast body
of uniform spiritual teaching on which to draw. One of the
many services which Mr. [W. A.] Pantin's recent work
[*The English Church in the Fourteenth Century,* 1955] has
accomplished for students of medieval English literature
is to make clear how the teaching of the Fathers and doctors had, by that time, become available to a very wide
public in a great number of semi-popular and popular
manuals and compendia.

Properly to understand the poet's use of this body of
teaching on the Christian life, which is essentially the
inner life of the individual, one must take into account the
scope and purpose of the poem. The one is indicated in the
Prologue; the other in Passus i. From the beginning, Langland shows that his subject is Christian society, or the
Church; and that his concern is with the reform of society.
It would seem that he largely takes for granted the traditional teaching on the spiritual life of the Christian; and
while using this as the framework of his poem in such a
way as never to distort its systematic character, he constantly modifies it to reflect his preoccupation with (*a*)
Christian society, and (*b*) the society of his own time and
its peculiar problems. Two examples may serve to illustrate the point.

The first is from Passus xix. Langland has here come to
the final stage of the spiritual life: we have moved from
Contrition, Confession, and Satisfaction through Patience
and Poverty to Faith, Hope, and Charity; and now to the
Cardinal Virtues. According to the traditional *schema,* the
final element of the spiritual equipment is the seven Gifts
of the Holy Ghost. But instead of describing these gifts—
Wisdom, Understanding, and the rest, which guide the
soul to the higher flights of mysticism—Langland describes the gifts of the Holy Ghost as the talents each man
receives for a particular work in the world; and he makes
the giving of these gifts the starting-point for building up
again at the end of his poem that composite picture of
Christian society we saw in the Prologue. This time, in
Passus xix, first the ideal; then, as in the Prologue, the contemporary. And so his end, like Mr. Eliot's, is in his beginning.

The other example is from the *Vita de Dowel.* This represents the beginning of the spiritual life proper; and a principal feature of such a beginning, according to all the spiritual writers, is coming to know oneself. In the *Benjamin
Major,* for instance, Richard of St. Victor points out in
some detail how the knowledge of oneself is first necessary
if one wishes to lead a spiritual life worthy of the name.
The diversity of our human faculties, the multiplicity of
affections, the perpetual mobility of the mind are elements
which must be understood if one wishes to control them.
Besides, concupiscence having veiled the eye of the intelli-

gence, how are we to distinguish the good from the bad, how can we judge the movements of the heart, how discern their provenance? A reconnaissance of the terrain where one is to exercise the inner life is indispensable. Richard judges that *discretio* and *deliberatio* take charge of that necessary work. It seems that Passus viii-xii really constitute that phase of the Christian's development where the dreamer comes to know himself. Scripture says at the beginning of Passus xii, "Multi multa sciunt sed seipsos nesciunt" [Many people know much, but they do not know themselves]; and the same point is underlined by Ymagynatyf throughout Passus xii. One might also refer to the effects of concupiscence on the intelligence, vividly described in Passus xi. This is, however, the framework. Within this framework, Langland has embodied two of the main intellectual preoccupations of his day: the place of learning in the good life and the problem of Predestination. These are represented as the chief clouds which obscure the dreamer's vision of the ground he has to cover.

Such manipulation of the body of traditional teaching presupposes among the poem's first readers a familiarity with the main lines of that teaching. The same assumption underlies the poem's outward structure. Its significance may be better understood by examining the terms "Contemplation" and "Action."

"The traditional doctrine of the two ways of life, the one of Action, the other of Contemplation, is so clearly suggested in the incident of Martha and Mary that it must be considered to have its origin in the Gospel itself." [H. Bérard, "Action et Contemplation," *La Vie Spirituelle,* XX (1929)]. Nevertheless, during the early centuries, especially at Alexandria, Christian thought on the subject was profoundly influenced by Neoplatonic philosophy. In the pagan tradition, the Contemplative Life meant a life of study, consecrated to philosophical speculation; the Active Life, one devoted to external works and especially to political affairs. The influence of this tradition on the Christian theologians at Alexandria may be seen in the high speculative quality they attributed to the Contemplative Life, by reason of the *gnosis,* which for them distinguished the perfect Christian. Cassian, on the other hand, in resuming the teaching of the Egyptian monks on Christian perfection, puts forward a somewhat different view. The life of the Egyptian coenobites was, in fact, not contemplative in the Alexandrian sense, being very little speculative and very much given up to manual labour. In his fourteenth *Conference,* Cassian divides the Contemplative Life into two parts, actual and theoretic. By the theoretic (*theoria*), he means the act of contemplation itself. He is quite clear that this act is not continuous: one cannot, as it were, *live* this kind of life. One achieves the act of contemplation from time to time. The actual life is the cultivation of virtues. This is, as it were, the setting of the contemplative life. Cassian does not seem greatly concerned with the precise character of this setting: it may be a hermitage; but it may also be the reception and care of strangers—what we should now call active good works.

It would seem that the teaching of St. Gregory on the spiritual life, from which the Western tradition chiefly derives, is a development of these ideas of Cassian. For "Gregory, the great clerk," as Langland calls him, the Active and Contemplative Lives are not lived separately by two distinct categories of people, but should be united in the lives of everyone; for the life of pure contemplation is quite beyond the power of human nature. In his view, contemplation is an act wherein the mind, having disengaged itself from the things of this world and fixed its attention on spiritual things, is by a great effort raised above itself to a direct and simple intuition of God, not by a process of reasoning but by a close union of love. This perception of the "unencompassed Light" "as through a chink" is momentary; and then the mind, exhausted by the effort and blinded by the vision of the Light, falls back wearied to its normal state, to recuperate its spiritual strength by exercising the works of the active life, till in due time it can again brace itself for the effort of another act of contemplation.

The Contemplative Life, then, in St. Gregory's mind, is not that solely which excludes the external works of the Active Life to devote the greater part of the time to actual contemplation: it is that which has Contemplation for its proper end, abstracting altogether from the amount of time given respectively to external works and to prayer. Contemplation is possible in a life crowded with external activity—as were, no doubt, the lives of many of those whom St. Gregory addressed; as were, for instance, the lives of St. Catherine of Siena and St. Bridget of Sweden and other contemporaries of Langland who achieved the highest Christian perfection. St. Gregory's distinction is based on the principle that in the moral order it is the end which specifies the acts. So was begun the great Western tradition of spirituality. St. Bernard, the Victorines, St. Bonaventure, and St. Thomas Aquinas are fully in accord with St. Gregory.

The importance of this teaching is that Contemplation is open to all: the Contemplative Life is conceived as the perfection of the ordinary Christian life, charity in a high degree. Some Christians, such as monks and hermits, lead a kind of life which is deliberately ordered towards Contemplation as its end: their state will be often referred to as "the Contemplative Life." Nevertheless, their lives, too, must necessarily be a blend of Action and Contemplation. And Contemplation is not confined to those in the monastic state.

The perfection for which man can hope on earth is, however, only relative, because "as long as we are on earth, there is always room in us for an increase of charity." Hence, "if the perfecting of our spiritual life be nothing else than growth in justice and charity, then its essential law will be progress." This concept of progress brings forward the notion of stages on the journey. These stages were discussed and analysed by the doctors from early Christian times; and by Langland's time the notion of three main stages in the progress of the soul towards God had become a traditional view. These stages constitute one aspect of the triple division Dowel, Dobet, and Dobest.

Since, in St. Gregory's view, the good Christian life at even its highest stage on earth is a blend of Action and Contemplation, in what sense can Dowel be considered to represent the Active Life? Or in what sense, if any, does the *Visio* represent the Active Life, as Mr. [Nevill] Coghill would have it?

It must be noted that the terms "Action," "Active Life," as used by St. Gregory, St. Bernard, St. Thomas, and other spiritual writers, refer to the *spiritual life:* the "action" denoted is not any kind of action, such as manual labour, but the active practice of virtue. The distinction is not between *otiosa* [leisure] and *negotiosa* [work]: the good works of the Active Life are works of religion and devotion. In other words, the Active Life is the ascetical life.

The Active Life may be considered under two aspects. First, these good works—vocal prayer, mortification, the service of the neighbour, the practice of the virtues—constitute the normal conditions under which the spiritual life is lived on no matter how high a plane. Whether the spiritual life of any individual have the character of Active or Contemplative does not depend on the absence of activity but on the presence of contemplation. Secondly, the term Active Life is used in a more restricted sense. The spiritual writers are agreed that to achieve union with God in prayer we must remove in ourselves the obstacles to the working of God's grace in us. This we do by severe self-discipline in the spiritual formation of our character—that is, by the good works of the Active Life. In this sense, the Active Life is a state in which contemplation is not yet present. And in this restricted sense, the Active Life is conceived as a stage of the spiritual life, the beginning of the spiritual life proper: Dowel. The transition from Dowel to Dobet is the transition from Action to Contemplation; this is indicated in Passus xv, the Prologue to Dobet, though Langland is careful also to indicate that the good works of the Active Life do not cease to be performed.

Now, there are other works which man must perform which are not works of the spiritual life at all. A consideration of this aspect of man's situation gives us the key to the *Visio.* As St. Paul says, "prius quod animale, deinde quod spirituale" [before, that which is physical; afterward, that which is spiritual] (1 Cor. XV. 46). Man is not a pure spirit, but a being composed of soul and body. He therefore finds himself compelled to take thought for the needs of the body. This primary necessity gives rise to the arts and crafts—the provision of food and clothing and all those major occupations which absorb most of the energies of men in civil society. We have only to live to become aware of the imperious demands of this necessity: and *necessitas* is the term St. Bernard, for example, uses for this care or love of the body: a necessity *quae urget nos* [which drives us]. It is to these facts of life Holy Church refers in Passus i, 17-57. This necessity must be distinguished—as Lady Holy Church points out—from another form of carnal love which arises from concupiscence and for which the technical term is *Cupiditas*—a cupidity *quae trahit nos* [which draws us]. "As the normal state of the body is health, so the normal state of the heart is purity," or *simplicitas* [guilelessness]. "It is unhappily a fact that human desire only very rarely observes the limits of either. Instead of remaining canalized in the bed of natural necessity"—within the limits, that is, set out by Holy Church

in Passus i, 20-60—"the will goes off in pursuit of useless pleasures; that is, of pleasures not desired because required for the due exercise (*in mesurable manere*) of the functions that preserve life, but pleasures desired for their own sake as pleasures." That the will has overstepped the limits of natural necessity may be recognized when it has no longer any right reason for its desires: "For rightful reson schulde rewle ghow alle."

The first stage, then, in the spiritual journey of man is the limiting of his natural appetites, by reason, within the limits of the *necessitas quae urget nos* [necessity which drives us]—"Measure is medicine," as Lady Holy Church says: and the rejection of Lady Meed, *quae trahit nos* [which draws us] by her meretricious beauty. Most of the folk in the field have been drawn to Lady Meed; but guided by Reason, they repent and go to Confession, and then set out in a body to seek St. Truth. Their guide is, appropriately at this stage, a poor ploughman, himself concerned with the provision of the basic necessities of life and whose condition is not one in which he is greatly tempted by cupidity. The way he outlines to Truth is the way of the Commandments, the first stage of the Active Life, the lowest plane of the spiritual life. But having been only just converted from servants of Meed to seekers after Truth, the folk in the field, before they can advance at all, must first be grounded in that carnal love which is of necessity and is therefore legitimate. They must be taught the lesson of Lady Holy Church's opening lines. And so, before the pilgrimage can start, we have in the ploughing of the half-acre an exposition of how the different ranks of society are to be provided with food and clothing in a measurable manner *so that* they may serve God. But the service of God in a positive fashion has not yet begun.

Two points may be noted at the end of B. Passus vi:

(*a*) It is true that Piers began by outlining a way to Truth; it is, however, merely the beginning of the way, the way of the Commandments, the way of those who, as Guillaume de St. Thierry says, "being either moved by authority or stirred by example . . . approve the good as set before them without understanding it" [*The Golden Epistle of Abbot William of St. Thierry,* 1930]. The next stage is where the spiritual life proper begins, when a man starts to progress along this way by beginning to understand the import of some of the truths in which he believes (an understanding that comes to Piers only as a result of Truth's "Pardon," at the very end of the *Visio*). Thus he moves from the *animale* to the *spirituale,* and becomes a "rational" man in the spiritual life, as Guillaume puts it. And he moves forward, not merely by the practice of virtues, but "by the progressive understanding of himself and of those things which in the teaching of the faith have been laid before him." This development takes place during the long debates of the *Vita de Dowel.*

(*b*) The second point to be noted is that the pilgrimage outlined by Piers does *not,* in fact, take place in the *Visio.* The reason is, I think, because the reform of society is not possible on a corporate basis: it is achieved when each individual reforms himself. For Langland, Christian society is the Church; and the reform of the Christian is the beginning and growth of a truly fervent spiritual life. Now the spiritual life by definition is the *inner* life of the individual. This pilgrimage to Truth must be made by each of the folk on his own. It is the *Vita de Dowel, Dobet, et Dobest.*

The Pardon episode in Passus vii seems to be clearly a call by God to Piers to lead a truly spiritual life—to move on from the way of the Commandments: to do well, in the sense in which St. Gregory and St. Bernard, St. Thomas and St. Bonaventure would interpret *bona agere:* to spend more time in prayer and penance; that is, to progress in Charity by the mortification of desires and the practice of virtue. And the message seems to bring to Piers in a flash a new understanding of old truths: *Fuerunt michi lacrime mee panes die ac nocte* [My tears have been for me my bread day and night]. . . . *Ne solliciti sitis* [Be not solicitous]. . . . The Pardon initiates a new kind of pilgrimage: the progress of the soul in the spiritual life.

The *Visio,* then, is concerned with the *animalis homo* and with the first stage in his regeneration. The *Vita de Dowel, Dobet, et Dobest* is concerned with the spiritual life proper. And at the end of Dowel, the people in the plain of Passus v are recalled in the person of Haukyn; and we are reminded that the pilgrimage to Truth has been, in fact, for

Depiction of the confession of Lady Meed from a manuscript of Piers Plowman *in the Bodleian Library.*

some time under way, but in a different mode—the only possible one. In this manner, the two parts of the poem are intimately bound together as one whole.

We now come to consider the significance in the poem of the threefold distinction of Dowel, Dobet, and Dobest. The poet has guided us here by a number of definitions, for the *Vita* begins with the Dreamer's search for Dowel and his questioning of various characters as to its nature. The definitions which are given may be divided into two main classes. Outside this division fall two definitions which may be termed accidental, and one rather mysterious definition given by Piers Plowman, who reappears in the *Vita de Dobet* as a symbolic figure, representing the human nature of Christ.

First, to consider the two definitions which I have termed "accidental," since they define Dowel in a particular case. The first of these is the tentative definition of the Dreamer towards the end of Passus xi. Dowel, he says, "is to see much and suffer more." Ymagynatyf, who has just appeared, tells him that if he *had* suffered, Reason would have further explained to him what had already been told him by Clergye. There is clearly no finality about this definition. The second comes in Passus xiv where Conscience identifies Dowel, Dobet, and Dobest with the three parts of the sacrament of Penance—Contrition, Confession, and Satisfaction. The meaning appears to be that at this stage the sacrament of Penance is what is most essential for Haukyn. For the sinful man, regeneration begins with this sacrament, which restores the infused virtues of Faith, Hope, and Charity, to the soul. And we note that immediately afterwards Conscience does in fact begin to exhort Haukyn to a higher life, to Patience, Poverty, and Charity—to the life to which Piers Plowman was called in the *Visio,* by the "Pardon."

To turn now to the two main classes of definitions. The first class consists of:

1. Definition of Friars, viii, 18 ff.
2. Definitions of Wit, ix, 94-97; 199-206.
3. Definitions of Study, x, 129-34; 187-88.
4. Definitions of Ymagynatyf, xii, 30-40.
5. Definitions of Patience, xiii, 136-71.

All develop the first definition of the Friars, for all define Dowel, Dobet, and Dobest as growth in Charity. Patience's definitions not merely end this series, but end the whole series (apart from a reference to Dowel, Dobet, and Dobest in the life of Christ in Passus xix, 104-93). These definitions, then, furnish one aspect—and the chief aspect—of the threefold division of the second poem in the *Liber de Petro Plowman.* The *Vita* is essentially concerned with spiritual reform; this must be the spiritual progress of the individual. We have reference here, then, to the distinction of three main stages in the Christian's progress in the love of God, whether considered, as St. Bonaventure considers them in his book *De Triplici Vita,* as the Purgative Way, the Illuminative Way, and the Unitive Way; or, in the terms of an earlier distinction, the condition of *incipientes* [beginning], of *proficientes* [progress], and of *perfecti* [perfection]. The Purgative Way of St. Bonaventure is concerned with the expulsion of error and sin, and leads to peace; the Illuminative Way is concerned with the deeper knowledge and more exact imitation of Our Lord; the Unitive Way is the achievement of union with God through the operation of the Holy Ghost.

The second class of definitions comprises:
1. those given by Thought in viii, 78-102;
2. Wit's first definition—leading on from Thought—in ix, 11-16;
3. the definitions given by Clergye in x, 230-65;
4. the definitions of the Doctor, xiii, 115-17.
To these may be added the distinction of Dowel, Dobet, and Dobest in the life of Christ, xix, 104-93.

In considering Langland's point of view in these definitions, we shall be helped by recalling that the phrase "Contemplative Life" may also denote a manner of corporate living ordered to the primary end of facilitating and promoting the exercise of contemplation; such a state of life is created by the stable observance of the evangelical counsels, by means of vows publicly taken. This objective state is referred to juridically as "religion" and the members of such a society as "religious." The contemplative life is not the exclusive prerogative of such persons; but in virtue of their vows they are constituted in an objective state of perfection: *in statu perfectionis acquirendae* [in the state of acquiring perfection]. Hence they are in the *Vita de Dobet,* but they are not the only persons there: Langland never identifies the *Vita de Dobet* with the religious state. (See Passus xv, Prologue to *Dobet,*)

A higher state than the religious life is the office of a bishop or abbot or other ecclesiastical prelate. This is the most perfect state of all. And here we come to the *only* sense in which the majority of the doctors will use the notion of a "Mixed" life of action and contemplation. As we have seen, the contemplative life as actually lived—even in religion—*is* a mixed life; but the relation between Action and Contemplation in the life of a prelate is a very special one. The function of a prelate is to exercise *spiritual* authority: it is, therefore, as John of Freiburg expresses it [in his *Summa Confessorum*], a *magisterium perfectionis* [office of perfection] and presupposes perfection. That is to say, it ought to be the overflowing of contemplation. *Contemplata tradere* [to deliver up to contemplation] is the phrase St. Thomas uses of true ecclesiastical government, and the phrase is often repeated in the *Specula* and *Compendia* used in the fourteenth century. Hence a prelate is said to be constituted in *statu perfectionis acquisitae* [the state of having acquired perfection]: in the *Vita de Dobest.*

Priests with the care of souls share in the authority of the bishop; but since they may resign their care at any time (and he may not, unless in very exceptional circumstances), they are not constituted in an objective state of perfection. Juridically, they are in the Active Life. However, by reason of their functions they are bound to be in a subjective state of perfection. Hence we meet them often in the *Vita de Dowel;* but their functions are discussed with those of religious in the Prologue to *Dobet.* (pp. 87-98)

If we now consider the second class of definitions of Dowel, Dobet, and Dobest, we may see, foreshadowed in them, the blending in the structure of the *Vita* of the two

traditional concepts: the three stages of the soul's progress in the love of God, and the three objective states of life—the Active Life, the Religious Life, and the Life of Prelates.

Thought distinguishes the three objective states clearly. In Wit's first definition, Dowel and Dobet are defined in subjective terms, but Dobest is "a bisschopes pere." We are moving towards the more important concept, that of progress in love; and Wit's further definitions in Passus ix belong to this class. Clergye again defines Dowel and Dobet in general fashion—the Contemplative Life is not the special prerogative of religious nor of priests—but Dobest includes "alle manere prelates." The Doctor's definition in Passus xiii is a general statement of the three juridical states, as we might have expected.

From this examination, it seems that Langland begins in the *Vita* by indicating the pilgrimage of the soul towards God. The first stage in the spiritual life of any individual is an emergence alike from intellectual error and moral disorder. This is the *Vita de Dowel.* I have earlier referred to the dissipation of intellectual error in the first part of *Dowel,* Passus viii-xii. In Passus xiii we meet moral disorder in the person of Haukyn, and the situation described in Passus v is recalled. As in Passus v, but now in a more explicit manner, this disorder is repaired by the sacrament of Penance. The moral virtues which will sustain Haukyn and also help him to make progress are put before him: Poverty, or the spirit of poverty in some degree; and Patience.

With the Prologue to *Dobet* (Passus xv) we have already progressed. Priests and religious come in for a large share of the discussion, for they make proclamation of leading the Contemplative Life. Langland summarizes the discussion conducted through Passus x-xii on the place of Learning in the good life and applies the conclusions to the obligations of the clergy in Christian society. The highest evangelical ideal of poverty, put by Patience before Haukyn, is here presented in practice, in the lives of religious, anchorites, and hermits.

We are thus led on to a more comprehensive view of Charity in the *Vita de Dobet.* Perfection is represented in the redemption wrought by Christ and is rightly conceived as a growth in Faith, Hope, and Charity in the speech of the Samaritan. Piers Plowman appears as the human nature which the Wisdom of God assumed to redeem mankind. (pp. 98-9)

> *T. P. Dunning, "The Structure of the B-Text of 'Piers Plowman',"* in Style and Symbolism in "Piers Plowman": A Modern Critical Anthology, *edited by Robert J. Blanch, The University of Tennessee Press, 1969, pp. 87-100.*

John Lawlor   (essay date 1957)

[*Lawlor was an English educator whose writings include* Piers Plowman: An Essay in Criticism *(1962) and a modern theatrical adaptation of Langland's poem entitled* The Vision of Piers Plowman *(1964). In the following excerpt, Lawlor attempts to find "the focus of imagi-*

native attention" in Piers Plowman, *or "the vantage-point from which we, with the writer, look out upon his world."*]

It is to be hoped that the considerations advanced by Fr. T. P. Dunning in a recent article ['The Structure of the B-Text of *Piers Plowman*', *Review of English Studies*, N.S. vii (1956)] will win general assent. Fr. Dunning has given in brief space an account of the unity of theme in *Piers Plowman* which should safeguard us from exploring false paths and repeating old errors. In particular, his identification of 'active life' with 'the spiritual life' will prevent that confusion of 'active life' with mere activity, action as opposed to contemplation, in which a good deal of comment upon *Piers Plowman* has been entangled. Much of the difficulty over the 'definitions' of the three lives might have been spared is those who followed [Henry W.] Wells's decisive lead had observed, as he did, that, in Fr. Dunning's words, 'the good works of the Active Life are works of religion and devotion'. There is thus room for the blending of two traditional triads—active, contemplative, and 'mixed' lives, and purgative, illuminative, and unitive ways. Indeed, so far from rejecting the one to provide for the other, we must see their very interdependence if we are to advance at all with the Dreamer. But confusion came from another source, Walter Hilton's special conception of 'mixed life': and here, too, Fr. Dunning does a notable service by showing that 'in regard to the meaning of Dowel, Dobet, and Dobest [Hilton] will bring only confusion'. The recent contribution of Mr. S. S. Hussey, in which Hilton's views are taken as authoritative, illustrates the difficulties which beset *Piers Plowman* criticism ['Langland, Hilton, and the Three Lives', *Review of English Studies*, N.S. vii (1956)]. Mr. Hussey perceives well enough that 'active life' must include 'much of what Langland's critics usually assign to Dobet'. But for him this serves only to throw doubt on any claim for the three lives as truly satisfactory equivalents of Dowel, Dobet, and Dobest, a doubt which is reinforced when 'the idea of mixed life' (that is, Hilton's idea of it) is correctly seen to be 'too limited' to apply to Dobest. The root cause is plain: it is the definitions of the active, contemplative, and mixed lives so far put forward by Langland's critics that are at fault. Mr. Hussey's contribution is more valuable for his criticism of those definitions than for any firm conclusions he himself can offer: for, correctly understanding the nature of 'active life', he cannot see its applicability to Langland's Dowel, a term which, he holds, 'must refer to the majority of Christians who have no special religious calling'. We are back, though by a less familiar route than usual, at that central stumbling-block of *Piers Plowman* interpretation, the connexion between the *Visio* and the *Vita.* There is no possibility of advance until we see that the 'doing well' which refers to *all* Christians consists in that conformity to the rule of 'rightful reson' which the Plowman of the *Visio* at once exemplifies and helps to bring about. This is the necessary condition of and the preparation for that further 'doing well' which, while it is open to all Christians, is essentially the progress of the individual soul in the spiritual life (and thus admits of degrees of 'perfection'). Mr. Hussey is, I am sure, wholly right to stress the penetrating simplicity which invests Langland's term Dowel (and hence the progression, Dobet, Dobest). It is

evident, above all, in that concern for the *practice* of the Christian life which I comment on below. But we shall be making an impossible demand if we insist that the Christian life, as the Dreamer begins to inquire into it in the *Vita,* must involve no complexities. The truth is that Langland's Dowel is no invariable term. His concern is with right conduct, a 'doing well' which, first apprehended as the obedience to God's law required of all men, is deepened into awareness of the spiritual life—that life which may be expressed as obedience to the Counsels rather than the Commandments, conformity to God's will in the spirit of a son rather than a servant. As such, Langland's 'doing well' joins with and becomes indistinguishable from the 'doing well' of the spiritual life; and the progression to a 'better' in this sphere is easily and naturally achieved. But it is the lasting appeal of Langland's work that in the conclusion he turns aside from the ideal, the 'best' of the spiritual life, to the real, the leadership which is required by the suffering and sinful humanity we first encountered in the Prologue. Langland's poem has thus a design all its own: and we rightly reject those 'definitions' that would 'provide a ready-made guide' to his thought. But we shall make no headway with Langland's thought until we grasp the connexion between the 'doing well' that is revealed to their leader, the Plowman. Fr. Dunning has, I believe, given us the firmest ground we have yet been offered for resolving the purely 'doctrinal' questions, What is the 'theme' or 'content' of the *Liber de Petro Plowman*?, and, What is the relationship in those terms between the *Visio de Petro Plowman* and the *Vita de Dowel, Dobet, et Dobest* ? Langland's theme is 'doing well', an insistent probing of man's capacity for the good life; and this is prepared for by presenting in the *Visio* the *animalis homo* and 'the first stage in his regeneration'.

If this is the relation between *Visio* and *Vita* in terms of Langland's thought we may be better enabled to ask, How is this relation effected in the poem?—and thus, of *Piers Plowman* as a whole, By what distinctive appeal to imagination does the poet initiate and conduct the 'argument' of his poem? Fr. Dunning has very well demonstrated how Langland, employing 'as the framework of his poem' 'the traditional teaching on the spiritual life of the Christian', modifies it to his purpose, 'his artistic preoccupation with (*a*) Christian society, and (*b*) the society of his own time and its peculiar problems'. What that 'artistic preoccupation' may be it is no part of Fr. Dunning's immediate purpose to inquire. But it should be a question worth raising; for *Piers Plowman* is not a treatise, remarkable only for clothing deep truth and penetrating observation in memorable verse. To be sure, some who have perceived poetry in *Piers Plowman* have yet withheld the designation 'poem'. Professor C. S. Lewis has praised Langland for 'sublimity', and for a 'largeness' of vision which pertains to 'the "intellectual imagination" ' [*The Allegory of Love*, 1936]. But Langland, he concludes, 'is confused and monotonous, and hardly makes his poetry into a poem'. Similarly, Professor G. Kane speaks of a 'paradox of total greatness and local failures' [*Middle English Literature*, 1951]. A unity of theme, or 'doctrine', and hence a mutual relationship of the major parts of the work, will not, assuredly, of themselves serve to counter these objections. We must try to clarify the imaginative appeal of Langland's work—to find, if we can, the focus of imaginative attention, the vantage-point from which we, with the writer, look out upon his world.

It should be the more useful to make this inquiry in as far as the poem, if there is one, may need to be rescued from overmuch elucidation. A work as long as *Piers Plowman* (in its B and C texts) and as comprehensive in its main issues may well reward approaches from widely differing standpoints. But critical evaluation is likely to fare ill in this pressure of interests. There is a further consideration. Readers—not always untutored—who have been conscious of the explorations as well as the affirmations that the work contains have thought of *Piers Plowman* as a kind of spiritual autobiography, in which the author hammers out his best understanding of what often appears to puzzle and even, sometimes, to elude him. Against these, there have not been lacking interpreters who, rightly insisting upon a body of traditional teaching informing Langland's thought, seem at times to come very close to suggesting that Langland is a writer of clear purpose, involving his readers in perplexities that were for him only apparent, in order to win their better understanding. It is, unless I am greatly mistaken, to the second group that Fr. Dunning belongs, in his maintaining that Langland 'largely takes for granted the traditional teaching on the spiritual life of the Christian'. The question here is not one of degree (the mere extent, covered by Fr. Dunning's 'largely', to which Langland might be thought *not* to 'take for granted' traditional teaching) but rather of kind, the kind of activity we are to envisage in the writer. It would require a considerable hardihood on our part to discredit Langland when he tells us of his setbacks and vexations, the problems he cannot solve, as well as the truths he can confidently affirm. Yet it is true that his 'teaching' at all points appears conformable to what had long been maintained and was more generally accessible in his own day than has always been realized. The question is, finally considered, insoluble: but in its present terms it is certainly ill put. The mere dichotomy, 'Poem or Autobiography?' will never take us very far; but with some kinds of poem we can hardly apply it all. If, then, we can see what imaginative unity *Piers Plowman* may have, we must go on to determine the kind of poem we have been dealing with.

It will be best to begin with the *Vita de Dowel:* not only because it is, by common consent, one of the most difficult parts of the whole work, but because in it we are given some account of the Dreamer himself, pondering the significance of what has been seen in the *Visio,* and in that pondering some of the problems which the Dreamer presents as vexing him are well to the fore. What deserves our notice at once is the series of rebuffs the Dreamer receives from the authoritative persons he interrogates after his first colloquy, that with the Friars. From the Friars he has received practical counsel in the parable of the man in the storm-tossed boat—counsel which is designed to turn the inquirer away from the high theoretical question, How shall a man avoid sin? to the humbler recognition of common experience implied in the distinction between sins of frailty and deliberate sins. The Dreamer is not content, and seeks to know more: but we should note, in view of the scoldings he is to receive, that all he seeks to know is

where he can find Dowel, so that, as he humbly says, he may learn of these high matters by direct observation: 'if I may lyue and loke. I shal go lerne bettere.' It is a sentiment which is repeated after Thought's 'explanation':

> I coueite to lerne
> How Dowel, Dobet, and Dobest. don amonges
> the peple.
>
> (viii. 108-9)

Wit's account of the matter is no more helpful to this Dreamer who seeks examples from practice. In the wooden allegory of Sir Dowel inhabiting the Castle of Kind, we may detect a similarity to the Plowman's allegory of the Ten Commandments, delivered to the Pilgrims of the *Visio.* In either case, the predicament of the listener is the same. Like the Pilgrims, the Dreamer seeks a living embodiment of the good, not mere discourse, however apt. It is therefore a striking irony that Dame Study, waiting with unconcealed impatience for the end of Wit's discourse, should soundly berate the Dreamer as a seeker after mere knowledge. But the irony is deepened when we perceive that the Dreamer is eventually drawn into debate, so that Study's warning against high speculation, unfairly levelled at the Dreamer on first encounter, is later amply justified. Her very words, 'Non plus sapere quam oportet' (x. 116), are repeated at the end of the *Vita de Dowel* by Anima, rebuking a Dreamer who has sought to know all (xv. 63-67). Similarly, Ymagynatyf is able to point, unopposed, the moral of the Dreamer's experience:

> for thine entermetyng. here artow forsake,
> *Philosophus esses, si tacuisses.*
>
> (xi. 406)

We see very readily that, in his being drawn into debate, the Dreamer has fulfilled Clergye's prediction:

> The were lef to lerne. but loth for to stodie.
> Thou woldest konne that I can. and carpen hit
> after,
> Presumptuowsly, parauenture. a-pose so manye,
> That hit myghthe turne me to tene. and Theolo-
> gie bothe.
>
> (A. xii. 6-8)

As Miss Maguire has remarked, in an article which firmly grasps the tension between the speculative and the practical in the *Vita de Dowel,* the Dreamer we meet at the beginning of Passus XIII 'still seems to hold to his faith in the possibility of an intellectual resolution of his problems' ['The Significance of Haukyn, *Activa Vita,* in *Piers Plowman', Review of English Studies,* XXV (1949)]. So, as she observes, the turning-point must come with the entry of a moral virtue, Patience, upon the scene of the Banquet. But we should not fail to notice that experience itself has already given the Dreamer a foretaste of patience. At his meeting with Ymagynatyf he could ruefully contribute his own finding concerning Dowel: 'To se moche and suffre more. certes', quod I, 'is Dowel!' (xi. 402). If we look back, we see that the Dreamer is one who has been drawn aside from his original purpose, from the question Where is Dowel? to discourse upon What is Dowel? But the situation in which he was placed, *vis-à-vis* Wit, Study, &c., is not simple; rather, it is one of cross-purpose. Just as his interlocutors mistrusted him, a seeker, as it appeared, after mere knowledge, so the Dreamer mistrusted them, the learned and authoritative. Christ was a carpenter's son; what, then, is the place of learning in the good life? In this, of course, Langland is echoing controversies of his own day, but it is his achievement to communicate the universal sense of unchangeable cross-purpose between authority and the ardent inquirer. So we follow a Dreamer who, meeting no direct answer to the over-simple question he proposes, finds himself involved in debate, to reach that point of ultimate weariness, foretold by Study, where all exercise of reason threatens to appear as profitless subtiliz-ing:

> The more I muse there-inne. the mistier it se-
>   meth
> And the depper I deuyne. the derker me it
>   thinketh;
> It is no science for sothe. forto sotyle inne.
>
>   (x. 181-3)

He must learn to be constant to his own initial purpose, the search for a truth revealed in practice: but it is no easy matter. It is his final lesson, at the hands of Anima, that the search for knowledge may be not merely immoderate but even positively harmful: for

> the more that a man. of good mater
>   hereth
> *But he do ther-after. It doth hym double scathe.*
>   (xv. 57-58)

In all this the Dreamer has been less fortunate than the repentant sinners of the *Visio.* They found a guide, in the Plowman who is 'of flessh oure brother'. The Dreamer's questioning will avail him little until, all subtilizing ex-hausted, he is brought to contemplate Incarnate Deity, the Saviour who

> wole Iuste in Piers armes,
> In his helme and in his haberioun. *humana na-*
>   *tura.*
>
>   (xviii. 22-23)

It is the last irony that those he had interrogated at the very outset of his journey had given a sufficient answer to his desire to find examples from practice:

> 'I have no kynde knowyng', quod I. 'to conceyue
>   alle ghowre wordes,
> Ac if I may lyue and loke. I shall go lerne bet-
>   tere'.
> 'I bikenne the Cryst', quod he. 'that on the
>   crosse deyde'.
>
>   (viii. 57-59)

The imaginative appeal of the *Vita* in its whole extent re-sides not in any answer to the Dreamer's inquirings, though there is, as we have seen, a decisive turn in the *Vita de Dowel* when the shift is made from speculative to prac-tical considerations. The truly imaginative appeal is in the very failure of inquiry so long as the initiative is with the Dreamer. It is he, who at the outset insisted on the prac-tice of the good life, who is in the end brought to under-stand what his earlier interlocutors had doggedly main-tained as the ground of their reserve towards him—that practice is all. Then, and only then, is he ready to appre-hend as vision what eluded him as discourse. And this, in

its turn, will mean that his search, so far from ending, must have a new beginning.

If this is the imaginative appeal, what is its focus? What particular aspect of human nature serves as an entry upon and sustains the *Vita*? To answer that question, we may with advantage turn back to the beginning of Langland's work as a whole, not only to see afresh the relation of *Visio* and *Vita,* but to place the rebukes of the *Vita de Dowel* in their full setting. In the Prologue, the Dreamer has acutely observed a world whose law is self-interest: now, in the first Passus of the *Visio,* Holy Church is to 'explain'. In doing so she will encounter questions from the Dream-er which are inappropriate to his understanding; for the Dreamer desires all-embracing answers, but his gaze is di-rected outwards, while the real situation requiring redress is within the heart of man. The colloquy deserves to be taken in some detail, for it contains indications which are central to our inquiry.

Holy Church, as yet unknown to the Dreamer, begins with the simple and sufficient statement that to do right is to live according to Truth's teaching, and this is at once given its particular application to the world the Dreamer has seen—men are to observe 'mesure' in the use of crea-ture comforts. The Dreamer at once asks a large ques-tion—and this is to be characteristic of him: To whom does the wealth of the world belong? The answer is, as was Holy Church's first statement, that the individual is to look to himself: he is to render unto Caesar the things that are Caesar's. As she concludes her 'explanation' of the 'field', the Dreamer asks her who she is: and the reply he receives carries its own mild reproof:

> 'Holicherche I am', quod she. 'thow oughtest me
>   to knowe,
> I vnderfonge the firste. and the feyth taughte'.
>
>   (i. 75-76)

The Dreamer at once cries to be taught how to save his soul. Holy Church's answer is in keeping with baptismal simplicity. Those who do good and purpose no evil to their fellow men shall have their reward. What she adds is very important for the implications that are later to come to the Dreamer of the *Vita de Dowel*; the truth she has uttered is common knowledge to all men, Christian and Pagan alike: 'cristene and vncristne. clameth it vchone' (i. 93). We should not miss the gentle rebuke that this implies. But it is not dwelt upon: Holy Church continues by em-phasizing the obedience to Truth which all men must give, and concludes that those whose actions show their true faith will go to heaven, where Truth is enthroned. Nothing simpler or more directly connected with the practice of the individual soul could be conceived. But the Dreamer re-sponds with another of his large questions, How does Truth come to man?, and disclaims any natural knowl-edge upon the point: he does not know 'By what craft in my corps. it comseth and where' (i. 137). Now Holy Church is less gentle: how stupid, she declares, to say he does not know something revealed by common experience! This is the first scolding the Dreamer receives, and the first of many that are to come in the *Vita de Dowel*. An apparently radical question has been asked: and the an-swer is, in effect, 'look in your heart'. Something known to all men has been overlooked by this searcher after knowledge:

> 'It is a kynde knowyng', quod he. 'that kenneth in thine herte
> For to louye thi lorde. leuer than thi-selue;
> No dedly synne to do. dey though thow shold-est.'

The Dreamer's question is foolishness indeed. But he is not left without one concession to his desire for knowledge. Holy Church concludes,

> 'This I trowe be treuthe. who can teche the bet-ter,
> Loke thow suffre hym to sey. and sithen lere it after.
> For thus witnesseth his worde. worche thow there-after.'

(i. 140-5)

The lesson should be clear to the reader, if it is long in coming to the Dreamer. There is something 'better' than this 'treuthe'—not better than truth, absolutely considered, but better than the truth that is all that can be revealed to the Dreamer in his present condition. And in the moment that Holy Church withholds the 'better' she gives her reasons for doing so: it is a teaching which must be carefully attended to, and it must be *practised*. At the outset of the work, the Dreamer is established for the purposes of the poem in one line by both the neat glance at his impetuosity—'suffer hym to sey'—and the sterner counsel to pass from theoretical inquiry to earnest application. We are prepared for the last lesson the Dreamer of the *Vita de Dowel* is to grasp. In him the desire to intervene, to search out the imagined heart of the problem, consistently overbears the simple and prior necessity of an individual attempt to practise the life about which he would know all. Again, the vexation of Holy Church with this inquirer who overlooks the knowledge written ineffaceably in his own heart may remind us of the 'pure tene' of the Plowman when realization breaks upon him. The focus of imaginative attention in **Piers Plowman** is upon our habitual incapacity to grasp that what we know as doctrine bears directly upon us, and hence our search for a truth which shall be comprehensive while in fact, and all unwittingly, we would exclude ourselves from the reckoning.

What I have called the 'focus' of imaginative attention is therefore perfectly adapted to the doctrines the poet communicates. As Fr. Dunning observes, a 'principal feature' of beginning 'the spiritual life proper' 'according to all the spiritual writers, is coming to know oneself'. Some men, at the outset, will 'approve the good as set before them without understanding it'; and progress is made when a man begins 'to understand the import of some of the truths in which he believes'. When the transition is made from the *animale* to the *spirituale,* man moves forward, 'by the progressive understanding of himself and of those things which in the teaching of the faith have been laid before him'.

We begin to see that Langland's work offers a remarkable combination. His theme is of the greatest solemnity: man is a creature destined for regeneration. Hence we have the distinctive appeal to imagination—vision must show forth what remains hidden to discursive thinking. But it is Langland's genius to initiate and conduct his poetic argument by showing us man as determinedly ratiocinative, seeking the causes of all things, and overlooking what lies nearest home. The kind of poem we are dealing with is thus not easily determined. If we approach it by asking what is the poet's dominant faculty, we must answer, in however unfashionable terms, the satiric intelligence.

The satire abounding in the *Visio* is not always squarely faced by critics elaborating a claim for the unity of **Piers Plowman.** True, there is general recognition that the perception of widespread wickedness prompts, by a natural reaction, the question 'How may I save my soul?' But the connexion between *Visio* and *Vita* may be thought to go deeper. Certainly, if we are to claim for **Piers Plowman** an imaginative unity, we must ask again how the work of the satirist is related to the thinker's task of construction. Some critics may feel that the satire of the *Visio* is an involuntary concession to the age in which Langland wrote: and it is noticeable that as scholarship has attended closely to **Piers Plowman** it has become increasingly absorbed in the matter of the *Vita* in its three great divisions. We are so much concerned with the issues Langland unfolds that we may be in danger of neglecting the simplicity with which he begins. Professor Lewis states clearly what is implied by others when he invites us to consider Langland in these terms:

> He is writing a moral poem, such as Gower's *Miroir de l'homme* or Gower's Prologue to the *Confessio Amantis,* and throwing in, as any other medieval poet might have done, a good deal of satire on various 'estates'.

This is a striking reaction from those earliest critics who, dwelling with satisfaction on the poet's more obvious satirical targets, hailed him as a great reformer and thus, in Fuller's phrase, 'by *Prolepsis* a Protestant'. But each side misses the mark: for Langland's satire is more radical than Professor Lewis allows, and covers a wider range than Fuller perceived. What is central to Langland's whole design is the observed discrepancy between what we believe and what in fact we are. His poem has its focus in this aspect of the human condition. He therefore proceeds at the outset of the poem by way of external observation—the misdeeds of others—until he has amply shown the necessity of repentance. At this stage, he advances a step farther in the whole inquiry, by bringing forward the one good man the world of his poem can produce in its deepest need—only to humble him. In the realization that comes upon Piers we may see that we have not reached a final limit when goodness is found—for the goodness is now seen to be relative: the only absolute is Perfection. The Plowman who began by instructing others in the way of law (the stiff, signpost-like allegory of the Commandments in Passus v) has perceived that the law condemns unless it is perfectly fulfilled. He therefore turns—or rather, he is turned—away from Justice to the Divine Mercy: and his 'confession of evil works' is, in St. Augustine's phrase, 'the beginning of good works'. For Piers there has opened a road to the Promised Land which leads beyond Sinai.

The satire of the *Visio* is emphatically not 'thrown in'. Langland, indeed, begins well within the customary usages of satire. But his genius is to carry the argument beyond those limits. If all men profess the truth and few appear to practise it, we must pass from censure to inquiry: for this universal condition must make us ask, What is man's capacity for the good life? It is in that light that we see the shortcomings of the best man the world of the *Visio* could produce, the Plowman whose Pardon brings an equal and undeviating assurance of reward and punishment. And it is thus that we are prepared for the next appearance of 'Piers Plowman'; for it is the Redemption, perfectly fulfilling inexorable law, which allows the Plowman to seek a Mercy which is also Justice. But the satiric intelligence has not done: what we have seen in the *Visio* is slow to declare itself to the Dreamer of the *Vita de Dowel.* In Langland imagination and logic are uniquely joined: his characteristic capacity is to imagine absolutely. The Pardon that is a 'pardon' only on condition that law can exact no punishment reveals the external world for what it is in the moment that we pass beyond it. There remains the Dreamer, hitherto the observer, on whom realization is yet to fall: and throughout the *Vita de Dowel* there is the continual play of a satiric intelligence, that comes upon us at many turns and with a varying range of effect—from tonic scorn and impassioned rebuke to the practised facility of the dialectician, in whose mind there is always ready to start up the *contra!* of swift objection. Langland appears to have solved a capital problem, to communicate in imaginative and poetic terms the central riddle of our experience. It is not only that we everywhere approve and seldom practise the good: much more, it is that the realization of our own predicament is the last discovery we make. The Dreamer searches long and confusedly for what the Plowman saw in a moment: but the Plowman was ready for this knowledge, by reason of his long perseverance in simple well-doing. The strength of the *Vita de Dowel, Dobet, et Dobest* is that the Dreamer in his turn is *brought* to know the truth when all his efforts have been apparently fruitless. He must contemplate Incarnate Deity before his ultimate questioning is at rest. But he is then freed to continue his own pilgrimage, long postponed, to find the human creature who comes closest to the ideal. Langland's poem propounds an answer not to the simple, though profound, question, How do we know ourselves?, but to the question which lies closer to real experience, How shall we be brought to know ourselves?

To put the primary difficulty in Fr. Dunning's words,

> . . . how are we to distinguish the good from the bad, how can we judge the movements of the heart, how discern their provenance? A reconnaissance of the terrain where one is to exercise the inner life is indispensable.

Langland's 'answer' is in effect twofold. Firstly, that we 'distinguish the good from the bad' all too easily—where others are concerned. This is his *Visio,* where the reader, with the Dreamer, is the spectator of vice and folly. But when we think we have found a good man, then the standard that is at once in question will surprise us into examining not the vices of others, but our own. The reader is involved in this development in a way comparable with that employed in *Gulliver's Travels.* In each instance, the standpoint of the observer is decisively shifted. Dislodged from a comfortable vantage-point, our guide, and thus we, find ourselves involved, no longer able to interpose between ourselves and reality that 'glass wherein beholders do generally discover everybody's face but their own'. But what for Gulliver comes as a progressive understanding in a world of sober discourse comes to the Dreamer all at once as action on the part of the Plowman—an action which continues to perplex the Dreamer until action is perfected in the Crucifixion and made triumphant in the Harrowing of Hell. The logical imagination of Langland can move easily from sardonic observation to exalted wonder. The quality of his poetry is an unswerving fidelity to the facts of particular experience: for its centre is in the hard fact that the human condition is to find self-knowledge the all-but-impossible undertaking. Of this kind of poem we are tempted to say that the poet succeeds by calling Reason to the aid of Imagination.

Piers Plowman, then, appears to traverse two major kinds of poetry to which we are accustomed. On the one hand, its greatest things, as Professor Lewis has observed, come from the region of 'the "intellectual imagination" '. So, we may add, does its continuing energy, the play of a logical imagination in a predominantly satiric mode. But this introduces us to the other aspect in which the poem must be viewed. The satire is concerned with the truths we claim to know and yet do not apprehend: so, at the turning-points, vision must play the decisive part. Thus, for some modern readers great Romantic poetry may be the best entry upon the complexity of experience to which *Piers Plowman* is faithful—the penetrating simplicity of 'realization', and its uncovenanted nature, the sharpness of the sense of defeat—which at once redoubles awareness of what we seek while it falsifies all our contriving—and, rarely but centrally, the exaltation of vision. We must not classify Langland's work with the poetry that merely expounds a system of beliefs. It is in its essentials more like that genuinely new 'kind' for which the treatise poem of the eighteenth century prepares a way—a poetry which is concerned not with the exposition of doctrine as a contribution to the reader's knowledge, but with the individual reader's apprehension of truth, his growing into awareness, as the poem proceeds, of a path inescapably opening before him. These different kinds may resemble each other at certain points; and we run the risk of confusing them whenever we paraphrase for discussion their 'content'. It could hardly be otherwise, when the poet himself cannot adequately safeguard from misinterpretation his theme of 'Imagination',

> Power so called
> Through sad incompetence of human speech.

But there is yet a difference between *The Pleasures of Imagination* and *The Prelude* which is not merely the difference between a greater poet and a less. Fr. Dunning does well to recall us from an unreflecting acceptance of *Piers Plowman* as spiritual autobiography. But we must not be diverted from the real centre of imaginative excitement, the difference between 'knowledge' and 'realization', between the doctrines so long accepted and the significances at last apprehended. We may well, if we choose, identify the poet behind the Dreamer, manœuvring the reader through his guide until vision is inescapable. But we should be very sure that we allow for the activity of the poem itself, bringing to the poet, in the act of telling, new relations and significances. Our criticism will be beside the mark if we do not see that the poem succeeds by communicating the mind, not behind, but *in* the poem—a poem which is always, in a sense, unfinished. As it is a poem piercingly clear in its central issues, so it is multiple in its implications.

It is with those 'implications' that we encounter the charge of passages that are 'confused and monotonous', the 'paradox of total greatness and local failures'; and we shall do well to heed Dr. Tillyard's warning that it is possible to be 'too tolerant of Langland's repetitions and irrelevant moralising' [*The English Epic and its Background,* (1954)]. Not everything in Langland can be defended: indeed, one would wish to hear less in some modern criticism of Langland as a master-craftsman of multiple allegorical meanings, perception of which will somehow enable us to see merit in what might otherwise appear otiose or redundant. But before judgement is given on such particular passages as appear faulty, it would be as well to place them in the setting of Langland's whole endeavour. His undertaking must be not merely to state the apparent perplexities and nearly insoluble difficulties, but to communicate the very sense of weariness and apparent purposelessness that any stage of the journey may afford, if it is looked at neither from the end nor the beginning, but as it was encountered. Perhaps, too, our modern practice of concentrating upon the **Vita de Dowel, Dobet, et Dobest** increases the difficulty of apprehending the whole work serially, experiencing its crises as they occur and not as they may be extracted from their setting for the purposes of cross-reference and detailed comparison. It is the merit of Langland's poem that we share the sense of confusion and apparent repetition of experience: for how otherwise shall we see that man must be brought to simple practice? But this is not to claim that Langland works of set purpose and in thorough detail, like a modern artist who would communicate the sense of reality as complex and ambiguous by fostering a degree of complexity and ambiguity in the very communication itself. There is no question of that capital verdict of criticism, *pauper videri Cinna vult et est pauper.* Langland is faithful to a central purpose, our blindness to what resists all our inquiry until we are brought to practise it: and for this fidelity we may be thankful. When penetrating clarity and largeness of vision are found side by side with the very taste of purposelessness we may feel that what is monotonous and confused is the necessary, but excessively rare, complement of those heights of 'intellectual imagination' which thereby gain in authenticity and are saved from any suspicion of the merely austere.

In the same way, our understanding of Langland will be sounder if, as we come to judgement, we can concern ourselves less with the doctrines with which the Dreamer wrestles, and more with the nature of his progress towards his goal. The poem deals in mysteries, but the focus of attention is not upon man's ignorance of what is too dark

for him; it is upon his insentience of what has been brought into the light of common day. Langland's poem thus succeeds in communicating not a cumulative effect of discursive thinking, but the very pressure of experience itself. However it may have been with Langland himself, his Dreamer is one who is forced, in the words of a later allegorist, 'not to propound, but to live through, a sort of ontological proof' [C. S. Lewis, *The Pilgrim's Regress,* 1943]. Langland's hand is there, certainly: but it is his greatest single achievement that at the turning-points we see that the preparation is not the creature's but the Creator's. Until the living example is set before us, all our inquiries serve only to mislead. So the Plowman, and after him the Saviour Himself, are sent to meet our need. It is thus fitting that the Dreamer goes forth at the end to seek a true exemplar. Langland's last and most individual stroke is in deepest conformity with his whole design. By it he draws that design conclusively away from a formal into a truly imaginative unity. (pp. 113-26)

John Lawlor, "The Imaginative Unity of 'Piers Plowman'," in The Review of English Studies, *n.s., Vol. VIII, No. 30, 1957, pp. 113-26.*

Robert Worth Frank, Jr.   (essay date 1957)

[*In the following excerpt, Frank disagrees with the popular critical conception that the B-text of* Piers Plowman *preaches the three ways to a Christian life through its description of Dowel, Dobet, and Dobest. Although he concedes that "the problem of salvation is the central issue of the poem," he sees the work as a reply to a question raised by the Dreamer: "How is man's soul lost, and how is it saved?"*]

A reader interested in the meaning of ***Piers Plowman*** has a variety of explanations to choose from, but one interpretation in particular, a composite work of several scholars, has achieved wide acceptance in Great Britain and the United States. The first expositor was Henry W. Wells. In a detailed analysis of the **B-text,** ["The Construction of *Piers Plowman,*" PMLA, (March 1929)], especially the second section, Wells argued that the definitions of the term "Dowel" describe the Active Life, and that this way of life is dramatized in the ***Dowel*** section. The definitions of Dobet describe the Contemplative Life, which is dramatized in the ***Dobet*** section. Dobest is the Mixed Life of both activity and contemplation, exemplified in the episcopal office, and the ***Dobest*** section treats of this way of life.

Building on Wells' views, Nevill K. Coghill then suggested that Dowel is "the life of the manual worker and layman," Dobet is the life of the contemplative or clerk, and Dobest is the life of the bishop, who "cares for the salvation of men through the right administration of the instituted Christian Church ["The Characters of Piers Plowman Considered from the B-Text," *Medium Aevum,* (June 1933)]. In addition, Coghill asserted that Piers himself is "the allegorical symbol" for these three ways of life, that his personal entries in the poem correspond to the divisions of the poem, and that the changes in his nature are relevant to those divisions. Here and in his suggestion that ***Dowel*** contains the moral argument of the poem and ***Dobest*** the anagogical, Coghill was to some extent influenced by Howard Troyer's proposal that in treating Piers, critics should use the medieval method of fourfold scriptural exegesis and look for the literal, the allegorical or typological, the moral, and the anagogical meanings ["Who is Piers Plowman?" *PMLA, 47* (1932)].

Although Wells objected to what he called Coghill's "too literal view" and maintained that the "three states are psychological rather than sociological," saying "Langland's three lives are not vocational callings but mental states," he concluded that he and Coghill were essentially in agreement ["The Philosophy of Piers Plowman," *PMLA, 53* (1938)]. To these views of Coghill, together with Wells' modifications, the late R. W. Chambers added the authority of his approval, both by direct recommendation and by a long essay on the poem in which he followed and elaborated upon their analysis. Since that time, most of the scholars who have discussed the meaning of *Piers Plowman* have accepted in greater or lesser degree the interpretation worked out by Wells, Coghill, and Chambers.

Inasmuch as I must express throughout this study my disagreement with their interpretation, let me respectfully acknowledge at once the obviously valuable contributions these students have made to an understanding of the poem. We have all profited enormously by Wells' conviction that a plan and principle animate the work, by Coghill's many felicitous observations on the overtones of particular scenes and the meaning of specific passages, by Chambers' lucid exposition of the narrative. To argue against their general thesis is by no means to dismiss their work or deny its value.

Curiously enough, however, years before these men advanced the thesis, it was put forward and rejected by the German scholar Otto Mensendieck. Mensendieck is usually remembered only for his suggestion [in his *Charakterentwickelung*] that *Dowel* is the poet's spiritual autobiography, a proposal which never met with acceptance. Few recall what he had to say about the message of *Dowel, Dobet, and Dobest.* His analysis of this message does not depend entirely on the autobiographical thesis and deserves consideration on its own merits. *Dowel,* according to Mensendieck, recounts the poet's belief in early years in three ways of life, the Active, the Contemplative, and the Episcopal (Dowel, Dobet, and Dobest), a view the poet later rejected because he came to believe that there was only one way of life for all men: to be followers of Christ in poverty and love. *Dobet* does not preach a way of life better than that described in *Dowel;* rather it shows examples of life lived by the principles stated at the conclusion of *Dowel,* primarily the example of Christ. *Dobest* dramatizes the founding of the Church and the Christian community. Dobest is the perfection of good on earth according to the example of Christ's life (Dowel) and through the strength of Christ's work of salvation (Dobet). What is particularly noteworthy here is Mensendieck's conclusion that the poet discards a belief in the Three Ways of Life and replaces it with a belief in one way of life for all; and that the *Dobet* and *Dobest* sections show not different ways of life but the one way preached in the final passus of *Dowel.* Important, too, are his comments on the content of *Dowel, Dobet, and Dobest.* Mensendieck, I believe, came closer to revealing the meaning of the poem than

anyone who has since written on it. My own interpretation, which has been worked out independently of Mensendieck's, is by no means identical with his, but it does proceed in the same direction. What he had to say about the poem deserves more attention than it has received, and I bring him forward as a fellow heretic who does not believe that *Piers Plowman* preaches the Three Ways of Life.

There are a number of weaknesses in the theory of the Three Lives. One weakness is Coghill's appeal to the fourfold method of biblical interpretation. There is not the slightest excuse for decking out a personification-allegory in the mystic garments of medieval scriptural exegesis. Personification-allegory, as I have observed already, is primarily literal and is not intended to carry more than two levels of meaning. The recent effort of Robertson and Huppé to apply the fourfold method in detail is unconvincing. Fortunately, Coghill, although he invokes the method, does not really apply it.

A more critical weakness is Coghill's treatment of the titles. *Dowel,* he says, is not really concerned with Dowel as a way of life. *Dowel* contains the moral argument of the whole poem. The Life of Dowel has been presented in the *Visio.* This imposes a most curious, halting plan on the work, for Dowel is exhibited first and then explained, but Dobet and Dobest are explained first and then exhibited. An embarrassment proceeding from the text seems to be responsible for this scheme: Coghill calls Dowel the Active Life, but there is much more of the active life in the *Visio* than in *Dowel,* where the action is largely an intellectual and moral quest. Since, however, the poet gave the title *Dowel* not to the *Visio* but to the later section, the conviction must remain that he was really talking about Dowel in the *Dowel* passus.

There are several objections to the thesis that the Three Lives are the poet's Dowel, Dobet, and Dobest. For one thing, the poet was not well-informed about the doctrine of the Three Lives. He apparently did not know the term "Mixed Life" or any equivalent term, for he never used it, not even in the two passages where he came closest to describing the Three Lives; Thought's speech and Clergy's. Nor does he use the terms "Active" and "Contemplative," which he knew, in Thought's speech. In Clergy's speech he uses the term "Active Life" with reference to Dowel, but does not apply the term "Contemplative Life" to Dobet, although Dobet seems to be the religious in part. The absence of the technical terms is puzzling if the doctrine of the Three Lives is of major importance.

Equally puzzling on this score is his treatment of the Tree of Charity scene, where Piers calls the three kinds of fruit on the tree marriage, widowhood, and virginity, although it seems a golden opportunity to introduce the doctrine of the Three Lives. Stranger yet, in the C-text version of this scene the Dreamer is *puzzled* to see three kinds of fruit, saying he thought Jesus taught "bote two lyues," Active and Contemplative. The passage suggests either that the poet did not know much about the Three Lives or that the doctrine did not much interest him.

His treatment of the Contemplative Life, again, is quite inadequate. In B he refers to the Active Life as the life of labor and the Contemplative Life as the life of prayer. In C the Active Life is wedded life and the Contemplative Life is the life of chastity. Chastity is one rule of the Contemplative Life, but only one. Of the Active Life the poet has much to say, for he was profoundly concerned about the salvation of those in the Active Life, the great majority of Christendom—indeed, it is the problem to which the poem as a whole speaks—but that is another question. What the poet does and does not say about the Contemplative and the Mixed Lives, I conclude, does not encourage one to believe that they were matters of much concern to him. (pp. 6-10)

It is . . . incorrect to think of the Active Life as a life of physical labor without any spiritual activity and to assume that a man in the Active Life could not be saved. Chambers seems to imply this when he says Piers realizes that following the Active Life of well doing "is not enough." True, the Contemplative Life, according to the teaching of the time, was more meritorious than the Active Life; but the Active Life could suffice for salvation. It did not comprise merely the activities of the workaday world, as the words of Gregory and pseudo-Bonaventura prove. The poet equates the Active Life with bodily labor, as in the figure of Haukyn the Actyf Man, but the lessons Haukyn learns from Patience and Conscience prove the poet knew that spiritual concerns were consonant with the Active Life and were, indeed, an integral part of it if mankind was to be saved. As I have said, throughout the poem he wrestles with the question of how active, working men shall attain salvation. His answer does not rest on wholesale abandonment of the Active Life for the Contemplative; rather, as Konrad Burdach's researches have shown, it rests in part on the idealization of labor, embodied primarily in the figure of Piers the Plowman.

As for the Contemplative Life, it does not consist of helping others, doing deeds of charity. Such actions are part of the Active Life, according to Gregory and the *Meditationes*. The Contemplative Life necessitated withdrawal from the world: its mode of life was to be quiet from all outward action; its goal was to see the face of God. The poet does not discuss these ideals, nor does he work them into the action of the poem. The narrative of Christ's life in *Dobet* is not a dramatization of the ideals of the Contemplative Life. *Dobet* concentrates on Christ's teaching of the doctrine of the Trinity, His example of charity to mankind by His sacrifice on the cross, and His release of man's soul from the devil by harrowing hell. This is action, not contemplation. Medieval writers on the Two or the Three Lives said Christ demonstrated the Contemplative Life, not in these activities, but in withdrawing to the hills to pray all night. This is never mentioned in *Dobet*.

These are the basic weaknesses I see in the interpretation of Wells, Coghill, and Chambers. While I agree that the problem of salvation is the central issue of the poem, my own interpretation differs sharply from theirs. I read the poem as a reply to the question which the Dreamer asks Holy Church in the first vision: How is man's soul lost, and how is it saved? The answer is divided into two main parts: the *Visio* is one, and *Dowel, Dobet, and Dobest* is the other. The two visions of the *Visio* present in narrative

form the two antithetical principles which determine, according to the poet's view, whether man's soul will be damned or saved. The evil principle which leads to damnation is the way of Falseness or Wrong: it is the life governed by Lady Meed, the uncharitable, selfish desire for reward, especially money reward. The good principle which leads to salvation is the way of Truth: it is the life governed by the law of love. (This is stated explicitly by Holy Church in the first vision but is only implied by the action of the second vision, where the poet is dramatizing the way of Truth. He is saving more direct statement for *Dowel, Dobet, and Dobest*, in which the law of love is his unifying theme.) The good life is, in part, obedience to one's feudal duties (which he portrays later as ordained by the Holy Ghost and governed by the principle of love) and obedience to the command to do well rather than reliance on pardons and indulgences purchased with silver.

In asserting at the conclusion of the *Visio* that doing well was the way to salvation, however, the poet had answered one question but raised another: What must man do in order to "do well"? And implicit in this is an even larger question: *can* man do well? Or perhaps it can be phrased more exactly and positively: how is it possible that weak, sinful man can do well? In *Dowel, Dobet, and Dobest* the narrative raises these issues and resolves them. Holy Church had already answered the first question: what must man do if he would "do well"?—but in *Dowel, Dobet, and Dobest* the answer is repeated many times and in a variety of forms. It is to obey the law of love. In analyzing the three terms "Dowel," "Dobet," and "Dobest" in the *Dowel* section I have concluded that they do not possess individual meanings but are divisions of the generic term "Dowel" and that when using them the poet had always a single, all-inclusive concept in mind, not three separate concepts or ways of life. My analysis of the *Dowel, Dobet,* and *Dobest* sections has led me to a similar conclusion: they do not show separate laws or ways of life. They show only how man has been enabled to obey the law of love to a greater and greater degree.

Implicit in the first question is a yet more disquieting query: *can* man do well? Can man obey the law of love, as he must do to be saved? The answer is that man can. The poet recognizes the dangers and difficulties; these provide the drama of his narrative. But he believes it is possible for man to do well and be saved. His positive faith rests on two insights. One is his belief that the Godhead in its Trinitarian aspect has by a series of acts enabled man to do well and so has made his salvation possible. The other is the belief that there is in human nature an inherent goodness, a semidivine quality, that implies man can do good and be saved. The first belief underlies *Dowel, Dobet, and Dobest;* it supplies the basic organization of the second section and is demonstrated there in detail. The second belief is assumed rather than demonstrated and pervades the entire poem. It is embodied in the figure of Piers the Plowman.

My own concern is primarily with the first belief; on the second I am content to follow Konrad Burdach's work on the figure of Piers. What he has to say about Piers, however, harmonizes so well with my own views about *Dowel,*

Dobet, and Dobest that I shall summarize his conclusions and adopt them in my analysis.

The significance of Piers in the second part of the work is far from clear. In the first part, the *Visio,* he is a symbol of the good man who performs his feudal duties faithfully and follows Truth rather than Lady Meed. But after the *Visio* the references to him are obscure, and some of them appear to suggest that Piers is divine rather than human. For example, Clergy tells Conscience that Piers has said the law of love is the only knowledge of any value. Soul says Piers alone sees into man's heart, quoting "Et vidit deus cogitaciones eorum" (probably Matthew ix: 4 and Luke xi: 17) and "Petrus, id est, Christus." Piers explains the Trinity to the Dreamer and uses it to protect men's souls from evil. Christ jousts with the fiend in Piers' armor, *humana natura.* Christ gives Piers power to absolve men of their sins. Grace makes Piers His reeve on earth. In the conclusion, Conscience sets out, after the triumph of sin, to seek Piers Plowman, who can rescue mankind.

There have been several attempts to wrest light from this darkness. [W. W.] Skeat explained Piers as a good man in the *Visio,* Christ in the latter part of *Dowel, Dobet, and Dobest.* To Howard Troyer he is a symbol with multiple meaning, but always he symbolizes man. Coghill analyzed Piers as a symbol for each of the Three Ways of Life. H. H. Glunz suggested he was first a godly king regulating the worldly concerns of his people in the *Visio,* then Christ before the Crucifixion, the Christ of the Crucifixion and the Harrowing of Hell, and finally the just God whose return on Judgment Day is awaited.

These explanations assume that Piers was the poet's own creation. But what if Piers was not a completely original figure? The poem itself does not explain him clearly. It treats Piers as though he needs no explaining. Perhaps he existed in some context outside the poem that made him more easily intelligible to fourteenth-century readers than he is today. And why did Piers give the poem its title? He appears infrequently in the action and, except for the second vision, rarely plays a leading role. But if the figure of Piers were, in some form, popular and important in his own right, there would be more reason for him to give the poem its name.

Although there are no references to Piers outside the poem that cannot be explained as derivative from it, Konrad Burdach has shown that certain popular ideas current in the fourteenth century could have been, without too much difficulty, suggested by a character named Piers the Plowman. His contention is that the figure of Piers embodies these ideas. The name "Piers," a form of Peter, was one of the commonest of names, and so could stand for Everyman. It also suggested the Apostle Peter, the mightiest servant of Christ. The name and role of plowman are even more significant. Because of its idealization in various passages in the Old and New Testament, particularly Ecclesiasticus vi:18-19 and II Timothy ii:6, and especially in Augustine, the plowman had become a symbol of human labor and primitive, uncorrupted human nature. A strain of mystical thought conceived of human nature as having originally possessed both a human and a divine

character. These speculations found this double nature in Adam. He was both the antithesis of Christ and like Christ. It is this belief in a divine or semidivine element in human nature that the tradition emphasizes. The semidivine element is revealed also in such figures as Moses, Jacob, Solomon, and Peter. Piers, Burdach believes, is created as an embodiment of this mysterious, half-divine essence in human nature. He is, however, always human, never divine. The concept of Piers is rooted in the poetical and religious idea that the original pure nature of man stands in close affinity with God, whose image he is, and that his nature is manifested most completely in active work, faithful trust in God, simple love. He is the confession of man's closeness to God and of pure, loving humanity, and grows out of the conviction that this pure humanity of labor and love in itself possesses the right to eternal life.

The figure of Piers, then, reveals the poet's belief that man can be saved because of, as well as in spite of, his human nature. Piers symbolizes the suprahuman or divine element in human nature, which is proof that man is savable. Because of this divine element, man can do well (Piers in the *Visio*) and know and obey the law of love; he can use the Trinity to ward off evil and lead the good life. Man's nearness to divinity is proved by the union of human nature with the divine in Christ and by God's entrusting to mankind the power of forgiveness of sins and the administration of the gift of grace. Individual men of the Church may abuse this trust, but the semidivine element in human nature is proof that good men can be found who will administer these gifts properly. The search for Piers Plowman with which the poem closes expresses both the poet's sense that the Church needs reforming and his conviction that there can be found in humankind someone to do this work of reform. A good pope would be one possibility. But what is important is that this rescuer will be human in nature, a man rather than God.

Side by side, then, with the many views of man's wickedness in the poem is the assertion, through the figure of Piers, that there is in human nature a power of goodness which enables man to do what he must do to be saved. The poem is called the **"Vision of Piers Plowman,"** therefore, because it gives us the poet's vision of man's capacity for salvation.

The poet, however, did not believe man would be saved solely because of his nature. Not only would this have been heresy, it would have been contrary to the poet's temperament. Such optimism about mankind was not for him. He had too keen an eye for man's darker nature. He believed he lived in an evil world among evil men, and he described this evil in almost loving detail. At the same time he clung to the belief that goodness, and consequently salvation, was possible. The tradition of the "divinity" of human nature helped keep him, one might say, from the sin of despair. Piers emerges in the poem when the way seems darkest.

The poet's hope that man can be saved does not rest exclusively, however, on any belief in the eternal goodness of his fellow men. What he devotes the body of his poem to showing is that man can achieve salvation because he is assisted by God. A divine plan, a scheme of salvation, exists for man. The "goodness" of human nature is a mystical hope, embodied in the fleeting figure of Piers Plowman. The divine plan is a more rational belief, more orthodox and more readily demonstrable. It shows God's love for man, and the poet's account of this plan is designed both to instruct man specifically in what he must do to be saved and also to evoke, in response to the evidence of God's love for man inherent in the plan, a corresponding love of man for God.

In this divine plan each person of the Trinity has made His specific contribution to man's salvation. It is this which gives the second part its threefold division into **Dowel, Dobet,** and **Dobest.** One of the most attractive features of the theory proposed by Wells was the fact that the Three Lives provided ready-made a threefold pattern to explain the tripartite division of the second part. But the Trinity is such another ready-made threefold pattern and was, of course, known to every member of medieval Christendom, as the doctrine of the Three Lives was not.

Every reader of **Dowel, Dobet, and Dobest** has probably observed that one Person of the Trinity figures in each of the three divisions: God the Father in **Dowel,** Christ in **Dobet,** and the Holy Ghost in **Dobest.** Wells called it "a further organizing factor" in the poem. This use of the Trinity means, Wells suggested, that the poet believed there was a spiritual trinity in man. But Wells never explained why the "state of mind" called Dowel should be associated with God the Father or why Dobet and Dobest are associated with the Son and Holy Ghost.

Rather than being "another organizing factor," the Trinity is, I believe, *the* organizing principle in the second part. It governs the order of events in this part, the theme of each of the three smaller divisions, and the use of the terms Dowel, Dobet, and Dobest as subtitles. We need not become involved in the doctrinal complexities of the Trinity; the poet uses it in a fairly simple fashion. Each Person of the Trinity is associated with a particular period of human history: the Father with the creation of the world and man; the Son with the events of Christ's life and death; and the Holy Ghost with the period after the Ascension. A kind of chronological order is achieved by making the Father dominant in **Dowel,** the Son in **Dobet,** and the Holy Ghost in **Dobest.** Moreover, the poet sees mankind assisted toward salvation by each Person of the Trinity. This gives a logical order to **Dowel, Dobet, and Dobest.** God the Father, in creating man, gave him an intellectual soul. It is by virtue of this intellectual soul that man is said to be created in God's image. It enables him to distinguish between good and evil and cleave to the good. This is the theme of **Dowel:** man's moral power, through God's gift of a rational soul, to know and obey the law of love, i.e. do well. God the Son released man from the bondage of hell, which was a consequence of Adam's sin. Moreover, this act, His Crucifixion, and His many acts of charity on earth gave mankind the supreme example of charity, to aid him in obeying the law of love. Christ also taught man the doctrine of the Trinity, which man had to know to be saved. And as the doctrine of the Trinity is explained in the poem, it becomes another counsel to obey the law of

love. Through God the Son, therefore, man is better able to know and obey the law of love, i.e. do better. This is the theme of **Dobet.** The Holy Ghost gives man the final gifts essential for salvation: grace, the various vocations in this world, the evangelists and the four great Church fathers, the four cardinal virtues, the Holy Church, contrition and confession, and the priesthood. These, together with the power of forgiveness of sins granted mankind by Christ after the resurrection, enable man to obey the law of love most completely, i.e. do best. The giving of these gifts and man's use and abuse of them is the theme of **Dobest.**

This does not mean that the poem was written to expound this scheme. What the poet focuses on is man and the drama of his salvation. The divine plan is in the background. It gives shape and organization to **Dowel, Dobet, and Dobest** and animates the fundamental conviction pervading the poem that salvation is possible for man. At moments this or that aspect of the divine plan may become the center of attention, as in the crucifixion scene or the scene in which the Holy Ghost distributes grace to mankind. But the poet is looking at man rather than at the Triune God; it is the implications of the divine plan for human salvation that give the poem its direction; and it is the spectacle of man now blundering and now moving forward within the framework of this plan that gives the poem its drama. (pp. 11-18)

Robert Worth Frank, Jr., "The Plan," in his "Piers Plowman" and the Scheme of Salvation: An Interpretation of Dowel, Dobet and Dobest, Yale University Press, 1957, pp. 6-18.

Rosemary Woolf (essay date 1962)

[*In the following excerpt, Woolf notes the lack of a sustained literal level in* Piers Plowman, *a quality which distinguishes it from other fourteenth-century allegories. She claims that the character of Piers "represents mankind, the Church, the Pope, St. Peter, Christ in His humanity, and other allied subjects" rather than any one figure; as the focal point of the poem, she concludes, he illustrates the allegory's intellectual uncertainty, a rare element in other works of the age.*]

Piers Plowman is most frequently discussed as a poem entirely typical of its period. But, whilst many of the ideas and arguments expressed in it are rooted in fourteenth century thought, as a poem it has a number of qualities which are startlingly new, and which indeed are far more 'modern' than anything to be found in the fifteenth century. The way in which **Piers Plowman** is untypical of Medieval literature can be most clearly seen in the handling of the allegory, and in particular in the treatment of the figure of Piers and of the dreamer himself. It has over and over again been said or implied that the allegory of **Piers Plowman** can be illuminated by reference to earlier traditions of Medieval allegory, but this is only self-evidently true, when all that is meant by it is that individual episodes can be shown to have sources. The well-known, rather brusque and grotesque passage, in which the procession is formed to take Lady Mede to London may seem slightly less odd and perfunctory if one recognises in it the kind of allegory which had been used by Nicolas Bozon in his

Anglo-Norman poem, *Le Char d'Orgueil.* Langland obviously borrowed some of his methods of allegory in a highly eclectic way, and probably more light could be thrown on individual passages by a farther investigation of them. But, when by the assumption that **Piers Plowman** is dependent on earlier traditions of allegory, is intended the well-known view that **Piers Plowman** appears a clear and well-organised poem once one understands the Medieval conception of allegory, and in particular the four levels of meaning, then this view can far less easily be substantiated.

One of the most obvious characteristics of the allegory of **Piers Plowman,** and that which often makes it so difficult to follow, is that the literal level of the allegory is so slight and poetically unimportant. The allegorisation of the Old Testament, however, had led to quite a different treatment, for every commentator began with the literal text which he normally held to be exactly true, and to be instinct with allegorical meaning. God was thought of as a master-allegorist, who had so guided the course of history, or so designed the natural world analysed in bestiaries and lapidaries, that in all of these man could discern allegories of the Redemption. The consequence of this view was that no writer had need to fear that he might disproportionately stress the literal level of his story, and a poetic emphasis upon it, as in the Old Testament mystery plays for instance, would be in no danger of detracting from the allegorical significance, for story and allegory were not arbitrarily joined, but formed, as it were, one organism. The particular Medieval capacity to respond to allegory, which distinguishes it from later periods, was the readiness to see through a story or object, however complete or interesting they might seem in themselves, to some moral or typological allegory.

Piers Plowman departs from this traditional style of allegory by its lack of a sustained literal level. Indeed there can be few Medieval poems in which the literal level is so tenuous and confused. The only approximate parallel, which comes easily to mind, is Jean de Meung's continuation of the *Roman de la Rose,* in which many of the figures exist chiefly as mouthpieces for argument, and in which the literal story of the lover's quest for the rose is treated in a perfunctory way. This continuation, however, seems to have been intended as a deliberate and satiric disruption of the clear and courtly allegory of Guillaume de Lorris, and it therefore cannot be considered a typical mode of allegory, though admittedly it might to Langland have seemed to set a precedent. This comparison between the allegorical methods of Jean de Meung and Langland is, however, an inadequate commentary upon **Piers Plowman.** Admittedly there can be seen in both works a body of thought which spills over from the meagre capacity of the literal level, but it is also clear from the figure of Piers Plowman himself that Langland was by design using allegory in a far more literary and subtle way than had done his predecessors.

The startling point about the figure of Piers Plowman is that it cannot be said clearly and indisputably what it is that he symbolises. It has been argued that Piers represents mankind, the Church, the Pope, St. Peter, Christ in

His humanity and other allied subjects. It is obvious of course that Piers changes in significance as the poem develops, and most of the suggestions can be shown to be relevant to one or two references. There is, however, no rational combination of allegorical significances which provides a simple key to the interpretation of the text or to the weight which is given to Piers. Over and over again he is referred to in the poem, or makes a momentary appearance, but from the time that he tears up the Pardon his significance is uncertain: yet he is the central figure of the poem, as the title, almost certainly given by Langland himself, shows. The figure of Piers has in fact the peculiar force of something which is only half understood. This kind of romantic uncertainty, however, was quite alien to the earlier Middle Ages. Panowsky has ingeniously elaborated a likeness in the quality of explicitness between the great theological *Summae* of the Middle Ages and the style of architecture of Gothic cathedrals [*Gothic Architecture and Scholasticism,* 1957]. But this even lucidity, this unwillingness to leave any detail or idea, however small, unstated, which is, incidentally so apparent in Medieval illumination, is perhaps also the most characteristic quality of the literature. Until the late fourteenth century there are never any shadows or half-light in Medieval poetry: everything that the poet wishes to say is set out clearly, exactly, and in detail. There are no ambiguities in allegory or language. This explicitness is delightful to imagination and reason, but it lacks the emotional insidiousness of a more allusive manner, the unique power of the half-stated. This clarity in literature and art obviously reflected the thirteenth century as an age of reason: it was the only Christian century in which there was a serene, intellectual certainty that every kind of knowledge and revelation, everything on earth—and indeed everything in heaven and hell—could be examined and set out in the light of reason, without there remaining any residue of mystery. In the fourteenth century, with the dissociation of philosophy and theology, this harmonious confidence disappeared. The effect of this on the character of the dreamer in **Piers Plowman** is, as we shall see later, unmistakable, but it surely also contributed to the imprecision of Piers, to the fact that he is the focal point of a sense of security in the poem, and yet cannot clearly be defined.

The combination in Piers of uncertain significance with deep emotional power is exactly the reverse of what is normally found in Medieval allegory. The imaginative impact of an object or an episode in a typical Medieval allegory was usually strictly limited by limits imposed by the common lack of moral or aesthetic concordance between the literal level and the allegorical. Well-known examples of moral inconsistency are of course Noah drunk symbolising Christ, and Orpheus looking back at Eurydice representing man looking back with longing at his former sins. The lack of aesthetic consistency, however, can be equally disastrous to a literary use of allegory: Christ could be typologically foreshadowed by David slaying Goliath or by Samson slaying the lion, but He could equally well be signified by the hydrus, a mythical little creature, which rolled itself in mud, and then slid down the throat of a crocodile to destroy it from within. In these examples, and in innummerable others, it is the pattern of the action rather than the dignity of the actor which is important.

For this reason it is only rarely that an image is used in which there is any point of correspondence apart from that explicitly set out. The Medieval method can perhaps be thrown into relief by a contrast with the Anglo-Saxon. In the elegiac poetry, for instance, the traditional Christian image of life as an exile is used technically for its Pauline point of comparison, that it is heaven and not the world which is man's proper home. But in the *Wanderer* and the *Seafarer* the image is so filled with emotional associations of the powerfully evocative ideas of transience and loneliness, that the reader's response to it is not limited by sharp lines drawn by the poet, but only by his individual capacity to respond to the evocative and nostalgic. The emphasis upon precise correspondence in Medieval allegory may also be illustrated in another way. There are very few Medieval allegories which could not aptly be given a visual illustration. Indeed for Biblical allegory, art with its isolated moment of time was usually a far better medium than poetic narrative, in which moral or aesthetic discrepancies were more likely to obtrude. It is, however, self-evident that *Piers Plowman* is insusceptible of illustration, a point borne out by the fact that none of the very numerous manuscript texts of the poem are illustrated. There is here a very striking contrast with the Ellesmere Manuscript of the *Canterbury Tales,* with the manuscript of the *Pearl* and *Sir Gawain,* with the many French manuscripts of the *Roman de la Rose* and of Guillaume de Guilleville's *Pèlerinage de la Vie Humaine.*

The absence of illumination surely drives home the point that *Piers Plowman* entirely lacks the visual quality which is so characteristic of Medieval literature. The lack of visualisation is a point which will later be amplified: its relevance here is that Piers himself is an important allegorical figure, whom it would be unhelpful and indeed impossible to illustrate, for, after his first appearance, it would be ludicrously irrelevant to imagine him as a ploughman. When, for instance, it is said that Piers 'lered hym [Christ] lechecraft his lyf for to save' (B Text, Passus xvi, 104), to imagine this scene visually would be almost blasphemously comic, and would quite clearly be at odds with the thought of Langland. This is a very obvious example of Langland's disregard for the literal level of his allegory: Samson or the hydrus became more intensely themselves through the reflected dignity of their relationship to Christ, but Piers, as he grows in allegorical significance, ceases to be a ploughman: all that remains of the literal level is a name. But, though Langland maintains no visual image of Piers, nor any consistent rational significance, yet by a skilful accumulation of references to him, he concentrates in the figure much of the emotional force of the poem. Piers Plowman does not appear in the poem between Passus 8-15 (B text), but in Passus 13-15 he is referred to a number of times, and is said to be a teacher of authority and the only guide to charity, and by this kind of reference Langland contrives an intense sense of expectancy, so that when in Passus 16 the dreamer is said to swoon with pure joy at hearing the name of Piers Plowman (II. 18-19), the reader shares a sense of joy and relief, so skilfully has Langland led up to this point. The role of Piers Plowman in this passus, where he presides over the tree of charity and in the subsequent passus where he becomes closely associated with Christ, is not at all clear,

and it is evident from the excision of many of these passages from the C text, that this lack of clarity was equally apparent in the fourteenth century. But with the diminishment of Piers in the C text there is lost a great deal of poetic force. As we have said before, it is possible to recognise in Piers at various points, Christ in His humanity, the Church, mankind, the virtuous life, etc., but the fact that all these can be signified by one symbol, and that there are other potent and enigmatic usages, gives to the figure a tremendous power as an intimation of security and perfection and as a promise of the Redemption. The power of the figure of Piers and the uncertainty of his significance is perhaps nowhere so clear as in the concluding lines of the poem which describes the beginning of a fresh search for Piers Plowman.

The other important character in the poem is the dreamer himself, and he too is presented in a manner which is not characteristic of Medieval literature. Langland had behind him a long tradition of poetry set in the form of a dream, and the aim of this much-used convention was obviously to give a rational framework to some phantasy, and to make it seem real and personal. Langland's use of the dream-vision, however, is far less straightforward than this. Normally the content of the dream, as in Chaucer's allegories or the *Pearl,* is quite clear: the scene is self-contained and the story as orderly as that of any other narrative. The relationship of the dream-world to the real world is not that of shadow to reality, but rather that of architype to copy. The dream-world of the *Pearl,* for instance, is the natural world heightened: colours are more intense, form and sound more perfect, everything more clear and ordered than it can be in the unselectiveness of every-day life. The extraordinary point about Langland's dreams, however, is that they show the bewildering indifference to time and place which is characteristic of real dreams. The effect of this unique modification of the convention may be seen in two ways. Firstly it may be seen in the absence of the visualisation of a scene, to which we have already referred. Often the background against which characters meet is quite unknown, and this gives an impression of vagueness and greyness to the poem, in contrast, for instance, with the precision and brilliance of the *Pearl.* This lack, however, is compensated for by the effect of movement. Whilst the dominant tone of the *Pearl* and *Sir Gawain* is set by their recurrent adjectives, that of **Piers Plowman** is set by the verbs, which constantly suggest abrupt and vigorous action—action such as leaping, jumping or rushing—in a way that could not be sensibly visualised, and which bear no relation to the static scenes of art. The well-known description of the triumph of death illustrates this point:

> Deth cam dryvende after and al to doust passhed
> Kynges and knyghtes kayseres and popes;
> Lered ne lewed he let no man stonde,
> That he hitte evene that evere stired after.
> Many a lovely lady and lemmanes of knyghtes
> Swouned and swelted for sorwe of Dethes dyntes.
>
> (B text, Passus XX, 99-104)

Though this theme was very familiar and traditional in art as well as literature, it is most unlikely that Langland could have seen an illustration of it before the end of the fourteenth century and in England, in which death swept upon man with such power and violence. Indeed the only approximate parallel to it at any date and anywhere in western Europe is the well-known fresco of the Campo Santo in Pisa. Certainly if Langland had seen the theme of the inevitability of death visually treated, he would have seen something like a nobleman and a skeleton confronting each other, a scene grotesque and motionless.

The second characteristic which derives from Langland's peculiar use of the dream-convention is the abrupt shifting of time and place, which is so familiar from actual dreams, and so extremely unlike any other Medieval use of the dream-convention. There are in fact many parts of the poem, in which one cannot tell where the action is taking place or at what point in time. There is, for instance, the episode in which the dreamer and Scripture argue learnedly about salvation, when suddenly Trajan (the great example of the righteous heathen) interrupts with his contemptuous exclamation 'Yee! baw for bokes!', and proceeds to discourse on his own situation (B Text, xi, 135 ff.). Here there is obviously the relevance to idea and the inconsequentiality of event, which is typical of dreams. This disregard for limits of time and place often quickens the pace of the narrative to a disconcerting speed, or perhaps it would be more accurate to say that the narrative progresses with an alternate dawdling and darting movement. Langland's avoidance of the common need to lay a foundation in reasonable plot for the appearance or conduct of any character is clearly related to his indifference to the literal level of his allegory, and his suggestion of the disorganised nature of real dreams gives at least a technical plausibility to the inconsistencies of the literal story of the poem.

It is necessary to give the first person narrator of *Piers Plowman* some title to distinguish him from Langland the poet. It is most obviously appropriate to call him the dreamer, but he could almost equally well be called the pilgrim or wanderer, for another peculiarity of the poem is that Langland has made an unusual conflation of two forms, that of the dream and that of the pilgrimage. By far the more obvious is that of the dream vision, or rather a series of them, and in these the dreamer meets allegorical characters, some of whom personify various of his intellectual qualities; dreams which also enable him to be present at various episodes of the Redemption, as they do later authors of the religious lyric. Between his dreams, however, the dreamer is also a pilgrim, wandering on his journey through life in search for Do-Wel. This allegory of life as a journey or pilgrimage was of course a common Medieval sermon theme, though now better known from its later use in the *Pilgrim's Progress.* In the first half of the fourteenth century this image had been used as the form for an extensive moral poem by the French Cistercian Guillaume de Guilleville in his *Pèlerinage de la Vie Humaine,* a poem later translated into English by Lydgate. In this poem the various points of man's life from birth to death are represented as stages on a journey: the dreamer at birth sets out for the heavenly Jerusalem, being provided with spiritual armour by Grace of God, but is thereafter impeded at every turning by Satan or one of the seven deadly sins, and

is confused by the wheel of fortune. At last, however, Grace of God intervenes to bring him to a Cistercian monastery, where he is later approached by old age and infirmity, the two messengers of death, and finally by death himself, whereupon he wakes up. In the clarity of its outline the *Pèlerinage de la Vie Humaine* is as different from *Piers Plowman* as all other Medieval allegories, but it can cast some light upon the kind of poem which Langland thought he was writing, and on the extension of time within the poem. Langland's conception of his poem was that of a journey, a journey in which the dreamer or wanderer was primarily engaged, not with virtue as in the *Pèlerinage,* but with knowledge, and in which, as he inquired farther, he grew older. In the A Text the dreamer at last meets with Fever, who says 'I am messenger of Deth', and who advises his victim in the traditional moral way to 'do after Do-Wel'. The poem then abruptly becomes a third person narrative, and we are told how the dreamer wrote the poem and then died. Whilst the fact that the A Text ends with the dreamer's death shows very pointedly that his journeyings are an allegory of life, the progress of growing old is more emphasised in the B Text. In the latter, before his dispute with Scripture, the dreamer finds himself pursued and enticed by fortune, with her attendants, lust and avarice, and though warned by old age not to trust in them, the dreamer finds their words too sweet for him to be able to dismiss them. Similarly in Passus 20 the dreamer meets with old age, whose effects are described in the traditional manner of Medieval moral satire: at age's blows the dreamer becomes deaf, toothless, stiffened by gout and impotent (xx, 188 ff.). One thread of Langland's allegory therefore is that of the dreamer as Everyman or the pilgrim through life, who is diverted from his search for virtue and heaven by the sins of the world, and, who, as the journey proceeds, in one version grows old and in the other dies.

This distinguishing of Everyman's journey as an important connecting thread in the poem brings us to the difficult but important point of the relationship of the dreamer to Langland himself. Up to the end of the fourteenth century one would not expect a poem set in the first person to contain any personal truth: the poet is not concerned with the individual, whether it be himself or another, but with what is common to everybody. In the religious lyric, for instance, the 'I' speaker expresses feelings which anybody could make their own, whilst in narrative poetry the 'I' character, as in Chaucer's *Prologue,* may be quite unlike the poet, indeed ironically his opposite. Modern critics seem sometimes to think that the use of a dramatic 'I' is sophisticated, and that the simple and natural thing for a poet to do is to express truthfully his own feelings. The course of English literature, however, suggests the exact opposite, for the development is from the impersonal or dramatic 'I' of Anglo-Saxon and Medieval poetry, through the semipersonal 'I' of Renaissance literature, to the completely personal 'I' of the Romantics. If Langland therefore was typical of his period, one would expect the dreamer to be as remote from the individual personality of the poet, as he is in the *Pèlerinage* or in the *Pearl.* The latter has admittedly been searched for autobiographical information, but the self-absorbed grief of the dreamer should properly be interpreted as that of anybody bereaved and unresigned. At first sight by analogy it might be supposed that the questionings of the dreamer in *Piers Plowman* are the questionings of any intelligent man of the fourteenth century: there is, however, a very striking difference between the 'I' character of the *Pearl* and that of *Piers Plowman.* In the *Pearl* the arguments of the maiden are very skilfully developed and timed, so that at each stage in his answers the dreamer becomes milder and more moderate, with the result that by the end he has emerged from his self-pitying possessiveness to a more tranquil understanding of loss and death. In *Piers Plowman,* however, the dreamer in this sense never learns, for there is no poetic resolution to the opposing arguments: they are merely accumulated and put on one side. It is hard therefore to avoid the inference that Langland, unlike the author of the *Pearl,* did not know which way his arguments were leading him, and that therefore, whilst his intention may have been to show Everyman seeking a solution to the moral corruption and philosophical problems of his own age, in fact he was exploring the perplexities of his own mind.

The setting out antithetically of opposing points of view was so common a method of Medieval theology and poetry, that it comes as quite a shock to find somebody, who either could not control the form or did not wish to do so. It has been pointed out that the second half of the fourteenth century was probably the first period in the Middle Ages in which laymen discussed philosophical problems, perhaps just as non-experts today take an interest in psychology. Langland seems to be an extreme example of a general tendency, for his inquiry into truth has the earnestness typical of the amateur and he does not write with the assurance of professional ease: at an earlier period he would surely not have concerned himself with problems such as those of grace or free-will. Langland's intellectual difficulties communicate themselves to the reader because there is no logical solution to them which is poetically emphasised. Until one has read the poem many times, and even then, it is difficult to remember which side in the various theological arguments prevailed: poetically the solution does not lie in a crowning argument, but in the figure of Piers and in the long and fine narrative of the Harrowing of Hell. It was not of course that Langland was intellectually feeble or that a man of sharper mind would not have shared his perplexity. In part his difficulties arose from a desire to reconcile current philosophical disputes with the issues of every day living, as, for instance, the relationship of Bradwardine's doctrine of predestination, which was the concern of philosophers, with the idea of personal moral choice, so vital an issue with preachers. Other people were not more successful than Langland in relating these two ideas, but rather with professional prudence they did not normally attempt it. It should, however, be added that the role of the plain man perplexed was not peculiar to Langland. Chaucer assumed it both for himself and for Troilus, and it is possible to think that this was not an attitude inconsistent with the depiction of Everyman in the second half of the fourteenth century. In Chaucer's work, however, such passages are minor asides, whilst in *Piers Plowman* they contribute to the dominant tone of the poem.

The extent to which we read the perplexity of the dreamer as being that of Langland himself depends finally upon the interpretation of a long passage of personal reference which was added in the C Text (Passus 6, 1-108). In this the dreamer describes himself as some kind of clerk in minor orders, who earns his living by saying the office for the dead, and who is reproached by reason for living the kind of life only proper to one in a religious order. This description obviously does not sum up Langland's career, for his poem shows him to have been a learned and well-read man, and of this the C Text says nothing. Yet the passage does not have the general relevance nor the unmistakable borrowing of previous commonplaces, which occurred in the passage describing the ageing of the dreamer, so that if it does not contain genuine personal description, it is difficult to account for it. But if it is personal description, then we can see clearly in it Langland's self-conscious concern and uncertainty over himself, of which the whole poem could in a sense be called a magnificent extension. It may well be that it was Langland's passionate concern with his own difficulties and their relationship to wider issues which was the driving force of the poem, contributing to both its merits and defects. The chief fault which it encouraged was confusion, for, since the subject-matter was the range of Langland's own mind, it had no inherent shapeliness which might have helped a poet whose power of imagination far exceeded his ability to organise his material. It is strikingly clear that there is a correlation between the dreamer's perplexity and the poet's confusion: that where the dreamer is most oppressed by the conflict between different philosophical arguments or by the antithesis between the contemporary world and the world as it should be, that there the poet is most likely to be diverted from his point, or to allow some allegorical figure to develop an argument inappropriate or irrelevant to his significance. This might be illustrated over and over again from the section on Do-Wel. There is here a strong contrast with the section on Do-Bet. In the section on Do-Wel Langland imitated the form of allegorical dream in which the dreamer is also one of the chief characters, but with the approach of the section on Do-Bet Langland gradually reverts to the kind which he had used for satiric purposes to begin with, that is the kind in which the dreamer is chiefly said to be present in order to give to the content an air of immediacy and reality. The very beautiful speech on poverty delivered by Patience in Passus 14 or the analysis of charity in Passus 15 are only listened to by the dreamer, whilst in the finest passus of the whole poem, that on the Harrowing of Hell (Passus 18), the dreamer is only present as an onlooker. The dream form here is no longer being used to explore the poet's mind, but as an external vision, and to this difference of method is related the confident tone of the poetry. As a poet Langland is at his greatest when not attempting an argumentative synthesis, but either when he is seeing the world through the eyes of a satirist as a place corrupted throughout by the seven deadly sins, or, by a reverse process, when he is seeing in it only Christ or His reflection.

In the development of this latter point there is a paradox, for, whilst as we said earlier, Langland disregarded the literal level of his allegory in a quite un-Medieval way, yet in isolated visionary passages he sees with extraordinary poetic insight some aspect of the real world combined with its farther supernatural significance. Whilst this was the basic theory of of Medieval allegory, Langland seems to have been the only writer who was stirred by it in his imagination rather than in his reason. This power of Langland is particularly evident in his descriptions of the poor, in whom he sees Christ most clearly reflected, and yet at the same time shows an acute and compassionate observation of their appearance and manners. The description, for instance, of the beggar, who, with his pack on his back (symbolising his good works), strides into heaven in front of the rich 'bataúntliche as beggeres done' (Passus 14, 213), shows a striking fusion of literal observation with allegorical significance.

Langland's allegorical method and in particular his treatment of the figures of Piers Plowman and the dreamer are the most obvious non-Medieval characteristics of the design and content of the poem. There remains, however, a concluding point about Langland's style, a point so important and deserving of analysis that is should properly be made the subject of an independent study. In so far, however, as it is related to the previous arguments it must be mentioned here. The relationship is this: it is not only Langland's manipulation of his allegory nor the absence of a visual imagination, which shows the lack of the typical Medieval virtue of clarity, but also his style, which has none of the lucid elegance of Medieval style at its best, but has on the contrary a subtle and complex texture. Associated ideas, for instance, are not set out one by one or side by side in the typical Medieval manner, but are interwoven and compressed together. A very fine illustration of this is the treatment of the image of drinking in Christ's speech to the devil in the account of the Harrowing of Hell:

> The bitternesse that thowe hast browe brouke it
>   thi-seluen,
> That art doctour of deth drynke that thow mad-
>   est!
>   For I, that am lorde of lyf loue is my drynke,
> And for that drynke to-day I deyde vpon erthe.
> I faughte so, me threstes yet for mannes soule
>   sake;
> May no drynke me moiste ne my thruste slake,
> Tyl the vendage falle in the vale of Iosephath,
> That I drynke righte ripe must *resureccio mort-*
>   *uorum,*
> And thanne shal I come as a kynge crouned with
>   angeles,
> And han out of helle alle mennes soules.
>   (Passus 18, 361-70)

The opening lines suggest the amplification of a common proverb of the kind, 'you have made your bed and now you must lie on it', and this brusque, colloquial retort is expressed in a tone of plain and righteous contempt, which nowadays recalls most strikingly that of *Paradise Regained.* With the devil's drink of death is then contrasted Christ's drink of love. In the amplification of this there are echoes of Mark xiv, 25, John xix, 28, and Matthew xx, 22, with the traditional commentaries upon them, in particular that Christ's thirst on the Cross was for man's salvation, and the whole is given a farther allegorical dimension by its incorporation within the image of the Christ-knight,

which had been developed earlier in the passus. Such disentangling, however, could at best cast light on Langland's method: the magnificence of the lines is scarcely illuminated by it. It is unfortunate that in some parts of *Piers Plowman* the style seems matted, turgid or flat, but in passages such as this, Langland writes with a profundity of imagination and a strength of style beyond the range of all other poets of the Middle Ages. (pp. 111-25)

> *Rosemary Woolf, "Some Non-Medieval Quali-*
> *ties of 'Piers Plowman',"* in Essays in Criti-
> cism, *Vol. XII, No. 2, April, 1962, pp. 111-25.*

Nevill Coghill   (essay date 1962)

[*In the following excerpt, Coghill praises Langland's unique talent as an allegorist, calling him "a visionary poet trying to discern the shape and meaning in our mortal predicament, through whatever kind of imagery rises to and is accepted by his mind."*]

It was Ymagynatyf who first recognized that Langland wrote poetry and he rebuked him for it. 'Thow medlest the with makynges,' he said, 'and mightest go sey thi sauter.' One may take this as the stricture upon himself of a religiously minded man, looking back over five and forty winters of a life he judged to have been largely wasted, 'for there ar bokes ynowe to telle men what Dowel is, Dobet and Dobest bothe'. He had let himself play about with poetry, only to form an incurable and time-consuming habit that led nowhere. He might have been better employed.

And indeed there were books enough about the good life and the way of salvation. What was unique in Langland's was the way it was 'made'. There had been dream-visions, allegories, pilgrimages, delineations of the Seven Sins, discussions of the Three Lives, satires and complaints before: nor was the rumbling grumble of alliteration anything new: in fact there had been almost everything that seems to make his poem. Yet it is unmatched because of the quite peculiar workings of his mind—the workings of *Ymagynatyf,* if by that phantom we may designate Langland's modes of memory, association of ideas and images, sense of perspective, and feeling for words.

He had many of the gifts that great poets commonly have: magnitude of design, passion, intuitions of things natural and supernatural, moral intensity, an instinctive ease in seeing one thing in terms of another, luck if not cunning in language, an obsessive theme. There are passages when his genius seems to fail him, as he flounders in the troublesome debates in which his quest involves him: but that is neither here nor there. What matters is that he has a great poet's stunning-power, and there are elements in it that I seem to meet nowhere but in him. They are not easy to account for, or even to describe, for this very reason; he breaks all convention and cannot readily be accommodated by the accepted language of criticism.

First among his unique creative gifts is a huge fluidity: *Piers Plowman* flows with powerful ease, up and down through Time and Space, with sudden tides that take unforeseeable directions without a word of warning: they carry the reader, sometimes protesting, from inner to

A sepia drawing by nineteenth-century painter and etcher Samuel Palmer entitled The Valley Thick with Corn. *Palmer's work, which depicts visionary landscapes, reflects the influences of medieval art and strong religious convictions on his life.*

outer worlds, natural and supernatural, with the arbitrary energies of a dream that has its secret purposes and destinations. In the end a reader perceives something of their organic shape, though no map that he can make of them is entirely satisfactory. To give example of the mobility of which I am speaking, the poem opens with the world at work in a field, moves swiftly to Westminster and back, undertakes a pilgrimage, but pauses to plough what is said to be a half-acre but seems to be another image for the working world. The Dreamer then awakes in the Malvern Hills, and turns inward into the life of the mind, moves once more to the life of London, then to the life of Nature in this middle-earth, and after many encounters in other places for the most part nameless, finds himself between Jericho and Jerusalem, stands at Calvary, descends into Hell, and returns thence to his cottage in Cornhill in time for Easter Mass. Beyond that it moves into an indeterminate Christendom, centred by implication in Rome, but yet is soon without a centre of any sort and is seen as a devastated area with no other confines than the world itself. In the course of this astonishing pilgrimage of his in space, the Dreamer is present at the coronation of Richard II, confers with Abraham and Moses, is an eye-witness of the Crucifixion, and of the Harrowing of Hell, and after watching the building of Holy Church, sees it torn down

by Antichrist. Present, Past, and Future are as instantly present to him as are the varied regions of his search, and though there is no logical pattern in these swift movements, there is a cogency in each as it happens. The fluidity and freedom of these shifting tides of dream result in a total form which could only come from a poet of archetypal or myth-creating power. However we analyse the detail of its structure, it has organic shape—the shape is of a spiritual hunger of search for some great epiphany that will show us what we are seeking, in a dream: the epiphany is granted and the Dreamer stumbles upon glory: but when it has been given into his hands to hold for ever, it is taken from him by an enemy and he is left in desolation and awake, with all his journey still to do. This is surely the shape of a universal experience.

Piers Plowman is often described as an allegory, even as the greatest of English allegories, and that will do well enough for ordinary purposes: no one will be greatly misled. But the poem is so exceptional in its modes of vision that when we look at it closely we are forced to revise this general account of it and consult our definitions. The most trenchant and authoritative description of allegory I know is that of C. S. Lewis, where he is speaking of the equivalences or correspondences, perceived by a poetic mind, between material and immaterial things:

This fundamental equivalence between the immaterial and the material may be used by the mind in two ways. . . . On the one hand you can start with an immaterial fact, such as the passions which you actually experience, and can then invent *visibilia* to express them. If you are hesitating between an angry retort and a soft answer, you can express your state of mind by inventing a person called *Ira* with a torch and letting her contend with another invented person called *Patientia*. This is allegory. . . . But there is another way of using the equivalence, which is almost the opposite of allegory, and which I would call sacramentalism or symbolism. If our passions, being immaterial, can be copied by material inventions, then it is possible that our material world in its turn is the copy of an invisible world. . . . The attempt . . . to see the archetype in the copy, is what I mean by symbolism or sacramentalism. [*The Allegory of Love,* 1936]

Pure allegory of this kind is nowhere better seen than in the *Psychomachia* of Prudentius, which Lewis instances. It must be among the finest of the mechanical operations of the spirit. (pp. 200-03)

Piers Plowman is a world and an age away from the *Psychomachia*. Gone are the modish rhetoric and the august Virgilian background, gone the notion of the soul as an orderly battlefield for the passions, where decisive victories in epic style smash, rather than probe, its problems. Who now can feel the manifold of moral tensions in any sort of temptation, sexual or other, in terms of a straight fight between two strapping amazons, whose sex is predetermined by purely grammatical considerations? (p. 203)

Langland's personified figures are of a different kind and, at their best, give no sense of having been fabricated: *Glutton* sounds as if he had been seen not once but many times in some Colwall pub, and *Coveytise* at any Winchester fair:

And thanne cam Coueytise, can I hym noughte
    descryue,
So hungriliche and holwe sire Heruy hym loked.
He was bitelbrowed and baberlipped also,
With two blered eyghen, as a blynde hagge:
And as a letheren purs lolled his chekes,
Wel sydder than his chyn: thei chiueled for elde:
And as a bondman of his bacoun his berde was
    bidraueled.

(B v. 188-94)

and, later,

'Repentedestow the eure', quod Repentance, 'ne
    restitucioun madest?'
'Yus, ones I was herberwed,' quod he, 'with an
    hep of chapmen,
I roos whan thei were arest, and yrifled here
    males.'
'That was no restitucioun,' quod Repentance,
    'but a robberes thefte,
Thou haddest be better worthy be hanged ther-
    fore
Than for al that that thow hast here shewed.'
'I wende ryflynge were restitucioun', quod he,
    'for I lerned neuere rede on boke,
And I can no Frenche in feith, but of the ferthest
    ende of Norfolke.'

(B v. 232-9)

(p. 204)

[But] unique in Langland's 'making' of personified abstractions is the character of Piers himself. The equivalences are kept shadowy and changeable: **Piers** is not a plain lable like *Pudicitia*.

Only gradually do we become aware of the significances the name includes and it is worth remarking that those who know the poem best differ among themselves over shades of meaning in him—a sure sign (since no one attributes this to incompetence in Langland) that Piers is a living character that can be argued over like Falstaff, and not an unmistakable abstraction like *Sodomita Libido,* whose nature is not in doubt, in spite of her grammatical sex. The meanings in Piers are the central meanings of the entire poem and we see them dissolve into one another at every fresh epiphany, with accumulated and ascending richness. The solid, simple farmer, honest worker, faithful son of the Church, who alone knows the way to Truth, returns long after as the Good Samaritan, a figure for Charity, and is seen at last in Christ, or Christ in him: into these meanings we must also pour others which Langland found in the gloss and adumbrated in his retelling of this parable: the man who fell among thieves is Fallen Man himself. The Priest and the Levite that passed by on the other side are the Patriarchs. The Good Samaritan is Christ in his humanity. To this gloss, Langland added identifications: the *patres antiqui* of Hugh of St Victor were to Langland Abraham and Moses, emblems of Faith and Hope: what else then could the Good Samaritan be but an emblem of Charity? All these meanings pass into Piers when we hear of the entry of Jesus into Jerusalem, to joust in Piers' arms, *humana natura,* and when Christ rises in triumph out of Hell, he still has some touch of Piers about him:

'Is this Iesus the Iuster?' quod I, 'that Iuwes did
    to deth?
Or is it Pieres the Plowman? . . . '

(B xix. 10-11)

Later still we are told that Jesus, while on earth, lived the lives of Dowel, Dobet, and Dobest: so these meanings, which are the quest-meanings of the whole poem, also pass into Piers and we are brought to realize that he has stood for them throughout and is their human custodian, the builder of Christ's church and House of Unity. If we are to 'lerne to loue and leue of alle othre', which is the last advice of Kynde, and sums the whole moral content of the poem, and of Christianity, we must seek Piers. No wonder, where so many significances crowd in, if critics differ in their emphasis when they interpret it! What I would at present stress, however, is not the *meaning* but the '*making*' of Piers: we recognize in him at first an allegorical figure, a visible, invented personification for an abstraction that we may call 'Dowel'. Next, an abstraction still personified, he teaches the Dreamer about the Tree of Charity. Then we see him identified with the Good Samaritan who is a figure from parable, not allegory, and in company with Abraham and Moses, who are neither abstractions nor fictions but historic people, used as symbols of Faith and Hope. Then he is Christ's humanity, visible and historical; the sum of Charity seen in person. When we look to our definitions, we see that all that is finest and most central in this figure is 'made' by a coalescence or fusion of allegory, parable, and symbol, and that is the poetic fact that volts it with imaginative power, unmatched in its own region of discourse. Langland is a visionary poet trying to discern the shape and meaning in our mortal predicament, through whatever kind of imagery rises to and is accepted by his mind, not an allegorical versifier at work upon a tidy little scheme, according to known rules.

We can see this same principle (the fusion of allegory and symbol) giving vigour to his sense of landscape, and even of action. To consider landscape first, the poem opens with one of the most memorable in English poetry: it was once believed to be an allegorical scene, invented to suit the poet's didactic intention. To the east, on high, a Tower of Truth. Below and to westward, a Dungeon of Care: in between, a fair field, full of folk. In these every reader can recognize an allegory of Heaven, Earth, and Hell, a fabricated theatrical set. But now it chances that this landscape has been identified and is as visible and as visitable as it ever was, in the Malvern hills. There stands the Herefordshire Beacon, high to the east; below it lies the dungeon-site of Old Castle, a little to the west: in between them the rolling fields of Colwall parish. These were the *visibilia* which came, for Langland, to symbolize our human situation and the choice between one or other of the eternities before us: many a church in Langland's time had a like image of Doom over its chancel arch: but Langland saw it in his native countryside. Yet from this symbolizing mountain in his poem there descends to the Dreamer a Lady, 'in lynene yclothid', who is an allegory, a figure invented to stand for Holy Church. An allegory has issued from a symbol.

This same mixture of kinds can be seen in actions as well as in people and places. Another of the memorable moments in the poem is the action of Kynde when he 'comes out of the planets' at the call of Conscience to protect the House of Unity, attacked by Antichrist and the Seven Sins. It is hardly possible to imagine an occasion that could sound more obviously allegorical: this is the action taken by Kynde:

> Kynd Conscience tho herde, and cam out of the
>   planetes,
> And sent forth his foreioures, feures, & fluxes,
> Coughes, and cardiacles, crampes, and toth-
>   aches,
> Rewmes, and radegoundes, and roynouse
>   scalles,
> Byles, and bocches and brennyng agues:
> Frenesyes, and foule yueles, forageres of kynde,
> Hadde yprikked and prayed polles of peple,
> That largelich a legioun lese her lyf sone.
> There was—'harrow and help!, here cometh
>   Kynde
> With Deth that is dredful, to vndone vs alle!'
>   (B xx. 79-88)

[W. W.] Skeat in fact believed this to be an allegory, invented to show how Nature will fail man and may even prove his enemy in his hour of need:

> Conscience supposes that Nature, for love of
> Piers the Plowman, will assist men against spiri-

tual foes. But the result is represented as being very different; for Nature also becomes man's enemy, afflicting him with various bodily diseases. . . . Yet Nature is, at last, man's true friend: see line 109.

When we take up this reference, we find line 109 to be as follows:

> And Kynde cessede tho to seon the peuple
>   amende.
>   (C xxiii. 109: B xx. 108)

But Skeat's interpretation is mistaken. Langland was not inventing an allegory to show the caprices of Nature, but showing how Nature serves God by putting the fear of death into man, if he cannot be brought to repent by any other means. Langland believed that he had witnessed a similar occasion in his own lifetime—in January 1362, to be precise—and had no need to invent an allegory: he recorded a fact and interpreted it as a symbol, *'in tokenynge of drede,* That dedly synne *at domesday* shal fordon hem alle'*:

> He preued that thise pestilences were for pure
>   synne,
> And the southwest wynde on Saterday at euene
> Was pertliche for pure pryde, and for no poynt
>   elles.
> Piries and plomtrees were puffed to the erthe,
> In ensample, ye segges, ye shulden do the bet-
>   tere.
> Beches and brode okes were blowen to the
>   grounde,
> Torned vpward her tailles in tokenynge of drede,
> That dedly synne at domesday shal fordon hem
>   alle.
>   (B v. 13-20)

Kynde, an allegorical figure, performs a symbolic action: he is coming to man's rescue on the Day of Antichrist by warning him of death. When he sees that the warning has been effective, he relents.

If I have laboured this matter of allegory and symbolism, it is not to deny the dichotomy, but to show that Langland, at his most Langlandian, and at the top of his powers as a poet, obtains his effects by blending or fusing them in his imagery: he may not have done this on purpose, but it was the way his mind worked. (pp. 205-09)

> *Nevill Coghill, "God's Wenches and the Light That Spoke," in* English and Medieval Studies: Presented to J. R. R. Tolkien on the Occasion of His Seventieth Birthday, *edited by Norman Davis and C. L. Wrenn, George Allen & Unwin Ltd., 1962, pp. 200-18.*

Elizabeth Salter   (essay date 1962)

[*Salter was an English educator and critic who completed a study of Langland's poem in* Piers Plowman: An Introduction, *as well as an edition of* Piers Plowman *(1967). In the excerpt below from the former work, she considers the allegory in the B-text as a social history, a medieval allegory, and an extensive versified sermon. Salter writes: "The fact that so many different ways of*

The most important reason for reading **Piers Plowman** is its magnificence as a work of religious art; conceived greatly, it contains a wider variety of fine poetry than any other work from the English Middle Ages. Langland's inquiry into man's relationship with God, set in the powerful allegory of the search which ends only to begin afresh, is not challenged for span and strength of execution by anything in English literature except *Paradise Lost.* Both poems have the same broad spiritual landscape. Milton's 'dungeon horrible' and 'opal towrs and battlements' are those which Langland saw as he passed from waking life on the Malvern Hills to his dream of 'a toure on a toft. trielich ymaked; a depe dale binethe. a dongeon there-inne', and their vision moves constantly between Heaven and Hell, with Earth as the battleground of divine and devilish agencies. Both, moreover, are shaped as the prelude to a further drama—a drama to be worked out within each responsible human being. In the closing lines of **Piers Plowman** and *Paradise Lost* we are certainly conscious of the immense backward stretch of all that has been suffered and achieved, and yet we know that this is only the beginning; great vistas of thought and action still open before us. As the poems end, new pilgrimages are about to take place; **Piers Plowman** shows us Conscience resolving upon a journey:

> 'Bi Cryste,' quod Conscience tho 'I will bicome
>   a pilgryme,
> And walken as wyde as al the worlde lasteth,
> To seke Piers the Plowman that Pryde may destruye,
> . . . . now Kynde me auenge,
> And sende me happe and hele. til I haue Piers
>   the Plowman.

In *Paradise Lost* two pilgrims set out:

> They looking back, all th' Eastern side beheld
> Of Paradise, so late their happie seat,
> Waved over by that flaming brand, the gate
> With dreadful Faces throng'd, and fierie Arms:
> Some natural Tears they drop'd, but wip'd them
>   soon:
> The world was all before them, where to choose
> Their place of rest, and Providence their guide:
> They hand in hand with wandering steps and
>   slow
> Through Eden took their solitarie way.

But if the basic purpose of both poets might be expressed in Milton's words—the need to 'assert Eternal Providence, And justifie the wayes of God to men'—their art offers no such grounds for comparison. It is Langland's peculiar distinction that, at one and the same time, he can keep us fully in touch with the great metaphysical consequences of human existence and with the tangible realities of our humorous, corrupt, frustrating and yet desirable life on earth. The language in which he conveys deep spiritual truths:

> For I, that am lorde of lyf loue is my drynke,
> And for that drynke to-day I deyde upon erthe.
>   (B.XVIII.363-4)

is often as simple and familiar as that in which he invites his reader to share the experience of the mediaeval peasant's harsh life in wintertime, the warm, raucous atmosphere of the alehouse:

> Kokes and here knaues crieden, 'hote pyes, hote!
> Good goos and grys go we dyne, gowe!'
> Taverners 'a tast for nouht' tolden the same,
> 'Whit wyn of Oseye and of Gascoyne,
> Of the Ruele and of the Rochel wyn the roste to
>   defy.'
>   (C.I.226-230)

Praising Christ who 'blewe alle thi blissed into the blisse of paradise', he achieves that blend of reverence and vigour which few religious writers after the mediaeval period were capable of, and which was not put to such high poetic uses by any of Langland's contemporaries. Sharp forthrightness of diction and spontaneity of verse-movement give us often a direct entry into **Piers Plowman**: much of the verse provides reading quite as unhampered as any we are likely to meet in the work of Chaucer, for instance, or in the Miracle Plays. And because of the return of many twentieth-century poets to the use of the free, unrhymed, accentual line which is Langland's verse norm, we can often respond to the movement of **Piers Plowman** as to a contemporary verse pattern. Familiarity with the characteristic rhythms of Pound, Eliot, Auden, means that lines such as these

> And that falleth to the fader that formed us alle,
> Loked on us with loue and lete his sone deye
> Mekely for owre mysdedes to amende us all;
>   (B.I.164-6)

need no special introduction as 'mediaeval verse': they come naturally and simply to the listener. Moreover the conviction that no theme and no vocabulary are to be debarred from poetry on account of their closeness to everyday, ordinary life, is one from which spring some of the finest passages in **Piers Plowman** as well as some of the finest in compositions nearer to our own day. 'For the modern poet nothing is inherently unpoetic'; this observation could be made equally well about Langland, as he presses sights, experiences and words, with little or no special selection, into the service of his urgent and dedicated purpose.

But it is not possible to recommend Langland as a poet who is always accessible to present-day readers. There *are* times when his work raises problems for us—problems only capable of partial solution by reference to contemporary thought and artistic methods. For **Piers Plowman** is 'English mediaeval' in ways that Chaucer's poetry, drawing strongly on French and Italian cultural traditions, could never be. If, therefore, we are to gain more than a partial understanding of Langland's art and meaning, we have to be prepared to meet a challenge almost as often as a welcome. It is easy to select and praise 'star' poetic passages, such as the splendid speech of Christ after the Harrowing of Hell:

> 'For I, that am lorde of lyf loue is my drynke,
> And for that drynke to-day I deyde upon erthe.

I faughte so, me threstes yet for mannes soule
   sake;
May no drynke me moiste ne my thruste slake,
Tyl the vendage falle in the vale of Iosephath,
That I drynke righte ripe must *resureccio mort-*
   uorum,
And thanne shal I come as a kynge crouned with
   angeles,
And han out of helle alle mennes soules.'

                     (B.XVIII.363-340)

There are many of equal dignity and beauty. It is also easy to find reasons for praising the whole work which are not sufficiently profound or comprehensive. *Piers Plowman* has been, and still is, read as a satirical commentary on the mediaeval scene, as a subtly performed exercise in religious allegory, or as a deepening analysis and correction of sin. It is much more difficult to grasp the poem as a total religious and artistic unit, operating extensively and harmoniously according to laws which may not be entirely familiar to us either from modern literature, or from the better known departments of mediaeval literature. The difficulty, however, should not deter us, for the rewards are unusually rich. *Piers Plowman* is a poem unique in its period. Connected with and resembling many other mediaeval literary forms, it is *exactly* like none of them; drawing fully upon the great common stock of mediaeval religious doctrines and images, it reinterprets and renews what it takes in the light of a highly personal vision.

The fact that so many different ways of approaching Langland's work can be recommended should be accepted as a sign of its wealth of content, and not as a persuasion to assert the exclusive truth of any one particular way. Each is justifiable, but not in isolation. The social-historical approach, for instance, which is the oldest-established, and uses the poem as a lively witness to the eventful years of the later fourteenth century, has a limited truth to convey. From the satirical, dramatic parts of the poem, comes information on life and manners in mediaeval days; scenes from ale-houses, from the courts of Kings and Bishops, from country cottages, churches and London streets crowd one against the other. On the many pilgrimages we make throughout the poem, we notice the faces and conditions of men of Langland's time—the wealth and corruption, Church and State laid ruthlessly open to our view. Here we can learn of the bare, staple diet of a mediaeval countryman:

   . . . two grene cheses,
   A few cruddes and creem and an hauer cake,
   And two loues of benes and bran . . . '

                     (B.VI.283-5)

of the elaborate dress of a mediaeval noblewoman:

   Hire robe was ful riche of red scarlet engreyned,
   With ribanes of red golde and of riche
     stones . . .

                     (B.II.15-16)

of the hunting parson, the deformed beggars, with their idle songs, 'How, trollilolli', and of the great, worldly Cardinals:

   'The contre is the curseder that cardynales come
     inne:'

                     (B.XIX.415)

Piers Plowman tells us what an intelligent man of the late fourteenth-century thought of politics and institutions in his day; Langland was deeply moved by such issues as social injustice, the responsibilities of kingship, and comments directly upon them.

But when we have realized the contemporary scene through his words, we are in a position to make only a superficial judgement of Langland's work as a poet; we have hardly begun to grasp his meaning and appreciate his art. Langland's whole intention is not to offer a faithful record of his time, to be used as documentary evidence by later historians, and we must enlarge our view of the poem if our reading and comment is not to be limited and often irrelevant.

At the opposite end of the scale, we can approach the poem as an exercise in interpreting mediaeval religious allegory. This is, of course, an extremely important element in our total experience of *Piers Plowman;* it is necessary that we should proceed further than the literal story and attempt to penetrate to deeper meanings. The knights, beggars, prelates, and above all, the main figure of the poem, the plowman Piers himself, are part of a larger pattern of significance than that immediately discernible from their discussions and actions. Our minds must be conditioned to expect and to find at many points in the poem, 'multiple meaning'. And we have received great help here in recent years from critics whose endeavour it has been to show us the unfolding and resolution of Langland's allegory.

There are signs, however, that we have perhaps turned too far away from the 'social-historical realism' to the complex symbolism of the poem. In many ways we are only slightly nearer to understanding its nature, and Langland's intentions, if we account for *Piers Plowman* as a consistently subtle exposition of spiritual truths, made in the many-layered fashion best exemplified by mediaeval Biblical commentary—literal, tropological, allegorical and anagogical senses packed tightly into the lines, only waiting to be released by the watchful reader. While there is no need to question multiple meaning as an element in the work, Langland's allegorical usages are varied and fluctuating, and we cannot easily generalize about the depth of significance in any given line of his verse. Moreover, we must be sure that we are not supporting the claims of the poetry by the interest of the allegory alone, and, in particular, that we are not excusing faulty art by the same means. Whether we are defending or attacking Langland's work, we must begin by acknowledging that an absorbing allegory need not necessarily be a great poem.

How, then, does the third commonly accepted way of reading *Piers Plowman*—as an extensive versified sermon—improve, if at all, upon these methods? There is no denying its strong sermon connections. The subject matter is often directly that of the mediaeval pulpit; the didactic impulse in Langland is powerful. Sermons are constantly being preached throughout the poem—by the poet, by his characters. But we must be careful how we express the relationship of *Piers Plowman* to sermon. A reduction of the poem to the status of a better-than-usual mediaeval homily, or series of homilies, is false and damaging; Langland utilizes homiletic material and form to a considerable extent, but his poem works through sermon to conclusions outside the reach of sermon. An investigation of general likenesses to homiletic language and procedure can, however, be of help in defining one particular aspect of the poem—its art.

A reading of *Piers Plowman* which neglects the fact that this is essentially a work of art, a product of the creative imagination, is seriously restricted. And this holds good even if we are reading for the sake of content only, for the impulses of the poetry, the varying sound of the language, the graph of rhythm, are sensitive guides to minute and important fluctuations of meaning. It has taken much longer for critics to come to terms with Langland's poetry than with the substance of his work. And it is not all the fault of critic and reader. Langland tells us frequently that he has vital matter to convey; only once does he speak of his 'poetic art'. While his best poetry asks for no defence, there are times when we may feel, initially, more doubtful about Langland's claims to the title of 'poet'. Here our assumptions about what we are likely to find in a work such as *Piers Plowman* need some thought. A man of Langland's time, training and temperament would accept without question that art must serve devotion; the lowering of purely artistic standards on some occasions will be sanctioned and deliberate. But we should remember that the religious impulse can also be expected to generate poetic energy. We must not be disposed, by criteria inappropriate to religious art, to find a tension in *Piers Plowman* between matter and form. Although we may ultimately be forced to accuse Langland of paying less attention to his art than to his meaning, of writing sense but failing to write poetry, we are not entitled to pass judgement unless we have prepared ourselves to receive a comprehensive work of a special poetic nature. We are not likely to feel deep and continuous pleasure in Langland's writing if we have not grasped the basic principle to which it works—the inseparability of religious and artistic forces—and, moreover, if we have not attempted to see it in its own context of space and time.

Approaching the poem, perhaps for the first time, we should take our directions from Langland himself. *Piers Plowman* is planned, as the opening lines tell us, on a cosmic scale: its dream province spans Earth, Heaven and Hell:

> And merveylously me mette as ich may yow
>   telle;
> Al the welthe of this worlde and the woo bothe,
> Wynkyng as it were wyterly ich saw hyt,
> Of tryuthe and of tricherye of tresoun and of
>   gyle,
> Al ich saw slepynge as ich shal you telle.
> Esteward ich byhulde after the sonne,
> And saw a toure, as ich trowede truthe was ther-
>   ynne;
> Westwarde ich waitede in a whyle after,
> And sawe a deep dale deth as ich lyvede.
> Wonede in tho wones and wyckede spiritus.
> A fair feld, ful of folke fonde ich ther bytwyne,

Alle manere of men the mene and the ryche,
Worchynge and wandrynge as the worlde as-
    keth.

(C.I.9-21)

And its theme is fittingly large; phrased many times over the course of the poem, it comes, in Passus I as a simple question, asked by the Dreamer:

> 'Teche me to no tresore but telle me this ilke,
> How I may saue my soule that seynt art yhol-
>   den?'

(B.I.83-4)

and answered by Holy Church:

> 'Love is leche of lyf and nexte owre lorde selue,
> And also the graith gate that goth into heuene;'
>
> ['Love is life's physician, and next to our Lord
> himself, and also the highway leading to heav-
> en.']

(B.I.203-4)

Clearly Piers Plowman will be more than a social commentary or a religious satire; the spiritual journey to which the dreamer, and reader, are being introduced will be different from a Canterbury Pilgrimage—they seek, not a 'holy blisful martyr' but God himself. Though there will be many halts and detours, the road they must travel is 'the graith gate that goth into hevene': it will be arduous and exhilarating.

Then, too, we see early on that the poem is cast allegorically. Langland will often intend more than at first he appears to do; there will be a special associative power in some, though not all, of his plainest words. While we need not press too consistently for 'multiple meaning', we can assume that nothing in the world of the poem rests in simple isolation. We must not be halted for overlong by the picture of grotesque sin—here, of Avarice:

> He was bitelbrowed and baberlipped also,
> With two blered eyghen as a blynde hagge;
> And as a letheren purs lolled his chekes,
> Well sydder than his chyn thei chiveled for elde;
> And as a bondman of his bacoun his berde was
>   bidraveled.
> With a hode on his hed a lousi hatte above,
> And in a tawny tabarde of twelve wynter age,
> Al totorne and baudy and ful of lys crepynge;
>   (B.V.190-197)

or the compassionate picture of beast and man, hungry and cold in winter time:

> 'And moche murthe in Maye is amonges wilde
>   bestes,
> And so forth whil somer lasteth her solace du-
>   reth.
> Ac beggeres aboute Midsomer bredlees thei
>   soupe,
> And yit is wynter for hem worse for wete-shodde
>   thei gange,
> A-fyrst sore and afyngred and foule yrebuked,
> And arated of riche men that reuthe is to here.
> Now, lorde, sende hem somer and some maner
>   Ioye,
> Hevene after her hennes-goynge that here han
>   suche defaute!'

(B.XIV.158-165)

These are good examples of realistic art, but they have not, in this poem, a separate existence; they are part of a larger web of allegorical significances, which Langland can only help us to understand if we will accept the initial premise—a potential though fluctuating richness of connected meanings.

And this is easier to accept if we remember that *Piers Plowman* is a dream poem. Within his 'merueilouse sweuene' Langland, the poet and thinker, is free to work as he wishes; if we, and his dreamer, seem to be subject to an unseen authority which moves us, sometimes inexplicably, from one scene or mode of meaning to another, this is surely nothing unusual for dream-experience. The events and thoughts in which we share will often, as in a *real* dream, have no more precise definition than that provided by the mere facts of sleeping and waking. Moreover, this is a dream whose religious nature becomes more significant as the poem continues; the abandonment of ordinary, rational logic is made more willingly when it is clear that deep spiritual revelation follows.

As for the nature, the quality of the poetry, we have only to attend closely as Langland introduces his themes, to realize that a man so oriented towards 'other heuene than here' will regard his art in a special way. He will demand that it achieve a blend of beauty and usefulness; its characteristic faults and excellences will depend intimately upon devotional needs. We must, therefore, understand how the mediaeval religious poet works—neither falling, on the one hand, into the error of supposing him to be hopelessly shackled by his faith, nor, on the other, ignoring the factors which may account for both his successes and limitations as an artist. More specifically, we can see how Langland drew upon certain long-established literary traditions to serve his vision. Born in a part of England where alliterative verse was a natural mode, he continued, even in the London of Chaucer's day, to write alliteratively. But he was equally indebted to the language and techniques of the mediaeval pulpit, and we can observe how both traditions combine, in an unusual, perhaps a unique way, to sanction his 'ars poetica'.

Piers Plowman has a large meaning which is accessible to us in its fullness provided that we are willing to use watchfulness and patience. It demands that we listen carefully to the poetry—the turn and flow of rhythm, the pattern of sound—and that we submit ourselves to the powerful working of the poet's imagination as phrase, image, and episode accumulate, enriching each other, and persuading us towards the acceptance of great general truths. For however absorbing it can become as an intellectual study, *Piers Plowman* claims out attention most strongly as a work of the religious imagination. Langland knows that

> . . . the painted slide, the imagined ideal is the real: but it is only actual, only operative, when we see its image projected upon the transience and terror of our world.

And his projection of the ideal onto the transient, terror-stricken world of the Field Full of Folk (which is our world too) calls out both art and devotion in a specially powerful way. So we see Gluttony, not simply as a vice or as a dramatic character, but as a principle of evil, able and

waiting to take innumerable forms of life. In addition to many abstract sermons on the value of Patience and Humility, we witness the feast to which Patience and the Dreamer go: there the pathetic and amusing sight of these two lowly ones enduring, while the great Doctor of Divinity crams food and wine into himself, is turned by a single arrogant gesture into a revelation of sin:

> 'What is Dowel? sire doctour,' quod I, 'is Dowel
>   any penaunce?'
> 'Dowel?' quod this doctour—. and toke the
>   cuppe and dranke—
>
> (B.XIII.102-3)

Moreover, in the central sections of the poem, Langland adds to the preacher's exposition of God's love, a vision of Piers—Christ, taken and crucified, and risen from the dead, speaking to us, and involving us in the everlasting sacrifice of love. The poet who dreamed himself into a wilderness, 'wiste I neuer where', is found, in the end, 'speaking no dream, but things oracular'. (pp. 1-11)

> *Elizabeth Salter, "The Approach," in her*
> *"Piers Plowman": An Introduction, Cambridge, Mass.: Harvard University Press, 1962,*
> *pp. 1-11.*

Morton W. Bloomfield (essay date 1962)

[*A Canadian-born American educator and critic, Bloomfield is interested in medieval studies and linguistics. In the following excerpt, he discusses Langland's language and style in* Piers Plowman. *He concludes that the poem is based on three genres—the allegorical dream narrative, the dialogue, and the encyclopedic satire—and that it was influenced by the complaint, the commentary, and the sermon genres.*]

That William Langland intended *Piers Plowman* to be a work of art is obvious from the form in which he cast it. He created characters, fashioned dialogue for them, and provided a narrative, even if at times the action seems bogged down in endless talk. But things do happen and do move, and there is a conclusion which, if puzzling, is nevertheless a conclusion. What form Langland was consciously using, what language and meter he employed, and what audience he was addressing are as vital and important problems as the problem of what he was saying. As an artist, even a not entirely successful one, he must have chosen his forms and language with some purpose and care. They must stand in some relation to what he was trying to say. This [essay] deals somewhat tentatively with these problems of rhetoric and art. . . . (p. 3)

Piers Plowman ends, as it begins, with a quest. At the conclusion of the poem, the seeker is Conscience, who, unlike the questing Will at the beginning, knows what and whom he is seeking. Whether or not he finds Piers Plowman, the reader is not told, but he may at least assume that Piers can, and some day will, be found. As a good Christian, the author certainly must have believed this. He has shown that Piers in the later part of the poem is the human manifestation of Christ—either as Jesus or as an ideal head of the Church, His continuing vicar—for it is only through Him that perfection may be found. Conscience and Will are in search of spiritual knowledge that will transform society and the self. The poem deals with the search not the finding; and although the quest has not been in vain, the goal is yet to be attained. More is known at the end than at the beginning—that there is a guide and principles to follow, that there are forces within men and within history working for Christian perfection—but the journey is not yet complete. *Piers* is a work whose artistic and moral claims on the reader reinforce each other. What is sought is a way to seek.

This study regards Christian perfection as the goal of Will, but it has been customary in the past forty years to speak of the poem, when it is recognized as more than a valuable social document, as being concerned with the problem of salvation. In the very important discussion between the dreamer and Lady Holy Church in Passus I, after the description of the field full of folk and the fable of the rats have been detailed in the Prologue, Will raises the question, "How I may save my soule" (I, 84), and is given a brief answer with instructions to teach Holy Church's lesson to unlearned men (I, 134). It is true that this question and answer, and the following action of the poem, seem to provide the poem's rationale. In modern times, however, salvation tends to be thought of in individualistic terms. One of the major themes of the poem is that true salvation is not only personal but social. The Gospel preaches a Kingdom, not a conglomeration of individually saved souls; and the Middle Ages, with its strong corporate sense, understood this message. As Etienne Gilson puts it [in his *Etudes de la philosophie médiévale,* 1944], "The Gospel had not only promised to the just a kind of individual beatitude, but it had announced to them entrance into a kingdom, that is to say a society, of the just, united by the bonds of their common beatitude. The preaching of Christ had been early understood as the promise of a perfect social life and the constitution of this society had been seen as the final purpose of His incarnation."

It is more appropriate, then, as this analysis will bear out, to say that the subject matter of *Piers* is Christian perfection, which is a broader term than salvation and which includes it. Valuable as many recent studies of the meaning of the poem have been, there has been a tendency to submerge the social, and elevate the individualistic, religious element in it. Fundamentally *Piers Plowman* is about social regeneration; and in this, the poem is in the main stream of the Judeo-Christian tradition.

Christian perfection is a well-known subject of Christian thought and endeavor, and it normally presupposes the existence of grades or levels. Salvation is an all or nothing proposition; but the poem is, as the section on the three Do's shows, closely concerned with levels of Christian living and with moral distinctions and subtleties. In every way, then, *Piers Plowman* is fundamentally concerned with the problem of Christian perfection.

The poem is divided into four major sections—the *Visio* and the *Lives of Do-wel, Do-bet, and Do-best,* the last three being known as the *Vita.* The whole *Visio* (from the

Prologue to Passus VII) may be regarded as an introduction in which the dreamer remains the observer. He locates himself and defines his self-image—a hermit and possibly a monk seeking after Christian perfection. He describes his contemporary world, which is full of sin and yet in a confused way longs to be free of sin. In this introduction, Langland also shows how men fail in their attempt to find salvation and perfection because they are fooled by Meed (cupidity) and because, even if cleansed of sin, they cannot find the way to the Saviour and fall into sin again. Their leaders betray them. The guide, Piers, who appears in the last few passus of the *Visio,* seems to be misled by a false pardon, and all ends in wrangling and despair. New complexities have opened up, and new distinctions must be made. Now the dreamer himself must undertake a pilgrimage and become active instead of passive, a seeker instead of an observer.

The *Vita* (Passus VIII-XX) consists of three parts, corresponding to three grades of perfection. Do-wel is concerned with the ordering of self to the natural world in terms of Christianity and raises questions about such topics as predestination, the value of learning, and the meaning of nature, natural man, and natural law. The quest in the first part of Do-wel (VIII-XII) is in general concerned with a burning fourteenth-century problem—that of authority. The movement of Will from one authority to another here dramatizes the problem of the relative authority of learning, reason, the Bible, and the Church. Possible autobiographical elements in this part of the poem may be present, but if they are here, they are secondary. After the search for an authority to answer these questions on perfection is satisfied at least on one level, by the clarifying speech of Imaginatif in Passus XII, we are finally led to the knowledge that patient poverty is Do-wel—the best way to lead the Christian life in the world, the lowest but by no means unworthy way of Christian perfection, which, perforce, must embrace the vast majority of Christians. The conclusion to this section is centered in the figure of Hawkin the Active Man and dramatized in his conversion and repentance.

Do-bet is concerned with the ordering of the self to Christ. The part centers on a discussion of the theological virtues, especially love, and culminates in a vision of the Harrowing of Hell. Do-best, coming back again, as in the *Visio,* to society and history, is concerned with the ordering of self to the Kingdom of God and to the regenerated society, centered in the cardinal virtues. The true Church is in the throes of "a time of troubles" and is being assailed by Antichrist at a time of crisis. Tribulation and persecution are the fate of the elect throughout the history of the world, and the betrayal of the ideals and doctrines of the Church by its adherents and leaders is the clearest sign of a coming renewal and of a further step towards the Kingdom of God.

How must a Christian live in order to attain as much perfection as possible within the limits of his human nature? What is the meaning of Christian perfection in general, and how can it be applied in Langland's own time? These are the basic questions of the poem and are closely related to the whole crisis of late medieval thought.

Unlike Marsiglio of Padua in his own century, Langland still believed in the Christianization of society and did not attempt to separate society (or the state) from religion. He went back to an older view of society and life to relieve the contending tensions of his age—the competing claims of society and the individual, of grace and free will, of piety and learning, and of this world and the next.

These contending claims, which are the sum and substance of the spiritual crisis of the age, appear throughout *Piers* in dialectical fashion as part of a dialogue in the broadest sense of the word between Will the dreamer and the exterior and interior worlds, the *saeculum* and the *anima,* under the overarching shield of the realm of grace. Langland fails, in part, to satisfy these claims completely and in perfect artistic form because his aim is to show the spiritual confusion of his own times. Spiritual confusion demands to some extent artistic confusion.

Today we have been taught to beware of reading autobiography into a work of art so as not to minimize the artifice and craft of the artist, although in some sense every work of art has some biographical significance however indirect; nevertheless, autobiography occupies a special role in a poem about the quest for perfection. One does not write such a poem in the first place unless one is committed personally and strongly to the subject; moreover, such a quest is not only for perfection but for a way in which the quest may be artistically presented. The artistic problem is closely related to the historical problem, and the historical problem is partly Langland's personal problem. Had Langland merely been presenting an ideal society so as to criticize contemporary society, he might have been able to find the right artistic form; but he is presenting the *search* for the ideal society in terms of the dilemmas of his time. His answer, therefore, is bound up with history, contemporary history and his own history, which is not complete until the end of time. Langland does believe that man can do something about the problem and indeed foreshadows his final answer; but, in effect, only history can give him the answer he is working for and of which he is convinced. *Piers Plowman* reflects in a very special way the dilemmas of its author.

All this is not necessarily to say that Langland and the dreamer are identical. But there is some of the one in the other. Evaluating the "I" of the poem is important in its interpretation, but certainly the "I" and the author are related to each other. Will is both William Langland and every Christian man. In brief, the dreamer is "both species and individual at the same time" [Ernest H. Kantorowicz, *The King's Two Bodies: A Study in Mediaeval Political Theology,* 1957].

Langland was well aware that he was a craftsman who had to work in the traditions of a craft possessed of styles and forms. Such awareness was not a hindrance to his creativity and originality, but the very presupposition of his art. The traditions provided the conditions of his art, and he could no more have conceived of himself as a rebel against them than he could have imagined nuclear physics. His task was to use them in the fittest way so as to produce what he had to produce with decorum. He was as free within these confines as a religious thinker could be free

within the limiting dogmas of Catholicism. Medieval theology shows a wide variety of attitudes and beliefs and many a clash of opinion; and medieval art similarly within its boundaries presents a wide range of works of different types and illustrating different points of view, some successful and some not. The limits gave strength to both theologian and artist, and within them all kinds of things were possible.

In what formal tradition of genre was *Piers Plowman* conceived? What kind of work was it, and in what form did the author choose to express himself? Actually, it seems that Langland never could decide what form he was using, and from beginning to end, part of the difficulty of *Piers* to its readers is its confusion and even clash of genres. Just as Langland could never come to rest in his search for perfection, so he could never find the one genre in which to express himself. In other literary works there is a mixing of genre—indeed it is a characteristic of much medieval literature, but a deliberate one—but in *Piers* it seems that the mingling is more extensive than in most and is intimately related to the quest for perfection that is the basic subject of the poem. And it is not entirely deliberate on the poet's part.

This is not the place to enter into a discussion of the importance of genre as one of the literary boundaries for the artist. Some have denied the validity of considering genre in assessing art; but without any reference to other periods, it is obvious that the medieval writer was very conscious of the kind of form in which he chose to present his artistic vision and that it is against the customary lines of this form that an author's innovations and uniqueness can best be understood. With a certain form went certain expectations which the writer felt he must at least satisfy.

Genre analysis is not a scientific subject. What is one man's genre may be another man's theme or motif. Some genres are artificially created by modern critics even when they have gone beyond the romantic notion that rhetoric implies insincerity. One must, however, accept as genres only literary forms defined as such before the time of the composition of the work being considered; for some forms are esoteric and others are so broad that they lose the distinguishing marks of a genre—a literary type that has a certain general organization and arouses certain definite expectations in its readers and listeners.

This problem of definition comes to the fore in connection with the quest around which *Piers Plowman* is mainly organized. The quest has been a most popular unifying principle in literature in all ages, but in the later Middle Ages it reached its apogee. "Then indeed," says R. W. Southern [in his *The Making of the Middle Ages,* 1953], "it meets us on all sides—in the Arthurian Romances, in allegories of love, in descriptions of the ascent of the soul towards God. The imagery of movement seemed at this time to lay hold on the imagination, and it invaded secular as well as religious literature." The quest is the literary counterpart of the new or revived twelfth-century conative attitude towards life, of the general Christian image of life as a pilgrimage, of actual travel, which increased as a result of the Crusades and greater wealth, and of what may be termed the idea of the Crusade itself, which seized all Europe. But

Mr. Southern's opinion, that it is a theme or dominant image rather than a genre, is probably correct. It is certainly the commanding image of *Piers.*

A simple answer to the question of the genre of *Piers Plowman* would be to say that it is an apocalypse. The classic Judeo-Christian apocalypse is cast in dream form, or consists of several dreams, is a revelation from some superior authority, is eschatologically oriented, and constitutes a criticism of, and warning for, contemporary society. In the Old Testament and Apocrypha, we may see such literary forms in Daniel and Second Esdras and in early Christian literature in Revelation, the *Shepherd of Hermas,* and in the *Visio sancti Pauli,* to take only a few examples. The form of the apocalypse owes something to the late classical aretalogy, a narration of the theophany of a god among men with emphasis on his miracles for the furtherance of his cult. But its actual origins are obscure, and the matter need not be pursued further.

These apocalypses and others were known to the Middle Ages, and there is even a parody of one, in the *Apocalypsis Goliae* of the twelfth century, possibly by Walter Map but certainly connected with the British Isles. It is fundamentally a satire on the Church, and the superior guide is Pythagoras. It is closely modeled on the Revelation of St. John.

In many ways *Piers Plowman* seems to fit the category of apocalypse, yet there are certain fundamental differences. The emphasis on the quest is foreign to the apocalypse as we know it. There is no single guide in *Piers,* but rather a search for guides, although Holy Church and Conscience have a certain authority. The use of personifications is not a characteristic of the apocalypse, and there is a strong vein of irony in the figure of Will that is not consonant with the apocalypse. Although *Piers* does criticize contemporary society, is in dream form, and is eschatologically oriented, these characteristics of the apocalypse can be accounted for otherwise.

The chief objection to taking the form of *Piers* to be an apocalypse is that it is doubtful whether such a literary form existed. I agree with Father H. Musurillo when he writes [in "History and Symbol: A Study of Form in Early Christian Literature," *Theological Studies,* XVIII, (1957)], "The form known as 'apocalypse' creates a problem, and perhaps no useful purpose is served in making the term a technical one applicable both to the Revelation of St. John and the so-called Shepherd of Hermas." He says that the *Shepherd* is rather "allegorical fiction disguised as a primitive Christian prophecy."

The problem of the genre of *Piers Plowman* is thus complex, but in some sense it can be said to be formally an apocalypse. The apocalypse as it appeared in the Bible and early Christian literature and in the occasional late parody of it may have prepared the way for *Piers* and made it possible in a very fundamental sense. However, the particular shifting organization of *Piers* can be understood only in terms of other and more common high medieval literary forms. In a basic sense, it is an apocalypse, but because we cannot clearly accept this form of literature as an established genre, we had better see it in another light.

It appears that *Piers Plowman* is based on three literary genres: the allegorical dream narrative; the dialogue, *consolatio,* or debate; and the encyclopedic (or Menippean) satire. And it is influenced by three religious genres (or forms): the complaint, the commentary, and the sermon. These genres are not mutually exclusive, and some are related. The *consolatio* in its classic medieval form is also a dream vision; the religious complaint owes something to classical satire and to the diatribe; and no doubt the sermon and complaint are difficult at times to keep apart. It is still true that in the Middle Ages these six forms were distinct in tradition, had a definite organization, and were designed to satisfy certain expectations in an audience. (pp. 3-10)

These six forms—three literary and three religious—are the genres in which Langland chose to work and with which he attempted to give structure to his poem. To them we may add the somewhat dubious literary form of the apocalypse. They were already to some extent intertwined before Langland's time, although I know of no writer who attempted to use them all. It is possible that Langland did not think of them all as separate, but in intellectual analysis they may be separated so as to see more clearly their impact on the poem. . . . That each of them existed and has its own tradition, we cannot deny; they are not the creation of modern scholars but actual medieval literary forms. Yet it is most unlikely that Langland himself sat down and took these six, one after the other, and mixed them up into his potion.

Rather, Langland was probably well aware of all these traditions; and in attempting to present his concern with perfection in the apocalyptic and prophetic frame of mind that was his, he could not properly solve his formal problem. The confusion of genre in *Piers* is a reflection of his concern with the quest for perfection. Langland combines in extraordinary degree a detachment and humor along with an intense involvement and unhappiness. He stood for a moderation—a balance between being a spectator and an actor—which he never could quite achieve.

All this is in Langland's style. Like most issues connected with the poem, the style of *Piers Plowman* presents a problem of considerable magnitude. Ostensibly it is written in the alliterative tradition, and certainly the chief poetic binding device is alliteration, yet the total effect of the poem is strikingly different from that of the ornate repetitive parallel style most other monuments of the "alliterative revival" display. Unlike their authors, Langland does not use an aristocratic "baronial" style; nor does his poem echo the heroic Old English alliterative line and vocabulary. In short, Langland is not, like perhaps the author of *Gawain and the Green Knight,* writing in high, but rather in middle, style, if one may accept these stylistic distinctions as laid down by Augustine and others, which were based on Cicero and the Roman rhetoricians. The *genus temperatum* could well describe Langland's style in the alliterative tradition.

The conclusion that *Piers Plowman* is written in the middle or moderate style is actually forced on us. The subject matter alone would eliminate the low or humble style, which for the most part could be used only in writing of erotic matters and of humble life or in simple religious instructions. The absence of long apostrophes and elaborate descriptions and ornamentation and the nature of the diction would seem to eliminate the high style.

The problem of the three literary styles in the later Middle Ages is not simple, because estimating the literary effect of the older stages of a language is not easy. England, with the struggle between English and French, had a complicating element. It is dubious whether a high style in English was at all thought possible until the last half of the fourteenth century. In any case French style had certainly differentiated itself by the thirteenth century and possibly earlier.

The tradition for a middle style was probably not well established by Langland's time, but everything we know of the work and a close analysis of its language, not merely the negative reasons given above, argue that *Piers* is written in this style. The vocabulary is not simple, imagery of an intellectual sort is present, and high ornamentation is absent. The contrast between the language and style of *Sir Gawain* and those of *Piers* is instructive in this matter.

There is no clash of style in *Piers* that could be used for special effects. Its tone and diction are remarkably stable; only occasionally does one find a heightening of effect, as in the last two Passus and here and there elsewhere. The heightening is obtained by a speeding-up of the action or by the sudden force of pathos or sincerity rather than by any analyzable change in diction or ornamentation. The stability of the author is found in his style; his uncertainty in his clash of genre.

As J. A. Burrow says, Langland can be accused of *circum-cogitatio* but hardly of *circumlocutio* or *gratuitous poeticism*. When he is narrating or when he is describing someone or some scene, his poetry moves briskly along, even though he indulges in word play or parallel clauses. The slowing down which is apparent, especially in the long speeches in the *Vita,* is largely due to Langland's difficulty in saying exactly what he means or to our inability to catch the scholastic or medieval mode of argument and allusion. The long-windedness of extensive sections of the poem arises from the long-windedness of Langland's thought or has this effect because of a lack of sympathy with the details of his argumentation.

It is possible that the very choice of the alliterative meter, as W. L. Renwick and H. Orton has suggested [in *The Beginnings of English Literature to Skelton,* 1940], "is indeed symbolic of opposition to the society and politics of which Chaucer was an apparently contented part." Langland, who lived in London, at least for part of his life, as his knowledge proves, even if we doubt the veracity of the autobiographical passages, must surely have been aware that this meter was not used over a vast part of the country. It is hard to think that deliberate choice did not enter into the selection of his verse form. And the choice may have been dictated by his disapproval of the current standards of the world about him. He may thus have harked back perhaps for his poetic meter to his youthful memories of baronial entertainment in Shropshire, Herefordshire, or

Worcestershire. Yet all this is speculative. We cannot penetrate his mind to this extent.

Looking at the poetry more closely, one must be immediately impressed by Langland's frequent use of quotations, mostly Latin, either worked into or merely deposited in the texture. "No work, whether literary production or dogmatic treatise, is so interlarded with Latin Scriptural quotations and Patristic *excerpta*—sometimes thrown in with utter disregard of rhetorical structure or easy comprehension of the sense, sometimes neatly incorporated into the flow of thought, now given in full, now forming a fragmentary tag—as the ***Piers Plowman*** [Sister Carmeline Sullivan in her *The Latin Insertions and the Macaronic Verse in "Piers Plowman,"* 1932]." Sometimes we find true macaronic lines, half English, half Latin, and sometimes whole lines of quotation inserted into the flow of the verse and sometimes whole lines or tags quoted in what is in effect an aside. As in theological writings, Langland often uses quotations to settle a dispute; he assumes a knowledge of the exegetical tradition. ***Piers Plowman*** is impregnated with the Bible and the writings of the Fathers, but more especially the Bible. It has been said of Bernard of Clairvaux that he speaks Bible as one might speak French or English. Langland speaks Bible too; phrases, echoes, and paraphrases crop out everywhere. His whole mind is steeped in the Bible; it is a real language to him.

This use of biblical (and Patristic) citation, besides giving Langland the authority he seeks for, reveals a remarkable sense of the power of language, which we see as well in his love of word play and puns. Acrostic and macaronic poetry are no longer much in fashion, yet they convey a respect for the magic power of language which is still not lost. Thought, serious thought, must always struggle against its medium, words. In using several languages or in writing acrostics, a poet is indicating his desire to pass beyond the limitations of his medium and at the same time indicating his belief, possibly subconscious, in the magic power, in a literal sense, of language.

This is all very general, and to apply it particularly to Langland and the problems he was struggling with would take up a great deal of space. The confusion of genres, the endless revisions of *Piers,* the struggle within the poem, are, however, all reflected in Langland's very choice of words and his dissatisfaction with one language. His movement from Lady Church to Conscience, to Reason, to the friars, to Dame Study, to Imaginatif, and all the others is a seeking for authority, for an answer to his own and his age's crisis; and this quest is duplicated in his reaching out for words that one language alone cannot satisfactorily supply, in his love of word play, and in his turning again and again to the Bible.

Part of his trouble is due to the inadequacies of English in Langland's own time. He was concerned with theological ideas, and "the fact that he quoted his authorities in Latin and not in English," not to speak of his choice of the content, "indicates that he regarded his poem as belonging rather to the theological than to the devotional type of religious literature" [Greta Hort, *"Piers Plowman" and Contemporary Religious Thought*]. English in the fourteenth century did not have an established learned vocabulary. In this, it was similar to Hindi or modern Hebrew. Latin provided the scientific and learned language, and the vernacular writers were as yet only groping towards a solution in their own terms. Chaucer and Gower might seem to be exceptions, but they were not struggling with theology and religious genres, as Langland was. This difficulty is not always recognized by modern scholars in dealing with Langland's diction. We can see it in the wideranging meaning carried by many of his technical words, like *inwit, conscience,* and *kind wit.* Latin, and more rarely French, provided Langland with the *mot juste* time and again.

But this is not the main reason for his use of Latin citations. The way Langland uses them shows they represented at one and the same time his desire for authority, his reaching after the absolute, and his way of dealing with intellectual perplexities. Above all, they were normal concomitants of the religious literary forms to which he was indebted. Langland's problem is not the struggle with the inexpressible, as a mystic might struggle, but the struggle to answer a very precise question—how to live the Christian life in society. The difficulty lies, not in the nature of what is to be communicated, but in the multiplicity of conflicting answers.

I do not wish to give the impression that Langland's style is tortured and ungainly. It is, on the contrary, relatively smooth and quick moving, even though there is a certain amount of afterthought and modification, such as is still characteristic of colloquial English and a certain negligence with regard to person, for frequently the language moves from second to third person, or vice versa.

In spite of the rhythm and alliteration, at times Langland's verse reads remarkably like blank verse. It is a segmented but smooth style, and its quality comes out very clearly when the complexities and tortuosities of his near contemporary Richard Rolle's Latin or English are compared with Langland's. It is difficult to find passages similar enough to make a fair comparison, yet there is an intensity in Rolle that Langland does not have. Rolle's violent sensuousness is lacking, and in its place one gets a coolness of development broken by occasional phrases or clauses in apposition and longer units interrupted by Latin quotations. It is the style, not of a fourteenth-century mystic, but of a puzzled man who is both detached and terribly involved in his problem, who is both spectator and actor. It is vivid with apt metaphors, appropriate pictures and images, and delight in word play. There is an intellectual rather than a sensuous perplexity in his long lines. Langland's problem is not, as with Rolle, essentially how to communicate, but what to communicate in the face of too many answers.

Langland's social and intellectual orientation may also be seen in his love of puns, half-puns, repetitions, and word play in general. They presuppose an audience, a certain society, and they reveal an intellectual perplexity and at the same time a fascination with that perplexity. This notable characteristic of his style has been studied by B. F. Huppé [in *"Petrus id est Christus*: Word Play in *Piers Plowman,* the B-Text,*" ELH,* XVII (1950)], and since his article has

appeared, students of the poem have been very much aware of it. Each careful reading of the poem uncovers more puns, and further discoveries in Langland's use of various forms of word play may well be expected.

Langland's balance, on the other hand, may be seen in the tendency for the rhetorical unit of his line to correspond with the semantic unit. It would be too much to say his lines are endstopped, for he writes in rather long sentences (if we may accept in general Skeat's punctuation) with parallel and parenthetical clauses; but the end of a line tends to be the end of a clause or at least a thought unit. When Langland does use, as on rare occasions he does (for example, in VI, 202-203, XI, 143-144 and 292-293), a violent enjambment dividing a syntactic unit in two, we are brought up short. In general his sentences are paratactic; he favors the extensive use of *and.* Here is a typical sentence:

> Saul, for he sacrifised sorwe hym be-tydde,
> And his sones al-so for that synne myscheued,
> And many mo other men that were no Leuites,
> That with *archa-dei* gheden in reuerence and in
>   worschippe,
> And leyden honde ther-on to liften it vp and
>   loren hir lif after.
>
> (XII, 117-122)

Or, again, two sentences:

> Lyf and Deth in this derknesse her one fordoth
>   her other;
> Shal no wighte wite witterly who shal haue the
>   maystre,
> Er Sondey aboute sonne-rysynge and sank with
>   that til erthe.
> Some seyde that he was goddes sone that so fair
>   deyde,
>   *Vere filius dei erat iste, etc.*
> And somme saide he was a wicche good is that
>   we assaye,
> Where he be ded or noughte ded doun er he be
>   taken.
>
> (XVIII, 65-70)

These excerpts give us typical Langland without the occasional striking image or metaphor and without the humor and irony that frequently play about his line. The colloquialism is marked in the appositions and repetition, especially by pronouns, and the general parataxis.

Langland's style is temperate, balanced, and clear, but its temperateness, balance, and clarity serve to reveal his fundamental intellectual complexity. His style, reconstructed from his poem, perfectly mirrors the movement of his mind. Following the tradition of the sermon, of exegesis, and of complaint, apparently tempered by scholastic literary forms, Langland uses texts as pillars of support both within and without the texture of his work. He reaches out after truth, the whole truth, which in abstract form the Bible and the Fathers give him, and hopes for the great bargain which God's grace can bring to him.

> And ghut, ich hope, as he that ofte haueth chaf-
>   fared,
> That ay hath lost and lost and atte laste hym
>   happed
> He bouhte such a bargayn he was the bet euere,

And sette hus lost at a lef at the laste ende,
Such a wynnynge hym warth thorw wordes of
　　hus grace:
　　　*Simile est regnum celorum thesauro abs-
　　condito*
　　　in agro & cetera:
　　　*Mulier que inuenit dragman unam, et ce-
　　tera;*
So hope ich to haue of hym that is al-myghty
A gobet of hus grace and bygynne a tyme,
That all tymes of my tyme to profit shal turne
　　　　　　　　　　　　(C, VI, 94-101)

A word or two about the stylistic effect of Langland's use of personifications may not be amiss. Their frequency can be accounted for by their presence in the genres discernible in *Piers,* but more must be involved. They must have corresponded to some inner artistic need of Langland and must be seen, at least partially, in this light. Personifications are essentially clarifying concepts, and they seemed to appeal to Langland because they afforded an objective and cool method of direct exposition. They are evidence of Langland's balance and temperateness and round out the presentation of his thought. Yet the endless dialogue and sometimes strife between various personifications and between them and Will reflect the other side of the coin, the perplexity and uncertainty of the seeker. His choice of genres and his style reveal a fundamental internal crisis that he cannot completely solve and at the same time demonstrate his admiration for moderation and clarity. His is the style of a moderate, clear-headed, but perplexed man.

Langland's use of personifications is the most potent force in the poem making for the strong sense of timelessness and spacelessness which it creates in the reader. Reading *Piers* gives one a feeling of being unlocalized and atemporal, in spite of Langland's strong concrete sense of human existence. We are in no particular time or place, yet Langland's lines are full of naturalistic detail and homely images. Personification is always a matter of nouns that are *per se* general; in personification the adjective and verb carry the particulars. Prosopopoeia thus is especially suited for portraying both the undifferentiated universal and the detailed concrete. Sharp lines separate one scene from another, but the background of depth seems missing. The scenes of *Piers,* vivid as they are, seem to move in an undifferentiated medium that makes the familiar strange. The concrete element seems to be at war with itself. The foreground is sharp; the background is vague.

One must be cautious in comparing works of literature with contemporary or near-contemporary works of art. Yet this sense of an empty stage on which the action of Langland's poem takes place is not unlike the bare or empty backgrounds in the paintings of Simone Martini or, to take an example closer in time, the Wilton diptych of the National Gallery. Against an empty background, or one in which space and depth are merely suggested, one sees in these paintings extremely naturalistic features. In the foreground, very real people and things are presented in an empty medium. Space and depth stop at the foreground; the background, without any or only the slightest suggestion of perspective, is out of time and space. Another splendid example is afforded by the Avignon *Pietà,* which is much later (1460) but is recognized by art histori-

ans as *retardataire.* Here, in moving detail, the naturalistic agony of the figures of the foreground is acted out against a background that is vacant except for the very small picture of the city of Jerusalem and a faint suggestion of a mountain. All these pictures suggest the combination of representationalism and nonrepresentationalism so characteristic of *Piers,* a combination much enhanced by the way Langland uses his personifications and also by his selective use of detail.

For whom was Langland writing? J. A. Burrow argues [in "The Audience of *Piers Plowman,*" *Anglia,* LXXV (1957)] that his audience consisted, not of the aristocracy or landed gentry, as was probably the case with the other poems of the "alliterative revival," but of clerics and the new, educated lay class. He gives convincing reasons for the argument. The evidence from wills and the contents of the codices in which *Piers* is found when it does not take up all the space bear this out. Although, as the autobiographical passages show, Langland was probably a member of what W. A. Pantin [in his *The English Church in The Fourteenth Century,* 1955] calls the "clerical proletariate," this need not mean that his audience were fringe clergymen in minor orders or wandering semi-goliardic clerics. It was probably otherwise. Unlike other alliterative poems, *Piers* is preserved in a large number of manuscripts—over fifty—and although this evidence is perhaps a little ambiguous, it argues for its popularity among serious-thinking people, religious and lay. It is hard to think of a large, popular audience for the work, in spite of John Ball's reference to *Piers* in his famous letter of 1381. The poem is too difficult and too allusive to have been enjoyed by the common people or by restless, uprooted clerics. The references to *Piers* and the poems influenced by it all argue for a medium-sized, literate, thoughtful audience.

Piers was widely read probably for the same reason that popular mysticism, anti-scholasticism, personal piety, and even heresy flourished in the late fourteenth and fifteenth centuries. The subsequent rapid rise and spread of Protestantism was possible because of the presence of a large number of people who were dissatisfied with the abuses of the Roman Church and its internal divisions and the conflict between ideals and reality, even though many were at first not prepared to go beyond an internal reformation. Yet when the logic of extreme censure and criticism carried the leaders of the Reformation to repudiate Catholicism completely, many Catholics were not prepared to fight for their faith or beliefs. The defenses had crumbled.

Within scholasticism itself we see in the fourteenth, fifteenth, and sixteenth centuries an increasing concern with minutiae, a growing skepticism and a rising emphasis on the will rather than reason. The dominant scholastic schools of the end of the Middle Ages were strongly voluntaristic. Reason, the very basis of scholasticism, was suspect, and we get evidence piled upon evidence of the desire for a new concept of Christian perfection that could be realized in action and life.

Piers attempted to analyze the ills of contemporary society and to redefine the ancient idea of Christian perfection, both desperately needed in the crisis of late medieval life.

It was for this reason, no doubt, that *Piers Plowman* had a wide, if not popular, audience and appeal. (pp. 34-43)

> Morton W. Bloomfield, "The Form of 'Piers Plowman'," in his "Piers Plowman" as a Fourteenth-century Apocalypse, *Rutgers University Press, 1962, pp. 3-43.*

J. F. Goodridge   (essay date 1966)

[*In the excerpt below from the 1966 revision of his introduction to his translation of the B-text of* Piers Plowman, *Goodridge explores Langland's thematic approach, his mastery of comic effects, and his unique use of allegory.*]

In common with Dante's *Divine Comedy* and Milton's *Paradise Lost,* **Piers Plowman** deals with the largest of all themes: the meaning of man's life on earth in relation to his ultimate destiny. Like Milton, Langland seeks to 'justify the ways of God to men'. But his perspective is different from either Dante's or Milton's. He does not take us on a journey through worlds other than this, or ask us to look back on life from the point of view of hell, purgatory or heaven. Nor does he remove us, as Milton does, to a distant vantage-point in time from which to survey human history. His poem is no epic in the ordinary sense of that word. Langland's cycle of visions begins and ends with fourteenth-century England. His pilgrimage, like Bunyan's, is that of man's individual life and his life in society, as it has to be lived on this middle-earth between the 'Tower of Truth' and the 'Dungeon of Falsehood'. Langland was concerned, as Blake was, both with the condition of society and with the history of the human soul struggling to 'cleanse the doors of perception' and come to terms with ultimate truth. But for Langland, this meant translating his visions, at every point, into an art that had an immediate application to practical life. Though epic in scope and constantly rising to a prophetic point of view, **Piers Plowman** is cast in the didactic form of medieval moral allegory—a spiritual journey which, though it takes place in a series of dreams dreamt by an imaginary dreamer, is constantly related to life as it has to be lived. The form allows various different time-scales, and with them different levels of meaning, to operate side by side, or be superimposed on one another. First there is the 'literal' life-span of the dreamer or poet. He is represented at the beginning as a lazy vagabond or ordinary human wayfarer whose interest in Truth amounts to little more than idle curiosity. But through his dreams he sees the world with fresh eyes, is bewitched into thinking seriously and is sent forth by Holy Church on a pilgrimage in search of Truth, which he can only find through learning the law of Love. So he must progressively meet and assimilate every aspect of reality, and rise from his preoccupation with physical, economic, social and political facts to the level of moral and spiritual vision.

Though the story of Will's growth in knowledge and understanding provides the poem's one consistent thread of narrative, it is no regular step-by-step progress. It is as irregular and unpredictable as life itself—there are moments that are crowded with vivid impressions, or flooded in solitude with the wonder of new realization, followed by long barren years of intellectual debate, uncertainty or, perhaps, complete unawareness. In Book XI the poet ironically allows forty-five years of the dreamer's life to drop out as if they had never existed, so that he passes in a moment from the struggles of early manhood to those of old age. Erratic, obstinate and often misguided, he constantly has to double back on his tracks to rediscover what he had half known before.

Unlike Milton or Blake, Langland was a master of comic effects. He could survey the world with humour, sometimes mocking or playful, more often wry and sardonic. So the pilgrimage is partly burlesque—the dreamer's over-eager curiosity and general lack of solemnity lead to many setbacks on his quest. Both he and the *personae* of his dreams bear witness, dramatically, to the absurdity of the human situation in the face of eternity's uncompromising demands. For Langland seems to combine opposite qualities—on the one hand, an almost exasperating sense of the absolute, that insists on following up every hint and will never leave a subject till the truth of it has been pursued to its final conclusions ('I shal tellen for treuth sake, take hede who so lyketh!'); on the other hand a sense of man's almost incurable folly and waywardness, and an awareness of the plain ungarnished facts of life as it has to be lived from moment to moment. He likes to show common sense confounding theory, but likes even better to show idealism confounding worldly common sense—as Conscience confounds Lady Fee, or Patience subdues the worldly Haukyn by showing him poverty. So the poem sometimes swings back and forth between extremes: harsh prophecy or solemn warning, and Rabelaisian satire that is not afraid to expose contradictions in terms of farce. These opposites are most effectively combined in the swift, sure satire of the final Book—and it is hard to see how such a resilient response to experience can ever have given rise to the idea of Langland as a grim pessimist. There is very little in his poem of the 'Nordic strain'.

One of the effects of Langland's self-mockery is to associate the dreamer, and ourselves, with the action, so that we are directly involved, and made to feel the difference between knowledge and full participation, which is one of the poem's main themes. But the dreamer seldom occupies the centre of the picture. The visions themselves, with their 'higher' time-scales, dominate his life, and the prime mover is an unseen providence that is always a little beyond the horizon of vision. So we gain from the poem a sense of reality as something objective and ineluctable, penetrating and overshadowing life as we know it in the world.

Superimposed on the time-scale of a single fourteenth century life-span, with its direct references to current political events, are the further time-scales apprehended in higher moments of vision. The painstaking allegorical expositions that describe the long way of the commandments are broken by sudden moments of illumination—hard surfaces of doctrine and argument dissolve into kaleidoscopic pictures, each revealing more than the last. One important scale that holds these dramatic variations together, especially in the last five Books, is that of the liturgical year, and we can observe in Langland the process of ritual being turned into drama. Beginning with the Nativity in the middle of Book XVI, the dreamer passes on rapidly through Epiphany and Lent to the climax of Passiontide and Easter (Book XVIII), then returns by way of Pentecost, in Book XIX, to Advent in the final Book. Coupled with this liturgical cycle run the main themes of sacred history—the story of the patriarchs and prophets followed by that of Christ and his church, which leads on inevitably to the *terminus a quo* of the present.

But in Langland the contemporary scene is itself shifting and multi-dimensional. Here, as in the realm of spiritual experience, his clairvoyance can penetrate beyond appearances and show us what lies behind the façade of church and state. He is one of the few writers in whose work it is difficult to distinguish between prophetic insight—that sometimes works on a historical or eschatological level—and plain truthfulness, especially (as John Lawlor has put it) his 'unerring eye for woes that are actual'. He did not sympathize with the poor at a safe distance; he felt need and hunger as immediate sensations and could express them in sharply physical and kinaesthetic terms. His denunciation of hypocrisy therefore carries conviction. We do not dismiss his prophetic role as a preacher's mannerism. At almost any stage in his narrative, he can rise easily to a point of view from which he can relate present facts to first causes and final ends. The present fulfils past warnings and shows portents of what is still to come. Christ and Antichrist are here and now. This gift of prophetic vision lends to the poem a time-scale vaster than that of any epic, and fills it with glimpses of a divine economy that may ultimately lead to the salvation of all mankind. Behind Langland's 'animated foreground', there is always 'the long vista of eternity'.

All these perspectives are present *within* the poem—in its flexible language and varied dramatic sequences: we need not look outside it to find the 'meaning'. Other medieval allegories are more formal and diagrammatic, but ***Piers Plowman*** does not depend on a fixed scheme of symbolic reference. There is little need, for example, to explain what 'Meed' (which I have translated 'Fee') is or was—her words and actions provide as full a context by which to judge her as any that Dickens could give. Allegory was for Langland a dynamic way of thinking or 'making out' the truth in pictorial and dramatic form, by intuition as well as by observation and logical argument. To do this, he freely used all the resources of the vernacular language, and the potentialities of the dream form. He moved easily from brisk reportage to grotesque nightmare, or from angry theological disputation to the dream-within-a-dream that is close to mystical vision. There is no infallible key to such dramatic poetry—we must be constantly alert to changes in tone and direction that would be impossible in the stately verse of a poem like *Paradise Lost*. We are required, in Book III, for instance, to move rapidly from a world that exhibits the perverse power of money, and jingles with thousands of florins, to a moving statement of the divine law of reward and restitution. This in turn is later associated with one Robert the Robber, who can never hope to repay his debts, and so is compared with the penitent thief on Calvary. The essence of Langland's

dream technique is its capacity for what Elizabeth Salter has called 'rapid contraction and expansion of reference'—where vivid realism can play its part within a progressively widening field of religious vision.

Langland's imagination was essentially visual and dramatic, and there are parts of his poem that might make good material for a film. We are struck at once by the fullness and variety of his picture of the Plain of the world, with its crowded panoramas and ugly close-ups, its noisy comings and goings and its intimate details. In the early books we witness a constant clash of opposing forces, and the truth about human society is revealed in the guise of a powerful and absorbing drama. Familiar vices and virtues no longer appear commonplace, but grotesque or disturbing. The 'real' characters—pardoners, lawyers, friars or thieves—are so placed alongside allegorical ones that the latter assume the semblance of life. Guile, Fee, Civil-Law, Conscience and Reason become the dynamic forces that move the world, and all the others fall under their direction.

A character like Sloth or Fraud is the personification of a propensity found in many men; and by embodying it in a single person, the poet shows us what shapes it assumes in human society. He reveals to us our moral qualities, stripped of all the conventions by which we seek to hide them. A schoolboy who uses a nickname, or the dramatist who gives one of his characters a name like Sir Francis Wronghead, is usually pointing to some social foible which characterizes a particular type. Langland employs a similar idiom, but places his types in surprising contexts that shock us out of our stock associations, so that we cannot mistake the enormity of the evils they represent and the perversions of truth that they bring about. By this method of contrast and opposition, familiar virtues also take on a dramatic interest which they rarely have in naturalistic drama or fiction.

Each of the Deadly Sins carries a load of sins greater than any man could possibly carry: the dominant vice is displayed in all its grossest forms. Sloth is not merely a lazy priest who goes hunting when he should be saying his Office; he is all kinds of sloth, lay and clerical, rolled into one. The world is foreshortened, and the gluttony of Glutton is reflected in a crowd of others whom he meets in the tavern. In the description of the soiled coat of Haukyn the Active Man, all the sins of the Plain are run together, flourishing under the cloak of self-important worldliness—and it is he whom Langland chooses to test the power of the Christian absolutes, Patience and Poverty. After the dreamer's frustrating struggles with a succession of intellectual faculties and pursuits (Thought, Study, Intelligence, Imagination, etc.), he meets a being, Anima, in whom all the powers of the human soul are combined; and when he has afterwards encountered the separate god-given virtues in incarnate form, he falls in with the Samaritan who unites all these graces in the one attribute of Love. The Samaritan in turn dissolves into the person of Piers-Christ; and it is important to bear in mind that Christ himself in this poem is also an 'allegorical' person, representing a god-like potentiality in the soul—for Langland shared something of the view of Meister Eckhart that 'a good man is the only-begotten Son of God'.

So the *dramatis personae* of **Piers Plowman** are not static abstract categories. Each is a mirror that reflects those aspects of life that stand out at a particular stage of mental or spiritual development, defining its categories of thought or modes of perception. They are the means by which the relevance of those categories and concepts to everyday life can be put to the proof. Langland does not offer us the 'plane mirror reflection' of the comedy of manners, but rather a comedy of humours, where single properties assume a life more powerful than that of ordinary individuals and gather into themselves a large number of observations and experiences. The great strength of such a method lies in its power to cut across habitual expectations—our conceptions, for example, of classes of people or individual 'character' types, or our common notions of what we ourselves are or may become. Langland's form of allegory reorganizes human experience according to new patterns. The cells of the dreamer's thoughts and perceptions keep dividing and coming together again around fresh nuclei. The simplicity of Holy Church's teaching gives way to the multiplicity of Falsehood's following; that of Piers into the contradictions of the mental faculties encountered in the search for Do-well, which is a kind of psychological drama: the dreamer's attention is turned inwards as he seeks the truth among the conflicting powers of the mind. Here the dramatic effect lies in the individual confrontation between the dreamer and his various *alter egos* ('single figures or incidents etched in sharp relief') and in the vigorous to and fro of intellectual debate and homily. What Learning, Study, Intelligence and the rest have to say to him is seldom more than he is capable of seeing for himself at the time. They all reflect his limitations. But as he increases in self-knowledge, the selves whom he at first had failed to recognize slowly coalesce, and their powers are gathered round new centres, the heavenly graces or virtues. The dramatic technique again changes, leaving the dreamer a passive spectator: in place of personal encounters we have dramatized narrative or parable, culminating in the ritualized drama of religious contemplation. The various narrative modes of picture and dialogue, action and comment are now combined, since all the faculties and virtues are concentrated on the person of Piers or Christ. But though the texture is here multi-layered and demands the reader's full attention on various levels, the poem never loses its dramatic and pictorial impact. At the climax of the Harrowing of Hell Langland's style still has much in common with that of the Miracle Plays that were performed in the streets.

Langland was never wilfully an obscure poet: he sought strenuously to make all his meanings clear, weaving all the glosses and explanations into the body of his narrative. He preferred simple similes to complex symbols and metaphors; he transposed abstruse doctrines into everyday terms or embodied them in dramatic dialogue so as to render them immediately applicable to practical life; he carefully spelt out each step in an argument and exhibited the truth from many different sides. If the resulting structure is still in places confusing and complex, this is only be-

cause, to him, the application of simple truth to actual experience was no simple matter.

Langland's willingness to follow, at times, wherever the spirit leads—a characteristic of most medieval devotional writing—occasions many digressions, stoppings-short and unexpected transitions. The pattern is incomplete in parts, yet unified on a higher level as the dreamer becomes caught up in the mystery of Christ and his spokesman, Piers. Piers represents the human ideal which is the ultimate object of the search. In Books VI and VII he is the good ploughman who alone knows how to obey the natural law. During the debates of Do-well he disappears, for the dreamer has lost sight of his ideal and only hears of him in hints and riddles. When he reappears, he has undergone a change corresponding to the change in the dreamer's understanding of what Truth is and where it is to be found. He is the perfect Christian and the representative of Christ mirrored in the soul of everyman. Having failed to discover him in the priesthood of his day, the dreamer must look for his image reflected in the powers of his own soul.

Allegory, as Langland employs it, is a way of testing and proving experience. It allows him almost unlimited scope to vary his modes of thought and feeling as the subject-matter demands. He can mix realism and fantasy in whatever proportion he chooses, and reinterpret for himself—in the concrete language of everyday life—traditional doctrines, symbols, legends and sacred histories. Since he did not write, like the 'court' poets, for a select audience of listeners, but rather for a wider literate public who were to read his poem in manuscript, he was able to employ every variety of speech, ranging from that of the theological lecture to the coarse vernacular of the street or tavern. There could be any number of *personae*—new ones might suddenly appear, while others merged together or disappeared. Through their mouths he could say whatever he wished, twisting the narrative this way and that as his mental and spiritual horizon expanded or contracted. The secret of the poem's appeal to a modern reader may lie partly in this irregularity of construction, for instead of giving us a finished picture of the Christian view of life, it registers all our 'uncertainties, mysteries, doubts' and shows a continuing process of thought: Truth is something to be appropriated to oneself, not merely understood by the mind.

Langland was not faced with the problem of finding a voice through which to project his response to the problems of his time. He had not to struggle for a style amid conflicting standards of poetic decorum. The alliterative verse that he used provided a comparatively easy, natural mode of utterance; its flexibility was perfectly adapted to the play and dramatic movement of the dream-allegory. In his day this form of verse seems to have been popular in the west and north of England—and though a court poet like Chaucer may have regarded it as provincial and old-fashioned, it is worth remembering that Langland was an educated cleric and also a Londoner, able to widen its range and assimilate into it many different traditions of speech. His was an age of oral learning and theological disputation, when the style of the homilist provided a matrix out of which writers could draw what they chose—even the Canterbury pilgrims tend to lecture one another. As Mr. [G. R.] Owst has shown, the medieval sermon was a repository of vernacular speech, where graphic similes and proverbial phrases jostled with learned terms. In Langland's day, the English language was not stratified according to class, function or level of literacy so much as it has been since. The reservoir on which he was able to draw contained no less than the whole spoken and written speech of his time. Glutton with his Great Oaths, Sloth with his ballads of Robin Hood, the lazy workmen singing a snatch from a bawdy French song did not seem out of keeping in a poem that drew much of its finest language from the Vulgate, the Fathers and the mystics. Religious discourse was not a solemn and mannered performance, remote from the common vernacular, and Langland's medley of tongues is the characteristic voice of fourteenth-century England. His art consists largely in deploying all its arresting combinations and contrasts. One of his favourite devices is to allow the hieratic and the demotic, the learned riddle and the popular joke, to fall out in quick succession or change places. At its simplest, this is the means by which a particular speaker turns the tables on his opponent, unexpectedly adopting his mode of talk. So Langland's two-edged irony repeatedly plays on the contrasts between Latin and English, clerical and lay, elaborate commentary and simple text, learned word-spinning and proverbial wisdom—seeking thereby to distinguish what is genuinely profound from specious sophistry. (pp. 11-19)

J. F. Goodridge, in an introduction to Piers the Ploughman *by William Langland, translated by J. F. Goodridge, revised edition, Penguin Books, 1968, pp. 9-21.*

Elizabeth Salter and Derek Pearsall   (essay date 1967)

[*Pearsall is an English medievalist and author of* Piers Plowman: An Edition of the C-Text *(1978). He also collaborated with Salter on* Landscapes and Seasons of the Medieval World *(1973). In the following excerpt from their* Piers Plowman, *Salter and Pearsall note the various allegorical techniques Langland used in writing the C-text of* Piers Plowman.]

A vast number of medieval works are usually described as 'allegorical': 'allegory' has to serve as a portmanteau-word for a range of compositions which require some degree of interpretation from the reader, and invite, through their fictions, an inner commentary on the events narrated. Often those are the only common factors: to see *Piers Plowman* and the *Divina Commedia* as allegories, a very flexible frame of reference indeed has to be allowed. Within such a frame, various attempts have been made to sort and regroup allegorical writings. For instance, one of the major methods of procedure in allegory is that of personification, and Langland's poem has been called, in company with other English and French poems, 'personification allegory'. In this, abstract qualities or faculties are given human form, and display their natures or re-enact some experience by means of a typical human activity—a debate, a fight, a feast, a trial, a journey. So, in the *Roman de la Rose,* the experience of falling in love is first abstracted from a particular human situation, and reshaped in terms of personified faculties—Reason, Shame, Jealousy, Idleness, Welcome—who meet, hinder and help the lover in his search for the rose of love. And in the English alliterative poem *Winner and Waster,* man's natural and opposed tendencies to extravagance and miserliness are set before the reader as two figures in debate about their ways of life.

But difficulties arise when we associate them with each other, and *Piers Plowman* with them, as 'personification allegories'. It is true that all three poems 'personify': Langland breaks down the lesson of preserving humility in the face of great provocation into its component parts of patience, reason, anger, and sets them up as characters at a feast. . . . But more important is a comparison of how each poet *used* the device of personification: Guillaume de Lorris's poem is a formal tableau of characters in an enclosed garden: *Winner and Waster* is a ceremonious encounter on a tournament field: Langland's Feast episode is a dynamic, wry scene of mounting tensions, insults, and reconciliations, which materializes and disintegrates before our very eyes. Not that this is always the case with *Piers Plowman:* Langland has static debates as well as bustling feasts—between Reason and the dreamer, Holy Church and the dreamer. The point to make is that the category 'personification allegory' is only of limited help in placing *Piers Plowman,* as, indeed, it may be in placing other medieval works. Personification is a weapon for many allegorists, but they can only be properly distinguished by their ability and inclination to handle it. And, as we shall see, personification is not the whole story: allegory has many faces.

The same difficulty arises when we try to assign *Piers Plowman* to any particular allegorical class or category, and it seems more useful to begin by recognizing its comprehensive allegorical span. This involves not only recognition of the variety of traditional methods Langland draws upon, but also his unique use and combination of those methods.

Usually—and rightly—singled out for attention is the kind of allegory we find in the Lady Meed episodes of *Piers Plowman* (C. III-V) or in the Feast of Patience (extract II: C.XVI). Here a central subject is investigated by means of an actively developing allegorical narrative, with conceptional and fictional elements in perfect, continuous adjustment. The whole sequence of events involving Lady Meed—the arranging of the marriage, the journey to Westminster, the arraignment at the king's court—is dramatically convincing, as well as deeply meaningful. No detail is imprecise in significance, or flat in design. Liar, for instance, evading the King's summons to judgment, is accurately analysed for us, but he leaps into the poetry with the sure energy of an English medieval line-drawing:

> Lyghtliche Lyere lep away thennes,
> Lorkynge thorw lanes, tologged of menye.
> He was nawher welcome for hus many tales,
> Oueral houted out and yhote trusse,
> Til pardoners hadden pitte and pullede hym to
>   house.

Thei woshe hym and wypede hym and wonde
　　hym in cloutes,
And sente hym on Sonnedayes with seeles to
　　churches . . .

　　　　　　　　　　　　　　　　　　(C.III.225-31)

It is visually satisfying as well as morally instructive that
Lady Meed—the essence of material reward—should be
fêted by a 14th-century court, and presented to society by
'a clerk—ich can nouht his name':

Cortesliche the clerk thenne, as the kynge hy-
　　ghte,
Toke Mede by the myddel, and myldeliche here
　　broughte
Into boure with blysse and by hure gan sitte,
Ther was myrthe and mynstralcy Mede to
　　plesen . . .

　　　　　　　　　　　　　　　　　　(C.IV.9-12)

All gestures are vividly realized, yet full of 'sentence'—
Meed, hard pressed, looks to the lawyers to save her from
Reason's logic:

Mede in the mote-halle tho on men of lawe gan
　　wynke,
In sygne that thei sholde with som sotel speche
Reherce tho anon ryght that myghte Reson
　　stoppe.

　　　　　　　　　　　　　　　　　　(C.V.148-50)

But her faded glamour comes under harsh scrutiny:

And alle ryghtful recordeden that Reson treuthe
　　seyde . . .
Loue let lyght of Mede and Leaute ghut
　　lasse . . .
Mede mornede tho, and made heuy cheere,
For the comune called hure queynte comune
　　hore.

　　　　　　　　　　　　　　　　(C.V.151,156,160-1)

Similarly, the description of the Feast of Reason, to which
the dreamer goes with Conscience, Clergy and Patience,
proceeds as a continuous and highly amusing narrative,
but skilfully utilizes every property or speech to convey a
bitter lesson of endurance. While the learned and pomp-
ous friar is fed on delicacies, 'mortrews and poddynges /
Braun and blod of the goos, bacon and colhoppes . . . ',
Patience and the impatient dreamer are more straitly and
healthily served by Scripture:

He sette a sour lof, and said, *'Agite penitentiam,'*
And sethe he drow us drynke, *diu-perseverans:*
'As longe,' quod he, 'as lyfe and lycame may
　　duyre.'
"This is a semely servyce!' saide Pacience.

　　　　　　　　　　　　　　　　(II.56-9:C.XVI.56-9)

We should not pass too quickly over the outraged astonishment of the dreamer as Patience accepts his fare *with
gratitude:*

Pacience was wel apayed of this propre service,
　　. . . ac I mournede evere.

　　　　　　　　　　　　　　　　(II.64-5: C.XVI.63-4)

It is a master stroke of dramatic writing, but it is also a
highly appropriate witness to the dreamer's unreformed,
and therefore rebellious, state of mind.

In both of these sequences—and in others like them—
Langland mingles personifications with 'real' figures:
Meed, Falsehood, Liar, Conscience, Peace, and Wrong
thread their way through undefined crowds of the medieval world—pardoners, lawyers, soldiers. The words spoken by personifications give glimpses of rough, authentic
life; Peace describes Wrong at work, and there behind the
personified figure, with his formal Bill of Complaint, is a
whole landscape overrun by men on aggressive, everyday
business:

'He menteyneth hus men to morthre myn hewes,
And forstalleth myn faires and fyghteth in my
　　chepynges,
And breketh up my bernes dore and bereth away
　　my whete'

　　　　　　　　　　　　　　　　　　(C.V. 58-60)

This mixture of personification and vivid local reportage
is not new; Langland would have known of it from many
earlier poems, in which Truth or Covetousness travel the
English countryside:

Coveytise upon his hors he wole be sone there,
And bringe the bishop silver, and rounen in his
　　ere.

Winner and Waster do not manage their debate in generalities, but by reference to the stuff of fourteenth-century living:

'. . . thy wyde howses full of wolle sakkes,
The bemys benden at the rofe, siche bakone
　　there hynges,
Stuffed　　are　　sterlynges　　undere　　stelen
　　bowndes . . . '

　　　　　　　　　　　　　　　　　　(El.250-2)

But such episodes in ***Piers Plowman*** modulate the 'real'
and the personified in an especially delicate and powerful
way; the details of the landscape behind Peace illustrate
but do not dominate the central moral theme of the passage—the tyranny of violence. In the Feast scene, the particular references to the friar preaching at St. Paul's lead
the eye out through an open window to the contemporary
scene:

Hit is nat thre daies don, this doctour that he
　　prechede
At Poules byfore the peple what penaunce they
　　soffrede . . .

　　　　　　　　　　　　　　　　(II.70-1: C.XVI.69-70)

Nothing outside, however, distracts attention from the essential moral drama indoors: the discovery of the very
basis of patience in willingness to listen to half-truths delivered by a corrupt man (see II.113n).

This is allegory at its most expansive—richly conceived,
precisely executed. But there are growing-points for such
writing all the way through the poem—embryonic allegory. Langland frequently rests on the very brink of 'realizing' an allegorical sequence. A quotation may suggest to
him a theme for development, and he makes a brief, telling
sketch for a larger design. The words 'Multi enim sunt vo-
cati, pauci vero electi' (*Matthew* 22:14) are rapidly set as
an allegorical feast-scene:

A field between the parishes of Colwall and Ledbury in England known as Longland or the Longlands and thought by some scholars to be both the setting for several scenes of Piers Plowman *and the origin of the author's surname.*

Multi to a mangerie and to the mete were sompned,
And whan the peuple was plener come, the porter unpynnede the gate,
And plyghte in *pauci* pryueliche and leet the remenant go rome.

(C.XIII.46-8)

'Iustus vix salvabitur' (*I. Pet.* 4:18) is dramatized, in simple but striking terms, as a court scene, with 'vix' personified, and interceding for 'justus':

> . . . how Ymaginatyf saide
> That *justus* bifore Jesu *in die judicii*
> *Non salvabitur* bote if *vix* helpe . . .

(II.21-3:C.XVI.21-3)

These little episodes, arrested between concept and allegorical action, and rich in potential, show how Langland was constantly drawn to allegory (cf. 16.84-5). But the fact that they remain undeveloped is interesting too: if Langland's movement towards allegory was instinctive, it was also controlled. For him, allegory vivified and clarified doctrine; its form and scope depended intimately upon the needs of the sense at any given moment. We can compare his compact treatment of these quotations with his elaborate drawing-out of a Biblical quotation in the 'Four Daughters of God' debate which prefaces the Harrowing of Hell (15.116 foll.) Here *Psalm* 85, verse 10, 'Misericordia et veritas obviaverunt sibi: iusticia et pax osculate sunt', is expanded into a fullscale encounter and debate on the reasons for man's salvation. The positioning of this debate is all-important: the length and detail of the allegory are closely related to Langland's concern for absolute clarity on the subject of atonement and salvation. Differences between such passages are those of extent rather than of nature: the minuscule sketches are capable of expansion into robust allegorical scenes—they cry out for lively development.

But there are forms of allegory in ***Piers Plowman*** which make no such claims upon us. By comparison, they are flat and unspectacular, and it is all the more important for us to understand their nature and function. Very frequently Langland uses an allegorical mode which is closely connected with a particular kind of medieval art: in fact, 'diagrammatic' is the best descriptive term to use of it. Although no exact sources have been identified, it seems possible that Langland was influenced by schematized drawings when he devised his allegory of the Tree of True-Love, growing in man's heart (13.6 foll.: C.XIX.6 foll.). Medieval moral treatises constantly used the image of the tree, formally divided into branches, leaves and fruit, as a way of expressing man's life, and his relationships to God. And Langland could easily have been familiar with some of the more popular handbooks of the Middle Ages, made probably for the clergy, which gave 'clear visual representation, that the reader, in the midst of a complicated world of abstractions, might see and grasp the essentials'. The description of the Court of Truth (5.86

foll.:C.VIII.232 foll.) and the Barn of Unity (C.XXII.320 foll.) which Piers Plowman builds for his spiritual harvest recall many manuscript drawings of allegorical buildings, quite as stiffly constructed and carefully labelled as Langland's:

> He made a maner morter and Mercy hit hihte.
> And therwith Grace bygan to make a good
>   foundement,
> And watelide hit and wallyde hit with hus
>   peynes and hus passion,
> And of alle holy writt he made a roof after . . .
>
> (C.XXII. 326-9)

It may be that Langland worked from purely literary materials, and not from the visual arts: allegorical buildings were favourite 'exempla' with medieval preachers, and a well-known 14th-century text such as the *Abbey of the Holy Ghost,* with its meticulous architectural symbolism, might very well have been read and used by Langland. Its stone walls are 'festenande togedir with the lufe of gode', its 'syment or morter' is the 'qwykelyme of lufe and stedfaste byleve . . . ', its foundations are laid by Meekness and Poverty, its walls raised by Buxomness and Misericord. Or, again, his debt may be double: he may have gone to illustrated texts which provided him with both 'mental images and actual forms'. His phrasing occasionally suggests direct debts to visual allegory; to a Tree of the Vices, for instance—

> 'Ac whiche be the braunches that bryngeth men
>   to sleuthe?'
>
> (C.VIII.70)

and to a Tree of the Vices compounded with a Tree of Life—

> . . . Pruyde hit aspide,
> . . . greuen he thenketh
> Conscience, and alle Cristene and cardinale uer-
>   tues,
> To blowen hem doun and breken hem and bite
>   atwo the rotes . . .
>
> (C.XXII.337-40)

Here Langland draws upon two iconographical features— Pride, traditionally at the base of the Tree of Vice, and animals (usually identified as Day and Night) gnawing at the roots of the Tree of life. The total image, built up from simple parts, is unusually complex.

But if our knowledge of particular sources must remain incomplete, we can still use art to help us define the character of Langland's diagrammatic allegory. For like the didactic illustrations of the period, it is static, precise, and formalized: what it lacks in evocative power it makes up in faithful accuracy of communication. The description of the way to St. Truth, offered by Piers Plowman (5.87: C.VIII. 157 foll.), illustrates this well. It is a route plan, laid before the 'thousand of men' who have been stirred by Repentance to 'go to Treuthe'. The passage has often been dismissed as dull and wooden. But like the maps and diagrams of medieval religious art, it is not meant to be visualized *in depth.* It is a blue-print for action, not a picture or a full description of the action itself. Similarly, the meticulous setting-out of the tree of 'Trewe-love', planted by the Trinity in man's heart, with its flowers of 'benygne-

speche', and its fruits of 'caritas', does not amount to a picture of a tree: it is nearer to an anatomical or botanical abstract of those physical entities, in which our observation is guided to general structural truths, rather than to variations within the species.

The same comment can be made about the final ploughing scene of the poem (C.XXII.262 foll.). Piers 'tilling truth', with a team of the four Evangelists, and sowing in man's soul four seeds of the cardinal virtues, only barely achieves any sort of dramatic presence—in contrast to an earlier ploughing scene (C.IX.112 foll.) when 'Perkyn with the pilgrimes to the plouh is faren' and we feel his sturdy personality directing the familiar activities of the land:

> Dykers and deluers diggeden up the balkes; . . .
> And somme to plese Perkyn pykede aweye the
>   wedes . . .
>
> (C.IX.114,118)

In the later passage, what matters above all is that each component part of the allegory should be accurately labelled and understood. For this vital account of the establishing of spiritual authority on earth, the fictional element is firmly disciplined. The idea that 'Grace gaf to Peers greynes, cardinales vertues / And sewe hit in mannes soule . . . ' (C.XXII.274-5) has visual and dramatic potential, but the poet is primarily concerned that we should understand what those grains were called, and what were their properties. Such allegory, in which nothing is left to chance, or to the reader's imagination, must be seen as the verbal equivalent of the elaborately inscribed and glossed art of medieval tract illustrations. In fact, it could be said that in its simple, linear quality it bears the same relationship to fully active and rounded allegory (the Meed episodes of C.III-V, for instance) as the diagram does to the picture, with its deep perspective and its more complex media of communication.

But Langland can, on occasion, deal even more severely with our visual expectations. The way to Truth may have to be 'realized' as a map, and not as a picture, but there are times when his allegorical writing is clearly not meant to be visualized in any form whatsoever. We should be mistaken in trying to make ordinary visual sense out of the descriptions of Book, Wit and Anima:

> Thenne was ther a wihte with two brode yes,
> Boke hihte that beau-pere, a bolde man of spe-
>   che.
>
> (15.239-40: C.XXI.240-1)

> He was long and lene, ylyk to noon other.
>
> (7.115: C.XI.114)

> Tyl I seigh, as it sorcerye were, a sotyl thinge
>   withal,
> One withouten tonge and teeth . . .
>
> (B.XV.12-13)

In these, the eye is refused any help: the details do not build up into a logically and visually acceptable whole, but are isolated symbolic features. Thus the protean shape of Anima—by turns Love, Conscience, Memory, Spirit, Reason—is properly denied a physical identity because this would limit and confine it: it is 'spirit specheles' (B.XV.36) and only assumes bodily form to operate God's will in man. The staring eyes of Book refer us directly to the double authority of the opened Gospel pages—an immediate confrontation with the revealed word of authority, rather than with 'a bold man' *representing* authority. Wit is a particularly interesting example; the blocking of a visual response in the second half of the line ensures that the details 'long and lene' are rapidly related to the judicious and sober nature of the faculty of Wit, and not allowed any physical reality.

If, to us, this seems a somewhat cold and intellectualized allegorical mode, we may be taking for granted that visual clarity and forcefulness are always the most effective means of communication for poet or artist. Langland's readers—many of whom were by no means unsophisticated—may have found the very impossibility of visualizing Book a short-cut to grasping its full significance. Clearly Langland could count upon a sensitive response to widely differing allegorical methods, and it is not surprising if, with his comprehensive and complex subject matter, he availed himself of all known devices to capture the understanding.

Somewhere between the full-scale allegorical sequence and the formal allegorical design lie numerous passages of illustrative material, presented very much like parables or 'exempla' in the sermon literature of Langland's time. They do not make use of personification, and they are not diagrammatic: occurring mostly within the speeches of allegorical characters, they are short narratives within narratives. Their function is essentially allegorical; the events they describe are meant to be translated into more significant conceptual terms—and, in fact, are often translated on the spot. But their most distinctive feature is their positioning, for they are experienced by the dreamer at one remove. They are reported allegory. And, like their counterparts in the sermon literature of the Middle Ages, they are vivid and authoritative. Their message is trenchant, but it is also limited: because of their special, circumscribed position in the poem, they can only be developed to a certain extent. Sometimes Langland uses them to make a moral point more tellingly than subtly: the rough effectiveness of the friar's 'forbisene' (in 7.32: C.XI. 32 foll.) is deliberate. Here sinful man is likened to a man in a boat in peril of the waves and the wind, and 'waggynge of the bote', but saved by the very condition of his humanity, which is set in faith and love. Man falls, but not into the sea; he only stumbles within the boat, and is saved: he sins, but only within the body, which, in its frailty, draws God's compassion to it:

> 'So hit fareth', quod the frere, 'by the ryhtful
>   mannes fallynge;
> Thogh he thorw fondynges falle, he falleth nat
>   out of charite . . . '
>   (7.41-2: C.XI.41-2)

It is immediately obvious that the 'equivalences' will not stand up to rigorous analysis—the boat as the body is a tricky concept and, indeed, Langland's purpose in the whole episode is to show us a spiritual teacher who is only superficially clever. The friars are a constant butt of his irony and anger for their glib, popular methods and their presumption. But Langland will also use the 'forbisene' in

a favourable context, as a swift means of clinching a protracted argument, or as a sudden—but not necessarily final—simplification of a complex debate. So Ymaginatif (in C.XV. 103 foll.) offers the puzzled dreamer a chance to resolve, temporarily, some of the long-worked-over problems of the debate on salvation by faith, good works, or learning. The man with learning, he says, can be compared to a man in the water who knows how to swim—he is more likely to be able to save himself from sinking, because of his knowledge:

> 'Ryght so,' quath that renke, 'reson hit sheweth,
> That he that knoweth cleregie can sonnere aryse
> Out of synne, and be saf, thow he synegy ofte.'
>   (C.XV. 110-12)

The sense of relief, shared by dreamer and reader, when they come upon what seems to be a neat and apt analogy, is short-lived. It soon becomes clear that there is much more to say about 'cleregie', and that Ymaginatif is certainly not envisaging it simply as a useful sort of expertise. Neither is he convinced that it is always as efficacious as his parable would have; his last words dwell upon truth, hope, and love, not upon learning:

> 'And where hit worth other nat worth, the byle-
>   yue is gret of treuthe,
> And hope hongeth ay theron to haue that treu-
>   the deserueth;
> *Quia super pauca fidelis fuisti, supra multa te*
>   *constituam:*
> And that is loue and large huyre yf the lord be
>   trewe,
> And cortesie more than couenant was, what so
>   clerkes carpen.'
>   (C.XV.213-16)

But as an interim comment, the parable had value: it helped to concentrate the dreamer's diffuse thoughts, and it encouraged him to use his reason as well as his feelings when tackling the thorny problem of salvation for the simple and the learned.

But if we can distinguish four or five allegorical methods at Langland's easy command, we should not think of them as operating independently of each other. Whatever approach is made—diagrammatic, exemplary, active—it is chosen to display or to investigate subject matter most effectively at that particular point, and may be preceded or superseded by an entirely different kind of approach. The merging of one type of allegory into another is a characteristic of *Piers Plowman,* not shared by many other poems of its time, though frequent enough in some types of devotional prose writing. The most striking example of this comes in extract 13 (C.XIX.106 foll.) when the static allegory of the Tree of Trewe-love quickens, and in the presence of the dreamer becomes an active allegorical drama of man's subjection to the devil—

> For evere as Elde hadde eny down, the devel was
>   redy,
> And gadered hem alle togyderes, bothe grete
>   and smale,
> Adam and Abraham and Ysaye, the
>   prophete . . .
>   (13.111-13:C.XIX.111-13)

and of the decision to save him—

> Thenne moved hym mod *in majestate dei,*
> That *Libera-Voluntas-Dei* lauhte the myddel
>   shoriar
> And hit aftur the fende . . .
> (13.118-20:C.XIX.118-20)

The passage from this to the actual historical moment of the Annunciation—

> And thenne spak *Spiritus Sanctus* in Gabrieles
>   mouthe
> To a mayde that hihte Marie . . .
> (13.124-5: C.XIX.124-5)

is, in one sense, a startling and brilliant move by Langland, but in another sense it is quite natural—a stage in a continuous process of evolution, from design to life, which in its turn is drawn back again to attitude and gesture. (pp. 9-19)

> *Elizabeth Salter and Derek Pearsall, in an introduction to their* Piers Plowman, *Northwestern University Press, 1967, pp. 1-58.*

David Mills   (essay date 1969)

[*In the following excerpt, Mills studies* Piers Plowman *on four levels: as a representation of medieval social and religious realities, as a dream experience reflecting either the Dreamer's confused mind or a prophetic vision, as a narrative, and in terms of its total structure.*]

It should be evident that a study of the rôle of the Dreamer in *Piers* is not merely the study of a particular aspect of a particular poem. A. C. Spearing has said that 'despite the great quantity of scholarly work that has been done on it [*Piers*], it appears that we are still at the stage of having to make up our minds what *kind* of poem it is'. Indeed, we must do even more. We must decide what we mean by *poetry* and whether *Piers* can justly be considered as a poem at all. Often it seems to be regarded as something requiring explanation rather than response, a philosophical argument made more obscure by being written in the form of a verse allegory, with certain passages being singled out for their poetic value. Perversely, its alleged poetic deficiencies are cited in justification of its extra-poetic interest. M. W. Bloomfield claims [in his *'Piers Plowman' as a Fourteenth-century Apocalypse,* 1961] that—

> Langland fails, in part, to satisfy these claims [the contending tensions of his age] completely and in perfect artistic form because his aim is to show the spiritual confusion of his own times. Spiritual confusion demands to some extent artistic confusion.

It is hard to believe that an impression of the spiritual confusion in the world can be effectively conveyed by a poem that is at all confused in its own structure. Rather, poetic confusion produces impatience and boredom, and it matters little whether we attribute that confusion to a confused poet or a confused Dreamer. *Piers* may be explained and even excused by this means, but it cannot be justified.

In *Piers Plowman,* I would claim, it is not possible to distinguish 'thought' from 'expression'. The work is a complete unity in which the poet explores the relationship between the finite and the infinite on a number of inter-related levels, and the Dreamer's rôle is to represent the finite on all these levels in contrast to Piers Plowman who represents the infinite. The resulting poem is complex and difficult, but it is nevertheless a poem, self-contained, whose structure is its meaning, and, like any work which has structural and thematic unity, it demands an emotional as well as an intellectual response from its readers. It is a poem with many aspects but, for the sake of convenience, it may be considered to have four levels— contemporary reality, dream-experience, narrative and total structure.

The contemporary world, with its social complexities and philosophies of life, is the starting point and 'raw material' of the poem. It is true that this reality is mostly presented through the vision-form, but the basic problems of the medieval world are not in doubt. Man has two inter-related obligations—to his fellow men in society and to God. Society presents an order which essentially is a moral order but which is overtly enforced by human law under the king. It also has an economic basis, again to be interpreted in terms of moral bligation, but overtly controlled by manufacture and trade and measured in terms of wealth. God is represented in society by His Church which is the means whereby Man is directed to God. From the Church Man learns his moral obligations which are consonant with the principles of social order, though wider reaching and of greater importance, and within the Church he can attain grace. Yet the reality to which *Piers Plowman* returns constantly is one in which human law and social order are overthrown by an excessive concern with material goods and in which moral obligations are ignored by laity and clergy alike in their desire for gain. In reality the unity envisaged in theocentric theory has been destroyed in every aspect.

The rôle of the Dreamer at this level is to represent contemporary man, almost the only 'real' person in the poem, and the opening lines of the poem go some way towards establishing this rôle:

> In a somer seson, whan soft was the sonne,
> I shope me in shroudes, as I a shepe were;
> In habite as an heremite, vnholy of works,
> Went wyde in this world wondres to here.
> Ac on a May mornynge on Maluerne hulles
> Me byfel a ferly, of fairy me thoughte.
> B Prol. 1-6

Burrow notes:

> For Langland, the dream is a structural device; and he does not exploit its decorative possibilities in the manner of *Wynnere & Wastoure, The Parlement of the Thre Ages,* or *Pearl.*

The result, however, is to divorce the preamble from a set literary convention; in this context the *May mornynge* is not only out of its conventionally decorative context but is allied to the precise *Maluerne hulles* and both suggest a definite time and place. They are the first of a number of precise and unexpected statements which relate the Dreamer to a background of space and time; e.g.:

. . . er I hadde faren a fourlonge, feyntise me
hente.

B v 5

Tyl it bifel on a Fryday two freres I mette.

B viii 8

. . . lened me to a lenten, and longe tyme I slep-
te.

B xviii 5

In myddes of the masse, tho men ghede to of-
frynge,
I fel eftsones aslepe.

B xix 4-5

And it neighed nyeghe the none, and with Nede
I mette.

B xx 4

The Dreamer is set against a precise background, never realized by detailed description but created by a few brief
references. The 'biographical' references to him living
with his wife Kit in a cottage on Cornhill (C vi 1-5) and
to *Kitte my wyf and Kalote my daughter* (B xviii 426) similarly serve to establish him in a precise context, and with
the same conciseness. Moreover, the Dreamer is presented
in the temporal context of his own life, as described by
Imaginative:

. . . of thi wylde wantounesse tho thow ghonge
were,
To amende it in thi myddel age, lest mighte the
faylled
In thyne olde elde.

B xii 6-8

and represented in his visions by the assaults of Elde upon
him (B xi 26-32; xx 182-197). These precise references,
both circumstantial and 'biographical', and the lack of accompanying conventional poetic descriptions help to establish the Dreamer as 'real' and enable him to fulfil the
function of dreamer noted by Gordon:

> Tales of the past required their grave authorities,
> and tales of new things at least an eyewitness, the
> author. This was one of the reasons for the popu-
> larity of visions: they allowed marvels to be
> placed within the real world, linking them with
> a person, a place, a time, while providing them
> with an explanation in the phantasies of sleep,
> and a defence against critics in the notorious de-
> ception of dreams.

Yet, if the Dreamer belongs to the real world, it is clear
that he stands outside society. What is less clear is the significance of his rôle as outsider, for even in the opening description he is an ambiguous figure. The physical comparison, *as I a shepe were,* is a grotesque and suggests the uneasy awareness of the absurdity of his position, considered
objectively, which the Dreamer shows elsewhere—for example, in his pose of social rebel (B XV 1-15)—and which
is also reflected in the rebukes which he receives—for example, from Dame Study (B x 1-134). But although the
Dreamer may often seem comic, there is a serious over-
tone in his absurdity. . . . The obvious sense here,
stressed by [D. W.] Robertson and [Bernard F.] Huppé [in
their *"Piers Plowman" and Scriptural Tradition,* 1951], is
the 'wolf in sheep's clothing' which is suggested by the ref-

erence to dress and the outward similarity to a hermit. Yet
at the same time the idea of a 'straying and lost sheep' is
present in the reference to wandering, and perhaps against
it stands the idea that the Dreamer wishes to be a 'sheep'
as opposed to a 'goat', one who is among God's chosen
and will be saved, and both these senses become stronger
as the poem progresses. Moreover, this ambiguity is continued in the next line by the play on *habite* which
strengthens the link between outer appearance and inner
nature. *Vnholy of workes,* as many critics have pointed
out, implies that the Dreamer is a wastrel masquerading
as a hermit, like the false hermits in the Field (B Prol. 53-
57). Yet the phrase could also imply the contrast of the
contemplative and the active life which is an important
concept in the poem. On the one hand, the Dreamer's
withdrawal from the world may mean that he does no evil
but also does no good works, is guilty of sins of omission.
On the other hand, it suggests his desire to fulfil the rôle
of a true hermit, standing apart from the world and relying upon prayer and contemplation; the Dreamer aspires
to a special faith, and perhaps a special grace and knowledge.

This initial ambiguity is never resolved and leaves some
doubt about the value of what the Dreamer says; his physical isolation from his fellow-men, reinforced by the absence of any definite indication of his social status, has a
counterpart in his critical attitude towards the contemporary world. Is he shirking his social responsibilities, living
upon society, like a false hermit or beggar? Is he preaching
false doctrine, like an evil preacher? Is he talking idle nonsense, like an entertainer or minstrel? The ambiguity may
be 'a defence against critics', but it contributes to the general sense of uncertainty that *Piers* leaves. The Dreamer
is seeking not only the answers to the problems around
him, but also the answers to his own identity and value,
and his request to Holy Church, *Kenne me bi somme
crafte to knowe the Fals* (B ii 4), has personal as well as
social reference. Is he a sinner, a guide to salvation, or
both?

In another way the Dreamer's 'real' situation can be related to his visionary situation, for he is like a pilgrim—like
all pilgrims—in search of Truth. Yet, as he recognizes,
there are true and false pilgrims, and pilgrimages may be
undertaken for idle pleasure as well as for true devotion.
Certainly it is in this spirit of idleness that the Dreamer
begins, for his journey seems motivated by nothing more
than the fine weather and consists in pointless wanderings
(*went wyde*). His avowed intent, *wondres to here,* suggests
an idle curiosity and a concern with hearsay rather than
deeds. This sense of aimlessness seems to appear whenever
the Dreamer awakes; e.g.:

> Thus yrobed in russet I romed aboute
> Al a somer sesoun for to seke Dowel.

B viii 1-2

> And I awaked therewith, witles nerehande,
> And as a freke that fre were, forth gan I walke
> In manere of a mendynaunt many a ghere after.

B xiii 1-3

> Wolleward and wete-shoed went I forth after,
> As a reccheles renke that of no wo reccheth,

And ghede forth lyke a lorel al my lyf-tyme.
B xviii 1-3

and at the very end, before his final vision, he is still in doubt and perplexity:

> Thanne as I went by the way, whan I was thus
>   awaked,
> Heuy-chered I ghede and elynge in herte;
> I ne wiste where to ete ne at what place.
B xx 1-3

The physical picture may well be an image of search, but it is also an image of aimlessness and one which becomes associated increasingly with despair. It may also be seen as an image of the Dreamer's own lack of steadfastness, of his own instability, which makes him incapable of progression. Yet it could be suggested that the abandonment of the idle gaiety of the opening is a sign of progression which is a counterpart to the Dreamer's spiritual growth in the visions. The parallels and contrasts of the physical journeys are evident, but the values to be set upon them are far from clear.

Yet these difficulties are small compared with those which the reader encounters in evaluating the dream-experience. Here the initial problem is to determine what kind of dream-experience this may be. This is not the place to attempt a detailed discussion of medieval dream-theory, but basically the problem is to decide if the dream has its origins in the Dreamer's own confused mind or if it is a prophetic dream impressed upon his mind by a celestial intelligence. If the dream is from the Dreamer's mind alone, it is unlikely to have any wider value and the Dreamer's rôle is to create his own dream. If it comes from outside him, however, his rôle is that of prophet, to receive a divine revelation and communicate it to his fellow-men. Even so, the two types are not totally distinct, and it is possible that the dream is part revelation, part personal creation, so that the problem of distinguishing between the various elements also arises.

These difficulties are clearly inseparable from those involved in the Dreamer's relation to society. Indeed, at the start of his dream, his position is comparable with his situation at the start of the poem:

> Thanne gan I to meten a merueilouse sweuene,
> That I was in a wildernesse, wist I neuer where.
B Prol. 11-12

The reference to the *wildernesse* takes up the earlier picture of the Dreamer as a hermit. He is outside the structure of his dream—tower, field and dungeon—and merely observes. At the same time the wilderness may suggest his inner aridity. Yet it also evokes the image of a desert-father, a prophet. The lack of purpose is taken up in *wist I neuer where,* but at the same time this contrasts with the firm reference to the Malvern Hills where the Dreamer falls asleep, suggesting both uncertainty and a liberation from earthly restriction.

If indeed there is a parallel between the Dreamer's relation to society and the Dreamer's relation to his vision, there is also an evident distinction between the vision and society. The dream is a form of escape, a kind of pleasant entertainment evoked by the pleasant natural scene. An image-pattern develops—'*wondres* to here', 'me byfel a *ferly*', 'it sweyued so *merye*', 'a *merueilouse* sweuene'. Initially the dream is a pleasant experience, but nothing more. Yet the value of the experience is still not clear. On the one hand, the Dreamer seems to suggest that the experience is an escape from doubt to certainty:

> . . . folke helden me a fole, and in that folye I
>   raued,
> Tyl Resoun hadde reuthe on me and rokked me
>   aslepe.
B xv 10-11

Here the dream is inspired by Reason as a means of leading the Dreamer from the folly induced by his misunderstanding of the previous vision. On other occasions the Dreamer sees his experience as a total renunciation of a hopeless world:

> . . . I wex wery of the worlde and wylned eft
>   to slepe.
B xviii 4

On other occasions, however, it is not clear if the dream represents a movement into a more meaningful experience or an escape from a personal duty:

> And so I babeled on my bedes thei broughte me
>   aslepe.
B v 8

> In myddes of the masse, tho men ghede to of-
>   frynge,
> I fel eftsones aslepe . . .
B xix 4-5

Does religious observance inspired a divine revelation, or is the dream a rejection of a meaningless ritual? Does the Dreamer fall asleep in church through boredom, or conveniently because he must make his offering, or in revolt against the worldly church, or because the worldly offering leads him naturally to think of God's offering for Man, the subject of his vision?

Perhaps most important of all, however, is whether the dream-experience can answer the Dreamer's questions. What the Dreamer seeks in the *Vitae* section is to know Dowel, Dobet and Dobest, but paradoxically this knowledge involves 'doing'. By his position outside society the Dreamer has cut himself off from the possibility of acting effectively, but by his further withdrawal from reality into a dream-experience he has cut himself off from the possibility of knowing what doing well may be. Perhaps the clearest statement of this dilemma is to be found in the C-text where the speaker is the Dreamer:

> . . . And sayde anon to myself: 'slepynge, ich
>   hadde grace
> To wite what Dowel ys, ac wakynge neuere!'
C xiv 218-19

It is difficult to see how the Dreamer can know Dowel when he is asleep and not when awake, although it is easy to translate this opposition into a contrast of the will and the deed such as St Paul makes. But such a contrast is made impossible by the Dreamer's continuation:

> And thenne was ther a wight—what he was ich
>   nuste—

'What ys Dowel?', quath that wight. 'ywys,
    syre,' ich seyde,
'To see muche and suffren al, certes, syre, ys
    Dowel.'

C xiv 220-222

The idea of activity is transformed into one of passivity—
to do well is to do nothing but observe uncritically; it is
a reinforcement of the Dreamer's withdrawal since, although the Dreamer would have 'done well' to have listened to Reason, he has made an absurd generalization
from a particular case. His act of dreaming is used as a
substitute for experience as well as an extension of experience and his medium of revelation is also a means of withdrawal.

Hence the Dreamer remains as uncertain of the value of
his dream as he is about his own rôle in the world. . . .
The Dreamer's difficulty is to find the prophetic element
in his vision, and heremains constantly unable to do so.
The dream may be prophetic but the Dreamer is not. (pp.
182-90)

The Dreamer has a dual rôle, as Dreamer and as a figure
in his own dream, but his function within his own dream
is to assert the primacy of the present and of the individual
against the denial which the dream-experience proposes of
any such primacy. It is this assertion which destroys the
unity of the vision but which also makes the vision uniquely the Dreamer's. It corresponds to the distinction between the prophetic and personal elements within the
dream and between the analogical correspondences and
'real' elements of the vision, for the Dreamer becomes the
means of asserting a sinful and worldly reality against the
advice and claims of the figures in the *Vitae.* For this reason, the dream must always return to reality, both because
the Dreamer must awake, and also because within the
dream there is always the assertion of a reality which con-
tradicts the ideal. But the great achievement of Langland
is to set against the figure of the Dreamer that of Piers who
epitomizes the fusion of time and space. Piers is timeless
and universal as the Dreamer is not. But Piers is also a
part of the social world which the Dreamer rejects, for
Piers has a definite social function—he is always Piers *the
Plowman.* As such—surprisingly, perhaps—he exemplifies action and involvement against the Dreamer's thought
and withdrawal.

It seems assumed that when the Dreamer asks questions,
he asks the right questions. Yet, given his attitude to society and the concepts of time and place which he represents, it would be strange if his questions were always
valid. His remarks to Holy Church are a case in point. He
has noted, it might seem, the concern of those in the Field
with money, and he asks a most pertinent question:

Ac the moneye of this molde that men so faste
    holdeth,
Telle me to whom, Madame, that tresore appen-
    deth?

B i 44-45

Yet this is a strange, childlike question which presupposes
that *someone* must own the treasure, and Holy Church's
answer, *Reddite Cesari,* never faces this presupposition; it
is merely a statement on the use of wealth. It is significant

*Pewtress or, in Langland's time, Promeswelle Spring, a little over
a mile from the Longlands, the source of a stream and possibly the
site of Will the dreamer's first rest in* Piers Plowman.

that the Dreamer supposes that his question can have an
absolute answer, for he continues, having discovered Holy
Church's identity, to question in a way which indicates
that he has not understood her answer:

Teche me to no tresore, but telle me this ilke,
How I may saue my soule, that seynt art yhol-
    den?

B i 83-84

Holy Church has already made it clear that worldly
wealth has a place in man's existence but must be governed by moral law. The Dreamer's new question is doubly childlike; it presupposes an opposition of worldly
goods and salvation which is only partially true and it suggests that Holy Church can tell him how to save his soul.
In fact, neither presupposition is correct. Holy Church patiently tries again:

'Whan alle tresores aren tried,' quod she, 'trew-
    the is the best.'

B i 85

where the 'treasure' image is an assertion of a comparative
scale of values against the Dreamer's totally exclusive categories—the things of this world cannot be totally rejected
but must be correctly valued. And as a counsel of salvation, it is unintelligible to the Dreamer:

. . . ghet mote ghe kenne me better,
By what craft in my corps it [Truth] comseth
and where.

B i 136-137

Small wonder that Holy Church, like an exasperated mother, loses control—*Thow dote daffe* (i 138)—and, after another attempt, concludes hastily 'I've had enough; I'm going!' (i 206-207) and to the Dreamer's howl of 'But *please!'* she replies hastily 'Look for yourself!' The Dreamer expects that there will be an absolute explanation and denies that he has any 'natural understanding' (*kynde witte*) to apply precepts to individual situations. He is therefore limited to a sequential vision, a system of logical and definable causes and effects, in which each answer is final.

Thus when he sees his visions, they correspond ostensibly to his questions and to Holy Church's answers. The trial of Meed follows the pattern of Holy Church's advice on worldly goods, while the pilgrimage to Truth is the answer to the Dreamer's demand for salvation. Yet the correspondence is only apparent, for the illogical division which the Dreamer made between wealth and salvation is made clear when the vision breaks down. In the trial of Meed, although the king, guided by Conscience and Reason, can limit the interference of Meed in the order of society under law and can help to enforce a *mesurable hire,* no one owns Meed—she owns them and she is more enduring than they are. At the end of the trial, Meed is still present and still has her supporters. And in the pilgrimage to Truth, the necessity to earn one's living in society becomes an important element in the pilgrimage and is a feature of the pardon. Although the individual may repent, the Sins, like Meed, are allegorical figures, enduring and incapable of change, and contrition and repentance are useless without obedience and love. Finally, the pardon episode is an example to the Dreamer that no simple definitive answer, of the kind which he expected from Holy Church, will suffice unless interpreted with 'natural understanding'. The priest is logically correct—good deeds are not enough; but from all that has gone before in the poem we know this. The text has to be set in its context—of the poem, or, as Robertson and Huppé point out, in its original context of the Athanasian Creed. The priest could certainly have done the latter, and every reader can do the former, but the priest treats the pardon in the isolating, definitive manner which we come to recognize as characteristic of the Dreamer himself.

The Dreamer, however, bound by his own experience in time and space, cannot escape from his sequential vision. From time to time he interposes, as Dreamer, his comments on the action showing that he is still no nearer an understanding of the true meaning of his vision. Thus, the incident of the shriving of Meed draws the trivial comment that the rich should not endow stainedglass windows (iii 64-99), while his conclusion on the pardonscene, that one should trust Dowel and not a paper pardon, is certainly true but misses the personal lesson to be learned from the priest's literalism.

The pardon-scene, however, marks a turning-point in the poem, since the quest for Dowel, Dobet and Dobest fol-

lows. If the questions with which the Dreamer directed the *Visio* were based on false assumptions, the suppositions underlying the *Vitae* are more obviously false. The Dreamer's quest originates, significantly, in the priest's comment on the pardon:

'Peter!' quod the prest tho, 'I can no pardoun
fynde,
But Dowel, and haue wel and god shal haue thi
sowle,
And do yuel, and haue yuel, hope thow non
other
But after thi ded-day the deuel shal haue thi
sowle!'

B vii 112-115

Dowel is very clearly a 'verb-adverb' construction suggesting a finite action, but the Dreamer, oddly, treats it as if it were a noun,

Thus yrobed in russet I romed aboute
Al a somer sesoun for to seke Dowel.

B viii 1-2

that is, as if it were a definite thing which could be sought out and found—like the person who owns all the treasure in the world. Then, to heap confusion upon confusion, Thought supplies a comparative and superlative:

'Dowel and Dobet and Dobest the thridde,'
quod he,
'Aren three faire vertues and beth naughte fer to
fynde.'

B viii 78-79

Dowel is a syntactical impossibility, a verbal phrase indicative of action frozen into a noun which implies an objective existence, an entity or state. One cannot seek Dowel, one can only *do* well, so that the Dreamer's lack of involvement has now been turned to the pursuit of the non-existent. Thought's comment erects a comparative and superlative upon a positive that has no objective existence. Every adviser that the Dreamer encounters can define Dowel for him only by limiting its reference to something which does exist, and hence provides only a partial definition. The Dreamer is looking for the impossible in his attempts to impose an order upon and direct the course of his own vision. (pp. 191-95)

Structurally, the concept of Dowel, Dobet and Dobest sets up an impression of progress towards an absolute goal which contrasts with the impression of balance created by the Dreamer's questions to Holy Church which are developed in the two episodes of the *Visio.* Ostensibly the Dreamer's rôle changes from that of observer to that of protagonist, since he is now a figure actively engaged in his own dreams. But just as Dowel, Dobet and Dobest develop from the pardon scene, so also does the idea of conflict and dispute, with the Dreamer taking over the priest's rôle and rigorously questioning the meaning of all that he encounters. Since the priest could not see the truth in the pardon sent by Truth, it is unlikely that the logical Dreamer can see the truth in his revelation. And since the Dreamer has begun by postulating a triad which has no objective existence, he cannot receive a satisfactory definition of it and hence progression becomes impossible, for he is asking the impossible. At the end of the poem he is still being given the same answers that Holy Church gave him—learn to love and do not set great store by worldly needs (B xx 206-210)—and from what we have seen of the Dreamer we can feel no confidence that he is capable of understanding these injunctions, particularly when his guide is not a perfect Holy Church but a disunited earthly church.

This is not to say that there is no concept of progression in *Piers,* but it is a 'progression' only in a limited sense. In the *Visio* there is an implied causative relationship between the trial of Meed and the pilgrimage to Truth; but with the breakdown of the pilgrimage it becomes clear that this is not a progression but a cycle, a sequence of aspiration and failure. In the *Vita*-section this concept of progression is more complex since it includes a historical perspective. The Fall of Man, the Harrowing of Hell, the Coming of Antichrist; Abraham, Spes (Moses) and the Good Samaritan exemplify a chronological progression, and the Dreamer's own position in a historical sequence, established by references to him in the real world, is assimilated to this pattern. Firstly, the introduction of his internal dialogues into the framework points a connexion between his situation and the historical pattern, and secondly, at the end of the dreams, the Dreamer is stricken by Elde and driven in fear to Unity (B xx 188-205); the coming of Antichrist preludes both the ordained end of the world and the physical end of the Dreamer. On the one hand, progression is progressive decline, but on the other hand it is increasing awareness of one's need; as [V. A.] Kolve says [in his *The Play Called Corpus Christi,* 1966]:

> For the most part, the Middle Ages was chiefly conscious of degeneration, of the times growing ever worse and worse. Only one medieval conception of present time had an affirmative tone, and its beginning is staged by the central story of the Corpus Christi cycle: whatever else 'now' might be, it was historically the time of mercy.

Yet this sequential concept of progress is secondary, for the sequence can only figure a unity. Thus Father, Son and Holy Ghost; Faith, Hope and Charity correspond to the historical triads above but represent a progression in degree, within a single unity, and are active, ever-present forces and principles. And Piers Plowman himself stands as an active, present force, the present manifestation of social man, spiritual man, Christ and St Peter. This rôle is something which the Dreamer cannot understand and he applies to Piers the same finite vision that he applied in his questions to Holy Church:

> 'Is Piers in this place?' quod I.
> B xviii 21

> 'Is this Iesus the Iuster?' quod I, 'that Iuwes did to deth?
> Or it is Pieres the plowman; who paynted hym so rede?'
> B xix 10-11

Piers for him must exist in one place and as one person (Iesus . . . *or* . . . Pieres) and this limited vision is the main barrier to the Dreamer's understanding. Basically, Dowel, Dobet and Dobest is a triad of unity, like the Trinity, not a triad of progression, like the historical groups. This is made quite clear by Clergy:

> For one Pieres the Ploughman hath inpugned vs alle,
> And sette alle sciences at a soppe, saue loue one . . .
> And seith that Dowel and Dobet aren two infinites,
> Whiche infinites, with a feith, fynden oute Dobest
> Which shal saue mannes soule; thus seith Piers the Ploughman.
> B xiii 123-124, 127-129

The Dreamer's false premises, like his earlier misguided questions, form the starting point for the exploration of a profound truth. Syntactically he has sought to define action as state, verb as noun, and has carried this further by establishing a progressive sequence of states which can be regarded only as a progressive intensity of action. The definitions which he receives are given in finite terms but the terms are infinites—syntactically incomplete and hence logically lasting for ever. The infinite can be approached and known only through the finite, and in one sense this is the progression of the *Vita,* but finite examples, existing in time and space, are inadequate manifestations since they are complete and cyclical. They represent the verbal aspect of the Dreamer's categories which must be reconceived in terms of the infinite noun-categories to which the Trinity and Faith, Hope and Charity belong. The recognition that states are subject to change is the basis of the poem's pessimism—the real world of change and corruption breaks in upon the 'ideal state' of the dream-experience with its unchanging allegorical figures, while the Dreamer hovers uncertainly between the two, demanding that a verb should be a noun and objecting because it cannot be. Meanwhile, Piers Plowman stands as the assertion of the nominal, himself an infinite in whom all triads meet and who unites time and space and defies change.

The Dreamer and Piers are in complementary rôles, but without the Dreamer there could be no poem, for one cannot dramatize a state. The conflicts of the *Vita* are foreshadowed in the *Visio* in a much simpler form. What the Dreamer sees is a physical picture, with the Tower of Truth, the Field of Folk and the Dungeon of Care, and when a pilgrimage to Truth is suggested one assumes that it will present the inhabitants of the Field ascending the hill to the Tower—a physical journey figuring a spiritual journey, with the duration of the journey being equivalent to the life of man. Piers, however, effects a characteristic fusion by destroying the Dreamer's physical picture. The people are to stay where they are and find Truth in their hearts and, as Burrow has pointed out [in 'The Action of Langland's Second Vision,' *Essays in Criticism* (July 1965)], a brief labour in the field becomes a substitute or an equivalent for the pilgrimage and an image of a lifetime's labour in the world. Yet the pilgrims cling to the physical image—they complain about the distance (vi 1-2), refuse to work in the field; and finally Truth's pardon is declared false on logical grounds by the priest. The intersection of the finite image of physical pilgrimage by the 'infinite' spiritual pilgrimage has its counterpart in the breakdown of the action. The point of the pilgrimage account is the sheer inadequacy of the image to sustain the meaning. The pilgrims are not first to 'honour their fathers' and next to 'swear not in vain' but are to do all these things simultaneously, and the spatial and temporal concepts of pilgrimage obscure the essential unity of Piers's message.

Piers's problem in directing the pilgrims is that of the Dreamer in his rôle of narrator, for although the dream-experience admits the infinite, any verbal expression, whether sentence or poem, is finite and limited. Just as dream-experience cuts the Dreamer off from reality, so the necessity of poetic expression prevents him from understanding or communicating the meaning of his dream. In contrast to the normal practice of a dream-poem, *Piers* presents a dream-experience in opposition to its verbal manifestation and demonstrates that an 'idea is translatable into words and fictions, but these may not faithfully represent the original [S. Delany, '"Phantom" and the *House of Fame', Chaucer Review*, ii (1967)] As narrator, the Dreamer sets a verbal barrier between the reader and his experience, and the poem becomes an expression of the limitations of poetry.

When Holy Church attempts to explain love to the Dreamer, she is compelled to use images, but shifts reference so frequently that the image breaks down. . . . . (pp. 196-200)

On a larger scale, the same inadequacy of imagery can be seen in the description of the Tree of Charity. . . . (p. 201)

[The account of Christ] . . . exemplifies the same inadequacies as Holy Church's account of love. The image is incapable of sustaining the two ideas of state and change simultaneously and hence breaks down. This breakdown is emphasized by the reference back to the starting point, so that the reader is made doubly aware that the image is inadequate, so that the breakdown is functional. But, above all, this breakdown of expression at narrative level corresponds to the breakdown of the dream-state by the Dreamer's logical interventions, and to the breakdown of an ideal reality by the forces of worldliness.

It is not surprising that the Dreamer's first question, *what is this to mene?*, is the most important, for it concerns not only the 'meaning' of life but also the 'meaning' of words. The Dreamer's problem in defining Dowel, Dobet and Dobest is essentially verbal, although verbal definition is impossible. In the same way, a number of terms are employed which cannot be verbally defined. *Truth* is used to refer to the owner of the tower on the hill, not *God*, for Truth is not only synonymous with God but also an active principle (contrast *False*) and its manifestation (contrast *Falsehood*). At the end of the poem Piers builds *Unity*, not *Holy Church*, for Unity is the harmony of God and Man, of man and man, and of man within himself; it is the manifestation of love, and hence wider than Holy Church. Yet because experience is fragmented, we can never understand these terms fully. The poem ends thematically where it should end—in Unity; but the real world in-

trudes, for there is disunity within the earthly unity. How then can the Dreamer come to Unity? How can he know Truth when all he sees is False? How can he know Charity when all that he can see is false charity and covetousness? He is faced with the problem of talking about an ideal infinite with the outlook, and language, of a corrupt finite. If language is inadequate to convey meaning, and experience is too limited and corrupt to give understanding, how can he attain salvation?

If we regard the Dreamer as the representative of reality, of logical reason, of definitive language, it is clear that his account of his visions is going to be weighted heavily in the direction of the very world which he is trying to reject. Thus, when we read the account of the Field of Folk, we are aware that it is an uneven account, and for two reasons. Firstly, there are far more evil-doers than virtuous men. This may be attributable to the actual state of society or to the selective nature of the Dreamer's vision which may or may not come from him; but it may be the result of the Dreamer, as narrator, selecting the evil element in society. This latter view is strengthened by the second reason, that the treatment of the figures endows the evil-doers with the greater poetic vitality. It is the friars, the beggars, the pardoner who remain in the mind. Even when he refers to the virtuous, it is the image of the bad which remains:

> Some putten hem to the plow, pleyed ful selde,
> In settyng and in sowyng swonken ful harde,
> And wonnen that wastours with glotonye destruyeth.
>
> Prol. 20-22
> (pp. 204-05)

This lack of poetic balance is a continuing problem in *Piers Plowman* and affects the reader's response. Meed contrasts with Holy Church in appearance and characteristics, but Meed is far more vital than Holy Church and emerges as a much stronger figure. As a vice she is necessarily dynamic, and as that particular vice she is concretely manifested in an interesting variety of forms and is capable of dramatic action. Having real manifestations, she serves as a vehicle for lively social satire, aided by the fact that she is an allegorical figure with no moral faculty and hence is completely unable to evaluate her actions. This gay immoral consistency is attractive and Meed is the one figure at the trial who holds our attention and captures our imagination. Yet Meed, as an allegorical figure, cannot question or change herself, but can only manifest herself and attempt to justify her existence. Even at the end of the trial, Meed has not been changed into something capable of reconciliation with Conscience, nor has she ceased to exist. She has only been denied control of one king for a moment, and her continuing existence is a justification both for her prominence in the real world and for her vitality in the scene which the Dreamer narrates. The visions of the ideal state put forward by Conscience and Reason lie in a future in which Meed does not exist and have no reference to the corrupt present, nor does the poem hold out any hope of the realization of the ideal by investing it with immediacy or conviction.

This lack of poetic balance is continued in the confessions

of the Deadly Sins. Many critics, following the 'thought' of the poem, would argue that the confessions of the sins represent the collective confessions of the people; thus [T. P.] Dunning says [in his *'Piers Plowman', an Interpretation of the A-text,* (1938)]:

> The Confessions are real confessions . . . they are the Sacrament of Penance and not mere self-declarations or public displays of their characters by the Sins. . . . The Confessions are made on behalf of, and stand for, the confessions of the folk.

But the dominant impression left by these confessions is not of repentance but of sin, and the vitality both of the manifestations of the sins and of the language in which they are described and describe themselves weights the poetic emphasis towards sin rather than repentance. As has been noted, part of the problem is the nature of allegory, for a sin is incapable of passing moral judgment upon itself; it may be sorry that it is a sin, but it cannot become a virtue, and indeed no absolution is pronounced upon the sins, and sinners appear among the crowd of pilgrims to Truth, unable to understand the nature of the 'journey' and finally disrupting the ploughing of the half-acre. But the other part of the problem is the vigour with which the sins are realized. Had all the sins been portrayed with the brevity of Superbia and Luxuria, the idea of repentance would have been realized, but other portraits are longer, with more varied manifestations. And the language has strong imaginative vitality, e.g.:

> 'I am Wrath,' quod he, 'I was sum tyme a frere,
> And the couentes gardyner for to graffe ympes;
> On limitoures and listres lesynges I ymped,
> Tyl thei bere leues of low speche, lordes to plese,
> And sithen thei blosmed obrode in boure to here shriftes.'
>
> B v 136-140

There is no penitent note here. The idea of grafting sprigs of lies is comically appropriate and is worked out skilfully, with none of the complexities of the expository images such as the plant of love. When sin is so vividly realized, the idea of penitence recedes, much as it does in the worst morality plays where the comic vice steals the scene. When a figure like Inuidia says:

> 'I am sori,' quod that segge, 'I am but selde other,
> And that maketh me thus megre, for I ne may me venge.'
>
> B v 127-128

we can see little hope of reformation. The breakdown of order in Pier's half-acre is a logical continuation of such sin-centred poetry which is explicable as an illustration of the Dreamer's own outlook.

In contrast to this vitality, Piers's own account of the journey to Truth is very poor poetry. Much can be said in favour of the simplicity and clarity of this 'signpost allegory' and there is no doubt that it occupies a key position in the development of the poem, but there is something in Ker's comment [in *English Literature, Medieval,* (1945)] that:

> It is tedious to be told of a brook named 'Be buxom of speech', and a croft called 'Covet not men's cattle nor their wives', when nothing is made of the brook or the croft by way of scenery.

It is still more tedious when compared with the racy, vital treatment of sin which has preceded this account. In fact, the inadequacy of the poetic method here parallels the inadequacy of the whole pilgrimage image which has been discussed above—it is comparatively simple to convey the idea of a sinful rebellion but extremely difficult to convey the concept of obedience. At a poetic level this unevenness is a further manifestation of the opposition between the dynamic and finite and the static and infinite. The Dreamer's account of the confessions of the sins presents a much more attractive and intelligible realization of sin than his report of Piers's address on the journey to Truth does for virtue.

At this point it is impossible to decide if the emphasis upon sin is intended to reflect a bias in reality, or in the dream, or in the Dreamer's account of the dream, but it is true to say that the Dreamer emerges as the representative of all the disruptive forces which he deplores. In a key passage, the dialogue with Anima, we find:

> 'Ghe, syre,' I seyde, 'by so no man were greued,
> Alle the sciences vnder sonne and alle the sotyle craftes
> I wolde I knewe and couth kyndely in myne herte!'
> 'Thanne artow inparfit,' quod he, 'and one of Prydes knyghtes;
> For such a luste and lykynge Lucifer fel fram heuene.'
>
> B xv 47-51

It is a culmination of the warnings given to the Dreamer by Study, Reason and Imaginative against seeking illegitimate knowledge and it provides the key to the Dreamer's widest rôle. He does not seek in a spirit of humility but in a spirit of speculative curiosity, and the basic failure of his questionings is the strong personal element—'How may *I* save *my* soul?' His quest for knowledge becomes sidetracked by irrelevancies. In passus xi he sees himself following Fortune through Lust of the Flesh and of the Eyes, but as old age approaches he demands burial in his parish church and is deserted by the friar-confessor; the thought of death should inspire remorse, but instead the Dreamer is sidetracked from self-knowledge into an attack upon the covetous friars. In passus xix he asks Conscience whether the figure he sees is Jesus or Piers, but instead of pursuing this key question, he is sidetracked into asking why Conscience calls Jesus 'Christ'. Even in passus xx, when beset by Elde once more, the Dreamer's cry is not for grace but for vengeance—'Awreke me' (202). The Dreamer's inability to understand the nature of his own need makes him unable to distinguish between necessary knowledge and idle speculation. It is ironic, then, that this figure who, as Dreamer, has persistently diverted and misdirected his own vision, and, as Narrator, has distorted his account by giving a misleading poetic emphasis to certain aspects of his subject, should now attempt to enter Unity, only to find that it no longer exists. The lack of unity in vision and poem are reflections of the Dreamer's own doubts about his identity, his rôle in society and his relationship to God—in fact, his own lack of unity. The sophistry and scepticism which he has expressed during the poem reflect the destruction of his means to salvation in his moment of greatest need.

Yet, if order and unity cannot be taught, they can be manifested, and Piers's rôle in the poem is this manifestation. He is a man in society, a ploughman in the real world with social and religious obligations, but he is also a figure in a dream who reappears at various times in various functions, and as such he becomes a figure in the Dreamer's allegorical poem. The analogical principle is a two-way principle—the man who conforms to the will of God manifests God in the world. Hence Piers, a ploughman, is also like Everyman, like an earthly ruler, like Christ, and the Good Samaritan, and St Peter. As the symbol of an ultimate Unity he is the fitting founder of Unity on earth and the mirror of the ideal pope. In a time of disunity, it is this unifying principle and agent that Conscience finally seeks. Piers is, apart from the Dreamer, the only figure to belong to all levels including the real, and he asserts the unifying principle of reality and of the poem against the Dreamer who at all levels disrupts the concept of order.

It is important to recognize the unity which Piers represents, since this constitutes the positive element of the poem. The Dreamer, as narrator, is bound by the demands of his poem's structure. Just as his first appearance, as a wanderer, seems to serve no purpose except a withdrawal from society, so his wanderings through the poem and dream in search of Dowel, Dobet and Dobest serve no purpose, since a dream is remote from the world of experience and no verbal statement can convey the meaning of Dowel. Ironically, the Dreamer's concern with the value or otherwise of learning reflects not only upon the ability of books to teach him, but also upon the ability of his book to teach his readers. If Piers, who has the certainty of Truth, cannot convincingly exhort the pilgrims, how can the Dreamer, without such certainty, ever convey the meaning of his vision?

The answer lies in the final level, the total structure of the poem, for both the Dreamer and Piers are figures in Langland's poem. It might seem so far as if the Dreamer's rôle in the total structure is that which he has in his own dream, to contrast with Piers. But although the Dreamer does contrast with Piers, it is evident that, in an allegorical poem, he need not contrast and that, indeed, because Piers is part of the Dreamer's vision, it is possible that the Dreamer has a part of him. A starting point may be Anima's statement:

> Therefore by coulore ne by clergye knowe shal-
>   tow hym neuere,
> Noyther thorw wordes ne werkes, but thorw
>   wille one.
> And that knoweth no clerke ne creature in erthe,
> But Piers the Plowman, *Petrus, id est, Christus.*
>   B xv 203-206

Clearly Piers is not Christ in the sense that he acted Christ's historical rôle, but only in the sense that in striving to be Christ-like he manifests Christ in the contemporary world. But is Piers then any different from any other

man? He knows Truth *kyndely* where no other man does, and he manifests Christ as *no creature in erthe* does, but Piers is then the realization of the potential in every man, differing only in degree from others. If Christ is the historical pattern, Piers is the contemporary reflection of that pattern and to be Piers-like is to be Christ-like. (pp. 206-11)

Piers knows and manifests Truth but cannot explain his knowledge, while the Dreamer expresses himself but does not know or manifest Truth. The division between the letter and spirit of the law is the key to the poem. If the Dreamer could attain Piers's knowledge, then he would manifest Truth, or, more simply, the Dreamer would be Piers. Yet finally, when the opportunity reaches the Dreamer, he is incapable of taking it and Conscience has to set off again in search of Piers. The picture of total disunity at the end of the poem is not unexpected, but Conscience, like all allegorical figures, is both collective and personal. It seeks the ideal leader, the successor of St Peter, but it seeks also the Piers-like quality in the individual, the promise of which Piers held out to the pilgrims in the *Visio* and which is available to the Dreamer himself.

But it is here that poetic structure takes over from philosophy. Paradoxically, although Piers is a creation of the Dreamer, Will cannot make the act of will which Anima says is necessary to knowledge. He must remain outside as well as inside his own vision, so that, while the identity of the Dreamer's own persona and Piers within the vision is possible, the Dreamer-narrator cannot step into the vision which he sees and sever his contact with the real world in which he began. Any man can be Piers-like, and hence Christ-like, for a moment, but no man can be Piers-like for ever, since the concept of a timeless, universal figure is a pattern imposed by a dream upon a changing reality. This is the final complexity of the poem—that the Dreamer and Piers are two sides of one man, William Langland, so that the poem represents the tension between the earthbound poet, imprisoned by his environment and language, and all his irrational hopes and visions which can never be known either through experience or through words. (pp. 211-12)

David Mills, "The Rôle of the Dreamer in 'Piers Plowman'," in "Piers Plowman": Critical Approaches, *edited by S. S. Hussey, Methuen & Co. Ltd., 1969, pp. 180-212.*

Mary Carruthers   (essay date 1973)

[*In the following excerpt, Carruthers discusses the difficulty of understanding the allegory in the prologue of the B-text of* Piers Plowman, *suggesting that "the problem of meaning in the Prologue presents itself as a problem in reading, the task of finding an adequate interpretive structure for the multifaceted world which Langland presents to us."*]

The belief that *Piers Plowman* does mean something is one that its readers and critics have clung to tenaciously, sometimes vainly, often desperately, through the poem's many incongruities, twists, and turns. It is a belief to which I subscribe as well, though I admit to attacks of doubt along the way. Indeed, I sympathize wholly with the confession of one of the poem's chief editors, who looked forward "to a year when the many incidental problems of editing *Piers Plowman* will, I hope, constantly distract me from the effort of understanding its meaning [E. T. Donaldson, "Patristic Exegesis: The Opposition," in *Critical Approaches to Medieval Literature,* ed. D. Bethurum, 1960]. Yet, in the effort to understand the problematical meaning of the poem, its readers have too often neglected the problem of meaning in the poem. For the meaning of *Piers Plowman* is at least as baffling to its characters as it is to its critics, and their efforts to understand what it all means give the poem its momentum and help to determine its form.

During the confessions of the Seven Deadly Sins in Passus V, the following exchange occurs between Repetance and Avarice:

> "Repentedestow [. . .] euere," quod
> Repentance, "[or] restitucioun madest?"
>   "Ghus, ones I was herberwed," quod he,
> "with an hep of chapmen, I roos whan thei
> were arest and yrifled here males."
>   "That was no restitucioun," quod
> Repentance, "but a robberes thefte,
> Thow haddest be better worthy be hanged
> therfore."
> [. . . . .]
>   "I wende ryflynge were restitucioun [. . .]
> for I learned neuere rede on boke,
> And I can no Frenche in feith, but of the ferthest
> ende of Norfolke,"
>
>   (V. 232-39)

This conversation is an echo of a similar one earlier in the scene in which Repentance is again misunderstood, this time by Envy:

>   "Ghus, redili," quod Repentaunce and
> radde hym to [goode],
> "Sorwe [for] synne is sauacioun of soules."
>   "I am sori," quod [enuye], "I am but selde
> other,
> And that maketh me [so mat] for I ne may me
> venge."
>
>   (V. 125-28)

These encounters are comic intensifications of a situation that is typical in *Piers Plowman.* Neither Avarice nor Envy can understand what Repentance is saying; they mistake his words. Avarice, without comprehension, hears in "restitution" only a mystifying French borrowing, and Envy understands "sorry" in quite another sense from the one Repentance has intended. Repentance uses a Latinate pedantry on the one hand and an ambiguous, unintended pun on the other, neither of which successfully communicates the intended meaning to its audience.

Neither of these misunderstandings involves a level of meaning more exaulted than that of the literal word itself. This is an important point to ponder, since the temptation for the reader is to leap to "read the allegory" of *Piers Plowman* without pausing to reflect upon the fact that *allegoria* needs a solid base in *littera* before it can mean anything. And the *littera* of this poem is slippery in the extreme. Verbal ambiguity, mistaken meaning, pun, hidden connotation, extreme compression or expansion of ordinary syntax—such devices are the hallmarks of Langland's language, and they define the situations which his characters face over and over again in the poem. I believe that this analysis of words as ambiguous tools of thought, capable not only of revealing a true cognition but also of generating a corruption of understanding, is the basic concern of the poem: *Piers Plowman* is an allegory which devotes its primary energies to redeeming its own *littera.* Poetry is a cognitive art, "in the service of wisdom," but the verbal medium in which it is conducted is full of traps, and to assume that the words of this poem are not inherently problematical is the mark of a fool.

Overconfidence in his own interpretive abilities is certainly the mark of the poem's biggest fool, Will. Indeed, it is the first mistake that he makes. After viewing the diverse procession of figures in the Prologue, Will assures his audience:

> What [þe] montaigne bymeneth and the merke
> dale,
> And the felde ful of folke I shal ghow faire
> schewe.
>
>   (I. 1-2)

The meaning is all perfectly evident to him. However, when Lady Holy Church approaches him, his confidence dissolves into a question about the very things he had been so sure of nine lines earlier: "Mercy, Madame, what [may] this [by] mene?" (I. 11). She proceeds to explain to him at great length and with considerable precision exactly what it all means, but as her explanation becomes fuller, Will's questions become more frequent and reveal less understanding. For instance, she states clearly that "treuthe is tresore, the triest on erthe" (I. 135). To which Will responds by asking, "By what crafte in my corps it comseth and where?" (I. 137). Lady Holy Church is angered at his dullness and tells him, "It is a kynde knowyng . . . that kenneth in thine herte / For to louye thi lorde" (I. 140-41). Yet her words to Will are less clear than she supposes—or than he does, for that matter. The "tresore" she refers to is spiritual treasure, the truth which is Truth. But by describing this treasure as the "triest on erthe" she creates a false impression of it, at least to an uninitiated listener. Lady Holy Church looks to the *allegoria* of words; Will cannot get beyond their *littera.* Will understands in the earthly sense; thinking of truth as knowledge of earthly things, he wants to know from what "craft" in his body it comes. In her answer, Lady Holy Church again uses ambiguous words—*kynde* and *herte. Kynde* could mean simply the earthly nature of man, or it could mean his spiritual one, man as the image of God. Similarly, *herte* either could mean the bodily organ or could be a metaphor for the spiritual one. It becomes quite clear, in fact, that Will and Lady Holy Church are speaking two quite different languages, though they are using the same lexicon. And unless they can agree upon the significance of the word, come to understand the exact reference of the verbal sign, it is useless as a cognitive tool. Thus, the initial situation in the poem seems to me to present succinctly its basic concern with the problem of meaning, particularly of verbal meaning. The meanings of mountain, dale, and field seem perfectly clear to Will; yet, in the next moment he has no idea of what they mean. This is the cognitive situation typical of *Piers Plowman,* both for its characters and for its critics. And the heart of this dilemma lies in the problematical nature of words themselves, as the poem perceives them.

There are three words which are particularly troublesome in *Piers Plowman,* as its narrator and nearly all of its critics have rightly perceived. They are three of the simplest words in the poem—*Dowel, Dobet,* and *Dobest.* The morphemic gradation of the adverb-suffix suggests that the three words make up an orderly, progressive revelation of meaning. Dowel is not an isolated term—it has degrees and aspects. As graded compounds, their relationship implies that they are aspects of a semantically unified concept, whose meaning will be revealed by their progressive structural relationship, as "-well" is progressively revealed in "-better" and "-best." Meaning is thus inextricably linked to the graded structural progression in the relationship of the three words. Moreover, the poem promises that this gradation bears a real relationship to its whole structure, by naming the chief sections which follow the *Visio,* the *Vita de Dowel,* the *Vita de Dobet,* and the *Vita de Dobest.* Unfortunately, most critics of the poem have chosen to regard the relationship of these three terms as conceptual and thematic rather than structural and formal.

Since Henry Wells published his article on "The Construction of *Piers Plowman*" [in *PMLA,* XLIV, 1929], most of the poem's commentators have argued that its structure depends on a progressive thematic relationship among these three words. But the attempt to define just what the informing concepts are has been most unsatisfactory, partly because the poet gives us so many definitions of them. (3-6)

The differences between the three terms are more apparent than real. Wells attempted to classify them (and the divisions of the poem) into characteristics appropriate to the Active, Contemplative, and "Mixed" or Prelatical Lives; in this he was followed with varying degrees of enthusiasm by [R. W.] Chambers, [Nevill] Coghill, and more recently [T. P.] Dunning, and [D. W.] Robertson and [B. F.] Huppé. But, as has often been pointed out, taken together, the definitions do not support this division. For example, the command *dilige inimicos* applies to all Christians, not just bishops, and the virtue of not wasting time is surely an aspect of living righteously. [R. W.] Frank writes with considerable understatement [in his *"Piers Plowman" and the Scheme of Salvation,* 1957] that "the relationship between the terms and their meanings is not very stable."

Other critics have more or less thrown up their hands at the prospect of wedding the definitions to the sections of the poem that bear their names and have attempted instead to characterize the sections themselves. Meroney has suggested that the terms refer to the mystic way of the Purgative, Illuminative, and Unitive states. This division is followed reluctantly by [E. T.] Donaldson [in his *"Piers Plowman": The C-Text and Its Poet,* 1949], on the grounds that Dowel, Dobet, and Dobest seem to refer more to inner states than religious vocations. And, indeed, the definitions given in the poem describe states of the soul at

least as frequently as they do religious actions; moreover, the *Vita de Dowel* and the *Vita de Dobet* are psychological and contemplative in nature. But, as Donaldson himself points out, "As it stands, Do-Best does not seem to contain much that is suggestive of the vision of God of St. Bernard." Frank rejects this scheme entirely on the grounds that the chaotic social vision which concludes the poem "can hardly be the poet's dramatization of the contemplative union with God." He suggests instead, as Wells did before him, that the three divisions are governed by the gifts of the Father, the gifts of the Son, and the gifts of the Holy Spirit. This scheme is somewhat more satisfactory than the other two, since at least it does not require that the three divisions of the poem be seen as getting conceptually "better," although again the poem does not really reflect it. The *Vita de Dobest* depicts a society lacking divine gifts of *any* sort; the contemplative vision of divine mysteries which concludes the *Vita de Dobet* should technically be one of the gifts of the Spirit; and if knowledge is one of the gifts of the Father, Will has not received it during the course of the *Vita de Dowel,* as he complains to Anima at the beginning of Passus XV. We are left with a multitude of ill-matching definitions, three sections of the poem named, with apparent arbitrariness, for three terms, and no clear relationship among them. S. S. Hussey has stated the case succinctly when he writes that Dowel, Dobet, and Dobest represent an equation with "one unknown and two multiples of it." Or as Piers Plowman himself says, reported by Clergy, "Dowel and Dobet aren two infinites, / Whiche infinites, with a feith, fynden oute Dobest" (XIII. 127-28).

It seems to me that all attempts to define the relationship among these terms clearly, or to relate them to the sections of the poem that bear their names, have been proceeding from the wrong assumptions. The important question is not how they are related. The fact that so much critical manipulation has been required to answer that question should be enough indication that it is misdirected. The important question, rather, is why those definitions are there at all, and why there are so many of them. Dowel, Dobet, and Dobest are self-evident terms—or should be. It has always struck me as curious that Langland's terms are so much simpler than those of his critics; Dowel means *doing well,* a far more commonplace concept than the Active Life, or the Purgative State, or the gifts of the Father. That Langland should feel the need to define the term at all is curious; the Bible, the preachers, the Fathers had laid out quite clearly what the life of doing well should be for a Christian. Evidently, he has far less confidence in the meaning of the word than do those critics who use it as a springboard to discover other levels of allegory. (pp. 7-9)

[Langland] not only defines Dowel but also redefines it and redefines it. He does so in ways that confuse more than clarify, and yet there is great urgency behind the definitions. Will keeps asking his question, though he has received many answers to it, all at least partially satisfactory. None of the definitions is rejected as wrong: the procedure suggests, rather, that they are all somehow inadequate, as though the verbal sign itself had no viable meaning for Will, pointed to no self-evident idea. It is surely significant that all of Will's teachers accept the fact that the term needs definition; not even the bluntest of them tells him that Dowel means doing well and that's the end of it. Such a process of continual definition suggests that the sign itself is being tested, explored, even stretched to the limits of its conceptual significance. In a very real sense Dowel is a word in search of a referent in this poem—hence the multitude of its definitions, the felt inadequacy of all of them, the confusion which results in a term which should be, by its very nature, perfectly clear.

Piers Plowman is a poem of searching, structured according to a series of pilgrimages—the pilgrimage of the folk on the field in the *Visio,* Will's pilgrimage in the *Vita de Dowel* and *Vita de Dobet,* which brings him at last to Unity-Holychurch, Conscience' pilgrimage at the end. And the pilgrimage motif early in the poem is cast in terms of a search for St. Truth. The central problem in *Piers Plowman* is not a moral one, though its moral application is apparent; it is one of knowing Truth. Doing well depends on knowledge, a knowledge which is no longer secure, as Will's persistent questions make clear. The cognitive concern of *Piers Plowman* is always basic to its moral and social concerns; even when the poem concentrates on social issues, these are inevitably recast as cognitive and perceptual problems, as the progress from the *Visio* to the *Vita* makes clear. This view of the problem of right action is venerably orthodox: "Ye shall know the Truth, and the Truth shall make you free." True understanding produces freedom of the will, which is the agent of moral action. Moreover, the interaction of understanding and will, according to Augustine, is God's image in the soul, an image man must fulfill and perfect in order to be saved. *Piers Plowman* is not basically a moral poem, or a social one, or even an apocalyptic one; it is an epistemological poem, a poem about the problem of knowing truly. Will's question to Lady Holy Church at the beginning of Passus I is the question of the entire poem: "Mercy, Madame, what [may] this [by] mene?" (pp. 9-10)

The search for St. Truth is conducted in terms of a search for and an analysis of the signs that truly express him. This concern with the truthfulness of signs, analyzed in terms of verbal forms and images, is evident in the devices which the poet uses—personification of concepts, elaborate and fluid metaphor—and in the choice of dream vision, the most symbolic of literary modes, as the medium for his poem. The multitude of allegorizing devices bespeaks a concern with the very process of allegory-making itself, and with the verbal medium in which Truth dwells, especially in poetry. Langland is in his own way searching for a truly Christian rhetoric as urgently as Augustine did, and for much the same reason—out of a sense that a rhetoric has failed and has led men away from Truth rather than toward him. Language is continually remade and reexamined by the poet. Indeed, one reason why so many of the schemes imposed upon it fail to explain *Piers Plowman* adequately is that they derive from an outside rhetoric, instead of addressing themselves to the language being forged by the poem itself.

An example of how the poem makes its own language is Passus IX, which is devoted to the definition of Dowel. Wit begins his discussion of the term with a description of the castle of Caro, whose mistress is Anima, who in turn is served by Dowel, Dobet, and Dobest. This fable is followed by a discussion of Inwit, of unkind godparents and unkind bishops, and by three more definitions of Dowel, Dobet, and Dobest (IX. 94-97). Next, there is a discussion of true marriage, followed by the story of Cain, who first brought care upon earth, the Flood, more discussion of marriage, counsel to young men to wed rather than sin, counsel to married couples, a few remarks on bastardy, and finally two more sets of definitions of Dowel, Dobet, and Dobest. All these devices—moral counsel, Biblical lessons, allegorical fable—are methods of defining Dowel. The passus circles back in on the term continually, each new spiral being another perspective on its meaning, another context in which to place the term. The so-called digressions in this passus are not really digressions at all but different angles of vision producing modified or new understanding of its key term. In this way a word like Dowel is constantly explored, tried out in new contexts, new relationships. The definitions of Dowel in Passus IX occur not only in those lines in which Langland mentions the word—the whole section is about the term, each topic being a step in forging its meaning. And by the end of the section it is clear that Dowel is a word of manifold complexity. No outside source can possibly tell us what the word really means; the concept is being created by the text of the poem itself.

Nor is the desire to make a new rhetoric confined to the poem's key terms; it informs its entire structural development as well. *Piers Plowman* explores many different kinds of concepts and forms of allegory, rejecting those it finds overly imperfect or misleading, seeking constantly for a more truthful kind of sign. This explains the many different, often confusingly various, types of allegorical language found in the poem; the same things keep being said, but always in somewhat different form, each change of form also revealing a new cognitive slant. As the structure of the sign changes, so does the understanding it produces of that which signifies it, sometimes for the better, more often, at least in this poem, for the worse. One of the most original features of *Piers Plowman* lies precisely in the changing forms of the poem's allegory, from the rapid variations of the Prologue, through the predominance of conceptual personifications in the *Visio* and the *Vita de Dowel,* to the gradual attempts, using figural allegory and language, to forge a fully redeemed speech in the *Vita de Dobet,* which then collapse, drawing the world with them, in the apocalypse of the *Vita de Dobest.* And the change of form both signals and expresses a progressively fuller understanding in the poem of the ineffable nature of that which makes significant all language and all action, the Word itself.

To see the poem in this way is to insist that Piers Plowman be taken seriously *as a poem,* not merely as an allegory. One of the major difficulties with much recent criticism has been the underlying assumption that, because *Piers Plowman* contains allegory, it is enough to translate its various allegorical devices into their "second level" of meaning, without examining the ways in which those devices embody, explore, and modify the concepts to which they point, and the ways in which they bring various concepts into relationship within the poem. It is as if one were to attempt an understanding of one of Keats's odes by looking up all the words in the dictionary and simply listing their meanings. Such an exercise may have its uses, but it does not get one very far into the experience of the poem. To read *Piers Plowman* is to be immediately and continually confused by a barrage of topics, figures, words; and no appeal to schemes of the Active, Contemplative, and Prelatical Lives, or to Augustinian, or Thomistic, or monastic, or Joachite theology will save the reader faced with the necessity of making sense of what he reads moment by moment. Any criticism of the poem which does not honestly start from this experience is doomed to failure, wholly or in part.

No one has yet denied that *Piers Plowman* is labyrinthine in structure, overly discursive, and badly organized. Yet, at least one of its apologists has insisted in the face of all the evidence that its author has "a strong architectural instinct for planning and carrying out a great composition. . . . It is not he who loses himself in a tangle of digressions" [Nevill Coghill, "The Pardon of Piers Plowman," *Proceedings of the British Academy,* XXXI (1945)]. This implied negative judgment of the reader seems to me to be wholly misdirected. For the fact is that the confusion *Piers Plowman* produces is inherent in the very nature of the experience it records; it is reflected by the fluidity of all its constantly changing and various elements. Will's experience in this poem is not to realize a design, but to explore a vision; its various forms of personification, figuralism, fable, metaphor, exegesis, social satire, and sermon are not the building blocks of a cathedral but are often inadequate tools for charting unseen and perhaps unseeable terrain (or so the ending of the poem would imply). If T. S. Eliot's characterization of great poetry as a raid on the unknown is at all true, *Piers Plowman* must rank highly indeed.

It is important to realize that *Piers Plowman* records the process of a particular mind dealing with problems of meaning in the form of a visionary poem. There are few poems which express such a strongly individual, even eccentric, intelligence. The best argument against the multiple-authorship theory, to my mind, is the extreme improbability that two (let alone four or five) people who lived in England in the later fourteenth century could have been enough alike in their oddity to have jointly written this poem. What is striking about the poem is the consistently extraordinary thought processes of its poet—how and why Langland thinks about things as he does, rather than what he thinks.

The poet's peculiarity is evident even in the simplest features of the narrative. For example, it is most unusual that Will wakes up and goes to sleep so frequently, at moments in the vision which often seem chosen out of pure whimsey. Indeed, the line between sleeping and waking becomes so hazy that the two blend into one another, as when Will, awake, meets the personification of Need in Passus XX of the **B-Text,** or is questioned by Reason at the beginning of Passus VI of the C-Text. But the fluidity of this relationship has a serious purpose, as it gradually merges dream with waking life, casting into doubt the ordinary perceptions of reality which are made possible only when there

A site just west of the Malvern Hills in England, possibly the "field of folk" mentioned by Langland in Piers Plowman.

is a secure division between being awake and being asleep. This particular effect could not have been achieved without waking Will up and sending him back to sleep so many times.

In defense of the poem's often haphazard movement, which he thinks is nonetheless controlled, one critic [John Lawlor in "Piers Plowman": *An Essay in Criticism,* 1962] reminds us that during the Middle Ages,

> there may coexist in the work of art both a formidable simplicity of main design and a degree of minor graphic representation in which the eye loses itself in detail.

The movement of medieval art tends to be circular or concentric, rather than linear. But this statement, useful though it is in defending Langland against a charge of total disorganization, does not account for the structural fluidity of *Piers Plowman.* The abundance of small sculptures in a cathedral like Chartres never detracts from the logically articulated movement of the building as a whole. There is no question about which is subordinate, no sense of conflict between the main forms and the details of style. But there are important structural features of Langland's poem which work against the emergence of a general and simple design. Indeed, these features preclude the possibility of a dominant form for the poem, and thus exhibit a quality not common in medieval art. In *Piers Plowman,* relationships of time and space, and of objects to one another, are indistinct. Things within the poem are not seen as coherent entities but are constantly in the process of changing into something else. The degree of distinction and coherence which marks characters and episodes in other medieval works, including allegorical visions, is simply not present in *Piers Plowman.*

Langland's disregard for naturalistic narrative structures can easily be seen when one examines the temporal progression of Will's visions, particularly of the two which contain inner dreams. The inner dream is not unique in medieval poems—what is remarkable is Langland's way of handling it. Dante, for instance, has several dreams during his ascent of the mountain of Purgatory. But Dante awakens exactly where he slept, after an appropriate time has elapsed. The inner dream is carefully distinguished from the main vision as a separate and distinct unit within it; it bears the same relationship to the main vision that a dream does to a person's waking hours. However, the secure structure which marks Dante's poem is not present in *Piers Plowman.* The first inner dream occurs in Passus XI. Scripture rebukes Will for his lengthy analysis of Dowel, and Will "for wo and wratth of her speche" (XI. 3) falls asleep. In the inner dream he receives instruction from several persons, one of whom is Scripture, the character in his main dream whose rebuke caused him to fall asleep in the first place. This may seem to be only a minor illogicality on Langland's part, but the point is that it is an illogicality which most poets—especially medieval ones—would never permit.

The second inner dream, the vision of the Tree of Charity, is even more interesting. When Will wakens from his first inner dream, he finds himself back in the time and place of the main dream. But the sequence of the second is continued into the main dream. Having witnessed the Incarnation and early life of Christ in the inner dream, Will awakens to meet Faith going to the Crucifixion, and his vision proceeds in time through the Resurrection. Inner dream and main dream have merged completely. The fact that Will wakes up at all seems to be a structurally unjustifiable concession to a conventional formula, since the two visions have ceased to be separate in any meaningful way. The blurring of these spatial dimensions with the vision is analogous to the hazy demarcation between sleeping and waking which I noted earlier, and it serves the same purpose. In contrast to *The Divine Comedy,* whose secure structural features provide solid ground for the reader's perceptions, even in a visionary world, **Piers Plowman** deliberately fuzzes the dimensions of reality. Time and space are the building blocks of Dante's cathedral; for Langland, they become the problematical dimensions of a world whose meaning is in the process of continual change.

The structural procedure typified in the handling of the inner dreams makes it difficult to tell one's physical location, something one rarely has trouble with in Dante or in Chaucer. Nor can the illogical progression of **Piers Plowman** be explained by "dream logic." The puppy which scampers from nowhere across the landscape of Chaucer's *The Book of the Duchess,* and abruptly disappears when his function is completed, may indeed be accounted for in that way, since dream characters have a way of entering without explanation and then suddenly disappearing when the dreamer is no longer thinking about them. This is the manner of dreams, and the manner of medieval dream visions, and there are many instances of it in *Piers Plowman.* The fluidity of the poem's dimensions, however, is another matter. For example, most medieval poets are faithful to some definite time sequence for their vision. Dante is the most scrupulous, of course, with his carefully orchestrated three-day vision, but even *The Romance of the Rose* is dreamed in one night.

Then, too, most dreamers are fairly careful to make clear the details of the physical progress of their dreams. The landscape itself may be peculiar, but its physical presence is always insisted upon, and the details of the dreamer's movement through time and space are accounted for with some regard to physical verisimilitude. Chaucer, for example, tells us how he gets places—there are gates through which he must walk (or be pushed), or there is an eagle to carry him around. But Langland's poem exhibits no regard at all for physical limitations. Scripture, for example, can hop between two visions without our being told how she got there. It is not just "dream logic" operating here, but Langlandian logic, or rather nonlogic, in which time does not impose a fixed sequence even upon visionary events, but is a fluid medium in which things can happen sequentially, or simultaneously, or take dizzying leaps backward and forward, however it suits the poet's thought. Indeed, nothing in this poem exists in solid dimensions. At any given moment, any given object is capable of extending itself in any direction, and frequently does.

Such fluidity of structure reflects the fact that *Piers Plowman* is not a designed poem, like *The Divine Comedy, The*

Parliament of Fowls, or even *The House of Fame.* It is rather a poem of searching, the record of a mental wandering to find a way to the soul's native country. Dante's poem records a journey through known territory, known always to his guides and eventually to the pilgrim as well. Langland is searching through unknown territory, his guides being the fluid, partially understood, often inadequate verbal signs of an insufficient rhetoric. Both *Piers Plowman* and *The Divine Comedy* seek understanding of Truth through the understanding of those signs which reveal it. But Dante's *signatum* is an object of thought which can be securely, if partially, known, while Langland's St. Truth becomes less and less apprehensible as the signs that lead to him prove to be more confused, inadequate, unknowable. To put the comparison in other terms, Dante's pilgrimage leads to a destination, Langland's only to another pilgrimage.

Both the fluidity and diversity of the devices which the poem employs in its search for St. Truth also reflect Langland's concern with making a new rhetoric. *Piers Plowman* is continually becoming meaningful rather than being so. No one device is adequate; Langland employs them all. Allegorical forms are forged in response to epistemological problems as they develop in the consciousness of the poet and dreamer, a fluid associative intelligence, whose reality is the movement of its own thought. If the poem lacks coherence, it is only because the Truth it so urgently seeks is not coherent in terms of those signs which Langland employs to conduct his search. Though its cognitive insecurity often results in tedium when the poem keeps circling back and back on itself in trying to invest its symbols with real meaning, this unsureness is also the source of its peculiar power. There is a St. Truth—if only we knew the way to get there.

The sense of emerging into unknown territory is strong at the beginning of the Prologue. It is clearly evident in its dream landscape and in the curious character of the narrator, yet it is seen more subtly but importantly in the fluid structural relationships created by the different kinds of symbols which the poet uses to describe his vision. Nearly every form of allegory used later in the poem is used also in the Prologue, and an examination of these various allegorical structures in their relationship to one another indicates the way in which Langland uses the fluid medium of his poem to raise and explore the question of meaning.

The poem opens in the familiar, conventional world of medieval dream visions—a leisurely walk on a May morning ending with a little nap by a burbling brook:

> In a somer seson when soft was the sonne,
> I shope me in [to a shroud] as I a shepe were,
> In habite as an heremite vnholy of workes,
> Went wyde in this world wondres to here.
> Ac on a May mornynge on Maluerne hulles
> Me byfel a ferly of fairy me thoughte;
> I was wery forwandred and went me to reste
> Vnder a brode banke bi a [borne] side,
> And as I lay and lened and loked in the waters,
> I slombred in a slepyng it [sweyed] so merye.
> (Prol., 1-10)

Yet certain details in this description ring curiously, intro-

ducing a note of uncertainty. The dreamer characterizes himself as a solitary man, probably a wanderer, "In habite as an heremite." This in itself is not so remarkable—many medieval dreamers have their visions while walking by themselves—but this dreamer is odd for two reasons. He suggests, first, that he is a habitual wanderer and, second, that there is something shady about himself. The phrase "as I a shepe were" has usually been taken to mean "I put on rough clothes like those of a shepherd," but it is quite possible that there is a pun on the word "shepe," in which case the phrase could also be a reference to the proverbial wolf in sheep's clothing. This additional meaning gains support from the next line, "In habite as an heremite vnholy of workes." Later on, Will consistently characterizes himself as a "lorel," a vagabond and an outcast from society, a role certainly suggested by these opening lines. He is a man who is not apt to be welcomed by, nor to feel at home in, ordinary society.

Will falls asleep at a particular time (though a conventional time, to be sure) "on a May mornynge," and in a particular place, "Maluerne hulles," but the dream occurs "in a wildernesse, wist I neuer where." Now, it is true that the unknown dream landscape is quite as conventional in this type of literature as is the May morning and the "brode banke bi a [borne] side." But the opposition here is sharply drawn. The reassuringly common and definite physical presence of the waking world makes more emphatic the indefinite nature of the dream world. The May morning, Malvern hills, the broad bank—these we know. They have definite shape and substance, and we have met them, or things very much like them, before, in countless other poems. But all we know about the dreamer is that he is not what he appears to be, and that this unknown character finds himself in his dream in an unknown landscape, "wist I neuer where." It is a world about which nothing is known; it could be, or become, anything at all.

Yet, this contrast is undercut by the fact that the unknown landscape is peopled with common contemporary folk, who are not at all unknown but are perhaps even more familiar than May mornings and burbling brooks. One is, after all, accustomed to meeting strange sights in visions, like the silver-leaved trees of Paradise in *Pearl* or the revolving wicker house of Rumor in *The House of Fame.* However, the field of folk is no stranger than a busy town street. Yet, the fact that it is part of the unknown landscape, "wist I neuer where," suggests that the everyday, known world itself is not nearly as reassuringly real as the opening contrast between waking and visionary, known and unknown worlds promises. The known world of contemporary life is called unknown; in light of this, the "real" world of literary convention with which the poem begins must also be called into question. Thus, Langland has doubly upset the conventional norms of reality, both literary and actual, bringing into focus the problematic nature of what things mean from the outset of his poem. Indeed, the strangeness of *Piers Plowman* is purely a function of the fluid nature of everything in it; it has no mysterious gates, strange gardens, mechanical birds, enameled meadows to signal to us that we are in a marvelous world. The opening world of *Piers Plowman* is, in fact, not marvelous at all, only profoundly ambiguous. Whatever structural lines it promises, it promptly dissolves.

The opening landscape of the dream is stark and unspecified:

> [Ac] I bihelde in-to the est an heigh to the sonne,
> I seigh a toure on a toft trielich ymaked;
> A depe dale binethe, a dongeon there-inne,
> With depe dyches and derke and dredful of
>   sight.
> A faire felde ful of folke fonde I there bytwene,
> Of alle maner of men, the mene and the riche,
> Worchyng and wandryng as the worlde asketh.
>
> (Prol., 13-19)

In its visual spareness, this description is reminiscent of the manuscript drawing of the stage-set for *The Castle of Perseverance,* a high tower in the center of the playing area, and various *sedes* representing such places as "Mundus," "Deus," "Belyal," and "Caro." It is a wholly allegorical landscape, in which the objects plainly represent something of a spiritual nature and are intended to be considered as simple signposts for something else. The folk wandering on the field, however, are not allegorical in this way; they do not fit into a schematized drawing but are as lively and random as everyday life itself. And their placement between the tower and the dungeon upsets the order embodied in the stark oppositions of the opening scene, suggesting on the one hand the possibility that the allegorical landscape gives the folk meaning, yet on the other hand that it may be too simple and severe to quite contain them. It is peculiarly difficult to pinpoint where metaphorical reality ends and the commonplace begins, difficult even to tell whether the structural lines suggested by the opposition of these terms have real meaning for the poem. Indeed, I would suggest that this opposition is one cognitive structure which Langland tests and discards as inadequate in the course of the Prologue.

Next the poet brings certain groups of folk into focus:

> Some putten hem to the plow, pleyed ful selde,
> In settyng and in sowyng swonken ful harde,
> And wonnen that [þise] wastours with glotonye
>   destruyeth.
>
> (Prol., 20-22)

The first group, plowmen, are typical of spiritual virtue, both by way of their place in the Christian exegetical tradition, and as they are described here. They win what wasters destroy through gluttony. And, to continue this opposition in even more specifically moral terms, the poet next contrasts those who apparel themselves after pride with those who live in prayer and penance. It is clear, however, that none of these types are specified—they inhabit a timeless, spiritual realm. They are "allegorical" in the simplest sense of the term, in which their physical relationships have total reference to another level of meaning.

But in line 28 the poet suddenly refers these allegorical types of good by contrast to a condition both contemporary and English:

> In prayers and in penance putten hem manye,
> . . . . .

As ancres and heremites that holden hem in here
    selles,
And coueiten nought in contre to kairen aboute,
For no likerous liflode her lykam to plese.

> (Prol., 25, 28-30)

The effect of this contrast is to pull the reader out of the schematic allegory to which he has become accustomed and into a fourteenth-century scene. The reference to abuses of the hermit's life specifies the unknown and generalized landscape, thus changing the nature of the allegory and the bases upon which the poem must be read. The description refers to no "other level": anchorites who roam the countryside are not traditional iconographic types nor generalized figures of Everyman. They are busy wanderers belonging to a contemporary scene. This same rapid shifting between typological moral allegory, in characters like the plowmen, and literally intended social comment, in characters like the unruly anchorites, continues throughout the Prologue. Thus, some beggars are described in concrete detail:

> Bidders and beggeres fast aboute ghede,
> [Til] her belies and her bagges [were bret] ful
>   ycrammed;
> [Flite þanne] for here fode, foughten atte ale;
>
> (Prol., 40-42)

And yet these same beggars are next discovered consorting with personified vices:

> In glotonye, god [. . .] wote, gon hij to bedde,
> And risen [vp] with ribaudye, [as] Roberdes
>   knaues;
> Slepe and [. . .] sleuthe seweth hem eure.
>
> (Prol., 43-45)

Shifts like these force a continuous change of perspective on the reader, from concrete description to metaphor and back again, without any clear borderline between them.

Some allegories can be relied upon to be consistently allegorical—that is, the narrative level points at all times to another level for which the story is the figure. Thus, in Alanus' *Anticlaudianus,* when Theology is made to conduct the chariot of the Seven Liberal Arts through the skies to Prudence, the reader makes the appropriate semantic translation of the literal level to its abstract meaning. The story demands that he do so and clearly directs him in the way to do it. But *Piers Plowman* defies most such efforts at the very level of the text, for it frequently varies the relationship between literal and metaphorical levels: literal statements change into metaphor, metaphors become different metaphors with startling and confusing ease.

Langland describes a pardoner preaching to the people:

> Lewed men leued hym wel and lyked his
>   [speche],
> Comen vp knelyng to kissen his [bulle];
> He bonched hem with his breuet and blered here
>   eyes,
> And raughte with his ragman rynges and bro-
>   ches.
>
> (Prol., 72-75)

These four lines contain a rapid jump from a literal to a metaphorical statement. The unlearned men kneeling about the pardoner are first described in naturalistic terms, visual and wholly concrete. But then the pardoner hits them with his official letter, hard enough to make their eyes water. In literal terms, this statement is absurd, as is the next line, describing him as gathering in rings with his sealed patent. Clearly, the terms of the description have shifted from a literal to a metaphoric level. Lines 74-75 cannot be read in the same way as 72-73, yet they occur as part of the description of the same scene. And the change occurs with such sharp contrast that it confuses the reader's apprehension of the scene—is the description literal, or figurative, or does it "exist" somewhere between the two? This blurring of levels is neatly accomplished by the word "blered," a pun which means literally "watered" and metaphorically "fooled." And the fact that the line makes sense either way dramatizes cogently the problem of meaning forced upon the reader by the verbal structure of the poem.

It is a strange group of people on the field, not only in terms of their mixed social class but also, more puzzlingly, at least to the reader, in terms of their degree of specificity. One never quite knows whether one is meeting an allegorical type or a particular figure drawn from Langland's familiar English scene. Those lean hermits going to Walsingham with their wenches are clearly in the latter mode, but the friars who succeed them in Langland's description, though they start as contemporary characters, end up by being assumed into an allegorical called Charity who is busily selling confessions to lords:

> Many of this maistres [. . .] mowe clothen hem
>   at lykyng,
> For here money and [hire] marchandise mar-
>   chen togideres.
> [. . .] Sith charite hath be chapman and chief
>   to shryue lordes,
> Many ferlis han fallen in a fewe gheris.
>
>   (Prob., 62-65)

After a description of more contemporary worldly clergymen (the pardoner, the lazy priests who neglect their parishes for soft livings in London, and churchmen who serve the temporal powers), the mode of the poem shifts again, this time to a wholly abstract level:

> I parceyued of the power that Peter had to kepe,
> To bynde and [. . .] vnbynde as the boke tel-
>   leth,
> How he [it left] with loue as owre lorde hight,
> Amonges foure vertues, [most vertuous of alle],
> That cardinales ben called and closyng ghatis,
> There crist is in kyngdome to close and to shutte,
> And to opne it to hem and heuene blisse shewe.
>
>   (Prol., 100-106)

This is allegory on a level even more abstract than the schematized landscape with which the poem begins. There the poet perceived physical objects which stood for conceptual values; here he perceives the abstraction itself, Peter's *power* to bind and unbind, and the leaving of that power not to his successors but to the four cardinal virtues. Indeed, this statement can hardly be called allegorical at all; only the use of the verb "perceive" makes it a figure rather than an outright statement of doctrine. Except for that tenuous link to the narrative, the poem has

left the realm of physical objects entirely and is contained within an abstract verbal frame.

The verbal nature of the allegory at this point is underscored by the fact that the poem proceeds to its next topic via a learned pun. "Cardinal" is related through the meaning of its Latin original, *cardo*, "a hinge," to the cardinals of the papal court. The pun serves here, as in the earlier pun on "blered," to effect a transition from a metaphorical statement to a literal situation (only in this case the transition is in the opposite direction). Once again the mode of the poem has shifted; these dozen lines cannot all be read from the same perspective, for we have on the one hand the abstract statement concerning the power of the keys (in itself a metaphor), and on the other a description of a historical situation. They are related to each other by means of a pun which itself plays off a literal against a more metaphorical meaning of a word.

Immediately following these lines, the Prologue describes a king, led by knighthood, whose clerks are counseled by Kynde Wit, and the *comunes* which he rules. The *comunes* contrive their crafts through the counsel of Kynde Wit, ordaining plowmen to till the land; and the king and Kynde Wit create law and loyalty. Then, suddenly, a lunatic looks up to beg the king to rule well, an angel leans down to him, speaking a warning in Latin, and a *goliardeys* shouts a verse in reply to the angel. The *comunes,* who have come together in some sort of parliamentary gathering (though this, like all the rest, is unclear) cry out to the king's council. And at that point a large herd of rats and mice rush out to consult among themselves on how best to deal with a cat that has been preying on them. After their debate ends in frustration, the dreamer describes sergeants of the law and others "in this assemble," though at this point it is very unclear *what* assembly is being referred to. The Prologue ends with a lively description of small tradesmen, diggers singing "Dieu . . . saue Dame Emme!," and cooks and taverners crying their wares.

The mysterious figures of the lunatic and the angel, the London taverners, and the parliamentary rats all coexist in the same visionary world. But the relationship of these figures is not at all clear. It is difficult to know how to read this allegory, what kind of sense, if any, it is supposed to make. Thus, the problem of meaning in the Prologue presents itself as a problem in reading, the task of finding an adequate interpretive structure for the multifaceted world which Langland presents to us, as his language constantly shifts its perspective among the temporal and eternal, literal and metaphorical, typological and specific modes of perception. The search for St. Truth is a search for the signs that reveal him—in the Prologue Langland utilizes many possible types of sign, many possible kinds of language, and produces a kaleidoscopic mirror, every piece of which promises clear vision, and none of which produces it. And his procedure focuses attention on the signs of intellection themselves; the world of the Prologue demands to be understood, by the very fact of its confusion. The signs used to give it order and understanding are inadequate, in conflict with one another rather than in harmony. The leaves of Langland's universe are not only scat-

tered; they seem to have come from unrelated volumes.
(pp. 19-33)

> *Mary Carruthers, "Chapter One," in her* The
> Search for St. Truth: A Study of Meaning in
> "Piers Plowman," *Northwestern University
> Press, 1973, pp. 3-33.*

Barbara Nolan   (essay date 1977)

[*In the following excerpt, Nolan focuses on the prologue
of the B-text, showing how* Piers Plowman *is unique in
its time period because of its emphasis on theological
skepticism. The critic finds that Langland "takes pains
to satirize the decadence of the established church, the
proliferation and confusion of its teaching, and the
moral formlessness of political and social life."*]

Both *Pearl* and **Piers Plowman** were produced in the latter
half of the fourteenth century, and both participate in the
great theological debates and spiritual difficulties of that
period. But the two poets differ widely, though they use
a common literary tradition, conventions, and techniques.
As if retreating to an earlier, calmer time, the *Pearl* poet
devises elaborate symmetries to represent a simple, almost
sweet trust in divine providence. By contrast, Langland's
long, wandering work—the last great visionary quest of
the Middle Ages—clearly defines a final stage in the
mode's history. In a poem which, like *Pearl,* ostensibly describes the way to salvation, the poet of **Piers** paradoxically chooses to emphasize late fourteenth-century theological skepticism: he takes pains to satirize the decadence of
the established church, the proliferation and confusion of
its teaching, and the moral formlessness of political and
social life.

The artistic order Langland manages in his poem reflects
a near breakdown of a familiar form in the face of impossible worldly pressures. Yet the poet also posits, perhaps
more forcefully than ever before, that eschatological idealism which is a hallmark of the later medieval visionary
quest. Piers (and Langland) war against human failure
and boldly point the way on a journey to an ultimate historical moment beyond the chaos of the contemporary
world. Langland's is finally a complex mode which defies
even as it employs the themes and techniques of the quest
form. His poetic voice represents a decisive, irreversible
shift in perspective from the sureness of a soul *in aevo* to
the linear uncertainties of a spirit *in medias res,* desperately dreaming of finality. Yet the tough-minded, hard won,
unifying optimism hidden in Langland's art may be, in its
way, no less potent than the *Pearl* poet's for those who will
"loke on boke and rede aryght." And this is particularly
true for the contemporary reader.

The continental visionary quests of thirteenth-century
France were . . . intended as guidebooks for the sinning
Christian, preparing him expressly for Easter and the celebration of man's redemption. Their purpose was formally
hortatory and their final success was explicitly the conversion of the listener to prayer, penance and a life of humility. Led by a dreaming narrator, the audience would encounter the deadly sins, pass through the houses of confession and mercy and arrive finally before the throne of the

Lamb in the New Jerusalem. At least some of the vision
quests were explicitly intended to be read aloud over the
course of several days but the poems are equally suited to
silent meditation. The poet's task, like the sculptor's or the
illuminator's, was to mark as clearly and forcefully as possible the way to salvation through examination of conscience, contrition, confession, and a firm purpose of
amendment. The stance of the listener or reader was to be
a meditative one. With devotion and concentration he
would hold the *series imaginum* in his mind, helped by the
"places" in which he found the images. Day by day during
Holy Week he would review the state of his soul, recall the
mercy of God, and look forward to the great feast of the
Resurrection.

In its basic outline, **Piers Plowman** follows the pattern of
its continental kin, setting out cumulatively enriching materials for a thorough examination of conscience. The **B-
text** (which will serve as the basis for this study) can be
divided into seven sections, providing seven interrelated
readings, each sixty to ninety minutes in length. . . . As
the narrator, Will moves through his visions, we can follow (albeit with difficulty) his gradual discovery of the way
to repentance and spiritual perfection. At the end of the
Vita Dobet (XVIII), after he has dreamed of Christ's redemption, he determines, as the audience should, to go off
to Easter Mass: "Ariseth and reuerenceth goddes resur-
rexioun, / And crepeth to the crosse on knees and kisseth
it for a Iuwel," (427-428) he orders his wife and daughter.

But while Langland used the basic form of the continental
penitential quest aimed at converting souls for the Easter
feast, he turned it to more complex use. Not only concerned with the conversion of the individual soul, he also
studies with prophetic urgency the need for converting the
whole society. His narrator is both Everyman of all ages
and fourteenth-century fallen man (perhaps quite like
himself) moving toward an imminent and much-needed
eschaton. Langland extends and complicates Will's field
of vision to include not only his own soul but the entire
world, both immediate and cosmic; and he designs his narrative to encompass all time in man's search for the Trinity, to be fully revealed at the end of the present age. In this
widening of perspective, Langland shared with prophets,
poets, historians and artists of the later Middle Ages a
sense of the special importance of his own place in the history of salvation.

Like Joachim of Fiore, St. Francis of Assisi, St. Dominic,
the designers of many an illustrated Apocalypse, Dante,
and his own later contemporary, St. Vincent Ferrer, the
poet could imagine for his audience the completion of
God's historical revelation to man: the coming and defeat
of Antichrist, a short time of peace on earth, and then the
eternal Sabbath. At the end of Passus XIX, the questing
Will shows us in vision an historical movement toward the
conversion of the world to Unity-Holichurch. After
Christ's resurrection, the apocalyptic harvest of the faithful becomes a critical concern (B.XIX, 314-330).

Once a personified house of humility has been built, Conscience and Kynde Wit draw all Christians to it:

> There nas no Crystene creature that kynde witte
> hadde,

Saue schrewes one suche as I spak of,
That he ne halpe a quantite holynesse to wexe.
Somme þorw bedes-byddynge and somme þorw
     pylgrymage,
And other pryue penaunce and some þorw
     penyes-delynge.
And thanne welled water for wikked werkes,
Egerlich ernynge out of mennes eyen.
Clennesse of the comune and clerkes clene
     lyuynge
Made Vnite holicherche in holynesse to stonde.
                                        (B.XIX, 370-378)

Even as this passage was being read by the faithful of the late fourteenth century, Vincent Ferrer had begun preaching of just such an age of peace near at hand:

> Aquarius figures the eleventh state of this world after the death of Antichrist, since then the sun of justice will be in Aquarius, for then all generations of the infidels will be baptized. Oh, there will be such a pressure for baptism, there will not be enough priests. Then the prophecy of Ezekiel will be completed: I will take you from among the peoples. I will gather you from the whole world and lead you into your land.

For Langland, both the perfection of the human race, and its converse, total degradation in love of the world had to be realized before mankind would enter the city of peace. In this last stage of human history, the good would be ruled by the Holy Spirit in an ideally spiritual church. Then Christ, who bridged the gap between fallen man and divine truth, would be joined by man renewed, spiritually free and living fully a life of unity and brotherhood. Then,

> . . . kynde loue shal come ghit and conscience
>   togideres,
> And make of lawe a laborere suche loue shal
>   arise,
> And such a pees amonge the peple and a perfit
>   trewthe,
> That Iewes shal wene in here witte and waxen
>   wonder glade,
> That Moises or Messie be come in-to this erthe,
> And haue wonder in here hertis that men beth
>   so trewe.
>   (B.III, 297-302)

It is in expectation of this moment that Langland measures Will's final achievement and extends the traditional form of his poem almost to the breaking point.

Langland begins his prologue, as we might have expected, by introducing his narrator. The protagonist's spiritual blindness at the opening of **Piers** is comparable to that of *Pearl*'s jeweler, though the particulars differ. With a guilelessness characteristic of souls unaware of their moral plight, Will presents himself as a wanderer who has given up all attachment to social forms, dressed himself in the costume (or disguise) of a shepherd-hermit, and begun a search for wonders "in this worlde:"

> In a somer seson when soft was the sonne,
> I shope me in shroudes as I a shepe were,
> In habite as an heremite vnholy of workes,
> Went wyde in this world wondres to here.
>   (1-4)

In a swift juxtaposition of significant images—the hermit's habit, the shepherd's shrouds, and the journey or pilgrimage—Langland's Will unwittingly draws together a rich, coherent framework through which the reader may both judge the wanderer's serious flaws and anticipate the necessary directions of the visionary poem.

A long and venerable tradition attached to the English hermit—including hermits roaming over the Malvern hills where Will locates his own adventures. Theirs was preeminently the responsibility of "seeing" and interpreting divine omens. While monastic writers habitually traced their lineage to Old and New Testament prophets—Elias, Eliseus, John the Baptist—hermits, who preferred the wilderness and solitude to human companionship, had particularly arrogated the prophetic role to themselves. Will, then, should have been especially fitted by virtue of the dress he had assumed, to interpret visions and lead Christians toward salvation. But his habit is a disguise. He has taken on the outer dress of eremitic life, yet has apparently given no thought to its meaning for his soul.

Such inattention to spirit in favor of outward show is not unusual in this world, as Langland will fully demonstrate in the prologue. But it has particular significance for those who profess to practice the highest Christian life. The earliest and most influential monastic literature had insisted on the importance of the monk's clothing as a sign of his spiritual state and a means of entering into God's mysteries. John Cassian devotes the first chapter of his seminal *Institutes* to a consideration of monastic dress as it reveals a man's special election and responsibility, "for when we have seen the external ornament, then we can explain their inner condition." Thus Will's costuming himself as a hermit reveals the possibility of a high vocation as prophet, but a possibility which our hero has carelessly—even unconsciously—rejected.

The narrator's second description of his garb—a shepherd's shroud—further defines the nature of his irresponsibility and seems to place him in an especially condemned class of spiritual drifters. St. Benedict had called attention to them in his rule: they were the "sarabaites" who are "without a shepherd, outside the Lord's flocks, but enclosed in their own" [*Benedicti regula*]. So Will, taking upon *himself* the dress and role of shepherd, rejects the true shepherd, Christ, as well as his surrogates, St. Peter and the abbot.

Finally, as a "wanderer," Langland's narrator falls into yet another class of false hermits decried by Benedict and often castigated in later spiritual literature. He is a "gyrovagus"—one of those who "all their life long, ever restless and never stationary, . . . are slaves of their own moods and love of luxury." While Will's pleasures are simple, they, rather than spiritual discipline, guide him. As a wanderer seeking wonders "in *this* world," he rejects the central and necessary pilgrimage of the soul *from* this world toward the heavenly city.

Will's attachment to this world also bears a clear resemblance to the singular fault of literary visionaries from the *De consolatione philosophiae* onward. Boethius, who created Will's most famous and authoritative ancestor in this plight, had defined the foolishness of taking up such aimless worldly wandering. But he had also demonstrated that it is an inevitable activity for Everyman confronted with himself in the world. Boethius, Huon de Méri's wandering soldier, *Amant* of the *Roman de la Rose*, Pearl's jeweler, Langland's shepherd—all have expected to find wonders in the world in neglect of the world within, the "treuth in hert," which is the only proper object of human searchings.

Like his comrades-in-quest, Will is sleepy and fallen, totally unprepared to discover Truth in his heart or to infuse it into the social order. He has gone out to hear "wondres," he tells us, but the day is so lovely and the sound of the stream where he lingers so enticing that he falls asleep:

> Ac on a May mornynge on Maluerne hulles
> Me byfel a ferly of fairy me thoughte;
> I was wery forwandred and went me to reste
> Vnder a brode banke bi a bornes side,
> And as I lay and lened and loked in the wateres,
> I slombred in a slepyng it sweyued so merye.
>
> (B. *Prol.* 5-10)

Yet like his literary forebears and contemporaries, this slightly absurd, slightly comic seeker after wonders also possesses just those qualities required to study a soul's halting movement toward grace—openness, optimism, above all, a *willingness* to see wonders.

But besides casting Will as Everyman of all time in his fallen state, Langland has also wedded him to his own historical moment in England of the later 1300s. As a Christian living in the evening of the world he cannot rest content with the salvation of his own soul. He has no choice but to accept his responsibility to convert society according to the ancient Christian and monastic ideals of social unity. By God's grace and the demands of his own time, Will must become a prophet. He is to discover the world in its absolute truth and falsehood. As he examines the fabric of history, he will learn how the three persons of the Trinity have been revealed to man through time and this temporal learning process will constitute an important basis for the long narrative. He will also perceive the arrival of Antichrist on the threshold of the eschaton. For in these last days of the world's history, absolute Truth and Falsehood have already begun to prepare for their final apocalyptic battle. Thus complexly characterized, Will is to serve as a filter for all our perceptions of his visionary experience. As a fallible self-deceiving pilgrim, he is not to be trusted entirely. Yet because he is also a prophet, his visions assume, at times, an authority and stability not unlike that of the scriptural prophets. Langland leaves it to the audience's judgment to discern and distinguish.

Will begins his first vision in the prologue as he reports the appearance of a surrealistic, nightmarish setting:

> . . . I was in a wildernesse wist I neuer where,
> As I bihelde in-to the est an hiegh to the sonne,
> I seigh a toure on a toft trielich ymaked;
> A depe dale binethe a dongeon there-inne,
> With depe dyches and derke and dredful of
>   sight.

> A faire felde ful of folke fonde I there bytwene,
> Of alle maner of men the mene and the riche,
> Worchyng and wandryng as the worlde asketh.
>
> (B. *Prol.* 12-19)

This scene bears some resemblance to the sun-capped hill and fearful valley of Dante's opening vision in the *Commedia*. But in its simplicity and symbolic directness, it more closely parallels an iconographical scheme which appears in contemporary Anglo-Norman and English Apocalypses. Illustrations show a tower on a hill next to which Christ in glory sits in a mandorla. At the bottom of the hill is a great hole with the feet of a fiend disappearing into the abyss and the seven-headed beast directing his progress. On either side stand the people of the world, those on the right dead, those on the left alive and militant. But whereas the Apocalypse illustrators give the scene clear eschatological significance, Langland witholds direct interpretation. Instead he relies on Will's pregnant silences to initiate a tone of unspecified anxiety—even terror—which will dominate the whole prologue.

In the next portion of the opening vision, the narrator's eyes take us from this panoramic overview to a close penetrating look at the folk who people the field. Good and evil members of human society appear in rapid succession, "worchyng and wandryng as the worlde asketh" (19). A melée of minstrels and merchants, farmers and hermits, pursue their manifold interests chiefly according to the dictates of greed. So great is the pressure of concrete detail in this catalogue that it seems scarcely reducible to the spiritual function proper to such prologues. The proud in their finery, worthless and false beggars, lying jongleurs, anchorites at home in prayer and penance, friars, parsons selling benefices in London to escape the penury imposed by the plague—all move confusedly across Will's field of vision.

Yet if we move back somewhat from Will's report, the crowded details in this scene assume a shape which is not without contemporary parallels. [Scriptural] commentators and designers of illustrated Apocalypses had been able to discover in the traditional eschatological scenes images of the society which had begun to embody them. Langland's illustrations likewise emphasize a dynamic tension between St. John's apocalyptic prophecy and the events of present history. Through Will's bitter, satiric comment on the vivid scene, the poet first exemplifies Everyman's dismay from the beginning of time, pondering the cruelty of his race, its injustice and avarice, aware in a bewildered way of a better society, but little able to effect it. Then his narrator imposes an eschatological interpretation on empirical experience, as if driven by desperation. His critique rises to an authoritative and prophetic level. With the assurance of a Wyclif, Will (certainly speaking for Langland and embodying with a vengeance the late medieval visionary perspective) condemns the greed and hypocrisy of clergy and laity alike. He calls at last on the judgment of Doomsday for comfort against his distress and anger:

>   drede is at the laste
> Lest crist in consistorie acorse ful manye.

Then, as if an inner curtain had been lifted, we are carried by the narrator's vision abruptly from the foreground of the fair field to its eternal presence in heaven and hell. Under the aegis of apocalyptic "dred," Will is given a glimpse of the Church's real power when it was ruled by Peter and the cardinal virtues, and then its failure in a court governed by imperfect cardinals:

> I parceyued of the power that Peter had to kepe,
> To bynde and to vnbynde as the boke telleth,
> How he it left with loue as owre lorde hight,
> Amonges foure vertues the best of alle vertues,
> That cardinales ben called and closyng ghatis,
> There crist is in kyngdome to close and to shutte,
> And to opne it to hem and heuene blisse shewe.
> Ac of the cardinales atte Courte that caught of
>   that name,
> And power presumed in hem a pope to make,
> To han that power that Peter hadde inpugnen I
>   nelle;
> For in loue and letterure the eleccioun bilongeth,
> For-thi I can and can naughte of courte speke
>   more.
>
>   (B. *Prol.* 100-111)

Through this abrupt shift from concrete detail to abstract "power," from creatures named to names, Langland deftly defines a twofold concern of the narrative: the movement inward and heavenward and the movement through time. For his complex literary and spiritual goal, the poet required terms to instruct the soul in its eternal aspect and also to represent humankind's historical progress toward salvation. Personifications and emblems could fill the first requirement: the tower, the dungeon and field, the cardinal virtues, Truth and Holichurch, Falsehood and Lady Mede, Conscience, Kynde Wit, Reason, Scriptures, Imaginatif, Gluttony, Lechery and the whole cast of abstract subjects depict the qualities or "places" for which their names stand eternally hovering over all human history as well as entering into it. On the other hand, the large troop of exemplary and scriptural personages—Will, cardinals, plowmen, minstrels and hawkers drawn from the streets, cathedrals, monasteries and courts of fourteenth-century England, angels, Abraham, Moses, Christ, Piers—meet the second need. Through them Langland shows the gradual historical realization of eternal good and evil at many points in time all through the course of salvation history. His complex intermingling of a double terminology allows the poet to reveal the qualities of Truth and Falsehood in abstract definition and also in individual souls within time's flow.

Langland also uses this twofold vocabulary to represent movements toward an historical merging of the temporal and eternal in anticipation of the grand apocalyptic conflict. When Truth has been fully realized in history and Antichrist has appeared as a man, then the final battle can be fought. In his stylistic entwining of "ideas" and history, Langland can prepare souls not only for a spiritually effective Easter but also for this last conflict. Will's double voice (or Langland's superimposed on Will's) in the prologue—as sleepy wanderer and doomsday preacher reviling the evil of the world—parallels the poem's verbal duality. The poet seems equally drawn by Everyman's lethargy and blindness and his paradoxical capacity to imagine a millennial society on earth.

Moving from Christ and the Church to Civil Justice, Langland now sets before Will's dreaming mind yet another mode of discourse and a bizarre tableau in which a Lunatic, a Goliard and an Angel teach the King what he must do in order to rule justly. This jarring sequence, as well as the fable of the belling of the cat which follows, belong to that enigmatic dream-art characteristic of prophetic and satiric literature. The narrative becomes riddling and parabolic: dark conceits cloak utopian idealism as well as cynical commentary on the actual King's and Commons' failures. At this point, the B-text poet prefers allusive drama to didactic glossing and does not interpret. Who are the Lunatic, the Goliard and the Angel? On what authority do they offer the King instruction?

The poet refuses to gloss the cat-rat fable. As Will says, "What this meteles (dream) bemeneth ghe men that be merye, / Deuine ghe, for I ne dar bi dere god in heuene!" (208-209) This whole complex inner dream from cardinals to cats, which carries the audience from surfaces to intimations of metaphysical order and disorder, does not clarify attainable goals but imposes a tone of mysterious foreboding and disturbing dissonance on the world of appearances. It also demonstrates that Will (and perhaps mankind generally), may have serious difficulty understanding pregnant dreams and prophecies.

As abruptly as it had begun, this metaphysical interlude ends, and Will returns the audience to his shallower vision of the field of folk. He describes a sample of civil population passing before him, those who rule and judge and those who toil with their hands. His last glimpse of the field in the prologue offers us a devastating image of society's pettiness and godlessness. Workers call out their empty salute, "Dieu vous saue, Dame Emme," and concentrate on their stomachs:

> Cokes and here knaues crieden, 'hote pies, hote!
> Gode gris and gees gowe dyne, gowe!'
> Tauerners vn-til hem tolde the same,
> 'White wyn of Oseye and red wyn of Gascoigne,
> Of the Ryne and of the Rochel the roste to defy.'
>   (B. *Prol.* 225-229)

For the audience who has looked on all the visionary scenes of the prologue from a late fourteenth-century perspective, the falsehood Will perceives in the busy field has special significance. It is not only an evil time but the worst of times, for "þe moste myschief on molde is mountyng wel faste" (67). The utter materialism of a world concerned with wine and hot pies instead of the bread and wine of the Eucharist can only presage the emergence of Antichrist and apocalyptic conflict. An urgency imposed by imminent cataclysm accounts for Will's (and the poet's) tone of anger culminating in these last lines of harsh alliteration and sharp monosyllables. (pp. 205-18)

> *Barbara Nolan, "Will's Dark Visions of Piers the Plowman," in her* The Gothic Visionary Perspective, *Princeton University Press, 1977, pp. 205-58.*

Maureen Quilligan   (essay date 1978)

[*Quilligan is an American educator whose works include*

The Language of Allegory (1979). In the following essay, she studies Langland's technique in the B-text of Piers Plowman, *focusing on his undermining of simplistic allegorical interpretations by sliding "tortuously back and forth between literal and metaphorical meanings of words, and therefore [making] moral use of the problematic tensions between them."*]

In his essay 'The Action of Langland's Second Vision' [*Essays in Criticism,* XV (July 1965)] John Burrow describes the workings of a pattern of narrative which is of fundamental importance to the nature of allegory, both medieval and modern. Although Mr. Burrow himself concludes that this pattern is itself 'foreign' to allegory, his mistake should not obscure the significance of his description, which can be extended into a distinctive definition of the genre of narrative allegory. So far from being foreign to its nature, the reflexive tension in the **Piers Plowman B-text** between literalness and metaphor which Mr. Burrow outlines is the essence of the genre.

Mr. Burrow's main point is that Langland's literal narrative 'actions' characteristically 'dwindle' into metaphor. At first Langland appears to be presenting a clearly defined series of actions in passus V-VII, which, as they proceed, inscribe the traditional 'arc of penitential action'. First, there is a sermon, next, a confession, then a pilgrimage, and finally a pardon, the usual object of fourteenth-century pilgrimages. According to Mr. Burrow, Langland chose this 'well-constructed plot' to show the kind of unapocalyptic change in society the poem itself was designed to instigate—a 'conversion that can be expected of people, here, now, and in England', or a conversion not unlike the one the pilgrims in *The Canterbury Tales* are supposed to experience. Yet, according to Mr. Burrow, Langland does not fulfil the expectations built up by this plot; rather he frustrates the shape of the arc, and disrupts the series by providing instead of successive actions, a series of substitutions. For example, the pilgrimage, which in Reason's sermon was to seek St. Truth (or God), is at first '*anything but an actual pilgrimage*', which like the Canterbury pilgrims', would normally have sought the actual shrine of a particular saint. It is essentially unlike a pilgrimage to 'God', who has no local habitation on earth. But beyond this subtle translation of the notion of pilgrimage into something less actual and more metaphorical, the fictional pilgrimage is itself frustrated. Piers does not lead the folk on any trip; Langland dispenses with the journey in the briefest kind of landscape allegory (Piers only describes the route, which goes over stiles and rivers, and around bends named from the ten commandments); instead Piers tells all the folk to stay at home and help him plough his half-acre. The pilgrimage is never resumed, either literally or metaphorically, for the image of pardon interrupts the image of ploughing, which had itself interrupted the image of pilgrimage. Mr. Burrow explains the reason for the interruption by the pardon: 'St. Truth himself, the very object of the proposed pilgrimage, commands his servant to stay at home'. Yet, as Mr. Burrow notes, 'at the same time, the fact that Truth obtains a plenary pardon for Piers . . . suggests equally clearly that the pilgrimage is, in another sense, completed'. What has happened to the idea of a pilgrimage, then, is that it 'first becomes an allegorical form or "vehicle", then dwindles into a mere metaphor'.

Mr. Burrow suggests that Langland drops the pilgrimage as an allegorical 'vehicle' simply because he did not believe in pilgrimages as forms of penance sufficient for salvation. They were external forms which could be abused (by wives of Bath, for instance) and because penance must be internally felt in order to operate, Langland insists on the image of ploughing, an action not so available to misinterpretation and one that stresses the notion of keeping oneself 'at home'. By frustrating the narrative, Langland makes an important moral point.

The problem of the pardon is, however, more complicated. If Langland believed in the efficacy of pardons more than that of pilgrimages, why does Piers, in the most notorious crux of the poem, tear up the pardon for 'pure tene'? Mr. Burrow explains that in trusting the unorthodox message of his pardon, Piers is, at the same time, 'rejecting bulls with seals'. This action, like the action of the pilgrimage, 'contains a message which is by implication an attack upon itself'. Reason's sermon had described an 'unreal' or 'impossible' pilgrimage; so too, the actual words of the pardon which Piers tears up are not the usual terms of a regular papal bull; it is not a real pardon. Langland does not stop with this paradoxical implication, however, but provides yet another substitution, a reversion to the ploughing metaphor which is, however, itself translated. Piers says that he will substitute prayers and penance for his plough: 'Of prayers and of penaunce my plow shal ben herafter' (VII. 119). It is almost as if Langland had become frustrated with each 'vehicle' in turn. In the same way that real pilgrimages and actual pardons can be subject to a too 'external' interpretation which belies the internal state necessary for the outward show to mean anything at all, Langland's metaphors can be abused. Thus, in tearing the pardon, Piers demonstrates against the 'form' of pardons, or the mere 'formality' which makes pardons spiritually meaningless. Langland is willing to sacrifice narrative coherence in order to make this point. According to Mr. Burrow, Langland is so morally bothered by the 'indeterminate degree of metaphor' in these literal actions that he allows 'interference' with the literal level of the poem. He agrees with Rosemary Woolf ([*Essays in Criticism*] XII, 1962) that a general 'lack of a sustained literal level' becomes among the 'chief non-medieval qualities of the poem'.

The basic process of allegory always involves the narrative in slippery switches of terms. Langland's practice in the **Visio** is only the most obvious form of allegory's tendency to slide tortuously back and forth between literal and metaphorical meanings of words, and therefore to make moral use of the problematic tensions between them. Thus, when Mr. Burrow goes on to conclude that Langland's characteristic lack of a 'sustained' literal level is not only *un*medieval but *unallegorical* as well, I must disagree. The problem derives from the difficulties of the term 'literal' in a discussion of allegory. Its general use is to mean 'actual', 'life-like', or 'real', and this is the sense in which Mr. Burrow primarily uses the term. Yet, paradoxically, when he explains that there is no 'sustained literal level', he is actually saying that there is no continuous fictional activity or 'plot' which can provide the basis for a continued, coherent allegorical interpretation. He is saying that there is no sustained *metaphor,* or there is no sustained base-line of literal action upon which the reader can build a consistent (metaphorical) interpretation.

No doubt it would have been easier to coordinate Langland's narrative with our traditional understanding of allegory as a neat set of parallel one-for-one correspondences had he given us an extended pilgrimage which we could translate into allegorical meaning, or which would have been translated for us into meaning by the tags attached to the outcroppings of the imaginary landscape (as Bunyan provides for us, for instance). Yet when Langland disrupts the literal level by his series of substituted images he specifically undermines this simplistic notion of allegorical reading. He interrupts the literal level specifically to hinder the reader's fascination with the operation of translating metaphors into 'allegory'. In effect, he signals that he does not want the operation of reading to proceed as easy, external, translation. He frustrates the reader's expectations in order to ram home to him that his very desire to read of a pilgrimage (or to read a sustained literal level) is the same as any literal-minded penitent's desire to substitute a physical pilgrimage for the internal understanding which only makes the travel worthwhile. He disrupts the literal level to remind the reader that he is reading too literally—and here I mean the word 'literally' metaphorically.

The literal meaning of 'literal' is, in fact, not 'actual' or 'life-like', but 'letteral'—having to do with letters and with the reading of words (as in the sense of 'literate'). When a reader is reading the 'literal' level (in traditional parlance), he is actually reading the 'metaphorical' level—that is, he watches the imaginary action in his mind's eye: the landscape flies by, the pilgrimage goes on with its bustle of noise. The only thing that will return a reader from imagining such a distracting 'level' of action to thinking about the significance this action ought to hold for him, is to deny him the colourful journey. Thus Langland frustrates his reader's normal desires for more interesting extensions of the literal level of the narrative, or for more 'plot'. By doing so the poet paradoxically insists that the reader read not *less* literally, but *more* literally, for, if the reader can no longer follow an imaginary event in his mind's eye, he must look at the words on the page. If the text does not sustain a movie-like image of action, he will be reminded that what he is reading is a text. It will be all he has left to read, for the imagined action will have disappeared. At that point Langland, like all allegorists (from Alain de Lille to Hawthorne), has got the reader doing what he wants him to do—looking carefully at those words, and the letters he uses to spell them, written out, on the page.

What, then, does Langland wish his reader to take away from the pardon scene? The function of the priest with whom Piers has his bitter argument, ended only by his tearing the pardon, is to impress upon the reader the vital problem of interpretation. As Hawthorne's focus in the *Scarlet Letter* is the problem of interpreting the letter 'A'

(which word—adultress, angel, able, art—does it stand for?), so Langland's focus in **Piers Plowman** is, for the same generic reason, the problem of interpreting the pardon. The priest offers to 'gloss' the pardon 'on Englisshe'—that is, to translate the latin words and to interpret them as words in an esoteric text. His conclusion from this 'glossing' is that the pardon is not an actual pardon because the words do not take the orthodox form. Mary Carruthers [in her *The Search for St. Truth,* 1973] points out that this priest is an example of blatant literal-mindedness; he rejects the pardon because it doesn't read like ones he has seen before. 'When he cannot discover the word "pardon" in the Latin statement, he says that it is no pardon at all.' Thus he is bounded by the 'literal statement of the words'. Yet, in a very fundamental sense, the priest's problem is not that he reads too literally, but that he does not read *literally* enough; he does not read the actual words of the pardon, nor think about what they mean, literally. Piers, however, understands that the pardon says simply 'do well', and his actions reveal that he takes these words in their most literal sense. The pardon does not say do any specific, 'literal' action. Piers is the only one to read the pardon literally for he remembers that 'do well' is an imperative verb with no immediate object; he says, therefore, that he is going to do well—he will cease ploughing and will make of his plough prayers and penance. He is not going to plough any longer, because it is not a sufficient outward sign of the spiritual understanding commanded by the pardon.

When Mary Carruthers explains that Piers 'sees the literal words as signs of a spiritual meaning, hidden within them, which can only be understood in relationship to the whole divine pattern', she wrongly assumes that Piers reads the pardon 'allegorically'. Langland, however, has taken great care to show that unlike anyone else, Piers reads *literally;* his 'pure tene' is a response to the fact that the words of Truth's pardon are not what he had expected. They are not, in fact, a pardon, for the text enjoins reward for good deeds and punishment for bad, or states the law one needs to be pardoned from. Yet the next text Piers quotes, the twenty-third Psalm, at least states the faith that man can be pardoned. In a few lines, Langland has condensed the central paradox of Christianity; to sum it up as the enduring conflict between Works and Faith is to simplify the paradox Langland spends much of the poem in developing; the conflict between the Law of Love and the Law of Justice *is* the crux of the pardon scene; and the 'breakdown' of the literal action is designed to make the reader become involved in the paradox. At the very least, the reader learns that the interpretation of the pardon is a puzzle.

Will's response to the pardon provides a specific foil to Piers's reading of it. Unlike Piers, Will reads the pardon literally, in the bad sense, for he transforms the terms of the pardon away from their literal, grammatical forms. 'Do well' in the pardon is a verb, yet Will's next action is to begin searching for a fully personified character named 'Do well'. By transforming the verb into a noun, and by personifying that noun, Will has involved himself in the same abuse of language Lady Meed represents simply by being the personification of a word that happens also to be a pun ('meed' may mean either bribery or reward). This is the normal process of allegory which operates most obviously by personifying nouns. Yet, just as there is a good punning, such as the sort of wordplay Holy Church uses, so there is a good literalness as well as a bad literal-mindedness. Will's literal-mindedness is bad at this point. He still prefers to treat the words of the pardon as concrete objects—as people; they become more than mere signs for some sort of specific, literal action he might perform, and by performing earn salvation. They become ends in themselves. Mrs. Carruthers concludes a similar argument about Will's response to the pardon scene by saying:

> Will has not yet realized that the problem of doing well is related to the problem of interpretation. . . . The problem of *intus legendum,* or inward reading is as pertinent to works as it is to words, for true works express an inner, spiritual meaning just as true words do. Thus the formulation which Will employs is a false one: it treats words and works as things in and of themselves, which can be judged absolutely on a moral scale, rather than understanding both as signs of a spiritual reality. And by casting the problem in terms of an irreconcilable conflict between words and works, Will demonstrates that he is just as wedded to a purely literal understanding as the priest is. He must understand, as Piers does, the true nature of words and works as signs, informed by the spiritual essence of kynde; they are not circumscribed, earthly things, but signs of the 'inner word', the understanding, and the will 'that shines within'.

The important point that this otherwise remarkable reading brushes over is that Piers's spiritual understanding is 'spiritual' only is so far as it is *literal*—in the good and literal sense of that term. Will reifies language and in turning 'do well' into a thing, he translates the term into metaphor; Piers does not. He allows the words their own proper meaning. Truly spiritual reading of allegory is paradoxically the most *literal* kind of reading.

Out of Will's literal-mindedness, however, Langland generates the next section of the poem, which develops in the most literal way possible, as a wrong-headed commentary on the text of the pardon. The relationship between the **Vita** and the **Visio** thus takes shape as the familiar connection between text and commentary. When Langland organizes Will's search in terms of an obsessive splitting of the verb 'do well' into other nouns, ranked furthermore in the degrees of adverbs—Dowell, Dobet, Dobest—he reveals the basic verbal nature of the problem which is at the heart of the last section of the poem. That his is the wrong kind of search, the wrong kind of interpretation, is part of Langland's point. Were is to be the right kind, the poem would end.

A major section of the **Vita** is designed to show that Will's interpretation of the words 'do well' is simply a manifestation of a much larger spiritual problem—a pervasive abuse of language which, in the process of trying to correct, allegory appears to 'unmake' itself. As a final example of Langland's frustrating refusal to supply continuous 'literal' action, John Burrow takes the dropping of another 'allegory' in the Dobet section—the allegory of Christ's

'jousting' in Jerusalem. Although, as Mr. Burrow point out, Langland makes elaborate preparations for this joust throughout three whole passus, when the reader finally arrives in Jerusalem fully expecting to be treated to the joust, he finds that it never happens. Again, Langland has simply 'dropped' the allegory, which again 'dwindles' into metaphor. Mr. Burrow takes Langland to task for capriciously dropping so promising an action: 'Langland could easily have sustained this allegory, as other medieval writers . . . had done before him'. Unlike his use of the allegorical actions of pilgrimage and pardon, Langland drops the allegory of the joust with no redeeming process of substitution; this is the kind of movement which Mr. Burrow finds 'foreign to the nature of allegory itself'. He reasons that

> An allegorical story is, in one very simple way, unlike a metaphor. A metaphor, however long it may be sustained, has no exclusive rights: the author is always free to dispense with it whenever he feels that his 'real' subject would be better served that way. An allegorical story, on the other hand, has itself a kind of 'reality'—the reality of the literal level—and for that reason, the author, however much he may digress and delay, cannot simply dispense with it.

Yet dispense with the jousting story is what Langland apparently does. Mr. Burrow concludes that by 'allowing intended meanings to interfere with . . . his chosen action' Langland simply violates the reader's expectation. 'The discarded parts of his allegory return to haunt him in the shape of metaphors', with the result that his literal level becomes 'hopelessly confused'. But confusion at the 'literal' level may not be a bad thing. Langland obviously did not assume it was, for he carefully orchestrates the narrative action of the joust in Jerusalem to frustrate not only the 'literal' level but the insufficiently *literal* kind of reading based upon it. With it he makes exactly the same point he had already made with his easy dispensations of the pilgrimage and pardon; with it he may be said to make the point of his poem, and to reveal as well a generically fundamental technique of narrative allegory.

Langland's careful artistry in this structural sleight-of-hand is neat but extensive; Langland uses three whole passus to force the transition from a metaphorical reading of a 'literal' level to a very word-conscious *literal* reading of the poem's *text*. This transition is the major purpose of the three passus, and the sheer amount of verse Langland devotes to the action of the joust indicates the importance of the theological point Langland hopes to make with it.

Significantly, the allegory of the joust is introduced by a pun. In passus XVI, after the image of the Tree of Charity has culminated in the disarray of Piers hitting at the Satanic 'raggman' who has stolen his fruit, Gabriel's voice breaks into the narrative to prophesy the coming of Christ:

> That one Ihesus, a *iustice* sonne most iouke in
>   her chambre
> Tyl *plenitudo temporis* fully comen were,
> That Pieres fruit floured and fel to be ripe.
> And thanne shulde Ihesus *iuste* there-fore bi iug-
>   gement of armes,

> Whether shulde fonge the fruit the fende or hy-
> mselue.
>
> (XVI, 92-96; my italics)

The pun is on the medieval term *just,* which here means both jousting and justice. Langland collapses the two terms through wordplay, implying that to joust is to do justice: a Son of Justice will joust with the devil to retrieve the stolen fruit of mankind. No mere bit of alliterative wit, this pun poses a serious question about the nature of Christian justice, which the whole jousting allegory devotes itself to answering. Gabriel's prophecy furthermore looks forward to the dramatic Harrowing of Hell in passus XVIII; it therefore anticipates the 'end' of the action, and the story of the 'joust' takes shape as the coherent narrative unit of Christ's life. As if to emphasize this fact, Langland gives a brief summary of that life stressing one particular incident, when Jesus raised Lazarus from the dead: 'Iewes iangled there-ageyne iugged laws, / And seide he wroughte thorw wicchecrafte' (XVI. 119-120). By referring to this incident, Langland alerts his reader to the central problem Jesus faced with the Pharisees—their literal-minded interpretation of the law, and consequent refusal to see his resurrection of its dead literalness into life—and also to the central problem he faces in writing of Christ's life in terms of the jousting allegory—the reader's literal-minded fascination with the details of the joust at the expense of what Christ's life means. Langland concludes this brief history with an account of Jesus's jousting on Good Friday:

> thus was he taken
> thorw iudas and iewes ihesus was his name;
> that on the fryday folwynge for mankynde sake
> *Iusted* in ierusalem a ioye to vs alle. . . .
>
> (XVI, 160-163; my italics)

After this vision, Will awakes from his dream-within-a-dream to meet Abraham (or Faith) described as an 'heraud of armes', who seeks a 'ful bolde bachelere', identified by a 'blasen' (179) which pictures the trinity. In this way the jousting terminology carries over into the next dream. While Abraham and Will walk toward Jerusalem, Will wonders with some surprise: 'what is in yowre lappe?'. With allegory's penchant for literalizing clichés, Langland imagines Abraham walking with his lap full of those who were traditionally supposed to be 'in the bosom of Abraham'. This impossible image is not meant to be visualized (no one could walk with a hell-full of people); however it is to be remembered, for it is another signal of the 'end' to the event and helps to keep the final shape of the narrative unit in the reader's mind. As he journeys to Jerusalem, Abraham looks forward to Christ's harrowing of Hell, which will free him from the burden he faithfully carries for God.

Will and Faith soon encounter Hope, a 'spye' who inquires 'after a knighte' and who carries a table given to him 'vpon the mounte of synay'; it contains, however, not the ten commandments, but the two—to love God and one's neighbour (XVII.11). This substitution, a bit like the kinds of substitutions Langland has given us in the *Visio,* bothers Will. A conservative, Will thinks the old laws are good enough, or that, at the very least, the new laws are too brief. He and Hope argue about the matter at length, nor is their disagreement resolved until the Good Samari-

tan appears, riding 'ful rapely . . . to a iustes in iherusalem' (XVII. 49-51). He settles the argument by action; he stops to help a man whom Abraham and Hope have passed by. As Will watches, he finally sees the need for the *lex Christi* which appears in the form of a farm-house where the Good Samaritan takes the wounded man, telling the hostler 'kepe this man til I come from the iustes' (XVII. 74).

This series of encounters not only creates a dramatic sense of the rush to judgment in Jerusalem, but also unfolds the complicated relationship between the Old and the New Laws. Critics who talk about the extensive pattern of punning on justice and jousting throughout these passus remark only the metaphor of the joust; they neglect the other part of the pun—justice—which provides the very concept which is continually redefined through Will's encounters with Faith, Hope, and Charity. Each of these three travellers has his own conception of sufficient 'law' and Faith and Hope try to help Will to understand the relationship between them:

> What neded it thanne a new lawe to bigynne,
> Sith the fyrst sufficeth to sauacioun & to blisse?
>
> (XVII. 30-31)

Faith's law (a belief in the trinity) is, according to Will, easier to obey; Will remarks with some irony to Hope 'Tho that lerneth thi lawe wil litel while vsen it!' (XVII. 46). Not only the action of the narrative, but such conversations as these, continually focus on the problem of law, and of justice.

At the opening of passus XVIII, Will falls asleep to find himself in Jerusalem in the midst of joyous tumult at the approaching joust. 'One semblable to the samaritan' arrives, looking lively, like a knight who comes to be dubbed and win gilt spurs. Will sees Faith again, who cries from a window a most significant welcome to the samaritan (whom we now recognize as Jesus) 'A! fili dauid! / As doth an Heraude of armes whan auntrous [adventurous knights] cometh to iustes'. And, Langland tells us, specifically the 'old iewes of ierusalem for ioye thei songen' (XVIII, 15-17). Abraham explains to Will that Jesus will 'iuste in piers armes . . . / In Piers paltok the plowman this pricker shal ryde' (XVIII. 22-25). In answer to Will's odd question, 'Who shal iuste with ihesus? iuwes or scribes?' Abraham answers, 'Nay'—Jesus will joust with 'the foule fende and fals dome & deth' (XVIII. 28). Yet Will's apparently stupid remark about the Jewish scribes is not so wide of the mark: the joust finally turns out to be not a joust at all but a trial. Just at the moment when any reader expects to be treated to the climactic jousting scene, Langland states instead

> Thanne cam *pilatus* with moche peple *sedens pro
> tribunali,*
> To see how doughtilich deth sholde do & deme
> her botheres righte
> *The iuwes and the iustice ageine ihesu thei were,*
> And al her courte on hym cryde *crucifige* sharpe.
>
> (XVIII. 36-39; my italics)

Here is the point at which, according to Mr. Burrow, Langland allows the 'literal' level to collapse into allegorical chaos, the biblical story of Christ's trial 'interfering' with the action of the joust. Langland has indeed frustrated the reader's expectation but he does so to a purpose. He forces him to abandon the 'literal' story of the joust so as to make him more sensitive to the true *literalness* of words. All Langland has done, in switching from joust to trial, is to return to the other term of the pun: justice. A trial is the *aptest* demonstration of the process of justice, and this biblical trial in particular is the unique, historic one which prepared for the total reorganization of divine law, or that redefinition of Old Testament justice which it was Christ's office to achieve, and toward which the allegory of the joust has always been pointing. (As if to underscore this point, Langland makes the main 'evidence' for Jesus's witchcraft quoted at the trial, his statement about tearing down and rebuilding the Temple in three days—an action which was not meant to be understood physically.) To dispense with the image of the joust is not, therefore, to drop the allegory, but to deepen it and to make it more immediately available to the audience who, while they may never have gone on pilgrimage, or obtained a pardon (or seen a joust), would surely have participated in the Good Friday liturgy, from which Langland takes the trial. The metaphorical shift from joust to trial then makes the theme of justice more immediate and more explicit. And again, the reality of the literal level, far from being violated by the shift in terms, itself decrees the legitimacy of such a switch. The most literal aspect of the literal level of the joust—the word 'just' itself—provides the image of a trial.

This sudden modulation is also Langland's paradoxical statement about the literalness of his allegory. In a sense, any reader who is disappointed by the trial scene must be faulted for the same Pharisaic literalness of interpretation as the Jews. The Jews and their Old Testament legality are arrayed against Jesus at the trial. Will was right: Jesus does indeed joust with scribes, and specifically with the Pharisaical attitude toward the literalness of the law. Abraham's correction of Will—that Jesus will joust with 'fals dome' and 'deth'—is only another way of saying the same thing, for Jesus does joust with false judgment, and with the kind of death a Pharisaic literalism brings—for, as we know, the letter killeth and the spirit giveth life.

Langland had carefully prepared for this point when he stipulated that it is only Abraham and the 'old iuwes of ierusalem' who rejoice at the sight of the knight Jesus. Langland's refusal to present Jesus as a warring knight in armour, as he seems to promise, and his substitution of Jesus's suffering at the trial for a triumphant joust, simply underscores the fact that Christ's mission was not to be a messianic leader of an army, but a sacrifice to fulfil, and to supersede the Old Law. Langland's transition from literal story of the joust, mediated by the switch from one meaning of the pun on 'just' to the other, forces the reader to realize again the paradoxical quality of Christian heroism which triumphs by being defeated. And Langland forces the reader to recognize this by disrupting the reader's own Pharisaic fascination with all the panoply of a medieval joust.

As social institutions in Langland's time, jousts were more archaic entertainments than the mock battles in preparation for war of the earlier middle ages, but they did retain their legal nature, in which God was assumed to give victory to the 'right' side of the duel. The lists at Coventry, scheduled for 16 September 1397 between Hereford and Norfolk, so honoured in the breach by Richard II, were not fabricated by Shakespeare; battle was a customary way of trying such matters at the time. Yet, as one of those once-again fashionable, formulaic entertainments, which were enjoying at the time a brief vogue among the bourgeoisie, a joust would have promised an even more romantic diversion to Langland's reader than a pilgrimage; to disrupt a story built on such an inherently escapist 'plot' would have been, no doubt, to risk even greater frustration in the reader than the simple evaporation of a pilgrimage. Of course, the greater intensity of the reader's disappointment is part of the point, and it would help to make the substitution of trial for joust even more forceful than the substitution of pardon for pilgrimage, especially with the direct reference of the trial to the actual historical details of Christ's life. The substitution is at once more jarring (because joust and trial are superficially farther apart than pilgrimage and pardon—which are both 'religious'), and also more *literally* appropriate because of the strict connection between the two in the pun on 'just'.

The return of the jousting terminology continues to make the same point about the reader's need to read *literally*, and Christ's translation of the problem of literalism into a new context. The Jews make Longinus, the blind chevalier, take 'the spere in his honde & iusten with ihesus'; when the spear pierces Christ's side, however, Langland explains that 'the blode sprong down by the spere & vnspered [opened] the knightes eyen. / Thanne fel the knighte vpon knees and cryed hym mercy' (XVIII. 86-87). The reader ought by now to be sensitive to the theological dimensions of the pun on the word 'spere'. Jesus's blood changes the blind notion of jousting justice to mercy; he opens Longinus's eyes. The pun on 'spere' shows by its own shift in meaning exactly what it is Christ has done; he has taken the instrument of death (a spear) and opened (unspered) men's eyes.

The episodes which immediately follow this 'joust'—the debate between the four daughters of God and the Harrowing of Hell—conclude the section of Dobet by continuing to consider the problem of justice and to extend the jousting allegory. The Harrowing of Hell has been called the real joust between Christ and Satan, yet it too is more a legalistic debate than a joust. The argument between Truth, Mercy, Righteousness, and Peace concerns whether or not Christ can rightfully overturn God's first law for man; it re-enacts the argument Will, Abraham, and Hope have about the two new commandments. Truth tells Mercy that her story about the undoing of death is 'but a tale of waltrot' (XVIII. 142). In the same way, Righteousness rebukes Peace for rejoicing that 'ihesus iusted well', because the 'dome' of God himself, decreeing death for man, cannot be undone.

The devils take up this same legalistic question when they defend their hegemony over the dead souls 'by right' (XVIII. 282), and, as Jesus himself explains, he releases the souls held in Hell only by fulfilling that Old Law:

Ergo, soul shal soule quyt & synne to synne
    wende,
And al that man hath mysdo I, man, wyl
    amende.
Membre for membre bi the olde lawe was
    amendes,
And lyf for lyf also & by that lawe I clayme it.
. . .
So leue it nougte, lucifer ageine the law I fecche
    hem,
But bi right & by resoun raunceoun here my
    lyges.

(XVIII, 338-347)

Morton Bloomfield has argued that Langland's decision to make the Harrowing of Hell rather than the Passion of Christ the climax of Dobet grew out of a need to reconcile love and charity with justice and reason: 'Christ's death is an act of love and an act of justice; but until the just are freed in hell and Satan bound and confined, His sacrifice is not complete'. Langland completes the sacrifice with the continued narrative of the Harrowing of Hell, and, furthermore, completes the jousting allegory which had always looked forward to Christ's release of those souls suffering bondage in hell, in Abraham's 'lappe'. Far from being a characteristic example of Langland's structural caprices, or the untidiness of his allegory, the story of the joust carefully and neatly unfolds the intricate relationships between the Old Law and the New, and points toward this last act of justice, when the New Law supersedes the Old, and brings in a necessary new way of interpreting the law.

Langland's theme in Dobet is the redemption of justice and of man. Yet, through the subtle manipulations of the jousting allegory and its insistence on the literalness of words, he seems to redeem language as well. Because of the polysemousness of such terms as 'just' and 'spere', Langland can legitimately switch the whole metaphoric basis of the narrative. The pun on 'just' itself makes the point about old definitions of justice—it is, in a sense, mere jousting, death for death, and therefore insufficient. The action of the narrative switches from the activity of jousting to the business of the Christian sacrifice executed by the biblical trial *at the exact moment* that sensitivity to the spiritual wisdom which transforms the letter of the law must be substituted for a facile reading of the 'literal' action. There is a clash between form and content initially: but after the reader understands the reason for his frustration, he perceives the true sense there is to the letter. Jewish justice is just jousting. Christ's kind is something other.

By managing to make so large a point (it is after all the basic outline of Christian history) with a word, Langland seems to assume the nearly sacred power of the polysemousness of words. Puns can be dangerous, as in Lady Meed's abuse of language; but puns can also provide the rationale for a subtly exfoliating pattern which extends over an immense stretch of narrative; the pun on 'just' helps, in fact, to correct the reader's tendency to misread. Language has definitely redeemed itself, or, as Langland himself might have said, Christ, who was the Word of God, has redeemed man's language and, therefore, the language of the poem. (pp. 95-111)

Maureen Quilligan, "Langland's Literal Allegory," in Essays in Criticism, *Vol. XXVIII, No. 2, April, 1978, pp. 95-111.*

John M. Bowers   (essay date 1986)

[*In the following excerpt, Bowers points to some of the theological controversies of Langland's day, suggesting that they periodically surface in the poem, adding to the "prevailing climate of anxiety" and "[contributing] to the general turbulence felt throughout* Piers Plowman.*"*]

Piers Plowman depicts a world in turmoil. Although Langland offers a vision not shared by all his contemporaries, the briefest look at fourteenth-century England shows how a writer might have felt that his country had suffered more upheavals than in previous ages. Recurrent outbreaks of plague carried off as much as a third of the population, a subsequent transformation of the ceremony caused widespread social unrest, political turmoil culminated twice in the murders of kings, and religious dissension bred heresies among learned theologians and spiritual doubts throughout the hierarchy of the Church. The Black Death, the Great Schism, the Hundred Years War, Lollardy, the Peasants' Revolt—an historical index of the century forms a litany of disasters.

Langland's poem reflects this prevailing climate of anxiety by enumerating problems, brooding over them, and railing against those felt to be responsible, but almost never does it offer any solid solutions. The poet seems to have discovered during the process of composition that complex problems have even more complex remedies. His struggle came to bear increasingly upon the twin realizations that ideal solutions can seldom be determined with absolute certainty and that these solutions are unlikely to be discovered and enacted by the individual, much less by Christian society as a whole. (p. 1)

It is not my intention to trace the precise ways in which Langland reacted to the great theological controversies of his century . . . but rather to point out some of the intellectual cross-currents that surface from time to time and thereby contribute to the general turbulence felt throughout **Piers Plowman.** Nor is it my intention to insist that the poem's confusion is the result of utter theological befuddlement in Langland's own mind. Compositional difficulty is suggested by the poet's apparent inability to complete the A-version, perhaps because the world that had at first seemed remediable with the proper corrections had become more problematic in the poem's second vision. If Langland became unsure how to proceed, he made the right artistic decision. He stopped writing, and took up the continuation of the B-version only after coming to terms with his problems—or rather discovering a way to integrate his sense of the problematic into the structure of the poem.

A major part of that artistic solution was to make the Dreamer, up to this point largely a passive observer, into the central actor, with *his* mind mirroring the confusions and contradictions of a world filled with too many plausible choices and too many contending claims—of society and the individual, of lofty learning and simple piety, of grace and free will, of this world and the next. If a portrayal of his mind's halting progress does not always result in satisfying poetry so that even an admirer like John Burrow [in "Words, Works and Will: Theme and Structure in *Piers Plowman*," *"Piers Plowman": Critical Approaches,* ed. S. S. Hussey, 1969] admits that "Langland can be boring," what does result is probably the first instance in a major English poem of the fallacy of imitative form. As Morton Bloomfield puts it [in his *"Piers Plowman" as a Fourteenth-Century Apocalypse,* 1962] "spiritual confusion demands to some extent artistic confusion."

The Middle Ages did not lack a sense that an artistic creation should have a planned and orderly arrangement. Augustine taught that the rules governing human institutions and creations would, ideally, be dominated by the same transcendent law that is manifested in number, weight, and measure. In *The City of God* (XI) he uses a verse from the Wisdom of Solomon (II 21)—"omnia in mensura, et numero, et pondere disposuisti"—to proclaim number as the form-bestowing principle in the divine work of creation; few verses were quoted so regularly in medieval Latin texts. Langland seems well aware of these standards when he has Conscience criticize the disarray of the Friars:

> And if ye coueite cure, Kynde wol yow telle
> That in mesure God made alle manere þynges,
> And sette it at a certain and at a siker nombre,
> And nempnede hem names, and noumbrede þe
> sterres.
>
> (B. xx. 253-56)

Guided by authorities such as the Bible and St. Augustine, as well as Boethius and Macrobius, medieval writers developed a sense that poetry should be an orderly creation whose structures, determined by the faculty of reason, paid tribute to the analogy between human and divine creation through number.

In sharp contrast to works like *The Divine Comedy* and *Pearl,* however, there is no sign of artificial construction in **Piers Plowman.** Langland's method of composition ignores proportion and shows no regard for numerology. The passus divisions are arbitrary and frequently jar with the action. Our poet does not even show an internal concern for demarcation equal to that of *Wynnere and Wastoure* where the first division concludes with the half-line "for here a Fitt endeth." This lack of structural self-consciousness carries with it implications that reach to the heart of Langland's poem. If the formal orderliness of *The Divine Comedy* emphasizes the harmony of the universe that Dante the pilgrim traverses from bottom to top, the structural irregularity of **Piers Plowman** accords with Will's experience of the disarrayed world in which he wanders.

Though indebted to a variety of formal resources—debate, sermon, satire, theological commentary, quest romance, and even apocalyptic literature—**Piers Plowman** is not finally controlled or explained by any of them. Yet the traditional genre to which Langland's poem most obviously belongs, the dream-vision, is also the form best able to create ambiguity and sustain a sense of uncertainty without any need of final resolution. Langland's contemporaries believed in unseen realities that framed and sometimes impinged upon their own: the Fair Field is bounded by the Dungeon of Hell and the Castle of Heaven, and from that castle a pardon is sent down to Piers and his followers. Dreams—though this point was constantly debated—might afford one way of seeing further, more deeply, more truly:

> Visions erased the sheer line between the known and the unknowable, the discoverable and the revealed. They interlocked the simultaneous realities; they made visible the unseen; they clarified the hidden shape of truth . . . [Carolly Erickson, *The Medieval Vision: Essays in History and Perception,* 1976].

This ingrained belief in the potential of dreams to open a portal into an invisible spiritual realm was inherited from the ancient world and granted special sanction in Macrobius' commentary on part of Cicero's *De Re Publica* ("The Dream of Scipio"), but inherited also was the suspicion that many dreams were empty and worthless. (p. 24-7)

Joining and mixing with the classical tradition was the Biblical account of how God had spoken to men in their dreams, as well as examples of how men like Joseph and Daniel correctly interpreted the dreams of others. With the large number of divine visions granted men in their sleep—the *Apocalypse of St. Paul* and the *Dream of the Rood* are two widely separated examples—it should come as no surprise to find such dreams discussed by later writers whose larger concern was mysticism. Working from the *Liber de Modo Bene Vivendi,* attributed to St. Bernard in the fourteenth century, Richard Rolle enumerates the various types and causes of dreams, again allowing for mixed visions. . . . (pp. 24-7)

[With] so many kinds and causes of dreams, the reader of a dream-poem might never be sure exactly what sort of vision he confronted, a perplexity made unusually acute in **Piers Plowman** where there is not a single dream but rather eight separate visions in the B-text, with two more dreams-within-dreams—a complication unique in all medieval literature.

Since so much uncertainty was possible, poets often provided themselves with various defenses for the truthfulness of their visions. Guillaume de Lorris begins his *Roman de la Rose* with a defense based casually on the authority of Macrobius. Relying on the Biblical tradition, the author of *Mum and the Sothsegger* responds to Cato's skepticism about dreams by asserting the positive example of Daniel. Other fourteenth-century poets, however, though appearing to follow a similar strategy, achieve quite a different effect. Chaucer prefaces *The House of Fame* with a rambling discussion of the nature of dreams in which he skeptically refuses to take a stand on either side of the question, and only hopes for the best.

Langland's passage on dreams (B. vii, 154-72) creates a comparable sense of ambiguity. Although it discredits Cato's *sompnia ne cures* (*Distichs,* II) by adducing the same Biblical authorities as *Mum and the Sothsegger,* it does not mention, as does *Dives and Pauper,* that many

Scriptural passages also reject the interpretation of dreams as a form of witchcraft. Furthermore, the contents of the dream are approved not by Langland but by the Dreamer, whose judgments are always open to suspicion. It is also worth noting that Will does not use these authorities to endorse the entire dream, only its conclusion—namely, that doing well is better than receiving a pardon from Rome (B. vii. 173-76). And finally, Will's approval applies only to this individual dream, the second vision of the poem, and not to any others before or after. The reader is placed in the uncomfortable position of having to remain alert for evidence with which to evaluate *each* later vision, evidence that does not always point to the same conclusion. When Will swoons for joy at hearing Piers' name (B.xvi, 18-22) or has a dream "as Crist wolde" (B.xiii.21-25), we feel that the dreams may well be sanctioned from above. But when the visions are described with phrases like "a ferly of Fairye" (B.prol.6) or "as it sorcerie were, a sotil þyng wiþ alle" (B.xv,12), then there is cause for doubt. The cumulative effect is one of pervasive uncertainty about the trustworthiness of these dreams, a sense of skepticism ably summed up in *Dives and Pauper:* "But forasmychil as dremys comyn on so many dyuers maner and it is wol hard to knowyn on what maner it comyn, weþer be God or be kende or be þe fend or be ony oþir wey, þerfor it is wol perlyous to settyn ony feyth þerynne."

There has been a growing consensus among critics that a narrator's eye-witness account of the events in his dream serves as an authenticating device, suspending disbelief and lending credence to what he tells. However weird and fantastical the dream, it really happened—the narrator really saw it in his mind's eye. Yet if the dreamer's testimony in poems like *Pearl* and *The Book of the Duchess* gives us the sense of a coherent visionary experience, the same cannot be said of *Piers Plowman.* Langland is masterful in his ability to weaken the integrity of the dream, blurring the distinction between dream and reality that otherwise gives the vision its special power to dazzle and convince. By moving between dreams and waking life, between dreams and dreams-within-dreams, the poem breaks down the familiar boundaries between types of experience, each with its own rules of action and perception. The audience is left confused as to where things happen, when and why.

The vision even ceases to be a vehicle for allegorical action. Familiar scenes from daily life occur in the first vision, and allegorical characters, like Need (B.xx) as well as Reason and Conscience (C. v.), appear in waking episodes. The warped logic of the dream—sometimes a mental wilderness where everything is slippery, everything problematic, nothing what it had seemed to be—begins to assert itself in Will's waking life, which comes to be equally characterized by abrupt shifts of time and place. Years pass in a few lines, a flash-back becomes the new present-moment of the action, and the Dreamer falls asleep in Malvern and wakes up in London.

If the conviction of the dream is based upon our confidence in the narrator as eye-witness, we grow increasingly uneasy with the inability of the poem, purportedly Will's attempt to set down his experiences in writing, to keep these experiences distinct. While the Dreamer is coping with his most important crises in private dreams, his life in the wide world of God's creation becomes vaguer, more confused, more and more dream-like. Rather than use the *Visio* merely to give authority to his poem as a real experience, Langland adapts the conventional features of this genre to create a sense of epistemological uncertainty, so that the reader comes away bewildered, unable to recall exactly what happened and in what order.

Another reason why the reader fails to form a clear recollection of the poem, and therefore comes away with the sense of having shared in a life of mental confusion, is the remarkable lack of visual imagery. Contrary to the various literary traditions to which *Piers Plowman* is otherwise indebted—sermons, personification allegory, and the poetics of the Alliterative movement—there is a general absence of visualization resulting in a shadowy drama of characters without attributes and names without faces. This lack of imagery would have seemed just as strange to a medieval audience—and probably more so. (pp. 27-31)

No true poet works without images, of course, especially one still writing in a Western tradition that harkens to that Horatian dictum *ut pictura poesis.* Yet when Langland invokes visual images in his use of simile or in his invention of allegorical figures like the Half Acre and Christ the Knight, he does so with scant regard for their integrity. They are likely to be juxtaposed with other images that jar with one another, or they are simply forgotten once the more important spiritual sense is revealed. David Mills points out [in "The Role of the Dreamer in *Piers Plowman,*" *"Piers Plowman": Critical Approaches,* ed. S. S. Hussey, 1969] that in Holy Church's explanation of love (B. i. 148-62), "she is compelled to use images, but shifts reference so frequently that the image breaks down." And John Burrow has observed [in "The Action of Langland's Second Vision," *Style and Symbolism in "Piers Plowman": A Modern Critical Anthology,* ed. Robert J. Blanch, 1969] that the typical piling up of similes, as in the description of Gluttony, creates a dizzying, phantasmagoric effect with shapes melting into shapes. Langland is no less cavalier in the way he abuses images which were initially invoked as vehicles for allegorical actions. Rather than sustain a coherent literal level, he creates constant interference that results in the disintegration or fading out of the image, to be replaced by the naked significance of the allegory or by a second image destined to suffer the same fate. When the Crucifixion is presented as a joust fought by Christ the Knight at Jerusalem (B. xviii), so much interference from the Biblical account creeps into the narrative that the joust is nearly forgotten, and the few remnants of the image that are left strike the audience as sustaining a metaphor rather than staging an allegory.

Even more confusing is Langland's habit of transforming and discarding images that had been part of the allegory. When he allows Piers to alter the notion of pilgrimage in the Half Acre—going on a pilgrimage is transformed into the act of plowing a field—the result is a characteristic fusion of images that destroys our mental picture, not only of the current images but also of allied images, in this case the Tower of Truth to which the pilgrims had been heading. Burrow sees all this as an entropic process in which images like the Half Acre, which seemed so full of all the right meanings at first, turn out to be too restrictive, merely provisional, "a way of putting it—not very satisfactory." As he says elsewhere, "It is as if the images which carry Langland along are consumed in the process." A certain amount of destabilization is inevitable when an allegorist tries to force a finite image like plowing to accommodate a rich spiritual meaning like pilgrimage, but Langland shows greater contempt than perhaps any other writer of the period for the limitations of images, specifically their inability to contain and communicate an elusive spiritual reality.

Langland's skeptical regard for images is evident in the ways he avoids concrete descriptions. When he does resort to imagery, he tends toward three major responses. First, as already mentioned, he moves away from the image and supersedes it with a statement of the naked spiritual truth—the jousting in Jerusalem becomes a narration of the Crucifixion—thus replacing the literal sense with the allegorical, directly stated. Next, he becomes dissatisfied with the fitness of an image and substitutes another which seems closer to the sense he is trying to establish: the pilgrimage to Truth becomes a season of plowing in the Half Acre. And thirdly, Langland capitalizes on the native ambiguity of images by creating figures whose quality *in bono* or *in malo* cannot be determined. The Dreamer himself is the supreme example of this studied ambiguity from the very beginning . . .. When he describes himself dressed as a *"sheep,"* for instance, are we to understand that he is a real shepherd, a pastor carrying on the work of the Good Shepherd, one of the lost sheep, or a wolf in sheep's clothing?

David Mills has also registered the ambiguity in Will's initial entry—"Is he a sinner, a guide to salvation, or both?"—and has felt that it contributes to the general sense of uncertainty in the poem. It is hard to know which, if any, of Empson's types of ambiguity best describes Langland's practice, whether an intention to mean several things or an indecision as to what he means, but since in subsequent waking episodes the Dreamer is described with details suggesting irreconcilable qualities of virtue and vice, I am tempted to place him in Empson's last and most disturbing category:

> . . . when the two meanings of the word, the two values of the ambiguity, are the two opposite meanings defined by the context, so that the total effect is to show a fundamental division in the writer's mind. [William Empson, *Seven Types of Ambiguity*, 1953]

Insofar as a word can be used to elicit an image in the reader's mind, it is flawed in being unable to insure that the image and its *intentio* will suit the meaning in the poet's mind—if indeed that mind is made up—and frequently it will be deficient since it cannot, by itself, embody and guarantee a spiritual lesson. I believe that the character of Piers the Plowman represents such a name, with elicited image, developed for the sake of just this limitation—Langland's fourth way of responding to the inadequacy of images—since no one can say clearly or indisputably who

he is or what he symbolizes. Mills phrases it more grandly: "Piers Plowman stands as the assertion of the nominal, himself an infinite in whom all triads meet and who unites time and space and defies change."

The poet's foredoomed hope of embodying all the spiritual meanings of his poem in the figure of a plowman finds its parallel in the Dreamer's error of thinking that Dowel is a man who resides in some inn beside the highway. Will confuses the verbal with a nominal. Irreducible in their capacity for meaning, Piers and the Three Do's are never meant to be fully knowable through the words used to describe them. Mary Carruthers is altogether convincing when she argues [in her *The Search for St. Truth; A Study of Meaning in "Piers Plowman"*, 1973] that while **Piers Plowman** may be ultimately concerned with the moral application of knowledge, its primary problem is epistemological rather than moral—and specifically that Will's mental quest is bedeviled by "the fluid, partially understood, inadequate verbal signs of an insufficient rhetoric."

Not only is Piers a nominal whose image is protean and whose essence unascertainable, he also embodies all of Langland's hostility toward the types of external show that contribute to a hollow formalism usurping the place of the inner spiritual reality and cluttering rather than illuminating the life of man. Piers sides with spirit against body, content against form, meaning against sign. His antagonism shows itself in the second vision through his work as the great substituter: he rejects the pilgrimage in favor of plowing, then tears the pardon in preference for the life of penance. In neither case does he reject the theory, only the debased form of its practice. Piers stands for a mode of perception that looks beyond the external and into the secret heart of things. Anima later explains more precisely the object of Piers' vision as the *wil* behind words and works, with another swipe at the scholastic method:

> "Clerkes haue no knowyng," quod he, "but by
> werkes and wordes.
> Ac Piers þe Plowman parceyueþ moore depper
> What is þe wille and wherfore þat many wight
> suffreþ:
> *Et vidit deus cogitaciones eorum . . .*
> Therefore by colour ne by clergie knowe shaltow
> hym neuere,
> Neiþer þorugh wordes ne werkes, but þorugh
> wil oone,
> And þat knoweþ no clerk ne creature on erþe
> But Piers þe Plowman, *Petrus id est Christus.*"
> (B. xv. 198-200 and 209-12)

Langland is concerned with a problem that had vexed Englishmen from the dawn of the Christian tradition. Bede had said that the quality of a man's will could be known by his deeds—"Per arborem intelligimus seu bonam seu malam voluntatem"—but elsewhere admitted to the impossibility of judging man's will and intent by external acts like the giving of alms. This doubt is echoed by a fourteenth-century mystic quoting St. Gregory ["Our Daily Work," *Yorkshire Writers: Richard Rolle of Hampole and His Followers*, ed. C. Horstman, 1895-96]: "Mani semes gode dedes & are noght gode, for þai are noght done with a gode wille." We find an enlargement of Augustinian skepticism, resembling Wyclif's own, applied to all human acts and institutions, as well as the transitory objects of the created world, that is, all the objects of human perception. "Because people cannot directly perceive the inner world of the spirit and the will," says Burrow, "they are inclined to forget about it, and become preoccupied with forms of words and external observances which in themselves have no value."

Langland's personal solution could have been the same one chosen by other souls beset by this crisis. He might have turned to a life of austere piety, devoid of ritual and occupied by a continual meditation according to the *via negativa,* looking beyond the jig-saw world of images and into the wordless purity of God's will. Fortunately for later generations of readers, this is not the alternative he chose. While he approves the life of the ascetic and the contemplative, he realizes that the vast majority of men must follow the active life of this world and struggle with all the encumbrances it imposes. To them he offers his poem.

Haukyn stands as the archetype of the active man whose soul is constantly soiled by contact with the world:

> "And kouþe I neuere, by Crist! kepen it clene an
>   houre
> That I ne soiled it wiþ sighte or som ydel speche,
> Or þorugh *werk* or þorugh *word* or *wille* of myn
>   herte
> That I ne flobre it foule fro morwe til euen."
>   (B. xiv. 12-15; emphasis mine)

Surely part of the solution to Haukyn's problem has already been included in Langland's previous discussion of the Three Do's. Patience, quoting a definition given by Charity, says that Dobest means to love God and keep His Commandments:

> "Wiþ *wordes* and *werkes,*" quod she, "and *wil* of
>   þyn herte
> Thow loue leelly þi soule al þi lif tyme.
> And so þow lere þe to louye, for þe lordes loue
>   of heuene,
> Thyn enemy in alle wise eueneforþ wiþ þiselue."
>   (B. xiii. 140-43; emphasis mine)

This adds to Clergy's earlier definition of Dobet as acting in strict accord with one's intent:

> "Loke þow werche it in *werk* þat þi *word*
>   sheweþ;
> Swich as þow semest in sighte be in assay
>   yfounde;
> *Appare quod es vel esto quod appares*;
> And lat no body be by þi beryng bigiled
> But be swich in þi soule as þow semest wiþoute."
>   (B. x. 260-63; emphasis mine)

And even earlier, the two friars had told the Dreamer that his wit and free will needed to work according to Dowel's instructions:

> "God wole suffre wel þi *sleuþe* if þiself likeþ,
> For he yaf þee to yeresghyue to yeme wel þiselue
> *Wit* and *free wil,* to euery wight a porcion,
> To fleynge foweles, to fisshes and to beestes.
> Ac man haþ moost þerof and moost is to blame
> But if he werche wel þerwiþ as Dowel hym
>   techeþ."
>   (B. viii. 51-56; emphasis mine)

In all four passages, and in many others that could be cited, Langland emphasizes the need for man to have a virtuous will and to act well according to its choices and assertions. A discrepancy between will and action would generate many of the difficulties already listed, such as focusing attention, ordering mental images, deciding, and actually doing. Yet the failure of the will, even a good will, to fulfill its duty in directing the actions of the body raised a problem of special concern to Langland: the problem of *acedia* or sloth, which the two friars in the passage quoted above hae singled out as the Dreamer's most prominent vice.

I have sought in the preceding pages to expose some of the tangled roots of fourteenth-century skepticism and to discuss some of its ramifications, both philosophical and artistic, as they appear in ***Piers Plowman.* . . .** [Most] of the poem's changes in direction, as well as its tensions, are created by the multiplication of alternatives, because instead of choosing among the possible precepts for moral action, Langland moves on to refine or redefine the alternatives without ever making clear-cut decisions. His sense of crisis would not have been so severe if he had accepted a basic "double-truth theory" as did Aquinas, so that the discoveries of the intellect could be considered merely provisional, forever open to revision if new evidence or a clearer theory were found, while the tenets of faith were left undisturbed. But Langland insists that there *is* a single Truth and that all the tools of the inquiring mind must be used in searching for it, for better or worse, even if the mind risks becoming so intent on inquiry that it loses sight of its goal.

Langland's opening vision shows the whole of humanity poised between the great alternatives of Truth and Falsehood—God and Satan, Heaven and Hell. Although the Dreamer is told that the foremost representative of falseness is Lady Mede, we later discover that there are *two* types of meed and that virtue lies in choosing the right one and rejecting the wrong (B. iii. 231-33). Later the people set out on a pilgrimage toward a destination called Truth, which had been defined by theologians as the accord between human will and the will of God, but the collective will of the folk wavers in the Half Acre, where all concludes in wrangling and despair. In the second vision we expect that the stalemate over the best way to reach Truth will be dispelled by the arrival of a pardon sent to Piers and all his followers. Instead of a resolution, however, the pardon gives rise to another conflict and another set of alternatives: the invalidity of the document argued by the Priest as opposed to the value of the message endorsed by Piers. Langland's skill in making the outcome ambiguous is evidenced by the heated debate among modern scholars. What has seldom been appreciated is that Langland chooses this episode to bring Will into the action and position him, significantly, midway between the Priest and Piers so that he can read over their shoulders. And Will remains suspended between these two alternatives even after he has awakened. Although he inclines toward Piers' position, he does not act upon it. Nor does he wholly reject the Priest's argument. He merely decides that trusting in pardons "is noght *so siker* for þe soule, certes, as is Dowel"

(B. vii. 186). Relative sureness is not tantamount to certainty, only to a refinement of doubt.

In setting off to search for Dowel, the Dreamer has made a choice of sorts, though it is no more successful than the decision of the folk to set out on a pilgrimage to Truth's Tower. In neither case is the chosen alternative completely known, and in neither case do the arbiters act fully upon their decisions. Both failures can be attributed specifically to the will, whose main function after judging between alternatives is directing the soul and body to act in favor of that choice. The search for Truth and the quest for Dowel are finally problems for the will—for the communal will of the folk and, more specifically as the poem progresses, for Will the Dreamer. And these problems were made more complicated for Langland and his audience by a host of conjectures raised during a fierce fourteenth-century debate over human volition, its powers, its limitations, and its role in the salvation of man's soul. (pp. 31-9)

> John M. Bowers, "Langland in an Age of Crisis," in his The Crisis of Will in "Piers Plowman," The Catholic University of America Press, 1986, pp. 1-39.

Laurie A. Finke   (essay date 1987)

[*In the following excerpt, Finke studies the elusiveness of meaning in the B-text of* Piers Plowman, *claiming that "the promise of a truth in, behind, or beyond the poem's language, and with it the possibility that Will's dreams actually mean 'something,' is from the beginning of the poem both proffered and withheld."*]

[The **B-text** of] ***Piers Plowman,*** at times, seems almost an allegory of the impossibility of discovering either significance or truth within language, whether one searches for divine or merely for human significance. Language in the poem . . . becomes "a vehicle for classification (of ways of life, of mental powers), a means of imposing order (the law), [and] a means of disorder and deception. More often than not . . . one cannot distinguish between these uses of language. . . . Man's language, although created in the image of the Logos, is capable of only an imperfect parody of it." The more human language strives to represent the world, the more it is trapped and frustrated by its own failure to assure referentiality.

Piers Plowman's resistance to interpretation inheres in its own interpretations of its difficulties. The dreamer's question "How may I save my soul?" leads him to search for Truth (Passus I-VII), for Dowel (Passus VIII-XIV), and finally for Piers himself (Passus XV-XX). These quests become, in one sense, the search for a transcendental signified that would legitimate all the human signs of the mundane world, the world of the "fair field" and the "half acre." Indeed, the promise of a truth in, behind, or beyond the poem's language, and with it the possibility that Will's dreams actually mean "something," is from the beginning of the poem both proffered and withheld. The opening tableau of ***Piers Plowman*** seems simple enough; Will, the poem's narrator, falls asleep and dreams:

> [Ac] as I biheeld into þe Eest, and heigh to þe
>   sonne,

> I seigh a tour on a toft treiliche ymaked,
> A deep dale byneþe, a dongeon þerInne
> Wiþ depe diches and derke and dredfull of
>   sighte.
> A fair feeld ful of folk fond I þer bitwene.
>   (Prologue 13-17)

The dreamer's sight here ("biheeld") is figurative rather than literal. What he sees are not things but representations of things. The dreamscape is composed of signifiers—tower, dungeon, and field—that seem to mean more than the poet tells us about them, that seem to point to other signifiers. The simplicity of the physical scene shades into the ambiguity of interpretation. The reader, like the dreamer, is compelled to ask, "What may it [by] meene?" The scene, in short, demands a gloss, an interpretation, additional text to explain the poetic utterance. The space that exists between the images of the tower, dungeon, and field and what they signify becomes the figural space of interpretation. It can be bridged or filled only by the attempt to understand it, by reading or creating a text that comments upon the text.

In the A and B versions the interpretation of this scene is deferred until Passus I, where the dreamer's first guide, Holi chirche, glosses these images. Of the "tour on þe toft" she tells the dreamer, "truþe is þerInne" (I, 8); in the dungeon, "Wonyeþ a [wye] þat wrong is yhote; / Fader of falsehed" (I, 63-64). The rhetoric of her commentary initially encourages the dreamer to believe that his vision "means" something, that he can pursue a rational account of the allegorical world in which he finds himself, and that the process of interpretation requires simply a translation or a substitution of one set of terms for another. The tower is Truth, the dungeon is Falsehood or Wrong. Holi chirche encourages the dreamer, in this regard, to believe that Truth is something within his reach, a goal, like the tower, at the end of a journey. Truth can be found simply by avoiding *temporalia* or the "tresor" of the world: "þat trusten on his tresor bitraye[d are] sonnest" (I, 70).

The literalness of Will's allegorical thinking, his belief that word and thing can coincide to create meaning, emerges in his request to Holi chirche to "Teche me to no tresor, but tel me þis ilke, / How I may saue my soule" (I, 83-84). But Holi chirche's answer undermines the dreamer's faith in the precision of allegorical language by troping on the very signifier he has rejected as false: "Whan alle tresors arn tried treuþe is þe beste" (I, 85). Neither meaning nor truth, it seems, is as unproblematic as Will had thought, nor the relationships between signs and signifieds nearly as simple or stable. In one instance, treasure is equated with the corruption of falsehood; in another, Truth is described as the best of all treasures. Apparently there are two kinds of treasure: one that is earthly and visible to the dreamer, and one that is invisible and not easily circumscribed by language, even the language of allegory. Each signifier—true treasure, false treasure—defines itself in terms of the other; each, therefore, exists only in opposition to its opposite.

The literal-minded dreamer, however, does not understand Holi chirche's explanation. What he wants is to lo-

A depiction of fourteenth-century London with London bridge in the background.

cate a simple means of identifying truth and to pass in silence over the problematics of representation.

> "Yet haue I no kynde knowyng," quod I, "ye
>   mote kenne me bettre
> By what craft in my cors it [truth] comseþ and
>   where."
>
>   (I, 138-39)

Will is interested in only half of the Augustinian dialectic; for him, allegory is a means of "comprehending the eternal and spiritual" by means of "corporal and temporal things" (*On Christian Doctrine*). Holi chirche cannot clarify what truth is, and her inability becomes a measure of the difference or the distance between language and what it represents. The dreamer desires a language that can express experience unequivocally and so allow him to dominate it. However, his guide's response generates not certainties, but more commentary, more opportunities for interpretation.

Holi chirche's response is a *dilatio* on truth. A rhetorical trope of amplification often cited in medieval *ars praedicandi, dilatio,* from the Latin *dilatare,* suggests both a deferral and a spreading out. In this respect, Holi chirche's answer simultaneously postpones the dreamer's inquiry and widens its perspective until it encompasses—or attempts to encompass—everything, including the divine.

> For truþe telleþ þat loue is triacle of heuene:

> May no synne be on hym seene þat vseþ þat
>   spice,
> And alle hise werkes he wroughte with loue as
>   hym liste;
> And lered it Moyses for þe leueste þyng and
>   moost lik to heuene,
> And [ek] þe pl[ante] of pees, moost precious of
>   vertues.
> For heuene myghte nat holden it, [so heuy it
>   semed,]
> Til it hadde of þe erþe [y]eten [hitselue].
> And whan it hadde of þis fold flessh and blood
>   taken
> Was neuere leef vpon lynde lighter þerafter,
> And portatif and persaunt as þe point of a nedle
> That myghte noon Armure it lette ne none
>   heighe walles.
>
>   (I, 148-58)

As this passage suggests, *Piers Plowman's* poetry is most eloquent—literally, most full of speech—when its language proclaims its own inadequacy. Here it attempts to describe and explain the mysteries of divinity by accumulating a series of highly antithetical images. Yet the allegory circles around the idea of God's highest expression of love and truth—the Incarnation—by calling that love "heuy" and light as "leef vpon linde," "triacle," and "portatif and persaunt," able to pierce any armor or wall. The same phrase, "For heuene myghte nat holden it," is used to describe both the Incarnation and Lucifer's fall from heaven. This passage is characteristic of the poem as a whole: language does not progress toward an illumination of truth but falls into the deferral of its own rhetoric. Each sign produces the next sign in a repetitive sequence that never arrives at anything but the next trope. The more the poem's language attempts to describe the divine, the less referential—and the more reflexive—it becomes.

I have quoted extensively from the poem's opening episode because it is typical of Langland's double-edged handling of allegory. The complications inherent in Holi chirche's explanation of the opening tableau are paradigmatic of the poem's repetitive, circular structure, its technique of *dilatio* to defer and expand on the referentiality of its language. Simple, apparently unequivocal figures—Truth and later Dowel and Piers himself—are complicated by the very attempt to define or explicate them. These terms, which de Man might call "primitive words," cannot be defined because their "pretended definitions are infinite regresses of accumulated tautologies"; in other words, they can be explained only by recourse to tropes that, like all attempts to represent the unrepresentable, proclaim absence instead of presence, darkness instead of light. Figures—truth is a tower, for instance, or divine love is "triacle"—offer similitudes in the place of definitions, what Derrida calls identity in difference, not the mystical identity that Coleridge located in the symbol.

The need to dilate—to explain, define, and distinguish—in *Piers Plowman* generates the endless monologues so characteristic of all three versions of the poem. These monologues seem to answer every question but the one that Will has asked precisely because it cannot be answered in human terms. His question is Augustine's: How can one distinguish the true or the divine in a fallen world? Yet the more Will seeks to learn (the more questions he asks, the more answers he seeks), the more text is generated and the more complicated the commentary becomes. Each gloss leads not to definitive answers or interpretations but to more glossing. Passus I ends with Holi chirche's reiterating "Whan all tresors ben tried treuþe is þe beste" (I, 207). But the dreamer is no more enlightened than he was before he asked his question. At the opening of Passus II he rephrases his inquiry and asks Holi chirche, "Kenne me by som craft to know þe false" (II, 4). Although the question changes, the rhetorical context does not. Commentary necessitates further commentary. Texts proliferate, but the substance, the thing that Will seeks, remains unattainable.

This "web of words" is the essence of allegory: "a textual plot of another text's tale, a figure of a figure." The nature of allegory, as de Man argues in "The Rhetoric of Temporality," always presents itself as repetition within both the temporal sequence of language—the syntagmatic succession of signs—and the temporal sequence of narrative—the metonymic succession of episodes. The sign always refers to and repeats a previous sign with which it can never coincide. The "meaning" that the allegorical sign constitutes consists only of repetition, which implies, in the Derridean sense of iterability, both identity and difference: "the identity of the *selfsame* [must] be repeatable and identifiable *in, through,* and even *in view of* its alteration." Repetition inscribes in allegory two senses of time: a progression from one manifestation or incident to the next, and a mere iteration of the same. This dual sense of time is what leads Miller to identify the irony of repetition as the trope of all narrative and de Man to privilege allegory as the trope of irony.

The allegorical narrative of **Piers Plowman,** in this respect, operates within two time frames: the temporal narrative of Long Will's quest for Truth (and later for Dowel and Piers), and the atemporal antinarrative of the dream which frustrates the dreamer's attempts to go forward. Dream visions and journeys are commonplace in medieval allegory precisely because they reflect the disjunction within allegory between sign and signified. In **Piers Plowman** these two allegorical strategies are "brought together" in such a way that, more often than not, they work at cross-purposes. The journey is metonymic and sequential; it imparts to the poem a sense of forward movement because it suggests that the signified, like the tower in the Prologue or the King at Westminster who arbitrates the marriage of Meed, may be what the dreamer seeks, even as it displaces his goal beyond wherever he happens to be. The dream, on the other hand, is metaphoric and ahistorical; it frustrates progression by making the goal into something else, by offering the endlessly referential web of words that lead only into labyrinthine repetition. The narrative pattern of the poem, then, creates a dialectical tension between the journey and the dream which simultaneously asserts and destroys the narrative's claim to linear progression.

The search for Truth which occupies the *Visio* illustrates this disjunction between the narrative's two displacements, the dream and the journey. After witnessing the confessions of the Seven Deadly Sins, the folk on the field set out, at Reason's urging, to "seken Seynt Truth, for he may saue yow alle" (V, 57). Their quest repeats Will's earlier quest for Truth, with a difference but with the same results: the forward impetus of the journey stalls as the dream repeats the symbols of desire. On the pilgrimage the folk encounter two guides, who, like Holi chirche, attempt to gloss the signs. The first is a pilgrim, or at least a "leode" "apparailled . . . in pilgrymes wise." His staff, bowl, and bag, his "Ampulles," "shelles," and "vernycle," are the "signes" of his pilgrimages, his quests for his "soules hele." But as signs they point only to other signs and other journeys: "Syney," the "Sepulchre," "Bethlem," "Alisaundre." He cannot tell the pilgrims the way to Truth, the way to pure signification, because his understanding does not extend beyond the signs themselves: "I [ne] seigh neuere Palmere wiþ pyk ne wiþ scrippe / Asken after hym [truth] er now in þis place" (V, 535-36).

The forward progression of the journey is halted; it repeats the sequence with the sudden dreamlike appearance of the second guide, Piers the Plowman, who offers to lead the folk to Truth. He conceives of the way to Truth as a series of signposts pointing the way in a moral landscape: a place called "swere-noght-but-it-be-for-nede-and-name-liche-on-idel-þe-name-of-god-almyghty," for example, or a croft called "Coueite-noght-mennes-catel-ne-hire-wyues-ne-noon-of-hire-seruantgh-þat-noyen-hem-myght." This allegorical description (V, 561-82) is no doubt long and dull, but its very lack of poetic immediacy—its plodding, one-to-one correspondence between physical place and spiritual state—comments on the failure of the epistemology of the **Visio,** its search for truth and transcendent meaning. The folk's encounters with the pilgrim and Piers again highlight the disjunction between outward signs and the always elusive inner meaning of truth.

In the last two passus of the **Visio,** Piers attempts to redeem the spiritual signification of the pilgrimage, to close the gap between outward forms and spiritual meaning, by transforming this trope into another trope.

> "And I shal apparaille me" quod Perkyn, "in pilgrymes wise
> And wende wiþ yow [þe wey] til we fynde truþe,"
> [He caste on] his cloþes, yclouted and hole,
> [His] cokeres and [hise] coffes for cold of his mailes,
> And [heng his] hoper at [his] hals in stede of a Scryppe.
>
> (VI, 57-61)

In this passage the image of the quest or journey gives way to the repetitive, circular action of plowing as Piers sets the folk to work. The "cokeres," "coffes," and "hoper," the signs of Piers's life of virtuous labor, replace the traditional signs of the pilgrimage: bowl, bag, and scrip. The simple life of labor, Piers assures the folk and the dreamer, will lead them at last to Truth. But all that this plowing of the fields leads them to is yet another dead end that requires more commentary, yet another textual *dilatio,* another attempt to redefine or resignify the *Visio*'s key terms. When the folk cannot persevere in their labor, Truth sends them a pardon, a document that emphasizes metaphorically the disjunction between temporal words and the allegorical incarnation of the spirit. The allegory of Truth's pardon . . . sets the pardon's spiritual significance as a reflection of God's grace against its debasement as an image of ecclesiastical corruption, a popular target of fourteenth-century satire. Piers's tearing of the pardon and his squabbling with the priest mark the end of the dream before the quest to find Truth has reached a satisfactory conclusion.

The interpretive difficulties that the *Visio* creates inhere, in large measure, in the oppositions between the *Visio*'s principal signs—between true treasure and false treasure, true meed and false meed, true pilgrimage and false pilgrimage, true pardon and false pardon. These dialectical oppositions exist symbiotically; each undermines and reinforces its opposite. The language of the poem's allegory is, to borrow Miller's description of Yeats's prose, "always forced to say the opposite of what it seems to want to say, as well as the opposite of that opposite." This "deconstructive" process of the allegorical text's undoing itself is not, however, nihilistic, nor does it become a simple reversal of dialectical hierarchies that privilege meaninglessness over meaning. The allegory of *Piers Plowman*—its reflexive questioning—is both an attempt to represent what is unrepresentable and an attempt to transcend the mundane world circumscribed by the folk on the field. Its image in the text is the quest, which, precisely because it can never reach a conclusion, must be repeated, for example in the *Vita*'s quest for Dowel and in the quest for Piers with which the poem breaks off. In essence, the rest of the poem unfolds as a repetition of the first two visions, the B and C versions as repetitions with a difference of the A version.

After tearing the pardon and abandoning the life of virtuous labor for that of prayer, Piers all but disappears from the poem until Passus XV, when Anima mentions him as the perfect exemplar of charity. His appearance and transformation at this juncture illuminate the way in which the action of the poem is now generated not by the quest but by language, by puns. This wordplay points to external and material coincidences between signifiers and distorts logocentric fictions about meaning. Piers himself becomes less a "character" than an instance of what happens to a fallen language in its attempts to define its own limitations. As Maureen Quilligan suggests, language becomes a principal actor in the poem—not simply a medium of expression, however imperfect, but an example of what happens to the spirit, to faith, when it is incarnated in the physical world. The actor in Passus XVI-XIX is not Piers the character but "Piers" the signifier, a deferral of the linguistic roots—the puns—that comprise its unstable identity.

When Anima mentions Piers in Passus XV, he is no longer the virtuous laborer who set the folk to work in Passus VI, no longer simply a plowman. His name, inscribed in Anima's phrase *"Petrus id est christus,"* has become a pun that harks back not only to Piers's namesake St. Peter but also to the etymology of Piers's name, from the Old

French *pierre* and the Latin *petrus* for rock, also for foundation or support. Anima's phrase, in this regard, becomes a kind of shorthand for Christ's words to Peter (Matt. 16.18): *"Tu es Petrus, et super hanc petram aedificabo ecclesiam meam"* [You are Peter, and upon this rock I will build my church]. The name Piers is embedded both in the logocentric tradition of etymology, of biblical exegesis, and in the nameless incidence of faith. From a description of the mundane rock, *petrus* achieves a figural significance—the foundation or support for the Church—gathering to itself a tradition of meanings that transcend any one interpretation. The allegorical significance of the name, then, goes beyond what language can possibly describe: the phrase *Petrus id est christus* becomes the incarnation of the divine as a pun on the dual nature of man-as-god.

The pun on Piers's name generates the plot of Passus XVI-XVIII by setting in motion biblical history. The dreamer learns that Piers, no longer a plowman, guards the tree of charity (B XVI). In the course of the dream, the tree becomes an elaborate metonymy for the tree of knowledge (the paradisaical *lignum vitae*) and the tree of the cross, both, as Gerhardt Ladner notes, "part of the metahistorical and historical economy of salvation" ["Medieval and Modern Understanding of Symbolism: A Comparison," *Speculum* 54 (1979)]. The tree is supported by three "piles," props or supports that, with Piers, protect the tree and its fruit from assault by the winds and by demons. The tree's "fruit" is postlapsarian mankind—Adam, Abraham, Isaias, Samson, Samuel, John the Baptist, and the like. When Piers shakes the tree to fetch an "apple" for the dreamer, this "fruit" falls and is gathered up by the Devil, initiating the temporal sequence of biblical history from the Fall to Christ's passion, death, and resurrection. The elaborate and bizarre allegory of the tree of charity, with Piers its gardener, is the first of a series of tropes centered on Piers's name which reenact the history of Christianity. These culminate in the allegory of the Christ-knight in which the Incarnation and Passion are figured as Christ jousting in "Piers armes" (B XVIII, 22) and in the final appearance of Piers in Passus XIX as the Church Militant, the institutional embodiment of faith and spirit as doctrine.

Yet this "sequence" in the poem is itself figural, a representation not of progression but of progressive revelation. Piers does not begin as one kind of signifier and "become" another; his name comprehends multiple meanings, none of which—not even *Petrus id est christus*—is definitive. "Piers" represents not an historical accretion of meaning but the mystery of the unchanging Word that cannot be interpreted, only made manifest. Will's final visions thus unfold in a temporal language that reveals, rather than represents in a more traditional sense, the timeless, ahistorical object of the dreamer's quest for faith. That this revelation can be only obscure and partial, that the essence of what stands behind and gives meaning to the signifier can never be certainly "known," is suggested by the way in which the poem simply breaks off. There is no conclusion, no end to the quest, but only the dreamlike repetition of Will still searching for the absent Piers.

In one sense, *Piers Plowman* becomes what de Man calls an allegory of reading; it explores the process of coming to terms with its own unreadability. Yet allegory—as the failure of literary language to demonstrate a one-to-one correspondence between signs and signifieds—also becomes the mode of faith. *Piers Plowman* does not fool around with literary language but with the inadequacy of theological language; it is an attempt to explore the generic limitations of allegory not simply as a vehicle for truth but as an epistemological exploration of the mysteries of the Incarnation, which, as Augustine suggests, enables truth. Such a reading of *Piers Plowman* posits an alternative to the authoritative procedure sanctioned by Augustinian hermeneutics:

> Whatever appears in the divine Word that does not literally pertain to virtuous behavior or to the truth of faith you must take to be figurative. . . . Scripture teaches nothing but charity, nor condemns anything except cupidity. (*On Christian Doctrine*, p. 88)

This reading of *Piers Plowman* promotes a knowledge—and a transcendence—that, far from enlightening the reader, forces him or her to take a "leap into darkness," a nearly Kierkegaardian leap of faith. The silence that Augustine maintains in the face of the divine, and the silence with which *Piers Plowman* breaks off, may be read as acts of faith as well as the "stillness of metaphysical irony." In this sense, the wandering and the wondering, the quest and the question, are the poem's mechanisms for trying to recover the signified; and the word "recover" suggests paradoxically the hiddenness and the discovery, the absence and the presence, of what lies behind the word. (pp. 57-68)

> *Laurie A. Finke, "Truth's Treasure: Allegory and Meaning in 'Piers Plowman',"* in Medieval Texts & Contemporary Readers, *edited by Laurie A. Finke and Martin B. Shichtman, Cornell University Press, 1987, pp. 51-68.*

Malcolm Godden   (essay date 1990)

[*In the following excerpt, Godden discusses some problems inherent in the critical perception of* Piers Plowman *as "an account of the spiritual progress or growth in understanding of the dreamer." He argues that this interpretation may overemphasize the search for coherence in the poem, thereby detracting from the work's most imaginative moments.*]

In recent years the view that has come to figure most prominently as an explanation of [*Piers Plowman*'s] central concerns and organisation is the argument that the poem is an account of the spiritual progress or growth in understanding of the dreamer, usually called Will for this purpose. The poem is thus to be seen as a kind of *Pilgrim's Progress* adapted to the first person, in which the dreamer functions as an everyman-figure undergoing an exemplary ascent from sin and ignorance to enlightenment. Characteristic expressions of this view are: 'this is substantially a poem about Will and his attempts to find out the truth about the human condition'; 'the story of Will's growth in knowledge and understanding provides the poem's one consistent thread of narrative'; 'Will's development

through his dreams and waking vicissitudes gives the poem linear progression'; 'the sequence depends for its continuity on the character of the dreamer; Will's presence alone holds this poem together. The quest for salvation is his personal quest'.

The difficulty with such views, as has several times been pointed out, is that they require a fair degree of extrapolation from occasional details in the poem. Though dream poems are common in the Middle Ages, *Piers Plowman* is unique in employing a series of dreams, and the interrelationships of the poet with his various personae are correspondingly complex. As we have seen above, Langland plays with varied and at times contradictory pictures of his persona's status and way of life. There are also important distinctions to be made in the authorial voice and stance. Thus in formal terms one can distinguish between the I-figure who is a character within the dreams, involved in the dream action and engaged in conversation with other characters in the dream—the dreamer—and the I-figure who has the dreams, reports them to the reader, comments on them himself, and acts and speaks outside the dreams—the narrator. The dreamer's main role is to question authority-figures and he is therefore presented fairly consistently as a naive and ignorant character, but his degree of prominence in the visions varies. In the first vision of the A version he questions Holy Church about the scene before him and acts as object for her teaching, but in the whole of the second vision he figures only in the single line reporting that he read the Pardon:

> And I behynde hem bothe beheld al the bulle.
> (A viii 92)

In the third he argues with a series of authority figures about the definition of Do-wel and finds himself the object of Study's criticisms. In the continuation of the third vision in the B version Langland begins with an account of the dreamer's life and makes him briefly the protagonist of a kind of fable or morality-play plot, as an exemplary sinner. The dreamer seems initially to be the protagonist of the fourth vision too, but he soon becomes a peripheral figure, with no role in the second half of the vision, and in the subsequent visions he reverts to a subordinate position, questioning authority-figures and guides about the vision and occasionally responding to events with emotion. In the final vision he is attacked by Elde and passes through penance to the House of Unity, but these moments seem incidental to the main concerns of the vision. Where the dreamer figure of *The Romance of the Rose* has the consistent aim of winning the rose and the figure in *Pearl* a consistent aim of understanding his daughter's situation, the dreamer in *Piers* takes his cue from events as they unfold. His questions vary from 'what is false?' in the first vision to 'what is Do-wel?' in the third and fourth and 'what is charity?' in the fifth.

The narrator is in some respects very like the dreamer: there is little difference, for instance, between the narrator questioning the friars about Do-wel in the prologue to the third vision and the dreamer questioning Thought and Wit within the vision. The representation of the narrator in the B version as 'witless' (B xiii I) and 'a fool' (B xv 3) chimes well with the presentation of the dreamer as naïve and ignorant within the dreams. But often the narrator speaks with much more authority, as if on behalf of the poet himself, both inside and outside the visions. The earliest example is a comment in the Prologue on the corruption of the friars:

> But holy chirche and hy holden bet togidere,
> The moste meschief on molde is mountyng up
> faste.
>
> (A Prol. 63-4)

This direct address by the narrator to the reader, warning of disaster if Church and the friars remain divided, clearly belongs to a quite different personality from the one sharply rebuked for his stupidity by Holy Church only a little later:

> 'Thou dotide daffe,' quath heo, 'dulle arn thine
> wittes.'
>
> (A i 129)

The narrator in the Prologue reflects the views of the poet, as revealed by the whole poem, rather than the stupidity of a straw man. Other examples of this authoritative voice are the description of the contents of the Pardon in the second vision and the commentary on the vision, some of the interventions in B xi (e.g. ll. 153ff), the passage on sloth at B xiii 409-56, the passage on the clergy at B xx 277-94, the address to Reason on the clergy and the state of society in C v. Thus while the narrator is sometimes represented as a naïve and foolish figure somewhat like the dreamer, at other times, both within the dream descriptions and outside them, he can address the reader directly in an authoritative voice, commenting on the issues on behalf of the author. At times, and no doubt for reasons linked with the poet's own uncertainties, it is difficult to tell which of these voices or masks Langland is using; the closing speech of the A version, for example, is assigned by one editor to the dreamer, by others to the narrator.

This complex interweaving of authorial personae and voices is something we are now familiar with from Chaucer: In *Troilus and Criseyde* too the narrator can speak as a *faux-naif* sympathising with Criseyde, as a poet struggling with his art and as a stern moralist condemning both his characters. A similar mix of voices is to be heard in the Pardoner's tale and the Merchant's. Langland's awareness of what he is doing, and pleasure in it, is nowhere more evident than in the witty lines in the A text version of the Pardon, where the merchants, delighted to find themselves included in the document, reward Will for writing it:

> Thanne were marchauntis merye; many wepe
> for joye,
> And yaf Wille for his writyng wollene clothis;
> For he copiede thus here clause, thei couden
> hym gret mede.
>
> (A viii 42-4)

Will appears here as a character in the dream-world with the merchants, but the person who has written the crucial clause of the Pardon is neither the dreamer, who has merely observed it, nor the narrator, who has merely dreamed about it, but William Langland the poet.

The I-figure contributes much of the sense of drama and debate, rather than mere exposition, which characterises the poem, but both within the dream and in the waking state he remains as full of questions and uncertainty at the end as he is at the beginning, and his own remarks and responses provide little evidence of a growth in understanding. Indeed, as the discussion above shows, he is really a complex of different identities and voices rather than a single personality. Those who see the poem as the story of Will seem in fact to be thinking of an imaginary figure lurking behind the action rather than the explicit I-figure. Thus Derek Pearsall writes in a recent study, 'the poem ends, full circle, with the dreamer going out once more in search of Piers Plowman' [*Old English and Middle English Poetry,* 1977]. In fact it is not the dreamer but the character Conscience who sets off to seek Piers; indeed, despite the 'once more' there are no instances at all in the poem of the dreamer seeking Piers. A. V. C. Schmidt implicitly recognises [in his *Piers Plowman*] that problem and corrects Pearsall when he says of the dreamer 'whilst at his final awakening it is not he but Conscience who sets out as a pilgrim, it has become clear that Will has advanced from identification with the folk of the field and later with their representative, the Active Man Haukyn, to a real if implied identification with Conscience'. The argument has a kind of cogency but the Will who is described here is not the figure called 'Will' or 'I' in the poem but a rather more hypothetical figure corresponding to the critics' own reconstructions of the poem's development.

If there are problems in making the story of the dreamer serve as the thematic centre and organising principle of the poem, it is admittedly hard to offer anything else in its place. Indeed, the desire to find such coherence may itself be a hampering modern obsession which distracts attention from the real strengths and attractions of the poem. It is at the moments of radical change in direction and thought that the poem is at its imaginative best. What the history of the poem suggests is that the successive versions and the individual visions grew gradually out of each other, not from any preconceived design but from a continued and intensely imaginative engagement with the issues of the time and the tensions of the poet's aspirations. As Langland himself tells us, if he had known the answers when he started he would not have written the poem:

> 'If ther were any wight that wolde me telle
> What were Dowel and Dobet and Dobest at the
> laste,
> Wolde I nevere do werk, but wende to holi chir-
> che
> And there bidde my bedes but whan ich ete or
> slepe.'
>
> (B xii 25-8)

The topics which Langland confronts were of vital importance for his time, and the whole tone of the poetry indicates a poet who cared passionately about them. If we can detect an overall pattern or progress in the later versions of the poem, it is because they record the development of Langland's own arguments with himself. (pp. 21-4)

*Malcolm Godden, "The Poem and the Poet,"
in his* The Making of Piers Plowman, *Longman, 1990, pp. 1-28.*

FURTHER READING

Aers, David. *"Piers Plowman" and Christian Allegory.* New York: St. Martin's Press, 1975, 141 p.
  Aims "to provide a sound basis for reading and interpreting *Piers Plowman*" through a determination of the elements of Christian and poetic allegory it contains.

———. *Chaucer, Langland and the Creative Imagination.* London: Routledge & Kegan Paul, 1980, 236 p.
  Attempts to "grasp the specific meaning and resonance" of the poetry of Chaucer and Langland by close attention to the historical context of each author.

Alford, John A., ed. *A Companion to "Piers Plowman."* Berkeley and Los Angeles: University of California Press, 1988, 286 p.
  Collection of critical essays surveying the critical heritage of *Piers Plowman,* its medieval context and poetic influences, and its textual and linguistic issues.

Baldwin, Anna P. *The Theme of Government in "Piers Plowman."* Cambridge: Boydell & Brewer, D. S. Brewer, 1981, 107 p.
  Aims to "set Langland's discussions of government in their precise context in the fourteenth century, and to relate them to each other and to the poem as a whole."

Bennett, J. A. W. "The Passion in *Piers Plowman.*" In his *Poetry of the Passion: Studies in Twelve Centuries of English Verse,* pp. 85-112. Oxford: Oxford University Press, Clarendon Press, 1982.
  Traces the allusive presentation of the passion of Christ in *Piers Plowman.*

Bertz, Douglas. "Prophecy and Apocalypse in Langland's *Piers Plowman,* B-Text, Passus XVI to XIX." *Journal of English and Germanic Philology* LXXXIV, No. 3 (July 1985): 313-27.
  Shows how and why a shift in emphasis occurs in *Piers Plowman* in passus XVI to XIX, from a concentration on the present to a focus on future events.

Blanch, Robert J., ed. *Style and Symbolism in "Piers Plowman": A Modern Critical Anthology.* Knoxville: The University of Tennessee Press, 1969, 275 p.
  Collection of critical essays whose authors attempt "to elucidate the literary value of *Piers Plowman* as poetry."

Bowers, R. H. "*Piers Plowman* and the Literary Historians." *College English* 21, No. 1 (October 1959): 1-4.
  Claims that *Piers Plowman* has been misinterpreted as a confused, structurally flawed poem of social protest, when it is actually "wholly traditional and finely attuned to medieval sensibility."

Bright, Allan H. *New Light on "Piers Plowman."* 1928. Reprint. London: Oxford University Press, 1950, 94 p.
  Investigation of the authorship controversy which concludes that William Langland is the sole author of *Piers Plowman.*

———. "Langland and the Seven Deadly Sins." *Modern Language Review* XXV, No. 2 (April 1930): 133-39.
  Demonstrates the evolution of Langland's treatment of the Seven Deadly Sins in *Piers Plowman.*

Burrow, J. A. *Ricardian Poetry: Chaucer, Gower, Langland and the "Gawain" Poet.* London: Routledge and Kegan Paul, 1971, 165 p.
  Places the four poets under the heading of Ricardian Poetry in an examination of their common stylistic and thematic characteristics.

Calí, Pietro. *Allegory and Vision in Dante and Langland.* Cork: Cork University Press, 1971, 198 p.
  Compares the *Divine Comedy* with *Piers Plowman* in search of similarities in theme and poetic expression.

Coghill, Nevill. "The Secentenary of William Langland." *The London Mercury* 26, No. 151 (May 1932): 40-51.
  Brief sketch of four of Langland's poetic attributes: his intensity of tone, his imaginative power, his awareness of the secular and religious worlds, and his ability to invent characters "spiritually alive."

———. Introduction to *The Vision of Piers Plowman,* by William Langland, translated by Henry W. Wells, pp. vii-xxix. 1935. Reprint. New York: Sheed and Ward, 1945.
  Examines the authorship controversy, comments on several aspects of Langland's style, and provides a summary of *Piers Plowman.*

———. *The Collected Papers of Nevill Coghill: Shakespearian & Medievalist.* Edited by Douglas Gray. Sussex: The Harvester Press, 1988, 292 p.
  Includes four essays on Langland's *Piers Plowman.*

Donaldson, E. Talbot. *"Piers Plowman": The C-Text and Its Poet.* Yale Studies in English, edited by Benjamin Christie Nangle, vol. 113. New Haven: Yale University Press, 1949, 257 p.
  Demonstrates the likelihood that the author of the C-text was the same as the author of the B-Text.

Dunning, T. P. *"Piers Plowman": An Interpretation of the A Text.* Rev. ed. Oxford: Oxford University Press, Clarendon Press, 1980, 178 p.
  Study of the A-text of *Piers Plowman* which concludes that "the *Visio* and the *Vita* in A are two distinct poems, each complete in itself."

Frank, Robert W., Jr. "The Conclusion of *Piers Plowman.*" *Journal of English and Germanic Philology* XLIX, No. 3 (July 1950): 309-16.
  Uses Conscience's last statement in *Piers Plowman* as a guide to understanding the conclusion of the poem.

Goldsmith, Margaret E. *The Figure of "Piers Plowman": The Image on the Coin.* Cambridge: Boydell & Brewer, D. S. Brewer, 1981, 128 p.
  Considers the "possible influences on Langland's conception of Piers" in *Piers Plowman.*

Griffiths, Lavinia. *Personification in "Piers Plowman".* Cambridge: Boydell & Brewer, D. S. Brewer, 1985, 125 p.
  Probes Langland's unique use of personification allegory in *Piers Plowman.*

Higgs, Elton D. "The Path to Involvement: The Centrality of the Dreamer in *Piers Plowman.*" *Tulane Studies in English* 21 (1974): 1-34.
  Concentrates on "Langland's artistry in using the dream as a literary technique."

Huppé, Bernard F. "*Petrus Id Est Christus*: Word Play in *Piers Plowman,* the B-Text." *ELH* 17, No. 3 (September 1950): 163-90.

Pursues "the possibility that word play," such as alliteration, consonance, and rhyme, "may supply a key to the structural plan" of *Piers Plowman.*

James, Stanley B. "The Neglect of Langland." *The Dublin Review* 196, No. 392 (January 1935): 115-23.

Examines the reasons behind the critical neglect of Langland's *Piers Plowman.*

Kane, George. "*Piers Plowman*": *The Evidence for Authorship.* London: University of London, The Athlone Press, 1965, 72 p.

Concludes that "all external and historical evidence of any authority attests that the three versions of *Piers Plowman* were written by a single man," William Langland.

———. "Langland and Chaucer: An Obligatory Conjunction." In *New Perspectives in Chaucer Criticism,* edited by Donald M. Rose, pp. 5-19. Norman, Okla.: Pilgrim Books, 1981.

Compares the work of Chaucer and Langland in order to identify the differences in their work and to "bring out unsuspected similarities."

Knott, Thomas A. and Fowler, David C. Introduction to *"Piers the Plowman": A Critical Edition of the A-Version,* by William Langland, edited by Thomas A. Knott and David C. Fowler, pp. 3-56. Baltimore: The Johns Hopkins Press, 1952.

Introduction to their A-text edition of *Piers Plowman,* providing background on the medieval Church in addition to stylistic, textual, and critical discussions of the poem.

Lawlor, John. *"Piers Plowman": An Essay in Criticism.* London: Edward Arnold (Publishers), 1962, 340 p.

Two-part study of *Piers Plowman* offering "a step-by-step reading of the poem," along with a discussion of such distinctive techniques as diction, rhythm, allegory, word play, and the role of the dreamer used by Langland.

Mills, David. "The Dreams of Bunyan and Langland." In *"The Pilgrim's Progress": Critical and Historical Views,* edited by Vincent Newey, pp. 154-81. Totowa, N. J.: Barnes & Noble Books, 1980.

Considers the ambigious attitudes of the author and the narrator towards their visions in two religious allegories: John Bunyan's *The Pilgrim's Progress* and *Piers Plowman.*

Monroe, Harriet. "Chaucer and Langland." In her *Poets & Their Art,* pp. 157-61. New York: The Macmillan Company, 1932.

Remarks that, although Chaucer's works have been more influential, Langland may still "bridge the centuries and clasp hands with the poets of the future" through his sympathy for the poor and suffering.

Owen, Dorothy L. *"Piers Plowman": A Comparison with Some Earlier and Contemporary French Allegories.* London: University of London Press, 1912, 173 p.

Notes resemblances between *Piers Plowman* and earlier French allegories, highlighting the vigor and originality of Langland's poetry.

Ryan, William M. *William Langland.* New York: Twayne Publishers, 1968, 166 p.

Biographical and critical introduction to Langland and *Piers Plowman.*

Scase, Wendy. *"Piers Plowman" and the New Anticlericalism.* Cambridge Studies in Medieval Literature, edited by Alastair Minnis, vol. 4. Cambridge: Cambridge University Press, 1989, 249 p.

Extended investigation of anticlericalism in *Piers Plowman.*

Schmidt, A. V. C. "The Inner Dreams in *Piers Plowman.*" *Medium Aevum* LV, No. 1 (1986): 24-40.

Analyzes two inner dreams, or dreams-within-dreams, contained in the B- and C-texts of *Piers Plowman.*

Schroeder, Mary C. "The Character of Conscience in *Piers Plowman.*" *Studies in Philology* LXVII, No. 1 (January 1970): 13-30.

Discusses Langland's expert treatment of Conscience in *Piers Plowman,* a character Schroeder calls the most complex personification in the poem.

Simpson, James. "From Reason to Affective Knowledge: Modes of Thought and Poetic Form in *Piers Plowman.*" *Medium Aevum* LV, No. 1 (1986): 1-23.

Highlights Mary Carruthers's study of poetic diversity in *Piers Plowman* in *The Search for St. Truth* (see excerpt above) by discussing the poem in relation to medieval literary theory.

Smith, A. H. *"Piers Plowman" and the Pursuit of Poetry.* 1951. Reprint. Folcroft, Penn.: Folcroft Press, Folcroft Library Editions, 1970, 24 p.

Provides a summary of *Piers Plowman* as well as a critical history. This essay was originally delivered as a lecture in 1950.

Stokes, Myra. *Justice and Mercy in "Piers Plowman": A Reading of the B Text Visio.* London: Croom Helm, 1984, 295 p.

Examines *Piers Plowman* in light of medieval concepts of justice and law.

Vasta, Edward, ed. *Interpretations of "Piers Plowman".* Notre Dame, Ind.: University of Notre Dame Press, 1968, 378 p.

Includes seminal critical studies of *Piers Plowman* "that assist in the study of the poem as a whole."

Williams, Margaret. Introduction to *Piers the Plowman,* by William Langland, translated by Margaret Williams, pp. 3-62. New York: Random House, 1971.

Considers several aspects of *Piers Plowman* including the authorship controversy and a discussion of its structure, and provides a critical history and summary of the poem.

The Legend of Robin Hood

INTRODUCTION

One of the most enduring legends in British culture, the body of stories recounting the adventures of Robin Hood has been in existence since at least as early as the fourteenth century. These stories generally feature the expert bowman Robin Hood and his Merry Men, a band of followers including Friar Tuck and Little John. They live in the woods, surviving off of the riches of dishonest clergy and nobility and assisting those whom they consider deserving of their aid. While some believe that the legend is based on the exploits of an actual medieval outlaw, historians have found it difficult to reach a definite conclusion regarding its origins. Most scholars instead focus on the transmission and proliferation of the legend, exploring the ways in which popular perceptions of Robin Hood reflect cultural attitudes toward the ideal of heroism, governmental and religious authority, and the relationship between humanity and nature.

The earliest literary reference to Robin Hood is found in the B-text of William Langland's poem *The Vision of William concerning Piers the Ploughman* (1377?), in which the allegorical character Sloth refers to "rymes of Robyn hood." The inclusion of the reference suggests that by the fourteenth century these "rymes" were well established in popular lore. Scholars have suggested three main theories concerning the origin of Robin Hood: that Robin Hood was an historical figure or a composite of a number of historical figures; that Robin Hood was a mythological figure, prominent in the medieval May rituals; and that Robin Hood is a fictional creation of medieval balladeers. After painstaking searches of the criminal records of Nottinghamshire and South Yorkshire, the two most likely regions of his activity, historians encountered many instances in which assorted variations of the surname "Robehod" were used as an alias to denote "fugitive" as far back as 1261-62. This evidence possibly suggests the existence of an earlier, more famous figure with that name. According to the historian J. C. Holt in his monograph *Robin Hood* (1989), the practice of criminals adopting the name "Robehod" has obscured the search for the original, and Holt, acknowledging that "by borrowing his reputation they dissolved his identity," has conceded that the investigations into this matter may never yield a definitive candidate. The case for Robin Hood originating in a mythological or religious context was endorsed in *Dictionary of National Biography* (1885-1900) by Sidney Lee, who portrayed Robin Hood as "a sprite or elf in Teutonic folk-lore." In this incarnation, Robin Hood figured as an allegorical icon representing Spring in the plays or games commemorating the month of May in medieval communities. Maid Marian, Robin Hood's companion in the legend, is especially prominent in the records of these festivals. The most notable advocate of the ballad theory of Robin Hood was the American historian Francis James Child, whose *English and Scottish Popular Ballads* (1893-98) remains the most comprehensive collection of medieval ballads, and who asserted that Robin Hood was "absolutely a creation of the ballad-muse." Many of the Robin Hood ballads share events and characters with the ballads of Eustace the Monk, Fulk Fitzwarin, and Hereward the Wake, leading some scholars to believe that they can be traced to a common source. Because of the nature of the ballad tradition—songs were spread orally by wandering minstrels—the identity of the original author has been lost over time.

The ballads and May game rituals influenced one another as each tradition evolved, and the intermingling of stories of Robin Hood's adventures and details of his character grew into a rich and complex legend. The most representative portrait of Robin Hood from the medieval age is a long poem titled *The Lytell Geste of Robyn Hode,* or *A Gest of Robyn Hode,* which Child dated to 1400 or earlier. This work is seen as a reworking of several smaller ballads, though, as David C. Fowler notes, its narrative is highly organized. In the *Gest,* Robin Hood is a highway robber who establishes and leads a forest community with its own code of ethics, the rules of which are simpler and more just than the laws followed by the rest of society. His opposition to the Sheriff of Nottingham and the Abbot of St. Mary's occupies much of the narrative, and historians observe that these enmities express a typical and widespread distrust for corrupt local law officers and dishonest clergymen. Robin Hood is nonetheless capable of great deeds of generosity, a trait he demonstrates when he takes pity upon a poor knight, Sir Richard at the Lee. Moreover, Robin Hood and his Merry Men love and honor King Edward, who surreptitiously infiltrates their party with the intention of capturing them, only to change his mind about their deeds, granting them a pardon and inviting Robin Hood to serve him. After a year in the King's service, Robin Hood grows restless and returns to his previous way of life in the forest. As John W. Hales and Frederick J. Furnivall assess him, "Robin, then, is the people's hero. He is the ideal champion of their cause—the helper of their extreme necessities—their great knight-errant and avenger—the representative freeman who spurns at the harshness of the laws . . . and stoutly upholds his independence—the more equal distributor of riches, transferring from the opulent to the indigent." While the notion of Robin Hood robbing from the rich and giving to the poor may in fact be a misinterpretation of a line from the *Gest,* it has become the hallmark of the Robin Hood legend.

As a yeoman in Medieval lore, Robin Hood existed in a class between the knights and the peasants. Two dramas from 1598 by Anthony Munday, *The Downfall of Robert Earl of Huntington* and *The Death of Robert Earl of Hun-*

tington, however, altered his social standing by giving him noble ancestry, and this detail, though relatively recent and having little basis in either fact or tradition, has become an ingrained characteristic of the Robin Hood legend. Munday further amended the Robin Hood legend by setting his escapades during the reign of Richard I (1189-99). The evolution of the ballad tradition is responsible for additional modifications of the Robin Hood legend in the seventeenth century. A marked rise in literacy among the English population during this period allowed for the tremendous increase in popularity of broadsides, one-sheet printed ballads sold at fairs. The anonymous authors of the broadsides took liberty with the Robin Hood legend, utilizing traditional elements where useful, but also amending it to suit their commercial needs, and in this manner Robin Hood was converted from a forceful pastoral hero to a mediocre urban artisan who entered archery contests with tanners, tinkers, and butchers, and often lost. R. B. Dobson and J. Taylor have written in the introduction to their *Rymes of Robyn Hood* (1976), "The Robin of the broadsides is a much less tragic, less heroic and in the last resort less mature figure than his medieval predecessor." For the remainder of the seventeenth century and much of the eighteenth, these distorted images of Robin Hood were perpetuated in ballad anthologies, called garlands.

In 1765, with the publication by Thomas Percy of *Reliques of Ancient Poetry,* also known as the Percy Folio, the heroic stature of Robin Hood began to be restored. By printing the medieval versions of the ballads "Robin Hood and Guy of Gisborne" and "Robin Hood His Death" Percy promoted the image of a courageous and just Robin Hood. Joseph Ritson's *Robin Hood* (1795) followed, collecting nearly all of the extant ballads relating to the Robin Hood legend, and becoming a popular and critical success. In his introduction, Ritson, who believed Robin Hood to be an historical figure active during the reign of Henry II (1517-55), portrayed him as a tireless rebel and implied a parallel between his heroism and that of the leaders of the French Revolution. Ritson's work also excited an interest in balladry itself among the writers of the English Romantic movement, who, in addition to sympathizing with Robin Hood's rebelliousness, emphasized his close association with the natural world. The novelist and poet Sir Walter Scott, a friend of Ritson's, augmented the popular appeal of Robin Hood by including him as a character in *Ivanhoe* (1819), and the poet John Keats in his "Robin Hood: To a Friend" (1818) perceived him as a symbol of England's vanished glory: "Gone, the merry morris din; / Gone, the song of Gamelyn; / Gone, the tough-belted outlaw / Idling in the 'greene shawe'." Children's stories of Robin Hood, the most successful of which was Pierce Egan's *Robin Hood and Little John; or, The Merry Men of Sherwood Forest* (1840), gained great popularity in Victorian England. In the twentieth century, scholars have continued to examine his character, suggesting, among others, interpretations of Robin Hood as a pagan divinity, a Christ figure, and a political revolutionary. Robin Hood has survived in children's adventure stories as well as several American films—a medium which has proven to be a highly suitable one for the legend. The most celebrated of these have been the silent movie *Robin Hood* (1922),

starring Douglas Fairbanks, and *The Adventures of Robin Hood* (1938), starring Errol Flynn, which Dobson and Taylor have called "perhaps the most vigorous of all twentieth-century treatments of the Robin Hood legend in any form."

ORIGINS AND DEVELOPMENT OF THE ROBIN HOOD LEGEND

R. H. Hilton   (essay date 1958)

[*Hilton is an English social historian and educator. In the following essay, he chronicles the development of scholarship pertaining to the origins of the Robin Hood legend.*]

Thomas Becket, Henry II's chancellor and later Archbishop of Canterbury, was an officially canonised saint, the most celebrated object of medieval English pilgrimages. Simon de Montfort, Earl of Leicester, a transplanted baron from the Île de France, was popularly and unofficially canonised for his part in the political upheaval and civil war of 1258-65. Another temporary, unofficial saint was Thomas, Earl of Lancaster, celebrated because of his rebellion against the government of his cousin, Edward II. But in spite of their official or unofficial sanctity, none of these, nor any other Englishman of the middle ages, ever became such a popular hero as Robin Hood. His popularity has never waned since we first hear of tales about his exploits in a version of Langland's *Piers Plowman,* probably composed towards the end of the seventies of the fourteenth century.

But Thomas Becket and the others really existed. Did Robin Hood ever live or was he a figment of popular imagination, or even the individual invention of a clever ballad maker? In this article I shall argue that probably there was no such individual, but that his historical significance does not depend on whether he was a real person or not. I shall suggest that what matters is that one of England's most popular literary heroes is a man whose most endearing activities to his public were the robbery and killing of landowners, in particular church landowners, and the maintenance of guerilla warfare against established authority represented by the sheriff. A man who would now, of course, be described as a terrorist. Perhaps a social historian can help to solve some Robin Hood problems which have so far mainly been considered by the literary historians.

On the face of it, the very scanty medieval evidence gives little grounds for supposing that Robin Hood was anything more than a literary creation. The reference made by William Langland occurs in his description of the allegorical character Sloth. In his famous dream the author sees Reason preach a sermon to the people, after which persons representing the seven deadly sins are led to repent. Sloth is a priest who has been a parson (that is, a parochial rector) for thirty years. He is ignorant of Latin and of the things of religion, but he is a skilled hunter of hares. He does not know his paternoster, but he knows rimes of Robin Hood and Randulf, Earl of Chester. The last Randulf (or Ranulf), Earl of Chester, died in 1232, so that while we need not conclude that the tales of the two heroes first began to be popular at the same time, the beginning of the Robin Hood legend may well be contemporary with the emergence of the ballad as a literary form in England, in the thirteenth century. Other medieval references to Robin Hood are later than that of Langland. They are in the Scottish chronicles of John Fordun [*Scotichronicon*] and John Major [*History of Greater Britain,* 1521]. The references are vague and it seems likely that their source material was, in fact, ballads that already existed. This is as we would expect, for the north of England and Scotland were the homes *par excellence* of the ballads, as any reader of Child's collection will have noticed, and the only identifiable location of Robin Hood's exploits is the West Riding of Yorkshire.

Another aspect of the Robin Hood legend, long known to literary historians, has been their association with the May Games of villages and towns in the sixteenth century. Troupes of May Day revellers dressed themselves up as Robin Hood and his outlaws, just as Morris Dancers included some grotesque or heroic character for the mime in their performance. The perfectly natural appearance of these popular personalities on May Day has, unfortunately, provoked over-enthusiastic folklorists into supposing that Robin Hood and his men have their roots in popular paganism, even in the witch cult. No doubt the May celebrations had a pre-Christian origin in the fertility rites of an agricultural people, and if Robin was known to us only in connection with these celebrations we might suppose, as Joseph Wright did in 1846 [*Essays on the Literature. . . of England in the Middle Ages,* Volume II], that he was no more than a woodland sprite. But when we come to analyse the earliest ballads themselves, we shall find abundant reference to the hard realities of thirteenth- and fourteenth-century secular existence, and only the most conventional references to religion. I do not propose to go further into this aspect of the matter, but to deal with a more important problem, the recurring effort to manufacture an authentic, documented, individual called Robin Hood.

Two sixteenth-century historians, Richard Grafton [in his *Abridgement of Chronicles,* 1572] and John Stowe [in his *Annales,* 1615], copying the Scottish chroniclers, introduced the idea, originally derived from the ballads, that Robin Hood had a real existence. Grafton even suggested that he was a nobleman fallen on evil times, and this was taken up by two court playwrights of the latter part of the century. Munday and Chettle's *Downfall and Death of Robert Earl of Huntingdon* (1601) started off a theory about Robin Hood which still goes the rounds of children's story books and films to-day. No doubt it was an attempt (probably unconscious) to make the popular hero acceptable to the snobbish and pedigree-conscious upper class of Tudor and Stuart England. The eighteenth-century antiquary, William Stukeley, fabricated a preposterous pedigree showing the descent of Robin (supposedly

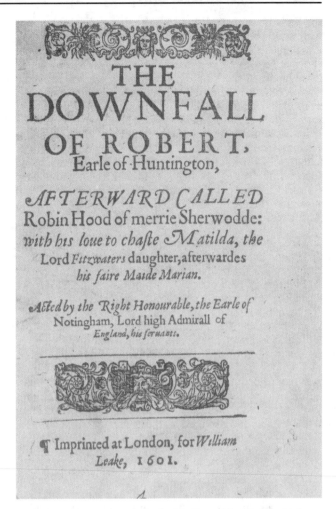

Recto of Anthony Munday's play The Downfall of Robert, Earle of Huntington.

a contemporary of Richard I) from the baronage of the Conquest period. Despite its dismissal by Percy, the great ballad collector [in his *Reliques of Ancient Poetry,* 1847], it was reproduced by an important early ballad editor, Joseph Ritson [in his *Robin Hood,* 1795]. But although no one seriously accepts the pedigree now, a curious by-product of the fabrication lives on in the assumption, by scholars and film producers alike, that the era of Robin Hood was that of Richard I (King of England, 1189-99). Sir Walter Scott, through *Ivanhoe,* is largely responsible for the popularity of this story, though it has support neither from contemporary sources nor from those ballads whose origin can safely be assumed to be medieval. Furthermore, none of the political or social upheavals of Richard's reign provide the same background of outlawry in the Midlands and the north which has been more plausibly associated with the Robin Hood legend in the reigns of Henry III and Edward II.

The development of accurate historical scholarship in the nineteenth century resulted in a number of rational attempts to account for Robin Hood, based on the study of authentic documents. The theory of fallen nobility was soon abandoned as some sort of chronological sequence of the ballads was established. Robin Hood's peasant origin was established. Some writers (such as the French historian Augustin Thierry [*History of the Conquest of England*]) thought he was a champion of Saxons against Normans, like Hereward the Wake. Unfortunately the ballads show no trace of this animosity. But such general notions were not satisfying, so historians tried to find events which were known to have resulted in large scale outlawries. Since the ballads seemed to have become popular in the fourteenth century (the latest date, as we have seen, being fixed by Langland's *Vision of Piers Plowman*), it seemed reasonable to examine the political history of the thirteenth and early fourteenth centuries. This examination produced the two principal theories held by those who think Robin Hood was a real man.

J. M. Gutch's 1847 edition of the *Lytell Geste of Robin Hood and* other Robin Hood Ballads was prefaced by a discussion of the problems of identification. Gutch rejected the theory of aristocratic origin, following Thierry—and also the idea that Robin Hood was contemporary with Richard I. Following an article in the *London and Westminster Review* for March 1840, Gutch suggested that Robin Hood was one of the disinherited supporters of Simon de Montfort who went into hiding after their defeat at Evesham in 1265. His evidence, apart from guesswork, was from Fordun, who associates Robin Hood and Little John with the disinherited. Fordun mentions that the people in his time celebrated the outlaws in tragedy and comedy, and as we have suggested, these were in fact his source of knowledge of the Robin Hood band. The association with the disinherited has been lately revived—cautiously, of course—by Sir Maurice Powicke in his *King Henry III and the Lord Edward*. There is, however, no positive evidence which links Robin Hood with the Disinherited, who were in any case members of the landowning nobility. They may have had followers of lower social status, but Robin Hood gives no appearance either of being any nobleman's follower or of being concerned with the political issues of the Barons' Wars.

More interesting and more convincing than Gutch's essay was Joseph Hunter's *Critical and Historical Tract no. IV* of 1852, entitled "The Ballad Hero, Robin Hood". Hunter was a historian and editor of records of some skill. He rejected the mythological explanation of Robin Hood, considered that he was not simply an abstraction of a number of outlaws, and suggested the reign of Edward II (1307-27) as the period of his activity. Hunter's merit is to have analysed with care the events described in those ballads which he considered to be of fourteenth-century origin, in relation to events for which there was documentary evidence. He came to the conclusion that Robin Hood and his friends were lesser members of the army which supported the rebel Earl of Lancaster, Thomas the king's cousin, who was defeated at Boroughbridge, Yorkshire, in 1322. The king confiscated the property of most of Thomas's supporters, referred to as the "contrariants". Among those mentioned in official records was a certain Godfrey of Stainton. This man, he suggested, was a relative of Elizabeth of Stainton, Prioress of Kirklees, traditionally supposed to have been the relative and murderess of Robin. The visit of the King to Robin in his greenwood home, de-

scribed in the ballads, recounts in poetic form the itinerary of Edward II in the north in 1323. To cap all, Hunter finds evidence in the accounts of the King's wardrobe wage payments to a porter called Robert Hood. This fits in with the sojourn of Robin at the king's court which is mentioned in the ballads.

This very circumstantial identification of Robin Hood with the contrariants has been repeated with some additions by Mr. J. W. Walker, in the *Yorkshire Archaeological Journal* for 1944. The principal new feature brought forward is the frequent mention in the Wakefield court rolls of a Hood family, one of whom was called Robert. And yet the whole reconstruction of Robin Hood as a fourteenth-century contrariant is based not simply on the evidence of the Wakefield court records, the royal wardrobe accounts and other public records, but on attempts to connect these evidences together by unjustifiable links of reasoning. The reasoning is based entirely on the assumption that various persons bearing the common name Robert Hood (Hade, Hod, Hodde or Hode) are in fact one person, and the same person as the ballad hero. It seems in fact to have been a common Yorkshire name, for another attempt to identify Robin Hood has been based on an entry in the Pipe Roll for 1230. This entry shows that the sheriff of Yorkshire was accountable to the royal exchequer for the value of the chattels of Robert Hood, a fugitive from justice. There are, however, important elements in the theory which lack verisimilitude. The ballads themselves contain no reference to Thomas of Lancaster, who, though a thoroughly unpleasant personality, did enjoy in the north a posthumous popular canonisation like Simon de Montfort—probably simply because he was a rebel against authority. Further, any genuine supporter of Lancaster would not have easily been reconciled to Edward II, who was widely hated and despised. Thirdly, the argument that Robin or Robert Hood would naturally be a follower of Lancaster as Lord of the Manor of Wakefield, falls to the ground since Lancaster had only two or three years earlier obtained Wakefield as a result of a private war waged against the Earl of Warenne, in whose family the manor had been for two hundred years. However, if the identification of the ballad hero with any one person is conceivable, it must be admitted that Joseph Hunter and his followers have so far produced the most likely case. The case, is, of course greatly strengthened by the fact that the earliest ballads refer to Barnesdale, between Wakefield and Doncaster, as the main scene of Robin Hood's exploits.

In view of the uncertain and elusive references to an individual "Robin Hood" in medieval records, it may be the best policy to leave for the moment the task of finding a precise setting in which to fit him and his outlaw band. The character of the hero and his associates has become so much of our tradition that it has been taken for granted. Closer attention to the internal evidence of the earliest ballads may give us a line on the external circumstances of their creation.

What can we say of the social milieu from which the legend emerged? It is, of course, generally accepted that the ballad audience was for the most part plebeian. Professor Entwistle [in his *European Balladry*] contrasts this audience with that of the epics of the preceding period, which, he says, was aristocratic. We cannot follow him in supposing that the ballad audience was "the whole people organised under its natural leaders", for the period of the European emergence of the genre, the thirteenth and fourteenth centuries, was one when we cannot talk of "the whole people" or of a "homogeneous folk". This, as we shall emphasise, was an era when society was the reverse of homogeneous, when peasants and landowners faced each other with mutual antagonism, when townspeople were regarded with suspicion by both, and when the peasantry itself was socially divided. However, the chasm which divided the landowners from the peasants and artisans was much deeper than those which were appearing amongst the people, and we must exclude the lords of manors from "the ballad people".

The "ballad people" lived in hard times, and if we are to recapture the authentic atmosphere of the first Robin Hood we must shed the common illusion that Robin and his fellows were simply a merry band of men who meant nobody any serious harm. "Apart from the particular history of his feud with the sheriff and abbot", says Professor Entwistle, "the episodes tend to repeat the tableau of good-humoured cudgellings". For Mr. A. L. Poole, in *From Domesday Book to Magna Carta,* Robin Hood is an "elusive and irresponsible sportsman" who "represents the cheerful side of the life of the forest, where merry and carefree men consorted in defiance of the law". For Professor Child the Robin of the *Gest* "yeoman as he is . . . has a kind of royal dignity, a princely grace and a gentlemanlike refinement of humour . . . for courtesy and good temper he is a popular Gawain" [*English and Scottish Popular Ballads,* Volume III, 1888]. This bland and fundamentally harmless character given to Robin and his men is probably derived from the numerous post-medieval broadsheet ballads, with their emphasis on one of the more harmless of the original themes—the way Robin dealt with his own class of people. These show him as a bold fighter with casual passers-by, usually artisans, such as the potter, the butcher and the tanner. In these ballads Robin usually loses, but with good temper, and invites the victor to join him in the greenwood. These ballads are on the whole later than the *Gest* and with their emphasis on artisan prowess may well be associated with the spirit of the May Games, which were as much urban as rural. But the *Gest* itself, and other indubitably early ballads show that Robin and his men are capable of a primitive ferocity against their enemies which ill fits the conception of good-humoured cudgelling and irresponsible sportsmanship. This physical cruelty is typically medieval. It occurs naturally in a society where any cross road might be furnished with a well-loaded gallows, where the heads and quartered bodies of traitors were nailed to city gates, and where quarrels over trifles amongst peasants, townsmen and nobles alike led to bloodshed and killing. Violence and cruelty were intensified when occuring as part of social conflict. If lords thought themselves justified in beating and hanging rebellious peasants, peasants replied when opportunity arose with similar cruelty.

And so at the beginning of the *Gest* Robin Hood's advice to Little John, should he meet bishop, archbishop or sher-

iff, is to "beat and bind". In the sixth "fytte" of the *Gest* Robin pierces the sheriff of Nottingham with an arrow and then cuts off his head with his sword. After the fight to the death between Robin and Guy of Gisborne, described in the ballad of that name, Robin cuts off the head of the dead Guy and sticks it on his bow's end so that he can mutilate the face beyond recognition with his knife. In *Robin Hood and the Monk,* Little John intercepts the monk who has betrayed Robin to the sheriff. He cuts off not only the monk's head but that of Much, "the little page", to ensure against betrayal. And the manner of Robin's own death at the hands of the wanton Prioress of Kirklees is as fierce and macabre as the tales of Robin's own doings. The woman bleeds him.

> And first it bled the thick, thick blood
> And afterwards the thin.
> And well then wist good Robin Hood
> Treason there was within

And her lover, stabbing him as he tries to escape, is himself slain and left for the dogs to eat.

Now we must see if we can, on the basis of the evidence of the ballads themselves, put Robin and the outlaws in their place in society. Robin is described frequently as a "yeoman" and in his own words shows that it is the yeomen who are his social equals whom he will cherish and protect above all. The word "yeoman" is one which has meant different things at different times. As it was commonly used in the sixteenth and seventeenth centuries it meant a wealthy peasant farmer, an employer of labour, holding most of his land freehold. He ranked socially above the mass of small copyholders and below the gentleman or squire. Two centuries earlier the word was not as clear in its meaning. Chaucer's yeomen in the *Canterbury Tales* are both serving men, the one attached to the knight and squire, the other to the canon. "Yeoman" in one of its meanings undoubtedly had the implication of service. But the knight's yeoman was also a forester, "yeomanly" accoutred. The fourteenth-century yeoman was not therefore necessarily in service, however honourable the service might be. The word as used in the ballads is almost certainly meant to imply neither a serving man (except in one place) nor a rich peasant, but simply a peasant of free personal status. And of course the first stanza of the *Gest* is addressed to an audience of free men:

> Lythe and listin, gentilmen
>   That be of free bore blode;
> I shall you tel of a gode yeoman,
>   His name was Robyn Hode.

The reference to gentility and free birth in the audience, and the emphasis on the yeoman class does not mean that the ballads were not in fact addressed to, and sung by, men whom the lords and the lawyers would consider servile. It is a persistent trait of thirteenth-century villeinage cases in royal courts that peasants (probably most often without success) considered themselves to be free men. Their heroes, consequently, will be as free as they themselves aspired to be. And so, although Sir Edmund Chambers [in his *English Literature at the Close of the Middle Ages,* 1945] makes a shrewd guess when he calls the Robin Hood and similar ballads the product of a "yeoman minstrelsy", we must not suppose with him that it was only the rich peasant lessees of manorial demesnes who enjoyed the tales of Robin Hood.

Social attitudes are better understood by attention to the relations between persons than by etymology. Let us consider the relations between Robin Hood and his men, and persons outside the woodland company, not as personal individual relations but as social relations, expressing the attitude of the outlaws to the various strata in society whom these persons represent. The Robin Hood band in a sense stood outside society since they were outlaws. Outlawry in Anglo-Saxon and Norman times had been the terrible lot of felons put outside the law. Their property was confiscated and any man could slay them with impunity. It was said of them that they "bore the wolf's head", they were to be treated as wolves by those within the law. By the thirteenth century outlawry was becoming less serious. An accused person who neglected to appear at four successive county courts for trial was automatically outlawed. Outlawry was becoming a sanction to compel attendance at court. But though it might no longer involve the lawful killing of the outlaw (except for resisting capture) it did involve the forfeiture of land and goods. Many a man who was not confident that law was the same as justice might prefer outlawry. At the Gloucester assizes in 1221 there were 330 homicide cases, but while only fourteen men were hanged, a hundred suspects had to be proclaimed outlaws in their absence.

The outlaws were not necessarily guilty homicides. They were often victims of oppression, especially when legal processes were subject to the pressure of powerful interests. An early fourteenth-century poem, written in the Anglo-Norman that was common in all literate circles and was used in the law courts, expresses this very vividly. The poem is about the way in which false accusers and interested persons could have a guiltless enemy flung into prison to await the travelling justices of "Trailbaston". The only remedy for the innocent was felt to be not to wait for the trial but to go to the woods:

> . . . suz le jolyf umbray
> La n'y a fauceté ne nulle mal lay
> En le bois de Belregard, ou vol le jay
> E chaunte russinole touz jours santz delay.
>
> [. . . in the beautiful shade
> There is no deceit there, nor any bad law.
> In the wood of Belregard where the jay flies
> And the nightingale always sings without ceasing.]

The poem is no lyric, however; life as an outlaw in the woods was not really merry or carefree. The outlaw wants to go home:

> Je pri tote bone gent qe pur moi vueillent prier
> Qe je pus a mon païs aler e chyvaucher.
>
> [I beg all good people they pray for me
> That I may go riding to my own country.]

Naturally the outlaw in the wood remembers those who are the oppressors and who are his friends. In the Robin Hood ballads these are classified with the greatest clarity—and treated accordingly.

The stories told in the older ballads very largely turn on the social attitude of the outlaws. Professor Child wrote that Robin Hood "has no sort of political character", and truly he takes no position with regard to the feudal faction fights which made up so much of medieval politics. We shall deduce this attitude from those ballads which are recognised as the oldest, that is mostly written down and even printed before 1500, and therefore probably derived from an oral tradition that goes back to the fourteenth century and beyond. These are the composite *Gest of Robyn Hode; Robin Hood and the Monk; Robin Hood and Guy of Gisborne; Robin Hood and the Potter.*

The *Gest* begins by Little John asking for instructions from Robin about how he and the others should treat various sorts of people.

> Where we shall robbe, where we shall reve,
> Where we shal bete and bynde?

The answer is

> But loke ye do no husbonde harme
> That tilleth with his ploughe.
> No more ye shall no gode yeman
> that walketh by grenë-wode shawe
> Ne no knyght ne no sqyer
> That wol be a gode felawe.
>
> These bisshopes and these archebishoppes
> Ye shall them bete and bynde;
> The hyë sherif of Notyngham
> Hym holde ye in your mynde.

Little John, Much the miller's son and William Scarlok then proceed to Watling Street somewhere in the Doncaster area and wait for a guest to take to dinner, preferably a rich guest who can be made to pay heavily for the privilege. In the event, the guest is poor, but the tale he tells is typical of the predicament of many a small landowner of the times.

Sir Richard at the Lee, to whom Robin plays host, has had to borrow money to get his son out of the consequences of a homicide. He borrowed the money from the Abbot of St. Mary's, York, and offered all his lands as security. The day for repayment has come and he has no money. Robin lends him more than enough, refits him with clothes, and sends Little John with him as attendant (as "knave" or "yeoman"). They arrive in the abbot's dining hall where the abbot is accompanied by his wealthy or subservient friends, including the high justice of England, retained by the abbot by fee and livery. The knight, concealing his money, asks for respite, is refused, and then, to the chagrin of the abbot, who coveted Sir Richard's land, throws the money on the table and leaves. Eventually, of course, Sir Richard comes again to the woodland home of Robin and repays the loan. The outlawed yeoman is shown to be possessed of Christian charity where the professed monk has none.

The sheriff of Nottingham figures on a number of occasions in the early ballads. In another of the stories in the *Gest,* Little John, disguised as Reynold Grenelefe from Holderness, is so successful in an archery competition in Nottingham that the sheriff takes him into his service. Reynold is an unruly servant, lies in bed when the sheriff is out and demands food and drink in such a way that after laying out the steward and the butler, he becomes involved in a fight with the cook. As so often in these stories, the fighters become friends and decamp with the sheriff's cash and silver. Still in his rôle as Reynold Grenelefe, Little John lures the sheriff to Robin's hiding place, where he is stripped to his breeches and shirt and made to lie out all night. Robin extracts from him a promise of immunity in return for his release. But the sheriff, of course, breaks the promise. This leads us to another section of the *Gest* (after a characteristic interlude involving the robbing of the high cellarer of St. Mary's Abbey). Robin and his men go to compete at archery at Nottingham, take all the prizes but are attacked by the sheriff's men. Little John is wounded and asks that his friends behead him rather than leave him alive in the sheriff's power. But they all escape and are sheltered by Sir Richard at the Lee in his castle. The knight defies the sheriff to inform the king of his protection of outlaws and the sheriff raises the siege. Robin and his fellows get away, back to the woods, but the sheriff surprises the knight out hawking and imprisons him. At the appeal of the knight's wife, Robin and seven score followers storm Nottingham, slay the sheriff and rescue the knight.

The sheriff has to die more than one death. In the ballad *Robin Hood and Guy of Gisborne* Robin dreams he is beaten and bound by two yeomen. On waking he determines to find them. He and Little John search the woods and eventually come on the sinister Guy of Gisborne, clad from head to foot in horse hide. Little John and Robin quarrel about who is to deal with Guy, and John departs to find some of the other outlaws killed in an encounter with the sheriff. John is taken by the sheriff after the failure of one of his arrows. Meanwhile Robin and Guy, as yet unknown to each other, compete at archery. Robin wins, and reveals his identity, for Guy has already said that he is searching for the outlaw. They fight and Robin kills and mutilates Guy of Gisborne. But since Guy is the sheriff's emissary, Robin puts on Guy's garment of horse hide and blows Guy's horn. The sheriff understands this to mean that Guy has killed Robin. The two meet and the sheriff offers the false Guy any reward he asks. Robin asks to be allowed to kill the captive Little John, but of course cuts John free with his "Irysh kniffe" The sheriff runs for his life, but Little John, with Guy of Gisborne's bow and rusty arrows

> Did cleave his heart in twinn.

Apart from any documentary or linguistic proof of medieval dating for these stories, the references to persons and situations imply a thirteenth or at the latest fourteenth-century origin. Such evidence as we have of peasant life in the century and a half before the rising of 1381 suggests that agrarian discontent was endemic throughout the country. Although economic conditions changed considerably during the period, the peasants at all times found themselves at odds either with the landlord or the state official, or with both. Villagers' grievances up to the middle of the fourteenth century were focussed on landlords' demands for rents and services. Quarrels about these matters—crucial for the countryman's standard of living—led

to issues of personal freedom. In a litigious age, the stage that was reached before riot broke out, was normally dispute in the courts. This, in numerous cases, touched on whether the peasants involved were free men or serfs, for if they were serfs they were legally liable for increased rents and services at demand. After the middle of the fourteenth century, though these issues were still alive, an additional bitter cause of complaint was the attempted wage-freeze of 1349 and 1351. This history of intertwined economic and social grievances, affecting rich and poor peasants, the servile, the would-be free and the free, seems more likely to have generated the Robin Hood ballads than the short-lived outbreaks of civil war, mainly affecting the upper classes, that have been quoted by Gutch and Hunter.

The sheriff, as the principal enemy, fits well into this context. In the thirteenth and early fourteenth centuries, before the Justices of Labourers and of the Peace come into prominence, the sheriff was the omnipresent representative of the power of the government. He was in the first place the principal local financial agent of the Crown and notorious as a past master in the art of extortion. It was he or his agents who performed all the administrative functions which led up to the appearance of litigants in court—delivery of writs, attachment of accused persons, distraint on property, empanelling of juries. He, furthermore, was the official whom the government instructed, on receipt of complaint from aggrieved landowners, to mobilise forces to compel tenants to pay rent, to perform services or to dispel and arrest rioters.

It could, on the other hand, be argued that the landlord does not seem to play a big enough part to support a theory of Robin Hood as a by-product of the agrarian social struggle. But this, of course, is the rôle of the Abbot of St. Mary's, York. The monks are not hated for their religion or for their lack of it. They are the exemplars of unrelenting landlordism, much more, one imagines, than the baron who, however extortionate, did not establish his presence in the shire as did the religious. St. Mary's, a Benedictine abbey, was the wealthiest religious house in Yorkshire, and indeed one of the first half dozen or so in the country. Abbots of such houses were among the greatest men of the kingdom, very apt to have a chief justice as an intimate (even on the pay-roll, as the ballad suggests) Furthermore it was the religious landowners who tended to be the most tenacious of their rights and the least sympathetic in face of social demands from below. The abbot of St. Mary's, in other words, is well cast, with the sheriff, as a target for peasant satire.

The attitude of the outlaws to authority as represented by the sheriff and the abbot is unmistakable. But it conflicts curiously with their attitude to the source of authority, the greatest landowner of them all, the King. In the *Gest* the King responds to the sheriff's appeal to come to punish Sir Richard at the Lee for sheltering the outlaw. The knight's lands are declared forfeit to the crown and offered to any man who could bring the king his severed head, for the king's wrath was further excited, as he travelled north, by the looting of the deer in his deer parks. But the king is warned that as long as Sir Richard is protected by

Robin, any man sent to capture him will lose his own head first. The king's next move, on advice from one of his intimates, is to go to the wood disguised as a monk, in the hope of tempting the outlaws' well-known greed for the riches of the church. The stratagem works, but after a competition in shooting and buffeting, the king is revealed. But Robin and the knight win the king's pardon, the king takes Robin's livery of Lincoln green, and Robin goes in the king's service for fifteen months to the king's court.

The king throughout is "our comely king" and shows himself in his visit to the wood as brave, strong, merciful and generous. Why the contrast between the king and his agents? In reality the king would have strengthened his officials' actions against peasant lawbreakers, especially poachers of deer in his parks and forests. But the medieval peasants did not see the king as one of the landlords, protecting landlord power and privilege. They thought of him as the fount of justice, and justice in their minds meant protection against those who oppressed them (their landlords) and those local officials who protected and helped the oppressor (chiefly the sheriff). Of course, the king and central government agents very often acted against overmighty subjects, not to protect the serfs of the overmighty, but to protect the interests of the crown. The people were confused, they had no powerful protectors, so they invented one. Their faith in the king led to their downfall in 1381.

The illusions of the medieval English peasant that the king was really on their side, reflected in the Robin Hood ballads, shows that their rebellious outlook was one of protest against immediately felt hardship. It was not critical of the established order. There was no conscious attempt to envisage a different England until the brief moment of their power and glory in the summer of 1381. And yet, while lacking political and social consciousness of a more modern type, they were not without aspirations. Perhaps it would not be exaggerated to suggest that the carefree merriment of the outlaws in the greenwood, so unlike the starved and hunted existence of real outlaws, was an unconscious invention in poetic form of the life that those who enjoyed the ballads would have liked to live. As we have seen, it was a life of peril at the hands of the sheriff and his open or secret emissaries. But it was also a life where the fat abbot or cellarer always comes off worse and has to disgorge his wealth to the representatives of the class from whom the wealth was taken in the first place. More important still, it was a life of abundance, of sportsmanship and without degrading toil. It was a life spent among friends and equals, under the direction of a leader chosen for his bravery, not imposed because of his wealth and power. (pp. 30-43)

*R. H. Hilton, "The Origins of Robin Hood,"
in* Past and Present: A Journal of Historical
Studies, *No. 14, November, 1958, pp. 30-44.*

J. C. Holt (essay date 1989)

[*Holt is an English historian and educator who served as historical adviser for the 1991 made-for-television movie* Robin Hood. *In the following excerpt from a revised edition of his book on the subject, Holt outlines some medieval legends analogous to the Robin Hood legend, describing the intermingling of these stories over time.*]

The stories of Robin Hood are a very mixed bag. It is now time to examine the mixture, to analyse the blend of fact and fiction and of original and borrowed material. This is an essential conclusion to the attempt to identify the outlaw, for the case must rest on the factual and original, not the fictional or derivative elements in the story. It is equally necessary as a preliminary to any discussion of the circumstances which shaped the legend, for both the remembrance of fact and the concoction of fiction reflect the concerns and tastes of the generations of tellers and listeners who fashioned the tales into the form in which they first survive.

The fiction is motley, derived from widely scattered sources. Some elements in it stem from the tales of real-life outlaw heroes. Some come from romantic literature which seems entirely fictional. Some are analogous to material in other stories which are roughly contemporaneous with the first versions of the Robin Hood legend, and in such instances it is far from clear whether the legend was the origin or the recipient of the shared material or whether it was dependent, along with the analogous story, on some common source.

Of these categories, the first, which links the legend with

E. J. Hobsbawm's nine traits of the "noblerobber" or Robin Hood hero:

First, the noble robber begins his career of outlawry not by crime, but as the victim of injustice, or through being persecuted by the authorities for some act which they, but not the custom of his people, consider as criminal.

Second, he 'rights wrongs'.

Third, he 'takes from the rich to give to the poor'.

Fourth, he 'never kills but in self-defence or just revenge'.

Fifth, if he survives, he returns to his people as an honourable citizen and member of the community. Indeed, he never actually leaves the community.

Sixth, he is admired, helped and supported by his people.

Seventh, he dies invariably and only through treason, since no decent member of the community would help the authorities against him.

Eighth, he is—at least in theory—invisible and invulnerable.

Ninth, he is not the enemy of the king or emperor, who is the fount of justice, but only of the local gentry, clergy or other oppressors.

Hobsbawm, in Bandits, *Delacorte Press, 1969.*

---

tales of earlier outlaws, is much the most important. There were three such: Hereward the Wake, Eustace the Monk and Fulk fitz Warin.

Of Hereward, who has become a national hero as leader of English resistance to the Norman conquerors, little need be said except that almost nothing certain is known of him. His turbulent career began before the Conquest of 1066, for it was recorded in the Domesday survey of 1086 that he had fled the land in the reign of Edward the Confessor. After 1066 he based himself on the Isle of Ely and in 1071 burned and looted Peterborough abbey. A year later William the Conqueror drove him from his stronghold in the Isle, where he had attracted others hostile to the Normans. He may subsequently have been reconciled with the king, and it is possible, but not certain, that he is one of the Herewards recorded in Domesday as a landholder in Lincolnshire and the Fenland in 1086. That is as far as fact and probability go. All other details come from legendary tales of his adventures which spread within the next century. The most important of these is the *De Gestis Herewardi Saxonis* (The Deeds of Hereward the Saxon), which survives in a compilation made by Robert of Swaffham, monk of Peterborough, in the middle of the thirteenth century. It is usually taken as a straightforward, if exaggerated and inaccurate account of English resistance to the Normans. In fact it is a peculiar and interesting literary amalgam which owes something to Norse saga and much to French epics of feudal resistance to an overlord, for Hereward's adventures started, not with a 'nationalist' rebellion against the invader, but earlier with his disinheritance by his father and Edward the Confessor.

Eustace the Monk was the son of a knightly house of the county of Boulogne. He entered a monastery but around 1190 abandoned it in order to avenge the murder of his father. He later became seneschal to the count, Renaud de Dammartin, but in 1203 fell foul of him and took to the woods as an outlaw. Thereafter he built up a reputation as a soldier of fortune and naval commander. He served in turn both King John of England and King Philip of France. He seized control of the island of Sark in 1205 and for the next decade organized piratical raids on shipping in the Channel, effectively dominating the passage at times. In 1217 he commanded a fleet bringing reinforcements to Prince Louis of France and his baronial supporters in England. He was defeated by the young Henry III's forces in a battle off Sandwich, Kent, on 24 August. His ships were taken and he was beheaded on the spot. His career was soon embellished in a romance, *Wistasse li Moine,* composed sometime after 1223 and surviving first in a manuscript written in or shortly after 1284. This is chiefly concerned with his feud with the count of Boulogne.

Fulk fitz Warin was a baron of the Welsh marches, born in the 1170s. On the death of his father in 1197 he took over a long-standing family claim to the barony and castle of Whittington, Shropshire. In 1200 the case went against him and he was outlawed; it is likely that he murdered the successful rival claimant. For the next three years he levied war against King John in the marches. He was pardoned in November 1203, recovered Whittington and remained in the king's peace until 1215 when he joined the baronial rebellion in support of Magna Carta. He was not reconciled until 1217. He recovered Whittington, of which he had been deprived during the rebellion, in 1223, and he lived on, increasingly venerable and appearing occasionally as a baronial spokesman, blind in his last years, to die in 1256-7. His deeds are the subject of a prose romance, *Fouke le Fitz Waryn,* first surviving in a compilation of a Hereford scribe of 1325-40. The prose version is based on an earlier verse romance, now lost, which was probably written in the late thirteenth century. The tale reviews the history of Fulk's claim to Whittington but is chiefly devoted to the three years between 1200 and 1203 when Fulk was an outlaw, engaged in a battle of wits with an enraged and vengeful King John.

The legends of these men contaminated the tale of Robin Hood. Two, Eustace and Fulk, live their life as outlaws in the forest, just as Robin does. Two, Hereward and Fulk, like Robin, are reconciled with the king. All show a remarkable prowess with arms. There is no one to resist them; they may be undermined by treachery or overpowered by numbers but, if so, they gain release through skilful ruse and the base stupidity of their captors. It is only in the last few lines of *Wistasse* that reality breaks in with the account of the hero's defeat and summary dispatch.

There is more to this than coincidence. Some of the analogous material must have been transmitted, by confusion of memory or literary borrowing, from one tale to another. All three heroes, in legend, are masters of disguise. Hereward, like Robin Hood, takes the disguise of a potter to make his way into King William's court and discover his plan of attack on Ely. His disguise is suspected, but not penetrated, until in the end he gives the game away when, like Little John in the *Gest,* he fights the kitchen staff while the king is out hunting. Eustace the Monk flits from one disguise to the next in bewildering fashion: monk, innkeeper, charcoal-burner, prostitute. He too makes a brief appearance as a potter.

There are other, equally significant parallels. Just as the sheriff is decoyed into the woods, captured and then re-

First page of an early copy of The Gest *of Robyn Hode.*

leased by Robin in fytte three of the *Gest,* so is the count of Boulogne lured into the woods, captured and released by Eustace, and so does Fulk, disguised like Eustace on one occasion as a charcoal-burner, entice King John into an ambush by promising to show him a fine stag. The king, like the sheriff and the count, is captured; he swears to restore Fulk to estate and favour and is then allowed to go. Again, just as Little John takes service with the sheriff in the *Gest,* so one of Fulk's men, John de Rampaigne, enters the castle and service of his enemy, Maurice fitz Roger, in order to discover his intentions. Subsequently in the lavish, unlikely guise of an Ethiopian minstrel, he rescues one of Fulk's men from King John. Fulk robs the king's merchants, at the king's expense, and forces them to dine with him. Eustace, even more significantly, asks those whom he had waylaid what they carry with them. A merchant of Boulogne who honestly admits that he has 40*l.* 5*s.,* is allowed to go in peace. The abbot of Jumièges, in contrast, is less direct. He admits to carrying no more than 4 marks; Eustace finds that his purse holds over 30; he returns four to the abbot who is sent on his way with the sentiment that he has lost the rest of his money just because he lied. This seems too close to the tale of Robin Hood, the knight and the abbot of St Mary's for the analogy to be accidental.

There is one other notable analogue, quite separate from these romances. In fytte seven of the *Gest* the king is only able to track down Robin by acting himself as a decoy. Disguised as an abbot he sets off into Sherwood, hoping and intending to be captured, and great play is made of his entertainment by Robin and of his subsequent revelation of his real identity. This theme of the king incognito is shared with the famous legend of King Alfred and the cakes which was interpolated into Asser's *Life of Alfred* in the twelfth century. Gerald of Wales, writing in 1216, also preserved a tale of King Henry II passing the night incognito at a Cistercian abbey after losing his company on a hunting expedition.

Taken as a whole, these analogues are numerous but limited in range. Only a few broad themes are shared between the romances and the Robin Hood stories: the greenwood, the honest outlaw, his ultimate reconciliation with authority. The rest is made up of bits and pieces, useful to string a tale together and to touch a familiar chord in the audience. Some notions of justice and injustice are shared; honour, trustworthiness, the keeping of oaths are set in sharp contrast to falsehood and treachery. But other themes important in the romances are not transmitted at all. The romantic hero seeks restitution. The grudge he bears is that the just claims of his family have been denied; he may even be dispossessed or disinherited. Hereward is an outlaw because he was rejected as heir by his father and King Edward; he is provoked to fight the Normans when his brother is slain and the family lands are seized; in his reconciliation with King William his lands are restored. Eustace the Monk is launched on his career by the murder of his father, killed in a dispute over a fief. In *Fouke* the family claim to Whittington informs the whole tale. In all three tales title to an inheritance plays a fundamental part. There is nothing of this in Robin Hood. Indeed, his presence in the greenwood as an outlaw is never explained and his restoration to royal favour is not accompanied by the

satisfaction of any grievance. Robin moves in a different world from that of the dispossessed feudal landowner. Equally it is a world in which Saxon resistance to the Norman conquerors must have seemed out of place for none of that element in *Hereward* is used to embellish Robin's story.

Those who first told tales of Robin were not just copying in simple fashion. They were building up and spreading a new cycle of stories by calling on dramatic situations made familiar in earlier tales cast in a different poetic mould about other heroes set in a different social context. The ballads are not bred in simple fashion from the romances. Mutation has intervened. Yet there is one characteristic common to all the situations which the ballads share with the romances: in both they seem to be drawn from the fictional rather than the factual elements in the tales. There was nothing so universally useful as a tall story, nothing so adaptable as the stock dramatic tricks of disguise or the simple moral rule of tit for tat. These elements made up much of the common ground.

If in one direction some of the characteristics of the legend of Robin lead back to the historical romances of earlier outlaw heroes, in another they look to other stories coeval with the legend and even less certain in their factual content. All of them may be entirely fictional. Some certainly are.

The most important of these deals with Adam Bell, Clim of the Clough and William of Cloudesley who, like Robin and his men, are outlaws.

They were outlawed for venyson, These three yemen everechone.	They were outlawed for venison, These three yemen everyone.

They are based not on Barnsdale, Sherwood and Nottingham, but on Inglewood in Cumberland and Carlisle. Their deeds are the subject of a lengthy poem of 170 stanzas which first survives in a printed fragment of 1536 and a fuller text of *c.* 1560, but the first certain reference to these Cumbrian outlaws belongs to 1432 and there is no real doubt that their story is medieval in origin.

Like the *Gest* the tale is divided into fyttes. It is a simple yarn of yeoman outlaws living off the royal deer in the greenwood and successfully outwitting the sheriff, the justice and even the king himself. But it has some important elements in which Robin's tale does not share. William of Cloudesley has a devoted wife, Alice, and three sons. It is the desire to see his wife and family which leads him to visit Carlisle, where he is betrayed by an 'old wyfe' of the household whom he had befriended for charity. On hearing her information the sheriff and the justice muster the townsfolk. William's house is burned down about his head and, after a notable fight, he is seized. New gallows are erected for his execution on the morrow but a small boy flees to the forest to tell Adam and Clim of the disaster to their comrade. So ends fytte one.

In fytte two Adam and Clim gain entry to Carlisle by persuading the porter that they carry the king's writ and seal. They are admitted and then:

(They) called the porter to a councell,	(They) called the porter to confer,
(And) wronge hys necke in two,	(And) wrung his neck in two,
(And) kest hym in a depe dongeon,	(And) cast him into a deep dungeon,
(And) toke the keys ym fro.	(And) took the keys from him.

They string their bows and proceed to the market-place to find William of Cloudesley ready for execution. They shoot the justice and the sheriff, release their friend and fight their way out leaving all the town's officials and many others dead. The second fytte ends with them safely back in Inglewood where William is reunited with his wife and family.

In the third fytte the outlaws travel to London to seek the king's pardon for shooting his deer. The king will not give it but the queen asks it as a boon and it is granted. No sooner done than messengers arrive bearing news of the outlaws' doings in Carlisle:

The kyng opened the letter anone,	The king opened the letter forthwith,
Hym selfe he red it tho,	Himself he read it then,
And founde how these thre outlawes had slaine,	And found how these three outlaws had slain
Thre hundred men and mo.	Three hundred men and more.
Fyrst the justice and the sheryfe,	First the justice and the sheriff,
And the mayre Of Caerlel towne;	And the mayor of Carlisle town;
Of all the constables and catchipolles	Of all the constables and catchpoles
Alyve were left not one.	Alive were left not one.
The baylyes and the bedlys both,	The bailiffs and the beadles both,
And the sergeauntes of the law,	And the sergeants of the law,
And forty fosters of the fe	And forty foresters in fee
These outlawes had y-slaw.	These outlaws had slain.

This report put the king off his food, but he has given them his pardon and nothing can be done:

When the kynge this letter had red,	When the king this letter had read,
In hys harle he syghed sore;	In his heart he sighed sore;
'Take up the table,'	'Take up the table,'
Anone he bad,	he bade at once,
'For I may eate no more'.	'For I can eat no more'.

The scene then shifts to an archery contest in the butts. William of Cloudesley demonstrates his skill by splitting a hazel-wand at 400 paces and then, like William Tell, by cleaving an apple placed on his son's head. The king promptly makes him his bow-bearer and 'chefe rydere' of all the north country. The queen makes him a gentleman of clothing and of fee, his two comrades become yeomen of her chamber, and his wife is summoned to become her chief gentlewoman and governess of the nursery. The yeomen, no longer outlaws, blessed indeed with office and fee, find a bishop to confess their sins and all live happily ever afterwards.

The similarities between this story and the tales of Robin Hood are striking and obvious. Throw together Robin Hood's capture and rescue in *Robin Hood and the Monk* and the reconciliation with the king in fytte eight of the *Gest,* and the result comes very close to *Adam Bell,* even in some detail. Adam tries to dissuade William of Cloudesley from his visit to Carlisle just as Little John does with Robin Hood. The sheriff and justice in *Adam Bell* raise the hue and cry against the outlaws in Carlisle just as the sheriff does against Robin in Nottingham. Adam and Clim gain entry to Carlisle by using a writ which they present to an ignorant porter as bearing the king's seal. Little John inveigles himself into the king's good graces and comes to Nottingham carrying a genuine royal writ. Clim, like John, takes the keys from the porter, Clim to ensure escape from the town, John to get access to Robin's cell. The social contexts of the two stories are similar. Adam Bell and his friends are 'Yemen of the north countrey'. The poetic techniques are identical, with introductory and concluding references to the greenwood, and the springtide of May. Each poet addressed his audience: 'Lyth and lysten, gentylmen'.

The two tales of Adam and Robin remained closely associated from their origin in the Middle Ages on to the eighteenth century. The first reference to Adam Bell is in the return of members of parliament for Wiltshire in 1432. The clerk responsible for the return was given to literary flourishes. For the 1433 parliament he arranged the sureties of the members returned for the county and boroughs of Wiltshire so that the initials of the names, which were entirely fictional, formed an acrostic making up a benign prayer for the well-being of those representing the local communities at Westminster. In 1432 he attempted something similar, but less consistently. The first eight surnames, read vertically, may or may not be genuine, but what followed was plainly fictitious for they run: 'Adam, Belle, Clyme, Ocluw, Willyam, Cloudesle, Robyn, hode, Inne, Grenewode, Stode, Godeman, was, hee, lytel, Joon, Muchette, Millersson, Scathelok, Reynoldyn.' Here, it should be noted, the Cumbrian outlaws take precedence over Robin Hood and his companions. At times there was some confusion between the two outlaw bands. Andrew de Wyntoun placed Robin in Inglewood as well as Barnsdale, and later, in broadsheets and chapbooks, identical illustrations were used for the two different tales. Indeed, in the iconography of Robin Hood, any frontispiece representing three men is likely to have been borrowed from the other tale for they usually stand for Adam, Clim and William. It is scarcely surprising that attempts were made to link the two legends. In *Robin Hood's Birth, Breeding, Valor and Marriage,* an unconvincing hotch-potch written probably no earlier than the seventeenth century and surviving first in eighteenth-century versions, the pinder of Wakefield arranges a shooting match between the three Cumbrian outlaws and Robin Hood's father. The author of this piece had plainly set himself up as a kind of literary marriage bureau for he made Robin's mother a niece of Guy of Warwick and gave her a brother called Gamwell, by whom presumably he intended Gamelyn.

Robin soon predominated over Adam Bell and his friends. The tale of Adam was still printed in broadsheet and chapbook in the seventeenth century, but it never proliferated into many different versions as did Robin's legend. There are several possible explanations. The legendary centres of Robin's activities, in Barnsdale and Sherwood, lay on or near to the Great North Road, one of the main arteries of medieval England. Inglewood, on the other hand, was isolated. The legend of Robin drew heavily on the thirteenth-century romances. In *Adam Bell* in contrast there are none of the familiar analogues with *Wistasse li Moine* or *Fouke*. Instead, for William's cleaving the apple from his son's head, it drew on Icelandic saga. That this should appear in a story associated with the hinterland of Carlisle, with access to the Irish Sea and the Isles, is scarcely surprising. But it reinforces the impression that Adam Bell is more peripheral than Robin, not only geographically but also in its literary sources, social context and potential audience.

There were other, less important, forest tales. *Johnnie Cock* is a Northumbrian and Border story, collected by Percy, in which the hero goes hunting dressed in Lincoln green and falls asleep with his dogs after slaying a dun deer. An old palmer reports him to the foresters against whom Johnnie's mother has already warned her son:

'There are seven	'There are seven
forsters at	foresters at
Pickeram Side,	Pickeram Side,
At Pickeram where	At Pickeram where
they dwell	they dwell,
They wad ride	They would ride
the fords of hell.'	the fords of hell.'

The foresters attack and wound him mortally. He shoots all but one who is left to bear news of his death to his mother. It is a brief story of some twenty stanzas, but has tragic, foreboding tones perhaps only matched in *Robin Hood his Death*. *Robyn and Gandelyn* is an older more enigmatic fragment of 17 stanzas surviving in a manuscript collection of the mid-fifteenth century. It opens simply with Robyn and Gandelyn going to the woods to hunt deer. It is not until eventide that they find a herd. Robyn shoots the largest of them and then is himself shot and killed. The assailant proves to be Wrennok of Donne. After verbal interchanges Wrennok shoots at Gandelyn and misses. Gandelyn in reply pierces Wrennok through the heart. The circumstances throughout are obscure. It is not clear whether Wrennok is a forester or a private enemy. It is uncertain whether Robyn and Gandelyn are outlaws. The reiterated theme is simply that Gandelyn must avenge the death of his master, Robyn. There is nothing to identify this Robyn with Robin Hood or Gandelyn with Gamelyn of *The Tale of Gamelyn*. The setting is the forest, but no specific forest is named.

The Tale of Gamelyn is the last parallel of any importance. It survives as a long poem running to nearly 1,000 lines, composed in its present form about 1350. Gamelyn is the youngest of three sons who is maltreated and deprived of his rightful share of his patrimony by his evil and treacherous elder brother, John. Gamelyn reacts with vigour. He defeats his brother's champion wrestler and kills his porter. He flees to the forest to escape arrest by the sheriff and there he becomes king of the outlaws. Meanwhile, his eldest brother is made sheriff. Gamelyn then seeks more legal forms of redress in court. He is arrested but is bailed by his second brother, Ote. When Gamelyn later appears for trial he finds Ote is in fetters. Gamelyn frees him and then takes the justice's place on the bench and sits in judgment on both him and his brother. Good triumphs over evil:

The Iustice and	The justice and
the scherreve bothe	the sheriff both
honged hye,	hanged high,
To weyven with the	To swing with the
winde drye.	the wind to dry.
And the twelve sisours	And the twelve jurors
(sorwe have that	(woe to those
rekke!)	who care)
Alle they were hanged	All were hanged
faste by the nekke.	firmly by the neck.

Gamelyn and Ote then seek pardon from the king. Ote is made a justice and Gamelyn achieves apotheosis as chief justice of the Free Forest.

There are parallels in this with Robin Hood. Gamelyn, like Robin, is an outlaw in the greenwood. Like Robin he makes his peace with and receives office from the king. Like Robin he expresses violent anti-monastic sentiments:

Cursed mot he worthe	Cursed may he be
bothe fleisch and blood,	both flesh and blood,
That ever do priour	That ever does prior
or abbot ony good.	or abbot good.

In *Gamelyn* a wrestling match plays an integral part in revealing the hero's strength and courage. In the *Gest* a wrestling match is interpolated incongruously at the end of fytte two as a means of delaying the knight's return to the greenwood.

Yet there are also important differences. *Gamelyn* is the more sophisticated piece of literature. Although it has some technical similarities with the *Gest* and with *Adam Bell* (at intervals the poet addressed his audience— 'Litheth and lesteneth and holdeth youre tonge'), it is a romance, not a ballad. It survives in some of the manuscripts of Chaucer. The poet may have considered it for the Canterbury Tales, perhaps as a Knight's Yeoman's Tale. Subsequently, Shakespeare drew on it for *As You Like It*. Moreover, Gamelyn and Robin move at different social levels. Gamelyn is of knightly family and is rewarded well beyond the expectations of mere yeomen such as Robin or Adam Bell. But the contrast lies not so much in Gamelyn's higher social status as in the feudal background to his tale. The plot is based on the division of an inheritance and on the wardship of the youngest son, Gamelyn, by his false and treacherous eldest brother. It is of great interest in that it carries over into the tales of outlawry of the later Middle Ages all the interest in rightful inheritance which is found in works like *Fouke le Fitz Waryn*. It preserves that part of the thirteenth-century tradition which the Robin Hood tales and *Adam Bell* never acquired. Perhaps for this reason Gamelyn focuses more sharply on the corruption of justice. In Robin's legend and *Adam Bell* the sheriff is simply the Law, the outlaws' natural enemy, and there is no need to explain their enmity. In *Gamelyn,* in contrast, the evil brother has become the sheriff, the justice has been suborned and the jurors have been bought. They connive in denying justice to a younger son and they must all hang. Only at one point does the *Gest* present a comparable picture of judicial corruption, in the scene where the justice supports the abbot of St Mary's rejection of the knight's plea for further delay on his mortgage. There, too, property was at stake. Nothing kindled a sense of injustice quite so effectively.

What conclusions are to be drawn from these varied analogues? There is no rule of thumb. Where they link Robin Hood with *Hereward, Wistasse* and *Fouke,* it seems inescapable that Robin is indebted to the earlier stories. Between the Robin Hood cycle and *Adam Bell,* in contrast, Robin could have been the source, or indeed they could have drawn from and given to each other, directly or indirectly. The significance of *Adam Bell* is not as a source for Robin Hood but as evidence that tales closely similar to those told of Robin were also told of other men in closely similar contexts. That puts the authenticity of both stories in doubt, but it does not utterly destroy it, for in an age when the king and his court emulated King Arthur and his knights and when genuine robbers took the name of Robin Hood and Friar Tuck, the possibility that outlaws might model their actions on legend cannot be ruled out. Yet doubt alone is enough, and it reduces the original and authentic element in the Robin Hood cycle to a small proportion of the total.

Robin Hood and the Potter is the most vulnerable to trial by analogue. The specific disguise had already been used in *Hereward* and *Wistasse,* and the luring of the sheriff into the forest is paralleled in both *Wistasse* and *Fouke. Robin Hood and the Monk* also rings hollow, for it runs too close to *Adam Bell.* In the *Gest,* fytte three, in which Little John takes service with the sheriff of Nottingham and then lures him into Sherwood, has to be classed as a tall story; there are too many similarities to it in both *Wistasse* and *Fouke.* The visit of the king in disguise to Sherwood is also suspect, for that was an old literary chestnut. The restoration of Robin to royal favour and his entry into royal service, on which Hunter built so much, is frail indeed for it has numerous parallels in *Hereward, Fouke, Adam Bell* and *Gamelyn.*

Some parts of the story are less easy to pin down. There is no general analogue to fyttes five and six of the *Gest* which tell of the sheriff of Nottingham's archery contest, the alliance of the outlaws with Sir Richard of the Lee and the rescue of Sir Richard and the slaying of the sheriff, but some of the detail of this section is reminiscent both of *Fouke* and *Adam Bell.*

Some parts of the story survive the test in whole or to a large degree. There is no obvious parallel to the tale of Robin Hood, the knight and the abbot of St Mary's, although one feature of it, Robin's test of a traveller's honesty through questions on the contents of his purse or baggage, is shared with *Wistasse,* and another, the wrestling match, has a more distant analogue in *Gamelyn.* Finally, there is no analogue to *Guy of Gisborne* or to *Robin Hoode his Death.*

It is improbable that all relevant analogues have survived. Hence there can be no certainty that those parts of the tale which lack obvious analogues are original. Even if they are, that is no guarantee of historical authenticity. It could well be that a real incident in which an outlaw gave aid to a knight in repaying a mortgage on land pledged to a monastery underlies the story of fyttes one, two and four of the *Gest.* But it is very doubtful whether real life was so nicely pointed as the tale. In *Wistasse* the confessions of resources, honest from the merchant, false from the abbot of Jumièges, are unrelated. In the *Gest* the honesty of the knight and the dissemblance of the monks are counterbalanced one against the other so that the monks' lie repays the knight's troth. That a real Robin recouped himself from monks of the monastery to which the land was pledged is possible. That the monks should appear on the very day appointed to the knight for repayment, and that they should come from St Mary's, thus rewarding Robin's devotion to the Virgin, presses coincidence altogether too far. Equally, an outlaw, even one called Robin Hood, may have died through treachery, even of a cousin who was a nun. Nevertheless, it would be surprising if much of *Robin Hoode his Death* were anything other than fiction.

However, the analogues provide only a very rough and ready test for the originality and authenticity of the tales of Robin Hood and, after making due allowance for all cautions and qualifications, one important point remains: on the whole, the stories based on Barnsdale and South Yorkshire, the tale of the knight and the abbot of St Mary's in fyttes one, two, and four of the *Gest, Guy of Gisborne* and *Robin Hoode his Death,* come through relatively unscathed; those which fail the test are based on Nottingham and Sherwood, fyttes three, seven and eight of the *Gest, Robin Hood and the Monk* and *Robin Hood and the Potter.* So the nearer Robin gets to Nottingham the less authentic he becomes. It is to Barnsdale and South Yorkshire that the greater part of the original tradition of Robin belongs. It is to Yorkshire too that the evidence of identification leads. And it is in Barnsdale that the tales are given their most detailed and exact locale.

These conclusions can be supported by an entirely different line of argument. Throughout the whole cycle, both in the original and derivative stories, the tales are presented to the listener in a realistic fashion which calls on everyday experience. If the weft of the fabric is spun from a mixture of legend and the doings of real outlaws, the warp is made up of themes and topics with which the audience would be familiar: archery, hunting and poaching, the iniquities of the sheriff and the like. These themes in turn are susceptible to a very rough and ready chronological examination: rough and ready because the warp, like the weft, is a mixture; the older threads were overlain by newer strands as the audience's interests and circumstances changed from one generation to the next. Such changes rarely lead to precise dates, and it was probably easier to bring in new themes than to jettison old; so the method yields probabilities, not certainties.

Even so, one striking coincidence is apparent. The analogues to the tale of Robin Hood, the knight and the abbot of St Mary's are few and incidental. The main theme of the story, the knight's debt by mortgage to the abbot and its repayment, the consequent loan from Robin and its repayment, is to all appearance original; there is certainly nothing similar in any of the obvious sources on which the legend called. It is also a theme which fits more easily into the circumstances of the thirteenth than the fourteenth century, for the Statute of Mortmain (*de viris religiosis*) of 1279 forbade alienation of feudal estates to the church or to churchmen by gift, sale or mortgage. Thereafter, in effect, it required a royal licence or dispensation. This might be obtained quite easily, but no such move was envisaged by the abbot of the *Gest*. Quite apart from the statute, the *Gest's* picture of the abbot as the hard-hearted mortgagee would be more readily and widely understood in a period when such monastic investment was at its height. By the end of the thirteenth century many houses had run into severe financial difficulties and were themselves heavily in debt; they were in no position to take up mortgages.

This seems reasonably firm ground. Some attempt has been made to circumvent it by suggesting that the knight's mortgage was arranged with the abbot as an individual, but even if this were so the prohibition of the statute would still stand for the abbot plainly intended that the knight should lose his land. Moreover, this is not what the story is getting at. The abbot was acting, not just for himself, but for his house. True, in fytte one the knight confesses that he has pledged his lands:

To a ryche abbot	To a rich abbot
here besyde	here nearby
Of Seynt Mari Abbey.	To St Mary's Abbey.

But in the second fytte the abbot explains the arrangement to the convent and it is plain that it is a matter for discussion between him, the prior and the cellarer. Indeed the prior objects:

'It were grete pyte',	'It were a great pity',
sayd the pryoure,	said the prior,
'So to have his londe;	'So to have his lands;
And ye be so lyght	If you are so easy
of your	with your
consyence	‡conscience
Ye do to hym	You do to him
moch wronge';	much wrong';

only to be met with the abbot's retort (91):

| 'Thou arte ever in my berde'. | 'Thou art ever in my beard'. |

It is difficult to see how the prior could hinder the abbot in a purely private matter, and indeed the cellarer puts the matter beyond doubt:

| 'He is dede or hanged', | 'He is dead or hanged', |

sayd the monke,	said the monk,
'By God that	'By God that
bought me dere,	bought me dear,
And we shall have	And we shall have
to spende in this	to spend in this
place	place
Foure hondred pounde	Four hundred pounds
by yere.'	a year.'

By 'we' the cellarer plainly meant the convent. Hence in fytte four it is through the cellarer, not the abbot, that the debt is repaid, and indeed he acts not merely for the abbey, but for St Mary, in whose name Robin's loan to the knight had been secured. Robin's devotion to the Virgin and the dedication of the abbey are both integral to the story. This is a well-wrought tale of right triumphing over evil conceived for an audience which was familiar with the reputation which some monastic houses had attracted to their order and was sympathetic to the plight of knightly landowners who got enmeshed.

Already, however, this particular complaint against the monks is embedded in more general anti-monastic sentiment. It is plain in all these tales that Robin reveres the Virgin Mother. In *Robin Hood and the Monk* his devotion is used to set the framework of the plot and even brings him to the edge of disaster. But it only does so because he is betrayed by a 'great headed monk', who suffers the proper penalty at the hands of Little John. The monk is the real villain of the tale, treacherous and untrustworthy. In *Robyn Hoode his Death* it is Robin's cousin, the worldly prioress. In some of the later stories the attack is broadened by casting bishops as Robin's enemies or victims. A

Frontispiece to an edition of The Geste of Robyn Hode, *dated between 1492 and 1534.*

friar, in contrast, becomes one of the leading figures of the band. Hence the sentiments which the tales express are not limited to those financial activities of monasteries that were at their most prominent in the thirteenth century. They also draw on a more general hostility to the monastic order characteristic of the later fourteenth century and, in that they leave room for a mendicant to become one of the heroes, do so in partisan fashion.

It may be that these more general sentiments helped to preserve the tales of the abbot of St Mary's as the miserly, monastic mortgagee. Even so, it is the one theme in the story where the balance of probability clearly favours an earlier rather than a later date of origin. In other cases the evidence is less certain. The difficulty is that it was easier to generate than to forget a grievance; and some grievances were enduring and widely shared.

Hostility to the sheriff is expressed in so deep-rooted but so generalized a fashion throughout the legend that it is difficult to pin down chronologically. It could embody the mistrust of local government which led county landowners in the thirteenth century to demand that sheriffs should be elected by the shire court. It could equally well express a more general discontent with shrieval corruption which ran through from the twelfth century to the later Middle Ages. There is nothing in the story in any way co-eval with the demand for the control of local office by local men as expressed in *The Song of Lewes,* written after Simon de Montfort's victory over Henry III in 1264. Equally, there is nothing in it which smacks at all of the abuses of purveyance which, in the fourteenth century, could be laid against the reputation of John of Oxenford, one of the many who have been advanced as the legendary sheriff of Nottingham. There is a timeless quality in the villainous sheriff. He is as evergreen as the forest in which he was condemned to his unavailing pursuit of the outlaw hero.

The attitudes expressed in the legend towards the forest and its deer are more suggestive chronologically. The forest of Robin Hood, as of Adam Bell and Gamelyn, is the royal forest, the deer slain are the king's deer, and in the *Gest* it is the state of his forest which brings King Edward north to seek the outlaw band. Now, while it is true that the royal forest remained a source of grievance throughout the Middle Ages, this was an area where the crown was on the retreat by the beginning of the fourteenth century. Edward I formally surrendered many of the forest areas in dispute with local communities in the forest ordinance of 1306. General circuits by the forest justices became less frequent; there was none in Sherwood, for example, between 1286 and the last of such visitations in 1334, when the justices recorded offences committed by men long since dead. Forests were being eroded from within by enclosure of land for cultivation. In Sherwood Edward I converted such 'assarts' into ordinary leaseholds which no longer shared rights of common within the forest, so that by the end of his reign a map of it would have been speckled with small estates no longer subject to the forest law. Meanwhile great landowners tried to absorb areas of forest which the crown had been forced to abandon. Among the lords against whom the first-known complaints were made by the men of Lancashire and Westmorland in 1225

were William de Warenne, lord of Wakefield and John de Lacy, lord of Pontefract and Clitheroe. As the thirteenth century advanced private chases were increasingly protected and private parks proliferated. At Wakefield in the early fourteenth century the Warennes had established two parks, the 'old' and the 'new'. There was also a 'great wood' where the trees and pasture were protected. At the head of the Calder valley they maintained the chase or forest of Sowerby which extended to the bounds of their lands on the watershed of the Pennines. At Sowerby Richard Hood was at loggerheads with the foresters in 1274-5. At Wakefield between 1308 and 1317 Robert Hood, like other tenants of the manor, made regular payments for firewood from the earl's woods.

Such preserves provoked widespread opposition. In 1302 a commission of *oyer and terminer* was issued to try persons who had entered the park, chases and warrens of the earl of Warenne at Wakefield with a multitude of armed men, while the earl was in Scotland fighting in the king's service, and had hunted there, carrying away deer, hares, rabbits and partridges, and had also taken fish from his fishery at Sandal. Between February 1322 and July 1324, a period whence the affairs of the forest penetrated the story of the *Gest,* there were fifteen commissions of *oyer and terminer* occasioned by raids on the royal forests and attacks on the king's foresters, a total which includes the parks of Queen Isabella and the forests, chases and parks which came to the crown with the forfeiture of Thomas earl of Lancaster. During the same period there were thirty-four similar commissions occasioned by attacks on chases, parks and warrens of other landowners, the great majority of them concerning parks. Forests and parks, royal and private, were all under attack. Yet in the tales of Robin Hood there is nothing even to suggest that such private preserves existed. They mention one park, 'Plumpton park', and that is a royal one. It will be argued later that the affairs of one particular private forest, that of Thomas of Lancaster, obtruded into the story, but that came into royal hands after the earl's defeat at Boroughbridge in 1322. This instance apart, the tales seem to reflect an earlier rather than a later stage in the interplay of royal and aristocratic interests in the forest law. The royal forest is their sole target. Private preserves, which enjoyed their greatest extension later, are ignored.

Another element in the story, the expert archery, has been thought to point to a later rather than an earlier date and also to a plebeian milieu. This has not proved convincing. It is natural enough to move from the tales of Robin's prowess to the victories achieved by the bowmen of England and Wales at Crécy (1346), Poitiers (1356) and Agincourt (1415), but the longbow was recognized as a highly penetrative long-range weapon centuries before. According to Gerald of Wales, writing at the end of the twelfth century, an arrow could pin a knight to his mount through both mail and saddle or penetrate an oak door a palm's width thick. The men of Gwent were already famed as archers in the twelfth century as were the archers of the Kentish weald in the civil wars of 1216-7 and 1264-5. In the legal records of the early thirteenth century the bow figures as a common household article, and one frequently used by robbers and in cases of assault. Outstanding accuracy might be alleged, even shooting out the light. Some historians have been misled by a semantic confusion. Almost inevitably the longbow has been contrasted with the 'short bow', which is alleged to have preceded it as the conventional weapon of the twelfth and thirteenth centuries. But the longbow was so described to distinguish it, not from a short, but from the crossbow. There were short bows. There were short men. Women also used the bow, and then, as now, children played with bows and arrows. But the short bow as a category of weapon and a necessary precursor of the longbow was invented by the military historian, Sir Charles Oman, in the nineteenth century. In the century after the Norman Conquest there may have been changes in the technique of bowmanship. The illustrations of the Bayeux tapestry present the archers of Hastings drawing their bows to the chest rather than to the ear in classic longbow style, but the bows of the archers depicted in the margins of the tapestry are clearly longbows in size. Whether any weight can be placed on such artistic conventions is problematical. Matthew Paris in contrast, in the middle of the thirteenth century, included archers with characteristic longbow actions in his drawings of the battles of Bouvines (1214) and Sandwich (1217). Robin Hood could have shot with a similar weapon and in similar fashion in Matthew's lifetime.

The sheriff, the forest and the archery are dominant themes in the story which reflected the enduring interests of the listeners: hence the difficulty of dating them. Also scattered throughout the tales are other allusions to everyday experience which are equally difficult to date. For example, when Robin first entertains the indebted knight, the impoverished condition of his guest leads him to wonder whether he was 'made a knyght of force', that is, compelled to take up knighthood. This reference to distraint of knighthood by the crown would strike a chord in the listener as early as the 1240s. It would be equally familiar more than a century later. Some allusions, on the other hand, are more likely to be derived from the fourteenth than the thirteenth century. In the *Gest* the justice has clearly been retained by the abbot—'I am holde with the abbot . . . Both with cloth and fee'; the sheriff of Nottingham offers to retain Reynold Grenelef, alias Little John, at a fee of 20 marks a year; and Little John promises the same fee to the cook if he will join Robin and his band. In *Robin Hood and the Monk* Little John receives a fee of £20 and becomes yeoman of the crown. All this was possible in the thirteenth century, but it was much more likely a century later when the permanent relationships of feudal tenure were decomposing into the more evanescent associations of 'bastard feudalism': livery, maintenance, the retinue and the money fee. But these instances are not many. They are not even consistent, for an earlier age seems to be reflected in *Guy of Gisborne* where Guy might have had a knight's fee for slaying Robin had he so wished. And they are incidental to the main themes of the stories: seasonal top dressing applied to keep them fertile.

In some respects the complexion of the ballads belongs entirely to the later Middle Ages. The author of the *Gest* addresses his audience as 'gentlemen'. Robin and his men are yeomen; so is Guy of Gisborne. Along with 'knight' and an occasional 'squire' and 'husbandman' these are the terms of social status on which the tales rely. 'Knight' apart, terms based on tenurial definitions, characteristic of the earlier Middle Ages, are entirely absent; there are no freemen or villeins, still less any sokemen or cottars; there is not even a franklin, a term which enjoyed some temporary importance in the later fourteenth century as the old social definitions declined. Hence the social categories of Robin's world belong to the early fifteenth century. For this there may be a simple explanation. The stories are in English. There is no evidence at all that Robin's deeds were told in any other language, Latin, Anglo-Norman or French. The new words went with the new literary language. (pp. 62-81)

> *J. C. Holt, in his* Robin Hood, *revised edition, Thames and Hudson, 1989, 223 p.*

REPRESENTATIONS OF ROBIN HOOD

John W. Hales and Frederick J. Furnivall   (essay date 1867)

[*Hales and Furnivall were English historians whose edition of* Bishop Percy's Folio Manuscript: Ballads and Romances *(1867-68) was an important source for ballad scholars, including the famous ballad historian Francis James Child. In the following excerpt from their introduction to that work, Hales and Furnivall chronicle the representations of Robin Hood in popular ballads, emphasizing his portrayal as a champion of the people and his closeness to nature.*]

There are those who represent [Robin Hood] to have been simply a famous robber chieftain, a great prince of outlaws—"latronum omnium humanissimus et princeps," to quote Mair's words—"prædonum mitissimus" in Camden's version of these words. Others insist that he was a great political leader, carrying on a perpetual guerilla warfare against his enemies, and finding refuge on occasion in the tangled labyrinths of the forests. A third theory denies him existence. According to it he is a mere creation of the Teutonic mind—a flesh-and-blood-less fancy. These are the three leading views entertained about him. The facts of the matter are, that he is first mentioned in literature in the *Vision of William concerning Piers the Ploughman*, written probably about 1362, and is there mentioned as the well-known hero of well-known popular songs. Says Sloth:

> "I kan noght parfitly my pater-noster
> As the priest it syngeth,
> But I kan rymes of *Robyn Hood*
> And Randolph Erl of Chestre."

His next mention is in Wyntoun's "Scottish Chronicle," written about the year 1420. Wyntoun, writing of the year 1284, says:

> Lytil John & *Robyn Hude*
> Waithmen ware commendyd gude;
> In Yngilwode & Barnysdale
> Thai oysyd all this time thare trawale.

Some thirty years afterwards one of the additions to Fordun's "Scotichronicon" (such, and not of the original work, Mr. Wright has shown the passage to be), speaking of the De Montfort period, informs us: "Hoc in tempore de exheredatis et bannitis surrexit et caput erexit ille famosissimus sicarius *Robertus Hode* et Littill Johanne cum eorum complicibus, de quibus stolidum vulgus hianter in comœdiis et tragœdiis prurienter festum faciunt et super ceteras romancias mimos et bardanos cantitare delectantur." (Goodall's "Forduni Scotichronicon, &c." Edinb. 1769. ii. 104.) Sir John Paston, in Edward IV.'s time, lets us know that games in honour of Robin Hood were then zealously celebrated. "I have kepyd hym," he writes of one of his servants, "thys iii yer to pleye Seynt Jorge, and *Robyn Hood* and the Shryf of Notyngham; and now," he adds complainingly, "when I wolde have good horse, he is goon into Bernysdale, and I without a keeper." Towards the end of the fifteenth century the Robin Hood ballads were collected and woven together into one long poem known as the *Lytel Geste,* printed by Wynken de Worde somewhere about 1490, reprinted in Scotland in 1508. At least two ballads relating directly to Robin Hood—to say nothing of several that allude to him—are found in MSS. of a certainly not later date than the oldest edition of the *Lytel Geste,* viz.: "Robyn Hode and the Potter," first printed by Ritson from a MS. among Bishop More's collections in the Cambridge University Library, and "Robin Hood and the Monk," first printed in Jamieson's "Popular Ballads" from a MS. in the same library, and, according to Mr. Wright, possibly as old as Edward II.'s time, but certainly not so old as the ballad which is, or is the basis of, the Fourth Fit of the *Lytel Geste,* as the spoiling of the monk there narrated is referred to in it.

In 1521 appeared Mair's "Historia Majoris Brittanniæ tam Angliæ quam Scotiæ," which may be said to contain the *locus classicus* on Robin Hood, inasmuch as the passage in it concerning him—whatever its sources—furnishes the earliest full description of him, and is adopted with scarcely any variation by Grafton and Stow and Camden, and along with the *Lytel Geste* forms the basis of that life in the Sloane MSS. No. 715 of which Ritson made so much use. Mair's therefore memorable words are:

> Circa hæc tempora [Ricardi Primi], ut auguror, *Robertus Hudus* Anglus, et Parvus Joannes latrones famatissimi [not famosissimi, as sometimes quoted] in nemoribus latuerunt, solum opulentorum virorum bona deripientes. Nullum nisi eos invadentem vel resistentem pro suarum rerum tuitione occiderunt. Centum sagittarios ad pugnam aptissimos Robertus latrociniis aluit, quos 400 viri fortissimi invadere non audebant. Rebus hujus Roberti gestis tota Britannia in cantibus utitur. Fœminam nullam opprimi permisit nec pauperum bona surripuit, verum eos ex abbatum bonis sublatis opissare pavit. Viri rapinam improbo, sed latronum omnium humanissimus et princeps erat.

About the middle and through the latter part of the sixteenth century and thenceforward allusions to Robin Hood abound. Especially worthy of note are Latimer's complaint, in his sixth sermon before Edward VI., how, when he proposed preaching in some country church, "one of the parish comes to me, and says 'Sir, this is a busy

day with us. We cannot hear you. It is *Robin Hood's* day. The parish are gone abroad to gather for *Robin Hood.* I pray you let them not,' " and the full description of the merry outlaws in Drayton's "Polyolbion," Song 26, and the notice given of Robin by Fuller in his "Worthies" in connection with Nottinghamshire. His story, we may add, was revised, and augmented again and again. The yeoman of the older ballads is transformed into an earl in the newer ones. A sentimental colour is given him. Maid Marian appears, and becomes a leading, absorbing part of the company. The fresh breezes of the greenwood are tainted with artificial odours. By Charles I.'s time the balladwriters have all, like sheep, gone astray. They have improved away the genuine old picture. In 1670 was published the first known edition of the "Garland." In 1678 appeared a prose version of it, with the title *The Noble Birth and gallant atchievements of that remarkable outlaw Robin Hood, together with a true account of the many merry and extravagant exploits he play'd, in twelve severall stories . . . Newly collected into one volume by an Ingenious Antiquary.* (Reprinted in Mr. Thomas' *Early English Prose Romances.*) Poor Robin's character sank sadly in the following century. He fell amongst mere thieves. About the middle of it came out *The lives and heroick atchievements of the renowned Robin Hood and James Hind, two noted robbers and highwaymen.* Nor did he recover his proper status till the year 1795, when Ritson put forth his hand and lifted him out of the mire. Ritson's *Robin Hood* is still the great treasure-house on the subject of the great outlaw. Not much of importance has been added to what his vigorous researches compiled some seventy years ago.

We know, then, nothing whatever of Robin Hood before he is the well-established favourite of the people. He is already a full-grown, most popular "fabula" when the first mention of him occurs. The first details about him are given some 150 years after the time at which they represent him to have lived. We cannot therefore attempt to make out from general literary or other sources the biography of Robin Hood. Some writers have essayed to eke it out with the assistance of the *Lytel Geste.* They have taken the last "Fytte" of that string of ballads to be a more or less sober historical narrative. We cannot praise them. Such treatment of the old ballads seems quite unjustifiable. But if it were not so, there is nothing whatever in any one of the ballads to countenance the theories that Robin Hood was the last of the Anglo-Saxons, or one of the Dispossessed (exheredati) of the battle of Evesham days, or one of the Contrariantes (the Lancastrians) of Edward II.'s time. There is no touch of political faction or national antagonism in any one of them. Robin's controversy is with the rich as rich, not as Normans. On the other hand, we are not inclined to deny the existence of Robin Hood. There is a certain local precision and constancy in the ballads. We can well believe that Hood existed as actually as the Earl of Chester, with whom he is coupled in the *Piers Ploughman*—that some outlaw of the name did make himself famous in the North Country, *i.e.* the country to the north of the Trent, and especially about Barnesdale, in or just before the thirteenth century—that his fame spread, and grew, and was fed from a thousand sources utterly disconnected with its origin, till his name became a household word, and himself the universal darling of the common people. Of a circumscribed renown to begin with, he was presently sung of throughout the length and breadth of the land. He was adopted as the hero of the people, and they delighted to honour him. In the darling of their fancy they soon forgot the original forester of the West Riding. He was made what they would have him be—a man after their own hearts. He was set up as their idol, and costumed and tricked out, no doubt, with ornaments and robes torn from the shoulders of less fortunate demigods. He absorbed the fames of his rivals. According to the poet,

> . . Mors sola fatetur
> Quantula sint hominum corpuscula.

But death sometimes makes the opposite confession. In Robin Hood's case his insignificance ended with his life. When that his body did contain a spirit, a single district was room enough, but afterwards a kingdom for it was too small a bound. Thus the outlaw of Barnesdale grew to be the acclaimed hero of the English commons.

He became the hero of the commons as King Arthur of the higher classes. As the aristocratic period passed away, and the third estate advanced in power and importance, the great yeoman rivalled the great knight. Robin Hood with his merry men of the greenwood, Little John and Scarlet and Much, displaced King Arthur with his Knights of the Round Table, Lancelot and Gawain and Tristram. The archery meeting presently superseded the joust as the national pastime. The lance is shivered, so to speak; the longbow wins the day. This great transition is taking place rapidly in Chaucer's time. He gives a full picture, not only of the knight but of the yeoman,—of the typical heroes of both times, the old and the new,—of the nobles' darling and of the people's. The older ballads speak of Robin Hood especially as the yeoman, and connect him with the yeomanry, as in "Robin Hood and the Potter:"

> Herkens, god yemen,
>   Comley, corteysse, and god,
> On of the best that yever bar bon,
>   Hes name was Roben Hode.
> Roben Hode was the yemans name,
>   That was boyt corteys and fre.

and again:

> God haffe mersey on Robyn Hodys solle,
>   And saffe all god yemanrey.

and in the *Lytel Geste:*

> Lithe and lysten, gentylmen,
>   That be of frebore blode;
> I shall tell you of a good yeman,
>   His name was Robyn Hode.

Robin, then, is the people's hero. He is the ideal champion of their cause—the helper of their extreme necessities—their great knight-errant and avenger—the representative freeman who spurns at the harshness of the laws, especially the Forest laws, and stoutly upholds his independence—the more equal distributor of riches, transferring from the opulent to the indigent.

> The widow in distress he graciously relieved,
>   And remedied the wrongs of many a virgin
>   grieved.

Observe the instructions he gives his men in the *Lytel Geste:*

> "Mayster," than said Lytell Johan,
>   "And we our borde shall sprede,
> Tell us whether we shall gone,
>   And what lyfe we shall lede;
>
> Where we shall take, where we shall leve,
>   Where we shall abide behynde,
> Where we shall robbe, where we shall greve,
>   Where we shall bete and bynde."
>
> "Thereof no fors," said Robyn,
>   "We shall do well ynough;
> But loke ye do no housband harme,
>   That tylleth with his plough;
>
> No more ye shall no good yeman,
>   That walketh by grene wode shawe,
> No no knyght ne no squyer,
>   That wolde be a good felowe.
>
> Thryes Robyn shot about,
>   And always he slist the wand,
> And so dyde good Gylberte,
>   With the whyte hande.
>
> Lytell Johan & good Scatheloke
>   Were archers good & fre;
> Lytell Much & good Reynolde,
>   The worste wolde they not be.
>
> When they had shot aboute,
>   These archours fayre & good,
> Evermore was the best
>   Forsoth, Robyn Hode.
>
> Hym delyvered the goode arow,
>   For best worthy was he.

In "Robin Hood's Progress to Nottingham,"

> "I'le hold you twenty marks, said bold Robin
>   Hood,
>   By the leave of our lady,
> That I'le hit a mark a hundred rod
>   And I'le cause a hart to dye."
>
> Robin Hood he bent up a noble bow,
>   And a broad arrow he let flye,
> He hit the mark a hundred rod,
>   And he caused a hart to dye.
>
> Some say hee brake ribs one or two,
>   And some say he brake three;
> The arrow within the hart would not abide,
>   But it glanced in two or three.
>
> The hart did skip, & the heart did leap,
>   And the hart lay on the ground.

Shortly afterwards, with the same fatal weapon, he brings down fifteen foresters who treated him badly; and when

> The people that lived in fair Nottingham
>   Came running out amain,
> Supposing to have taken bold Robin Hood
>   With the foresters that were slain,
>
> Some lost legs & some lost arms,
>   And some did lose their blood;
> But Robin hee took up his noble bow,
>   And is gone to the merry green wood.

In his extreme hour, according to the "Garland,"

"Give me," says Robin, "my bent bow in my
    hand,
And a broad arrow I'll let flee;
And where this arrow is taken up
    There shall my grave digg'd be.

Lay me a green sod under my head,
    And another at my feet;
And lay my bent bow by my side,
    Which was my music sweet."

Lastly, Robin Hood was dear to the English imagination as the representative of the forest life—as the joyous tenant of the greenwood—the spirit not to be cribbed and cabined in towns and cities, but rejoicing in entire unrestraint and the wildest freedom. For him too, in his rough way—

αζυ τι ψιθυρισμα και α πιτυσ αιπολε
    τηνα
α ποτι ταισ παγαισι μελισδεται

The greenwood is the home of his heart. The ballads that celebrate him are redolent of it. They are inspired by the breath of its breezes. They re-echo with the songs of its birds. They rejoice with a great joy in its abundant beauty. There is nowhere in our literature a heartier delight in the woodland than in these ballads. Take the opening lines of "Robin Hood and the Monk:"

In somer when the shawes be sheýne,
    And leves be large & longe,
His is full merry in feyre foreste
    To here the foulys song,

To se the dere draw to the dale,
    And leve the hilles hee,
And shadow him in the leves grene,
    Under the grene-wode tree.

Hit befell on Whitsontide
    Early in a May mornyng,
The son up faire can shyne,
    And the briddis mery can syng.

"This is a mery mornyng," said Litulle Johne,
    "Be hym that dyed on tre;
A more mery man than I am one
    Lyves not in Christianté.

Pluk up thi hert, my dere mayster,
    Litulle Johne can sey,
And thynk hit is a fulle fayre tyme,
    In a mornynge of May."

What bright, healthful happiness in a May morning! "Oh evil day, if I were sullen!" says with all his heart this outlaw of the fourteenth century. No wonder if Robin Hood came to be the type of such happiness; and that Shakespeare, when portraying it with an exquisite grace and sympathy in the sweetest of all pastoral poems, recalls him to mind, and makes Charles the Wrestler answer in this wise Oliver's question, "Where will the old duke live?" *"They say he is already in the forest of Arden, and a many merry men with him; and there they live like the old Robin Hood of England: they say many young gentlemen flock to him every day, and fleet the time carelessly, as they did in the golden world."* (pp. 1-12)

> *John W. Hales and Frederick J. Furnivall,*
> *"Introduction to the Robin Hood Ballads," in*

Bishop Percy's Folio Manuscript: Ballads and Romances, Vol. I, *edited by John W. Hales and Frederick J. Furnivall, N. Trübner & Co., 1867, pp. 1-12.*

David C. Fowler (essay date 1968)

[*Fowler is an American literary historian who specializes in Middle English texts. In the following excerpt, he argues that* The Gest of Robyn Hode *is a poem of carefully balanced structure rather than a disjointed collocation of miscellaneous ballads.*]

It is often remarked that *A Gest of Robin Hood* is made up of a group of separate Robin Hood ballads "stitched" or "strung" together. To some extent this may simply echo Child's theory [in *English and Scottish Popular Ballads,* 1893-98] that it is "A popular epic composed from several ballads" and "A three-ply web" of adventures. But I suspect that theoretical considerations are not entirely absent, and that the form of this remarkable narrative is being interpreted in such a way as to establish the early existence of popular Robin Hood ballads. That earlier metrical narratives of Robin Hood existed may well be true; but to say that *A Gest of Robin Hood* is merely a stringing together of such tales is unfortunate, since it fails to recognize the poem's remarkable unity and above all its narrative symmetry.

The narrative symmetry of the early minstrel ballads is not something unique, but rather it is a phenomenon often found in various forms of narrative art, from medieval romance to the modern novel. One thinks immediately of the formal repetitions of a folktale like "Kulhwch and Olwen," which give the Welsh story a rather rigid symmetrical form. But the use of patterned repetitions in narrative structure is by no means confined to folk tradition; it can be found, admittedly in highly sophisticated form, in the work of such gifted narrators as Chrétien de Troyes and Chaucer.

One of the greatest poems of the twelfth century was Chrétien's *Perceval,* the first Grail narrative and the model for numerous later romances of the Arthurian cycle in both France and England. It chronicles the career of Perceval from his rustic home in the forest of Wales to the moment of his success as a knight of King Arthur's court, and concludes his story at a hermitage in the forest where the young hero learns to submit his worldly ambition to a higher, spiritual authority. The poem has a remarkable symmetry which reinforces its religious theme. It begins in spring, moves through the "winter" of Perceval's worldly prestige and acclaim, and returns to springtime (Easter) in the hermitage, the scene of the hero's spiritual rebirth. The contrast between the spirituality of Perceval and the worldliness of Gauvain is underscored by parallel adventures in the other world, Perceval at the Grail castle and Gauvain at Escavalon. The parallel lameness of Perceval's father and the fisher king point toward an identification of the two. Finally, similar incidents at the beginning and end of the narrative dramatize a change in the hero's values. When the story opens in the forest of Wales, Perceval meets a group of knights, magnificently clad in armor, and this experience leads him to seek knighthood at Arthur's court. At the end of the story, in the forest near the hermitage, he meets a group of knights and ladies barefoot and in ragged clothes (because it is Good Friday), and on their advice he is led to seek spiritual counsel at the hermitage.

The example of *Perceval* shows that in the hands of a skilled poet like Chrétien narrative repetition rarely means identical recurrence. Instead there is usually some dramatic change designed to introduce by contrast a new increment of meaning, as when the knights first appear to Perceval in shining armor, then in rags. Readers of Chaucer will recall a similar skilled use of repetitions to produce an admirable narrative symmetry in "The Knight's Tale," the relevance of which to Chaucer's theme has been well described by Charles Muscatine [in "Form, Texture, and Meaning in Chaucer's *Knight's Tale*," *PMLA*, LXV (1950)].

The fact that there has been little discussion of narrative symmetry in the ballads is perhaps due to the notion that the latter are lacking in art and therefore cannot be supposed to possess features in common with the poetry of a Chrétien or a Chaucer. But . . . the "new minstrelsy" which we are considering is patterned after medieval romance, and it can be expected to reflect its motifs and narrative structure. Hence it is not surprising, and probably not coincidental, that *A Gest of Robin Hode* displays the kind of narrative symmetry that we normally associate with medieval romance.

A Gest of Robyn Hode begins in the Arthurian manner. Robin Hood, the most courteous of outlaws, refuses to eat until he has some "vnkouth gest." He sends Little John and two other outlaws to find someone, and they return with a poor knight, Sir Richard at the Lee, who dines with Robin Hood and tells of his misfortune and his debt of four hundred pounds, owed to the abbot of Saint Mary's. Robin lends him the money on the security of Our Lady (sts. 1-81).

The poor knight, Sir Richard, finds the abbot at dinner and first pleads for an extension of time, but is cruelly refused. He then pays the debt to the consternation of the abbot and sets out to return to Robin Hood his money (sts. 82-143). Meanwhile, Little John secretly takes service with the hated sheriff of Nottingham. One day, after quarreling with the sheriff's butler, who refused to serve him any dinner, John makes friends with the cook (after fighting him to a draw), and the two of them join Robin in the greenwood, bringing with them much of the sheriff's silverware and a considerable amount of money. The sheriff, meanwhile, is in the forest hunting, and Little John tricks him into an ambush, with the result that he is forced to have dinner and spend the night with Robin Hood and the outlaw gang before being allowed to return to Nottingham (sts. 144-204).

In the greenwood Robin Hood refuses to dine until he has sent Little John and two other outlaws to find some uncouth guest. They return with a monk of Saint Mary's abbey, who dines with the outlaws and then is forced to surrender his money. Robin sends the monk on his way and says that Our Lady has discharged the knight's debt;

when Sir Richard returns to the greenwood and attempts to repay the outlaw, Robin will take nothing (sts. 205-280).

When Robin Hood and his men come to Nottingham to participate in an archery contest, the sheriff tries to capture them but they escape and are given protection by their friend Sir Richard (sts. 281-316). The frustrated sheriff seeks the help of King Edward and furthermore captures the knight with a view to executing him quickly. But Sir Richard's wife appeals to Robin, who rescues the knight and kills the sheriff (sts. 317-353).

At last the King arrives with the intention of capturing Robin Hood, and, disguised as an abbot, he is stopped by the gang and forced to dine on his own deer before he is recognized by the outlaws, who ask forgiveness. The King grants them a pardon, on condition that Robin Hood and his men will come into the King's service (sts. 354-417). For sport the King and his men are clothed in Lincoln green and all return happily to Nottingham. Robin Hood is unhappy in the King's household, and after little more than a year he returns to the greenwood and never again enters the King's service. Eventually he is treacherously slain by the prioress of Kyrkesly (sts. 418-456).

Even this brief summary of the plot of *A Gest of Robyn Hode* indicates the central theme and its relationship to the sequence of events. Robin Hood is a courteous outlaw, with a passion for justice, who therefore hates the exploiting, greedy monks of Saint Mary's and the treacherous sheriff of Nottingham, but who loves good knights like Sir Richard and is unfailingly loyal to his king.

It will be noted that one of the most frequent events in the *Gest* is a dinner. This is perhaps understandable as a form

Robin Hood and his Merry Men, by Daniel Maclise, painted between 1839 and 1845.

of wish fulfilment with considerable appeal to a popular audience of the poor and needy, but it serves in this poem primarily as an occasion for the testing of character. Robin Hood has dinner with the knight, the sheriff, the monk, and the King, which is to say nearly all of the major figures in the story, and each time, in various ways, the dinner provides an opportunity for some kind of test or disclosure. Even Sir Richard's interview at Saint Mary's takes place while the abbot is having his dinner. It is possible, I suppose, to assume that the various Robin Hood ballads "stitched together" to form the *Gest* all simply happened to contain these commonplace eating episodes. But this assumption should not be allowed to obscure the fact that our author has used these scenes with great skill to dramatize the courtesy of Robin Hood's friends and the avarice and cruelty of his enemies.

Instances of the courtesy of Robin Hood and his companions are to be found almost from the very beginning of the poem. Little John is quite correct in his first approach to the knight, Sir Richard at the Lee (sts. 243-244):

> Litell Johnn was full curteyes,
>   And sette hym on his kne:
> 'Welcom be ye, gentyll knyght,
>   Welcom ar ye to me.
>
> 'Welcom be thou to grene wode,
>   Hende knyght and fre;
> My maister hath abiden you fastinge,
>   Syr, al these oures thre.'

Robin is equally courteous in receiving the knight, and their conversation throughout the meal could be taken as a model of courtly behavior (sts. 29-31):

> They brought hym to the lodge-dore;
>   Whan Robyn hym gan see,
> Full curtesly dyd of his hode
>   And sette hym on his knee.
>
> 'Welcome, sir knight,' than sayde Robyn,
>   'Welcome art thou to me;
> I haue abyden you fastinge sir,
>   All these ouris thre.'
>
> Than answered the gentyll knight,
>   With wordes fayre and fre;
> 'God the saue, goode Robyn,
>   And all thy fayre meyne.'

This scene contrasts sharply with that which takes place in the dining hall of the abbey where Sir Richard comes to plead for an extension of time for repaying his loan (sts. 102-103):

> Lordes were to mete isette
>   In that abbotes hall;
> The knyght went forth and kneled downe,
>   And salued them grete and small.
>
> 'Do gladly, syr abbot,' sayd the knyght,
>   'I am come to holde my day:'
> The fyrst word the abbot spake,
>   'Hast thou brought my pay?'

The knight pleads vainly for mercy in turn to the high justice, the sheriff, and again to the abbot, who villainously tells him to "spede the out of my hall." The good knight at last loses patience (st. 115):

> Vp then stode that gentyll knyght,
>   To the abbot sayd he,
> "To suffre a knyght to knele so longe,
>   Thou canst no curteysye.'

When the knight suddenly confronts the abbot and his men with the money for payment of the loan, he also points the moral (st. 121):

> 'Haue here thi golde, sir abbot,' saide the knight,
>   'Which that thou lentest me;
> Had thou ben curtes at my comynge,
>   Rewarded shuldest thou haue be.'

At this news the abbot seems to have lost his appetite (st. 122):

> The abbot sat styll, and ete no more,
>   For all his ryall fare;
> He cast his hede on his shulder,
>   And fast began to stare.

In a subsequent dinner scene less satiric than comic, the sheriff of Nottingham, faced with the necessity of eating a meal with his own stolen silverware, suffers a similar loss of appetite (st. 191):

> Sone he was to souper sette,
>   And served well with silver white,
> And when the sherif sawe his vessell,
>   For sorowe he myght nat ete.

By far the most elaborate repetition of the dinner scene is that involving the monk in the fourth fytte, which is closely modeled after Robin's dinner with the knight in the first fytte. This is one of our best illustrations of the minstrel's technique, for it has enough close repetition to show how such a device could serve as a memory aid, while at the same time there is enough significant variation to dramatize an important contrast between the knight and the monk. Whole passages are repeated: stanzas 17-20, telling how Little John, Uruch, and William Scarlok go in search of a dinner guest, are repeated almost exactly in stanzas 208-212, with the exception of one stanza (211) in which Little John girds on a sword. [Fowler adds in a footnote: "The girding on of the sword in stanza 211 of the *Gest* is added deliberately, I think, to foreshadow the hostility and threat of violence implicit in the meeting of the outlaws with the monk and his party. A similar function can be assigned to stanza 245, in which Robin warns the monk that he will lose his money if he is lying about the amount."] Then the passages diverge at that point where the dinner guests arrive (sts. 21, 213):

> But as they loked in to Bernysdale
>   Bi a derne strete,
> Than came a knyght ridinghe;
>   Full sone they gan hym mete.
>   . . . . .
> But as they loked in Bernysdale,
>   By the hye waye,
> Than were they ware of two blacke monkes,
>   Eche on a good palferay.

Even the slight variations here point a contrast. The knight takes a sidestreet, the monks ride (proudly? apprehensively?) on the highway; he rides alone "in symple aray" (st. 23), while the monks ride each on a good palfrey in the company of fifty men (st. 216).

Our attitude toward the monk is determined somewhat by the behaviour of the outlaws toward him. Whereas Little John had been very courteous to the knight, he speaks sharply to the monk when he orders him to have dinner with his master. But there is likewise a contrast in the reply of the guests (sts. 26, 221):

> 'Who is thy maister?' sayde the knyght;
> Johnn sayde, Robyn Hode;
> 'He is a gode yoman,' sayde the knyght,
> 'Of hym I haue herde moche gode.'
>
> . . . . .
>
> 'Who is your mayster?' sayd the monke;
> Lytell Johan sayd, Robyn Hode;
> 'He is a stronge thefe,' sayd the monke,
> 'Of hym herd I neuer good.'

Like the knight before him, the monk is brought to the outlaws' lodge, but unlike Sir Richard he fails the test of courtesy (sts. 226-227):

> Robyn dyde adowne his hode,
> The monke whan that he se;
> The monke was not so curteyse,
> His hode then let he be.
>
> 'He is a chorle, mayster, by dere worthy God,'
> Than sayd Lytell Johan:
> 'Thereof no force,' sayd Robyn,
> 'For curteysy can he none.'

But perhaps the most skilful use of repetition here is in the passage describing the outlaws' search of their guest's personal effects (sts. 39-43, 243-248). A basic contrast is of course seen in the fact that the knight tells the truth when asked how much money he has, whereas the monk lies. The one extra stanza in the repeated passage, however, warns the monk that he will lose his money if he is lying (st. 245), and the outcome of the search points a dramatic contrast between the knight and the monk (sts. 42-43, 247-248):

> Lyttell Johnn sprede downe hys mantell
> Full fayre vpon the grounde,
> And there he fonde in the knyghtes cofer
> But euen halfe a pounde.
>
> Littell Johnn let it lye full styll,
> And went to hys maysteer full lowe;
> 'What tidynges, Johnn?' sayde Robyn;
> 'Sir, the knyght is true inowe.'
>
> . . . . .
>
> Lytell Johan spred his mantell downe,
> As he had done before,
> And he tolde out of the monkes male
> Eyght hondred pounde and more.
>
> Lytell Johan let it lye full styll,
> And went to his mayster in hast;
> 'Syr,' he sayd, 'the monke is trewe ynowe,
> Our Lady hath doubled your cast.'

John's leisurely obeisance in the first passage is in contrast with his haste in the second, and a nice distinction in the meanings of "true" is implied. The knight spoke the truth;

the monk is a "true" messenger of Our Lady—he has brought the money—which is indeed a courteous interpretation of the monk's duplicity.

From what has been said of the narrative symmetry employed by the poet it should be evident that *A Gest of Robyn Hode* is the work of a skilled artist, and that the stitching that binds the various episodes together is more significant than the assumed vestigial remains of earlier Robin Hood ballads. That the repetitions we have examined occurred independently in earlier ballads and then converged accidentally to reinforce the poet's theme is extremely unlikely; but if on the other hand it is supposed that the poet changed the form of the ballads which he strung together so as to achieve a narrative symmetry, then this supposition merely implies that his poem utilizes earlier narrative sources, a fact which has long been known. Hence it is not really possible to speak of sources for the poem *in ballad form*. All this leads me, in the absence of other evidence, to the conclusion that the separate Robin Hood ballads often supposed to be the sources of the poem actually did not come into being until well after 1400, which is the date usually assigned to *A Gest of Robyn Hode*. (pp. 72-9)

David C. Fowler, "Rymes of Robyn Hood," in his A Literary History of the Popular Ballad, *Duke University Press, 1968, pp. 65-93.*

Maurice Keen   (essay date 1961)

[*Keen is an English historian who specializes in Medieval culture. In the following excerpt, he discusses how the Robin Hood ballads—along with other "outlaw ballads," including those of Gamelyn, Hereward, and Fulk Fitzwarin—express discontent among medieval peasantry, a trend which culminated in the Peasant Revolt of 1381.*]

The characteristic plot of the Robin Hood ballads, and indeed of all the later outlaw stories, is very simple. It is a tale in which wicked men meet a merited downfall, and the innocent and the unfortunate are relieved and rewarded. As the wicked are always the rich and powerful and the innocent the victims of poverty and misfortune, they may be said to be in essence stories of social justice. Though an occasional episode may have nothing to do with this theme, this is only the result of uneclectic borrowing by authors who only half understood the demands of their material. In fact the general drift of nearly all the stories is the same; clearly it was not only their traditional source which was shared by the ballad makers, the circumstances which inspired them were common to them also.

Their theme is the righting of wrongs inflicted by a harsh system and unjust men. It is this that raises the stature of Robin Hood above that of the common thieves who lurked about every highway in a lawless age; he was no ordinary robber:

> Strong thievys were tho childerin none
> But bowmen good and hende.

He stole from the rich only to feed the poor. It is this that gives point to his ferocity; he was dreaded only by those whose wealth was undeserved. It is also this that gives point to his liberality; there is more in it than the traditional medieval loyalty of master to man, for he was open-handed also to all those in real need, the victims of misfortune and the oppressed poor. For he was essentially the people's hero. His friends were to be found among the pindars and potters of the world, or with knights whom fraud or mischance had reduced to penury; he belonged to a different social world to exiled nobles like Hereward and Fulk Fitzwarin, whose companions were high born like themselves. The lowly people whom he befriended responded to his championship of their cause; always in the ballads and stories they are the outlaws' staunchest allies. Richard atte the Lee lowered his drawbridge to let in Robin Hood's men as they fled from the sheriff, though by his act he risked his life and lands; it was the swineherd's boy whom they had helped who slipped away to the forest to warn Adam Bell and Clym of the Clough that Cloudisley was a prisoner in Carlisle. So it was too with Gamelyn; the simple folk stood steadfastly by him:

> There was no lewde man in the hall that stod
> That wolde do Gamelyn anything but good.

It was people such as these that were embraced in Robin Hood's 'good yeomanry', and their rewards were tangible. The potter went away paid for his wares three times over; Sir Richard had again not only his four hundred pounds but the interest thereon that doubled it. Alan-a-Dale in another ballad had back his bride who had been 'chosen to be an old knights delight'; the widow in the ballad of *Robin Hood and the Three Squires* not only saw her sons who had been condemned to die for poaching free once more, but also avenged upon their enemies. Robin Hood was true to his own maxim, 'Look ye do non housbonde no harme'; he was the man to right the wrongs of the poor:

> What man that helpeth a gode yeman
> His frende then will I be,

he declared. Where he acted, moreover, justice was not only done but was seen to be done.

Martin Parker, who compounded his *True Tale of Robin Hood* out of old ballads, was near enough to the mark when he sketched the character of his hero:

> The widow and the fatherlesse
> He woulde send means unto,
> And those whom famine did oppresse
> Found him a friendly foe.

But the poor man of Robin Hood's story is not the traditional toiling, suffering peasant of so much medieval literature, whose cry of woe, unheard on earth, goes up to heaven where his reward is prepared for him. There is hardly a hint of pathos in the ballad-makers' treatment of those victims of want and injustice whom the outlaw helped in need. The peasant people with whom Robin Hood mingled were yeomen, independent and with a pride in themselves and their free status, who would brook interference from no man. Robin himself was a yeoman 'corteys and free'; Little John when he first met his master was a young giant, 'brisk' and 'lusty', already famed far and wide for his strength; Alan-a-Dale was a bold youth clad in a scar-

let cloak and with a bow in his hand. When in the ballad of *Robin Hood and the Tinker* the outlaw asked the man what knave he was, the answer was proud and defiant:

> 'No knave, no knave', the tinker said,
> 'And that you soon shall know;
> Whether of us hath done most wrong
> My crab tree staff shall show'.

It was his independence of speech, his demand that he be not trifled with, that won the potter Robin Hood's friendship and the freedom of his and the outlaws' society:

> 'By my trowet, thou says soth' sayde Roben
> 'Thou says goode yemanrey.'

There is nothing menial about the bearing of Adam the Spencer in *Gamelyn;* Adam Bell and Clym of the Clough 'had dread for no man', even in the King's hall. Their independence of spirit is an essential part of the atmosphere of the outlaw ballads; the whole theme of the 'free forest' revolves around it. The life of those who dwell in the woods may be harder than that of hermit or friar, as the *Geste* declares, but at least it is free; the men of the forest choose their own law and live untrammelled. With their bows in their hands and the waste of woodland about them, these are the freest spirits in the land; they are not bound to any soil or to the whim of any master:

> Mery it was in grene forest,
> A'mong the leves grene,
> Where that men walke bothe east and west,
> Wyth bowes and arrows keen.

They belong to a society of their own, and in their own territory they speak on equal terms with whoever comes, be he bishop or baron. There is nothing humble about the yeomen of the ballads; poor they may be, but they hold themselves erect and proud, 'comely, corteys and good'.

On the one side in the ballads stands Robin Hood and the great brotherhood of good yeomen, independent and defiant. Against them on the other side are ranged all those who use their rank and possessions to cheat and oppress, to hold down the poor in unwilling thraldom. Two classes of men in particular earn the undying enmity of the outlaws, the officers of the law and the rich churchmen. The retribution which always overtakes them in the end reveals their incorrigible villainy. It is in the ferocious verse of the *Tale of Gamelyn* that the bitterness of the hatred in which these men were held finds its fiercest expression; in it we can almost hear the groans of the maimed clergy who were carried home from Gamelyn's hall in 'carts and waynes', and the rattle of the bones of the sheriff and justice upon their windy gallows. But the same theme runs consistently through all the outlaw poems.

It is strange to find in the guardians of the law the villains in a poetic cycle whose undercurrent theme is the triumph of justice. Yet it is consistently so: the sheriff, the King's justice, and the foresters who enforce the arbitrary precepts of the law of the King's forest, are the men who are singled out to be the victims of an exemplary retribution. It is significant, therefore, that the ballad makers are always careful to particularize the abuse which these men have made of their position. The sheriff is a man in whose word no one can put the slightest trust; no trickery or injustice is too despicable for him to stomach. Though the case between them is *sub judice* and Sir Richard atte the Lee has sworn to answer for his conduct before the King, the sheriff will have him ambushed when he is hawking alone by the river, and do his damnedest to see him hanged before any questions can be asked. If he takes an outlaw in the wood, there will not even be the mockery of a trial; Guy of Gisborne or the first-comer may crave his death for a boon and will be satisfied. The sheriff in *Gamelyn* does not shrink from shedding the innocent blood of his own brother:

> 'If he have not that oon, he will have the other.'

It is the same with the justice. His judgements have been bought almost before a tale begins. What hope had Sir Richard of obtaining a delay at the law when his judge was already the abbot's man?

> 'I am holde with the abbot' sayde the Justice
> 'Both with cloth and fee.'

Judge and jury alike in *Gamelyn* had been hired to hang Sir Ote; the process in their court provided not justice but a legal travesty thereof. These men have earned the fate that overtakes them in long careers of crime, and when the end comes no pity is wasted on them, for only by their death will men ultimately be free from their oppression. So when finally in the ballad of *Robin Hood and the Three Squires,* the Sheriff of Nottingham is hanged on his own gallows 'in the glen', we may speak justifiably of the poem having a happy ending. The tale of his misdeeds has already revealed him to be incorrigible in wickedness.

This care to particularize the crimes of sheriff and justice explains the curious attitude of the outlaw poems towards the law's officers. They are not hated because of the law which they administer, but because their administration of it is corrupt. Before justice's guardians are attacked it is made clear that their justice is a mockery. There is no animus against the law itself; did not Sir Ote in the *Tale of Gamelyn* himself end his days as the King's justice? Significantly in the case of the foresters the treatment is not the same. They are slain indifferently; Adam Bell and his companions had forty dead foresters to account for, and Robin Hood is said to have killed fifteen of them single-handed as he went to Nottingham:

> 'You have found mee an archer' saith Robin
> Hood
> 'Which will make your wives for to wring'.

There are no tears shed over Guy of Gisborne or Wrennock of the Dunne, though the story of their crimes remains untold. The reason is not far to seek, and it lies in the nature of the law the foresters administered. The forest law was arbitrary and tyrannical; it threw men into prison on suspicion to await trial at the convenience of the forest justices. It knew no equity, and those who lived on lands where it ran had no recourse to common law to protect them from its injuries. For the venial sin of poaching the penalty could be death. It was not for any real crimes committed, the widow told Robin Hood, that her three sons were condemned to die; it was:

> ' . . . for slaying of the King's fallow deer,

> Bearing their long bows with thee.'

It was because they enforced without mercy a merciless law which had its foundation not in custom nor equity but in arbitrary will that the foresters were hated, as the dying words of the Scots outlaw, Johnnie Cock, whom they shot as he hunted in the woods, tell us:

> 'Woe be to you, foresters,
> And an ill death may you die!
> For there would not a wolf in a' the wood
> Have done the like to me.'

Here it is the law itself which is resented, because there was no shadow of justice in it. The crimes of sheriffs and men of law are retailed because in the ballad-makers' ideal world the sheriffs and justices would be better men; those of the foresters are not because their calling itself is unjust and in an ideal world they would be out of work.

The case of Robin Hood's other traditional enemies, the rich churchmen, is very similar to that of the men of law. Once again their misdeeds are particularized. Their greed, their frauds and their lying have been proven to the hilt before they come to grief. Indeed there is not much of the priest about them in the ballads. They are hard, pitiless men, who in their covetousness have forgotten the Christian quality of mercy. To the pleas of Gamelyn, chained to the post of his brother's hall, they were deaf as the post itself; Sir Richard atte the Lee begged in vain to the Abbot of St. Mary's for a delay to pay his debt:

> The abbot sware a full grete othe;
> 'By God that dyed on tree,
> Get the londe where thou may,
> For thou getest none of me'.

It was no wonder that Robin Hood gave his famous bidding to his men:

> 'These bishoppes and these arche bishoppes
> Ye schal hem bete and bynde.'

Their conduct deprived them of any claim which their religious calling might make on his mercy, or that of any other of their fellow Christians. But once again, as in the case of the men of law, it is noticeable that Robin Hood's animus is against particular churchmen and not the Church itself. When the King came to Sherwood disguised as an abbot, Robin would only take half the alms that he offered him, and his conduct was courtesy itself; he took the abbot 'full fayre by the hond' and spread a royal feast before him 'under his trystel-tree'. He himself was always the model of conventional piety. His own sorrow in the forest was his enforced absence from the mass:

> 'Yea, on thyng greves me' seid Robin,
> 'And does my hert mych woo;
> That I may not no solemn day
> To mass or Matyns go.'

According to the *Geste*, he built a chapel in Barnesdale dedicated to the Magdalene. Our Lady was his patron saint; when Guy of Gisborne wounded him, his prayer to her 'that was both mother and may' gave him strength for the riposte. It was not against religion that he fought, as the mythologists who see in him a devotee of the witch religion, would have it; it was against the rich cleric whose insatiable hunger for land would not stop short at fraud. It is as landlords, not as priests, that abbots and monks play a part in the outlaw ballads, and it is as unjust and ungenerous landlords that they are robbed, beaten and bound.

It is the churchmen of rank whom the outlaws persecute, the bishops and archbishops, the abbots and the officers of the great monasteries. Against the lesser clergy they have no animus, and in the friars, significantly, they find their friends. Though he does not come into any of the early outlaw ballads, Friar Tuck seems to have been long associated with the outlaws. In the fragment of a play of Robin Hood among the Paston papers, which dates from 1475, he has a part to play, and before that in the reign of Henry V, there was a real outlaw, Richard Stafford, who went under the alias of 'Frere Tuk'. The friars were just the kind of persons whom one might expect to be the outlaws' friends. They were vowed to poverty, and their rule made them the natural critics of the monks who could enjoy privately the profits of their wide estates in the seclusion of their cloisters. As mendicant preachers they mingled with the poor, and many of them shared the same humble origins with the people of the countryside. Whether or not he was really the same man as Tuck, it need not surprise us that the *Ballad of Robin Hood and the Curtal Friar of Fountains Abbey* should end with the latter bound for the greenwood in the company of Robin's merry men.

Though it is among those who have riches and high rank that Robin's enemies, both in the religious and in the secular worlds, are to be found, it is important to note that the poems about him reveal no animus against wealth or rank as such. The poems do not just divide the world into rich and poor, and describe the struggle of their champions. To hereditary rank Robin Hood payed the respect which his age regarded as appropriate. Richard atte the Lee was justly proud that he was a knight, and what the ballad maker is anxious that we should know is that he enjoyed that rank by a right of birth which he does not attempt to question:

'A hundred wynter here before
  Myn auncestres knyghtes hath be.'

For him there was something essentially wrong about the idea that the son of an old family should lose his inheritances, and the attempt to wring it from him is contributory to the injustice of the abbot's part. Robin Hood and Little John by contrast honoured Sir Richard as was due:

'It were great shame' sayde Robin
'A knight alone to ryde'

and for just that reason he gave him Little John to be his knave and go with him. Knights and lords seemed to the ballad makers to be an essential part of the social system, and they did not question their right to a high social status. They even reproduced in the ranks of the outlaw's own society a graded hierarchy; Gamelyn was 'King of the Outlaws', and the crown that he is said to have borne shows that this was not an empty euphemism for the leadership of a robber band, but a title which set him apart, giving him duties towards his men as well as the right to their obedience. As soon as he was free of prison he must hurry back to his subjects in the wood, to see how they went about their business and to judge their quarrels:

'To see how my yonge men ledyn her lif
Whether thy live in joye or ellys in stryf.'

Gamelyn, like Sir Richard, belonged to the hereditary knightly class, and he too was proud of his breeding. His brother's slurs on his legitimacy roused him to the quick: he was no 'gadelyng',

'But born of a lady and gotten of a knyght.'

It was only meet that the king of the outlaws should be a man of high birth. In some stories Robin Hood himself is made out to be a noble, though he is more usually a proud yeoman. One tradition makes him an outlawed Earl of Huntingdon; another makes him the child of 'Earl Richard's daughter', born in the greenwood, out of wedlock it is true, but of a father who was also of gentle blood:

O Willie's large O'lith and limb
And come o' high degree

The object of the ballad maker here is quite clearly to increase the stature of his hero, and like others of his age he took it that nobility of blood gave a man a right to special status and consideration. The middle ages were profoundly respectful to hereditary rank and they did not question its title to homage. They did on the other hand question the right of those whose actions belied any nobility of mind to the enjoyment of the privileges of noble status. They were not indignant against an unjust social system, but they were indignant against unjust social superiors. The ballad makers accepted this contemporary attitude and echoed it in their poems.

This explains why the ballads have nothing to say of the economic exploitation of the poor, of the tyranny of lords of manors whose bondmen were tied to the soil and bound by immemorial custom to till their land for him. For we might expect, from what we know of the social system of the countryside in the middle ages, to find Robin, as the champion of the poor, freeing serfs from bondage, harbouring runaway villeins in his band, and punishing the stewards of estates whose conduct was every whit as harsh and unjust as that of the officers of the law. But the middle ages did not view social injustice, as we do, in terms of the exploitation of one class by another; they admired the class system as the co-operation for the common wellbeing of the different estates of men. They recognized three different classes in their society; the knights and lords, whose business it was to protect Christendom in arms, the clerks who had charge of its spiritual well-being and whose duty was prayer, and the common men whose business it was to till the soil. Each rank had its obligation to discharge its proper duties without complaint, and, in the case particularly of the first two classes, not to abuse the privileges which its function gave it. That they were made to 'swink and toil' gave the peasants no ground for complaint; their occupation, as one preacher quaintly put it, lay in 'grobbynge about the erthe, as erynge and dungynge and sowynge and harwying' and 'this schuld be do justlie and for a good ende, withoute feyntise or falshede or gruechynge of hire estaat'. But those who failed to discharge their duties and abused their position had no right to a place in the system, nor to the profits of association. 'They neither labour with the rustics . . . nor fight with the knights, nor pray and chant with the clergy; therefore,' says the great Dominican, Bromyard, of such men 'they shall go with their own abbot, of whose Order they are, namely the Devil, where no Order exists but horror eternal.'

The law's object is ultimately to uphold social justice, and to the middle ages social justice meant a hierarchical social system. The trouble came when those who belonged to a high class used the wealth, which was given them to uphold their proper rank, to corrupt the law and abuse it for their own profit. Their ultimate sin was the use of their originally rightful riches to purchase more than was their due. For this reason, those who were shocked by flagrant injustice into attacking the accepted system criticized not the economic oppression which it almost automatically implied, but the corruption of evil men whose personal greed destroyed the social harmony of what they regarded as the ideal system. The method which these men employed was to buy the law, and to control by their position its application. It is for this reason that the outlaw ballads, whose heroes are the champions of the poor, are silent about the multitudinous economic miseries of the medieval peasant, and are concerned only or at least chiefly with an endless feud against the corrupt representatives of the law. Contemporary opinion diagnosed the disease which was gnawing at society as the personal corruption of those in high rank; that such disease was the inevitable accompaniment of their hierarchic system they simply could not see. This is why the animus in the outlaw ballads is against oppression by those who own the law, not against exploitation by those who own the land.

The cast of contemporary thought also explains the immunity from criticism of one particular lord in the outlaw ballads, that is, the King. Because they accepted that the law, with all its hierarchical implications, was ultimately just, and confined their attacks to those who administered it to wrong ends, men had to accept the justice of the law's ultimate fountain head, the King. Reverence for the King stood upon a basis even firmer than respect for high rank in medieval thought. He stood apart from the social system, in it but not born of it like the baronage, hallowed and anointed but not of the hated race of clerks, God's minister in the land, made sacred by the mysteries both of religion and tradition. He was its guardian, God's vicar in whose hand was placed the sword of temporal power, and from whose court no appeal lay in this world. We are trespassing here upon the edge of one of the great unsolved problems of medieval thinking, that of the powers of the King who in person is human, but the authority of whose office is divine. Whether as the Roman law declared the laws were in the King's mouth, or whether, as ancient custom implied, he was but the guardian of a law to which he and his people alike owed obedience, was a question over which the subtle doctors of the schools were themselves divided. The fiction of the King's two bodies, the corporal body which was mortal, the phenomenal shell of regality, and the mystic body which was undying, explained the problem posed by his office but did not solve it. About the answer a thousand problems revolved, as the

question of tyrannicide and the right to depose an erring monarch, and the question of prerogative and the force of the King's arbitrary will; but these were problems far beyond the understanding of the humble minstrels who sang the outlaw ballads and of the simple men who heard them. They only knew that the King was the ultimate repository of a law whose justice they acknowledged, and they saw treason against him as a betrayal of their allegiance to God himself. If they could only get past his corrupt officers, whose abuse of the trust reposed in them amounted to treason in itself, and bring their case before the King, they believed that right would be done. Their unshakeable faith in the King's own justice was the most tragic of the misconceptions of the medieval peasantry, and the ballad makers and their audiences shared it to the full.

Thus it is that just as the outlaws love the God whose servants they persecute, so they honour as truly as any of his subjects the King against whose officers they war:

> 'I love no man in all the worlde
> So well as I do my King'

declares Robin in the *Littel Geste.* In that ballad, indeed, comely King Edward is treated as almost as much a hero as Robin Hood himself. There is another ballad on this same theme where it is 'King Henry' who comes to the forest in disguise and is made welcome by the outlaws. All sorts of variant stories of the King's mixing in disguise with poachers of the forest and being entertained by them were once known, and several survive. There is one which tells of how Edward IV met with a tanner when he was out hunting, which has significantly opening lines very similar to the traditional summer setting of the scene in the ballads of Robin Hood; another tells of the King's clandestine feasting on poached meats with a shepherd in Windsor forest, in which the King adopts the name of Joly Robyn; another, which is incomplete, of his meeting a friar in Sherwood who combined the roles of hermit and forest archer. All these men are ultimately forgiven for their offences by the King and admitted to his intimacy. So also, when they finally come to him, the King always sees the justice of the outlaws' case and pardons them. He took Robin Hood with him to serve at his court; he pardoned, at his Queen's entreaty, Adam Bell and his companions; he forgave Gamelyn. Over the deaths of his servants he seldom shed any false tears. To Sir Richard he returned his lands which were confiscated; Ote and Gamelyn became his justices; Robin Hood and Adam Bell became his yeomen and exchanged their Lincoln green for the King's livery. The King is the *Deus ex machina* of the outlaw stories; by his authority the righting of wrongs done which has been the theme of the poems is stablished fast, and those who have served him loyally, if illegally, are rewarded. Occasionally, as in the ballad of *Adam Bell,* pardon is wrung from him unwillingly, but one knows that his word, unlike the sheriff's, cannot be broken when it is once given. Robin Hood in the ballads is the arbiter of an unofficial justice which accords with the unrecognized moral law; the King is authority, which ultimately endorses the moral law and makes its justice official.

The concept of justice is one which has held different meanings for different ages, and we should not, because it is said to be based in the moral law, read too modern an interpretation into it. The medieval picture of the day of judgement, with its vivid, hideous detail of the suffering of damned souls in a nether world of bestial demons, stands to remind us that for this age justice was retributive. It is this that explains the callousness, amounting almost to brutality, of some of the outlaw stories. Medieval man saw nothing tragic in the downfall of the wicked; awful and exemplary it might be, but not poignant. Justice, moreover, was in no way impaired by the fact that it could only be achieved by violent means, for the resort to force was ultimately nothing less than an appeal to the judgement of God, which does not err. The levying of war in a just cause was a duty, not a last resource forced on one by dire necessity. The shedding of innocent blood was of small moment provided the cause had absolute justice; had not God himself been forced by the exigences of nature, when he visited his wrath on the sins of Sodom and Gomorrah, to consume three other cities in the same storm of fire, although their inhabitants had not run up a more than average debit balance of sin? After all, the innocent had their reward laid up for them in heaven. If through mischance their fate was caught up on this earth in the retribution which overwhelmed the wicked, it was not a matter for undue regret, since death to them was but the gate to a better world. For an age of faith such as was the medieval period, there was nothing incongruous about justice and violence going hand in hand: they were familiar bedfellows.

The wildness of their life and the violence of their deeds cannot therefore be made a reproach to the outlaws. In taking the law into their own hands they were only falling back upon the ancient right of those who could not obtain justice to use force, and to use that force in the cause of others could only be altruism. When they shed the blood of their enemies, they were performing meritorious acts of retributive justice. Hence the endless tale of death and bloodshed which runs through the ballads. There are few holocausts so dramatic as the bloodbath with which the *Tale of Gamelyn* is rounded off; but it will not do to forget the forty foresters of the fee killed by Adam Bell, or the bloody mutilated head of Guy of Gisborne which Robin set on his bow's end, or the rotting corpses of the monk and his 'little page', hidden in the moss by the wayside in Barnsdale in *Robin Hood and the Monk*. Nor should one forget Gandelyn's words of triumph over the body of Wrennock of the Dunne, or Robin Hood's exultant cry in the *Geste,* as he stands over the sheriff's body in the square of Nottingham:

> 'Lye thou there, thou proude sheriffe,
>   Evyll mote thou cheve!
> There myght no man to thee truste
>   The whyles thou were alyve.'

Face to face with their enemies, one will find the outlaws pitiless enough, for one cannot spare thought for pity in the cause of justice.

This streak of violence does not, of course, run through all the ballads. There are some, like that of *Robin Hood and the Potter,* which preserve the gay mood of their opening lines throughout. But it is important not to overlook it in other ballads, because it is so much taken for granted that it can quite easily pass unnoticed. There are the exultant moments which strike one, as those quoted above, but there are plenty of deaths which are recorded without comment. The monk and his page are assassinated and quickly forgotten; the sheriff in *Guy of Gisborne* is shot down running and his death is dismissed in a line; in the ballad of *Robin Hood and the Three Squires* the drama of the sheriff's execution is quite undeveloped (by contrast, for instance, with the same scene in *Gamelyn*). This might be taken for callousness, but it is hardly even that. It is simply the recognition of the fact that in the cause of justice, blood must most probably be shed; indeed, that it ought to be. This is the second tragic misconception of the common man of the middle ages, that because his cause was just and force was an appeal to the judgement of God, his ends would be served by recourse to violence.

Behind the matter of the later outlaw stories, therefore, there seems to lie the common man's demand for social justice. This is the only consistent theme which runs through most of the poems. We have seen that the manner of its presentation accords well with what we might expect to be the prevalent attitudes of the times. What we have still to see is whether history will bear out this interpretation and show that in the fourteenth and fifteenth centuries, the period which seems from their background to be the setting of the ballads, there was a real demand from the common people for social justice. If there was, we must further examine whether or not it was framed in terms which accord with the recurrent grievances urged in the ballads.

By and large, the earlier middle ages seem to have been a period of oriental passivity among the common people. We know a great deal about the terms of their bondage, about the number of days in a week on which a villein had to work on his lord's land and about the fines and reliefs which he had to pay; we know plenty too about the economic organization of manors, the methods of tilling the soil, the function of lords' officers such as bailiffs and reeves and haywards. But of the peasants' attitude to all this we know very little. We can imagine that he grumbled, for the burdens put upon him seem to us to have been almost intolerable, but history has left no witness to his complaining of his hard fate. Once in a while we hear of the angry tenants of some specially tyrannical lord suddenly breaking into revolt and assassinating their master or burning his house; or of some body of peasants withdrawing their services from their lord in protest against some particularly harsh innovation. But these revolts and protests are confined to one estate at a time, and one and all seem to fizzle out in failure. They are not part of any great movement. The average peasant does not seem to have had much to say to the conditions which bound him to poverty and ancestral thraldom, and in the history of the age he plays his passive role in sullen silence.

But in the last centuries of the middle ages the giant who strides through modern times, the labouring man, collective and impersonal, seems to be stirring for the first time in his sleep. He is only half awake as yet, and with only glimmerings of political consciousness his efforts are doomed to failure. But from all over Europe comes the same story. Suddenly the passive peasant is in arms, and his wrath breaks upon his oppressors like a thunderstorm. In 1359 it was the peasants of France who rose in revolt in the hour of national disaster, when the King was a prisoner in England and the country was riven with civil war, and for a moment they caught their masters off their guard. The quelling of this rebellion of the *Jacquerie* was the one good deed for France of Charles the Bad, King of Navarre. In 1381 it was the peasantry of England who rose in the great Peasants' Revolt, and marched with Wat Tyler and John Ball to London. Their rising too, was relentlessly put down. In 1525 it was the peasants of Germany who took to arms, inspired by the preaching of Luther, only to be betrayed when their hero, horrified at the effect of his words, threw in his hand with the princes. In England at the end of the middle ages there seems to have been a permanent subcurrent of popular discontent, 1381 was the first occasion when it flamed up into widespread revolt, but there had been rumblings of the coming storm for years before that, and there had been scattered outbreaks of violence up and down the land. Stories were abroad of gatherings of recalcitrants in the woods at night, and of men banding together to support one another in a struggle for justice. In the very year after 1381 there were rumours of revolt in the West Country; there was open revolt in Cheshire in the 1390s, and there were many scattered local outbreaks over the succeeding years. Jack Cade's revolt in 1450 saw peasants marching on London once more, though there were others too, of higher rank, among the rebels. In Robin of Redesdale's revolt in the North in 1469 poor men again had their part. Down to the time of the Pilgrimage of Grace in 1536 and Kets rebellion in 1549 there seems to be a constant simmering of popular discontent just below the surface. But the same tragic sequel of repression follows all these outbreaks. They are bursts of sleepy-eyed wrath; half-blind, the peasant does not quite know what it is he is fighting for, except for a world in which his lot shall be less harsh. There is no realism about the aims he professes, and his leaders have not the understanding of politics to make realistic plans for the event of success. But though these risings were doomed to failure before they started, they do reveal just that background of widespread popular unrest which would make men listen, and admire the stories of an outlaw whose defiance of the law was more successful than their own.

Modern historians who have examined the causes of these revolts have diagnosed them in economic terms. But because the rebels were medieval men living in an age which tended to see everything in terms of law their demands were largely legal, which is what we would expect from the outlaw poems with their persistent bitterness against the men of law. Let us take the example of 1381. The revolt began when the Essex men rose against the King's officers and put Chief Justice Bealknap, who was sitting at Brentwood, to flight. At Bury, where there was a fierce outbreak, Chief Justice Cavendish was among the first to be assassinated. When the rebels reached London, they broke into the Temple and burned all the books of the lawyers that they could lay hands on. When Wat Tyler presented the demands of the rebels to the King at Smithfield

they were couched in legal terms. This is the account of them which is given in the *Anonimalle Chronicle:*

> And the said Wat then listed the matters which were in question, and he demanded that there should be no law but the law of Winchester, and that sentence of outlawry should not be pronounced in any case at law henceforth, and that no lord should have seigneurial jurisdiction . . . but that all should be in the King's lordship . . . and that there should be no bondmen in England, and no serfdom, but that all should be free and of one condition.

What a bondman meant was a villein, and villeinage was a legal status, not an economic one. The lord's rights over his villeins were again legal, for he could tax them at his will; they were his justiceables and against him, and him only, they had no recourse to common law. To be sure he could and did use his legal advantages for the purpose of economic exploitation, but what the peasant felt and hated were the legal disabilities of his position, and his first demand was that they should be abolished.

What the rebels of 1381 demanded was in effect not a review of the whole system but reform on particular points in it which bore harshly on them. Once satisfied of this and issued with new charters, most of them were content to return to their estates. Their aims were bounded by local horizons, and this was in part the reason for their downfall. The rebels of St. Albans, for instance, were not particularly concerned to aid a general movement; they were concerned to get Wat Tyler's aid in wringing from their abbot the concessions which he had consistently denied them, the right to use handmills in their own homes, the right to hunt in the chases and warrens, of the liberty and the right to govern their borough through their own corporation. Significantly, the rebels put their case in terms of the restoration of old liberties of which they had been illegally defrauded by tyrannous masters in the past. Rumours were running about of ancient charters which had been conveniently lost; at Bury it was the terms of a charter of Canute which the rebels demanded, at St. Albans they set the abbot hunting his muniments for a long charter written in golden letters and said to have been granted by King Offa in the eighth century, six hundred years previously. Significantly again, the peasants were careful by their conduct to prove the justice of their cause: they would not demean it by indiscriminate looting. When they set light to John of Gaunt's vast palace in London, the Savoy, its priceless treasures were carried away and cast into the Thames; those who were caught thieving were thrown into the flames and were consumed with the house. They ravaged and burned but they did not steal, for they were God's avengers of injustice, and what they did, they did in the name of the Father, Son and Holy Ghost, and King Richard. All this is just what we might expect from the tone of the outlaw ballads.

Besides the men of law, Robin Hood's other traditional enemies were the rich clerks, and they were the other enemies also of the peasants of 1381. If ever anyone followed to the letter Robin Hood's advice to his men:

'These bishoppes and these arche bishoppes,

Ye schal hem bete and bynde,'

it was Wat Tyler's men who beheaded Simon of Sudbury, the Archbishop of Canterbury, on Tower Hill. He was not the only cleric to suffer at the hands of the rebels: John of Cambridge, Prior of Bury, was killed in Suffolk along with Sir John Cavendish, and so was the Abbey's steward, John de Lakingheth. All up and down the areas affected, monasteries were attacked, and the court rolls and manorial extents which recorded the terms of their tenants' services solemnly burnt; at Canterbury in Kent, at St. Albans in Hertford, at Bury in Suffolk, at St. Benet's Holm and Benham and Carrow in Norfolk. The peasants had good cause to hate the possessionate clergy. A corporate landlord always tends to be harsher than a personal one, because its officer cannot, as an individual owner can, take account of cases of special hardship, because his duty is to the corporation, not the tenant. The medieval church was no exception to this rule. They had besides the reputation of being particularly conservative landlords; where for instance a borough lay within an abbey's liberty, the monastery often clung to its rights of jurisdiction over the affairs of the inhabitants long after all the neighbouring towns had obtained royal charters giving rights of self-government.

Deep resentment of the Church's vast wealth and especially that of the monasteries, was in any case a widespread feeling in this period and shared by many of higher rank than the peasants. In the later middle ages the monasteries were ceasing to play the prominent part which had once been theirs in the religious and intellectual life of the kingdom. Comparatively few bishops of the fourteenth and fifteenth centuries were monks, and intellectual leadership had switched by then to the rising universities. More and more the monasteries' public role seemed to be limited to that of influential landlords; it was as landlords that their abbots' voices had weight in the parliaments and councils of the realm, while their work of prayer was carried out unseen in the cloister—if indeed it was carried out. The habits of many monks were becoming lax, and their outlook more secular; Chaucer's monk was known better as a huntsman than a man of God. Of course, there were exceptions by the legion, and the monasteries still doubtless housed many men of saintly life and thinking; but men were already beginning to wonder whether these multitudinous religious houses were really serving sufficient religious purpose to justify the vast estates which they were constantly and carefully extending. They were the butt of a great troop of satirists; Wycliffe castigated their unmerited riches in his fierce rhetoric. In the Parliament of 1371 a move was made to seize the land of monasteries, and there were many even among the great who were ready to support it. Rumblings of the storm which broke upon the English monasteries in Henry VIII's time could be heard nearly two hundred years before. We need not be surprised to find Robin Hood's preying on the rich clergy regarded as an act of elemental justice.

Among the lower clergy the discontented peasants found many sympathizers. John Ball, the mad priest of Kent, was one of their leaders; John Wrawe, leader of the Suffolk rebels, was the Chaplain of Ringsfield. In particular the friars were accused of being in league with them; their in-

surrectionary sermons were said by many to be at the back of the revolt. William Langland, writing his *Vision of Piers Plowman* only a few years before, had complained of the social anarchy which they preached:

> They preche men by Plato and proven it by Seneca,
> That alle thinges under hevene ought to be in comune.

One can see in the ecclesiastical demands of the peasants the influence of the ideas of the medicant orders, with their doctrine of evangelical poverty for the Church. This is what Wat Tyler asked for in this matter: 'That the goods of Holy Church be no longer left in the hands of men of religion . . . and that there shall be no bishop or prelate in England save one, and that their goods and lands and all their possessions be divided among the Commons, saving to Churchmen enough to live on.' Jack Cade's rebels in 1450 showed the same animus against the rich clergy, but Sir Thomas More exaggerated when he wrote that they intended 'to kyll up the clergie, and sel priestes heddes as gode chepe as shepes heddes, thre for a peni, bie who would'. The peasant rebels had their friends among the clergy, in the poorer of the friars and parsons and the hedge-priests like John Ball; it was rich clerks who abused their wealth and oppressed the poor that they hated.

It will not do to overlook the deep undercurrent of religious feeling in the minds of the peasants; 'We are men formed in Christ's likeness and they handle us as beasts.' Echoes of the sermons of the great homilists run all through the sayings attributed to the rebels. Even John Ball's famous catch

> When Adam delved and Eve span,
> Who was then the gentleman?

was not new; the same rhyme is found in a poem written on the hermit's life by an English anchorite in the early fourteenth century. John Ball's letter to the peasants opens with a call to them to stand together in Christ:

> John Balle seynt Marye prist gretes wele alle maner men and byddes hem in the name of the Trinite, Fader and Sone and Holy Ghost, Stande manlyche togedyr and in trewthe, and helpeth trewthe, and trewthe shall helpe you.

The *Continuator of Knighton's Chronicle* collected a series of other 'letters' of this kind which were said to have circulated, curious little pastiches of catch phrases, and nearly all have a religious tinge. 'John Mylner asketh helpe to turne his mylne aright. He hath grounden smal smal; the King's son of Heven he schal pay for alle.' Rygt and mygt, wylle and skylle; God spede every dele.' 'God do bote, for now is time.' Behind these snatches culled largely from contemporary pulpit literature, one sees the same conventional, trusting piety that is a feature of the Robin Hood ballads, and which here is combined with strong anticlericalism. (pp. 145-66)

Maurice Keen, "The Outlaw Ballad as an Expression of Peasant Discontent," in his The Outlaws of Medieval Legend, *Routledge and Kegan Paul, 1961, pp. 145-73.*

David Wiles (essay date 1981)

[*In the following excerpt, Wiles documents the represen-*
tations of Robin Hood, Maid Marian, Friar Tuck, and
Little John in the medieval May games and rituals.]

It is remarkable how often Robin Hood appears in the ancient records in close association with a Lord of the May
or Summer King. At Amersham in 1530 we find money
received 'of the lord for Robin Hood'. In Croscombe the
reckonings from the 'sport' or 'revel' of Robin Hood are
handed in almost every year, but in 1477/8 and 1503/4,
when Robin Hood makes no appearance, we find instead
receipts from a 'King's revel'. At Kingston, from the point
when the records begin in 1503, we read of a may-game
called the 'Kingham', involving the election of a male as
king and female as queen; and since a crown was supplied
to the morris dancers in 1516, it appears that they were
closely involved in the ceremony. Robin Hood and the
king alike make gatherings at Whitsuntide, and often their
costs and receipts are accounted together. The morris men
never gather money themselves, for only their lords may
do so. In 1525 the word 'Kingham' is struck out, and
'Church Ale' substituted: it seems from this entry, the last
time a Kingham is mentioned, that the king and queen became passive presidents at the feast, while all active gathering of money came to be done by Robin Hood.

At Reading, in the parish of St Lawrence, a 'king play' re-

Robin Hood and Friar Tuck, in Howard Pyle's illustration from
his Merry Adventures of Robin Hood, *1883.*

places the 'May play called Robin Hood' for a single year
in 1502. In 1504 and 1505 we find that the church-
wardens themselves are gathering at Whitsun in addition
to Robin Hood. In 1506 there are no Whitsun entries, for
the parish seems to have put all its efforts into mounting
a Corpus Christi pageant. Then in 1507, when Robin
Hood makes his last appearance, we have an additional
'gathering in money' at Whitsun, and the mention of a
'king play'. In subsequent years money is regularly received 'of the young men for the king play at Whitsuntide'.
We do not know what motivated the wardens to set up a
rival or alternative gathering; perhaps Robin Hood the
outlaw proved more uncontrollable than an orthodox
May King. It is hard to believe that the young men of the
parish—a much smaller one than Kingston—would have
kept up the Robin Hood game on an unofficial basis in addition to the king game, and we must conclude that Robin
Hood and his men either vanished or transformed themselves into morris dancers. The morris men later involved
themselves in the king game, for in 1530, the year after
Maid Marian and the morris dancers were re-equipped by
the parish, we find a joint receipt entered for 'the king
game and morris dancers that year'. It is most improbable
that the parish would have supported two Lords at Whitsun, for rivals must already have existed in the other two
parishes of Reading. The young men of St Giles' have a
king play every Whitsun from the year records begin in
1518; we have no early records for St Mary's, but there
were morris dancers and a 'lord' at Whitsun 1556.

A final piece of evidence for identifying the Robin Hood
game with the king game is provided by the borough records of Henley-on-Thames. The Council resolved in September 1499 that money remaining in the hands of those
who gathered at the recent Robin Hood game should be
spent upon a silver censer. In 1500 and in subsequent years
we have receipts from a 'king game'—a Whitsun may-
game played by the young men. The proceeds of 1501 and
1502 were put towards the same silver censer, which was
then finally purchased. For the year 1520 we again have
an entry for 'Robin Hood's money' in place of the usual
'king's money'. The most interesting piece of data, however, is the fact that Robin Hood of 'Hendley'—which can
only be Henley-on-Thames—visited Reading in 1505, a
year in which the 'king game' took place as usual. Robin
Hood and the Whitsun king must surely be one and the
same.

There is good reason, then, for believing that the Robin
Hood game is a version of the king game, and that Robin
Hood is a variant of the May King or Summer Lord. If
we study the form and purpose of a Summer Lord game,
we will have a good basis for understanding the Robin
Hood game. (pp. 7-8)

The *locus classicus* for the study of Tudor may-games . . .
is the attack upon them in Philip Stubbes' *Anatomy of*
Abuses, published in 1583. A close study of Stubbes' description of the activities of a Summer Lord—under the
title 'Lord of Misrule'—gives us an insight into many facets of the Robin Hood game. Since the passage is well
known, I shall quote only the salient points of the description.

First, all the wild-heads of the parish, conventing together, choose them a Grand-Captain (of all Mischief) whom they ennoble with the title 'my Lord of Misrule', and him they crown with great solemnity, and adopt for their king.

Once chosen, the Lord/king himself selects anything from twenty to a hundred men to attend upon him. All of these 'he investeth with his liveries of green, yellow or some other light wanton colour'. His young attendants also don ribbons, lace, jewels and dancing bells. The Lord and his company then . . .

> march towards the church and churchyard, their pipers piping, their drummers thund'ring, their stumps dancing, their bells jingling, their handkerchieves swinging about their heads like madmen, their hobby-horses and other monsters skirmishing amongst the rout.

We have here a vivid picture of a troupe of morris men in full spate. Even though a service is in progress, the men perform their dance inside the church itself. Having duly entertained the congregation, the dancers eventually go . . .

> forth into the churchyard, where they have commonly their Summer Halls, their bowers, arbours and banqueting houses set up, wherein they feast, banquet and dance all that day and peradventure all the night too.

The halls, bowers and arbours are presumably the same as those Stubbes mentions as standing 'hard by' the maypole, and set up at the same time as the pole was erected—an event which might take place during 'May, Whitsunday or other time'. The Lord's banquet is provided by parishioners who bring along bread, ale, cheese, custards and cakes—a sacrifice to the devil, in Stubbes' eyes. The Lord and his men gather money as well as food and drink from the spectators:

> They have also certain papers, wherein is painted some babblery or other of imagery work, and these they call 'my Lord of Misrule's badges'. These they give to everyone that will give money for them.

Those who refuse to purchase these paper livery badges are 'mocked and flouted at not a little'. Others, however, not only part with their money but 'also wear their badges and cognizances in their hats or caps openly'. Finally, Stubbes roundly condemns church-wardens' involvement in organising parish feasts. The fact that Church Ales finance the purchase of vestments and service books does not make them morally admissible. (pp. 10-12)

A Scottish poet in 1568 recalled the era when Robin Hood helped to bring in the may:

> In May quhen men zeid everichone
> With Robene Hoid and Littill Johne
> To bring in bowis and birkin bobbynis . . .

The symbolism of the may-pole, and more particularly of the boughs which decked it, was enhanced by the fact that the boughs were by convention stolen from the lands of the wealthy. In 1480 the Mayor of Coventry responded to a complaint about this custom by stating:

> . . . that the people of every great city—as London and other cities—yearly in summer do harm to divers lords and gentles having woods and groves nigh to such cities by taking of boughs and trees; and yet the lords and gentles suffer such deeds oft-times of their good will.

In Leicester, there was legislation to curb such practices by 1551. In order to steal the flowers and branches which were to deck both pole and bower, the young—and Stubbes adds that old men and wives would join them—by tradition went out into the woods before dawn. This annual, half-illicit entry into the greenwood, with its ritualised trespass and theft, is an event which helps us to understand how the legend of Robin Hood adapted itself so easily to the may-games, and how the legend in its turn was nourished. The famous Robin Hood's Gate into Richmond Park must commemorate forays, whether real or imagined, made into forbidden territory by the Kingston-upon-Thames outlaw, questing boughs for the may. For in the figure of Robin Hood two elements are combined, the outlaw who ignores the requirements of society, and the green man, the incarnation of spring. (pp. 18-19)

. . . . .

We have seen how Stubbes' description of a Summer Lord game is confirmed in detail by the early records of performance, and we have gained a clear enough picture of the structure of a may-game for us to examine those aspects of a Robin Hood game that differentiate it from a conventional king game—in particular, the individual characters of the outlaws and the close link with the morris dance. Perhaps the most obvious general difference is the fact that Robin Hood is by definition an outlaw, a rebel against authority. In a conventional king game, the real world can either be forgotten or be imitated, so that, temporarily but completely, the real world vanishes; but in a may-game of Robin Hood the real world is incorporated into the mythical world, and a measure of overt defiance becomes, inescapably, an ingredient in the game.

Arcadian pastoral literature gives us a picture, albeit idealised, of earlier practice. An interesting example is the may-game woven into Peele's *Edward I*. The hero of the play is a Welsh prince, who, when his real kingdom is threatened, declares: 'I'll be Master of Misrule, I'll be Robin Hood!' He appoints a Friar Tuck and a Little John, and dubs his beloved Elinor 'Maid Marian'. He will sell a chain to raise money, he says, 'to set us all in green; and we'll all play the pioneers, to make us a cave and a cabin for all weathers'. 'Robin Hood' and 'Little John', having duly dressed in green and built their bower, leave 'Marian' inside the bower making garlands while 'Friar Tuck' sings to her. Peele's play is clearly based upon a memory of folk practices, according to which the Summer Lord would erect a bower as the palace for his Lady or Queen. A real-life parallel can be found in the Summer Game which took place at Wistow in Yorkshire in 1469. From among the unmarried of the parish, Margaret More and Thomas Barker were elected as Summer King and Queen. On the third Sunday in June, from before mid-day until after sunset, the Queen sat in a kind of 'barn' known as the 'Summer-House' which lay next to the churchyard. She was accompanied by the King and by two young men termed 'soldiers', besides a crowd of others. One learns from Peele's play that when the Summer King or Master of Misrule went by the name of Robin Hood, his lady or May Queen would go by the name of Maid Marian; and when two attendants were selected, these were given the names Little John and Friar Tuck.

Maid Marian is often Robin Hood's companion in sixteenth-century may-games, but she does not enter the ballad tradition until the seventeenth century. A study of the Kingston accounts can do much to clear up the enigma of her origins.

Dobson and Taylor [in *Rymes of Robyn Hood,* 1976] follow [W. E.] Simeone's belief, that Marian and Tuck were absorbed into the may-game from the morris. Robin Hood, they assert, 'assimilated into his own legend the jolly friar and Maid Marian, almost invariably among the performers in the early sixteenth-century morris dance'. The situation is in fact more complicated than this, and I have pointed out already that the Robin Hood game is older than the morris dance. It is abundantly clear from Marian's absence in the earlier ballads that she entered the legend via the may-games, but it is not clear that she, any more than Robin, makes her first appearance as a dancer. In the case of the friar, we cannot with such confidence attribute his place in the legend to the may-games, for the ballad which tells of Robin's encounter with a friar is an early one.

In the Elizabethan period we find two quite contradictory concepts of Maid Marian: on the one hand we have Peele's idealised May Queen, and on the other Nashe's man-woman—the clownish character who features in the Elizabethan morris and whom Falstaff cites as a proverbial instance of immorality. Our task must be to trace two distinct characters to their origins. *Prima facie* evidence for the greater antiquity of the courtly Marian is provided by her etymology, for she seems to derive her name from the *Marion* who is mistress to *Robin* in the French *pastourelles.* From the first quarter of the sixteenth century, we have only two pieces of evidence which permit us to link Maid Marian—and alongside her, Friar Tuck—to the morris dance: one is the Kingston account book, the other is the so called Betley window.

The window from Betley is of painted glass and depicts morris dancers in costume of the period 1490-1520, dancing round a may-pole. At the bottom of the picture, a friar, apparently dancing, is placed next to a stationary lady. The friar wears red stockings beneath his russet habit. The lady, often identified as Marian, is elegantly dressed, and her golden crown shows that she is the May Queen. She holds a red flower in her hand like a sceptre. Her physique and flowing hair leave no room for doubt that this is a woman, and not a man in disguise. The Maid Marian who first appeared at Kingston was likewise a woman: in 1509 she is paid two shillings for *'hir'* labour for the two years past, and in 1506 the character is referred to simply as 'the lady'. She is paired with Robin in 1509, for there is a purchase of '2 pair of gloves for Robin Hood and Maid Marian', and like Robin in that year she wears the green cloth known as Kendal. Her annual fee, set at a shilling, is the

same as Robin Hood's in 1516, and more than Little John's (10d.) or Friar Tuck's (8d.). Her *'huke'* or cloak is trimmed with the rich type of satin called Cypress, so it appears that some attempt is being made at elegance. There is evidence enough for us to be confident that the Marian of 1508-9 is a version of the May Queen, the traditional companion of the Summer Lord, and the figure depicted in the Betley window.

The Kingston inventory of 1538 includes, in addition to a worsted kirtle trimmed with red, a *'mowrens cote of Buckerame'.* The worsted kirtle is the one made up for Maid Marian in 1536; the buckram coat must be the *'morenys'* coat for which four yards of buckram was purchased in 1523. As we have seen already, the morris troupe at Kingston consisted of six dancers together with two supernumeraries who wore bells but did not have the benefit of regular new shoes; these two supernumeraries were the *'dizard'* or fool, and the *'mowren'.* It is tempting to see this *mowren* as a prototype of the Elizabethan Marian. Writing in 1575, Laneham discribed how Elizabeth watched a rustic bride-ale in the course of which there featured *'a lively morisdauns, according to the auncient manner: six dauncerz, mawd-marion and the fool'.* The ancient manner seems to be exemplified by the Kingston may-game in which six dancers, the *mowren* and the *dizard* formed the troupe. There is no evidence from Kingston to suggest what the *mowren* looked like, but etymologically the word must derive from 'moor'—as indeed does the word 'morris' or 'morisco'. We can safely identify the Kingston *mowren* clad in his *morenys* coat with the *'yonge morens'* whom Machyn saw processing with their Sultan in the may-games of 1557. It is easy to imagine how the flowing Moorish skirts of such a character could cause him to be reinterpreted as a woman, once his original racial identity had been either forgotten or disregarded.

References to a male Marian are exclusively Elizabethan. We have, however, to account for the Marian who appears at St Lawrence's in 1529, and for the later Marians at Kingston. Again at Kingston evidence is provided by the purchase of shoes—that most perishable yet most essential piece of a dancer's equipment. For the year 1516 we have a list of 'shoes for morris dancers . . . ' and in another ink are added the words 'and Robin Hood and his company'. Nine men's names are listed, next the cost of riband for tying the shoes, and then 'Robin Hood', followed by three more men's names. We may reasonably deduce that the last three names are those of the players of Little John, Friar Tuck and Maid Marian. Marian and Tuck both qualify for shoes in 1520, so there is no reason for Marian to be omitted on this occasion. Unlike John and Tuck, however, Marian received no payment in 1516, so in all probability it was *'paulmares man'* who played the part. An anonymous servant would not need to be paid, and would be either young or humble enough to play a woman's part.

The part of Marian was given over to a male in 1516. To this we may add a second and more important deduction, that Robin Hood and his company began to dance in that year. In earlier years, the evidence suggests a procession. There is mention of gloves (1509, 1515), arrows (1508,

1509) and a banner (1506), but shoes are provided only for the morris dancers. After the 1509 entry of costumes for Robin, Marian and the Friar, and before the remainder of their expenses, we find a payment made to 'a luter for luting in the Whitsun week': this is a more romantic or courtly type of music than the taboring which always accompanied morris dancing, and which took place on 'fair eve and fair day' 1516. There is, finally, the fact that over the four years 1508-11—and we have no records for the three following years—new coats are provided annually for Robin, John and Friar Tuck. The newly elected Robin Hood created a new version of the character, and the spectators' interest lay in what appearance he and his company would assume. In the later records, clothes are kept from one Whitsuntide to the next, and have to be sponged or mended to make them ready for the coming year; it is the characters' actions that have become important. Before 1516, shoes were not purchased for Robin and his three associates, but from that date they replace costume as the main expense. The purchase of six pairs of double soled shoes together with six pairs of single soled shoes in 1536 makes it clear that the most vigorous dancing was expected of the six morris men, but implies also that some dancing was expected of the fool, the *mowren,* Robin, and his three associates. The wearer of the thirteenth pair of shoes, purchased in 1516 and 1538, remains a mystery, but perhaps in 1516 it was the wearer of the crown, the 'king'. If, as all the evidence suggests, Robin and his company did begin to dance in 1516, we have a logical explanation of why a man should have taken over the role of Marian. It would have been socially unacceptable for a girl to dance alone with a group of males; while it was traditional for a maiden to serve as May Queen, the morris dance, then as now, was a male preserve.

With the growing popularity of the morris dance in the sixteenth century, other figures were attracted to dance in loose association with it—'skirmishing amongst the rout' in Stubbes' phrase. We see the logical conclusion of this process in the medley of clowns who participate in the may-game performed in *Two Noble Kinsmen.* The hobby-horse and the fool were two early adjuncts to the morris, and the Marian became a third. When Marian's part was first given to a man at Kingston, there was probably no thought of the coarse Elizabethan clown that the Marian was to become. But the appearance of Maid Marian dressed in a robust coat of canvas alongside the morris men at Reading indicates that by 1529 the character had already begun a process of dissociation from the legend. I have suggested that a degree of confusion between the 'May *moren*' and the 'Maid Marian' helped to distance the character from Robin Hood, and to give him/her an independent identity. By the end of the sixteenth century, the divorce between the outlaw band and the man-woman of the morris was well advanced, but not complete; at the same time, a vogue for nostalgic pastoral literature caused the memory of the original female Marian to be preserved and idealised.

The evolution of Friar Tuck's character seems no less complex than that of Maid Marian's. A Jonsonian character expects Marian and the Friar to figure together in a morris dance. By the end of the Elizabethan period, the convention was well established that Friar Tuck was both a lecher and a dancer; he was a lecher because he danced opposite the Marian. Peele's Friar plays out a wooing scene with Maid Marian, but he sings rather than dances. [The Friar in *The Downfall of Robert, Earl of Huntingdon,* by Anthony Munday] refers to a tradition of 'merry morrises of Friar Tuck', and himself performs a dance; but he courts Jinny the serving-wench rather than the idealised Marian. When we turn back to the play-script of c.1562, we find that the performance ends with the lecherous friar dancing opposite an unnamed 'trull of trust' who must be the Marian. Documentary evidence for the dancing friar is provided by the parish of St Columb Major, which possessed a set of 'Robin Hood's clothes'. The inventory of 1585 makes no mention of Robin, but includes five coats for morris dancers, a friar's coat, and twenty-four bells. Since the bells make up six sets for arms and legs, we infer that the friar is the sixth dancer. The Kingston accounts inform us that the Friar travelled to Croydon in 1536 accompanied only by the piper, so he must have gone to perform some dance or song advertising the Kingston fair. An entry for 1520 records payment for '8 pair of shoes for the morris dancers, the Friar and Maid Marian', thereby associating both with the dance, and suggesting that by 1520 Marian is paired with the Friar rather than Robin. Perhaps there is some significance in the Friar's change of costume: for when he attended the female, green-clad Marian in 1509 he wore an innocent white, but by 1520 he is wearing the familiar russet. The final piece of evidence for the Friar's early and independent existence as a dancer is the Betley window, which portrays him, chaplet in hand, attending on the May Queen.

The earliest reference to Friar Tuck occurs in 1417. The name was assumed by a cleric of Lindfield in Sussex who was outlawed for repeatedly trespassing in parks, for hunting deer and other forms of game, and for burning the houses of park-keepers. Some popular campaign against enclosers was no doubt involved. It is inconceivable that the nick-name of such a minor outlaw could have been perpetuated in legend, and it was probably the established place of Friar Tuck in the Robin Hood legend that caused the name to be lent to this individual. The absence of the name 'Tuck' from the northern ballads is curious, however, and Robin has no chaplain in the ballads but visits Nottingham for his devotions. Our other fifteenth-century reference derives from a southern game, for Friar Tuck plays a part in the Norfolk playlet of 1475. It is likely, therefore, that the character of Friar Tuck owes more to the May Queen's chaplain than to the unnamed 'curtal friar' of the ballad. The enigma posed by the historical Sussex outlaw is best resolved if we posit the great antiquity of Robin Hood's place in the may-games; but it is quite possible also that Friar Tuck originally had an independent place in the games.

The mock cleric certainly had an ancient and important role to play in may-games. Robin Hood of Wednesbury, for instance, timed his visit to Willenhall in 1497 to coincide with a gathering made by the 'Abbot of Marham' of Wolverhampton. There are often links between Robin Hood and a game based around a mock Abbot. In Shrewsbury, an 'Abbot' in a painted cloak, under a variety of names, appears regularly in the May-time festivities throughout the reigns of Henry VIII and Edward VI. Then, in the first year of Mary's reign, the 'Abbot' vanishes, and payment is made 'for jackets and other vestments and the painting of the same for Robin Hood'. Anticlerical satire must have become anti-Catholic during the Reformation, and could no longer be tolerated; Robin's treatment of corrupt abbots in the ballads may have helped suggest him as a natural replacement. The same kind of substitution took place in Scotland. In Aberdeen in 1508 Robin stepped into the shoes of the 'Abbot of Bonaccord', and Little John took over the functions of the 'Prior'. In Edinburgh, likewise, by 1518 Robin and John had replaced the penniless 'Abbot of Na-rent'. The Robin Hood game and the Mock Abbot game involve, in exactly the same manner, a formalised reversal of the social order. The step from a mad abbot to a mad friar is not a great one. Skelton in 1520 associates Friar Tuck with the preaching of sermons, so his role was not originally confined to dancing. If the Robin Hood game was to present a complete image of inverted reality, the presence of a mock cleric was indispensible.

It is perhaps fortunate that few enigmas surround the development of Little John. He is at Robin's side in the earliest ballads, and he appears in records of the game by the end of the fifteenth century. In Scotland his function is 'to make sports and jocosities in the town', and probably in England also he takes on the role of organiser. These four—Robin Hood and Little John, Friar Tuck and Maid Marian—are the only ones who appear as named characters in Tudor records of the game. It is highly likely that some kind of dance evolved in which they worked as two pairs or a foursome, but information here is lacking.

The ancient records have yielded a clear picture of the form and structure of the Robin Hood game, and of its principal characters. The picture may be completed by some account of the organisation of the game. In most of the instances that we have, the church provides costumes and pays for the hire of musicians; profits from the game are then paid back into church funds. Sometimes the profits were directed to particular areas of need. The game at Chagford in 1555, for instance, helped finance the reintroduction of music in church services: the organist's fees were paid, and four prick-song books, a hymnal and two processionals were purchased, while other books were repaired. But relationships between the young men and the parish authorities did not always run smoothly, as the case of the Somerset village of Croscombe serves to illustrate.

In the market town of Wells in 1498, the burgesses authorised the master of the corporation to make an official inquiry 'into whose hands the moneys of the church and commonalty were unjustly held—viz. money hitherto deriving from Robin Hood . . . ' and several other sources of revenue are cited. At Croscombe, a mere two miles distant, we have an example of such money going astray, for the pattern of payments is highly erratic. Robin Hood and Little John were supposed to appear in person at the annual audit in February to pay over the proceeds from their revels, but the time lapse over the winter may have put temptation in their way. Alternatively, local politics may

have been involved—as was the case just after the Reformation, when the church-wardens used parish funds to sue their unreformed parish priest. We find in the Croscombe accounts an increasingly large sum being presented through the 1470s and 1480s, rising to a record £3.7.8d. in 1487/8. Then comes a series of lean years with often no payment entered covering the period when complaints are being made at Wells. In 1504/5 a large sum appears again—£2.13.4d.—but the wardens note that the money 'resteth in the hands of W. Carter', and in the following year an entry of £2.3.4d. is made but then crossed out. Evidently the young men were prepared to show the wardens how much money had been gathered, but refused to hand it over. The next year the wardens tried to make other arrangements, for they hand in the money themselves—a mere 9/8d. Two years later, the situation improves dramatically: parish unity seems to have been restored by the project of building a chapel to St George, a saint of some interest to the theatrically inclined. With the completion of the chapel, the entries cease, apart from one in 1525/6: here the sum of £4.0.4d. is firmly labelled 'a gift' and seems connected with the parish's need of money to repair the steeple and build almshouses. This last entry indicates that the game was flourishing, but had completely passed out of parish control. When the Robin Hood game gains, or retrieves, this kind of independence, it vanishes from our records, so that we cannot measure the scale on which it took place, or establish what the normal pattern was.

The case of Shrewsbury, where the borough organised the game, is unusual in England. But in Scotland it was almost always the secular authorities rather than the church which took control, and this represents the most important difference between the southern and northern traditions. In Aberdeen the Council in 1508 decreed that a fine of twenty shillings was to be paid by any burgess, merchant or craftsman who failed to carry bow and arrows and ride dressed in green and yellow behind Robin Hood and Little John; the Sundays in May and the patronal feast day in November were given over to these processions. In Edinburgh, though the Council controlled the game, some of the money for it was put up by the guilds. And in Ayr, the extent to which the borough managed to institutionalise the game is shown by the fact that town treasurers often took the parts of Robin and John, receiving a fee of five marks apiece. All such official sponsorship of the game vanished after a repressive statute of 1555 ordained:

> that in all times coming no manner of person be chosen Robert Hood nor Little John, Abbot of Unreason, Queens of May, nor otherwise, neither in borough nor to landward in any time to come.

Any corporation choosing people for these offices was to lose its freedom for five years, and anyone taking on such an office was to be fined ten pounds. Fear of disorder seems to lie behind the statute—a fear perhaps justified by the Edinburgh riots of 1561, when a group of apprentices and craftsmen got together *'efter the auld wikit maner of Robene Hude'*. The rioters elected a tailor as Robin Hood, and dubbed him 'Lord of Inobedience', before storming through the city gates, past the magistrates and up Castle Hill. As always, when official organisation is stripped away, the strength of popular sentiment which inspired the game comes momentarily into view.

While in Scotland the secular sponsors of the game were curbed by Parliament, in England the task of stopping church sponsorship fell to the bishops. In Kingston and other parishes within the ambit of London the game vanished with the Reformation. Latimer's famous attack on the Robin Hood game, though delivered in 1549, relates to an incident in the period 1535-9 before local church authorities had been forced to capitulate to the new attitude of the hierarchy. It was only in remote Devon and Cornwall, where strength of Catholic feeling triggered the 'Prayer Book Rebellion' of 1549, that traces of the game can be found in the 1540s. The accession of Mary provided the opportunity for a renaissance. In Chagford, for instance, the game began to be played annually from 1554, but in 1562 a new task was allocated to the young men of the community, wardenship of the store of St George. In Protestant England, patriotism had to be the key-note. Many were unhappy with the change, for in 1564, the year following the last appearance of Robin Hood, no less than five young men paid fines for refusing to play the new role. Though morris dancing flourished in Elizabeth's reign, the games declined, surviving longest in remote parishes safe from archiepiscopal visitations. It is impossible to define exactly when the game vanished. Some continuity of tradition must lie behind Robin Hood's re-emergence in a processional may-game at Wells in 1607. And in the most remarkable instance of the game's survival, at Enstone in royalist Oxfordshire a foreign visitor was able to watch it during the Commonwealth.

A Scottish example illustrates the manner in which, in unsupervised villages, the game was able to sustain an underground existence. The Presbytery records of Kelso tell us of a Robin Hood play performed in April 1610 in the parish of Linton in the Cheviot foothills. The event formed part of 'the May plays used by them called Lord or Abbot of Unreason'. The 'chief actors and authors' of the plays were George Ker of Linton village who played Robin Hood, the inn-keeper who played Little John, the goodman of Schaipsrig—presumably an independent shepherd—who played the Sheriff, and a ploughman in the service of the Laird who played the 'lord', that is to say, the regular elected Lord of Unreason. The four received a public summons from the ecclesiastical court, under threat of excommunication. When they finally put in an appearance, they were not sufficiently apologetic, for the summoner was sent off to Sir William Cranston—who must have been the local J. P.—asking him to enforce the Act of 1555 and exact the statutory fine of ten pounds. Sir William promised to help, but did nothing. The Presbytery set in motion the procedure for excommunicating the foursome, who countered by pointing out a technical irregularity in their trial, and, in June 1611, by appealing to the Bishop of Glasgow. In November the excommunication was finally implemented. As the one most in the public eye, the inn-keeper made some sort of apology at once, but was told to return 'when God shall touch his heart with repentance'. It was not until May 1612, when another season of maygames was safely over, that written

apologies were accepted, and the four men were readmitted to church.

In England, urbane seventeenth-century writers speak of the Robin Hood game as a thing of the past. A Jacobean poet typically laments the passing of an era for which the may-pole alone remains as a symbol:

> Let us talk of Robin Hood
> And Little John in merry Sherwood,
> Of poet Skelton with his pen
> And many other merry men,
> of May-game Lords and Summer Queens
> And milk-maids dancing o'er the greens,
> Of merry Tarlton in our time
> Whose conceit was very fine,
> Whom death hath wounded with his dart,
> That loved a may-pole with his heart.

It is Tarlton, the witty comedian of the Elizabethan playhouse, whom the poet himself recalls from his youth. He knows, however, that Tarlton's humour was rooted in the anarchic, inverted world of the early Tudor maygames—a world which he associates with Skelton and the time of Henry VIII. The players of the professional theatre replaced the amateur players of games in the answering to the imaginative needs of men on holiday. In the Elizabethan period, the conventional setting of stage comedy remained the countryside, and links with the pre-Reformation past remained. But in the Jacobean period the setting of comedy became the city, and, for Londoners at least, Robin Hood had no place outside the bounds of self-conscious pastoral literature. (pp. 20-30)

David Wiles, in his The Early Plays of Robin Hood, *D. S. Brewer, 1981, 97 p.*

R. B. Dobson and J. Taylor   (essay date 1976)

[*Dobson and Taylor are English historians whose* Rymes of Robyn Hood: An Introduction to the English Outlaw *collects treatments of the legend from several diverse sources. In the following excerpt from their introduction to that work, they explore the various depictions of Robin Hood in the nineteenth and twentieth centuries, stressing the somewhat mysterious but universal appeal of the legend.*]

In providing his readers with the opportunity to read *Robin Hood and Guy of Gisborne* [Thomas Percy, in his *Reliques of Ancient English Poetry*, 1765] made available the first printed text of a ballad 'of much greater antiquity than any of the common popular songs on this subject'. Much more important was the general stimulus of the *Reliques* in creating the ballad mania of the late eighteenth century, a mania out of which a substantially new and recognizably 'modern' Robin Hood eventually came to be born. In the course of their search for poetry that would be popular rather than aristocratic, and 'natural' rather than artificial, the poets and scholars of the period developed a much greater interest in Robin Hood ballads than any of their predecessors. One sign of changing attitudes to the outlaw legend was the inclusion of large numbers of ballads from the Garlands in Thomas Evans's popular collection of *Old Ballads, Historical and Narrative* (1777).

Nevertheless literary as well as social prejudice against 'foolish tales of Robin Hood' died hard: for a contributor to the *Critical Review* in January 1792, Robin Hood ballads were still by definition 'the refuse of a stall'.

The rehabilitation of Robin Hood was essentially the work of one man, the eccentrically indefatigable Joseph Ritson (1752-1803), whose *Robin Hood: A Collection of all the Ancient Poems, Songs and Ballads, now extant, relative to that celebrated Outlaw* appeared in 1795. As an already well-established collector of local verse noted for the rigour of his critical standards, as the acquaintance of Dr Johnson as well as the friend of Sir Walter Scott, Ritson had the best possible credentials for his task. He was triumphantly successful. With the single important exception of the ballad of *Robin Hood and the Monk*, the first edition of Ritson's comprehensive anthology made available reliable texts of all the major works in the Robin Hood canon. Frequently reprinted in revised and extended form during the course of the nineteenth century, Ritson's *Robin Hood* remains an indispensable handbook to the outlaw legend even now. Perhaps the greatest tribute to its value is that it has only had two successors. John Mathew Gutch's two-volumed collection of 1847 is largely based on Ritson's and displays considerably less critical acumen than its model. Nor did it ever attain the commercial success of Ritson's work. Only in 1888 with the appearance of Francis Child's edition of the *Gest* and the Robin Hood ballads was Ritson's achievement surpassed by a scholar whose learning was even greater than his own.

One of the greatest of Child's many virtues was his ability, as an American, to approach the study of England's greatest outlaw myth in a spirit of critical detachment, a quality which Ritson and his many disciples inevitably found it hard to achieve. Nevertheless it is salutary to remember that Child's formidable scholarship has exercised comparatively little influence outside the world of learning. Ritson's *Robin Hood,* on the other hand, is itself a critical document in the history of the legend. By providing the English poets and novelists of the Romantic and Victorian periods with a convenient source-book, Ritson gave them the opportunity to re-create Robin Hood in their own imagination. So extensive was the effect of his anthology that it may even have influenced the 'folk' traditions dear to the hearts of the lovers of popular ballads. Is it altogether a coincidence that the famous Mrs Brown of Falkland provided Robert Jamieson with a song on *The Birth of Robin Hood* in 1800, only five years after the publication of Ritson's *Robin Hood* revealed a surprising absence of any existing ballad on that important theme? More important still, it was Ritson who gave pride of place in his collection of Robin Hood songs to the *Gest* and established that poem as the central work in the outlaw saga, a position it has held ever since. Above all perhaps, the sheer weight of learning Ritson brought to his self-imposed task of rehabilitating Robin Hood (most evident in his prefatory 'Life' with accompanying 'Notes and Illustrations') made Robin Hood intellectually as well as socially respectable for the first time in his long history. As Sir Walter Scott wrote, with his usual perspicacity, Ritson 'had an honesty of principle about him, which, if it went to ri-

diculous extremities, was still respectable from the soundness of the foundation'.

However, Joseph Ritson's contribution to the development of the greenwood legend went further still. Not only did he popularize and legitimize the study of Robin Hood, he also produced a highly influential interpretation of the hero. In the first place the fact that Ritson himself actually believed in the existence of a historical Robin Hood ('just, generous, benevolent, faithful, and beloved or revered by his followers or adherents for his excellent and amiable qualities') had an incalculable effect in promoting the still continuing quest for the man behind the myth. More specifically, Ritson was the first writer to convert Robin Hood into a thoroughgoing ideological hero, a repository for his own extremely complex and at times idiosyncratic revolutionary opinions. For Ritson Robin Hood was 'a man who, in a barbarous age, and under a complicated tyranny, displayed a spirit of freedom and independence, which has endeared him to the common people, whose cause he maintained (for all opposition to tyranny is the cause of the people); and, in spite of the malicious endeavours of pitiful monks, by whom history was consecrated to the crimes and follies of titled ruffians and sainted idiots, to suppress all record of his patriotic exertions and virtuous acts, will render his name immortal'. The sentiments here are of course those of the French Revolution (Ritson was one of the few Englishmen to adopt the French revolutionary calendar) and, more specifically, of Tom Paine. Only three years before the publication of Ritson's *Robin Hood,* Paine had converted another famous medieval English rebel, Wat Tyler, into a revolutionary hero in exactly the same manner ('his fame will outlive their falsehood'). The relevance of Robin Hood, like that of Wat Tyler, to modern revolutionary movements is perhaps questionable and certainly ambiguous; but the long and still continuing interpretation of the forest outlaw as an apostle of popular liberty only seriously began with Joseph Ritson. 'What better title king Richard could pretend to the territory and the people of England, than Robin Hood had to the dominion of Barnsdale or Sherwood, is a question humbly submitted to the political philosopher'.

That particular question remains a relevant one. Interestingly enough it was taken up, in very different ways, by the two greatest 'Robin Hood novels' both written in 1818. Although Thomas Peacock's *Maid Marian* was not published until 1822, three years after the appearance of Walter Scott's *Ivanhoe,* each book was based on an independent reading of Ritson's Robin Hood anthology. The two most forceful and imaginative contributions of early-nineteenth century Romanticism to the Robin Hood legend, *Maid Marian* and *Ivanhoe* illustrate to perfection the complexities and ambiguities of the Romantic movement. Of the two novels *Maid Marian* is at the same time much more subtle and much the less successful. Peacock's light-hearted and astonishingly cavalier re-telling of the Robin Hood story has been rightly categorized as 'an in-between book: half comic opera, half novelistic idyll; or half social satire, half genuine, if humorous, romance' [C. Dawson, *His Fine Wit: A Study of Thomas Love Peacock,* 1950]. When compared with his famous 'conversation novels', *Maid Marian* seems a disappointing commentary on Peacock's inability to handle the material he had pillaged from Ritson. Yet this is perhaps to miss the important point that Peacock's failure is as much symptomatic as personal: *Maid Marian* reveals, better than any other work in Robin Hood literature, the impossibility of reconciling the medieval outlaw legend with a modern literary sensibility. To put the problem in its simplest possible terms, Peacock could never decide exactly how seriously to regard Robin Hood; and it is this uncertainty which accounts for his novel's inconsistency of tone and discontinuity of structure. *Maid Marian*'s most obvious feature to the modern reader is its mock-violent buffoonery, a quality so apparent that it ensured the work's commercial success at Covent Garden when converted into a comic opera for Christmas entertainment at the end of 1822. Yet what Peacock thought he was writing, as he remarked in a letter to Shelley, was 'a comic Romance of the Twelfth Century, which I shall make the vehicle of much oblique satire on all the oppressions that are done under the sun'. Peacock's satire failed because it had too many targets, not only the reactionary political forces of the day but also Ritson's Cobbett-like radical agrarianism, caricatured as the view that 'Robin Hood is king of the forest both by dignity of birth and by virtue of his standing army'. In the last resort Peacock was content to present the forest outlaw as a figure of nostalgic and idyllic 'romance', to be remembered

Errol Flynn in the 1938 film The Adventures of Robin Hood.

(as he remembered Old Windsor Forest itself) with resigned regret.

Sir Walter Scott approached the Robin Hood legend in a much more positive and less qualified spirit. Robin Hood had long been 'no small favourite of mine' when in *Ivanhoe* he triumphantly fulfilled his promise 'to excite an interest for the traditions and manners of old England, similar to that which has been obtained in behalf of those of our poorer and less celebrated neighbours'. The correctness of Scott's belief that 'the name of Robin Hood, if duly conjured with, should raise a spirit as soon as that of Rob Roy' is vouched for by the phenomenal popularity of this first venture into medieval English history on the part of the author of the Waverley Novels. Scott's *Ivanhoe* can fairly be said to have re-created the world of the English middle ages. The appearance, as important if subsidiary characters, of Robin Hood and Friar Tuck (alias Locksley and the Hermit of Copmanhurst) consequently did more than anything else to ensure their continued fame throughout the rest of the nineteenth century. As recent reassessments of Scott have revealed, his historical novels are more complex than most of his contemporary readers were aware. The Robin Hood of *Ivanhoe*, like Cedric the Saxon and even Ivanhoe himself, is a character compelled to sacrifice at least part of his idyllic freedom in the cause of order and strong government. Despite his personal bravery and the loyalty of his men, Scott's Robin Hood is a figure condemned to extinction by the inexorable laws of the historical process. This is the chord, sounded by both Peacock and Scott, which continued to reverberate throughout the Robin Hood literature of the nineteenth century. In 1818, the very year in which *Maid Marian* and *Ivanhoe* were being written, John Keats had produced his own slight 'dirge of a national legend' in the form of a Robin Hood poem. At the very time when the long tradition of the popular Robin Hood Garland was finally coming to its end, the outlaw hero had been rescued from oblivion by the professional novelist and poet. For this survival he has admittedly had to pay a heavy price. Of the many Victorian and Edwardian men of letters to have taken up the outlaw's bow, from Leigh Hunt to Alfred Tennyson and from John Drinkwater to Alfred Noyes, not one proved able to make Robin Hood seem relevant to the issues of his own day. The writers of the Romantic period and after popularized Robin Hood only at the cost of converting him from a real outlaw into a literary symbol of a vanished and largely illusory medieval Arcadia. 'Playing Robin Hood and Maid Marian' became an appropriately light diversion for the leisured classes of Victorian society—in fact as well as fiction.

Much more significant than the sporadic and nostalgic interest in Robin Hood displayed by various English men of letters during the last century and a half has been the growth of a vast juvenile audience for the greenwood legend. Indeed many of the features of the traditional Robin Hood saga which have made it irresponsive to sophisticated literary treatment—its loose and episodic structure, its lack of pronounced characterization, the absence of any strong sexual connotations—are exactly those guaranteed to ensure its appeal to the young. The ability of children throughout the world to identify with the forest outlaw hero-figure is now, as it has been for many years, the most important single reason for his immortality. It is clear enough that a series of short adventure stories which are linked together by readily identifiable heroes and villains can readily mirror the fantasies of the child. In particular, the concept of a gang or fellowship which triumphantly undergoes different tests or ordeals on successive appearances provides the standard framework for much conscious 'day-dreaming' experienced by children now and presumably at all times in the past. The juvenile audience for Robin Hood certainly existed long before *Ivanhoe*. As early as the seventeenth century it is evident that a taste for the heroes of medieval romance, King Arthur and Guy of Warwick, Bevis of Hampton and Robin Hood, was regarded as a characteristic of old women, the servant classes and children. Despite the advice provided by such manuals as Thomas White's *A Little Book for Little Children* ('When thou canst read, read no Ballads and foolish Books, but the Bible'), there is similarly no doubt that children were amongst the most avid readers of, or listeners to, the Robin Hood Garlands of the eighteenth century. It was as a young boy that William Stukeley, later the ingenious fabricator of Robin Hood's most fraudulent pedigree ["Robin Hood Earl of Huntingdon"], listened 'enraptured to an old man who remembered the traditional ballads of Robin Hood'; and as a boy too that William Wordsworth first encountered in the chapbooks those nostalgically remembered joys of 'the Wishing-Cap / of Fortunatus, and the invisible Coat / Of Jack the Giant-Killer, Robin Hood / And Sabra in the forest with St George!' [*The Prelude*, V].

Nevertheless it was during Wordsworth's own life-time that a decisive change occurred—less perhaps in the history of juvenile enthusiasm for Robin Hood than in the readiness and ability of writers and publishers to produce versions of the Robin Hood tales addressed specifically to young readers. The innumerable Robin Hood Garlands of the late eighteenth century may have been read by more children than adults; but with their traditionally coarse humour, they were clearly not written specifically for children. Not long after 1800, partly in response to an extension of literacy as well as to improvements in the production and distribution of printed matter, the situation began to alter. The emergence of a Robin Hood ballad anthology in folding toy-book form, the appearance of more and bigger illustrations, and (above all) the increased popularity of connected prose narratives rather than the traditional verse garlands were the harbingers of the impending revolution in book-production for children. One indication of the change was the appearance in 1820 of the second edition of Ritson's *Robin Hood* collection, now abridged into a single volume 'which could with propriety be put into the hands of young persons'. Children's editions of the traditional chapbooks were still produced here and there in the 1840s; but by that decade they were being rapidly replaced in popularity by a new genre of Robin Hood literature—the children's novel, often appearing in weekly penny serial instalments, which handled the characteristic themes of the Robin Hood tales with an unprecedented freedom and made a deliberate appeal to middle-class Victorian juvenile taste. It could be argued that Pierce Egan the younger's *Robin Hood and Little John; or, The Merry Men of Sherwood Forest* (first published in 1840) has exercised more influence on the development of the outlaw legend than any other work since *Ivanhoe*. Like his father of the same name, Pierce Egan (1814-80) was a leading pioneer in the development of cheap literature for the Victorian public; and it is characteristic of his approach as well as of the predilections of his audience that his book begins with Robin Hood as an abandoned baby in the cottage of a humble forester named Gilbert Head or Hood. Egan introduced new characters into the story such as Roland Ritson of Mansfield, the brother of Gilbert Head's wife. As he confessed in his introduction, 'the Author had no material for the early portions of Robin Hood's life but such as his imagination supplied him with'!

Perhaps the greatest tribute to the exceptional popularity of Egan's *Robin Hood and Little John* was its use by Alexandre Dumas as the basis for his own two Robin Hood novels, *Le Prince des Voleurs* (1872) and *Robin Hood Le Proscrit* (1873), themselves later to be widely read in English translation as well as in France itself. The popular French cult of *Robin des Bois,* now nearly always naturalized as a hero of the medieval French maquis, derives in all its essentials from Dumas's adaptation of the legend. Much more spectacular was Robin Hood's conquest of late nineteenth-century America, a conquest which reached its climax with Howard Pyle's superbly illustrated *The Merry Adventures of Robin Hood of Great Renown in Nottinghamshire,* first published by Charles Scribner's Sons of New York in 1883. The quality of Pyle's illustrations, and the genuine literary skill with which he forged an integrated story out of the traditional ballad episodes, account for that work's enduring success. Although Pyle's deliberate archaisms now often strike a jarring note, his refusal to write down to his audience could well have been emulated to advantage by his countless successors in this country as well as the United States. Much the most popular prose re-tellings of the Robin Hood stories in the first half of this century were Henry Gilbert's *Robin Hood and the Men of the Greenwood* (various editions since 1914) and E. Charles Vivian's *The Adventures of Robin Hood* (1927), neither of particular distinction despite their laudable attempt to stir 'the hearts of healthy boys and girls' and their common emphasis on Robin as a benevolent patron of the poor serfs. More recently still the writing of a version of the Robin Hood legend has shown unfortunate signs of becoming almost a compulsory obligation imposed by their publishers upon the writers of children's stories. Despite the occasional attempt to provide a novel emphasis, for example by means of an overtly political interpretation of the story in Geoffrey Trease's *Bows Against the Barons* (1934), few of the countless modern re-tellings of the greenwood tales display any real originality or distinction. On the whole, the most successful recent versions of the Robin Hood saga for children are those, like R. L. Green's *The Adventures of Robin Hood* (London, 1956), which have treated the original ballad stories with the greatest sensitivity and respect.

The children's story may not however always continue to hold its present place as the primary vehicle for the diffusion of the Robin Hood legend. Indeed the most enterprising recent publicists of the outlaw have shown greater interest in soliciting the attentions of the film producer or television director rather than those of the book publisher. The adaptation of the medieval outlaw legend to the screen is almost as old as the history of film itself. For obvious reasons, the story of Robin Hood lent itself particularly well to the requirements of the silent cinema. At least five British or American Robin Hood screen 'spectacles' on the subject had been produced before the outbreak of the First World War. This tradition reached its greatest and most fabulously expensive climax with Douglas Fairbanks's Hollywood version of *Robin Hood* in 1922. Sixteen years later, and with the added attractions of Technicolor as well as sound, Erroll Flynn and Olivia de Havilland starred in *The Adventures of Robin Hood,* perhaps the most vigorous of all twentieth-century treatments of the Robin Hood legend in any form. Although no later director has ever come close to rivalling the panache displayed by Michael Curtiz when he made that film in 1938, films based on the legend have continued to proliferate. [In a footnote, Dobson and Taylor list: "*The Bandit of Sherwood Forest* (U.S.A., 1946); *Prince of Thieves* (U.S.A., 1948); *Rogues of Sherwood Forest* (U.S.A., 1950); *Tales of Robin Hood* (U.S.A., 1950); *The Story of Robin Hood and his Merrie Men* (U.S.A., 1952); *Men of Sherwood Forest* (G.B., 1954); *Sword of Sherwood Forest* (G.B., 1961); *Robin Hood and the Pirates* (Italy, 1964); *A Challenge for Robin Hood* (G.B., 1967). The most curious of all films on the subject are however *The Son of Robin Hood* (U.S.A., 1958), in which the outlaw hero becomes a heroine, Robina Hood; and the recent Disney production of *Robin Hood* (U.S.A., 1973), in which Little John appears as a bear, Friar Tuck as a badger and their leader as a fox."] The special requirements of the film medium as well as the preconceptions determining the aims of the film industry have undoubtedly had an important influence in determining the contemporary characteristics of the legend. It is by now a convention of the genre that Robin Hood will be an unjustly dispossessed nobleman, the leader of 'free Saxons' against their oppressive Norman masters, finally restored to his title and united to his equally aristocratic Maid Marian at the hands of a grateful monarch. Rather more seriously, the need to compress the action of a film into ninety or so minutes of running time has led to the replacement of the traditional episodic quality of the Robin Hood story into a more closely structured and tightly organized form. How far this will be a permanent legacy of the cinema to the Robin Hood legend is altogether less certain. In recent years no treatment of the outlaw stories has proved more popular with children than a B.B.C. television series which reverted in several ways to the episodic, cyclical world of the traditional ballads. An even more interesting sign of the times is the new vogue for portraying Robin Hood as a personally disillusioned as well as socially alienated exile in the greenwood.

As a folk hero, portrayed successively in the medieval ballads, the May Games, the broadsides and garlands, the Victoria penny weekly and the modern film, Robin Hood inevitably retains the characteristics of his kind. If 'to become a public legend a man must have simple outlines' [E. J. Hobsbawm, *Bandits,* 1969], then Robin Hood was and is ideally qualified for his role. Like other popular heroes, Robin must be clever, brave and resourceful and can

only die (if he dies at all) by treachery. Yet it is not his personality nor his physical appearance but his prowess with the longbow which identifies him through the ages. Indeed the very absence of any serious attempt at positive characterization of the outlaw leader in the late medieval ballads has proved a positive advantage in allowing him to appear a different kind of hero to different generations. With the one possible exception of the stained glass window now at Minsterley in Shropshire, which may date from the reign of Edward IV, there survive no medieval representations of Robin Hood. As the woodcuts which preface the Lettersnijder printed edition of the *Gest* were derived from existing blocks not originally intended to illustrate the outlaw legend at all, the iconography of Robin Hood only properly begins with the broadsides and chapbooks of the seventeenth century. For many decades the outlaw was depicted in contemporary dress of the Stuart period, for example in a long gown and a shovel hat. By the early nineteenth century, in the various editions of Ritson's *Robin Hood* anthology, he was usually portrayed as a woodman. Not until the high Victorian period did a distinctive 'medieval' image emerge, the work of illustrators in England and America who depicted the forest hero as a bearded figure, clad in his familiar suit of Lincoln green. The occasional attempts of twentieth-century artists and sculptors to diverge from this tradition and to portray Robin Hood in a more contemporary idiom (James Woodford's statue on Castle Green in Nottingham for example) have failed to displace the Victorian conventions. In so far as the outlaw hero is ever visualized at all precisely, he still conforms to the stereotype originally created by Walter Scott's *Ivanhoe.*

Though he possessed qualities that appealed to a contemporary audience, Robin Hood was not of course the only medieval hero figure to survive the passing of the middle ages. To sixteenth- and seventeenth-century observers his peers were men like Guy of Warwick and Bevis of Hampton, Hereward the Wake and Fulk Fitz Warin. As a swashbuckling adventurer whose exploits could be celebrated as easily in song as prose, as a rudimentary symbol of protest against a corrupt ruler or form of government, Robin Hood's attributes were certainly not unique. The fact remains that the hero of the English greenwood has outlasted all his rivals to become the ideal standard by which all outlaws, real and imaginary, past and future, tend to be assessed. Why has an obscure highwayman earned immortality when it is the inevitable lot of most bandits to be forgotten (except by the historian) within a relatively short space of years? To this, the most important of all questions to do with Robin Hood, there can never be a simple answer. But one possible explanation can at least be put firmly out of court. To several students of the legend, admittedly more common in the late nineteenth than the twentieth century, Robin Hood was not so much a historical character as a mythological figure, one 'whose name but faintly disguises either Woden in the aspect of a vegetation deity, or a minor wood-spirit Hode, who also survives in the Hodeken of German legend'. To this hypothesis have been added such modern variants as the identification of Robin with Robin Goodfellow, or Hood with a mysterious 'log cut from the sacred oak'. The last word on these ingenious notions still belongs to Francis

Child: 'I cannot admit that even the shadow of a case has been made out by those who would attach a mythical character either to Robin Hood or to the outlaws of Inglewood'.

While such mythological theories bear indirect witness to the immense appeal of the legend, and to its part in popular folk culture, against them all it must be said that when we first meet Robin Hood in the ballads he is firmly anchored in the historical world. Mythological characters like Woden and Balder generally belong to a much earlier period of European history. As we have seen, what evidence there is suggests that Robin Hood was, in fact, based upon the memory of one or a number of Barnsdale outlaws. The association of Robin Hood with various English place-names and natural features, often quoted in favour of his mythological origin, can only be dated to periods long after the first literary development of the legend. Similarly the connection of Robin Hood with the May Games came after, and probably because of, the popular appeal of the 'rymes'. The student of Robin Hood is therefore encountering not mythology which became literature, but a literary phenomenon which attained exceptionally wide currency. It is clear from what we know of developments in the sixteenth century that the legend of Robin Hood was one capable of moving out of the ballad world into a broader cultural setting. At an early date Robin Hood became in fact not simply a character in literature but a folk hero, and it is this which distinguishes him most from other literary and historical figures of the middle ages and later.

As an outlaw figure who became a folk hero, Robin Hood has never completely lost the attributes of his origins in the social and economic world of late medieval England. He is the familiar archetype of the 'social bandit' found in most pre-industrial peasant societies. In such societies the bonds of lordship may have weakened but gentry and popular cultures still intermingled. In his general outlines Robin Hood is therefore the product of a period when the state was relatively weak, and when local power groups could be portrayed in the form of the sheriff and the abbot. In this society the 'noble bandit' could redress social wrongs, and justice be done by one man's heroism and audacity. Like those other heroes of twentieth-century fantasy, the Westerner and the gangster, Robin Hood also poses a fundamental problem in its simplest possible outlines: he too, 'exhibits a moral ambiguity, which darkens his image and saves him from absurdity' [R. Warshow, 'The Westerner', *Film: An Anthology,* ed. D. Talbot, 1959]. Under what conditions is a man justified in leaving the society of his fellow men and taking the law into his own hands? That important question duly considered, the limitations of the social bandit's role must also be recognized. From the viewpoint of the inhabitants of modern industrialized societies the deeds of Robin Hood are too circumscribed to solve complex social problems, while he himself is perhaps too simplistic a hero to engage deeply the sympathies of a modern adult audience. Yet for centuries Robin Hood was a real hero to simple and unlettered people: his perennial popularity shows that, transcending its historical context, his myth had in it some element of universal appeal. This we may possibly ascribe to 'a dream

of justice' latent in all peoples at all stages of historical development, allied to the fact that with the passage of time the land of Robin Hood came to hold its own particular brand of nostalgia. It became a 'spiritual Indian territory', an escape from the monotony of the urbanized present into a medieval 'Sherwood' that was itself largely the creation of the ballad writers and never really existed elsewhere. (pp. 53-64)

> *R. B. Dobson and J. Taylor, in their* Rymes of Robyn Hood: An Introduction to the English Outlaw, *William Heinemann Ltd., 1976, 330 p.*

ROBIN HOOD AS HERO

G. H. Radford   (essay date 1894)

[*Below, Radford discusses what Robin Hood's heroic standing reveals about the English national character.*]

[What] sort of man was the Robin Hood of the ballads in which our forefathers delighted for many generations? and what was the story they heard from the minstrels and read before printing was invented? If you know a people's hero you know something important about them. The hero will not have qualities that his worshippers despise. His exploits will be such as they would perform if they could, and his faults will be such as they are tolerant of. When an indictment of the kind that Edmund Burke shrank from is prepared against this people, Mr. Mudie's library will afford a large part of the incriminating material. We are not, of course, asserting that Robin Hood was Old England's only hero. But that he was one of them, and one of the most popular, will not be denied by the critics who deny that he ever existed. The *Lytell Geste* enables us to give some answer to the question we have propounded. First as to the story. Robin Hood was an outlaw and a bandit who lived in the green-wood with a trusty troop of followers and had a lodge at Barnysdale. There he one day entertained Sir Richard at the Lee, whose estate was at Wierysdale and was worth £400 a year. Sir Richard was exceeding sorrowful, and the cause of his sorrow was that he had borrowed £400 of the Abbot of St. Mary's, at York, and had set his lands in pledge to him to secure the return of the money at a certain day, which fell on the morrow of his dining in the forest. Robin Hood no sooner knew of his distress than he lent him £400, and Little John told it out to him by "two-and-twenty score." This liberal reckoning with a borrower pleased our forefathers, as it does our children now. But Robin had some instinct of business, and before he parted with the money he suggested sureties for its repayment. Sadly the knight replies that he has none to offer except Our Dear Lady. This is enough for Robin, and he declares that if you search all England through he knows not "a moch better borowe." So the knight rides away to St. Mary's Abbey with the money, and arrives there before the day for payment is spent. In the hall is the Abbot, eagerly hoping that the knight will make default, the Prior, and the High Cellarer. Moreover, the "High Justice of England" is there, and he has been retained by the Abbot, "both with cloth and fee," to do justice between the Abbot and Sir Richard. The latter conceals his money and professes poverty. He has come to pray for a longer day. The Abbot is delighted, for he looks forward to acquiring the lands of Sir Richard in discharge of his loan. They are worth £400 a year, and he will thus acquire them at one year's purchase! He refuses to extend the time, and the High Justice tells Sir Richard that his "day is broke," and that he will not get his land.

The legal reader will observe that the law thus laid down is extremely unfamiliar and archaic, but it is quite sound. There was no "equity of redemption" in the good old days. The borrower granted his land to the lender on condition that it should be granted back by the latter if the loan was repaid on the day agreed. If the money was not repaid on the day, the condition was not complied with, and the land, however great in value, remained the absolute property of the lender. It was to prevent extortion in such cases as this that the Chancellor intervened with doctrines of Equity, and laid down the maxim, "Once a mortgage always a mortgage." Sir Richard lived before the Chancellor's intervention so he can only beg the Abbot to hold the lands until he has raised the £400 out of the rents. This, too, the Abbot refuses. . . . The Justice is on his side, but proposes that he shall advance a further sum, and that Sir Richard in return shall give him a "release," else the Justice thinks the Abbot will never hold the lands in peace. The Abbot is reluctant, but consents to advance another £100. The Justice suggest £200, but before the Abbot has time to reply the affair takes a new turn. The Knight, who has all this time been kneeling as a suppliant before his creditor, now starts up, goes to a round table and shakes out of a bag the £400 required. The Abbot is bitterly disappointed. He has mentally appropriated the Knight's lands and now that he only gets his money back he feels that he is robbed and plundered. Then to save something out of the wreck of his hopes, he begs the Justice to return his gold. "Not a penny!" says the Justice with an impressive oath. Sir Richard has the last word at this conference:—

> "Syr Abbot, and ye men of lawe
>   Now have I holde my daye,
> Now shall I have my londe agayne
>   For ought that you can saye."

So he departs singing to his home, and there lives quietly till he has saved out of his rents enough to repay Robin Hood the £400. He has his year for repayment, and the place for repayment is under the same tree in Barnysdale where the money was lent. The day has come and Robin Hood sends Little John, Much, and Scathelock out to look for Sir Richard and bring him home to dine. They do not meet Sir Richard, but fall in with two Black Monks (Benedictines), one of whom is the "fat-heded monke," the High Cellarer of St. Mary's, York, and they are on their way to London accompanied by fifty-two men and seven sumpter horses. After a little skilful archery on the part of Much and Little John the escorts take to their heels, and the obese monk is led back to dine with Robin Hood. After dinner Robin Hood suggests, as he generally did, that his

guest shall pay for his entertainment. The monk says he has only "twenty marke." Robin Hood says if this is true he will not take a penny, and will lend him any more that he may need, but he does not accept the statement without verifying it. The monk's "mail" is searched and found to hold £800 and more. Robin asks the monk whence he comes, and he replies from St. Mary's. This reminds Robin that She was surety for a little money he lent a year ago to Sir Richard, and he trusted to Her for payment. She has been an excellent surety, and sent her servant the Cellarer with double the amount. Robin Hood accepts, or rather retains, it thankfully, and sends away the Monk empty but heavy of heart. He says:—

> "Me reweth I cum so nere
> For better chepe I myght have dyned
>   In Blythe or in Dankestere."

Later in the day Sir Richard arrives. He has been delayed by stopping to save from foul play a notable wrestler. He has brought the money and "a poor present" for Robin Hood and all his merry men: a hundred bows, and a hundred sheaves of arrows, each an ell long, feathered with peacock and notched with silver. Robin assures him that the money has been already paid, and tells him with laughter the story of the fat-headed monk. It would be a shame to take the money twice, so he will have nothing from Sir Richard. Indeed he will take nothing more than his loan, and as Our Lady of her bounty has overpaid him £400 he makes him a present of this sum. Robin will take no refusal, so Sir Richard takes the money, and the two part the best of friends. Sir Richard proves himself a fast friend when Robin Hood is in need of one later on.

We have given the outline of the story thus far to show the kind of tale that pleased our forefathers in the fifteenth century or earlier. In our opinion the plot is ingenious, and the story at least as diverting as that of some of our present novels and comedies.

We pass on now to the character of Robin Hood, again not so much for his sake as for the sake of the characters of our forefathers. It has been said that only Germany could make a professor a hero. England has certainly never done so. But she has made a hero of a forester and an outlaw, who adorns his profession with excellent qualities, being not only brave, playful, adventurous, humane and chivalrous, but extremely loyal and pious to a fault. His piety was perhaps, all things considered, his most striking quality. He built a chapel at Barnysdale, and dedicated it to Mary Magdalene, and it was a longing to get back there to worship that induced him to leave the King's Court where he was highly honoured. Notwithstanding the arduous duties of his profession, he observed punctually in the green-wood the offices of religion.

> A good maner then had Robyn,
>   In londe where that he were,
> Every day or he woulde dyne
>   Three messes wolde he here:
> The one in worship of the fader
>   The other of the holy goost
> The thyrde was of our dere lady
>   That he loved of all other moste.

And so punctilious was he in this matter that he refused

to leave mass half-said merely because the Sheriff had discovered his retreat and surrounded him while at prayers with the *posse comitatus.* This story is told by Fordun, who wrote about the middle of the fourteenth century; and he adds that Robin Hood after the service was ended overcame his enemies with extraordinary facility and endowed with their spoils the church where he had worshipped.

The Virgin was especially his patron saint, and the immunity of women in his forays is connected with this fact.

> Robyn loved our dere lady.
>   For doute of dedely synne
> Wolde he never do company harme
>   That ony woman was ynne.

It will be remembered that he lent Sir Richard liberally on his proposing "our dere lady" as surety, and he says very frankly that he would have declined the operation if the security proposed had been that of some other saint of good standing, such as "Peter, Poule or Johan." When Sir Richard goes away to keep his day with the Abbot, Robin Hood gives him a good horse for the reason that "he is our ladyes messengere." In another place he says:—

> "For god is holde a ryghtwys man.
>   And so is his dame."

But there was something idiosyncratic, and as it were eclectic, about Robin Hood's piety. While he dedicated his chapel to the Magdalene, and while Our Lady was his special patroness, when he had occasion to swear his usual oath was "by dere worthy god." This expression may be criticised by some of the disciples of St. Ernulphus, the great master in this art, as slight and thin, but on the whole it will be regarded by most amateurs as ample and dignified. It compares favourably in tone and volume with the King's "By St. Austyn!" and Sir Richard's "By St. Quinton!" Robin Hood's devotion was accompanied by an aversion to the Clergy, especially of the higher orders. Whether he hated them, as Tennyson suggests, "for playing upside down with Holy Writ," we do not know. But while he warns his followers to do no harm to husbandman or knight or squire "that wolde be a good felawe," he does not bid them spare the Clergy. On the contrary he says:—

> "These bysshoppes, and thyse archebysshoppes
>   Ye shall them bete and bynde."

And in his raids and expeditions he always considered as fair game an Abbot or a fat-headed monk. There is no necessary inconsistency here, for the lives of the clergy may not have been blameless. Robin Hood was in this matter like the great majority of our French neighbours of to-day, *Catholic but Anti-clerical.*

Though an outlaw his loyalty was genuine and unquestionable. To the Stranger in a cowl he says:—

> "I love no man in all the worlde
>   So well as I do my kynge."

and he kneels, not only before the King when there is opportunity, but before the King's seal which the stranger produces, and welcomes and entertains him "for the love of my kynge." When the King is made known to him in the Forest, Robin does him no harm, though the King has only five knights and Robin seven-score archers, all men of whom the King said:—

> "His men are more at his byddinge
>   Then my men be at myn."

Robin Hood begs grace of the King for himself and his men. This is granted, and Robin Hood and all his merry men enter the King's service and return with him to his Court. It must be confessed that this loyalty to the King's person did not produce any respect for the King's game laws, nor prevent Robin Hood and his band from living on the King's deer. He confesses it:—

> "We be yemen of this foreste
>   Under the greene wode tre,
> We live by our kynges dere,
>   Other shyft have not we."

Nor did this loyalty extend to the King's officers, or protect the Sheriff of Nottingham from Robin Hood's just revenge.

> He smote of the sheryves hede
>   With his bryght bronde.

saying, after the decapitation:—

> "Lye thou there, thou proud sheryf
>   Evyll mote thou thryve,
> There might no man to the trust
>   The whyles thou were alyve."

If this combination of loyalty and turbulence is not chronic with our countrymen, it is perhaps characteristic of the age when Robin lived.

But it is Robin Hood's practical experiments with the problem of property that have attracted more attention than anything else that is recorded of him. He is said to have robbed the rich to give the poor. Tennyson makes him say:—

> "I am a thief, ay, and a king of thieves
> Ay! but we rob the robber, wrong the wronger
> And what we wring from them we give the
>   poor."

His method is thus described by Major in his *Britanniæ Historia,* printed at Paris in 1521.

> About this time, as I think Robert Hood and Little John the notorious thieves lurked in the forests only plundering the goods of the rich. They killed no one unless he attacked them or resisted them in protection of his property. Robert maintained a hundred archers very apt for rapine, whom four hundred of the strongest men dared not attack. He allowed no woman to be maltreated; nor ever took anything from the poor, but charitably fed them with the wealth he drew from the Abbots. I disapprove of the robbery of the man, but he was the most humane and the prince of all robbers.

The last lines of the *Lytell Geste* are:—

> Cryst have mercy on his soule
>   That dyed on the rode!
> For he was a good outlawe

And dyde pore men moch god.

It is clear that in following his profession he showed some discrimination and did not consider all booty legitimate profit. His revenues were derived from those who could supply funds without suffering distress, and his expenditure was designed to alleviate the distresses of the poor.

If any inference may be drawn from the character of their hero to that of our forefathers, we may take it that they were Catholic but anti-clerical, loyal but rowdy, and disposed to redress somewhat roughly the inequalities of fortune. (pp. 37-54)

> G. H. Radford, "Robin Hood," in his Shylock and Others: Eight Studies, *Dodd, Mead & Company, 1894, pp. 29-54.*

Luke Parsons   (essay date 1957)

[*In the following essay, Parsons explores Robin Hood's significance as an archetypal hero, concluding that "he is neither pure pagan nor pure Christian," but rather a blend of two traditions.*]

Robin Hood existed as a significant figure in the consciousness of Englishmen for upward of two centuries before the Reformation, of which, as we shall see, he was in some sense a prophet. His name, of course, is still proverbial. That his fame as a legendary hero was wide-spread is shown by the references to him we may find outside of the ballads; in the title of a poem, reputedly of 1304, in which he is compared with Sir William Wallace; in the pages not only of Stow but of the Scottish historians Fordun and Major; and in the work of poets as varied as Langland, Shakespeare and Michael Drayton. A reference in *The Vision of Piers Plowman,* opposing rhymes of Robin Hood to the *Pater Noster,* reflects the traditional hostility to him as a rival of the church; a hostility in itself indicative of his importance as myth, though we may deem him undeserving of such clerical anathemas. Shakespeare, more in sympathy with the popular view of him, in *As You Like It* equates him with Saturn as representative of a Golden Age. Drayton, in his *Polyolbion,* presents the homespun hero in more elegant attire. Keats's light, occasional lines come nearer to the spirit of the ballads, having in them something of their simple spontaneity. We may compare them with Elizabeth Barrett Browning's evocative elegy for Pan, in which dead pagan gods paradoxically inspire the Christian poetess to her finest flights. But where Mrs. Browning conscientiously condemns, Keats does well to honour, for though Robin may recall a lost, pagan harmony with Nature, he does not typify a reversion to paganism.

The fashion set by such early editors as Ritson and Gutch, even where otherwise they disagreed, of a purely historical, even biographical approach to the central figure of the Robin Hood ballads has inhibited later writers from a more rewarding study of the nature of his significance. The hero of the ballads was a superhuman bowman who lived through several centuries, and to reduce him to the stature of a particular individual living through a particular span of mediaeval time—whatever the truth about the historic Robin—is no more than a speculative exercise, however intriguing. Fresh light on the existence of such an individual would not alter the fact that the Robin of the ballads is a mythical conception and, as such, he is at once alive for us and larger than life; like all gods and legendary heroes, he is greater than any one historical great man.

Robin Hood—the mythical Robin—is above all the ideal of rustic as opposed to courtly chivalry. If we compare the description of him at the start of the *Lytell Geste* with that of the knight in the Prologue to *The Canterbury Tales,* the "good yeman" appears a more life-like and lovable figure than Chaucer's rather neutral exemplar. His reverence and humility and his simple moral code reveal a person, not a type. He is also, of course—an aspect of him popularized by *Ivanhoe*—the legendary last champion of the Saxons against the Norman invader. As such he is the successor of Alfred in his struggle against the Danes, of Harold Godwinson and of the historical but also legendary Hereward. Robin, the good yeoman, may also be compared with the nonpareil of kingship, Arthur—for his place in the national consciousness is to some extent complementary. Against the hero of *Morte d'Arthur* and the *Idylls* whose "last, weird battle in the west" has a timeless, allegorical significance—the foe is Sin as well as Modred—we may put the hero of the ballads who is the eternal champion of the oppressed. As Arthur appealed to Malory's courtly patrons, so Robin stirred the imagination of the Balladist's wider, if humbler audience; of those for the most part below the salt at the feudal table.

The Arthurian Legend was French as well as English, and in its association with Joseph of Arimathea and the story of the Grail became more overtly religious than any native "ryms of Roben Hode." Arthur, we may say, owing less perhaps to the Welsh *Mabinogion* than to Chrestien de Troyes, is part of the general European consciousness, whereas Robin, though Puck and even Pan may have some place in his ancestry, is essentially a yeoman hero of mediaeval England. Just as he is more of a person than Chaucer's nameless knight, so also he is recognizably more human than the half-magical, mistily delineated Arthur. He is good, bold and merry, even jolly, where Arthur is pure and noble and brave. He also has a sense of humour, which is not a notable attribute of Arthur, and is manly and natural where the latter is kingly and formal, which may explain why he does not lose *his* Guinevere—Marian—to some woodland Lancelot. Another reason, of course, is that he has less reason to fear adultery since he is divorced from the tradition of courtly love. Arthur's queen is fair and false; the courtly pattern of "merciles beaute." Robin's love, if hoydenish in the may-games, is bonny and true. Like Shakespeare's Rosalind, she dresses as a boy and goes off to the forest but, unlike Rosalind, she takes to the wild, outlaw life in earnest and turns her back for ever on that of "painted pomp." Her mating with Robin, natural as the confluence of forest rivers, contrasts with the courtly coupling, joylessly sophisticated, of Lancelot and Guinevere.

Marian's origins may date back to early French pastoral drama and she has been speculatively identified with Matilda or Maud Fitzwalter whose relations with King John, according to Stow, suggest a more virtuous counterpart of Henry II's Fair Rosamond. Because the figure of Robin's love does not feature prominently in the ballads, her significance in relation to the myth has largely been ignored, although she is constantly associated with the hero in songs and plays and in the may-games and the morris-dance. There is something of the elemental dryad in her; something, too, of the huntress chaste and fair. Her reputation has waxed and waned according to whether she was vaguely associated with a holier Mary or crowned queen of the May in a pagan succession. No doubt the mediaeval mind would also associate her with another Mary—Magdalene—since she became, in the greenwood, an outcast from society. Her pagan aspect, as with Robin himself, is really more complementary than opposed to the Christian. Her love for Robin, as we have seen, is distinct from the courtly tradition but it has, in common with that tradition, a heretical acceptance of ecstasy. Robin and Marian as passionate lovers would be sinners in the eyes of the church who held physical joy in union, even within marriage, to be lechery. Their love tale refutes a dogma out of touch with human nature and provides a less sophisticated alternative, that is at once older and more modern, to the artificial tradition of courtly love. They mate for life—akin, equally, to true Christians and wild forest birds:

> In solid content together they liv'd,
> With all their yeomen gay.

It is in what we may call their romantic domesticity in their woodland bowers that they are singular; before their time both in relation to church dogma and to poetic convention.

As Robin is a new kind of lover, he is also, by contemporary standards, a different sort of hero. His position among his followers contrasts with the old Norse and Teutonic conception of leadership that was common to both Saxons and Normans. In this tradition, wind-sown with the long ships of the Vikings, the hero imposed his will on his fellows partly by superior wisdom and cunning but chiefly by superior strength and prowess in arms. Boasting, if not vain, was admired, and was done for fun and for effect. Beowulf was the pattern of such a hero. Robin's authority among the tough and motley band we know as his "merry men" is from a different source and of another kind. Often his conqueror in battle elects to become his liegeman. Little John himself is thus typically recruited. Primarily, we must conclude, it is Robin's personality that induces men to follow him. The impulse to give him an earldom is probably similar to the desire to make Shakespeare a de Vere; at its shallowest romantic snobbery; at best an instinctive recognition that the one as nobly typifies the human spirit as the other portrays humanity. Robin is "one of Nature's gentlemen" in the sense that he represents a moral or spiritual aristocracy that transcends that of the feudal system. This new conception of leadership owes much to Christianity but derives, too, from rustic intuition made articulate by the balladists. It postulates a "natural selection" in human affairs that owes as much to moral as to physical fitness. Both as leader and lover Robin is more than an allegorical abstraction. Perhaps earlier than Chaucer he exemplifies the emergence of per-

sonality in literature. Unlike Ben Jonson's Everyman, he is integrated rather than synthetic. Unlike most characters in modern novels, he is more than just a creature of circumstance and environment. His nature is human nature; his fate paradoxical as human destiny. Miscalled a landless man, half England is his hunting-ground. Exiled to the forest, he regains something of Eden.

Robin's merry men, it has been claimed, were originally his merry "meinie" or retainers. However this may be, the substitution of men for meinie—whether or not a corruption of later usage—is more in keeping with the spirit of the ballads. Robin's followers are rather martial than menial, though we may see in them both disciples and companions at arms. One of them has a sad and lovely name—Gilbert with the white hand—and of him Gavin Douglas writes in lines emotive as Dunbar's *Lament of the Makaris:*

> Thair saw I Maitlaind upon auld Beird Gray,
> Robene Hude, and Gilbert with the quhite hand
> How Hay of Nauchton slew, in Madin land.

The merry men choose the forest life freely, for its own sake, and not because they are fugitives. Robin befriends anyone in need, whatsoever his degree, but poverty and rags are a better passport to his favour than power and riches. In his association with lowly and outcast men we discern a parallel with him who consorted with publicans and sinners. Men follow Robin out of hope, because they find in the greenwood a natural and fulfilling concept of society. If they are merry, it is because they are free. It is not that Sherwood is less perilous, though it may well be less envious, than town or court. Robin offers hard knocks rather than soft living. It is not that all men are equal in the forest. Robin is no anarchist, though an outlaw, and his rule in the greenwood is not the law of the jungle. Men, under him, are heroic, not brutish. He demands of them a dedicated life and a valorous one. Perhaps there is a Mithraic element in its appeal. They are happy warriors as well as merry men.

In the greenwood, we find, it is always summer. This should not lead us to confuse ballad Sherwood with pastoral Arden—in many respects it is a wild, mediaeval forest—but the convention serves to establish a mental climate. It relates to our view of the outlaw life; in one of its aspects, as a glimpse of Eden. Often a conventional portrayal of the sunlit forest precedes a story of robust action that confounds our expectation of pastoral peace. The best-known of such introductions, at once to be followed by an unseemly but very human quarrel between Robin Hood and Little John, we find in the opening lines of *Robin Hood and the Monk:*

> In somer when the shawes be sheyne,
> And leves be large and longe,
> Hit is fulle mery in feyre foreste
> To here the foulys song.
>
> To se the dere draw to the dale
> And leve the hilles hee,
> And shadow hem in the leves grene,
> Undur the grene wode tre.

This is pastoral, even paradisal, but the petty quarrel that ensues reminds us that, though Man may approach Eden, he is, through his own nature, outside it. The two heroes squabbling over five shillings recall Achilles sulking in his tent. Like Homer, the Balladist is aware of the heroic potentialities of Man without forgetting the depths of sin, of meanness and sensuality, into which at any moment he may fall. There is also, of course, a quite prosaic and practical reason why Robin Hood's season should be summer. The opening lines of *Robin Hood and the Ranger* speak of Robin venturing abroad once the snow and ice have melted, and we may conclude that, during the long, dark nights, he and his men retire to winter quarters in the depths of the forest—where they have few opportunities for adventure—and do not "frolick abroad" till warmer weather. Akin to forest animals, they acquire, we may say, the habit of hibernation.

Robin loses most of some dozen encounters with local champions and itinerants recorded in the ballads and we may see in him, in these essentially sporting contests, the original Good Loser who has become so popular a mythical figure in English games-playing. Against jolly tinkers and tanners, fellow-mortals with souls and sinews, Robin is a friendly foe, but against an enemy that symbolizes Evil, embodied in such figures as Guy of Gisborne and The Sheriff, he is implacable. He strives against the powers of darkness in a greenwood become a moral battle-ground. Without appreciation of this allegorical element in the ballads, common to so much mediaeval writing, Robin's hatred of one type of his enemies—though he loves others—seems extravagant and shocking. *Robin Hood's Progress to Nottingham,* for instance, seems but a saga of savagery in which Robin reverts to the inhuman type of hero of the *Edda,* unless we view it as we would that other *Progress* of Christian; unless we realize that in this ballad Robin is the personification of Fate, as the fifteen foresters whom he slays personify Pride, Wrath, Envy and Avarice; in fact all uncharitableness and most of the deadly sins. The people of Nottingham fare ill, too, because they side with Might against Right in this moral struggle. In *Robin Hood and Guy of Gisborne* the disfigurement of a dead foe is also partly allegorical:

> "Thou hast beene a traytor all thy life,
> Which thing must have an end".

With Guy's death, the evil thing—Treachery—is effaced. We may ascribe to rustic humour the ribald bathos in the last line of this grim tale through which blows the chill wind of mortality if not of winter. The awful and elemental nature of such ballads we must relate to the standards of their time. Mediaeval Man, as he emerges from the Dark Ages, grows out of the unimaginative and therefore amoral cruelty of his forebears. If he still holds life cheap, it is because he sees so clearly its transience. If he has fear of hell, he has hope of heaven. Unlike post-Renaissance Man—unlike, for example, Donne and Webster—he takes the physical fact of death in his stride. Neither the Vulgate nor the recurring theme of the old Moralities lets him forget that he is but a wayfarer on the face of the earth. The ballad Robin does not forget it. Historically he is mediaeval—but no thrall of the *Zeitgeist.* In the greenwood he escapes from the otherworldliness preached by worldly prel-

ates whom, at least figuratively, he would "bete and bynde."

Robin's position as a devout Christian but an opponent of the mediaeval church is clearly stated at the beginning of the *Lytell Geste.* His respect for women stems from his attitude towards Mary, the mother of Jesus—and this is both filial and superstitious; the love of a Christian "mother's son" for the most blessed among mothers; worship, essentially pagan, of a kindly goddess who will intervene on behalf of her idolaters. To Robin, as to so many Romanists, there is a homeliness as well as holiness about Mary that seems less awful and remote than the mystical conception of the Trinity. Indeed, she replaces the Son in the three masses he hears before meals. She is his household god of the forest. Robin is a man of simple, child-like faith who opposes not the more complex theology of the church but its worldliness and corruption. Ostensibly the church disapproves of Robin because it fears he will seduce the faithful into old ways of paganism or new ways of unbelief. In fact, in the ballads, "bysshoppes and archebysshoppes"—and, of course, abbots—fear him as a menace to their wealth and power; and because of his refusal to be priest-ridden. In the *Lytell Geste* he saves the estate of a poor knight from falling into covetous clerical hands. He attacks the church rather for its politics than its doctrines; for allocating unto itself, in the name of God, the things that are Caesar's. When, in *Robin Hood and Allin a Dale,* Robin prevents the bishop from conducting a mockery of marriage between Allin's love and a wealthy, old knight, he is protesting, vigorously and successfully, against the unholy alliance of Priest and Mammon. His capture in church and subsequent escape, in *Robin Hood and the Monk,* we may see as the struggle for freedom of the individual conscience. If the "gret hedid munke" in this old ballad is the hierarchical church, his little page is the servile laity involved in the consequences of the Judas-priest's betrayal. Robin's own moral testing comes towards the end of the *Lytell Geste* when, in the eighth "fytte," he tastes the flesh-pots of the court and the king would keep him there—that is, bind him to Caesar—and he realizes, almost too late, that he must flee the corruption of the world. He is saved by returning to the greenwood in the name of Mary Magdalene who, we need not doubt, here symbolizes Repentance.

The characters associated with Robin in the may-games, though not without individuality, are recognizable, too, as recurring types of literature and legend. Maid Marian as the presiding female deity of the may-day revels is perhaps the last of the ancient goddesses. Or we may hail her first of our modern beauty queens. Little John is of the pattern of faithful companion from *fidus* Achates to Doctor Watson. Friar Tuck to some extent prefigures Falstaff. Those who, with unimaginative exactitude, would make the "curtall fryer" of Fountains Abbey a Cistercian monk miss his symbolic significance. He is a friar because the friar, alone among priests, is of the church but outside its man-made walls. With Robin in the greenwood Tuck has "new orders taken" and in the may-games his bibulous and bucolic figure recalls another forerunner of Falstaff—Silenus. He ridicules in his person clerical dignity as the old pagan and the tavern knight mock all convention and pomp. They would show us that a man is still the son of Adam behind his social mask; even despite the hoar of age. One aspect of Robin himself, as we have seen, is as a pattern of the hero patriot, historical or mythical, such as William Wallace or William Tell. He is also in the tradition of "mighty hunters" and Wild Huntsmen from Nimrod and Woden to the saintly Hubert and the sinister Herne. In recent times he has become quite erroneously associated in popular imagination with fictional "gentlemen cracksmen" such as Raffles and Blackshirt who rob the rich, it is suggested, for fun rather than from greed; who may even claim a social conscience. The difference, of course, is that such types accept the protection of the society they batten on, while Robin uncompromisingly rejects Norman tyranny. The modern counterparts of the heroic Robin are in the forests of Poland; under terror rule in Eastern Europe. Perhaps the nearest to an embodiment of him was General Mihailovitch. Among the improbable and often repulsive "heroes" of contemporary popular press mythology—the sub-, called super-, men, for example, of the strip cartoons—only Tarzan has an archetypal significance akin to that of Robin Hood. This modern "noble savage," whose Sherwood is the African jungle, represents, as Robin does, Man's lost harmony with Nature. He, too, sides with Right against Might; Good against Evil; often with unspoiled natives against a corrupted invader. (He is born, we may suspect, of America's bad conscience about her native Redskins). It is fair to conclude that the appeal of the mediaeval "wolf's head," as of the modern ape-man, is more than just a siren call of the wild to the animal side of Man's nature. As with Robin and Marian, the mating of Tarzan with his Jane is pastoral. Despite the worst Hollywood and horror comics can do, they seem as unself-conscious as Adam and Eve first were in their primordial innocence. They exemplify in their relations neither the sublimation of sex nor D. H. Lawrence's submergence in it, but its natural fulfilment. As symbols of Natural Man, untrammelled and unsophisticated, such heroes attract alike the victims of tyrannical régimes and of a tyrannical industrialism.

If we may call the ballads the scripture of the Robin Hood myth, the may-games provide its ritual. To mediaeval churchmen and even to the Lutheran Latimer these represented either a reversion to paganism or a rejection of the spiritual for the profane. They condemned them as would a modern parson the sad contrast of full cinemas and empty pews. Though most clerical writers dismissed the may-games as mere secular junketing—the sort of empty Fellowship of *Everyman*—they doubtless disapproved of them more as symptomatic of a return to paganism, though they would be loath overtly to grant them religious significance. The spring "gatherynge" for Robin seemed to reverse the process by which pagan festivals had been transformed into Christian holy days. With the exception of "Robin Hoodes daye," this had been a sure and subtle process of conversion and accretion that had led to the synthesis of Yule and Christmas, the retention of Woden's and Saturn's days in a Christian calendar, and even—the Venerable Bede tells us—the adoption for the Christian festival of Easter of the name of a Teutonic goddess of spring. The church no doubt rightly suspected that some pagan element—perhaps an instinctive pantheism—

inspired, as much as did zeal for archery, the rustic revels dedicate to Robin, but it failed to realize that such primitive joy in the rebirth of spring—renewal on earth—was an enduring religious emotion and supplementary rather than hostile to the Christian hope in the Resurrection with which it sought to supplant it. As it contemplated the drama of life, both human and divine, the church's absorption with heaven and hell led it to neglect the background of Nature for the prospect of Eternity. The may-games we may see as a neo-pagan protest at this neglect and a reaffirmation of Man's age-old faith in the awfulness of Nature as the handywork, perhaps the very essence, of God. In rejecting the pantheistic doctrine of immanence, the mediaeval church was led, as the modern mystic Aldous Huxley has been, to view Nature rather in horror than with awe. Pastoral harmony is lost as much by an otherworldliness that ignores Nature as by the *hubris* that would exploit it solely for worldly ends. But perhaps only a Saint Francis would have sensed the underlying reverence of country folk a-maying in God-created woods and meadows. To most churchmen the may-games seemed an excuse for rustic revelry that might degenerate into bacchanalian frenzy or into the devilish hysteria of the sabbat. Robin to them was incarnate Pan. And was not the pagan god, with his horns and goat's feet, the very pattern of the Christian Sathanas?

We do not find in the ballads the atmosphere of magic and faerie of which Arthurian romances such as *Sir Gawain and the Green Knight* are redolent nor much evidence of the supernatural, of an explicit acceptance of miracle, that might derive from the New Testament. Unlike the Greek heroes who were half gods, it is Robin's naturalness, his mortal strength and weakness, that makes him so appealing and convincing a character. In so far as Yeoman and Balladist saw in him *imitatio Christi* it was in human, not divine attributes, and the feats he achieves, if we except, perhaps, those of archery, are marvellous but not miraculous. He cannot raise from the dead, but he saves from the very gallows. He cannot divinely heal, but he restores fallen fortunes. He cannot intercede for the soul of his murderess, but he forbids that her body be harmed. His treacherous kinswoman, the prioress who lets his life-blood, has elements in her both of Judas and Caiaphas. The hero's death at the hands of a female priest we may see as the consummation of the anti-clericalism that recurs, as a sort of *Leitmotif,* throughout the ballads.

> Syr Roger of Donkestere
> By the pryoresse he lay,
> And there they betrayed good Robyn Hode,
> Through theyr false playe.

Behind this anti-clericalism of the ballads and their incidental social criticism there is not only a *mystique* of primal innocence such as we find traces of in modern nudism or "naturism," but also something of the reforming zeal of the Lollards. As we may learn from Winifred Bryher's great novel *The Fourteenth of October,* the Saxon Balladist's dislike of the church no doubt stems, too, from its backing of William against Harold and its collaboration, after Hastings, with the Normans. The ballads look backward to the Conquest—but also forward to the Reformation. Where else in mediaeval literature do we find a comparable challenge to the power and infallibility of the church? Secular writing such as Malory's runs parallel to the sacred literature of the monastic age whereas the ballads cut across it. Malory, we may say, is profane; the Balladist is heretical. Were Robin historical, we might deem him one of the earliest of Protestant martyrs. Certainly his myth opposes, not the spirit of the Gospels, but the pretensions and corruption of the mediaeval church. His death, attended at the last by a solitary companion, bears only a superficial resemblance to the passing of Arthur. His bow, unlike *Excalibur*, is of English yew and not magical. It returns with him to English earth in the greenwood where he is buried. The ballads do not perpetuate the recurring pagan myth of a sleeping god or hero who will come again. Robin does not lie dreaming in Sherwood as Merlin does in Broceliande and Arthur in Avalon. He is heroic but mortal; immortal only in the Christian sense that all of us may hope to be:

> Cryst have mercy on his soule,
> That dyed on the rode!
> For he was a good outlawe,
> And dyde pore men moch god.

Whatever the truth about the historic Robin—were he churl or earl, royal retainer or rebel—he became for English yeomen an archetypal figure; the type of Old Saxon, just emerging from paganism, with whom they associated a heroic past; with whom, in their aspiring moments, they identified themselves. He is Dunbar's "weild Robeine under bewch" and Shakespeare's old Robin Hood of England. He has survived even to this day, if only in children's books and Hollywood films, because he symbolises some eternal strain, both heroic and rebellious, in the mind and heart of Man. He is neither pure pagan nor pure Christian. The pagan strain in him can perhaps best be seen in his at-homeness in the forest; a pastoral harmony, cherished by Saint Francis and the eremites, that the mediaeval church had lost sight of. The Balladist considers in the greenwood the lilies of the field. The Cloistered Monk views Nature only as "the wilderness" of Exodus and the Forty Days; as symbolic of doubt or temptation. Robin's myth, we may say, restates certain truths both of paganism and primitive Christianity. If in some aspects he has affinity with Pan, we should remember that, to Milton's shepherds, the pagan god and the Christian Saviour are synonymous. Perhaps because he is a figure of two worlds, of mythology as well as of history, he has been curiously neglected by English historians—though Trevelyan and Wingfield-Stratford acknowledge him—and it has been left to a Frenchman, Augustin Thierry in his *Norman Conquest,* seriously to consider him as throwing light on the English genius. A rustic Arthur, our native Odin, he is heir both to the martial virtues of the old gods and to the values of Christendom that give his acts moral significance; make a person out of a hero. From among the shadowy figures on the far side of the Renaissance and the Reformation he stands out as recognizably human. We discern in his lineaments those of our remote and wild forebears, yet sense behind his words a mind not wholly strange. The ballads that tell of him are the rustic scripture of our race. They come to us out of the dark, mediaeval forest. They are an outpouring of the yeoman soul. (pp. 268-77)

Luke Parsons, "The Meaning of Robin Hood," in The Hibbert Journal, *Vol. LV, April, 1957, pp. 268-77.*

Joseph Falaky Nagy (essay date 1980)

[*Here, Nagy characterizes Robin Hood as an outlaw from society residing in "an in-between world, where separate categories are blended and liminal figures abound."*]

The narrative tradition about Robin Hood, which throve in the folklore and the popular literature of England from the medieval period to the nineteenth century, reflects the worldwide fascination with the figure of the outlaw, the man who exists beyond human society and has adventures which would be impossible for normal members of society in their normal social environments. In this [essay] I present an analysis of the 'mystique' of Robin Hood the outlaw and an examination of the Robin Hood ballads as myth—that is, as an expression of basic social issues. I will attempt to demonstrate that Robin Hood is not so much a figure outside society as one who exists *between* culture and nature, and several other pairs of opposed categories as well. The liminal world of Robin Hood, a construct of narrative, provides a context in which social values and realities are mirrored and redefined. To examine the function of the narrative tradition about Robin Hood is to examine a specific instance of the function of liminality in myth.

One of the most prominent characteristics of the Robin Hood figure, from the earliest extant Robin Hood narratives—such as the fifteenth-century *Gest of Robin Hood*—to the broadside ballads of the eighteenth century, is that he and his men are devoted hunters; it is both a means of survival in the forest and a pastime for them. Robin Hood describes their situation to the disguised king in the *Gest* thus:

> We be yemen of this foreste,
> Under the grene wode tre;
> We lyve by our kynges dere,
> Other shyft have not we.

Robin's general attitude is that of a professional hunter, who lives in the woods and has no taste for the 'civilized' life of town and court. After Robin spends some time with the king in civilization, he becomes restless (and destitute). The reformed outlaw returns to the forest, where he reflects:

> It is ferre gone, sayd Robyn,
> That I was last here;
> Me lyste a lytell for to shote
> At the donne dere.

He slays a deer, summons his men, and returns to the life of the hunter. Thus, Robin Hood *can* survive for periods within the civilized world: he spends some time in the king's court, and in the ballads Robin is frequently sneaking into the town of Nottingham. But he prefers to live in the wilderness far from normal human habitations. In

'Robin Hood and the Butcher' the hero, disguised as a butcher, does business with his mortal enemy, the sheriff of Nottingham, who inquires whether Robin has any cows:

> Hast thou any horn-beasts, the sheriff repli'd,
> Good fellow, to sell unto me?

Robin does have 'horned beasts' to show the sheriff, but they turn out to be wild deer in the forest:

> How like you my horned beasts, good Master
>   Sheriff?
> They be fat and fair for to see.

(The sheriff replies:)

> I tell thee, good fellow, I would I were gone,
> For I like not thy company.

The point made in Robin's joke on the sheriff is that a great gap exists between the civilized man, for whom 'horned beasts' are cattle, and the hunter, for whom they are game.

Robin and his men dress in green, the colour of their natural environment, and live among the game on which they depend, to the point that there is almost identification of hunter with hunted. In the *Gest* Little John, Robin's trusty companion, lures the sheriff out into the forest by offering to show him a herd of deer, but leads him into an ambush laid by the outlaws and jokingly introduces Robin as the 'mayster herte.' This playful confusion of human with animal indicates the liminality of Robin and his men, who live in a world where identity is fluid and separate categories of identity can blend.

Closely linked to his role as a hunter is Robin's role as a robber who attacks members of society travelling through the wilderness. He disrupts their travel; he has dominion over roads and those who use them. In the earlier Robin Hood Ballads he is generally not associated with Sherwood Forest in Nottinghamshire but with the less forested area of Barnsdale in Yorkshire. It has been noted that the latter association is consistent with the image of Robin as a robber, a 'highwayman,' for Barnsdale was 'the most frequented passage into the Vale of York and in a real sense the gateway to north-eastern England and Scotland.' In 'Robin Hood and the Potter' the hero attempts to exert his dominion over roads and travellers not really as a robber but as a kind of informal toll-taker: he demands 'pavage' from the travelling craftsmen. Robin first meets Little John on a narrow bridge, where Robin demands the right of way. In both of these instances Robin is bested by his victims; nonetheless, his association with roads and travelling is apparent. In one of the versions of the ballad about Robin Hood's death, the dying hero asks that his body be taken 'to yonder streete' and buried there. Robin is a figure of the road, and he materializes in the context of travelling. The action of the *Gest* begins with Robin's men interrupting the journey of a knight; at the centre of the action in the *Gest* there occurs another disruption of a journey—this time, the journey of a monk; and towards the end of the *Gest* the king meets Robin Hood 'stondynge on the waye,' and the two arrive at a rapprochement. Robin's association with roads and with the period of passage between locations makes him a figure 'in-between,' a liminal figure.

Robin Hood is an outlaw—in English medieval legal terms, one who does not appear in court for his trial, who places himself beyond the grasp of the forces of law and authority, such as the sheriff, and who is therefore deprived of his social identity and status. The outlaw abandons society and the latter disavows him. Society and the events which occur within it become irrelevant for the person outlawed. From society's point of view, he is a creature of nature: the outlaw 'bears the wolf's head,' in the language of medieval English law. Yet social values, issues, and events are of great concern to the figure of Robin Hood. He is no longer a member of society (in the traditional ballads it is never explained why he was outlawed), but in several of his adventures Robin the outlaw is drawn into society, where he wants to trick the sheriff, rescue someone in danger, stop a marriage, or even attend church services. Robin commutes between the world of culture and the world of outlawry; he exists between the normal social order and the asocial void that the concept of outlawry suggests.

Sherwood Forest, where Robin and his outlaw band dwell according to some strands of tradition, functions in the narratives as a place of nature, juxtaposed with the town of Nottingham, a place of culture, where the sheriff has dominion. But, at least in the medieval context of the tradition, Sherwood forest is also an anomaly existing between culture and nature, for it is one of the king's forests—nature owned, protected, and theoretically controlled by the most powerful and representative member of society. Therefore, the world of Robin Hood is a distinctly liminal one, whether it is Barnsdale—a passageway, a place of travel—or Sherwood Forest.

There has been scholarly controversy over whether the figure of Robin Hood is a projection of some late medieval social class, and whether he has a special affinity with the peasantry or the gentry. (This controversy implicitly confirms the anomalous nature of this figure, an outlaw who appears to be linked with a sector of society.) In the *Gest,* one of the surviving Robin Hood narratives that is closest to the medieval world, the hero and his companions are frequently referred to as 'yemen'; Robin forbids his men to harass yeomen, and he states:

> What man that helpeth a good yeman,
> His frende that wyll I be.

Thus, the outlaw is the defender, and paradoxically even a member, of the yeomanry—the class of free peasantry which was emerging in late medieval English society. Also in the *Gest,* however, Robin orders his men not to attack

> . . . . knyght ne no squyer
> That wol be a gode felawe.

The main tale of the *Gest* features Robin saving a destitute knight from ecclesiastics who want to take all his property. The outlaw gives the knight money, clothes, a horse, and even Little John as a temporary servant so that he may keep the dignity fitting to a member of the gentry. Robin clearly has an interest in the welfare of this class; in 'Robin Hood Rescuing Three Squires' he enters Nottingham in disguise to rescue three members of the gentry from execution. Of course, this link between Robin and the gentry does not necessarily mean that the hero is, or was before he was an outlaw, a member of this class; in the *Gest* Robin is really supporting a social superior, not a peer, and he reveals an awareness of a hierarchical distinction between knight and yeoman when he asks the knight to give something in return for the dinner which Robin gave him:

> It was never the manner, by dere worthi God,
> A yoman to pay for a knight.

Robin is not actually a member of the gentry, but he is noted for his 'courtesy,' a quality characteristic of a knight. Perhaps this confusion in the figure of Robin Hood is a reflection of the breakdown of the boundary between rich peasantry and impoverished gentry in late medieval English society. But then, Robin is not member of any social class inasmuch as he is an outlaw. Thus, we see that Robin Hood as a sociological phenomenon is confusing, anomalous, and liminal.

Not only is Robin Hood a liminal figure but so are his companions, and even some of his enemies. His most famous companion in the greenwood is Little John, who, despite the name, is a giant—he is, therefore, a contradiction, both 'little' and 'big.' John receives his paradoxical nickname (his original name is John Little) as part of his initiation into Robin's band: joining the men in the greenwood means, for John, becoming an anomaly. This is true also for Maid Marian in the only surviving Robin Hood ballad which features her: when she comes from society into the wilderness to join Robin, she is dressed like a man, and Robin even fights with this 'man-woman' before they recognize each other.

Marian and most other females who appear in the Robin Hood ballads are depicted as liminal figures. Thus Robin's devotion to women, an important theme in the ballads, is another indication of his own liminal nature. Robin is especially devoted to the Blessed Virgin, the most important female in the Christian tradition, who performs an essential liminal function: she mediates between God and man by interceding on behalf of humanity. In the *Gest* Mary is chosen as the surety for the loan which Robin gives to the knight. Robin says:

> To seche all Englonde thorowe,
> Yet fonde I never to my pay (i.e. satisfaction)
> A moche better borrowe (i.e. surety).

Mary mediates between the knight, a member of society and of the gentry, and Robin, a figure who suggests yeomanry but who, more importantly, is a figure outside society. Females in Robin Hood narratives cross the boundary between culture and nature—society and the world of the outlaw—easily. In the *Gest,* after the knight has been seized by the sheriff, his wife goes out into the wilderness, finds Robin, and tells him the news. A woman whom the outlaw meets 'along the highway' tells him of the plight of the three squires about to be executed by the sheriff in 'Robin Hood Rescuing Three Squires.' It is a female messenger sent from London who finds Robin in the forest and gives him the mission of saving the princess from her

undesirable suitor in 'Robin Hood and the Prince of Aragon.' The outlaw is invited to the king's court and pardoned through the efforts of the queen in 'Robin and Queen Katherine.' The sheriff of Nottingham's wife invites the disguised Robin to dinner and thus introduces him to the sheriff in 'Robin Hood and the Potter.' All these narratives present women as mediators between Robin, an extra-social figure, and society. In 'The Noble Fisherman' the land-based outlaw decides to go to sea; it is a woman who makes this radical transition possible for Robin by giving him a job as a sailor on her ship. Thus, females effect passage between all kinds of realms and identities in the Robin Hood ballads—they exist between categories, like their devotee Robin. In 'Robin Hood and the Bishop' the outlaw actually exchanges identities with an old woman in order to escape from an ecclesiastic; Little John does not recognize his master in the woman's clothing, and the bishop mistakes the old woman in green for Robin Hood. There is a deep affinity between the outlaw and women: both are ubiquitous and liminal.

Females are Robin's allies usually, and they share with him an anomalous quality. Anomaly is something that Robin has in common with his main enemies as well—clerics. By definition they too are mediators, between God and man. According to Christian ideology, the ecclesiastic lives a life different from, and closer to the 'sacred' than, the life of secular people. Yet, as depicted in the Robin Hood ballads, clerics are exceptionally greedy and worldly. Therefore, the cleric exists between God and man; also, in the context of the Robin Hood ballads, he leads both a sacred and secular life. Although one of Robin's companions, Friar Tuck, is a cleric, in general these liminal figures are Robin's enemies, as opposed to women, who are equally liminal figures but are usually on his side. The outlaw's death, however, is brought about by the treachery of a figure *both* female and ecclesiastical—the prioress of a nunnery, who is not celibate, as nuns theoretically are, but has a lover. Liminality proves to be both Robin's way of life and also his way of death.

The 'surprise' of the Robin Hood narrative tradition is that the figure who appears to be Robin's greatest enemy, the king (on whose land the outlaw poaches), becomes Robin's benefactor and friend. But the king as a social figure intimately associated with nature (the king's forests) is a liminal figure himself, and so he has an anomalous characteristic in common with the outlaw: both figures suggest a transcendence of the boundary between culture and nature. With liminality in common, we would expect the king and the outlaw to be either very good friends or mortal enemies: in the shifting world of Robin Hood, relationships between liminal figures can go either way.

The king's friendship with the outlaw is thus not so surprising after all in this narrative tradition full of paradoxes. Towards the end of the *Gest* there is a climactic scene of anomaly and confusion: the reconciled king and outlaw ride together into Nottingham dressed in green, so that the townspeople think that the outlaw has slain the king and has come to ravage the town. But the king remains the king, and the outlaw ultimately returns to being an outlaw. Nonetheless, Robin stays in the king's court for a while, and temporarily the distinction between the 'centre' and 'periphery' of society is blurred.

As one who exists between several opposed categories—man and animal, culture and nature, knight and yeoman, even man and woman—Robin Hood's identity is unfixed and malleable. This lack of definition gives the outlaw a distinct advantage. Robin is a master of disguise; he attains his goals by assuming various identities—incognito he enters Nottingham easily, joins the world of sailors and ships, and strikes up relationships with all kinds of people. Robin is characterized by his hood, which perhaps suggests the concealment of identity which is a way of life for him. In 'Robin Hood and the Monk,' when the hero attempts to enter Nottingham without disguise, he places himself in mortal danger. Robin's effectiveness lies in his liminality, his ability to assume different identities and thus penetrate different levels of social or natural reality. Little John, who also has a knack for disguises, conceals his identity and penetrates both Nottingham and the king's court in the process of rescuing Robin in the same ballad.

Robin Hood not only disguises himself frequently: he can disguise others as well or confuse their identities. In *The Gest,* after the outlaw captures the sheriff in the greenwood, the paradigmatic enforcer of law is dressed in the green clothes of Robin's men and the outlaw threatens to change the sheriff's identity altogether:

> All this twelve months, sayde Robin,
> Thou shalt dwell with me;
> I shall thee teche, proude sheriff,
> An outlawe for to be.

When in the forest with Robin, the king asks the outlaw to give him some green to wear, so that the king too experiences a confusion of identity in Robin's company. In 'Robin Hood and Guy of Gisbourne,' the outlaw assumes his enemy's identity and mutilates the latter's corpse so that it will be unrecognizable. The lack of identity which is a reflection of the outlaw's anomaly is clearly infectious in the greenwood.

The world depicted in the Robin Hood ballads is a shifting, dangerous world, where identity and relationship can change very suddenly. The story pattern in several of the ballads features Robin confronting a stranger in the wilderness; their relationship changes from one of intense antagonism to one of friendship in the course of the story. The stranger is revealed to be a sturdy fellow, who can defeat Robin in combat, and he becomes a member of the outlaw band; sometimes the stranger turns out to be an unrecognized kinsman. The world of Robin Hood is one where appearances are deceiving and where the regularity of normal life is non-existent.

Oddly, together with this fluidity there exists a kind of stability in Robin's world, for the ethos of Robin Hood, an outlaw living beyond society, is actually based on essential social concepts and values, which at times in the ballads seem to be more operative in the world of outlaws than in the social world of the sheriff and the church establishment. As mentioned above, the Robin of the *Gest* is a model of gentility—he doffs his hood or kneels in the pres-

Kevin Costner in the 1991 film Robin Hood: Prince of Thieves.

ence of the knight, the monk and the king, while the monk shows his rudeness by not doffing his hood in front of his 'host' Robin, and the sheriff reveals his deceitful nature when he has Robin and his men attacked, despite the sheriff's pledge not to harm them. In his time of need the knight is abandoned by all of his friends within society, but he finds a true friend in the outlaw Robin. Unlike his ecclesiastical enemies, Robin Hood is sincerely devout: he attends Mass regularly and has a chapel in the greenwood. Even though he defies the sheriff, the outlaw respects and loves the ultimate symbol of social authority, the king. Robin does not really revolt against social order; indeed, he even supports it, and he exemplifies several cultural values. The centre of his world in the wilderness is the 'trystell tree,' where Robin meets with his men or with others, such as the knight, who goes there to repay his debt to the outlaw, or the sheriff, who swears friendship to Robin there. The 'trystell tree' is a symbol of both the natural environment in which the outlaws live and also of the agreements which exist among them or between Robin and others—it is paradoxically a symbol of both nature and social order.

Robin Hood and his band in the wilderness function as a paradigm of the proper relationship between master and man. In the *Gest,* when the king observes how Robin's men serve him he thinks:

> Here is a wonder semely syght
> Me thynketh, by Goddes pyne,
> His men are more at his byddynge
> Than my men be at myn.

In 'Robin Hood and the Monk' the outlaw leader acts unfairly towards Little John, but, despite a period of alienation, John remains faithful to his master and rescues him. When Robin and his men join the king's retinue in the *Gest,* he loses most of them because Robin cannot support them within society; he returns to the greenwood and reassembles his band. The paradigm of Robin and his men functions only in their liminal world. Robin in the wilderness, as opposed to Robin in the king's court, is such a popular employer that he can lure members of society away from their social masters into his world of outlawry.

In many of the ballads, Robin, a master of disguise and deception, ironically is very concerned about exposing falsehood and finding out the truth. In the *Gest* he takes from his victims only the valuables which they do *not* declare—thus he points out the truth or falsehood of their statements, or he makes false statements 'true' by taking away what the victims claim not to have. The outlaw wants the travellers whom he meets to tell the truth; and those who do, he does not molest. In 'Robin Hood's Golden Prize,' the hero refuses to take the word of two clerics who claim to have no money:

> I am much afraid, said bold Robin Hood,
> That you both do tell a lye;
> And now before that you go hence,
> I am resolvd to try.

After Robin has exposed them as liars, he even 'reforms' them:

> You shall be sworn, said bold Robin Hood,
> Vpon this holy grass,
> That you will never tell lies again,
> Which way soever you pass.

The result of most of the confrontations between Robin (or his men) and people passing through the wilderness in the ballads is that the travellers' true natures are revealed. In the *Gest* Robin's first 'guest,' the knight, demonstrates his integrity in his dealings with the outlaw. Another 'guest,' the monk, proves, on the other hand, to be a 'chorle.' The king goes into the forest disguised as a cleric, but when he becomes Robin's guest in the greenwood, his true identity is soon revealed. The sheriff, another 'guest,' swears to be Robin's friend; afterwards, the outlaw enters the sheriff's archery contest to test his word, finds the sheriff to be treacherous, and ultimately slays him. Those who keep their word, such as the knight, prosper in the world of Robin Hood—the knight's status and property are restored to him. But those who break their word, such as the sheriff, perish. Robin Hood himself is captured by the sheriff soon after he breaks his word to Little John in 'Robin Hood and the Monk.' Little John, a master of deceit like Robin, can see through the deceit of others and expose their true selves in 'Little John a Begging,' where he reveals some infirm beggars to be actually neither infirm nor poor. John's own true nature, specifically his strength, is revealed in his first meeting with Robin Hood, who declares before they fight:

> And now, for thy sake, a staff will I take,
> The truth of thy manhood to try.

In the ballads which feature a confrontation between Robin and a mysterious stranger, the outlaw is usually beaten, but at least he attains his goal of testing the stranger's mettle.

Closely linked to Robin Hood's desire for the truth is his insistence on 'fair play,' or on sharing and reciprocity between himself and the people whom he meets in the greenwood. After the outlaw has found the money which the clerics denied having in 'Robin Hood's Golden Prize,' he says:

> We will be sharers now all alike
> Of the money that we have;
> And there is never a one of us
> That his fellows shall deceive.

In the *Gest* Robin expects the knight, the monk, and the king—his 'guests'—to share their money with him, just as he shares his dinner with them; when the sheriff is captured in the greenwood and forced to eat with Robin and his men, he is served on dinnerware stolen from his own home.

Rarely in the ballads do Robin or his men commit an outright act of theft; the taking of goods is often described, albeit whimsically, as the collecting of a debt, or a matter of indirect reciprocity. In the *Gest* Robin takes the monk's money as payment of the debt which the knight owes the outlaw—the monk is from an abbey dedicated to Mary, who is the surety in the transaction between Robin and the knight. Thus, Robin is taking what belongs to him. In 'Robin Hood and the Potter,' the outlaw does not want to rob the craftsman but only claim the toll which is due to him as a kind of 'guardian' of the road; when Robin assumes the potter's identity and goes into Nottingham, he virtually gives his wares away, yet he collects his 'payment' when he robs the sheriff. The latter's wife says to her husband after he returns from the greenwood a poorer man:

> Now haffe yow payed ffor all the pottys
> That Roben gaffe to me.

When Robin takes, there is at least a pretence of a justification for the action. The outlaw is 'collecting debts' more than he is 'stealing;' and Robin gives nothing without expecting something in return, as the victim invited to sup with the outlaw realizes in 'Robin Hood and the Bishop of Hereford:'

> Call in the reckoning, said the Bishop,
> For me thinks it grows wondrous high.

Nothing comes free or without obligations attached in the world of Robin Hood; services are rendered in return for past services or as payment of debts. In 'Robin Hood and the Bishop,' the old woman with whom Robin exchanges clothes owes the outlaw:

> For I well remember, one Saturday night

Thou bought me both shoos and hose;
Therefore I'le provide thy person to hide,
And keep thee from thy foes.

When Robin takes someone's clothes in order to disguise himself, he gives his own clothes in return; when the takes the potter's or the butcher's goods in order to assume their roles in society, he pays them. The various adventures and crimes of the outlaw paradoxically revolve around the concepts of fairness and reciprocity.

In this [essay] I have emphasized two aspects of the world of Robin Hood in the traditional ballads. It is an in-between world, where separate categories are blended and liminal figures abound; the greenwood is rife with confusion and sudden change, elements that set it apart from society proper, which, however, is occasionally 'infected' by the anomaly of the greenwood, in the person of Robin Hood. The world of the outlaw is peripheral to society. Yet it is to an extent a mirror of society, for the world of Robin Hood is based on essential social values such as truth, loyalty, honesty, reciprocity, and religiosity; the outlaw's adventures are a context for the reaffirmation of these values, which seem in the ballads to be barely operative in society proper.

In his study of initiation rituals, the anthropologist Victor Turner [in *The Forest of Symbols: Aspects of Ndembu Ritual,* 1967] has noted that the liminal period of time during the initiate passes from one social state to another is marked by the ritual representation of important cultural concepts and values, which the initiate experiences as part of his social education. Liminality, a state in which normal distinctions and order are transcended, is a context for the recreation and reformulation of order, a 'clean slate' upon which culture is rewritten. In the context of liminality cultural concepts and values appear in unique, paradoxical, almost chaotic forms. This confusion of separate categories is a means of reinforcing the separateness of those categories in the mind of the initiate:

> During the liminal period, neophytes are alternately forced and encouraged to think about society, their cosmos, and the powers that generate and sustain them. Liminality may be partly described as a stage of reflection. In it those ideas, sentiments, and facts that had been hitherto for the neophytes bound up in configurations and accepted unthinkingly are, as it were, resolved into their constituents. These constituents are isolated and made into objects of reflection for the neophytes by such processes as componental exaggeration and dissociation by varying concomitants.

This reaffirmation of social values in a liminal context through paradox is apparent in the Robin Hood tradition, though, of course, what we are dealing with here is a liminal context communicated by a narrative tradition and not a unit of liminal space or time marked out by ritual. The Robin Hood ballads present a liminal world where basic social values are juxtaposed or even mixed with their seeming opposites: truth with deceit, honesty with thievery, gentility with outlawry. Thereby these values are highlighted and endowed with new richness and complexity. In such a context of paradox fundamental aspects of

society can stand out more clearly than they do in everyday social life.

The Robin Hood narrative tradition originated in medieval English society; but the values which these narratives communicated were relevant in the post-medieval world as well, and the liminal context in which they were expressed continued to exert a fascination. Thus, though some of this liminality (e.g. Robin as existing between the yeomanry and the gentry) became outmoded with the changes that society underwent, the Robin Hood narratives remained popular down to the eighteenth century. They continued to function as a myth, featuring a liminal world that mirrors and interacts with the social world and characters whose adventures are an indirect expression of the values of the world from which they are seemingly so alienated. (pp. 198-207)

> *Joseph Falaky Nagy, "The Paradoxes of Robin Hood," in* Folklore, *Vol. 91, No. 2, 1980, pp. 198-210.*

FURTHER READING

"Robin Hood." *The Atlantic Monthly* I, No. II (December 1857): 156-66.
    Presents many of the theories of Robin Hood's origins.

Behlmer, Rudy, ed. *The Adventures of Robin Hood.* Madison: The University of Wisconsin Press, 1979, 235 p.
    Contains the screenplay and production credits, as well as illustrations of the 1938 film version of the Robin Hood legend. In his introduction, Behlmer chronicles the making of the film.

Bellamy, John. *Robin Hood: An Historical Enquiry.* Bloomington: Indiana University Press, 1985, 150 p.
    Concise introduction to the progress of scholarship pertaining to the Robin Hood legend.

Bessinger, J. B., Jr. "Robin Hood: Folklore and Historiography, 1377-1500." *Tennessee Studies in Literature* 11 (1966): 61-9.
    Observes the ways in which the fifteenth-century Scottish historians Andrew of Wyntoun, Walter Bower, and John Major influenced the development of the Robin Hood legend.

——. "*The Gest of Robin Hood* Revisited." In *The Learned and the Lewed: Studies in Chaucer and Medieval Literature,* edited by Larry D. Benson, pp. 355-69. Cambridge: Harvard University Press, 1974.
    Assesses the literary merit of *The Gest of Robin Hood* and speculates about its genre.

Child, Francis James, ed. *The English and Scottish Popular Ballads.* 5 vols. New York: Cooper Square Publishers, 1965.
    Seminal edition of the ballads, including several versions of the Robin Hood legend, originally published in 1893-98.

Crook, David. "Some Further Evidence Concerning the Dating of the Origins of the Legend of Robin Hood." *The English Historical Review* XCIX, No. 392 (July 1984): 530-34.

> Supplements J. C. Holt's discovery of a thirteenth-century Robin Hood from a writ dated 1262 naming a William "Robehod."

————. "The Sheriff of Nottingham and Robin Hood: The Genesis of the Legend?" In *Thirteenth Century England,* Vol. II, edited by P. R. Coss and S. D. Lloyd, pp. 59-68. Suffolk, England: The Boydell Press, 1988.

> Suggests that the identity of the Sheriff of Nottingham can be traced back to Eustace of Lowdham, a thirteenth-century sheriff.

Cross, P. R. "Aspects of Cultural Diffusion in Medieval England: The Early Romances, Local Society and Robin Hood." *Past and Present* 108 (August 1985): 35-79.

> Discusses the Middle English romances of the first half of the fourteenth century, focusing on the transmission of the Robin Hood ballads.

Gensler, Howard. "The Sharpshooter of Sherwood Has Stayed on Target with Audiences throughout the Ages." *TV Guide* 39, No. 19 (11-17 May 1991): 24-6.

> Focuses on the differences between the made-for-television movie *Robin Hood* (1991), directed by John Irvin, and the Kevin Costner film of the same year.

Goodman, Mark. "A Hood for the Ages." *People Weekly* 35, No. 26 (8 July 1991): 47-8.

> Brief summary of the search for the original Robin Hood on the occasion of the 1991 film. Goodman remarks, "A dozen times or so in our day, Hollywood has dusted off the enduring story (with the ironic result that the outlaw prince of Sherwood has filled to overflow the coffers of the already rich)."

Graves, Robert. "The Triple Muse." In his *The White Goddess: A Historical Grammar of Poetic Myth,* pp. 383-408. London: Faber and Faber, 1952.

> Includes an interpretation of the symbolic meaning of Maid Marian.

Harris, P. Valentine. *The Truth about Robin Hood: A Refutation of the Mythologists' Theories, with New Evidence of the Hero's Actual Existence.* London: Privately printed, 1951, 93 p.

> Relies on the findings of Joseph Ritson and Joseph Hunter to defend the theory of Robin Hood's historical existence.

Hilton, R. H., ed. *Peasants, Knights and Heretics: Studies in Medieval English Social History.* Cambridge: Cambridge University Press, 1976, 330 p.

> Contains material published in the periodical *Past and Present* between 1958 and 1973, including essays on Robin Hood by Hilton, J. C. Holt, and Maurice Keen.

Hobsbawm, E. J. "The Noble Robber." In his *Bandits,* pp. 41-57. Middlesex: Penguin, 1985.

> Defines the qualities of "the noble robber"—an historical type exemplified by Robin Hood—and provides several other examples from different periods.

Kirtley, Bacil F. "Theories and Fantasies Concerning Robin Hood." *Southern Folklore Quarterly* XIX, No. 2 (June 1956): 108-15.

> Disparages much of the Robin Hood scholarship of the nineteenth and twentieth centuries for attempting to explain the origins of popular legends with untenable theories.

Lee, Sidney. "Robin Hood." In *Dictionary of National Biography,* Vol. IX, edited by Leslie Stephen and Sidney Lee, pp. 1152-55. New York: Macmillan, 1908.

> Asserts that Robin Hood's origins can be traced to an English "mythical forest-elf" and summarizes the debate over his historical existence. The *Dictionary* was originally published between 1885 and 1900.

Maddicott, J. R. "The Birth and Setting of the Ballads of Robin Hood." *The English Historical Review* XCIII, No. 367 (April 1978): 276-99.

> Discusses *The Gest of Robin Hood,* maintaining that the "*Gest*'s vocabulary and frame of reference place its origins in a period well before the early sixteenth century, when it first emerges, while the antique middle English literary forms which it preserves indicate that the whole poem had been put together by 1400 at the latest."

Nelson, Malcolm A. *The Robin Hood Tradition in the English Renaissance.* Salzburg Studies in English Literature: Elizabethan Studies, edited by James Hogg, Vol. 14. Salzburg, Austria: Institut für Englische Sprache und Literatur, 1973, 269 p.

> Studies representations of Robin Hood in the literature of the English Renaissance as a means of understanding the society out of which they emerged.

Raglan, Lord. "Robin Hood," In his *The Hero: A Study in Tradition, Myth, and Drama,* pp. 45-53. Westport, Conn.: Greenwood Press, 1956.

> Maintains that Robin Hood was originally a hero in fifteenth-century ritual dramas.

Ritson, Joseph. *Robin Hood: A Collection of All the Ancient Poems, Songs, and Ballads, Now Extant, Relative to that Celebrated English Outlaw.* London: John C. Nimmo, 1885, 400 p.

> Important scholarly work that provides background material on the Robin Hood legend.

Simeone, W. E. "The May Games and the Robin Hood Legend." *Journal of American Folklore* 64, No. 253 (July 1951): 265-74.

> Questions the conclusion of Lord Raglan (see above) that the Robin Hood legend originated with the medieval May rituals.

————. "Still More about Robin Hood." *Journal of American Folklore* 65, No. 258 (October 1952): 418-20.

> Defends his position that Robin Hood's origins lie in the popular ballad.

————. "The Historic Robin Hood." *Journal of American Folklore* 66, No. 262 (October 1953): 303-08.

> Presents several sides of the dispute over the origins of the Robin Hood legend, maintaining that he is a fictional creation of the balladeers.

————. "Robin Hood and Some Other Outlaws." *Journal of American Folklore* 71, No. 279 (January 1958): 27-33.

> Comparison of the Robin Hood legend to those of Hereward the Saxon, Fulk Fitz Warine, and Wistasse le Moine.

————. "Renaissance Robin Hood Plays." In *Folklore in Action: Essays for Discussion in Honor of MacEdward Leach,* edited by Horace P. Beck, pp. 184-99. Philadelphia: The American Folklore Society, 1962.

Examines the dichotomy between the "historical Robin Hood" and the "pastoral Robin Hood."

Spence, Lewis. "The Supernatural Character of Robin Hood." *The Hibbert Journal* XL (April 1942): 280-85.

Casts the Robin Hood legends as "a reminiscence of an early departmental deity or godling associated with afforested places . . . [whose] festival would be celebrated at the season of vernal growth."

Steadman, J. M., Jr. "The Dramatization of the Robin Hood Ballads." *Modern Philology* 17, No. 1 (May 1919): 9-23.

Explores the influence of the Robin Hood ballads upon the Robin Hood plays of the fifteenth century.

Wawn, Andrew. "Robin Hood and the Elizabethans: A Propagandist Note." *Cahiers Elisabéthains,* No. 22 (October 1982): 87-91.

Brief inquiry into a late sixteenth-century Robin Hood fragment which portrays Robin as pro-clerical.

Williams, Jay. "More about Robin Hood." *Journal of American Folklore* 65, No. 257 (July 1952): 304-05.

Affirms the medieval May Games as the origin of the Robin Hood legend.

Mary Sidney

1561-1621

(Full name Mary Sidney Herbert, Countess of Pembroke)
English poet and translator.

A prominent figure in sixteenth-century literary circles, Sidney is best known for her verse translations of the biblical psalms, a project begun in conjunction with her brother Sir Philip Sidney and completed by her after his death. Although psalm translations were common during the Renaissance, the Sidneian psalms are considered poetically superior to other versions, incorporating energetic rhythms and diverse stanzaic forms skillfully chosen to mirror the content of each psalm. Critics have also praised Sidney's psalm translations for their emotional power and personal tone, and they are widely viewed as a major contribution to Elizabethan poetry.

Sidney was born in 1561 at Tickenhall, Worcestershire, to a renowned and powerful family; the marriage of her parents, Mary Dudley and Henry Sidney, had united two prominent families in what was known as the Dudley/Sidney alliance, an integral force in Protestant politics. Her maternal grandfather, John Dudley, Duke of Northumberland, was executed in 1553 for his part in the attempt to put the Protestant Lady Jane Grey on the throne in place of the Catholic Mary Tudor. As Lord President Council of the Marches of Wales and Lord Governor of Ireland, Sidney's father administered one-quarter of all land under Queen Elizabeth, the Protestant successor to Mary; Sidney's mother was lady-in-waiting to the queen. Sidney was educated privately at home, studying literature, religion, and science, as well as learning several languages. She went to court at thirteen and in 1577 married Henry Herbert, second Earl of Pembroke, who had also been involved in the Lady Jane Grey affair and was thirty years Sidney's senior. Their marriage was a pre-arranged political alliance, but despite this and the age difference, Sidney gave no indication of unhappiness with the match. After her marriage, her home at Wilton House, Pembroke's ancestral estate, became the most important literary center outside Elizabeth's court. With her brother Philip, one of the most renowned and respected writers of the time, Sidney cultivated and patronized what became known as the Sidney Circle, a group of literary figures praised for their theological learning as well as their artistic talents. Sidney was described by John Aubrey as "the greatest Patroness of witt and learning of any Lady of her time," and Wilton House was the gathering place of such noted writers as Samuel Daniel, Nicholas Breton, Fulke Greville, Edmund Spenser, and Michael Drayton.

Philip's death in 1586 was the impetus for Sidney to begin writing on her own. Sidney's first literary projects were translations of Philippe de Mornay's essay *Discours de la vie et de la mort* (1576), Robert Garnier's play *Marc-Antoine* (1579), and Petrarch's poem *Trionfo della Morte* (1353?). In addition to editing Philip's works *The Count-*

ess of Pembrokes Arcadia (1593) and *Astrophel and Stella* (1598), Sidney wrote "The Dolefull Lay of Clorinda," which was published in *Colin Clouts Come Home Againe* (1595), a collection of elegies for Philip edited by Edmund Spenser, and a pastoral poem for Elizabeth entitled "A Dialogue Between Two Shepheards, Thenot and Piers, in Praise of Astraea." However, she devoted most of her energies to the verse translations of the psalms. Sidney revised forty-three poems Philip had left unfinished and translated the remaining psalms in addition to writing two accompanying dedicatory poems, "To the Angell Spirit of Sir Philip Sidney" and "Even Now that Care which on thy Crown attends," the latter addressed to Elizabeth. Sidney also used her influence to continue the patronage of those writers who had been Philip's friends and colleagues. After her husband's death in 1601, Sidney was less active in public life, and her sons, William and Philip, continued the tradition of patronage she had established at Wilton House. She died of smallpox in 1621.

In "To the Angell Spirit," Sidney credited Philip as her sole inspiration and motivation to write: "To thee pure spirit, to thee alone addres't / this coupled worke, by double int'rest thine: / First rais'de by thy blest hand, and what is mine / inspir'd by thee, thy secrett power imprest." However, critics agree that her work was also influenced to a considerable extent by her interest in Protestant politics. In "To the Angell Spirit," for example, Sidney praised her brother not only for his nobility of character, but also for his dedication to the cause of Protestantism. In "Even Now that Care," a conventional adulatory poem for Elizabeth, Sidney combines praise for the queen with a strong political message, equating Elizabeth with the biblical King David and implying that it is her duty to protect and further the cause of Protestant Christianity, which Sidney viewed as the one true faith. The most direct and skillful expression of Sidney's Protestant sentiment is found in her translation of the psalms. Although she consulted numerous French, Latin, and English versions of the psalms, her work is based primarily on a Protestant French psalter of 1562 by Clément Marot and Théodore de Bèze and relies heavily on the commentary of John Calvin.

However, critics note that Sidney's poetic skills enabled her to transcend mere polemics in her psalms. Using conversational syntax and powerful images drawn from her own experiences, Sidney created a personal tone in her psalms which subtly reinforces her concept of religion as a deeply felt connection with God. Beth Wynne Fisken described her technique as "a mixture of translation and interpretation which allowed for additions based on personal reflection and experience," and G. F. Waller assessed her distinctive approach to the text as "communicated experience, not as encapsulated doctrine." Critics often explain the emotional urgency of Sidney's psalms in the context of Renaissance restrictions on women's writing; although translation of religious material was permitted, women were not expected to articulate any personal commentary. The exclusion of women from other forms of discourse forced Sidney to express herself through the voice of the psalmist, and the distinctive style and poetic force of her psalms originate in this sense of personal commitment. While Philip's psalms focus on the subject matter from a position of detached examination, his sister's convey an intense involvement with the psalmist and an intimate expression of piety. Critics have also noted that Sidney's translations represent a major stylistic advancement over earlier versions, stressing in particular her use of numerous stanzaic forms and metrical patterns to match her structure to the content of her sources. Such an attempt to unify form and content had never before been undertaken by psalm versifiers. She used 164 stanzaic forms and 94 metrical patterns; for example, she expressed a psalm's lyric mode in a sonnet, but employed a narrative form for psalms that contain stories. On the title page to the collection, Sidney expressed her intention to achieve poetic variety, describing the work as "divers and sundry kindes of verse, more rare and excellent, for the method and varietie then ever yet hath bene don in English."

Though intended for private devotion, the psalms were distributed beyond the Sidney Circle, and contemporary poets referred to them frequently. John Donne's poem, "Upon the translation of the Psalms by Sir Philip Sidney, and the Countess of Pembroke his sister," in which he claims "They tell us why, and teach us how to sing," expresses the admiration and respect the Sidneian psalms generated among her peers. However, during her life, the psalm translations were thought to be primarily the work of her brother and her own contribution was largely overlooked. Most praise directed to Sidney emphasized her role as patroness: Edmund Spenser addressed her as "most Honourable and bountifull Ladie . . . to whome I acknowledge my selfe bounden, by manie singular fauours and great graces," and Samuel Daniel praised her as "the happie and iudiciall Patronesse of the Muses (a glory hereditary to your house)." Critics speculate that perhaps Sidney's humility prevented her contemporaries from identifying her more closely with the psalms; her signature, "Sister of that Incomparable Sidney," emphasizes her relation and debt to Philip rather than pride in her own achievements. An 1823 edition of the psalms spawned only a brief revival of interest in her work, and though A. B. Grosart acknowledged in his 1873 edition of Philip's poems that Sidney's work was "infinitely in advance of her brother's in thought, epithet and melody," hers were not published until 1963 in a collection edited by J. C. A. Rathmell. Since that time, critics have acknowledged Sidney's importance as a bridge between traditional psalm translators and religious lyric poets; some even suggest that seventeenth-century poets used her psalms as a model for their own work. More recently, her work has generated interest among feminist scholars who see her, in the words of Elaine V. Beilin, as a "turning point in the development of the woman writer," surpassing the achievement of her predecessors. Examining her work in the context of Renaissance conventions that generally silenced women, these critics have praised her personal and poetic self-assertion.

Long overshadowed by her brother's reputation, Sidney is now recognized for her contribution to the development of religious poetry, and she is currently recognized as one of the first important English women poets. Her psalms are considered the most significant precursor to the prodigious production of religious verse in the seventeenth century, as well as the finest example of that genre from the Elizabethan era.

PRINCIPAL WORKS

Antonius: A Tragoedie [translator] (drama) 1592
A Discourse of Life and Death [translator] (essay) 1592
The Countess of Pembrokes Arcadia [editor] (poetry) 1593
"The Dolefull Lay of Clorinda" (poem) 1595; published in *Colin Clouts Come Home Againe,* edited by Edmund Spenser
Astrophel and Stella [editor] (poetry) 1598
"A Dialogue Between Two Shepheards, Thenot and Piers, in Praise of Astraea" (poem) 1602; published in *A Poetical Rhapsody,* edited by Francis Davison
The Triumphe of Death [translator] (poetry) 1912; published in journal *PMLA*

†*The Psalms of Sir Philip Sidney and the Countess of Pembroke* (poetry) 1963
The Triumph of Death and Other Unpublished and Uncollected Poems by Mary Sidney, Countess of Pembroke (1561-1621) (poetry) 1977

*This work was completed in 1593.

†The *Psalms* were written before 1600 and were first published in a limited edition in 1823.

John Donne   (essay date 1633)

[*Donne is renowned by scholars as the greatest Anglican divine, as well as one of the most accomplished if controversial poets of the seventeenth century. He was at the head of the metaphysical school of poetry, which is characterized by complex, witty conceits, sudden paradoxes and contemplations melding the natural world with the divine. In the following poem, he praises the Sidneian psalms.*]

Eternal God, (for whom who ever dare
Seek new expressions, do the circle square,
And thrust into strait corners of poor wit
Thee, who art cornerless and infinite)
I would but bless thy name, not name thee now;
(And thy gifts are as infinite as thou:)
Fix we our praises therefore on this one,
That, as thy blessed spirit fell upon
These Psalms' first author in a cloven tongue;
(For 'twas a double power by which he sung
The highest matter in the noblest form;)
So thou hast cleft that spirit, to perform
That work again, and shed it, here, upon
Two, by their bloods, and by thy spirit one;
A brother and a sister, made by thee
The organ, where thou art the harmony.
Two that make one John Baptist's holy voice,
And who that psalm, *Now let the Isles rejoice,*
Have both translated, and applied it too,
Both told us what, and taught us how to do.
They show us Islanders our joy, our King,
They tell us why, and teach us how to sing;
Make all this all, three choirs, heaven, earth, and
     spheres;
The first, heaven, hath a song, but no man hears,
The spheres have music, but they have no
     tongue,
Their harmony is rather danced than sung;
But our third choir, to which the first gives ear,
(For, angels learn by what the church does here)
This choir hath all. The organist is he
Who hath tuned God and man, the organ we:
The songs are these, which heaven's high holy
     Muse
Whispered to David, David to the Jews:
And David's successors, in holy zeal,
In forms of joy and art do re-reveal
To us so sweetly and sincerely too,
That I must not rejoice as I would do
When I behold that these Psalms are become
So well attired abroad, so ill at home,
So well in chambers, in thy church so ill,

As I can scarce call that reformed until
This be reformed; would a whole state present
A lesser gift than some one man hath sent?
And shall our church, unto our spouse and king,
More hoarse, more harsh than any other, sing?
For that we pray, we praise thy name for this,
Which, by this Moses and this Miriam, is
Already done; and as those Psalms we call
(Though some have other authors) David's all:
So though some have, some may some psalms
     translate,
We thy Sidneian Psalms shall celebrate,
And, till we come th' extemporal song to sing,
(Learned the first hour, that we see the King,
Who hath translated these translators) may
These their sweet learned labours, all the way
Be as our tuning, that, when hence we part
We may fall in with them, and sing our part.
                                        (pp. 332-34)

John Donne, "Upon the Translation of the Psalms," in his John Donne: The Complete English Poems, *edited by A. J. Smith, Penguin Books, 1971, pp. 332-34.*

The Gentleman's Magazine   (essay date 1845)

[*In the following excerpt, the critic surveys Sidney's accomplishments.*]

As it is the care of a faithful servant to wipe away the dust which time has heaped on the tombs and escutcheons of the illustrious dead, so it is the duty of those who devote themselves to the service of literature to preserve a just remembrance of the departed by recording their lives as either eminently good, great, or deserving well of letters. Alas! how often has this sacred duty been neglected. How many names of the good do we find now adorning the page of history, and now disappearing to be mentioned no more, as though, forsooth, death, the common lot, were a crime, and its punishment oblivion! They appear on the stage of life, they perform their parts with the approbation of all; they depart, and none are found to chronicle their praises—none of those who before were loading them with high-sounding compliments and fulsome adulation.

This complaint can with justice be uttered by him who searches for memorials of Mary Sidney, Countess of Pembroke, mentioned in the history of her day as a bright ensample of all that is good, beauteous, and learned; and celebrated by Spenser [in *Colin Clout's Come Home Again*] as

Urania, sister unto Astrophel,
In whose brave mind, as in a golden coffer,
All heavenly gifts and riches locked are,
More rich than pearls of Ind or gold of Ophir,
And in her sex more wonderful and rare.

Few circumstances connected with her are now retained; no history of her life exists, and she may be said, like the luminary of the night, to shine in the eyes of the many by a lustre derived from her brother, to be remembered but as the beloved sister of Sir Philip Sidney, and to live in our memory by her beauteous epitaph recorded in the pages of Addison. But at the same time it is just to bear in mind that her own merits were great, and that for her own sake her memory deserves to be cherished; that she was the presiding spirit of "the Arcadia" of Sidney, the patroness of Daniel, the lyric poet, the sweet translator of the Psalms, and the mother of William Earl of Pembroke, celebrated by Clarendon for his many virtues. (p. 129)

In [1580] her brother, Sir Philip Sidney, being insulted by Vere Earl of Oxford, who had called him "puppy," and being deprived by the Queen of the power of obtaining satisfaction from his adversary, was unwilling to endure this slight upon his honour in the eyes of the court, and retired to Wilton, where his sister was then residing. Here, reposing from the splendid fatigues of pomp and pageantry, tranquilized by the placid enjoyments of a rural life, and listening to the suggestions of his talented sister, he began the composition of his *Arcadia*. Tradition tells us that a great portion of this pastoral romance was written in the neighbouring woods; and, if this be true, it would appear from the dedication to her that the Countess was the companion of his excursions, and assisted him with the suggestions of her lively fancy. A desire to give all the scanty information that we can respecting this illustrious lady, and the very active part which she took in bringing this work before the public, will plead as an excuse for the insertion of the dedication of "The Countess of Pembroke's Arcadia."

> To my dear lady and sister the Countess of Pembroke.
>
> Here now have you (most dear, and most worthy to be most dear, lady) this idle work of mine, which I fear, like the spider's web, will be thought fitter to be swept away than worn to any other purpose. For my part, in very truth, (as the cruel fathers among the Greeks were wont to do to the babes they would not foster,) I could not find in my heart to cast out in some desert of forgetfulness this child which I am loth to father. *But you desired me to do it;* and your desire to my heart is an absolute commandment. Now it is done only for you, only to you; if you keep it to yourself, or to such friends who will weigh errors in the balance of good will, I hope for the father's sake it will be pardoned, perchance made much of, though in itself it have deformities. For indeed, for severer eyes it is not, being but a trifle; and that triflingly handled. Your dear self can best witness the manner, being done in loose sheets of paper, most of it in your presence, the rest by sheets sent unto you as fast as they were done. In sum, a young head, not so well staid as I would it were (and shall be, when God will), having many, many conceits begotten in it, if it had not been in some way delivered, would have grown a monster, and more sorry might I be that they came in than that they got out. But his chief safety shall be the not walking abroad, and his chief protection the bearing the livery of your name, which, if much good-will do not deceive me, is worthy to be a sanctuary for a greater offender. This say I, because I know the virtue so, and this say I because it may be ever so, or, to say better, because it *will* be ever so. Read it then at your idle times, and the follies your good judgment will find in it, blame not,

but laugh at. And so, looking for no better stuff than, as in a haberdasher's shop, glasses or feathers, you will continue to love the writer, who doth exceedingly love you, and most heartily prays you may long live to be a principal ornament to the family of the Sidneys.

> Your loving brother,
> PHILIP SIDNEY.

It was perhaps at this period that Sir Philip and his sister commenced that translation of the Psalms which is generally considered a joint production of these noble relatives. The latter part was most probably translated by her after the death of her brother, at intervals of retirement, when, now alone, with a melancholy pleasure, she completed a work once entered upon in conjunction with a beloved relative tied by similarity of sentiment and mutual affection. (p. 133)

Of the *Arcadia,* to which, if not a joint production of herself and her brother, she can lay some claim as having given it finishing touches, and relieved it of many blemishes, we are justified in pronouncing that it promises to bestow on its author an immortality in the literary annals of this country. That it is by no means so universally perused at this period as it was two centuries since, is attributable rather to a change in the public taste than to any defect in the work itself. In so extensive a volume it is surprising how the interest is maintained throughout, and with how much discrimination the various features of character are developed. Without degenerating into pedantry or affectation, the morals inculcated are of the highest tone, and the sentiments are of the most refined nature. The beauty of the descriptions affords ample testimony of the vigour and fertility of the poet's imagination. It would be presumptuous, knowing as we do that Sir Philip Sidney was an elegant poet, to say that many of the beauties of the *Arcadia* are owing to the assistance which he received from the Countess of Pembroke; but some of them doubtless, in her revision of it, were matured by the conceptions of her wellstored fancy. This work, however, has not escaped the frigid censure of Horace Walpole. In his *Royal and Noble Authors* he styles it "a tedious, lamentable, pedantic romance." But his dispraise sinks into insignificance when compared with the commendations of such men as Sir William Temple, Heylin the cosmographer, and the poet Cowper, who highly applauds its beauty and morality.

The virtuous Lord Plessis de Mornay was an intimate and dear friend of Sir Philip Sidney, who translated that nobleman's defence of christianity, entitled *The true Use of the Christian Religion.* This translation was published in the year 1587, about seven months after the death of Sir Philip. True to the congeniality of taste which had always existed between her and her brother, the Countess had imbibed a love for the works of his illustrious friend, and at Wilton, May 13, 1590, she finished a translation of his work styled, *A Discourse of Life and Death,* which was printed in 1592, and again in 1600, with the following title: *A Discourse written in French by Philip de Mornay, done into English by the Countess of Pembroke, printed for W. Ponsonby.* The witty Gabriel Harvey, in his *Letter of Notable Contents,* 1593, says, speaking of this translation, that it is "a restorative electuary of gems, the author of which

I do not expressly name, not because I do not honour her
with my heart, but because I would not dishonour her
with my pen, who I admire, and cannot blazon enough."
Park, in his edition of Lord Orford's *Royal and Noble Authors,* considers this translation to have been a joint production of Lady Pembroke and Sir Philip Sidney. It may,
indeed, have been suggested to her by him, but it is not
probable that she would have usurped the merit of being
the sole translator, if she could possibly, in truth, have reminded the world of their mutual affection by proclaiming
it as the result of their common labours. A melodious softness and a graceful simplicity characterize her style, and
afford additional grounds for a belief that she had a greater
share in the composition of the *Arcadia* than has been generally imagined. Lodge, who in his *Portraits* is severe upon
her merits as a writer, acknowledges that her prose composition has great merit, and that it is far better than her
verse; "it is more ornamented," he says, "yet more graceful; more metaphorical, yet more simple and intelligible."
(pp. 258-59)

In November, 1590, at Ramsbury, in Wiltshire, [Mary
Sidney] completed a translation from the French of a tragedy called *Antony,* by Robert Garnier. It was printed in
12mo. in 1592, and in 4to. and 12mo. in 1595, with the following title: *Antonie, done into English by the Countess of
Pembroke, Ramsbury, 26th November, 1590. Imprinted at
London for W. Ponsonby, 1595.* In this translation are to
be found interwoven some verses of her own composition.
It is remarkable as being one of our earliest specimens of
blank verse: Sir E. Brydges, in his "Restituta," says, that
"it shews much facility and skill in versification." The dialogue is maintained in rhyming couplets and blank verse,
and the choruses present a great variety of metres, some
very rarely to be met with. The opening affords a fair sample of her merits as a writer of blank verse; it is a soliloquy
spoken by Antony.

> Since cruel heaven's against me obstinate;
> Since all mishaps of this round engine do
> Conspire my harm; since men, since powers di-
>   vine,
> Air, earth, and sea, are all injurious;
> And that my queen herself, in whom I liv'd,
> The idol of my heart, doth me pursue;
> It's meet I die. For her have I foregone
> My country, Cæsar unto war provok'd,
> (For just revenge of sister's wrong, my wife,
> Who mov'd my queen, aye me! to jealousy);
> For love of her, in her allurements caught,
> Abandon'd life, I honour have despis'd,
> Disdain'd my friends, and of the stately Rome
> Despoil'd the empire of her best attire;
> Contemn'd that power that made me so much
>   fear'd,
> A slave become unto her feeble face!
> O cruel traitress, woman most unkind!
> Thou dost, forsworn, my love and life betray,
> And giv'st me up to rageful enemy,
> Which soon (oh fool!) will plague thy perjury.

The following extract from a chorus is more remarkable
for the singularity of the measure than its intrinsic beauty.

> Nature made us not free,
> When first she made us live;

> When we began to be,
> To be began our woe,
> Which growing evermore,
> As dying life doth grow,
> Do more and more us grieve,
> And tire us more and more.

The chorus from which the following lines are taken is eminently beautiful, exhibiting simplicity, ease, and melody.

> Lament we our mishaps,
> Drown we with tears our woe,
> For lamentable haps
> Lamented easy grow.
> And much less torment bring
> Than when they first did spring.

> We want that mournful sound
> That prattling Progne makes,
> On fields of Thracian ground,
> On streams of Thracian lakes.
> To empt her breast of pain,
> For Itys by her slain.
> We want that woful song
> Wherewith wood-music's queen
> Doth ease her woes among
> Fresh spring-time's bushes green,
> On pleasant branch alone,
> Renewing ancient moan.

It was in compliment to Lady Pembroke on her translation of this play that Daniel wrote his "Cleopatra." In his
dedication to her he says,

> Lo! here the labours which she did impose
> Whose influence did predominate my muse,
> The star of wonder my desire first chose,
> To guide their travels in the course I use.
>   • • • • •
> I (who contented with an humble song)
> Made music to myself that pleas'd me best,
> And only told of Delia and her wrong,
> And prais'd her eyes, and plain'd mine own un-
>   rest,
> A text from which my muse had not digrest.
> Madam, had not thy well-grac'd Antony
> (Who all alone having remained long)
> Requir'd his Cleopatra's company.

In the "Astrophel" of Spenser, which contains a number
of elegies on the death of Sir Philip Sidney, we find one
written by his sister. It consists of sixteen stanzas, com-
mencing thus:

> Ay me! to whom shall I my case complain,
> That may compassion my impatient grief?
> Or where shall I unfold my inward pain,
> That my enriven heart may find relief?
> Shall I unto the heavenly powers it show,
> Or unto earthly men that dwell below?

Her lamentation concludes in the following strain:

> But live thou there still happy, happy spirit,
> And give us leave thee thus to lament;
> Not thee that dost thy heaven's joy inherit,
> But our own selves that here in dole are drent,
> Thus do we weep and wail, and wear our eyes,
> Mourning in others our own miseries.

It must be confessed that these lines, resembling the humble effusions of Sternhold and Hopkins, cannot bear the test of criticism. We must in justice coincide with the censure of Lodge, that the elegy is unworthy of the subject. But we must bear in mind that it was the desire of the writer herein to pour out "her own heart's sorrowing," rather than to attend to the niceties which a critical taste would demand; if it is not the language of a poetical imagination, it is that of an aching heart; and, as her sole wish here was to "unfold her inward pain," and to pay the tribute of affection, we may in this instance be content to allow the end to atone for the inefficiency of the means.

The pastoral dialogue in praise of Queen Elizabeth, under the name of "Astræa," in Davison's "Poetical Rhapsody," 1602 and 1611, is below mediocrity. Its singularity will be an excuse for inserting a portion of it. The speakers are two shepherds, Thenot and Piers.

> T.—I sing divine Astræa's praise,
> O muses, help my wits to raise,
> And heave my verses higher.
> P.—Thou need'st the truth but plainly tell,
> Which much I doubt thou canst not well,
> Thou art so great a liar.
>
> T.—If in my song no more I shew,
> Than heaven, and earth, and sea do know,
> Then truly I have spoken.
> P.—Sufficeth not no more to name,
> But being no less, the like, the same,
> Else laws of truth be broken.
>
> T.—Then say she is so good and fair,
> With all the world she may compare,
> Nor Momus self denying.
> P.—Compare may think where likeness holds,
> Nought like to her the earth enfolds;
> I look'd to find you lying.
>
> T.—Soon as Astræa shews her face,
> Strait every ill avoids the place,
> And every good aboundeth.
> P.—Nay, long before her face doth shew,
> The last doth come, the first do go:
> How loud this lie resoundeth.

Were it not for the serious disposition of the Countess, we might almost imagine that the spirit of irony, or "Momus" himself, the god of nonsense, had prompted the composition of these lines. If they were really intended for the praise of the queen, we can only account for their fulsomeness and coarseness by supposing that the genius of poetry refused to inspire the writer when engaged in the task of adulation, one which she should have left to those unfortunate bards who are fated to subsist on patronage. She erred in common with the subjects of Elizabeth, who seem to have wished to persuade her that she was something more than human.

With regard to the Sidney translation of the Psalms, Antony Wood and Sir R. Steele (*Guardian,* No. 18) ascribe it solely to Sir Philip Sidney; Sir John Harington (*Nugæ Antiquæ,* vol. iii.) and Dr. Thomas (*History of the Bishops of Exeter*) say that it was the joint composition of Lady Pembroke and her chaplain, Dr. Gervase Babington, successively Bishop of Worcester and Exeter. Sir John Harington's reason for thinking thus is by no means satisfacto-

ry, as he seems to take it for granted that she could not have translated from the Hebrew without the aid of the divine. Speaking of Babington, he says, "He was sometime chaplain to the late Earl of Pembroke, whose noble Countess used this her chaplain's advice, *I suppose,* for the translation of the Psalms, (of which I have seen some,) for it was more than a woman's skill to express the sense so right as she hath done in her verse, and more than the English or Latin translation could give her." Æmilia Lanyer, addressing her in her "Salve Deus," 1611, says that she was unaided: Daniel seems to imply the same; in the dedication of his "Cleopatra," speaking of this translation, he says,

> By this, great lady, thou must then be known,
> When Wilton lies low levell'd with the ground,
> And this is that which thou may'st call thine
>   own,
> Which sacrilegious time cannot confound.
> Here thou surviv'st thyself; here thou art found,
> Of late succeeding ages, fresh in fame,
> Where in eternal brass remains thy name.

Dr. Donne is, however, correct in considering it as a joint production of Sir Philip and his sister. He styles it, in his eulogy on the work, "The Translation of the Psalms, by Sir Philip Sidney and the Countess of Pembroke his sister"

> —as thy blest spirit fell upon
> These Psalms' first author in a cloven tongue.
>   • • • • •
> So thou hast cleft that spirit to perform
> That work again, and shed it here upon
> Two by their blood and by thy spirit one,
> A brother and a sister made by thee
> The organ where thou art the harmony.

Other circumstances would seem to point her out as having had a great share in this translation. The original manuscript was given to the library at Wilton by the Countess, in the hand-writing of Sir Philip Sidney and herself, bound in crimson velvet. There exists a copy of it in folio, written by James Davies, writing-master to Prince Henry, for whose use, perhaps, it was prepared. His brother, Davies of Hereford, addressed her in his "Wit's Pilgrimage," accompanied with a translation of Eight Psalms, probably knowing her taste to be directed that way. In Simon Pass's portrait of her she is represented with a book of Psalms in her hand; perhaps it was intended as a frontispiece to a contemplated publication of her translation. In Dr. Woodford's MS. copy in the Bodleian Library, he has written at the end of Psalm xliii. "In the margin (that is, of the original MS.) hitherto, Sir Philip Sidney," implying that Sir Philip had translated up to that Psalm, and that the remaining portion was translated by his sister. Sir Richard Hoare, in his History of Wiltshire, erroneously assigns the translation to Anne, second wife of Philip, Earl of Pembroke and Montgomery. This translation appears to have been greatly multiplied by manuscripts, and much used by private families at that period. Donne, complaining of the inefficient version of Sternhold and Hopkins, says,

> —I must not rejoice, as I would do,
> When I behold that these Psalms are become
> So well attir'd abroad, so ill at home;

So well in chambers, in thy Church so ill,
As I can scarce call that reform'd until
This be reform'd.

It remained unpublished until 1823 (when 250 copies were printed by Whittingham for Robert Triphook), with the exception of a few to be found in the *Nugæ Antiquæ* of Harington, and the 137th, somewhat altered, in the 18th Number of the *Guardian*. Some specimens will show the merits of this translation to be of a high character.

From Psalm xliv.—

Lord, our fathers' true relation
Often made hath made us know,
How thy power on each occasion
Thou of old for them didst show,
How thy hand the pagan foe
Rooting hence, thy folk implanting,
Leafless made that branch to grow,
This to spring, no verdure wanting.

Psalm lxxviii. begins—

A grave discourse to utter I intend,
The age of time I purpose to renew;
You, O, my charge! to what I teach attend,
Hear what I speak, and what you hear ensue.
The things our fathers did to us commend,
The same are they I recommend to you.

From Psalm lxxxii.—

All gladness gladdest hearts can hold,
In merriest notes that mirth can yield,
Let joyful songs to God unfold,
To Jacob's God, our sword and shield.
Muster hither music's joys,
Lute and lyre and tabret's noise,
Let no instrument be wanting,
Chasing grief and pleasure planting.

Psalm cxxxvii. commences—

Nigh seated where the river flows
That wat'reth Babel's thankful plain,
Which then our tears in pearled rows
Did help to water with their rain,
The thought of Sion bred such woes,
That, though our harps we did retain,
Yet useless and untouched there
On willows only hang'd they were.

Now, while our harps were hanged so,
The men whose captives then we lay
Did on our griefs insulting go,
And more to grieve us thus did say:
'You that of music make such show,
Come sing us now a Sion lay.'
O, no! we have nor voice nor hand
For such a song in such a land.

If anything was wanting before the publication of these Psalms to bestow on the Countess of Pembroke the merit of having a truly poetical genius, these specimens will show how well that want is now supplied. For melodious cadence, variety of metre, and faithfulness of translation, they will hardly be found to be equalled by any other English version. The first extract flows with all the ease of a well-told narrative. In the second, with what striking gravity is the admonition conveyed! What gladness of heart is portrayed in the choice of expressions and rapid measure of the next! In the last how admirably are painted the remembrance of bygone happiness and the melancholy feelings arising thence, in feelings of which nature, alas! the translator had been taught by experience keenly to participate. (pp. 364-68)

As a poetess Lady Pembroke has not had her claims to superiority justly laid before the world. Her translation of the Psalms has been but recently made public, and on that work she must chiefly rely for the proof of her poetical merits. Although much applauded by the poets and wits of her own time, and highly complimented by them upon her abilities and poetical vein, her merits are much curtailed by most of the few who at the present day have bestowed a transitory notice upon her works. Lodge, in his *Portraits,* has gone so far as to say that "as a poet she was spoiled by adulation, and complimented into conceit and carelessness;" and Drake "on Shakespeare" has styled her a writer of mediocrity. That a woman of her sense was spoiled by adulation is a matter much to be doubted, and persons are less frequently complimented into carelessness than into a desire more justly to deserve those compliments. After perusing her translation of the Psalms, we would decide on her merits rather by improving on the opinion expressed by Drake, than concurring with the severe criticism of Lodge.

Besides the poets already mentioned who have complimented her, she has been celebrated by Thomas Churchyard in his "Pleasant Conceit."

Pembroke, a pearl that orient is of kind,
A Sidney right, shall not in silence sit,
A gem more worth than all the gold of Ind,
For she enjoys the wise Minerva's wit,
And sets to school our poets everywhere,
That do presume the laurel crown to wear;
The muses nine, and all the graces three,
In Pembroke's books and verses you shall see.

These lines, replete with glowing hyperbole, were at that time but the ordinary expressions of civility and politeness, and as such, whatever effect they might now produce on an author, were not likely to compliment her into conceit and carelessness.

Stradling the poet, who was related by marriage to her brother Sir Robert Sidney, in his "Epigrammata," also compliments her. Ben Jonson in his lines to an anonymous person, the Countess of ——, but doubtless really addressed to the Countess of Pembroke, approaches her in terms of high approbation. The following lines will show how her time was employed:

For you admit no company but good,
And when you want those friends or near in
blood,
Or your allies, you make your books your
friends,
And study them unto the noblest ends,
Searching for knowledge, and to keep your mind
The same it was, inspir'd, rich, and refin'd.

On her character no lengthened comment is required. Educated by her parents in the strict observance of her religious duties, and attached to the reformed religion, she appears in her afflictions to have been distinguished by pious resignation. Attentive to her social duties, she was a tender sister and an affectionate mother: her ears were not deaf to the calls of benevolence and charity, nor were her eyes closed to the tattered garb of neglected and suffering talent. She appears in her declining years to have been of a melancholy habit of mind, and how could she be otherwise than melancholy who had survived her parents, brother, uncles, husband, and daughter? losing them all in the space of twenty years. But her refuge seems to have been in the Scriptures, and her comforts to have arisen from a firm confidence in the merits of her Saviour. The dart of Time, since her well-spent pilgrimage closed here, though hurled at death, has swept away all but a few fragments relating to her; and much is it to be regretted that, though no chronicler of her life and virtues arose immediately on her departure hence, some one has not appeared in that lengthened lapse of time who could more skilfully put together those fragments than the hand which has compiled this memorial of her life and merits. (pp. 369-70)

> *H. T. R., "Lady Mary Sidney and Her Writings," in* The Gentleman's Magazine, *Vol. XXIV, August, September, and October, 1845, pp. 129-36; 254-59; 364-70.*

J. C. A. Rathmell   (essay date 1963)

[*Rathmell is an English educator and critic. In the following excerpt, he appraises the literary significance and poetic qualities of the Sidneian psalms.*]

Shortly after the death of the Countess of Pembroke in 1621, John Donne in a long and characteristically fanciful poem paid tribute to what he called the "Sydnean Psalmes"—that is, the series of 150 verse-translations of the Psalms begun by Sir Philip Sidney and completed after his death by his sister Mary, Countess of Pembroke. These poems (for they are more than translations) were known in manuscript not only to Donne, but to Fulke Greville, Samuel Daniel, Ben Jonson, Joseph Hall, and Sir John Harington, among others, yet they remained unprinted for more than two centuries and were only finally published, in a limited edition of 250 copies, in 1823. The collection has not been reprinted in its entirety since that date, with the result that a fine example of Elizabethan psalmody, justly admired in its day, is now largely unknown. Sidney's editors (Grosart, Feuillerat, and most recently Professor William Ringler) have quite properly printed only that portion of the collection which is the work of Sidney himself—the first forty-three Psalms. Inevitably this has meant the omission of the major part of the collection— major not only in bulk, but in quality. For, as Grosart himself ventured to suggest, the Countess of Pembroke's Psalms (44-150) are "infinitely in advance of her brother's in thought, epithet and melody." Briefly, I wish to suggest that they demand to be considered not only in the context of Elizabethan psalmody, but as significant and attractive poems in their own right. Those written by the Countess, 128 in all, had been begun by 1593 and were completed before 1600. Donne, we know, was familiar with the collection, and there is an inherent likelihood that Herbert— who was related, and owed his living at Bemerton, to the

Pembroke family—also knew it. Professor Louis Martz [in *The Poetry of Meditation,* 1954] goes so far indeed as to suggest that Sidney's translation of the Psalms (his remark applies equally to his sister's share in the work) represents "the closest approximation to the poetry of Herbert's *Temple* that can be found anywhere in preceding English poetry."

The "Sydnean Psalmes" are not, in any useful sense of the term, "metaphysical"; but their strong, energetic rhythms, the expressive stanza forms, the insistent verbal play, and the preference for a packed, concise line immediately differentiate them from conventional Elizabethan psalmody. The intention of Sidney and his sister is in fact strikingly and consciously different from that of those earlier versifiers of the Psalms whose chief purpose was to "suite the Capacitie of the Vulger." The Countess plainly avows an artistic intention when on the title page to the joint work she recommends the "divers and sundry kindes of verse" as "more rare and excellent, for the method and varietie then ever yet hath bene don in English." The claim is by no means extravagant. Donne in celebrating the "Sydnean Psalmes" scarcely disguises his contempt for the metrical versions officially "allowed" in the Church ("shall our Church . . . More hoarse, more harsh than any other, sing?"). Indeed, many writers at this period complained of the poetic poverty of English psalmody when compared with what Bishop Hall described as the "diligence and exquisitenesse" of the versions sung by French and Dutch congregations. Nor did it seem any adequate excuse to Hall that the universally employed versions of Sternhold and Hopkins were written at a time when English poetry was still "rude & homely."

The congregational singing of versified psalms had of course been an integral part of the church service since the early years of Elizabeth's reign. It was a practice that had been vigorously promoted by the Marian exiles at Geneva, and as early as March 1560, one of their number, John Jewel, Bishop of Salisbury, reported on his return to England that the Genevan custom had been very rapidly adopted in London and the provinces. "As soon as they had once commenced singing in public, in only one little church in London," he wrote, "immediately not only the churches in the neighbourhood, but even the towns far distant, began to vie with each other in the same practice. You may now sometimes see at Paul's Cross after the service, six thousand persons old and young of both sexes, all singing together and praising God." At this early date the congregation presumably used what was then the largest generally available psalm-book, the Anglo-Genevan psalter of 1556, a collection of fifty-one metrical psalms by Sternhold, Hopkins, and Whittingham. By 1562 all 150 Psalms had been "versified" and *The Whole Booke of Psalmes,* although of little or no poetic merit, was soon employed in cathedrals and parish churches throughout the country—for it had the virtue, important politically in the early days of the Elizabethan settlement, of being acceptable to both Anglican and Puritan elements within the church. It had already gone through forty editions at the time of Sidney's death, and by 1621, the year in which the Countess died, close on one hundred and fifty editions had been published. Its place in the church service remained unchallenged in fact until Tate and Brady's "New Version" appeared in 1696. By 1828, when it finally ceased to be reprinted, *The Whole Booke of Psalmes* had achieved more than six hundred editions.

The Sidneian Psalms differ in three obvious and important respects from the Sternhold-Hopkins psalter. In the first place, stylistically they have an energy, intensity, and emotional piquancy which are conspicuously absent from the popular version—inventive metres and a vigorous syntax vividly inform and enforce the sense in a way which the stereotyped forms of Sternhold and Hopkins manifestly cannot. Secondly, whereas in congregational psalmody the necessity to provide a simple and easily memorable text virtually precludes any attempt at subtlety, the Sidneian versions, which were intended primarily for use in private devotions, constantly bring out and point the underlying "allegoricall sense." Sidney and the Countess of Pembroke have clearly made intelligent use of a wealth of scholarly commentary that was not so readily accessible to the earlier psalmodists. Finally, instead of straitjacketing the Psalms into a narrow range of simple stanza patterns they have devised a quite extraordinary variety of forms, each conformable to the emotional tenor of the individual psalm. The Sidneian collection, in brief, is an attempt to answer the need, increasingly voiced both within and outside the Church, for a more adequate and expressive form of psalmody.

A comparison of the Countess of Pembroke's version of Psalm 55 with the Sternhold-Hopkins rendering will bring out most effectively the differences. The psalm, as it appears in the Geneva Bible of 1560, ends: "And thou, O God, shalt bring them downe into the pit of corruption: the blooddie, & deceitful men shall not live halfe their dayes: but I wil trust in thee." In the lifeless end-stopped lines of Hopkins this becomes:

> But God shall cast them deep in pit,
> That thirst for blood always:
> He will no guileful man permit
> To live out half his days.
> Though such be quite destroid and gone,
> In thee O Lord I trust:
> I shall depend thy grace upon,
> With all my heart and lust.

In contrast, the Countess not only retrieves the latent poetical qualities of the biblical verse but gives it a dramatic and personal authority:

> But, Lord, how long shall these men tarry here?
> Fling them in pitt of death where never shin'd
> The light of life; and while I make my stay
> On thee, let who their thirst with bloud allay
> Have their life-holding threed so weakly twin'd
> That it, half spunne, death may in sunder sheare.

The poetic urgency of the original is redeemed in a way that patently isn't in the Sternhold-Hopkins version; the pressure of the lines even suggests something of Donne's angular strength. (pp. xi-xv)

The significance of the Sidneian collection, I am suggesting, is primarily literary; it represents one of the earliest and most ambitious attempts to grace English psalmody with the fully developed resources of the Elizabethan lyric

while at the same time preserving the "fulnes of the Sence and the *relish* of the Scripture phrase." Sidney and his sister sought to translate the Psalms so that they might stand up as poems in their own right, and for the purposes they had in mind neither the Sternhold-Hopkins version nor the Scottish psalter of 1564 can be regarded as having any significant relevance. Both were designed primarily for congregational use and by design restricted themselves to a limited vocabulary and to simple, obvious rhythms. (More than a hundred of the psalms in the English version of 1562 also occur in the Scottish psalter, which differs chiefly in the inclusion of a rather larger number of psalms by Kethe, Craig, Whittingham, and Pont.) Like the metrical paraphrases of Crowley (1550) and Matthew Parker, Archbishop of Canterbury (c. 1567), they offer no literary interest.

Sidney and his sister took their bearings, rather, from the work of two court poets, Sir Thomas Wyatt and Clément Marot, both of whom had died at an early age in the 1540s. They were writing, that is to say, in a consciously sophisticated tradition, and yet one that belonged to a period that had not been affected by the full impact of the lavish, ornamentalized Italianate style. Wyatt's *Seven Penitential Psalms,* posthumously published in 1549, were almost certainly known to Sidney and his circle. They are frankly personal, exhibit a wide and sophisticated vocabulary, and are plainly, and in the best sense, the work of a "courtly maker." Wyatt's terza rima is continually animated by the acting out of a personally experienced struggle. In his version of Psalm 130, a judiciously controlled rhetoric enforces dramatically the halting utterance of an anguished plea to God:

> Ffor, lord, if thou do observe what men offend
> And putt thy natyff mercy in restraint,
> If just exaction demaund recompense,
> Who may endure, O lord? Who shall not faynt
> At such acompt? Dred, and not reverence
> Shold so raine large. But thou sekes rathr love,
> Ffor in thy hand is mercys resedence,
> By hope wheroff thou dost our hertes move.

It is a similar strength, the conjunction of a formal Hebrew complaint with the vital presence of a baffled, distinctively Elizabethan voice, that gives the Countess of Pembroke's psalmody its peculiar vigour:

> Who but such caitives would have undermin'd,
> Nay overthrowne, from whome but kindness
>   meare
> They never found? who would such trust betray?
> What buttred wordes! yet warr their harts be-
>   wray;
> Their speach more sharp than sharpest sword or
>   speare
> Yet softer flowes than balme from wounded
>   rinde.
>
>   (Psalm 55)

The colloquial strength of these lines, the deliberate avoidance of mere fluency suggest something of Wyatt's characteristic strenuousness. But the work that most obviously served as a model to the Sidneys is the French psalter of 1562, a collection that had been completed at Geneva by Théodore de Bèze on the foundation of fifty psalms composed between 1532 and 1543 by Clément Marot. Marot, like Sidney, was a court poet and never envisaged initially that his versified psalms would be put to congregational use. It was no doubt the accomplishment and variety of the French poet's work that first suggested to Sidney the poetic potential of the Psalms. Sidney has done no more than Marot in bringing to bear on his psalmody all the verbal and rhythmical subtlety of his lyric art. It is significant, for instance, that there is not a single example among the Sidneian Psalms of the simple ballad stanza or "fourteener" so monotonously employed by Sternhold and Hopkins. What Sidney and the Countess have attempted to do is to create for every one of the 150 Psalms a unique combination of stanza pattern and rhyme scheme. There are in fact only four instances in the entire collection of the exact repetition of any one combination. . . . Admittedly there may be an element here of virtuosity for virtuosity's sake, but the wide variety of form is intended also to reflect the diversity of the Psalms themselves. Sidney and his sister have attempted to devise appropriate forms for poems which in the original Hebrew are variously psalms of rejoicing, of lamentation, of triumph, of imprecation, and in some cases of historical narrative. Like Wither, a later versifier of the Psalms, they have done so not "out of any speciall affectation of variety; but with an intent to sute the matter of each Psalme . . . to such Numbers as might most aptly expresse it." In the imprecatory Psalm 59, for example, a stanza of varying line lengths ingeniously reflects the restless movement of hounds "whom hunger enforceth to run gadding about without ceasing":

> Abroad they range and hunt apace
> Now that, now this,
> As famine trailes a hungry trace;
> And though they miss,
> Yet will they not to kennell hye,
> But all the night at bay do lye.

Whereas in the versions of Sternhold and Hopkins alternating lines of eight and six syllables are made to serve all purposes, the Countess of Pembroke varies her stanza form according to the nature of her subject. Psalm 78, a long historical narrative, is appropriately cast in ottava rima, the stanza that Drayton chose to use in *The Barons' Warres* because of its "majesty, perfection, and solidity." On the other hand, another group of psalms (among them 64, 72, 74, 88, and 139) have an almost Herbertian deftness of touch. There is, for instance, an obvious continuity between the sort of effect the Countess achieves in Psalm 88:

> Alas, my Lord, will then be tyme,
> When men are dead,
> Thy truth to spread?
> Shall they, whome death hath slaine,
> To praise thee live againe,
> And from their lowly lodgings clime?
>
> Shall buried mouthes thy mercies tell?
> Dust and decay
> Thy truth display?
> And shall thy workes of mark
> Shine in the dreadful dark?
> Thy Justice where oblivions dwell?

and the deceptively simple form employed by Herbert in "Affliction" (IV):

> Oh help, my God! let not their plot
> Kill them and me,
> And also thee,
> Who art my life: dissolve the knot,
> As the sunne scatters by his light
> All the rebellions of the night.

"Your ocular proportion," writes Puttenham, "doeth declare the nature of the audible." It is quite clear that the authors of the Sidneian collection, no less than Herbert, have deliberately attempted to accommodate the contour of the strophe to the sense of the words.

The Sidneian Psalms, it has been said, "constitute a school of English versification," and Theodore Spencer has described them [in "The Poetry of Sir Philip Sidney", *Journal of English Literary History* 12, December 1945] as examples in "Art, Imitation, and Exercise"; but clearly they are something very much more than this. One of the most significant features of the collection lies in the way the two poets, especially the Countess of Pembroke, attempt to reveal by an accurate and intelligent use of the scholarly commentaries the latent meaning of the Hebrew originals, and to convey within the conventions of Elizabethan verse the sense of intimate, personal urgency that gives the Psalms, even in prose form, their poetic force. There is no reason to believe that either Sidney or the Countess of Pembroke could read Hebrew (Ballard's assertion to the contrary is unsubstantiated), yet it is clear that they carefully compared the versions of the Psalms found in the Prayer Book psalter and the two current versions of the Bible, the Geneva Bible of 1560 and the Bishops' Bible of 1568. They also consulted (in the English translations of Golding and Gilby) the elaborate commentaries on the Psalms of Calvin and Bèze; we frequently find the Countess of Pembroke, in particular, expanding and developing a biblical image where the commentaries give her authority to do so. In Psalm 139, for instance, which is concerned with the marvel of creation, the fifteenth verse of the version on which Calvin's commentary is based reads simply: "My strength which thou hast made in secret is not hid from thee, I was woven together in the lowest parts of the earth." Calvin's commentary, however, expands the significance of the weaving metaphor and explains at length the comparison of the mother's womb to what he calls the "dark denne" of the tailor's workroom. It is this elaboration of the biblical image that gives rise to the metaphors of "embrod'ry" and "shopp" in the Countess of Pembroke's bold version:

> Thou, how my back was beam-wise laid,
> And raftring of my ribbs, dost know:
> Know'st ev'ry point
> Of bone and joynt,
> How to this whole these partes did grow,
> In brave embrod'ry faire araid,
> Though wrought in shopp both dark and low.

The Countess has, in a devotional sense, *meditated* on the text before her, and the force of her version derives from her sense of personal involvement; she has taken into account Calvin's interpretation of the verse, and it is her capacity to appreciate the underlying meaning that vivifies her lines. For, as Wither comments [in *A Preparation to the Psalter,* 1619], "they who are ignorant of the *Allegoricall* senses of the *Psalmes* . . . are no wiser than such as are ignorant of all that appertaines unto them." What is so striking about the Countess of Pembroke's versions is the way in which they convey, alive as it were, the impulse and the force of the Hebrew originals. By recreating the Psalms as Elizabethan poems, the Countess compels us to read them afresh. Consider, for instance, the syntactical compression of her rendering of Psalm 58 which, despite its insistent alliteration and the formal balance of phrase, remains challengingly unconventional:

> So make them melt as the dishowsed snaile
> Or as the Embrio, whose vitall band
> Breakes er it holdes, and formlesse eyes do faile
> To see the sun, though brought to lightfull land.

The image of the stillborn embryo has an immediacy that is certainly not present in the formal metaphor of the "untimely frute" that we find in both the Geneva and the Bishops' Bible. It is a figure that takes its vitality from the Elizabethan poet's capacity to identify herself with the Hebrew lyrist's desire for the destruction of his enemies: in the images of the crushed snail and the disintegrating embryo that desire is made palpable to the imagination. The Countess, too, while adhering closely to the meaning of the originals, has given her psalms strength by contriving to provide them as poems with an argumentative momentum. In this Fifty-eighth Psalm, for instance . . . , the parallelistic structure of the Hebrew verse has been abandoned, and a deft redistribution of emphases has given the poem a compelling rhetorical structure. The challenging question with which the poem opens, "And call yee this to utter what is just . . . ?" is rebutted with equal force by the scathing "O no . . . " of the fifth line—the insertion of the exclamatory "O" gives a characteristically personal weight to the merely connective "Nay" of the Bishops' Bible reading. All the subtle art of the Elizabethan lyrist contributes to the effect. The hissing alliteration of "skillful'st spells" is not simply ornamental; it has, in the context of the snake imagery, a peculiar appositeness. Similarly the taut antithesis of "Just to your selves, indiff'rent else to none" provides a tension that is both dramatic and decisive. What Professor Martz has characterized as the peculiar significance of Sidney's forty-three psalms—"the attempt to bring the art of the Elizabethan lyric into the service of psalmody, and to perform this in such a way that it makes the psalm an intimate, personal cry of the soul to God"—applies, it must be emphasized, with even greater force to the psalms of the Countess of Pembroke. (pp. xv-xxi)

It is through her heavily accented metres and artfully marshalled phrasing that the Countess enforces a sense of anguish that is not generalized, but personal and individual:

> Surelie Lord, this daily murther
> For thie sake we thus sustaine:
> For thy sake esteem'd no further
> Than as sheepe, that must be slaine.
>
> (Psalm 44)

I as I can, think, speake, and doe the best:

> They to the worst my thoughts, wordes, doings wrest.
> All their hartes with one consent
> Are to worke my ruine bent,
> From plotting which, they give their heads no rest.
>
> (Psalm 56)

Although later poets completed verse translations of the Psalms, notably George Wither (1632), Sandys (1636), Watts (1719), and Smart (1765), there is nothing in these works precisely comparable to the vivacity and syntactical energy of the Elizabethan version. The sense of involvement that gives the finest of the Countess of Pembroke's psalms their force is already lost in the paraphrases of Wither and Sandys; nor can it find expression, except in a very modified form, in the comparatively formal idiom of Watts and Smart. The reasons for this are not hard to seek. The practice of singing versified psalms in church gradually gave way during the eighteenth century—especially among the Nonconformists—to the custom of hymn singing. Watts's preface to his *Psalms of David Imitated in the Language of the New Testament* (London, 1719) helps to explain how this came about. The Psalms of David, Watts argued, "express nothing but the Character, the Concerns, and the Religion of the *Jewish King.*" How, he asked, can a Christian worshipper assume the words of David "when our Condition of Life, our Time, Place, and Religion, are so vastly different from those of David?" In versifying the Psalms, Watts felt bound to blunt the edges of David's "sharp invectives" against his personal enemies, and to bring the sublimer expressions of faith and love "within the Reach of an ordinary Christian." Moreover, he deliberately modified words that implied "some peculiar Wants or Distresses," giving them a broader application suited "to the general Circumstances of Men." Within the terms of this stated design, Watts's psalms and hymns, like those of the later eighteenth-century hymn writers, Charles Wesley, Smart, Newton, and Cowper, are, at their best, admirable achievements. Unfortunately, however, the gradual displacement of psalm singing by an increasingly sentimental hymnody ushered in a vastly inferior form of church song. When in 1861 *Hymns Ancient and Modern* was published, the distinguished hymns of poets of earlier centuries were but meagrely represented.

It was in fact the poverty of Victorian hymnody that caused Ruskin to value so highly what he called the "Sidney Psalter." He possessed a copy of the 1823 edition and spoke of it with pardonable extravagance as "a classical model of the English language at the time of its culminating perfection." In 1877 he published a selection of the Sidneian Psalms in a volume entitled *Rock Honeycomb.* He does not distinguish between the work of Sidney and that of the Countess of Pembroke, but his comments are no less cogent for that. He wrote:

> Whereas a modern version, if it only clothe itself in what the author supposes to be genteel language, is thought perfectly satisfactory, though the said genteel language mean exactly the contrary of what David meant,—Sir Philip will use any cowboy's or tinker's words, if only they help him to say precisely in English what David said

in Hebrew: impressed, the while, himself so vividly by the majesty of the thought itself, that no tinker's language can lower it or vulgarize it in his mind. And, again, while the modern paraphraser will put in anything that happens to strike his fancy, to fill in the fag-end of a stanza, but never thinks of expanding or illustrating the matter in hand, Sidney, if the thought in his original appears to him pregnant, and partly latent, instantly breaks up his verse into franker and fuller illustration; but never adds a syllable of any other matter, to fill even the most hungry gap of verse.

In an early issue of *Fors Clavigera* (November 1872) he expressed his admiration more tersely: "You may not like this old English at first; but if you can find anybody to read it to you who has an ear, its cadence is massy and grand." (pp. xxiii-xxv)

> *J. C. A. Rathmell, in an introduction to* The Psalms of Sir Philip Sidney and the Countess of Pembroke, *edited by J. C. A. Rathmell, New York University Press, 1963, pp. xi-xxxii.*

G. F. Waller   (essay date 1979)

[*Waller is an Australian educator, critic, and poet who has written extensively on sixteenth-century English literature. In the following excerpt, he examines the psalms in the context of Renaissance religious writing, praising Sidney's poetic improvement of the originals.*]

> At home, abroad most willingly I will
> Bestow on God my praises utmost skill:

The opening lines of the Countess' Psalm 111, a 20-line alphabetical poem, may serve to introduce the spirit in which her psalms were written. As she expressed it near the conclusion of the vow of personal commitment she made from Psalm 104:

> As for my self, my seely self, in me
> While life shall last, his worth in song to show
> I framed have a resolute decree,
> And thankfull be, till being I forgoe.

Typically here she turns a joyful, but somewhat general, hymn of praise into an expression of deeply personal commitment. In what was a continuous exercise of personal piety, a prolonged tribute to her brother's memory, and an increasing dedication to poetry itself, Mary Sidney must have lived constantly with these poems for over a decade. . . . [She] probably started by working over her brother's versions, gradually discovering her own considerable talents. Wilton itself would have had the psalms very much at the centre of its religious and cultural life: no doubt, in the chapel, the Earl and Countess' chaplains would read through the Psalter, as the Prayer Book instructed, "once every Month, as it is there appointed, both for Morning and Evening Prayer" in " . . . the Translation of the great English Bible, set forth and used in the time of King *Henry* the Eight, and *Edward* the Sixth"—although the Sidneys' reverence for the Geneva version might well have meant that was preferred, especially as Wilton had a private chapel. Psalm 101, in its original a

ritual communal expression of a king's vow of service, contains an evocation of the ideals upon which Wilton was undoubtedly centered. Although they were the Queen's loyal servants, both Mary's brothers had intense yearnings to abandon the court and Elizabeth's wars for their own homes and families. She too virtually retired from the court in the 1590s to cultivate poetry and the inner virtues at Wilton and her determination is echoed in the psalmist's vow, that

> Deepe study I on vertue will bestow:
> And pure in hart at home retired lyve.

Typically, here the Countess gives her original a personal directness and relevance. By contrast, Geneva's version reads: "I wil do wisely in the perfite / waie til thou comest to me: I wil / walke in the uprightness of mine / heart in the middes of mine house." Other likely sources for her version are no more specific, although the gloss to the Geneva version obviously provided a hint for the specific direction her poem takes, with its relevance to the ideal of life at Wilton. Sidney's retirement to Wilton in the late seventies anticipates a significant counter-movement in the late decades of the century: the infighting at court became more frenetic and the older generation of Elizabethan statesmen and courtiers died or became disillusioned in the years following the defeat of the Armada. The source of the traditional virtues seemed to be shifting from the court to the great country families, just as the dynamic literary movements of the future were to come from the periphery rather than from the centre of the court.

The fundamental claim that I am making for the Countess' Psalms . . . is that, in Rathmell's words, "they demand to be considered not only in the context of Elizabethan psalmody, but as significant and attractive poems in their own right." Although, as with most lengthy collections of poems, their quality varies, at their best the Countess' psalms, even more than Sidney's, display a remarkable intensity of poetic evocation, formal inventiveness and intellectual subtlety. They represent "one of the earliest and most developed resources of the Elizabethan lyric" and, especially, constitute a landmark in the development of the English religious lyric. In Rathmell's words, "when recognition is accorded to the Sidney psalter the history of the metaphysical revival of our time will have to be rewritten." They are thus as important a part of the late Elizabethan literary revolution as *The Shepheards Calender* and *Astrophel and Stella*.

In the 1580s and 1590s we can see evidence of a growing tradition of narrative religious verse, partly inspired by and partly written in reaction to the tradition of secular love-lyrics. Central to this development are the Sidney psalms. To recognize their importance calls into question many common assumptions about the development of the post-Reformation religious lyric in English. We are accustomed to seeing the Counter-Reformation providing a crucial influence on the development of meditational verse. But there develops, as well, a Protestant tradition of devotional poetry in the 1580s and 1590s in which the Sidney psalms have a central place. The tradition is seen especially in the fashion for Biblical verse paraphrases, the culminating achievement of which is the Sidney Psalms themselves, which uniquely merge two distinct poetic traditions, that of the courtly lyric and of Reformation psalmody. Before Coburn Freer's study of Herbert and the Psalm tradition, the poetical psalms of the sixteenth century had been overlooked as the seedbed for the seventeenth century's flowering of religious poetry in England partly because of their lack of merit, and because they were translations. In an age that rightly views the *Imitations* of Robert Lowell as major poetry we should surely be able to appreciate the inherent merits of a tradition that eventually produced the Sidney Psalms and which deeply influenced the poetry of Herbert. (pp. 179-82)

The Psalms show that [Mary Sidney] taught herself the subtleties of poetic craftsmanship which she so admired in her brother, until she was able, in religious verse at least, to match him. Many of her psalms are moving and superbly constructed devotional lyrics in their own right, and are among the high points in English post-Reformation religious verse before Herbert's in the 1620s. As well, the Psalms provide further intimate glimpses into the mind of the Sidney Circle, with its characteristic tension between Protestant piety and courtly neo-Platonism and its place in the shifting social and intellectual realities of the 1590s.

When we consider the riches of the post-Reformation religious lyric, we are struck by two important characteristics. The first is the apparently belated development in England of a tradition of religious verse to rival the secular tradition. I am suggesting that the Psalm paraphrase movement, seen at its best in the Sidney Psalms, helps us fill out the tradition that culminates in Herbert and Vaughan. Second, it is interesting to note that the keenness of sensibility and individuality of voice so often praised as characteristic of late Elizabethan and Metaphysical verse is already present in the Psalm metaphrases and, behind them, in the Psalms themselves. We look, for instance, at Donne's restless, dislocated sensibility and we perhaps see the prototype of the insecure, secular sensibility of our own time. But the voices of Donne's poetry, both secular and divine, are as much a product of the Reformation as they are of Renaissance secularization. His self-analysis, often neurotic although usually the basis for an eventual affirmation of self, is an echo of the Psalmist's self-obsession and restlessness in continual debate with the self or with God. If, as Paul Tillich remarks, the characteristic mark of the post-Reformation era is that of anxiety and self-doubt, then we see the first literary manifestations of it not in Shakespeare's sonnets or Donne's songs and sonnets, but in the Sidney Psalms. There, for the first time in English, we can sense an awareness that religious verse demanded a vigorous, flexible, and perhaps above all a dramatic and varied voice. When we set Herbert's "Easter," first, alongside the metaphrases made of Psalm 57, verses 7-11, by Sternhold and Hopkins, and second, compare the Countess' flexible and intense version of the same Psalm, we can see in miniature a process of maturation and self-realisation that is as much a literary development as it represents a tradition of devotional piety. Reformation commentators pointed out how the Psalms spoke to men caught in the trials of the world and opened their consolation most especially to those under affliction and anguish. The root of their appeal to the Reformation seems to have been this deeply subjective sense of a soul wrestling with God. David, wrote Donne, "had an harmonious, a melodious, a charming, a powerfull way of entring into the soule, and working upon the affections" of his hearers, and thus provided the basis of a poetic as well as becoming the inspiration of the introspective spirit of post- and Counter-Reformation devotion and meditation. Catholics and Protestants alike used the Psalms as the basis of private meditation, public praise, and poetical inspiration. Although the fashion was European-wide, in England alone more than one hundred psalm translations or paraphrases appeared between 1500 and 1640; the most popular, that by Sternhold and Hopkins, the so-called "Old Version," went through over 300 editions, in less than a century.

Attitudes to the translation of the Psalms and to their status as poetry varied greatly. Many versifiers, such as Sternhold, Hopkins and their collaborators, attempted to translate the biblical original as closely as possible, avoiding erroneous denotations, and if necessary sacrificing metrical form to doctrinal orthodoxy. In the words of the authors of the Bay Psalm Book:

> Neither let any think, that for the meetre sake wee have taken liberty or poeticall licence to depart from the true and proper sense of Davids words in the hebrew verses, noe; but it hath beene one part of our religious care and faithfull indeavour, to keepe close to the originall text.

And yet, translators were uncomfortably aware that in such an exercise "the sence of the author is oftentimes corrupted and depraved; and neyther the grace of the one tongue nor yet of the other is truely observed or aptlie expressed." As Harington pithily expressed it in his translation of Ariosto (1591), it would be a mark of "simplicity . . . to go word for word." Hence there developed an increasing number of writers who appreciating the psalms as poetry tried to avoid the ludicrous literality of so many versions, like those in the Old Version or the Bay Psalm Book. Therefore many, in Dryden's terminology, can more properly be termed "imitations," in which primary emphasis is laid upon verse form, rhetorical effectiveness, and the underlying experience (rather than simply the doctrines) found in the Psalms. So Wyatt experimented with *terza rima* and *ottava rima* and Surrey attempted to make poulter's measure adaptable to the Psalms. But it was not until Philip and especially Mary Sidney took up the task that the psalm imitations can be said to join with the developing traditions of English lyric verse. Indeed, of all those writers (to call all "poets" is to stretch the word's meaning somewhat) who attempted to versify the psalms in English, the Sidneys were the most sensitive to their originals as evocations of religious experience and as poetry. Indeed, looked at strictly in an English context, their versions stand slightly aside, in both intention and quality, from the main line of Biblical paraphrases. Their versions are unambiguously designed for private enjoyment and meditation, and they approach their sources with considerations very different from translators concerned with congregational worship, as were Sternhold and Hopkins, or the overwhelming majority of other translators who were usually intent on expressing the doctrinal unity and orthodoxy of the Psalms. (pp. 182-86)

The Countess' virtuosity in experimenting with stanzaic and metrical forms is most striking. Overall, not counting Sidney's original 43 translations or those to which she made only minor revisions, her Psalms contain 164 distinct stanzaic patterns, with only one repeated. There are, as well, 94 quite distinct metrical patterns. Early versifiers of the Psalms tended to write fairly unvaryingly in ballad metre, poulter's measure or fourteeners, and were generally careless of tone or meaning. Sternhold and Hopkins, for instance, usually chose the ballad stanza, written in fourteeners, with a thumping caesura almost invariably after the eighth syllable. Crowley's 1549 Psalter is in the same measure, and even the contemporary miscellanies of secular verse like Tottel's, *The Paradise of Dainty Devices* or *The Phoenix Nest* are equally limited metrically. It is only with *England's Helicon* that anything approximating the Countess' virtuosity is reached: Rathmell observes that by comparison with the Countess' 162, Tottel has 32, *The Phoenix Nest* 25, and it is *England's Helicon* with 105 that comes closest to the Countess' virtuosity. Thus her psalms anticipate the metrical and stanzaic variation which becomes such a standard feature of early seventeenth-century religious verse. (p. 190)

While not entirely consistent, the Countess of Pembroke clearly endeavoured to match form, meaning, and tone. In her version of Psalm 56, for instance, she employed an *aabbcc* stanza, with lines of 10, 10, 7, 7, and 10 syllables. The metre is basically trochaic, but with some contrasting anapaests to convey the rising indignation of one falsely accused and looking to God for rescue:

> Fountaine of pitty now with pitty flow:
> These monsters on me daily gaping goe,
> Dailie me devoure these spies,
> Swarmes of foes against me rise,
> O God that art more high than I am lowe.

Psalm 100 is a sonnet, rhyming *ababbcbccdcdee,* the form used by Spenser, and possibly consciously borrowed by the Countess. The long, 176-verse, alphabetical Psalm 119 is rendered by a miscellany of inventive stanzas, with a different pattern for each of its 22 parts. . . . Psalm 57 is an especially interesting example, as the Countess cleverly varies line length and metrical stress much in the way Herbert does in a poem with a similar tone, "Affliction." She seizes very acutely the underlying mood of her original, with its sense of mounting threat countermanded by a cry for rescue. She combines unobtrusive, idiomatic diction with an insistently varied stanza pattern, *abbcca,* with lines of 10, 4, 4, 7, 7, 6 syllables, using mainly iambics with occasional shifts of stress for emphasis. The pattern creates a highly appropriate impression of urgency:

> Thy mercie Lord, Lord now thy mercy show,
> On thee I ly
> To thee I fly
> Hide me, hive me as thine owne,
> Till these blasts be overblown,
> Which now doe fiercely blow.

The emphatic repetition of line one, the urgent echoing of

lines two to four with their accumulation of muscular vowel sounds, are simple but effective techniques indicative of a poet's precise control over mood and movement. The tone of urgency is further underlined by the way the Countess alters her original in the fourth and fifth lines (cf. until this *tiranny* be overpast—Great Bible, Bishop's; *afflictions*—Geneva; *wickednesse*—Coverdale). The lines are rendered much more concretely in the added imagery of the storm. It is probably the gloss to Geneva which gives her the hint for the amplification—a typical way in which she works, as we shall see—since it reads: "He compareth the afflictions, which God layeth upon his children, to a storme." (pp. 193-94)

The Countess' technical virtuosity is, then, important and remarkable for her time; with few models available in English, she extends the technical range of English versification, and thus contributed to the revolution in both form and sensibility observable in poetry over the next forty years or so. Her technical ambitiousness has, however, been generally recognized, even by detractors of her poetical skills, and I shall enumerate no further examples. What is more important is the impressive range of appropriate tones and the variations in stylistic level that her virtuosity affords. Wither suggested that he was trying to suit his forms "to the matter of each *Psalme*," and, as C. A. Huttar points out, "the main difference between the Sidneys and their colleagues can be stated in one word—perception. Before launching forth on a paraphrase of a psalm they took the trouble to understand it as a poem." Usually, the Countess is not indulging in formal experimentation for its own sake, but matches form with tone. Psalm 67, for instance, exemplifies the direct, terse style of the Elizabethan plain lyric; into Psalm 65, by contrast, she brings the golden lyrical amplification of the high Elizabethan age:

> Thy eie from Heav'n this land beholdeth,
> Such fruitfull dewes down on it rayning,
> That, storehowse-like her lap enfoldeth
> Assured hope of plowmans gayning.
> Thy flowing streames her drought doe temper so,
> That buried seed through yelding grave doth grow.
>
> Drunk is each ridg of thy cup drincking,
> Each clodd relenteth at thy dressing:
> Thy cloud-born waters inly sincking,
> Faire spring sproutes foorth blest with thy blessing.
> The fertile yeare is with thy bounty crown'd:
> And where thou go'st, thy goings fatt the ground.
>
> Plenty bedewes the desert places:
> A hedg of mirth the hills encloseth:
> The fields with flockes have hid their faces:
> A robe of corn the vallies clotheth.
> Desertes, and hills, and feilds, and valleys all,
> Rejoyce, shout, sing, and on thy name doe call.

The mixture of iambics and anapaests with the characteristic Sidneian use of feminine rhyme creates a serene, dancelike vision of order which is exactly appropriate for one of the most beautiful word-pictures of the Psalms.

Her most pervasive influence is, of course, her brother. Frequently she echoes quite specific sonnets from *Astrophel and Stella*. Psalm 73 commences "It is most true that God to Israell . . . ," echoing Sidney's "It is most true that eyes are form'd to serve . . . " (Sonnet 4). Line four similarly echoes Sidney's, "Most true, I see . . . ," and the ratiocinative structure continues to the stanza's end:

> Nay, so they guarded are with health and might,
> It seemes of them death dares not claime his
>   right.

Other incidental echoes abound: "Nay ev'n within my self, my self did say" (Psalm 73, 37) seems to pick up "But to myself my self did give the blow" (*Astrophel and Stella,* 33); like Sidney, the Countess often employs feminine rhyme and shows a fondness for compound epithets "which," Sidney claimed, are among "the greatest bewties can be in a language."

If the sophistication of the Elizabethan courtly lyric enriches the Psalm metaphrase tradition in the Countess' psalms, the reverse is also true. As Rathmell remarks [in his introduction to *The Psalms of Sir Philip Sidney and the Countess of Pembroke,* 1963], "to read through this Elizabethan paraphrase is to realize afresh the impact on English verse of the audacious and often bizarre imagery of the ancient Hebrew poets." The elements of verbal surprise, the arresting openings, and the personalized emotions, which characterize the Countess' poems anticipate the typical tensions of Metaphysical poetry—and perhaps one source for Metaphysical "wit" may well be in Hebrew poetry. The vigorous first lines of Donne's lyrics are anticipated by such openings as the Countess' "Tyrant, why swel'st thou thus" (52), "Not us I say, not us" (115), "Sure, Lord, thy self art just", (119, s), "Upp, up my soule, advaunce Jehovas praise" (146), while the mixture of Sidneian wit and Metaphysical surprise which characterizes Herbert's poems is anticipated by such openings as the Countess' Psalm 77:

> To thee my crying call,
> To thee my calling cry
> I did, O God, adresse,
> And thou didst me attend.

The Countess is especially confident in handling the muscular plain lyric stanza and bringing in a note of personal urgency to sharpen the particularities of the original. Unlike the naive diction of Sternhold and Hopkins, the simplicity of such psalms as 67 or 69 reflects the peculiar degree of personal joy or anguish she seems to bring to the most emotionally charged psalms. Like Herbert in *The Temple,* she constantly finds analogies with her own spiritual experiences. Psalm 139 deserves some attention in this respect. It is, [E. A. Leslie notes in *The Psalms,* 1949], "one of the most spiritually profound psalms in the Psalter. It is the awed utterance of individual thanksgiving . . . on the part of one of the noblest thinkers of Israel." The Psalm is a meditation on the awesome powers of God, who sees, follows, and knows the speaker's most intimate movements of mind and body; his presence upholds the whole universe and penetrates to the earliest and most secret recesses of the personality. Modern commentators see verses 19-22 (stanzas 11-12) as later interpo-

lations, and Reformation scholars were also somewhat uneasy with their sudden turn from awed meditation to a cry for divine vengeance, although no translation or commentator would have doubted their authenticity.

The Countess chooses a 7-line stanza, rhyming abccbab, with lines 1-2 and 5-7 generally in iambic trimeters and two short lines between. She uses the contrasting rhythms thus set up very skilfully, as in the opening stanza:

> O Lord in me there lieth nought,
> But to thy search revealed lies:
> For when I sitt
> Thou markest it:
> No lesse thou notest when I rise:
> Yea closest closet of my thought
> Hath open windowes to thine eyes.

Similarly effective in its control and contrast of tone is the opening of stanza two, which builds up a sense of God's presence; here the short couplet is used as for succinct emphasis:

> Thou walkest with me when I walk,
> When to my bed for rest I go,
> I find thee there,
> And ev'rywhere . . .

To give the urgent speaking voice further particularity, the Countess brings into the psalm a strand of domestic imagery, to suggest the speaker actually meditating in his (or her) room. The original psalm had simply emphasized that God is present at one's rising and sleeping; her version has a tone of endearing quaintness, in a stanza again anticipating Herbert:

> Thou, how my back was beam-wise laid,
> And raftring of my ribbs, dost know:
> Know'st ev'ry point
> Of bone and joynt,
> How to this whole these partes did grow,
> In brave embrod'ry faire arraid,
> Though wrought in shopp both dark and low.

The emphasis in 139 is, as with Herbert, not to versify the doctrine of God's omnipotence, but to evoke the experiential roots of the doctrine, to dramatize mood and emotion rather than theology.

She is often at her best when dealing with strongly personal emotions of anguish or deep revulsion, when her vocabulary is usually appropriately sparse and the syntax flexible. The concluding stanza of Psalm 63 is one such example. The beginning of the poem suffers in contrast with the inspired simplicity of most contemporary English prose versions, but by the end, the Countess has built to a superbly ringing climax to stress God's inevitable retribution on the wicked:

> But such as seeke my life to ruinate,
> Them shall the earth in deepest gulph receave.
> First murdring blade shall end their living date,
> And then their flesh to teeth of foxes leave;
> As for the king, the king shall then conceave
> High joy in God, and that God adore,
> When lying mouthes, shall, stopped, ly no more.

The threatening movement and slightly formal diction mount to a forceful effect in the muscular, emphatic climax of the last lines. Here her control of tone is impressively confident.

She is also usually adept at evoking a tone of joy or celebration appropriate to a courtly festivity in a note to which she responds well, as in Psalm 81:

> All gladness, gladdest hartes can hold,
> In meriest notes that mirth can yeld,
> Lett joyfull songues to God unfold,
> To Jacobs god our sword and shield.
> Muster hither musicks joyes,
> Lute, and lyre, and tabretts noise:
> Lett noe instrument be wanting,
> Chasing grief, and pleasure planting.

Here the lilting tripping effect is achieved especially by the combination of falling rhythms and light vowels, the succession of iambs and trochees all rounded off by the measured formality of the final couplet.

In incidentals, in the changing moods or tones within particular psalms, too, the Countess is concerned with finding an appropriate variety—by underlining the drama of a situation (as in the opening of 50), constantly breaking up the syntax with a question, or a sudden change of mood. Such variety stands as a constant rebuttal to Coburn Freer's dismissal of the Countess' skills [in *Music for a King,* 1972] that "when she strikes on a natural phrasing in her psalms, it is as much by accident as by design." Usually, rhetorical effectiveness coincides with idiomatic movement, and while undoubtedly there is unevenness in her verse, nevertheless her technical achievements are deliberately striven for, an impression reinforced . . . by a study of her revisions.

I want now to move on to the question of the Countess' originality. Discussing Psalm 139, Rathmell observes that the Countess "*meditated* on the text before her, and the force of her version derives from her sense of personal involvement . . . it is her capacity to appreciate the underlying meaning that vivifies her poems." Usually, if not exclusively, it is the "underlying meaning" that the Countess is concerned to evoke. She is at her best when direct expressions of subjective emotion are involved: her approach to her text is usually as communicated experience, not as encapsulated doctrine. Many of the longer narrative or historical psalms fail and frequently degenerate into formally competent but mechanical translation. (pp. 198-204)

While comparison with her sources is obviously crucial in understanding her intentions and achievements, it would be a mistake to read the majority of the Countess' psalms alongside her sources as an attempt to check her accuracy. Her usual procedure, especially with the shorter psalms, is to keep the general drift of the original in mind, and develop—from hints in her sources, from commentaries, or the deep reservoir of Elizabethan theological and rhetorical commonplaces—a consistency of tone. This involves using metaphorical amplifications, often, though not exclusively, derived from the original. Geneva 44.2, for instance, reads:

> How thou hast driven out the
> heathen with thine hand, and

> planted them: *how* thou hast destroyed
> the people, and caused them to grow.

In this case the Countess extends the imagery of planting and growing, and further evokes the process of organic development with the feminine rhyme moving the verse on:

> How thy hand the Pagan foe
> Rooting hence, thie folke implanting,
> Leavelesse made the braunch to grow,
> This to spring, noe verdure wanting.

A similar development of the original imagery is seen in Psalm 80. 8-11:

> Thou hast brought a vine out of Egypt:
> thou hast cast out the heathen, and planted it.
>
> Thou madest roume for it, and didest cause
> it to take roote, and it filled the land.
>
> The mountains were covered with the
> shadow of it, and the boughs there of *were
> like* the goodlie cedres.
>
> She stretched out her branches unto the
> Sea, and her boughes unto the River.

In the single stanza that is based upon these four verses, the Countess both develops and tightly links together the original imagery of planting and growth—and as well emphasises the typological significance of the original which is referring back to such passages as Genesis lxix.22 and forward to Isaiah 27.2-6, and Jeremiah 2.21, 12.10:

> A Vine thou didst translate from Zoan playnes,
> And weeding them that held the place of old,
> Nor planting care didst slack, nor pruning
>   paines,
> To fix her rootes, whom fieldes could not enfold.
> The hills were cloked with her pleasing cold:
> With Cedars state her branches height contend-
>   ed:
> Scarse here the sea, the River there controld
> Her armes, her handes, soe wide she both ex-
>   tended.

Other developments may be more dramatic. Into the relatively formal threat of 50.22—"Oh consider this, ye that forget God, lest I teare you in pieces . . . "—she imports a vigorous muscular evocation of a very personal struggle between God and the elect soul:

> In vaine to others for release you flie,
> If once on you I griping fingers sett.
> And know the rest: my dearest worship I
> In sweete performe of offred praise doe place:
> And who directs his goings orderlie,
> By my conduct shall see Gods saving grace.

Such expansions usually occur when the Countess can draw on the stock areas of Elizabethan metaphor and simile—nature, the heavens, various political commonplaces. In successive stanzas of Psalm 77, she tightens her original's meaning by bringing in an appropriate Elizabethan commonplace. "Are all the conduites dry / of his erst flowing grace?", she asks, echoing verse 9 of the Psalm. Then, amplifying, she asks:

> Could rusty teeth of tyme
> To nought his promise turne?

Exactly the same technique is used at the same point in the following verse:

> Then lo, my wrack I see,
> Say I, and do I know
> That chang lies in his hand,
> Who changlesse sitts aloft?

Again, the image is not hinted at in the original, and the Countess has effectively underlined the theological point she wants to bring out of the Psalm. She has an especial preference for the sharply ironical or paradoxical reference and on occasions her verse can resemble that of Greville or Ralegh in terseness of tone or sparseness of illusion. In other psalms, her rhetoric can be elaborate and rich. To Psalm 148.8-12, she adds a picture, typical of the most serene of Elizabethan cosmological thought, of the universe moving mysteriously at God's command in a complex, courtly dance:

> You boisterous windes, whose breath fullfills
> What in his word, his will setts down:
> Ambitious mountaines, curteous hills:
> You trees that hills and mountaines crown:
> Both you that proud of native gown
> Stand fresh and tall to see:
> And you that have your more renown,
> By what you beare, than be.
>
> You beastes in woodes untam'd that range:
> You that with men famillier go:
> You that your place by creeping change,
> Or airy streames with feathers row;
> You stately kings, you subjects low
> You Lordes and Judges all:
> Your others whose distinctions show,
> How sex or age may fall;

The original passage adapts itself harmoniously to a melodious and serene expression of the commonplace view of nature as a cosmic dance. Like her brother, she brings a highly acute musical ear to the Psalms, and many of the celebratory lyrics are superbly light and joyful in tone. Her version of Psalm 72. 2-3 is, for instance, much richer and more elaborate than the original, as she turns a rather solemn invocation of political responsibility into an evocation of the joyfully patterned movement of an ordered and harmonious commonwealth:

> Then fearelesse peace,
> With rich encrease
> The mountaynes proud shall fill:
> And justice shall
> Make plenty fall
> On ev'ry humble hill.

She further reorganizes the psalm to continue the note of joyful harmony in the following stanza:

> And thou againe
> Shall blessings rayne,
> Which down shall mildly flow,
> As showres thrown
> On meades new mown
> Wherby they freshly grow.

However close to the original any Renaissance translator of the Psalms might attempt to keep, one important difference between Hebrew and Renaissance poetry had to be struggled with. The parallelism typical of Hebrew poetry is habitually an expression of a cultic approach to poetry, so the internal structure of a psalm is formulaic rather than logical, with many discontinuities and logical gaps. Hence the common post-Reformation reading of the psalms as meditational in tone and akin to the ode in form meant that the apparent gaps and discontinuities had to be smoothed out, usually by expansion of material or the use of unifying strands of imagery. In part, Calendar argues, this process of expanding the matter of the Psalms in paraphrases is "simply Europeanizing or 'Ciceronizing' of the Psalms, ignoring the 'Attic' style of the Hebrews." Poets struggled to find a unity of purpose and tone in the psalm that might not have been there in the original. Consequently, often a totally new poem emerges, for the thought becomes less communal and more personal, and the poem takes on an intellectual unity not found in the Hebrew original. The Countess' concern with concrete evocation and distinctively urgent voice is therefore typical of the whole paraphrase movement. The best of her poems are meditations on complex but distinct religious moods, not embodiments of ritual or community cults. They provide examples of a fruitful cultural give-and-take which, in the poetry of Donne and Herbert eventually creates some of the high points of English poetry.

I want now to extend my analysis of the Countess' skills as a poet by looking at the intellectual structure of her Psalms. So far as the majority of them is concerned, of course, her interpretation stays close to the Geneva version which was the Sidneys' main doctrinal guide. But there are Psalms which gave strong support to certain key Protestant doctrines and which were stressed by the Geneva Bible translators. There are, too, Psalms where the Countess herself has found or added a further Protestant note—sometimes taking up a suggestion from Beza or Calvin, sometimes quite independently as if realizing the possibility of extending the force of her original by a distinctive doctrinal emphasis. And there is, most significantly, a final group where a possible Calvinistic interpretation is firmly rejected and a deliberately contrary position adopted which clearly reflects her neo-Platonic interests. . . . In many cases, these intellectual contrasts reflect contrasting intellectual drives in the originals that more dogmatic translations smooth out; but as well, they often bring out the recurring intellectual preoccupations of the Countess.

The first category, where the Countess is faithful to her strong Reformed piety, is, understandably, by far the dominant group. Psalm 74, ll. 79-84 stresses God's transcendence of "natures lawes" in nourishing the Israelites with a fountain springing "from thirsty flynt." She stresses strongly the dependence of God's elect on his inexplicable mercies in Psalm 73, and in Psalm 143, takes up a hint in the Geneva gloss, which notes that "in Gods sight all men are sinners" to faithfully ask: "For Lord what living wight / Lives synnlesse in thy sight?" Equally orthodox, although more than usually succinct, is her opening for Psalm 127:

> The house Jehova builds not,
> We vainly strive to build it:
> The towne Jehova guards not,

We vainly watch to guard it.

The matter-of-fact directness of her four lines contrasts strongly with Beza's prose paraphrase (an art, he says, which puts the "full sence and meaning of the holy ghoste in other words") which runs to some 300 words. The Countess, although doctrinally orthodox enough, is here typically concerned primarily with the mood of unchallengeable authority evoked in the psalm.

There are, akin to this first group, Psalms which lent themselves to Calvinist emphases and thus frequently became key texts in Reformation controversies. Here, too, usually the Countess faithfully echoes an orthodox reading. However, the reliance by both the Countess and in his psalms, her brother, is somewhat more complicated than Ringler suggests [in his edition of Sir Philip Sidney's *Poems*] when he claims that precedence was consistently given to the Geneva version. There are certainly many examples where Ringler's claim does hold true, but there are other examples where the Countess especially is drawing upon other sources for her doctrinal guidance.

Examples where the Countess clearly follows Geneva, either the text or the marginal glosses, include such passages as Psalm 59.10: Geneva has "My merciful God will prevent me," and her words follow closely: "Thou ever with thy free grace / Prevented hast." By contrast, Coverdale and the Great Bible have "God sheweth me his goodness plenteously," while the Bishops' Bible follows Geneva. In Psalm 94.10, the Countess is even more clearly bowing to the Geneva version, where she follows its expansion of the original Hebrew. "He that chastiseth the nations, shall he not correct? he that teacheth man knowledge, shal he not know?" is the Geneva rendering. The last clause is added by the translators to complete the analogy, which Coverdale, the Great Bible and the Bishops' Bible leave hanging awkwardly. The Countess here follows Geneva in the structure of her verses:

> Who checks the world, shall he not you reprove?
> Shall knowledge lack, who all doth knowledge
> lend?

An interesting instance is at Psalm 147.20, "He hathe not dealt so with everie nacion, neither have they knowen his judgements" (Geneva). The Countess emphasises even more strongly the Calvinist note of election:

> No Nation els hath found him half soe kind,
> For to his light, what other is not blynd?

Here she is echoing not the text but rather the dogmatic fervour of the Geneva marginal gloss which stresses that "the cause of this difference is Gods fre mercie, which hathe . . . appointed the reprobate to eternal damnation." The strong note is reinforced by contemporary Protestant commentators. The verse "teacheth us," writes Thomas Wilcox, "that God will have mercy upon whomsoever he will have mercie, and he will show compassion to whomsoever he will show compassion, as for the other he will harden them." Geneva's translation of the last line is "because God hathe cast them off " (Coverdale, Great Bible, and Bishops read "despised them"). Neither the gloss of the Geneva version nor any of the standard commentators give a hint of anything so harsh, although the concept is

common enough in Calvinist theology. Elsewhere an orthodox reading may be reinforced by a handy Elizabethan commonplace. Thus the despairing question of Psalm 77, verse 9, "Are all the conduites dry / Of his erst flowing grace?"—is underlined by the following lines, which are introduced by the Countess' own brooding on the experience behind the psalm rather than on its words: "Could rusty teeth of tyme / To nought his promise turne?" Another similar instance is the image which she brings into Psalm 119, Part C: "A Pilgrim right / On earth I wandring live." The image of Man as a Pilgrim was a favourite Biblical image, although here it is derived not from the original Psalm, but perhaps from Genesis 17 v.8 or 23 v.4.

It ought to be added that there are similar emphases which occur in Sidney's Psalms. There is, for instance, a strong stress upon election at Psalm 43, which echoes both Beza's and Calvin's glosses; upon imputed rather than inherent righteousness in Psalm 32 v.1; upon the total depravity of mankind and the vanity of works of supererogation in Psalm 14 vv.1-2 where man:

> . . . and all his mates
> Do workes, which earth corrupt, and Heaven
>   hates:
> Not one that good remaineth.

Beza's paraphrase of the verse is similarly emphatic: "all doe make them selves abhominable and not one of them doth lead his life aright." In Sidney's version of Psalm 17, the typical Calvinist stress on God's close providential control of time is evoked by the description of "the firmament so strangely bent" which "showes his hand-working wonders."

In these examples the close reliance on Geneva's text or glosses makes the Countess' psalms orthodox enough in doctrine. But in the next category of Psalms I have isolated something different that is occurring. There are occasions where the Countess is attempting to reach into the experiential core of the psalm, and her enthusiasm to find a vigorous phrase emerges in a theological stress strikingly different from her sources. One striking example is the ringing conclusion to 58:

> The good with gladness this reveng shall see,
> And bath his feete in bloud of wicked one
> While all shall say: the just rewarded be,
> There is a God that carves to each his own.

It is an effective evocation of the mood, if not the text, of the original, but however appropriate its vindictiveness may be, none of the standard translations or glosses make much of the line. Beza's paraphrase of the lines in Gilby's translation comes closest in words although not in tone: " . . . surely ther is a God in the earth, that doth also give every man his owne"; Thomas Wilcox turns the almost malevolent glee of the original into moral torpitude by annotating the lines as teaching "that the execution of Gods judgements upon the wicked, is a matter of great comfort to the godly." The available translations are no less tame. Coverdale and Geneva simply have: "there is a God that judgeth the earth," although once again the Geneva gloss spells out part of the doctrine the Countess is concerned to evoke when it states that "seeing God governeth all by his providence, he must needs put difference between the godlie, and the wicked." The difference between her version and these others lies in that she is concerned with the religious energies that lie behind what her sources express as doctrine; her poem consequently lacks the ideological weight of say, the Geneva version, but it has far more evocative power. It has passed beyond mere translation and become a poem in its own right.

A similar example of the Countess' power of evoking the feelings that lie behind such commonplaces is her stress upon God's actively hardening the hearts of the reprobate in Psalm 53, where her poem impressively builds up a curse upon the depraved, culminating in an assertion of one of the great Calvinist sureties that echoes through the literature of denunciation of the sixteenth century:

> But on their bones shall wreaked be
> All thy invaders force and guile,
> In vile confusion cast by thee,
> For God him self shall make them vile.

Other examples are readily found. An element of doctrinal stiffening is introduced into Psalm 76 vv.1-2, where Geneva reads:

> 1. God is knowen in Judah: his Name is great in Israel
> 2. For in Salem is his Tabernacle, and his dwelling in Zion.

The Geneva gloss adds that God's power is seen "in prefering his people and destroying his enemies," while the Countess expands on a similar note of exclusiveness:

> Only to Juda God his will doth signify;
> Only in Jacob is his name notorious;
> His restfull tent doth only Salem dignify;
> On Syon only stands his dwelling glorious.

Oddly enough, Calvin overlooks the exclusiveness implicit in the Hebrew; Beza, however, brings it out. God, he paraphrases, "is only knowne in Judea . . . and he doth there only declare him selfe. . . . "

An interesting example of the Countess' procedure in selecting different commentaries or glosses to back up a particular mood she feels to be in the psalm is at Psalm 62 v.11:

> All powre is Gods, his own word showes,
> Once said by him, twice heard by me:
> Yet from thee, Lord, all mercy flowes,
> And each manns work is paid by thee.

The original of these lines was the subject of some controversy. Coverdale's version, although less definite, is close to the Countess' and for once she may have preferred it over the Geneva translation which states that God spoke an indefinite number of times i.e. "once or twice. . . . " Beza glosses this reading as signifying "both with wordes and by the ende of thinges." Calvin, however, strongly rejects any such implication of divine hesitancy in his commentary. His translation, doctrinally more in accord with the Countess', is: "once hath God spoken it, I have heard it twice, that power belongeth unto God." He further comments that "once or twice" in the sense understood by Beza is too indefinite to be applied to God since "God ea-

teth not his word when he hath once spoken it"; it is on the contrary "our dutie to think leyzurely and advisedly uppon what soever is proceeded out of his mouth."

These are all fairly random examples of ways in which the Countess is more concerned with poetical rather than doctrinal unity—although it is obviously true that as she read them she found evoked in the Psalms experiences that accorded with her own piety. The randomness of course points up the crucial nature of her psalms, that she realised the variety of experience depicted within what was by too many commentators welded into a false unity. Other examples can reinforce the point. A particularly interesting example, indicating not merely a judicious selection among commentators but a marked degree of meditational independence is found at Psalm 103 v.14:

> Our potter he
> Knowes how his vessells we
> In earthly matter lodg'd this fickle forme.

The image of God as a potter and man as his clay, derived from Romans 9.21, is of course a favourite Calvinist commonplace:

> If thou and thousands perish, it is
> nothing to him; hee cares no more
> for the destruction of the whole
> world, than thou does for the
> throwing away of a little dust . . .
> Therefore do not thou disputeth with
> *God,* and aske, why are so many
> damned . . . shall the clay say to
> him that fashions it, what makest thou?

But neither Geneva nor any of the commentators bring out the rhetorical possibilities of the image as explicitly as does Mary Sidney. Calvin's translation is "he knoweth whereof wee bee made, he remembered that we are but duste." Beza's paraphrase is closer without being explicit: "for he knoweth that we are but earthen vessels, he knoweth that our substance is made of the earth." In evoking the doctrinal implications of the image, Mary Sidney is not only going back to the root meaning of the Hebrew, but she is enriching the meaning of her translation by bringing in a New Testament reference to which the Psalm obviously points forward. The example reinforces Rathmell's comment on her poetic practice that, at best she "meditates on the text before her, and the force of her version derives from her sense of personal involvement."

So far, in analysing the intellectual structure of the Countess' translations I have shown how in the process of discovering the religious experience expressed by the psalm, she frequently reinforces their impact by adding an insistent Calvinist stress. With many psalms, her reading of Calvin's and Beza's commentaries, and of the text and glosses of the Geneva version suggested to her certain possible points of emphasis or development. But there is another group of psalms in which something different is happening. Indeed, in both the Countess' and in some of her brother's there is evidence of the other pole of the tension I perceive in the Sidneian spirit as a whole. In what Louis L. Martz [in *The Poetry of Meditation,* 1954] has called the Sidneys' "attempt to bring the art of the Elizabethan lyric into the service of the psalmody," they imported not only the rhetorical vigour and flexibility of the court lyric, but also some of the sophisticated courtly philosophy that the secular lyric served to express. The Countess' expansion of Psalm 104.19, "He appointed the moone for certeine seasons: the sunne knoweth his going downe" (Geneva) is an obvious example on a superficial level of the way the lyrical riches of the golden Elizabethan lyric are being brought into her verse:

> Thou makest the Moone, the Empresse of the
>   night,
> Hold constant course with most unconstant
>   face:
> Thou makest the sunne the Chariot-man of
>   light,
> Well knowe the start and stop of dayly race.

The elaboration comes straight from the conventional figures of the Elizabethan lyric. The tone is serene, rich, and elaborate—an appropriate and convincing expansion of the original. But there are more profound and revealing examples. The opening of 81 is a case in point. The Geneva translation reads:

> 1 Sing joyfully unto God our strength: sing loude
> unto the God of Jaakob.
>
> 2 Take the song and bring forthe the timbrel, the
> pleasant harpe with the viole.

The Geneva marginal gloss to the psalm describes it as a psalm for "solēne feaste and assemblies of the people, to whome for a time these ceremonies were ordeined, but now under the Gospel are abolished." The same firm distrust of frivolity and ceremony is found in Calvin's and Beza's commentaries. God, says Calvin, is not to be "worshipped . . . with idlenesse," and Beza emphasizes that godly celebration must be "voyde of all wantonesse, so that your joy may tend to the glory of God." In the Countess of Pembroke's version however, a joyful, musical, even frivolous, note is sounded:

> All gladness, gladdest hartes can hold,
> In meriest notes that mirth can yeld . . .
> Muster hither musicks joyes,
> Lute, and lyre, and tabretts noise:
> Lett noe instrument be wanting,
> Chasing grief, and pleasure planting.

The emphasis is on wholehearted celebration, a rich assemblage of music, colour and spectacle—again, the Countess meditates on the poetical level of the psalm, and the poem takes on an independent life beyond the stern boundaries of Reformed piety. Courtliness has triumphed over Calvinism.

The Countess' delight in ornamentation is also illustrated by an interesting elaboration of Psalm 45.13-14:

> This Queene that can a King her father call,
> Doth only shee in upper garment shine?
> Naie under clothes, and what she weareth all,
> Golde is the stuffe the fasshion Arte divine.

The translation is alive with the swirl of robes, the celebration of what might well pass for a courtly marriage ceremony of a costly bedecked Elizabeth lady and an ideal *uomo universale* of the Renaissance:

> Fairer art thou than sonnes of mortal race:
> Because high God hath blessed thee for ay,
> Thie lipps, as springs, doe flowe with speaking
>   grace.

The Psalm was a crucial one for the Reformation understanding of the nature of the Messianic King. It praises Solomon and then turns to admonish his bride on her place and duties. But as Calvin put it "under this image, the majestie, welthiness, and far spredding abroade of Christes kingdom are adorned with their tytles." In tone the original psalm can be unambiguously read as a celebration of the nobility and even the divine potential of man. It is instructive to note that on this point it caused Calvinist commentators some difficulty. Beza asserts that the "whole Psalme is altogether allegoricall," and devotes five earnest pages to unravelling its significance for the duties and rights of kings. Calvin is worried about the misapplication of such costly finery to church decoration and the sober service of God. He glosses it, predictably enough, as an allegory of the church—a reading which is not denied by Mary Sidney's translation but which is, certainly on the most direct level, startlingly at odds with the tone of sensual celebration. Rather than being bogged down by doctrinal constraints, she has gone back to the original, and in her expansion, greatly added to the force of her version.

Where this courtly strain is most evident and most at odds with Calvinism is in Sidney's version of Psalm 8, especially vv. 4-6, verses which the Countess significantly left strictly alone in her detailed revision of her brother's work, thus stressing her acceptance of its clear philosophical implications:

>   Ah, what is this man
> Whom that greate God remember can?
> And what the race, of him descended,
> It should be ought of God attended?
>
> For thou in lesse than Angells state
> Thou planted hast this earthly mate;
> Yet hast thou made ev'n hym an owner
> Of glorious crown, and crowning honor.

Predictably, this apparent paean of man also gave Reformed commentators some trouble. Beza describes the psalm as a thanksgiving to God for man's creation in Adam and redemption in Christ, and stresses that the Psalm underlines that "man by his owne fault did fall" from his first high dignity. But the Psalm, on a very plausible reading, speaks of more than man's fallen state. Psalm 144.3, verbally similar in some respects, certainly lends itself to such a reading, and both the Geneva gloss and the Calvinist commentators make much of its unambiguous assertion of man's depravity. But Psalm 8 is another matter. It is actually quoted by Pico della Mirandola near the beginning of his famous *Oration on the Dignity of Man,* not as Calvinists saw it as proof of man's prelapsarian state, but as a tribute to man's manifest excellence. It thus becomes the starting point for his glorification of man's infinite powers of self-transformation. From Calvin to Pico almost encompasses the whole spectrum of Renaissance thought on the nature of man, and the stress on man's autonomy which underlies Pico's *Oration* or is found in

Bruno's celebration of man as magus, is both faithful to the tone of the Psalm in question—and antipathetic to the Calvinist doctrine of man's depravity. Hence Calvinist commentators have a great deal of difficulty with the Psalm. The Geneva gloss on Psalm 8 v.4 is unconvincingly in line with that on Psalm 144 v.3, that God had no need to come "so low as to man, which is but dust." It is especially uneasy on the Psalm's stress on the "crowning" of man which is glossed as only "touching his first creation." Calvin is in even more difficulties. First of all, he disapproves of the Psalm's rhetorical extravagance—God, he comments on Psalm 8.3, has no great need of great rhetoricians, but merely of distinct speech. He then argues that the Psalm stresses the miseries of man, "this miserable and vyle creature" and comments "it is a woonder that the creator of Heaven . . . submitteth himselfe so lowe, as to vowtsafe too take uppon him the care of mankind." Such a conjunction of divine grace and what Calvin sees as the depravity of man evidently worries him—he describes it tellingly, once again, as "this matching of contraries." The affinities between Calvin and the Renaissance neo-Platonists perceived some years ago by Professor Roy W. Battenhouse [in "The Doctrine of Man in Calvin and in Renaissance Platonism," *Journal of the History of Ideas* IX (1948)] is not evident here, where Calvin sees a neo-Pelagian misinterpretation of the Psalm as a distinct possibility.

The Sidneys' version, certainly, has the appropriate wonder that man, a fallen creature, should be thus elevated by God, but at the same time there is an almost hellenistic note of glorification that obviously reflects the sophisticated courtliness of the Elizabethan aristocrat. They turn the Psalmist's wonderment at man's privilege into a celebration of his possibilities, "attended" by God, an "owner" of regal status and "crowning honour." There is no sense of imputed glory, no acknowledgement of man's fallen nature. Man emerges, by implication, as a free and wondrous being, as capable on his own level of existence as his creator of "freely raunging within the Zodiack of his owne wit." Courtly philosophy here is neatly combined with the celebration of man's creative autonomy to balance the Calvinist view of man as a sinful and limited being. Uniquely, the contraries coexist. (pp. 207-25)

> *G. F. Waller, in his* Mary Sidney, Countess of Pembroke: A Critical Study of Her Writings and Literary Milieu, *Universität Salzburg, 1979, 296 p.*

Beth Wynne Fisken   (essay date 1985)

[*In the following essay, Fisken studies the development of Sidney's poetic voice, suggesting that she taught herself to write poetry through her revisions of Philip's unfinished psalms.*]

Mary Sidney's verse translations of the Psalms began as an education in how to write poetry and ended in a search for wisdom. Through close work with her brother Philip's translations as well as painstaking revision of her own efforts, she slowly gained the confidence to develop an individual style which stressed the immediacy of God's power

and presence and dramatized the quandary of the psalmist seeking God's grace in adversity. Eventually Sidney's growing confidence in her work encouraged her to develop original patterns of imagery, reflecting her public experiences as lady-in-waiting at court and manager of her husband's estate as well as her individual perceptions as a woman and a mother. In doing so, she transformed her verse translations into independent poems and exercises in private meditation, teaching herself not only how to write poetry, but ultimately, how to speak to God.

Mary Sidney's process of composition revealed her dedication to the classical ideal of the education of a poet. As Gary Waller has demonstrated in his study of the extant manuscripts of her psalms [*Mary Sidney, Countess of Pembroke: A Critical Study of Her Writings and Literary Milieu,* 1979], she began by revising her brother Philip Sidney's versions of Psalms 1 to 43, and then undertook the rest of the psalms, working between two copy-texts and constantly reworking and revising, at times arriving at varying independent versions of the same psalm. This process of composition, begun sometime after her brother's death in 1586, continued steadily until 1599, when the presentation copy was readied for a projected visit from Queen Elizabeth. Mary Sidney learned first from imitating a master, her brother, and then through perseverance and laborious revision, she discovered her own style. Certainly the dazzling variety of stanzaic forms and metrical patterns she experimented with constituted a course in the discipline of suiting sound to sense that led to a technical mastery of poetic forms.

The Sidneian psalms, with their inventive structure and extended imagery, were a significant departure from the unadorned literalism which was found in, for example, the prose paraphrases of the Book of Common Prayer and the Geneva Bible, or in the simple metrical psalms in common measure of the Sternhold-Hopkins psalter, a literalism which was deemed necessary for the congregational use of psalms as communal expressions of Christian devotion. Rather, the Sidneian psalms addressed a parallel tradition of reading and reciting the psalms in solitary, meditative sessions, examining the relationship between the individual spirit and God. Certainly, Mary Sidney's choice of the Psalms as the basis for her poetic endeavors reflects her intense commitment to this introspective Protestant tradition which stressed the role of the psalms as meditative paradigms; yet perhaps it also reveals a shrewd understanding on her part that religious translations were a sanctioned form of intellectual exercise for noblewomen of her time, Queen Elizabeth herself having tried her hand at them. Writing without models of serious, committed women poets for her to emulate, Mary Sidney erected her version of the Psalms on the foundations of her brother's work, plumb with the religious practices and social conventions of her time. Thus, by doubly buttressing her work, she was gradually able to build sufficient self-confidence to develop a poetic voice that would fully express the richness of her interior spiritual life.

Although Mary Sidney's poetic efforts were nourished in the security of the socially accepted forms of her time which sanctioned modest displays of scholarly attainment when subordinated to pious endeavors, she soon surpassed the conventional boundaries of mere ladylike accomplishment. Her scholarship was thorough; she consulted many available sources such as the Prayer Book Psalter to Coverdale's Great Bible of 1539, the Geneva Bible of 1560, the Bishops' Bible of 1568, and the Marot-Bèze psalter of 1562, as well as Golding's translation of Calvin's commentaries and Gilby's version of de Bèze. Mary Sidney was a learned and sensitive exegete, seeking to dramatize the predicament of the psalmist and through her reconstruction of the psalmist's voice to establish her own relationship to the spiritual issues of her time, defining her views by selecting or rejecting the glosses offered by others and then adding comparisons and elaborations unique to her. In these verse translations she discarded the literalism of her previous translations of Garnier's *Antonie* and Mornay's *Discours* in favor of a mixture of translation and interpretation which allowed for additions based on personal reflection and experience. This freer translation made her psalms exercises in the classical mode of imitation, in which Sidney strove to reconstruct the style and matter of the original within a context that would carry weight and meaning, first for her contemporary society, and ultimately, for herself as an individual. As such, her psalms are grounded in the Protestant tradition which stressed the application of the Scriptures to the situation of the individual. The psalms were interpreted simultaneously as the "emotional history of all the faithful, and . . . the particular spiritual autobiography of every particular Christian." Hence, by reworking them, Mary Sidney sought to become [in the words of Barbara K. Lewalski in her *Protestant Poetics and the Seventeenth-Century Religious Lyric,* 1979] a "correlative type," a new David forging "a new work in the same spirit, under the impress of the same emotions." Yet, for her, it was equally important that the meaning of the originals be adhered to faithfully, because to do otherwise would be to set one's own work above that of God—the very antithesis of wisdom. To personalize the meaning of the Psalms without distorting it was a delicate and demanding task, requiring both judgment and sensitivity to tone and connotation.

The Psalms were a particularly appropriate choice for models in poetic composition, as Philip Sidney himself urged in his *Defence of Poesie.* The best English scholars of that time recognized that the Hebrew originals were themselves remarkable poems, and they deplored the lack of an English hymnal the equal of the French Marot-Bèze psalter at reconstructing the beauty of the originals. The complex voice of the psalmist, David's "often and free chaunging of persons," as Philip Sidney described it in his *Defence,* contributed to the immediacy and intensity of the psalms as dramatizations of the conflicts of the spirit wrestling with itself in search of God. Consequently, the Psalms were thought to be a Bible in miniature, a searching "Anatomy of all the partes of the Soule," revealing "all the greefes, sorowes, feares, doutes, hopes, cares, anguishes, and finally all the trubblesome motions wherewith mennes mindes are woont to be turmoyled." Therefore, the psalmist's voice subsumes all our individual voices and private concerns, and as a result, the voice of the translator becomes our voice and "translates" our hopes and desires into his or her expression of David's petitions and

prayers. Not only was Mary Sidney as translator of the Psalms encouraged by her material to speak in many voices, but also to speak in her own voice when her voice was congruent with the meaning of the text. The translator, as well as the reader in private meditation, is continually urged to apply the psalms to his or her own situation for the full revelation of their meaning. Not only did her material challenge Sidney to stretch her poetic repertoire to dramatize the psalmist's many personations, but also it ultimately threw her back on herself, to develop the confidence to find a poetic equivalent for her own small, personal voice, "my self, my seely self in me."

By examining some of the revisions Mary Sidney made when reworking and condensing the final stanzas of seven of her brother's psalms, we can see how specific exercises in versification led to the eventual development of a style independent of her brother's influence, reflecting her own ideas, tastes, and experiences. By setting herself the task of condensing and tightening her brother's stanzas, Mary Sidney taught herself how to sharpen an image by eliminating superfluous expressions and how to dramatize rather than explain. For example, at the end of Psalm 26, she changed "That hand whose strength should help of bribes is full" to "With right hands stain'd with gifts," permitting us to supply the moral connotations of "right hands." She chose to emphasize the force of the speaker's righteousness reflected in his carriage, his physical pride in standing erect and walking a straight path, in her revision of

> But in integrity
> My stepps shall guided be,
> Then me redeem Lord then be mercifull,
> Even truth that for me sayes
> My foot on justice stayes,
> And tongue is prest to publish out thy prayse,

to:

> But while I walk in my unspotted waies,
> Redeeme and show mee grace,
> So I in publique place,
> Sett on plaine ground, will thee Jehovah praise.

Everyday routine is luminous with signs of grace if we only know how to see them. Mary Sidney's emphasis on action rather than abstraction, her speaker's foot "sett on plaine ground" rather than "on justice stayes," make the present material sphere seem laden with spiritual significance without the need for extrapolation.

This commitment to the palpable and perceptible objects and events of the daily routine defines the essence of the meditative self "that speaks constantly in the presence of the supernatural, that feels the hand of the supernatural upon himself and upon all created things." There is urgent drama in every hour of the day, as the human spirit struggles to sustain its belief in God's grace; and it was the desolation of the soul, cut off from God and crying for a sign of forgiveness, that most engaged Mary Sidney as a writer.

In fact, throughout her *Psalmes,* Mary Sidney tended to view affirmations of grace as precious gifts—awarded only after intense grappling and soul searching—which are in imminent danger of loss because of the incapacity to sustain faith through testing and ordeal. It is the intimate relationship between the supplicant spirit and God which is the focus of her psalms and which is italicized by her style. God as portrayed by her psalmist's prophetic voice is familiar and plainspoken, often brusque and impatient with human foibles:

> Bragg not you braggardes, you your saucy horne
> Lift not, lewd mates: no more with heav'ns
>   scorne
> Daunce on in wordes your old repyning mea-
>   sure.
>
> (Ps. 75, ll. 10-12)

Yet, Mary Sidney's God is ever-present at the psalmist's elbow, available to comfort as well as to discipline, and in the following memorable passage from Psalm 50, both voices are counterpointed:

> Invoke my name, to me erect thy cries,
> Thy praying plaints, when sorow stopps thy
>   waie,
> I will undoe the knott that anguish tyes,
> And thou at peace shalt glorifie my name:
> Mildly the good, God schooleth in this wise,
> But this sharpe check doth to the godlesse
>   frame:
>
> How fitts it thee my statutes to report?
> And of my covenant in thy talk to prate
> Hating to live in right reformed sort,
> And leaving in neglect what I relate?

In this dramatic monologue Sidney transformed the spare assurance of the original—"And call upon me in the time of trouble: so will I hear thee, and thou shalt praise me"—into an active, sympathetic engagement with the tortured spirit of the petitioner: "I will undoe the knott that anguish tyes." The God imaged in these psalms penetrates the recesses of our souls and speaks to us in our own language to make us understand His will.

Mary Sidney not only personalized and dramatized the psalmist's relationship with God but also the internal conflicts of her speaker and, by extension, of all of us. She favored a complicated, conversational syntax studded with questions, exclamations, interruptions, and parenthetical interjections to dramatize her speaker's fits and starts of anxiety, despair, and renewed hope. At times this syntax underlines the speaker's bitterness when estranged from God and His healing grace:

> Shall buried mouthes thy mercies tell?
> Dust and decay
> Thy truth display?
> And shall thy workes of mark
> Shine in the dreadful dark?
> Thy Justice where oblivions dwell?
>
> (Ps. 88, ll. 50-54)

These headlong, tumbling questions measure the psalmist's loss of self-possession, the extent to which he is obsessed with his own suffering and self-importance, unable to wait for or even hear an answer to his complaints. At other times the speaker realizes that he has lost control and chastises himself for presumption: "What speake I? O lett me heare / What he speakes for speake he will." Often the speaker's exclamations underscore the intensity of his pleas for pardon and renewed favor: "Ah! cast me not from thee: take not againe / Thy breathing grace! againe thy comfort send me." In Psalm 62 Sidney paralleled the gradual change in her speaker's attitude from provisional to total faith in his capacity to withstand all trials, by repeating the line, "Remove I may not, move I may," with some crucial syntactical changes: "Remove? O no: not move I may."

Mary Sidney's use of vigorous, colloquial language to personalize God's voice and emphasize His nearness recreates before the reader's eye the spiritual drama of the psalmist in relation to the God who raises and crushes him. An illusion of spontaneity is sustained by her conversational syntax which depicts the conflicts of a mind "quailed in mind-combats manifold," continually revising and reassessing, despairing and then disciplining itself, channeling its frustrated energies into new petitions and assertions of faith. These techniques define Mary Sidney's style—both what she chose to preserve and stress from her sources and models and how she chose to do so.

Not only does a characteristic style emerge from examination of Mary Sidney's versions of the psalms, but it is also possible to sketch an outline of her personality, temperament, tastes, and interests, particularly in those passages in which she permitted herself greater freedom to develop or elaborate on her text, as the voice of the psalmist became distinctively her own. Psalm 45, an epithalamium on the marriage of Solomon, is one of the most striking examples of this fusion of translation with personal experience. In it, she drew on her own brief career as lady-in-waiting, during which she witnessed Elizabeth's progress to Kenilworth and the ceremonial welcome to the queen and attendant ladies at Woodstock. Despite the suggestions of Calvin and de Bèze that the lavish pomp and ceremony of this psalm should be contemplated in light of its allegorical significance as the prefiguration of Christ's union with the Church, Sidney chose to elaborate on the pageantry of the original as visual demonstration of the king's power and authority, unrolling the scene as if it were occurring before her eyes during her own time—one of the most effective ways to achieve a composition of place to dramatize and enliven her material. In her hands Psalm 45 became an exposition of the divine rights of monarchs as well as the duties that these rights entailed, and she emphasized in it a chain of prerogatives and obligations issuing from God to king to his new queen and the members of his court.

> The king is beyond other men, a reflection of
>   God on earth:
> Fairer art thou than sonnes of mortall race:
> Because high God hath blessed thee for ay,
> Thie lipps, as springs, doe flowe with speaking
>   grace.

Sidney stressed the trappings of power in Psalm 45, not just for their magnificence, but because they are resonant symbols in a ceremony revealing the links between God and monarch. The sceptre held in the right hand is an emblem or "ensigne of thie kingly might, / To righteousness is linckt with such a band, / That righteous hand still holds thie Sceptre right." Therefore, it is a constant reminder that the king must dispense justice as well as inspire awe and fear. The formulaic repetition of "righteous" and "righteousness" transforms this psalm into an invocation to God to make this ideal representation of the monarchy a reality on earth. Likewise, with her counterpoised repetition of "terror" and "mortall," emphasizing the two spheres linked in the image of the monarch, Sidney created an awesome incantation of power and majesty:

> Soe that right hande of thine shall teaching tell
> Such things to thee, as well maie terror bring,
> And terror such, as never erst befell
> To mortall mindes at sight of mortall king.

This focus on the king's terrifying power might reflect the underlying insecurity of the Sidneys' fortunes at Elizabeth's court. Mary Sidney's father was overworked as Lord President of Wales and Governor and Lord Deputy of Ireland and consistently underpaid with insufficient allowance for his public expenses. The family was often in financial difficulty, to the extent that Henry Sidney was forced to refuse a peerage as too expensive without an accompanying pension or land grant. Philip, of course, was in brief disfavor with Elizabeth for formally protesting her marriage to the Duc d'Alençon and d'Anjou, as was her brother, Robert, for marrying Barbara Gamage over the queen's objections. Lurking always in the Sidneys' minds, perhaps, was an uneasiness born out of the past complicity of the families of both Mary Sidney's husband and her mother in the abortive attempt to place Lady Jane Grey on the throne, a history that would make them doubly vulnerable to Elizabeth's whims.

When Mary Sidney describes in Psalm 45 the position of the royal women in the king's cortege, who "By honoring thee of thee doe honor hold," she gives us a brief glimpse of the dependency of these women on the monarch's good will. Similarly, in a vignette sketching the situation of the queen's maids-of-honor, who "shall on her attend / With such, to whome more favoure shall assigne / In nearer place their happie daies to spend," we are permitted a glance backstage at the politics and ambition governing the hierarchy of court life. As Mary Sidney knew, however, there could be unfortunate consequences to being a queen's favorite. Her mother's devotion in nursing Elizabeth through her bout with smallpox ruined her own appearance and health. At times, also, there was simply not enough "favoure" to go around at court, as was attested to by her mother's frequent petitions for less cramped quarters with adequate heating. In this psalm, there are no overt references to the potentially unpleasant consequences attendant on the subordinate position of these women, but certainly the repeated emphasis on the terror inspired by the monarch was rooted in the experiences of Mary Sidney and her family.

Sidney's verse paraphrase of Psalm 45 is a rich tapestry of interwoven privilege and obligation, as the rights and duties of the king, the noblewomen of the court, and the maids-of-honor are carefully outlined. It is the queen, however, whom the psalmist wishes to instruct by explaining her position, the homage due her by the court and other nations, as well as her corresponding duty to leave behind memories of her family and home to concentrate on producing an heir to guarantee the perpetuation of the hierarchy. Sidney's advice to the queen on how to main-

tain her husband's love, for example, is practical and unromantic. She should remember that:

> Soe in the king, thie king, a deere delight
> Thie beautie shall both breed, and bredd, maintaine:
> For onlie hee on thee hath lordlie right,
> Him onlie thou with awe must entertaine.

Beauty, fidelity, and the proper demeanor of awe are the queen's calling cards; appearance and subordination are all. This perspective on marriage recalls the Mary Sidney who conformed to the expectations of her family and the court by marrying, when she was but fifteen years old, Henry Herbert, the second Earl of Pembroke, a man twenty-five years her elder. Yet there is an ambiguity in these lines which suggests a more intimate link between the king and his new bride. If her beauty breeds in him a "deere delight," the syntax of these lines makes it equally possible to read them as saying that it is his delight in her that nourishes her beauty, a beauty based on internal contentment rather than external show. As such, the delight is mutual and reciprocal, and the gold in the "fasshion Arte divine" she wears under her clothes becomes a metaphor for the rare wealth and beauty of her soul.

There is, indeed, an "Arte divine" which fashions Psalm 45. The color and magnificence of the pageantry of the original psalm is captured so well that the procession seems to advance slowly before the reader; however, Mary Sidney was always careful to place the pomp and material splendor within the perspective of God's decrees, as but symbols of His righteousness and the ordination of His monarch over earth. This monarch's rule, reflective of God's justice, is nevertheless a rule over fallible humans, and as such requires a constant show of strength to instill a terror which then makes possible "justice, truth, and meekness." There is a tough-minded political pragmatism informing Sidney's elaboration of the following lines from the Book of Common Prayer: "Thy arrows are very sharp, and the people shall be subdued unto thee: even in the midst among the King's enemies." Her version of these lines gives a Machiavellian slant on how to maintain power:

> Sharpe are thie shaftes to cleave their hartes in twaine
> Whose heads do cast thy Conquestes to withstand
> Good cause to make the meaner people faine
> With willing hartes to undergoe thie hand.

Here is revealed an aristocratic contempt for the people's capacity for political judgment; if the masses are to be content, "with willing hartes" to be ruled, it can only be as a result of a grim demonstration of power. Sidney knew that the enemies of the state, when subjected to its will, always "frown in heart" although "they fawn in sight" (Ps. 66, l. 8).

Sidney's version of Psalm 45 is one of her most inspired imitations, as well as one of her most independent. Her emphasis is on the problem of power, how to reconcile God's mandate with the realities of an imperfect earth. She herself was no stranger to the difficulty of distinguishing between the use and abuse of power. As a result of her husband's poor health in the mid-1590s, Mary Sidney gradually undertook more and more responsibility for the management of his estate. For example, in a letter written August 3, 1602, to Sir Robert Cecil, she enclosed an exasperated, yet thoroughly practical assessment of the appropriate punishment suited to the different behavior of two rebellious bailiffs:

> Now for this sedisious beggerly wretche whom it pleasd yow to bring downe under my mercy & now seemes most penetent, I must confess it were no conquest to his utter ruein & yet thinke it not fitt to take his present submission to retorne him to be disposed of according to yr will, if please yow in regard of his missery to be released of his imprisonment. The other his barbarus demeanur hath bin so odious & therein so obstinate as this hand may in no reason consent to become any meane for his release till by a more thorow fealing of his fowle offence others lykewise will be better tought by his smart. . . .

The blunt self-assurance of her statement, her stern invective, reminiscent of the scornful voice of the prophet in her *Psalmes,* demonstrate a show of power essential for a woman in her position. These lines reveal an experienced pragmatism. She remains suspicious of the seeming penitence of the first prisoner, but the appearance of reform is sufficient for her purposes. Rather, it is the obstinate unregeneracy of the second prisoner that is most threatening to peace and discipline because it poses a potentially dangerous example for others.

If publicly Mary Sidney was a tough-minded pragmatist, a firm supporter of the divine right of monarchs and the aristocratic traditions of government, we must remember that privately Mary Sidney chose to live at Wilton, in retirement from the court. Certainly she knew firsthand the sordid opportunism and factionalism that defined life at court, and it would seem that she chose to withdraw from the arena, arranging her life at Wilton so she could use her hospitality and influence to attract the fine minds of her society and through them affect the literature of her age. It was not just weariness and intellectual ambition that motivated her retirement from court, however. The privacy of her life at Wilton enabled the concentrated meditation that prepares the soul for the "searching sight" of God: "Search me, my God, and prove my hart, / Examyne me, and try my thought" (Ps. 139, ll. 85-86). The discipline of private prayer and meditation, far from the distractions and intrigues of court life, schools the soul to submit itself as naturally and unself-consciously as a child to God's examination.

One facet of this private Mary Sidney shines through in her images of birth and child care. This comparison did not originate with her, of course, but Sidney invested a unique tenderness in her use of it which renders those sections of the *Psalmes* softly luminous. She never forgot the reality of the experience behind the comparison. Even in the midst of a long passage calling for the destruction of David's enemies, her tone of relentless indignation is momentarily softened by the pathos of her stillbirth comparison:

> So make them melt as the dishowsed snaile

> Or as the Embrio, whose vitall band
> Breakes er it holdes and formlesse eyes do faile
> To see the sun, though brought to lightfull land.
> (Ps. 58, ll. 22-25)

The specific details of "vitall band" and "formlesse eyes," as well as the beautifully alliterative "lightfull land" in the explorer image, were added by Sidney to heighten the tragedy of a baby brought senseless out of the womb. As the only one of three daughters to survive past childhood, and as a mother who lost her own daughter, Katherine, at the age of three, it was perhaps impossible for her to exploit such a metaphor merely as a display of wit.

Similarly, there is an authenticity in her amplification of the standard image of God as a merciful father in Psalm 103: "Yea like as a father pitieth his own children: even so is the Lord merciful unto them that fear him." The father she envisions is fond of His refractory child:

> And looke how much
> The neerly touching touch
> The father feeles towards his sonne most deare,
> Affects his hart,
> At Ev'ry froward part
> Plaid by his child:
> Soe mercifull, soe mild,
> Is he to them that beare him awfull feare.

The charming and clever polyptoton, "touching touch," has an incantatory, yearning quality, capturing the tug of parental love by conjuring the image of a father holding out his arms to a toddling child.

In Psalm 139, in one of Mary Sidney's strongest, most arresting stanzas, the development of the fetus is used as an image of the conflation of spiritual and physical growth. The theme of the psalm is God's absolute knowledge of men and women. Stanza after stanza reveals yet another layer of God's penetrating understanding until the very formation of the body in the womb is laid bare to His scrutiny:

> Thou, how my back was beam-wise laid,
> And raftring of my ribs, dost know:
> Know'st ev'ry point
> Of bone and joynt,
> How to this whole these partes did grow,
> In brave embrod'ry faire araid,
> Though wrought in shopp both dark and low.

The image of the embroidery wrought in a dark shop came from suggestions made in the commentaries of Calvin and de Bèze, but the taut, tortured extension of "back was beam-wise laid" and "raftring of my ribbs" was original to Sidney. Calvin mused upon the "inconceivable skill which appears in the formation of the human body," inspiring Sidney to reenact the stress and strain of growth. The images are ambiguous in that they suggest both the expanding pressure on the ribs and back of the mother, as well as the developing fetus. Her choice of the embroidery comparison suggests the texture of sinew and muscle, the woven skin that covers and knits "ev'ry point / of bone and joynt." The "inconceivable skill," the miraculous workings of God on earth, are described in terms of a painful distension of body and spirit, naked before God's scrutiny.

Mary Sidney's version in Psalm 51 of the psalmist's meditation on his own conception centers around the repetition of the word "cherish," chosen from Calvin's commentary. She then added a gloss from de Bèze found in *Chrestiennes Méditations* (1582) in order to capture the spiritual dilemma posed by parenthood:

> My mother, loe! when I began to be,
> Conceaving me, with me did sinne conceave:
> And as with living heate she cherisht me,
> Corruption did like cherishing receave.

Here the standard declaration of original sin voiced in the Book of Common Prayer, "Behold, I was shapen in wickedness: and in sin hath my mother conceived me," is transformed into a striking portrait of frustrated maternal energy that is not only helpless to save the child from sin, but actually generates the child's fate. The instinctive animalism of "living heate" emphasizes our sensual origins, while the alliterative connection between "conceave," "corruption," and "cherishing" underlines the irony that this physical bond between mother and child reflects the spiritual peril that is our birthright from conception.

Perhaps it was Mary Sidney's commitment to a poetry which sought to reconcile our imperfect origins with our spiritual aspirations that led her to develop a style juxtaposing a sweet lyricism celebrating the inexhaustible bounty of nature with a plain realism reminding us of our mortal roots. She gives the commonplace figure of Mother Earth some new twists:

> Earthe, greate with yong, her longing doth not
>   lose,
> The   hopfull   ploughman   hopeth   not   in
>   vayne . . .
> All things in breef, that life in life maintaine,
> From Earths old bowells fresh and yongly
>   growes.
>   (Ps. 104, ll. 43-48)

The image of the earth as an aging mother, once again pregnant, underscores the miraculous renewal of spring and suggests the potential for regeneration in all of us. In Psalm 65 she chose her words carefully to convey the exuberant vitality, as well as the barren and withered source of that new life which only God can quicken. The antithetic "buried seed" and "yelding grave" epitomize the resurrection of the land:

> Thy eie from heav'n this land beholdeth,
> Such fruitfull dewes down on it rayning,
> That, storehowse-like her lap enfoldeth
> Assured hope of plowmans gayning.
> Thy flowing streames her drought doe temper
>   so,
> That buried seed through yelding grave doth
>   grow.

This cycle of birth and death can be made explicit, as in the above example, or can be merely suggested: "Even then shall swell / His blossoms fatt and faire, / When aged rinde the stock shall beare" (Ps. 92, ll. 40-42). Here the opposition of "fatt and faire" prepares the reader for the "aged rinde" that generates the flower. Similarly, in the description of Jehovah, "By whom the rayne from cloudes to dropp assign'd / Supples the clodds of sommer-

scorched fields" (Ps. 147, ll. 25-26), the blunt force of "clodds" and the ominous threat of "scorched" attest to the glory of God who causes this dead land to be fertile, and yet serve as reminders that this soft abundance is ephemeral. The ample wisdom of these counterpoised images reflects, perhaps, Mary Sidney's hard-earned ability to come to terms with private sorrow. While writing these psalms, she was looking back on the deaths of her daughter, father, mother, and brothers Philip and Thomas, as well as working through the progressive decline of her husband's health—losses which were counterbalanced by the births of her children. By alternating sweetly alliterative language with the plain and vulgar diction of "fatt," "aged rinde," "bowells," "grave," and "clodds," Sidney played one vocabulary off the other to reveal the inseparability of life from death, natural beauty from aged and gnarled roots.

Throughout her *Psalmes* Mary Sidney contrasted the foolish pretensions of earthly endeavors with the wise paradoxes of heavenly wisdom. This theme is developed most clearly in her legal and business metaphors which were undoubtedly inspired by direct experience in managing her husband's estate. In her handling of this strain of imagery, the practical knowledge of the public woman was reinterpreted in light of the wisdom gleaned from private meditation, usually to emphasize the inadequacy of a merely legalistic point of view. Her comparisons continually remind us that this is how affairs are conducted on an imperfect earth, rather than in heaven. God's covenant with us is referred to as a "league" in which the land of Canaan is promised "in fee," yet we are reminded that the limited scope implied by such contractual arrangements cannot encompass the omnipotence and omnipresence of God:

> The daies bright guide, the nightes pale gover-
>   nesse
> Shall claime no longer lease of their enduring:
> Whome I behold as heav'nly wittnesses
> In tearmlesse turnes, my tearmlesse truth assur-
>   ing.
>   ˙(Ps. 89, ll. 93-96)

"Tearmlesse" refers to both timelessness as well as freedom from restrictive legal and financial conditions. Day and night serve not as earthly witnesses to a testament of our inevitable decay, but rather as "heav'nly wittnesses" of the eternal glory of God. A lease, of course, cannot designate "tearmlesse truth," and all our contracts and stipulations only demonstrate our foolish distrust that would make conditions with that which must be unconditional.

Mary Sidney employed a major strain of antithetical repetition throughout her translation of the Psalms which contrasts the limitations of human understanding with the infinite power and wisdom of God: "O Lord, whose grace no limits comprehend; / Sweet Lord, whose mercies stand from measure free" (Ps. 51, ll. 1-2). Human arrogance "would in boundes that boundless pow'r contain" (Ps. 78, l. 128), but God always reminds us that "speciall bonds have bound" us (Ps. 145, l. 32), that we have a clearly defined position with accompanying duties outlined in the universal plan:

All formed, framed, founded so,
Till ages uttmost date
They place retaine, they order know,
They keepe their first estate.

                    (Ps. 148, ll. 21-24)

The emphatic resonance of Sidney's alliteration and parallel syntax, as well as the legal, political, and class connotations of estate, would seem to suggest a confining rigor to God's arrangements on earth, but that is true only from the human perspective narrowed by a mind accustomed to operating in terms of leases and contracts. The best indication of God's grace is the free acceptance of His will; the faithful soul does not feel straitened but rather chooses freely to occupy the ordained place: "Who uncontrol'd / Sure league with him doe hold, / And doe his lawes not only understand" (Ps. 103, ll. 78-80). Once again legal imagery is used ironically to reveal its own limitations; the only genuine league is that which is "uncontrol'd." This pattern of imagery urges us to learn the distinctions between an earthly contract and our covenant with God. The one is null and void upon our death, at which time we lose all that we vainly sought to preserve as our own under its protection. The other is eternal and our only security against oblivion.

Throughout Mary Sidney's *Psalmes,* therefore, we find a sophisticated use of sacred paradox that attempts to illuminate the unknowable and yet maintain the integrity of God's mystery, to emphasize both the potential and the limit of human knowledge. Sidney chose her comparisons carefully to remind us that the soft abundance of our world can scorch and shrivel in a moment, that it is wrung from withered bowels, that the cherishing animal warmth of our mother's womb incubates the seeds of our sinfulness, and that our terms, contracts, and leases but reflect our powerlessness and the transitory nature of all earthly goods and arrangements. These paradoxes underline the folly of all human attachments and measure the vast distance between earth and heaven.

This distance is bridged in a handful of Mary Sidney's psalms where we find the peace and serenity, the simple, hopeful confidence of the soul in concert with the universe. These psalms are distinguished by a simple eloquence that is at once subdued and ecstatic:

Looke how the sunne, soe shall his name re-
    mayne;
As that in light, so this in glory one:
All glories that, at this all lights shall stayne:
Nor that shall faile, nor this be overthrowne.
The dwellers all
Of earthly ball
In hym shall hold them blest:
As one that is
Of perfect blisse
A patterne to the rest.

                    (Ps. 72, ll. 71-80)

The preponderance of one-syllable words joined with the lack of qualifiers ("earthly" and "perfect" are counterpoised as the only two descriptive adjectives) create an aura in which single words are able to convey absolute meaning, reflecting the oneness of the divine spirit. There is no need here for the involved syntax, the paradoxes and

wordplay that usually characterize Mary Sidney's writing. Such displays of wit are inappropriate and unnecessary in those rare moments when faith is spontaneous rather than labored. In such moments the infused state of contemplation which reveals the "single viewe of the eternall veritye" supersedes the self-conscious, analytic process of meditation, as wordplay and extended comparisons can only measure the extent to which we approximate rather than know the ways of God. In this transcendent phase, reliance on the mere "Wisdom of Words" obscures the stunning simplicity of the "Word of Wisdom."

It is Mary Sidney's commitment to "the wandering voices of the fallen world," however, which marks her greatest poetic achievement. Her best passages dramatize the dilemma of her speaker, who represents all of us, sinking in an apprehension of unworthiness, yet calling for a renewal of special favor from God. Her psalms are centered in the world as we know it; God speaks to us in our own words, but too often we do not hear and our pleas to Him are confused and troubled. The very effort we make to understand God's will marks our failure to do so, since such understanding must come simply and naturally without effort. Education can be inimical to wisdom and obscure the unitive way to special grace, blinding the restless spirit to the correspondences underlying diversity, the essential rightness of the way things are. However, Mary Sidney's dedication to her verse translations of the Psalms is a testimony to her faith in human effort in general and in our capacity for self-education in particular. During her many years working with the psalms, she taught herself both how to write poetry and how to speak to God. In fact, it is her insistence on the validity of applying to the psalms knowledge and understanding gained from study and personal experience that makes them exemplary models for private meditation. In the fusion of Mary Sidney's voice with that of the psalmist, the process of education and the purpose of wisdom coincide. Wisdom is gained neither by the suppression of individual energy and intelligence, nor by a vainglorious display of these qualities, but rather by an abiding appreciation that God's spirit works through individual talent which reflects the capacity of all humankind. (pp. 166-83)

> *Beth Wynne Fisken, "Mary Sidney's 'Psalmes': Education and Wisdom,"in* Silent But for the Word: Tudor Women as Patrons, Translators, and Writers of Religious Works, *edited by Margaret Patterson Hannay, The Kent State University Press, 1985, pp. 166-83.*

Rivkah Zim   (essay date 1987)

[*In the following essay, Zim examines Sidney's modifications of the psalms, emphasizing her ornamental style and expression of personal emotion through the psalmist's voice.*]

More than two thirds of the Sidney-Pembroke psalter is the work of the Countess of Pembroke. A. B. Grosart [in *The Complete Poems of Sir Philip Sidney,* 1873] regarded her psalm versions as 'infinitely in advance of her brother's in thought, epithet and melody', and later modern assessments of the two psalmists have tended to favour the Countess's literary achievement. However, since the sample of her work is about twice as large as his, it inevitably provides more examples of stylistic and interpretative felicities. Not enough attention has been paid to the similarities in their processes of imitating the Psalms.

In her dedicatory poem, addressed to the 'Angell spirit' of her dead brother, the Countess proclaimed her 'zealous love' which was unfolded in the 'world of words', for no 'other purpose but to honor thee'. To Sidney's psalms

> (Immortall Monuments of thy faire fame,
> though not compleat . . .
> Yet there will live thy ever praised name)

she added her own, describing them as

> theise dearest offrings of my hart
> dissolv'd to Inke . . .
> sadd Characters indeed of simple love

The Countess mingled Christian and familial pieties, since her completion of his psalter was an act of devotion not only to God but also to her brother: 'the wonder of men',

> sole borne perfection's kinde,
> Phoenix thou wert, so rare thy fairest minde
> Heav'nly adorn'd, Earth justlye might adore,
> where truthfull praise in highest glorie shin'de

(She signed herself 'the Sister of that Incomparable Sidney'.) She may also have had another, more personal interest in his project. In 1586 the Countess lost not only her brother but also her parents: her father died on 5 May, her mother on 11 August, and Philip on 17 October. The Sidneys had been a close family, they wrote affectionate letters to each other and enjoyed each other's company. In these circumstances the Countess may also have turned to the Psalms for her own spiritual guidance and solace. There is no evidence that she was actively involved with Sidney's psalms before his death, but she had completed drafts of all her psalms by 1594.

Sixteen manuscripts of the Sidney-Pembroke psalms survive. The best witness to the texts of Sidney's forty-three psalms is Samuel Woodford's incomplete but careful transcript (now Oxford, Bodleian Library, Rawlinson poet. 25) of one of the Countess's working copies. This working copy had contained thirty-seven psalms (by Sidney or his sister) which she had crossed out or marked for revision. Since all the deletions and annotations have been reproduced by Woodford, it is possible to trace the processes of the Countess's many revisions and emendations of her own psalms as well as those of her brother's. She made substantial and repeated revisions to her own psalms, and is aptly described in Ringler's often-quoted phrase as 'an inveterate tinkerer'. Comparison of the texts in Woodford's transcript with those in the Penshurst manuscript copied by John Davies of Hereford for presentation to the Queen, shows that the Countess's revisions of Sidney's work were relatively limited and tentative. Her respect for Sidney's achievement is evident not only in the pattern of her revisions of her work but also in the way she adopted his methods for her own imitations of psalms.

The Countess was not an innovator: she did not try to change her brother's conception of the work, and she used the same biblical and scholarly sources. Like Sidney, she also adapted the metres, stanza forms and rhyme schemes of the French metrical psalter. She recognized that her contribution to their psalter was 'inspired' by him and she referred to it as

> this coupled worke, by double int'rest thine:
> First rais'de by thy blest hand, and what is mine
> inspird by thee, thy secrett power imprest

The Countess's own versions do not represent any further significant development in the English metrical psalm as a literary kind. She accepted and adopted her brother's view of the Psalms as 'holy Davids . . . divine Poeme' in which the psalmist's 'heavenly poesie' could best find expression in the best contemporary English verse: 'that Lyricall kind of Songs and Sonets'. She also adopted certain features of Sidney's poetic practice in an attempt to make their psalter into a single work bearing the impression of Sidney's eloquence.

However, because of the sort of thing which Vives said was natural to mankind (*quod genus sunt homini naturalia*), like every other psalmist the Countess has her own personal eloquence and literary personality. Samuel Daniel assured her that the psalms had given 'Eternitie' 'Unto thy voyce':

> And this is that which thou maist call thine
> owne

Her perceptions and imitations of Psalms 44-150 are often remarkably individual and forceful. A characteristic strength of her poetry arises from the ways in which she ruminated on literal translations, with the help of glosses and commentaries on the Psalms, in order to build (usually extensively) on implicit themes. J. C. A. Rathmell has commented on the vitality of her interpretations, which derives from her sense of personal involvement with the procedures in the models of her imitations:

> it is her capacity to appreciate the underlying meaning that vivifies her lines . . . By recreating the Psalms as Elizabethan poems, the Countess compels us to read them afresh

Nevertheless, the quality of her work is uneven, and it often appears that her understanding of and sympathy with the psalmist's divine poem exceeded her own proficiency as a writer. While Sidney's psalms may be seen as a fulfilment of his 'unelected vocation' as a Christian poet, her psalms exemplify the self-education of a novice poet. G. F. Waller [in *The Review of English Studies* xxvi (1975)] has suggested that those most heavily revised and abandoned versions among Psalms 44-80 were practice pieces in which the Countess discovered and developed her own skills as a metrical psalmist.

The Countess's personal eloquence as a poet is characterized by her response to and handling of suggestive metaphors in her models. Like Sidney, she turned to Calvin's commentaries on the Psalms and to Beza's paraphrases for guidance on the meaning and significance of the biblical models.

Calvin's commentaries, which draw attention to the metaphorical qualities of the Hebrew poetry, provided a stimulus to her own imagination and wit. Ps. 44 marks the beginning of the Countess's section of the psalter, and illustrates some of her characteristic methods. Her treatment of verse 2 (in lines 5-8) is particularly interesting:

> Lorde, our fathers true relation
> Often made, hath made us knowe
>
> How thy hand the Pagan foe
> Rooting hence, thie folke implanting,
> Leavelesse made that braunch to grow,
> This to spring, noe verdure wanting
>   (Ps. 44, lines 1-2, 5-8)

The biblical psalmist had contrasted the position of the heathen, who (according to the Geneva Bible) were 'driven out' and 'destroyed', with that of his own fore-fathers who were 'planted in' and 'caused to growe'. The Countess's imitation extends this biblical metaphor of planting and growth under the influence of Calvin's explanation that the psalmist

> compareth the old inhabiters of the land of Canaan to trees, bicause they had taken root there by long continued possession. Therfore the sodein alteracion that happened, was like as if a man should *pluck up trees by the rootes, and plant other in their steedes*

Calvin's tree metaphor is subsumed in the Countess's image of the two branches (in lines 7 and 8) which correspond to the progeny of the 'Pagan foe' and 'thie folke'. Her meaning is made clearer by reference to Calvin once again:

> there is added another Metaphor, wherby the faithfull shew how it came to passe through the blissing of the Lord, that the chozen people multiplyed: like as in process of time a tree is the more strengthened in the place that hee hath gotten, by spredding forth farre, aswell his boughes, as his rootes

The Countess's earlier draft of this psalm made the parallel between the image of physical destruction and that of fertility more obvious:

> Our fathers Lord by hearing
> Have made us understand
>
> How rooting nations, them thy hand
> Did plant and planted nourish
> The stock prophane did leafelesse grow
> The faithfull branch did flourish

Her revised version is denser, with more varied rhythms, but lines 7 and 8 are consequently more obscure. She was over-ingenious in changing the point of contrast from the simple antithetical parallelism: 'stock prophane . . . faithfull branch' to '*that* braunch' and '*this*'. However, the revision makes a more complex rhetorical figure, and demonstrates that the dislocated syntax in the later version was deliberate.

Some of the Countess's most striking figurative language is derived from Beza's prose paraphrases in the English translation by Gilby, which had been dedicated to her aunt. Several notable passages in her version of Ps. 139

provide insights into her processes of imitation, and her literary tastes. The Geneva Bible translation of verses 7 and 8:

> Whether shal I go from thy Spirit? or whether shal I flee from thy presence?
>
> If I ascend into heaven, thou art there: If I lie downe in hel, thou art there

provided the substance and structure of the Countess's imitation.

> To shunn thy notice, leave thine ey,
> O whither might I take my way?
> To starry spheare?
> Thy throne is there.
> To dead mens undelightsome stay?
> There is thy walk, and there to ly
> Unknown, in vain I should assay
>   (Ps. 139, lines 22-8)

The Countess found scholarly precedents for her exploitation of the antithetical parallelism in lines 24 and 26, and for her figurative periphrasis (line 26), in Gilby's translation of Beza's paraphrase:

> If I shal even go up and flie up into *the verie heavens,* verelie there shal I find thee: contrariwise, if I lie downe in *the close places of the grave,* behold againe there shal I perceive thee

Like Beza, and unlike all the translators of the English Bibles, she restricted the range of her psalmist's reference to the physical universe. In the same vein she contributed the metaphors which connote God's 'presence' in anthropomorphic terms: 'Thy throne . . . thy walk'. As Coburn Freer has said [in *Music for a King: George Herbert's Style and the Metrical Psalms,* 1972] (in a different context), she is careful of observed detail and rigorously logical. Although the binary structure of each of the two biblical verses is represented in her double parallelism, 'To . . . ? To . . . ? There . . . and there . . . ', the Countess made the complete stanza her sense unit, combining the two verses into a single entity. The form and varied rhythms of her stanza are well matched with the sense; for example, 'Unknown' (line 28) completes the sense of the previous line, but receives an appropriate emphasis from its position at the beginning of the last line of the stanza.

The influence of Beza's paraphrase is particularly evident in the Countess's version of the next verse:

> Let me take the wings of the morning, & dwell in the uttermost partes of the sea
>   (Geneva Bible, Ps. 139:9)

since it supplied her with the figure of the rising and setting sun and the verbs 'lend' and 'flee'

> the sunne it selfe arising up, should lend me his most swift wings, whereby I might flee even into the farthest part of the west

Her own literary taste encouraged her to develop the witty play on 'light' and 'flight' in lines 29 and 30:

> O Sun, whome light nor flight can match,
> Suppose thy lightfull flightfull wings
> Thou lend to me

And I could flee
As farr as thee the ev'ning brings:
Ev'n ledd to West he would me catch,
Nor should I lurk with western things
(Ps. 139, lines 29-35)

In verse 15, the biblical psalmist 'expresse[s] metaphorically' what Calvin referred to as 'the inestimable woorkmanshippe whyche appeareth in the shape of mannes bodye':

My bones are not hid from thee, thogh I was made in a secret place, & facioned beneth in the earth
(Geneva Bible, Ps. 139:15)

Characteristically the Countess developed Calvin's emphasis on craftsmanship with well-visualized images of building and embroidery in her imitation.

Thou, how my back was beam-wise laid,
And raftring of my ribbs, dost know:
Know'st ev'ry point
Of bone and joynt
How to this whole these partes did grow,
In brave embrod'ry faire araid,
Though wrought in shopp both dark and low
(Ps. 139, lines 50-6)

Gilby's translation of Beza's 'compāges', 'the joining of my bones', provided the basis of the Countess's 'raftring of my ribbs', but not for the house-building metaphor which her imitation implies. Beza's simile 'as it were with needle worke' was also the basis for her embroidery metaphor depicting the physical beauty of the human body. The final detail in line 56 of the dark workshop was probably derived from Golding's translation of Calvin's commentary on this verse, which refers to a 'craftesman . . . with a peece of worke in some darke denne'.

In Ps. 141:7 the Countess developed a metaphor from Beza's paraphrase to represent the contrary sense of the worthlessness rather than the beauty, of the psalmist's frame or bones which are broken and disperst by death.

Mean while my bones the grave, the grave expects my bones,
Soe broken, hewn, disperst, as least respected stones,
By careless Mason drawn from caves of worthless quarry
(Ps. 141, lines 19-21)

(Our bones lie scattered at the graves mouth, as he that heweth wood or diggeth in the earth)
(Geneva Bible, Ps. 141:7)

Here too the Countess responded to the biblical simile by emphasizing the physical action which dominates the sense of Beza's paraphrase:

In the meane season, we do lie not onlie as dead men: but also even as the hewers of stone do cut here and there the peeces of stones, so are we scattered, and our bones cast to and fro, at the mouth of the grave

The carelessness of the mason was suggested by 'here and there' and 'to and fro' in Gilby's translation of Beza. But she has personalized and dramatized the situation on her own initiative both by using a singular pronoun and by personifying the grave through the effect of zeugma in line 19

. . . my bones the grave, the grave expects my bones

The additional figures of chiasmus and epizeuxis (or 'the coocko spel') in this line also demonstrate her taste for those rhetorical ornaments which were considered poetical.

The Countess, like her brother, always restricted the most inventive features of her imitations to the detail of her interpretative paraphrase, and used the resources for imagery which she found in her scholarly sources in order to make the truth 'more palpable'. She then developed these resources according to her own capacities to comprehend, evaluate and regenerate David's 'heavenly poesie' as late Elizabethan poetry. She was most successful when she was able to develop images which were already explicit or implicit in the biblical verses and the commentaries.

In this respect her imitation of Ps. 73:6-7 may be contrasted with Surrey's more inventive methods. The Countess's practice was to extend rather than expound the biblical similes

Therefore with pride, as with a gorgious chaine
Their swelling necks encompassed they beare;
All cloth'd in wrong, as if a robe it were:
So fatt become, that fattness doth constraine
Their eies to swell
(Ps. 73, lines 16-20)

(Therefore pride is a chaine unto them & crueltie covereth them as a garment. Their eyes stand out for fatnes)
(Geneva Bible, Ps. 73:6-7)

The Countess's inventive detail in line 17 of the 'swelling necks encompassed' elaborates on Beza's interpretation:

they . . . testifie with how great pride and fiercenes their heart swelleth, by the verie apparel of their bodie adorned with chaines, with gold, and pretious stones

Her imitation generates a vivid impression of bloated self-importance and self-indulgence; the laboured rhythm of line 17 enhances the associations of the visual image, all the essential features of which were inherent in her usual sources: Calvin had commented

fatnes maketh folkes eyes to swell outward . . .
David . . . Metaphorically expresseth the pryde, wherewith the ungodly be puffed up by reason of too much fulnes

By contrast, Surrey's imitation of verse 7 had expounded the biblical simile and transformed it into a vehicle for his sharp criticism of the misuse of power by those

Whose glutten cheks slouth feds so fatt as scant their eyes be sene.
Unto whose crewell power most men for dred ar fayne
To bend and bow with loftye looks, whiles they vawnt in their rayne

And in their bloody hands, whose creweltye
  doth frame
The wailfull works that skourge the poore with
  out regard of blame

(Ps. 73, lines 14-18)

As with Surrey's sonnet 'Th' Assyryans king . . . ' it 'is tempting, but not necessary, to see in this poem a covert allusion to Henry VIII'. However just as the interpretations of Calvin and Beza informed the Countess's imitation so the paraphrase by Campensis had provided the stimulus to Surrey's imagination:

Every man that meteth them, is afrayde of them
by reason of theyr power, whych is waxen so
greate, that they gyve no force whether theyr
wyckednesse and vyolence (wherby they op-
presse the poore) be knowne or no

Thus the differences between the versions by the Countess and by Surrey reflect not merely differences of intention and personal eloquence but also the nature of the different scholarly sources which informed their understanding and interpretation of the biblical models.

The weaknesses of the Countess's psalms like her strengths often arise from her characteristic literary tastes and powers of expression. She has a tendency to overdo the surface detail of rhetorical ornamentation, and to lose control of the larger imaginative infrastructure of her own

Sidney's translation of Psalm 117.

psalm imitations. The application of her usually good attention to detail is occasionally too localized. Coverdale had translated Ps. 73:16,

Then thought I to understande this, but it was
  to harde for me

Surrey's psalmist explains his dilemma in terms of intellectual failure to penetrate divine mysteries:

And as I sought wherof thy sufferaunce, Lord,
  shold groo,
I found no witt cold perce so farr, thy holly
  domes to knoo,
And that no mysteryes nor dought could be distrust

(Ps. 73, lines 35-7)

The Countess independently generated images with visual qualities and implying physical action:

So then I turn'd my thoughtes another way:
Sounding, if I, this secrets depth might find;
But combrous cloudes my inward sight did
  blynd

(Ps. 73, lines 46-8)

The visual image is apt, given the traditional reference to intellectual perception as 'inward sight', but in the larger context of the psalm verse, the associations of her mixed metaphors lead to incongruity: while sounding the depths (sea, understood) the psalmist was blinded by 'combrous cloudes' (sky, understood). (Gilby had translated Beza's paraphrase ' . . . howbeit, I could not rid my selfe of these most troublesome cogitations'.) In Ps. 88:1, the biblical psalmist had cried day and night before God; the Countess dissipated this sense of intense continuous action by periphrasis,

Both when the sunn the day
The treasures doth display
And night locks up his golden wealth

(Ps. 88, lines 4-6)

Such a poetical device of ornamentation is contrary to the mood of the poem. The 'treasures' and 'golden wealth' represent the sunlit universe of the God of creation, and are out of place. They import irrelevant associations thereby changing the tone of the psalmist's voice from lament to praise at the point where the tone of penitential lament needs to be firmly established.

The Countess often reveals her inexperience as a writer by improvising her own metaphorical details, rather than developing those she found in her usual sources. She was more dependent on Calvin and Beza than Sidney appears to have been, and she was more elaborate and copious in her treatment of borrowings from these commentators. Sidney had used these same sources but had also observed more carefully the terse quality of the biblical psalmists' styles. The differences between his uses of the sources and hers arise from differences in taste and from the disparity between their practical experience as writers.

Coburn Freer has commented that the Countess's rhythms are not as subtle and varied as her brother's, and that the variety of metrical forms in her psalms appears to have been chosen more arbitrarily. The brief example from Ps. 139 demonstrates that she could vary her rhythms with interest and subtlety. In her imitation of Ps. 100 (*Jubilate deo*) the Countess matched form and content very deliberately: she represented this psalm's lyric mode of praise and prayer by exploiting a form more traditionally associated with a secular convention for praise and devotion: the sonnet.

> 1 O all you landes, the treasures of your joy
> In mery shout upon the Lord bestow:
> Your service cheerfully on him imploy,
> With triumph song into his presence goe.
> 2 Know first that he is God; and after know
> This God did us, not we our selves create:
> We are his flock, for us his feedings grow:
> We are his folk, and he upholds our state.
> 3 With thankfullnesse O enter then his gate:
> Make through each porch of his your praises
>   ring,
> All good, all grace, of his high name relate,
> 4 He of all grace and goodnesse is the spring.
> Tyme in noe termes his mercy comprehends,
> From age to age his truth it self extends
>
> (Ps. 100)

There is a close correspondence between the structure of the biblical psalm (which in the Bishops' Bible is divided into four verses) and the argument of the Countess's sonnet. She rejected the opportunity to make the opening phrases of her first two quatrains parallel each other in the manner of several of Sidney's secular sonnets, or of some of the biblical translations of this psalm. Her final couplet lends an apt weightiness to the concluding *sententia,* and the last word—'extends'—is a triumphant summary of the psalmist's teaching: mercy and truth stretch into eternity.

There is often a wistful quality to the Countess's imitations of those psalm verses which depict the emotional states of the speaker—a quality which distinguishes her work from both Surrey's and Sidney's. In Ps. 73 the biblical psalmist is troubled because the wicked prosper, and God, who is truly 'lovynge unto Israel', apparently allows the wicked to oppress the righteous.

> Lo, these are the ungodly, these prospere in the
> worlde, and these have ryches in possession
> (Great Bible, Ps. 73:12)

Surrey had paraphrased this verse

> In terrour of the just thus raignes iniquitye,
> Armed with power, laden with gold, and dred
>   for crueltye
>
> (Ps. 73, lines 27-8)

While Surrey's psalmist sees prosperity and riches as adjuncts of a power maintained by fear, the Countess's psalmist relates this prosperity to a state of personal happiness:

> See here the godlesse Crue, while godly wee
> Unhappy pine, all happiness possesse:
> Their riches more, our wealth still growing lesse
> (Ps. 73, lines 34-6)

Her rhetorical manipulation of syntax has introduced an implied relationship between the godly and the godless, like that between the two pans of a balance for weighing gold: so as the riches of the 'godlesse Crue' increase, the

'wealth' of the godly grows less. Whereas Surrey had realized the physical properties of weight and colour in his image of iniquity 'laden with gold', the Countess made 'riches' into a metaphor for a psychological state, and thereby offered a new reading of the psalm verse.

All the English Bibles translate the final clause of Ps. 88 as a statement that, either God hid the psalmist's friends from him, or else the friends hid themselves. The Countess's imitation of this verse softens the resentful tone of the biblical psalmist by emphasizing the distance, rather than the cause of the separation:

> Who erst to me were neare and deare
> Far now, O farr
> Disjoyned ar:
> And when I would them see,
> Who my acquaintance be,
> As darknesse they to me appeare
> (Ps. 88, lines 73-8)

> (Thou hast removed al my friends and companions farre from me, that I see nothing aniewhere, but meere darknes)
>
> (Beza, tr. Gilby)

Beza supplied the two distinctive elements of her imitation: the references to distance and darkness. However, whereas Beza had focussed on the situation of the psalmist, the main subject of the Countess's stanza is the psalmist's lost nearest and dearest. This emphasis gives her imitation a wistful quality as the psalmist reflects on the friends, 'Far now, O farr', and on the nature of their relationship; the final impression is of personal loss and fading memories. The mood she has successfully evoked is a reflexion of her personal eloquence.

As she developed the potential of the figurative language in the Psalms, the Countess did not scruple to borrow imagery associated with a pagan, classical tradition. This had not been Sidney's practice in his psalms. In her imitation of Ps. 73:10 the Countess conspicuously substituted the classical metaphor of the cornucopia for the biblical metaphor of a cup running over:

> Their horne of plenty freshly flowing still
> (Ps. 73, line 29)

> (waters of a ful cup are wrung out to them)
> (Geneva Bible, Ps. 73:10)

Similarly, at the end of her version of Ps. 55 she introduced a metaphor of death (but not specifically of the Fates), shearing the half-spun thread of man's life:

> their life-holding threed so weakly twin'd
> That it, half-spunne, death may in sunder sheare
> (Ps. 55, lines 71-2)

The usual biblical figure of speech for a man's life is the number of his days, thus all the contemporary English Bibles translate this verse '. . . shall not lyve out halfe their dayes' (Great Bible, Ps. 55:23). Although Sidney's psalms do not employ such classical imagery, these two *topoi* are so commonplace in literature that there was no breach of decorum in the Countess's application of them here; their general 'literary' quality is matched by such phrases as 'Zephyrs nest' (Ps. 67, line 30) and 'sweete Auroras raine'

(Ps. 110, line 16). By utilizing such figures the Countess helped to revitalize biblical poetics according to a tradition by which Orpheus was seen as a figure for David and Urania had become a Christian muse.

The Countess imitated her brother's secular poetry as well as his imitations of David's 'heavenly poesie'. She began her version of Ps. 73 by incorporating an allusion to the fifth *Astrophil and Stella* sonnet.

> It is most true that God to Israell
> I meane to men of undefiled hartes
> Is only good, and nought but good impartes.
> Most true, I see, allbe allmost I fell
> From right conceit into a crooked mynd;
> And from this truth with straying stepps de-
> clin'd
> (Ps. 73, lines 1-6)

> It is most true, that eyes are form'd to serve
> The inward light . . .
> It is most true . . .
> True, and yet true
> (*Astrophil and Stella* 5, lines 1-2, 5, 14)

This is sacred parody. The biblical psalmist's assertion of truth and the qualification 'Neverthelesse', must have helped to put Sidney's sonnet into the Countess's mind:

> (Truly God is lovynge unto Israel: even unto soch as are of a cleane hert? Neverthelesse my fete were almost gone, my treadynges had well nye slypte)
> (Great Bible, Ps. 73:1-2)

There are implicit thematic links here between Astrophil's notion of 'inward light' (reason or understanding) and the emphasis of the Countess's psalmist on 'undefiled hartes' which think 'right conceit[s]'. Similarly, there are links between on the one hand, the psalmist's praise of God's goodness and his fear of error or physical slipping, and on the other hand, Astrophil's rational, moral argument and his own failure to sustain it ('True, and yet true that I must Stella love', line 14).

In her imitation of Ps. 51:6,

> My trewand soule in thy hid schoole hath
> learned
> (Ps. 51, line 21)

> (therefore hast thou taught me wisdome in the secret of mine heart)
> (Geneva Bible, Ps. 51:6)

the Countess has developed Calvin's reference to 'a froward scholer' from Golding's translation. But in doing so she seems to have recollected the penultimate line of *Astrophil and Stella* I, in which Astrophil—the novice poet—having studied 'inventions fine', bites

> My trewand pen

and is told by his muse 'looke in thy heart and write'. The Countess too was a novice poet when she began her psalm imitations. In her version of Ps. 73:25 the psalmist asks,

> O what is he will teach me clyme the skyes?
> (Ps. 73, line 73)

For the reader who recognizes her allusion to the opening line of *Astrophil and Stella* 31,

> With how sad steps, ô Moone, thou climb'st the
> skies

the implication must be that Sidney was her teacher in the art of poesie of 'that Lyricall kind'. Such allusion was probably deliberate; it is partly an indication of the Countess's regard for her brother as a poet. It is also, more importantly, part of her effort to give their 'coupled worke'— the whole psalter—the character or 'marke' of Sidney's 'sweet sprite':

> So dar'd my Muse with thine it selfe combine,
> as mortall stuffe with that which is divine

The Countess saw her brother as having established the canons of a poetic suited to the most cultivated Protestant sensibilities in late Elizabethan England. Sidney had defended poetry against the abuse of hostile critics: by arguing in *The Defence* that 'the end & working of [poetry] . . . being rightly applied, deserveth not to be scourged out of the Church of God'; and by setting a standard for the 'right' application of poetry in his forty-three psalms. John Donne, who lamented that the Psalms were 'So well attyr'd abroad, so ill at home' in those holy songs used in Church, celebrated the 'Sydnean Psalmes' by 'this Moses and this Miriam' for the way in which they 're-reveal[d]', 'In formes of joy and art', those songs 'which heavens high holy Muse' had 'Whisper'd to David'. When she addressed her brother's 'Angell spirit', the Countess expressed her belief that

> all of tongues with soule and voice admire
> Theise sacred Hymns . . .
> thy works so worthilie embrac't
> By all of worth

The example of Sidney's 'divine' Muse provided, she thought, 'lightning beames' which gave 'lustre' to her own psalms. She completed his psalter by combining her own 'mortall stuffe with that which is divine', and by producing a full repertoire of psalms in a heavenly poesie for the most cultivated of Christian souls in devotion. Her 'mortall stuffe'—her concentration on poetic detail in the elaboration of metaphor, and the introduction of images based on *topoi* familiar to the cultivated reader—is part of her higher purpose in developing Sidney's poetic ideal. The nature of her achievement cannot be appreciated in isolation from the literary ambitions and achievements of her brother, and from the whole tradition of English psalm versions. In combining her Muse with Sidney's and completing the psalter as his memorial, she helped to set the seal on her contemporaries' expectations of psalms as the best kind of lyrical poetry. Thereafter, the English archetype of devotional poetry was the Sidneys' idea of a psalm. (pp. 185-202)

Rivkah Zim, " 'A Heavenly Poesie . . . of That Lyricall Kind': Part Two—The Countess of Pembroke," in her English Metrical Psalms: Poetry as Praise and Prayer, 1535-1601, *Cambridge University Press, 1987, pp. 185-202.*

Elaine V. Beilin   (essay date 1987)

[*In the following excerpt, Beilin traces Sidney's evolution as a lyric poet through an examination of her original poems and studies the psalms in relation to her other works.*]

As the first woman in [the Renaissance] period who sought a clear literary vocation and who, as a poet, far surpassed any of her predecessors, Mary Sidney, Countess of Pembroke, presents a turning point in the development of the woman writer. While her piety and her commitment to the Reformed cause ally her closely to figures like Katherine Parr or Anne Dowriche, her devotion to poetry and her studied development as a literary artist distinguish her from her precursors and contemporaries. And while the didactic spirit of writers like Whitney and Dowriche brought them apologetically into the domain of public poetry, with each succeeding work, Mary Sidney addressed an ever-widening circle of readers, beginning with private translations, proceeding to an elegy for her brother, Philip Sidney, and concluding with her translation of the Psalms, a text intended narrowly for the devotions of court and queen, and more broadly for the comfort of all the godly. Yet, despite her considerable growth as a poet and despite her widened audience, these "good works" still characterize the Countess of Pembroke as a learned and virtuous woman writer aware of her limitations.

Mary Sidney's most significant achievement was her evolution as a lyric poet. Either because the education of most women did not encourage imitation and composition of lyric poetry or because their weighty subject matter seemed best expressed in plain style, Mary Sidney was the first to embark on a course of imitation and experimentation which led her through varied personae and a wide range of lyrical forms. That she in particular should have progressed beyond the ubiquitous ballad meter or rhymed couplets is probably the result of a combination of circumstances: her talents; her education in French and Italian; a familial environment of humanist parents and two literary brothers, one among the most accomplished writers of his time; the interest of her class in lyric poetry; and the circumstances of her life which led her particularly to the lyrical topics of praise and elegy. While her writing career begins and ends with translation, her final version of the Psalms far surpasses the ingenious literalness of her first efforts in conception, execution, and effect. In the process, she established herself as both a divine poet and a fresh voice for the Reformed cause.

Few writers unwaveringly improve from one work to the next, and where accurate dating is problematic, an overall assessment is even more difficult. With such cautions in mind, we may find in the *oeuvre* of the Countess of Pembroke, if not an absolute progress from apprenticeship to mastery, a clear series of trials in form and voice on the countess's three related interests, the godly life, the relationship between poetry and divine truth, and the role of the pious female poet. Her works include three translations: the doctrinaire prose of Philippe de Mornay's *A Discourse of Life and Death;* Robert Garnier's play, *Antonius,* and Petrarch's *Triumph of Death;* an elegy on her brother, Philip Sidney, **"The Dolefull Lay of Clorinda"**; the pasto-

ral dialogue, **"Thenot and Piers in Praise of Astraea"**; two long dedicatory poems, one to Queen Elizabeth, one to Philip Sidney; and her greatest and most self-defining work, a metrical version of the Psalms. Each reveals how she worked to articulate her piety, first by experimenting with the works of others—by ventriloquizing—and then by developing her own literary personae. In the Psalms, she seems to have found the voice most suited to her religious and poetic vocation. (pp. 121-22)

Probably the first of Mary Sidney's occasional poems was her fine elegy for her brother, published in Spenser's collection of elegies for Philip Sidney which included his own "Astrophel." Generally known as **"The Dolefull Lay of Clorinda,"** it is a pastoral with obvious classical antecedents, but also a pastoral with specific Christian connotations. As the grieving shepherdess, Clorinda not only inhabits an earthly rural landscape but translates that landscape into a vision of heaven. Her poetry encompasses the mutable, fallen world and the bliss of the eternal, redeemed one, because the pastoral traditionally represents both. The death of the shepherd Astrophel provokes her "impatient griefe" and "inward paine" (stanza 1) and causes her to look both to heaven and to earth for consolation. However, realizing that heaven ordained her loss and that men "like wretched bee" (stanza 3) and are themselves in need of comfort, Clorinda is forced to confront herself and her landscape. Through the description of a "desolate" pastoral world, she presents a cleareyed vision of fallen nature, now clarified for her by the immediate presence of death. In hollow, echoing lines, "all the fields do waile their widow state, / Sith death their fairest flowre did late deface" (stanza 5), and "shepheards lasses" must break their garlands and wear "sad Cypres" and "bitter Elder" (stanza 7). Following such vivid images of "Death the devourer," Clorinda asks the crucial question: what has become of Astrophel? "Can so divine a thing be dead?" (stanza 11).

Her answer, while no immediate remedy for those left behind in the fallen world, affirms the hope of "blisfull Paradise" in the life to come. Astrophel, that spirit from the "hevenly quires select" will be serenaded by celestial birds, "In bed of lillies wrapt in tender wise. / And compast all about with roses sweet, / And daintie violets from head to feet" (stanza 12). The delicate beauty of the celestial pastoral, expressed in soft sibilants and balanced lines, represents Astrophel's initiation into immortality through divine love, and contrasts with the mournful appearance and hollow laments of earthly nature, where love is finite and therefore painful.

By adopting the persona of the grieving shepherdess, Mary Sidney can make pastoral convention convey both her view of human beings "that here in dole are drent" and the hope of immortal life. In this poem, she begins with the heavy rhetorical grief of "Ay me, to whom shall I my case complaine . . . " but finds consolation only in understanding the real source of her woe, human sin and helplessness, and the ultimate remedy for human misery in God. The identification of herself as the shepherdess sister of the shepherd Astrophel suggests several poetic connotations. Spenser had introduced her as "most resembling both in shape and spright / Her brother deare," and her guise as shepherdess might confirm her succession to Astrophel's role as poet. But more significantly, in the context of Christian pastoral, the role of shepherd designates the follower of Christ, and so the persona of Clorinda expresses not only a poetic identity but a religious one. Mary Sidney ends her poem as a true Christian, not by lamenting her brother, whom she believes is now a divine soul, but by mourning for all those left on the wretched earth. Here, her assurance of Philip Sidney's divinity is crucial to her assertion of faith; in future poems, it will also give her a way to define her poetic mission.

In light of Mary Sidney's devotion to the Reformed cause and her experiments with poetic voice, her two poems to Queen Elizabeth, **"A Dialogue betweene two shepheards, Thenot and Piers, in praise of Astraea"** and the dedication of the Psalms, **"Even now that Care which on thy Crown attends,"** are noteworthy for their presentation of the queen and their further experiments with persona. Both draw on current mythology to glorify Elizabeth at a time when many English Reformers identified their country as the militant champion of the Protestant cause. Many writers had associated Elizabeth with Astraea the virgin, and the return of a golden age of justice; just as insistent was the Reformist propaganda that identified her as the ruler of the new Israel, an England redeemed from the Catholic Antichrist. In this guise, she was equally a Deborah, a David, and a Solomon, but for Mary Sidney the queen's association with the divine virgin, Astraea, and with David—king, poet, and forefather of Christ—were the most significant.

In each of these poems, Sidney uses the occasion of praise to explore the poetic expression of divine or ineffable truth. Developing the idea of the divine lady, whom she cannot address as Petrarch did his Laura, she seeks nevertheless a voice and a language appropriate to her sense of mission. The solution in the **"Dialogue betweene two shepheards, Thenot and Piers, in praise of Astraea,"** is to present two contrasting voices which articulate the problems inherent in poetry about divine truth. Certainly the poem flatters Elizabeth, but more important, it depends on the exalted connotations of "divine Astraea" to demonstrate how the praiser needs "the truth" but can only use words that fall so far short of divinity as to prove him "so oft a lier" (stanza 1). Because the fallen world and heaven are so completely divided, whenever Thenot praises Astraea's divinity by relating it to something on earth, he will fail to express her:

> Thenot. Then say, she is so good, so faire,
> With all the earth she may compare,
> Not *Momus* selfe denying.
>
> Piers. Compare may thinke where likenesse
>   holds,
> Nought like to her the earth enfolds,
> I lookt to finde you lying.
>
> (stanza 3)

Even to praise her by saying that "Astrea sees with Wisedoms sight, / Astrea workes by Vertues might" (stanza 4) is to reverse the reality, because both Wisdom and Virtue emanate from the divine and do not exist as inde-

pendent earthly entities. Comparison itself becomes an impossible technique because the divine Astrea is unique, "to us none else but only shee." Like the sonnet-lover, Thenot uses all his rhetorical techniques in an attempt to define his lady and his love. Like Clorinda, Piers emphasizes the chasm between worldly and heavenly vision by pointing out that darkness often clouds light, but "*Astreas* beames no darknes shrowdes. . . ." The inadequacy, of course, extends to language, and Piers's final verse explains to Thenot why his words lie, and "strive in vaine to raise her":

> Words from conceit do only rise,
> Above conceit her honour flies;
> But silence, nought can praise her.

The human imagination must suffer too from the Fall which totally cut off humankind from its original divinity. Thenot may sense what he wants to say, "my meaning true," but nothing in human experience is now adequate to express that understanding. Although Elizabeth would still be pleased by a poem asserting how far beyond mortal expression Astraea was, nevertheless, for a poet, the problem remained of finding the words to convey the nature of divinity.

To pose this artistic and religious problem, Mary Sidney chose two male voices in dialogue, reminiscent perhaps of Sidney's Arcadian Eclogues, and even more of Spenser's *Shepheardes Calender* where both a Thenot and a Piers appear. In the February, April, and November eclogues, Thenot, the old commentator, represents experience from which the younger shepherds can learn, as revealed by his parable of the Oak and the Briar, by his upbraiding of Colin's foolish love, and by his encouragement of Colin's true poetry. The countess's Thenot reverses this role by learning through his attempts at praise of the insufficiency of human "conceit" and language. But more significantly, Spenser's Piers, appearing in May and October, heralds the specific concerns of Mary Sidney's Piers. In May, pitted against the Catholic priest, Palinode, he is the Protestant pastor inveighing against the pastors or shepherds who care for worldly pleasure and not their flocks. A "shepheard muste walke another way, / Sike worldly sovenance he must foresay"; he must act righteously to be ready to account to Christ, the "great Pan." In the October eclogue, in dialogue with Cuddie, "the perfect paterne of a Poete" who laments the age's contempt for poets and poetry, Piers confirms the argument that poetry is a "divine gift and heavenly instinct," despite its present degeneracy, and he praises the kind of love that lifts mankind's mind "up out of the loathsome myre . . . above the starry skie." The countess's Piers closely resembles the May Piers, advocating as a good Protestant that Thenot "the truth but plainely tell" and "speake in measure"; and if he denies the ability of Thenot's poetry to express the divine, he, like the October Piers, may only be admitting the failure of contemporary poets.

But more important, at its core, the dialogue expresses disappointment in the insufficiency of human language, or the sense of fallen inadequacy, to express faith. But while she composes a poem about the failure of poetry in two male voices, thus distancing her personae from herself in number and gender, Mary Sidney reserves the celebration of poetry for a persona who more nearly resembles Clorinda, sister of Astrophel, who is actually enabled as a poet by her perception of the divine. The two poems she wrote to dedicate the Psalms, one to the queen, one to her brother, indicate how she achieved her vocation as poet of the truth.

In her second poem to Queen Elizabeth, **"Even now that Care which on thy Crown attends,"** the speaker is the poet, now defining herself as the faithful and reverent subject praising her queen as God's chosen ruler, the present-day analogy to David himself. Addressing the queen first as the earthly prince bound by the unending cares of state, she at once strikes the theme of Elizabeth's divine right:

> What heav'nly powrs thee highest throne assin'de,
> assign'd thee goodnes suting that Degree:
> and by thy strength thy burthen so defin'de,
> To others toile, is Exercise to thee.
>
> (stanza 2)

The analogy between Elizabeth and David follows, justifying the presentation of his "English denizend" Psalms to the woman synonymous with England, "what English is by many names is thine" (stanza 6).

However, the comparison of Elizabeth to David is not merely the witty conceit or flattery of a dedicator. For Sidney's belief that Elizabeth is a David builds a vision of England as the new Israel, a vision fervently espoused by other godly writers. Indeed, the countess may have remembered a text like Thomas Bentley's *Monument of Matrones,* the third part of which clearly makes David Elizabeth's archetype, as he was of her father, Henry VIII. In "The Kings Heast, or GODS familiar speech to the QUEENE: Collected out of the holie Psalmes of good king DAVID, as they are learnedlie expounded by THEODORE BEZA," God speaks to Elizabeth "as he sometimes did unto David, though not in so mysticall maner," declaring how Providence guided her preservation from her enemies, and promising to bless her and her realm. In "The Queenes Vow, or selfe-talk with GOD," also collected out of Beza's Psalms, we hear how "the Queenes Majestie, after a most Christian maner, even with Davids spirit, his sweet words, and divine sentences, first inciteth and prepareth her hart and mind to devotion."

In carefully balanced clauses, Mary Sidney herself draws the analogies between David's rule and Elizabeth's:

> For ev'n thy Rule is painted in his Raigne:
> both cleere in right: both nigh by wrong opprest:
> And each at length (man crossing God in vaine)
> Possest of place, and each in peace possest.
> Proud Philistines did interrupt his rest,
> The foes of Heav'n no lesse have beene thy foes;
> Hee with great conquest, thou with greater blest;
> Thou sure to winn, and hee secure to lose.
>
> (stanza 9)

This remarkable phenomenon of a woman ruler extending her power over male heads of state, "Kings on a Queene enforst their states to lay . . . Men drawne by worth a woman to obay" (stanza 11), derives its legitimacy from her ordination by God himself. Elizabeth's sacred right is

in fact demonstrated by her great success as a ruler, although the poet claims that such workings of divine providence are too exalted a topic for her muse. But what her muse can contribute is an English voice for an English queen. The poet's legitimacy as a divine maker comes, not because she herself is God's chosen, but because she provides a song for the chosen, for God's new David, Elizabeth. Her belief in the queen's divine right, her "thrice sacred" nature, underpins her own vocation as *vates,* the divine poet. For Mary Sidney the problem of how a woman poet may sing divine truth is solved first by recasting King David as Queen Elizabeth:

> And who sees ought, but sees how justly square
> his haughtie Ditties to thy glorious daies?
> How well beseeming thee his Triumphs are?
> his hope, his zeale, his praier, plaint, and praise,
> Needles thy person to their height to raise:
>
> (stanza 8)

And second, she offers the English Psalms to be the queen's voice, so that Elizabeth may "Sing what God doth, and doo What men may sing"—praise God and enact her subjects' praise of her.

If she believed as fervently as the other Reformers that England was the new Israel, then no greater task existed for the poet than glorifying Israel's and England's God. By rendering the Psalms in English verse, Sidney would be simultaneously following divine authority and identifying herself as a true poet. Significantly, she was also following the authority of all the Reformed commentators who gave the Psalms vital importance in the new faith, suggesting that her decade of writing and revising may have been motivated by more than a desire to finish her brother's work.

From Thomas Becon's *Davids Harpe* (1541) to the key commentaries of Calvin and Beza, both of which were available in English, the English Reformers took the Psalms to be a text central to the new spiritual life of their church. They were the source and inspiration of private meditation available for every Christian to use, and the most applicable scriptural text representing an unmediated path to God: as a record of human suffering, conflict, guilt, repentance, faith, and joy, they were particularly appropriate to the Reformers' perception of fallen humankind in continual war against itself, with only God's grace to offer the hope of salvation.

Addressing Katherine, Countess of Huntingdon (Mary Sidney's aunt), Anthonie Gilbie, translator of Beza's *Paraphrase and Commentary on the Psalms,* invokes the Psalms as a path to righteousness at a time when he trembles for the safety of England beset by "general plagues" and the threat of God's wrath for her sins. All English people need to pray for mercy, "that so by earnest praiers, either we may turne away his fearce wrath from us altogither, or at the least with our Hezekias (our gracious Queene I meane) to obteine that it come not in our daies." Every Christian must daily "meditate them in their hearts," in order to learn "what we shal saie unto God."

Expressing the goal of the Reformers to purify the Church of England and to universalize the new faith, these writers turn to the Psalms as an all-encompassing text to aid private prayer and public renovation. By translating the Psalms into a wide range of verse forms, experimenting with meter and rhyme to find the most apt expression of emotion and faith for each song, Mary Sidney sought to play her part in the encouragement of godliness among her peers. To provide them with more memorable forms than might be found, for instance, in the Sternhold-Hopkins Psalter, was to subscribe to the ancient dictum, *utile et dulce,* and to make the songs even more attractive to an audience whose ears were attuned to the variety and subtlety of lyric poetry.

At the same time that she was creating the language of Antony and Cleopatra, Laura, and Clorinda, Mary Sidney worked on her version of the Psalms, editing the first 43 by her brother, and composing Psalms 44 through 150 herself. The seventeen extant manuscripts reveal a long process of writing and revising over ten years, suggesting that the countess considered this work worthy of considerable serious effort in order to accomplish her goals. And if her other poetry had ranged through passion, divine love, grief, and praise, in the Psalms, all these were placed in the perspective of "what we shal saie unto God," an attempt to express both human fallibility and the longing for God, to recognize the gulf between humanity and the divine, yet attempt to bridge it through praise.

Basing her version on a variety of contemporary sources, from the glosses of the Geneva Bible to Marot's translation to the commentaries of Beza, Mary Sidney embarked on a pious work that was essentially scholarly, and yet still poetically inventive. All readers of the Sidneian Psalms have remarked upon the variety of verse forms—Rathmell [in his introduction to *The Psalms of Sir Philip Sidney and the Countess of Pembroke,* 1963] notes only four instances in all the Psalms that exactly repeat the same stanza pattern and rhyme scheme—suggesting that both Sidneys, but to a greater extent, Mary, saw the fulfillment of their task to lie in conveying received doctrine through the individual expression of the poet. To write "heavenly poesy" required not only theological knowledge to make readers think about doctrinal matters, but appropriate forms to make them feel the griefs and joys the poet-prophet experiences.

This [essay] permits but a brief focus on how the countess handled one of the central subjects of the Psalms as interpreted by the Reformers, but it will clarify the continuities between her other poetry and this work, and confirm the direction of her growth as a poet. In the countess's other work, the central Reformist doctrine of the insufficiency of humankind unaided by God's grace appears both as a theme and as a technical problem of language. In the Psalms, however, instead of clinging to her Biblical text or authorities, she uses metaphor and stanzaic form to convey doctrine; in other words, by marrying form and content, her writing escapes the safety and disguise of being mere doctrine, and becomes poetry. While clearly not the first time that a woman poet has recognized the importance of form, still it is the first time that form has been elevated to the central role of moving readers' minds and penetrating their consciences.

In the countess's Psalm 51, for example, a penitential psalm that has received some attention for its merits, the fourth stanza enlarges upon verse 7 of the Psalter, "Purge me with hyssope, and I shal be cleane: wash me, and I shalbe whiter then snowe," and verse 8, "Make me to heare joye and gladnes, that the bones, which thou has broken maie rejoyce." Adopting the Geneva gloss of hyssop as a cleanser of leprosy (Leviticus 14:6), Sidney introduces the image of leprosy, thus doubling the significance of whiteness and intensifying the joy of cure:

> Then as thy self to leapers hast assign'd,
> With hisop, Lord, thy Hisop purge me soe:
> And that shall clense the leaprie of my mind;
> Make over me thy mercies streames to flow,
> Soe shall my whiteness scorn the whitest snow.
> To eare and hart send soundes and thoughts of
>   gladness,
> That brused bones maie daunce awaie their sad-
>   ness.

The repetition in the second line of "hisop, Lord, thy Hisop," emphasizes the teaching that the cure of such a deadly diseased soul is all God's. Connotative of purification and also of a lowly plant, the hyssop reminds the reader that redemption is possible and that humility is the way. And the following image of the dread white scabs of leprosy miraculously vanishing in the healing waters, leaving instead the pure whiteness of natural health, vivifies and dramatizes the simpler scriptural "wash me, and I shal be whiter than snow." Implied in "mercies streames to flow" is the abundance of God's grace and its immediate ability to turn *in malo* to *in bono,* human deformity into divine beauty. Such miraculous cure prompts the final prayer of the stanza, that the sinner may rejoice in salvation. Adding "thoughts" to the "soundes" of gladness of the Biblical text marks the improvement from "leaprie of my mind," while the image of "brused bones" now dancing underlines the joy of spiritual regeneration for which the sinner longs. The weak endings of the couplet provide a final lift to the stanza, a lighter touch indicative of the poet's hoped-for gladness.

A more dramatic example of the function of stanza form in the countess's Psalms is Psalm 57. In the Geneva version, verse 1 reads, "Have mercie upon me, o God, have mercie upon me, for my soule trusteth in thee, and in the shadow of thy ways wil I trust, til these afflictions overpasse." Mary Sidney's stanza appears:

> Thy mercie Lord, Lord now thy mercy show,
> On thee I ly
> To thee I fly
> Hide me, hive me as thine owne,
> Till these blasts be overblown,
> Which now doe fiercely blow.

Here, the urgency of the sinner's plea for mercy evolves from the short, intense lines, from the staccato rhymes of "ly" and "fly" and the near-rhyme of "Hide" and "hive," and the explosiveness of "blasts . . . overblown . . . blow." Building on the Geneva gloss, "He compareth the afflictions, which God layeth upon his children to a storme, that commeth and goeth," in this brief stanza, Sidney's diction conveys both the vehemence of the sinner's woes which "fiercely blow" and the close protection sought with God, "Hide me, hive me as thine owne." Everything seems in chaotic motion, except the implied still point of safety—and salvation—within the hive, thus evoking the distance between the mutable world and the unchanging heavens.

Such attention to language and form typifies much of Mary Sidney's writing in the Psalms. Although they were never published in her lifetime, the wide currency of manuscripts in court circles suggests that they did indeed fulfill a need and achieve some measure of success. The Psalms may be seen, then, both as a public act of devotion and a private dedication of Mary Sidney to the role of divine poet. The prefatory address to the queen confirms the first, and the dedication to her brother bears witness to the second.

The intense fervor of **"To the Angell spirit of the most excellent Sir Phillip Sidney"** might suggest a "sincere" outpouring of the countess's personal grief, but its emotional energy should not obscure its essential elegiac and self-dedicatory purposes. Like **"The Dolefull Lay of Clorinda,"** this poem is an elegy and displays Mary Sidney's awareness of the elegy's classical components of praise, lament, and consolation. But while Clorinda found consolation in believing that Astrophel was immortal, she also emphasized the insuperable division between paradise and earth. In **"To the Angell spirit,"** however, while the poet still laments her terrible loss—"Deepe wounds enlarg'd, long festred in their gall/fresh bleeding smart; not eie but hart teares fall:"—and still acknowledges the gulf between his "pure Sprite" and earth dwellers, almost all her praise concerns Sidney the poet, and thence evolves her consolation and her inspiration. As an elegy that is also a dedication, praise is the dominant mode, but it does not simply arise from fraternal and personal affection. Instead, the belief in her brother's divinity allows her to find a bridge between earth and heaven through the "sacred Hymnes" which he began and which she has finished:

> So dar'd my Muse with thee it selfe combine,
> as mortall stuffe with that which is divine,
> Thy lightning beames give lustre to the rest.
>
> (stanza 1)

If this is "presumption too bold/if love and zeale such error ill-become," yet her act grows from "zealous love, Love which hath never done, / Nor can enough in world of words unfold" (stanza 4). "Zeal" is, of course, a key word in the Puritan lexicon for the devotion of the elect to God, and the repetition here with "Love" suggests that Sidney composed her Psalms as a direct response to divine love, represented by her apotheosized brother. In addressing her brother's celestial being as "fixt among thy fellow lights" where "Thy Angell's soule with highest Angells plac't / There blessed sings enjoying heav'n-delights / thy Maker's praise," she herself imitates the divine, likewise singing God's praise, albeit with the shadowy language of earth. Her Psalms echo heavenly music, praising God to whom Sidney is near, and so simultaneously erecting a monument to her brother's "ever praised name." The Psalms will be both God's "Hymnes" and Sidney's "obsequies," because her belief in Sidney's divinity makes hymns and obsequies identical in the poet's mind.

If the countess consulted Sidney's discussion of *vates* in *The Defence of Poesie,* she would have found his definition of the poet as "diviner, foreseer, or prophet," and his designation of David's Psalms as a "divine poem" or a "heavenly poesy, wherein almost he showeth himself a passionate lover of that unspeakable and everlasting beauty to be seen by the eyes of the mind only, cleared by faith." In response, she took up a role for herself hitherto unique among women writers, to become that divinely inspired poet, legitimized by a divinely ordained queen and a sanctified brother.

In the context of Mary Sidney's poetic development, **"Thenot and Piers, in praise of Astraea"** and **"Even now that Care which on thy Crown attends"** seem not merely flattery of Elizabeth, but rather the poet's expression of her true lyrical subject. Similarly, the poems about Philip Sidney reveal little about the actual sibling relationship; instead, they are metaphoric celebrations of Mary Sidney's idea of her brother, animated by his death. Poetically, Queen Elizabeth and Philip Sidney share the greatness that Petrarch attributed to Laura, the function of leading the poet to a divine vision and dedication to God's Word. Mary Sidney wrote good, and sometimes very fine, lyric poetry partly because she created in her brother and her queen rich emotional and intellectual sources of language and imagery, and clearly defined her poetic personae in relation to them. Instead of merely translating doctrine into verse, she trained herself as a poet devoted to her sovereign's rule and worthy of her brother's immortality.

Unlike Anne Dowriche or Rachel Speght, Mary Sidney did not write prefaces apologizing for or defending her sex. More like Elizabeth Melville Colville, she devoted herself entirely to the writing itself. She was both innovative and conservative. On the one hand, she considerably extended the range of women's literary accomplishments by following less the conventions of humanist education for women and more the path of her own experiments with language and persona; on the other hand, she by no means broke with feminine literary decorum, but indeed represented to her own and succeeding generations the essence of learning and virtue. By choosing wisely her subjects and points of view, from the de Mornay translation and *Antonius,* through Clorinda to the Psalms, she could write about a variety of situations, locations, and characters without challenging the implied limitations on women's writing. Because the essence of her work was her piety, she could transcend the treatise writers and versifiers without sacrificing her legitimacy. (pp. 137-50)

> *Elaine V. Beilin, "The Divine Poet: Mary Sidney, Countess of Pembroke," in her* Redeeming Eve: Women Writers of the English Renaissance, *Princeton University Press, 1987, pp. 121-50.*

Beth Wynne Fisken   (essay date 1989)

[In the following essay, Fisken analyzes Sidney's psalms in the context of Renaissance restrictions on women's writing, stressing her expression of a female poetic voice within the religious form. Fisken views Sidney's translations of the psalms as the poet's attempt to circumvent societal restrictions on women's expression.]

When Mary Sidney undertook the completion of her brother Philip Sidney's verse-translations of the Psalms, she developed a style markedly different from that demonstrated in the forty-three psalms he was able to finish before his death. Rather than using his psalms as models for her writing, she looked to secular poetry, in particular the sonnet sequence, for poetic techniques that would actualize the urgency and insecurity of her speaker's quest. Consequently, her psalms claim for the sincerely religious spirit the same tortured intensity of involvement traditionally associated with the profane rather than the sacred lover. As such her versions of Psalms 44 through 150 demonstrate what Louis Martz calls "the art of sacred parody," which exploits the conventions of love poetry to convert the spasms of earthly passion into the consummation of divine love.

"Sacred parody" was devised as a form of literary religious propaganda, setting up a rival tradition of sacred verse to counter the popularity of love poetry and encourage the individual to worship God with the intensity of romantic love, in fact, to use one as training for the other. Hence, "sacred parody" is a continuation of the neo-Platonic extension of Plato's ladder, reaching from admiration of earthly beauty to divine fusion with God, a progression described in Ficino's tracts and Bembo's monologue at the end of Castiglione's *The Courtier* and realized in the sonnets of Dante and Petrarch. What Mary Sidney emphasized were the parallel functions served by the sonnet cycle and the Psalms, the resemblances between the anxiety of the lover beseeching his beloved and the anguish of the worshiper pleading with God. Quoting C. S. Lewis, William Ringler reminds his readers [in *The Poems of Sir Philip Sidney,* 1962] that the sonnet sequence was not meant to tell a story but rather to be " . . . a form which exists for the sake of prolonged lyrical meditation," a meditation conducted in monologues revealing the varied moods and voices of the lover in relation and reaction to his love, who encourages and rejects him. Similarly, the Psalms were generally accepted as "the prime models for the soul in meditation." The Psalms taken as a whole formed what Luther called "a little Bible," thought to be the "epitome of human emotions, a searching analysis . . . of each and every Christian," or as Calvin explained: "An Anatomy of all the parts of the Soul . . . all the griefs, sorrows, fears, doubts, hopes, cares, perplexities, in short, all the distracting emotions with which the minds of men are wont to be agitated." To dramatize this agitation experienced by the psalmist upon speaking to the God who raises and crushes the individual soul, the Psalms contain a variety of modes of address: meditations, soliloquies, laments, prayers, and petitions; in an encyclopedia of poetic kinds—lyrical, heroic, satiric, elegiac, and ritualistic. The psalmist becomes a symbol of the struggle of all Christians, who are invited to apply their own uneven spiritual history to what they read in an education in how to speak to God, just as the lover in the sonnet sequence represents the experience of all lovers analyzed through interior monologue and debate. As Alan Sinfield points out [in "Sidney and Astrophil," *Studies in English Literature* 20 (1980)], the sonnets, like the Psalms, become aids to self-examination, "involving the reader in a range of emotional states so that he [or she] comes to appreciate his [or her] own fallibility."

Yet it is possible to conjecture certain private reasons for Mary Sidney's use of the conventions of "sacred parody," reasons arising from the position of a sixteenth-century woman with ambitions to write poetry. Even from the more progressive humanists such as Sir Thomas More and Juan Luis Vives, the message to a Renaissance woman was to use her intellectual potential privately to perform her wifely and maternal duties. Both More and Vives advised that a woman's intelligence could never equal a man's; and, overwhelmingly, religious leaders, educators, philosophers, and writers concurred that a woman's natural inferiority and moral instability necessitated restrictions on her encounters and activities. A woman should remain at home, shunning common entertainments; most importantly, she should never push herself forward or be seen conversing at length in public. By selectively quoting Paul's injunctions, male figures of authority cautioned women again and again never to presume to teach—to remain silent. Women's reading, even under the most liberal system of education, was to be restricted to the Bible and the writings of church fathers, Christian poets, and moral philosophers—largely to protect their chastity, deemed their chief defining virtue. Women were prescribed an educational regimen of copying the moral *sententiae* they read; they were never encouraged (as were men) to comment on what they read or to undertake original writing. Religious translation was the farthest extent of literary ambition considered suitable to a woman's position or capacity.

However, the breadth of scholarship revealed in Mary Sidney's translations of the Psalms clearly overstepped the modest bounds of scholarly attainment allowed aristocratic women of her time to expand their marital horizons. For her versions, Mary Sidney consulted a variety of contemporary sources, ranging from the Prayer Book Psalter in Coverdale's Great Bible of 1539, the Geneva Bible of 1560, and the Bishop's Bible of 1568, to the Geneva Marot-Beza Psalter of 1562, as well as Golding's translation of Calvin's commentaries and Gilby's version of Beza. It seems unlikely that Mary Sidney could have read Hebrew and consulted the originals; rather her psalms are the result of extensive and judicious comparison of other translations and commentaries. Even though they are not new translations in the modern sense, however, in the process of selecting which nuance to accentuate, which image to expand, which gloss to elaborate, Mary Sidney developed her own moral vision. Fluent in French and Italian, probably trained in Latin and possibly in Greek as well, Mary Sidney was not content merely to recopy the words of others; rather, through her versifications of the Psalms she used her scholarship to enable her to establish her own relationship to the spiritual issues of her time.

Despite her deep and abiding commitment to scholarly endeavors, Mary Sidney must have felt constrained by contemporary injunctions against love poetry and romantic tales, whether classical or contemporary, as inappropriate reading material for women. As Suzanne Hull sensibly points out, apparently the upper classes of Renaissance women disobeyed these social constraints, as indicated by the increasing publication of such works specifically addressed to women readers. Still, the distance between reading such literature and writing it would have been nearly unbridgeable if the official line remained that even reading it was an immoral act. To write in such a mode was to convict oneself of an unchaste imagination. Indeed, the most notorious example of a woman writing love poetry prior to Mary Sidney's work on the Psalms was Mary Stuart, Queen of Scotland, who composed privately a series of love sonnets to Bothwell while he was still married to another woman, sonnets that were later discovered and used publicly against her in her trial for possible complicity in the murder of Darnley, her second husband. Later, after Mary Sidney's writing career had ended, Lady Mary Wroth, who bore two illegitimate children to her first cousin, William Herbert, the Earl of Pembroke, appended the sonnet collection, *Pamphilia to Amphilanthus,* to *The Countesse of Mountgomeries Urania* (1621). For her temerity in publishing such a work, Wroth was vilified by one courtier as a "hermaphrodite" and a "monster"; her writing was judged to be as sinful as her private life. It would seem that such literature was undertaken only by women who had already scandalously flaunted society's conventions in their private lives. If anything these notable exceptions confirmed the axiomatic link between amatory poetry and loose morals as promulgated by the male establishment.

Indeed, the sonnet tradition itself excluded women as speakers and writers of their own experience. It is difficult to master a discourse that, as Gary Waller has argued, "masters" you, that renders you passive and silent, a shadowy projection or worshipped object valued most for a mysterious aloofness, an "absent presence," as Philip Sidney himself described it in Sonnet 106 of *Astrophil and Stella.* The speaker of the sonnet is normally a man exploiting the occasion of his lady's rejection to anatomize, in an exercise in self-aggrandizement, his own feelings as what matter most. He is created by her silence. When Mary Stuart and Mary Wroth struggled with the form, they spoke in the personae of women who experience themselves as passive and incomplete without the affirmation of their lovers; they can neither actively pursue nor initiate a confrontation but must wait, enumerating their sacrifices and protesting their constancy. They are depreciated by the silence of their men.

What was a woman to do in the sixteenth century, who felt that inner compulsion to write but was denied access to the dominant modes of literary expression by her internalization of society's limits on what she should be thinking, reading, and writing—who was, in fact, marginalized and silenced by the very conventions of the reigning poetic genre? Mary Beth Rose [in "Gender, Genre, and History," in *Women in the Middle Ages and Renaissance,* edited by Mary Beth Rose, 1986] labels the strategies of female autobiographers in the late seventeenth century "devious self-assertion . . . disguised as self-deprecation," and, indeed, that label could apply equally to Mary Sidney's situation a century earlier when she versified her translations of the Psalms. Religious translations demonstrated a twofold submission to male authority, first to the traditional

patriarchal image of God and then to the male religious establishment that perpetuated this image. In addition, in Mary Sidney's case, tribute was paid to her brother's memory by completing his work. She displayed the pious devotion her society endorsed in the mode permitted her. Yet the mere fact that she composed poetic versions in an impressive array of sophisticated meters and stanzaic forms gave her a latitude to visualize, intensify, and amplify the existing text—to express as well as translate.

In the traditional Protestant understanding of the role of the psalmist-persona, the identity of the speaker and translator were fused. The Psalms were interpreted simultaneously as the "emotional history of all the faithful, and . . . the particular spiritual autobiography of every particular Christian." By reworking them, Mary Sidney sought to become a "correlative type," a new David forging, as Lewalski explains, "a new work in the same spirit, under the impress of the same emotion" [Barbara K. Lewalski, *Protestant Poetics and the Seventeenth-Century Religious Lyric,* 1979]. In the Renaissance understanding of the Psalms, David assumes many roles, subsuming a variety of individual voices and concerns; similarly, the voice of the translator becomes our voice and "translates" our hopes and desires into his or her expression of the psalmist's petitions and prayers. The translator, as well as the reader, is urged to apply the Psalms to his or her own situation in private meditation for the full revelation of their meaning. As translator of the Psalms, Mary Sidney was encouraged by her material not only to speak in many voices, but also to speak in her own voice when congruent with the text.

This sanctioned flexibility of poetic persona effectively liberated Mary Sidney (at least imaginatively) from the restraints placed on her sex by her society. She was free to speak as a prophet or a king, a sinner or a seer—as a man as well as a woman. She could speak with authority and explore a wide range of complex emotions. She could reenact lives and experiences outside the narrow sphere circumscribed for women by her society and then pursue her own spiritual odyssey within that ambit. She could become an active participant in her verse-translations of the Psalms in a way that would have been impossible for her within the conventions of the sonnet form, where even a woman speaker imagined by a woman writer is limited to passive suffering and endurance. It is illuminating that Mary Sidney was recommended to Mary Wroth by one male critic as a model of what a woman writer should be. In short, Mary Sidney could explore the emotive range of the love lyric without sacrificing the authorized respectability of the religious translation by means of "sacred parody."

Indeed, it was Mary Sidney's depiction of the psalmist as a passionate, frustrated, often desperate wooer of God's favor that most distinguished her versions of the Psalms from those of her brother. His psalms, rather than highlighting the turmoil of his speaker, focus on the subject matter from a more distant, encompassing, and abstract perspective; they seem like poems created out of events recollected in tranquility, the speaker reflecting back on difficulties that have since been resolved. In distinct contrast,

Mary Sidney's psalms chart the erratic progress of the feverish soul, the current peaks and valleys of the psalmist's alternating fits of despondency and hope. Philip's psalms emphasize the bounty and power of God as envisioned by a confident prophet, who perhaps contemplates that "unspeakable and everlasting bewtie to be seene by the eyes of the mind, onely cleared by fayth," while Mary's psalms dramatize the difficulty of maintaining that faith and the confusion of her speaker, wedded to this earth and searching for signs of God's favor in the here-and-now.

Perhaps the main reason Philip Sidney's versions of the Psalms are more serene and less dramatic than his sister's is that he had the entire gamut of literary forms available to him to explore other levels of feeling. Mary Sidney stretched the latitude permitted her as far as she could—she had to compress all that she felt and thought and imagined into the additions and elaborations authorized by the challenges of versification. It is scarcely surprising that her psalms are at once more forced and forceful than her brother's, her conceits more strained and elaborate, her syntax more twisted and turbulent, her lines in general more packed; from the evidence of her manuscripts, she reworked the same psalms over and over obsessively. They were all she had and constituted already the furthest extent of what the male establishment thought she should be allowed in all decency to attempt.

Possibly she feared that she had gone too far. While for Philip, the exercise of versifying the Psalms could only be viewed by his society as a praiseworthy act of piety, for Mary, the same undertaking might be judged a well-intentioned but excessive show of intellectual pride compromising the modest reticence that should define a woman in all her actions, private and public. Despite the fact that she had previously published her more literal translations of Robert Garnier's *Antoine* and Philippe de Mornay's *Discourse of Life and Death,* her ***Psalmes*** remained unpublished, as did her terza rima translation of Petrarch's *Triumph of Death* and two lengthy dedicatory poems, **"To the Angell spirit . . . "** and **"Even now that Care. . . . "** Mary Sidney's poetic ambitions remained largely a private affair. Perhaps a guilty uneasiness with her own use of the Psalms as a means of "devious self-assertion" also explains, at least in part, why she chose so often to emphasize the peril of the earthly sinner rather than the confidence of the righteous elect.

That this was a characteristic stylistic choice is clearly demonstrated by contrasting examples taken from parallel passages in the two Sidneys' psalms. For instance, when they describe the awesome storm-making power of God, Philip emphasizes the storm as a manifestation of God's great majesty, whereas Mary's depiction underscores the terrifying destruction endured on earth. In Psalm 18, Philip's alexandrines slow the turbulent activity to a sonorous and solemn pageant, a stately show of authority:

> Then out his arrowes fly, and streight they scatterd been,
> Lightning on lightning he did for their wrack augment,
> The gulfs of water then were through their Chanels seen,

The World's foundations then lay bare because he shent
With blasting breath O Lord, that in thy chiding went.
Then sent he from above, and took me from below,
Ev'n from the Waters' depth my God preserved me so.

For Mary, in Psalm 77, the storm is raging around her, its rage regenerated by the urgency of her trimeter lines and heavy alliteration:

> The waves thee saw, saw thee,
> And fearefull fledd the field:
> The deepe with panting brest.
> Engulphed quaking lay:
> The cloudes thy fingers prest,
> Did rushing rivers yield;
> Thy shaftes did flaming flee
> Through firy airy way.
> Thy voices thundring crash
> From one to other pole,
> Twixt roofe of starry Sphere
> And earths then trembling flore,
> While light of lightnings flash
> Did pitchy cloudes encleare,
> Did round with terror role,
> And rattling horror rore.

The epanados, "thee saw, saw thee," recreates the crash and recoil of the waves, and the repeated "r" and "t" sounds in lines 81-88 simulate the rattling thunder. The reader is buffeted—a frightened victim caught in the midst of the storm rather than seated as a removed spectator at an exhibition.

Again and again, Mary Sidney's choice of syntax and stanza magnify the guilty distress of her speaker, cut off from God's manifest grace and crying for a sign of forgiveness, as can be seen in such opening stanzas as the following from Psalm 74 with its breathless, tumbling questions:

> O God, why hast thou thus
> Repulst, and scattred us?
> Shall now thy wrath no lymmitts hold?
> But ever smoke and burne?
> Till it to Asshes turne
> The chosen folk of thy deare fold?

These anxious moments provoked some of Mary Sidney's most inspired lyrics. For example, she transformed the brief opening of Psalm 130—"Out of the deep have I called unto thee; O Lord: Lord hear my voice"—into a stanza form that mimics the effect of a wailing plea chased by short, quick sobs:

> From depth of grief
> Where droun'd I ly,
> Lord for relief
> To thee I cry:
> My earnest, vehement, cryeng, prayeng,
> Graunt quick, attentive, hearing, waighing.

Generally, Philip's translations did not elaborate as extensively as Mary's on the original text. In his version of Psalm 28, he reproduced faithfully the initial lines ("Unto thee will I cry, O Lord my strength: think no scorn of me;

lest, if thou make as though thou hearest not, I become like them that go down into the pit.''):

> To thee Lord my cry I send.
> O my strength stop not Thine eare,
> Least, if answer Thou forbeare,
> I be like them that descend
> To the pitt where flesh doth end.

As a result, the speaker in Philip's psalms seems calmer, more declarative, as if he were recalling past misery that he has conquered with present faith.

Unlike her brother, Mary Sidney chose to emphasize the tortured uncertainty of the psalmist in what Calvin referred to as the "time of his affliction." Perhaps the terrors of God's wrath seemed more immediate and real to her in anxious projection of censure by the male religious establishment, which decreed that a woman should never presume to comment on or alter the sacred word because her faulty understanding would only confuse and mislead others. Yet inevitably such an ambitious versification would transform the original meaning. It is entirely appropriate for Philip to undertake these psalms in the accomplished manner of the Geneva Marot-Beza Psalter but a very different matter for Mary to demonstrate skillful mastery of the lyrical and rhetorical conventions of secular verse.

While Mary Sidney's psalms reveal a tendency to focus on and magnify the guilty fear of her speaker, the dramatic exuberance of the style in which that fear is portrayed must have been both challenging and liberating. As Ruth Kelso demonstrates in *Doctrine for the Lady of the Renaissance,* the virtues urged on women were those of passive accommodation; women were supposed to prevent storms by acts of peace-making conciliation, not release them by onomatopoeic reenactment. The expression—indeed, the experience of emotion—was supposed to be muted; sober moderation and disciplined temperance defined the ideal standard of behavior. Public outbursts of vehement protestation and wailing despair would be judged unseemly for men and women alike; for a woman, however, these displays would be doubly condemned as acts of prideful self-assertion, which would not only weaken her necessary resignation to her lot as God's will but also undermine her primary function, obedient submission to the needs of her husband and family. Male writers could use the conventions of the love sonnet to indulge in a culturally sanctioned and artistically controlled testing of unruly passions, to play with such desires in the "safe" context of non-serious recreational literature. In her versions of the Psalms, Mary Sidney, too, could experiment with the expression of turbulent emotions that were conventionally muffled and censored by her society but could be savored, anatomized, and intensified in her writing. She also found a "safe" context for these experiments, safe in this case because of the grave seriousness of her undertaking, which would sanctify the heightened emotionalism of such passages as faithful enactments of the psalmist's prostration before God's power.

On the simplest level, "sacred parody" involves appropriating the amorous language of love poetry to emphasize the compelling bonds between God and humankind. The speaker in Mary Sidney's version of Psalm 86 pleads,

"And hold me fast thy fearing lover", and God's irrestible power takes on distinctly orgasmic overtones in Psalm 88:

> Ay me, alas, I faint, I dy,
> So still, so still
> Thou dost me fill,
> And hast from yongest yeares,
> With terrifying feares,
> That I, in traunce, amaz'd doe ly.

Estranged from God, the speaker in Psalm 44 languishes like the lover in the lyrics of the *Arcadia,* outward persecution mirroring inward torment:

> By reviling slaundring foe
> Inly wounded thus I languish:
> Wreakfull spight with outward blow
> Anguish adds to inward anguish.

Certainly such language was impossible for a woman in its customary sense, and one suspects that even its use on the sublimated, idealized level of "sacred parody" was a risky endeavor for a woman writer. Even in marriage (or especially in marriage, as some moral philosophers saw it), the conventional wisdom was that a husband should avoid arousing too much ardor in his wife to insure that her moral and intellectual chastity would not be compromised. To describe the languishing, fainting trances of a lover, even in a spiritual context, was to suggest a sensual knowledge that was supposed to be repressed and even absent.

Mary Sidney enacted the distress of her "fearing lover" by frequent use of enjambment in a complicated conversational syntax studded with questions, interjections, and exclamations that mirror the psalmist's changeable emotions. In particular, she used the interrogative mode to recreate the impatience, doubt, and insecurity of her speaker, a strategy commonly found in the sonnet form as well. For example, in Sonnet 31 of *Astrophil and Stella,* Philip Sidney's exasperated lover inveighs against his love's silent indifference:

> Is constant *Love* deem'd there but want of wit?
> Are Beauties there as proud as here they be?
> Do they above love to be lov'd, and yet
> Those Lovers scorne whom that *Love* doth possesse?
> Do they call *Vertue* there ungratefulnesse?

In the person of the psalmist, Mary Sidney transforms herself into one who can petition and demand through the interrogatory mode; she is released from the imprisoning image of woman as mute immovability. Indeed, she assumes an active, aggressive stance, as demonstrated in Psalm 88, in which she uses questions to convey the mounting frustration of the psalmist, who has the presumption to berate God for His silence. In her verse-paraphrase she intensifies the cumulative agitated effect of the questions taken from the original version of this psalm by varying her line length and by opening lines 50 and 53 with unexpected trochaic substitutions:

> Shall buried mouthes thy mercies tell?
> Dust and decay
> Thy truth display?
> And shall thy workes of mark

Shine in the dreadfull dark?
Thy Justice where oblivions dwell?

In another application of the interrogative mode, Mary Sidney makes a bold departure from the plain declaration of the original version, "I will hearken what the Lord God will say," by transforming Psalm 85 into a dramatic monologue in which her speaker attempts to curb his or her panic to listen for God's reply:

Wilt thou thus for ever grieve?
Wilt thou of thy wrathfull rage
Draw the threed from age to age?
Never us againe relieve?
Lord yet once our hartes to joy
Show thy grace, thy help employ.

What speake I? O lett me heare
What he speakes: for speake hee will.

This syntactical strategy encourages the reader to share the confusion and distress of the speaker, who tests and revises possible interpretations of experience while losing and then regaining self-control. As a result, the speaker's turmoil seems contemporaneous with the experience of reading the poem.

To emphasize this illusion of performative speech, Mary Sidney uses colloquial invective that enlivens her speakers as fallible and recognizable people. In her version of Psalm 75, she turns the Prophet's projected vision of God's wrath ("I said unto the fools, Deal not so madly: and to the ungodly, Set not up your horn") into an exasperated explosion, in which God is imagined as a coarse fellow comrade:

Bragg not you braggardes, you your saucy horne
Lift not, lewd mates: no more with heav'ns
    scorne
Daunce on in wordes your old repyning mea-
    sure.

In other examples Mary Sidney's psalmist exclaims, "No light, no law; fy, fy, the very ground / Becomes unsound", and mimics the conceited folly of those who doubt God's existence: "They prate and bable voide of feare, / For, tush, saie they, who now can heare?". For a woman to exploit artistically such vigorous colloquialism could only be acceptable as part of the dramatic ventriloquism that required her to speak as a man and to recreate with fidelity the multiple personae of the Psalms in her translation.

This ventriloquism enabled Mary Sidney to play a variety of characters; her protagonist assumes several representative roles, striking diverse attitudes in the guise of a heartfelt petitioner. Similarly, in the sonnet cycle the various moods of the lover are dramatized by the chameleonic postures of the speaker. In *Astrophil and Stella,* the speaker becomes a poet denouncing artifice (Sonnets 1, 3, 15) or a rationalizer only half-convinced by his own arguments (4, 10, 52, 61, 71). He is a man addressing his friends (14, 20, 21, 51, 69) or an exasperated fellow beset by busybodies and gossips (23, 27, 54, 104). Most of all, he is a lover embodying the experiences of all lovers, pleading for mercy and reproaching his lady for her coolness (36, 40, 45, 59, 107), using every argument and approach to sway her, no matter how transparently manipu-

lative and sophistical (62, 64, 68). The lover in *Astrophil and Stella* is at times hopeful and joyful, divided and in conflict, perplexed and frustrated, resigned and despairing.

Mary Sidney's psalmist assumes as many roles as Philip Sidney's Astrophil. It is in the extended exploration of a reader's interactions with the text—encouraged by this strategy of multiple speakers—that the sonnet most resembles the psalm as a poetic form, and Mary Sidney chose to emphasize this strategy in her verse-paraphrases. Her use of multiple personae recognizes and takes advantage of the multiple authorship of the originals and so was entirely consistent with the religious thought of her time. Philip Sidney commented on David's "often and free chaunging of persons" as both ruler of his nation and representative voice of its church and congregation. In Renaissance exegesis of the Psalms, David serves simultaneously as an allegorical figure aware of his prophetic function as a prefiguration of Christ, as a private individual pleading his own case before God, and as a public spokesman for all supplicants, whether confident of God's grace or apprehensive of His judgment. The psalmist becomes a visionary projecting the words of God (Psalms 50, 75, 110), a pattern of virtue who assumes the right to lecture kings (45, 52, 72, 82), a member of the congregation asking for a sign of favor (74, 94) and praising God's constant care (44, 81, 95, 96, 100, 113), a desperate individual besieged by enemies (57, 59), or a penitent sinner pleading for mercy and forgiveness (51, 69, 119D, 130). The speaker entreats God as a ruler, a suitor, or a servant, as a pilgrim, a poet, or a student. In her translations, Mary Sidney experiments with all these roles, speaking in tones ranging from energetic to reflective, outraged to delighted, doubtful to confident, despondent to expectant—often within a single psalm.

Not only do the varying personae in psalms and sonnets speak for us, but they speak to us as well, thrusting us into different roles signaled by changing modes of address. The reader of *Astrophil and Stella* becomes the lady who enthralls the lover (Sonnets 40, 45, 59, 86), attempting in vain to curb his passion by appealing to reason (62, 64, 68). At other times, the reader is chided as a well-meaning but officious friend who disapproves of the poet's love (14, 21, 51) or is hailed as a more sympathetic comrade, equally vulnerable to love's ambush (20), willing to listen to the poet's outbursts (69). The reader turns into an envious gossip (54, 104), a dull fellow who will not tell the speaker news of his love (92), or an allegorist and poetaster who would spoil it all with over-interpretation and vulgar embellishment (15, 28).

Similarly, in the Psalms the reader is characterized alternatively as friend or enemy, saved or damned. We are members of the congregation—rich and poor alike—who require instruction (Psalms 49, 78), citizens of rejoicing nations (107, 122), or God's servants and priests (134, 135). We are sinners (50, 79, 103, 130), arrogant heathens (115, 129), tyrants (52), or princes in need of correction (82). Mary Sidney, while addressing us, can assume the rhetorical trappings of authority. If not in her own voice, then at least in the guise of her speaker, she is permitted to lecture, advise, and instruct, not merely to listen and submit. As a woman, she can only be a silent member of the congregation, but in her psalms she can experience the challenge of preaching at least by proxy.

When Louis Martz affirms that "the sighs and groans and tears of the afflicted lover form the ground-tone of the Psalms," he reveals a major connection between these two seemingly disparate forms, the sonnet sequence and the Psalms. Both emphasize the psychological complexity of the experience of love, whether sacred or profane. At the heart of both the Petrarchan sonnet and the Protestant lyric based on the Psalms, according to Gary Waller, is a "discontinuous" and "decentered self," beseeching a sign of recognition from an all-powerful, unapproachable, and too-often silent beloved—an uncertain self anxious to forge a coherent and cohesive sense of identity through the hopeful fabrication of language. The difficulty of sustaining faith despite the silence of the beloved, of maintaining reason and control despite disappointment, of affirming belief despite confusion and temptations to despair is central to both the Psalms and the sonnet sequence; and such difficulty is one reason Mary Sidney chose the unsettled and bewildered voice characteristic to "sacred parody" as the dominant note in her verse-translations, rather than the secure equanimity of the chosen prophet that prevails in Philip Sidney's psalms. Mary Sidney's versions focus on the drama of the embattled spirit "quailed in mind-combats manifold" (Psalm 94, 1. 35), a drama in which the psalmist, like the lover in the sonnet, is a bewildered victim, not a master of his or her experience. Mary Sidney taught herself well the art of "sacred parody" to record what David Kalstone describes as "the wandering voices of the fallen world"—voices that are amplified through the media of complex syntax, multiple speakers, and direct and specific characterization of the audience common to both the psalm and the sonnet form. The reader of the psalm both listens to and participates in the speaker's struggle to discipline him or herself to know and love God, just as the reader of the sonnet sequence witnesses the throes of obsessive passion and is encouraged to confront the potential for those delicious and destructive emotions in him or herself as well. Both the sonnet and the psalm are essentially meditative forms that stimulate in the reader the capacity for direct application of self to the rich and varied experiences dramatized by the speakers of those poems.

Yet at the heart of Mary Sidney's decision to emphasize these links between the psalm and the sonnet through "sacred parody" might very well be the oblique personal and poetic self-assertion enabled by that mode of presentation. Cloaking her efforts in the security of translation absolves Mary Sidney from the censure of the male establishment. The act of translation is inevitably an act of submission to the authority of the text, religious translation a mark of dutiful reverence. After all, Mary Sidney is not presuming to speak in her own voice; rather she is humbly assisting in the perpetuation of the sacred documents of patriarchal power. In this instance, the aggressiveness of her scholarship is offset by her decision not to publish. Still, in translating the Psalms into the challenging meters and stanzas of her poetic versions, inevitably she must change the

words and embroider on the ideas of the originals. In adopting the stance of the male psalmist, she is free to experiment, as a woman, with a variety of personae, to speak in many voices beyond those allowed by her society. Even though she is speaking as a man, she is authorized to draw parallels to herself as part of the meditative tradition of individual application to the rhetorical situation of the psalm. Thus, by implication, she asserts a woman's right to speak within the canon. Assuming the guise of a man, she strikes a wide range of dramatic attitudes, varying from vehement despair to guilty terror to sublime passion, expressed in tones stretching from insistent interrogation to angry invective to imperious assertion. She can enjoy the poetic and emotional latitude permitted the speaker of the sonnet by hiding behind the speaker of the psalm, projecting her voice and pulling the strings.

In these translations, Mary Sidney possibly invents on a literary level an androgynous identity analogous to that offered in the ambiguous modes of self-address used by Queen Elizabeth to defuse male discomfort at being ruled by a woman. Elizabeth combined avowals of individual womanly weakness with symbolic political references to herself as an all-powerful prince and king. Mary Sidney speaks as a man, simultaneously suggesting the inappropriateness of such tones for a woman while demonstrating a woman's competence as a poet and capacity for speaking with many voices. In speaking as a man, Mary Sidney allows herself to express the unrecognized potential of a woman. "Sacred parody" empowers her to step down from her pedestal, as the frozen "absent presence" of the sonnet, to become the active, controlling presence of the psalm, even if she must do so indirectly from backstage. Only in the psalm, through the words of another, is Mary Sidney able to begin to speak as herself; only by translating the Psalms can she write a sonnet. (pp. 223-36)

> *Beth Wynne Fisken, " 'The Art of Sacred Parody' in Mary Sidney's 'Psalmes',"* in *Tulsa Studies in Women's Literature, Vol. 8, No. 2, Fall, 1989, pp. 223-39.*

Mary Ellen Lamb   (essay date 1990)

[*In the following excerpt, Lamb considers the theme of the "good death" in Sidney's translations of Mornay, Garnier, and Petrarch, linking the stoicism implicit in this theme to the condition of women during the Renaissance.*]

Taken as a group, Mary Sidney's translations from Mornay, Garnier, and Petrarch suggest an interest in the art of dying which apparently gained strength not only from her grief over the death of her brother Philip, but also from her mother's impressive death, from her husband's expressed desire to die, and from the preoccupation with the topic evidenced by her culture in general. In the common representation of the countess's literary activities as motivated entirely by her love for her brother, critics are drawing upon a perception that she herself was partly responsible for conveying. Like Spenser's elegiac version of Clorinda, Mary Sidney's own version of her authorship functions to deny the existence of dangerous sexuality or of a desire for worldly power. Her representation of her various literary activities as an extended elegy for her famous brother enabled her writing at a time when the boundaries were tightly drawn around women's public speech or published words. While her participation in the *ars moriendi* tradition was no doubt sincere, the desire for death permeating her authorship also accomplished two related functions: first, it provided a means of heroism accessible to Renaissance women through their constancy to their husbands, and second, this heroics of constancy was also able to serve as a mask for anger simultaneously elicited and denied.

Since no reasons were usually required for a woman's translating religious works for her own perusal, the countess's construction of a version of authorship was perhaps necessitated by her preparation of a copy of the Psalms translated by her brother and herself for presentation to the queen in 1599. Accompanying (and accounting for) this presentation copy were two dedicatory poems, both composed by the countess, one to Queen Elizabeth and the other to the spirit of her deceased brother, Philip. Margaret Hannay has written ably on the political messages embedded in both poems, which exhort the queen to support the Protestant cause on the mainland espoused by Sir Philip Sidney. Despite, or more likely because of, this political agenda, these presentation poems portray a modestly unpolitical version of the countess's authorship. In the requisite dedicatory poem to Queen Elizabeth, Mary Sidney presents her translation as rent owed to the queen; and, as befits a woman author, this rent takes the form of cloth. Together she and her brother have woven a livery robe which they now present to Her Majesty as her due in exchange for those "nighe feelds where sow'n [her] favors bee."

The dedicatory poem **"To the Angell spirit of the most excellent Sir Philip Sidney"** sets up a split audience for the translation, written not only for Queen Elizabeth but for the late Philip Sidney. In fact, in oblivious contradiction to the previous poem addressing her work to the queen, the first line of **"To the Angell spirit"** claims her deceased brother as the countess's only audience, to whom the work "alones addres't." Since this second poem was not required, as was the first, for this presentation copy, its inclusion represents a strong statement. Its primary function seems to be the invention of an acceptable version of the countess as an author-translator; her version of authorship in this poem is notable for its use of several of the authorial strategies created for Clorinda in Spenser's *Astrophel.* After deflecting any anxieties about her attempt to influence a royal audience through her writing, the countess (like Clorinda) also disclaims any "Art or skill" on her part, attesting to the source of her poetry as "simple love" for her brother.

Like Spenser's Clorinda, the countess creates her authorship as a form of mourning. Not only is Philip the countess's only meaningful audience, but he is also her poetry's real author, inspiring her after his death:

> To thee pure sprite, to thee alones addres't
> this coupled worke, by double int'rest thine:
> First rais'de by thy blest hand, and what is mine

inspir'd by thee, thy secrett power imprest.

Merely completing what her brother would have finished had "heav'n spared" his life, she is not a "real" poet asserting the independent subjectivity of an author. Far from serving as a means of self-display, her writing serves only to express her love for her dead brother, according to this striking image:

> To which theise dearest offrings of my hart
> dissolv'd to Inke, while penns impressions move
> the bleeding veines of never dying love:
> I render here.

In using her blood for ink, she represents her writing as almost a physical rather than an intellectual act, literally writing from the heart's feelings rather than from the head's thoughts. The next lines make clear that her work proceeds from love, not from learning:

> These wounding lynes of smart
> sadd Characters indeed of simple love
> not Art nor skill which abler wits doe prove,
> Of my full soule receive the meanest part.

Far from desiring worldly recognition, Mary Sidney's representation of herself as wishing only to join her brother in death forms a poignant conclusion to this poem:

> I can no more: Deare Soule I take my leave;
> Sorrowe still strives, would mount thy highest
>   sphere
> presuming so just cause might meet thee there,
> Oh happie chaunge! could I so take my leave.

The countess's concluding desire for death implies her absolute detachment from any desire to influence the affairs of this world through her writing. This yearning for death is the fitting conclusion for her dedicatory poem, which constructs her translation of the Psalms, produced through Philip's inspiration and addressed solely to his eyes, as a conversation with her deceased brother, as an intermediate stage of communion with the dead for which her own death represents the only wholly satisfactory fulfillment. This desire for death will be shown to permeate her version of authorship, exerting powerful control over the other works which she not only translated, but allowed to be published.

With what seriousness can we take Mary Sidney's version of her authorship? The dedicatory poem to her brother's spirit suggests that her self-representations can neither be taken at face value nor wholly discounted. While her devotion to her brother and even her desire to join him in death cannot be denied, the contradictions which fissure her representation of her authorship make visible the pressure exerted against women's writing at that time. Poetry proceeding from "simple love" does not require meticulous consultation with numerous versions of the Psalms and their commentaries; an artless expression of love does not "extend the technical range of English versification," as [G. F. Waller] claims for her translations. Poetry intended solely for the reading of an "Angell spirit" is not presented formally to the queen, nor does it advocate even subtly the political policy of supporting Protestants on the Continent. If her translations were informed primarily by her goal to die well, why, then, did she allow their publication? It is not clear whether these unresolved contradictions proceed from a gap between the countess and the mask of authorship she assumes or more deeply within her character, from a conflict posed by her dual identity as woman and as writer. What is clear, however, is that in the Psalms as in her other translations, her representation of herself as wishing to die formed an integral and necessary condition for her presentation of her work to the public eye, for her presentation of herself as an author.

Mary's own expressions of devotion for her brother Philip were no doubt partially responsible for the conventional understanding of her other literary projects as motivated by sisterly dedication. But this attribution of motive does not go very far in explaining her actual choice of works to translate. Critics who generally agree that she translated Philippe du Plessis Mornay's *Discours de la vie et de la mort* because her brother had begun a translation of another work by that author do not speculate upon why the countess chose to translate that particular work instead of another. Scholars' claims that her translation of Robert Garnier's *Marc Antoine* supposedly forwarded Sir Philip Sidney's attempt to reform the English stage along the principles laid out in his *Apology for Poetry* never seem to wonder why, if she wished to reform the English stage, she chose a notable example of closet drama, never intended for the stage at all? If her translation of Petrarch's *Trionfo della Morte* was truly an embodiment of her "idealized love" for her brother, why did she choose a poem which depicts the excellent death of a woman, rather than of a man?

Mary Sidney's representation of her desire to die expressed at the end of her poem **"To the Angell spirit of the most excellent Sir Philip Sidney"** suggests an additional discourse underlying her version of authorship, which she shared not only with her brother Philip but also with her mother, her husband, and many other late-sixteenth-century Elizabethans. Taken together, these three translations by the countess of Pembroke—her *Discourse of Life and Death* (1590) from Philippe du Plessis Mornay's *Discours de la vie et de la mort,* her *Antoine* (c. 1590) from Robert Garnier's *Marc Antoine,* and her *Triumph of Death* from Petrarch's *Trionfo della Morte*—reveal an interest in the art of dying, particularly by beautiful heroines who die for love. Mornay's essay is an explicit *ars moriendi* tract that develops its argument against the fear of death along a peculiarly stoicized version of Christianity, while Garnier's play and Petrarch's poem feature appealing female protagonists who demonstrate their heroism by dying well.

The countess's translations of the works by Garnier and Petrarch reveal her struggle to apply Mornay's insights to the specific situation of women. These three translations demonstrate her response to the *ars moriendi* literature and to the heroics of constancy as these concerned women at the end of the sixteenth century. By exalting the ability to suffer without complaint, to endure any affliction with fortitude, Stoicism was consonant with other models in the Renaissance that recommended silence and obedience in the face of adversity as praiseworthy female behavior. Similarly, the scene of the noble death repeatedly portrayed in the *ars moriendi* tracts offered a model of heroism that women might emulate without violating the dominant sexual ideology. The countess's translations embody a female literary strategy through which women could be represented as heroic without challenging the patriarchal culture of Elizabethan England.

Not only did translating works about women who die well provide the countess with viable women heroines, but her subject also worked to absolve her as author from the charge of attempting to seduce or to gain power through her writing. Presenting women who die well as models to emulate strongly implied her own involvement in making a good death. After all, a woman who studies methods of dying has, it would seem, declared her distance from such transient concerns as illicit sexuality or other forms of control over men.

This creation of heroines who demonstrate their purity by their willingness to die well draws power from the captivity episode in Philip Sidney's revised *Arcadia,* which presented a revaluation of women and of passionate love. Rather than sharing in the guilty sexuality of the "fair ladies" addressed in the *Old Arcadia,* the princesses become constant heroines in the *New Arcadia.* Through their passionate love for their princes, they show control over, rather than capitualtion to, their emotions; for through their love they conquer their fear of death. From this model Mary Sidney may well have constructed a form of authorship, also heroized by the willingness to die, exonerating her from the sense of sexual contamination surfacing with special strength in episodes of female authorship in Sidney's work.

Heroizing women for their willingness to die was hardly limited to the Sidneys. This form of heroism was a cultural cliche, set forth in a multitude of works read in the Renaissance, from Boccaccio's *De Claris Mulieribus* to Chaucer's *Legend of Good Women* to Castiglione's *Book of the Courtier.* In all of these works, the willingness to die was represented primarily as a means of exonerating women from the charge of sexual guilt. In Castiglione's work, for example, Cesare Gonzaga mounts an impassioned defense of women by demonstrating their continence through an array of grisly examples of women who "have chose rather to dye then to lose their honesty" not only in the "olde time" but even in his day.

These gory accounts of glorious female deaths, usually suicides, were explicitly offered for imitation in the lives of young women in tracts on women's education in the Renaissance. Vive's influential *Instruction of a Christian Woman* (1592) recommends that girls be informed about the examples of virtuous women. The kind of virtue he intends becomes apparent in the no fewer than twelve stories he recounts of women who preferred death, usually by suicide, to submitting to sexual dishonor. These women represent only a small portion of those "infinite in number, that had leaver be killed, headed, strangled, drowned, or have their throtes cut, then loose their chastitie." Vives was not unique in his approach to female education. In recommending appropriate readings for young girls in his *Mirrhor of Modestie,* Thomas Salter elevates "Lucres, Portia, Camma," and Christian martyrs, all of whom preferred ghastly deaths to dishonorable lives, as examples of "vertuous Virgines and worthie Women" through which an Elizabethan girl "maie increase and augmente her vertue by immytatyng their lives." How did these examples affect young Elizabethan girls? The lesson was clear, even if few women were actually offered the necessary conditions for an exemplary suicide in their personal lives. By preferring death to dishonor (should it be offered), they could attain the stature of heroines, cleansed from the possibility of contamination from unauthorized sexuality. This lesson may well have influenced Mary Sidney's version of authorship, as well. Through translating works about women who died well, she cleansed her writing from the contamination of the illicit sexuality inherent in female authorship.

The countess's decision to translate Mornay's *Discours de la vie et de la mort* sets her writing within an additional discourse which presented an opportunity for heroism more capable of enactment within the actual lives of its adherents. From the late Middle Ages, the *ars moriendi* tradition provided a means of attaining or proving spiritual worth. Numbers of Elizabethans attempted to implement its lessons in their lives by making a good death, although what was considered to be a good death depended upon which version a dying person chose to follow. Nancy Lee Beaty [in *The Craft of Dying: A Study in the Literary Tradition of the Ars Moriendi in England,* 1970] traces how, by the late sixteenth century, authors of *ars moriendi* tracts had rung at least three separate changes upon the original fifteenth-century source, which offered practical advice to arm dying persons against the devil's final temptations, especially the temptation to despair. First, several Protestant tracts adapted a Catholic technique of meditation to inspire the dying person with the religious devotion fitting for an exemplary death. Second, and less satisfactorily, Calvinist tracts included expositions of dogma not always directly helpful to the act of dying itself; this strategy reflected the strain the *ars moriendi* tradition created within the Calvinist theology, according to which a person was already elect or damned, despite deathbed behavior.

When the countess chose to translate Mornay's *Discours de la vie et de la mort,* she was turning to a somewhat Christianized version of the third form of *ars moriendi* tract, which ignored the deathbed to focus instead on philosophical arguments persuading the reader not to fear death. Even in its most classical form, this third, humanistic version developed a Stoic view that need not have conflicted with church doctrine; for its pervasive sense of the illusory nature of worldly fortune was thoroughly present in church teachings as well. But in practice this classical perspective drastically deemphasized the personal relationship between man and God, the sense of sin, and the recognition of Christ as Redeemer that composed the cornerstones of both Catholic-influenced and Calvinist tracts on dying. Despite the introduction of a Christian emphasis in its final quarter and despite its occasional scriptural allusions scattered throughout, Mornay's tract is characterized by all of these aspects of the humanistic form of *ars moriendi.* An avid Calvinist, Mornay seems an unlikely author of a primarily humanist, as opposed to a Calvinist, tract. His *Vindiciae contra tyrannos* posits reason as a ser-

vant of faith, not as a source of belief in itself. Yet, as Diane Bornstein shows in the introduction to [*The Countess of Pembroke's Translation of Philippe de Mornay's "Discourse of Life and Death",* 1983], the major portion of Mornay's work is so permeated by Stoic philosophy that when Mornay refers to Christian immortality at the end of the work, "it almost strikes a jarring note." This perception of Mornay's work as primarily Stoic in emphasis is confirmed by Mornay's addition of selections from Seneca's letters in its 1576 edition. (pp. 115-22)

While an interest in Seneca was by no means confined to any one gender, there are indications of the felt applicability of the Stoic ideal to the situation of women in the Renaissance. By the seventeenth century, moralists had made the usefulness of Stoic philosophy to women's domestic situation explicit, but the particular appropriateness of Seneca's letters to women was apparently sensed earlier. For example, a 1589 portrait of the countess of Cumberland holding the works of Seneca along with a Bible and a book of alchemy represents the centrality of the Stoic ideal to the presentation of a well-known Elizabethan woman. Even the restrictive Luis Vives encouraged women to read Seneca. Writings of Seneca were translated by various women, including, apparently, Queen Elizabeth.

The reason for the attractiveness of Seneca to Renaissance women is not difficult to comprehend. Perhaps more than any other contemporary philosophy, Stoicism was consonant with the sexual ideology of the time. The Stoic ideal as expressed in Mornay's *Discours de la vie et de la mort* is as follows: the apparent "goods" of this life—love, wealth, fame—are illusory, for they cannot bring true satisfaction. Instead, they subject one to the destabilizing emotions of hope and fear, joy and sorrow, which attend the revolutions of the wheel of Fortune. Only by disengaging from earthly desires can one gain a sense of what is real and enduring; from this detachment one achieves the equanimity of soul to bear any misfortune, even death, without complaint. Death, in fact, provides a welcome release from the miseries of life; and the calmness with which one greets one's own death measures the extent to which one has achieved a superior understanding of the illusory nature of the pleasures of this life.

This Senecan ideal ennobled the behavior that was hoped for from women. It heroized the enforced nonparticipation of ordinary women (as opposed to queens) in the public arena; for one who understands the transitory nature of worldly events, detachment from the hustle and bustle of public affairs was to represent true wisdom. Stoicism's emphasis upon passive endurance over heroic action and its privileging of inner composure as a positive virtue provided a powerful model for heroism that was accessible to women. If they could not fight on the battlefields, if they could not administer justice in the law courts, if they could not gain properties by charming an aging queen, yet they could prove their worth, if only in their own eyes, by enduring whatever fortune sent without resistance or discontent.

This ability to endure misfortune without complaint was consonant with the passivity that had been associated with women from the time of Aristotle, who allowed women excellence in the "imperfect" or passive virtues of *continentia, verecundia,* and *tolerantia,* or chastity, modesty, and long-suffering. While the story of Eve rendered women's chastity suspect by the time of the Renaissance, women's superiority in endurance, or long-suffering, was reinforced by biblical precedent, especially in Proverbs. Perhaps the most important factor contributing to Stoicism's appeal to women proceeded from its unusual structure as a discourse, in the way in which its creation of a view of the ideal man was not predicated upon his superiority to women. Unlike other Renaissance discourses, which defined the ideal man in opposition to irrational and/or sinful women, the Stoic discourse defined its hero, the sage, in opposition to the powerful, those whom Fortune raised up and cast down. Its villain was not Eve, but Alexander. Predictably, Stoicism, the one text which did not strongly construct a view of women as a weak or sinful Other, became in fact the discourse which enabled the countess's writing.

Mary Sidney's *Discourse of Life and Death* was a close translation of Mornay's tract, which until its final quarter based its argument more on reason than on faith or Scripture, to move inexorably towards the conclusion that death is to be welcomed, not feared. After an introductory collection of soothing metaphors for death—the haven for the toiling mariner, the end of a weary journey, "our true home and resting place"—Mornay embarks on a thorough disquisition of the ills endemic to each stage of life. A baby or small child is miserable, "neither receiving in his first yeeres any pleasure nor giving to others but annoy and displeasure"; as he grows, he "falleth into the subjection of some Schoolemaister" to study only with "repining." As a youth, he becomes subject to the bondage of passion, which aims only to "cast him into all viciousness."

While the miseries of the first stages of life were endured by aristocratic little girls as well as boys, the illusory ambitions of middle age for which Mornay saves his special fervor refer almost exclusively to male experience. Money, that "vile excrement," can never content the covetous. Worldly honor repays us only with "smoke and winde," as those "great about Princes" or "commanders of Armies" can witness. Soldiers hazard their lives, often losing an arm or leg, for princes who do not love them. Courtiers lose their ability to command themselves through their constant flattery of the prince. If a courtier is raised to a "great height," the prince "makes it his pastime . . . to cast him downe at an instant." Especially subject to the wheel of fortune, courtiers endure the envy of their inferiors at their height and then, "disrobed of their triumphall garment," are known by no one. Even at their height, their pleasure is spoiled by their fear of loss and their ambition to climb yet higher. Even princes are the most miserable of men, and numerous monarchs have attested to the anxiety which attends the crown. Escape from the world provides no respite. The world follows us even into the desert, and if it does not, "we finde greater civill warre within our selves." Even learning is an empty vexation of the spirit leading to no self-knowledge, for it brings "on the minde an endlesse labour, but no contentment," failing to pacify

"the debates a man feeles in himselfe." The only stage easily applicable to ordinary women is old age, which gathers in only the "plentifull harvest of all such vices as in the whole course of their life, hath held and possessed them." Death provides a welcome release.

Despite occasional references to Lot and Solomon, this first three-quarters of Mornay's tract is essentially secular. His Senecan approach is so strong that the Christian hope for heaven is temporarily forgotten: "Tell mee, what is it else to bee dead, but to bee no more living in the worlde? Absolutelie and simplie not to be in the worlde, is it anie paine?" The classical orientation of most of his argument becomes explicit in Mornay's introduction to the final, Christian fourth of his tract: "But unto us brought up in a more holy schoole, death is a farre other thing: neither neede we as the Pagans of consolations against death." Christians who have faith in God need not fear death. We should neither seek death (for that is cowardice) nor flee it (for that is childish). Through death, God will provide us "true quietnesse" and "pleasures whiche shall never more perish." We must "die to live" and "live to die." This Christian ending did not substantially alter Mornay's perception of this work as imbued with Stoic philosophy, for he issued the work in 1576 with selections from Seneca's letters, which were later appended to an edition of Mary Sidney's translation in 1606. In his preface to Seneca's selected letters, Mornay explains his use of Seneca's views: Seneca arrived at a perception of "le vanite de l'homme . . . seulement avec son jugement natural et quelque connoissance et experience." Christians, then, should be all the more able to attain the same knowledge and resignation to God's will.

Mornay's treatise applied the Stoic ideal primarily to the life course led by men, not by women. Sheltered at home, aristocratic young Englishwomen seldom had the opportunity to be cast into any dramatic, immediately recognizable forms of viciousness by their passion. More strikingly, few women had the chance to experience the emptiness of being "great about Princes" or commanding armies. While they could enjoy the fruits of the wealth of their fathers and husbands, women did not, as a whole, have the opportunity personally to strive in the world, attempting to climb higher, becoming ever more thirsty for worldly honors. Instead, their rise or fall depended for the most part upon the rise or fall of their close male relatives. While dying to live and living to die would seem to represent a goal women could attempt to reach, the specific application of Mornay's Senecan philosophy to the lives of women was yet to be made.

Strong evidence suggests the the countess's translation of Garnier's *Marc Antoine,* with its heroic portrait of a female protagonist, Cleopatra, is an attempt to apply Mornay's philosophy to the situation of Renaissance women. First, the translations of Mornay's treatise and Garnier's play were probably intended as a pair, for they were published in the same volume. Secondly, the content of the two works is strikingly similar. The chorus of act 1 of *Antonie,* for example, reads like a versified *Discourse of Life and Death.*

Nature made us not free

When first she made us live:
When we began to be,
To be began our woe:
Which growing evermore
As dying life dooth growe,
Do more and more us greeve,
And trie us more and more.

The chorus to act 3 recites a virtual paean to death:

> *Death* rather healthfull succor gives,
> *Death* rather all mishapps relieves,
> That life upon us throweth:
> And ever to us doth unclose
> The doore whereby from curelesse woes
> Our wearie soule out goeth.
> What Goddesse else more milde than she
> To burie all our paine can be,
> What remedie more pleasing?

But it is the central figure of Cleopatra herself who most prominently employs Stoicism in her heroics of constancy. From Antony's opening speech, the suspense of the play revolves around whether or not Cleopatra will betray him to Caesar to save her own kingdom and her life. Much of the middle of the play consists of debates between Cleopatra's followers, who attempt to dissuade her from her decision to die, and Cleopatra, whose contempt for life and desire for death would impress any Stoic philosopher. The play ends with Cleopatra's ringing resolution to die as soon as she has performed the proper obsequies for Antony's corpse. In her absolute rejection of the possibility of saving her life and perhaps her crown by living subject to Caesar, Cleopatra attains the stature of a constant heroine in her insistence on death.

Cleopatra's desire to die for love would not have been endorsed by Seneca or Mornay. Neither writer makes any distinction between mature love and the "tyrannical passion" felt at the height of youth. An Elizabethan explication of Seneca asserts that love is madness, although not as severe a madness as the lust for riches. Love, according to Seneca, is one of those passions that bind a human to Fortune's wheel; emotional dependence on another person's affections prevents the attainment of complete calm. For Cleopatra, however, love is the agency through which she rises above the caprices of Fortune, as she declaims to the absent Antony:

> And didst thou then suppose my royall hart
> Had hatcht, thee to ensnare, a faithles love?
> And changing minde, as Fortune change cheare?

For Cleopatra, the prospect of loyalty to a defeated Antony, even a dead Antony, outweighs her realm, her children, her own life. And it is her love for Antony, not just her ability to face death, that motivates her bravery. Far from a beastly passion, this love is an integral part of her humanity, as she exclaims to one of her women: "Without this love I should be inhumaine."

Cleopatra's renunciation of her ability to protect the interests of her children and her realm as well as her own life understandably displeases her fellow Egyptians; and much of the central portion of *Antonie* is composed of their attempts to dissuade her. Her exchange with Charmion is typical:

CHARMION: Live for your sonnes.
CLEOPATRA: Nay for their father die.
CHARMION: Hardhearted mother!
CLEOPATRA: Wife kindhearted I.

Diomede soliloquizes his wish that the queen would cease mourning and charm Caesar to gain back her crown, saving them all from disaster. But despite the wishes of her followers and despite Antony's suspicions that she will betray him, Cleopatra never wavers in her resolve. As the curtain falls, she bends weeping over Antony's corpse, her own suicide delayed only until she can give Antony his "due rites."

Cleopatra's determination to die provides two means through which ordinary women could demonstrate their heroism. Cleopatra's loyalty to the defeated Antony heroizes the domestic virtue of a wife's loyalty to her husband despite the vicissitudes of fortune. Representing this usually passive attribute as heroic ennobles a wifely response perhaps often taken for granted. Second, just as the countess's mother compensated, according to Holinshed, for the obscurity of her life with a noteworthy death, any woman could die well. But there is a difference between Cleopatra's orientation towards death and that of the elder Mary Sidney. Holinshed represented the elder Mary Sidney's speeches as demonstrating Christian virtues, as she exhorted those standing around her deathbed to "repentance and amendement of life," persuading them "from all sin and lewdness" and proving herself a virtuous Christian in much the same manner as a man would do. In contrast, Cleopatra combines the attributes of Stoic and wife. By defining herself in terms of her relationship with a man, Cleopatra represents a specifically female deviation from the Stoic ideal as it applied to men, who died declaiming philosophical, political, or moral sentiments, not their love for their wives.

Repeatedly calling Antony "husband," Cleopatra is portrayed as a faithful wife instead of the adulteress of legend. The absence of any hint of illicit sexuality or even of Egyptian sensuality suggests the way in which Cleopatra's willingness to die cleanses her from sexual taint. Her overtly sexual lines are delivered only over Antony's dead body. These lines, which conclude the play, represent her wished-for death as an erotic act:

> A thousand kisses, thousand thousand more
> Let you my mouth for honors farewell give;
> That in this office weake my limmes may growe,
> Fainting on you, and fourth my soule may flowe.

This eroticization of death was hardly novel in a period when "to die" signified the act of intercourse. Yet the confinement of Cleopatra's sexual impulses to an expression of desire for death represents a striking deviation from the conventional representation of this.exotic queen of the fertile Nile.

This unusual suppression of Cleopatra's sexual nature suggests insights into the way in which the resolve to die cleanses a heroine of sexual taint. The intent to die well apparently cannot coexist with a desire for sexual love in one woman character. These two kinds of woman protagonists—the ascetic, loyal heroine who proves her heroism through her resolution to die and the alluring, seductive heroine who demonstrates her sexual power through attracting men with her abundant charms—are not combined until the stunning death scene of Shakespeare's Cleopatra. Quite possibly these diers and seducers are polarized because of their represented differences in their control over their emotions. It would seem that, in theory, a dying woman who can control her fear of death can also be expected to control her sexual appetites; a woman who cannot control her sexual appetites cannot be expected to control her fear of death. Yet whether they make love to them or die for them, both kinds of female protagonists define themselves in terms of their love for their men. (pp. 126-32)

Mary Sidney's translation of Petrarch's *Triumph of Death,* which she was working on in 1599 but never published, provides another powerful model for female self-effacement. Petrarch's prominent placement of Laura among a troop of women whose chastity has just won a victory over love inserts Laura securely in the tradition of women like Lucrece who were willing to sacrifice their lives for their chastity. While Laura does not actively choose death, her brave anticipation of the news of its arrival demonstrates her sexual purity in much the same way as this often-cited female suicide. Her resignation probably provided a more usable model for Renaissance women readers than the willed deaths of other heroines held up to young Elizabethan girls for imitation.

Like Cleopatra and the other constant heroines, Laura defines herself even in death in terms of her relationship with a man, as she tempers her welcome of death with regret for the sorrow it will bring the poet:

> This charge of woe on others will recoyle,
> I know, whose safetie on my life depends:
> For me, I thank who shall me hense assoile.

The passivity of Laura's death, surpassing even the sacrifice fantasy of Brandon's Octavia, represents a striking departure from the *ars moriendi* tradition. While after her death Laura admits that "the crosse / Preeceding death, extreemlie martireth," her death scene, "deservedly famous for its serene beauty," conveys no sense of her physicality or of her pain. She fades like a flame; her whiteness resembles snow. Taking no active role, neither exhorting her friends to repentance as did the countess's mother, nor engaging in Cleopatra's lengthy internal debates, Laura gains admiration through her beauty:

> Right lyke unto som lamp of cleerest light,
> Little and little wanting nutriture,
> Houlding to end a never-changing plight.
> Pale? no, but whitelie; and more whitelie pure,
> Then snow on wyndless hill, that flaking falles:
> As one, whom labor did to rest allure.
> And when that heavenlie guest those mortall walles
> Had leaft: it nought but sweetlie sleeping was
> In hir faire eyes: what follie dying calles
> Death faire did seeme to be in hir faire face.

In the *Triumph of Death,* "making a good death" has been radically revised. The scene of Laura's death demonstrates not her religious fervor, not her detachment from the illusory pleasures of the world, but her beauty. Laura's beauty

is in fact best displayed in death, in its affirmation of her recumbent passivity, of her ethereal insubstantiality, of the absolute erasure of her person. All of these had already occurred in the *Canzoniere,* in which she had always represented an externality, a projected fiction by which the male poet measured his fame, his work, his ontology. While the depiction of Laura in *Triumph of Death* was perfectly understandable according to the artistic goals of Petrarch, who was not writing an *ars moriendi* poem or even a biographical statement about Laura, the countess's apparent acceptance of Petrarch's perspective implied in her choice to translate this *Triumph* is disturbing.

Perhaps the representation of Laura functions less as a model for dying well than, like the versions of Octavia, a model for living heroically. Her example shows how any woman can fulfill the function of spiritual guide, molding her words and actions to benefit her man on his pilgrimage to heaven. Returning to the poet as a spirit after her death, Laura exposes the elaborate fiction she had created to mold his behavior, encouraging him when he despaired, appearing angry with him when his suit became too hot, all out of her loving concern for his spiritual health:

> A thousand times wrath in my face did flame,
> My heart meane-time with love did inlie burne,
> But never will, my reason overcame.

Laura's modulation of her display of emotion to respond to the poet's needs rather than to her own feelings demonstrates a control of her passions far exceeding the poet's. Ironically, she reverses the pattern presented by Octavia. Laura controls her love to make it appear as anger, rather than controlling her anger to emerge victoriously loving. But the principle remains the same. Laura, like the Stoic heroines, creates her heroism through the absolute mastery of her feelings. Yet this mastery represents a form of self-erasure, for her inner drama is determined solely by the needs of the poet. While the idealized and insubstantial character of Laura herself does not admit ambiguity, her model for heroism represents the same mixture of anger and love, the same self-effacement disguised as self-mastery, as that offered by the constant heroines.

The art of dying emerging from the countess of Pembroke's translations bears varied fruits; its roots reach deeply into several substrata of soil. Most immediately, her intellectual and accomplished family provided fertile topsoil for her creation of the Stoic heroine. Written up by an eminent historian, her mother achieved an excellent death; writing a somewhat Senecan letter of condolence, her husband revealed a more Stoic preoccupation with death; her brother influenced her or, perhaps even more generously, let himself be subject to her influence when he created the princesses as constant heroines in the captivity episode of the *New Arcadia.* In addition to her family, Mary Sidney was no doubt also influenced by wider cultural trends, by the popularity of the *ars moriendi* tradition, by the Senecan revival, and by the numerous Christian Stoic sages making good and even learned deaths at the end of the sixteenth century. Beneath these lay the barren clay of the sexual ideology of the Renaissance, according to which she twisted both *ars moriendi* and Stoicism to create heroines who not only perceived themselves in terms of their men, but who also demonstrated their willingness to annihilate their inner selves by effacing their anger.

Perhaps the deepest influence on Mary Sidney's translations was a fundamental need to find a form of heroism applicable for her time and gender. Her translations held up mirrors in which Renaissance women could be perceived as heroic. Cleopatra's constancy to Antony exalts the domestic virtue of a wife's loyalty to her husband despite the turnings of the wheel of Fortune. Through this representation of Cleopatra, women could view themselves, in their simultaneous love for and anger at their husbands, as worthy protagonists in the drama of their own lives. Through Laura, women could perceive themselves as spiritual authorities, bearing upon their virtuous shoulders the responsibility for their husbands' immortal souls. If women could not win public admiration for remarkable deeds in the outside world, they could at least attain dignity in their own eyes as constant heroines, giving of themselves, submerging their rage and sorrow beneath the smooth surface of equanimity. And when the time came, they all had the opportunity to die gracefully.

Both Cleopatra and Laura are, finally, models of negation. Each model defines women as important solely in terms of their relationships with men, even in the most private and solitary act of death. Militant images of self-aggression and self-enclosure characterizing the adaptations of the constant heroine by authors connected with the countess of Pembroke reveal the destructive potential of this means of channeling rage. These negative aspects of the constant heroine remind us that the Countess was a translator, not an author in her own right. In both the literal and the broad sense, she translated a male perspective on women. The Cleopatra of the *Antonie* is the creation of Robert Garnier; Laura is the creation of Petrarch. Both of these female heroines bear striking resemblances to Lucrece, Portia, Iphigenia, and the other women who "died well" to prove their sexual purity to a patriarchal culture.

We should not be too quick to criticize Mary Sidney for the disturbing implications of her constant heroines. There were few alternatives. The Renaissance offered women few healthy models for encouraging the expression of justified rage or for acknowledging the heroism of their ordinary lives as they bore with husbands whose marital infidelities were so generally condoned within the culture that these infidelities could not even be effectively protested. The countess made good use of her limited material to enable not only her writing, but even more astonishingly, her publication of her translations. A woman's publication of her work without apology or subterfuge was extremely rare in the Renaissance. Unlike the learned Anne Bacon, the countess did not first submit her translation to the discerning eye of male authority. No sympathetic friend obliged her by "betraying" her work to the press. She presented her work to the world in her own person, even marking the date and place of completion at the end. The countess of Pembroke's publication of her translations presents a model if not of heroism, then at least of courageous intellectual assertion that was made possible by her creation

of these Stoic heroines, from whose very self-effacement and beautiful deaths she created a viable version of authorship. (pp. 138-41)

 Mary Ellen Lamb, in her Gender and Authorship in the Sidney Circle, *The University of Wisconsin Press, 1990, 297 p.*

Margaret P. Hannay (essay date 1990)

[*Hannay is an American educator and critic who has remarked that she is "intrigued by that brief period in sixteenth-century England when women . . . were esteemed for their learning." In the following excerpt, Hannay discusses the political message encoded within Sidney's dedicatory poems and the psalms.*]

When the countess prepared the presentation volume of her *Psalmes,* she followed the example of the Geneva Psalter and the Gilby translation of Bèze by including pointed political comments in her two prefatory poems, **"To the Angell Spirit"** and **"Euen now that Care."** These original works were confined to the margins of discourse, to the minor genres of dedications and epitaphs, but we hear her own voice most clearly in these two poems, which had limited circulation. Nathaniel Baxter, Aemelia Lanyer, Michael Drayton, and John Davies of Hereford apparently referred to **"Angell Spirit."** Baxter, for example, in dedicating *Ourania* to Mary Sidney, says that Sir Philip's praise "is paynted with an Angels quill." Similarly, Michael Drayton speaks of the praises, "Pend with the quill of an Archangels wing." Both the dedicatory poem and the accompanying epitaph, **"To the Angell Spirit of the most excellent Sir Philip Sidney,"** mourn the loss of the countess's beloved brother, who had begun the Psalm translation; this was decorous and expected. What is more surprising is the political subtext of these two poems.

In **"To the Angell Spirit,"** Mary Sidney continued the partisan glorification of Sir Philip Sidney, who had been not only her brother, but also the hope of the more militant Protestants in England and particularly on the Continent. It was only in his own country of England and with his own queen that Sidney had had little recognition, a situation that the family attributed to envy at court. Envy, a theme that runs throughout *Astrophel,* including **"The Dolefull Lay of Clorinda,"** is an absent presence in **"Angell Spirit":** Sir Philip is portrayed at a heavenly court "where never Envie bites."

Although the *Psalmes* are officially dedicated to the queen, Mary Sidney declares that they are written only for her brother:

> To thee pure sprite, to thee alones addres't
> this coupled worke, by double int'rest thine:
> First rais'de by thy blest hand, and what is mine
> inspird by thee, thy secrett power imprest.

In a statement more accurate than most dedications, the countess acknowledges a double debt to Sidney. He had begun to translate the Psalms before he left for the Netherlands, possibly during one of his visits to Wilton. Since he had given her copies of the Psalms, they may have been written on "loose sheetes of paper" and sent to her, as had been the first drafts of the *Arcadia*. When he died from wounds received at the battle of Zutphen, he had translated just 43 of the 150 Psalms. The countess, as she says, completed the **Psalmes** as a memorial to her brother; through him she found her voice. As Gary Waller [in *Mary Sidney, Countess of Pembroke: A Critical Study of Her Writings and Literary Milieu,* 1979] and Beth Wynne Fisken [in "Mary Sidney's Psalms: Education and Wisdom," in *Silent But For the Word* edited by Margaret P. Hannay, 1985] have demonstrated, she learned her craft by following his model and by revising his drafts of the early Psalms. Given Mary Sidney's deprecation of her own abilities, it is probable that Sidney had discussed his Psalms with her and indicated the alterations that he had planned to make. The rest of the work was her own, although inspired by him.

Had he not died and so "reft the world of all / what man could showe, which wee [in our imperfection] perfection call," she declares, then "this half maim'd peece had sorted with the best." Her motivation in writing is clearly stated: "it hath no further scope to goe, / nor other purpose but to honor thee." Although more than two-thirds of the **Psalmes** are hers, she takes the humble place, comparing her contribution to his works as "little streames" that "flowe / to their great sea."

The next stanzas praise Sir Philip as a Phoenix adorned by heaven, fit to be adored by earth. Her loss is such that it strikes her dumb, as it would other writers: "who knewe thee best doeth knowe / There liues no witt that may thy praise become." Now that he is placed in heaven "among thy fellow lights," she mourns that day has been "put out, my life in darkenes cast." As he sings with the heavenly choir in a court where he finally receives the honor he deserves, on earth his works are "Immortall Monuments of thy faire fame." Although they remain incomplete, yet "there will liue thy ever praised name." Concluding with a prayer that he will "Receiue theise Hymnes," she signs the poem "By the Sister of that Incomparable Sidney," her habitual self-designation.

Although **"Angell Spirit"** is primarily a lament for personal loss, the conjunction of this epitaph with the dedication to the queen makes a powerful political statement. All eyes "which are not blindely madde," Elizabeth is told, praise Sidney's words "Beyonde compare." Had he been spared to peace, he would have completed these "Immortall Monuments"—a reminder that he had died in Elizabeth's service, in a war that the Sidneys believed doomed by her withholding of money and supplies. In the **"Angell Spirit"** the countess was reminding the queen that she had not favored "the wonder of men, sole borne perfection's kinde" as she ought, and, by implication, that she was not fulfilling her godly duties by defending the faith as Sidney had done.

The dedication to Queen Elizabeth is even more pointed. In the tradition of those relegated to the margins of society, the countess uses flattery to instruct, but **"Euen now that Care"** does not contain the fulsome praise of Elizabeth that one would expect from the title, from her obsequious 1601 letter to the queen, and from the decorum of the cult of the Faerie Queene. The relatively subdued compliments of the opening stanzas flatter her scholarship but serve primarily as a reminder that the fate of Europe rests in her hands: she is the one "On whom in chiefe dependeth to dispose / what Europe acts in theise most active times." The significance of this statement is clarified by Fulke Greville's usage: *active* means "busy in the Protestant cause." In his "Dedication to Sir Philip Sidney" "those active times" is a code phrase referring to the Protestant interventionism of Elizabeth's reign, as contrasted with "the narrow salves of this effeminate age," the Stuart period in which Greville wrote. Similarly, he described the Dutch as "this active people, which held themselves constantly to their religion and freedom." Like her family and like the Genevan Protestants, Mary Sidney believed that Elizabeth herself was the key to the establishment of the Protestant faith, in Continental Europe as well as England. If she functioned as a godly monarch, these would become "active times." To the Sidneys, her efforts were feeble, inadequate to the task; to Greville, looking back from what he perceived as the effeminate pacifism of the Stuart era, her days had indeed been "active."

After her opening salutation to Elizabeth, the countess once again mourns for her co-author, Sidney. The topic is deftly introduced; the senders "which once in two, now in one Subject goe, / the poorer left, the richer reft awaye." (These lines indicate that she had worked on the **Psalmes** from the beginning: once there had been two authors; now there is only one.) In a most accurate metaphor, she declares that "hee did warpe, I weau'd this webb to end"; that is, he set up the loom with the structural warp threads, while she supplied the pattern of the weave. "I the Cloth in both our names present, / a liuerie robe to bee bestowed by thee." Once again, the countess is reminding the queen that Sidney died wearing her livery and that, had she chosen rightly, he would have lived to wear it in her service. Now the countess must weave a web of words to create a livery with which to adorn Elizabeth, a livery that would emphasize the queen's own position as servant to God and to the Protestant cause. The queen can then bestow this livery on others, those who serve her cause and God's.

"The Dolefull Lay" and **"To the Angell Spirit"** are primarily personal laments, but in the dedication to Queen Elizabeth, the full intent of these epitaphs becomes clearer. Not only will Sidney's memory be sustained by the countess's completion and publication of his work, but his efforts to establish a Protestant League will be carried on. If the countess is barred by her sex from political councils and from the battlefield, she will use her pen. Thus by reminding the queen of Philip's death in the first half of the dedication, Mary Sidney was continuing the family tradition of seeking to influence Elizabeth toward a more radical Protestant stance. By comparing her to the Psalmist in the second half of the dedication, she was continuing the tradition of admonitory flattery, which was a standard element in the dedication of Scripture to sovereigns in both England and France. Although relegated to the margins of discourse by her gender, she found a model in the vernacular translations by exiles, relegated to the margins by their religion and politics: flattery is their safest weapon. (pp. 88-91)

By the time the countess wrote her own dedication to Elizabeth, the "Protestant David" (the David found in the commentaries of Luther, Philip Melanchthon, Calvin, Bèze, and Martin Bucer) was already well established in France as a paradigm for the reformed church. In England, the David comparison was deemed particularly appropriate to Elizabeth, as Mary Sidney recognizes when she declares, "how justly square / his haughty Ditties to thy glorious daies," elaborating the comparison in stanza 9:

> For eu'n thy Rule is painted in his Raigne:
> both cleere in right: both nigh by wrong opprest:
> And each at length (man crossing God in uaine)
> Possest of place, and each in peace possest.
> Proud Philistines did interrupt his rest,
> The foes of heau'n no lesse have beene thy foes;
> Hee with great conquest, thou with greater blest;
> Thou sure to winn, and hee secure to lose.

Like David, Elizabeth had been menaced by an ungodly ruler; like David, she had been vindicated by God and blessed with a triumphant rule. The countess did not make explicit the equation of Philistines with Catholics, but she did not have to; the text had become self-explicating. That equation was already as familiar a trope in the Protestant literature as the comparison of the Protestant monarch (Elizabeth or Henri de Navarre) to David. For example, in his *Coronation of David* (1588), Edmund Bunny of York compares "the late unnatural practices" against Elizabeth with the various attempts on David's life, predicting that as David at last overcame his foes, so Elizabeth would possess the land in peace. Similarly, Greville looks back nostalgically on Elizabeth as England's "she-David" and, for Jacobean eyes, makes explicit his identification of the Philistines: "I mean Spain and the Pope."

The countess was astute in choosing the David comparison, because Elizabeth herself had implied an identification with David in her own youthful translation of Psalm 13, appropriately a call for succor and revenge in time of affliction by "the foes of heaven." When her translation of the Psalm was printed in 1548, John Bale's dedication interpreted it as an anti-Catholic statement:

> By thys do your grace vnto us sygnyfye, that the baren doctryne and good workes without fayth of the hypocrytes, which in their . . . latyne ceremonyes serue their bellyes and not Christ, in gredly devourynge the patrymony of poor wydowes and orphanes, are both execrable in themselues, and abhomynable afore God.

Whether or not this reading was intended by the queen, this Psalm may explain the penultimate phrase of the countess's dedication, asking that the queen may "sing what God doth"—as she had once before. Even more telling is Elizabeth's reputed reaction on hearing of the death of her sister, Queen Mary. Appropriating the words of the Psalmist, she cried, "This is the Lord's doing; it is marvellous in our eyes." (pp. 92-3)

Psalms have always been a standard part of Judeo-Christian worship, but the Psalms of medieval missals were far from the Psalms sung as battle cries by the Huguenots. Identifying their cause with that of the Psalmist, the Huguenots adapted the Psalms to their own conditon, finding in them a strong—even militant—sense of identity, as W. Stanford Reid has demonstrated. When they went into battle, the Huguenots sang Psalm 68, "Let God arise, let his enemies be scattered." When the Prince of Condé arrived in Orléans, people sang in the streets, "If it had not been the Lord who was on our side, now may Orléans say. . . ." Martyrs in England went to the stake singing Psalm 130; in Antwerp, a sermon delivered by Dr. Hermanus was followed by Psalm singing and then a riot, during which the crowd demolished all the church images; Mary, Queen of Scots, was welcomed home to Scotland in 1561 by crowds singing Psalms under her bedroom window. Some twenty years later, when the exiled John Durie returned to Edinburgh, some 2,000 of his followers paraded to St. Giles Church while singing Psalm 124 ("Now may Israel say") and so terrified Esmé Stuart, Duke of Lennox, that he fled Scotland, "more affrayed of this sight than anie thing that ever he had seen before in Scotland." (pp. 93-4)

Although the Psalms were not used as a battle cry in England until the Civil War of the seventeenth century, the returning Marian exiles brought back the custom of singing Psalms "after the Geneva fashion," gathering at St. Paul's Cross in London, to Elizabeth's dismay. These Psalm-singing Protestants were a constant worry to Elizabeth, for they threatened her careful religious compromise by continuing to use every possible occasion to instruct her on the means necessary to maintain the true faith, just as the Genevan dedication on her accession had done: such pointed application of the Psalms to current political issues was a very different matter from daily readings of Psalms in the *Book of Common Prayer*.

Elizabeth herself had used a French Psalter early in her reign; nevertheless, Mary Sidney's gift of a Psalter modeled on the Huguenot Psalms could itself be interpreted as a political statement in 1599. When prefaced with a lament for Sir Philip Sidney, already acknowledged as a Protestant martyr, and a dedicatory poem that began with a reference to the Continent, the political intent of her gift would be unmistakable.

While the countess is certainly not advocating either slaughter of heretics or regicide, unlike the more radical Huguenot works, her reference to the early adversities of Elizabeth does emphasize the prudence of a stalwart defense of the Protestant faith; like Philip's letter, Mary Sidney's dedication is a reminder that for Elizabeth, the Catholics can only be the Philistines. In his peroration, which Elizabeth could not have forgotten, Sidney had echoed the Genevan dedication: "You must take it for a singular honour God hath done unto you, to be indeed the only protector of his church." If "you make that religion, upon which you stand . . . [your] only strength" and maintain alliance with those abroad of similar faith, then "your Majesty is sure enough from your mightiest enemies." If the queen is steadfast, Sidney promises, then Protestants will continue to support her, and her reign will be glorious: "doing as you do, you shall be, as you be: the example of princes, the ornament of this age . . . and the perfect mirror to your posterity." The conflating of present and future tenses does not quite mask the imperative that underlies them; Philip Sidney's statement is a more guarded version of Samuel Daniel's dedication to "most hopefull" Prince Henry, "not as you are / but as you may be." That Elizabeth knew how to interpret such flattery is clear. During one of the early progresses, she had responded to the usual fulsome praise by saying, "I now thank you for putting me in mynd of my duety, and that should be in me."

Mary Sidney's own flattering comparison of Elizabeth to David is carefully connected to her concluding prayer that the aging queen will be granted years "farre past hir living Peeres / and rivall still to Iudas Faithfull King." Like her use of the tradition of admonitory flattery and of the David comparison, this prayer for the sovereign is part of the partisan tradition. As Bèze declares in his preface to Psalm 72, "When God does raise vp such kings [as David], one must recognize that they are singular . . . gifts of God . . . so that they may know that it is for themselves that they pray when they pray for their Lords and Magistrates." This Psalm is a prayer that God will teach "the king, whome thou hast appointed, the rules of right government . . . That he may justlie gouerne, not his people, but thine." If the monarch governs justly, "his memorie shal be for euer, euen durable as the Sunne: and this king shall be an example of al felicitie vnto al nations." Despite Elizabeth's negligence toward her brothers, the countess probably agreed with Bèze's earlier conclusion that "England is the happiest (kingdom) in the world today" because the authority of the English monarch is founded on the consent of Parliament: "the happy repose the English have enjoyed . . . under the mild and beneficent government of their most gracious Queen Elizabeth, as compared with the wretched . . . condition of so many other countries, shows . . . what happiness . . . there is in moderation of royal power if it is rightly observed." But royal power can be correctly moderated only when the monarch listens to her subjects, as the countess is asking her to do.

Thus as the last strong voice of the Dudley/Sidney alliance left in Elizabethan England, the countess not only supported the Protestant cause through her translation of a work by the Huguenot leader Mornay and through her encouragement of a hagiography that elevated her brother Philip to the status of Protestant martyr, but also attempted to address the queen, decorously but directly. Like her *Psalmes,* Mary Sidney's dedicatory admonitions are far more subtle and literary than most of their predecessors. Nevertheless, it is clear that the countess is not merely praising Elizabeth by the David comparison; like the Genevan Protestants and like her brother Philip, she also is exhorting her to fulfill her obligations as monarch, defend the true faith, and so "doo What men may sing."

The countess did not need to add a political cast to her original. In the first place, the Hebrew Psalms themselves contain a cry for deliverance and vengeance. In the second place, we have little evidence that either Philip or Mary Sidney knew Hebrew; they worked primarily from the best scholarly editions in Latin, French, and English. Because the very concept of translating and elucidating the

Scriptures was one of the strongest elements in the Reformation, the commentaries most readily available to them were intensely partisan. This means that when they read a Psalm like 82, all the identifications of Elizabeth with David and the Philistines with the Catholics were present for them in the text. Just as medieval readers could not read a narrative without perceiving it as allegory, so someone raised in the Protestant alliance could not read the Psalms without recognizing contemporary political parallels. (pp. 94-6)

Even before the completion of the French Psalter of 1562, the countess's own family had used the Psalms in a pointed personal attack on enemies. Both John and Robert Dudley translated Psalms of vengeance while they were imprisoned in the Tower for having taken part in their father's conspiracy to put the Protestant Lady Jane Grey on the throne. Although it was as clear to Northumberland's enemies as it is to modern historians that political ambition was his primary motivation, he was also attempting to maintain the "one true faith" in England against the Catholicism of Mary Tudor. It would not take more than the usual mental dishonesty for the Dudleys to identify their enemies with the enemies of God. John Dudley's paraphrase of Psalm 55 becomes a cry for vengeance against friends who had betrayed him:

> ffor yf they had bene foes / that wold display
>   their yre
> Then warn'd thearby I might have bene / as by
>   the flambe from fyre
> but even my mates they weare / that seem'de to
>   holde me deere
> When vnder face of frendlye faithe / they bredd
>   this doulefull cheere
> Synce so: devoure them Lorde / consume them
>   everye chone
> And throwe them in the dredfull pitt / wheare
>   they shall stintles mone.

Robert Dudley's paraphrase of Psalm 94 is even more emphatic in the identification of his cause with God's:

> But yet in time beware / you froward blooddie
>   band
> What thinges against the Lord your god / you
>   seeke to take in hand.

Sir Henry Sidney made the same identification of his cause with the cause of God and his enemies with the enemies of Israel in his quotation of Psalm 114 as he left Ireland, "In exitu Israel de Aegypto, and domus Jacob de populo barbaro." Lest we miss the implication, John Hooker interprets the citation for us: Sidney is "alluding thereby to the troublesome state of Moses in the land of Egypt." (p. 98)

[This] identification of the Sidneys' cause with God's was present in the primary sources for the Sidneian Psalms. Mary Sidney's Psalter retains the political cast of these sources, although her version is technically and poetically superior to all of them but the best of Marot. Three Psalms will serve as examples: Psalms 82, 83, and 101. Like Bèze and the translators of the Geneva Bible, Mary Sidney interprets Psalm 82 as a condemnation of the corrupt judgment of earthly rulers, Psalm 83 as a prayer to save the true faith from the machinations of the Amalekites and the Moabites (who were, like the Philistines, identified with the Catholics in the Protestant literature), and Psalm 101 as David's portrait of the ideal ruler, with particular emphasis on rewarding the righteous and punishing the ungodly.

The standard Protestant reading of Psalm 82 is boldly stated in Calvin's heading:

> Forbicause Kings and such as be endewed with authoritie being blinded with pride, doo for the moste parte take libertie to do what they list: he giueth them warning, that they must render an account before the souerein iudge, which surmounteth all worldly highnesse. And after he hath put them in minde of their duetie and estate: forasmuche as he perceiueth himself to talk to deafe folke, he calleth vpon God for vengeance.

In her version, the countess retains this traditional interpretation; her main alteration of her sources is to dramatize the situation: while "poore men plead at Princes barre," the judges themselves are being judged by God. Mary Sidney, "meditating" on the Psalm before her, condensed an entire sentence of Bèze's commentary on the "gods" (as God's vice regents) and gives a sense of another court "pight" (pitched) over the visible one, a court with a supreme judge who not only hears the case, but also judges plaintiff and magistrate alike. Stanzas 2 to 5 are presented, as they are in her sources, as the direct words of that superior judge, God. Clarifying the speech available to her, she shapes an oration that relies heavily on parallel structure and repetition. "How long will ye just doome neglect? / How long saithe he, bad men respect?"

Her version sharpens the political emphasis. Like Marot (and unlike her English sources), she sets up a list of imperatives for magistrates:

> You should his owne vnto the helplese giue,
> the poor releeue,
> ease him with right, whom wrong doth greeue.
>
> You should the fatherlesse defend:
> you should vnto the weake extend
> your hand, to loose and quiet his estate
> through lewd mens hate
> entangled now in deepe debate.

As judges, their duty is to help the weak—the poor, and widows and orphans—whose estates are entangled in litigation. The entire passage is summarized by the sentence "This should you doe" before the judgment is given, "but what doe ye?" The judges' failings are succinctly analyzed: "You nothing know, you nothing see," although they are supposed to see and to weigh. The following phrase, "no light, no law," is an extraordinarily concise statement of Bèze's interpretation, one that draws on the Law as lamp (Psalm 119) and on the New Testament association of God with light. The ungodly judges turn their backs on God's Law and oppress the poor. This concern for the poor is evident in the countess's life, if we can believe Nicholas Breton's description of Wilton as a paradise where "the poor [are] blessedly relieued." (pp. 98-9)

As Psalm 82 speaks of the oppression of the poor by unjust judges, so Psalm 83 speaks of the oppression of the godly by foreign enemies. The translators of the Geneva version designate Psalm 83 as referring to the time of Jehoshaphat, a comparison they had already used for Queen Elizabeth in their dedication. The Bèze and Gilby commentary, although assigning the Psalm to David, also emphasizes the contemporary application: "[I]t declareth, that there shal neuer want neither foreine nor domestical enimies unto the Church, and by what weapons they are chieflie ouercome: the which doctrine how necessarie it is to our times especiallie, would God that al, to whome it belongeth, would consider." Calvin's heading, again conflating Israel and the true church, stresses God's vengeance: "The Prophet calleth for Gods helpe against the enemies of the Churche . . . he sheweth by allegation of many examples, how mightely God hathe benne wonte to succour his seruantes."

Mary Sidney's version of the Psalm emphasizes that political reading through original imagery. To stress the hunting of God's people by their enemies, for example, she develops an extended metaphor from falconry. The only hint of such imagery in her usual sources is Bèze's description of God's own people "flieng vnder thine onlie shadowe of defence." The countess portrays the enemies of God filing sharp points for their "trapps and traines"; *traines,* a technical term from falconry, here has a secondary meaning of "treachery" or "stratagem" as well as the primary "snare." God's people are his "hid ones," shrouded (concealed and sheltered) under his wings, in an echo of her own translation of Psalm 91:

> From snare the fowler laies
> He shall thee sure unty: . . .
> Soft hiu'd with wing and plume
> thou in his shrowd shalt ly.

The repetition of the words *shroud* and *wing* from Psalm 91 emphasizes the same context of refuge. God's people are hidden in the truth, safe from the "serching sight" of their enemies. The enemies therefore "forge in busy braines" the snares and lures that will draw God's people out from the shadow of God's wing. When God's people refuse to leave his protection, the hunters change their strategy. Stanza 3 presents their plan in direct dialogue:

> Come lett us of them nothing make:
> lett none of them more a people see:
> stopp we their verie name
> within the mouth of fame.

That is, they plan to take this quality of being hidden and turn it into annihilation. Because of the dramatic irony inherent in the Protestant Psalms, however, the readers know that David's prayer was heard, and his enemies themselves were destroyed. Thus without departing from the sense of her original, the countess has introduced the Protestant appeal to history, particularly the history of Israel, to demonstrate that God's chosen people have always been avenged; the readers, identifying with David, know that this—their own—prayer for vengeance will be answered as well.

Her Psalm concludes with another striking metaphor, that

of God as a painter who portrays the downfall of the wicked. "So paint their daunted face" expands the hint of the French *teinte* to present God as an artist using a "pencell of disgrace," an image that becomes a pun in her plea to "confound them quite, and quite deface," used both in the old sense of "discredit" or "defame" and as a glance back at the artist damaging the portrait. The enemies of God will literally lose face in the heavenly court.

Like Psalm 82, Psalm 83 ends with a plea that God's enemies be forced to recognize his legitimate authority. In retribution for their attempts to erase the name of the godly, their own names will be publicly discredited, and they will be forced to acknowledge that the name of Jehovah is "high plac't aboue all earthly place." Both Psalms focus on the tyrannical enemies of God's people, presenting negative images of kingship; Psalm 101, in contrast, focuses on the duties of the godly ruler.

Psalm 101 is traditionally interpreted as David's meditation on the responsibilities of kingship, composed between the time he was anointed and the time he ascended to the throne, "not thinking so much of the great honour . . . as of the greevous burthen that should be laide vpon him," as the Geneva heading declares. Sternhold and Hopkins amplify this reading in their own heading: "David describeth what gouernement he will obserue in his house and kyngdome. He will punish and correct by rooting out the wicked, and cherishing the godly persons." The Psalm is particularly useful because, as Bèze observes, "al the office of a king with maruelous breuitie is explaned, though generallie, yet verie exactlie." Stressing mercy and judgment as the two requisite qualities for kingship, David is careful not to "arrogate vnto himselfe the gouernement of this kingdome promised, but onelie receiue it of the hand of GOD himselfe deliuering it vnto him." In other words, like Psalms 82 and 83, Psalm 101 stresses the concept of kingship as vice regency under God.

Like Bèze, Calvin stresses that David would not presume to thrust himself into kingship: "he acknowledgeth himself to haue bene appoynted . . . by the benefite of God." This humility is necessary, Calvin says, "because it commonly falleth out that such as haue the soueraintie shoulde be fooles and doltes." Although they are not born so, "yet doothe their dignitie blynde them, so as they think they are no whit indetted to their subiects" and "welter themselues carelesly in their owne vices." When David vows "I will deale wisely," he is promising to avoid these common abuses of rulers.

The political reading is even clearer in Mary Sidney's version of Psalm 101, although it keeps closer to her sources than do Psalms 82 and 83. In the first line, she incorporates the notes of the Geneva Bible and of Calvin into a single clause: "When, now appointed king, I king shall be." As in her sources, David's song becomes also his vow. Knowing that it is not yet time for him to assume his public duty, he vows to study virtue and live at home pure in heart. The emphasis of this line is not so much on the disillusioned retreat from the court to the country house, as Waller suggests, as on the utilization of enforced retreat as preparation for destined return as king. In this, Mary Sidney follows her Genevan sources, reading "Till thou

comest to me" as a subordinate clause instead of the more traditional interrogative reading (as in the Great Bible, "When wilt thou come unto me?"). What David is waiting for is most explicit in Marot: "Quand viendras-tu me rendre Roi paisible?" Calvin declares "that althoughe Dauid continue styll a priuate person, and enioy not as yet the princely estate that was promised him, yet ceaseth he not to folow vprightnesse, all the meane whyle." Bèze interprets verses 1 and 2 as a recognition that by governing first himself and then his family (with a note on Joshua 7 and 8), he will learn to govern the kingdom. In either case, David is not retreating from the court, but preparing for his destined return. This reading underlies the countess's rendering:

> Till that day come thou me the crowne shalt
>   give,
> deepe study I on vertue will bestow:
> and pure in hart at home retired lyue.

Contemplation does not take the place of action, but serves as preparation for kingship. This interpretation may imply a glance back at Sidney's retirement at Wilton, time spent in frustration and in preparation for public service.

As in Mary Sidney's poems on Sir Philip, Psalm 101 emphasizes the problem of envy and slander, developed here through a cluster of images: heart, eye, and tongue. Expanding the image of *cœur,* or heart, she draws on Marot as well as English translations. Her reference to David's pure heart in line 6 is contrasted with the "malicious hartes" that he will not admit into his court and with the "puffed hartes" of stanza 5, wherein the swelling appears as a diseased growth. Calvin rendered this verse, "Whosoeuer is haultye of countenance, and wide of harte, him can not I abyde." The countess derived her image of "puffed hartes" from Calvin's commentary: "they must needs be puft up and swolen which gape after great things. For nothing is inough with them, onlesse they may swalowe up the whole world." Adapting her sources, she develops the poetic possibilities of another image cluster, contrasting the Psalmist's lowly, or humble, eye with those whose "eyes looke high" and with the promise that when David *sees* (her addition) "a wicked wretch" he will hate him and free Jehovah's city of that evil.

To eyes and hearts, the countess adds another image cluster on tongues, emphasizing the passages on slander. . . . [The] slander of the envious plagued her life. . . . In Psalm 101, the just king promises that "the cunning coyning tongue shall in my sight / be not endur'd, much lesse accepted well." He will overthrow "whisp'ring biters," wherein the term *whispering* clearly bears its secondary meaning of "secret slander," and *biter* its obsolescent sense of "deceiver" or "con artist," in addition to the emphasis on a devouring mouth. The slanderer's eyes will not be endured in David's sight; instead, David's eyes will "for truth-tellers seeke and search the land." Calvin interprets slander as a synecdoche of all types of wickedness, since "backbiting is a noysome plague aboue all others. For it is all one as if a man should kill a body by treason: nay rather, a backbiter dispatcheth menne unwares no lesse than a poysoner." Certainly in Mary Sidney's version, the "mischieuous heads" and "malicious hartes" are the source of the "whisp'ring biters." This emphasis on slander and envy echoes that of the epitaphs on Sidney, which claimed that he had been slain by envy, and of Book VI of *The Faerie Queene,* in which Sir Calidore (traditionally believed to represent Sidney) pursues the Blatant Beast. Thomas Moffett's *Nobilis* says that Sidney himself turned flatterers out and received only "learned and pious men," exactly what David promises to do in this Psalm.

Mary Sidney's use of political discourse is evident in her interpretation of verse 6. Most translations show David choosing the virtuous "within my house to dwell," as Sternhold and Hopkins put it, and expelling the wicked, missing the implications of kingship present in even the Vulgate: "hic mihi ministrabat." In the Crowley Psalter, for example, David promises "such wyll I teke to dwell wyth me." The Great Bible comes closer, saying of the virtuous that "he shalbe my seruaunt." and Parker stresses that he "Who walketh more strayt / Shall serve me bet." In the Psalms of Marot and the commentaries of Bèze and Calvin, the countess found the explicitly political interpretation, that David is speaking of his counselors and ministers. Marot says that the wicked "à ma maison point ne trouuera place," making explicit the definition of his "maison" as David's "court royalle" in stanza 4. Such identification signals the political context of the words *serve* and *favor:* David says that only he who follows the right "me servira" and refuses to give "faueur" to the wicked. Bèze says that David speaks of ordering himself, his family, and his kingdom. He will "most carefullie eschue men of corrupt manners." Since princes are "compelled of necessitie to use the seruice of manie others . . . he promiseth that he wil receiue no man, whome he shal knowe to be of an euil conscience." Yet in Bèze's rendering of verses 4 to 6, David promises, "I wil put far from me the authors of euil counsels. . . . I searching out on euerie side men that loue the truth, wil take them to be my familiar companions," obscuring the political implications of his own commentary. Calvin's commentary is more pointed: the Psalm refers to "all the magistrates that execute publike iudgements, as of household seruants," particularly those "of the kyngs trayne." Such care in choosing ministers is essential, Calvin continues, for "although the Prince be neuer so good, yet shal his subiects hardly be parttakers of his vncorruptnesse, except his officers be according to himselfe." This political interpretation is clearly present in Mary Sidney's rendering:

> Such men with me my Counsailors shall sitt:
> such euermore my Officers shall be,
> men speaking right, and doing what is fitt.

Although Psalm 101 delineates the duties of the godly monarch instead of castigating the wicked, as do Psalms 82 and 83, the net result is the same: the godly are to be rewarded, and the wicked pursued with hatred. If Queen Elizabeth ever received the 1599 presentation copy of these Sidneian *Psalmes,* she would undoubtedly have recognized the political intentions of the family that had so vehemently objected to her proposed marriage to the Catholic Duke of Alençon, a family that supported the Huguenot cause in their lives and in their writings. Like the Geneva Bible, dedicated to Elizabeth at her accession, the Sidney *Psalmes,* dedicated to Elizabeth at the close of her long reign, served as a reminder of the duties of the godly monarch. Protestants would accept her as their David only as long as she emulated his example, ruling with justice and mercy, punishing the wicked and rewarding the godly. (pp. 101-05)

> *Margaret P. Hannay, in her* Philip's Phoenix: Mary Sidney, Countess of Pembroke, *Oxford University Press, Inc., 1990, 317 p.*

FURTHER READING

Bornstein, Diane. "The Style of the Countess of Pembroke's Translation of Philippe de Mornay's *Discours de la vie et de la mort.*" In *Silent but for the Word: Tudor Women as Patrons, Translators, and Writers of Religious Works,* edited by Margaret Patterson Hannay, pp. 126-48. Kent, Ohio: Kent State University Press, 1985.

> Praises Sidney's translation of the *Discours* and discusses the personal reasons behind her attraction to its stoic message.

Brennan, Michael. *Literary Patronage in the English Renaissance: The Pembroke Family.* London: Routledge, 1988.

> A comprehensive survey of the patronage system focusing on the Pembrokes' literary influence.

Costello, Louisa Stuart. "Mary Sidney, Countess of Pembroke." In her *Memoirs of Eminent Englishwomen,* Vol. I, pp. 334-69. London: Richard Bentley, 1844.

> Discusses Sidney's family, focusing on her relationship with Philip.

Hogrefe, Pearl. "Mary Sidney Herbert, Countess of Pembroke." In her *Women of Action in Tudor England: Nine Biographical Sketches,* pp. 105-35. Ames: Iowa State University Press, 1977.

> Studies Sidney's influence on Renaissance literature with an extensive discussion of works dedicated to her.

Lamb, Mary Ellen. "The Countess of Pembroke's Patronage." *English Literary Renaissance* 12, No. 2 (Spring 1982): 162-79.

> Claims that Sidney's patronage has been greatly exaggerated and criticizes the "second-rate nature of much of the writing" produced at Wilton.

Young, Frances Berkeley. *Mary Sidney, Countess of Pembroke.* London: David Nutt, 1912.

> The first full-length biography of Sidney. It includes all her known letters, complete ancestral background, and the first, though incomplete, published copy of her translation *The Triumph of Death.*

Sir Philip Sidney

1554-1586

English poet and prose writer.

Sidney is regarded as one of the most prominent and influential literary figures of the Elizabethan period. Famous during his lifetime for his noble character and political connections, he is primarily remembered today as an imaginative and adept writer whose works—all published posthumously—represent a variety of genres including fiction, essays, and poetry. His *Countess of Pembroke's Arcadia* (1590), a prose romance, presents a unique textual history and a euphuistic style that has evoked both admiration and censure, while his *Defense of Poesie* (1595) represents one of the first English discourses on poetry. *Astrophil and Stella* (1591), his most highly esteemed work, is celebrated for its innovations in poetic style and structure. As Theodore Spenser observed, "It is Sidney . . . who is the most central of English poets in the generation that was soon to know Shakespeare."

Born in Kent to Sir Henry Sidney, the Lord Deputy of Ireland, and Mary Dudley, sister of the Earl of Leicester, Sidney received the financial, social, and educational privileges of the English nobility. In 1564 he entered the Shrewsbury School on the same day as Fulke Greville, who became his lifelong friend and later gained renown as an esteemed scholar and Sidney's biographer. Sidney matriculated at Christ's Church, Oxford, in 1568 but left three years later without taking a degree, possibly due to an outbreak of plague that forced the university to close temporarily. He then continued his education in Europe, traveling extensively and studying languages, music, and astronomy. During this time, he became acquainted with some of the most prominent European statesmen, scholars, and artists; he dined regularly with royalty, sat for a portrait by the Italian artist Veronese, and exchanged ideas with important thinkers of his day, including Hubert Languet, with whom he shared a correspondence which is a valuable source of information about Sidney's life and career. Languet's censure of Catholicism and his espousal of the Protestant religion, as well as his attempts to encourage Queen Elizabeth I to further this cause in England, are believed to have strongly influenced Sidney's religious and political convictions.

On returning to England in 1575, Sidney established himself as one of Queen Elizabeth's courtiers and began to pursue literary interests, associating with such prominent writers as Greville, Edward Dyer, and Edmund Spenser. He wrote poetry and completed a masque in 1578 entitled *The Lady of May,* a popular entertainment performed for Elizabeth which required her participation. His chief ambition, however, was to embark on a career in public service. Aside from acquiring some minor appointments, he was never given an opportunity to prove himself as a statesman. Critics speculate that his diplomatic career was deliberately discouraged by Elizabeth, whose policy of

caution in handling domestic and religious matters conflicted with Sidney's ardent support of Protestantism in England.

In 1580 Sidney was dismissed from court, probably as a result of a letter he wrote to Elizabeth advising against her proposed marriage to the Duke of Anjou. Upon his dismissal he retired to Wilton, the estate of his sister Mary, Countess of Pembroke. Critics speculate that at Wilton Sidney began writing the prose romance *Arcadia,* which he intended for the entertainment of his sister, and that after completing a first version, he began expanding and revising the manuscript. The composition of his treatise *A Defense of Poesie* and the sonnet sequence *Astrophil and Stella* is also dated to this period. In 1585 Sidney was summoned back to court and was appointed governor of Flushing, an area comprising present-day Beligum and the Netherlands, where the English were involved in the Dutch revolt against Spain. During this time he served in battle alongside his uncle, the Earl of Leicester. The following year, in a skirmish near the town of Zutphen, he was mortally wounded by a musket ball and died several days later.

Although Sidney died before completing his revisions to

the *Arcadia* and requested on his deathbed that the manuscripts be burned, an edition was published in 1590 containing the revised chapters. Three years later, Mary Sidney published a version that retained the material of the 1590 edition and appended the concluding chapters which she had revised based on notes in her possession. This 1593 edition remained the authoritative text until the twentieth century. In 1908, Bertram Dobell discovered one of the manuscripts of the original, complete version that Sidney presented to his sister at Wilton; it was published for the first time in Albert Feuillerat's 1926 edition of Sidney's complete works. Since then, critics refer to the original unrevised version as the *Old Arcadia* and the 1593 text as the *New Arcadia*. Drawing on elements of Italian pastoral romance and Greek prose epic, the plot of the *Arcadia* is essentially the same in both versions: two princes embark on a quest for love in the land of Arcadia, fall in love with two daughters of an Arcadian king, and eventually, despite a series of mistaken identities and misunderstandings, marry the princesses. While the *Old Arcadia* presents events in a simple and relatively brief prose narration, the *New Arcadia* is elaborate, featuring several subplots and a nonchronological structure interspersed with sections of poetry—additions that nearly double the length of the original text.

Opinion is sharply divided on the issue of which approach produced the superior work. Characterized by extensive alliteration, similes, paradoxes, and rhetorical devices, Sidney's euphuistic style in the *New Arcadia* is artificial and extravagant by modern standards. In an early comparison of the style of the two versions, Mario Praz noted that "almost each sentence of the first draft has been subjected to a process of stucco decoration, until the once clear outline has disappeared behind the fashionable finery of a tortuous phraseology." Similarly, the interweaving of subplots in the *New Arcadia* is regarded by some as confusing and superfluous. These critics favor the *Old Arcadia* as the more coherent and less pretentious text. However, some commentators, such as E. M. W. Tillyard, argue that the *New Arcadia* represents the maturation of Sidney's abilities, as evidenced by its greater detail and realistic characterizations, and that a proper appreciation of the romance may be reached through careful consideration of Elizabethan literary tastes and conventions. Furthermore, these critics contend, the creativity and concern for literary detail intrinsic to Sidney's prose style in the *New Arcadia* is a valuable innovation, encouraging experimentation and greater attention to craftsmanship among Renaissance writers. Sidney Lee observed that "the *Arcadia* is a jumble of discordant elements; but, despite its manifold defects, it proves its author to have caught a distant glimpse of the true art of fiction." Sidney's *Defense of Poesie* responds to Stephen Gosson's *School of Abuse* (1579), which charges that modern poetry exerts an immoral influence on society by presenting lies as truths and instilling unnatural desires in its readers. Sidney answered Gosson's invective by asserting that the poet provides a product of his imagination, which does not pretend to literal fact and therefore cannot present lies. The *Defense* also purports to describe the nature and purpose of poetry, maintaining that while individual poets may abuse the literary form by producing an immoral work, poetry itself

is not corrupt because its purpose is to instruct and delight. In addition, the *Defense* provides an unfavorable assessment of English drama, a perspective later substantiated by critics who have noted that in Sidney's lifetime, prior to the works of Christopher Marlowe and William Shakespeare, the English stage seemed an improbable forum for literary achievement.

While generally commending the witty and incisive style of the treatise, critics have debated its intent and the validity of its argument. George Saintsbury observed that Sidney's defense offered encouragement for poets during the Elizabethan period and is valuable as a reflection of "the temper of the generation which actually produced the first-fruits of the greatest Elizabethan poetry." Acknowledging that the essay chiefly functions as a refutation of Gosson's argument, some critics have examined ways in which the *Defense* operates on a more ambitious and complex level as an attempt to construct an original theory of poetics. Forrest G. Robinson, for example, has proposed that the essay reflects Sidney's "firm conviction that poetry is a science" and that it should be regarded "not so much a handbook on poetry as . . . a scientific theory of communication." The success of Sidney's defense is also debated. Ronald Leavo has asserted that despite evidence of faulty logic, the *Defense* is "one of the most daring documents of Renaissance criticism." However, in a series of lectures addressing the question of whether or not Sidney may be considered one of the earliest literary critics, H. A. Mason has concluded that "if we ignore his manner and persist in demanding that he prove his assertions by real critical judgment, he has nothing to offer."

Astrophil and Stella represents the first sonnet sequence in English literature and is regarded by many critics as Sidney's masterpiece. A series of thematically connected verses, the work consists of 110 sonnets written from the perspective of Astrophil, a poet and courtly lover who chronicles his passion for Stella, her conditional acceptance of his advances, and finally, his plea to be released from his obligation to her. The sonnets are generally modelled after the Italian or Petrarchan sonnet form which consists of an octave (eight lines that present a question or problem) and a sestet (six lines that resolve or comment on the foregoing proposition). Stylistically, the sonnets also feature such Petrarchan conventions as exaggerated comparison, ornate imagery, and elaborate metaphor.

Until the twentieth century, *Astrophil and Stella* was primarily appreciated as a powerful reflection of Sidney's romantic life; biographical elements have been traced in *Astrophil and Stella,* suggesting that the sonnets were inspired by Sidney's love for Penelope Devereaux, a noblewoman to whom he was briefly engaged but who, for unknown reasons, married another man. Maintaining that Astrophil's impassioned speeches reflect Sidney's frustration over his unrequited love for Devereaux, such critics regarded sincerity as the greatest strength of the sonnets. Commenting on the enduring appeal of the sonnets, Charles Lamb observed that they are "full, material, and circumstantiated." Later critics rejected the biographical interpretation, arguing that formal rather than biographical analysis provides a better understanding of Sidney's technical achievements. Such critics attribute the success of *Astrophil and Stella* to Sidney's adept manipulation of language, meter, and imagery, noting his often ironic presentation of Petrarchan conventions. In a seminal study of Sidney's poetry, Theodore Spencer cited his "direct and forceful simplicity, his eloquent rhetoric, his emotional depth and truth, [and] his control of movement, both within the single line and throughout the poem as a whole" as innovations to poetic form which exerted a profound impact on subsequent poets during the Renaissance. Such achievements were also examined by C. S. Lewis, who remarked that *Astrophil and Stella* "towers above everything that had been done in poetry . . . since Chaucer died," and that "the fourth [sonnet] alone, with its hurried and (as it were) whispered metre, its inimitable refrain, its perfect selection of images, is enough to raise Sidney above all his contemporaries."

PRINCIPAL WORKS

The Countess of Pembroke's Arcadia   (prose) 1590
Astrophil and Stella   (poetry) 1591
The Defense of Poesie   1595; also published as *An Apologie for Poetrie*, 1595
The Correspondence of Sir Philip Sidney and Hubert Languet   (letters) 1845
**The Complete Works of Sir Philip Sidney*   (poetry, essays, letters) 4 vols. 1912-26

*This work includes Sidney's drama *The Lady of May*.

Philip Sidney   (essay date 1581?)

[*In the following excerpt from the preface to the* Arcadia, *Sidney encourages his sister Mary, Countess of Pembroke, to regard the narrative as an imperfect entertainment rather than as a serious literary effort.*]

Here now have you (most deare, and most worthy to be most deare Lady) this idle worke of mine: which I fear (like the Spiders webbe) will be thought fitter to be swept away, then worn to any other purpose. For my part, in very trueth (as the cruell fathers among the Greekes, were woont to doo to the babes they would not foster) I could well find in my harte, to cast out in some desert of forgetfulnes this child, which I am loath to father. But you desired me to doo it, and your desire, to my hart is an absolute commandement. Now, it is done onelie for you, only to you: if you keepe it to your selfe, or to such friendes, who will weight errors in the ballaunce of good will, I hope, for the fathers sake, it will be pardoned, perchance made much of, though in it selfe it have deformities. For indeede, for severer eyes it is not, being but a trifle, and that trifling lie handled. Your deare selfe can best witnes the maner, being done in loose sheetes of paper, most of it in your presence, the rest, by sheetes, sent unto you, as fast as they were done. In summe, a young head, not so well stayed as I would it were, (and shall be when God will) having many many fancies begotten in it, if it had not

ben in some way delivered, would have growen a monster, & more sorie might I be that they came in, then that they gat out. But his chiefe safetie, shalbe the not walking abroad; & his chiefe protection, the bearing the liverye of your name; which (if much much good will do not deceave me) is worthy to be a s[an]ctuary for a greater offender. This say I, because I knowe the vertue so; and this say I, because it may be ever so; or to say better, because it will be ever so. Read it then at your idle tymes, and the follyes your good judgement wil finde in it, blame not, but laugh at. And so, looking for no better stuffe, then, as in an Haberdashers shoppe, glasses, or feathers, you will continue to love the writer, who doth excedinglie love you; and most most hartelie praies you may long live, to be a principall ornament to the familie of the Sidneis. (pp. 3-4)

> *Philip Sidney, in a letter to the Countess of Pembroke, in 1581? in his* The Countess of Pembroke's Arcadia, *edited by Albert Feuillerat, Cambridge at the University Press, 1912, pp. 3-4.*

Thomas Moffett   (essay date 1592?)

[*Moffett was an English physician and scholar who associated with Sidney and several of his friends and family members. His* Nobilis Or a View of a Sidney's Life and Death *is addressed to Sidney's nephew, William Herbert, for whom Moffett chronicled the poet's childhood, experience as a courtier, and military service. In the following excerpt from that work, which was probably written toward the end of 1592, Moffett describes Sidney's intellectual ambitions and praises his integrity and literary skill.*]

Hence it twice occurred that, overstimulated by his prolonged studies in early adolescence, he fell ill of a fever attended by the greatest peril; and he was forced to slacken the reins in sports, until, the breakdown of his health having been repaired, more fit and more active he returned to the Muses. Let them who may have the power tell how, meanwhile, unsettled spirits strove within that single soul; for at one moment he judged it inhuman to abjure the care of the body; at another moment not to proceed with his studies he deemed a reproach; he considered that care could not be given to both without impairing one or the other; he reckoned that a higher consideration could not be given to one and at the same time the soundness of the other be complete. And, to be sure, since he craved to be wise rather than to be strong, he would almost have failed in both had he not given himself over, though unwillingly, to recreation, and mingled, by way of spice, certain sportive arts—poetic, comic, musical—with his more serious studies. He amused himself with them after the manner of youth, but within limits; he was somewhat wanton, indeed, but observed a measure and felt shame. On that account he first consigned his ***Stella*** (truly an elegant and pleasant work) to darkness and then favored giving it to the fire. Nay, more, he desired to smother the ***Arcadia*** (offspring of no ill pen) at the time of its birth. And in it he so cultivated the comic that he avoided the scurrilous; he so pursued the dramatic that he shunned the obscene; he so composed satires that he nicely ridiculed satyrs full of vices and their little grandsons full of wantonness. The blindness, vanity, and fickleness of Cupid, the harlots (allurements and banes of adolescents), parasites evilly gained, procurers evilly conditioned, the slippery ways of adolescence, the weak ways of youth, the wretched ways of age (upon which we cannot enter without peril, stand without irksomeness, or run without falling)—how cleverly in that work, most illustrious Herbert, has he presented these for us, decked out and made odious! How, and with how sharp a sting, in a sort of dithyramb he has described, and censured, those Demaenetuses with white hair, goatish beard, phlegmy nostrils who pursue pleasures of love at an unseasonable age and do not put away voluptuousness from them until their property, business, love, and lust are at once extinguished, together with life! Having come to fear, however, that his *Stella* and *Arcadia* might render the souls of readers more yielding instead of better, and having turned to worthier subjects, he very much wished to sing something which would abide the censure of the most austere Cato. For, truly, let us read the *Week* of the great Bartas, made English by Sidney; let us contemplate the psalms of the Hebrew poet, ah, how choicely set forth, first explicitly and then paraphrastically, and distinguished, each one, by a new meter! When others, with dirty hands, strive to cleanse these psalms, they seem to seek a knot in a bulrush and (to put the matter in a word) while they polish they pollute. I pass over letters of most elegant style, in metrical and prose form, which he addressed to the Queen, to friends, but particularly to your honored mother (inheritor of his wit and genius); if it shall be deemed well to let these epistles go into the everlasting memory of his race and of the republic of letters, may I die if, compared to them, Horace will not seem stupid, Cicero mediocre, and Ovid simply nothing at all, or weak. (pp. 73-4)

> *Thomas Moffett, "Translation: Adolescence of Philip Sidney," in his* Nobilis or a View of the Life and Death of a Sidney and Lessus Lugubris, *translated by Virgil B. Heltzel and Hoyt H. Hudson, The Huntington Library, 1940, pp. 73-4.*

Fulke Greville   (essay date 1628?)

[*Greville was an English poet, a prominent public official, and a lifelong friend of Sidney. His biography,* The Life of the Renowned Sr Philip Sidney *(1652), probably composed in the 1590s, represents the first extensive examination of Sidney's life and served as an authoritative source throughout the seventeenth and eighteenth centuries. In the following excerpt from that work, Greville praises Sidney's sense of moral and civic responsibility as reflected in the* Arcadia. *Because the composition date of Greville's work is unknown, the author's death-date has been used.*]

[Though Sidney] purposed no monuments of books to the world, out of [his] great harvest of knowledge; yet doe not his Arcadian Romanties live after him, admired by our foure-eyed Criticks? who, howsoever their common end upon common arts be to affect reputation by depraving censure; yet where nature placeth excellencie above envy,

there (it seemeth) she subjecteth these carping eyes to wander, and shewes the judicious reader how he may be nourished in the delicacy of his own judgement.

For instance; may not the most refined spirits, in the scope of these dead images (even as they are now) finde, that when Soveraign Princes, to play with their own visions, will put off publique action, which is the splendor of Majestie, and unactively charge the managing of their greatest affaires upon the second-hand faith, and diligence of Deputies, may they not (I say) understand, that even then they bury themselves, and their Estates in a cloud of contempt, and under it both encourage and shaddow the conspiracies of ambitious subalternes to their false endes, I mean the ruine of States and Princes?

Again, where Kingly Parents will suffer, or rather force their wives and daughters, to descend from the inequality and reservednesse of Princely education, into the contemptible familiarity, and popular freedome of Shepherds; may we not discern that even therein they give those Royall birthes warrant, or opportunity, to break over all circles of honor, safe-guards to the modesty of that sex; and withall make them fraily, apt to change the commanding manners of Princely Birth, into the degrading images of servile basenesse? Lastly, where humor takes away this pomp, and *apparatus* from King, Crown, and Scepter, to make fear a Counsellor, and obscurity a wisdom; be that King at home what the current, or credit of his former Goverment, for a while, may keep him: yet he is sure among forrain Princes to be justly censured as a Princely Shepherd, or Shepherdish King: which creatures of scorn seldome fail to become fit sacrifices for home-born discontentments, or ambitious forrain spirits to undertake, and offer up.

Againe, who sees not the chanceable arrival of *Euarchus* into *Arcadia;* his unexpected election to the temporary Soveraignty of that State; his sitting in a cloudy seat of judgement, to give sentence (under a mask of Shepherds) against his Son, Nephew, Neeces, the immediate successors to that Scepter; and all accused and condemned of rape, paricide, adulteries, or treasons, by their own Lawes: I say who sees not, that these dark webs of effeminate Princes be dangerous forerunners of innovation, even in a quiet, and equally tempered people? So that if Sir *Philips* had not made the integrity of this forrain King an image of more constant, pure, and higher strain, than nature makes those ordinary mouldes, wherein she fashioneth earthly Princes, even this opportunity, and map of desolation prepared for *Euarchus,* wherein he saw all the successors of this Province justly condemned under his own sentence, would have raised up specious rights, or pretences for new ambition in him; and upon the never-failing pillars of occasion amasednes of people, and sad offer of glorious novelties, have tempted him to establish this Election for a time, successively, to him and his for ever?

To be short, the like, and finer moralities offer themselves throughout that various, and dainty work of his, for sounder judgements to exercise their Spirits in; so that if the infancie of these *Ideas,* determining in the first generation, yield the ingenuous Reader such pleasant & profitable diversity, both of flowers, and fruits, let him conceive,

Title page of Fulke Greville's biography of Sidney.

if this excellent Image-maker had liv'd to finish, and bring to perfection this extraordinary frame of his own Common-wealth: I meane, the return of *Basilius,* from his dreames of humor, to the honor of his former Estate; the marriage of the two sisters with the two excellent Princes; their issue; the warres stirred up by *Amphialus;* his marriage with *Helena;* their successions; together with the incident Magnificences, pompes of state, providences of councells in treaties of peace, or aliance, summons of warres, and orderly execution of their disorders; I say, what a large field an active able spirit should have had to walk in, let the advised Reader conceive with grief. Especially if he please to take knowledge, that in all these creatures of his making, his intent, and scope was, to turn the barren Philosophy precepts into pregnant Images of life; and in them, first on the Monarch's part, lively to represent the growth, state, and declination of Princes, change of Government, and lawes: vicissitudes of sedition, faction, succession, confederacies, plantations, with all other errors, or alterations in publique affaires. Then again in the subjects case; the state of favor, dissavor, prosperitie, adversity, emulation, quarrell, undertaking, retiring, hospitality, travail, and all other moodes of private fortunes, or misfortunes. In which traverses (I know) his purpose was to

limn out such exact pictures, of every posture in the minde, that any man being forced, in the straines of this life, to pass through any straights, or latitudes of good, or ill fortune, might (as in a glasse) see how to let a good countenance upon all the discountenances of adversitie, and a stay upon the exorbitant smiling of chance.

Now, as I know this was the first project of these workes, rich (like his youth) in the freedome of affections, wit, learning, stile, form, and facilitie, to please others: so must I again (as ingenuously) confess, that when his body declined, and his piercing inward powers were lifted up to a purer Horizon, he then discovered, not onely the imperfection, but vanitie of these shadowes, how daintily soever limned: as seeing that even beauty itself, in all earthly complexions, was more apt to allure men to evill, than to fashion any goodness in them. And from this ground, in that memorable testament of his, he bequeathed no other legacie, but the fire, to this unpolished Embrio. From which fate it is onely reserved, until the world hath purged away all her more gross corruptions.

Again, they that knew him well, will truly confess, this **Arcadia** of his to be, both in form, and matter, as much inferior to that unbounded spirit of his, as the industry and Images of other mens works, are many times raised above the writers capacities: and besides acknowledge, that howsoever he could not choose but give them many aspersions of spirit, and learning from the Father; yet that they were scribled: rather as pamphlets, for entertainment of time, and friends, than any accompt of himself to the world. Because if his purpose had been to leave his memory in books, I am confident, in the right use of Logick, Philosophy, History, and Poësie, nay even in the most ingenuous of Mechanicall Arts, he would have shewed such tracts of a searching, and judicious spirit; as the professors of every faculty would have striven no less for him, than the seven Cities did to have *Homer* of their Sept. But the truth is: his end was not writing, even while he wrote; nor his knowledge moulded for tables, or schooles; but both his wit, and understanding bent upon his heart, to make himself, and others, not in words or opinion, but in life, and action, good and great. (pp. 13-21)

> *Fulke Greville, in his* The Life of the Renowned Sr Philip Sidney, *1652. Reprint by Scholars' Facsimiles & Reprints, 1984, 255 p.*

William Hazlitt   (lecture date 1820)

[An English essayist, Hazlitt was one of the most important critics of the Romantic age. He was a deft stylist, a master of the prose essay, and a leader of what was later termed "impressionist criticism"—a form of personal analysis directly opposed to the universal standards of critical judgment accepted by many eighteenth-century critics. For Hazlitt the ideal of any critical endeavor is not an ultimate judgment regarding a work of literature; instead, the critic serves as a guide to help determine the reader's response to certain works, or passages within those works. Perhaps the most important thing to remember when reading Hazlitt is that he was a journalist who wrote for the general public and lived from the proceeds of his pen. He was acutely aware of

*the abstract nature of literature as well as the limitations
of his audience in understanding questions of aesthetics
and style. For this reason he purposely made his criticism palatable by using illustrations, digressions, and
repetitions. Below, in an excerpt from a lecture delivered
in 1820, he finds Sidney's use of language ineffective,
particularly in the* Arcadia.]

Sir Philip Sidney is a writer for whom I cannot acquire a
taste. As Mr. Burke said, "he could not love the French
Republic"—so I may say, that I cannot love the **Countess
of Pembroke's Arcadia,** with all my good-will to it. It will
not do for me, however, to imitate the summary petulance
of the epigrammatist:

> I do not love thee, Dr. Fell;
> The reason why I cannot tell,
> But this alone I know full well:
> I do not love thee, Dr. Fell.

I must give my reasons, "on compulsion," for not speaking well of a person like Sir Philip Sidney:

> The soldier's, scholar's, courtier's eye, tongue,
>   sword,
> The glass of fashion, and the mould of form:

the splendour of whose personal accomplishments, and of
whose wide-spread fame, was, in his lifetime:

> ————Like a gate of steel,
> Fronting the sun, that renders back
> His figure and his heat:

a writer, too, who was universally read and enthusiastically admired for a century after his death, and who has been
admired with scarce less enthusiasm, but with a more distant homage, for another century, after ceasing to be read.

We have lost the art of reading, or the privilege of writing,
voluminously, since the days of Addison. Learning no longer weaves the interminable page with patient drudgery,
nor ignorance pores over it with implicit faith. As authors
multiply in number, books diminish in size; we cannot
now, as formerly, swallow libraries whole in a single folio:
solid quarto has given place to slender duodecimo, and the
dingy letter-press contracts its dimensions, and retreats
before the white, unsullied, faultless margin. Modern authorship is become a species of stenography: we contrive
even to read by proxy. We skim the cream of prose without any trouble; we get at the quintessence of poetry without loss of time. The staple commodity, the coarse, heavy,
dirty, unwieldy bullion of books, is driven out of the market of learning, and the intercourse of the literary world
is carried on, and the credit of the great capitalists sustained, by the flimsy circulating medium of magazines and
reviews. Those who are chiefly concerned in catering for
the taste of others, and serving up critical opinions in a
compendious, elegant, and portable form, are not forgetful
of themselves: they are not scrupulously solicitous, idly in-
quisitive about the real merits, the *bonâ fide* contents of
the works they are deputed to appraise and value, any
more than the reading public who employ them. They
look no farther for the contents of the work than the title-
page, and pronounce a peremptory decision on its merits
or defects by a glance at the name and party of the writer.
This state of polite letters seems to admit of improvement

in only one respect, which is to go a step farther, and write
for the amusement and edification of the world, accounts
of works that were never either written or read at all, and
to cry up or abuse the authors by name, though they have
no existence but in the critic's invention. This would save
a great deal of labour in vain: anonymous critics might
pounce upon the defenceless heads of fictitious candidates
for fame and bread; reviews, from being novels founded
upon facts, would aspire to be pure romances; and we
should arrive at the *beau ideal* of a commonwealth of letters, at the euthanasia of thought and millennium of criticism!

At the time that Sir Philip Sidney's **Arcadia** was written,
those middle men, the critics, were not known. The author
and reader came into immediate contact, and seemed
never tired of each other's company. We are more fastidi-
ous and dissipated: the effeminacy of modern taste would,
I am afraid, shrink back affrighted at the formidable sight
of this once popular work, which is about as long (*horresco
referens!*) as all Walter Scott's novels put together; but besides its size and appearance, it has, I think, other defects
of a more intrinsic and insuperable nature. It is to me one
of the greatest monuments of the abuse of intellectual
power upon record. It puts one in mind of the court dresses and preposterous fashions of the time, which are grown
obsolete and disgusting. It is not romantic, but scholastic;
not poetry, but casuistry; not nature, but art, and the
worst sort of art, which thinks it can do better than nature.
Of the number of fine things that are constantly passing
through the author's mind, there is hardly one that he has
not contrived to spoil, and to spoil purposely and maliciously, in order to aggrandise our idea of himself. Out of
five hundred folio pages, there are hardly, I conceive, half-
a-dozen sentences expressed simply and directly, with the
sincere desire to convey the image implied, and without
a systematic interpolation of the wit, learning, ingenuity,
wisdom, and everlasting impertinence of the writer, so as
to disguise the object, instead of displaying it in its true
colours and real proportions. Every page is "with centric
and eccentric scribbled o'er;" his muse is tattooed and
tricked out like an Indian goddess. He writes a court-
hand, with flourishes like a schoolmaster; his figures are
wrought in chain-stitch. All his thoughts are forced and
painful births, and may be said to be delivered by the Cae-
sarean operation. At last, they become distorted and rick-
ety in themselves; and before they have been cramped and
twisted and swaddled into lifelessness and deformity.
Imagine a writer to have great natural talents, great powers of memory and invention, an eye for nature, a knowledge of the passions, much learning, and equal industry;
but that he is so full of a consciousness of all this, and so
determined to make the reader conscious of it at every
step, that he becomes a complete intellectual coxcomb, or
nearly so;—that he never lets a casual observation pass
without perplexing it with an endless running commentary, that he never states a feeling without so many *circu-
mambages,* without so many interlineations and parenthetical remarks on all that can be said for it, and anticipa-
tions of all that can be said against it, and that he never
mentions a fact without giving so many circumstances and
conjuring up so many things that it is like or not like, that
you lose the main clue of the story in its infinite ramifica-

tions and intersections;—and we may form some faint idea of the *Countess of Pembroke's Arcadia,* which is spun with great labour out of the author's brains, and hangs like a huge cobweb over the face of Nature! This is not, as far as I can judge, an exaggerated description: but as near the truth as I can make it. The proofs are not far to seek. Take the first sentence, or open the volume anywhere and read. I will, however, take one of the most beautiful passages near the beginning, to show how the subject-matter, of which the noblest use might have been made, is disfigured by the affectation of the style, and the importunate and vain activity of the writer's mind. The passage I allude to, is the celebrated description of Arcadia:

> ———So that the third day after, in the time that the morning did strew roses and violets in the heavenly floor against the coming of the sun, the nightingales (striving one with the other which could in most dainty variety recount their wrong-caused sorrow) made them put off their sleep, and rising from under a tree (which that night had been their pavilion) they went on their journey, which by-and-by welcomed Musidorus' eyes (wearied with the wasted soil of Laconia) with delightful prospects. There were hills which garnished their proud heights with stately trees: humble valleys whose base estate seemed comforted with the refreshing of silver rivers; meadows enamelled with all sorts of eye-pleasing flowers; thickets which, being lined with most pleasant shade, were witnessed so, too, by the cheerful disposition of many well-tuned birds; each pasture stored with sheep feeding with sober security, while the pretty lambs with bleating oratory craved the dam's comfort: here a shepherd's boy piping, as though he should never be old; there a young shepherdess knitting, and withal singing, and it seemed that her voice comforted her hands to work, and her hands kept time to her voice-music. As for the houses of the country (for many houses came under their eye) they were all scattered, no two being one by the other, and yet not so far off, as that it barred mutual succour; a show, as it were, of an accompaniable solitariness, and of a civil wildness. I pray you, said Musidorus (then first unsealing his long-silent lips), what countries be these we pass through, which are so divers in show, the one wanting no store, the other having no store but of want. The country, answered Claius, where you were cast ashore, and now are past through, is Laconia . . . . . . But this country (where you now set your foot) is Arcadia. . . . .

One would think the very name might have lulled his senses to delightful repose in some still, lonely valley, and have laid the restless spirit of Gothic quaintness, witticism, and conceit, in the lap of classic elegance and pastoral simplicity. Here are images, too, of touching beauty and everlasting truth, that needed nothing but to be simply and nakedly expressed to have made a picture equal (nay superior) to the allegorical representation of the Four Seasons of Life by Giorgione. But no! He cannot let his imagination or that of the reader dwell for a moment on the beauty or power of the real object. He thinks nothing is done, unless it is his doing. He must officiously and gra-

tuitously interpose between you and the subject as the cicerone of Nature, distracting the eye and the mind by continual uncalled-for interruptions, analysing, dissecting, disjointing, murdering everything, and reading a pragmatical, self-sufficient lecture over the dead body of Nature. The moving spring of his mind is not sensibility or imagination, but dry, literal, unceasing craving after intellectual excitement, which is indifferent to pleasure or pain, to beauty or deformity, and likes to owe everything to its own perverse efforts rather than the sense of power in other things. It constantly interferes to perplex and neutralise. It never leaves the mind in a wise passiveness. In the infancy of taste, the froward pupils of art took Nature to pieces, as spoiled children do a watch, to see what was in it. After taking it to pieces, they could not, with all their cunning, put it together again, so as to restore circulation to the heart, or its living hue to the face! The quaint and pedantic style here objected to was not, however, the natural growth of untutored fancy, but an artificial excrescence transferred from logic and rhetoric to poetry. It was not owing to the excess of imagination, but of the want of it, that is, to the predominance of the mere understanding or dialectic faculty over the imaginative and the sensitive. It is in fact poetry degenerating at every step into prose, sentiment entangling itself in a controversy, from the habitual leaven of polemics and casuistry in the writer's mind. The poet insists upon matters of fact from the beauty or grandeur that accompanies them; our prose poet insists upon them because they are matters of fact, and buries the beauty and grandeur in a heap of common rubbish, "like two grains of wheat in a bushel of chaff." The true poet illustrates for ornament or use: the fantastic pretender, only because he is not easy till he can translate everything out of itself into something else. Imagination consists in enriching one idea by another, which has the same feeling or set of associations belonging to it in a higher or more striking degree; the quaint or scholastic style consists in comparing one thing to another by the mere process of abstraction, and the more forced and naked the comparison, the less of harmony or congruity there is in it, the more wire-drawn and ambiguous the link of generalisation by which objects are brought together, the greater is the triumph of the false and fanciful style. There was a marked instance of the difference in some lines from Ben Jonson which I have above quoted, and which, as they are alternate examples of the extremes of both in the same author and in the same short poem, there can be nothing invidious in giving. In conveying an idea of female softness and sweetness, he asks:

> Have you felt the wool of the beaver,
> Or swan's down ever?
> Or have smelt o' the bud of the briar,
> Or the nard in the fire?

Now "the swan's down" is a striking and beautiful image of the most delicate and yielding softness; but we have no associations of a pleasing sort with the wool of the beaver. The comparison is dry, hard, and barren of effect. It may establish the matter of fact, but detracts from and impairs the sentiment. The smell of "the bud of the briar" is a double-distilled essence of sweetness: besides, there are all the other concomitant ideas of youth, beauty, and blushing modesty, which blend with and heighten the immediate feeling; but the poetical reader was not bound to know even what *nard* is (it is merely a learned substance, a nonentity to the imagination), nor whether it has a fragrant or disagreeable scent when thrown into the fire, till Ben Jonson went out of his way to give him this pedantic piece of information. It is a mere matter of fact or of experiment; and while the experiment is making in reality or fancy, the sentiment stands still; or, even taking it for granted in the literal and scientific sense, we are where we were; it does not enhance the passion to be expressed: we have no love for the smell of nard in the fire, but we have an old, a long-cherished one, from infancy, for the bud of the briar. Sentiment, as Mr. Burke said of nobility, is a thing of inveterate prejudice, and cannot be created, as some people (learned and unlearned) are inclined to suppose, out of fancy or out of any thing by the wit of man. The artificial and natural style do not alternate in this way in the **Arcadia;** the one is but the helot, the eyeless drudge of the other. Thus even in the above passage, which is comparatively beautiful and simple in its general structure, we have "the bleating oratory" of lambs, as if any thing could be more unlike oratory than the bleating of lambs; we have a young shepherdess knitting, whose hands keep time not to her voice, but to her "voice-music," which introduces a foreign and questionable distinction, merely to perplex the subject; we have meadows enamelled with all sorts of "eye-pleasing flowers," as if it were necessary to inform the reader that flowers pleased the eye, or as if they did not please any other sense; we have valleys refreshed "with *silver* streams," an epithet that has nothing to do with the refreshment here spoken of; we have "an accompaniable solitariness and a civil wildness," which are a pair of very laboured antitheses; in fine, we have "want of store, and store of want."

Again, the passage describing the shipwreck of Pyrochles, has been much and deservedly admired; yet it is not free from the same inherent faults:

> But a little way off they saw the mast (of the vessel) whose proud height now lay along, like a widow having lost her mate, of whom she held her honour" [this needed explanation]; "but upon the mast they saw a young man (at least if it were a man) bearing show of about eighteen years of age, who sat (as on horseback) having nothing upon him but his shirt, which being wrought with blue silk and gold, had a kind of resemblance to the sea" [this is a sort of alliteration in natural history], "on which the sun (then near his western home) did shoot some of his beams. His hair (which the young men of Greece used to wear very long) was stirred up and down with the wind, which seemed to have a sport to play with it, as the sea had to kiss his feet; himself full of admirable beauty, set forth by the strangeness both of his seat and gesture; for holding his head up full of unmoved majesty, he held a sword aloft with his fair arm, which often he waved about his crown, as though he would threaten the world in that extremity.

If the original sin of alliteration, antithesis, and metaphys-

ical conceit could be weeded out of this passage, there is hardly a more heroic one to be found in prose or poetry.

Here is one more passage marred in the making. A shepherd is supposed to say of his mistress:

> Certainly, as her eyelids are more pleasant to behold than two white kids climbing up a fair tree and browsing on his tenderest branches, and yet are nothing compared to the day-shining stars contained in them; and as her breath is more sweet than a gentle south-west wind, which comes creeping over flowery fields and shadowed waters in the extreme heat of summer; and yet is nothing compared to the honey-flowing speech that breath doth carry; no more all that our eyes can see of her (though when they have seen her, what else they shall ever see is but dry stubble after clover grass) is to be matched with the flock of unspeakable virtues, laid up delightfully in that best-builded fold.

Now here are images of singular beauty and of Eastern originality and daring, followed up with enigmatical or unmeaning common-places, because he never knows when to leave off, and thinks he can never be too wise or too dull for his reader. He loads his prose Pegasus, like a pack-horse, with all that comes, and with a number of little trifling circumstances, that fall off, and you are obliged to stop to pick them up by the way. He cannot give his imagination a moment's pause, thinks nothing done, while any thing remains to do, and exhausts nearly all that can be said upon a subject, whether good, bad, or indifferent. The above passages are taken from the beginning of the **Arcadia,** when the author's style was hardly yet formed. The following is a less favourable, but fairer specimen of the work. It is the model of a love-letter, and is only longer than that of Adriano de Armada, in *Love's Labour's Lost:*

> Most blessed paper, which shalt kiss that hand, whereto all blessedness is in nature a servant, do not yet disdain to carry with thee the woeful words of a miser now despairing: neither be afraid to appear before her, bearing the base title of the sender. For no sooner shall that divine hand touch thee, but that thy baseness shall be turned to most high preferment. Therefore mourn boldly my ink: for while she looks upon you, your blackness will shine: cry out boldly my lamentation, for while she reads you, your cries will be music. Say then (O happy messenger of a most unhappy message) that the too soon born and too late dying creature, which dares not speak, no, not look, no, not scarcely think (as from his miserable self unto her heavenly highness), only presumes to desire thee (in the time that her eyes and voice do exalt thee) to say, and in this manner to say, not from him—oh no, that were not fit—but of him, thus much unto her sacred judgment. O you, the only honour to women, to men the only admiration, you that, being armed by love, defy him that armed you, in this high estate wherein you have placed me" [*i.e.* the letter], "yet let me remember him to whom I am bound for bringing me to your presence: and let me remember him who (since he is yours, how mean soever he be) it is reason you have an account of him. The wretch (yet your

wretch), though with languishing steps, runs fast to his grave; and will you suffer a temple (how poorly built soever, but yet a temple of your deity) to be rased? But he dieth: it is most true, he dieth: and he in whom you live, to obey you, dieth. Whereof, though he plain, he doth not complain: for it is a harm, but no wrong, which he hath received. He dies, because in woeful language all his senses tell him, that such is your pleasure; for if you will not that he live, alas, alas, what followeth, what followeth of the most ruined Dorus, but his end? End, then, evil-destined Dorus, end; and end thou, woeful letter, end: for it sufficeth her wisdom to know that her heavenly will shall be accomplished.

This style relishes neither of the lover nor the poet. Nine-tenths of the work are written in this manner. It is in the very manner of those books of gallantry and chivalry, which, with the labyrinths of their style, and "the reason of their unreasonableness," turned the fine intellects of the Knight of La Mancha. In a word (and not to speak it profanely), the *Arcadia* is a riddle, a rebus, an acrostic in folio: it contains about four thousand far-fetched similes, and six thousand impracticable dilemmas, about ten thousand reasons for doing nothing at all, and as many more against it; numberless alliterations, puns, questions, and commands, and other figures of rhetoric; about a score good passages, that one may turn to with pleasure, and the most involved, irksome, improgressive, and heteroclite subject that ever was chosen to exercise the pen or patience of man. It no longer adorns the toilette or lies upon the pillow of maids of honour and peeresses in their own right (the Pamelas and Philocleas of a later age), but remains upon the shelves of the libraries of the curious in long works and great names, a monument to show that the author was one of the ablest men and worst writers of the age of Elizabeth.

His sonnets, inlaid in the *Arcadia,* are jejune, far-fetched, and frigid. I shall select only one that has been much commended. It is to the Highway where his mistress had passed; a strange subject, but not unsuitable to the author's genius:

> Highway, since you my chief Parnassus be,
> And that my Muse (to some ears not unsweet)
> Tempers her words to trampling horses' feet
> More oft than to a chamber melody;
> Now blessed you bear onward blessed me
> To her, where I my heart safe left shall meet;
> My Muse, and I must you of duty greet
> With thanks and wishes, wishing thankfully.
> Be you still fair, honour'd by public heed,
> By no encroachment wrong'd, nor time forgot;
> Nor blamed for blood, nor shamed for sinful
> deed;
> And that you know, I envy you no lot
> Of highest wish, I wish you so much bliss,
> Hundreds of years you Stella's feet may kiss.

The answer of the Highway has not been preserved, but the sincerity of this appeal must no doubt have moved the stocks and stones to rise and sympathise. His *Apology for Poetry* [1595] is his most readable performance; there he is quite at home, in a sort of special pleader's office, where his ingenuity, scholastic subtlety, and tenaciousness in ar-

gument stand him in good stead; and he brings off poetry with flying colours; for he was a man of wit, of sense, and learning, though not a poet of true taste or unsophisticated genius. (pp. 201-12)

> *William Hazlitt, in a lecture delivered in 1820,*
> *in his* Lectures on the Literature of the Age
> of Elizabeth, and Characters of Shakespear's
> Plays, *Bell & Daldy, 1870, pp. 172-212.*

Charles Lamb   (essay date 1833)

[*Lamb was an English essayist who, along with William Hazlitt, developed the personal essay into an important literary form in English literature. Written under the pseudonym "Elia," his essays are considered by many critics to epitomize the "familiar" style. This style is also apparent in Lamb's critical writings, in which his self-professed method was to point out fine passages in particular works and convey his enthusiasm to his readers. In the following excerpt from an essay originally published in 1833, he offers an appreciation of Sidney's work, particularly the sonnets, which he finds admirable for their passion.*]

Sydney's Sonnets—I speak of the best of them—are among the very best of their sort. They fall below the plain moral dignity, the sanctity and high yet modest spirit of self-approval, of Milton, in his compositions of a similar structure. They are in truth what Milton, censuring the *Arcadia,* says of that work (to which they are a sort of aftertune or application), "vain and amatorious" enough, yet the things in their kind (as he confesses to be true of the romance) may be "full of worth and wit." They savor of the Courtier, it must be allowed, and not of the Commonwealthsman. But Milton was a Courtier when he wrote the *Masque* at Ludlow Castle, and still more a Courtier when he composed the *Arcades.* When the national struggle was to begin, he becomingly cast these vanities behind him; and if the order of time had thrown Sir Philip upon the crisis which preceded the revolution, there is no reason why he should not have acted the same part in that emergency, which has glorified the name of a later Sydney. He did not want for plainness or boldness of spirit. His letter on the French match may testify he could speak his mind freely to princes. The times did not call him to the scaffold.

The Sonnets which we oftenest call to mind of Milton were the compositions of his maturest years. Those of Sydney, which I am about to produce, were written in the very heyday of his blood. They are stuck full of amorous fancies—far-fetched conceits, befitting his occupation; for True Love thinks no labor to send out Thoughts upon the vast and more than Indian voyages, to bring home rich pearls, outlandish wealth, gums, jewels, spicery, to sacrifice in self-deprecating similitudes, as shadows of true amiabilities in the Beloved. We must be Lovers—or at least the cooling touch of time, the *circum præcordia frigus,* must not have so damped our faculties as to take away our recollection that we were once so—before we can duly appreciate the glorious vanities and graceful hyperboles of the passion. The images which lie before our feet (though by some accounted the only natural) are least natural for the high Sydnean love to express its fancies by. They may serve for the loves of Tibullus, or the dear Author of the "Schoolmistress;" for passions that creep and whine in Elegies and Pastoral Ballads. I am sure Milton never loved at this rate. I am afraid some of his addresses ("Ad Leonoram" I mean) have rather erred on the further side; and that the poet came not much short of a religious indecorum, when he could thus apostrophize a singing-girl:

> Angelus unicuique suus (sic credite gentes)
> Obtigit æthereis ales ab ordinibus.
> Quid mirum, Leonora, tibi si gloria major,
> Nam tua præsentem vox sonat ipsa Deum
> Aut Deus, aut vacui certè mens tertia cœli
> Per tua secretò guttura serpit agens;
> Serpit agens, facilisque docet mortalia corda
> Sensim immortali assuescere posse sono.
> QUOD SI CUNCTA QUIDEM DEUS EST, PER CUNC-
>   TAQUE FUSUS,
> IN TE UNA LOQUITUR, CAETERA MUTUS
>   HABET.

This is loving in a strange fashion; and it requires some candor of construction (besides the slight darkening of a dead language) to cast a veil over the ugly appearance of something very like blasphemy in the last two verses. I think the Lover would have been staggered if he had gone about to express the same thought in English. I am sure Sydney has no flights like this. His extravaganzas do not strike at the sky, though he takes leave to adopt the pale Dian into a fellowship with his mortal passions.

I.

> With how sad steps, O Moon, thou climb'st the
>   skies!
> How silently; and with how wan a face!
> What! may it be, that even in heavenly place
> That busy Archer his sharp arrow tries?
> Sure, if that long-with-love acquainted eyes
> Can judge of love, thou feel'st a lover's case;
> I read it in thy looks, thy languished grace
> To me, that feel the like, thy state descries.
> Then, even of fellowship, O Moon, tell me,
> Is constant love deem'd there but want of wit?
> Are beauties there as proud as here they be?
> Do they above love to be loved, and yet
> Those lovers scorn, whom that love doth pos-
>   sess?
> Do they call *virtue* there—*ungratefulness!*

The last line of this poem is a little obscured by transposition. He means, Do they call ungratefulness there a virtue?

II.

> Come, Sleep, O Sleep, the certain not of peace,
> The baiting-place of wit, the balm of woe,
> The poor man's wealth, the prisoner's release,
> The indifferent judge between the high and low;
> With shield of proof shield me from out the
>   prease
> Of those fierce darts despair at me doth throw;
> O make in me those civil wars to cease:
> I will good tribute pay if thou do so.
> Take thou of me sweet pillows, sweetest bed;
> A chamber deaf to noise, and blind to light;
> A rosy garland and a weary head.
> And if these things, as being thine by right,

> Move not thy heavy grace, thou shalt in me,
> Livelier than elsewhere, STELLA'S image see.

III.

> The curious wits, seeing dull pensiveness
> Bewray itself in my long settled eyes,
> Whence those same fumes of melancholy rise,
> With idle pains, and missing aim, do guess.
> Some, that know how my spring I did address,
> Deem that my Muse some fruit of knowledge
>   plies.
> Others, because the Prince my service tries,
> Think, that I think state errors to redress;
> But harder judges judge, ambition's rage,
> Scourge of itself, still climbing slippery place,
> Holds my young brain captiv'd in golden cage.
> O fools, or over-wise! alas, the race
> Of all my thoughts hath neither stop nor start,
> But only STELLA'S eyes, and STELLA'S heart.

IV.

> Because I oft in dark abstracted guise
> Seem most alone in greatest company.
> With dearth of words, or answers quite awry,
> To them that would make speech of speech arise;
> They deem, and of their doom the rumor flies,
> That poison foul of bubbling *Pride* doth lie
> So in my swelling breast that only I
> Fawn on myself, and others do despise;
> Yet *Pride,* I think, doth not my soul possess,
> Which looks too oft in the unfaltering glass;
> But one worse fault—*Ambition*—I confess,
> That makes me oft my best friends overpass,
> Unseen, unheard—while Thought to highest
>   place
> Bends all his powers, even unto STELLA'S grace.

(pp. 264-67)

XII.

> Highway, since you my chief Parnassus be;
> And that my Muse, to some ears not unsweet,
> Tempers her words to trampling horses' feet,
> More soft than to a chamber melody;
> Now blessed You bear onward blessed Me
> To Her, where I my heart safe left shall meet,
> My Muse and I must you of duty greet
> With thanks and wishes, wishing thankfully.
> Be you still fair, honor'd by public heed,
> By no encroachment wrong'd nor time forgot;
> Nor blamed for blood, nor shamed for sinful
>   deed.
> And that you know, I envy you no lot
> Of highest wish, I wish you so much bliss,
> Hundreds of years you STELLA'S feet may kiss.

Of the foregoing, the first, the second, and the last sonnet, are my favorites. But the general beauty of them all is, that they are so perfectly characteristical. The spirit of "learning and of chivalry," of which union, Spenser has entitled Sydney to have been the "president," shines through them. I confess I can see nothing of the "jejune" or "frigid" in them; much less of the "stiff" and "cumbrous," which I have sometimes heard objected to the *Arcadia.* The verse runs off swiftly and gallantly. It might have been tuned to the trumpet; or tempered (as himself expresses it) to "trampling horses' feet." They abound in felicitous phrases—

O heav'nly Fool, thy most kiss-worthy face—
                              —*Eighth Sonnet.*

———— Sweet pillows, sweetest bed;
A chamber deaf to noise, and blind to light;
A rosy garland and a weary head.
                              —*Second Sonnet.*

———— That sweet enemy, France—
                              —*Fifth Sonnet.*

But they are not rich in words only, in vague and unlocalized feelings—the failing too much of some poetry of the present day—they are full, material, and circumstantiated. Time and place appropriates every one of them. It is not a fever of passion wasting itself upon a thin diet of dainty words, but a transcendent passion pervading and illuminating action, pursuits, studies, feats of arms, the opinions of contemporaries and his judgment of them. An historical thread runs through them, which almost affixes a date to them; marks the *when* and *where* they were written.

I have dwelt the longer upon what I conceive the merit of these poems, because I have been hurt by the wantonness (I wish I could treat it by a gentler name) with which W. H. [William Hazlitt] takes every occasion of insulting the memory of Sir Philip Sydney. But the decisions of the Author of *Table Talk,* etc. (most profound and subtle where they are, as for the most part, just), are more safely to be relied upon, on subjects and authors he has partiality for, than on such as he has conceived an accidental prejudice against. Milton wrote sonnets, and was a king-hater; and it was congenial perhaps to sacrifice a courtier to a patriot. But I was unwilling to lose a *fine idea* from my mind. The noble images, passions, sentiments and poetical delicacies of character, scattered all over the ***Arcadia*** (spite of some stiffness and encumberment), justify to me the character which his contemporaries have left us of the writer. I cannot think with the *Critic,* that Sir Philip Sydney was that *opprobrious thing* which a foolish nobleman in his insolent hostility chose to term him. (pp. 269-71)

> *Charles Lamb, "Some Sonnets of Sir Philip Sydney," in his* The Essays of Elia, *National Book Company, 1893? pp. 264-72.*

Robert Southey   (essay date 1843?)

[*Southey was an English poet and critic. His poetry includes short verse, ballads, and epics which feature experiments in versification and meter. His prose writings include ambitious histories, biographies, and social commentary known for its conservative viewpoint. In the following excerpt from a series of biographical essays on Sidney which remained unfinished at the critic's death in 1843, Southey assesses the strengths and weaknesses of Sidney's experiments with verse.*]

[Sidney's retirement from court] happily gave him leisure, which otherwise he was little likely to have found, for those literary pursuits to which his better genius inclined him. At court he was continually called upon for the display of external accomplishments, and to exhibit himself rather for the admiration and applause of others than to his self-improvement. He was tempted and almost necessi-

tated there to incur expenses beyond what his father's means could justly afford; he was incited to vanity, exposed to envy, and compelled to lose time the value of which he understood, and the mispenditure of which he lamented. To all these considerations he refers in verses which are on that account deserving of notice, and would have had some value in themselves if the author had not cast them in a metre ill adapted to the English language, and composed also upon an erroneous system of adaptation. They were written during his retirement at this time:

> O sweet woods, the delight of solitariness,
> O how much I do like your solitariness!
> Here no treason is hid, veiled in innocence;
> Nor Envy's snaky eye finds any harbour here;
> Nor flatterers' venomous insinuations,
> Nor cunning humourists' puddled opinions,
> Nor courteous ruin of preferred usury,
> Nor time prattled away—cradle of ignorance,
> Nor causeless duty, nor cumber of arrogance;
> Nor trifling title of vanity dazzleth us,
> Nor golden manacles stand for a paradise.
> Here Wrong's name is unheard; Slander a monster is:
> Keep thy sports from abuse, here no abuse doth haunt,
> What man grafts in a tree dissimulation?

These verses, which he called 'Asclepiads,' were written in pursuance of a scheme for naturalising in English the Latin forms of versification. With some of the Latin metres this is impracticable, because no skill in our language can make them metrical to an English ear; and it was rendered impracticable in others by the preposterous attempt at naturalising with them the rules of Latin prosody, for this occasioned a forced accentuation, which could not be introduced unless the very fashion and character of our speech were changed. The attempt, therefore, necessarily failed, and its failure has led to a most unjust depreciation of Sydney himself as a poet; as if he had written no better poems than his exercises in this kind, and as if his intention had been altogether to supersede our vernacular measures. But that he never entertained so absurd a thought is made evident by what he says in his ***Defence of Poesy,*** which treatise, if he had written nothing else, might alone have sufficed to obtain for him a distinguished name in English literature. In that beautiful treatise he says, upon the subject of versifying:

> There are two sorts, the one ancient, the other modern. The ancient marked the quality of each syllable, and according to that, framed his verse; the modern, observing only numbers, with some regard of the accent, the chief life of it standeth in that like sounding of the words, which we call rhyme. Whether of these be the more excellent would bear many speeches. The ancient, no doubt, more fit for music, both words and time observing quantity, and more fit lively to express divers passions by the low or lofty sound of the well-weighed syllable; the latter likewise with his rhyme stocketh a certain music to the ear, and in fine, since it doth delight, though by another way, it obtaineth the same purpose, there being in either sweetness, and wanting in neither majesty. Truly the English, before any vulgar language I know, is fit for both sorts.

No Englishman before Sydney had taken so philosophical a view of the nature and scope of poetry as is presented in this treatise, nor has any later critic treated the subject with more wisdom, or with equal felicity of expression. Ben Jonson, whose critical discernment none but a witling would presume to question, classes him as a prose writer with Hooker, saying that 'in different matters' they 'grew masters of wit and language,' and that in them 'all vigour of invention and strength of judgment met.' Jonson held his poetry also in high estimation:

> Youth [he says] ought to be instructed betimes, and in the best things; for we hold those longest we take soonest: as the first scent of a vessel lasts, and the tinct the wool first receives. And as it is fit to read the best authors to youth first, so let them be of the openest and clearest: as Livy before Sallust, Sydney before Doune.

When Sydney composed his defence of poetry, it seems as if he had not yet entertained the ambition of becoming a poet himself. The purport of the treatise was to show the uses and dignity of an art (in his just estimation the noblest of all arts) which, 'from almost the highest estimation of learning,' had been in England, he says, 'fallen to be the laughing-stock of children.' In this country alone it 'found a hard welcome,' when in all others it was honoured according to its deserts. (pp. 104-05)

[Sidney's sonnets have] a character of their own, which distinguishes his amatory poems from most, if not all, other effusions of the same kind, whether of English or of foreign growth. No man was better versed in the contemporary literature of other countries; but he was as little infected by the prevalent vices of Italian, or Spanish, or French poetry as by the alliterative affectation of his own countrymen, who in their eager pursuit of sound did not always remember to keep sight of sense, and provided they found the fit initials troubled themselves little concerning the fitness of the word in other and more material respects. But Sydney aimed at something higher than the vulgar mark. Seldom have any such poems been so free from conceits and prettinesses, from exaggeration and extravagance, from anything forced either in thought or expression. There is nothing meretricious in his verses. He regarded poetry, not as a mere sport of fancy, the light effusion of idle hours, but as the highest employment of the human mind; as that which, 'in the noblest nations and languages that are known, had been the first light-giver to ignorance and first nurse whose milk by little and little enabled them to feed afterwards of tougher knowledge.' How 'high and incomparable a title' that of poet is, 'wherein,' he says, 'I know not whether by luck or wisdom we Englishmen have met with the Greeks in calling him a maker,' he shows by comparing the scope of poetry with that of other sciences and arts, all which were founded upon nature and subordinate to it. . . . (p. 113)

As he had well considered the nature of poetry, so did he make a diligent study of the art. Verse he looked upon, not as essential to it, but as an ornament. There had been many most excellent poets who had never versified, and his own country swarmed at that time with versifiers who never, he said, needed answer to the name of poets. To that name he thought Xenophon entitled, and Heliodorus, and

the author of *Amadis;* but 'the senate of poets,' he said, 'had chosen verse as their fittest raiment; meaning that as in matter they passed all, in all, so in manner to go beyond them; not speaking table-talk fashion, or, like men in a dream, words as they chanceably fall from the mouth, but poising each syllable of each word, by just proportion, according to the dignity of the subject.' No other English poet has ever made so many experiments in versification; a fact which, important as it is in Sydney's history, has never before been stated. His hexameters and other verses composed upon the rules of Latin prosody are the only ones which have heretofore attracted notice; it was seen at a glance that they were absolutely worthless, and few persons even of those who most admired the author troubled themselves to inquire what should have made them so. The attempt, as I have before observed, proceeded upon an erroneous principle, because Sydney and his associates in the experiment adopted the rules of a foreign prosody, instead of adapting the Latin metres to a language in which accentuation and not quantity is regarded. But there was nothing preposterous in the scheme itself; the absurdity would be in supposing that the same cadence which in Greek or Latin is agreeable to an Englishman, should not be agreeable in his mother tongue. It may be made offensive if violence is done to established usage either in the pronunciation of words or in their collocation; but if they are accented in the verse as they would be in common speech, and if there be no wider deviation from the usual construction of our language than we are accustomed to in our vernacular forms of verse, then can there be no other reason for condemning it than an unreasonable prepossession.

No such prejudice existed against it in the Elizabethan age; there was rather a disposition to favour the experiment among those scholars who did not think the literature of their mother tongue beneath their notice, and it was tried about the same time in France and Italy and Spain as well as in England. Here it would be out of place to inquire what were the causes of its failure in other countries; with us the mistaken principle upon which it was undertaken sufficiently explains it. It was moreover made ridiculous by the portentous absurdity of Stanihurst's Virgil; and Sydney's own productions of this kind were almost without any merit whatever. But they are few in number, and it ought to be remembered that none of them were published during his life, and it may well be doubted whether, if he had lived some years longer, they would ever have been published at all. For evidently they were written as exercises in metre,—so entirely so that matter and thought and expression were things of secondary consideration, the first and almost only care of the writer being, not to 'poise his syllables by just proportions according to the dignity of the subject' (his own rule), but to measure their quantity.

With a very few exceptions, Sydney's verses of the kind are included in the Eclogues of his *Arcadia* which are pastoral interludes consisting of prose and verse, being indeed the only pastoral parts of the work. Readers who are not conversant with the foreign literature of the sixteenth century would feel it difficult to conceive how small a modicum of invention was required for pastoral compositions of any kind. The flimsiest narrative in prose served to introduce poems as flimsy, as florid, and as inane as the prose that connected them. Yet they had their day, and some not inconsiderable reputations were made by them, which, though the books are no longer read, retain as by prescription their place. The language was mellifluous and lulled the ear, the images were agreeable and soothed the mind, birds warbled, lambs sported, heaven smiled, streams glittered as they flowed, and fountains gurgled, and earth was redolent of flowers. There was no lack of fruit, neither of curds and cream. Shepherds and shepherdesses tended their flocks, all alike amiable, alike poetical, and alike in love, some with the right object and some with the wrong. They piped, they danced, they sung; they contended with each other in amœbean verses, or uttered their complaints to the listening groom in sonnets, tercets, quatrains, or other stanzas, or in more fantastic sestines rung the appointed set of changes upon the everlasting theme. From the beginning to the end all was dulcet, emulsive, and soporiferous; the gentle reader was never put to the trouble of thinking, and he might fall asleep over the book in perfect complacency with the author and with himself.

On such subjects it was that Sydney chose to make his experiment in the classical metres, as if he wished to be encumbered as little as possible with meaning in his task. He tried the heroic hexameter, the elegiac long and short, anacreontics, sapphics, phaleucians, and asclepiads. As might be expected, the anacreontics are the least uncouth, the pentameters the most so. But that all are uncouth to an extraordinary degree may be seen from the most favourable and not least characteristic specimen that could be selected: a passage in which having hit upon a vein of conceit he works it as far as it leads him.

> When I meet these trees, in th' earth's fair livery
> cloathed,
> Ease do I feel (such ease as falls to one wholly
> diseased),
> For that I find in them part ōf my state repre-
> sented.
> Laurel shows what I seek; by the Myrrh is
> shown how I seek it;
> Olive paints me the peace that I mūst āspire to
> by conquest;
> Myrtle makes my request; my request is crown'd
> with a Willow;
> Cypress promiseth help, but a help where comes
> no comfort.
> Sweet Junipēr saith this, 'Tho' I burn, yet I burn
> in a sweet fire.'
> Yew doth make me think what kind ōf bow the
> Boy holdeth
> Which shoots strongly without any noise, ānd
> deadly without smart.
> Fir-trees, great ānd green, fixt ōn a hǐgh hill but
> a barren,
> Like to my noble thoughts, still new, well
> placèd, to me fruitless.
> Fig thǎt yields most pleasant fruits, his shadow
> is hurtful.
> Thus be her gifts most sweet, thus more dangēr
> to be near her.
> Now in a Palm, when I mark hǒw hě dōth rise
> under a burden,

> And may I not (I say then) get up, tho' grief be
> so weighty? . . .
>
> (pp. 115-17)

I cannot but think that if Sydney had lived to revise the work in which these verses were introduced he would have discovered in what this system of metrification was erroneous; that he would have remedied that error by following the common laws of accentuation instead of attempting to introduce rules of quantity, which are not in accord with the character of our language, and that the hexameter would then have been naturalised in England at that time as successfully as it was, two centuries afterwards, in German and other of the northern tongues.

He introduced other metrical experiments in the same ecologues, trying most of the forms of composition and varieties of measure which were to be found in Italian and French poetry, madrigals, songs as he translated the Italian word canzoni, sestines (an invention of the troubadours, which might well have been left where it was found, were it not that it is desirable to be in some degree acquainted with even the preposterous fashions of other nations in literature as in other things), and tercets, or the trinal verse of Dante, a grave and majestic metre which has recently, and for the first time upon any great scale, been exhibited in this country by Mr. Heraud with exuberant powers both of imagination and diction in his poem of the *Descent into Hell.* Sydney, to render it more exactly upon the Italian model, tried it also with double, or trochaic rhymes, and with the *sdruccioli,* or dactylic termination—this latter being, like the sestines, a mere trial of skill. (pp. 117-18)

> *Robert Southey, "Life of Sir Philip Sidney," in*
> Fraser's Magazine for Town & Country, *Vol.*
> *LXXVIII, July, 1868, pp. 96-118.*

Edmund Gosse   (essay date 1886)

[*Gosse was a prominent English scholar of the late nineteenth century. A prolific literary historian, biographer, and critic, he is primarily remembered for his translations of Scandinavian literature and for his* Father and Son: A Study of Two Temperaments *(1907), one of the most distinguished examples of Victorian spiritual autobiography. In the following excerpt from an overview of Sidney's life and career, Gosse discusses the poet's principal works, concluding that the study of his poetry is less rewarding than that of his life.*]

The years 1578 and 1579 were quiet ones in Sidney's career, and they mark his first serious attention to literature. His masque of *The Lady of the May* belongs to May, 1578, and is even below what men like Gascoigne and Churchyard had been producing. The moment was a critical one in English poetry. The hour was darkest just before the dawn, and, though England was full of boys of genius, there was only one living poet of recognized position—namely, Sackville, who had long ceased to write. Everything seemed dead; Spenser, writing to Cambridge from London, could hear of no new books except "The School of Abuse." For some reason or another, all lovers of literature, all the young men who desired to excel and had not found a voice, looked to Sidney as the pioneer who should open a way into the kingdom of poetry. This is the secret of Sidney's extraordinary interest to the poetical student; he is the leader of the Elizabethan chorus, elected by popular acclaim to point the way for Spenser and Marlowe and Shakespeare. Very hard things have been said about the affectation of his earliest efforts, and the lovers of Sidney have tried . . . to evade the facts as regards his leadership of the Areopagus. But something may be said to justify action the responsibility of which must remain on his head. The English verse which he saw about him was the verse of Turberville and Churchyard, of Tusser and of the blood-and-thunder translators, the verse which he himself attempted in *The Lady of the May.* There was no structural vigor in English versification, no knowledge of prosody, no ambition for a fine style. Gascoigne had feebly and tamely hinted at better things; and, now Gascoigne was gone, and Whetstone had celebrated him in the old dreadful manner, Sidney and Dyer determined upon the "general surceasing and silence of bald rimers," and the adoption of fixed rules for quantitative metre. It could not be achieved, the genius of the language being opposed to it, but it did the poets no harm to try. They learned from these experiments a great deal about the value of syllables and the general ductility of the language which no other apprenticeship would have given them.

In the very midst of the Areopagus period there appeared "The Shepheard's Calendar," with its pretty, timid triplets of dedication to Sidney. All through 1580 Spenser, as much the greater poet as Sidney was the greater man, was breaking away from the bondage of his friend, while Sidney was still pursuing the vain attempt, as the asclepiads and anacreontics of the *Arcadia* are enough to prove. But, indeed, that famous pastoral is, in a certain sense, one of the most interesting books that ever were published; in the eyes of the literary historian it is a belvidere from which he looks up and down the whole range of English literature. It is the great transitional or probationary book, in which the old is passing away and the new is coming in. In verse it contains specimens of all the styles then fashionable, or defunct, or about to come into vogue. There are the quantitative failures of the Areopagus, there are long swinging pieces in the Golding or Turberville manner, there are sextains and sonnets in the new Italian fashion, there are rhyming dialogues, octosyllabics in the form that Greene and his friends were to adopt, all meeting in the verse-divisions of the *Arcadia.* The prose bears the same transitional character, except that it leans more to one model, and is less original. I am afraid that the *Arcadia* would never have been written, in the style that now characterizes it at least, if Lyly's "Euphues" had not preceded it by a year. There seems to me to have been a distinct effort made by Sidney's numerous admirers to assert his originality in opposition to that of Spenser in poetry and Lyly in prose. It is difficult to see what else Nash meant by his diatribe against Lyly's "miserable hornpipes" in his preface to the first edition of *Astrophel and Stella.* Into this question, or into any critical consideration of the romance of the *Arcadia,* it is impossible to go within such space as is here at my command. I would only venture to indicate it as deserving more patient attention than has yet been given to it, both in its relation to Spanish and Italian pastoral, and in its position as a precursor of the romantic tragi-comical drama in England ten or fifteen years later.

If the *Astrophel and Stella* belongs entirely to 1581, as I suppose, and as has been generally admitted until lately, it marks a further advance in Sidney's power. Very little of the verse in the *Arcadia* is even tolerable; Mrs. T. H. Ward, who is the latest and the most indulgent of the critics of Sidney's poetry, admits that here he is "undeniably dry and artificial." There is in this fact an important element of internal evidence to rebut the notion that much of *Astrophel and Stella* belongs to a period earlier than Lady Penelope Rich's marriage. If it had been so, there would have been a sensible incongruity between the style of the various sonnets, as there is between that of the earlier and later sections of the verse in the *Arcadia.* But no such incongruity can be discovered. The sonnets of the *Astrophel and Stella* differ very singularly in merit, but they are written in the same mode. Mrs. Ward has claimed that the cycle is second as a series of sonnets only to Shakespeare's. She speaks, of course, of Elizabethan competitors only; but it is no very great praise to say that the *Astrophel and Stella* is better than "Delia" or "Idea" or "Fidessa." The Elizabethans loved to compose cycles of sonnets, repertories of affected and often very careless work, in which only one or two pieces possess lasting merit. Sidney did better than this; of his one hundred and ten there are perhaps fifteen that are very good. Charles Lamb admitted twelve into his selection of the best; Mrs. Ward quotes twenty-three, but amongst her favorites there are several which evidently owe their admission only to a happy phrase or a touch of natural feeling. By far the best are the two most famous—the one to the moon, and the other to sleep. It is strange that Lamb did not happen to light on the following sonnet, one which admirably exemplifies the qualities he claims for Sidney's poetry, the swift and gallant run of the verses, the full, material, and circumstantial color:—

I might! unhappy word—O me, I might,
And then would not, or could not, see my bliss;
Till now wrapped in a most infernal night,
I find how heavenly day, wretch! I did miss.
Heart, rend thyself, thou dost thyself but right;
No lovely Paris made thy Helen his;
No force, no fraud robb'd thee of they delight,
Nor Fortune of thy fortune author is;
But to myself myself did give the blow,
While too much wit, forsooth, so troubled me,
That I respects for both our sakes must show;
And yet could not, by rising morn, foresee
How fair a day was near: O punished eyes,
That I had been more foolish, or more wise!

This is astonishingly like Shakespeare, and it was written when Shakespeare was a lad of seventeen.

Still better than any but the very best passages in the *Astrophel and Stella* are the occasional verses first printed in 1598 as an appendix to the *Arcadia.* These are doubtless mainly later than the Stella cycle; and here we have Sidney at his highest as a poet. They contain the lovely ode or madrigal entitled **"Philomela"**; and **"The Dirge,"** Sidney's first lyric, isolated from the rest of his verse as strangely as Raleigh's "Pilgrimage" is from the rest of his. In the same category I would place the two pastorals addressed to Dyer and Greville, and the very charming allegorical **"Child-Song,"** or Lullaby, which I may be permitted to quote here:—

> Sleep, baby mine! Desire's nurse, Beauty, singeth;
> Thy cries, O Baby, set mine head on aching.
> The babe cries, " 'Way, thy love doth keep me waking."
> Lully, lully, my babe! Hope cradle bringeth,
> Unto my children alway good rest taking.
> The babe cries, " 'Way, thy love doth keep me waking."
> Since, baby mine, from me thy watching springeth,
> Sleep then a little! pap Content is making!
> The babe cries, "Nay, for that abide I waking."

It is difficult, however, to date any of Sidney's poems later than 1582, and during the last four years of his short life he seems to have been silent. He died as a poet at twenty-eight, younger than Shelley or Collins. He was eminently an "inheritor of unfulfilled renown," and yet it is very hard to tell whether he would ever have come back to literature from diplomacy and sword-craft. His poetry was but an accident of his leisure. So universally gifted a man, in that age, was bound to write verses, and, being Sidney, we may say, was bound to write them well. But we have only to compare his work with that of Spenser to see the difference between the most brilliant amateur and the artist who made verse the sole business of his life.

To us, perhaps, in summing up, Sidney is most interesting as a radiating centre of sympathy, intelligence, brightness. He was singularly modern, a little ahead of every one else about him, full of ideas and wishes, which he strewed around to fructify when he himself was dead. As a great author, surely, we must never venture to regard him. The positive merit of the bulk of his writings is almost pathetically inadequate to any excess of praise. Even Lamb perhaps, in his generous indulgence, says a little too much. Yet it would be an error to overlook the original flavor or perfume which gives a charm to his work, even where it is a little thin and uninteresting. There is always to be found in it the "Sidneian sweetness," the purity, the grace of thought. In the beautiful **Apology for Poetry** we see these qualities at their best, clarified from their author's occasional affectation and triviality; and this essay seems to hold a middle position between his verse and prose. After three hundred years, however, Sir Philip Sidney has become more important to us than his poetry. We perceive that he was one of the most gifted and engaging persons that ever lived, and we admit that he was a very pleasant poet also. (pp. 585-87)

> *Edmund Gosse, "Sir Philip Sidney," in* Littell's Living Age, *Vol. CLXXI, No. 2215, December 4, 1886, pp. 579-87.*

J. A. Symonds (essay date 1886)

[*Symonds was an English poet, historian, critic, and translator who wrote extensively on Greek and Italian* history and culture. *In the excerpt below from his full-length study of Sidney, he examines* The Defence of Poesy, *tracing the development of the treatise's arguments and praising its originality and conciseness.*]

Fulke Greville, touching upon the **Arcadia,** says that Sidney "purposed no monuments of books to the world."

> If his purpose had been to leave his memory in books, I am confident, in the right use of logic, philosophy, history, and poesy, nay even in the most ingenious of mechanical arts, he would have showed such tracts of a searching and judicious spirit as the professors of every faculty would have striven no less for him than the seven cities did to have Homer of their sept. But the truth is: his end was not writing, even while he wrote; nor his knowledge moulded for tables or schools; but both his wit and understanding bent upon his heart, to make himself and others, not in words or opinion, but in life and action, good and great.

"His end was not writing, even while he wrote." This is certain; the whole tenor of Sidney's career proves his determination to subordinate self-culture of every kind to the ruling purpose of useful public action. It will also be remembered that none of his compositions were printed during his lifetime or with his sanction. Yet he had received gifts from nature which placed him, as a critic, high above the average of his contemporaries. He was no mean poet when he sang as love dictated. He had acquired and assimilated various stores of knowledge. He possessed an exquisite and original taste, a notable faculty for the marshalling of arguments, and a persuasive eloquence in exposition. These qualities inevitably found their exercise in writing; and of all Sidney's writings the one with which we have to deal now, is the ripest.

Judging by the style alone, I should be inclined to place **The Defence of Poesy** among his later works. But we have no certain grounds for fixing the year of its composition. Probably the commonly accepted date of 1581 is the right one. In the year 1579 Stephen Gosson dedicated to Sidney, without asking his permission, an invective against "poets, pipers, players, and their excusers," which he called *The School of Abuse.* Spenser observes that Gosson "was for his labour scorned; if at least it lie in the goodness of that nature to scorn. Such folly is it not to regard aforehand the nature and quality of him to whom we dedicate our books." It is possible therefore that *The School of Abuse* and other treatises emanating from Puritan hostility to culture, suggested this Apology. Sidney rated poetry highest among the functions of the human intellect. His name had been used to give authority and currency to a clever attack upon poets. He felt the weight of argument to be on his side, and was conscious of his ability to conduct the cause. With what serenity of spirit, sweetness of temper, humour, and easy strength of style—at one time soaring to enthusiasm, at another playing with his subject,—he performed the task, can only be appreciated by a close perusal of the essay. It is indeed the model for such kinds of composition—a work which combines the quaintness and the blitheness of Elizabethan literature with the urbanity and reserve of a later period.

Sidney begins by numbering himself among "the paper-blurrers," "who, I know not by what mischance, in these my not old years and idlest times, having slipped into the title of a poet, am provoked to say something unto you in the defence of that my unelected vocation." Hence it is his duty "to make a pitiful defence of poor poetry, which from almost the highest estimation of learning, is fallen to be the laughing-stock of children." Underlying Sidney's main argument we find the proposition that to attack poetry is the same as attacking culture in general; therefore, at the outset, he appeals to all professors of learning: will they inveigh against the mother of arts and sciences, the "first nurse, whose milk by little and little enabled them to feed afterwards of tougher knowledge?" Musæus, Homer, and Hesiod lead the solemn pomp of the Greek writers. Dante, Petrarch, and Boccaccio in Italy, Gower and Chaucer in England came before prose-authors. The earliest philosophers, Empedocles and Parmenides, Solon and Tyrtæus, committed their metaphysical speculations, their gnomic wisdom, their marital exhortation, to verse. And even Plato, if rightly considered, was a poet: "in the body of his work, though the inside and strength were philosophy, the skin as it were, and beauty, depended most of poetry." Herodotus called his books by the names of the Muses: "both he and all the rest that followed him, either stole or usurped of poetry their passionate describing of passions, the many particularities of battles which no man could affirm." They also put imaginary speeches into the mouths of kings and captains. The very names which the Greeks and Romans, "the authors of most of our sciences," gave to poets, show the estimation in which they held them. The Romans called the poet *vates,* or prophet; the Greeks ποιητηζ or maker, a word, by the way, which coincides with English custom. What can be higher in the scale of human understanding than this faculty of *making?* Sidney enlarges upon its significance, following a line of thought which Tasso summed up in one memorable sentence: "There is no Creator but God and the Poet."

He now advances a definition, which is substantially the same as Aristotle's: "Poesy is an art of imitation; that is to say, a representing, counterfeiting, or figuring forth: to speak metaphorically, a speaking picture; with this end to teach and delight." Of poets there have been three general kinds: first, "they that did imitate the inconceivable excellences of God;" secondly, "they that deal with matter philosophical, either moral or natural or astronomical or historical;" thirdly, "right poets . . . which most properly do imitate, to teach and delight; and to imitate, borrow nothing of what is, hath been, or shall be; but range only, reined with learned discretion, into the divine consideration of what may be and should be." The preference given to the third kind of poets may be thus explained: The first group are limited to setting forth fixed theological conceptions; the second have their material supplied them by the sciences; but the third are the makers and creators of ideals for warning and example.

Poets may also be classified according to the several species of verse. But this implies a formal and misleading limitation. Sidney, like Milton and like Shelley, will not have poetry confined to metre: "apparelled verse being but an ornament, and no cause to poetry; since there have been

many most excellent poets that have never versified, and now swarm many versifiers that need never answer to the name of poets." Xenophon's "Cyropædia," the "Theagenes and Chariclea" of Heliodorus, are cited as true poems; "and yet both these wrote in prose." "It is not rhyming and versing that maketh a poet; but it is that feigning notable images of virtues, vices, or what else, with that delightful teaching, which must be the right describing note to know a poet by." Truly "the senate of poets have chosen verse as their fittest raiment;" but this they did, because they meant, "as in matter they passed all in all, so in manner to go beyond them." "Speech, next to reason, is the greatest gift bestowed upon mortality;" and verse "which most doth polish that blessing of speech," is, therefore, the highest investiture of poetic thought.

Having thus defined his conception of poetry, Sidney inquires into the purpose of all learning. "This purifying of wit, this enriching of memory, enabling of judgment, and enlarging of conceit, which commonly we call learning, under what name soever it come forth, or to what immediate end soever it be directed; the final end is to lead and draw us to as high a perfection as our degenerate souls, made worse by their clay lodgings, can be capable of." All the branches of learning subserve the royal or architectonic science, "which stands, as I think, in the knowledge of a man's self in the ethic and politic consideration, with the end of well-doing, and not of well-knowing only." If then virtuous action be the ultimate object of all our intellectual endeavours, can it be shown that the poet contributes above all others to this exalted aim? Sidney thinks it can.

Omitting divines and jurists, for obvious reasons, he finds that the poet's only competitors are philosophers and historians. It therefore now behoves him to prove that poetry contributes more to the formation of character for virtuous action than either philosophy or history. The argument is skilfully conducted, and developed with nice art; but it amounts in short to this, that while philosophy is too abstract and history is too concrete, poetry takes the just path between these extremes, and combines their methods in a harmony of more persuasive force than either. "Now doth the peerless poet perform both; for whatsoever the philosopher saith should be done, he giveth a perfect picture of it, by some one whom he presupposeth it was done, so as he coupleth the general notion with the particular example." "Anger, the Stoics said, was a short madness; but let Sophocles bring you Ajax on a stage, killing or whipping sheep and oxen, thinking them the army of Greeks, with their chieftains Agamemnon and Menelaus; and tell me if you have not a more familiar insight into anger than finding in the schoolmen his genus and difference?" Even Christ used parables and fables for the firmer inculcation of his divine precepts. If philosophy is too much occupied with the universal, history is too much bound to the particular. It dares not go beyond what was, may not travel into what might or should be. Moreover, "history being captivated to the truth of a foolish world, is many times a terror from well-doing, and an encouragement to unbridled wickedness." It cannot avoid revealing virtue overwhelmed with calamity and vice in prosperous condition. Poetry labours not under the same restrictions. Her ideals, delightfully presented, entering the soul with the enchanting strains of music, "set the mind forward to that which deserves to be called and accounted good." In fine: "as virtue is the most excellent resting-place for all worldly learning to make his end of, so poetry, being the most familiar to teach it, and most princely to move towards it, in the most excellent work is the most excellent workman."

Sidney next passes the various species of poems in review: the pastoral; "the lamenting elegiac;" "the bitter but wholesome iambic;" the satiric; the comic, "whom naughty play-makers and stage-keepers have justly made odious;" "the high and excellent tragedy, that openeth the greatest wounds, and showeth forth the ulcers that are covered with tissue—that maketh kings fear to be tyrants, and tyrants to manifest their tyrannical humours—that with stirring the effects of admiration and commiseration, teacheth the uncertainty of this world, and upon how weak foundations gilded roofs are builded;" the lyric, "who with his tuned lyre and well-accorded voice giveth praise, the reward of virtue, to virtuous acts—who giveth moral precepts and natural problems—who sometimes raiseth up his voice to the height of the heavens, in singing the lauds of the immortal God;" the epic or heroic, "whose very name, I think, should daunt all backbiters . . . which is not only a kind, but the best and most accomplished kind of poetry." He calls upon the detractors of poesy to bring their complaints against these several sorts, and to indicate in each of them its errors. What they may allege in disparagement, he meets with chosen arguments, among which we can select his apology for the lyric. "Certainly, I must confess my own barbarousness: I never heard the old song of 'Percy and Douglas' that I found not my heart moved more than with a trumpet; and yet it is sung but by some blind crowder, with no rougher voice than rude style; which being so evil-apparelled in the dust and cobweb of that uncivil age, what would it work, trimmed in the gorgeous eloquence of Pindar?"

Having reached this point, partly on the way of argument, partly on the path of appeal and persuasion, Sidney halts to sum his whole position up in one condensed paragraph:

> Since, then, poetry is of all human learnings the most ancient, and of most fatherly antiquity, as from whence other learnings have taken their beginnings; since it is so universal that no learned nation doth despise it, nor barbarous nation is without it; since both Roman and Greek gave such divine names unto it, the one of prophesying, the other of making, and that indeed that name of making is fit for him, considering, that where all other arts retain themselves within their subject, and receive, as it were, their being from it, the poet only, only bringeth his own stuff, and doth not learn a conceit out of a matter, but maketh matter for a conceit; since neither his description nor end containeth any evil, the thing described cannot be evil; since his effects be so good as to teach goodness, and delight the learners of it; since therein (namely in moral doctrine, the chief of all knowledges) he doth not only far pass the historian, but, for instructing, is well nigh comparable to the philosopher; for moving, leaveth him behind him; since the Holy Scripture (wherein there is no uncleanness) hath

whole parts in it poetical, and that even our Saviour Christ vouchsafed to use the flowers of it; since all his kinds are not only in their united forms, but in their severed dissections fully commendable; I think, and think I think rightly, the laurel crown appointed for triumphant captains, doth worthily, of all other learnings, honour the poet's triumph.

Objections remain to be combated in detail. Sidney chooses one first, which offers no great difficulty. The detractors of poetry gird at "rhyming and versing." He has already laid it down that "one may be a poet without versing, and a versifier without poetry." But he has also shown why metrical language should be regarded as the choicest and most polished mode of speech. Verse, too, fits itself to music more properly than prose, and far exceeds it "in the knitting up of the memory." Nor is rhyme to be neglected, especially in modern metres; seeing that it strikes a music to the ear. But the enemy advances heavier battalions. Against poetry he alleges (1) that there are studies upon which a man may spend his time more profitably; (2) that it is the mother of lies; (3) that it is the nurse of abuse, corrupting the fancy, enfeebling manliness, and instilling pestilent desires into the soul; (4) that Plato banished poets from his commonwealth.

These four points are taken seriatim, and severally answered. The first is set aside, as involving a begging of the question at issue. To the second Sidney replies "paradoxically, but truly I think truly, that of all writers under the sun the poet is the least liar; and though he would, as a poet, can scarcely be a liar." It is possible to err, and to affirm falsehood, in all the other departments of knowledge; but "for the poet, he nothing affirmeth, and therefore nothing lieth." His sphere is not the region of ascertained fact, or of logical propositions, but of imagination and invention. He labours not "to tell you what is, or is not, but what should, or should not be." None is so foolish as to mistake the poet's world for literal fact. "What child is there, that cometh to a play, and seeing Thebes written in great letters upon an old door, doth believe that it is Thebes?" The third point is more weighty. Are poets blamable, in that they "abuse men's wit, training it to a wanton sinfulness and lustful love?" Folk say "the comedies rather teach than reprehend amorous conceits; they say the lyric is larded with passionate sonnets; the elegiac weeps the want of his mistress; and that even to the heroical Cupid hath ambitiously climbed." Here Sidney turns to Love, and, as though himself acknowledging that deity, invokes him to defend his own cause. Yet let us "grant love of beauty to be a beastly fault," let us "grant that lovely name of love to deserve all hateful reproaches," what have the adversaries gained? Surely they have not proved "that poetry abuseth man's wit, but that man's wit abuseth poetry." "But what! shall the abuse of a thing make the right odious?" Does not law, does not physic, injure man every day by the abuse of ignorant practisers? "Doth not God's Word abused breed heresy, and His name abused become blasphemy?" Yet these people contend that before poetry came to infect the English, "our nation had set their heart's delight upon action and not imagination, rather doing things worthy to be written than writing things fit to be done." But when was there that time when the Albion nation was without poetry? Of a truth, this argument is levelled against all learning and all culture. It is an attack, worthy of Goths or Vandals, upon the stronghold of the intellect. As such, we might dismiss it. Let us, however, remember that "poetry is the companion of camps: I dare undertake, Orlando Furioso or honest King Arthur will never displease a soldier; but the quiddity of *ens* and *prima materia* will hardly agree with a corselet." Alexander on his Indian campaigns left the living Aristotle behind him, but slept with the dead Homer in his tent; condemned Callisthenes to death, but yearned for a poet to commemorate his deeds. Lastly, they advance Plato's verdict against poets. Plato, says Sidney, "I have ever esteemed most worthy of reverence; and with good reason, since of all philosophers he is the most poetical." Having delivered this sly thrust, he proceeds: "first, truly, a man might maliciously object that Plato, being a philosopher, was a natural enemy of poets." Next let us look into his writings. Has any poet authorised filthiness more abominable than one can find in the "Phaedrus" and the "Symposium?" "Again, a man might ask out of what commonwealth Plato doth banish them." It is in sooth one where the community of women is permitted; and "little should poetical sonnets be hurtful, when a man might have what woman he listed." After thus trifling with the subject, Sidney points out that Plato was not offended with poetry, but with the abuse of it. He objected to the crude theology and the monstrous ethics of the myth-makers. "So as Plato, banishing the abuse not the thing, not banishing it, but giving due honour to it, shall be our patron and not our adversary."

Once again he pauses, to recapitulate:

> Since the excellencies of poesy may be so easily and so justly confirmed, and the low creeping objections so soon trodden down; it not being an art of lies, but of true doctrine; not of effeminateness, but of notable stirring of courage; not of abusing man's wit, but of strengthening man's wit; not banished, but honoured by Plato; let us rather plant more laurels for to ingarland the poets' heads (which honour of being laureate, as besides them only triumphant captains were, is a sufficient authority to show the price they ought to be held in) than suffer the ill-favoured breath of such wrong speakers once to blow upon the clear springs of poesy.

Then he turns to England. Why is it that England, "the mother of excellent minds, should be grown so hard a stepmother to poets?"

> Sweet poesy, that hath anciently had kings, emperors, senators, great captains, such as, besides a thousand others, David, Adrian, Sophocles, Germanicus, not only to favour poets, but to be poets: and of our nearer times, can present for her patrons, a Robert, King of Sicily; the great King Francis of France; King James of Scotland; such cardinals as Bembus and Bibiena; such famous preachers and teachers as Beza and Melancthon; so learned philosophers as Fracastorius and Scaliger; so great orators as Pontanus and Muretus; so piercing wits as George Buchanan; so grave counsellors as, besides

many, but before all, that Hospital of France; than whom, I think, that realm never brought forth a more accomplished judgment more firmly builded upon virtue; I say, these, with numbers of others, not only to read others' poesies, but to poetise for others' reading: that poesy, thus embraced in all other places, should only find, in our time, a hard welcome in England, I think the very earth laments it, and therefore decks our soil with fewer laurels than it was accustomed.

The true cause is that in England so many incapable folk write verses. With the exception of the *Mirror of Magistrates,* Lord Surrey's Lyrics, and *The Shepherd's Kalendar,* "I do not remember to have seen but few (to speak boldly) printed, that have poetical sinews in them." At this point he introduces a lengthy digression upon the stage, which, were we writing a history of the English drama, ought to be quoted in full. It is interesting because it proves how the theatre occupied Sidney's thoughts; and yet he had not perceived that from the humble plays of the people an unrivalled flower of modern art was about to emerge. *The Defence of Poesy* was written before Marlowe created the romantic drama; before Shakespeare arrived in London. It was written in all probability before its author could have attended the representation of Greene's and Peele's best plays. *Gorboduc,* which he praises moderately and censures with discrimination, seemed to him the finest product of dramatic art in England, because it approached the model of Seneca and the Italian tragedians. For the popular stage, with its chaos of tragic and comic elements, its undigested farrago of romantic incidents and involved plots, he entertained the scorn of a highly-educated scholar and a refined gentleman. Yet no one, let us be sure, would have welcomed *Othello* and *The Merchant of Venice, Volpone* and *A Woman Killed with Kindness,* more enthusiastically than Sidney, had his life been protracted through the natural span of mortality.

Having uttered his opinion frankly on the drama, he attacks the "courtesan-like painted affectation" of the English at his time. Far-fetched words, alliteration, euphuistic similes from stones and beasts and plants, fall under his honest censure. He mentions no man. But he is clearly aiming at the school of Lyly and the pedants; for he pertinently observes: "I have found in divers small-learned courtiers a more sound style than in some professors of learning." Language should be used, not to trick out thoughts with irrelevant ornaments or to smother them in conceits, but to make them as clear and natural as words can do. It is a sin against our mother speech to employ these meretricious arts; for whoso will look dispassionately into the matter, shall convince himself that English, both in its freedom from inflections and its flexibility of accent, is aptest of all modern tongues to be the vehicle of simple and of beautiful utterance.

The peroration to *The Defence of Poesy* is an argument addressed to the personal ambition of the reader. It somewhat falls below the best parts of the essay in style, and makes no special claim on our attention. From the foregoing analysis it will be seen that Sidney attempted to cover a wide field, combining a philosophy of art with a practical review of English literature. Much as the Italians had recently written upon the theory of poetry, I do not remember any treatise which can be said to have supplied the material or suggested the method of this apology. England, of course, at that time was destitute of all but the most meagre textbooks on the subject. Great interest therefore attaches to Sidney's discourse as the original outcome of his studies, meditations, literary experience, and converse with men of parts. Though we may not be prepared to accept each of his propositions, though some will demur to his conception of the artist's moral aim, and others to his inclusion of prose fiction in the definition of poetry, while all will agree in condemning his mistaken dramatic theory, none can dispute the ripeness, mellowness, harmony, and felicity of mental gifts displayed in work at once so concise and so compendious. It is indeed a pity that English literature then furnished but slender material for criticism. When we remember that, among the poems of the English Renaissance, only Surrey's Lyrics, *Gorboduc,* the *Mirror of Magistrates,* and *The Shepherd's Kalendar* could be praised with candour (and I think Sidney was right in this judgment), we shall be better able to estimate his own high position, and our mental senses will be dazzled by the achievements of the last three centuries. Exactly three centuries have elapsed since Sidney fell at Zutphen; and who shall count the poets of our race, stars differing indeed in glory, but stars that stream across the heavens of song from him to us in one continuous galaxy? (pp. 155-69)

> *J. A. Symonds, in his* Sir Philip Sidney, *1886. Reprint by Gale Research Company, 1968, 205 p.*

William Ernest Henley   (essay date 1890)

[*Henley was an English critic and poet. As an important figure in the counter-decadent movement of the 1890s and the leader of an imperialistic group of young British writers, including Rudyard Kipling, H. Rider Haggard, and Robert Louis Stevenson, Henley stressed the relevance of action, virility, and inner strength over alienation, effeminacy, and despair. These latter characteristics he attributes to Sidney's poetry in the following negative assessment, originally published in 1890.*]

Sidney's prime faults are affectation and conceit. His verses drip with fine love-honey; but it has been so clarified in metaphysics that much of its flavour and sweetness has escaped. Very often, too, the conceit embodied is preposterously poor. You have as it were a casket of finest gold elaborately wrought and embellished, and the gem within is a mere spangle of paste, a trumpery spikelet of crystal. No doubt there is a man's heart beating underneath; but so thick is the envelope of buckram and broidery and velvet through which it has to make itself audible, that its pulsations are sometimes hard to count, while to follow it throb by throb is impossible. And if this be true of that *Astrophel and Stella* series in which the poet outpours the melodious heyday of his youth—in which he strives to embody a passion as rich and full as ever stirred man's blood—what shall be said of the *Arcadia*? In that 'cold

pastoral' he is trying to give breath and substance to as thin and frigid a fashion as has ever afflicted literature; and though he put a great deal of himself into the result, still every one has not the true critical insight, and to most of us, I think, those glimpses of the lofty nature of the writer which make the thing written a thing of worth in the eyes of the few are merely invisible.

In thinking of Sidney, Ophelia's lament for Hamlet springs to the lips, and the heart reverts to that closing scene at Zutphen with a blessed sadness of admiration and regret. But frankly, is it not a fact that that fine last speech of his has more availed to secure him immortality than all his verse? They call him the English Bayard, and the Frenchman need not be displeasured by the comparison. But when you come to read his poetry you find that our Bayard had in him a strong dash of the pedant and a powerful leaven of the euphuist. Subtle, delicate, refined, with a keen and curious wit, a rare faculty of verse, a singular capacity of expression, an active but not always a true sense of form, he wrote for the few, and (it may be) the few will always love him. But his intellectual life, intense though it were, was lived among shadows and abstractions. He thought deeply, but he neither looked widely nor listened intently, and when all is said he remains no more than a brilliant amorist, too supersubtle for complete sincerity, whose fluency and sweetness have not improved with years. (pp. 94-5)

> *William Ernest Henley, "Sidney," in his* Views and Reviews: Essays in Appreciation, *Macmillan and Co., Ltd., 1921, pp. 94-5.*

Francis Thompson   (essay date 1901)

[*Thompson was one of the most important poets of the Catholic Revival in nineteenth-century English literature. Often compared to the seventeenth-century metaphysical poets, especially Richard Crashaw, he is best known for his poem "The Hound of Heaven" (1893), which displays Thompson's characteristic themes of spiritual struggle, redemption, and transcendent love. Like other writers of the fin-de-siècle period, Thompson wrote poetry and prose noted for rich verbal effects and a devotion to the values of aestheticism. In the following excerpt from an essay originally published in 1901, he assesses the strengths and weaknesses of Sidney's prose.*]

Among prose-writers a peculiar interest attaches to the poets who have written prose, who can both soar and walk. For to this case the image will not apply: of the eagle overbalanced in walking by the weight of his great wings. Nay, far from the poets being astray in prose-writing, it might plausibly be contended that English prose, as an art, is but a secondary stream of the Pierian fount, and owes its very origin to the poets. The first writer one remembers with whom prose became an art was Sir Philip Sidney. And Sidney was a poet.

If Chaucer, as has been said, is Spring, it is a modern, premature Spring, followed by an interval of doubtful weather. Sidney is the very Spring—the later May. And in prose he is the authentic, only Spring. It is a prose full of young joy, and young power, and young inexperience, and young melancholy, which is the wilfulness of joy; full of young fertility, wantoning in its own excess. Every nerve of it is steeped in deliciousness, which one might confuse with the softness of a decadent and effeminate age like our own, so much do the extremes of the literary cycle meet. But there is all the difference between the pliancy of young growth and the languor of decay. This martial and fiery progeny of a martial and fiery age is merely relaxing himself to the full in the interval of his strenuous life's campaign, indulging the blissful dreams of budding manhood—a virile Keats, one might say. You feel these martial spirits revelling in the whole fibre of his style. It is, indeed, the writing of a child; or, perhaps, of an exceptional boy, who still retains the roaming, luxuriant sweetness of a child's fancy; who has broken into the store-closet of literary conserves, and cloyed himself in delicious contempt of law and ignorance of satiety, tasting all capricious dainties as they come. The *Arcadia* runs honey; with a leisurely deliberation of relish, epicureanly savoured to the full, all alien to our hurried and tormented age.

Sidney's prose is treasurable, not only for its absolute merits, but as the bud from which English prose, that gorgeous and varied flower, has unfolded. It is in every way the reverse of modern prose. Our conditions of hurry carry to excess the *style coupée,* the abrupt style, resolved into its ultimate elements of short and single sentences. Sidney revels in the periodic style—long sentences, holding in suspension many clauses, which are shepherded to a full and sonorous close. But with him this style is inchoate: it is not yet logically compacted, the clauses do not follow inevitably, are not gradually evolved and expanded like the blossom from the seed. The sentences are loose, often inartificial and tyro-like, tacked together by a profuse employment of relatives and present participles. At times the grammar becomes confused, and falls to pieces.

"Even as a child is often brought to take most wholesome things," etc.; "which if one should begin to tell them the nature of the aloes or rhubarbum they should receive, would"—and so forth. Either Sidney should have written "children" instead of "a child," or "if one should tell it," and so throughout the remainder of the sentence. This is a mild specimen of the reckless grammar into which he often lapses. The piling up of relatives and present participles we need not exemplify: it will be sufficiently seen in the quotations we make to exhibit his general style. But this looseness has a characteristic effect: it conduces to the general quality of Sidney's style. Here, truly, the style is the man. The long, fluctuant sentences, impetuously agglomerated rather than organic growths, have a copious and dissolving melody, quite harmonious with the subject-matter and the nature of the man. Jeremy Taylor, too, mounds his magnificent sentences rather than constructs them: but the effect is different and more masculine; nay, they are structural compared with Sidney's—so far had prose travelled during the interim.

The *Arcadia* is tedious to us in its unvarying chivalrous fantasy and unremittent lusciousness long drawn-out. Yet it has at moments a certain primitive tenderness, natural and captivating in no slight degree. No modern romancer could show us a passage like this, so palpitating in its

poured-out feminine compassion. The hero has attempted suicide by his mistress's couch:

> Therefore, getting with speed her weak, though well-accorded limbs out of her sweetened bed, as when jewels are hastily pulled out of some rich coffer, she spared not the nakedness of her tender feet, but, I think, borne as fast with desire as fear carried *Daphne,* she came running to *Pyrocles,* and finding his spirits something troubled with the fall, she put by the bar that lay close to him, and straining him in her well-beloved embracements; "My comfort, my joy, my life," said she, "what haste have you to kill your *Philoclea* with the most cruel torment that ever lady suffered?"

What a delicate chivalry of heart there is in it all! How exquisitely felt that phrase, "her sweetened bed"! How charmingly fancied the image which follows it; and how beautiful—"she spared not the nakedness of her tender feet"! How womanly Philoclea's outburst, and the tender eagerness of the whole picture! In other passages Sidney shows his power over that pastoral depiction dear to the Elizabethans—artificial, if you will, refined and courtly, yet simple as the lisp of babes.

> Thyrsis not with many painted words nor falsified promises had won the consent of his beloved Kala, but with a true and simple making her know he loved her, not forcing himself beyond his reach to buy her affection, but giving her such pretty presents as neither could weary him with the giving nor shame her for the taking. Thus, the first strawberries he could find were ever, in a clean-washed dish, sent to Kala; the posies of the spring-flowers were wrapt up in a little green silk, and dedicated to Kala's breasts; thus sometimes his sweetest cream, sometimes the best cakebread his mother made, were reserved for Kala's taste.

Naturally, his youthful efflorescence spreads itself in description when the chance comes his way: for the Elizabethans had not our monomania for description *per se:*

> There were hills which garnished their proud heights with trees; humble valleys, whose bare estate seemed comforted with the refreshing of silver rivers; meadows, enamelled with all sorts of eye-pleasing flowers; thickets, which, being lined with most pleasant shade, were witnessed so, too, by a cheerful disposition of many well-tuned birds; each pasture stored with sheep, feeding with sober security; while the lambs, with bleating oratory, craved the dam's comfort. Here a shepherd's boy piping, as though he should never be old; there a young shepherdess knitting, and withal singing; and it seemed that her voice comforted her hands to work and her hands kept time to her voice-music.

Sidney is not without that artificial balance and antithesis which, in its most excessive form, we know as euphuism. This, and the other features of his style, appear where we should least expect them; for his style has not the flexibility which can adjust itself to varying themes. How shall an age accustomed to the direct battle-music of Kipling and

Stevenson admit such tortuous narratives of conflict as this?

> Both being thus already allied by blood, yet did strive for a more strict affinity: wounds, in regard of their frequency, being no more respected than blows were before. Though they met in divers colors, now both were clad in one livery, as most suitable to their present estate: being servants to one master, and rivals in preferment. Neither could showers of blood quench the winds of their wrath, which did blow it forth in great abundance, till faintness would have fain persuaded both that they were mortal, and though neither of them by another, yet both overcomable by death. Then despair came to reinforce the fight, joining with courage, not as a companion but as a servant: for courage never grew desperate, but despair grew courageous; both being resolved, if not conquering, none of them should survive the other's conquest, nor owe trophy but to death.

Assuredly Sidney might have learned much from the forthright old Northern sagas, if he had known them, in the art of warlike narrative. But his best prose is, after all, to be found, not in the romantic **Arcadia,** but in the **Defence of Poesy.** There he has had a set purpose of conviction, of attack and defence before him, and is not constantly concerned with artistic writing. The result is more truly artistic for having less explicit design of art. We get not only melodiously-woven sentences, but also touches of true fire and vigor: he is even homely on occasion. It is from the **Defence of Poesy** that critics mostly choose their "Sidneian showers of sweet discourse."

Here is one well-known passage:

> Now, therein, of all sciences (I speak still of human, and according to the human conceit) is our poet the monarch. For he doth not only show the way, but giveth so sweet a prospect unto the way as will entice any man to enter into it. Nay, he doth, as if your journey should lie through a fair vineyard, at the very first give you a cluster of grapes, that, full of the taste, you may long to pass further. He beginneth not with obscure definitions, which must blur the margin with interpretations and load the mind with doubtfulness; but he cometh to you with words set in delightful proportion, either accompanied with, or prepared for, the well-enchanting skill of music; and with a tale, forsooth, he cometh unto you—with a tale which holdeth children from play and old men from the chimney corner; and, pretending no more, doth intend the winning of the mind from wickedness to virtue, even as a child is often brought to take most wholesome things by hiding them in such other as have a pleasant taste, which, if one should begin to tell them the nature of the aloes or rhubarbum they should receive, would sooner take their physic at their ears than their mouth. So is it in men—most of whom are childish in the best things till they be cradled in their graves. Glad they will be to hear the tales of Achilles, Hercules, Cyrus, Aeneas; and hearing them, must needs hear the right description of wisdom, valor, and justice; which, if they had been bare-

ly—that is to say, philosophically—set out, they would swear they be brought to school again.

Very plainly, Sidney was no believer in that modern fanaticism—art for art's sake. But from his own standpoint, which is the eternal standpoint, no finer apology for poetry has ever been penned. The reader will note passages which have become almost proverbial. One ought to be proverbial: "Most of whom are childish in the best things, till they be cradled in their graves." The construction has not the perfection of subsequent prose—of Raleigh at his best, or Browne. The sentences do not always stop at their climax, but are weakened by a tagged-on continuation. A modern writer would have made a period after "wickedness to virtue," and greatly strengthened the effect. But, for all the partial inexpertness, it is splendid writing, with already the suggestion of the arresting phrase and stately cadences presently to be in English prose. He is specially felicitous in those sayings of direct and homely phrase which have become household words: "A tale which holdeth children from play, and old men from the chimney-corner," or that other well-known saying that Chevy-Chase moved him "like the sound of a trumpet." It was a great and original genius, perhaps in prose (where he had no models) even more than in poetry, which was cut short on the field of Zutphen; even as the Spanish Garcilaso, also young, noble, and a pastoral poet, fell in the breach of a northern town. (pp. 227-39)

> *Francis Thompson, "The Prose of Poets: Sir Philip Sidney," in his* A Renegade Poet and Other Essays, *The Ball Publishing Co., 1910, pp. 227-39.*

George Saintsbury   (essay date 1902)

[*Saintsbury has been called the most influential English literary historian and critic of the late nineteenth and early twentieth centuries. He adhered to two distinct sets of critical standards: one for the novel and the other for poetry and drama. While he maintained that "the novel has nothing to do with any beliefs, with any convictions, with any thoughts in the strict sense. . . [and is] mainly and firstly a criticism of life," he was a radical formalist in his poetry criticism, frequently asserting that subject is of little importance and that "the so-called 'formal' part is of the essence." René Wellek has praised Saintsbury's critical faculties: his "enormous reading, the almost universal scope of his subject matter, the zest and zeal of his exposition," and "the audacity with which he handles the most ambitious and unattempted arguments." In the excerpt below, Saintsbury examines the style and content of Sidney's* Apology for Poetry.]

[Sidney's main object in his **Apology for Poetry**] is the defence, not so much of Poetry as of Romance. He follows the ancients in extending the former term to any prose fiction: but it is quite evident that he would have, in his *mimesis,* a quality of imagination which Aristotle nowhere insists upon, and which is in the best sense Romantic. And of this poetry, or romance, he makes one of the loftiest conceptions possible. All the hyperboles of philosophers or of poets, on order, justice, harmony, and the like, are

THE
COVNTESSE
OF PEMBROKES
ARCADIA,
WRITTEN BY SIR PHILIPPE
SIDNEI.

SOIT·QVI·MAL·Y·
HONI   PENSE
QVOFATA   VOCANT

LONDON
Printed for William Ponfonbie.
Anno Domini, 1590.

Manuscript page of Sidney's An Apology for Poetrie.

heaped upon Poetry herself, and all the Platonic objections to her are retorted or denied.

It has been said that there is no direct reference to Gosson in the **Apology,** though the indirect references are fairly clear.

Sidney begins (in the orthodox Platonic or Ciceronian manner) somewhat off his subject, by telling how the right virtuous Edward Wotton, and he himself, once at the Emperor's Court learnt horsemanship of John Pietro Pugliano, the Imperial Equerry, and recounting with pleasant irony some magnifying of his office by that officer. Whence, by an equally pleasant rhetorical turn, he slips into a defence of *his* office—his "unelected vocation" of poet. Were not the earliest and greatest authors of all countries, Musæus, Homer, Hesiod, in Greece (not to mention Orpheus and Linus), Livius Andronicus and Ennius among the Romans, Dante, Boccaccio, and Petrarch in Italy, Chaucer and Gower for "our English"—were they not all poets? Even the philosophers in Greece used poetry, and Plato himself is a poet almost against his will. Herodotus called his nine books after the Muses; and he and all historians have stolen or usurped things of poetry. Wales, Ireland, "the most barbarous and simple Indians," are cited. Nay, further, did not the Romans call a poet *vates,* a "prophet"? and, by presumption, may we not call

David's psalms a divine poem? Whatever some may think, it is no profanation to do so. For what is a poet? What do we mean by adopting that Greek title for him? We mean that he is a *maker.* All other arts and sciences limit themselves to nature; the poet alone transcends nature, improves it, nay, brings himself ("let it not be deemed too saucy a comparison") in some sort into competition with the Creator Himself whom he imitates.

The kinds of this imitation are then surveyed—"Divine," "Philosophical," and that of the third or right sort, who only imitate to invent and improve, which neither divine nor philosophic poets can do. These classes are subdivided according to their matter—heroic, tragic, comic, &c.—or according to the sorts of verses they liked best to write in, "for, indeed, the greatest part of poets have apparelled their poetical inventions in that numerous kind of writing which is called verse—indeed but apparelled, verse being but an ornament and no cause to poetry." And again, "it is not rhyming and versing that maketh a poet." Xenophon and Heliodorus were both poets in prose.

Now let us "weigh this latter part of poetry first by works and then by parts," having regard always to the "Architectonice or mistress-knowledge," the knowledge of a man's self, ethically and politically. Philosophy, history, law, &c., are then "weighed" against poetry at some length: and the judgment of Aristotle that Poetry is *philosophoteron* and *spoudaioteron* than history, is affirmed chiefly on the odd ground of poetical justice,—the right always triumphing in poetry though not in fact. Instances of the moral and political uses of poetry follow. Then for the parts. Pastoral, comedy, tragedy, &c., are by turns surveyed and defended; and it is in the eulogy of lyric that the famous sentence about *Chevy Chase* occurs ["I must confess my own barbarousness: I never heard the old song of Percy and Douglas that I found not my heart moved more than with a trumpet."]. After this, and after a stately vindication of Poetry's right to the laurel, he turns to the objections of the objectors. Although repeating the declaration that "rhyming and versing make not poetry," he argues that if they *were* inseparable, verse is the most excellent kind of writing, far better than prose. As to the abuses of poetry, they are but abuses, and do not take away the use, as is proved by a great number of stock examples.

Why, then, has England grown so hard a stepmother to poets? They are bad enough as a rule, no doubt; though Chaucer did excellently considering his time. The *Mirror for Magistrates* is good; so is Surrey; and *The Shepherd's Calendar* "hath much poetry," though "the old rustic language" is bad, since neither Theocritus, nor Virgil, nor Sannazar has it. And what is the reason of our inferiority? The neglect of rule. From this point onwards Sidney certainly "exposes his legs to the arrows" of those who ignore the just historic estimate. He pours ridicule on all our tragedies except *Gorboduc,* and still more on our mongrel tragi-comedies. We must follow the Unities, which, as it is, are neglected even in *Gorboduc,* "how much more in all the rest?" Whence he proceeds (unconscious how cool the *reductio ad absurdum* will leave us) to the famous ridicule of "Asia on the one side and Africa on the other," of "three ladies walking to gather flowers," and how the same place which was a garden becomes a rock, and then a cave with a monster, and then a battlefield with two armies—of the course of two lives in two hours' space, &c. And he concludes with some remarks on versification, which we should gladly have seen worked out. For he does not now seem to be in that antagonistic mood towards rhyme which Spenser's letters to Harvey discover in him. On the contrary, he admits *two* styles, ancient and modern, the former depending on quantity, the latter depending on "number," accent, and rhyme. He indeed thinks English fit for both sorts, and denies "neither sweetness nor majesty" to rhyme, but is, like almost all his contemporaries and followers (except Gascoigne partially), in a fog as to "numbers" and cæsura. The actual end comes a very little abruptly by an exhortation of some length, half humorous, half serious, to all and sundry, to be "no more to jest at the reverent title of a rhymer."

The importance of this manifesto, both symptomatically and typically, can hardly be exaggerated. It exhibits the temper of the generation which actually produced the first-fruits of the greatest Elizabethan poetry; it served as a stimulant and encouragement to all the successive generations of the great age. That Sidney makes mistakes both in gross and detail—that he even makes some rather serious mistakes from the mere "point of view of the examiner"—is of course undeniable. He has a good deal of the merely traditional mode of Renaissance respect for classical—and for some modern—authority. That, for instance, there is a good deal to be said, and that not only from the point of view of Ben Jonson, against Spenser's half-archaic half-rustic dialect in the *Calendar,* few would refuse to grant. But Theocritus *did* use dialect: it would not in the least matter whether either he or Virgil did not; and if it did, what has the modern and purely vernacular name of Sannazar to do with the matter? It can only be replied that Spenser, by permitting "E. K.'s" annotation, did much to invite this sort of criticism; and that Englishmen's reluctance to rely on the inherent powers of the English language was partly justified (for hardly any dead poet but Chaucer and no dead prose-writers but Malory and perhaps Berners deserved the title of "great"), partly came from very pardonable ignorance.

It has been already observed that Sidney is by no means peremptory about the "new versifying"; and in particular has absolutely none of the craze against rhyme as rhyme which animated persons of every degree of ability, from Stanyhurst to Milton, during more than a century. His remarks on versification are, however, too scanty to need much comment.

There remain his two major heresies, the declaration that verse is not inseparable from poetry, and the denunciation of tragi-comedy. In both the authority of the ancients must again bear good part of the blame, but in both he has additional excuses. As to the "pestilent heresy of prose poetry," he is at least not unwilling to argue on the hypothesis that verse *were* necessary to poetry, though he does not think it is. He is quite sure that verse is anyhow a nobler medium than prose. As for the plays, there is still more excuse for him. His classical authorities were quite clear on the point; and as yet there was nothing to be quoted

on the other side—at least in English. Spanish had indeed already made the experiment of tragi-comic and anti-unitarian treatment; but I do not think any of the best Spanish examples had yet appeared, and there is great difference between the two theatres. In English itself not one single great or even good play certainly existed on the model at Sidney's death; and, from what we have of what did exist, we can judge how the rough verse, the clumsy construction, or rather absence of construction, the entire absence of clear character-projection, and the higgledy-piggledy of huddled horrors and horseplay, must have shocked a taste delicate in itself and nursed upon classical and Italian literature. And it is noteworthy that even *Gorboduc,* with all its regularity and "Senecation," does not bribe Sidney to overlook at least some of its defects. He is here, as elsewhere,—as indeed throughout,—neither blind nor bigoted. He is only in the position of a man very imperfectly supplied with actual experiments and observations, confronted with a stage of creative production but just improving from a very bad state, and relying on old and approved methods as against new ones which had as yet had no success.

And had his mistakes been thrice what they are, the tone and temper of his tractate would make us forgive them three times over. That "moving of his heart as with a trumpet" communicates itself to his reader even now, and shows us the motion in the heart of the nation at large that was giving us the *Faerie Queene,* that was to give us *Hamlet* and *As You Like It.* What though the illustrations sometimes make us smile? that the praise of the moral and political effects of poetry may sometimes turn the smile into a laugh or a sigh? Poetry after all, like all other human things, has a body and a soul. The body must be fashioned by art—perhaps the body *is* art; but the soul is something else. The best poetry will not come without careful consideration of form and subject, of kind and style; but it will not necessarily come with this consideration. There must be the inspiration, the enthusiasm, the *afflatus,* the glow; and they are here in Sidney's tractate. (pp. 171-76)

George Saintsbury, "Elizabethan Criticism," in his A History of Criticism and Literary Taste in Europe, from the Earliest Texts to the Present Day: From the Renaissance to the Decline of Eighteenth Century Orthodoxy, *Vol. II, 1902. Reprint by William Blackwood & Sons Ltd., 1934, pp. 144-210.*

Sidney Lee   (essay date 1904)

[*Lee is best known as an accomplished Shakespearean scholar and as the exacting editor of the* Dictionary of National Biography. *In the latter capacity, he oversaw the writing of most of the* Dictionary's *sixty-three original volumes as well as its first two supplements. In the following excerpt from his* Great Englishmen of the Sixteenth Century, *a work based on research done for the* Dictionary, *he discusses the style and structure of Sidney's* Arcadia *as well as the literature that influenced its content.*]

Sidney affected to set no value on [*Arcadia*], which exile from the central scene of the country's activities had given him the opportunity of essaying. He undertook it, he said, merely to fill up an idle hour and to amuse his sister. 'Now, it is done only for you, only to you:' he modestly told her, 'if you keep it to yourself, or to such friends, who will weigh errors in the balance of goodwill, I hope, for the father's sake, it will be pardoned, perchance made much of, though in itself it have deformities. For indeed, for severer eyes it is not, being but a trifle, and that triflingly handled.'

The work is far more serious than the deprecatory preface suggests. Sidney's pen must have travelled with lightning speed. Whatever views may be entertained of the literary merits of his book, it amazes one by its varied learning, its wealth of episode and its exceptional length. It was eulogised in its own day by Sidney's friend, Gabriel Harvey, as a 'gallant legendary, full of pleasurable accidents and profitable discourses; for three things especially very notable—for amorous courting (he was young in years), for sage counselling (he was ripe in judgment), and for valorous fighting (his sovereign profession was arms)—and delightful pastime by way of pastoral exercises may pass for the fourth.' The commendation is pitched in too amiable a key. The *Arcadia* is a jumble of discordant elements; but, despite its manifold defects, it proves its author to have caught a distant glimpse of the true art of fiction.

The romance was acknowledged on its production to be a laborious act of homage to a long series of foreign literary influences. In his description of character and often in his style of narration he was thought to have assimilated the tone of the Latin historians Livy, Tacitus, and the rest, and the modern chroniclers, Philippe de Comines and Guicciardini. The *Arcadia* is a compound of an endless number of simples, all of which are of foreign importation. Sidney proves in it more than in his sonnets or his critical tract his loyalty to foreign models and the catholicity of taste which he brought to the study of them.

The corner stone of the edifice must be sought in a pastoral romance of Italy. A Neapolitan, Sanazzaro, seems to have been the first in modern Europe to apply the geographical Greek name of Arcadia to an imaginary realm of pastoral simplicity, where love alone held sway. Sanazzaro, who wrote very early in the 16th century, was only in part a creator. He was an enthusiastic disciple of Virgil, and he had read Theocritus. His leading aim was to develop in Italian prose the pastoral temper of these classical poets. But he brought to his work the new humanism of the Renaissance and broadened the interests and outlook of pastoral literature. His Italian *Arcadia* set an example which was eagerly followed by all sons of the Renaissance of whatever nationality. In Spain one George de Montemayor developed forty years later Sanazzaro's pastoral idealism in his fiction of *Diana Inamorada,* and the Spanish story gained a vogue only second to its Italian original. Sidney was proud to reckon himself a disciple of Montemayor the Spaniard, as well as of Sanazzaro the Neapolitan.

But it was not exclusively on the foundations laid by Italian or Spaniard that Sidney's ample romantic fiction was based. Two other currents merged in its main stream. Sidney knew much of late Greek literary effort which produced, in the third century of the Christian era, the earliest specimen of prose fiction. It was the Græco-Syrian Heliodorus, in his 'Aethiopian Tales,' who first wrote a prose novel of amorous intrigue. Heliodorus's novels became popular in translation in every western country, and Sidney familiarised himself with them. But his literary horizon was not bounded either by the ancient literature of Greece or by the contemporary adaptations of classical literary energy. Feudalism had its literary exponents. Mediæval France and Spain were rich in tales of chivalry and feudal adventure. The tedious narrative, for example, of *Amadis of Gaul,* which was mainly responsible for the mental perversion of Don Quixote, fired the Middle Ages with a genuine enthusiasm. That enthusiasm communicated itself to Sidney.

To each of these sources—the pastoral romances of the Renaissance of Italy and Spain, the Greek novel, and the mediæval tales of chivalry—Sidney's *Arcadia* is almost equally indebted. But his idiosyncrasy was not wholly submerged. Possibly Sidney originally thought to depict with philosophic calm in his retirement from the Court the life of shepherds and shepherdesses, and thereby illustrate the contrast between the simplicity of nature and the complex ambitions of princes and princesses. But the theme rang hollow to one who had studied closely life and literature, who sought, above all things, to be sincere. To credit rusticity which he knew to be coarse, ignorant, and sensual, with unalloyed innocence was little short of fraud. To confine himself solely to pastoral incident, however realistically treated, was to court tameness. On his pastoral groundplan, therefore, he grafted chivalric warfare of a mediæval pattern, and intrigue in the late Greek spirit.

Chivalric adventure is treated by Sidney for the most part with directness and intelligibility. At the outset of his *Arcadia,* two princely friends, Musidorus of Macedon and Pyrocles of Thessaly, who enjoy equal renown for military prowess, are separated in a shipwreck, and find asylum in different lands. Each is entertained by the king of the country which harbours him, and is set at the head of an army. The two forces meet in battle. Neither commander recognises in the other his old friend, until they meet to decide the final issues of the strife in a hand-to-hand combat. Peace follows the generals' recognition of one another. The two friends are free to embark together on a fantastic quest of love in Arcadia. Each seeks the hand of an Arcadian princess, and they willingly involve themselves in the domestic and dynastic struggles which distract the Arcadian court and country.

Sidney developed the design with bold incoherence. The exigences of love compel his heroes to disguise themselves. Musidorus, the lover of the Arcadian Princess Pamela, assumes the part of a shepherd, calling himself Dorus; while Pyrocles, the lover of the Arcadian Princess Philoclea, with greater boldness, metamorphoses himself into a woman; he arrays himself as an Amazon, and takes the feminine name of Zelmane. Out of this strange disguise is evolved a thread of story which winds itself intricately through nearly the whole of the romance. The Amazonian hero spreads unexpected havoc in the Arcadian court by attracting the affections of both the Princess's parents—of Basilius, the old king of Arcady, who believes him to be a woman; and of Synesia, the lascivious old queen, who perceives his true sex.

The involutions and digressions of the plot are too numerous to permit full description. The extravagances grow more perplexing as the story develops. Arcadian realms exhibit in Sidney's pages few traditional features. The call of realism was in Sidney's ears the call of honesty, and his peasants divested themselves of ideal features for the ugly contours of fact. His shepherds and shepherdesses have long passed the age of innocent tranquility. Their land is a prey to dragons and wild beasts, and their hearts are gnawed by human passions. Sidney had, too, a sense of the need of variety in fiction. New characters are constantly entering to distort and postpone the natural *dénouement* of events. The work is merged in a succession of detached episodes and ceases to be an organic tale. Parts are much more valuable than the whole. Arguments of coarseness and refinement enjoy a bewildering contiguity. At one moment Platonic idealism sways the scene, and the spiritual significance of love and beauty overshadows their physical and material aspects. At the next moment we plunge into a turbid flood of abnormal passion. The exalted thought and aspiration of the Renaissance season Sidney's pages, but they do not exclude the grosser features of the movement. There are chapters which almost justify Milton's sour censure of the whole book as 'a vain and amatorious poem.'

The *Arcadia* is a prose tale and Milton only applied to it the title of poem figuratively. But one important characteristic of the *Arcadia* is its frequent introduction of interludes of verse which, although they appeal more directly to the historian of literature than to its æsthetic critic, must be closely examined by students of Sidney's work. Shepherds come upon the stage and sing songs for the delectation of the Arcadian King, and actors in the story at times express their emotions lyrically. Occasionally Sidney's verse in the *Arcadia* seeks to adapt to the English language classical metres, after the rules that the club of 'Areopagus' sought to impose on his pen. The sapphics and hexameters of the *Arcadia* are no less strained and grotesque than are earlier efforts in the like direction. They afford convincing proof of the hopeless pedantry of the literary principles to which Sidney for a time did homage, but which he afterwards recanted. Sidney's metrical dexterity is seen to advantage, however, in his endeavours to acclimatise contemporary forms of foreign verse. In his imitation of the sestina and terza rima of contemporary Italy he shows felicity and freedom of expression. He escapes from that servile adherence to rules of prosody which is ruinous to poetic invention. Sidney's affinity with the spirit of Italian poetry is seen to be greater than his affinity with the spirit of classical poetry.

No quite unqualified commendation can be bestowed on the prose style of his romance. It lacks the directness which distinguishes the *Apologie for Poetrie.* It fails to give much support to Drayton's contention that Sidney rid the English tongue of conceits and affectations. His metaphors are often far-fetched, and he overloads his page with weak and conventional epithets. The vice of diffuseness infects both matter and manner. But delightful oases

of perspicuous narrative and description of persons and places are to be found, although the search may involve some labour.

The unchecked luxuriance of Sidney's pen, and absence of well-wrought plan did injustice to the genuine insight into life and the descriptive power which belonged to him. Signs, however, are discernible amid all the tangle that, with the exercise of due restraint, he might have attained mastery of fiction alike in style and subject-matter. (pp. 132-39)

Sidney Lee, "Sir Philip Sidney," in his Great Englishmen of the Sixteenth Century, *1904. Reprint by Thomas Nelson & Sons, 1908, pp. 95-152.*

Mario Praz (essay date 1927)

[*Praz was an Italian critic, translator, and authority on the literature of the Baroque and Romantic periods. Here, he compares Sidney's original* Arcadia *with its 1590 revision, arguing that the former is superior in style and content. Praz also suggests that Sidney's work benefits from a biographical rather than a literary interpretation.*]

Times, one would think, are fairly propitious for the revival of pastoral romances. 1926 saw the first edition of the older form of Sidney's *Arcadia* through the industry of Professor A. Feuillerat, and the second volume of the reprint (in progress) of d'Urfé's *Astrée,* due to another French scholar, M. Vaganay. Both romances have enjoyed, in their time, a success only paralleled by that of their predecessors and models in Italy and Spain. Is it possible, then, that current opinion be right, when it proclaims as unreadable (except by antiquarians) works which delighted generation after generation of readers, and were warmly praised by high and low? The style and happy invention of Montemayor's *Diana* which pleased no less a judge than Cervantes, the "Sidneian showers of sweet discourse" with which Richard Crashaw was daily conversant, and d'Urfé's monumental work, worshipped like a new gospel by Mme. de Rambouillet and her friends—should they stir no other muscles in our faces than those reserved for yawning?

M. Louis Mercier, in his preface to *Astrée,* most emphatically denies that the glamour of that famous romance has entirely faded, and, after having reminded us of the homage paid to d'Urfé, *homme divin,* by no fewer than forty-eight German princes on March 1st, 1624, invites us to read *Astrée,* aloud and by short stages, and defies us to be insensible to the delicate scent of days of yore exhaling from the pages of the French pastoral. Professor Feuillerat, on the other hand, feels not so sure about the first *Arcadia,* and seems to regard it as "at best the immature work of a young man of great promise who is trying his hand at romance writing"; but the critic of the *Times Literary Supplement,* having duly rebuked Sidney's editor for such a lukewarm defence of his author, takes up the cudgels in his place and asserts that we can not only read *Arcadia,* but positively enjoy reading it. To him the first *Arcadia* reads like a good, exciting story, likely to have a fair chance of being a popular success even to-day, if suitably modernised in language. One would almost be led to think that what in recent years Joseph Bédier has done for the romance of *Tristan* and Carmen de Burgos for *Amadis de Gaula,* a writer of the ability of Mr. George Moore might successfully accomplish for the first *Arcadia.*

I am afraid we are not justified in feeling as sanguine as that. Not because, as is usually maintained, *Arcadia* lacks humour. This withering accusation has been levelled at so many worthy authors that it is almost bound to recoil boomerang-wise on the accusers, and argue in them lack of understanding. Moreover, Sidney has been credited by the critic of the *Times Literary Supplement* with nothing less than irony! Of course Sidney showed lack of humour in recasting laboriously a story he had first considered to be no better than "a trifle, and that triflinglie handled"; but this is another matter. One thing is, however, beyond remedy in *Arcadia,* as in other pastoral romances: the slowness of its *tempo.* We are decidedly out of tune with it, and for page after page we starve for something substantial, to the point of almost imploring Sidney with his own words:

> But ah! DESIRE still cries, "Give me some food!"

Is it our fault if, reading the old *Arcadia* as a story, we find that it is not subtle enough to let us forget its sluggishness, not poignant enough to enable us to get over its crudity? A suspicion of *âge ingrat* hangs about its psychology. Characterisation is rudimentary in earlier romances, but then everything there is rudimentary, primitive, and, in its barren outline, direct and forceful. But the world of *Arcadia* is the world of polite society, of convention and refined manners; its people are too sophisticated to keep any childish charm, and not mature enough to appeal to our complex taste. The question is not one of verisimilitude. The people in *Arcadia* may even be granted the epithet of real; but doubtless they are lanky.

This shortcoming is less apparent in *Astrée.* The characters in *Astrée* know the rules of the artificial world so nicely that, though we do not make more account of them than of puppets, yet we are amused at their gracefulness and pretence of naivety. But social customs in France had gone far more ahead than in England. In *Astrée* we can foreshadowed the incomparable refinement of the rococo society; love-letters, there, are really sugary *billets-doux.* On the other hand, *Arcadia* is limbo: the less pleasing features of the Middle Ages are still there, with bodily tortures and callous contempt for the multitude; its dancers dance with their boots on, its lovers do not write *billets-doux,* but make speeches, nay, harangues as in a war-assembly or at a Court mission. The absurd play of equivocation finds accomplished actors in d'Urfé's puppets:

> Celadon mesme eut opinion que j'aymois Lycidas, et moy je creus qu'il aymoit Phillis, et Phillis pensa que Lycidas m'aymoit, et Lycidas eut opinion que Phillis aymoit Celadon.

The ultimate sense of many a pastoral romance hardly conveys to us more than what is meant by the foregoing sentence; d'Urfé, however, succeeds in keeping our attention for a quarter of an hour with preposterous tricks of that kind. Sidney's puzzles are not as clever as that, and,

when all has been said, the only thing we care to remember of *Arcadia* is perhaps the passage about the shepherd boys who piped as though they should never be old, and even this we probably remember because of its Keatsian flavour.

But whatever one thinks of the old *Arcadia,* one must agree that, as a whole and in details, it is really superior to its successor. Why the man who wrote **The Defence of Poesie** should have thought his trifling pastoral such a momentous affair as to summon up an almost incredible skill in reweaving his story upon the loom of Heliodorus, as Dr. S. L. Wolff has shown [in his *The Greek Romances in Elizabethan Prose Fiction,* 1912], and that without dropping a single thread in the whole enormous design, is an instance of perversion which can find a parallel only in Tasso's garbling his masterpiece into a lifeless Counter-Reformation epic.

In the first *Arcadia* Sidney has kept clear of the Spanish fashion of dovetailing many side-stories into the main plot. Such a taste for nests of boxes may be condoned in the Spaniards. After all, that taste is to be traced back to the Arab strain in their blood, and is instanced in every branch of Spanish art. In the same way as *plateresque* style and Churriguerra's architectural wedding-cakes are after all reincarnations of the Alhambra, so side-plot and frame-story are as old as the Arabian Nights. To the nation which invented such encyclopædias of savours as the *olla podrida* and the *puchero,* a maze of stories has positively an attraction which is entirely lost upon us.

But in rewriting *Arcadia* Sidney did even worse than clogging a straight enough story with under-plots. He took to that kind of style which, after Cervantes, we might well define *la razon de la sinrazon* style. From jingles of words he had been singularly free in the first version. Quite by exception, there, we come across timid oxymora like "unjust Justice" or "extremity of cruelty grewing to be ye stopp of cruelty" or "Fortune . . . that will graunte mee no fortune to bee unfortunate." But the new *Arcadia* literally teems with elegances like this:

> exceedingly sorry for *Pamela,* but exceedingly exceeding that exceedingness in fears for *Philoclea.*

Surely Sidney thought he had achieved perfection when he was able to write in the following manner:

> But when the messenger came in with letters in his hand, & hast in his countenance, though she knew not what to feare, yet she feared, because she knew not; but she rose, and went aside, while he delivered his letter and message; yet a far of she looked, now at the messenger, & then at her husband: the same feare, which made her loth to have cause of feare, yet making her seeke cause to nourish her feare. And wel she found there was some serious matter; for her husband's countenance figured some resolution betweene lothnesse and necessitie: and once his eie cast upon her, & finding hers upon him, he blushed; & she blushed, because he blushed; & yet streight grew paler, because she knew not why he had blushed. But when he had read, & heard, & dispatched away the messenger (like a man in

whom Honour could not be rocked on sleepe by Affection) with promise quickly to follow; he came to *Parthenia,* and as sorie as might be for parting, and yet more sorie for her sorrow, he gave her the letter to reade. She with fearful slownesse tooke it, and with fearefull quicknesse read it; and having read it, *Ah, my Argalus* (said she), &c.

Having mastered this kind of style through the study of Greek and Spanish romances, Sidney proceeded to embellish his trifle. Telling comparisons may be drawn between the first and the second version of numberless passages. Professor Feuillerat has considerably facilitated our task by his final table of relations.

In the old *Arcadia,* Gynecia's falling in love with Pyrocles-Cleophila is described with remarkable penetration:

> at the first sighte shee had of *Cleophila,* her harte gave her, shee was a man . . .

No more than a few words, but Sidney hardly approached such directness a second time. In the new version, Pyrocles himself is caused to narrate Gynecia's love at first sight, thus:

> For she (being a woman of excellent witte, and of strong working thoughts) whether she suspected me by my over-vehement showes of affection to *Philoclea* (which love forced me unwisely to utter, while hope of my maske foolishly incouraged me) or that she had taken some other marke of me, that I am not a woman, or what devil it is hath revealed it unto her, I know not, &c.

Here Sidney tries to be deep, and to imagine all possible reasons for Gynecia's behaviour, and of course misses the mark he had already hit so successfully in the first instance. In the old version he depicts life, in the new one he gives us a barren casuistry. Similarly he contrived to spoil his mustering of *Philoclea's* first love-thoughts. The old *Arcadia* has:

> Shee founde a burning affection towardes *Cleophila,* an unquyet desyer to bee with her, and yet shee founde that the very presence kyndled her desyer; and examening in her self the same desyer, yet coulde shee not knowe to what the desyer enclyned, sometyme shee woulde compare the Love she bare to *Cleophila,* with the naturall good will shee bare to her sister, but shee perceyved yt had an other kynde of worcking: Sometyme shee woulde wish *Cleophila* had bene a Man, and her Brother, and yet in truthe yt was no Brotherly Love shee desyred of her. But, thus lyke a sweete mynde, not muche traversed in the Cumbers of these greffes she woulde eeven yeelde to the burthen, rather suffering sorowe, to take a full possession, then exercysing any way her mynde, how to redress yt.

This becomes in the new *Arcadia:*

> then streight grew an exceeding delight stil to be with her, with an unmeasurable liking of al that *Zelmane* [*Cleophila*] did: maters being so turned in her, that where at first, liking her manners did breed good-wil, now good-wil became the chiefe

cause of liking her manners: so that within a while *Zelmane* was not prized for her demeanure, but the demeanure was prized because it was *Zelmanes*. [And so on for another page of would-be psychology, until we reach the passage:] At last she fell in acquaintance with loves harbinger, wishing. First she would wish, that they two might live all their lives together, like two of *Dianas* Nimphes . . . Then would she wish, that she were her sister . . . But against that, she considered, that though being her sister, if she happened to be married, she should be robbed of her. Then growne bolder, she would wish either her selfe, or *Zelmane* a man, that there might succeed a blessed marriage between them. But when that wish had once displaied his ensigne in her minde, then followed whole squadrons of longings, that so it might be, with a maine battaile of mislikings, and repynings against their creation, that so it was not. Then dreames by night . . .

And so forth, and so forth, with a pretty intricacy in the place of the comparative simplicity of the old text, and squadrons of longings and battles of mislikings and repinings, and blushing, and paling, and being hot and cold in turns, in brief, the whole glittering arsenal of Petrarchian paraphernalia summoned up in order to make the trifle look a really serious concern. Almost each sentence of the first draft has been subjected to a process of stucco decoration, until the once clear outline has disappeared behind the fashionable finery of a tortuous phraseology. Thus one would hardly recognise the following passage:

> When *Cleophila* streight embracing her, (and warranted by a womanly habite ofte kissing her) desyered her to stay her sweete speeche . . .

in the successive form:

> When *Zelmane* (making a womanish habite to be the Armour of her boldnesse, giving up her life to the lippes of *Philoclea,* and taking it againe by the sweetenesse of those kisses) humbly besought her to keepe her speach for a while within the Paradise of her minde.

Reading . . . the old *Arcadia* (in the Feuillerat edition) side by side with . . . the 1590 *Arcadia* affords a good illustration of euphuistic technique:

> *Old Arcadia:* The Joy whiche wroughte into *Pygmalions* mynde whilest hee founde his beloved Image waxe by little and little bothe softer and warmer in his folded armes . . .

> *1590 Arcadia:* The joy which wrought into *Pygmalions* mind, while he found his beloved image was softer, & warmer in his folded armes . . .

Here apparently very little is changed; still how much is lost by substituting the growing sense of rapture expressed in "waxe by little and little," with the certainty of the sudden transformation, "was"! Of course there is no question of euphuism here, but, a few lines further, we read:

> *Old Arcadia:* Suche Contradictions there must needes growe in those myndes whiche neyther absolutely embrace goodnes, nor freely yelde to evell . . .

1590 *Arcadia:* with all the other contradictions growing in those minds, which nether absolutely clime the rocke of Vertue, nor freely sinke into the sea of Vanitie.

Old Arcadia: as hee whiche newly findes muche treasure ys moste subject to Doubtes . . .

1590 *Arcadia:* as he that newly findes huge treasures, doubtes whether he sleepe or no; or like a fearfull Deere, which then lookes most about, when he comes to the best feede . . .

Old Arcadia: How harde ys yt to bringe shame to owteward Confessyon . . .

1590 *Arcadia:* How harde it is to bring inward shame to outward confession . . .

Here the word "inward" is entirely superfluous, but helps to balance the sentence according to the rules of rhetorical speech.

Old Arcadia: yf my Castle had not seemed weyke you woulde never have broughte these disguysed forces . . .

This sounds already euphuistic enough, but the new version refines upon it:

1590 *Arcadia:* the weakenesse of my government before, made you thinke such a maske would be gratefull unto me: & my weaker government since, makes you to pull of the visar.

Old Arcadia: Shall I laboure to lay Coloures over my galled thoughtes . . .

This is pretty bad, but the "improvement" is hardly better:

1590 *Arcadia:* Shall I labour to lay marble coulours over my ruinous thoughts?

We turn a few pages and reach the episode of the Arcadian uprising. On the whole, this scene is better handled in the new version, both from the point of view of verisimilitude and from that of characterisation. Obviously Sidney knew more about the moods of the rabble when he rewrote the episode, and he was well advised in making Clinias expound the source of the tumult. But in dealing with particulars, he could not resist the temptation of embellishing:

Old Arcadia: But bothe shee and the Duke so wearyed with the excessive number of them, yt were bothe resolved to sell theyre lyves at a deare pryce. When *Dorus* comming in . . . made so fayre way among them, that hee wann tyme for them all to recover the Lodge and to give the Rebells a face of wood on the owteside.

1590 *Arcadia:* Yet the multitude still growing, and the verie killing wearying them (fearing, lest in long fight they should be conquered with conquering) they drew back toward the lodge; but drew back in such sort, that still their terror when forwarde: like a valiant mastiffe . . . though his pace be backwarde, his gesture is forward . . . Yet among the rebels there was a dapper fellowe a tayler [An entire page is inserted to describe various amazing deaths] . . . In this manner they recovered the lodge, and gave the rebels a face of wood of the out-side.

The newly inserted page dedicated to a would-be funny account of the slaughter is foreshadowed in a passage of the Fourth Book of the old *Arcadia* about the fellow who is killed while running head foremost: *Musidorus* chops off his head, and the head

falling betwixt the handes and the body and the body falling upon yt, yt made a shewe as thoughe the fellow had had greate haste to gather up his heade ageane.

There is very little originality about this would-be ironical death. Classical epigrams, such as the one of Callimachus on the boy killed by his stepmother's statue tumbling down on him, another of Martial on the boy killed by the piece of ice, and a few in the Greek Anthology relating prodigious cases gave the lead to such *macabre* fun as Sidney's and, later on, to the monstrous absurdities of Marino's *Strage degl'Innocenti,* where one finds the trick, passable enough for an epigram, mechanically repeated over and over again throughout a long poem. Sidney must have relished those gruesome *concetti.* Has he not himself anticipated the pun which made the French poet Théophile for ever famous as a paragon of ridicule?

1590 *Arcadia* (p. 424): woundes, which made all his armour seeme to blush, that it had defended his master no better.

Pyrame et Thysbé: Ha! voicy le poignard qui du sang de son maistre
S'est souillé laschement: il en rougit, le traistre!

Such is the kind of puns which were looked at by Sidney as purple patches to be inserted at all costs, whenever possible. Accordingly, in order to "improve" the account of the peasants' revolt, Pyrocles is caused to cut off the nose of a tailor, who stoops down to pick it up, "but as his hand was on the grounde to bring his nose to his head, *Zelmane* with a blow sent his head to his nose"; and *Dorus* is caused to cut off both hands of a painter who had come to the battle in order to see some notable wounds and be able to express them more lively: so that the painter became well skilled in wounds, "but with never a hand to perform his skill." In the description of another battle Sidney indulges once again this *macabre* strain, after this witty foreword:

the earth it selfe (woont to be a buriall of men) was nowe (as it were) buried with men: so was the face thereof hidden with deade bodies, to whom Death had come masked in diverse manners.

A comparison of the last three books of the old *Arcadia* with the 1593 completion of the new *Arcadia* affords less interest. As is well-known, the Countess of Pembroke completed the romance with a part of the third book, and all of the fourth and fifth books of the original version. Lady Pembroke did not alter the early text, apart from a few significant omissions already on the whole pointed out by Mr. Bertram Dobell [in his essay in the *Quarterly Review,* July 1909]. The most noteworthy of these omissions consists in the deleting of all the expressions apt to convince the reader of the sensual quality of the love of Pyrocles and Musidorus for the two sisters. Musidorus' attempt at taking advantage of Pamela asleep and

Pyrocles' and Philoclea's "mutuall satisfaction" are sternly bowdlerised in the 1593 *Arcadia.* A number of passages appear modified in consequence, and Sidney's moral purpose, as expounded at the beginning of the Fourth Book of the old *Arcadia,* is made void. In fact, Sidney's aim was to show how:

> The everlasting justice (using oure selves to bee the punishers of oure faultes, and making oure owne actions the beginninge of oure Chastisement, that oure shame may bee the more manifest, and oure Repentance followe the sooner,) tooke *Dametas* at this present (by whose folly the others wysdome might receyve the greater overthrowe) to bee the instrument of reveyling the secrettst Connyng: So evill a grounde dothe evell stande upon, and so manifest yt ys, that no thing remaynes strongly but that whiche hathe the good foundacyon of goodnes.

This morality, which by the way is common also to Manzoni's *Promessi Sposi,* is illustrated by Sidney with the sensual behaviour of Pyrocles and Musidorus, and the ensuing punishment. Lady Pembroke, by leaving out the mention of the fault, was aware that she was depriving the romance of its moral conclusion, and had to rewrite the beginning of the Fourth Book as follows:

> The almightie wisedome evermore delighting to shewe the world, that by unlikeliest meanes greatest matters may come to conclusion: that humane reason may be the more humbled, and more willinglie geve place to divine providence: as at first it brought in *Dametas* . . .

The publication of the old *Arcadia* is also expected to throw light on the development of Sidney as a thinker. Professor Feuillerat believes that "this entirely unexplored field will fully reward those who undertake it." Though the study of poets not as such, but rather as thinkers, seems to be pretty much the vogue of to-day—a vogue against which a recent book on Keats ought to be a sufficient warning—still one can hardly deny that such a study would be justified in the case of Sidney. In the persons of Pyrocles defending solitariness and Musidorus urging him, instead, to follow that knowledge, in which consists the bettering of the mind, and to go back to the service of his own country, we at once recognise Sidney himself seeking for peace at Wilton, after the turmoil of the Court, and his friend and adviser Languet reminding him how his duty should have kept him in public life. The argument is resumed when Basilius is blamed for having withdrawn from public life, and is contrasted with the active Evarchus:

> the treasures of those inward giftes hee had were bestowed by the goddes upon hym to bee beneficiall, & not idle.

Passages like these, or the meditation on self-murder, or the one on pardon and reward, supply sufficient material to sketch a profile of Sidney as a thinker. And a comparison of the treatment, in the two versions, of such episodes as the peasants' revolt, enables us to gauge how far Sidney had meanwhile progressed in practical wisdom. But too often the subtlety of thought instanced in the 1590 *Arcadia* is leading to such conceits as not even Aristotle would

be able to make head or tail of, should he come back to life. Let, therefore, everyone who prepares to study Sidney as a thinker keep in mind the opening pages of the immortal book of Cervantes. (pp. 507-14)

Mario Praz, "Sidney's Original 'Arcadia'," in The London Mercury, *Vol. XV, No. 89, March, 1927, pp. 507-14.*

Mona Wilson   (essay date 1931)

[*In the following excerpt from her biography of Sidney, Wilson comments on contemporary responses to the* Arcadia *and the work's influence on English literature.*]

[The] *Arcadia,* which has for so long been relegated to the shelf inscribed "For students only," was by far the most successful book of the whole Elizabethan age. Its vogue recalls the popularity of Erasmus's *Colloquies* and anticipates that of *Robinson Crusoe.* Until the invasion of French romances it held its own because no rival appeared. It drew housewives from their duties, and set a standard for the behaviour of their children. Graver readers, who felt that every work of fiction required a moral justification, occupied themselves with the examples of vice and virtue, devices of policy and stratagems of war to be found in its pages. Sidney himself might maintain that it was only glass and feathers, a toy, written to work off a boy's fancies; Molyneux might repeat that it was "a mere fancy, toy, and fiction"; Greville knew better. If we are to believe him, Sidney contemplated a still further elaboration of the story, and meant not only to rewrite the old *Arcadia,* but to trace the fortunes of his personages, their subjects, and descendants, after Basilius resumed his crown. "In which traverses (I know) his purpose was to limn out such exact pictures of every posture in the mind, that any man being forced, in the strains of this life, to pass through any straits, or latitudes of good or ill fortune, might (as in a glass) see how to set a good countenance upon all the discountenances of adversity, and a stay upon the exorbitant smilings of chance." In short the *Arcadia* was to be a code of behaviour, an encyclopædia of moral and political science. An analytical index would certainly have been required, and Greville's chapter headings, so unkindly rejected by the Countess, are well-fitted for the purpose. In Book III, Chapter V, a modest niece may find an ensample of maidenly resistance to a shameless aunt's shrewd temptations to love and marriage: in a later chapter she will learn how an aunt's atheism can be refuted by a niece's divinity. But Sidney may be credited with intentions less portentous and rather more artistic. The *Arcadia* eludes the classification of Polonius. Harvey's description is enough. "Here are amorous courting (he was young in years), sage counselling (he was ripe in judgement), valorous fighting (his sovereign profession was arms), and delightful pastime by way of pastoral exercises."

To the unjaded taste of those early readers the long procession of tapestry figures, woven in the vert of pastoral and the sanguine of chivalry—eighty-eight are named without the minor personages—did not seem lifeless. To our more experienced eyes most of them are types rather than persons. Sidney was a painstaking psychologist. But he cannot suggest: his working is always given: his characters never take on flesh and blood spontaneously. Gynecia, for instance, with a little more and a great deal less, would have been a fine creation. The way is prepared by our first introduction to her. A beautiful creature and many years younger than her husband, she was "a woman of great wit, and in truth of more princely virtues than her husband, of most unspotted chastity, but of so working a mind, and so vehement spirits, as a man may say it was happy she took a good course, for otherwise it would have been terrible." Her passion for Pyrocles, her remorse and restoration to dignity, are all well thought out. A French critic has even done Sidney the honour of comparing her with Phèdre. But the final projection is missing.

Euphuism and Arcadianism were rivals for the favour of the Elizabethan public, and the prize fell to Arcadianism. By 1590 when the revised *Arcadia* was published people were becoming weary of Lyly, and still more weary of his followers. The chief defects of Euphuism, the tiresome alliteration and prodigality of similes from natural and unnatural history, censured by Sidney in the *Defence,* lent themselves with fatal ease to unconscious parody by his imitators, and masterly reproduction by Falstaff. Unhappily, in rejecting what was bad in Euphuism, Sidney sacrificed also its saving virtue, substituting for the compactness and balance of Lyly's prose a fluid style in which paragraphs and sentences lose all shape and structure. This loose web he decorated with every ornament, rhetorical or pictorial, that his reading or imagination could suggest. Dazed by the spectacle of so much industry failing of its purpose and so much ingenuity missing its effect, the modern reader murmurs—

> Endless labour all along,
> Endless labour to be wrong.

Contemporaries felt otherwise. "Is not the prose of Sir Philip Sidney, in his sweet *Arcadia,* the embroidery of finest art and daintiest wit?" asks Harvey, "always gallant, often brave, continually delectable, sometimes admirable?" For nearly a hundred years the public answered yes.

In the *Defence of Poesie* Sidney writes—

> Undoubtedly (at least to my opinion undoubtedly), I have found in divers smally learned courtiers a more sound style than in some professors of learning: of which I can guess no other cause but that the courtier, following that which by practice he findeth fittest to nature, therein (though he know it not) doth according to art, though not by art: where the other, using art to shew art, and not to hide art (as in these cases he should do), flieth from nature, and, indeed, abuseth art.

The *Defence* itself and the *Discourses* on the Anjou marriage and Irish Affairs exemplify his meaning. The style is that of a good talker, watchful of his audience: neither rhetorical nor fantastic. Before he went to the Netherlands Sidney translated part of Du Plessis Mornay's *Vérité de la Religion Chrétienne.* The style is admirable: terse, lucid, and so much in the manner of the *Discourses* that it reads like a maturer work of Sidney's own. But other influences were at work while he was elaborating the style of the *Ar-cadia.* The Renaissance had created an unnatural appetite for better bread than is made of wheat, and Sidney's vogue helped to delay the creation of such a prose style as his better judgment preferred, a style for which he himself shewed a natural aptitude. But for this unhappy deviation from his right path, he might have set such a standard for English prose as *Astrophel* has set for English poetry.

In fact Sidney often seems to be wasting in cumbrous prose the raw material of poetry. Take her lover's description of Pamela—

> But this cruel quietness, neither retiring to mislike, nor proceeding to favour; gracious, but gracious still after one manner; all her courtesies having this engraven in them that what is done is for virtue's sake, not for the party's; ever keeping her course like the sun, who neither for our praises nor curses will spare or stop his horses. This (I say) heavenliness of hers, (for howsoever my misery is I cannot but so entitle it), is so impossible to reach unto, that I almost begin to submit myself to the tyranny of despair, not knowing any way of persuasion where wisdom seems to be unsensible

It is a sonnet in all but form, and what a beautiful sonnet it might have been. Again, the picture of the ship-wrecked Pyrocles, lovely as it is, just lacks that gem-like quality which verse would have given it—

> But a little way off they saw the mast, whose proud height now lay along, like a widow having lost her make of whom she held her honour: but upon the mast they saw a young man (at least if he were a man), bearing shew of about eighteen years of age, who sat (as on horseback), having nothing upon him but his shirt, which being wrought with blue silk and gold, had a kind of resemblance to the sea, on which the sun (then near his western home) did shoot some of his beams. His hair (which the young men of Greece used to wear very long) was stirred up and down with the wind, which seemed to have a sport to play with it, as the sea had to kiss his feet; himself full of admirable beauty, set forth by the strangeness both of his seat and gesture, for, holding his head up full of unmoved majesty, he held a sword aloft with his fair arm, which often he waved about his crown, as though he would threaten the world in that extremity.

Constantly we are surprised by some touch of pure poetry, the effect of which is smothered by the surrounding conceits. Such are the footprints where Urania left "the farewell of all beauty," Parthenia's cheeks "like roses, when their leaves are with a little breath stirred," and the southwest wind "creeping over flowery fields and shadowed waters." The most famous passage in the *Arcadia* is to-day a garland of withered fancies with one flower alive and fragrant—

> There were hills which garnished their proud heights with stately trees: humble valleys whose base estate seemed comforted with refreshing of silver rivers: meadows, enamelled with all sorts of eye-pleasing flowers: thickets which, being lined with most pleasant shade, were witnessed

so to by the cheerful deposition of many well-tuned birds: each pasture stored with sheep feeding with sober security, while the pretty lambs with bleating oratory craved the dams' comfort: here a shepherd's boy piping, as though he should never be old: there a young shepherdess knitting, and withal singing, and it seemed that her voice comforted her hands to work, and her hands kept time to her voice's music.

That chorus of birds, all testifying in tune, no longer reaches our ears, the young shepherdess has dropped beneath her burden of antithesis, but the boy pipes forever and his songs are forever new.

When Sidney aims at beauty he too often topples into absurdity. Before the princesses enjoyed a bathe their handmaids "(like a couple of forswat melters) were getting the pure silver of their bodies out of the ore of their garments." When they retired for the night "they impoverished their clothes to enrich their bed." His masterpiece in this kind is the behaviour of Pamela's sewing materials.

> For the flowers she had wrought carried such life in them, that the cunningest painter might have learned of her needle: which with so pretty a manner made his careers to and fro through the cloth, as if the needle itself would have been loth to have gone fromward such a mistress, but that it hoped to return thenceward very quickly again: the cloth looking with many eyes upon her, and lovingly embracing the wounds she gave it: the shears also were at hand to behead the silk, that was grown too short. And if at any time she put her mouth to bite it off, it seemed that where she had been long in making of a rose with her hand, she would in an instant make roses with her lips.

He can be dainty, as in the scene labelled by the overseer conjugal happiness.

> The messenger made speed, and found Argalus at a castle of his own, sitting in a parlour with the fair Parthenia, he reading in a book the stories of Hercules, she by him, as to hear him read; but while his eyes looked on the book she looked on his eyes, and sometimes staying him with some pretty question, not so much to be resolved of the doubt, as to give him occasion to look upon her. A happy couple, he joying in her, she joying in herself, but in herself because she enjoyed him: both increasing their riches by giving to each other; each making one life double, because they made a double life one; where desire never wanted satisfaction, nor satisfaction never bred satiety; he ruling because she would obey, or rather, because she would obey, she therein ruling.

It is fitting, after this, that the dying Argalus should address Parthenia as "my better half," the only relic left in common parlance of "all Arcadia's golden creed."

Sometimes our attention is caught by an unexpected crispness, as in the shameless aunt's praise of marriage—

> For believe me, niece, believe me, man's experience is woman's best eye-sight. Have you ever seen a pure rose-water kept in a crystal glass;

how fine it looks, how sweet it smells, while that beautiful glass imprisons it? Break the prison, and let the water take its own course, doth it not embrace dust, and lose all his former sweetness of fairness? Truly, so are we if we have not the stay rather than the restraint of crystalline marriage.

Or malice—"She was a queen, and therefore beautiful"—a demure observation, which has elicited from a German critic the comment that it illustrates the author's profound respect for royalty. Sometimes he gives us a welcome scrap of humour or reality. Here is a morning's hunting in Clarendon Park:

> Then went they together abroad, the good Kalander entertaining them with pleasant discoursing, how well he loved the sport of hunting when he was a young man, how much in the comparison thereof he disdained all chamber delights; that the sun, how great a journey soever he had to make, could never prevent him with earliness, nor the moon, with her sober countenance, dissuade him from watching till midnight for the deer's feeding. O, said he, you will never live to my age without you keep yourself in breath with exercise, and in heart with joyfulness: too much thinking doth consume the spirits: and oft it falls out that while one thinks too much of his doing he leave to do the effect of his thinking. Then spared he not to remember how much Arcadia was changed since his youth: activity and good-fellowship being nothing in the price it was then held in, but according to the nature of the old-growing world, still worse and worse. Then would he tell them stories of such gallants as he had known: and so with pleasant company beguiled the time's haste and shortened the way's length till they came to the side of the wood where the hounds were in couples staying their coming, but with a whining accent craving liberty: many of them in colour and marks so resembling that it shewed they were of one kind.

The master of Pied Pepper and Grey Synott had an eye for a dog too. The water spaniel hunting duck in cold Ladon was bred much nearer home. He

> came down the river shewing that he hunted for a duck, and with a snuffling grace, disdaining that his smelling force could not as well prevail through the water as through the air: and therefore waiting with his eye to see whether he could espy the ducks getting up again: but then a little below them failing of his purpose he got out of the river and shaking off the water inweeded himself so as the ladies lost the further marking his sportfulness.

But such things are all too rare. The peace of Wilton and Penshurst, and the memory of some garden-house on the Brenta, hung with the pictures of Titian and Veronese, pervades the Arcadian landscapes, but the topography like the history is that of the golden age.

It will be noticed that in this, as in all the other passages I have quoted, Sidney's diction, in the narrow sense, his choice of words and idioms as contrasted with the use he makes of them, is masculine and sober. In his preface to the *Dictionary* Johnson wrote—

> But as every language has a time of rudeness antecedent to perfection, as well as of false refinement and declension, I have been cautious lest my zeal for antiquity might drive me into times too remote, and crowd my book with words now no longer understood. I have fixed Sidney's work for the boundary, beyond which I make few excursions. . . . If the language of theology were extracted from Hooker and the translation of the Bible; the terms of natural knowledge from Bacon; the phrases of policy, war, and navigation from Raleigh; the dialect of poetry and fiction from Spenser and Sidney; and the diction of common life from Shakespeare, few ideas would be lost to mankind, for want of English words, in which they might be expressed.

Johnson, as usual, was right. The *Arcadia* is the earliest example of a book written throughout in standard English speech. Hardly any word that Sidney uses has become obsolete: but, unlike the Pléiade, he was satisfied with his mother tongue as he found it. Of his one excess, the compound epithet,

> That new elegance
> Which sweet Philisides fetched of late from
> France,

the worst that can be said is that he sometimes went further than English prose, though not English poetry, has chosen to follow him. A fine instinct for language kept him equally distant from the archaizers and the ink-hornists, and against the mischief of the Arcadian style must be set its merit as an exemplar of the Illustrious and Courtly Vernacular.

Greville held that, apart from poetry, Sidney's true bent was for logic, philosophy and history. Evarchus' judgment is a fine piece of judicial reasoning which might have been delivered with effect at the Council table or in the House of Commons, when the fate of Mary Stuart was under discussion.

> The first doubt ariseth because they give themselves out for Princes absolute, a sacred name, and to which any violence seems an impiety. For how can any laws, which are the bonds of all human society, be observed if the law givers and law rulers be not held in an untouched admiration? But hereto although already they have been sufficiently answered, yet thus much again I will repeat unto you. That, whatsoever they be or be not, here they be no Princes, since betwixt Prince and Subject there is as necessary a relation as between father and son. And as there is no man a father but to his child, so is not a Prince a Prince but to his own subjects, therefore is not this place to acknowledge in them any principality, without it should at the same time, by a secret consent, confess subjection. Yet hereto may be objected that the universal Civility, the Law of Nations (all mankind being, as it were, Coinhabiters or world citizens together) hath ever required public persons should be (of all parties) especially regarded: since not only in peace, but in wars, not only Princes, but heralds

> and trumpeters, are with great reason exempted from injuries. This point is true, but yet so true as they that will receive the benefits of a custom must not be the first to break it, for then can they not complain if they be not helped by that which they themselves hurt. If a Prince do acts of hostility without denouncing war, if he breaks his oath of Amity, or innumerable such other things contrary to the Law of Arms, he must take heed how he falleth into their hands whom he so wrongeth, for then is courtesy the best custom he can claim.

This is from the old *Arcadia.* There are frequent traces in the new version of the graver interests which were to occupy Sidney's last years.

The speech with which Pyrocles quells the insurrection might have come from the lips of a young Lord Deputy confronting his father's enemies in the Irish Parliament:

> Imagine, what could your enemies more wish unto you, than to see your own estate with your own hands undermined? O what would your fore-fathers say, if they lived at this time, and saw their off-spring defacing such an excellent principality, which they with so much labour and blood so wisely have established? Do you think them fools, that saw you should not enjoy your vines, your cattle, no, not your wives and children, without government; and that there could be no government without a Magistrate, and no Magistrate without obedience, and no obedience where every one upon his own private passion, may interpret the doings of the rulers? Let your wits make your present example. Under whose ensign would you go, if your enemies should invade you? If you cannot agree upon one to speak for you, how will you agree upon one to fight for you? But with this fear of I cannot tell what, one is troubled, and with that passed wrong another is grieved. And I pray you did the sun ever bring you a fruitful harvest, but that it was more hot than pleasant? Have any of you children, that be not sometimes cumbersome? Have any of you fathers, that be not sometimes werish? What, shall we curse the sun, hate our children, or disobey our fathers? But what need I use these words, since I see in your countenances (now virtuously settled) nothing else but love and duty to him, by whom for your own only sakes the government is embraced. For all what is done, he doth not only pardon you, but thank you; judging the action by the minds, and not the minds by the action. Your griefs, and desires, whatsoever, and whensoever you list he will consider of, and to his consideration it is reason you should refer them. . . . If now you end (as I know you will) he will make no other account of this matter, but as of a vehement, I must confess over-vehement affection: the only continuance might prove a wickedness. But it is not so, I see very well, you began with zeal, and will end with reverence.

Sidney's political faith as revealed in the *Arcadia* was as simple as his religion. He accepted as heartily as Spenser or Shakespeare the Tudor ideal of a nation united in love and allegiance to its natural prince, and a throne supported by "a loyal nobility, a dutiful gentry, an honest, industrious and obedient commonalty." Once the narrative is interrupted to make room for a scornful picture of democracy in action—

> When they began to talk of their griefs, never bees made such a confused humming: the town dwellers demanding putting down of imposts: the country fellows laying out of commons: some would have the Prince keep his court in one place, some in another. All cried out to have new councillors: but when they should think of any new, they liked them as well as any other that they could remember; especially they would have the treasure so looked unto as that he should never need to take any more subsidies. At length they fell to direct contrarieties. The artisans, they would have corn and wine set at a lower price, and bound to be set so still: the ploughmen, vine labourers and farmers would none of that. The countrymen demanded that every man might be free in the chief towns: that could not the burgesses like of. The peasants would have the gentlemen destroyed, the citizens (especially cooks, barbers and those that lived most on gentlemen) would but have them reformed. No less ado was there about choosing him who should be their spokesman: the finer sort of burgesses as merchants, printers and cloth workers, because of their riches, disdaining the baser occupations, they because of their number as much disdaining them: all they scorning the countryman's ignorance, and the countryman suspecting as much their cunning.

While he was revising his book Sidney had grown up: perhaps this is why he abandoned it and wished the manuscript to be burnt. He had been in love: he had sat in the House of Commons: he was thinking of marriage and a career. In the management of the plot the revised *Arcadia* is distinctly maturer than the old: the characters, especially Pamela, are fuller and more solidly drawn. Perhaps, too, that vein of chivalric Platonism, which Sidney shared with Spenser, had been enriched by his own experience. In the old *Arcadia* Desire is too strong for Honour. Musidorus is only prevented by the accidental arrival of a band of robbers from violating the sleeping Pamela, and the union of Pyrocles and the gentle Philoclea is consummated. From the new *Arcadia* these incidents have disappeared. There can be little doubt that the alteration, though made by the Countess of Pembroke, follows Sidney's general directions. He had recognised that his heroes' readiness to take advantage of their charges is a flaw in the story. In the novella, to be happy in haste and marry at leisure is the natural course of affairs: true romance reserves the constant lover's reward till the day when he leads "the beauty of the world" into his father's home in far-off Pella.

Milton the poet acknowledged his debt to the moral teaching of the sage and serious Spenser: Milton the politician assailed the unhappy Charles for stealing from a vain amatorious poem the words of a heathen woman praying to a heathen god.

> O all-seeing Light, and eternal Life of all things, to whom nothing is either so great, that it may

resist, or so small, that it is contemned: look upon my misery with thine eye of mercy, and let thine infinite power vouchsafe to limit out some proportion of deliverance unto me, as to thee shall seem most convenient. Let not injury, O Lord, triumph over me, and let my faults by thy hands be corrected, and make not mine unjust enemy the minister of thy justice. But yet, my God, if, in thy wisdom, this be the aptest chastisement for my inexcusable folly; if this low bondage be fittest for my over-high desires, if the pride of my not-enough humble heart be thus to be broken, O Lord I yield unto thy will, and joyfully embrace what sorrow thou wilt have me suffer. Only thus much let me crave of thee, (let my craving, O Lord, be accepted of thee, since even that proceeds from thee) let me crave even by the noblest title, which in my greatest affliction I may give myself, that I am thy creature, and by thy goodness (which is thyself) that thou wilt suffer some beam of thy Majesty so to shine into my mind, that it may still depend confidently upon thee. Let calamity be the exercise, but not the overthrow of my virtue: let their power prevail, but prevail not to destruction: let my greatness be their prey: let my pain be the sweetness of their revenge: let them (if so it seem good unto thee) vex me with more and more punishment. But, O Lord! let never their wickedness have such a hand but that I may carry a pure mind in a pure body.

But even Milton acknowledges the *Arcadia* to be "a book of worth and wit."

Worth and wit is measured praise for a book which had kept the ear and formed the sentiments of sixty changing years. The *Arcadia* is one of the three great monuments of that early Anglican culture, part chivalrous, part Protestant, part classical, which, formed in the peace of Elizabeth, survived the assaults of Calvinism and the corruption of the Restoration, the culture of Herbert and Falkland and Evelyn. The others are the *Faerie Queene* and the *Ecclesiastical Polity.* The *Arcadia* perpetuated and diffused the ideal which Sidney's life had created. It transmitted to the next age his conceptions of spirited and delicate manhood, loyal and intelligent womanhood, justice, government, friendship and piety: it was [according to Gabriel Harvey] "the silver image of his gentle wit and the golden pillar of his noble courage." (pp. 142-55)

Mona Wilson, in her Sir Philip Sidney, *Duckworth, 1931, 328 p.*

Virginia Woolf (essay date 1932)

[*An English novelist, essayist, and critic, Woolf is one of the most prominent figures of twentieth-century literature. Like her contemporary, James Joyce, with whom she is often compared, Woolf employed the stream-of-consciousness technique in the novel. Concerned primarily with depicting the life of the mind, she rebelled against traditional narrative techniques and developed a highly individualized style. Woolf's works, noted for their subjective explorations of characters' inner lives and their delicate poetic quality, have had a lasting effect on the art of the novel. Her critical essays, which cover almost the entire range of English literature, contain some of her finest prose and are praised for their insight. In the following excerpt from an essay originally published in 1932, she discusses the twentieth-century reader's reaction to the* Arcadia, *concluding that while the narrative offers "romance and realism, poetry and psychology," the modern reader is eventually alienated by Sidney's overly elaborate language and careless narrative construction.*]

If it is true that there are books written to escape from the present moment, and its meanness and its sordidity, it is certainly true that readers are familiar with a corresponding mood. To draw the blinds and shut the door, to muffle the noises of the street and shade the glare and flicker of its lights—that is our desire. There is then a charm even in the look of the great volumes that have sunk, like the **Countess of Pembroke's Arcadia,** as if by their own weight down to the very bottom of the shelf. We like to feel that the present is not all; that other hands have been before us, smoothing the leather until the corners are rounded and blunt, turning the pages until they are yellow and dog's-eared. We like to summon before us the ghosts of those old readers who have read their **Arcadia** from this very copy—Richard Porter, reading with the splendours of the Elizabethans in his eyes; Lucy Baxter, reading in the licentious days of the Restoration; Thos. Hake, still reading, though now the eighteenth century has dawned with a distinction that shows itself in the upright elegance of his signature. Each has read differently, with the insight and the blindness of his own generation. Our reading will be equally partial. In 1930 we shall miss a great deal that was obvious to 1655; we shall see some things that the eighteenth century ignored. But let us keep up the long succession of readers; let us in our turn bring the insight and the blindness of our own generation to bear upon the **Countess of Pembroke's Arcadia,** and so pass it on to our successors.

If we choose the **Arcadia** because we wish to escape, certainly the first impression of the book is that Sidney wrote it with very much the same intention: '. . . it is done only for you, only to you', he tells his 'dear lady and sister, the Countess of Pembroke'. He is not looking at what is before him here at Wilton; he is not thinking of his own troubles or of the tempestuous mood of the great Queen in London. He is absenting himself from the present and its strife. He is writing merely to amuse his sister, not for 'severer eyes'. 'Your dear self can best witness the manner, being done in loose sheets of Paper, most of it in your presence, the rest, by sheets sent unto you, as fast as they were done.' So, sitting at Wilton under the downs with Lady Pembroke, he gazes far away into a beautiful land which he calls Arcadia. It is a land of fair valleys and fertile pastures, where the houses are 'lodges of yellow stone built in the form of a star'; where the inhabitants are either great princes or humble shepherds; where the only business is to love and to adventure; where bears and lions surprise nymphs bathing in fields red with roses; where princesses are immured in the huts of shepherds; where disguise is perpetually necessary; where the shepherd is really a prince and the woman a man; where, in short, anything may be and happen except what actually is and happens

here in England in the year 1580. It is easy to see why, as Sidney handed these dream pages to his sister, he smiled, entreating her indulgence. 'Read it then at your idle times, and the follies your good judgment will find in it, blame not, but laugh at.' Even for the Sidneys and the Pembrokes life was not quite like that. And yet the life that we invent, the stories we tell, as we sink back with half-shut eyes and pour forth our irresponsible dreams, have perhaps some wild beauty; some eager energy; we often reveal in them the distorted and decorated image of what we soberly and secretly desire. Thus the **Arcadia,** by wilfully flouting all contact with the fact, gains another reality. When Sidney hinted that his friends would like the book for its writer's sake, he meant perhaps that they would find there something that he could say in no other form, as the shepherds singing by the river's side will 'deliver out, sometimes joys, sometimes lamentations, sometimes challengings one of the other, sometimes, under hidden forms, uttering such matters as otherwise they durst not deal with'. There may be under the disguise of the **Arcadia** a real man trying to speak privately about something that is close to his heart. But in the first freshness of the early pages the disguise itself is enough to enchant us. We find ourselves with shepherds in spring on those sands which 'lie against the Island of Cithera'. Then, behold, something floats on the waters. It is the body of a man, and he grasps to his breast a small square coffer; and he is young and beautiful—'though he were naked, his nakedness was to him an apparel'; and his name is Musidorus; and he has lost his friend. So, warbling melodiously, the shepherds revive the youth, and row out in a bark from the haven in search of Pyrocles; and a stain appears on the sea, with sparks and smoke issuing from it. For the ship upon which the two princes Musidorus and Pyrocles were voyaging has caught fire; it floats blazing on the water with a great store of rich things round it, and many drowned bodies. 'In sum, a defeat, where the conquered kept both field and spoil: a shipwreck without storm or ill footing; and a waste of fire in the midst of the water.'

There in a little space we have some of the elements that are woven together to compose this vast tapestry. We have beauty of scene; a pictorial stillness; and something floating towards us, not violently but slowly and gently in time to the sweet warbling of the shepherds' voices. Now and again this crystallises into a phrase that lingers and haunts the ear—'and a waste of fire in the midst of the waters'; 'having in their faces a certain waiting sorrow'. Now the murmur broadens and expands into some more elaborate passage of description: 'each pasture stored with sheep, feeding with sober security, while the pretty lambs with bleating oratory crav'd the dam's comfort: here a shepherd's boy piping, as though he should never be old: there a young shepherdess knitting, and withal singing, and it seemed that her voice comforted her hands to work, and her hands kept time to her voice-music'—a passage that reminds us of a famous description in Dorothy Osborne's *Letters.*

Beauty of scene; stateliness of movement; sweetness of sound—these are the graces that seem to reward the mind that seeks enjoyment purely for its own sake. We are drawn on down the winding paths of this impossible landscape because Sidney leads us without any end in view but sheer delight in wandering. The syllabling of the words even causes him the liveliest delight. Mere rhythm we feel as we sweep over the smooth backs of the undulating sentences intoxicates him. Words in themselves delight him. Look, he seems to cry, as he picks up the glittering handfuls, can it be true that there are such numbers of beautiful words lying about for the asking? Why not use them, lavishly and abundantly? And so he luxuriates. Lambs do not suck—'with bleating oratory [they] craved the dam's comfort'; girls do not undress—they 'take away the eclipsing of their apparel'; a tree is not reflected in a river—'it seemed she looked into it and dressed her green locks by that running river'. It is absurd; and yet there is a world of difference between writing like this with zest and wonder at the images that form upon one's pen and the writing of later ages when the dew was off the language—witness the little tremor that stirs and agitates a sentence that a more formal age would have made coldly symmetrical:

> And the boy fierce though beautiful; and beautiful, though dying, not able to keep his falling feet, fell down to the earth, which he bit for anger, repining at his fortune, and as long as he could, resisting death, which might seem unwilling too; so long he was in taking away his young struggling soul.

It is this inequality and elasticity that lend their freshness to Sidney's vast pages. Often as we rush through them, half laughing, half in protest, the desire comes upon us to shut the ear of reason completely and lie back and listen to this unformed babble of sound; this chorus of intoxicated voices singing madly like birds round the house before anyone is up.

But it is easy to lay too much stress upon qualities that delight us because they are lost. Sidney doubtless wrote the **Arcadia** partly to while away the time, partly to exercise his pen and experiment with the new instrument of the English language. But even so he remained young and a man; even in Arcadia the roads had ruts, and coaches were upset and ladies dislocated their shoulders; even the Princes Musidorus and Pyrocles have passions; Pamela and Philoclea, for all their sea-coloured satins and nets strung with pearls, are women and can love. Thus we stumble upon scenes that cannot be reeled off with a flowing pen; there are moments where Sidney stopped and thought, like any other novelist, what a real man or woman in this particular situation would say; where his own emotions come suddenly to the surface and light up the vague pastoral landscape with an incongruous glare. For a moment we get a surprising combination; crude daylight overpowers the silver lights of the tapers; shepherds and princesses suddenly stop their warbling and speak a few rapid words in their eager human voices.

> . . . many times have I, leaning to yonder Palm, admired the blessedness of it, that it could bear love without sense of pain; many times, when my Master's cattle came hither to chew their cud in this fresh place, I might see the young Bull testify his love; but how? with proud looks and joyfulness. O wretched mankind (said I then to myself) in whom wit (which should be the governor

of his welfare) become's the traitor to his blessedness: these beasts like children to nature, inherit her blessings quietly; we like bastards are laid abroad, even as foundlings, to be trained up by grief and sorrow. Their minds grudge not at their bodies comfort, nor their senses are letted from enjoying their objects; we have the impediments of honour, and the torments of conscience.

The words ring strangely on the finicking, dandified lips of Musidorus. There is Sidney's own anger in them and his pain. And then the novelist Sidney suddenly opens his eyes. He watches Pamela as she takes the jewel in the figure of a crab-fish to signify 'because it looks one way and goes another' that though he pretended to love Mopsa his heart was Pamela's. And she takes it, he notes,

> with a calm carelessness letting each thing slide (just as we do by their speeches who neither in matter nor person do any way belong unto us) which kind of cold temper, mixt with that lightning of her natural majesty, is of all others most terrible unto me. . . .

Had she despised him, had she hated him, it would have been better.

> But this cruel quietness, neither retiring to mislike, nor proceeding to favour; gracious, but gracious still after one manner; all her courtesies having this engraven in them, that what is done, is for virtue's sake, not for the parties. . . . This (I say) heavenliness of hers . . . is so impossible to reach unto that I almost begin to submit myself unto the tyranny of despair, not knowing any way of persuasion. . . .

—surely an acute and subtle observation made by a man who had felt what he describes. For a moment the pale and legendary figures, Gynecia, Philoclea, and Zelmane, become alive; their featureless faces work with passion; Gynecia, realizing that she loves her daughter's lover, foams into grandeur, 'crying vehemently Zelmane help me, O Zelmane have pity on me'; and the old King, in whom the beautiful strange Amazon has awakened a senile amorosity, shows himself old and foolish, looking 'very curiously upon himself, sometimes fetching a little skip, as if he had said his strength had not yet forsaken him'.

But that moment of illumination, as it dies down and the princes once more resume their postures and the shepherds apply themselves to their lutes, throws a curious light upon the book as a whole. We realize more clearly the boundaries within which Sidney was working. For a moment he could note and observe and record as keenly and exactly as any modern novelist. And then, after this one glimpse in our direction, he turns aside, as if he heard other voices calling him and must obey their commands. In prose, he bethinks himself, one must not use the common words of daily speech. In a romance one must not make princes and princesses feel like ordinary men and women. Humour is the attribute of peasants. They can behave ridiculously; they can talk naturally; like Dametas they can come 'whistling, and counting upon his fingers, how many load of hay seventeen fat oxen eat up on a year';

but the language of great people must always be long-winded and abstract and full of metaphors. Further, they must either be heroes of stainless virtue, or villains untouched by humanity. Of human oddities and littleness they must show no trace. Prose also must be careful to turn away from what is actually before it. Sometimes for a moment in looking at Nature one may fit the word to the sight; note the heron 'wagling' as it rises from the marsh, or observe the water-spaniel hunting the duck 'with a snuffling grace'. But this realism is only to be applied to Nature and animals and peasants. Prose, it seems, is made for slow, noble, and generalized emotions; for the description of wide landscapes; for the conveyance of long, equable discourses uninterrupted for pages together by any other speaker. Verse, on the other hand, had quite a different office. It is curious to observe how, when Sidney wished to sum up, to strike hard, to register a single and definite impression, he turns to verse. Verse in the *Arcadia* performs something of the function of dialogue in the modern novel. It breaks up the monotony and strikes a high-light. In those snatches of song that are scattered about the interminable adventures of Pyrocles and Musidorus our interest is once more fanned into flame. Often the realism and vigour of the verse comes with a shock after the drowsy langour of the prose:

> What needed so high spirits such mansions
> blind?
> Or wrapt in flesh what do they here obtain,
> But glorious name of wretched human kind?
> Balls to the stars, and thralls to fortune's reign;
> Turn'd from themselves, infected with their
> cage,
> Where death is fear'd, and life is held with pain.
> Like players plac't to fill a filthy stage. . . .

—one wonders what the indolent princes and princesses will make of that vehement speaking? Or of this:

> A shop of shame, a Book where blots be rife,
> This body is . . .
> This man, this talking beast, this walking tree.

—thus the poet turns upon his languid company as if he loathed their self-complacent foppery; and yet must indulge them. For though it is clear that the poet Sidney had shrewd eyes—he talks of 'hives of wisely painful bees', and knew like any other countrybred Englishman 'how shepherds spend their days. At blow-point, hot-cockles or else at keels',—still he must drone on about Plangus and Erona, and Queen Andromana and the intrigues of Amphialus and his mother Cecropia in deference to his audience. Incongruously enough, violent as they were in their lives, with their plots and their poisonings, nothing can be too sweet, too vague, too long-winded for those Elizabethan listeners. Only the fact that Zelmane had received a blow from a lion's paw that morning can shorten the story and suggest to Basilius that it might be better to reserve the complaint of Klaius till another day.

> Which she, perceiving the song had already
> worn out much time, and not knowing when
> Lamon would end, being even now stepping over
> to a new matter, though much delighted with
> what was spoken, willingly agreed unto. And so

of all sides they went to recommend themselves to the elder brother of death.

And as the story winds on its way, or rather as the succession of stories fall on each other like soft snowflakes, one obliterating the other, we are much tempted to follow their example. Sleep weighs down our eyes. Half dreaming, half yawning, we prepare to seek the elder brother of death. What, then, has become of that first intoxicating sense of freedom? We who wished to escape have been caught and enmeshed. Yet how easy it seemed in the beginning to tell a story to amuse a sister—how inspiriting to escape from here and now and wander wildly in a world of lutes and roses! But alas, softness has weighed down our steps; brambles have caught at our clothing. We have come to long for some plain statement, and the decoration of the style, at first so enchanting, has dulled and decayed. It is not difficult to find the reason. High-spirited, flown with words, Sidney seized his pen too carelessly. He had no notion when he set out where he was going. Telling stories, he thought, was enough—one could follow another interminably. But where there is no end in view there is no sense of direction to draw us on. Nor, since it is part of his scheme to keep his characters simply bad and simply good without distinction, can he gain variety from the complexity of character. To supply change and movement he must have recourse to mystification. These changes of dress, these disguises of princes as peasants, of men as women, serve instead of psychological subtlety to relieve the stagnancy of people collected together with nothing to talk about. But when the charm of that childish device falls flat, there is no breath left to fill his sails. Who is talking, and to whom, and about what we no longer feel sure. So slack indeed becomes Sidney's grasp upon these ambling phantoms that in the middle he has forgotten what his relation to them is—is it 'I' the author who is speaking or is it 'I' the character? No reader can be kept in bondage, whatever the grace and the charm, when the ties between him and the writer are so irresponsibly doffed and assumed. So by degrees the book floats away into the thin air of limbo. It becomes one of those half-forgotten and deserted places where the grasses grow over fallen statues and the rain drips and the marble steps are green with moss and vast weeds flourish in the flower-beds. And yet it is a beautiful garden to wander in now and then; one stumbles over lovely broken faces, and here and there a flower blooms and the nightingale sings in the lilac-tree.

Thus when we come to the last page that Sidney wrote before he gave up the hopeless attempt to finish the *Arcadia,* we pause for a moment before we return the folio to its place on the bottom shelf. In the *Arcadia,* as in some luminous globe, all the seeds of English fiction lie latent. We can trace infinite possibilities: it may take any one of many different directions. Will it fix its gaze upon Greece and princes and princesses, and seek as it might so nobly, the statuesque, the impersonal? Will it keep to simple lines and great masses and the vast landscapes of the epic? Or will it look closely and carefully at what is actually before it? Will it take for its heroes Dametas and Mopsa, ordinary people of low birth and rough natural speech, and deal with the normal course of daily human life? Or will it brush through those barriers and penetrate within to the anguish and complexity of some unhappy woman loving where she may not love; to the senile absurdity of some old man tortured by an incongruous passion? Will it make its dwelling in their psychology and the adventures of the soul? All these possibilities are present in the **Arcadia**—romance and realism, poetry and psychology. But as if Sidney knew that he had broached a task too large for his youth to execute, had bequeathed a legacy for other ages to inherit, he put down his pen, midway, and left unfinished in all its beauty and absurdity this attempt to while away the long days at Wilton, telling a story to his sister. (pp. 19-27)

> *Virginia Woolf, "The Countess of Pembroke's 'Arcadia'," in her* Collected Essays, Vol. 1, *The Hogarth Press, 1966, pp. 19-27.*

Theodore Spencer   (essay date 1945)

[*In the following excerpt, Spencer defends Sidney's experiments in poetic form and content.*]

[Sidney's] poetry deserves close attention, not only because of its historical importance, but also because it is a striking example, one of the most striking in existence, of the relation between form and content, convention and passion, experiment and accomplishment. Its historical importance, its value for Sidney's own generation were, to be sure, great, but it can have importance and value for other generations as well, generations in which, like Sidney's and our own, poetry needs awakening and guidance.

When, at the end of his noble **Defence of Poesie,** written in the early 1580's, Sidney makes a rapid survey of recent English poetry, he cannot find much to praise. He admires Chaucer's *Troilus,* though he does not mention *The Canterbury Tales;* he admires Surrey, though he does not mention Wyatt; he admires the *Mirror for Magistrates* and Spenser's recent *Shepheardes Calendar.* That is all; "besides these," he says, "I do not remember to have seen but few (to speak boldly) that have poetical sinews in them. For proof whereof," he continues, "let but most of the verses be put in prose, and then ask the meaning, and it will be found, that one verse did but beget another, without ordering at the first what should be at the last, which becomes a confused mass of words, with a tingling sound of rhyme, barely accompanied with reasons."

Sidney is even more specific in sonnet XV of **Astrophel and Stella,** where he describes what seem to him (and to us) the three chief faults of his poetic contemporaries; they seek for meaningless pseudo-classical decoration, they rely too much on alliteration, and they too slavishly imitate Petrarch:

> You that do search for every purling spring
> Which from the ribs of old Parnassus flows,
> And every flower, not sweet perhaps, which grows
> Near thereabouts, into your poesy wring;
> Ye that do dictionary's method bring
> Into your rhymes, running in rattling rows;
> You that poor Petrarch's long-deceasèd woes
> With new-born sighs and denizen'd wit do sing:
> You take wrong ways; those farfet helps be such

> As do bewray a want of inward touch,
> And sure, at length stol'n goods do come to light. . . .

It was the "inward touch" which, as we shall see, Sidney most prized, and which, in his own best poetry, he so admirably reveals. But before it could be expressed English poetry needed to do some hard work; it needed leadership and practice. "Yet confess I always, that as the fertilest ground must be manured, so must the highest flying wit have a Dedalus to guide him. That Dedalus, they say both in this and in other, hath three wings to bear itself up into the air of due commendation: that is Art, Imitation and Exercise."

Those three words, Art, Imitation, and Exercise, which he uses in their precise critical sense, sum up admirably the first part of Sidney's brief poetic career. From 1576 to 1580, by which latter date the first draft of the **Arcadia** was finished, Sidney practiced his art by imitating every verse form he could think of, and by exercising every available linguistic and rhetorical device. He evidently realized that it was not enough to attack the Parnassian flowers, or weeds, of Gascoigne, the Petrarchanism of Thomas Watson, and the alliterative monotony that stumped on wooden feet through the contemporary anthologies; both he and his contemporaries—Spenser, Greville, Dyer, and Harvey—were aware that something more positive must be accomplished. They were enthusiastic about the prospect. To them poetry itself was, in Sidney's words, "full of virtue-breeding delightfulness," and, like the Italian followers of Aristotle, Sidney extolled poetry as greater than either of its rivals, philosophy and history, for it combined the wisdom of the one with the concrete examples of the other.

The young men of the late 'seventies had an equal enthusiasm for the English language. Throughout the correspondence on poetry between Spenser and Gabriel Harvey there is a feeling of excitement for what Harvey calls "so good and sensible a tongue as ours is," and their discussion of details is more than irrelevant pedantry. The interest shown by Spenser and Harvey in such matters is an example of how the English vocabulary was being re-examined, with a loving as well as a pedantic concern. And Sidney himself claims that English is superior to any other modern language as a medium for either quantitative or rhyming technique; it is of all vulgar tongues, the "most fit to honour Poesie." The art of poetry and the native language in which it was to be expressed were both worthy of all the art and exercise which could be devoted to them. It is with this conviction that Sidney began his poetic career.

Sidney's earliest important poetic task was a metrical version of the first forty-three Psalms. Although, as Miss Mona Wilson points out [in her *Sir Philip Sidney,* 1931], "Donne professed to admire them, and Ruskin really did," other critics, including Miss Wilson herself, dismiss them as having little or no importance. It is true that their intrinsic merit is small, for they almost never rise from the ground of ordinariness, but the student of Sidney's poetry should not ignore them. For they are, in two respects, examples of "Art, Imitation and Exercise." They are experiments in metrics and, in a smaller degree, experiments in vocabulary. With the exception of Psalms VII and XII, both of which are in terza rima, each psalm is translated in a different stanza form, and this in itself indicates, though in a mechanical way, Sidney's creative energy. There are stanzas which have only one rhyme throughout, there are stanzas of various lengths, from three lines to ten, and there are stanzas in which short lines are contrasted in various ways with long ones. A number of the rhyme schemes are original with Sidney, and if only for this fact the Psalms are worth notice. Furthermore several of the verse forms are early experiments in a kind of metrical music, as yet undeveloped and by no means yet enchanting, which Sidney was later to explore with much greater success: the music which is produced by a contrast between masculine and feminine rhymes. The device, of course, was nothing new in itself; the novelty consists in the deliberate self-consciousness and consistency with which Sidney employs it. In Psalm VI, for example, the second and fourth rhymes are invariably feminine:

> But mercy, Lord, let mercy thine descend,
> For I am weak, and in my weakness languish;
> Lord help, for ev'n my bones their marrow
>   spend
> With cruel anguish.

And there are a number of other examples where the same, rudimentary but effective, device occurs.

The vocabulary of the Psalms is simple, limited, and commonplace. It is no way remarkable, which is why it is well worth observing. For much of Sidney's later success as a poet comes from his ability to express himself in the most ordinary and everyday words, words that have all affectation and decoration stripped off them, that go straight to the center of meaning:

> Fool, said my Muse to me, look in thy heart and
> write.

And in translating the Psalms, Sidney was almost forced to use simplicity; the original required it, and it was congenial to his nature.

> But ever, ever shall
> His counsels all
> Throughout all ages last.
> The thinkings of that mind
> No end shall find
> When times, Time shall be past.
>
>   (XXXIII)

Such a stanza is, to be sure, unusual. Most of them are much more clumsy:

> The Lord, the Lord my shepherd is,
> And so can never I
> Taste misery.
> He rests me in green pastures his;
> By waters still and sweet
> He guides my feet.

But even in something as awkward as this, in which directness of expression has to be inverted and cramped into a preconceived pattern, there is metrical experiment and simplicity of diction.

When Sidney wrote the poems in the ***Arcadia*** (I am thinking of both versions), he was not only educating himself, he was educating a whole generation. They may be academic, like work done at a university, but universities can play an essential role in society. The poems in the ***Arcadia*** played that role for the poets of the sixteenth century. By them, to change the figure, a whole poetic landscape, hitherto unexplored, was revealed. It was not, to be sure, exactly natural; it was clustered with wax models, dressed in the hired costumes of shepherds and arranged in the languorous poses of conventional artifice; the water in its streams was pumped and the flowers in its fields were of paper. But it was a landscape which Englishmen had seen before, if at all, only in occasional glimpses, and it had one peculiarity which kept it from being merely a scene on the stage; at any moment a breath of fresh wind might strike it; the wax figures might come to life, the water might run by itself over the pebbles, and the flowers might suddenly be real.

The poems in the ***Arcadia*** represent an astonishing variety of forms. At least forty-five different metrical devices or stanzas are used; English, classical, and Italian. There are couplets, six-line stanzas, and rhyme-royal; there are elegiacs, hexameters and hendecasyllabics; there are sonnets,

Engraving of Sidney from the frontispiece of a 1624 edition of Arcadia.

canzone, sestinas and, above all, terza rima; no form seems to have been too foreign or too difficult for Sidney to attempt. It is—what Gabriel Harvey called it—a "gallant variety," an attempt to make available for English poetry the entire technical range of the craft; it is "Art, Exercise and Imitation" on the most comprehensive scale.

But, with the exception of one or two poems, the whole collection has been damned by nearly all modern critics as—to quote Miss Wilson—"a deservedly forgotten mass." This is not just. A great number of the poems, to be sure, are undistinguished in diction, monotonous in technique, and boring in subject matter; they are exercises and nothing else. But there are others—more than is commonly recognized—which are something more than exercises, which are important not merely from the historical point of view, but which are examples of a kind of poetry that is as original as we look back on it now as it seemed to Sidney's own contemporaries.

The poets of Sidney's circle have been severely rebuked for wasting their time in trying to write English poetry in classical meters. Their "versifying," as they called it, has been regarded as an intrepid march up a hopelessly blind alley, and its results dismissed as both futile and barbarous. Yet those who have spoken of it in these terms have, I believe, looked at it from too absolute a point of view. For the experiments in classical meters, though rarely successful in themselves, were just what English poetry, in the 'seventies, most needed. After the accomplishment of Wyatt and Surrey, English poetry, though the work of Sackville is an exception, had apparently lost its ear. Technically speaking, it was in the doldrums. Its sense of ryhthm had become half paralyzed, and the only meter it seemed to be aware of was the iambic. The blank verse of *Gorboduc* (1561), for example, is unenlivened by any metrical variation; the invariable iambs march five abreast implacably down the page. When Gascoigne uses anything but an iamb, which he rarely does, it happens by accident, not intention. The metrical disease known as *poulter's measure,* which was endemic in the 'sixties and 'seventies, aggravated the situation. Sidney himself uses it once—for purposes of parody—in the first poem in the revised *Arcadia;* perhaps he puts it there to show what sort of poetry he was anxious to displace:

> Her forehead jacinth-like, her cheeks of opal
>   hue,
> Her twinkling eyes bedeck'd with pearl, her lips
>   as sapphire blue;
> Her hair like crapal-stone; her mouth O heaven-
>   ly wide,
> Her skin like burnish'd gold, her hands like sil-
>   ver ore untried.

And the only device used to alleviate this tuneless monotony, the device of alliteration, had nothing to do with rhythm; it was merely another kind of clog put upon a way of writing that was badly clogged enough already. The general impression we get of most English poetry in the 'sixties and early 'seventies is that of dullness, flatness, and cowardice; it is as if the writers did not dare to vary from the iambic foot for fear of losing their sense of ryhthm altogether. This is true even of Sidney's translation of the Psalms; hardly a single foot in all the poems varies from the iambic norm.

If English poetry were ever to have any music in it, if the rhythm of the lines were rightly to echo the rhythm of the thought, if there were ever to be any of that essential *drama* in English verse technique, by which a resolved conflict occurs between the basic metrical pattern and the necessary rhythm of the meaning—if all this were to happen, the situation which existed before 1576 had drastically to be changed. The practice of verse technique needed a violent wrench to get it out of its dusty rut. And this wrench, this virtual dislocation, was, I suggest, largely accomplished by the experiments in classical meters. To a modern reader the prolonged discussion between Spenser and Harvey as to whether "heaven" is a monosyllable or a disyllable, seems a waste of time, but actually it was not. What such discussions did was to make people *think* about words; in order to "versify," words had to be broken up, each syllable had to be weighed and considered, and new rhythmical combinations had to be found which were as far removed as possible from the unthinking jog-trot of the prevalent iambic habit.

To take an example. One of the classical forms which Sidney uses in the *Arcadia* is what he calls "Asclepiadickes"—lesser Asclepiad Verses. As used by Sidney this requires a five-foot line. . . . [There] are no iambs at all; instead we have feet of three different kinds; a spondee, three dactyls and a monosyllable. The result is a rhythm which may, perhaps, be foreign to the character of the English language, yet which is interesting not merely as an experiment but also delightful as an accomplishment:

> O sweet/ woods, the de/light/of soli/ tariness
> O how much I do like your solitariness,
> Where man's mind hath a freed consideration,
> Of goodness, to receive lovely direction.

The "versifying" experiments re-inforced one very important metrical lesson, namely that the same kind of foot did not necessarily have to be repeated throughout the line. Perhaps the most valuable part of the lesson was the practice gained in employing the spondee. This heaviest of metrical feet is rare in Sidney's immediate predecessors (with the notable exception of Wyatt), but in the classical meters it has to be widely used, for a wide variety of effects. An ear trained by experiments with spondees was able to give the conventional iambic thump the variation, the weight, that it needed, and Sidney frequently transfers to his rhymed accentual poetry the spondaic experience he had learned from his quantitative exercises:

> Earth, brook, flow'rs, pipe, lamb, dove
> Say all, and I with them,
> Absence is death, or worse, to them that love.
> Since stream, air, sand, mine eyes and ears con-
>   spire;
> What hope to quench, where each thing blows
>   the fire.

But this is only one detail. When Sidney came to write *Astrophel and Stella* he had at his command many other devices for varying the feet in a given line; he no longer beats out continuous iambs as he does in his translation of the psalms; he is various, dramatic, and musical. And he was able to be these things more readily, there can be little doubt, because of his classical experiments.

How far from iambic monotony, for example, is the first line of Sonnet XX:

> Fly, fly, my friends, I have my death's wound, fly!

or the dramatic last line of LXXI:

> But ah, Desire still cries,—"Give me some food!"

or the spondees that begin XLIII:

> Fair eyes, sweet lips, dear heart, that foolish I. . . .

or the cretics in LXXVIII:

> Beauty's plague, virtue's scourge, succor of lies.

or the effective emphasis on the word "plant" in LXXVII:

> That voice which makes the soul plant himself in the ears.

Few of Sidney's classical experiments are successful as complete poems; the asclepiads quoted above dry up as they progress, and the hexameter Echo verses, which begin so charmingly—

> Fair rocks, goodly rivers, sweet woods, when shall I see peace? Peace.
> Peace? What bars me my tongue, who is it that comes me so nigh? I.

—these degenerate, as was perhaps inevitable with so artificial a device, into mere mechanics. But there is one example of Sidney's versifying which is successful almost throughout, and, because it is little known, I quote it entire. It is written in what Sidney himself calls "Anacreon's kind of verses". . . . It was first published in the 1598 folio of the *Arcadia,* but was not, apparently, meant to be a part of that work.

> When to my deadlie pleasure,
> When to my lively torment,
> Lady, mine eyes remained
> Joined, alas, to your beams.
>
> With violence of heav'nly
> Beauty tied to virtue,
> Reason abasht retired,
> Gladly my senses yielded.
>
> Gladly my senses yielding,
> Thus to betray my heart's fort,
> Left me devoid of all life.
>
> They to the beamy suns went,
> Where by the death of all deaths,
> Find to what harm they hastned.
>
> Like to the silly Sylvan,
> Burn'd by the light he best lik'd,
> When with a fire he first met.
>
> Yet, yet, a life to their death,
> Lady, you have reserved,
> Lady, the life of all love.
>
> For though my sense be from me,

> And I be dead who want sense,
> Yet do we both live in you.
>
> Turned anew by your means,
> Unto the flower that aye turns,
> As you, alas, my Sun bends.
>
> Thus do I fall to rise thus,
> Thus do I die to live thus,
> Changed to a change, I change not.
>
> Thus may I not be from you:
> Thus be my senses on you:
> Thus what I think is of you:
> Thus what I seek is in you:
> All what I am, it is you.

The poem starts slowly and somewhat laboriously, for the spondees at the end of each line are not always happily chosen, and the conceit which is the framework of the poem may seem at first to be too heavily ground out by the mind. But even in the first part of the poem there is a weight of both concept and rhythm, and without the conceit the poem could not develop, as it so movingly does, to the depth and haunting intensity of the last eight lines. At the end we have writing which is purely characteristic of Sidney at his best; the language is very simple, the verbal paradox ("changed to a change I change not") is the expression of a deeply embedded truth, and there is a cumulative intensity through repetition, combined with a control of rhythmic movement, which conveys, by its slow weightiness, the conviction of passion. There had been nothing quite like this in English poetry before, and there has been nothing quite like it since.

The *Arcadia* contains four or five times as many poems in Italian verse forms as it does poems in classical meters. There is a double sestina and a single sestina, there are seventeen sonnets, four poems in octaves, three canzone, and nine poems—the longest are among them—in terza rima. Once more a whole new range of expression is opened to English poetry.

When, in *The Defence of Poesie,* Sidney discusses the relative merits of quantitative and rhyming verse, he praises each for separate reasons: "Whether of these be the more excellent, would bear many speeches. The ancient (no doubt) more fit for music, both words and tune observing quantity, and more fit, lively to express divers passions by the low or lofty sound of the well-weighed syllable. The latter likewise with his rhyme striketh a certain music to the ear; and in fine, since it doth delight, though by another way, it obtaineth the same purpose, there being in either sweetness, and wanting in neither, majesty. Truly the English before any vulgar language, I know is fit for both sorts."

The lesson to be learnt from the Italian, as Sidney suggests, was different from that taught by the classics. The classical experiments were valuable chiefly as showing what variations could be made inside the individual line; the Italian gave practice in variations from one line to another. Both provided exercises in movement, but the movement in the Italian forms was of a broader kind. It was stanzaic, not linear; it could train the ear in a more elaborate melody and counterpoint.

Consequently Sidney set himself to experiment with rhyme as fully as possible. His enthusiasm for the resources of the English language had been already richly illustrated in his own practice by the time he wrote the *Defence,* and what he there says about the advantages of his native tongue were generalizations from his own experience. He is specific concerning one important detail. The Italian language, he observes, is handicapped by not having masculine rhymes; Italian rhymes are always either feminine rhymes or triple rhymes, which the Italians call "*Sdrucciola:* the example of the former is *Buono, Suono;* of the *Sdrucciola* is *Femina, Semina.* The French of the other side, hath both the male as *Bon, Son;* and the Female as *Plaise, Taise.* But the *Sdrucciola* he hath not: where the English hath all three, as *Due, Trew, Father, Rather, Motion, Potion.*"

This particular advantage of the English language Sidney deliberately exploited at least three times in the *Arcadia,* and the technical possibilities it reveals are so awakening to the ear that the result is worth examining in some detail. A good example is the long duet between Lalus and Dorus in the first book.

As far as its rhyming technique is concerned, the poem has six movements. It begins in terza rima with triple rhyme:

> Come *Dorus,* come, let songs thy sorrows signi-
>   fy:
> And if for want of use thy mind ashamed is,
> That very shame with love's high title dignify.
> No style is held for base, where love well named
>   is.

This continues for some seventy lines, and then modulates into double rhyme:

> Her peerless height my mind to high erection
> Draws up; and if hope-failing end life's pleasure,
> Of fairer death how can I make election?
> Once my well-waiting eyes espied my
>   treasure . . .

Then, in a third modulation, the rhyme becomes single:

> This maid, thus made for joys, O Pan bemoan
>   her,
> That without love she spends her years of love:
> So fair a field would well become an owner.
> And if enchantment can a hard heart move,
> Teach me what circle may acquaint her sprite,
> Affections charms in my behalf to prove.

This continues for a few lines more, and then, the poem having, as it were, anchored on the monosyllabic rhyme, it rides there in a different rhythm. The fourth movement abandons terza rima for an internal chime of monosyllables:

> Kala at length conclude my lingering lot:
> Disdain me not, although I be not fair,
> Who is an heir of many hundred sheep
> Doth beauties keep, which never sun can burn.

The fifth movement consists of four five-line stanzas of five- and three-beat lines, rhyming *abccb,* the last line of one stanza being also the first line of the next:

> Such force hath love above poor Nature's power,

> That I grow like a shade,
> Which being naught seems somewhat to the
>   eyne,
> While that one body shine,
> Oh he is marred that is for others made.

And the poem concludes by returning, with a kind of technical leap, to the triple-rhyme terza rima with which it began:

> Oh he is marred that is for others made,
> Which thought doth mar my piping declaration,
> Thinking how it hath marred my shepherd's
>   trade.
> Now my hoarse voice doth fail this occupation,
> And others long to tell their love's condi-
>   tion. . . .

It is clear enough that this is not great poetry; the content is conventional, monotonous, and dreary, and the demands of the rhyme scheme are so exacting that only by accident is the phrasing ever felicitous. Furthermore, in spite of Sidney's enthusiasm, triple rhyme in English is something of a tour-de-force; it calls more attention to itself than any technical device should, and we too frequently ask ourselves, as we read, how the poet is going to pull it off instead of accepting it as a thing done. It is a means become too obviously an end.

But the exercise, for the healthy growth of English poetry, was extremely valuable: a pianist practices arpeggios which he will not duplicate when he plays an actual composition, yet he could not play the composition so well if he had not first practiced the arpeggios. And Sidney's experiments with different kinds of rhyme are not always mere muscular exercises; sometimes, if only briefly, the modulation from one kind to another produces an extra rhythmical vibration which is musically effective—as in the following passage from the terza rima dialogue between Basilius and Plangus in the second book:

> Thy wailing words do much my spirits move,
> They uttered are in such a feeling fashion,
> That sorrows work against my will I prove.
> Methinks I am partaker of thy passion,
> And in thy case do glass mine own debility . . .

But though Sidney's exercises in terza rima are highly interesting from the technical point of view, and though they were valuable for showing the poets of the sixteenth century what could be done with English rhyme, they are not his most successful imitations of Italian art. His real triumph is with the sestina, and the most beautiful of the poems in the *Arcadia* is the double sestina in book one which begins:

> You goat-herd Gods, that love the grassy moun-
>   tains.

The poem has been well described by Mr. Empson:

> Nowhere in English literature can [the] use of diffuseness as an alternative to, or peculiar brand of, ambiguity be seen more clearly than in those lovely sestines of Sidney, which are so curiously foreign to the normal modes or later developments of the language. . . . This form has no direction or momentum; it beats, however rich its

orchestration, with a wailing and immovable monotony, for ever upon the same doors in vain. . . . Limited as this form may be, the capacity to accept a limitation so unflinchingly, the capacity even to conceive so large a form as a unit of sustained feeling, is one that has been lost since that age.

The poem is admirably constructed. For ten stanzas the two shepherds Strephon and Klaius lament their desolation with increasing passion, the repetitions become weightier and weightier, sinking more and more deeply into grief; then the cause of their grief—their lady's absence—is revealed in the climactic eloquence of the eleventh and twelfth stanzas, and the poem ends in the three-line coda required by the sestina form, a coda which reiterates the permanence of their sorrow:

> Our morning hymn is this, and song at evening.

A musical analogy, as so often with Sidney's poetry, is almost inevitable. The first ten stanzas swell with a slow and steady crescendo, and the language and the rhythm gradually acquire an extraordinary force:

> *Strephon:*
> I wish to fire the trees of all these forests;
> I give the Sunne a last farewell each evening;
> I curse the fidling finders out of Musicke:
> With envie I doo hate the loftie mountaines;
> And with despite despise the humble vallies:
> I doo detest night, evening, day, and morning.
>
> *Klaius:*
> Curse to my selfe my prayer is, the morning:
> My fire is more, then can be made with forrests;
> My state more base, then are the basest vallies:
> I wish no evenings more to see, each evening;
> Shamed I have my selfe in sight of mountaines,
> And stoppe mine eares, lest I growe mad with
>   Musicke.

After this intensity comes the resolution or revelation, the statement which clarifies and relieves the despairing darkness by explaining its cause. The stanzas must be quoted in full, for only quotation can show how carefully they are made. In each the verb is held back till the beginning of the fifth line so as to produce the maximum rhetorical effect; it is an example of the precise and necessary craftsmanship which underlies all of Sidney's work, and which controls so authoritatively the movement of his verse. The metrical variations are also masterly.

> *Strephon:*
> For she, whose parts maintainde a perfect mu-
>   sique,
> Whose beautie shin'de more then the blushing
>   morning,
> Who much did passe in state the stately moun-
>   taines,
> In straightness past the Cedars of the forrests,
> Hath cast me wretch into eternall evening,
> By taking her two Sunnes from these darke val-
>   lies.
>
> *Klaius:*
> For she, to whom compar'd, the Alpes are val-
>   lies,

> She, whose lest word brings from the spheares
>   their musique,
> At whose approach the Sunne rose in the eve-
>   ning,
> Who, where she went, bare in her forhead morn-
>   ing,
> Is gone, is gone from these our spoyled forrests,
> Turning to desarts our best pastur'de moun-
>   taines.
>
> *Strephon:*
> These mountaines witnesse shall, so shall these
>   vallies,
>
> *Klaius:*
> These forrests eke, made wretched by our mu-
>   sique,
> Our morning hymne is this, and song at evening.

To find his own voice, to discover his own poetic idiom and his own rhythm, is the main business of a poet. It is not a simple matter, and the discovery occurs in various ways, ways which vary according to the character (both personal and poetic) of the poet and according to the character of the age which surrounds him. But there is one constant fact which is true of all poets and at all times; the discovery of oneself depends on an act of submission. For the poet, as for the human being, to lose one's life is to find it. In our time this fact has been widely recognized, though it has been expressed in widely differing terms. In a minor way it is what Pound means when he calls his poems "Personae"; it is what Housman discovered when he spoke through the mouth of the Shropshire Lad. It is the fact that lies behind the search of W. B. Yeats for the antimask—the discovery of the self by contemplation of its opposite; it is what T. S. Eliot expresses by his theory of the "objective corelative" and by his requirements that poetry should be as "impersonal as possible."

In the sixteenth century this saving loss of personality, this discovery of self through submission to an "other," could be accomplished to a considerable extent through convention. Convention is to the poet in an age of belief what the *persona* is to the poet in an age of bewilderment. By submission to either the poet acquires authority; he feels that he is speaking for, is representing, something more important than himself—or, in the case of the *persona,* he is at least representing something different from his own naked and relatively insignificant ego; in both cases he has taken the first step toward universality.

But the submission to convention is by no means a passive process, even if the poet does it so naturally that he never thinks of doing anything else. The convention, whether it involve setting, as in the pastoral, or tone, as in the elegy, or technique, as in the sestina, must obviously be freshened by continual re-examination so that it is remade every time it is used. This is what Sidney did with the double sestina which I have just quoted. The pastoral setting, the traditional tone of lament, the rigorous form of the verse have been revitalized not merely by Sidney's superb technique, but by the fact that he has put into them something more than the purely conventional emotion. In a way that does not often happen in the ***Arcadia*** the external conventions have here become a *persona,* an objective corelative, for Sidney's own projected feelings.

Or, perhaps more accurately, the convention has stimulated, has even created, those feelings. Once the poet has set himself the task of writing an amorous complaint, that deep melancholy which lay beneath the surface glamour of Elizabethan existence and which was so characteristic of Sidney himself, begins to fill the conventional form with a more than conventional weight. It surges through the magical adagio of the lines; they have that depth of reverberation, like the sound of gongs beaten under water, which is sometimes characteristic of Sidney as of no other Elizabethan, not even Shakespeare.

The most famous of the poems in the *Arcadia,* in fact the only one which is at all well known, is the sonnet in book three beginning "My true love hath my heart and I have his." The theme of the poem, the exchange of hearts, is a common one, and in the sestet, at least, it is expressed in a commonplace fashion, but there are two things about it which make it memorable: the monosyllabic simplicity of the diction (only twelve words are not monosyllables), and the flawless movement of the rhetoric. The poem is a perfectly drawn circle, ending most contentedly where it began: "My true love hath my heart, and I have his." This particular movement is something new in English sonnet writing; it is one more example of the continual experimenting which make the poems in the *Arcadia* such a striking revelation of what could—and sometimes of what could not—be done with the English tongue.

I have spoken of the value of convention as a means of poetic release, and I do not want in any way to slight its importance; but convention is, after all, only a means to an end, the great and difficult end of direct and accurate expression. To catch, in the words of T. E. Hulme, "the exact curve of the thing," whether it be an external object, a thought, an emotion, or, more likely, a combination of all three, to make the glove of verbal expression skin-tight, this is what all poetry aims for. Only by finally achieving this honesty, this truth, can the poet discover his own idiom, his own rhythm, his own voice. Consequently all poets have, like Shakespeare, consistently attacked affectation (the spotted underside of convention), and none more vigorously than Sidney. In *Astrophel and Stella* Sidney tries deliberately to put convention aside, and to speak out for himself. He is by no means always successful, and one of the first things a critic must do in discussing this third and obviously most important part of his poetic work is to determine where and how the success does or does not occur. But Sidney's attempt, whether invariably successful or not, is the significant thing, his attempt to be himself, to find a richer and more exacting freedom than that given by the *persona* of convention, the attempt that was to be Sidney's legacy, not only to the generation of poets which immediately followed him, but to all poets since.

Sidney states his aim at the beginning of the sequence. The famous first sonnet of *Astrophel and Stella* is a manifesto of sincerity, an eloquent rejection of anything but the strictest devotion to honest feeling. It is also characteristic of Sidney at his mature best: the structure is perfect, the single movement rises to its climax through a flawless logical progression as well as through a rhythmical pulsation, the

language is very simple, the images are strikingly exact, and—what is here first fully developed in Sidney's poetry and is to distinguish many of the finest sonnets in the sequence—the climax is presented dramatically:

> Loving in truth, and fain in verse my love to
>   show,
> That she, dear she, might take some pleasure of
>   my pain,
> Pleasure might cause her read, reading might
>   make her know,
> Knowledge might pity win, and pity grace obtain,
> I sought fit words to paint the blackest face of
>   woe,
> Studying inventions fine, her wits to entertain,
> Oft turning others' leaves, to see if thence would
>   flow
> Some fresh and fruitful showers upon my sunburnt brain.
>
> But words came halting forth, wanting invention's stay,
> Invention, Nature's child, fled step-dame
>   Study's blows,
> And others' feet still seem'd but strangers in my
>   way.
> Thus great with child to speak, and helpless in
>   my throes,
> Biting my truant pen, beating myself for spite,
> "Fool!" said my Muse to me, "Look in thy heart
>   and write."

At least six other sonnets are on the same theme; Sidney rejects all decoration, all exaggeration, all borrowing; he will write only of Stella, for to copy nature is to copy her, and he will, he says,

>   in pure simplicity
> Breath out the flames which burn within my
>   heart,
> Love only leading me into this art.

Who Stella was, and whether or not Sidney as a man felt a genuine passion for her, are puzzling questions, but not worth much conjecture. All that matters is that she was a symbol around which were mustered a set of important emotions, emotions which were multiplied and intensified, sometimes perhaps even induced, by Sidney's desire to express them. Everyone who writes poetry knows that once a subject matter is accepted, or an object of potential emotion set up in the mind, all sorts of previously unnoticed emotional iron-filings flow toward it as to a magnet, and new patterns are formed the shape of which had been unexpected until the act of composition has made them mysteriously appear. The conscious act of deliberation which focuses the mind on fulfilling the requirements of a given poetic form invokes hitherto subconscious relationships and intensifications which may produce a final result that is quite different, and much richer, than anything planned at the start. Such a process had already occurred, as we have seen, in Sidney's double sestina in the *Arcadia;* the convention of the love sonnet, in spite of all that Sidney has to say against its artificiality, gave a further opportunity. A Laura, a Stella, a dark lady, has only a thin and shadowy "reality" as a biographical fact compared to her reality in the poetry ostensibly written about her. Whether

Stella was Lady Rich or somebody else (she was in all probability Lady Rich) is of no importance to the student of Sidney's poetry. Her symbolic value is all that matters.

Sometimes this value is unhappily small, and we feel, as in sonnet LXXIV, that Stella—or in this instance Stella's kiss—is too trivial a matter to justify the weight of rhetoric that Sidney crowns it with. But even in so anticlimactic a sonnet as this one there are lines which exemplify Sidney's admirable simplicity and force:

> And this I swear by blackest brook of hell,
> I am no pickpurse of another's wit.

These qualities are common throughout the sequence, and many illustrations of them could be given, but they appear perhaps most clearly in the eighth of the interspersed songs, a love poem which has very few equals in the language, and which no one but Sidney could have written. It has not only force and simplicity, but also intensity and passion. It is a dialogue, a presentation in dramatic terms of that conflict between chaste and passionate love with which all sixteenth century art, both visual and verbal, was so much concerned, and to which Sidney's richest love poetry gave so full and deep an expression: "The argument cruel chastity, the prologue hope, the epilogue despair."

The verse form is as simple as the diction; octosyllabic couplets with alternate masculine and feminine rhymes, a triumphant result of Sidney's earlier experimentation:

> In a grove most rich of shade,
> Where birds wanton music made,
> May, then young, his pied weeds showing
> New perfumes with flow'rs fresh growing,

> Astrophel with Stella sweet
> Did for mutual comfort meet,
> Both within themselves oppressed,
> But either in each other blessed.

> Him great harms had taught much care,
> Her fair neck a foul yoke bare;
> But her sight his cares did banish,
> In his sight her yoke did vanish.

For a time they are silent, till love makes Astrophel speak. He praises Stella's beauty in exquisite language, and presents as delicately as possible the arguments for the satisfaction of their love. When he is finished,

> There his hands (in their speech) fain
> Would have made tongue's language plain;
> But her hands his hands repelling,
> Gave repulse, all grace expelling.

> Then she spoke. Her speech was such
> As not ears but heart did touch,
> While such wise she love denied,
> As yet love she signified,

Her refusal is as gracious, as courtly, as simply expressed, as Astrophel's invitation, but what she says is no mere following of convention, it is universally right and true. She does not deny her passion, as a more conventionally minded poet would make her do; her passion is as genuine, as burning, as Astrophel's. But she will not submit to it lest the submission spoil her love by shame:

> "Astrophel," said she; "my love
> Cease in these effects to prove;
> Now be still, yet still believe me,
> Thy grief more than death would grieve me.

> If that any thought in me,
> Can taste comfort but of thee,
> Let me, fed with hellish anguish,
> Joyless, hopeless, endless, languish.

> If those eyes you praised be
> Half so dear as you to me,
> Let me home return, stark blinded
> Of those eyes, and blinder minded.

> If to secret of my heart,
> I do any wish impart
> Where thou art not foremost placed,
> Be both wish and I defaced.

> If more may be said, I say,
> All my bliss in thee I lay.
> If thou love, my love content thee,
> For all love, all faith, is meant thee.

> Trust me while I thee deny,
> In myself the smart I try;
> Tyrant Honor doth thus use thee—
> Stella's self might not refuse thee.

> Therefore, dear, this no more move,
> Lest (though I leave not thy love,
> Which too deep in me is framed)
> I should blush when thou art named."

> Therewithal away she went,
> Leaving him to passion, rent
> With what she had done and spoken,
> That therewith my song is broken.

It is interesting to compare this poem with "The Ecstasie" of Donne. Both are love poems, both are concerned with the conflict, or at any rate the balance, between physical and spiritual love, both use for the most part simple and colloquial language, both—for what the fact is worth—are in octosyllabic couplets. But otherwise they are very different. Donne's performance is much more brilliant; the Platonic and the Aristotelian traditions, botany, physiology, cosmology, and theology, are all brought to bear on the situation; Donne's Briareus-like mind takes hold of virtually all the available knowledge of his time as material to weave into his texture. The result is a very fine poem, admirably planned and frequently superbly phrased. But it is a little inhuman; unlike the song of Sidney it does not bleed.

Sidney's poem is more elemental, more direct, than Donne's; compared to Donne's brilliant sophistication Sidney's straightforward and graceful strength seems almost archaic, like Greek sculpture of the sixth century B.C. or the painting of Duccio. Donne writes, as he and his lady look into one another's eyes:

> Our eye-beams twisted, and did thread
> Our eyes upon a single string. . . .

Which is very clever. But when Sidney wants to express the same idea, though he uses paradox, he is much more simple:

Wept they had, alas the while;
But now tears themselves did smile,
While their eyes by love directed
Interchangeably reflected.

It is, in fact, a relief to turn back, after reading Donne, to Sidney, for in Sidney there is a baring of the heart rather than an exercise of the mind, and we feel that for the healthy life of English poetry it is the example of Sidney that is more central and more sound.

In *Astrophel and Stella* there is much more, of course, than simplicity and directness, though simplicity and directness are the foundations on which the other qualities are built. There is an occasional magic:

A rosy garland and a weary head. . . .
(XXXIX)

Wise silence is best music unto bliss. . . .
(LXX)

—my soul which only doth to thee
As his sole object of felicity
With wings of love in air of wonder fly. . . .
(LXXXVI)

And, perhaps more important, there is very frequently, as in the opening sonnet, drama. The thought is introduced by a dramatic question: "Come, let me write, and to what end?" (XXXIV) or it is put in the form of a quoted speech:

Because I breath not love to every one,
Nor do not use set colors for to wear,
Nor nourish special locks of vowed hair,
Nor give each speech a full point of a groan,
The courtly nymphs acquainted with the moan
Of them who in their lips love's standard bear;
"What? He?" say they of me, "Now I dare swear
He cannot love. No, no; let him alone."

Or a sudden dramatic turn is given to the situation or the thought in the final couplet. Sonnet XVII, for example, is largely a fanciful one, it seems a typical piece of Renaissance mythological decoration. It tells how Cupid's bow and arrows were broken and how Nature made him new ones from Stella's eyebrows and eyeglances. Nothing could be more apparently artificial. And yet at the end Sidney rescues the sonnet from emptiness by bringing it back to life with dramatic simplicity. Cupid, he says, was delighted with his new weapons:

Oh how for joy he leaps, Oh how he crows!
And straight therewith, like wags new got to
play,
Falls to shrewd turns; and I was in his way.

This quality of drama helps to give the impression of reality which we get from the best of the sonnets. They are not, said Lamb, "rich in words only . . . they are full, material and circumstantiated. Time and place appropriates every one of them. It is not a fever of passion wasting itself upon a thin diet of dainty words, but a transcendent passion pervading and illuminating action, pursuits, studies, feats of arms, the opinions of contemporaries and his judgment of them."

The drama lies not only in the external manner of presentation; it is also inherent in the conflict between virtue and desire which is so important an aspect of the subject matter. When the matter and the manner are both dramatic, Sidney is at his best (LXXI):

Who will in fairest book of Nature know
How virtue may best lodg'd in Beauty be,
Let him but learn of love to read in thee,
Stella, those fair lines which true goodness show.
There shall he find all vice's overthrow,
Not by rude force, but sweetest sovereignty
Of reason, from whose light those night birds fly,
That inward sun in thine eyes shineth so.
And not content to be perfection's heir,
Thyself dost strive all minds that way to move,
Who mark in thee, what is indeed most fair;
So while thy beauty drives my heart to love,
As fast thy virtue bends that love to good.
But ah, Desire still cries, "Give me some food!"

This sonnet illustrates another of Sidney's excellencies, his admirable control over movement, a control which had already been firmly practiced in the poems in the *Arcadia.* Each quatrain has its own idea, the second being a development of the first, and the third an extension and universalizing of the first and second, while the conclusion locks the whole together with its exclamatory and dramatic cry. This firmness of logical progression is always present in Sidney, but in a few of the finest sonnets he transcends it, and we have that slow, haunting, reverberating Sidneian music, a music both full and broad, which occurs in the double sestina in the *Arcadia,* and which reappears with a deeper richness in the greatest of the sonnets in *Astrophel and Stella:*

With how sad steps, O Moon, thou climb'st the
skies!
How silently, and with how wan a face!
What, may it be that even in heavenly place
That busy Archer his sharp arrows tries?
Sure, if that long-with-love acquainted eyes
Can judge of love, thou feel'st a lover's case;
I read it in thy looks; thy languish'd grace,
To me that feel the like, thy states descries.
Then even of fellowship, O Moon, tell me,
Is constant love deem'd there but want of wit?
Are beauties there as proud as here they be?
Do they above love to be lov'd, and yet
Those lovers scorn whom that love doth possess?
Do they call virtue there, ungratefulness?

This same mastery of movement appears in another poem—not a sonnet—which shows once more how Sidney profited by the strictness of the early training he gave himself. The stanzas to the Nightingale are each divided into three sections which musically contrast lines of five beats with lines of three, and which, following an Italian model, invariably have feminine rhymes. The language is simple, and once or twice—as more frequently in the sonnets—has the succinctness of an epigram. The variations in the feet are also notable, and emphasize the theme, so common in Sidney, of the melancholy of unsuccessful love. And, as usual, the movement is ordered by a firm logical structure; it is a poem that could have been composed only by a master of technique, yet it is more than a merely technical success, for in spite of the somewhat literary conceit on which it is based, its lovely modulations convey real feeling.

The nightingale as soon as April bringeth
Unto her rested sense a perfect waking,
While late bare earth proud of new clothing springeth
Sings out her woes, a thorn her song-book making,
And mournfully bewailing,
Her throat in tunes expresseth
What grief her breast oppresseth
For Tereus' force on her chaste will prevailing.
O Philomela fair, O take some gladness,
That here is juster cause of plaintful sadness;
Thine earth now springs, mine fadeth;
Thy thorn without, my thorn my heart invadeth.

Alas, she hath no other cause of anguish
Than Tereus' love, on her by strong hand wroken,
Wherein she suffering, all her spirits languish
Full woman-like complains her will was broken.
But I who daily craving,
Cannot have to content me,
Have more cause to lament me,
Since wanting is more woe than too much having.
O Philomela fair, O take some gladness,
That here is juster cause of plaintful sadness:
Thine earth now springs, mine fadeth;
Thy thorn without, my thorn my heart invadeth.

Sidney wrote two love sonnets which were not printed as part of *Astrophel and Stella,* but which were evidently planned to conclude the sequence. In them he at last resolves the long conflict between desire and virtue which, in the last half of the sequence at least, is expressed with such force and intensity and which seems to have been the cause of more than ordinary suffering. Desire is at least repudiated, and the love which "reacheth but to dust" is spurned in favor of love that is eternal. After the last one are printed the words, "Spendidis longum valedico nugis."

Both of these sonnets are very fine; among all of Sidney's work they offer the clearest justification for the claim put forward by one modern critic that Sidney rediscovered, for English poetry, the "grand style." The finest is perhaps the first, and less well known of the two, though it is hard to choose between them. It is a triumphant example of Sidney's best qualities—his direct and forceful simplicity, his eloquent rhetoric, his emotional depth and truth, his control of movement, both within the single line and throughout the poem as a whole; and a discussion of Sidney's craft may appropriately end with its slow reverberant music sounding in our ears.

Thou blind man's mark, thou fool's self-chosen snare,
Fond fancy's scum, and dregs of scattered thought,
Band of all evils, cradle of causeless care,
Thou web of will, whose end is never wrought,
Desire, desire! I have too dearly bought
With price of mangled mind thy worthless ware;
Too long, too long, asleep thou hast me brought,
Who should my mind to higher things prepare.

But yet in vain thou hast my ruin sought,
In vain thou mad'st me to vain things aspire,
In vain thou kindlest all thy smoky fire;

For virtue hath this better lesson taught,
Within myself to seek my only hire,
Desiring nought but how to kill desire.

What Sidney accomplished in his own poetry and what he did for English poetry in general have both been somewhat overshadowed by the more ambitious and apparently more professional work of Spenser. The poems in the *Arcadia* have been neglected in favor of the contemporary poems in *The Shepheardes Calendar,* and the comprehensive width of *The Faerie Queene* has tended to relegate *Astrophel and Stella* to the position of minor poetry. For this Sidney himself is partly responsible, and for two reasons; in spite of his superb defense of the importance of poetry, he subscribed too readily to the silly contemporary notion that no gentleman should be a professional writer, and, partly because of this notion, the content of his poetry was too narrowly limited to the subject of love. Even the most devoted admirer of Sidney finds it something of a chore to read through all the poems in the *Arcadia* because they are virtually all about the same thing; one lover after another—men and women, shepherds and kings—all rejoice or lament (chiefly the latter) about the condition of their affections. Spenser was wiser; more than half of the eclogues in *The Shepheardes Calendar* are concerned with other topics—with religion, politics, poetry, and morality. And in *The Faerie Queene* he created an entire world, where love is only one among many other motivating passions. It is most unlikely that Sidney, if he had lived, would have written anything so extensive; he was too much in the center of active political life to have had the desire, or the time, for such a task. Spenser, fortunately, was only on the fringes of society.

But if we accept the limitations of Sidney's subject matter, and set his love poetry by that of Spenser, it is Spenser—if we except the "Epithalamion"—who suffers by the comparison. Spenser has justly been called a master of melody, his lines move with wonderful sweetness and grace, they carry the reader along with as little effort as that with which they were apparently composed. But, compared to Sidney, they are thin; their language, however musical, lacks weight. Spenser's style, compared to Sidney's, has two deficiencies: it is rarely pungent, and it is almost never dramatic. The reader is soothed, not challenged; enchanted, not awakened to a new reality.

This reality, this depth and pungency, we recognize as belonging not only to Sidney's awareness, but—as happens with all great poetry—as creative of a new awareness in ourselves. The art, exercise, and imitation which Sidney so assiduously practiced throughout the Psalms and the *Arcadia,* resulted, in the best of the sonnets in *Astrophel and Stella,* in poetry to which all lovers of honesty and directness must continually return. In this essential respect, it is Sidney—not Spenser—who is the most central of English poets in the generation that was soon to know Shakespeare. (pp. 73-99)

Theodore Spencer, "The Poetry of Sir Philip Sidney," in Theodore Spencer: Selected Essays, *edited by Alan C. Purves, Rutgers University Press, 1945, pp. 73-99.*

John F. Danby   (essay date 1952)

[*In the excerpt below, from an essay assessing Sidney's influence on the later works of William Shakespeare, Danby defends Sidney's* Arcadia *against critical contentions that it lacks unity and coherence, arguing that the narrative achieves unity through Sidney's celebration of virtue.*]

In *The Use of Poetry and the Use of Criticism* Mr. Eliot wrote: 'The works of Sir Philip Sidney, excepting a few sonnets, are not among those to which one can return for perpetual refreshment; the *Arcadia* is a monument of dullness.'

Miss Mona Wilson, too, finds the *Arcadia* something of a trial: 'But the more we appreciate Sidney's ingenuity the more full-heartedly shall we echo Hazlitt's judgement that the result is one of the greatest monuments of the abuse of intellectual power on record.'

Miss Wilson is referring particularly to Sidney's revised version of the original story. And Book II, it must be admitted, is both complex and involved. The stories proliferate, and one story will intersect another at times unnecessarily. Fresh characters are constantly making appearance, old ones reappear after we have forgotten the parts they have already played. Sidney can be over-elaborate. His involutions can both confuse and exasperate. At the same time, however, Mr. Eliot's and Miss Wilson's disparagement is rather excessive. . . . [The] *Arcadia* has a grand design. The various stories introduced into Book II are not merely random concatenations of incident. They are, on the contrary, planned *exempla,* necessary parts of the map Sidney was constructing. They are articulated into the large scheme, and *belong.* They give the *Arcadia* its distinctive range, variety, and scope—the compendiousness which recommended it to Greville and the whole of the seventeenth century. (p. 74)

Besides letting us see 'how to set a good countenance upon all the discountenances of adversitie', Greville also claimed that the *Arcadia* could provide an almost complete guide to political wisdom. Concern with the question of good government runs through the whole of the book. The two princes are themselves as it were serving an apprenticeship in the art of ruling well. 'Politic matters', Sidney was well aware, 'receive not geometrical certainties', so there is no text-book presentation of political maxims. The general picture that can be composed is one of enlightened aristocracy. Sidney has no reverence, however, for 'degree' except as it is grounded in virtue. That is the 'natural imperiousness' which 'rests in a well-formed spirit'. The aristocracy will submit to a monarch—but the monarch will be limited by his own defects of virtue, and the caution he must always exercise not to unleash those powerful forces that wait all the time to break out the moment he shows himself weak or unwise. Sidney has a cool eye, and always we get the impression of a man who can look down on the machinery of government from above, whose perceptiveness is the result of first-hand acquaintance, and whose dry light is that of a mind that can not only see but see through. Here, for example, is his account of the confusion attendant on a king's death when the succession is not decided:

> Altogether like a falling steeple, the parts whereof, as windows, stones, and pinnacles were well, but the whole mass ruinous. And this was the general cause of all, wherein notwithstanding was an extreme medley of diversified thoughts, the great men looking to make themselves strong by factions, the gentlemen some bending to them, some standing upon themselves, some desirous to overthrow those few which they thought were over them; the soldiers desirous of trouble, as the nurse of spoil, and not much unlike to them though in another way, were all the needy sort, the rich fearful, the wise careful. This composition of conceits brought forth a dangerous tumult, which yet would have been more dangerous, but that it had so many parts that nobody well knew against whom chiefly to oppose themselves.

This is typically Sidneian. First we get the brilliant visual image so well capable of carrying a moral—the steeple falling, still maintaining the appearance of cohesion, none of the parts broken 'but the whole mass ruinous'; then the translation of the image into terms of confusion in the commonweal, great men, gentry, soldiery, and 'all the needy sort'; finally, the use of his favourite dialectic in the last sentence (an abstract statement of what the image of the falling steeple implied) showing how absolute lack of cohesion has itself a kind of safety in it or can at least indefinitely postpone disaster—the steeple now falling for an indefinitely long time, a perfect form in the air that the least touch will dissipate utterly.

Pyrocles and Musidorus will ultimately be ideal governors like Euarchus. They are plentifully supplied in the *Arcadia* with knowledge of bad rulers. Sidney varies his examples, but the variations are all on the theme of a wrenching away from the frame of nature. Plexirtus, for example (he is Shakespeare's Edmund), ousted his brother Leonatus (Shakespeare's Edgar) by machiavellian practice. The parallel story of Plangus and his step-mother gives almost a recipe for perversion of a king's mind so that the truth will seem to him a lie, and the rightful heir be forced to flee the country. The queen in this instance makes use of a tool-villain:

> Then took she help to her of a servant near about her husband, whom she knew to be of a hasty ambition, and such a one, who, wanting true sufficiency to raise him, would make a ladder of any mischief. Him she useth to deal more plainly in alleging causes of jealousy, making him know the fittest times when her husband already was stirred that way. And so they two, with divers ways, nourished one humour, like musicians, that singing divers parts, make one music. He sometimes with fearful countenance would desire the king to look to himself, for that all the court and city were full of whisperings and expectations of some sudden change, upon what ground himself knew not. Another time he would counsel the king to make much of his son, and hold his favour, for that it was too late now to keep him under. Now seeming to fear himself, because, he said, Plangus loved none of them that were great about his father. Lastly, breaking with him directly, making a sorrowful counte-

nance, and an humble gesture bear false witness for his true meaning, that he found not only soldiery but people weary of his government, and all their affection bent upon Plangus; both he and the queen concurring in strange dreams, and each thing else, that in a mind already perplexed might breed astonishment: so that within a while, all Plangus's actions began to be translated into the language of suspicion. Which though Plangus found, yet could he not avoid, even contraries being driven to draw one yoke of argument. If he were magnificent, he spent much with an aspiring intent, if he spared, he heaped much with an aspiring intent; if he spoke courteously, he angled the people's hearts; if he were silent, he mused upon some dangerous plot. In sum, if he could have turned himself to as many forms as Proteus every form should have been made hideous . . . the more he protested, the more his father thought he dissembled, accounting his integrity to be but a cunning face of falsehood.

Counterpointing this story of the uxorious king and his baseborn wife there is the story of Erona and Antiphilus—the overfond queen who married beneath her. Antiphilus had been helped originally by Pyrocles and Musidorus. When 'the two paragons of virtue' leave him his nature is unable to withstand the temptations of absolute power:

> Antiphilus I say, being crowned and delivered from the presence of those two, whose virtues, while they were present, like good schoolmasters, suppressed his vanities, he had not strength of mind enough in him to make long delay of discovering what manner of man he was. But straight like one carried up to so high a place that he loseth the discerning of the ground over which he is, so was his mind lifted so far beyond the level of his own discourse, that remembering only that himself was in the high seat of a king, he could not perceive that he was a king of reasonable creatures who would quickly scorn follies and repine at injuries. But imagining no so true property of sovereignty as to do what he listed, and to list whatsoever pleased his fancy, he quickly made his kingdom a tennis-court, where his subjects should be the balls, not in truth cruelly, but licentiously abusing them, presuming so far upon himself, that what he did was liked of everybody: nay, that his disgraces were favours, and all because he was a king. For in nature not able to perceive the bounds of great matters, suddenly borne into an unknown ocean of absolute power, he was swayed withal, he knew not how, as every wind of passion puffed him.

The stories of Erona and Antiphilus, and of Andromana and Plangus are only two of the episodes of Book II. Their adjectival force and relevance are apparent. Adjusted to the main theme, they suggest the dark side of Arcadia—the evil that the lovers must overcome in the world and in themselves in order that their mutual perfections might be maintained. The lapse from virtue, the surrender of the will to passion, sets up an inward tempest that soon brings about external disorder, and 'an evil mind in authority doth not only follow the sway of the desires already within

it, but frames to itself new desires not before thought of '. A striking thing about the Sidneian universe is its similarity to Shakespeare's in structure. The technique whereby Plangus is blackened to his father is familiar to us in Iago and Edmund. Shakespeare's villains too are either the slaves of passion or the resolved rejectors of the frame of Nature. Defection in the private world leads, for both, to dissolution of the public amities and concord. And the strategy of flight—the only possible one in such circumstances as Plangus finds himself surrounded by—is the strategy Edgar adopts, and Pericles, Polixenes, and Camillo after him. Sidney and the later Shakespeare would both agree on the moral mechanisms at work. They are embraced by the same community of ideas.

The Sidneian heroical poem is, then, compendious. Its material is deliberately moralized. Nothing is included which does not exhibit the intellectual scheme Sidney has in mind—a scheme which must treat of Virtue in relation to politics; Virtue in 'the school of affection' where desire will be taken up into an ideal wholeness of mind maintained by two; Virtue, finally, set in the wider frame of adversity, confronted by the irrationals of chance as well as by the irrationals of wrong choice, Virtue tried by Fortune until it arrives at the transcendent patience and is transformed into a reason above reason: for Virtue is not enough:

> man's virtue is but part of man,
> And part must follow where whole man doth go.

We have already quoted Milton's adverse comment on the Sidneian world. Another and more equable Miltonic statement is also appropriate. In *Paradise Lost,* Book IX, Milton deplores the degenerate notions of heroical poetry, and holds up against these his loftier conception:

> Warrs, hitherto the onely Argument
> Heroic deem'd, chief maistrie to dissect
> With long and tedious havoc fabled Knights
> In Battels feign'd; the better fortitude
> Of Patience and Heroic martyrdom
> Unsung.

Sidney would undoubtedly agree. Milton is almost echoing the 'patience and magnanimitie' of the *Apologie.* Sidney's own poem covers the better as well as the worse fortitude. Its most characteristic moments are such climaxes as when captive good must maintain its ground against captive ill: as when the three prisoners are brought out and threatened with beheading:

> A sight full of pity it was, to see these three (all excelling in all those excellencies wherewith nature can beautify anybody: Pamela giving sweetness to majesty; Philoclea enriching nobleness with humbleness, Zelmane setting in womanly beauty manlike valour) to be thus subjected to the basest injury of unjust fortune. One might see in Pamela a willingness to die, rather than to have life at other's discretion; though sometimes a princely disdain would sparkle out of her princely eyes, that it should be in other's power to force her to die. In Philoclea a pretty fear came up, to endamask her rosy cheeks: but it was such a fear, as rather seemed a kindly child to her innate humbleness, than any other dismayedness; or if she was dismayed it was more

for Zelmane, than for herself; or if more for herself, it was because Zelmane should lose her.

This is a nice example of Sidney's art. The verbal pattern
never remains a matter of merely verbal play. The external
formalism reflects a vital inner unity of thought. Virtue in
the romance world is the apex of a pyramid, or the point
of intersection of two worlds. It is comprehensive, a consummation. So one way of expressing it is by accumulation amounting to hyperbole, 'giving sweetness to
majesty . . . enriching nobleness with humbleness . . .
setting in womanly beauty manlike valour'—the reconciliation of opposites that erected wit can achieve and express. But another way is just as possible: a *via negativa*,
such as the fine series of discriminations that suggest so
exactly Pamela's willingness to die that is not a wish to be
rid of life, or Philoclea's fear and dismay that are neither
timidity nor depression. The spiritual experience, the intellectual lucidity, and the literary gift displayed in passages such as this remind us of those similar ones responsible for Cordelia, Samson, or St. Thomas refuting the
Fourth Tempter. (pp. 75-80)

> *John F. Danby, "Sidney and the Late-
> Shakespearian Romance," in his* Poets on
> Fortune's Hill: Studies in Sidney, Shake-
> speare, Beaumont & Fletcher, *Faber & Faber,
> 1952, pp. 74-107.*

E. M. W. Tillyard   (essay date 1954)

[*Tillyard was an English scholar of Renaissance literature who remains highly esteemed for his studies of John
Milton, William Shakespeare, and the epic form. In the
following excerpt, he examines the new* Arcadia, *arguing that through its embellished style Sidney sought to
produce an heroic poem or epic.*]

Old Arcadia (and if the old, still more the new) is not a
pastoral, contrary to the still current assumption. There
are shepherds in it, but that is because Basilius has retired
to the country. The king's chief herdsman is called Dametas, but he is a genuine herdsman and unlike his aged
namesake in *Lycidas,* who, in the genuine pastoral convention of the Renaissance, stands for one of the Cambridge
dons. The political structure is clear and simple. Basilius,
the king, once efficient but grown foolish and culpably
negligent, is contrasted with Euarchus, the perfect ruler.
Euarchus did not seek war but was a fierce fighter when
attacked. In restoring the state of *Arcadia* he shows perfect
impartiality and disregard of personal feeling, for he condemns his own son and nephew to death when the evidence is apparently against them. Musidorus and Pyrocles
are perfect kings in the making. Nevertheless, the chief
substance of the *Old Arcadia* concerns friendship and
love, ethics not politics. Musidorus and Pyrocles fulfil the
Renaissance code of bosom friends, and the game of love
is played with all the ceremony of extreme sensibility and
high rhetoric and with all the complications and cross-
purposes that the age held dear. The telling is straightforward apart from the narratives within the eclogues; and
the plot progresses evenly to its various climaxes and to
their solutions. In its kind it is a harmonious and well-

proportioned composition; but that kind is the romantic
novel not the epic. (p. 296)

Structurally the old *Arcadia* had been straightforward in
the romance manner. The new *Arcadia* is constructed on
the classical model of Heliodorus, with the action beginning in the middle and previous action narrated. It also
has resemblances with Xenophon's *Cyropedia.* There can
be no doubt that Sidney was glancing at his revised *Arcadia* when he wrote about the prose-poem in general in his
Defence of Poesie:

> The greatest part of Poets have apparelled their
> poeticall inventions in that numbrous kinde of
> writing which is called verse: indeed but apparel-
> led, verse being but an ornament and no cause
> to Poetry; sith there have beene many most ex-
> cellent Poets that never versified, and now
> swarme many versifiers that neede never aun-
> swere to the name of Poets. For *Xenophon,* who
> did imitate so excellently as to give us *effigiem
> iusti imperii,* the portraiture of a just Empire,
> under the name of *Cyrus,* made therein an abso-
> lute heroicall Poem. So did *Heliodorus* in his su-
> gred invention of that picture of love in *Thea-
> gines* and *Cariclea.* And yet both these writ in
> Prose: which I speak to shew, that it is not rim-
> ing and versing that maketh a Poet, no more
> then a long gowne maketh an Advocate; who
> though he pleaded in armor should be an Advo-
> cate and no Souldier. But it is that fayning nota-
> ble images of vertues, vices, or what els, with
> that delightfull teaching, which must be the
> right describing note to know a Poet by.

The new *Arcadia* corresponds to this passage not only
through its imitating the *Cyropedia* and the *Ethiopica* but
in its heightened didactic tone, its far more emphatic
'fayning notable images' of virtues and vices. The truth of
this becomes evident if we consider the main additions.

To go into this matter of additions in any detail would take
far too long, for Sidney added many new motives. But his
principal additions are two: much more ample information about the earlier deeds of Musidorus and Pyrocles
and the very long and important episode of Cecropia, sis-
ter-in-law to Basilius, inciting her son Amphialus to wrest
the throne of Arcadia from his uncle. The first addition
serves to make the new *Arcadia* relatively more martial
and political and less erotic than the old. The second not
only has the same effect but serves to alter the whole balance and tone of the novel. I must explain briefly how it
does this. In *Old Arcadia* no major character was a villain;
by adding the villainous Cecropia to the major characters
Sidney almost added a new dimension to his novel. Cecropia is boundlessly ambitious and quite ruthless and unscrupulous. She dominates her son Amphialus and distorts his naturally good character a long way (but not
quite irredeemably) to evil. We hear of her evil nature first
through the adventure of the lion and the bear. In *Old Arcadia* these beasts had broken into Basilius's country
quiet, to be killed by the two princes. They served,
through the princely valour that went to their killing, to
promote the course of true love; Pamela and Philoclea naturally warming towards their protectors. We are not told
how the beasts got there. In the revised *Arcadia* we have

the same episode but with the added information that Cecropia had them let loose from her menagerie in the hope that they would harm Basilius and his family. Later she succeeds by a stratagem in capturing Pamela, Philoclea, and Zelmane (as Pyrocles called himself in his Amazonian disguise) and holds them prisoner in her castle. Cecropia subjects the captive princesses to torture both physical and mental and persuades Amphialus, in love with Philoclea, to force his suit on her. Zelmane is nearly driven to suicide by the exhibition of the pretended execution of Philoclea. Cecropia is an atheist of the Lucretian school and she tries to argue Pamela out of her religion. The theme of a supreme test of character and of martyrdom is added to *Arcadia* through this episode. Naturally the Arcadians rouse themselves to deal with Cecropia's crimes, and there result battles more closely and lengthily described than any in *Old Arcadia.* This testing of character and these battles not only give *Arcadia* a new and different type of seriousness but structurally they constitute the climax. They turn *Arcadia* into a different kind of novel, one dealing principally with the ultimate problems of man's destiny and in its scope competent to be an epic. The question whether these very serious additions blend with the predominantly erotic character of the first version must wait till I consider the success of the structure. All I seek to assert now is that the ingredients of the revised *Arcadia* admit of the epic dignity.

Having made that assertion I can leave *Old Arcadia* and ask whether the *Arcadia* of 1590, as far as it goes, realises the epic potentialities of its ingredients.

At the outset we are confronted with the style, for according to some of its critics it could certainly not be the vehicle of the most serious kind of feelings. The popular conception of the style is of the high fantastic, and Hazlitt gave the most brilliant as well as the most hostile account of it at the end of his sixth lecture on the *Literature of the Age of Elizabeth.* Recent writers on *Arcadia* do not regard Hazlitt's attack as important; at any rate they mostly ignore it. But Hazlitt says things about *Arcadia* that have enough truth in them to make it perilous not to heed them. What Hazlitt cannot abide and what no reader can ignore is a persistence in amplifying the plain sense of a thing. Sidney, says Hazlitt,

> never lets a casual observation pass without perplexing it with an endless running commentary, he never states a feeling without so many *circumambages,* without so many interlineations and parenthetical remarks on all that can be said for it, and anticipations of all that can be said against it, and he never mentions a fact without giving so many circumstances and conjuring up so many things that it is like or not like, that you lose the main clue of the story in its infinite ramifications and intersections.

Hazlitt will not even have it that Sidney's habit of amplification springs from poetic vitality; on the contrary it shows only a low poetic vitality in subservience to an irrelevantly high intellectual one. . . . Hazlitt's attack, so reminiscent of Johnson's on the Metaphysicals, whether justified or not, goes, again like Johnson's, to the heart of the matter. There are many stretches of the *Arcadia* where

every sentiment is qualified in some way or another; and Sidney did exert his dialectical faculty extensively in composing them. In fact, he wrote a great deal of prose in a style that anticipated the Metaphysical style in verse. Of such a style, whether in prose or verse, we are now rightly more tolerant. But there are certain natural limits to its use. In Donne it graces the individual *Songs and Sonettes* better than it does the sustained length of the *Anniversaries.* In reading certain parts of *Arcadia* and the *Anniversaries* alike the reader not excessively prejudiced in favour of the Metaphysical style is forced to exclaim to himself something like, 'the damned fellow can't keep off it', or 'if only he would spare us for a few minutes'. The wit browbeats the reader and ends by dulling his faculties. Here is a passage containing samples of the kind of writing in *Arcadia* I am thinking of:

> Then fell she to so pitiful a declaration of the insupportablenes of her desires, that *Dorus* eares (not able to shew what woundes that discourse gave unto them) procured his eyes with teares to give testimonie, how much they suffered for her suffering: till passion (a most cumbersome guest to itselfe) made *Zelmane* (the sooner to shake it off) earnestly intreate *Dorus,* that he also (with like freedom of discourse) would bestow a Mappe of his little worlde, upon her; that she might see, whether it were troubled with such unhabitable climes of colde despaires, and hot rages, as hers was. And so walking under a fewe Palme trees, (which being loving in their own nature, seemed to give their shadow the willinger, because they held discourse of love) *Dorus* thus entred to the description of his fortune.

> Alas (said he) deare Cosin, that it hath pleased the high powers to throwe us to such an estate, as the onely entercourse of our true friendshippe, must be a bartring of miseries. For my parte, I must confesse indeede, that from a huge darkenes of sorrowes, I am crept (I cannot say to a lightsomnes, but) to a certain dawning, or rather, peeping out of some possibilitie of comfort: But woe is me, so far from the marke of my desires, that I rather thinke it such a light, as comes through a small hole to a dungeon, that the miserable caitife may the better remember the light, of which he is deprived: or like a scholler, who is onely come to that degree of knowledge, to finde him selfe utterly ignorant.

The first paragraph of this passage is typical of what maddened Hazlitt: who would have complained that instead of mentioning the palms and allowing them to do their own work Sidney must needs complicate the effect and hold up the action by attributing to them gratuitously a kind of life they do not in fact possess; that instead of asking plainly for a summary of Dorus's state of mind—the real point—Zelmane drags in the commonplace of the great world of nature and the little world of man and frigidly puts human feelings in terms of physical geography, of arctic ice and desert heat. Now in one sense Hazlitt was wrong in attacking such a loading of the plain action. He failed to see that Sidney wanted to write like this, that his emotions dictated these intellectual parentheses. He failed also to see that to any Elizabethan it was natural to introduce the symbolism of the palm and to go beyond its mere physical, vegetable self; and that Sidney delighted to compare microcosm to macrocosm because he was greatly aware that God's creation was, for all its diversity, yet of a piece. Lamb, in fact, knew better than Hazlitt when he said that for a Sidney it was natural to be unnatural. But in another sense Hazlitt was right; for there is a limit to the amount of this parenthetical writing the ordinary reader can endure on end. It is no use justifying the parts of a long passage if they offend when taken together. And there are stretches in *Arcadia* that weary. But I must add the immediate qualification that their number is far smaller than Hazlitt and his school imagine. That the school of Hazlitt still flourishes is clear from T. S. Eliot's statement that 'the *Arcadia* is a monument of dulness'. And the only way I can account for such flourishing is to suppose that an immediate dislike for such paragraphs as I have been discussing clouds the reader's vision and persuades him to see all the rest of *Arcadia* (except for a few habitually anthologised passages) in the same guise. This process of obfuscation can be illustrated by turning to the second paragraph of the extract under discussion. Here there is more imagery and less circumlocution. When in the first paragraph Dorus's ears pass on to his eyes the job of showing sympathy with Zelmane's grief, Sidney is indeed in the region of rhetoric, of preconceived decorum, of manners not of feeling. But when in the next paragraph Dorus tries to define the 'huge darknes' of his sorrows and feels his way from one comparison to another, Sidney has stopped being rhetorical and is seeking to describe as well as he can the motions of a human heart. Now it would not be difficult for a reader, hating the literary climate of the first paragraph, to read the second so slackly as not to see the change, to consider the progression from a 'lightsomnes' to 'a certain dawning' and then to a 'peeping out' to be mere rhetorical amplification, when it is actually a search for ever more and more precision. Having missed the greater naturalness and directness of the second paragraph, such a reader must miss another thing: the contrast between the two paragraphs; the first resembling a stilted recitative, the second a freely melodic air.

This last observation brings me to the principal thing I have to say about the style of *Arcadia.* In spite of some stretches where the rhetorically parenthetical style is sustained too long for the reader's comfort, Sidney in his revised *Arcadia* showed a variety and a contrast of styles with which, popularly, he has never been credited. Further, this variety is much greater and more evident in the new than in the old *Arcadia;* corresponding with the maturer power of Sidney's mind.

The first few pages of the revised *Arcadia,* which are new writing, furnish an evident example of contrasted styles: an example particularly significant too, because here, if anywhere, in his revision, Sidney would have sought to establish his tone and demonstrate his method. *Arcadia* opens with the two shepherds, Strephon and Claius, haunting the coast of Laconia at the spot whence their adored mistress, Urania, embarked for the island of Cythera. These two are a superior sort of shepherd and they lack all jealousy in their hopeless common passion for

Urania. Urania is a mysterious figure, just mentioned in *Old Arcadia* as being 'thought a Shepherdes Daughter, but in deede of farr greater byrthe'. In the new *Arcadia* on a later page she is the subject of one of the most thrilling short passages Sidney ever composed, itself an instance of a style far removed from the ample and parenthetical. Among the descriptions of the pictures carried in triumph by Phalanthus after his defeat of the champions who fought for the different subjects of these pictures occurs the following:

> It was of a young mayd, which sate pulling out a thorne out of a Lambs foote, with her looke so attentive upon it, as if that little foote coulde have been the circle of her thoughts; her apparell so poore, as it had nothing but the inside to adorne it; a shephooke lying by her with a bottle upon it. But with al that povertie, beauty plaid the prince, and commanded as many harts as the greatest Queene there did. Her beautie and her estate made her quicklie to be known to be the faire shepheardesse, *Urania.*

Whether Strephon and Claius represent actual people or symbolise a contemplative kind of man I do not know; but plainly Urania is not named so for nothing and represents something heavenly towards which a chosen few aspire. After referring to the other shepherds and their ordinary shepherdish occupations, Strephon says:

> Ah you base minded wretches, are your thoughts so deeply bemired in the trade of ordinary worldlings, as for respect of gaine some paultry wooll may yeeld you, to let so much time passe without knowing perfectly her estate, especially in so troublesome a season? to leave that shore unsaluted, from whence you may see to the Island where she dwelleth? to leave those steps unkissed wherein *Urania* printed the farewell of all beautie?

However, the present point is not the precise meaning of the two shepherds' adoration of Urania; it is the style in which they couch it. And this is one of high and strained rapture, built up with elaborate artifice. It is as fully intended as the suddenness with which Sidney in this passage interrupts it with a very different theme expressed in a very different style:

> But in deede as wee can better consider the sunnes beautie, by marking how he guildes these waters and mountaines then by looking upon his owne face, too glorious for our weake eyes: so it may be our conceits (not able to beare her sunstayning excellencie) will better way it by her workes upon some meaner subject employed. And alas, who can better witnesse that then we, whose experience is grounded upon feeling? hath not the onely love of her made us (being silly ignorant shepheards) raise up our thoughts above the ordinary levell of the worlde, so as great clearkes do not disdaine our conference? hath not the desire to seeme worthie in her eyes made us when others were sleeping, to sit vewing the course of heavens? when other were running at base, to runne over learned writings? when other marke their sheepe, we to marke ourselves? hath not shee throwne reason upon our desires, and,

as it were given eyes unto *Cupid?* hath in any, but in her, love-fellowship maintained friendship betweene rivals, and beautie taught the beholders chastitie? He was going on with his praises, but *Strephon* bad him stay, and looke: and so they both perceaved a thing which floted drawing nearer and nearer to the banke; but rather by the favourable working of the Sea, then by any selfe industrie. They doubted a while what it should be; till it was cast up even hard before them: at which time they fully saw that it was a man.

And there follows the vivid account of the burning ship and the blood-stained sea. One of the most sympathetic critics of *Arcadia* says that it begins with the shipwreck, thus having failed to remember that it begins with a contrast, both of substance and of style, between the idea of man's 'erected wit' and the pitiful spectacle of what in crude fact man has made of man. And if a sympathetic critic can thus go wrong, is it surprising if ordinary readers still assume that Sidney uses a style of unvarying ornateness through which to tell an unprofound though complicated and improbable set of tales?

Here is a second example of deliberate stylistic contrast. To while away the time in their country retreat Basilius and his company tell one another stories. They draw lots, and it falls out that the sluttish Mopsa, daughter of Dametas the king's herdsman, tells her story before Pamela tells hers. Mopsa's story is a beautifully ludicrous version of common folk-lore and romance matter. It begins like this:

> And so being her time to speak (wiping her mouth, as there was good cause) she thus tumbled into her matter. In time past (sayd she) there was a King, the mightiest man in all his country, that had by his wife, the fairest daughter that ever did eat pappe. Now this King did keepe a great house, that everybody might come and take their meat freely. So one day, as his daughter was sitting in her window, playing upon a harpe, as sweete as any Rose; and combing her heade with a comb all of precious stones, there came in a Knight into the court, upon a goodly horse, one haire of gold, and the other of silver; *and so* the Knight casting up his eyes to the window, did fall into such love with her, that he grew not worth the bread he eate; till many a sorry day going over his head, with Dayly Diligence and Grisly Grones, he won her affection, so that they agreed to run away togither. *And so in May, when all true hartes rejoyce,* they stole out of the Castel, without staying so much as for their breakfast.

After some more in the same style,

> Now good *Mopsa* (said the sweete *Philoclea*) I pray thee at my request keepe this tale, till my marriage day, and I promise thee that the best gowne I weare that day shal be thine.

Mopsa accepts the bargain and refrains, leaving the field to Pamela and her tale of Plangus. This tale, dealing with the machinations of Plangus's wicked step-mother, resembles Mopsa's in springing from the stock of immemorial folk-lore. Through this resemblance the exquisite art of the telling is made to contrast the more sharply with Mopsa's ridiculous ineptitude.

I give a final example of Sidney's variety of style; and from a different and more tragic context. The culminating scenes of the revised *Arcadia* are those that describe the imprisonment of Pamela, Philoclea, and Pyrocles (still disguised as the Amazon Zelmane) and the cruelty Cecropia uses towards them. Cecropia's maltreatment of Philoclea culminated in physical violence, which is thus described:

> At length, abhominable rage carried her to absolute tyrannies, so that taking with her certaine olde women (of wicked dispositions, and apt for envie-sake to be cruel to youth and beautie) with a countenance impoysoned with malice, flew to the sweet *Philoclea,* as if so many Kites should come about a white Dove, and matching violent gestures with mischievous threatnings, she having a rod in her hand (like a fury that should carry wood to the burning of *Dianas* temple) fel to scourge that most beautifull body; Love in vaine holding the Shield of Beautie against her blind cruelty. The Sun drew clouds up to hide his face from so pitiful a sight; and the very stone wals did yeeld drops of sweate for agonie of such a mischiefe: each senselesse thing had sense of pittie; only they that had sense, were senseles.

This is a high point of the book; and many readers may think it ruined by the intrusion of Diana's temple, the comparison of beauty to a shield, and the imparting to the sun and the stone walls the feelings of persons. They might also think that Sidney thus elaborated through sheer cold-blooded habit. They would be wrong. Sidney feels keenly but he remembers contemporary decorum and that a queen must not scourge a princess in the style a cook boxes the ears of a scullery-maid. And that his elaboration is not cold-bloodedly habitual but intended is made evident by the simplicity of a passage that comes very soon after. When the scourging is over and Philoclea is once more in her solitary confinement, Sidney describes the feelings of her and of her lover, Pyrocles, captive also and separated from her. Although Pyrocles did not yet know of Philoclea's scourging, yet his measure of grief was full because he was powerless to help:

> for well he knew the confidence *Philoclea* had in him, and well he knew *Philoclea* had cause to have confidence: and all troden under foot by the wheele of senselesse Fortune. Yet if there be that imperious power in the soule, as it can deliver knowledge to another without bodilie organs: so vehement were the workings of their spirites, as one mette with other; though themselves perceaved it not, but only thought it to be the doubling of their owne loving fancies. And that was the onely worldly thing, whereon *Philoclea* rested her minde, that she knewe she should die beloved of *Pyrocles,* and should die rather than be false to *Pyrocles.*

This high speculation on the telepathy of souls and the dignity of Philoclea's single-hearted love were so far from any possibility of being vulgar that Sidney can safely put them into simple language. And in its simplicity the passage is both moving and deliberately contrasted with the mannered account of the scourging itself.

To sum up my argument so far, I have sought to show by examples that in his revised *Arcadia* Sidney commands a style of considerable range, a range that admits the possibility of the work attaining to the rank of epic.

I come now to the nature of *Arcadia* as a whole. Like Spenser, Sidney had current critical theory in mind when he wrote *Arcadia,* however little the reader is aware of such a remembrance. His claim that a poem need not be in verse and that Xenophon wrote a prose epic had been made already by Trissino and Cinthio. Scaliger and Tasso had approximated the *Ethiopian History* to the epic. When Sidney revised *Arcadia* on the model of Xenophon and Heliodorus he knew, and meant others to know, that he followed the critical lead of western Europe. Trissino and other Italians had demanded the marvellous; and Sidney in recounting the amazing feats of valour performed by Pyrocles and Musidorus, the shipwrecks, the disguise of Pyrocles as an Amazon (destined to be the subject of a king's and a queen's infatuate love), the drugging of Basilius and his supposed death, and the accident of Euarchus having to condemn his own son to death sought not merely to delight his readers but to fulfil the epic obligation to astonish. Tasso thought the epic amplitude should not exceed what the average human memory could deal with; and Sidney's revised *Arcadia,* though it defeats the average modern memory, would have just been within the power of the better-exercised Elizabethan. Tasso thought too that the characters should represent a single quality of mind; and it would be easy to see, for instance, in Basilius foolish curiosity, in Cecropia pride, in Pyrocles courtesy, in Philoclea sweetness of disposition, and so on. K. O. Myrick has written on Sidney's knowledge of the Italian critics [in his *Sir Philip Sidney as a Literary Craftsman,* 1935], and it may well be that he was especially aware of Minturno. But one must not forget that debts of English writers to Italian critics may derive just as well from a kind of common pool of their ideas known through talk and detached from any particular critic. Sidney may have contributed to that pool himself, but he may also have drawn from it notions the contributors of which are unknown. The main point is that Sidney was aware of the gist of Italian theories of the epic and that he revised his *Arcadia* in the light of that awareness. And the most important single conclusion from the drift of this paragraph is to confirm the evidence of the *Defence of Poesie* that Sidney meant his new *Arcadia* to be a heroic poem.

Like Spenser, Sidney classicised: only more effectively and more extensively. Spenser claimed to have begun his action in the middle but intended to postpone any account of the beginning so long that the effect of his act would have lacked force. Sidney too begins at a far advanced stage of his story, but he does not wait too long before informing us of the past history of Basilius, Euarchus, and the two princes by related narrative. Much of the fighting is medieval, but the great battle between the forces of Basilius and Amphialus is predominantly Virgilian. The same kind of thing is true of the characters. Euarchus, the two princes, and two princesses are, humanly speaking, perfect. They do not conform to Aristotle's definition of the tragic hero. Cecropia, on the other hand, is un-Aristotelian in her complete badness. But Sidney makes Basilius and Amphialus Aristotelian. Basilius was a good king but corrupted by a foolish curiosity about the future: a curiosity that led him to deplorable acts and much trouble in compensation. Amphialus was naturally noble but he had the failing of being too much under his mother's influence. He becomes greatly but not irretrievably corrupted. It looks as if in revising *Arcadia* Sidney wished to cross the medieval unmitigatedness of most of his characters by Aristotelian elements. The resultant mixture of medieval and classical elements has a strange air today but caused no surprise to the Elizabethans.

In another way, too, Sidney is more modern and less medieval than Spenser. Though there may be incidental references to actual persons, though for instance Philisides and Myra may be Sidney and Penelope Devereux, there is no large allegory dominating the book. The characters are firmly attached to the story; none of them even begins to turn into a personification of a quality. Spenser's Malbecco, once a jealous old man, ceased to be human and became Jealousy, living in a cave on a cliff. There is nothing in the least like this in *Arcadia;* and if, as said above, Basilius, for instance, can be made to stand for foolish curiosity, this happens not in the reading but by a process of deduction after having read. Again, *Arcadia* is like the *Lusiad* and unlike the *Faerie Queene* in having nothing to do with the theme of the soul's pilgrimage. Some of the characters may be educated by experience; but no one of them stands for Everyman, and the experiences are not arranged in the pattern of partial success, failure, repentance, regeneration, and triumph. Pamela and Philoclea are indeed tested in prison and through the test perfected; but they do not have to retrace their steps to the true road they had forsaken. They have never left that road and merely proceed further along it.

But in one principal matter the *Faerie Queene* and *Arcadia* are alike: they are both concerned with the fashioning of a gentleman. Indeed, whatever the difference between the two in their actuality, their authors had the same intentions. Spenser said his aim was 'to fashion a gentleman or noble person in vertuous and gentle discipline' and he divided his discipline into the ethical and the political. Sidney's aim was the same, but in what he completed of *Arcadia* he included that political education which Spenser said he might one day demonstrate in action through his Arthur after he had succeeded to the throne.

It is important to be clear on this main aim of *Arcadia,* for usually it has been missed. In the first paragraph of this [essay] I mentioned the recent change of opinion on the book's nature. For some two hundred years opinion, with some notable exceptions, thought of *Arcadia* as remote and fantastic, as presenting a world of make-believe, once enjoyed as an entertaining refuge from the realities of ordinary life. Scholars have denied this opinion and have especially stressed the work's political seriousness. But if you do so too earnestly, you risk falling into another error.

And for this error there are reasons. For one thing, Fulke Greville is very emphatic about the politics of *Arcadia,* and he, as Sidney's intimate friend, possesses authority. Greville spoke of *Arcadia* as an absolute repertory of every kind of political example. For another, the *Old Arcadia,* though more romantically erotic than the new, is, where it is serious, relatively more political. There, the main theme, apart from the love-making, is the political disaster of Basilius's retirement, the consequent insurrection, the ultimate chaos, and the final intervention of Euarchus. The political chaos is indeed the climax of the plot; and the contrast between Basilius, the king in name but not in deed, and Euarchus, the perfect ruler, not seeking war but tested in wars not of his own choosing, is the grand contrast that gives reason to the whole book. Some scholars write as if the same was true of the revised *Arcadia;* but they are wrong. It is too easy to include in the revised *Arcadia* the portions of the old attached to it by the Countess of Pembroke for the 1593 edition. But Sidney might have altered these drastically, including the end with its main stress on the unflinching political justice of Euarchus. Anyhow, in the authentic *Arcadia* Sidney did alter the main stress of seriousness from politics to ethics and religion, and I cannot conceive that he would not have carried this process through. In the revised *Arcadia* the culminating episodes concern Pamela and Philoclea in prison and the perfecting of their characters through their display of Christian patience and fortitude in unjust persecution. When the revised version breaks off, Pyrocles and Musidorus have not yet reached the degree of perfection to which their betrothed princesses have arrived. Musidorus was impatient in his courtship and attempted to kiss Pamela before that stage had been reached, incurring her indignant censure. Pyrocles attempted suicide in captivity, when he thought he saw Philoclea's execution. It is probable that if Sidney had carried through his revision he would have made the patience of Musidorus and Pyrocles under the mistaken sentence of Euarchus match the patience of Pamela and Philoclea when in captivity to Cecropia. In *Old Arcadia* it is the ethical theme of friendship that is most prominent at this place, each prince begging for his own death in place of the other's. Not that Sidney need have removed this theme in revising; but I believe he would have introduced a more definitely religious tone in accordance with the powerfully religious tone of the culminating episode of Pamela and Philoclea in prison. Only when the two princes had cleansed themselves of worldly desires and even transcended their passionate friendship would they be worthy husbands of the two female 'confessors.' Through such a cleansing they would be the dominant figures of the last scene; Euarchus, still important, would become relatively less so; and the purely political contrast between Basilius and Euarchus would be subordinated to the theme of educating two princes and two princesses in the virtues—ethical, political, and religious—appropriate to their sex and rank. And the example of this educational process would be the supreme justification of the book and the means of raising it to the epic height.

This interpretation of the ground of *Arcadia* seems to me undoubted. It also approximates Sidney to Spenser. Like Spenser, Sidney passed from pagan ethics to Christian; from the realm of Nature to the realm of Grace. And in so doing he fulfilled what his contemporaries would undoubtedly have considered the duty of the most serious kind of poet. It is here that we should remember that Greville spoke not only of the political didacticism of *Arcadia* but . . . of its comprehensive moral virtue. Such virtue could not but include the ethics of the Christian religion.

As Sidney makes the education of the four princely young people his central theme, so he carefully arranges them in a pattern. Musidorus, the elder prince, is a more purely masculine character than Pyrocles, the younger. Pamela, the elder princess, has more male pride and resolution in her than her entirely feminine younger sister, Philoclea. (Surely Goldsmith modelled his account of Olivia and Sophia at the beginning of the *Vicar of Wakefield* on the corresponding account of Pamela and Philoclea in *Arcadia.*) As J. F. Danby noticed, Pamela combines woman-and-man, and Pyrocles man-and-woman. But Sidney does not pair these two. It is the more purely masculine Musidorus who is set to cope with the more powerful woman, Pamela; and the more sensitive Pyrocles to understand and manage the more feminine woman, Philoclea. Danby points out that Pyrocles's disguise as an Amazon is not a mere piece of romantic ornament but expresses a symbolic truth: the genuinely feminine element in Pyrocles. And he claims, I think rightly, that this symbolic significance disinfects, as it were, the queer complication of events—the infatuation of Basilius and Gynecia—this disguise occasions. Certainly, this disguise is the nearest approach to the Spenserian habit of making characters shift along the scale from realism to abstraction. Anyhow, it warns us to be chary of approximating the conditions governing the acts it occasions, to those of ordinary life. If we do so approximate them, the double infatuation of the king and queen, the one old the other no longer young, is both ridiculously improbable and slightly disgusting. Kept in the more abstract realm dictated by the emblematic nature of the disguise, it qualifies as a series of moral examples of what to avoid. To revert to the treatment of the four main characters, Danby puts the education which they undergo in terms of Sidney's pronouncement in the *Defence of Poesie* that Homer's Ulysses exemplified the virtues of patience and magnanimity. And these terms suggest aptly enough that combination of the active, Aristotelian, virtues with the Christian virtues of patience and humility which the Christian humanism of the Renaissance postulated. This double process of education proceeds briefly as follows. Musidorus and Pyrocles are intensely active men, whether in war or in peaceful government. And one of the principal themes of the book is the contrast between this activity and the fugitive and cloistered life of Basilius. In the revised *Arcadia* Sidney inserted quite near the beginning a long new episode, that of the war between the Helots and the Lacedemonians. It occurs immediately after the account of Basilius's retirement and it contains a duel between the two princes, each unknown to the other and now the principal fighters on opposite sides, and an account of their masterly statesmanship in settling the war, once they recognise each other. Having thus proved themselves in magnanimity, they fall victims to the discipline of love, a passion uniting the provinces of action and contemplation, and they end by having to submit in Christian humility to the prospect of abandoning the fruits of all their virtuous active elements. Pamela and Philoclea have less scope in action; yet they make themselves felt as great ladies, condemning the course their father has chosen and ready to take their part, when called to do so, in the exacting life of head of a great married establishment. The great lady of Tudor times was in her way as much a governor as her husband. Their ordeal and their Christian conduct in prison have already been mentioned.

In making the education of the princes and princesses the central theme of **Arcadia** I have no wish to minimise the amount of political doctrine it contains, or the zest with which Sidney writes of politics. Out of many possible illustrations of this zest I choose a passage from the end of Musidorus's account of the state into which the kingdom of Macedonia had fallen, through misgovernment, when his uncle Euarchus came to the throne:

> Hence grew a very dissolution of all estates, while the great men (by the nature of ambition never satisfied) grew factious among themselves: and the underlings, glad indeede to be underlings to them they hated lest, to preserve them from such they hated most. Men of vertue suppressed, lest their shining should discover the others filthines; and at length vertue itself almost forgotten, when it had no hopefull end whereunto to be directed; olde men long nusled in corruption, scorning them that would seeke reformation; yong men very fault-finding; but very faultie; and so to newfanglenes both of manners, apparrell, and each thing els, by the custome of self-guiltie evill, glad to change though oft for a worse; merchandise abused, and so townes decayed for want of just and naturall libertie; offices, even of judging soules, sold; publique defences neglected; and in summe, (lest too long I trouble you) all awrie, and (which wried it to the most wrie course of all) witte abused, rather to faine reason why it should be amisse, then how it should be amended.

But Sidney's zest for politics was not just vague and general; it was founded on detailed knowledge and conviction. Greenlaw has written well on this topic. He points out, for instance, how well diversified are some of the bad political characters and how well grounded in Machiavelli are some of their acts. There is Plexirtus, bastard son of the King of Paphlagonia and brother of Leonatus (corresponding to Edmund, Gloucester, and Edgar in *King Lear*), who usurps the throne, uses foreign mercenaries to keep it, blinds his father, and seeks to murder his brother. By carefully hiding his faults he gets the service of good men. And he ends as the completely bad ruler, the cunning Machiavellian tyrant. Then there is Clinias, the plotting coward, once an actor and hence a master of insincere oratory, the venal tool of wicked employers. And then there is Amphialus, a more important and a more complicated figure. He is not radically bad but accepts the results of his mother's plotting. Acting on this he holds the rightful heirs to the throne of Arcadia, to which he aspires, in captivity. He then foments rebellion and in particular gathers the various malcontents of the realm around him. In his strategy he follows the advice of Machiavelli, paying especial attention to his citadel, his supplies, and the kind of

men he has near him. In choosing these men he is careful to turn their vices to his own advantage. In arranging tournaments he is careful to preserve the outward appearance of courtesy, but he actually uses them to advertise his own powers and to establish his own influence: in accordance with the principles laid down in the twenty-first chapter of the *Prince*.

The mention of these three characters from outside the range of Basilius's household prompts my next observation. Although the education of the four princely young people with the important though subordinate theme of the contrast between Basilius and Euarchus constitutes a powerful central theme and although the main structural lines may be classical, there is a vast wealth of subordinate detail. To describe this adequately is impossible in a small space; and the most I can do is to present a few samples.

For all the classicising there is a great amount of detail derived from the medieval romance. Sidney may copy Virgil in the big battle scene between the forces of Amphialus and Basilius he inserted in the revised **Arcadia,** but much of the fighting and the jousting is in the style of the medieval romances, for instance the duel already mentioned between Musidorus and Pyrocles unknown to each other, Phalantus's beauty challenge, and Amphialus's reputation for being 'the best knight in the world'. Or take this sentence:

> And so went they, making one place succeed to an other, in like uncertaintie to their search, manie times encountring strange adventures, worthy to be registered in the roulles of fame.

The evident desire here to amplify, to swell the lake of adventure into a sea, is characteristically medieval and quite different from the classical desire to omit everything that does not promote the business in hand.

But in spite of much remote medievalising, close observation of nature, human and animal, is constantly breaking in. Sidney is not a whit behind contemporary drama in this respect. When near the beginning Musidorus, weak from the shipwreck and dulled with grief at his loss of Pyrocles, walks with the shepherds to Arcadia, at first he cannot listen, but gradually their talk penetrates his consciousness. When Basilius and Gynecia are both in love with Pyrocles in his Amazon disguise, Gynecia one night, while Basilius slept, gave vent to her grief:

> More she would have said but that *Basilius* (awaked with the noise) tooke her in his armes, and began to comfort her; the goodman thinking, it was all for a jealous love of him: which humor if she would a little have maintained, perchance it might have weakned his new conceavd fancies. But he finding her answeres wandring from the purpose, left her to her selfe.

That is nature indeed. Or take this description of a spaniel hunting duck:

> There the Princesses determining to bath themselves, though it was so priviledged a place, upon paine of death, as no bodie durst presume to come thither, yet for the more surety, they looked round about, and could see nothing but

a water spaniell, who came downe the river, shewing that he hunted for a duck, and with a snuffling grace, disdaining that his smelling force coulde not as well prevaile thorow the water, as thorow the aire; and therefore wayting with his eye, to see whether he could espie the duckes getting up again: but then a little below them failing of his purpose, he got out of the river, and shaking off the water (as great men do their friends, now he had no further cause to use it) inweeded himselfe so, as the Ladies lost the further marking his sportfulnesse.

There is no doubt here of the reality of the animal.

'Separate your selfe a little (if it be possible) from your selfe, and let your owne mind looke upon your owne proceedings', said Musidorus to Pyrocles, rebuking him for having assumed the disguise of an Amazon; and Sidney himself had the faculty of self-criticism. Having it, he is naturally able to see things in a comical as well as in a serious light. Some of his comedy falls flat today; some gets home. Basilius, old but in love with Zelmane, is at times truly ludicrous, as when he sings her a sonnet,

> which being done he looked verie curiously upon himselfe, sometimes fetching a little skippe, as if he had said, his strength had not yet forsaken him.

The romance of Phalantus and Artesia ends in comedy. Theirs was an adolescent, exhibitionist passion. Phalantus had been touring Greece upholding his beauty-challenge on behalf of Artesia in tournaments. He prospered until beaten by the ill-apparelled knight, who was Pyrocles disguised.

> But the victorie being by the judges given, and the trumpets witnessed to the ill apparelled Knight; *Phalantus* digrace was ingrieved in lieu of comforte by *Artesia;* who telling him she never lookt for other, bad him seeke some other mistresse. He excusing himselfe, and turning over the fault to Fortune, Then let that be your ill Fortune too (saide she) that you have lost me. Nay truely Madame (saide *Phalantus*) it shall not be so: for I thinke the losse of such a Mistresse will proove a great gaine: and so concluded; to the sporte of *Basilius,* to see young folkes love, that came in maskt with so great pompe, goe out with so little constancie.

The satisfaction of Basilius, doomed from the beginning both as elderly lover and as lover of a girl who is really a man, adds irony to straightforward comedy.

Such are some of the strains of *Arcadia,* and there are others. Sidney had a brilliantly varied mind, and it is not on the side of variety that any weaknesses as an epic writer are likely to be found.

In the matter of structure we have to distinguish between what Sidney did accomplish and what he could have accomplished. Sidney had a massively powerful as well as a brilliantly active brain and a will capable of the highest efforts. If he had dedicated brain and will exclusively or even principally to literature he could have carried through the structure of a serious long work with full suc-

cess. Even with the partial attention he gave to literature he accomplished a good deal in his fragmentary revised *Arcadia.* He had a firm conception of his main scheme, the education of four princely persons, and he had all his details firmly in mind. And, in view of the number and diversity of the details, this was a great feat. But he did not achieve the further structural feat of keeping all the details in suspension and not finally settled till the very end, so that every addition and subtraction of detail was made with reference to its influence on all the rest. Sidney does indeed suffer from a lack of moderation in his structure. He is a bountiful writer and he does not sufficiently heed the effect of his bounty on the aims he most has in view. And that effect, though certainly not to obliterate, is partly to blur those aims. Sidney did not make his supremely difficult task of structure any easier by revising old work instead of writing something quite new. He begins brilliantly, as I have already indicated, by two large contrasts; those between the high Platonic passions of the two shepherds and the ugly actuality of the shipwreck, and between the politically irresponsible retirement of Basilius and the martial prowess and political sagacity of Musidorus and Pyrocles in the part they take in the war between the Lacedemonians and the Helots. Most of this is new writing. But as soon as Sidney begins incorporating large portions of *Old Arcadia,* his grasp becomes less comprehensive and more confined to whatever detail he has in hand. Ben Jonson in his talks with Drummond recorded the legend that Sidney intended to turn his *Arcadia* into an Arthuriad. He had better have done so. To amalgamate old and new material into an organic whole was more difficult than to write a new work. Anyhow, this is certain: if Sidney had lived and had found the leisure to bend all his powers to the epic task, he could quite have transcended what of *Arcadia* there now survives.

I come now to the question of *Arcadia*'s choric character. . . . In England, as in no other European country after the collapse of Portugal in the Battle of Alcazar, national sentiment was likely to be a principal subject of epic writing. And it was the subject likely to spread its appeal to the widest extent of the community. Shakespeare in his History Plays best satisfied such a demand. But there was another epic theme appealing to another kind of public. To repeat words I used when writing on Shakespeare [in *Shakespeare's History Plays*],

> it is the idea of education or 'nurture'. The political theme, in the form adopted by Shakespeare, was peculiarly English: a set of generalisations given special vitality through the favoured position in which by good luck England found herself. The idea of education was the great Renaissance motive, applicable equally to Christian and Stoic, Protestant and Catholic, translatable into terms as well of knowing yourself as of losing your life to gain it.

Arcadia is absolutely at one with its age in dealing primarily with this great theme. Its English vogue would not have extended as far down the social scale as Shakespeare's Histories. But for the educated classes it was their book from the start. They hailed it with astonishing rapidity and they were astonishingly faithful in their admiration. Before ever *Arcadia* was printed, in 1588, Abraham Fraunce chose Sidney as one of the seven authors through whom to illustrate the use of rhetorical figures, the others being Homer, Virgil, Tasso, Du Bartas, Boscan, and Garcilasso. His editor has noted that Fraunce habitually gives Sidney the place of honour after Homer and Virgil and that half the quotations are from the prose of *Arcadia.* About eleven years later John Hoskins published his *Directions for Speech and Style,* which his editor says 'remains chiefly as a document witnessing to the charm exerted by the person and writings of Sir Philip Sidney'. In this book it is *Arcadia* that above all provides the model of good writing and of the instructive creation of character. In its substance and its style alike the late Elizabethans found it to speak with their own authentic voice. It was soon translated into other tongues, a diffusion which no play of Shakespeare enjoyed by anywhere near so early a date. A further sign of the hold *Arcadia* had on men's minds is the persistent attempts to complete and continue it. There were six of these in the first half of the seventeenth century, not to speak of the narrative poems deriving from it.

I have not yet committed myself to saying how Sidney ranks among the great literary figures, of what quality is his work . . . , how deeply he moves us. The answer is

that, besides impressing us by his commanding intellectual grasp, as shown by the grand basic scheme of *Arcadia,* he can achieve writing of great beauty and intensity, though through means now unfamiliar, and that he can build up characters who have it in them to acquire the kind of proverbial quality that marks one kind of distinguished character-creation. The taste which in recent years would judge a long and ambitious narrative rests unconsciously on works whose highest places consist of dialogue or rumination at moments of intense mental action or development: Andromache saying farewell to Hector; Dido blaming Aeneas; Lady Macbeth goading her husband; Jeanie Deans pleading for her sister's life; Dorothea Casaubon talking on the meaning of marriage; Anna Karenina caught in the transports of jealousy. And such taste is apt to miss intensity reached by other means. Now Sidney in places corresponding to those just mentioned seems to let us down. Instead of allowing his characters to say the words their passion appears to dictate he fills their mouths with rhetoric apparently fabricated on a preconceived code of decorum. In compensation he touches his greatest heights through the isolated display made by this or that character. He had what you could call a heraldic mind and when he writes most intensely he does so in a manner more plastic or pictorial than literary and progressive. I have given one example in the description of the shepherdess Urania pulling the thorn from the lamb's foot. To establish my point I give two more; and it is worth noting that none of the three occurs in the old *Arcadia.* While Musidorus was posing as the shepherd Dorus, in order to secure Pamela's attention, he procured a horse and made her a display of his horsemanship. This is how Pamela, in talk with Philoclea, builds up the picture of him riding:

Title page of the first edition of Sidney's *Arcadia.*

But oh how well it did with *Dorus,* to see with what a grace he presented him selfe before me on horseback, making majestie wait upon humblenes? how at the first, standing stil with his eies bent upon me, as though his motions were chained to my looke, he so staide till I caused *Mopsa* bid him doo something upon his horse: which no sooner said, but (with a kinde rather of quick gesture, then shew of violence) you might see him come towards me, beating the ground in so due time, as no daunce can observe better measure. If you remember the ship we saw once, when the Sea went hie upon the coast of *Argos;* so went the beast: But he (as if Centaur-like he had bene one peece with the horse) was no more moved, then one is with the going of his own legges: and in effect so did he command him, as his owne limmes, for though he had both spurres and wande, they seemed rather markes of soveraintie, then instruments of punishment; his hand and legge (with most pleasing grace) commanding without threatning, and rather remembring then chastising, at lest if sometimes he did, it was so stolen, as neyther our eyes could discerne it, nor the horse with any chaunce did complaine of it, he ever going so just with the horse, either foorth right, or turning, that it seemed as he borrowed the horse's body, so he lent the horse his minde: in the turning one might perceive the bridle-hand somthing gently

stir, but indeed so gently, as it rather did distill
vertue, then use violence.

That is no mere supererogatory description but the distillation into a single self-sufficient picture of Sidney's passionate belief in the chastening discipline that elevates the natural gifts of both beast and man to the highest reaches of which they are capable. It is eloquence but of very powerful significance, and very moving if properly understood.

And here is the description of Pamela during her supreme testing-time in prison doing embroidery work:

> Cecropia threatning in her selfe to run a more ragged race with *Philoclea,* went to her sister *Pamela:* who that day having wearied her selfe with reading, and with the height of her hart disdaining to keepe companie with any of the Gentlewomen appointed to attende her, whome she accounted her jaylours, was woorking uppon a purse certaine Roses and Lillies, as by the finenesse of the worke, one might see she had borrowed her wittes of the sorow that owed them, and lent them wholy to that exercise. For the flowers she had wrought, caried such life in them, that the cunningest painter might have learned of her needle: which with so prety a maner made his careers to and fro through the cloth, as if the needle it selfe would have bene loth to have gone fromward such a mistres, but that it hoped to return thenceward very quickly againe: the cloth loking with many eies upon her, and lovingly embracing the wounds she gave it: the sheares were also at hand to behead the silke, that was growne to short. And if at any time she put her mouth to bite it off, it seemed, that where she had beene long in making of a Rose with her hand, she would in an instant make Roses with her lips; as the Lillies seemed to have their whitenesse, rather of the hande that made them, then of the matter whereof they were made; and that they grew there by the Sunnes of her eyes, and were refreshed by the most in discomfort comfortable ayre, which an unwares sigh might bestow upon them. But the colours for the grounde were so well chosen, neither sullenly darke, nor glaringly lightsome, and so well proportioned, as that, though much cunning were in it, yet it was but to serve for an ornament of the principall woorke; that it was not without marvaile to see, howe a minde which could cast a carelesse semblant upon the greatest conflictes of Fortune, coulde commaunde it selfe to take care for so small matters. Neither had she neglected the daintie dressing of her selfe: but as it had ben her marriage time to Affliction, she rather semed to remember her owne worthinesse, then the unworthinesse of her husband. For well one might perceyve she had not rejected the counsaile of a glasse, and that her handes had pleased themselves, in paying the tribute of undeceyving skill, to so high perfections of Nature.

Here most readers would echo Johnson's condemnation of *Lycidas:* that 'it is not to be considered as the effusion of a real passion; for passion runs not after remote allusions and obscure opinions'. And like him they would be

wrong. For Sidney has elaborated a passionately felt emblem of fortitude dressing it in the *sprezzatura,* or nonchalance, which in the opinion of Castiglione put the last touch of perfection on the courtier. By concentrating so entirely on her embroidery when her life was in peril, Pamela both manifested a consummate power of will and achieved the height of aristocratic irony by being lighthearted over great things and serious over small. And though in other places Sidney may elaborate for no better reason than bare decorum, he does so here in the very manner of his own Pamela, clothing a tragic feeling in the artifice of fine writing. One may best get the sense of Sidney's picture of Pamela embroidering by imagining the scene painted: the girl dressed in exquisite finery, her attention quite riveted to her work, and some symbol of death drawn faintly in the background.

If people habitually read **Arcadia** they would find certain characters drawn powerfully enough to become as it were proverbial. These do not include the two princes, who, though differentiated up to a point, have both to be such impeccable soldiers and politicians and such faithful friends to each other that they end by lacking great individual emphasis. But Pamela and Philoclea could well become classic examples of two feminine types, not inferior in their way to Rosalind and Celia in *As You Like It.* The other two great characters are Cecropia and her son Amphialus. In Cecropia, born princess of Argos, Sidney created a convincing picture of declared pride and forthright ambition. She has not the least doubt that she had the right to all that she wants; and she uses words that well express her confidence. This is how she describes to Amphialus her state when she married Amphialus's father, then heir presumptive of Arcadia, Basilius having given out his intention of remaining a bachelor:

> for else you may be sure the King of *Argos,* nor his daughter would have suffered their Royall bloud to be stained with the base name of subjection. So that I came into this countrie as apparant Princesse thereof, and accordingly was courted, and followed of all the Ladies of this countrie. My porte and pompe did well become a King of *Argos* daughter: in my presence their tongues were turned into eares, and their eares were captive unto my tongue. Their eyes admired my Majestie, and happy was he or she, on whom I would suffer the beames thereof to fall. Did I goe to church? it seemed the very Gods wayted for me, their devotions not being solemnized till I was ready. Did I walke abroad to see any delight? Nay, my walking was the delight it selfe: for to it was the concourse; one thrusting upon another, who might shewe him selfe most diligent and serviceable towards me: my sleepes were inquired after, and my wakings never unsaluted: the very gate of my house full of principall persons, who were glad, if their presents had received a gratefull acceptation. And in this felicitie wert thou borne, the very earth submitting it selfe unto thee to be troden on as by his Prince.

Energy pulses through this speech; and though her lofty pride degenerates into furious spite Cecropia never ceases to be a woman on a grand scale. Amphialus is a truly tragic character, well intentioned but dragged against his will and finally without his knowledge into a position that he abhors. His genuine and honourable love of Philoclea cheats him into misguided agreement with his mother's prompting to court her while in captivity. Sidney presents his consequent plight with great power.

Sidney thus shows himself able to shape comprehensively, to write greatly, and to create great characters. He was a man of epic capacity. On the other hand he died young; and of his short life he put much of the best into action. He could not therefore achieve a true epic; and *Arcadia* is no more than an epicising fragment, successful in part and of great promise. It is not for us to complain that he did not distil all of himself drop by drop into literature. We are lucky enough to know much about his life; and there is every reason why we should think of his life and writings together. So thinking, we shall acknowledge that he did much in each and that the sum leaves no doubt of the great height of human distinction to which he rose. (pp. 297-319)

> *E. M. W. Tillyard, "Sidney," in his* The English Epic and Its Background, *Oxford University Press, 1954, pp. 294-319.*

C. S. Lewis   (essay date 1954)

[*Lewis is considered one of the foremost Christian and mythopoeic authors of the twentieth century. He is regarded as a formidable logician and Christian polemicist, a perceptive literary critic, and—most highly—as a writer of fantasy literature. Lewis also held instructoral posts at Oxford and Cambridge, where he was an acknowledged authority on medieval and Renaissance literature. A traditionalist in his approach to life and art, he opposed the modern movement in literary criticism toward biographical and psychological interpretation. In place of this, he practiced and propounded a theory of criticism that stresses the importance of the author's intent, rather than the reader's presuppositions and prejudices. Here, he assesses strengths and weaknesses in* Astrophil and Stella *and the* Arcadia, *suggesting that a proper appreciation of Sidney's works depends on the reader's ability to sympathize with the literary and social customs of the sixteenth century.*]

[Sidney] is dazzling. He is that rare thing, the aristocrat in whom the aristocratic ideal is really embodied. Leicester's nephew, Pembroke's brother-in-law, an eligible *parti* for a princess, painted by Veronese, poet and patron of poets, statesman, knight, captain—fate has dealt such hands before, but they have very seldom been so well played. Little of the Spenser whom we love is to be found in the letters to Harvey or the *View of the State of Ireland;* but the Sidney revealed in his life and letters is just what the author of the *Arcadia* ought to have been. He is a young man ambitious of learning, anxious to read Aristotle in the Greek, though French will do for Plutarch, sufficiently of his age to like the *Imprese* of Ruscelli and to quote Buchanan, yet independent enough of its worst folly to call Ciceronianism 'the cheife abuse of Oxford'. He is a serious-minded young man, zealous for the whole European *respublica Christiana* (of which he thinks Rome a *putridum membrum*) and fervent as Ascham against the

corruptions of Italy. He is a keen student of affairs, policies, constitutions, but also of 'the true points of Honour', best learned from the French and Spaniards 'wherein if they seeme ouer curious, it is an easie matter to cutt of, when a man sees the bottome'. He complains (perhaps yielding somewhat to the fashion) of melancholy, but there is little of it to be found in his letters; least of all when he is once launched on his utterly hopeless command in the Netherlands. It is then, as one critic rightly says, that his words breathe a certain exaltation. If the Queen were the fountain, he would see nothing ahead but despair. But she is only a means. Even if she cried off altogether 'other springes would ryse to help this action'; for we are engaged against 'the great abusers of the world'. Before he sailed he had 'cast his count' not of danger only, but of 'want and disgrace'. In those last few months the man rises above the author. His care for 'the miserable souldier', and the famous sacrifice of the cup of water at Zutphen, are traits we might not have anticipated from the *Arcadia.*

Apart from the *Lady of May* (1578), a trifle now chiefly remembered for the possible connexion between its Rombus and Shakespeare's Holofernes, Sidney's poetical output consists of the Arcadian pieces and the *Astrophel and Stella,* with some poems added to it in the folio of 1598.

It is not on the Arcadian group that Sidney's lasting fame depends, but they establish his position as the pioneer of Golden poetry. This is best seen by comparing him with one of his predecessors. Here are three lines of Sackville:

> O Sorrow, alas, sith Sorrow is thy name,
> And that to thee this drere doth well pertaine,
> In vayne it were to seeke to cease the same . . .

And here three of Sidney's:

> You Gote-heard Gods that love the grassie
>   mountaines,
> You Nimphes that haunt the springs in pleasant
>   vallies,
> You Satyrs joyde with free and quiet
>   forrests . . .

Everyone feels the clogged, laborious movement of the first, the sense of liberation and ease in the second. And some of the causes are obvious; the hissing alliterations in Sackville, and the lack of vocalic melody; against this, in Sidney, the admirable variety of vowels (*Nimphes* and *springs* being the only exception) and the sub-alliterations of G-GR, FR-F. But there is a difference even more important than this. In the Sackville the words which make any appeal to the emotions or imagination are almost lost in dull connectives. Thus in the second line the noun *drere* is the only live word. In Sidney every single word, except the inevitable *that*'s and *the*'s and *with,* does something for us; there are gods, nymphs, and satyrs who love and haunt and enjoy, grass on the mountains, water and pleasure in the valleys, and, best of all, liberty and silence in the woods. There are no non-conductors. (pp. 324-26)

In his Arcadian poems Sidney offers a much wider range of metrical experiment than Spenser. He has a more delicate ear and is more learned in the art. The poems which stand out will usually be found to do so by some novelty or other excellence in their music. Such are 'The ladd

Philisides', which may have suggested the stanza of Milton's *Hymn* on the Nativity, 'Get hence foul grief', which pleases by its metre alone, and the stately 'Why dost thou haste?' Even the pieces in classical metres, which Sidney understands far better than either Harvey or Spenser, are not all failures. The Asclepiads ('O sweet woods') have real charm.

Since *Astrophel and Stella* is the first full-blown sonnet-sequence we have met, something must be said about that misunderstood Form. The difference between the *Vita Nuova* and Petrarch's *Rime* is that Petrarch has abandoned the prose links; and it was they that carried the narrative. The first thing to grasp about the sonnet sequence is that it is not a way of telling a story. It is a form which exists for the sake of prolonged lyrical meditation, chiefly on love but relieved from time to time by excursions into public affairs, literary criticism, compliment, or what you will. External events—a quarrel, a parting, an illness, a stolen kiss—are every now and then mentioned to provide themes for the meditation. Thus you get an island, or (if the event gives matter for more than one piece) an archipelago, of narrative in the lyrical sea. It is not there in order to interest you in the history of a love affair, after the manner of the novelist. To concentrate on these islands, and to regard the intervening pieces as mere links between them, is as if you valued a Mozartian opera chiefly for the plot. You are already turning away from the work of art which has been offered you. To go further and seek for the 'real' (that is, the biographical) story is to turn your back on it altogether. To go further still and to start rearranging the pieces in the hope of mending the story or squaring it with other biographical data is, in my opinion, to commit yourself to unresisted illusion. If you arrange things to make a story, then of course a story will result from your rearrangement; have we not all done it as a parlour game with pictures torn at random from the daily papers?

Facts may, of course, lie behind (and any distance behind) a work of art. But the sonnet sequence does not exist to tell a real, or even a feigned, story. And we must not listen at all to critics who present us with the preposterous alternative of 'sincerity' (by which they mean autobiography) and 'literary exercise'. The only poet (unless I am mistaken) who has edited Sidney, Mr. Drinkwater, makes short work of that dichotomy. 'Look in thy heart and write' is good counsel for poets; but when a poet looks in his heart he finds many things there besides the actual. That is why, and how, he is a poet.

The narrative, still more the biographical, reading of a sonnet sequence may obscure its real qualities. Where the poet (thinking symphonically, not historically) has put in a few lighter or more reflective sonnets for relief or variety, the reader who wants a 'human document' will thrust them aside as frigid and miss any structural fitness they may really have. Something like this has happened with Sidney. Scholars draw a distinction between the first thirty-two sonnets and the rest. At XXXIII the 'real' (that is, the historical) passion is supposed to begin. The change, we are told, coincides with the marriage of Penelope Devereux to Lord Rich; and XXIV, which does not fit the theo-

ry, must have been put in (as God, in some anti-Darwinian theologies, put in the fossils) to deceive us. My concern is not with the truth or falsehood of the theory, but with its inutility. Grant it true, and what have we gained? Nothing, apparently, but an obstacle to our appreciation of the first thirty-two sonnets. These seem dull only because they do not fit into the story. Read without the perverse demand for story, they will not be found to differ much from the others either in subject or merit. They introduce most of the themes on which the sequence is built. We have in them sonnets about sonnet-writing (why not? Milton writes about the epic in his epic, Pindar about odes in his odes) as we shall have again in XXXIV, L, LVI, and XC. We have glances at the outer world of moralists, *losengiers,* and impertinents; we shall meet them again in XXXV and XLVIII. The 'Platonic' solution which occupies us from LXIX to LXXI has already been hinted in XI. The direct or conceited celebration of the lady's beauty occurs as often after the thirty-third sonnet as before it. That none of the most passionate sonnets come before XXXIII is true. I know no reason why they should. The earlier pieces deal with the conflict between Love and Virtue (or 'Reason'). Structurally it is very proper that this theme should come at the beginning. Such a conflict may not interest all modern readers so much as the pictures of passion triumphant, but it interested Sidney. Pyrocles and Musidorus talk about it at great length in the *Arcadia.* It is significant that the poet makes no attempt to explain what particular circumstances threw Love and Virtue into opposition. He takes the opposition for granted. Everyone knew that Passion and Reason, or Will and Wit, were antagonists. It was assumed that they would be at loggerheads, as we assume that a dog will go for a cat. Similarly, when he deals with a lovers' quarrel (Song 10 to Sonnet XCV) he does not say what the quarrel was about. Everyone knows that lovers have quarrels. He is writing not a love story but an anatomy of love.

There is so much careless writing in *Astrophel and Stella* that malicious quotation could easily make it appear a failure. Sidney can hiss like a serpent ('Sweet swelling lips well maist thou swell'), gobble like a turkey ('Moddels such be wood globes'), and quack like a duck ('But God wot, wot not what they mean'). But *non ego paucis.* With all its faults this work towers above everything that had been done in poetry, south of the Tweed, since Chaucer died. The fourth song alone, with its hurried and (as it were) whispered metre, its inimitable refrain, its perfect selection of images, is enough to raise Sidney above all his contemporaries. Here at last a situation is not merely written about: it is created, presented, so as to compel our imaginations. Or consider Sonnet LXXI. In almost any other poet the first thirteen lines would have the air of being a mere 'build up' for the sake of the last. But Sidney's sonnet might have ended quite differently and still been equally, though diversely, admirable. Nearly all the trochaic songs hint at the incantatory music of the *Phoenix and the Turtle.* They do not quite achieve it. Lines rhythmically dead, such as 'But when their tongues could not speake' always break in and mar the spell. But to have gone so far is immense praise.

Considered historically, then, and in relation to his predecessors, Sidney is one of our most important poets. Nothing which that century had yet produced could have led us to predict the music, passion, and eloquence of *Astrophel and Stella.* It is not all in the 'sugared' manner. Sidney can come down to earth when he chooses—'He cannot love: no, no; let him alone', or even 'Is it not ill that such a beast wants hornes?' And these passages may please the modern reader as much as any. The historian . . . is more likely to notice what is unprecedented, the conceits that 'with wings of love in aire of wonder flie', the 'golden sea whose waves in curles are broken' or the

> shafts of light
> Closed with their quivers in Sleeps armorie.

Notice again how few of these words exist only for the sake of other words; notice the variety of the vowels; notice the hint, the finer spirit, of alliteration. Then consider how far it overgoes the common (though excellent) equation of eye-glances with arrows, and yet preserves it. There had been nothing like this in English before. There had hardly been anything like it in Latin; you must go back to Greeks, whom Sidney almost certainly did not know, to find a parallel.

Poetry still has its militant, though tiny, audience: but the taste for romance seems in our age to be dead, and the very corpse mutilated and mocked. Yet if we are ever to enter into the life of our ancestors we must try to appreciate the *Arcadia* as well as the *Astrophel and Stella.* For those (I am not one of them) who find it unattractive the first step must be to replace it in its setting. It was not, when Sidney wrote it, a *bizarre,* irrelevant book. Its style may not be what they now call 'functional'; no more were the architecture, clothes, furniture, and etiquette of the period that begot it. As we read it we must have in mind the ruffs, the feathers, the tapestries, the rich carvings, the mannered gardens, the elaborate courtesies. Even its sentiment was at no such distance from life as we suppose. How near it came to Sidney's own life we know; when he threw away his cuisses at Zutphen, by which he got his death wound, he was obeying a heroic punctilio worthy of Argalus or Amadis. But love could be as romantic as war. 'He told him of a gentleman who not long before found all the people bewailing the death of a gentlewoman that had lived there, and grew so in love with the description that he grew desperately melancholy and would goe to a mount where the print of her foote was cutt and lie there pining and kissing of it all the day long, till at length death concluded his languishment.' You would think that was from a heroic romance: actually, it comes from Lucy Hutchinson's memoir of her husband, and his own passion, a few pages later, is almost of the same kind. Many readers may ask whether the reality is not as foolish and tasteless as the fiction. It is a good question; and sympathetic reading of the *Arcadia* will enrich our data for answering it. To judge between one *ethos* and another, it is necessary to have got inside both, and if literary history does not help us to do so it is a great waste of labour.

Some time between 1577 and 1580 Sidney wrote for his sister a prose romance; an 'idle worke', partly written in her presence and partly sent to her sheet by sheet. In 1581

or 1582, as we know from a letter of Greville's, he began to re-write it in a more serious spirit and on a much larger scale, but left off in the middle of a sentence in Book III. This fragment was published by Ponsonby after Sidney's death in the quarto of 1590. Such a truncated text must have tormented all gentle hearts, and in 1593 the best that could now be contrived was given them in Ponsonby's folio: this reprints the fragment which had appeared in the quarto and adds Books III to V 'out of the Authors owne writings and conceits'. This composite text is the *Arcadia* which our ancestors knew. But the original 'idle worke' had not perished, and in the present century several manuscripts of it have been discovered. It was then found that this 'old *Arcadia*' differed in some respects not only from the revised fragment (as we knew it would) but also from those later parts of the Ponsonby folio which had been 'supplied' from Sidney's 'owne writings and conceits'. It thus comes about that, instead of the work which Sidney intended to leave us, we have three things: (1) The 'old' or cancelled *Arcadia* in its entirety, (2) the fragment of revised *Arcadia,* (3) the last three Books (III-V) of the cancelled *Arcadia* modified for inclusion in the folio.

The difference between the first and second is structural. The cancelled *Arcadia* had told a fairly simple tale; in the revised fragment Sidney complicated it by a labyrinth of interwoven stories in conformity with the epic practice of his time. He turned, in fact, from something like the technique of the modern novel to the technique of Spenser, Ariosto, Malory, the French prose romances, and Ovid's *Metamorphoses.* It was therefore to be expected that many modern critics, bred on the novel, should prefer the cancelled *Arcadia* to the revised; but to say that it was better, that Sidney in his revision was spoiling his work, would be rather ingenuous. Our own taste in fiction has not yet lasted as long as the taste for the interwoven sort lasted. When we find ourselves rejecting a method in which so many spirited and polished generations took pleasure, it requires great boldness—or impudence—to assume that we are in the right.

The differences between the cancelled *Arcadia* and the later parts of the folio are small but important: the two that matter most are these. In the cancelled *Arcadia,* at the end of Book III, Philoclea (under very extenuating circumstances) surrenders her virginity to Pyrocles without marriage; and earlier in the same book (under circumstances of most aggravated treachery) Musidorus is restrained from the rape of Pamela only by a timely interruption. In the corresponding parts of the folio the honour of Philoclea and the good faith of Musidorus are both preserved. This does not imply any change of morality, for the acts which are omitted in the folio had been condemned in the cancelled version. The artistic value of the change is very difficult to judge. For those of us who have been early steeped in the traditional version, the difficulty is not one of morals but of credibility. We cannot suspend our disbelief in a Musidorus who commits indecent assaults: it is as if, in some re-discovered first draft of *Emma,* we were asked to accept a Mr. Woodhouse who fought a duel with Frank Churchill. Philoclea's lapse is in comparison a trifle; and in the folio text, where so much of the scene is retained and the main purpose of the scene omitted, the result is certainly inferior.

It is tempting to assume that Lady Pembroke made these changes with no authority, in obedience to what some call her 'prudery'. But this is by no means certain. Ponsonby said that the later books were derived not from Sidney's writings only, but from his 'writings and conceits'. This may, no doubt, be merely a redundant expression; but it is equally possible that Ponsonby means what he says, and that Lady Pembroke retouched the 'writings' or manuscripts in the light of the 'conceits'—that is, of alterations which, to her knowledge, Sidney had intended to make. In revising his romance, he was turning it from a 'toyfull booke' into a prose epic which would have no need to shun 'severer eyes'. This might well have involved heroines more chaste and heroes more heroical than he had previously intended, and it would be natural enough that he should discuss these changes with his sister. It was, after all, her book.

But these questions, however interesting to the student of Sidney, do not much concern the literary historian. To him 'the **Arcadia**' must mean the composite text of 1593: it, and it alone, is the book which lived; Shakespeare's book, Charles I's book, Milton's book, Lamb's book, our own book long before we heard of textual criticism. If the recovery of the cancelled version is to prevent our looking steadily at the text which really affected the English mind, it will have been a disaster.

The two great influences on Sidney's romance are the *Arcadia* (1501) of Sannazaro and the *Ethiopian History* (fourth century A.D.) of Heliodorus. There are of course others; Malory possibly, *Amadis* probably, and Montemayor's *Diana*. But Montemayor is himself largely a disciple of Sannazaro: it is from Sannazaro and Heliodorus that the two kinds of fiction which Sidney is fusing really descend.

Sannazaro's work belongs formally to an extinct species, the Varronian *Satura Menippea* in alternating proses and metres, as used by Boethius and Alanus. Since it was originally entitled *Ecloghe* we may perhaps conclude that for Sannazaro the poems were the important thing and the intervening proses were intended merely as links. If so, his actual achievement is different from, and better than, his design. The thread of narrative in the proses, though enriched with epic material (the funeral games in XI) and romantic (the subterranean journey in XII or the Wood of Dreadful Beauty in X) is indeed very slight. But it has a momentous effect. It creates for the singing shepherds a landscape, a social structure, a whole world; a new image, only hinted by previous pastoralists, has come into existence—the image of Arcadia itself. That is why Sannazaro's work, though in one sense highly derivative—it is claimed that almost every phrase has a classical origin—is, in another, so new and so important. If Pope was able to take it for granted that 'Pastoral is an image of what they call the Golden Age', this was largely the result of Sannazaro's *Arcadia*. It was Sannazaro, more than any one else, who turned pastoral away from the harshness of Mantuan (or our own Barclay), made of it something to be pictured not in grotesque woodcuts but in the art of Poussin, and

so created one of the great dreams of humanity. To that extent he is a founder.

Heliodorus, translated by Thomas Underdowne in 1569, not from the Greek but from an intermediate Latin version, had in Sidney's time an importance which the successive narrowings of our classical tradition have since obscured. In order to see that importance we must once more remind ourselves that the word 'poesie' could cover prose fiction. We must remember the taste for interlocked and endlessly varied narrative to which the medieval romances and Italian epics equally bear witness. These facts, taken together, explain why Scaliger cites the *Aithiopica* as a model of epic construction; why Sidney and Tasso both mention it among heroic poems, and Racine (it is said) thought of turning it into a tragedy. And though it is not literature of the greatest sort, it partly deserved Scaliger's praise. The plot is cleverly devised so as to combine a breathless variety of adventure with an ultimate unity of action. This supplied the *delectare;* the *docere* was provided by the constancy, lawfulness, and (almost medieval) courtesy of the love between Theagenes and Chariclea. It was widely read. Shakespeare makes Orsino remember its 'Egyptian thief'. Fletcher in his *Shepherdess* borrows from it the taper that will not burn the chaste. Details about the 'church' and priesthood of Isis reappear in Spenser's story of Britomart. Its elaborate descriptions of dress may have encouraged an existing Elizabethan taste for such things.

From Sannazaro Sidney took over the Menippean form (though he made his proses so long that we hardly notice it) and the idea of Arcadia itself. From Heliodorus he took over the conception of the prose epic, filling his story with shipwreck, disguise, battle, and intrigue. For the battles he drew upon Homer (but no doubt, Homer strained through Virgil). The first thing we need to know about the **Arcadia** is that it is a heroic poesy; not Arcadian idyll, not even Arcadian romance, but Arcadian epic.

To call it a pastoral romance is misleading. The title seems to promise that, and the first few pages keep the promise. But almost at once Sidney leads us away from 'the shepherdish complaynts of Strephon' to a shipwreck, to the house of a country gentleman, to affairs of state, and to the royal family. The shepherds sink to the rank of minor characters, their eclogues to a recurrent interlude. It is true that Basilius and his court for the sake of the plot are in rustic retirement. But they are not figures in an idyll; their complicated domestic life contains both tragic and comic elements. The loves of the major characters are not 'shepherdish'. Those of the heroes are heroical, that of Basilius, senile and ridiculous, that of Gynecia, a sinister obsession like the love of Phèdre, and felt as such by its victim. But as the **Arcadia** is not mainly pastoral, so neither is it wholly amatory. Already in the first two books we are struck by the high proportion of chivalrous adventure to amorous complaint. When we reach the third the epic quality increases. There is less interweaving of separate stories in the medieval manner. There is an increasingly tragic atmosphere. The battles, though no less chivalrous, are more filled with Homeric echoes. The main story, now marching steadily forward, holds us for its own sake.

But even when we have added the heroic to the amatory and realized that the pastoral is quite subordinate, we have still left out one of the elements that go to make the *Arcadia.* Sidney is not merely a lover and a knight; he is also a moralist, a scholar, and a man of affairs. He aspires to teach not only virtue but prudence. He often exchanges his poetical prose for that style which the ancients called *politike;* and he dearly loves a debate or a set speech. No one has really tasted the *Arcadia* who does not remember the epistle of Philanax in Book I, Zelmane's speech to the rebels in Book II, the discussions on beauty and on the existence of God in Book III, or that on suicide in Book IV— not to mention the maxims of law, government, morals, or psychology, which are scattered on nearly every page. It is significant that the whole story moves neither to a martial nor an amorous, but to a forensic, climax; the great trial scene almost fills the fifth book. We are expected to enjoy the rhetoric of the chief speakers and (what is really part of their rhetoric) their carefully chosen dress. We are expected to revere the inflexible gravity of Euarchus. It was only the conventional modesty of a 'gentle' author that led Sidney to describe even his cancelled version as a 'toyfull booke'; and to the real *Arcadia* such words have no application at all. Beyond all doubt he was intending to express *totius vitae imaginem.* If he offers sweets in plenty for the young and amorous reader, he also provides solid nourishment for maturer stomachs.

This many-sided appeal can easily be misrepresented by a one-sided choice of quotations. We can paint Arcadia all 'humble vallies comforted with refreshing of siluer riuers', all trees that 'maintaine their flourishing olde age with the onely happinesse of their seat, being clothed with a continual spring because no beautie here should euer fade'. We can people it with lovers who 'stoppe their eares lest they grow mad with musicke' and who, on seeing their mistress in an orchard, exclaim 'the apples, me thought, fell downe from the trees to do homage to the apples of her breast'. We can mention the war horse 'milk white but that vpon his shoulder and withers he was fretned with red staines as when a few strawberries are scattered into a dish of creame', his mane and tail 'died in carnation' and his harness 'artificially made' like vine branches. Such is the *Arcadia* we know from popular tradition before we open the book. And all this is really there. But it is not there alone. Against these passages we can quote almost as many of a sterner and graver kind. 'Judgement', says Euarchus (as if he had been reading Burke), 'must vndoubtedly bee done, not by a free discourse of reason and skill of philosophy, but must be tied to the lawes of *Greece* and municipall statutes of this kingdome'. 'Hope', says Pamela, 'is the fawning traitour of the minde, while vnder the colour of friendship, it robbes it of his chiefe force of resolution'. Noble youths 'looke through loue vpon the maiesty of vertue' and 'the journey of high honour . . . lies not in plaine wayes'. If Charles I used Pamela's prayer in prison, he was not ill advised: even the less known prayer of Musidorus, if somewhat unregenerate in its object, is noble in style and rhythm. The fantastic equipage of the knights does not mean that Sidney ignores the reality of battle. He draws both sides of that picture and himself points the contrast:

For at the first, though it were terrible, yet Ter-

ror was deckt so brauelie with rich furniture, guilte swords, shining armours, pleasant pensils, that the eye with delight had scarce leasure to be afraide; But now all vniuersally defiled with dust, blood, broken armours, mangled bodies, tooke away the maske, and sette foorth Horror in his owne horrible manner.

Quotation to illustrate this less Arcadian side of Sidney could be endless, but I must content myself with one more specimen, the magnificent *viximus* of Musidorus and Pyrocles in their condemned cell:

We haue liued, and liued to be good to our selues and others: our soules, which are put into the sturring earth of our bodyes, haue atchieved the causes of their hither coming: They haue knowne, and honoured with knowledge, the cause of their creation, and to many men (for in this time, place and fortune, it is lawfull for vs to speake gloriously) it hath bene behouefull that we should liue.

The elaboration of the style, always, of course, most noticeable to those who have no taste for the matter, seems to me to lessen as the book goes on. But even at its most elaborate it does not exclude reality, though it is usually a heightened reality. Most of the characters are, no doubt, types and much that happens is improbable; but Sidney contrives to let us know very well the sort of people he is talking about. His artificiality is not of the kind which needs to be carefully protected; whenever he pleases he can drop into simplicity and no shock is felt; as in the sentence 'At that Philoclea smiled with a little nod'. He can afford to let us hear Zelmane stuttering or Kalander lecturing the young men on early hours. He can show us Zoilus 'turning up his mustachoes and marching as if he would begin a paven', or old Basilius 'stroking vp' his stockings and nodding his head 'as though they mistook him much that thought he was not his wiues maister'. The comic relief supplied by Dametas and his family is by no means contemptible; at the end of the old fourth, in the story of the buried treasure and the ash-tree, it is really good. Sidney does not, like Shakespeare, love his clowns, but he has made me laugh.

Of the characters, Basilius is a stock comic type and the two heroes, though adequate in their context, do not live on in the mind. It is in his women that Sidney shows himself a true maker. Gynecia I have already compared to Phèdre, not, of course, because there is any equality of art between Sidney and Racine, but because both are studies of the same thing, and against the same background of Augustinian theology. Each pictures the tormented human will, impotent against the depravity of fallen human nature. The horror of Gynecia's state is that, while the will is instantly enslaved, the judgement of good and evil remains clear. Her very virtues, being merely natural, and therefore only *splendida vitia,* give her no help against the 'hideous thing', nay rather aggravate her fall: in Sidney's terrible words she had been 'guiltie of a long exercised virtue which made this vice the fuller of deformitie'. In defiance of the supposed paganism of Arcadia he allows her to make the theology explicit when she says, 'strange mixture of humaine mindes! Only so much good left as to make vs languish in our owne euills'.

Pamela and Philoclea, on the other hand, are true natives of Arcadia. They can be praised without reservation. English literature had seen no women to compare with them since Chaucer's Crisseid; and, apart from Shakespeare, was to wait centuries for their equals. They are, of course, idealized; but then they are lifelike as well. It is easy to produce lifeless idealisms; it is perhaps easier than we suppose to paint people (think of Trollope's Johnny Eames) as real, and also as dull, as some people we meet. But to idealize discreetly, to go beyond Nature yet on Nature's lines, to paint dreams which have not come through the ivory gate, to embody what reality hints, forms such as 'Nature, often erring, yet shewes she would faine make'—this is a very rare achievement. And Sidney has almost done it. I do not think that the majesty of Pamela is ever strained or the simplicity of Philoclea ever insipid. The contrast between the two cynosures, worked out in every detail, down to the difference of their toilets in prison, helps to save them from abstraction. Here are great ladies; the first fruits of returning civilization and an earnest that this civilization will rise high and last long.

Yet characterization is not Sidney's main interest. The heart of the *Arcadia,* the thing for which it exists, which wrung from Milton even in his anger an admission of its 'wit and worth', is its nobility of sentiment. We can almost say of Sidney as Johnson said of Richardson, 'You must read him for the sentiment.' Sidney assumes in his readers an agreed response to certain ideals of virtue, honour, friendship, and magnanimity. His conception of love is a Platonic elaboration of medieval *Frauendienst*—the theory, later expressed by Patmore, that erotic love can be a sensuous appetite of intelligible good. Hence he can speak of noble women as having 'throwne reason vpon our desires and, as it were, giuen eyes to Cupid'. We are meant to feel as an unpurchasable grace that single kiss which Pamela vouchsafes to her lover, 'either loue so commanding her, which doubted how long they should enjoy one another; or of a liuely spark of noblenes, to descende in most favour to one when he is lowest in affliction'. And the second alternative is to be taken seriously. A lover is not to be suspected of self-deception when he says

> the roote of my desire
> Was vertue cladde in constant loues attire.

At the same time, there is no notion that love has a right to override all claims. Infinite, so to speak, in one direction, it is, in another, rigidly bounded by different parts of the pattern of honour. It leaves the laws of friendship sacred. 'Life of my desires,' says Musidorus to Philoclea, 'what is mine euen to my soule is yours; but the secret of my friend is not mine.' And the friendship of which we here speak is 'a child and not the father of Vertue'. Everything proposed for our admiration in the *Arcadia* is on that level, everything is good and fair and beyond the common reach. It was not written for a democracy. And though this exaltation may strain a modern reader it is never itself strained, never rings false like the later heroic drama. We can hardly doubt that it was among the lofty romances which Milton acknowledged as his textbooks of

love and chastity, replete with those beauties whereof 'not to be sensible argues a gross and swainish disposition'.

In that way the *Arcadia* is a kind of touchstone. What a man thinks of it, far more than what he thinks of Shakespeare or Spenser or Donne, tests the depth of his sympathy with the sixteenth century. For it is, as Carrara says of the earlier Italian *Arcadia,* a work of distillation. It gathers up what a whole generation wanted to say. The very gallimaufry that it is—medieval, Protestant, pastoral, Stoical, Platonic—made it the more characteristic and, as long as that society lasted, more satisfactory.

The style is not one that naturally appeals to most modern ears. Its essence is fullness, its danger, overfullness. Every rift is loaded with ore; this 'ore' mostly consisting of descriptive detail, simile, metaphor, or conceit. The sentences are usually long: whether too long, may be disputed. A sentence is too long either when length makes it obscure or unpronounceable, or else when the matter is too little to fill it. Sidney seldom offends against the first canon; about the second it is not so easy to decide. Much that seems otiose if we consider only the necessities of plot and character, may yet be necessary to the atmosphere. The looks and clothes and retinues of the characters, and the scenes in which they appear, are really essential to the Arcadian quality. The world which Sidney is imagining could not, perhaps, be described without conceits. Even the real world, as he saw it, was allegorical, emblematic: Arcadia, of course, more so. I believe we should seldom blame Sidney for saying too much if we were in full sympathy with his mode of appreciating external nature. When the princesses are drying after their bathe, 'the water (with some drops) seemed to weepe that it should parte from such bodies'. We are apt to regard such conceits as a frigid substitute for real observation and enjoyment. More probably they are fantasies wrought upon an observation and enjoyment which were real but very different from ours. I remarked before that the Elizabethans had neither the romantic, nor the scientific, reverence for nature. Her beauties were, for them, not degraded but raised by being forced into real service to, or fanciful connexion with, the needs and moods of humanity. Their outlook was anthropocentric to a degree now hardly imaginable. This comes out well in a place where Sidney is not writing fantastically at all. He tells us that the shepherds' arena was surrounded by 'such a sort of trees as eyther excellency of fruit, statelines of growth, continuall greennes, or poeticall fancies haue made at any time famous'. Every one of these qualifications is illuminating. Sidney likes things to be useful, healthy, and perfect in their own kinds. To that extent he is at one with Jane Austen's Edward Ferrars; 'I do not like crooked, twisted, blasted trees. I admire them much more if they are tall, straight and flourishing. . . . I am not fond of nettles or thistles or heath blossoms.' But, unlike Ferrars, he is a poet, a mythologist, and a scholar. He wants 'poeticall fancies' and 'fame' as well as fruit and shade. He values, in fact, those parts of nature which, for whatever reason, have already made good their claim on man's attention. His 'Nature' is a nature thoroughly humanized, thoroughly subjugated to man's pleasure, and now, after so many centuries of planting, pruning, mowing, myth-making, after so many physic gardens, emblems, languages of flowers, and topiary, almost an extension of ourselves. He would not understand our objection to the conceits. The Romantic poet wishes to be absorbed into Nature, the Elizabethan, to absorb her.

The case against the *Arcadia* does not rest upon its style. Doubtless it is no perfect style, but it has its own appropriateness and admits more vigour and variety than is popularly supposed. Probably no man, qualified in other respects to enjoy the book, was ever really deterred by its style. Those who dislike Sidney's manner also dislike his matter. A simple style could not carry that matter at all. In that sense his decorations can be called 'functional', if not in each particular sentence, yet in their total effect. Jonson placed him beside Hooker as a master, not only of invention and judgement, but of language.

A more serious criticism against him might be that the elements he has taken from Sannazaro do not really lie down at ease with those he has taken from Heliodorus. Sannazaro's Arcadia was a golden world; Heliodorus offers us a world of battle, murder, and sudden death. When Sidney has blended the two, some may ask how Arcadia can admit such disorders, or what was the use of taking us to Arcadia at all if this is what we find there. But I think such criticism would reveal a misunderstanding. Sidney by no means commits himself to the claim that his Arcadia represents the state of innocence in any strictly Christian or Stoical sense. Its woods are greener, its rivers purer, its sky brighter than ours. But its inhabitants are 'ideal' only in the sense that they are either more beautiful or more ugly, more stately or more ridiculous, more vicious or more virtuous, than those whom we meet every day. The world he paints is, in fact, simplified and heightened; because it is the poet's business to feign 'notable images' of virtues and vices. But we must not exaggerate the extent to which he intends his heroes and heroines for images of virtue. Their faults are conceived, no doubt, as the faults of noble natures: yet still as faults. Musidorus exhorts Pyrocles against the 'base affection' of love as a thing which will 'divert his thoughts from the way of goodnesse'; when conquered himself, he apostrophizes love as a 'celestial or infernal spirit'. Not that Sidney thinks thus of love *simpliciter;* but he sees in these loves an element of 'ill governed passion' and they lead to actions which he does not approve. In that respect the expurgation of Philoclea's weakness and Musidorus' attempted rape alter the nature of the story only in degree. Imperfection, not condoned because it is lovely imperfection, remains and is rebuked by Euarchus: 'Loue may have no such priviledge. That sweete and heavenly vniting of mindes, which properly is called loue, hath no other knot but vertue, and therefore if it be a right loue, it can never slide into any action which is not vertuous.' The 'uniting of mindes' does not here, of course, exclude the uniting of bodies in marriage; what is condemned is disguise, trickery, hypocrisy, and abduction—and probably marriage without parents' consent. These things bring his heroes within an ace of death under the sentence of a just judge.

Theoretically we are all pagans in Arcadia, and there is nothing necessarily foreign to paganism in the judgement of Euarchus. Nevertheless, Christian theology is always breaking in. Thus a single phrase like 'Since neither we made ourselves nor bought ourselves' casually and perhaps unconsciously lets in the whole doctrine of the Redemption. Pamela's prayer is Christian in all but name. This superficial discrepancy does no more harm here than in *Comus* or in the *Winter's Tale,* where Leontes consults the Delphic oracle but Polixenes knows all about original sin, 'the imposition hereditary ours'. The convention was well understood, and very useful. In such works the gods are God *incognito* and everyone is in the secret. Paganism is the religion of poetry through which the author can express, at any moment, just so much or so little of his real religion as his art requires.

The *Arcadia,* as I have said, is a work of sentiment. It expresses an ideal. Whatever we think of that ideal, we must not mistake it for a mere emotional indulgence. The balance and tension within it of many diverse ardours—erotic, heroic, political, ethical, religious—save it from that charge. In Dryden's heroic plays all is subordinate to love, in Mackenzie, all to 'feeling', in Kipling, all to discipline. Sidney is not like that. His ideal is not a reverie but a structure. A sane man could—I think sane men did—attempt to live by it. His constancy to so builded an ideal gives to him, as to the young Milton, the quality of joyful seriousness. And that, to some tastes, compensates for many faults. (pp. 327-42)

> *C. S. Lewis, "Sidney and Spenser," in his* English Literature in the Sixteenth Century, Excluding Drama, *Oxford at the Clarendon Press, 1954, pp. 318-93.*

David Daiches   (essay date 1956)

> [*Daiches is a prominent English scholar and critic who has written extensively on English and American literature. He is especially renowned for his indepth studies of Robert Burns, Robert Louis Stevenson, and Virginia Woolf. His criticism is generally characterized as appreciative in content and attached to no single methodology. In the excerpt below, he analyzes* The Defense of Poesie, *particularly as it relates to Aristotle's defense in his* Poetics.]

In 1595, after its author's death, appeared Sir Philip Sidney's critical essay, **The Defence of Poesie,** which had been written over ten years before. Sidney was concerned to defend poetry—by which term . . . he meant imaginative literature in general—against the charge brought against it by the Puritans that it was immoral, debilitating, lying, and provocative of debauchery. He was thus faced with a problem similar to that of Aristotle in meeting Plato's charges, though the arguments to which Sidney was replying were less coherent and less well argued than Plato's had been. Nevertheless, the knowledge that Plato had expelled poets from his ideal republic was used by the Puritans in their attack, and Plato's prestige, which was formidable in the Renaissance, lent weight to his opinion even though the reasons underlying it were not fully appreciated.

If Aristotle in his *Poetics* had demonstrated the essential truth, seriousness, and usefulness of imaginative literature, one might have thought that Sidney had arguments ready to hand with which to demolish the Puritan opposition. However, the circumstances under which the *Poetics* was rediscovered and used in the Renaissance, as well as the whole Christian tradition of defense of works of imagination by treating them allegorically which had intervened between classical times and the editing and translating of the *Poetics* by sixteenth century Italian humanists, meant that for Sidney Aristotle's arguments were available in a context which gave them a meaning rather different from anything Aristotle had intended. We are not here concerned with the sources of Sidney's **Defence,** but with its method and the critical position it takes up: to demonstrate that Sidney was putting together a host of arguments common to renaissance critics and through them deriving from a variety of classical and Christian sources is not necessarily to show their critical significance, which is our present purpose. By what arguments, then, does Sidney defend poetry?

His opening arguments strike us at first sight as singularly irrelevant. He stresses the antiquity of poetry and its early civilizing function. The first philosophers and scientists wrote in verse. But is not this to ignore Aristotle's warning that "Homer and Empedocles have nothing in common but the metre, so that it would be right to call the one poet, the other physicist rather than poet"? Indeed, Sidney cites Empedocles among the early Greek philosophers who "durst not a long time appeare to the worlde but under the masks of Poets." It soon becomes clear, however, that Sidney does not call them poets merely because they write metrically. "For that wise *Solon* was directly a Poet it is manifest, hauing written in verse the notable fable of the Atlantick Iland, which was continued by *Plato.*"

"Hauing written in *verse* the notable *fable*"—we see two criteria of poetry here, with the latter clearly the more important. Solon conveyed his wisdom not only in verse but through a fable, through an invented story; and he shrewdly adds (for later he has to deal with Plato's embarrassing attack on poets) that this same invented story was also used by Plato. Poetry is verse, but, more important, it is invention, the telling of a story which is not literally true. The reference to Solon, the great Greek lawgiver, in this context thus suggests that untruths may be valuable as means of communicating wisdom. This is not Aristotle's position; he never suggests that poetry is an effective way of communicating a kind of knowledge that could also be communicated (but less effectively) by other kinds of discourse. But for Sidney lies can be shown to be good and valuable if they are used as allegorical ways of teaching moral doctrine.

This is in essence the old doctrine of allegory which goes back to Philo, the Jew of Alexandria, who in the first century A.D. endeavored to reconcile the Hebrew Bible with Platonic philosophy by interpreting parts of the biblical narrative allegorically. It is perhaps an obvious way of defending imaginative literature, and one eagerly seized on by Christian writers who wanted to keep parts of pagan classical literature from ecclesiastical proscription. But Sidney goes further than this. He proceeds to point out

that Plato himself used invented situations in his philosophical works:

> And truely, even *Plato,* whosoever well considereth, shall find that in the body of his work, though the inside and strength were Philosophy, the skinne as it were and beautie depended most of Poetrie: for all standeth vpon Dialogues, wherein he faineth many honest Burgesses of Athens to speake of such matters, that, if they had been sette on the racke, they would neuer have confessed them. Besides, his poetical describing the circumstances of their meetings, as the well ordering of a banquet, the delicacie of a walke, with enterlacing meere tales, as *Giges* Ring, and others, which who knoweth not to be flowers of Poetrie did neuer walke into *Apollos* Garden.

Poetry is the record of imaginary events, but it is more: the events must be described in a lively and persuasive style. And when Sidney goes on to cite the historian Herodotus as a poet because "both he and all the rest that followed him either stole or vsurped of Poetrie their passionate describing of passions, the many particularities of battailes, which no man could affirme" he is adding passion, forceful and moving expression, to his criteria, so that by poetry he now means fiction plus liveliness plus passion. If a lively and passionately expressed invention can be employed as a means of conveying historical or moral truths, then poetry is justified—but not as an art in itself so much as one among many ways of communicating kinds of knowledge which are themselves known independently to be valuable. At this stage in Sidney's argument, poetry is simply a superior means of communication, and its value depends on what is communicated. And to determine that value we have to go to other arts—to history or moral philosophy.

Sidney is here expressing a view that has long been popular and is still very common among lay readers of poetry. Imaginative literature can be justified if it communicates historical or philosophical or moral truths in a lively and pleasing manner, and if this means telling things which are not literally true, the untruths can either be interpreted allegorically as ways of representing an underlying general truth, or, in the case of the historical poet, as plausible reconstructions of what might well have occurred. This latter point brings us fairly close to Aristotle's notion of probability, but it stops short of it. Sidney does not go on to say that the "fained" speeches of the historian can give a more fundamental insight into the truth of the human situation than the factual historical record; he does not, in fact, at this stage in his argument go further than to say that the historian, in his search for a means of communicating what he has to say in a lively and convincing manner, is led to draw on his own invention and thus to become a poet. When Herodotus describes "the many particularities of battailes, which no man could affirme" he is behaving like a poet, but the only conclusion Sidney seems to be drawing from this fact is that if historians use poetry then poetry must be a good thing. This is a curious kind of *argumentum ad hominem*—the worth of an art depends on the intentions and purposes of its user—and is far from a justification of poetry (in the sense of fiction plus liveliness plus passion) for its own sake. One can only begin to justify poetry for its own sake if one can isolate its differentiating qualities and consider what unique function poetry serves. Are fiction plus liveliness plus passion good in themselves, or good only if they serve as means to communicate kinds of knowledge which are known independently to be good? Sidney does not here answer this question, and although the tone of his argument suggests that they *are* good in themselves he does not tell us why. Later on, however, he gives this argument a new turn.

Before he does so he pauses to remind us of the universality of poetry. He has already mentioned its antiquity, and now he points out—with illustrations from Ireland and Wales, and from Romans, Saxons, Danes, and Normans—that it is to be found in every nation. The universality and antiquity of an art is perhaps no necessary proof of its value—many patently harmful activities are both long established and widespread—but some notion of the implications of this kind of argument can be seen if we put beside Sidney's remarks some observations made nearly two hundred years later by Dr Johnson in his preface to his edition of Shakespeare:

> To works . . . of which the excellence is not absolute and definite, but gradual and comparative; to works not raised upon principles demonstrative and scientifick, but appealing wholly to observation and experience, no other test can be applied than length of duration and continuance of esteem. What mankind have long possessed they have often examined and compared; and if they persist to value the possession, it is because frequent comparisons have confirmed opinion in its favour. . . . The reverence due to writings that have long subsisted arises therefore not from any credulous confidence in the superior wisdom of past ages, or gloomy persuasion of the degeneracy of mankind, but is the consequence of acknowledged and indubitable positions, that what has been longest known has been most considered, and what is most considered is best understood.

The appeal to antiquity and universality may thus be considered as the appeal to the verdict of many different kinds of people over a long period of time. This kind of argument is not, of course, drawn from any further insight into the special nature of poetry, but is general and *prima facie:* it is not likely that what has been long and widely esteemed should be worthless. It is rather a further reason for pursuing the investigation into the nature and value of poetry than a further step in that investigation. It is nevertheless a point of some importance in that it implies (however indirectly) an underlying humanist position. The appeal is to what all sorts of men have always done and have always considered valuable: this makes poetry an activity essentially appropriate to man, what the Greeks called αυθρωπινον and the Romans, translating the Greek term, *humanum.* If one takes the Christian position on Original Sin, one cannot of course take the view that what is *humanum* is good—the Latin proverb *humanum est errare,* "to err is human," would be the appropriate one there rather than the famous declaration *"homo sum, et nihil humani a me alienum puto,"* "I am a man, and noth-

ing human is alien to me"—certainly there is no overt suggestion in Sidney that he accepts the complete humanist position. But he does make the appeal to human nature, which later critics were to develop much further. That could only be done by an age which had become much more optimistic about the nature of man.

Sidney then proceeds to consider the significance of the title given to the poet by the Greeks and Romans. The Romans called him *vates* "which is as much as a Diviner, Fore-seer, or Prophet," and that poetry can be (but not that it must be) "divine" is shown by the Psalms of David. The Psalms are songs, written in meter, argues Sidney. But meter alone does not make poetry; we must have the lively invention. So he reminds us that the Psalms are full of vigorous figures of speech—David tells "of the Beastes joyfulness and hills leaping," which is to tell literal untruths—and can so be considered poetry in the sense of his earlier discussion. Again, however, it is the non-poetic objective which gives the poetry its ultimate value. This is simply an extension of what he had said earlier about the philosopher and the historian.

When he comes to the name the Greeks gave to the poet, *Poietes,* maker, he has found a channel that leads to an important new argument, and a new justification for poetry. The poet is indeed a "maker," and this distinguishes him from the practitioners of other arts and sciences:

> There is no Arte deliuered to mankinde that hath not the workes of Nature for his principall obiect, without which they could not consist, and on which they so depend, as they become Actors and Players, as it were, of what Nature will haue set foorth. So doth the Astronomer looke vpon the starres, and, by that he seeth, setteth downe what order Nature hath taken therein. So doe the Geometrician and Arithmetician in their diuerse sorts of quantities. So doth the Musitian in times tel you which by nature agree, which not. The naturall Philosopher thereon hath his name, and the Morall Philosopher standeth vpon the naturall vertues, vices, and passions of man. . . . The Lawyer sayth what men haue determined. The Historian what men haue done. The Grammarian speaketh onely of the rules of speech; and the Rhetorician and Logitian, considering what in Nature will soonest proue and perswade, thereon giue artificiall rules, which still are compassed within the circle of a question, according to the proposed matter. The Phisition waigheth the nature of a mans bodie, and the nature of things helpfull or hurtfull vnto it. And the Metaphysick, though it . . . be counted supernaturall, yet doth hee indeede builde vpon the depth of Nature. Only the Poet, disdayning to be tied to any such subiection, lifted vp with the vigor of his own inuention, dooth growe in effect another nature, in making things either better than Nature bringeth forth, or, quite a newe, formes such as neuer were in Nature, as the *Heroes, Demigods, Cyclops, Chimeras, Furies* and such like: so as hee goeth hand in hand with Nature, not inclosed within the narrow warrant of her guifts, but freely ranging only with the Zodiack of his owne wit.

The poet does not imitate or represent or express or discuss things which already exist: he *invents* new things. We have already seen that Sidney, in an earlier stage of his argument, stressed the fact that the poet made things up, so that philosophers turn poet when they use illustrative fables or imaginary dialogues in order to bring home their points, and historians turn poet when they draw on their imagination for details of events they could not have known. Here he is approaching this point more directly. Invention is the distinguishing character of the poet; he creates new things by drawing on "his owne wit." Is this an exaltation of the inventive imagination? Is Sidney claiming that the creative aspect of the poet's art is in itself valuable? Is there a splendor in the very process of creation, in the exercise of the imagination, without any ulterior motive? Sidney certainly seems to be emphasizing this differentiating quality of the poet and holding it up to be admired. Is he then the first English protagonist of the imagination as such? Note how he proceeds:

> Nature neuer set forth the earth in so rich tapistry as diuers Poets haue done, neither with plesant riuers, fruitful trees, sweet smelling flowers, nor whatsoeuer els may make the too much loued earth more louely. Her world is brasen, the Poets only deliuer a golden. But let those things alone and goe to man, for whom as other things are, so it seemeth in him her vttermost cunning is imployed, and knowe whether shee haue brought foorth so true a louer as *Theagines,* so constant a friende as *Pilades,* so valiant a man as *Orlando,* so right a Prince as *Xenophons Cyrus,* so excellent a man euery way as *Virgils Aeneas:* neither let this be iestingly conceiued, because the works of the one be essentiall, the other, in imitation or fiction; for any vnderstanding knoweth the skil of the Artificer standeth in that *Idea* or fore-conceite of the work, and not in the work it selfe. And that the Poet hath that *Idea* is manifest, by deliuering them forth in such excellencie as hee hath imagined them. Which deliuering forth also is not wholie imaginatiue, as we are wont to say by them that build Castles in the ayre: but so far substantially it worketh, not onely to make a *Cyrus,* which had been but a particular excellencie, as Nature mught haue done, but to bestow a *Cyrus* vpon the worlde, to make many *Cyrus's,* if they wil learne aright why and how that Maker made him.

Sidney is here making many interesting points. In the first place, he is saying that the world invented or created by the poet is a *better* world than the real one. It is not the mere exercise of his imagination that justifies the poet, but the exercise of his imagination in order to create this better world. The real world "is brasen, the Poets only deliuer a golden." Only the poet can, by his invention, produce something that goes beyond nature. The lovers of fiction are truer than those of real life; its friends are more constant, its warriors more valiant, its princes more "right," its heroes more "excellent in euery way." Note that for Sidney the poet's world is not better than the real world in some special poetic way, in that it is more probable in the Aristotelian sense, for example, but it is better on standards we apply in ordinary life. Flowers smell sweeter in the works of the poets than they do in real gardens.

The next point Sidney makes in the paragraph quoted above is one which might well have been used by Aristotle in an endeavor to turn Plato's own notions against his attack on the poets. In creating this better world, the poet has in view the *Idea* (in the Platonic sense, clearly) of the quality he is representing; he is not imitating the idea as reflected palely in real life, but is directly embodying his own vision of the ideal. The poet's embodiment can then in turn be imitated by the poet's readers, just as, for Plato, any human instance of constancy, courage, or any other virtue, represents an imitation of the idea of that virtue. The poet makes direct contact with the world of Platonic ideas, and thus Plato's charge against the poet, as someone who merely imitates an imitation, is dismissed. But Sidney does not seem to realize that he has here disposed of one of Plato's main charges against poets, and when, later on in his essay, he comes to defend the poet against Plato, he seems unaware of the relevance of this argument.

What is Sidney getting at here, and why does he not develop his second point much further? The answer seems to be that, fighting as he is on his enemy's ground (defending poetry against the Puritan charge that it is conducive to immorality) he is so anxious to prove the perfection (both moral and in every way) of the world created by the poets that he lays his main emphasis on the difference between the poet's world and the imperfect real world, slurring over the implication that what the poet creates is not so much different from reality as the very essence of it, the original undimmed Platonic idea of it. Aristotle had met Plato's charge that the poet painted imitations of imitations by showing how, by concerning himself with fundamental probabilities rather than with casual actualities, the poet reaches more deeply into reality than the historian. Sidney is on the point of answering Plato in more purely Platonic terms. But, carried away by his enthusiasm for *creation,* and anxious to vindicate the quality of the world created by the poets against the charges of the Puritans, he ends by striving to show that *the imagination does not give us insight into reality, but an alternative to reality,* the alternative being in every way superior.

This development leads Sidney away from the Aristotelian notion of imitation; even though he uses the term "imitation" later on in his discussion, he is not really concerned to prove that poetry imitates anything—indeed, its glory is that it is the only one of the arts that does not imitate, but creates. He almost proceeds to develop a theory of "ideal imitation," the notion that the poet imitates not the mere appearances of actuality but the hidden reality behind them, but stops short of this to maintain the more naive theory that the poet creates a better world than the one we actually live in. He does not, however, rest content with a mere escapist position. The function of imaginative literature is not to provide us with an escape world in which our imaginations can seek consolation for the difficulties and imperfections of real life. It is true that this view of literature as simple escape is often held, and that the great majority of ordinary readers of popular magazine stories today have some such view of the function of fiction, but for Sidney this would be a far from adequate defense of poesy, and would certainly not meet the Puritan charge. No; for Sidney the ideal world of the poet is of value because it is both a better world than the real one and it is presented in such a way that the reader is stimulated to try and imitate it in his own practice. Thus the Aristotelian notion of imitation is transferred from the poet to the reader. The poet does not imitate but creates: *it is the reader who imitates what the poet creates.*

This is a most interesting development of the argument. Taking from the Roman poet Horace the view that the poet both delights and teaches, Sidney goes on to show that the poets "indeede doo meerely make to imitate, and imitate both to delight and teach, and delight to moue men to take that goodnes in hande, which without delight they would flye as from a stranger; and teach, to make them know that goodnes whereunto they are mooued, which being the noblest scope to which euer any learning was directed, yet want there not idle tongues to barke at them." He then proceeds to point out that verse "is but an ornament and no cause to Poetry" and "it is not riming and versing that maketh a Poet, no more than a long gowne maketh an Aduocate . . . But it is that fayning notable images of vertues, vices, or what els, with that delightful teaching which must be the right describing note to know a Poet by: although indeed the Senate of Poets hath chosen verse as their fittest rayment, meaning, as in matter they passed all in all, so in maner to goe beyond them: not speaking (table talke fashion or like men in a dreame) words as they chanceably fall from the mouth, but peyzing [weighing] each sillable of each worde by iust proportion according to the dignitie of the subiect."

The poet, then, teaches by presenting an ideal world for the imitation of the reader. But if the poet's world is, as he had earlier maintained, a perfect world, where all rivers are pleasant, all trees fruitful, all lovers faithful and all friends constant, how can the poet's activity be described as "fayning notable images of vertues, *vices, or what else*"? Should not they all be virtues? The answer to this is that when Sidney asked earlier where such perfect lovers, friends, princes, and heroes as one finds in the works of the poets were to be found in real life, he did not really mean that *all* characters in fiction were ideal; he meant that when they were good they acted in accordance with the full perfection of that kind of goodness, and when they were bad their badness was equally unmixed, obviously ugly, and inevitably leading to appropriate punishment. The perfection of the poet's world, it emerges later in Sidney's argument, does not consist in its being peopled with wholly virtuous characters, but in its heroes always being perfect in behavior and successful in fortune and its villains always thoroughly and obviously villainous and doomed to a certain bad end. In the poet's world the righteous always prosper and the wicked are never left unpunished. It is from this conception that we get the term "poetic justice."

In this lies the superiority of the poet to the historian who, sticking to what really happened, must often show us the wicked prospering and the righteous suffering. *That* is no way to teach people to be good, says Sidney. If we should reply that it is not the function of the poet to make people good, Sidney might retort that he is arguing against Puritans who held that no activity is justified unless it conduces directly to moral improvement—and he might add that Plato held this position also. Sidney accepts the assumption that unless we can show that poetry leads to moral improvement in its readers it cannot be really justified. Its two chief rivals in this claim (on the purely human level, excepting revealed religion and divinity) are moral philosophy and history:

> . . . the ending end of all earthly learning being vertuous action, those skilles that most serue to bring forth that haue a most iust title to bee Princes ouer all the rest. Wherein if wee can shewe the Poets noblenes, by setting him before his other Competitors, among whom as principall challengers step forth the morall Philosophers, whom, me thinketh, I see comming towards mee with a sullen grauity, as though they could not abide vice by day light, rudely clothed for to witnes outwardly their contempt of outward things, with bookes in their hands agaynst glory, whereto they sette theyr names, sophistically speaking against subtility, and angry with any man in whom they see the foule fault of anger: these men casting larges [largesse, abundance] as they goe of Definitions, Diuisions, and Distinctions, with a scornefull interogatiue doe soberly aske whether it bee possible to finde any path so ready to leade a man to vertue as that which teacheth what vertue is? and teacheth it not onely by deliuering forth his very being, his causes, and effects; but also by making known his enemie vice, which must be destroyed, and his cumbersome seruant Passion, which must be maistered; by shewing the generalities that contayneth it, and the specialities that are deriued from it; lastly, by playne setting downe, how it extendeth it selfe out of the limits of a mans own little world to the gouernment of families, and maintayning of publique societies.

The Historian scarcely giueth leysure to the Moralist to say so much, but that he, loden with old Mouse-eaten records, authorising himselfe (for the most part) vpon other histories, whose greatest authorities are built vpon the notable foundation of Heare-say, hauing much a-doe to accord differing Writers and to pick trueth out of partiality, better acquainted with a thousande yeeres a goe then with the present age, and yet better knowing how this world goeth then how his owne wit runneth, curious for antiquities and inquisitiue of nouelties, a wonder to young folkes and a tyrant in table talke, denieth, in a great chafe, that any man for teaching of vertue, and vertuous actions, is comparable to him. . . .

'The Phylosopher' (sayth hee) 'teacheth a disputatiue vertue, but I doe an actiue: his vertue is excellent in the dangerlesse Academie of *Plato*, but mine sheweth foorth her honorable face in the battailes of *Marathon, Pharsalia, Poitiers,* and *Agincourt.* Hee teacheth vertue by certaine abstract considerations, but I onely bid you follow the footing of them that haue gone before you. Olde-aged experience goeth beyond the fine-witted Phylosopher, but I giue the experience of many ages. Lastly, if he make the Songebooke, I put the learners hande to the Lute: and if hee be the guide, I am the light.'

Then woulde hee alledge you innumerable examples, conferring storie by storie, how much the wisest Senatours and Princes haue been directed by the credite of history, as *Brutus, Alphonsus of Aragon,* and who not, if need be? At length the long lyne of theyr disputation maketh a point in thys, that the one giueth the precept, and the other the example.

This is in Sidney's best style, and his vivacious and mocking portrait of the historian (which is directed against the claims of history, then being so strongly pressed in England as elsewhere in Europe, to be the best "mirror for magistrates" and instructor of princes) is itself a good example of that liveliness of presentation which he lists as one of the qualities of a good work of literary art. But the attractiveness of the style must not distract our attention from what is happening to his argument here. He is making quite clear that the arts are valuable only in so far as they are conducive to virtuous action, and the claims of poetry must stand or fall on this criterion. Moral Philosophy teaches virtue by abstract precept and theoretical argument, whereas the historian claims to do better since he teaches by concrete example, drawn from history. But both are defective:

> The Philosopher therfore and the Historian are they which would win the gole, the one by precept, the other by example. But both not hauing both, doe both halte. For the Philosopher, setting downe with thorny argument the bare rule, is so hard of vtterance, and so mistie to be conceiued, that one that hath no other guide but him shall wade in him till hee be olde before he shall finde sufficient cause to bee honest: for his knowledge standeth so vpon the abstract and generall, that happie is that man who may vnderstande him, and more happie that can applye what hee dooth vnderstand. On the other side, the Historian, wanting the precept, is so tyed, not to what shoulde bee but to what is, to the particuler truth of things and not to the generall reason of things, that hys example draweth no necessary consequence, and therefore a lesse fruitfull doctrine.

The philosopher is too abstract to be persuasive, while the historian is tied to "the particuler truth of things" so that his examples are not always the most suitable for his purpose. There is an echo here of Aristotle's argument that poetry is more "probable" than history, but it is only an echo, and Sidney's argument is bound in a very different direction. Note how he proceeds:

> Nowe dooth the peerelesse Poet performe both: for whatsoeuer the Philosopher sayth shoulde be doone, hee giueth a perfect picture of it in some one, by whom hee presupposeth it was doone. So as hee coupleth the generall notion with the particuler example. A perfect picture I say, for hee yeeldeth to the powers of the minde an image of that whereof the Philosopher bestoweth but a woordish description: which dooth neyther

stroke, pierce, nor possesse the sight of the soule so much as that other dooth.

> For as in outward things, to a man that had neuer seene an Elephant or a Rinoceros, who should tell him most exquisitely all theyr shapes, cullour, bignesse, and perticular markes, or of a gorgeous Pallace the Architecture, with declaring the full beauties, might well make the hearer able to repeate, as it were by rote, all hee had heard, yet should neuer satisfie his inward conceits with being witnes to it selfe of a true liuely knowledge: but the same man, as soone as hee might see those beasts well painted, or the house wel in moddel, should straightwaies grow, without need of any description, to a iudicial comprehending of them: so no doubt the Philosopher with his learned definition, bee it of vertue, vices, matters of publick policie or priuat gouernment, replenisheth the memory with many infallible grounds of wisdom, which, notwithstanding, lye darke before the imaginatiue and iudging powre, if they bee not illuminated or figured foorth by the speaking picture of Poesie.

> *Tullie* taketh much paynes, and many times not without poeticall helpes, to make vs knowe the force loue of our Countrey hath in vs. Yet vs but heare old *Anchises* speaking in the middest of *Troyes* flames, or see *Vlisses* in the fulnes of all *Calipso's* delights bewayle his absence from barraine and beggerly *Ithaca.* Anger, the *Stoicks* say, was a short madnes: let but *Sophocles* bring you *Aiax* on a stage, killing and whipping Sheepe and Oxen, thinking them the Army of Greeks, with theyr Chiefetaines *Agamemnon* and *Menelaus,* and tell mee if you haue not a more familiar insight into anger then finding in the Schoolemen his *Genus* and difference. See whether wisdome and temperance in *Vlisses* and *Diomedes,* valure in *Achilles,* friendship in *Nisus* and *Eurialus,* euen to an ignoraunt man carry not an apparent shyning: and, contrarily, the remorse of conscience in *Oedipus,* the soone repenting pride of *Agamemnon,* the selfe-deuouring crueltie in his Father *Atreus,* the violence of ambition in the two *Theban* brothers, the sowre-sweetnes of reuenge in *Medœa,* and, to fall lower, the *Terentian Gnato* and our *Chaucers Pandar* so exprest that we nowe vse their names to signifie their trades: and finally, all vertues, vices, and passions so in their own naturall seates layd to the viewe, that wee seeme not to heare of them, but cleerely to see through them. But euen in the most excellent determination of goodnes, what Philosophers counsell can so redily direct a Prince, as the fayned *Cyrus* in *Xenophon?* or a vertuous man in all fortunes, as *Aeneas* in *Virgill?* or a whole Common-wealth, as the way of Sir *Thomas Moores Eutopia? . . .* Certainly, euen our Sauiour Christ could as well haue giuen the morrall common places of vncharitablenes and humblenes as the diuine narration of *Diues* and *Lazarus;* or of disobedience and mercy, as that heauenly discourse of the lost Child and the gratious Father; but that hys through-searching wisdome knewe the estate of *Diues* burning in hell, and of *Lazarus* being in *Abrahams* bosome, would more constantly (as it were) inhabit both

the memory and iudgment. Truly, for my selfe, mee seemes I see before my eyes the lost Childes disdainefull prodigality, turned to enuie a Swines dinner: which by the learned Diuines are thought not historicall acts, but instructing Parables. For conclusion, I say the Philosopher teacheth, but he teacheth obscurely, so as the learned onely can vnderstande him, that is to say, he teacheth them that are already taught; but the Poet is the foode for the tenderest stomachs, the Poet is indeed the right Popular Philosopher, whereof *Esops* tales giue good proofe: whose pretty Allegories, stealing vnder the formall tales of Beastes, make many, more beastly then Beastes, begin to heare the sound of vertue from these dumbe speakers.

But now may it be alledged that if this imagining of matters be so fitte for the imagination, then must the Historian needs surpasse, who bringeth you images of true matters, such as indeede were doone, and not such as fantastically or falsely may be suggested to haue been doone. Truely, *Aristotle* himselfe, in his discourse of Poesie, plainely determineth this question, saying that Poetry is *Philosophoteron* and *Spoudaioteron,* that is to say, it is more Philosophicall and more studiously serious than history. His reason is, because Poesie dealeth with *Katholon* that is to say, with vniuersall consideration; and the history with *Kathekaston,* the perticuler: 'nowe,' sayth he, 'the vniuersall wayes what is fit to bee sayd or done, eyther in likelihood or necessity, (which the Poesie considereth in his imposed names), and the perticuler onely marks whether *Alcibiades* did, or suffered, this or that.' Thus farre *Aristotle:* which reason of his (as all his) is most full of reason. For indeed, if the question were whether it were better to haue a perticular acte truly or falsly set down, there is no doubt which is to be chosen, no more then whether you had rather have *Vespasians* picture right as hee was, or at the Painters pleasure nothing resembling. But if the question be for your owne vse and learning, whether it be better to haue it set downe as it should be, or as it was, then certainely is it more doctrinable the fained *Cirus* in *Xenophon* then the true *Cyrus* in *Iustine,* and the fayned *Aeneas* in *Virgil* then the right *Aeneas* in *Dares Phrigius.* As to a Lady that desired to fashion her countenance to the best grace, a Painter should more benefite her to portraite a most sweet face, wryting *Canidia* vpon it, then to paynt *Canidia* as she was, who, *Horace* sweareth, was foule and ill fauoured.

Poetry, Sidney claims, is superior as a moral teacher to both philosophy and history, because it does not deal with mere abstract propositions, as philosophy does, but with the concrete example, and as its examples are not tied to fact it can make them more apt and convincing than anything found in history. The true nature of virtue is painted vividly and attractively, while vice, with equal vividness, is made to appear always ugly and unattractive. Though he cites Aesop's fables as examples of effective moral teaching by the poet, it would be unfair to Sidney to say that his argument implies that the beast fable is the highest form of literature, for, in the first place, he has already em-

phasized the importance of liveliness and passion, which are no necessary qualities of a fable, and, second, he has also, more than once, cited the epic as an especially effective kind of poetry since it gives us, in the persons of its heroes and villains, those "notable images of vertues, vices, or what els, with that delightful teaching which must be the right describing note to know a Poet by."

In the last of the paragraphs quoted above, Sidney refers to Aristotle, quoting his famous dictum that poetry is more philosophical and more serious than history because it deals with the universal rather than with the particular. Nevertheless, Sidney's position is not Aristotelian at all. When he argues that the fictitious rendering of the poet is more effective than the true report of the historian, his point is that the ideal world of the poet shows things as they *ought* to be rather than as they *are* and is thus more conducive to virtuous action in the reader. "If the question be for your owne vse and learning, whether it be better to haue it set downe as it should be, or as it was, then certainely is it more doctrinable the fained *Cirus* in *Xenophon* then the true *Cyrus* in *Iustine.*" The key word here is "should." *Sidney has changed Aristotle's probable "should" to a moral "should."* To Aristotle, the poet wrote of what "should" be in the sense of what was most probable; his "should" was a "should" of probability. To Sidney, the poet wrote of what ought to be, in a purely moral sense. The world created by Sidney's poet is more edifying than the real world, not more true to the fundamental probabilities of the human situation or probable in terms of the self-consistent world which it creates.

Thus though Sidney, like Aristotle, is concerned with replying to the kind of arguments against poetry that Plato brought forward, his defense is basically different from Aristotle's. For Sidney the poet is the creator of a world which leads those who view it to follow virtue and shun vice:

> If the Poet doe his part a-right, he will shew you in *Tantalus, Atreus,* and such like, nothing that is not to be shunned; in *Cyrus, Aeneas, Vlisses,* each thing to be followed; where the Historian, bound to tell things as things were, cannot be liberall (without hee will be poeticall) of a perfect patterne, but, as in *Alexander* or *Scipio* himselfe, shew dooings, some to be liked, some to be misliked. . . .

> For see wee not valiant *Milciades* rot in his fetters? The iust *Phocion* and the accomplished *Socrates* put to death like Traytors? The cruell *Seuerus* liue prosperously? The excellent *Seuerus* miserably murthered? *Sylla* and *Marius* dying in theyr beddes? *Pompey* and *Cicero* slaine then when they would haue thought exile a happinesse? See wee not vertuous *Cato* driuen to kyll himselfe? and rebell *Caesar* so aduanced that his name yet, after 1600 yeares, lasteth in the highest honor? . . . I conclude, therefore, that hee [the poet] excelleth Historie, not onely in furnishing the minde with knowledge, but in setting it forward to that which deserueth to be called and accounted good: which setting forward, and moouing to well dooing, indeed setteth the Lawrell crowne vpon the Poet as victorious, not

onely of the Historian, but ouer the Phylosopher, howsoeuer in teaching it may bee questionable.

The poet not only exceeds the philosopher in his ability to
create the perfect example, but also in his ability to move
the reader to follow that example. 'I thinke that no man
is so much *Philophilosophos* [a lover of philosophy] as to
compare the philosopher, in moouing, with the Poet."
This comes close to identifying poetry with rhetoric, the
art of persuasion, as Sidney himself realizes later on in his
argument. But at the same time it enables Sidney to find
room in his didactic theory of poetry for the qualities of
liveliness and vigor which he had already commended.
However ideal the poet's world may be, however virtuous
its heroes and however much "poetic justice" may prevail
in the course of the action, no reader is going to be
"moved" to imitate that world in his own behavior unless
it be presented with such life and passion that he finds it
irresistible. The delight which the reader has in reading of
this ideal world and in responding to its vitality depends
not on content but on form and style. Thus by his theory
of moving Sidney finds a way of including the purely esthetic qualities of form and style in his criteria of the good
work of literary art.

It is perhaps question-begging at this stage to use the word
"esthetic" at all, for are we not concerned to discover what
kinds of meaning can be given to this term? But all that
is meant by the term here is those qualities which provide
for the reader pleasure in the reading regardless of the content—qualities which derive from the way in which language is handled. (Whether in the last analysis form and
content can be distinguished in this way is a profound
question . . . . : Sidney's critical thought was hardly sophisticated enough to reach this question.) The point to
be made here is the important one that Sidney frames a
didactic theory of poetry in such a way that he includes
style among his interests and "good style" among his
criteria for a good work of literature, though he does not
use the actual word. In doing so he makes it possible to
separate a purely stylistic judgment from a total judgment
of the value of a poem as something which both teaches
and delights and teaches by delighting; when, later on in
his essay, he condemns the love poetry of his day because
it is written in too cold and artificial a style, he is being
perfectly consistent. What is cold and artificial can never
carry conviction, can never be, in Wordsworth's much
later phrase, "carried alive into the heart by passion."
"The Poet binds together by passion and knowledge the
vast empire of human society," Wordsworth was to claim
more than two hundred years after Sidney, and Sidney
would have at least agreed that the poet combines passion
and knowledge, the knowledge being moral knowledge
and the passion manifesting itself in the vigor and liveliness of the style.

One can hardly emphasize too much Sidney's insistence
that the poet's world should be presented delightfully, and
that the delight comes from the passionate vitality of the
expression, for this gives him a criterion which, if necessary, he can abstract altogether from his total view of poetry as the most effective way of moving to virtue and apply
to a work of literary art whatever its subject matter and

whether it has a moral purpose or not. If you say that poetry both teaches and delights, and have separate criteria for
what is good doctrine and what constitutes delight in the
way of expression, then you have prepared the way for the
emergence of a purely esthetic point of view. You have
also, however, oversimplified the relation between form
and content and paved the way for the kind of criticism
which talks about "a bad book, but so well written"—an
approach which, as we shall see, involves a far too mechanical view of the nature of literary form.

We have seen that for Sidney the world created by the poet
is not an "imitation," in any sense, of the real world we
live in, but an improvement on it, presented so persuasive-
ly that the reader will wish to imitate that improvement.
The limitations of this point of view come out most clearly
when Sidney uses the sister art of painting as an analogy.
"As to a Lady that desired to fashion her countenance to
the best grace, a Painter should more benefite her to portraite a most sweet face, wryting *Canidia* vpon it, then to
paint *Canidia* as she was, who, *Horace* sweareth, was foule
and ill fauoured." The implication here is clearly that it
is the function of portrait painting to help people to improve their own faces by imitating the portrait. This is the
difficulty one gets into if one transfers the Aristotelian notion of imitation from the artist to his public, so that the
artist does not imitate the world but invents a better one
for the public to improve itself by imitating. On the other
hand, later critics who maintained that the function of art
was to imitate human nature and who at the same time demanded that art be morally instructive were caught up in
another kind of dilemma if they were honest enough to
admit that human nature as we know it in real life is far
from edifying. If poetic justice does not prevail in life as
it is and men in their actual lives are far from models of
moral perfection, how can one at the same time imitate nature (which, to the seventeenth and much of the eighteenth century, meant human nature) and lead your readers to the paths of virtue? Dr Johnson, who had no illusions about life as it is and men as they are, at the same
time praised Shakespeare for knowing and imitating
human nature and blamed him for not having sufficient
poetic justice in his plays. You cannot have it both ways,
and it is more consistent, if you wish the poet's picture of
man to be morally edifying, to insist (unless you want to
edify solely by a series of awful warnings) that the poet is
not concerned with the real world at all. There is, of
course, a third way, which is to maintain that the "real"
world is not the everyday world but the patterns underlying that world as seen by the poet's imagination. Only in
this last way can an imitative theory of art be reconciled
with a didactic one, and, though there are (as we have
noted) traces of such an argument in Sidney, he never
really develops it.

We have seen that for Sidney the world created by the poet
can be "golden" in more than one way. It can present ideal
heroes so vividly that one will wish to imitate their virtues.
It can present a world in which virtue always triumphs
and vice is always punished. Or it can present a world in
which evil, whether it triumphs or not, is made to appear
so ugly that the reader will in future always wish to avoid
it. In the latter part of his essay, in which he discusses the

objections made by the Puritans to the different kinds of literature, he suggests other ways in which the poet can "move to virtue." The satirist "sportingly neuer leaueth, vntil hee make a man laugh at folly, and, at length ashamed, to laugh at himselfe." Similarly, "Comedy is an imitation of the common errors of our life, which he representeth in the most ridiculous and scornefull sort that may be; so as it is impossible that any beholder can be content to be such a one." And tragedy "openeth the greatest wounds, and sheweth forth the Vlcers that are couered with Tissue; that maketh Kinges feare to be Tyrants, and Tyrants manifest their tirannical humors; that, with sturring the affects of admiration and commiseration, teacheth the vncertainety of this world, and vpon how weake foundations guilden roofes are builded"—a definition which, using some of Aristotle's terminology ("admiration and commiseration" represent a modification of Aristotle's fear and pity, admiration being used in its earlier sense of mingled wonder and reverence), changes Aristotle's psychological explanation of the therapeutic function of tragedy to a straight moral theory.

It is in his discussion of lyric poetry that Sidney places such emphasis on the importance of "moving"—whose relation to the moral function of poetry we have already discussed—that he seems for the moment almost to be resting his case on this quality alone:

> Is it the Liricke that most displeaseth, who with his tuned Lyre, and wel accorded voyce, giueth praise, the reward of vertue, to vertuous acts? who giues morrall precepts, and naturall Problemes, who sometimes rayseth vp his voice to the height of the heauens, in singing the laudes of the immortall God. Certainly I must confesse my own barbarousnesse: I neuer heard the olde song of *Percy* and *Duglas* that I found not my heart mooued more than with a Trumpet; and yet is it sung by some blinde Crouder, with no rougher voyce then rude stile. . . .

Earlier, Sidney had emphasized the poet's ability to "move" as the factor which contributed most to the didactic effect of a poem: not only was the reader shown the ideal world, but, in virtue of the way in which it was presented, he was moved to imitate it. But the word "move" is ambiguous, and while most of the time Sidney uses it to mean "spur on" or even simply "persuade," in the passage just quoted he seems to be talking of emotion without any regard to its results in action; the thrilling sounds of a trumpet affect the hearer emotionally, and though of course the implication is that he is stirred to acts of greater courage the immediate suggestion here is that the "affective quality" (to borrow a term from some modern critics) in itself is what matters. At any rate, later critics have seen such an implication in this passage and have based on it a claim for Sidney to be a "romantic" critic in the sense that he is interested in the arousing of emotion for its own sake. But if virtue results from the subduing of passion by reason—a point agreed by both Plato and the Christian Platonists of Sidney's day—to say that poetry arouses passion is to concede one of Plato's main objections and to yield an important point to the Puritans. Sidney, then, cannot have intended any overt suggestion of the kind we cannot help seeing in the passage quoted. His whole case depends on his enlisting passion on the side of virtue: he shows how by a passionate picture of an embodied ideal the poet can move men to follow it. We have noted that this means that he has a criterion of style, that "passionate describing" becomes important for him, and we have seen that Sidney is content to keep his criteria of style and of moral content separate. But nowhere does he come right out and say that passionate describing *of anything* is poetically valuable, even though we may sometimes feel that if he had not been constrained to fight on his enemy's ground he might have said something like this. The most he does in the argument he overtly presents is to show that passion need not be on the Devil's side—"I don't see why the Devil should have all the good tunes," as a later moralist was to put it—but could be enlisted in the cause of virtue to make poetry, by its passionate teaching, the most effective of all didactic instruments. Richardson, said Dr Johnson in a later century, talking of the mixture of psychological realism and moral teaching in the former's novels, "taught the passions to move at the command of virtue." Sidney might have reversed this, and said that the poet teaches virtue to move at the command of the passions. One must not forget that, while Sidney was replying to a Puritan attack on poetry, he, like Spenser, was a Puritan himself. He was also, like Spenser, a neo-Platonist, a humanist, and a poet. His defense of poetry was a noble attempt to combine all these positions.

If the rhetorical side of Sidney's theory enables him to lay such emphasis on "moving" and thus insist on the importance of a lively and passionate style, it should also be noted that his insistence that the function of poetry is to show forth an ideal golden world instead of imitating the brazen one of actuality enables him to construct a hierarchy of literary forms. He can defend satire as the kind of poetry that laughs a man out of his folly, comedy as making the common errors of life seem ridiculous, and tragedy as showing the awful consequences of tyranny so that kings will fear to be tyrants (this last being perhaps the most inadequate of all Sidney's definitions), but the kind of poetry which paints directly the kind of virtue to which the readers are to be drawn will be the highest kind. That is heroic or epic poetry, "for by what conceit can a tongue be directed to speake euill of that which draweth with it no lesse Champions than *Achilles, Cyrus, Aeneas, Turnus, Tideus,* and *Rinaldo?* who not onely teach and moue to a truth, but teacheth and moooueth to the most high and excellent truth; who maketh magnanimity and iustice shine throughout all misty fearfulness and foggy desires. . . . But if any thing be already sayd in the defence of sweete Poetry, all concurreth to the maintaining the Heroicall, which is not only a kinde, but the best and the most accomplished kinde of Poetry."

Sidney, then, is able to answer the Platonic and the Puritan objections, he can find room for a criterion of style while insisting on a didactic content, and he has some ideas of a hierarchy of literary *genres*. He does all this, however, at the expense of making a dangerously clear-cut division between manner and matter and by making the ultimate objective and function of poetry not something unique, with a "peculiar pleasure" (in Aristotle's phrase) of its own and differentiating qualities in terms of which its very essence is to be recognized and valued, but as something shared with all other worthy human activities. Unlike Aristotle, Sidney does not justify poetry by singling out and justifying what is uniquely poetic and like Plato he applies a single value standard to all products of the human mind and imagination. He gets out of the Platonic dilemma by showing that passion is not the Devil's prerogative but can be used to implement virtue and by insisting that what the poet creates, if like nothing in the world of actuality, is morally better than the world of actuality and portrayed in such a way that the reader will want to try to bring it into being. But his triumph is won at the cost of poetry's independence. Though poetry for Sidney is a more effective moral teacher than philosophy or history, the critic of poetry has to wait for the moral philosopher or the man of religion to tell him what is morally good and what is morally bad before he can proceed to judge a poem. Aristotle's *Poetics* had been a declaration of independence for poetry as well as a justification of it; Sidney is content to achieve the latter at the expense of the former. And if—with some justice—we think Sidney's position naive, we might remember that from his day to ours the vast majority of readers of imaginative literature have taken substantially his view and generally applied it with less cunning and sensitivity. (pp. 50-72)

> David Daiches, "The Poet as Moral Teacher,"
> in his Critical Approaches to Literature, *Pren-*
> *tice-Hall, 1956, pp. 50-72.*

William A. Ringler, Jr.   (essay date 1962)

[*In the excerpt below, Ringler provides a detailed analysis of Sidney's structural and metrical poetic innovations.*]

The *Arcadia,* in both its old and new forms, is the most important original work of English prose fiction produced before the eighteenth century. It has an ingenious plot, a series of strong situations, a varied cast of characters, and a surprising denouement. There is a deal of high-flown language and much dallying with the gentle passion of love, which is treated sometimes sentimentally, sometimes voluptuously, and at other times wittily. But it is much more than a mere love story, for it deals also with kingship and its duties, the proper conduct of public affairs, and vexed problems of personal ethics. Basilius, the Duke of Arcadia, is a ruler who shirks his duties; Euarchus of Macedon is the perfect pattern of the just judge and righteous king. The heroes, Pyrocles and Musidorus, and the heroines, Philoclea and Pamela, struggle with the demands of personal desire and rational conduct, the avoidance of consequences and the maintenance of personal integrity. It is a fundamentally serious romance, concerned with problems of conduct in both public and private life, but fraught with emotion and humour—full of 'delightful teaching'.

In composing it Sidney did not follow the loose structural patterns of the romances of his own and earlier times, but produced an entirely new and original literary form. His strictures on the English plays of his day, which he said were 'neither right Tragedies, nor right Comedies, min-

gling Kinges and Clownes, not because the matter so carrieth it, but thrust in the Clowne by head and shoulders to play a part in majesticall matters, with neither decencie nor discretion,' have led some critics to assume that he was a neo-classicist who upheld the separation and preservation of the conventional genres in all their theoretical purity. But those critics have not noticed the qualifying phrase 'with neither decencie nor discretion', and have not examined the *Arcadia.* In point of fact Sidney approved the mingling of genres, for he said that 'some Poesies have coupled togither two or three kindes, as the Tragicall and Comicall, whereupon is risen the Tragicomicall, some in [like] maner have mingled prose and verse, as Sanazara and Boetius; some have mingled matters Heroicall and Pastorall, but that commeth all to one in this question, for if severed they be good, the conjunction cannot be hurtfull.' This precisely describes his own *Arcadia,* a mixed kind combining tragic and comic, prose and verse, heroic and pastoral.

Sidney's artistic ideal was to achieve a maximum of variety and complexity within a clearly articulated structure. He achieved this, and overcame the formless meandering of late Greek, medieval, and renaissance long prose tales, by embodying the diverse materials of romance in dramatic form. The *Old Arcadia* is a tragi-comedy in five acts, with a serious double plot (the two pairs of noble lovers with Basilius, Gynecia, and Euarchus) combined with a comic underplot (Dametas and his wife and daughter). The action is carried on by a small group of characters (there are only eighteen major actors) and is unified in both place and time—most of the events take place in the area around the two country lodges in Arcadia (the travels and other adventures of the princes are reported) and the plot unrolls within the limits of a single year. The renaissance Terentian five-act structure is followed with its movement of protasis, epitasis, and catastrophe. The various strands of action are cleverly intertwined; there is a climax in the third act, a counter-movement in the fourth, and a denouement in the fifth with a totally unexpected anagnorisis and peripeteia. Sidney produced in prose a pastoral tragi-comedy before the earliest examples of the genre, the *Aminta* and *Pastor Fido* of Tasso and Guarini, were available in print.

In addition to giving his prose narrative a dramatic structure, Sidney accentuated the division into acts by placing after each of the first four a set of pastoral pastimes or 'eglogues', in the manner of the *intermezzi* of the learned comedies of Italy. But his eclogues are much more than mere inter-act entertainments, for though they for the most part have a separate cast of characters and do not themselves advance the plot, they nevertheless set the tone and establish the themes that control the action of the main narrative. Here in the remote and abstract world of the pastoral the actions of the princely characters of the courtly world are mirrored and given perspective in the rural songs of the shepherds.

The eclogues, though they contribute to the design of the main action, also form an isolable unit with a structure of its own that can perfectly well stand by itself. But because they are embedded in the prose of the *Arcadia* as an integral element of a larger whole, they have never been considered by themselves and Sidney has never received his due as a pastoral poet. Discussions of English verse pastoral have always been focused upon Spenser's *Shepheardes Calender,* with never more than a brief reference to an isolated poem or two in the **Arcadia.** But Sidney's four sets of eclogues, containing twenty-seven poems totalling more than 2,500 lines, form a more extensive and varied pastoral work than Spenser's and one that equally deserves attention for its artistic merit. One of the most striking things about Sidney's eclogues is their carefully integrated structure. Each of the four groups develops a situation and explores a theme: the first presents the pangs of unrequited love, the second the struggle between reason and passion, the third the ideals of married love, the fourth the sorrows of lovers and the sorrows of death; and through them all moves the figure of Philisides (Sidney himself), whose identity and full story are not revealed until the very end.

The first two sets of eclogues each contain eight poems arranged in precisely parallel order. In each of the two sets the first poem announces the theme with which all the following poems are concerned, the second begins the development of the theme, the third is a comic interlude satirizing the theme, the fourth returns to the theme, the fifth deals with Philisides and his love, and the last three, recited by the disguised princes Pyrocles and Musidorus, exemplify the application of the theme.

The third set, containing only five poems celebrating the marriage of the shepherds Lalus and Kala, has a different structural pattern. It begins with a formal epithalamium wishing joy to the newly married pair, continues with a humorous fabliau illustrating the effects of unfounded jealousy, follows with a sonnet describing the ideal husband, proceeds with a beast fable about the origins of monarchy narrated by Philisides, and ends with an exhortation to marriage and the proper bearing of the double yoke of wedded life with mutual consent. The beast fable might on a superficial view appear to break the unity of this group; but a little reflection shows that it is entirely appropriate, for it is concerned with discovering the proper form of sovereignty in the state, just as the other marriage poems are concerned with indicating the proper form of sovereignty in the home, which is the point made in the last poem:

> But let us pick our good from out much bad,
> That still our little world may know his king.

The fourth eclogues, coming after the supposed death of Basilius and the imprisonment of the princes, exploit the double nature of the renaissance elegy as a song of the sufferings of lovers or a lament for the dead. The set consists of six paired poems. In the first two Strephon and Klaius lament the absence of their beloved Urania, in the second two Philisides tells how he first saw his Mira in a dream and how he bade her farewell after she rejected him, and in the last two Dicus and Agelastus bewail the death of Basilius in a formal pastoral elegy and a rhyming sestina.

Though each of the four sets of eclogues is concerned with a single theme, the individual poems are considerably more varied, both in form and in metrics, than are Spenser's. The conventional pastoral kinds appear—the sing-

ing match, the debate, the love lament, the funeral elegy; and also a number of other kinds that are not found in the classical pastoral—the beast fable, the epithalamium, the fabliau, the impresa. The metrics also are amazingly varied, from tetrameter, pentameter, and Alexandrine couplets, terza rima, sixain stanzas, rhyme royal, a nine-line stanza of varied line lengths with refrain, a sonnet, and an echo poem, to a corona of dizains and a double sestina, with polymetric poems containing three or more forms in intricate progression. Each participant is assigned a rhythm appropriate to his character; the native Arcadians recite in the common (that is common for English readers) accentual iambics, the noble strangers use artificial quantitative measures.

In addition to the eclogues there are fifty-one other poems interspersed in the prose narrative of the **Old Arcadia,** for most of the characters, from the members of the Court to the lowliest shepherds, break into song at moments of tension or when they wish to be emphatic. These poems too are varied in form, kind, and mood. There are answer poems, madrigals, blasons, a mock encomium, a hymn, nine varieties of sonnet, &c., some tender, some mocking, some merely ingenious. They have been called experiments, and they were, for Sidney was exploring many of the ways by which language can be patterned. Several were quite successful experiments, and a measure of the esteem with which contemporaries at least regarded his productions can be gained from the first anthology of pastoral lyrics in English, *Englands Helicon* published in 1600, which contains three selections from Spenser, fourteen from Sidney.

Most of these poems gain their full effect only when viewed in the prose contexts in which they occur, which is the reason why I have included in the Commentary a brief account of the situation out of which each arises. The one Arcadian poem that has a place in all the anthologies is the song of the shepherdess Charita:

> My true love hath my hart, and I have his.

The late Theodore Spencer, who in 1945 published the best essay that had been written on Sidney's poetry, praised this sonnet for 'the monosyllabic simplicity of the diction . . . and the flawless movement of the rhetoric. The poem is a perfectly drawn circle, ending most contentedly where it began.' It is a pretty poem, not a great one; though it is superior in technique to most of the verse that had been produced in England during the preceding thirty years because of the finish of its form. But people reading it only in anthologies have taken it much too seriously, because the context in which it appears is entirely humorous and it is actually an elaborate *tour de force.*

The narrative episode of which the poem is a part is as follows. The young prince Musidorus has disguised himself as a shepherd in order to gain access to the princess Pamela, who is continually watched by the ugly hag Miso, wife of the lecherous old herdsman Dametas. In order to elope with Pamela Musidorus must somehow get Miso out of the way, so he plays upon her jealous disposition by telling her a completely made-up story of overhearing her husband make an assignation with a young shepherdess.

So ys yt, Mistris (sayde hee) that, yesterday dry-
ving my Sheepe up to the stately Hill, whiche
liftes his heade over the fayre City of Mantinea,
I hapned upon the syde of yt . . . to perceyve
a younge Mayde, truely of the fynest stamp of
Beuty. . . . In her Lapp there lay a Shepeheard
so wrapped up in that well liked place, that I
coulde discerne no peece of his face . . . [and]
her Angelike voyce, strake myne eares with this
Songe:

> My true love hath my hart, and I have his . . .

Whereupon the shepherd 'recorded to her Musick this
Rurall Poesy':

> O words which fall like sommer deaw on
> me . . .

'O sweete Charita saide hee . . . when shall youre Blisfull
promyse now Due be verifyed with Just performance.'
And then, Musidorus continued, he recognized the shepherd as Miso's decrepit husband Dametas, and heard the
young shepherdess agree to meet him that night at her
house in the Oudemian street. Miso, completely taken in
by this story, rushes off to prevent the supposed assignation, and Musidorus is left free to pursue his own courtship.

But the reader is not taken in, and enjoys the comedy of
the situation in which the witty prince gulls the stupid
countrywoman and deceives her while telling her plainly
that she is being deceived—for the Oudemian street means
a street without inhabitants, and the songs by their juxtaposition and their stylistic devices mock one another and
themselves. Dametas's 'Rurall Poesy' is just as sophisticated a composition as Charita's song, and gains its effect
through the clash of its form and content. The images are
those that an ignorant country fellow might be expected
to use in courtship—'breath more sweete, then is the
growing beane', 'haire more gaie then straw', 'flesh . . .
as hard, as brawne'; but the ingenious rhetorical structure
is completely at variance with the homely imagery. It is
built upon the formula of correlative verse, by which a series of terms are distributed and then at the end recapitulated, and the device is carried almost to the ultimate limits of complexity by combining three different sets of distributed terms and their recapitulations. The conclusion
makes a complete mockery of Charita's song, because
while the young shepherdess sings prettily of the courtly
dream of two hearts in one, the old shepherd cares nothing
for such idealistic imaginings—for him it is 'skinne' and
'flesh' that 'must pay, the gage of promist weale'.

Sidney did not devote his entire time to the composition
of the *Old Arcadia,* for during the years that he was engaged upon it he also wrote a variety of other pieces. Probably in the spring of 1578 he composed *The Lady of May,*
a pastoral entertainment devised for Queen Elizabeth
when she visited his uncle the Earl of Leicester at Wanstead. He also continued to play the game of Philisides and
Mira, and wrote other poems about their courtship for
which he did not find a place in the *Arcadia.* One of these
he later inserted in a different work and another was rescued from his loose papers by his sister and inserted in the
composite version of the *New* and *Old Arcadia* that she

published in 1593. In addition he wrote a number of other
poems, totally unconnected with the *Arcadia,* that he later
collected under the title *Certain Sonnets,* all but two of
which were composed before the end of 1581.

The *Certain Sonnets* is a gathering of thirty-two poems of
various kinds. Five are translations from Latin and Spanish, the rest are original; most are love poems, and though
the collection is miscellaneous in nature Sidney gave it
some semblance of structure by beginning with two sonnets yielding to love and ending with two others bidding
farewell to love. Only thirteen of the poems are properly
sonnets; the others are in a variety of metrical forms which
show the range and variety of Sidney's poetical experiments even beyond the multiplicity of kinds he had essayed in the eclogues and songs of the *Old Arcadia.* Several of his best poems are here—especially the song on the
nightingale with the refrain, 'Thy thorne without, my
thorne my heart invadeth'; and the song beginning 'Ring
out your bells' with its carefully equipoised passion, the
recoil of rage upon itself at the end accentuated by the
shift in the refrain, and the whole held together by a stanzaic form whose lines of varying length give just the right
pace, pause, and surge to the angry epithets.

Five of the *Certain Sonnets* show his continued preoccupation with quantitative metres. Eight others derive their
stanzaic structure and rhythms from contemporary
tunes—one Dutch, one English, five Italian, and one
Spanish. The only one of these whose music can now be
identified (CS 23) shows that Sidney, though changing the
sense, patterned his stanza syllable by syllable upon the
words of the original, and that the syllables of the original
are directly proportioned to the notes of the music. An especially tantalizing problem is raised by CS 7, 26, and 27,
the first to a Spanish and the last two to Neapolitan tunes,
for they bring a new rhythm into Elizabethan verse:

> This you heare is not my tongue,
> Which once said what I conceavëd,
> For it was of use bereavëd,
> With a cruell answer stong.

These, with one exception, are the first regularly sustained
accentual trochaics in English. (pp. xxxvi-xliii)

[*Astrophil and Stella*] is a collection of 108 sonnets and
eleven songs that tells of the love of a young courtier for
a married woman. Sidney went out of his way to identify
himself as Astrophil and Stella as Lady Rich, and even
wrote three sonnets to reveal her married name. But
though the poems are ostensibly autobiographical they do
not form a versified diary, for the details are highly selected and most of Sidney's known public and private activities are passed over in silence. Nor are they, like many
other collections of sonnets, a series of verse epistles designed to gain the favour of the lady. There is no evidence
that the sonnets were ever sent to Stella herself; indeed,
many of them were inappropriate for her eyes—there
would have been no point to having her guess her own
name, and no lover attempting to gain favour would tell
his mistress of his cynical resolve to break her covenants.
Stella herself is not directly addressed until sonnet 30, and
she is only occasionally addressed thereafter. Astrophil is
the central figure, everything is presented from his point

of view, and he addresses a variety of persons (a friend, other poets, lordings, envious wits), or things (the moon, a sparrow, his bed), or personifications (Virtue, Reason, Cupid), or he communes with himself. The poems then are a series of conversations or monologues which the reader overhears. The reader and not the lady is the audience, while Astrophil and those he addresses are the actors. As the principal actor Astrophil is also able to observe himself with wry self awareness, or even to play a patently sophistical part. The mode of presentation is essentially dramatic.

The dramatic development of Sidney's individual poems can be illustrated from the great majority of them—song iv for example, or even from sonnet 54, 'Because I breathe not love to everie one', which is narrated. In this latter piece we are given a little tableau with Astrophil on one side and the young ladies of the Court on the other. Astrophil is dressed and acts in a perfectly normal fashion, he wears no lovelocks for a token and heaves no melancholy sighs. The ladies, accustomed to the protestations of conventional courtly lovers, chatter among themselves in charmingly colloquial fashion:

> What, he? say they of me, now I dare sweare,
> He cannot love; no, no, let him alone.

The chatter of the ladies causes Astrophil to recoil, to withdraw within himself and soliloquize:

> And thinke so still. So Stella know my mind,
> Professe in deed I do not Cupid's art.

The word 'art' suggests to him its opposite, the unaffected simplicity of true affection; and he addresses the ladies, telling them what he has learned in the instant, and what they may never feel: the silent swan, not the noisy magpie, is the type of the true lover, who is afraid to express his affection. Astrophil's discovery is scarcely new, is no more than the rephrasing of a proverb; so it is not the thought but the process by which it is arrived at, the way it results from and is developed by a situation, that strikes our attention.

Sidney grouped his poems to mark definite stages in the progress of Astrophil's courtship and gave his work a greater over-all unity than most renaissance collections of sonnets possess. The songs, however, present something of a problem. The six songs in trochaic metres narrate the more important events of the sequence—the stealing of the kiss, the night-time courtship at Stella's window, the climactic episode in which Stella admits her love for Astrophil but at the same time refuses his advances, his lament at her refusal, and his thoughts of her while absent. The other five songs, in conventional iambic metres, are little more than fillers, and the grouping, between the trochaic songs iv and viii, of sonnet 86 and the iambic songs v, vi, and vii, shows clumsy joinery. Sidney obviously saw the necessity of separating the two important lovers' meetings described in iv and viii; but in order to provide the needed interval he contented himself with selecting one sonnet he had written to Stella and adding to it three songs, at least one of which he had written earlier for quite a different purpose. The results are not very happy, for though the 'change of lookes' of sonnet 86 provides an ad-

equate occasion for the reproaches of song v, it follows strangely upon Stella's inadvertant revelation of her affection in song iv, and though songs vi and vii on the lady's voice and face are related in subject to one another, they again follow strangely after the reproaches of v and do not in any way prepare for the May-time meeting in viii. Neither are all the trochaic songs entirely consistent with the sonnets and with one another, for all the poems are in the first person, except song viii which is narrated in the third person, and Astrophil is consistently portrayed as a courtier, except in song ix where he surprisingly appears as a shepherd. A possible explanation of these inconsistencies is that Sidney first began to write about Astrophil's love for Stella in a set of detached songs in the new trochaic metres he had recently been experimenting with in the *Certain Sonnets,* and that not until after he had written the songs did he think of writing the sonnets and of combining them with the songs in a single sequence. Aside from these slight inconsistencies, Sidney's work is more carefully structured than that of any other Elizabethan sonnet collection.

Though there is some physical action in *Astrophil and Stella*—accounts of tournaments, a stolen kiss, clandestine meetings—the essential action is internal and concerns the play of thought and the workings of emotion. The poem appears to be divided into three parts, which are marked by shifts in the attitude of Astrophil himself. The first part presents the first reactions to being in love of a sensitive, intelligent, and highly principled young man. He does not find it in the least pleasant because for the first time in his life he is experiencing an emotion he cannot control, and like most young men who value their independence he rebels at being under its sway and calls it slavery, hell, and poison. He debates the conflicting claims of will and wit, passion and reason; but though he can rationally believe that reason should prevail over the senses, that worship of the loved one is an idolatry that destroys the worshipper, that physical beauty is no more than a dim shadow of the Platonic Good, that our duty is not to regard this life but to prepare for the next, though all this is true, it is 'yet true that I must Stella love.' Unlike many other sonneteers who had attempted to transform their emotions by processes of Platonic or religious sublimation, or to escape from their mistresses with cries of 'the Devil take her', Astrophil remains a realist and accepts the power of emotion as an empirical fact that cannot be denied.

He is aware that his love is 'vaine' and brings 'shame' upon him, but he cannot free himself from it; so he at first attempts to maintain a measure of self-respect by inventing sophistical arguments to justify his thraldom, to prove by 'reason good, good reason her to love,' and to equate passion with virtue. He insists that it was the lady's 'knowne worth' that first caused him to love her, and that in her 'Vertue is made strong by Beautie's might,' while to the charge that love plunges him 'in the mire Of sinfull thoughts' he replies instead that it ennobles and breeds 'A loathing of all loose unchastitie.' All this, the reader soon realizes, is an elaborate game of self-deception.

The mask is dropped in the 52nd sonnet, which marks the

beginning of the second part of the sequence, where Virtue and Love argue for the possession of Stella, Love claiming her body and Virtue her soul, whereupon Astrophil gives judgement:

> Let Vertue have that Stella's selfe; yet thus,
> That Vertue but that body graunt to us.

The consequences of his change in attitude are shown in the immediately following second tournament sonnet. In the first tournament sonnet he had gained the prize, he said, because he was inspired by Stella's eyes; but in this second tournament he is so bemused at her sight that he forgets to fight and makes a complete fool of himself. His change of attitude is made even more emphatic by contrast with the earlier sonnets. Formerly he had at least given intellectual assent to his friend's arguments:

> Your words my friend (right healthfull caustiks)
>   blame
> My young mind marde, whom Love doth
>   windlas so,
>   . . . that to my birth I owe
> Nobler desires, least else that friendly foe,
> Great expectation, weare a traine of shame.

But in the second part he gives over all protestation and goes in active pursuit of Stella:

> No more, my deare, no more these counsels trie,
> O give my passions leave to run their race:
> Let Fortune lay on me her worst disgrace,
>   . . . . .
> Let all the earth with scorne recount my case,
> But do not will me from my Love to flie. (64)

A change also occurs in Stella. Previously she had been presented as distant and unresponsive; but one day she blushes when he looks at her, and finally she gives him the monarchy of her heart, though only on condition that he maintain a virtuous course. Her admission of affection, instead of ennobling as he had earlier pretended it would, causes him to throw aside all principle and to remark cynically:

> And though she give but thus conditionly
> This realme of blisse, while vertuous course I
>   take,
> No kings be crown'd, but they some covenants
>   make.

Thereafter, until the eighth song, he gives his sensual race the rein. He steals a kiss from her while she sleeps, and thinks what a fool he has been for not taking more than a kiss; he sophistically praises the lecherous Edward IV as the greatest of English kings; he hopes Stella will go to bed in a more receptive mood; he composes a blason of her visible charms, suggestively concluding with the remark that his 'Mayd'n Muse doth blush to tell the best'; and he writes a denunciation of her husband suggesting that it would be no more than justice to cuckold him.

The climax of the drama occurs in the eighth song, in which Astrophil urges his suit, and Stella, though admitting her affection, says they must part:

> Trust me while I thee deny,
> In my selfe the smart I try,
> Tyran honour doth thus use thee,

Stella's selfe might not refuse thee.

> Therefore, Deere, this no more move,
> Least, though I leave not thy love,
> Which too deep in me is framed,
> I should blush when thou art named.

She leaves him 'passion rent', and the final section of the poem deals with Astrophil's despair, his sorrow at her absence, and his attempts to see her again. He finally by an act of will gives over the active pursuit of Stella; but he does not and cannot cease to love her, for he never frees himself from or sublimates his emotion. It is a fact that must be lived with.

Thomas Nashe, in the preface he wrote for Newman's unauthorized edition of *Astrophil and Stella* in 1591, characterized it as 'the tragicommody of love . . . performed by starlight. . . . The argument cruell chastitie, the Prologue hope, the Epilogue dispaire.' In calling it a tragicomedy Nashe meant that it was comic only in the technical sense 'in respect it wants deaths', for otherwise the action is tragic. Astrophil attains no serenity, and is left alone with 'most rude dispaire' as his 'daily unbidden guest.' There is no solution. The interest of the poem lies in its presentation of the emotional states and the psychology of Astrophil himself. Its artistic merit, beyond the excellence of the individual sonnets and songs, resides in its over-all structure. This structure is not rigidly planned, for the *Astrophil and Stella* poems do not have the intricate complication of incident of the plot of the *Arcadia*, nor are the individual poems arranged with the same regard for parallelism and unity of theme that we find in the first two sets of Arcadian eclogues. Instead they present us with a succession of scenes that illustrate emotional attitudes. There are some inconsistencies in the songs, and some of the sonnets could with more appropriateness occupy different positions; but in general there is an orderly progression of mood, the focus of attention remains fixed upon Astrophil as the lover of Stella, no irrelevancies are allowed to intrude, and the courtship is presented as having a beginning, a middle, and an end.

Probably either shortly before or after composing *Astrophil and Stella* Sidney wrote his *Defence of Poesy.* In this, especially in the digression on the contemporary state of English poetry, he describes the principles he had followed and many of the technical innovations he had introduced in his own verses. Thereafter he appears to have written no more than a handful of original poems. (pp. xliv-xlix)

Sidney did not write any poems about his campaigns in the Netherlands, or if he did no record of them survives. His poetry is remarkable for what he did not write about. He was a courtier, but except for some passages in *The Lady of May* he never wrote in praise of the Queen. He was sincerely religious, but he never wrote a poem of personal devotion. He placed a high value upon friendship, but except for his 'Two Pastoralls' and a single mention of Languet he never wrote a commendatory or memorial poem for a real person. The major interest of his life was politics, but only once did he deal with problems of government, and then under the veil of a beast fable. Except for *Astrophil and Stella* his verse was neither official nor personal and dealt almost entirely with imagined situations. Most of it was concerned with love; but even in his love poetry when he spoke as 'I' he usually did so through a created character, Philisides—and even Astrophil. He remained aloof, and so could view both his productions and himself with a sometimes quizzical detachment.

Until he attained complete mastery of his medium in *Astrophil and Stella*, he devoted his attention more to manner than to matter. When in his idlest times he looked upon the poetry of his own country he did not find it good, and he determined to make it better. He believed that 'the highest flying wit' must have 'a Dedalus to guide him'; and he felt that the greatest defect of his fellow English poets was that with 'neither Artificiall Rules, nor imitative paternes, we much comber our selves withall.' So he set out to be a Daedalus to his countrymen, to teach them rules of right writing, and to provide them with models to follow. His contemporary Spenser, who was also a reformer and proclaimed as 'this our new Poete', sought to revitalize English poetry by amalgamating the native and continental traditions; but Sidney turned his back almost completely upon the English past. Though he admitted the appeal of the old song of Percy and Douglas, he never wrote a ballad; and though he was acquainted with stories of King Arthur, he modelled his own romance upon works from Greece, Italy, and Spain (Heliodorus, Sannazaro, and Montemayor). He had spent his formative years studying the classics at Shrewsbury and Oxford and travelling upon the Continent; so when he commenced poet he followed classical and continental styles and forms more than he did those of his own country.

The Tudor poets had been faced with three major technical problems—forging a poetical language, discovering effective rhythms, and creating new poetical forms—for which they had found various but not always entirely satisfactory solutions. In language Sidney took a middle way, for he avoided both the ink-hornisms of the neologizers and the archaisms of the patriotic purists. 'I have found in divers smally learned courtiers', he said, 'a more sound stile, then in some professors of learning.' He therefore did not attempt to create a special poetic diction, but was content to use the language of everyday polite conversation. His verse contains no unusual words, no strange forms; only once did he indulge in Chaucerisms, and that was a single experiment in the manner of Spenser that he never repeated. So restrained was his vocabulary that, again except for isolated experiments, he avoided the excessive use of polysyllables, and preferred the commonest and shortest words. And yet he made a virtue of the prevailing monosyllabic quality of English. AS 31, for example, opens with ten words in a ten-syllable line—

> With how sad steps, ô Moone, thou climb'st the
> skies—

but the words are not low, nor is the line dull.

Almost the only departures from ordinary prose usage that he permitted himself, aside from tight logical and rhetorical structure, were the occasional use of compound epithets and the frequent use of inversion. Some years after Sidney's death Joseph Hall called the compound epithet

> . . . that new elegance,
> Which sweet Philisides fetch't of late from
> France.

But Sidney himself had noted in his *Defence* that English 'is perticularly happy in compositions of two or three wordes togither, neare the Greeke, farre beyond the Latine,' so he probably cultivated the device more in emulation of ancient classical than of contemporary continental writers. His compounds are usually made up of two elements only, as 'thanke worthie frends,' but on occasion they are extended to considerable length, as 'long with Love acquainted eyes.'

Sidney also used inversion, occasionally in his earlier and with increasing frequency in his later poems. Sometimes the device is a mere ornamental mannerism, and sometimes it produces puzzling ambiguities, as 'Not though thereof the cause her selfe she know'; but usually it provides subtle modulations of rhythm and sense, as 'Indeed O you, you that be such of mind,' or gives needed emphasis to the most important words: 'And to old age since you your selfe aspire,' 'For even the hearbes our hatefull musique stroyes,' 'But him her host that unkind guest had slaine.'

Though Sidney was conservative in his choice of words, he was an innovator in his handling of rhythm. In the earlier years of the sixteenth century English prosody had been in a state of anarchy with no generally accepted principles of structure. Followers of the degenerate Lydgate tradition, like Stephen Hawes and William Nevill, wrote verse whose lines had no equivalence in length and no established pattern of stresses, only a tinckle of rhyme at the end. But by the middle decades of the century the earlier anarchy had been reduced to mechanical regularity. As a result George Gascoigne, whose *Certain Notes of Instruction* published in 1575 is the earliest formal treatise on English metrics, recognized only one rhythm, the iambic, and knew of only one way to write English verse: count syllables, have a regular alternation of stresses, and place a caesura in the same position in every line. Absolute regularity had thus become the primary virtue, and Gascoigne and most of his contemporaries maintained in their verses a fixed and never-varying pattern. . . . (pp. li-liv)

Sidney set about to combat the monotony of the English verse of his time; but he allowed himself only moderate and not excessive freedom, for he maintained a strict syllable count and an equal number of stresses as the basic pattern of all equivalent lines. To maintain an equal syllable count he made full use of the orthographic schemes that permitted each syllable of a word to receive full pronunciation or to be suppressed at will by elision, apheresis, syncopation, or apocopation, 'as thadvantaige of the verse best serves'; but his scribes were not at all consistent in indicating the suppression of syllables by spelling or apostrophes, and Sidney himself may not have been consistent in using graphical devices for this purpose in his holographs. Since the pronunciation of the lines is made the responsibility of the reader, there is room for a certain amount of individual variation. Whether the last three feet of a line such as, 'Since sorow is the follower of evill fortune', should be read as 'the fóll'wer 'f évil fórtune' or as 'the fóll'wer óf 'ill fórtune' is something of an open question; but since Sidney had a more formal conception of metre and was not as disturbed as we are today at a stress falling on an unemphatic word, he may have preferred the second reading. On the other hand, he scarcely ever wrenched pronunciation by diastole to fit his metre. A couplet such as,

> With neighing, blaying, braying, and barking,
> Roring, and howling for to have a King,

in which the rhyme demands that the last word of the first line be pronounced 'barkíng', is extremely rare.

Some of Sidney's earliest verse is as mechanical as that of Gascoigne; but he almost at once began to vary the tempo of his lines by inversion of feet and shifting of caesuras:

> And keep it joynde, fearing your seate's consumption.
>
> . . . . .
>
> Thus Painters *Cupid* paint, thus Poets do,
> A naked god, young, blind, with arrowes two.

He introduced variations of this sort sparingly at first, but more frequently as he went on; until in *Astrophil and Stella* he resolved mechanical regularity to a controlled freedom by allowing the rhythms of speech to have an increasing part in introducing variations in the fixed pattern—

> 'Foole,' said my Muse to me, 'Looke in thy heart and write.'

Sidney never achieved the elaborate harmonies of Spenser, but he helped to free English metre from the strait jacket to which poets of the mid century had confined it, and he also sought other rhythms besides the ubiquitous iambic. Following the lead of Ascham and Drant, he for awhile experimented with adapting classical quantitative metres to English. But his greatest triumph was naturalizing an entirely new rhythm, the accentual trochaic. He made his first tentative experiments in this new form in three of the *Certain Sonnets,* and brought it to perfection in the songs of *Astrophil and Stella.*

In his handling of rhyme also he was both a meticulous craftsman and an innovator. He almost always rhymed with complete phonetic accuracy. Apparent variations, such as 'bear-were' and 'far-stir', were actually perfect rhymes in Elizabethan pronunciation (in Sidney's holographs they would have been spelled 'bear-wear' and 'fur-stur', but the scribes seldom preserved his phonetic spelling). He sometimes took advantage of variant current pronunciations, but he hardly ever allowed himself the common licence of creating entirely new rhymes by the figure antisthecon, such as 'seech' for 'seek'.

His great innovation was to bring feminine rhyme back into English verse and to make it a formal structural element in the shaping of his stanzas. After the early years of the sixteenth century the Tudor poets had confined themselves almost exclusively to masculine rhyme. Surrey has at most five, and probably only two, pairs of genuine feminine rhymes in all his verse, and an analysis of the selections in a standard anthology such as that of Hebel and Hudson reveals only three pairs of feminine rhymes between Wyatt and Sidney. But Sidney used feminine rhyme in one out of every five of his poems, and even used trisyllabic (*sdrucciola*) rhyme in four poems. He only occasionally introduced it haphazardly as an ornamental variation; most of the time he made it a regularly recurring structural element of his stanzaic patterns. Thus each quatrain of OA 57 has feminine rhyme in its second and fourth lines, and each stanza of CS 23 maintains a pattern of regularly alternating feminine and masculine rhymes. He used feminine rhyme in all of his trochaic poems and in all of his sestinas; but he avoided it in all but three of his early sonnets—none of the *Astrophil and Stella* sonnets contains feminine rhyme, though it regularly appears in the songs. This distinction in its use may be the result of some privately formulated and as yet unexplained principle of decorum. Though feminine rhyme almost never appears in the poetry of the mid century, by the 1590's, probably in part as a result of Sidney's example, it had become an accepted feature of English verse.

But though Sidney introduced important innovations in rhythm and rhyme, he was even more interested in larger structural patterns which he created by a compact and complex combination of the devices of logic and rhetoric within established or newly invented fixed forms. He prided himself on being 'a peece of a Logician', and his poems are notable for the orderly progression of their ideas. Some of them are concatenations of arguments, others are debates, and in all the images are controlled by their logical function and the feeling is guided by thought.

His handling of rhetorical devices also shows a great advance over his predecessors. Though the earlier Tudor poets had been conscious of rhetoric, their range of figures was limited, and they usually contented themselves with the repetitive use of a few simple schemes such as anaphora or alliteration. Sidney structured his verse with an intricate interlacing of the whole panoply of both schemes and tropes. As a result, Abraham Fraunce in his *Arcadian Rhetorike* could illustrate the entire range of figures in the Talaean manual from Sidney's poems. Sometimes he used only a few devices, as in OA 35—

> Sweete glove, the sweete despoyles of sweetest hand,
> Fayre hand, the fayrest pledge of fayrer harte,
> Trew harte, whose trewthe dothe yeeld to trewest bande—

where the controlling scheme gradation is emphasized by polyptoton and some subsidiary devices of repetition. At other times he used tropes as well as schemes in greater variety and related in a more complex manner. In OA 21 the 'brookes', 'aier', and 'sande' on which Cleophila looks, with which he speaks, and in which he writes are the elements water, air, and earth which combine with the fire of his passion; the enumeration is recapitulated in the next to the last line, and the phrases are further related and elaborated by synecdoche, anadiplosis, prosopopoeia, antithesis, and a variety of other figures. In the *Old Arcadia* the rhetoric is sometimes obtrusive, in the best of the *Astrophil and Stella* sonnets it is less obvious because more completely functional. His special contribution was the use, not of one or two figures in isolation, but of a wide variety of figures in intricate combination.

Sidney also enhanced the structure of his poems by following the patterns of the established genres, and by imitating or devising an astonishing number of stanzaic forms. His critical preoccupation is shown by his being the first to introduce into English many of the terms which today are part of our basic vocabulary when talking about poetry— 'couplet', 'lyric', 'madrigal', 'masculine rhyme', 'octave', 'stanza', &c. He was also the first Englishman to give a formal list of the traditional classical kinds—pastoral, elegiac, iambic, satiric, comic, tragic, lyric, and heroic. He himself, if we include the mixed forms appearing in his prose fiction, produced examples of all of these except the personal invective of the iambic; and in addition he wrote poems modelled on a number of the subsidiary kinds, such as the blason, epithalamium, fabliau, and hymn.

But his greatest innovations were in the variety and number of verse forms that he used and introduced. His 286 poems contain 143 different line and stanza patterns, 109 of which he used only once. Most of these were entirely new to English—fewer than 20 appear in Tottel's *Songes and Sonettes*. His lines vary in length from 3 to 14 syllables, his stanzas from 3 to 15 lines; for rhythms he used iambics, trochaics, and 7 varieties of quantitative metre. His *Old Arcadia* contains half a dozen polymetric poems; but in all his later poems, except for introductory quatrains or concluding couplets and partial stanzas, he strictly maintained the same stanza form with which he began, even to the exact patterning of masculine and feminine rhymes. Among the more technically difficult forms that he first introduced were the sestina, the crown, and the canzone. No previous English poet, from Old English to Tudor times, even approached Sidney in the variety and complexity of metrical forms that he used.

The form that he cultivated most assiduously was the sonnet, which after its introduction by Wyatt and Surrey had been strangely neglected by later English poets except Gascoigne. Approximately half of Sidney's poems are sonnets, of which he produced thirty-three different varieties. His handling of the form shows a definite direction of experimentation. He began with the Surreyan form of three quatrains and a couplet—20 of his 34 early sonnets are patterned on that model, though he never used it later. The canard that English poets avoided the Italian form because of the difficulty of finding rhymes is effectively refuted by his practice, for sixteen of his earliest sonnets have five rhymes or less—indeed three have only three rhymes, two have two, and one repeats the same rhyme sound in all 14 lines. But he soon began to prefer an octave with only two rhymes, though only once in the *Old Arcadia* did he imitate the strict Italian form (the Petrarchan rhyme scheme and hendecasyllabic lines of OA 69 make the Italian source of his inspiration obvious). The form he eventually found most satisfactory combined an Italian octave with a *cdcdee* sestet, a combination he used in his later composed CS 1 and 2 and in 60 of his *Astrophil and Stella* sonnets. Since Wyatt had written two sonnets of this type, his model in this case, as Lever observed, may have been English rather than continental. Sidney's earlier sonnets are excellently constructed rhetorical forms exemplifying the Erasmian doctrines of copiousness. His later and better sonnets, instead of being static rhetorical statements,

frequently contain a dynamic interaction of feeling and thought by which something is made to happen and through which a discovery is made by both the speaker and the reader.

The poet, Sidney said, is a 'maker,' and from his own practise we can see that he considered him not only as a creator of an ideally ordered world, but also as a creator of artistic forms. His own central preoccupation was with structure, and in his search for form he not only produced single excellently fashioned poems, but also sought to relate them to one another to produce larger and more complex unities. He closely related the verses in the narrative portion of his *Arcadia* to the contexts in which they occur by making them appropriate to the situation and the speaker, and he even so grouped his miscellaneous *Certain Sonnets* that they have a clearly defined beginning and end. But his greatest triumphs in creating larger architectonic patterns are in the between-the-act eclogues of the *Old Arcadia* and in *Astrophil and Stella.* He unified each group of eclogues by making the individual poems illustrate a single theme in different ways, and he related the four groups to one another so that they form an artistic whole that is fully capable of standing by itself. In *Astrophil and Stella,* instead of collecting a mere aggregate of sonnets and songs, he arranged them to provide a narrative and psychological progression, and so produced a sequence that is more dramatic and highly ordered than any other in the renaissance.

Sidney taught his countrymen that a poet should be neither an artisan mechanically performing a task nor an undisciplined enthusiast, but an accomplished craftsman, and in his own poetry he provided both technical models to be followed and examples of excellence. He introduced new techniques of rhythm and rhyme, new stanzaic patterns, and new examples of poetic kinds. What he taught his countrymen in the 1580's, many of them were practising in the 1590's. (pp. liv-lx)

> *William A. Ringler, Jr., in an introduction to* The Poems of Sir Philip Sidney, *edited by William A. Ringler, Jr., Oxford at the Clarendon Press, 1962, pp. xv-lxvi.*

S. K. Orgel (essay date 1963)

[*Orgel is an American educator and critic who has written extensively on Elizabethan and Renaissance drama. In the essay below, originally published in the* Journal of the Warburg and Courtauld Institutes *in 1963, Orgel examines Sidney's masque* The Lady of May, *characterizing it as an experiment in the pastoral form and contending that, due to its rhetorical nature, it is better read than performed.*]

Sidney's *The Lady of May* has gone largely unnoticed since its inclusion—apparently at the last moment, and in the interests of completeness—in the 1598 folio of his works. It had been commissioned by Leicester as an entertainment for Queen Elizabeth, and was presented before her at Wanstead, probably in 1578. It merits attention on a number of grounds, not the least of which is its obvious interest as a dramatic piece by the author of *Arcadia* and *Astrophel and Stella*. It is characteristic of Sidney in its treatment of literary convention, its concern with examining and reassessing the underlying assumptions of pastoral; in the unique way, in short, that its creator thinks about literature. Every new form posed a set of new problems for Sidney: although he employed conventional modes, he took nothing for granted, and *The Lady of May* provides us with a brief and excellent example of the way his mind worked. In this entertainment, Sidney used the monarch in a functional way in the action of his drama. This device, which had been the central characteristic of the English court masque after 1513, serves to define the genre even more than the formal dances, which were often but not inevitably present. Sidney, as usual, adds a new depth to the old device, but his use of it at all in such a context links him with Jonson and the Milton of *Comus* in treating the masque as primarily a literary form. The work has an additional point of interest which has also gone unnoticed for almost four centuries. It provides us, as we shall see, with an account of what must have been for Sidney and a few other alert observers (among whom no subsequent commentator may be numbered), a surprising fiasco.

> Her most excellent Majestie walking in Wansteed Garden, as she passed downe into the grove, there came suddenly among the traine, one apparelled like an honest mans wife of the countrey, where crying out for justice, and desiring all the Lords and Gentlemen to speake a good word for her, she was brought to the presence of her Majestie, to whom upon her knees she offred a supplication, and used this speech.

So begins *The Lady of May* in the 1598 folio, the basis of all our texts. The title is a modern invention appearing in none of the sixteenth- or seventeenth-century editions. Though running heads are used throughout the 1598 volume, there are none for this work, which concludes the book. And though the work starts on the verso of the last page of *Astrophel and Stella,* there is no catchword for it on the recto. Typographically, in fact, it accosts us with the same abruptness which must have characterized the performance itself. What we possess is a text which is intended as a description of the actual production: no re-writing seems to have been done, and it remains as a unique record of an audacious experiment which went wrong.

From the outset, Sidney insists that the action of his drama has the same kind of reality as everything else at Wanstead. We are turned without warning from a country garden to the world of pastoral; turned, as it were, on a pivot; for, as in the masque, the centre is constant, the Queen cannot change. But deliberately, there is no artifice; no frame for the drama; no theatre; the actors bring their world with them and transform ours; they deny that they are "characters", treating their audience exactly as they treat each other; and we, as spectators, find we cannot tell them apart from ourselves. We need look no further than this to realize the extent to which *The Lady of May* is conceived in terms of the masque.

So the distraught suppliant makes her entreaty directly to the monarch standing before her. The catastrophe is a nuptial; the country-woman's daughter, the May Lady, has two suitors, a shepherd and a woodsman; and she cannot decide between them. The country people have taken sides, and the Lady's choice now has the aspect of a judgment on the relative merits of two ways of life, the contemplative and the active. It is the Queen who must settle the controversy, and the woman urges her to continue her walk; for "your owne way guides you to the place where they encomber her".

"And with that", the text continues, "she went away a good pace", leaving with the Queen a formal supplication. The ensuing poem is a traditional invocation with this difference: the muse, the inspiration of the work, is literally present. The poem must have been written out and handed to Elizabeth; presumably it was also read aloud for the benefit of the other spectators. In invokes and defines the monarch by first adducing a set of conventional attributes for her, and then qualifying these with another set. The Queen is, it says, exalted beyond the reach of ordinary people, but her greatness is also their comfort and protection. Though her countenance may be dangerous to look at, it is also beautiful. Her mind is matchless in argument, but also wise and understanding. The point to be stressed here is that both sets of tropes, both the initial descriptions and what subsequently qualifies them, represent traditional attitudes toward the sovereign. The qualification does not weaken or deny the original metaphor, it only shows us another aspect of it; and the conventions, therefore, remain intact. The poem, in fact, examining a number of commonplaces about royalty, speaks wholly in terms of literary conventions, of stock tropes. It is an apt introduction to the work, in that its rhetorical method, a kind of dialectic of metaphor, is to be repeated in each of the several debates around which the drama is built; but we might also note that the masque itself is conceived as an examination of literary convention—of one of the basic assumptions of the traditional pastoral.

And yet the work *is* a pastoral. Let us remark from the outset, then, how characteristic it is of its author. Here, as everywhere in his writings, Sidney is above all a critic, and so we find this masque returning constantly to basic questions of its own form. *The Lady of May* is concerned with only a single aspect of the pastoral mode, the assumption that the contemplative life is intrinsically more virtuous than the active life. We may see the critique extended and deepened in the larger pastoral world of *Arcadia,* that wild country where the retired life of the contemplative man is full of deception and misery, and the innocent lover, that indispensable figure of pastoral, is met with sudden and violent death. *Arcadia* is about what happens if we consider the real implications of pastoral romance, about the abrogation of responsibility in a world where nature is not friendly nor chance benign. Similarly, Sidney creates, in a Petrarchan sonnet sequence, a beloved who is literally unattainable, and a lover for whom the sense of loss and separation approaches the Calvinist sense of original sin. Both *Arcadia* and *Astrophel and Stella* are, obviously, serious in a way in which the Queen's entertainment at Wanstead cannot be. Nevertheless, the same intelligence is at work, the same sorts of questions are being asked; and the solutions, when they come, are arrived at only after all the traditional assumptions have been discarded. In *The Lady of May,* the validity of the conventional antithesis of pastoral—contemplation versus action—is to be questioned, thought through again from the beginning, debated and judged.

As the action proceeds now, the antithesis appears dramatically before us. Immediately after the supplication, "there was heard in the woods a confused noyse, and forthwith there came out six sheapheards with as many fosters haling and pulling, to whether side they should draw the Lady of May, who seemed to encline neither to the one nor the other side". We may wish to call this entry of rough country folk, juxtaposed with the rigid decorum of the opening poem, a dramatic antimasque; and certainly we can hardly imagine a more striking representation of the central conflict of the drama than a tug-of-war with the prize in the middle. We become aware at once, however, of the efficacy of the royal presence:

> But the Queene comming to the place where she
> was seene of them, though they knew not her es-
> tate, yet something there was which made them
> startle aside and gaze at her.

Let us beware of calling this flattery: its name is convention. There is, simply, that in her countenance which they would fain call master. The validity of the debate—and indeed, the whole drama—here hinges on Authority, inherent in the nature of the monarch.

Two of the country people now attempt to explain the problem to the Queen, Lalus, "one of the substantiallest shepheards", and Maister Rombus, a pedant schoolmaster. Shepherds are traditionally the heroes of pastoral, and Lalus has been a successful enough shepherd to grow rich at the work. What enlightenment we may justly expect from him, however, is lost in the pretentious ignorance of his euphuism, and he soon yields his place to Rombus, who, he says, "can better disnounce the whole foundation of the matter".

Rombus is a scholar. If the shepherd is a conventional exemplar of the contemplative life, Rombus is the contemplative man in person. And yet, far from expounding the basic issues of the masque, his "learned Oration" only succeeds in adding burlesque Latinisms and bombast to the shepherd's periphrases. He barely reaches his subject, taken as he is with both his rhetoric and his accomplishments; and the true and tedious burden of his address turns out to be the local contempt for "the pulcritude of my virtues". If the contemplative man is without honour in his own country, then this pastoral land of Sidney's is a most unfamiliar one. In any traditional pastoral, Lalus and Rombus would in some way at least be at the centre of their world, would express at least some truth, embody some virtue which the work may ultimately assert. Here, on the contrary, we find that they cannot even express what the masque is about.

Both are dismissed by the clear, balanced, characteristically Sidneian prose of the May Lady, who proceeds to describe her two suitors, "the one a forrester named *Therion,* the other *Espilus* a sheapheard". Espilus is rich, but Therion is lively; Therion "doth me many pleasures", but has a nasty temper, whereas Espilus, "though of a mild dispo-

sition", has done her neither any great service nor any wrong. "Now the question I am to ask you", she concludes, "is whether the many deserts and many faults of *Therion,* or the very small deserts and no faults of *Espilus* are to be preferred."

The Lady's prose is superseded by a more formal rhetoric as the two adversaries enter to speak for themselves. Therion challenges Espilus to a singing contest, the staple controversy of this most artificial form. The ideological conflict is now presented as verbal and musical as well. Since the argument must be discussed in some detail, I quote the poem in full:

ESPILUS

Tune up my voice, a higher note I yeeld,
To high conceipts the song must needes be high
More high then stars, more firme then flintie
    field
Are all my thoughts, on which I live or die:
Sweete soul, to whom I vowed am a slave,
Let not wild woods so great a treasure have.

THERION

The highest note comes oft from basest mind,
As shallow brookes do yeeld the greatest sound,
Seeke other thoughts thy life or death to find;
Thy stars be fal'n, plowed is thy flintie ground:
Sweete soule let not a wretch that serveth
    sheepe,
Among his flocke so sweete a treasure keepe.

ESPILUS

Two thousand sheepe I have as white as milke,
Though not so white as is thy lovely face,
The pasture rich, the wooll as soft as silke,
All this I give, let me possesse thy grace,
But still take heede least thou thy selfe submit
To one that hath no wealth, and wants his wit.

THERION

Two thousand deere in wildest woods I have,
Them I can take, but you I cannot hold:
He is not poore who can his freedome save,
Bound but to you, no wealth but you I would:
But take this beast, if beasts you feare to misse,
For of his beasts the greatest beast he is.

The singing match is also a formal debate. Therion, the man of action, has issued the challenge. Espilus begins, "as if he had been inspired with the muses", but the rebuttal always offers the stronger position in a debate, and Therion clearly knows what he is about. Rhetorically, this duet is set up in the same way as the earlier supplication: Espilus states his case through a series of metaphors; Therion shows that any trope is only a partial truth.

The shepherd opens in the Petrarchan manner: his love is higher than stars, firmer than earth; he is a slave to his mistress; she is a treasure. The world he adduces is severely limited, and "my thoughts, on which I live or die" turn out to be a set of perfectly conventional conceits. It is precisely the limitations of these metaphors—of this view of the world—that Therion, in his reply, exposes. High notes do *not* imply high thoughts, and neither are the stars so immutable nor the earth so solid as Espilus imagines. The forester has from the outset a much firmer grasp on the physical facts of this pastoral world than the shepherd has: Therion's conceits are related directly to apprehensible phenomena—the noise brooks make, falling stars, ploughed fields. Indeed, he even has a deeper understanding of the realities of Espilus' life than the shepherd appears to have. Therion uses Espilus' own characterization of himself as a "slave" to point out that his bondage is more real than he thinks: he is bound to his wealth, his flock. This is Espilus' "treasure", and his metaphor, says Therion, has thus equated his lady with his sheep.

And in his second turn, the shepherd goes on to make the comparison perfectly explicit:

> "Two thousand sheep I have as white as milke,
> Though not so white as is thy lovely face . . . "

The simile, happily, works out to the detriment of the sheep. But the limitations of Espilus' apprehension are now apparent. He boasts of his possessions and conceives of his mistress as one of them; "thy grace" is something he will add to his treasure. Finally we find that it is no longer the lover but the lady who is a slave, for he warns her against *submitting* to the wrong master, "one that hath no wealth".

To Therion, however, possession is a denial of humanity, and his reply, "Two thousand deere in wildest woods I have", is a statement not of his riches, but of his potentialities as a man. Instead of Espilus' wealth, he offers his own freedom and hers; one may keep beasts, "but you I cannot hold." His description of their marriage ("Bound but to you . . . ") implies not her submission, but their mutual union; and the apostle of wealth, the shepherd, is ultimately seen as only a beast of the higher orders.

Throughout this exchange, the forester has continually undercut what is for the shepherd his only mode of thought, and hence of expression. It is clear that in every way Therion has the better of it. The argument, in fact, progresses with such ease that we may tend to credit the forester with an easy victory, and overlook its significance in the work as a whole. Surely it is unusual to find Espilus, the contemplative man, preaching the virtues of worldly wealth; we had thought it was only in the forest of Arden that shepherds were concerned with economics. But Sidney, like Shakespeare, is redefining the convention behind his work, examining and judging the values it implies. Therion has charged Espilus with using conventions he does not understand, with being unaware of the implications of his own metaphors. And the charge is directed as well at the audience at Wanstead, and at us. Essentially, this is the warning of a first-rate critic against abstracting literary devices from their contexts; and it is to become a warning against the dangers of asserting the traditional advantages of the contemplative life, without understanding the function the assertion served in the individual pastorals from which the tradition grew.

The case is discussed more fully in the debate which follows, a prose parallel to the singing match; "the speakers were Dorcas an olde shepheard, and Rixus a young foster, betweene whom the schoolemaister Rombus came in as moderator." Dorcas speaks for the contemplative view. He cites the legal profession—"the Templars"—as evidence that "templation" is "the most excellent", and sees in the shepherd the man best fitted to a life of contemplation. So, he continues, courtiers leave the court to sit in the country and write pastoral complaints about their mistresses. And here, for the first time, we see that the shepherd need not be a literal one: "So that with long lost labour finding their thoughts bare no other wooll but despaire, of yong courtiers they grew old shepheards." Their thoughts—contemplation—are their sheep; but in this work, even Dorcas is wary of metaphor. Unlike real sheep, he points out, these are unproductive. And finally, the best Dorcas can say for them is that they are utterly harmless; his case rests on sentiment: "he that can open his mouth against such innocent soules, let him be hated as much as a filthy fox . . . "

This is not, even in itself, a very strong argument. But Rixus's rebuttal goes far beyond answering the shepherd's meagre claim. Dorcas's life has, he says,

> "some goodnesse in it, because it borrowed of the countrey quietnesse something like ours, but that is not all, for ours besides that quiet part, doth both strengthen the body, and raise up the mind with this gallant sort of activity. O sweet contentation to see the long life of the hurtlesse trees, to see how in streight growing up, though never so high, they hinder not their fellowes, they only enviously trouble, which are crookedly bent. What life is to be compared to ours where the very growing things are ensamples of goodnesse? we have no hopes, but we may quickly go about them, and going about them, we soone obtaine them . . . "

Again, simply by his position in the debate, the foster has the advantage. But more than that, we are aware that no case at all has been presented for the shepherd, and that it is Rixus, who, in this speech about the virtues of a life of action, is the one really concerned with the life of the mind. "This gallant sort of activity," he says, asserting its inherent nobility, "doth both strengthen the body and raise up the mind"; and his "ensamples of goodnesse" are drawn, like Therion's in the earlier debate, from the observable facts of the pastoral world. One would, I suppose, be hard put to find a *less* active "ensample" of the active life than "the hurtlesse trees", but the point is that the man of action is receptive to all experience; he is living as a part of nature, and everything in nature offers him an exemplary lesson; and consequently he, and only he, possesses the contemplative virtues as well. Indeed, we find that for Sidney there can be no dichotomy, between contemplation and action: the one necessarily leads to the other. So, what we may call "original sin" in **Arcadia** is the renunciation of an active political life for a pastoral dream—which ultimately cannot be realized. We may compare with this the Elizabethan version of a classic invitation to give up the world, couched in the language of Espilus and rejected by the Renaissance prototype of wisdom:

> Come, worthy Greek, Ulysses come.
> Possess these shores with me . . .

There can by this time, I take it, be no question about

where the choice between Espilus and Therion must lie. The time for the judgment has come, and the May Lady submits her fate to the Queen, reminding her and us explicitly "that in judging me, you judge more than me in it". The answer should, then, be a statement about the nature of a whole convention, an apprehension of the kinds of values pastoral may validly assert. And since the case is so clear, we will find it amusing enough that Elizabeth should have picked wrongly, but astonishing that no one since then should have noticed the error.

> It pleased her Majesty to judge that Espilus did the better diserve her: but what words, what reasons she used for it, this paper, which carrieth so base names, is not worthy to containe.

The omission of the reasoning is perhaps fortunate. Elizabeth, versed in the convention, picked Espilus because shepherds are the heroes of pastoral. But this is a most unconventional pastoral, and how wrong the Queen's choice was is apparent from the song of triumph which follows:

> *Silvanus* long in love, and long in vaine,
> At length obtaind the point of his desire,
> When being askt, now that he did obtaine
> His wished weale, what more he could require:
> Nothing sayd he, for most I joy in this,
> That Goddesse mine, my blessed being sees.
>
> When Wanton *Pan* deceiv'd with Lions skin,
> Came to the bed, where wound for kisse he got,
> To wo and shame the wretch did enter in,
> Till this he tooke for comfort of his lot,
> Poore *Pan* (he sayd) although thou beaten be,
> It is no shame, since *Hercules* was he.
>
> Thus joyfully in chosen tunes rejoyce,
> That such a one is witnesse of my hart,
> Whose cleerest eyes I blisse, and sweetest voyce,
> That see my good, and judgeth my desert:
> Thus wofully I in wo this salve do find,
> My foule mishap came yet from fairest mind.

"Espilus", we learn, "sang this song, tending to the greatnesse of his owne joy, and yet to the comfort of the other side, since they were overthrowne by a most worthy adversarie." But the song recounts how Silvanus, the archetypal fo(re)ster, *won* his love, and Pan, the archetypal shepherd, *lost* his, defeated moreover by Hercules, the archetypal man of action. Only the final couplet properly belongs to Espilus, who is clearly the loser.

We may muse a little on the mechanics of this fiasco. The judgment was obviously left entirely in the Queen's hands, and it is certainly possible that she was asked to deliver it on the spot. If she saw a text of the work beforehand and prepared her reply, it must have seemed somewhat impolitic for Sidney to tell the learned Eliza that she had missed the point. But why at least was the final song not revised?—or did the queen withhold her decision even from the author until the performance? And if so, did Espilus know Therion's victory song? Or—one final speculation—is the text we have, which was presumably owned by the Countess of Pembroke, simply an original script of the masque, with the Queen's decision indicated, but not including any alterations made for the actual performance?

At last, with a brief valediction, the masquers depart. No curtain closes, there is no theatre to leave; nothing has changed, and the Queen continues her walk through Wanstead garden. Sidney's problem had been to make a queen who was not a masquer the centre of his masque. His solution was to conceive his work as a series of addresses to the monarch, and its resolution as her reply—which is also her critique of the work. So rhetoric, not the traditional dance and spectacle, is the vehicle for the action of the drama; and the masque, then, is conceived entirely in literary terms. This looks forward to what Jonson tried to do with the form, to the assertion that if the masque was a spectacle, it was also a poem. Milton's *Comus* is even more obviously literary, and like *The Lady of May* it is highly rhetorical, centres around a debate and assumes—perhaps equally rashly—that its audience is capable of making the right choice between the contestants. Sidney's essay in the form is a worthy step on the way toward these. If it was a fiasco in production, its success, for those who care to look, is apparent on the page. (pp. 61-71)

> *S. K. Orgel, "Sidney's Experiment in Pastoral: 'The Lady of May'," in* Essential Articles for the Study of Sir Philip Sidney, *edited by Arthur F. Kinney, Archon Books, 1986, pp. 61-71.*

Richard A. Lanham   (essay date 1965)

[*Lanham is an American educator and critic. Below, he attempts to determine the genre of the* Old Arcadia, *the first unrevised version of Sidney's prose romance, concluding that it is best regarded as a comedy and a precursor to the Shakespearian comic drama.*]

[The *Old Arcadia* is] a prose-fictional tragi-comical-heroic-politico-pastoral drama. It is an awkward title, to be sure, but one which does full justice to the complexity of the work. The reader appreciates immediately that Sidney (to use Amos Alonzo Stagg's memorable phrase) "gave of the fullness of his best." Scholarly description can go no further.

Starting from the rear and working our way forward we can fit it into each genre in turn. Perhaps when we reach the front of the line we shall know whether to laugh or cry, whether to confirm our souls in self-control or turn the whole romance over to Momus. First, consider the *Old Arcadia* as a drama, a genre in the forefront of Sidney's mind when he wrote his toyful book. Its five divisions are "books or acts." Characters and narrator frequently refer to the story in theatrical terms. The final personification of the first book is explicit: "For in deede, Fortune had framed a very stage play of Love amonge these fewe folkes, making the Olde age of *Basilius* the vertue of *Ginecia,* and the simplicity of *Philoclea,* all affected to one." Again, later in the romance: "The Sunne beginning now to sende some promyse of his Cominge Lighte, making haste (as I thinke) to bee *Spectator* of the following tragedyes. . . ." Dametas "thoughte certeynly all the Spirittes in hell were come to play a Tragedy, in those woodes." Gynecia too is apt to dramatize her troubles, as when she taunts the scornful Cleophila: "There ys a fayrer Scene prepared for thee, to see the Tragicall ende of thy hated Lover?"

In Sidney's life there is no dearth of evidence of a strong interest in the stage. Shrewsbury, where Sidney was at school, emphasized drama:

> Allusion has already been made to Ashton's [the headmaster] partiality for dramatic performances, and his skill in arranging them. With such predilections it is not surprising that he should have made them a prominent feature of school life at Shrewsbury. He left it a standing regulation of the school that, on every Thursday, the highest form should, before going to play, "declaim and play one Act of a Comedy"; and the celebrity of the Whitsuntide Plays at Shrewsbury in Ashton's time is strong evidence of the pains he must have taken in training the boys for their performance.

That Sidney's aroused interest persisted the digression on drama at the end of the *Defence* attests.

Several critics have noted Sidney's interest in drama. F. S. Boas [in *Sir Philip Sidney*] describes a stage simile as "an incidental illustration of Sidney's critical interest in the stage of his day." Tucker Brooke, too, noticed [in his *A Literary History of England*] that: "The main story, handled in the 'acts,' has much the quality and structure of one of the tragicomedies which Sidney's namesake, Philip Massinger, later wrote for the seventeenth-century stage." Other subsequent influence has been at least mentioned. H. W. Hill, in an imperceptive study of the relation between the *Arcadia* and Elizabethan drama ["Sidney's *Arcadia* and the Elizabethan drama," *University of Nevada Studies,* 1-3 (1908-11)], vaguely points to the great debt later writers of romantic comedy owe to Sidney: "Further investigation on the part of the reader will, I think, convince him that the more general influence of the *Arcadia* on the Elizabethan drama was to encourage love of nature, lofty conceptions of duty, and refined courtesy." Further investigation, unfortunately, shows none of these influences. As a matter of fact, there has not been much further investigation of Sidney's relationship with the drama of his time. It must have been close. The *Old Arcadia* alone draws on current drama heavily. Not simply Dametas' mock-Senecan rants or the tragic-heroine characterization of Gynecia, but the romance's whole structure shows his knowledge of contemporary and classical drama. The rigorous five-act structure, the choric role which the narrator often plays, the symmetrical division into oracular involvement and dénouement, all betray it. The contemporary drama must have contributed the double plot, but the stock character of the foolish husband and the travesty of the good blunt man which Dametas plays out seem to owe more to the Commedia dell'Arte. The element of masque is strong, too; witness the elaborate staging of the trial scene. Clearly much of this concern with setting may have come from the Greek romances, but it is a mistake to overlook the more obvious pageants that offered a vivid "source" closer to home. The interpolated songs, too, owe much to contemporary stage practice. Finally and obviously, many passages of the *Old Arcadia* strike the reader as designed for quick, easy, and successful transfer to the stage. The basic stylistic unit seems to be not chapter or book but scene; it is individual scenes which impress themselves graphically on the memory.

The extent to which the *Old Arcadia* is a pastoral has been much debated. Sidney's intention has generally been viewed as the antithesis of the pastoral impulse to withdrawal and retreat; and action—heroic or not—is undeniably stressed in the romance. The pastoral elements often strike one as stage setting. In spite of Hill's contention that Sidney's romance encouraged a love of nature, and in spite of the ink spilled over the famous descriptive passages (the "leaves of grass of an equal height" is probably the best known), the modern reader is not likely to put the author down as a nature lover. Sidney is far more interested in Arcadians than in Arcadia. The details of a dress, the wanton disarray which exposes a patch of white skin, these details catch his attention. His eye for nature seems much more conventionally limited. Outside the eclogues (this is, of course, a large exception) the elements of pastoral are kept to a minimum. Only the setting, the forest, is clearly pastoral, and even here Sidney is different. For Arcadia is not only the forest, the place of retreat; in Sidney's romance, it is the whole country. And a real country, too, not a fairyland. Critics who overlook this important distinction are likely to miss the unity of the *Old Arcadia,* thinking Sidney's political didacticism foisted on his romance. F. S. Boas, for example, writes: "For a time the *Arcadia* turns from a romance into a political treatise on that perennial Elizabethan bogy, the difficulties and dangers of a disputed succession to the throne." In the sense in which he uses the word, the *Old Arcadia* had never been a "romance." Arcadia had never been a pastoral paradise exempt from the political constraints of everyday life in real kingdoms. The political lesson Sidney embodies in Basilius' folly depends upon a fundamental political normality. And it is a lesson offered directly to the reader; there is no allegorical transfer of political realities to the shepherd and his flock. The only purely pastoral transformation—that of Prince Musidorus into Dorus the shepherd—has a quite practical motive, the seduction of Pamela. No one even suggests that Dorus is attempting to escape from the cares of the great world. As for Basilius' escape, it is called folly and cowardice by everyone concerned with the kingdom; the most knowledgeable, Philanax and Euarchus, are the strongest against it. It is not exaggerating to maintain that Sidney's fundamental political concern caused him to write an antipastoral. If the *Old Arcadia* was actually written during a rustication at Wilton, we can only infer from the so-called pastoral temper of the work that the idleness was enforced and uncomfortable. He was bored with the idyllic peace of the Elizabethan countryhouse, not bathing in its golden glow.

Interesting as they are, the political and pastoral facets of the *Old Arcadia* do not pose the crucial question for the modern reader: With what degree of seriousness are we to regard Sidney's romance? It is easy, of course, to call it a comedy. It has a happy ending. Forget that, and one can as easily make it out a tragedy. Its superficial similarities to classical tragedy are apparent. The oracle prompts Basilius to seek out a security which the gods do not permit and he is punished for his folly. The classical structure has

2

been remarked above. The romance has obvious affinities with a political tragedy like *Gorboduc* (a play that Sidney singles out for special praise in the *Defence of Poesie*), which shows the consequences of folly at the apex of the state. Without Euarchus and the happy ending the same kind of civil war which plagues *Gorboduc* (and later *Lear*) could have arrived with Musidorus and his army. This type of sophisticated political morality play stems, of course, from the earlier medieval notion of tragedy as the "fall of illustrious men," and Sidney seems aware of this tradition as well. Basilius, had he died as a result of his folly, might have qualified for inclusion in the *Mirror for Magistrates*. The two princes, leaving their high careers for a commoner's life and a degrading death, would have fitted without trouble. None of these parallels is exact, certainly. But several elements of the older conception of tragedy are demonstrably included in the final effect of the romance. Tragedy in its fullest Shakespearean sense is more difficult to isolate. Pyrocles and Musidorus are prepared, it is true, to give up all for love, and many readers have found them modeling heroic virtue in one guise or another. They unabashedly cast themselves in a tragic role (especially in their dialogue on immortality). Yet even if we regard them with high seriousness, it is questionable whether their heroism, brought into the Arcadian world from the outside as it is, would give them sufficient dignity for a tragic ending had Sidney desired it. Nothing indicates that he did. Euarchus is potentially the most tragic character in the romance once he learns the identity of the prisoners he has just condemned, but this tragic potentiality is neglected entirely.

Even without the quick-release ending, the comic intent in much of the *Old Arcadia* is unmistakable. Sidney does not merely introduce comic relief into a tragic drama; his serious figures are ironically undermined as well. If this be admitted, then our conception of Sidney's two heroes will have to be radically modified. For it is undeniable, as one critic writes [L. J. Potts in his *Comedy,* 1949], "that a comic character must not finally seem to us heroic, and that it must as a whole invite critical judgment rather than arouse strongly sympathetic feeling." Critical judgment has been aroused by the *Old Arcadia* less frequently than sympathetic feeling, to be sure, but the romance demands both, and neither exclusively. If the two are mutually exclusive, then the *Old Arcadia* is fundamentally weakened by demanding both at once.

One way out of this dilemma is to call the romance a tragicomedy. Sidney, of course, expresses opinions on the subject of tragicomedy in the *Defence.* He writes, first:

> Now in his parts, kindes, or *species,* as you list to tearme them, it is to be noted, that some *Poesies* have coupled togither two or three kindes, as the *Tragicall* and *Comicall,* whereupon is risen the *Tragicomicall,* some in the manner have mingled prose and verse, as *Sanazara* and *Boetius;* some have mingled matters *Heroicall* and *Pastorall,* but that commeth all to one in this question, for if severed they be good, the conjunction cannot be hurtful.

Later, he maintains:

> But besides these grosse absurdities, howe all their Playes bee neither right Tragedies, nor right Comedies, mingling Kinges and Clownes, not because the matter so carrieth it, but thrust in the Clowne by head and shoulders to play a part in majesticall matters, with neither decencie nor discretion: so as neither the admiration and Commiseration, nor the right sportfulnesse is by their mongrell Tragicomedie obtained.

Here, as elsewhere, the precepts of the *Defence* are of limited use in evaluating Sidney's imaginative work. Such a work as the *Old Arcadia* could conceivably include both the tragic and comic consequences of being stricken by love. The primary sin in the *Old Arcadia,* if sin is the right word, is a loss of self-control in the throes of love. Such a loss can lend itself easily to either serious or comic treatment for, though potentially the greatest of social dangers, its first and most immediate consequences are almost always ludicrous.

The comic version of *hubris*—frequent in romantic comedy—also works in Sidney's romance. The *Old Arcadia* contains many instances of the punishment Cupid exacts from those who resist him. The First Eclogues are the most obvious extended example, but Dorus, Gynecia, and Philoclea all pay for their various degrees of resistance. The perception behind the myth, that a man seeking to deny the passionate half of his nature courts disaster, is at the heart of Sidney's quarrel with the pastoral attempt at escape. There, too, one attempts to avoid the unavoidable and brings it down upon oneself all the more quickly. The symbol which most fully expresses this foolish attempt to escape the inevitable limitations of man's nature—the oracle—is thus fitting for tragic or comic development, or for both at the same time. There seems to be no intrinsic reason why Sidney should not have attempted such a parallel development. If this purpose were to present the "triumph of love" from Mopsa to Basilius, he could hardly have avoided presenting both the tragic and the ludicrous. If he attempted to show as well the consequences to the body politic of such a triumph, then his plot would have to include the basic elements of the didactic political or historical work, of tragedy, and of comedy. Reduced to barest essentials, the plots of the three types show a basic—perhaps unavoidable—similarity. In each case the status quo (taken for granted as the preferable arrangement) is broken by an eruption of passion which works itself out at human expense leaving, finally, personal happiness or disaster and a society hopefully resolving itself again into a normal civil order. The plot of the *Old Arcadia* follows this pattern exactly; it does seem to try to include (if the anachronism will be pardoned) the essential elements of Shakespearean tragedy, comedy, and history.

Yes, the reader will say, but they do not all fit. They *cannot* all fit. They are mutually exclusive. L. J. Potts states the case precisely:

> There are only two literary modes of thought: tragedy and comedy. The nearest other species of literature to these two is the epic. . . . There is an eclectic form of fiction, borrowing certain of the superficial or accidental features of tragedy and comedy, but containing none of the es-

sence of either, and lacking both their pedigree and their philosophical justification: tragi-comedy . . . has a popular appeal, and has commended itself to dramatists who like to please their public. There is no great harm in a play or novel that pains and frightens us superficially and not in full earnest, adding yet another thrill—of artificial felicity—by an inappropriate stroke of good fortune in the last act or chapter. But it is not the happy ending that makes a comedy; nor merely the pity and fear that make a tragedy.

I hope that by this stage of our investigation we can dismiss the epic possibility without further consideration. The New may be an epic of sorts, but the *Old Arcadia* certainly is not. But even if we admit the justice of Potts' charge in reference to the *Old Arcadia*—as to an extent we must—we can still make out a rationale for the *Old Arcadia* as a tragicomedy, inferior though it may be. The type from which the *Old Arcadia* most directly derives, the Greek romance, does not demand the whole-hearted emotional commitment which tragic suffering calls forth. Its pathos is highly stylized and highly rhetorical. We are meant to enjoy the language as a tour de force, to be titillated but not profoundly moved. To an extent this is true of the *Old Arcadia.* In such an atmosphere, one feels as less offensive the ironic juxtaposition of fool and suffering woman (Basilius and Gynecia), each speaking the same pathetical rhetoric. We are not meant to feel either amusement or pity deeply because we are not meant to think of the characters as fully three-dimensional. They are types—at best, actors—and we are not to be wholly caught up in their feelings. They certainly are not; they constantly play for effect and we are meant to see it. This artificiality persists, and indeed is greatly developed, in Jacobean tragicomic drama. Eugene M. Waith, in his study of Beaumont and Fletcher [*Pattern of Tragicomedy*], comments on *The Maid's Tragedy:* "For however inferior *The Maid's Tragedy* may be when compared to *Hamlet,* it is an amazing piece of dramatic contrivance. Admiration for the sheer virtuosity of the play is an important part of the spectator's response." So in the *Old Arcadia.* We are not meant to pierce the artifice to the real world behind it. There is no real world behind it. We do not feel that a contrived surprise ending does real violence to life as we know it, because life as we know it is not what the genre purports to represent. Rather, the world of romance is primarily one of conventions—conventional action, character, and ethics. We accept the fantastic ending as we do in a fairy story. Euarchus' lecture is chastening, and after giving the reader a sufficient scare and pressing the moral, the princes are to be given their fondest desires.

Sidney's fundamental didacticism seems well served by such a reading of the romance. Tragicomedy, though willing to punish the utter villain (Tymantus) and the complete fool (Dametas and company), insists for its protagonists only that they learn their lesson in an egregiously melodramatic scene, thus leaving the reader with a moral taste in his mouth. So Pyrocles and Musidorus, who hold our sympathy throughout, must be chastened but not destroyed. The reader needs to be frightened but not finally disappointed. Such a work, we may suppose, would be cal-culated to please the delicate sensitivities of Sidney's fair ladies.

An interpretation such as this is very inviting and, provided one is willing to play down the heroic element, seems borne out to some extent by the romance. Certainly it accurately describes what goes on in the Greek romances, which Wolff and others have held to be the immediate ancestors of the *Old Arcadia.* Sidney's version of the genre it fits less well. For if we are not, finally, to accept the work as seriously meant, we are more puzzled than ever by the obvious labor which went into it. Its political philosophy is unavoidably cheapened by such an inconsequential context. The moralizing of narrator and characters loses both depth and application, becomes merely a collection of old saws to be quoted at random. The triumph of love becomes tear-jerking melodramatic pathos. In the end Potts is right—the price of manipulated plot and character is unavoidable triviality. We cannot mix mirth and sadness without creating nostalgic sentimentality. The final prohibitive reason why Sidney could not show the same force of love leading to a tragic conclusion in some cases and a ludicrous one in others is the cosmic injustice, the moral (and artistic) chaos such an unraveling would bring about. His conclusion had to be either a general tragedy or an arranged comic release. His choice of the latter gratifies our tender-heartedness but at the risk of our thinking Sidney the moralist had lost his nerve.

There is another solution to the dilemma. The most profitable attitude toward Sidney's romance, I would suggest, refuses to make allowances for it, reads it as much as possible as we would a comic novel. For it was toward this form that Sidney was groping. That he was occasionally maladroit should not surprise us, since the comic novel as we know it did not yet exist. His successes are considerable, but to see them we must clear our minds of the misapprehensions which have obscured Sidney's prose for so many years. Although elements of realism, topical allegory (conjectural, to be sure), even autobiographical allusions have been pointed out, almost no one has been willing to acknowledge that the *Old Arcadia* deals with life in any manner directly. To a reader of Elizabethan romance, Tillyard's voice [in *Shakespeare's Last Plays,* 1954] is quite alone: "The notion, so widespread to-day, that Elizabethan drama dealth with life while Elizabethan romance escaped from it, is as alien to Elizabethan opinion as it should prove itself false to any modern who troubles to read *Arcadia* with sympathetic attention."

Let us take first a brief but broad look at the romance as we have described it thus far. On one level it is a serious explanation of the consequences, public and private, of unbridled passion. On another, it is a sympathetic spoof of the extravagant behavior and inflated language of the traditional literary lover. From Sannazaro, Sidney takes a form which allows him ample opportunity for prose and verse experiment, from the Greek romances the incidents with which to illustrate the effects of love. His heroes look to the medieval romances for their unrelieved heroism. Such syncretism runs the danger of becoming a potpourri, a great jumble; but we have seen how Sidney's cleverly integrated plot avoids this danger.

Still remaining is the problem of conflicting elements, comic spoof and serious passion. We are led to be sympathetic—if smilingly so—toward the princes and princesses, and then we are clubbed by Euarchus' condemnation of them in the last book. As one student of the work has put it: "The result is that the reason is divided while the sympathies remain intact, and the *Arcadia* ends on an effect of ethical confusion." But if we look at the characters of the two princes as in some sense intended to be consistent and credible, this difficulty disappears. If the reader is intended to penetrate their most idealistic declarations of feelings and motives to a base of self-seeking lust beneath, then he is prepared for the condemnation when it comes. It has been building up in his subconscious for some time. Sidney's characters are not, of course, the fully three-dimensional people of modern fiction. But they are not pasteboard rhetorical mouthpieces either. The reader is clearly meant to see them as people with recognizable motives. He is meant to hold them responsible for what they do. They are playing roles, to be sure, and their motivation is often simple: satisfaction of physical passion. But they are sufficiently rounded to serve for a use beyond caricature. So the levity which seems to characterize the early books of the romance does not become serious all of a sudden. To the perceptive reader there is a gradual modulation.

What of the serious true love in the romance? As the comic elements become more serious, the serious passion takes on a steadily increasing ludicrous coloration. The two grow closer together in a unified but steadily and frankly ambiguous definition of the nature of love which would not surprise us in modern fiction but which seems unlikely coming from Sidney. What we expect Sidney to offer us is love as the medieval romances present it. The *Old Arcadia* does not wholly oblige. Once we grant the conventions of falling in love at first sight, the use of an oracle, and the change of identity, then Sidney does not depend on miraculous happenings to show us the triumph of love. Sidney's pairs of lovers are quite as realistically motivated as a character in one of O'Hara's novels. There are, except for Philanax, no radical discontinuities of character, and even in Philanax' case Sidney takes care to supply a realistic motivation. What misleads us is the language the characters use to accomplish their purpose. Once we recognize its complex use we can see Sidney the novelist more clearly.

He stands back from the scene he creates, thereby making it difficult for us to determine precisely what he thought of it. But he clearly was not uncritical. He was not writing simply a love fantasy as that sort of thing was understood in his day. He was trying to make a more profound comment on the enduring paradoxes of passion, and this we hold the legitimate province of the novelist and not of the romancer. Beneath the various kinds of stylization, beneath the burlesque of the language and situations of courtly love in his own time, his purpose was serious. Golden poetic nowithstanding, he was not making men but using "men according as men were." Admittedly he is sometimes carried away with the excess he is gently mocking, as Shakespeare later was. John Palmer has remarked [in his *Comic Characters of Shakespeare,* 1946]: "Shake-speare will so easily lose the satirical purpose with which he started, and so often provoke us to wonder whether he is ridiculing excess in his characters or sharing their intoxication." It is easy to spot instances where Sidney does the same thing, but they hardly invalidate his pervasive detachment from the full-blown rhetoric. Nor does his love of language compromise his didacticism. Sidney had written in the *Defence,* one remembers:

> For the representing of so straunge a power in Love, procures delight, and the scornefulnesse of the action, stirreth laughter. But I speake to this purpose, that all the ende of the Comicall part, bee not uppon suche scornefull matters as stirre laughter onelie, but mixe with it, that delightfull teaching whiche is the ende of *Poesie.*

At the heart of modern discontent with the *Arcadia* in either of its forms lies, I would maintain, a suspicion that it has really nothing to offer except traditional morals pointed in obvious ways, and characters who are merely vehicles sagging under the weight of an ideal virtue and orante rhetoric they are forced to carry through life. The romantic chivalric derring-do of the New, the extravagant passions of the Old, are just what we would expect from the cynosure of chivalry. The average reader, who has read "parts of" the *Arcadia,* Old or New, would probably come away with this impression. If he read as far as the trial scene he would be puzzled by the contradictions implied in Euarchus' verdict but would finally ascribe it to the cheap thrills of tragicomedy.

A further acquaintance with the *Old Arcadia* shows the reader that something more than an obvious Greek or chivalric romance is offered. A few especially credulous students may continue to seek for heroics amidst the many qualifications, but most will be willing to grant Sidney a greater subtlety. Myrick's description of the *Old Arcadia* [in *Sidney as Literary Craftsman*] as "largely a story of love and lovers' devices, thrown against a background of politics in a Greek province" would probably gain general agreement, though here the agreement ends. Some have seen a clearly expressed philosophy in the romance. John F. Danby, for example [in *Poets on Fortune's Hill*], remarks:

> Sidney's romance is important because it has such inner coherence—a large, mature, and conscious philosophy. We are protected, with him, from projecting on to him meanings of our own, or finding in him answers to needs of ours he himself did not share and did not intend to answer. In his storm we can confidently follow his own moralizations.

But can we? The narrator is, as we have shown, far from reliable, sometimes frankly self-contradictory. If Sidney's philosophy is so plain as Danby would have us believe, why have most readers been unable to agree on what this philosophy is? Sidney's conscious philosophy may be large and mature, but that part which is incorporated into the *Old Arcadia* is far from clear. Is he in favor of heroic self-assertion or against it? Is he defending romantic love or repudiating it? Was he a great admirer of chivalry or its severest critic?

"The whole chivalrous culture of the last centuries of the Middle Ages," Huizinga tells us [in *The Waning of the Middle Ages* 1924], "is marked by an unstable equilibrium between sentimentality and mockery. Honour, fidelity and love are treated with unimpeachable seriousness; only from time to time the solemn rigidity relaxes into a smile, but downright parody never prevails." By the late sixteenth century, the progressive decay of chivalry had advanced still further, mockery and seriousness had drawn further apart. Love in this later stage is described by Burckhardt [in his *The Civilization of the Renaissance in Italy*]:

> When we come to look more closely at the ethics of love at the time of the Renaissance, we are struck by a remarkable contrast. The novelists and comic poets give us to understand that love consists only in sensual enjoyment, and that to win this, all means, tragic or comic, are not only permitted, but are interesting in proportion to their audacity and unscrupulousness. But if we turn to the best of the lyric poets and writers of dialogues, we find in them a deep and spiritual passion of the noblest kind, whose last and highest expression is a revival of the ancient belief in an original unity of souls in the Divine Being. And both modes of feeling were then genuine, and could co-exist in the same individual.

The two modes clearly did coexist in Sidney. In the *Old Arcadia* he forces them to live side by side in the same plot. The rhetorical style and Petrarchan sentiment which characterize the heroes from beginning to end, the standard situations in which the lovers find themselves, bring the whole panoply of traditional courtly love before the reader's eye. But it is introduced only to be gradually undermined and finally wholly repudiated. The language is so gorgeous that it often makes the speaker seem ludicrous or insincere or both. Behind it we see a love which "consists only in sensual enjoyment" and a pair of heroes whose heroism seems to consist primarily of just the audacious unscrupulousness which Burckhardt describes. When Goldman writes [in his *Sidney and the Arcadia*] that the *Arcadia* shows Sidney's "complete consecration to the ideal of fortitude and honor," and that "The real heroes of the *Arcadia,* Pyrocles and Musidorus, unquestionably represent Sidney's ideal of young manhood," he is contradicting the whole meaning of the *Old Arcadia* and (as we shall see) a good deal of that of the New. He is taking their word for their own worth and their word, as Euarchus makes clear, is wholly unreliable. All the Petrarchan elements upon which this mistaken judgment is based are ironically weakened. The Neo-Platonism each hero affects is constantly belied by his single-minded concentration on bedding his chosen woman. Pyrocles, for example, jumps out of Philoclea's bed, "Having first with earnest kissing the Pereles *Philoclea*, (who then soundly sleeping) was the naturall Image of exact Beuty receyved into his sence." So much for Platonic love. Pyrocles' change of sex, which has bothered Boas and others, was really a stroke of genius which enabled Sidney to focus the silly contradictions of the Petrarchan code on a single character. Boas complains:

> Thus the tangle of loves [in the Old] arising out

of the confusions of sex is completed. This had an irresistible fascination for the Elizabethans which we find it difficult to appreciate today. On the stage it had its origin and partial justification in the acting of women's parts by boys. But in the long-drawn-out narrative of a romance, even Sidney's skill and delicacy of touch find it difficult to make the equivocal 'he she' situation fully palatable.

Actually, the change of sex becomes the center of an increasingly strong ironic comment on the constant pleas for aid and succor which are so strong an element in the psychology of courtly love. The noble impulse to action so often praised as the very mark of Sir Philip is here directed to the agreeable but hardly noble business of seduction. Both heroes, in the end, get caught with their heroic pants down. They constantly deceive themselves as well as their inamoratas. In one of a hundred instances, Pyrocles, after seducing Philoclea, justifies his action with "And as for shame, howe can I bee ashamed of that, for which my well meaning Conscyence will answer for mee to god, and youre unresistable beuty to the worlde." Yet when that "worlde" knocks at the door, he readily confesses, "I was fettered in the moste guilty shame that ever Man was, seeyng what a Paradyse of unspotted goodnes my filthy thoughtes soughte to defyle." When is he lying?

It is the juxtaposition of a rhetorical language moving in one direction and a plot constantly moving in another which gives us our main clue to Sidney's final intention. The language is extremely ornate, always idealistic, crammed with emotional fervor, constantly calling attention to itself. The plot is plain, unobtrusive, moving slowly from sin to retribution. If we strip the idealistic language used by the participants from their behavior, the picture is sordid enough. It seems almost willful misinterpretation to think Sidney unaware of this.

The self-reliance so often seen in the two princes may have once been laudable, but in Arcadia it is clearly not. It has strayed so far, as a matter of fact, that the behavior it prompts lends itself readily to the most dire interpretations. The princes really are brave, there is no doubt of that; and bravery, whatever historians have said since, had always been the working definition of chivalric honor. Cleophila does brave the mob, Dorus defends Pamela against the band of outlaws. But why do they do so? Sidney had rather a higher conception of honor than simply physical courage, one by which his heroes are tried and found wanting. And, obviously enough, the code of courtly love is sentenced guilty with them.

In the sudden reversal of the reader's judgment embodied in Euarchus' verdict is contained the central "moralization" of the *Old Arcadia*— the substitution of marriage for the adulterous intercourse of the Petrarchan code. Dramatically, the substitution was a gamble. Would the reader's sensitivities be led into a trap he would resent so strongly that he would reject the moral offered? Or would he, his suspicions properly aroused, have foreseen the final justice of such a decision? The crucial factor for an author in a decision like this is perceptively pointed out by Wayne Booth [in his *The Rhetoric of Fiction*]:

Finally, some of the most powerful literature is based on a successful reversal of what many readers would "naturally" think of as a proper response. Such reversals can only be achieved if the author is able to call to our attention relationships and meanings that the surface of the object obscures.

My opinion is that Sidney's gamble paid off, that he did succeed in calling attention to relationships and meanings beneath the surface of his narrative. Certainly the last two books provide a compelling demonstration of the effects of uncontrolled passion. At one point in the Second Eclogues Cleophila sings:

> The Lyfe wee Leade ys all Love,
> The Love wee holde ys all deathe.

This is the text which the two concluding books of the romance gloss. They do it well enough so that the final verdict is far from a complete surprise.

The alternative Sidney provides for passion—the stability of Christian marriage—presumably would not be necessary for heroic paragons. Such perfect princes, their self-control taken for granted, could be heroes utterly uninhibited. It is characteristic of the real "idealization" of the two heroes that such a Platonic course is never even suggested. For men as they are, marriage seemed to Sidney the only plausible alternative to the destruction promised by passion. Faced with the implications of such a solution to the problems of passion, Sidney could hardly avoid a happy ending. It is the only way the solution could be put into practice.

Such at least I conceive to be the "message" Sidney sought to convey. It seems plausible that Sidney, lacerated as he was by his passion for Penelope Devereux, should seek the solace of a rehearsal of his problem and an explanation for it, in writing the *Old Arcadia.* (I hardly see how we can avoid concluding that Sidney was fully in love with her when he wrote the *Old Arcadia,* whatever final dating may be decided upon.) Marriage was for him, I have no doubt, the just and proper solution for such an infatuation.

As a moral man, yes, but as an artist? One wonders. Marriage as a solution certainly fails to satisfy the modern reader, especially as an artistic conclusion to the *Old Arcadia.* For, in fact, it solves nothing. Sidney must have been aware of this too. Who more so? Penelope Devereux was, after all, engaged to marry somebody else—perhaps actually married to him. What then? What if she were unmarried but unwilling too? She seems to have been so. Sidney must have been thrown back on his dilemma as we are today. The melancholy conclusion that eternal frustration is the price of order, fit him though it did, must have offered meager comfort. And besides this, how was he to end the romance? He must marry them off—if marriage was to be the conventional moral drawn—but he could at least show that it was a contrived solution, applied to a problem that in life has no end and no painless solution. This would explain the obvious haste and aplomb with which he wraps things up in a very few pages. Here, as in the lesser *sententiae,* the moral is drawn a little too obviously to carry complete conviction, though in each case the convention is fundamentally irrefutable.

But conventional wisdom does not always fit life. Though reason wins the rhetorical victories, passion actually determines what happens in Arcadia. It is Sidney's reluctance to provide the conventional, easy answer which many students of the romance have overlooked. Danby, for example, thinks Christian patience emerges as the final lesson from the trial. It brings about, he feels, a kind of spiritual illumination for the princes. One looks vainly for evidence of such illumination in the *Old Arcadia.* Is the marriage more than a pious hope? What are they going to do after the marriage? Would all the patience in the world channel desire into the path of moderation? Sidney was idealistic, perhaps, but not naïve. To preach patience to the lover is, as the *Old Arcadia* demonstrates repeatedly, to charge hell with the proverbial bucket of ice water. The lover has lost control of himself, has ceased—as Sidney makes crystal-clear—to be a moral human being at all. What, after all, brings the happy ending about? Patience? Persistence? No, construed realistically, it is chance, pure chance. Is it oversubtle to think Sidney capable of relishing this final irony?

That passion is at war with society is an ancient profundity, but a profundity nonetheless of the sort upon which real works of art are built. Sidney's *Old Arcadia* does face honestly one of life's insoluble paradoxes. It may even be said to face two, for to Sidney the reality of passion conflicted not only with society but with the conventional means of expressing passion. One of the concerns of the *Old Arcadia* is the language of love.

It was Sidney's saving grace as an artist that he was willing to admit to a strong streak of plain physical desire in his makeup. His work would have been so much cant had he idealized this strong sex drive. For the most part he refused to do so, and his refusal has embarrassed his admirers. Dobell manfully faced the problem when he said, "It can hardly be denied that there was in Sidney's mind a somewhat undue predominance of the sexual element." On a wooden hero of chivalry such evidence of our common humanity doubtless sits uncomfortably, but it is the very making of Sidney as an artist and perhaps even as a man. For the undeniable fact of his physical passion constantly conflicted with his ideals, sharpening their edge and making him hold them with a more than conventional depth of feeling. When in Sonnet 72 of *Astrophil and Stella* he cries out:

> DESIRE, though thou my old companion art,
> And oft so clings to my pure love, that I
> One from the other scarcely can descrie . . .

he is admitting frankly that the Petrarchan pose does not fit love as he knows it. The idealization of the poet fundamentally opposes the desires of the man.

It is easily seen how this opposition has been built into the *Old Arcadia.* The woods are full of Petrarchan lovers, all spouting devotions set up to the highest note. As men and women, though, they act according to the drives Sidney saw to be common to all creatures. The tension between speech and action, a primary one in the romance, thus proceeds from a basic cleavage in Sidney's own personality. The easy outpourings of exaggerated passion were bound to offend a man who really felt the power of a passion which most only professed. It is in the light of this recognition that we must read the passages where he declares his dissatisfaction with the fashionable language of love. In the **Defence,** for instance, he writes:

> But truly many of such writings, as come under the banner of unresistable love, if I were a mistresse, would never perswade mee they were in love: so coldly they applie firie speeches, as men that had rather redde lovers writings, and so caught up certaine swelling Phrases, which hang togither like a man that once tolde me the winde was at Northwest, and by South, because he would be sure to name winds inough, then that in truth they feele those passions, which easily as I thinke, may be bewraied by that same forciblenesse or *Energia,* (as the Greeks call it of the writer).

Significantly, he does not rule out the possibility of expressing real passion. But it must be done energetically, directly. "Give me some food!" may be an extreme example, but it is that kind of language which seems sincere to Sidney, not the elaborate pattern of double talk which Pyrocles and Philoclea act out before they can climb into bed.

What one really sees in the **Old Arcadia** is an early indication in Elizabethan literature that the rhetorical language of love cannot always be taken seriously, that it is subject to persistent ironical qualification on a large scale. The attitude of Sidney in the **Old Arcadia** is different from the momentary trivializing of a major concern—the "Much ado there was, God wot, / He would love and she would not" of a Nicholas Breton. It is an elaborately patterned questioning of the possible sincerity of an elaborate speech. For the questioning does not stop at the language of love. Ornate language of all sorts is held up to question.

The reader who suspects this to be an oversubtle reading into the romance of a meaning not intended by Sidney must explain the trial speech of Euarchus. We have called attention to the realism of much of the formal oratory of the **Old Arcadia,** but anyone who has read an Elizabethan legal or even quasi-legal document will know that Euarchus' speech is really far too clear to be decretal. Sidney has intentionally put the truth as he saw it in plain and unadorned words. Plain truth does not need rhetoric. Sidney is Aristotelian: "All such [rhetorical] arts are fanciful and meant to charm the hearer. Nobody uses fine language when teaching geometry." It is not an accidental irony that Euarchus comes to the kingdom of Arcadia with a direct proposal of marriage for his son and nephew. *His* wooing would have been as plain as his speech.

Though Sidney admitted to a strong physical desire, his attraction to the idealism of traditional courtly passion was undiminished. He could smile at its obvious artifices while at the same time feeling their power. For he needed the rhetoric of passionate love to express his real feelings quite as much as the poseur needed it to enliven his. Denis de Rougemont has described this predicament very well [in *Love in the Western World,* 1957]:

> The more a man is given to sentiment, the more likely is he to be wordy and to speak well. Like-

wise, the more passionate a man is, the more likely is he to reinvent the tropes of the rhetoric, to rediscover their *necessity,* and to shape himself spontaneously according to the notions of the 'sublime' which these tropes have indelibly impressed upon us.

The aristocratic impulse in Sidney's nature may have contributed, probably subconsciously, additional force to his need for the traditional rhetoric of love. For lust is a great leveler, and it depends upon the grace and polish of the language with which it is offered to us for its final evaluation. How else, after all, are we to distinguish the fine feelings of the aristocrat from those of the peasant? Whether or not Sidney really thought physical desire the lowest rung on the ladder of love we shall never know. The modern reader is sorely tempted to dismiss the whole ladder as "rationalization," but even if he resists this error there are few unequivocal clues in the **Old Arcadia.** We are meant clearly to sympathize with the characters, stricken as they are by a power beyond their control; the reader is supposed to see that there is genuine feeling behind the flowery protestations of the two princely pairs. Otherwise the tension between speech and action loses its point. But what this real feeling is, we are not told.

One thing is certain. It is not the affectionate companionship which seems to us the stuff of a lasting marriage. Of this there is not a trace in the **Old Arcadia.** Love, for Sidney, was still the grand passion of the chivalric past, and this passion was not built on affection. The lovers are trained for contest not cooperation. Sidney's attitude toward love is far more erotic than domestic, and the infusion of irony in no way lessens its erotic force. Knowing the inglorious end of one's passion seems only to intensify it. Seized as Gynecia is, they would all die a hundred deaths to gain satisfaction. Many of Sidney's later commentators attribute to him a domestic sentimentality more characteristic of Dickens.

Sidney, it appears, was caught in a social and philosophical contradiction not of his own making. Marriage, to a man of his time, provided no alternative to passionate love. It was a matter of dynasty, of money, too important even in the lower strata of society to permit any real deference to the parties concerned. Sidney's own dickering for a wife certainly shows none. Marriage was, in any case, impossible for Sidney with the woman he desired. But—and here we see the man in all his basic honesty—the alternatives of passion were even worse. He did not idealize or romanticize them. Theoretically love of one's lady spurred one on to deeds of prowess, toward glorious adventure, toward fame. But this depended on a passion wholly stylized, on a desire strictly "Platonic." For a really passionate lover, the much more probable rewards were enervated frustration if he failed to win the lady, and slothful ease were he successful.

Thus the struggle between reason and passion, between duty and love in the **Old Arcadia** is built on a fundamental contradiction within the theory of chivalry, an impossible choice between bed and sword. The two heroes make their choice, or rather love makes their choice for them, at the very beginning of our acquaintance with them. They thus renounce the call of duty before we are able to see how ardently they formerly followed it. Half of their chivalry is lopped off before we know them, and makes them to our eyes more the insipid heroes of Greek romance than Sidney intended. In the original romance at least, the values of chivalric honor are not seriously questioned. It is on the love half of the chivalric code that he concentrates in the *Old Arcadia,* love and the havoc it often makes of the more important questions of life.

It has not to my knowledge been remarked that love in the *Old Arcadia* is strangely sterile. Within the romance at least, it prompts no deeds, not even a single generous impulse which reaches beyond lover and beloved to the welfare of mankind. Cleophila saves the state for love, and is willing to make war for the same reason. Dorus fights the outlaw band for love and makes peace with them for the same reason. For their loves, the princes will give their all, a noble sentiment without doubt, but in the context of the *Old Arcadia* a vain, misdirected sacrifice. For finally, to Sidney the public world must predominate over the private; personal glory must be harnessed for service to the state. Passionate love in the last analysis can only detract from such a larger goal.

Sidney was not the first to be aware of this internal inconsistency of the chivalric code. Chaucer's *Troilus* would probably be the earliest incontestable example, and there too the focus is on love rather than honor. One would like to think that Sidney saw, in Chaucer's infinitely subtle exegesis of the courtly love drama as it was played in real life, the tragic difference between fine words and fine deeds. So I choose to construe his remark in the *Defence:* "*Chawcer* undoubtedly did excellently in his *Troilus* and *Creseid:* of whome trulie I knowe not whether to mervaile more, either that hee in that mistie time could see so clearly, or that wee in this cleare age, goe so stumblingly after him." In the last quarter of the sixteenth century the problems of adapting the code to a world which it fitted even less well than it had the Europe of the late Middle Ages drew the attention of some of the greatest minds England has ever known. A series of Shakespearean figures, from Falstaff to Thersites, probe chivalric honor. Falstaff's positive, hopeful counterpart is the Red Cross Knight, learning a code of honor that would have astounded his robberbaron ancestors. That Spenser's alternative to passionate love was the same as Sidney's, however different their methods, needs no elaboration here. I do not mean to imply that the *Old Arcadia* is among peers in this company: it is not. But it addresses itself to the same set of problems which troubled greater minds and greater talents. Its fundamental concern is a major concern of its age. It is not simply a latter-day *Amadis,* or a domesticated Greek romance. Nor is it a compendium of fine sentiments for all occasions; if we read it for the sentiment we should hang ourselves.

At all events we cannot call Sidney a romancer. The title novelist fits him far more nearly. But serious novelist though he is, he has written what finally we must read as a comic novel. As things turned out, it was the drama and not prose fiction which was to bring romantic comedy to full flower, but the bud clearly emerges in the *Old Arca-*

dia. It is not, fundamentally, a tragicomedy, which is wholly serious until the ending, when the author intrudes and solves all problems. Its ironic undercutting, sometimes humorous, sometimes not, is present from the beginning. The comic ending, here as in all high comedy, poses more questions than it answers.

For the first time in the sixteenth century, the contrast between the literary psychology of the lover and his true feelings is made the subject of comedy. When Cleophila tells Basilius: "These bee but those swelling speeches which give the uttermoste Name to every Tryfle . . . Truly Love were very unlovely yf yt were half so deadly as yow Lovers still Living terme yt," she is the direct antecedent of Rosalind, saying: "No, faith, die by attorney. The poor world is almost six thousand years old, and in all this time there was not any man died in his own person, videlicet, in a love-cause . . . men have died from time to time and worms have eaten them, but not for love." If romantic comedy can be said to stem from the decay of the Petrarchan tradition, or more largely to be the end product of the roughly thousand years of courtly love between the late Greek romances and Sidney's lifetime, then the *Old Arcadia* is the first appearance of the last stage. Gynecia and Basilius in the cave are acting out the first comic death of grand passion.

So the dramatic elements of the *Old Arcadia* with which this discussion began were in the long run to prove the most fruitful for later times. Rhetorical fiction as such reached a dead end with *Menaphon,* modulating into either the jagged but vivid mockery of *The Unfortunate Traveller* or expiring into insipidity. Its tragic potentialities have perhaps a distant descendant in the many heroes who give all for love. Its epic potentiality lived on in the *New Arcadia.*

The reader may be reluctant to concede to the *Old Arcadia* the seriousness of the Shakespearean comedy to which it contributed. Faced with Sidney's didacticism, he is tempted to dismiss it as an overlay of frivolity. Sidney has done something more. He has tried, I feel, to penetrate his own easy advice to an awareness of the paradox of passion with which his moral solution only insufficiently deals. He has made his heroes not only mistaken but necessarily so. The lovers in the *Arcadia* are not their own masters, and they are condemned for their slavery. Necessary as such a condemnation is, it is made with full knowledge of its ultimate futility. Sidney is a realistic moralist. We should think him naïve neither in the results he expects nor in his awareness that exhortation must still be tried. (pp. 358-83)

Richard A. Lanham, "Comedy-Tragic and Romantic," in Sidney's Arcadia: A Map of Arcadia, Sidney's Romance in Its Tradition/ The Old Arcadia *by Walter R. Davis and Richard A. Lanham, Yale University Press, 1965, pp. 358-83.*

David Kalstone   (essay date 1970)

[*Kalstone was an American educator and critic who specialized in sixteenth-century literature. In the following excerpt from a work originally published in 1970, he em-*

Sidney's work—posthumously published—was part of the literary ferment of the 1590's; but his achievement properly belongs to a more barren decade. When he began writing in the late 1570's, he was to find little in contemporary English literature to admire; his *Defence of Poesie* names Spenser's *Shepheardes Calender,* but the other works praised—*Gorboduc, A Mirror for Magistrates,* and 'the Earle of Surreis Lirickes'—belong to the mid-century, all of them well-known when he was a boy. At his death in 1586, he himself had contributed to the renewal of English literary life the heroic romance and pastoral lyrics of the *Arcadia,* a pastoral entertainment (*The Lady of May*), a series of metrically inventive translations of the Psalms, the first and most energetic of the English sonnet sequences in *Astrophel and Stella,* and in *The Defence of Poesie* the noblest and most acute literary criticism of the age. In all his work the critic's prescriptive intelligence is close to the surface, almost as if to direct contemporary readers and writers to the nature of his accomplishment. For if he helped to domesticate European literary conventions in England—he was to Elizabethans the 'English Petrarke,' and his *Arcadia* borrowed its title from the Italian begetter of the great Renaissance pastorals—he was also alive to the ways energetic writing might extend traditional meanings or call values into question.

So, in his *Arcadia,* when the noble princes and princesses set out to inspect a grove where shepherds are to perform pastoral eclogues, they find a scene as extravagantly appropriate as any in Sannazaro's *Arcadia,* the romance from which Sidney drew his title. It has its brook, its streams, its roses:

> about it (as if it had bene to inclose a *Theater*) grew such a sort of trees, as eyther excellency of fruit, statelines of grouth, continuall greennes, or poeticall fancies have made at any time famous.

But the deliberate theatricality of the scene, first to be savoured for the delicacy and harmony of presentation, invites further questions about the nature of poetical fancies. The princes' identities are as yet unknown to the princesses they would like to woo; Musidorus is disguised as the shepherd, Dorus, and Pyrocles is dressed as an Amazon, Zelmane, but the courtly nature of their distressed gestures is unmistakable:

> the Ladies sate them downe, inquiring many questions of the shepheard *Dorus;* who (keeping his eie still upon *Pamela*) answered with such a trembling voice, and abashed countenance, and oftentimes so far from the matter, that it was some sport to the young Ladies, thinking it want of education, which made him so discountenanced with unwoonted presence. But *Zelmane* that saw in him the glasse of her owne miserie, taking the hande of *Philoclea,* and with burning kisses setting it close to her lips (as if it should stand there like a hand in the margine of a Booke, to note some saying worthy to be marked) began to speake these wordes. O Love, since thou art so changeable in mens estates,

how art thou so constant in their torments? when sodainly there came out of a wood a monstrous Lion, with a she Beare not far from him, of little lesse fiercenes . . .

The prince disguised as a shepherd answers questions in a trembling voice; the prince disguised as an Amazon recognizes in him a mirror of his own unhappiness. But Sidney underlines the very literary nature of their poses. With everyone frozen into position, the action becomes a tableau before our eyes. The hand being kissed becomes the pointing hand in the margin of a book. What it points to, and what Pyrocles' apostrophe to love invokes, is the appearance of a monstrous lion and bear—in this context a comic reminder that we may have been tempted to misinterpret this pastoral scene. It is almost as if we need the beasts to complete the picture, suggesting as they do the appetites being hidden under the guise of a golden setting and high rhetorical invocations to love.

The hand in the margin is a characteristically Sidneyan touch, the critic's prose pointer. It marks a connection between literary conventions and the emotions they are designed to represent, and suggests that any divorce between the two is a source of comedy. Sidney, discouraged with the state of English writing ('idle *England,* which now can scarce endure the pain of a pen') recommends the pursuit and understanding of classical and European literary models: 'as the fertilest ground must be manured, so must the highest flying wit have a *Dedalus* to guide him . . . that is, Art, Imitation and Exercise.' But those three are not to be empty graces; the poet must sense the vitality of his literary guides. What Sidney deplores in the '*Lyrical* kinde of Songs and Sonets' of his period, he takes care to avoid in his own *Astrophel and Stella:*

> But truly many of such writings, as come under the banner of unresistable love, if I were a mistresse, would never perswade mee they were in love: so coldly they apply firie speeches as men that had rather redde lovers writings, and so caught up certaine swelling Phrases, which hang together like a man that once tolde me the winde was at Northwest, and by South, because he would be sure to name winds enough, than that in truth they feele those passions, which easily as I thinke, may be bewraied by the same forciblenesses or *Energia* (as the Greeks call it) of the writer.

The aim, then, is a truly animated use of conventions, not a random collection of devices. In most of his works Sidney makes the point explicitly, allowing, for example, a declaration of liveliness to launch his sonnet sequence ('Foole, said my Muse to me, looke in thy heart and write.') or a pointed metaphor in the *Arca*dia (the hand in the margin) to alert us to the dangers of stylized lament. In one sense, the *Arcadia, Astrophel and Stella,* and *The Lady of May* are literary manifestoes which complement *The Defence of Poesie;* they shape and attune a reader's response, and also represent Sidney's own developing effort to come to terms with the governing voices of literature.

The chief virtue of poetry, as Sidney sees it in the *Defence,* is that it delivers a golden world; 'since our erected wit maketh us know what perfection is, and yet our infected will keepeth us from reaching unto it.' And the form that comes closest to fulfilling this mission is the heroic poem: 'the loftie image of such worthies, most inflameth the minde with desire to bee worthie'; epic poetry 'maketh magnanimitie and justice, shine through all mistie fearfulnesse and foggie desires.' Heroic obligation and heroic education are never far from the centre of Sidney's work, though these concerns play against competing values in his pastoral masque, pastoral romance, and sonnet sequence, the genres in which he chose to write. The clear power of epic, voiced in the **Defence,** is in Sidney's verse and fiction more often poised against the lively presence of 'infected will' or the competing energies of love. One way of seeing his career—dangerous though it is to look for too much 'development' in so short a literary life—is in terms of the growing difficulty his protagonists have envisioning and attaining the perfection of the exemplary heroes mentioned in the **Defence.** The wit of Astrophel is at once more various and more clearly a 'fallen' power than the 'erected wit' of the visionary poet in Sidney's critical manifesto.

Questions of heroic energy are posed in what was probably Sidney's earliest work, the brief pastoral entertainment which came to be known in the eighteenth century as **The Lady of May.** Devised for one of Elizabeth I's visits to Sidney's uncle, the Earl of Leicester, at Wanstead (probably the visit of May 1578), the piece asks the Queen to make one of those choices so popular in Elizabethan and Jacobean masques. She is to award a husband to the young and beautiful May Lady, who has two suitors; in asking the Queen to choose, the Lady makes clear that 'in judging me, you judge more than me in it.' The rivals are Espilus, a rich shepherd with 'verie small deserts and no faults' and Therion, a forester with 'many deserts and many faults.' Like his comic ancestors, the bumptious Polyphemus of Theocritus and Corydon of Virgil's second eclogue, Espilus assumes that his weight in wool will recommend him. But as the debate moves to a more general level, to a choice of life, it is clear that the mere force of literary tradition will guarantee victory to the shepherd, whose supporters press his claim as representative of the contemplative life. The forester's followers present a more inclusive and original alternative:

> I was saying the shepheards life had some goodnesse in it, because it borrowed of the country quietnesse something like ours, but that is not all, for ours besides that quiet part, doth both strengthen the body, and raise up the mind with this gallant sort of activity. O sweet contentation to see the long life of the hurtlesse trees, to see how in streight growing up, though never so high, they hinder not their fellowes, they only enviously trouble, which are crookedly bent. What life is to be compared with ours where the very growing things are ensamples of goodnesse?

The appeal was lost on the Queen, who chose Espilus, perhaps not recognizing the unexpected turn the masque had taken, or perhaps seeing in it a covert appeal for the activist Protestant policies of Leicester. It is, however, clear from the text that Sidney expected Therion to win and had composed for the conclusion a song consoling the shep-

herd's god Pan for his defeat at the hands of the forest god Silvanus: 'Poore *Pan* (he sayd) although thou beaten be, / It is no shame, since *Hercules* was he.' The triumph of Hercules, archetypal man of action, in a pastoral masque suggests Sidney's playful reinterpretation of bucolic virtue and retirement; in the image of the forester's life he takes a momentary pleasure in the vision of an undivided life, a free twinning of action and contemplation, of reason and an exemplary ease—conjunctions not so happily accomplished in the works to follow.

No reader of **The Lady of May** would then be surprised to find heroes introduced into the forest retreats of Sidney's **Arcadia.** Though it takes as a point of departure the entirely pastoral romance of Jacopo Sannazaro, and though much of the heroic material was added when Sidney came to revise the work sometime after 1580, a concern for heroic control dominates both the original and 'new' Arcadias. The later version (and the only one known until our century when the unrevised **Arcadia** was discovered and published) opens with the entrance of the princes Pyrocles and Musidorus into that pastoral world where they are to test and be tested by love. But a great deal of energy and attention—almost all of Book II—is devoted to their heroic education and exploits, recounted by the disguised princes themselves as part of their wooing. Sannazaro provides a setting and his eclogues provide material for the pastoral games which serve as interludes between each 'act' of the romance, but the larger subject—the princes' wanderings—reflects Sidney's admiration for Greek and chivalric romance, for the *Aethiopica* of Heliodorus, the *Diana* of Montemayor, and the sprawling *Amadis de Gaula.* Eclogues, performed by the 'real' shepherds of Arcadia, are carefully framed; when they are past, the narrative again places them and reflects upon the princes' joining in: 'In these pastorall pastimes a great number of dayes were sent to follow their flying predecessours, while the cup of poison (which was deeply tasted of this noble companie) had left no sinewe of theirs without mortally searching into it. . . . ' Though landscapes are described in terms of the traditional and golden pastoral world, Pyrocles and Musidorus, the heroic princes, cannot simply escape to Arcadia and pursue their loves with absolute immunity. The **Arcadia** brings forth the 'golden world' of poetry not simply by creating ideal settings, but by teaching its readers and characters *how* to see the pastoral world in relation to a whole range of earthly settings which encircle it.

An incident in Book II suggests Sidney's critical intention. The inhabitants of Arcadia have begun a mutiny. A painter is standing by—and, in introducing him, Sidney stresses that he is not a good one—

> This painter was to counterfette the skirmishing betweene the *Centaures* and *Lapithes,* and had bene very desirous to see some notable wounds, to be able the more lively to express them; and this morning (being carried by the streame of this companie) the foolish felow was even delighted to see the effect of blowes.

The painter is so rapt in observing the wounds of others that he does not see a sword directed against himself and loses both hands. 'And so,' Sidney tells us, 'the painter returned, well skilled in wounds, but with never a hand to performe his skill.' This gruesome and pointed interruption reminds us not simply—as Ascham said—that experience is the worst teacher; it also suggests something about the superiority of stylized narrative and description to the crude use to which the copyist painter was about to put his artistic powers.

So, for example, when Sidney describes a disaster, the technique is less that of the photograph than of the foreshortened painting. The *Arcadia* opens with a shipwreck from which one of the heroes, Musidorus, is washed ashore and rescued. He persuades a fisherman to ferry him back to the wreckage in hope of catching sight of his comrade-in-arms Pyrocles:

> but when they came so neere as their eies were ful masters of the object, they saw a sight full of piteous strangenes: a ship, or rather the carkas of the shippe, or rather some few bones of the carkas, hulling there, part broken, part burned, part drowned: death having used more than one dart to that destruction. About it floted great store of very rich thinges, and many chestes which might promise no lesse. And amidst the precious things were a number of dead bodies, which likewise did not onely testifie both elements violence, but that the chief violence was growen of humane inhumanitie: for their bodies were ful of grisly wounds, and their bloud had (as were) filled the wrinckles of the seas visage: which it seemed the sea woulde not wash away, that it might witnes it is not alwaies his fault, when we condemne his crueltie: in summe, a defeate, where the conquered kept both field and spoile: a shipwrack without storme or ill footing: and a wast of fire in the midst of water.

This moving and stylized description proclaims itself from the beginning as one observed by those whose eyes are 'ful masters of the object.' Our attention is directed inevitably to the way that mastery is performed: movement is almost suspended ('a ship, or rather the carkas of the shippe, or rather some few bones of the carkas'), and the increasing precision of Sidney's metaphor leaves us with a vision of the ship as if it had been picked dry by vultures. Then again, the blood from the wounds of the dead 'filled the wrinckles of the seas visage.' Far beyond the observed detail—waves appear furrowed—the intensity and horror depend upon our feeling that something human has been defiled, the sea personified as ancient and as victim. In other words Sidney's descriptive powers force us again and again to remember that human beings in this shipwreck had been more death-dealing to one another than either fire or water had been. They had made themselves victims of their own panic and their own appetites. The eye becomes 'ful master of the object' when it grasps that essential point. Sidney's description is what he would call in *The Defence of Poesie* a 'speaking picture': what the educated eye ought to understand about what it sees.

There is a fuller, a more complex example in a later seascape. Book II is devoted to the adventures of Pyrocles and Musidorus, recounted against Arcadian settings as part of the wooing of the princesses Philoclea and Pamela. Musidorus is explaining how he and his cousin first set out

on their exploits. The passage includes an elaborate description which begins with their calm embarkation and proceeds through a fierce storm, the ship driven upon the rocks, the crew panicked, only the princes emerging as survivors. The passage is too long for quotation here, but the events may be told, as they just have been, in a single sentence. The impression one carries away is of an intense narration in which every stage of the adventure, every detail of the action, is ornamented and amplified by metaphors that touch other areas of the princes' experience. It is almost as if, as Musidorus retells his story, he is able to see the connections of this initial adventure to the high expectations and inevitable trials of love and politics in Arcadia. Setting sail, the ships 'kept together like a beautifull flocke, which so well could obey their maisters pipe.' Another comparison refers to expectations in love:

> the seeming insensible Loadstone, with a secret beauty (holding the spirit of iron in it) can draw that hard-harted thing unto it, and (like a vertuous mistresse) not onely make it bow it selfe, but with it make it aspire to so high a Love, as of the heavenly Poles.

With that introduction the mood of the comparisons changes; the events which follow are narrated with constant reminders of their likeness to civil and personal treachery. The sea that receives the heroes has already been marked as having 'so smooth and smiling a face, as if *Neptune* had as then learned falsely to fawne on Princes.' The winds become 'fittest instruments of commaundement' in a 'tumultuous kingdome'; night 'usurped the dayes right'. Such phases contribute to an elaborate parallel between this scene and moments of public and private treachery. Above all, amid this concentration of analogies, Sidney introduces the theatrical metaphors which frame the action of the *Arcadia* at its critical moments: 'a mournefull stage for a Tragedie to be plaied on'; 'lest the conclusion should not aunswere to the rest of the play. . . .' At climactic moments we are reminded that we constitute an audience. Spectators are essential to the drama being played out: the princes who are characters undergoing the experience, one of whom is retelling it; and, of course, the reader of the romance. Our attention is focused on the *images* which remain from the adventure, images which convey its lasting effect and meaning:

> Certainly there is no daunger carries with it more horror, than that which growes in those flowing kingdomes. For that dwelling place is unnaturall to mankind, and then the terriblenesse of the continuall motion, the dissolution of the fare being from comfort, the eye and the eare having ougly images ever before it, doth still vex the minde, even when it is best armed against it.

The drama—and this is what makes it essentially Sidneyan—is finally and explicitly centered in the mind, in images which forever haunt it and in the effort of will to arm against them. It is no coincidence that Musidorus recounts this episode when he tells Pamela of the princes' education, and it is no surprise that his terms recall Sidney's language in the *Defence:* the princes received 'conceits not unworthy of the best speakers'; 'images . . . being then delivered to their memory, which after, their stronger judgements might dispens. . . . ' What happens to them is what happens to the reader of literature described in the **Defence:** 'this purifying of wit, this enriching of memorie, enabling of judgement, and enlarging of conceit, which commonly we call learning.' The categories are those of Musidorus: images delivered to memory and judgement. Sidney's emphasis is never on simple participation in the stream of events, or even simple delight in or fear of the images before one, but rather on control and mastery. His heroes become *read*ers of their experience. Sidney's narrative is, in other words, the exact opposite of something like Miranda's wondering, uncomprehending description of the tempest in Shakespeare's last romance, or of the Clown's fragmented account of the storm in *The Winter's Tale:* 'now the ship boring the moon with her main-mast, and anon swallowed with yeast and froth, as you'ld thrust a cork into a hogshead.'

Sidney's description, while it registers the full horror and fear of the shipwreck, is governed by and comes to a full stop with the measured assurance of the prepared mind: 'a monstrous crie begotten of manie roaring vowes, was able to infect with feare a minde that had not prevented it with the power of reason.' The whole episode has been distanced, paced by the certainty of a mind prepared by reason, and witnessed by an eye which is 'ful master of the object.' Musidorus, all along, has been demonstrating in his way of telling the story a memory well-stored, rich in images, drawing likenesses to courts and pastures, stepping back theatrically to remind us that this is a stage for the education of princes. It is all much more explicit, much more self-consciously acted out for the reader than the adventures of Spenser's knights. Britomart and Redcrosse do not interpret themselves aloud for us; much more is discovered to the reader through their participation in the welter of experience. In the **Arcadia** the retrospective narratives of the princes and the highly directive prose of the third-person narrator are constantly demonstrating analytic powers, rich in images which 'enable the judgement.' For example, the memory of shipwreck crops up at important moments. Musidorus, discovering that his cousin Pyrocles is in love, registers this as a threat to their heroic ambitions:

> What have I deserved of thee, to be thus banished of thy counsels? Heretofore I have accused the sea, condemned the Pyrats, and hated my evill fortune, that deprived me of thee; But now thy self is the sea, which drounes my comfort, thy selfe is the Pirat that robbes thy selfe of me: Thy owne will becomes my evill fortune.

The true pitfalls and most potent dangers in Sidney's world are within. When Musidorus says 'thy self is the sea,' he means *self* in the strongest sense, one which he equates with *will.* Its failure is like the failure to stand against the fiercest natural powers; the forces released are as turbulent as those 'flowing kingdomes' whose images forever vex the mind. Musidorus, referring metaphorically to their own shipwreck, makes such connections explicitly and self-consciously. He brings into play images and associations alive in his memory, part of his heroic education. What is so special here is the degree to which described actions and landscapes so quickly become landscapes of

the mind, and the extent to which heroes are both participants in and interpreters of their experience. When Musidorus enters Arcadia, he does not take on his shepherd's role with the easy wit of Marlowe's passionate shepherd in 'Come live with me and be my love,' nor with the initial relaxation of Spenser's Calidore in Book VI of *The Faerie Queene*. Rather he welcomes the disguise with a judicious appraisal of his fallen state: 'Come shepheard's weedes, become your master's mind.' Pastoral details are almost immediately taken up as psychological markers, ways in which the heroes describe and test their own feelings.

It is in that light that we can understand the essentially static poetry of the **Arcadia.** The lyrics scattered through the text (this does not apply to the eclogues between the books, which belong principally to the Arcadian shepherds) have a choric function, the pursuits of love for a moment stilled in verse that bears the pressure of judgement: the princes lament their transformed state; the Queen Gynecia laments her lack of self-control (she is in love with Pyrocles, who in turn loves her daughter). To the shepherds Sidney gives more colloquial singing contests, an epithalamium, fabliaux taking comic delight in lust and adultery. But the norm for the aristocrats of the **Arcadia**—even when they join in pastoral dialogues or singing contests with the shepherds—is verse, self-conscious in its devotions, using the props of pastoral to express, understand, and, to some extent, control their feelings: 'My sheepe are thoughts, which I both guide and serve'; 'Transformd in shew, but more transformd in minde'; 'Over these brookes trusting to ease mine eyes.' The forms chosen are deliberately repetitive, the most extreme example being the beautiful double sestina 'Yee Goatheard Gods, that love the grassie mountaines.' But even sonnets are divided into quatrains with strictly repeating verbal patterns, so as to reinforce the impression of plangent lament, of an unbreakable circle of desire and strong feeling. Only in Book III does Sidney start to use sonnets in which changes of tone transform the sestet and lead emotions in unexpected directions.

The emphasis on self-mastery and control should not, of course, suggest that Pyrocles and Musidorus are consistently perfect interpreters of their experience or their pastoral surroundings. The book's splendid comedy is often bound up with moments when the heroic eye is not entirely master of its object. The appearance of the lion and bear in Book I—an episode already discussed—is only one of many examples. At a turning point in the book, the princesses are taken off into captivity by their wicked aunt Cecropia because of just such a misreading of their surroundings. 'Devising how to give more feathers to the winges of Time,' they follow a troop of shepherdesses into the forest and at an innocent picnic are lulled by the 'pleasantest fruites, that Sun-burnd *Autumne* could deliver unto them.' The scene is completed this time not by a lion and a bear, but by twenty armed men who carry them off to Cecropia's castle.

Sidney's princes, already alert interpreters of their martial adventures, must learn how to read these pastoral scenes, how to include love within the circle of their experience, making it compatible with the responsibilities of their active lives. Characteristically their days are full of conflict, their golden scenes often filled out by crouching attackers representing appetite.

> O heaven and earth (said *Musidorus*) to what a passe are our mindes brought, that from the right line of vertue, are wryed to these crooked shifts? But o Love, it is thou that doost it: thou changest name upon name; thou disguisest our bodies, and disfigurest our mindes. But in deed thou hast reason, for though the wayes be foule, the journeys end is most faire and honourable.

Oddly enough—and perhaps Sidney would have made it clearer if he had lived to revise the *Arcadia* beyond Book III—the princes are only freed from their predicament by a comic accident. The king, Basilius, supposedly dead but really only set asleep with a love potion, awakens just in time to save the princes from being punished for their 'lustful' attempts on the princesses. It is perhaps the only way out of a book where love is construed as a necessary lapse, one eventually leading to virtue, but where heroes self-consciously

> goe privately to seeke exercises of their vertue: thinking it not so worthy, to be brought to heroycall effects by fortune, or necessitie (like *Ulysses* and *Aeneas*) as by ones owne choice, and working.

No writer could set a higher standard for heroism, and none could have a sharper sense of our resources for self-bafflement.

In the *Arcadia* Sidney paid his strictest tribute to the heroic ideal and to the *Defence*'s epic vision of literature. Pyrocles and Musidorus win their princesses and return to their public responsibilities and the unrelenting demands of heroic vigilance, the 'journeys end . . . most faire and honourable.' *Astrophel and Stella,* beginning as well with a young hero's truancy to the world of love, never grants the rewards of the *Arcadia.* Astrophel continues his 'wailing eloquence,' neither winning Stella nor wishing to re-enter the hollow world of chivalry and 'great expectation.' Thomas Nashe's breezy summary—in a preface to the first (and unauthorized) edition of 1591—tells only part of the story when he describes it as the 'tragicommody of love . . . the argument cruell chastitie, the Prologue hope, the Epilogue dispaire. . . .' The sequence indeed follows the plot line of the great tales of courtly love (*Troilus and Criseyde* was, reportedly, one of 'Astrophel's cordials'). And there are moments of dramatic confrontation in the interspersed songs when the voices of both lovers are heard, Astrophel facing Stella, entreating and ruefully refused. But in general the sequence of 108 sonnets directs us not to narrative excitements but to Astrophel's complicated and changing reactions, to an inner dialogue in the course of which we glimpse fragments of a familiar curve of events: Astrophel's falling in love, his expectations and victories and disappointments. Unlike the Arcadians, whose prose and verse demonstrates their awareness of heroic control and mastery, Astrophel in his poems conveys an incomplete and developing experience. He is a puzzled participant in his love for Stella and is engaged in a series of rich encounters with authority, testing the formulas with which others characterize experience. Assertions and distinctions of feeling challenge and qualify precept at every turn. Sometimes he encounters books: poets' phrases which do not seem adequate to the true voice of feeling (sonnets 1, 3, 6, 15, 74); the lessons of Reason, Virtue, and 'great expectation' (4, 10, 21) which trouble his growing allegiance to Stella; and finally Stella herself, 'fairest booke of Nature,' whose lessons are confusing and do not accommodate his strong desires (62, 71). The sequence is filled with personifications from a textbook for lovers, figures whose importance Astrophel is continually challenging: Hope (67); Patience (56); 'traytour absence' (88); Doctor Cupid (61). His chafings and probings create the pattern of *Astrophel and Stella*—its definitions, its declarations against adversaries. Sidney, who helped domesticate the Petrarchan mode in England, also carried its habitual introspection to an extreme which helped undermine the tradition. The immediacy with which he follows the lover's turn of mind—from line to line or from sonnet to sonnet—draws us away from visions of the ideal mistress (like Petrarch's Laura) to an individualizing energy, impatient with the worshipful stance the lover finds himself assuming. Where Petrarch's poet-lover, imagining his mistress, is drawn by the brilliance of her image, his turbulence balanced and transformed by intense lyric presentations of Laura, Astrophel can only fitfully, without strain, transport himself into these moods. By the end of the sequence, unlike Petrarch and unlike the idealized heroes at the end of the *Arcadia,* Astrophel is irrevocably, even joyfully, committed to the confusions of the fallen world. His understanding of love is not the purifying, gradual refinement of Petrarch's *Rime,* but rather an emerging clarification of and commitment to his own fallen nature as an earthly lover.

Charged with truancy to his heroic training, Astrophel moves from an opening series of harried defences against Reason and Virtue to redefine those words and claim their power for love. Sometimes jaunty, sometimes guilty and rueful, allowing full strength to 'Reason's audite,' he relies on energetic conversions:

> If that be sinne which doth the maners frame,
> Well staid with truth in word and faith of deed,
> Readie of wit and fearing nought but shame:
> If that be sinne which in fixt hearts doth breed
> A loathing of all loose unchastitie,
> Then Love is sinne, and let me sinfull be.
>
> (Sonnet 14)

Once committed to love, he alternately invokes the Petrarchan contraries ('Where *Love* is chastnesse, Paine doth learne delight'—Sonnet 48) and bristles at the artificialities of courtship ('Alas, if Fancy drawne by imag'd things, / Though false, yet with free scope more grace doth breed / Than servant's wracke . . . '—Sonnet 45). The pressures of desire challenge easy literary definitions of love: Stella imposes 'a Love not blind,' one anchored 'fast . . . on *Virtue's* shore,' so leading Astrophel to new discriminations:

> Alas, if this the only metall be
> Of *Love,* new-coind to helpe my beggery,
> Deare, love me not, that you may love me more.
>
> (Sonnet 62)

The sequence follows Astrophel from one crossroad to another, each of his bright distinctions proving not to be the irresistible gesture he had hoped it would be. New paths branch off constantly; new frustrations are discovered in his love until, wearily, he acknowledges the irreducible element of desire, by sonnet 72 greeted as his 'old companion': 'But thou Desire, because thou wouldst have all, / Now banisht art, but yet alas how shall?' Late in the series, sonnets give way to lyric confrontation in eleven songs, both characters now directly on stage, the impossibility of their love crystallized as Stella, regretfully, banishes him in honour's name. *Astrophel and Stella* ends with what amounts to a ceremony of grief; the last sonnets, more like songs than any others in the series, invoke personifications of Woe, Sighs, Thought, and Grief. After this clarification of feeling, the sequence can do nothing but end, with little truly resolved though emotions have been exhausted.

Astrophel's probing and puzzlement demand techniques which make these sonnets far different from the Arcadian poems. Many of them are pitched toward an unexpected conclusion, the sonnet form filled out as if, while Astrophel speaks, his counter feelings are gathering and burst out in the final lines. Majestic praise of Stella as the 'fairest booke of Nature' drawing him forcibly to Virtue (71) is suddenly challenged:

> So while thy beautie drawes the heart to love,
> As fast thy Vertue bends that love to good:
> But ah, Desire still cries, give me some food.

Or the eloquent claims of the 'inward light' (5)—'True, that on earth we are but pilgrims made, / And should in soule up to our countrey move'—crystallize a quiet countering resolve: 'True, and yet true that I must *Stella* love.'

But the true departure of *Astrophel and Stella*—what points ahead to Shakespeare and to Donne—is its more intense verbal activity: a liberated control of sound, rhythm, and syntax which vividly transmits the sense of Astrophel as participant in rather than heroic master of his experience. One can pose, for example, Pyrocles' judicious lament, 'Transformed in shew, but more transformd in minde,' against Astrophel's urgent discovery of what it is like to fall in love:

> Flie, fly, my friends, I have my death wound; fly,
> See there that boy, that murthring boy I say,
> Who like a theefe, hid in darke bush doth ly,
> Til bloudie bullet get him wrongfull pray.
> (Sonnet 20)

Familiar as the scene of Cupid's ambush may be in Renaissance poetry Astrophel's sonnet still manages to sound urgent and irritated. He is experiencing in the present tense, what Pyrocles has already weighed and assimilated before he begins his poem. A traditional conceit is in the later sonnet animated by all the rhythms of surprise, above all by the penetrating sounds (Flie, fly, my . . . I . . . fly / See . . . say / . . . like . . . theefe . . . ly . . . pray), the long *e's* and *i's* and *a's*, which keep these opening cries echoing through the poem (in all the rhyme words of the octave, for example) until the urgency is slowly damped down by the closed rhymes of the last lines.

Syntax, too, follows the hesitations and pressures of feeling rather than marking and controlling emotions as the Arcadian sonnets do.

> Wo, having made with many fights his owne
> Each sence of mine, each gift, each power of
>   mind
> Growne now his slaves, he forst them out to find
> The thorowest words, fit for woe's selfe to grone,
> Hoping that when they might find *Stella* alone,
> Before she could prepare to be unkind . . .
> (Sonnet 57)

These words have the quality of breathy yet considered speech. It is possible to read the phrases of line 2 as intensified objects of 'made . . . his owne'; or, as spilling over into the following line, any or all of them as the subject of 'growne now his slaves.' Such deliberate fluidity makes it seem as if the battles and slavery to Woe are now, wearily and firmly, a part of life, telescoped quickly behind the redundant 'he' as if to put these experiences in place. The rapid movement calls us back to the present, to new frustrations: as Stella receives his 'plaints,' she sings his poem and so removes the sting of his strong feelings. We must be alive to these syntactical pleasures which, slowing and quickening the flow of the sonnets, give privileged renditions of particular moments of feeling.

Astrophel and Stella often invites attention to such details; its resources, its more intense verbal activity allow a psychological subtlety which would have been inappropriate to the willed evaluations of the *Arcadia.* The movement of mind, so often praised in Donne, is already present in many of the sonnets of Sidney's sequence, though perhaps without so intricate a representation of the snares of thought. The pattern of *Astrophel and Stella* is one that both Donne and Shakespeare would have understood: exploring the possibilities of sustained praise and lyric vision leads to a shattered awakening and a recall to the desiring, unsatisfied self.

Auden has referred to Sidney as a poet's poet. Ambiguous praise, it highlights an important truth: that Sidney's range is not great and that many of his self-conscious efforts at formal effects are of interest only to those, like poets, whose concerns are highly technical. It was Auden and Empson who called attention to the wonderful double sestina, 'Yee Gote-heard Gods', reprinting it for an audience which might never have looked for it among the self-absorbed, sometimes drab lyrics of the *Arcadia.* Surely it suggested for their own poetry an example of the heightened effects of form divorced from the individualized, errant, probing voices of modern poetry. Yet Sidney himself was moving away from those patterned achievements. In *Astrophel and Stella* he discovered, triumphantly, that very different kind of voice which was to be fully at home in the spacious achievement of the Elizabethan stage: dramatic speech, committed to the wandering voices of the fallen world, the high road of English poetry ever since. (pp. 41-56)

David Kalstone, "Sir Philip Sydney," in English Poetry and Prose: 1540-1674, *edited by Christopher Ricks, revised edition, Sphere Reference, 1986, pp. 41-59.*

A. C. Hamilton   (essay date 1977)

[*In the following excerpt, Hamilton explores Sidney's* Defense of Poetry, *particularly as it is informed by religious convictions.*]

In his poetry Sidney shows his contemporaries how poetry should be written. In so doing, he seeks to counter its abuse by the poet-apes through whose work, as he argues in the second part of the **Defence of Poetry,** England had come to despise poetry. Yet he needed to counter also the poet-haters, the μισομουσοι, through whose influence England had come to despise the art itself. Accordingly, in the first part of the **Defence** he describes the nature and working of the 'right poets'. In showing why poets write and how their works should be read, he provides a manifesto for the major Elizabethan writers.

Sidney may have written the **Defence** between 1580 and 1582. From Spenser's letter to Harvey in October 1579 announcing that Sidney and Dyer had proclaimed 'a general surceasing and silence of bald rhymers' by experimenting in quantitative verse, one infers that Sidney had reached the position, expressed in the **Defence,** that verse is 'but an ornament and no cause to poetry' but not what he goes on to say here, that verse remains its fittest raiment. The **Defence** may have been occasioned by the attack on poetry in Gosson's *School of Abuse* (1579), or by the dedication of that work to Sidney, which provoked him not to answer Gosson specifically but Plato and all after him who had spoken against poetry. For all we know—and we know little—the **Defence** may also have been prompted by Spenser's lost critical treatise, 'The English Poet'. Sidney may have wanted to complement that work by treating the art of poesy itself; or even to counter its doctrine: that poetry is 'a divine gift and heavenly instinct . . . poured into the wit by a certain ενθουσιασμος and celestial inspiration' is exactly contrary to his own doctrine that the poet is 'lifted up with the vigour of his own invention'. The close relationship between Sidney's creative and critical faculties suggests that the **Defence** was prompted by his own work: he came to understand the art of poesy by practising it. The modest reference to himself as one who 'having slipped into the title of a poet, am provoked to say something unto you in the defence of that my unelected vocation' shows pride in some substantial work, which may well be **Astrophel and Stella.** The **Defence** may be dated after that work and before the **New Arcadia,** that is, between 1580 and 1582, because it is not necessary to our understanding of the former but illuminates our reading of the latter. While it could be earlier, a later date is likely because of its mastery of matter and manner. To write the **Defence,** Sidney had to assimilate an extensive body of contemporary learning and then integrate the major traditions of literary doctrine from Plato, Aristotle, and Horace to the sixteenth-century Italian critics into a profound and original argument on the idea of the 'right poet'. The sustained brilliance of its style—it is surely the best written treatise of its kind in any language—supports a later date. A later date may explain why Sidney should write a defence of poetry while his friends were writing political and religious treatises. (George Buchanan's *De Fure Regni apud Scotos* and Duplessis's *Vindiciae contra Tyrannos* appeared in 1579, the year in which Sidney began to take a

strong interest in poetry.) Evidently he had concluded that his future lay in writing rather than in politics.

The **Defence** is characterized by its style. Swift remarks scornfully, though truly, that Sidney argues 'as if he really believed himself'. Even more, Sidney convinces his readers that they, too, should believe what he says. His persuasive intent becomes clear if the opening of the **Defence** is compared to the opening of the *Poetices* by Scaliger, his chief Italian counterpart. The latter begins with a division of *oratio* according to its three ends, each with its own type of expression:

> Everything that pertains to mankind may be classed as necessary, useful, or pleasure-giving, and by an inherent characteristic of all these classes the power of speech was implanted in man from the very beginning, or, as time went on, was acquired. Since man's development depended upon learning, he could not do without that agency which was destined to make him the partaker of wisdom. Our speech is, as it were, the postman of the mind, through the services of whom civil gatherings are announced, the arts are cultivated, and the claims of wisdom intercede with men for man.'

It is clear even in translation that, to use his own category, Scaliger's language may be classified as 'useful': he argues logically, to convince us by reason. In contrast, Sidney begins with a personal, and apparently casual, recollection of the time 'when the right virtuous Edward Wotton and I were at the Emperor's court together' (assuming that we know who that Emperor was), and relates an anecdote about a certain John Pietro Pugliano who so over-praised horses that Sidney concludes: 'if I had not been a piece of a logician before I came to him, I think he would have persuaded me to have wished myself a horse' (thus wittily alluding to his own name, Philip, *philippos,* one fond of horses), and concludes with a disarming 'disabler', apologizing for his own apology for poetry: 'if I handle [it] with more good will than good reasons, bear with me'. Anyone who continues to read will be persuaded by Sidney's 'good will' before ever he may entertain his 'good reasons'.

Sidney's style may be illustrated in the passage in which he answers the second charge against poetry, that poets are liars:

> To the second . . . that they should be the principal liars, I will answer paradoxically, but truly, I think truly, that of all writers under the sun the poet is the least liar, and, though he would, as a poet can scarcely be a liar. The astronomer, with his cousin the geometrician, can hardly escape, when they take upon them to measure the height of the stars. How often, think you, do the physicians lie, when they aver things good for sicknesses, which afterwards send Charon a great number of souls drowned in a potion before they come to his ferry? And no less of the rest, which take upon them to affirm. Now, for the poet, he nothing affirms, and therefore never lieth . . . Though he recount things not true, yet because he telleth them not for true, he lieth not—without we will say that Nathan lied in his speech before-alleged to David; which as a wick-

ed man durst scarce say, so think I none so simple would say that Aesop lied in the tales of his beasts; for who thinks that Aesop wrote it for actually true were well worthy to have his name chronicled among the beasts he writeth of. What child is there, that, coming to a play, and seeing *Thebes* written in great letters upon an old door, doth believe that it is Thebes? If then a man can arrive to that child's age to know that the poets' persons and doings are but pictures what should be, and not stories what have been, they will never give the lie to things not affirmatively but allegorically and figuratively written.

This extended passage answers a stock charge familiar from the time of Plato: it is a re-statement, as Shepherd notes, of the Aristotelian handling of Plato's position. Clearly Sidney has a purpose beyond conveying a mere argument. It is startling that he should lead so casually and humorously to the concluding sentence, which is central to the argument of the *Defence.*

The opening conveys the accents of a man speaking, and thinking as he speaks: 'I will answer paradoxically, but truly, I think truly'. 'I think' indicates hesitation as much as it does confirmation, forcing us to follow Sidney's process of thinking rather than his thoughts, so that by the end we will think as he does. Although he argues paradoxically, we agree readily that an astronomer will prove a liar if he tries to measure the distance to a star. The Renaissance reader would consider the attempt both vain and forbidden. After this persuasive example we are ready to join Sidney in mocking the medical profession. The phrase, 'How often, think you', draws us fully to his side, particularly when he continues with the witty metaphor of patients drowned in doctors' potions before they come to Charon's ferry. The charge against doctors is a commonplace, but Sidney may have taken it from Agrippa's *Of the vanity and uncertainty of arts and sciences:* 'Well near always there is more danger in the physician, and the medicine, than in the sickness itself.' When the charge is so expressed, we may agree or not, as we believe it to be true or false. As expressed by Sidney, however, all will agree, being persuaded by his wit, without pausing to quibble over just how many were drowned. Only when Sidney has persuaded us does he affirm his central doctrine that 'the poet . . . nothing affirms'. He then anticipates a reader's possible protest, namely, that the poet affirms things not true, not by logical argument but by an *argumentum ad hominem:* such a reader would place himself among those worse than the wicked or among beasts, and show less percipience than a child not to allow that the poet describes things not as they are, but as they ought to be. So readers are entertained, cajoled, even tricked, into accepting the argument that 'they will never give the lie to things not affirmatively but allegorically and figuratively written'.

The *Defence* is deeply and powerfully persuasive throughout, not because its argument immediately convinces us, but because Sidney convinces us that we should believe *him.* Not to be convinced would be to place oneself among the enemy, the unnamed because unnamable μισομουσοι whose one great spokesman, Plato, attacks only the abuse of poetry (so Sidney shows) because he hon-

ours its proper use. Sidney impresses any reader as honest, passionate, witty, civilized, and, above all, fully human. His voice speaks for the best in us and the best in human society. It is personal in that it records Sidney's own commitments, and public in that it conveys the values and aspirations of his age. As a result, the *Defence* gained central authority among contemporary writers. Lewis notes that the greatness of Sidney's theory is that 'it is the form into which the actual taste and ethics and religion and poetic practice of his age and class . . . naturally fell when reflected on and harmonized'. Shepherd concludes that 'the more closely the *Apology* is studied the more astonishing appears Sidney's sensitivity to contemporary intellectual development, in the arts, in religion, in politics, and in science'.

The persuasiveness and authority of Sidney's style might suggest that the *Defence* is a gracious expression of the ideas of others, 'what oft was thought, but ne'er so well expressed'. Whatever Sidney took from others, however, he made his own, and his style conveys an argument that is closely reasoned and logical in all its parts. Since he possessed an eclectic and synthesizing mind, that originality appears as a simple rightness and central wholeness rather than a uniquely personal judgment. One paradox of the *Defence* is that it is both personal as it is dominated by the immediate and constant presence of Sidney as narrator, and impersonal as it expresses the truth about the essential nature and working of poetry. Another paradox is that despite its central authority, it proposes a revolutionary poetic.

The argument of the *Defence* arises from a division of poets into three kinds. The first 'imitate the unconceivable excellencies of God': 'such were David in his Psalms; Solomon in his Song of Songs . . . Orpheus, Amphion, Homer in his Hymns'. The second deal with philosophical matters: 'either moral, as Tyrtaeus, Phocylides, Cato, or natural, as Lucretius and Virgil's *Georgics;* or astronomical, as Manilius and Pontanus; or historical, as Lucan'. The third are set apart as 'indeed right poets': 'they which most properly do imitate to teach and delight, and to imitate borrow nothing of what is, hath been, or shall be; but range, only reined with learned discretion, into the divine consideration of what may be and should be'.

Sidney's source is Scaliger, who divides poets into three kinds according to their subject-matter. Yet Scaliger also divides poets into kinds according to inspiration and the age in which they wrote, and allows that there are as many kinds of poets as there are subjects. What is for him a convenient classification becomes in Sidney an absolute distinction. The first kind are not really poets at all but 'may justly be termed *vates*'; of the second kind he remarks: 'whether they properly be poets or no let grammarians dispute'; only the third kind are 'indeed right poets'. Thus Scaliger classifies poets differently as they are divinely inspired or aroused by strong wine, while Sidney keeps the same division to describe the inspiration of the three kinds of poets. The first kind is divinely inspired; a poet of the second kind cannot be inspired because he is 'wrapped within the fold of the proposed subject, and takes not the course of his own invention'. Only the right poet is properly inspired, not in the Platonic sense of inspiration as that suppression of intellect by which the poet is akin to the lunatic, but in the Christian sense of 'breathing into' by which he is 'lifted up with the vigour of his own invention'. Thus Sidney rejects Plato's notion that the poet receives 'a very inspiring of a divine force, far above man's wit', for he holds that the poet freely ranges 'only within the zodiac of his own wit'. He was well aware of how he had transformed his source. Scaliger classifies the poets in order to claim that Lucan is a poet because he wrote verse; Sidney adds Lucan to the second kind, those who are not true poets, and goes on to claim that 'it is not rhyming and versing that maketh a poet'.

Sidney went behind Scaliger to the source of the critical tradition in Plato. He adopts the adroit strategy of directing Plato's attack on poetry against the first two kinds of poets, leaving the right poet free. In this way he can absorb Plato—'whom, the wiser a man is, the more just cause he shall find to have in admiration'—and go beyond him.

The first kind, the divine poet, Plato denounces for telling false things about the gods; only if he praises the gods may he be admitted into the ideal state. Sidney allows only that the divine poet may cheer the merry and console the troubled. While he honours this 'most noble sort', he is not concerned to defend him. The second kind, the poet who takes his material at second-hand from philosophical or historical matters, Plato attacks because his poetry is twice removed from reality. Sidney allows Plato's argument when he claims that such poets 'retain themselves within their subject, and receive, as it were, their being from it', and when he calls them 'takers of others'. As Plato compares such poets to the painter whose work is a copy of a copy, Sidney compares them to 'the meaner sort of painters, who counterfeit only such faces as are set before them'. Plato banishes them, but Sidney questions their right even to the name of poet.

Sidney allows, as Plato does not, a third kind of poet who 'bringeth his own stuff, and . . . maketh matter for a conceit', for 'all only proceedeth from their wit, being indeed makers of themselves'. Such poets may not be compared to the meaner sort of painter but only to 'the more excellent, who having no law but wit, bestow that in colours upon you which is fittest for the eye to see'. While the first two kinds of poets take their matter from nature, the right poet 'bringeth things forth surpassing her doings'. He imitates not by copying nature but by creating another nature; and being a maker, he may be compared to the heavenly Maker. For Plato, such a comparison explains the creative role only of the first two kinds of poets. As the Demiurge shapes the world out of pre-existing matter according to Ideas apart from him, Plato's poet struggles with matter taken from others. Lacking its Idea, he must yield himself to his subject in admiration (as the first kind) or render it sweetly (as the second kind). For Sidney, however, the comparison illuminates the right poet's creative power. As God creates *ex nihilo* according to Ideas within himself, the right poet 'with the force of a divine breath . . . bringeth things forth' for he 'borrow[s] nothing of what is, hath been, or shall be'. Further, 'that the poet hath that *idea* [of perfect man] is manifest, by delivering them forth in such excellency as he had imagined them'.

Sidney's views on the nature and working of poetry are epitomized in a passage which Dorsten calls the 'most fundamental paragraph of the *Defence*':

> Neither let it be deemed too saucy a comparison to balance the highest point of man's wit with the efficacy of nature; but rather give right honour to the heavenly Maker of that maker, who having made man to His own likeness, set him beyond and over all the works of that second nature: which in nothing he showeth so much as in poetry, when with the force of a divine breath he bringeth things forth surpassing her doings— with no small arguments to the credulous of that first accursed fall of Adam, since our erected wit maketh us know what perfection is, and yet our infected will keepeth us from reaching unto it. But these arguments will by few be understood, and by fewer granted.

This paragraph deserves to be examined closely not only because it illustrates the cogency and clarity of Sidney's argument but also because it reveals the firm Christian basis of his poetic.

Sidney is supporting his claim that all arts and sciences follow Nature, and are therefore subject to her—all except the right poet, who remains free to create another nature. Since Nature is fallen, her world is brazen; but the poet's world, being unfallen, is golden. Sidney illustrates this by comparing Nature's skill and the poet's at their greatest, in producing man. As one example, he cites Cyrus: fallen Nature has never produced 'so right a prince as Xenophon's Cyrus'. He allows two objections to his placing the poet over Nature. The first is that the works of Nature are 'essential', while those of the poet are 'in imitation or fiction'. To this he replies that the skill of any artificer stands 'in that *idea* or foreconceit of the work, and not in the work itself'. So judged, the excellence of what he creates proves that he has the idea in his mind. Again, the work of the poet is essential because he not only makes a Cyrus, which Nature may do, but 'bestow[s] a Cyrus upon the world to make many Cyruses, if they [the readers] will learn aright why and how that maker made him'. The second objection, that the poet's creative power would far exceed Nature's, is answered in the paragraph cited above. Having concluded cryptically that 'these arguments will by few be understood, and by fewer granted', he turns to 'a more ordinary opening' of the nature of poetic creation in which the truth is obvious to all.

Sidney challenges his more discerning readers to understand his arguments, and clearly he desires that of these some will grant them. The distinction between what may be understood and what may be granted seems to refer to his arguments on the nature of poetry and those on its working. Some few in the age would understand his claims for the poet's creative power in relation to Nature, but far fewer (and none in our age?) would grant his claim for the poet's creative power over his readers.

A poet may create an image of Cyrus as 'so right a prince' exceeding what Nature may create because, in making man in His image, God first 'set him beyond and over all the works of that second nature'. Sidney alludes to Hebrews 2:7: in creating man, God 'didst set him over the works of thy hands' (the Geneva text reads: 'above the works of thine hands'). His phrase, 'beyond and over' asserts that entire dominion over Nature which man enjoyed in his unfallen state when he was commanded to 'subdue' the earth (Gen. 1:28). When man fell, his relationship to Nature was inverted: he became subject to 'all the works of that second nature', by which Sidney means fallen Nature. Accordingly, the arts which imitate Nature 'become actors and players, as it were, of what nature will have set forth'. Sidney's case against the arts and sciences is that they serve only to confirm man in his fallen state. The right poet alone claims man's former dominion over Nature by creating a golden world, which is the first, or unfallen, Nature. For this reason, the fallen reader, remaining subject to Nature, may hardly believe that the poet enjoys man's unfallen dominion over Nature. Yet proof that he does is shown in the images of perfection he creates: 'so true a lover as Theagenes, so constant a friend as Pylades, so valiant a man as Orlando, so right a prince as Xenophon's Cyrus, so excellent a man every way as Virgil's Aeneas'. Sidney implies that poetry derives from that element in man which remains unfallen, and he identifies that element with the poet's capacity to imagine states of perfection which existed only before the fall.

Sidney allows that perfection is known to fallen man by his 'erected wit', although his 'infected will' keeps him 'from reaching unto it'. His arguments will be understood by few because they are involved in religious controversy over man's fallen nature. That man's will had become infected was generally accepted by Christians of all faiths. Protestant emphasis upon man's total depravity extended to his wit. The Calvinist position is expressed by William Tyndale: 'the will of man followeth the wit, and is subject unto the wit; and as the wit erreth, so does the will; and as the wit is in captivity, so is the will; neither is it possible that the will should be free, where the wit is in bondage'. Yet Calvin himself allows that man's depravity is not absolute:

> For even though something of understanding and judgment remains as a residue along with the will, yet we shall not call a mind whole and sound that is both weak and plunged into deep darkness. And depravity of the will is all too well known. Since reason, therefore, by which man distinguishes between good and evil, and by which he understands and judges, is a natural gift, it could not be completely wiped out; but it was partly weakened and partly corrupted, so that its misshapen ruins appear.

This view that man is not totally fallen was seized upon by the Christian humanists who emphasized man's erected wit—what Sidney calls in the **Defence** man's 'own divine essence' and in a letter to Languet, 'that particle of the divine mind', and what Milton names as 'some remnants of the divine image [that] still exist in us, not wholly extinguished by . . . spiritual death'. The poet's creative power displayed in his images of perfection manifests this 'divine image'.

More difficult to understand, and even more difficult to grant, is the poet's creative power over his readers, how he may 'bestow a Cyrus upon the world to make many Cyruses, if they will learn aright why and how that maker made him'. Evidently readers must do more than read Xenophon: from Sidney's poetic they must learn—and learn aright—both how and why the poet creates the image of perfection in Cyrus.

From that poetic, one may learn *why* the poet makes his images. Sidney accepts Horace's familiar concept of the end of poetry when he defines poesy as 'an art of imitation . . . with this end, to teach and delight'. These two ends become one when he goes on to claim that 'delightful teaching . . . must be the right describing note to know a poet by'. Yet he defends poetry on the ground that it teaches and delights in order to move. For him, 'moving is of a higher degree than teaching', for the end of all knowledge is virtuous action. Since 'the poet, with that same hand of delight, doth draw the mind more effectually than any other art doth', he concludes that 'as virtue is the most excellent resting place for all worldly learning to make his end of, so poetry, being the most familiar to teach it, and most princely to move towards it, in the most excellent work is the most excellent workman'. While this rhetorical end of moving was allowed by earlier critics—Scaliger speaks of poetry *'docendi & mouendi, & delectandi'*—none anticipates Sidney's emphasis. His defence of poetry rests upon its power through delight to move men to virtuous action.

Sidney's poetic is based on the Protestant emphasis on the doctrine of the Fall, and particularly on the Augustinian-Calvinist doctrine of the infected will. Since his will is infected, man must be moved to virtuous action. He may best be moved, Sidney believes, by the delight given by poetry. Horace's concept of the two ends of poetry implies that poetry teaches the reader by addressing his reason and delights him by appealing to his emotions. It combines the two ends when it delights in order to teach. For Sidney, however, poetry delights the reader in order to move his will. Since the will is radically infected, the reader must be ravished with delight. 'Delight' becomes a key word in what Sidney calls his 'defence of sweet poetry'. In the peroration he sums up his view of poetry when he speaks of it as 'full of virtue-breeding delightfulness' (120). Poetry teaches by delighting the readers with images of perfection, and by this means achieves the 'final end' of learning which is 'to lead and draw us to as high a perfection as our degenerate souls, made worse by their clayey lodgings, can be capable of '.

The second part of Sidney's argument, that the poet may 'make many Cyruses, if they will learn aright . . . how that maker made him', may be inferred from his own reading of poetry. His practical criticism is limited to the concluding pages of the **Defence** for he writes a defence of poesy, not of particular poets: as he says, 'I speak of the art, and not of the artificer'. Since that art is most fully realized in the genre of the heroic poem, his art of reading may be inferred from his comments on the heroic poets:

> If the poet do his part aright, he will show you in Tantalus, Atreus, and such like, nothing that

is not to be shunned; in Cyrus, Aeneas, Ulysses, each thing to be followed.

The poet nameth Cyrus or Aeneas no other way than to show what men of their fames, fortunes, and estates should do.

So is it in men (most of which are childish in the best things, till they be cradled in their graves): glad will they be to hear the tales of Hercules, Achilles, Cyrus, Aeneas; and, hearing them, must needs hear the right description of wisdom, valour, and justice.

Who readeth Aeneas carrying old Anchises on his back, that wisheth not it were his fortune to perform so excellent an act? Whom doth not these words of Turnus move, the tale of Turnus having planted his image in the imagination, *Fugientem haec terra videbit? / Usque adeone mori miserum est?*

Only let Aeneas be worn in the tablet of your memory, how he governeth himself in the ruin of his country; in the preserving his old father, and carrying away his religious ceremonies; in obeying God's commandment to leave Dido, though not only all passionate kindness, but even the human consideration of virtuous gratefulness, would have craved other of him; how in storms, how in sports, how in war, how in peace, how a fugitive, how victorious, how besieged, how besieging, how to strangers, how to allies, how to enemies, how to his own; lastly, how in his inward self, and how in his outward government—and I think, in a mind not prejudiced with a prejudicating humour, he will be found in excellency fruitful.

Reading becomes a way of possessing poetry so actively that the reader is himself possessed. The poet's image is mnemonic and heuristic: it 'replenishes', 'inhabits', and 'enriches' the memory, and the knowledge it provides teaches man how to act. Yet Sidney refers to the knowledge that poetry provides as 'heart-ravishing', for it inspires rather than instructs. The poet fashions his image not to teach directly but to 'strike, pierce, [and] possess the sight of the soul'.

Aeneas carrying Anchises on his back is adduced by Alciati as an emblem, with the motto *'Pietas filiorum'*. For Sidney, Virgil's image does not illustrate a moral tag but inspires a reader to similar virtuous action. It combines the philosopher's precept and the historian's example in a way that cannot be broken down into moral abstraction or historical event. What the poet imagines, he transplants directly into the reader's imagination. Hence Sidney speaks of the virtues, vices, and passions presented by the poet 'so in their own natural seats laid to the view, that we seem not to hear of them, but clearly to see through them'. If the reader heard of the virtues directly, poetry would supply knowledge of good and evil, as do the other arts and sciences. By seeing the virtues, and seeing through them, the reader reaches a higher state of illumination, which only poetry may provide. The distinction may be compared to that which Plato makes between knowledge which clarifies the world around us and that which illuminates a world of higher reality; and to Augus-

tine's distinction between *scientia* and *sapientia*, that is, between the experiences that man's senses provide and what the mind provides by transcending experience through its contact with a higher reality.

Sidney regards all learning in religious terms: its final end is 'to lead and draw us to as high a perfection as our degenerate souls, made worse by their clayey lodgings, can be capable of', and its scope is 'by knowledge to lift up the mind from the dungeon of the body to the enjoying his own divine essence'. As the highest form of learning, poetry lifts man from the brazen world of things as they are to a vision of the golden world of things as they should be. Accordingly, the illumination it provides suggests a religious vision. One may compare the wisdom which Agrippa urges his readers to find in Holy Scripture by rejecting the vanity of the arts and sciences:

> If ye desire to attain to this divine and true wisdom, not of the tree of the knowledge of good and ill, but of the tree of life, the traditions of men set apart, and every search and discourse of the flesh and blood. . . . For the knowledge of all things is compact in you . . . Even as he [God] then hath created trees full of fruits, so also hath he created the souls as reasonable trees full of forms and knowledges; but through the sin of the first parent, all things were [concealed] and oblivion, the mother of ignorance, stepped in. Set you then now aside, which may, the veil of your understanding, which are wrapped in the darkness of ignorance. Cast out the drink of Lethe you which have made yourselves drunk with forgetfulness: await for the true light you which have suffered yourselves to be taken with unreasonable sleep; and forthwith when your face is discovered ye shall pass from the light to the light: for (as John saith) ye are anointed.

In its revelation of the golden world, poetry provides a secular analogue to such religious vision. Accordingly, Sidney uses metaphors of light to describe how poetry affects the reader: it possesses the 'sight of the soul'; by its images, wisdom is 'illuminated or figured forth'; its pictures give 'insight' into the virtues and vices to make us 'see the form of goodness'; and he is prepared to entertain Plato's view that 'who could see virtue would be wonderfully ravished with the love of her beauty'.

For Plato, the teacher serves as a midwife to help give birth to man's innate virtues, or as a gardener to quicken the seeds of virtue within him. For Renaissance Platonists, man could fashion his virtues as he pleased. In *The heroic frenzies,* a work dedicated to Sidney, Giordano Bruno writes that nature has endowed him with an inward sense by which he 'can discern the most profound and incomparably superior beauty', that is, divine beauty. But Sidney reserves such language for the divine poet: he refers to David 'almost' (i.e. indeed) showing himself in the Psalms as 'a passionate lover of that unspeakable and everlasting beauty to be seen by the eyes of the mind, only cleared by faith'. He refers to 'the inward light each mind hath in itself' only after he has noted that reason must overmaster passion before the mind has 'a free desire to do well'. He prefaces Plato's view that man may be moved by the sight of virtue with an 'if': 'if the saying of Plato . . . be true', for that mere 'saying' conflicts with religious doctrine on man's infected will.

Sidney's view of poetry remains stubbornly anti-mystical and severely practical. He avoids the extravagant claims made by some of his contemporaries, by Chapman, for example, who declares that poetry provides the means 'to the absolute redress, or much to be wished extenuation, of all the unmanly degeneracies now tyrannizing amongst us' by rooting out original sin. He ignores the esoteric meanings claimed by the allegorists, such as Abraham Fraunce, who writes that in poetry the 'better born and of a more noble spirit, shall meet with hidden mysteries of natural, astrological, or divine and metaphysical philosophy, to entertain their heavenly speculation'. Characteristic of his poetic is his claim that poetry is to be preferred to history on grounds of 'your own use and learning'. For him, poetry is rooted in man's life in this world, and the poet is concerned how best to move his infected will to lift him out of it.

For Sidney, poetry leads or draws the reader, always persuading him through delight. Its ethical and aesthetic functions are one and the same. It does not scold or harass the reader; even a lower poetical kind, such as tragedy, which 'maketh kings fear to be tyrants', does so by 'stirring the affects of admiration and commiseration'. It does not point to the guilt of man's fallen nature, but to the innocence of his unfallen nature, to that part of him which may be awakened by delight. Its way is 'sweet' as its means is delight, and its end is rapture and release.

Sidney says little about the way in which the poet makes his image. When he writes that the poet gives 'a perfect picture' of what man should do, he implies that the poet seeks to convey his vision of the virtues clearly and exactly. Since the poet may persuade his readers to 'steal to see the form of goodness (which seen they cannot but love)', it would seem that he tries simply to make them see the goodness which he has seen.

When Sidney defines the work of the right poet, he compares him to the painter who shows 'the constant though lamenting look of Lucretia, when she punished in herself another's fault, wherein he painteth not Lucretia whom he never saw, but painteth the outward beauty of such a virtue'. Usually this comparison is made to claim that the poet does not set down the particular and individual but the general and universal. Shepherd compares Fracastorius's argument in *Naugerius:* other writers 'are like the painter who represents the features and other members of the body as they really are in the object; but the poet is like the painter who does not wish to represent this or that particular man as he is with many defects, but who, having contemplated the universal and supremely beautiful idea of his creator, makes things as they ought to be'. Yet Sidney's point is not that the poet and painter present the appearance of an ideal, and ideally chaste, Roman matron but that her outward beauty reveals her inner state. More pertinent, then, is Lomazzo's argument in *Trattato dell' arte della pittura* (1584-5), that the poet and painter represent the *moti* or *passioni dell' animo,* showing outwardly what the soul suffers inwardly. Further, Sidney points to Lucrece's conflicting passions: 'the constant though la-

menting look . . . when she punished in herself another's fault'. That she should punish herself for Tarquin's fault led Augustine to challenge her legend: in Christian terms, she chose honour in the world before honour in the eyes of God. Since her body was polluted, she chose to pollute her soul by suicide. Her story may be contrasted with Chaucer's tale of Virginia, the maiden who chose death at the hand of her father rather than be violated by the lustful judge. While Virginia stands as an emblem of virginity, there is no moral abstraction to which Lucrece, as described by Sidney, may be reduced. In the terms in which Greville read the *Arcadia,* she is shown rather as a 'pregnant image of life'. Her contradictory action of punishing herself for another's fault expresses a complex inner moral state that reveals both innocence and guilt. That image cannot be reduced to precept or example but as a whole is planted in man's imagination for him to see and live by. When Sidney refers to 'the outward beauty of such a virtue', there is strangeness in the beauty, which arouses man's admiration and wonder at her act, and a complexity in her virtue, which leads him to understand her nature and his own.

Sidney does not extend the comparison between poet and painter because he recognizes clearly that to call a poem 'a speaking picture' is 'to speak metaphorically'. What the painter shows in Lucrece, the poet shows in a poem, such as Shakespeare's *Lucrece.* Yet his chief reason for not explaining further about the way in which the poet makes his image may well be that he had decided to show how such images are made by rewriting his *Old Arcadia.* 'The outward beauty of . . . virtue', such as the painter may show in Lucrece, is expressed only diffusely in that work. For example, after Philoclea has been seduced, she is first described in sleep as 'the natural image of exact beauty' and then her inner state is expressed by Pyrocles's claim that she 'had in truth never broken the bands of a true living virtue'. Yet that virtue is not expressed in her beauty, so she remains an admirable, yet pathetic, figure. In the *New Arcadia,* however, beauty and virtue become one as Sidney displays each virtue in its own outward beauty. (pp. 107-22)

A. C. Hamilton, in his Sir Philip Sidney: A Study of His Life and Works, *Cambridge University Press, 1977, 216 p.*

Katherine Duncan-Jones   (essay date 1989)

[*In the excerpt below, Duncan-Jones assesses the strengths and weaknesses of Sidney's works, noting that they reflect the frustration and melancholia that characterized Sidney's life.*]

The question of audience—for whom did Sidney write?—is an important one to ask, though a hard one to answer, for it must have a bearing on a yet more fundamental question: why did Sidney write at all?

There is no evidence that he intended any of his works except his intemperate *Defence* of his uncle, the Earl of Leicester, to see print: it is to the accident of his death that we owe the fact of their publication during the 1590s. Sidney's nearest contemporaries, writers such as Gascoigne,

Spenser, and Lyly, wrote and published poetry in the hope of attracting or consolidating patronage, or of gaining secure employment and/or reputation at Court. Sidney did not need these things in quite the same way. He had plenty of 'business', as he often complains in letters, and if writing poetry and fiction was one of the things that kept him frequently for longish spells away from Court, . . . literary activity may even have hindered his chances of lucrative preferment. While other Elizabethans, Shakespeare included, wrote at least partly for money, Sidney may actually have lost money by writing, in so far as absorption in literary projects kept him out of the Queen's eye when offices were being filled. A sense of career opportunities lost filters into several of the sonnets of *Astrophil and Stella,* such as *AS* 18:

> . . . my wealth I have most idly spent.
> My youth doth waste, my knowledge brings
>   forth toys,
> My wit doth strive those passions to defend
> Which for reward spoil it with vain annoys.
> I see my course to lose itself doth bend . . .

As a young courtier, rather than as a poet, Sidney appeared to have everything to play for. Unlike Spenser, who had to carve out a career for himself through diligent and loyal service to his employers (one of whom may have been Sidney's father), Sidney was from birth beset by more 'great expectation' than can have been altogether comfortable. Philip II, his godfather, is said to have enjoyed dandling his infant namesake on his knee, and as he grew up into a period in which many courtiers of the older generation were either unmarried, like Hatton or Dyer, or, like Leicester and Walsingham, had the utmost difficulty in producing male heirs, Sidney became a kind of universal 'nephew' figure. He was actual nephew to his two childless uncles, the Earls of Warwick and Leicester; and later son-in-law and heir to Sir Francis Walsingham. He filled similar roles abroad. William of Orange hoped that he might marry one of his daughters; and he clearly inspired more than fatherly devotion in the bachelor diplomat Hubert Languet. It is not clear that any of these avuncular figures knew that the promising young Protestant courtier wrote poems and stories, or would have thought the better of him if they had. In imagination, at least, the 'heir apparent' role extended yet further. Reaching adulthood in the period of Queen Elizabeth's advancing middle age, with the last hopes of her producing either a consort or an heir to the throne collapsing at the end of the second Alençon courtship in 1582, Sidney became in the eyes of some almost a crown prince. In a surprisingly frank elegy in which he admits that in life he refrained from praising Sidney, as 'the rising sun', Sir Walter Ralegh was to celebrate his 'princely lineage'. For much of his life Sidney's father, Sir Henry Sidney, was Lord Deputy Governor of Ireland, which came out in Latin as 'Pro-Rex'. As the son of a quasi-king he could be viewed, and on the Continent often was, as a quasi-prince. It also probably did not escape the notice of his Continental admirers that one of Sidney's aunts by marriage, Lady Jane Grey, had actually ascended the throne, albeit briefly. However, it does seem largely to have escaped their notice that the young 'baron Sidney'

(he was given the title in Paris when he was only 17) was a poet.

Why, then, did Sidney write poetry? In *A Defence of Poesy* he describes himself as having, in his 'not old years', 'slipped into the title of a poet', and there may be some truth in this. He hints elsewhere in the *Defence,* and suggests more explicitly in both the *Old Arcadia* and *Astrophil and Stella,* that it was the experience of falling passionately in love that compelled Sidney/Philisides/Astrophil to relieve pent-up anguish in verse. There may be truth in this, too; we shall probably never know. But whether love or other factors were the catalyst, there may indeed have been something partly accidental in Sidney's self-discovery as a poet. What we know for sure is that after his return from three years of European travel in 1575 Sidney played an increasingly public role in Elizabethan high society as a deviser of and participant in what Molyneux calls 'royal pastimes.' These included tiltyard appearances, playlets, and allegorical displays of lesser or greater sophistication, ranging from the probably very early 'pastoral show' at Wilton in which the love-lorn rustic Dick lamented his woes in poulter's measure to his even more naïve companion Will, by way of the attractive pastoral mini-drama *The Lady of May* (1578 or 1579) to the elaborate, and in detail rather mysterious, *Triumph of the Four Foster Children of Desire* (1581), which made use of elaborate machinery, lavish costumes and armour, caparisoned horses, and 'special effects' on a grand scale. . . . Sidney's fame as a tilter and a deviser of courtly spectacles spread well beyond the circle of those who actually saw them. If he had left no other literary works, his fame as an up-market Master of the Revels would probably have lingered. But despite such minor legacies from the entertainments as the possible influence of the pedantic schoolmaster Rombus in *The Lady of May* on Shakespeare's Holofernes in *Love's Labour's Lost,* Sidney would scarcely have qualified as an 'Oxford Author' on the strength of these alone.

More obliquely, Sidney's 'public entertainer' role penetrated most of his other literary works. For instance, the four sets of Ecologues or 'pastorals' in the *Old Arcadia* . . . consist of elegant poetic recreations before an assembled audience which may reflect real-life debates and discussions between Sidney and his friends on such issues as love, marriage, the social order, and versification. Though Philisides, the Sidney figure, is by no means central, his role is comparable with that of Chaucer the pilgrim—the poor or limited versifier who is, on another level, the versatile author of the whole wide-ranging entertainment. In *Astrophil and Stella* the poet-lover Astrophil shares many of Sidney's public functions and is, in particular, an outstanding tilter, who claims that Stella's presence on occasion makes him perform even better. The *New Arcadia* is full of spectacular armed combats of lesser or greater degrees of seriousness, such as the 'Iberian jousts', which probably reflect the actual Accession Day Tilts in which Sidney participated. In Book 3 of the revised *Arcadia* Sidney develops a new and more momentous kind of theatricality, as, for instance, when the heroine Philoclea gazes down, as so many unhappy courtiers did in the sixteenth century, at a solemnly staged execution in the courtyard below her window. The relatively lightweight and conventional discussions of love and friendship that characterized earlier books of the *Old Arcadia* give way, in the final book of the *New Arcadia,* to serious debates on marriage and on the existence of Divine Providence, not the least remarkable feature of which is that they are conducted by female characters.

Although in the *Defence* Sidney seems to align himself more or less with the Puritan Stephen Gosson in his disapproval of the licentiousness of the public theatres—the 'abuse' of poetry—a feeling for drama and dramatic effect characterizes many of his own works. Such a feeling may have been fostered early on by his education at Shrewsbury School, where the regular acting of comedies was part of the curriculum for older boys, and where scholars also took part in the annual outdoor staging of morality plays in a large natural arena, 'The Quarry'. Under the direction of Sidney's headmaster, Thomas Ashton, these Whitsuntide plays drew audiences of thousands. Sidney's Oxford college, Christ Church, was also rich in dramatic activity, and included the dramatist George Peele among its members while Sidney was there.

Yet much of Sidney's most powerful and characteristic writing has little to do with public displays, whether at school, college, Court, or in great houses such as Wanstead and Wilton. Early requirements to participate in public entertainments of various kinds—learned, sporting, or courtly—may have helped Sidney to discover his own extraordinary creative facility. But he soon developed it in other directions, and for much more restricted audiences. There seems little doubt that the *Arcadia,* in its earliest form, was for family entertainment only, among the younger Sidneys and Herberts. As he said to his sister, 'Now it is done only for you, only to you'. The audience he envisaged for *Astrophil and Stella* may have been smaller still. We do not know to what extent it was composed for the immediate perusal of Stella's real-life model, Penelope Rich—she would certainly have been capable of appreciating it. But characteristically the 'felt' audience within individual sonnets is intensely private. Astrophil seems frequently alienated both from his friends and from Stella, hammering out his obsessions in neurotic solitude—'As good to write, as for to lie and groan'—— which brings us back to the subject of love. Whether or not it dominated Sidney's life as a young man, it certainly dominated his poetry.

To one of the earliest and best of Sidney's modern critics [Theodore Spencer], it seemed that Sidney wrote too much about love and that his verse was not sufficiently varied, especially as compared with Spenser's. Yet he saw the power and originality of Sidney's lyric gift as inseparable from his emotionality:

> Once the poet has set himself the task of writing an amorous complaint, that deep melancholy which lay beneath the surface of glamour of Elizabethan existence, and which was so characteristic of Sidney himself, begins to fill the conventional form with a more than conventional weight. It surges through the magical adagio of the lines; they have that depth of reverberation, like the sound of gongs beaten under water,

which is sometimes characteristic of Sidney as of no other Elizabethan, not even Shakespeare.

This is an eloquent account of a paradox at the heart of Sidney's writing. The splendid rhetorical show of the public courtier conceals inward torment, though for some of his audience the concealment may be effective. As Sidney said bitterly of the Queen, 'so long as she sees a silk doublet upon me her Highness will think me in good case'. But the attentive reader will find that time and again deep misery is welling up beneath the bright, witty, metrically assured surface of Sidney's verse lines. His literary theory, in the *Defence,* celebrates artistic freedom and joyous creativity—the free imagination of the poet 'ranging only within the zodiac of his own wit' as he delivers the 'golden world' of art. But this is not how it feels in many of his own lyrics or passages of prose fiction, which offer us repeated images of paralysis and stagnation. Tellingly, Sidney's own persona, Philisides, is described on his first appearance as disabled by unhappiness:

> Another young shepherd named Philisides . . . neither had danced nor sung with them, and had all this time lain upon the ground at the foot of a cypress tree, leaning upon his elbow, with so deep a melancholy that his senses carried to his mind no delight from any of their objects.

The avuncular Geron attempts to rouse him to activity with a store of good advice, but is rejected as a tedious old fool, rather as Polonius is snubbed by the love-madseeming Hamlet. Time and again in Sidney's lyrical poems, culminating in *Astrophil and Stella,* the speakers lock themselves into positions of emotional and rhetorical impasse. Gifted, like Sidney/Philisides, with exceptional linguistic skills, they are left either with nothing to say or no one to say it to, or both.

For instance, *Lamon's Tale,* a poem which forms a bridge between the *Old Arcadia* and *Astrophil and Stella,* describes the two shepherds Strephon and Klaius falling in love with the celestial-sounding shepherdess Urania. Having come, rather slowly, to apprehend the nature of their own feelings, they proceed to bewail their inner torment at great length and with astounding emotional intensity. But like so many of Sidney's literary projects, *Lamon's Tale* is unfinished, breaking off before Klaius has had his say, which, to match that of Strephon, needs to be at least a hundred lines long. The compiler of the Eclogues in the 1593 composite text tells us that the hearers, 'not knowing when Lamon would end, being even now stepped over to a new matter', decide it is time for bed. It is not surprising that even other characters in the fiction are imagined as lacking patience to hear the 'tale' out, since Strephon and Klaius, alarmingly solipsistic, seem to be going nowhere unless towards bedlam (rather than bed). In their long and intricate outpourings, both here and in the Fourth Eclogues, they use hyperboles which travel close to the verge of madness, as their minds' landscapes blot out external reality:

> Me seems I hear, when I do hear sweet music,
> The dreadful cries of murdered men in forests.

Astrophil and Stella, unusual among Sidney's works in being apparently finished and fully shaped, ends likewise with emotional impasse. In the Eleventh Song, Astrophil is forced to 'run away' from Stella's window, his dialogue with her unresolved; and in the last sonnet the final image given us is of Astrophil's everlasting and inescapable emotional imprisonment:

> Ah what doth Phoebus' gold that wretch avail
> Whom iron doors do keep from use of day?

The only escape, as the penultimate sonnet hints, is for Sidney to drop the 'Astrophil' persona altogether and begin writing in a quite different genre.

This he clearly tried to do. The dates of his various works of translation—from Aristotle's *Rhetoric,* Du Plessis Mornay's treatise on the truth of the Christian religion, Du Bartas's *Sepmaine sainte,* and the Psalms—are not known; but he may have undertaken them at various times to channel his writing energies into serious, un-amorous projects. If so, the attempt was probably not very successful. All that survive are metrically skilled versions of the first forty-two Psalms. . . . If the other translations had been anything like finished they would surely have been preserved and published by Sidney's literary executors, who were all only too anxious to provide evidence of his moral seriousness: it seems likely that he did not get very far with any of these enterprises. Writing **A Defence of Poesy,** which lays so little stress on love poetry and so much on the freedom and power of heroic or epic modes, might perhaps be expected to unlock Sidney, as a writer, from his compulsive drift towards emotional paralysis. Certainly it is, *per se,* a confident, celebratory, in many ways prophetic work, which lays down the theoretical basis for a richly inventive heroic narrative. Yet it does not seem fully to have released Sidney from his habitual tendency to journey towards deadlock. The revised *Arcadia* certainly has a wealth—perhaps even an excess—of interlaced and inset narratives, such as the story of the 'Paphlagonian unkind king', which was to provide Shakespeare with the sub-plot of *King Lear;* but it also has yet more images of impasse. Amphialus, a character newly conceived in the revised *Arcadia,* is yet another tragic lover, an 'accidental man' trapped in concentric circles of impossible situations, the inmost of which is an agonized love melancholy even more intense than that of his predecessors in Sidney's work, Dick, Philisides, Strephon, Klaius, or Astrophil. It provokes him to an extreme never considered by them: suicide. The **New Arcadia** breaks off with three of its five principal characters (Pamela, Philoclea, Pyrocles) literally in prison, as well as locked emotionally in the toils of love. The other two, Musidorus and Amphialus, also in love, are trapped in misguided and violent conflict based on misunderstanding, and both are grievously wounded, Amphialus near death. A recent critic, John Carey, has written powerfully of the 'constant impulse towards deadlock in the rhetoric' in the **New Arcadia,** and of Sidney's accounts of 'the space in which the characters move, full of vacillation and ambivalence'. Cruelty, misunderstanding, corruption, and a besieged fortress seem strangely to prefigure situations that Sidney was to experience in real life in the Netherlands in 1585-6, except that in the **New Arcadia** love is the central source of all these things. If Sidney tried to bid farewell to the

splendid trifles of human passion in his latest literary work, he clearly did not succeed.

The melancholy and stagnation of Sidney's lovers may have psychological roots which will never yield themselves to our scrutiny; they may form part of an artistic strategy to lend 'forcibleness' to his poetry; or they may express a deliberate pose, part aesthetic, part didactic, assumed to show the vanity of human wishes and the emptiness of merely human longings. Fulke Greville, who played down the dominance of love in Sidney's writings, would no doubt have supported the last view:

> The truth is, his end was not writing even while he wrote . . . but both his wit and understanding bent upon his heart to make himself and others, not in words or opinion, but in life and action, good and great.

However, there may be yet another reason for the recurring images of deadlock in which Sidney's young men find themselves. They may echo the frustrations of his own unique personal position in Elizabethan society. Despite, or even because of, the high hopes placed on him both at home and abroad, life was not particularly comfortable for Sidney. He does not seem, for instance, to have had a house he could call his own. He clearly spent as much time as possible at Wilton, his brother-in-law's house, and after his marriage he lived in the house of his father-in-law, Sir Francis Walsingham. He was always short of money. The enormous wealth of his uncles, Leicester and Warwick, was not freely available to him; his immediate resources as a young man were most often determined by the poverty and consequent frugality of his father, Sir Henry Sidney. The office of Royal Cup-bearer, which he held from 1576, was poorly remunerated and carried little status. His embassy to the Holy Roman Emperor Rudolph II was splendidly successful, but was not followed up with any further commission of comparable status. The glittering career as the Queen's ambassador which seemed to lie before him at the age of 22, never really took off, for several reasons. One was the Queen's caution. Sidney may have been rather *too* successful on the Continent for her liking, as he could not be trusted not to take independent initiative. Another handicap was the modified admiration felt for him by the Queen's favourite, the Earl of Leicester. Greville describes a conversation with Leicester after Sidney's death:

> [He] told me . . . that when he undertook the government of the Low Countries . . . he carried his nephew over with him as one among the rest, not only despising his youth for a counsellor, but withal bearing a hand upon him as a forward young man.

Letters written in the immediate aftermath of Sidney's wounding and death make it poignantly clear that it was only during the Netherlands campaign that Leicester came fully to appreciate his nephew's worth. As a recurrent reminder to him of his own childlessness (his only legitimate child, Lord Denbigh, died in July 1584 at the age of about 6) Sidney must inevitably have aroused rather mixed feelings in Leicester's ambitious bosom, and he may well have put a damper on some of Sidney's bids for preferment. In addition to all this, an element of sheer bad luck seemed often to frustrate his chances of worthwhile employment.

For instance, in July 1584 Sidney was commissioned to visit the King of France to negotiate with him over the protection of the Low Countries and was allocated an unusually generous £1,500 for the expenses of this important mission. However, news came that the King was travelling to Lyons, where he would be unable to receive ambassadors, and the project terminated after only eight days without Sidney and his train leaving British soil. It was only in 1583 that Sidney was knighted (his French barony was not recognized in England), and this was more part of a diplomatic mopping-up operation than a tribute to his worth. Someone was needed to stand proxy for the installation, *in absentia,* of the German Prince Casimir as a Knight of the Garter, and Sidney, as a friend of Casimir's, was suitable. The honour done to him personally was almost accidental.

There is no need, then, to suggest that Sidney foresaw his early death in order to explain the recurrent melancholy and frustration evoked in his literary works, which may have had multiple causes, internal and external. By the last months of his life, as he said to Walsingham, he had indeed foreseen the inglorious collapse of Leicester's Netherlands campaign: 'be not troubled with my trouble, for I have seen the worst in my judgement beforehand, and worse than that cannot be'. But we should not read the weary tone of this letter back into the years of Sidney's creativity, from 1577 to 1584/5. During these seven years he was rich in promise but—for a man of his exceptional talent and energy—severely underemployed and underappreciated, at least in England. His greatest happiness was probably experienced in the company of his sister, for whom he wrote the first *Arcadia.* He is said also to have written her numerous letters, both in prose and verse. If these were ever to come to light they might show us a more relaxed, humorous Philip than the one we meet in correspondence with statesmen and humanists. We probably come nearest to their tone in surviving letters to his younger brother Robert—'Lord, how I have babbled!'—and in some of the lyrics in *Certain Sonnets,* such as the sonnet on a naïve satyr written in answer to one by his friend Edward Dyer. However, 'that deep melancholy which lay beneath the surface glamour of Elizabethan existence', as Theodore Spencer called it, remains the prevailing mood of Sidney's surviving work.

If obsessive melancholy and a tendency to write himself into a corner are negative features of Sidney's writing, something should be said, briefly, of its abundant positive characteristics. The first and perhaps most overwhelming is his use of language. It was not for nothing that Dr Johnson chose Sidney as his earliest quarry for examples in the *Dictionary,* especially for 'the dialect of poetry and fiction'. The breadth, originality, and flexibility of Sidney's diction is scarcely surpassed even by Shakespeare. Often, like Chaucer, he uses words which seem easy and accessible to us, so that we may not readily appreciate the fact that he is using them for the first time, or for the first time in a still-current sense. His linguistic legacy to English language and culture is not now often acknowledged or noticed, yet is considerable, ranging from the popular phrase 'my better half', to denote a spouse, which comes from a passage of high tragedy in the *New Arcadia,* to the name 'Pamela', adopted from Sidney by Richardson, or such a half-explicit allusion as Dickens's use of the title *Great Expectations* for a novel overshadowed by the obsessive passion of a hero called Philip for an unattainable lady called [E]stella. More recent titles derived from Sidney are Philip Larkin's 'Sad Steps', a meditation on moonlight and the unreachableness of love whose title and initial point of reference come from *Astrophil and Stella,* and a recent travel book on France, *That Sweet Enemy,* derived from *Astrophil and Stella.*

Also easy to overlook is Sidney's originality in genre. The two *Arcadia*s are so innovatory, in fact, that they have never been satisfactorily pigeon-holed either as 'novel', 'romance', 'comedy', or 'heroic poem'. The difficulty of classification, along with the problem of the disunity of the composite text, has probably been one of the factors contributing to their long period of neglect from the eighteenth to the early twentieth centuries. Because of its date of publication, *Astrophil and Stella* does not look so original as it was. It was to be followed by dozens of sonnet sequences in the 1590s, but it must be remembered that when Sidney wrote it there were no other sonnet sequences in English, unless we count the pedantic and wholly un-'forcible' *Hekatompathia* of Thomas Watson (1581/2), in eighteen-line stanzas, which may indeed have stimulated some of Sidney's attacks on derivative and unconvincing love poets. Sidney's is not only the earliest English sonnet sequence properly so described: it is also arguably the best, in terms of assured poetic technique, richness of tone, and subtlety of organization.

Then, again, *A Defence of Poesy* stands head and shoulders above all the other theoretical treatises of the Elizabethan period, such as those of Gascoigne, Webbe, Puttenham, Campion, and Daniel, both because it is consistently entertaining, which the others are not, and because Sidney carries the debate back to first principles—the value of the imagination itself—and tackles Plato head-on. If some of his critical assumptions, most notably those about drama, seem somewhat limited, we should remind ourselves that his own death was not the only event on the horizon that Sidney could not foresee. The *Defence* was probably written, or at least begun, in 1580, when Shakespeare was 16. At this date others who were to light up the literary landscape in the last years of Elizabeth's reign were Marlowe, who was also 16; Nashe, who was 13; Donne, who was 8; and Ben Jonson, who was 7. If Sidney had lived to be 60, he could have seen all of Shakespeare's plays. Dying, as he did, at 32, he saw none. (pp. vii-xviii)

Katherine Duncan-Jones, in an introduction to Sir Philip Sidney, *edited by Katherine Duncan-Jones, Oxford University Press, 1989, pp. vii-xviii.*

Joan Rees   (essay date 1991)

[*In the following excerpt from her full-length study of*

C. S. Lewis wrote of the princesses Pamela and Philoclea that "They can be praised without reservation. English literature had seen no women to compare with them since Chaucer's Crisseid; and, apart from Shakespeare, was to wait centuries for their equals." John Danby also praised the characterization of the princesses and made a good critical point in reference to them: "Sidney's discriminations are finer than we have been in the habit of making for three hundred years." To engage in discrimination is to take characters and their moral stature seriously, and Sidney prepares the way for his extensive studies of female natures by placing near the beginning of *Arcadia* a justification of so much and so careful attention to subjects by no means inevitably found worthy of it.

Very early in *Arcadia,* Pyrocles confesses to Musidorus that he has fallen in love, and Musidorus is horrified at the news. Implicated in the debate that follows about the nature of love is a crucial question concerning the nature of women. Musidorus, who has not yet seen Pamela and who scorns the state of being a lover, attempts to shame Pyrocles out of his passion by reminding him that he is a *man* and that to partake of anything "womanish" is to be disgraced. Pyrocles has adopted a female disguise, in itself shameful, and risks adopting female characteristics too. " 'You must resolve,' Musidorus tells him, 'if you will play your part to any purpose, whatsoever peevish imperfections are in that sex, to soften your heart to receive them.' " Pyrocles in his reply defends love, and claims that it is compatible with virtue, but first he defends women and has evidently given his arguments some thought: " 'I am not yet come,' he says 'to that degree of wisdom to think light of the sex of whom I have my life, since if I be anything . . . I was, to come to it, born of a woman and nursed of a woman.' " Men by "their tyrannous ambition," he goes on, "have brought the others' virtuous patience under them" and, not content to have done so, then insult them with "unmanlike cruelty." Reason should teach that women "are framed of nature with the same parts of the mind for the exercise of virtue as we are. . . . And truly, we men and praisers of men should remember that if we have such excellencies, it is reason to think them excellent creatures of whom we are, since a kite never brought forth a good flying hawk."

Musidorus, when he sees Pamela, recants, and to make the reversal of his views all the more striking, Sidney comments, in *Old Arcadia,* "that he was wounded with more sudden violence of love than ever Pyrocles was," the agonies he suffers being perhaps, Sidney suggests, love's revenge on him for "the bitter words he had used." The point that retribution is exacted remains the same in *New Arcadia* but is developed with greater finesse. The characters of the princesses have larger room to develop in the revised text, and by an irony that Sidney must have planned with amusement, the girl who wins Musidorus's heart gives ample evidence of her majesty of demeanor and her "high heart." Pyrocles, who praises women's capacity for Amazonian valor, loves the shy and gentle Philoclea, but Musidorus, who dispraises their idle hearts and weak hands, falls at the feet of one who, even when

she returns his love, insists that he treat her with the most punctilious respect. His humiliation and remorse following his attempt to kiss her are evidently a punishment for his masculine arrogance and insensitivity in earlier days.

In the *New Arcadia* version of their adventures, Pyrocles and Musidorus arrive at different times in Arcadia, having been shipwrecked on their way to Greece and separately rescued. Musidorus gets there first and is given hospitality by a noble lord, Kalander. Among other amenities of Kalander's splendid mansion is a room full of pictures, including a large painting of Basilius, ruler of Arcadia, his wife, Gynecia, and their younger daughter, Philoclea—Pamela, the elder, is not with them. The picture rouses Musidorus's curiosity, and Kalander obligingly gives him (and the reader) an account of the state of affairs in the country. Together with this brief history, Kalander also gives Musidorus thumbnail sketches of the women of Basilius's family. Gynecia he describes as beautiful and intelligent "and in truth of more princely virtues than her husband . . . but of so working a mind and so vehement spirits as a man may say it was happy she took a good course, for otherwise it would have been terrible." His account of Pamela and Philoclea balances and compares: "more sweetness in Philoclea but more majesty in Pamela . . . love played in Philoclea's eyes and threatened in Pamela's . . . Philoclea so bashful . . . so humble . . . Pamela of high thoughts, who avoids not pride with not knowing her excellencies, but by making that one of her excellencies to be void of pride; her mother's wisdom, greatness, nobility but . . . knit with a more constant temper." Having introduced the royal ladies by way of the painting, Sidney turns from them to set in motion the stories of other women whose lives will to some degree interlock with theirs and, more importantly, whose experiences will contribute to rounding out the world of feminine action and choice as *New Arcadia* presents it. Parthenia is a type of womanly excellence as Argalus is of manly, and her story before her marriage anticipates aspects of the later story of Philoclea. Like Philoclea persecuted by the unwelcome love of Amphialus, she is importuned by Demagoras, a man who loved "nobody but himself and, for his own delight's sake Parthenia." Parthenia's mother favors his suit, and as Cecropia torments Philoclea and Pamela, so Parthenia's mother, "witty and hard-hearted," does all she can to break Parthenia's spirit. She employs Argalus in dangerous enterprises, in the hope that he will be killed, but his valor is equal to all trials and, similarly, "to Parthenia, malice sooner ceased than her unchanged patience." Despairing of success, Demagoras resorts to "unmerciful force," the smearing of the poisoned ointment that ruins her beauty, and the story then develops as has already been described. As Argalus stands to the male characters in the book, so stands Parthenia to the female, giving an example of unimpugnable excellence. She is obedient to her mother until she meets Argalus, and then, knowing what love is, she refuses Demagoras firmly, though with sympathy for the pain she must inflict. She endures patiently all the ill treatment that follows at the hands of her mother, and when her beauty is lost she thinks only of Argalus's welfare not her own, just as he, in the crisis, rises above all selfish feeling and cares only for her.

Portrait of Sidney dated 1578 given to his sister, Mary, Countess of Pembroke.

The marriage of Argalus and Parthenia is the immediate prelude to the first signs of Pyrocles' falling in love, but the development of this situation is deferred while the story of Helen, Queen of Corinth, intervenes. She is unhappily in love with Amphialus, and her love story is again a triangular one, the unwanted suitor being this time Amphialus's friend and foster-brother Philoxenus. Philoxenus is no villain like Demagoras, but, equally, Amphialus is no paragon like Argalus. Neither is Helen as faultless as Parthenia. She confesses that before she knew Amphialus, her heart was "utterly void" of affection, "as then esteeming myself born to rule and thinking foul scorn willingly to submit myself to be ruled." When she falls in love, she retains still some hardness of heart. Unlike Parthenia, who treats the unworthy Demagoras with consideration, Helen is indifferent to the feelings of the amiable Philoxenus and makes a cruel response to his offer of love. With more thought and care her on part, the fight that takes place between the friends, and that results in the deaths of Philoxenus and his father, might never have occurred. The blood then shed marks both Helen and Amphialus.

Helen's behavior shows a culpable pride and selfishness and evidently contrasts strongly with that of Parthenia. Both she and Amphialus fail to make an adequate response to love, she in her unfeeling dismissal of Philoxenus, he in his bitter repudiation of her, and the result is suffering and long estrangement. During this time, Am-

phialus's pursuit of Philoclea leads to the kidnapping and the bloody siege, but for Helen it is a period of penitential pilgrimage. She has come to a different understanding of what love is and requires and has learned to temper pride with penitence and patience. Sidney thereafter speaks of her with respect and admiration, as indeed he does of her behavior before Philoxenus wooed her and brought Amphialus to help him in his suit. Her failure to rise to the demands of that situation is the one blemish in an admirable life, but its consequences bring great unhappiness. Fulke Greville tells us that Amphialus and Helen were to marry at the end, and this must be assumed to have been Sidney's intention since Amphialus, though desperately wounded in body and mind, is not actually dead after his suicide attempt and Helen arrives to take him to Corinth to be healed. We do not know how, on the other side of near death and nursed back to life by Helen, Amphialus would have voiced his experience. The reader does know that *she* has come a long way from her first arrogant queenliness to her lament over Amphialus's barely living body: "Alas, why should not my faith to thee cover my other defects, who only sought to make my crown thy footstool, myself thy servant?" Her love and self-abnegation save him from the destructive path of self-will on which he was set. Clearly the contrast in their responses to unrequited love is a major point of their stories as Helen emerges out of initial selfishness to become a major force of regeneration through love selflessly offered.

The story of Parthenia's love for Argalus shows that gentleness like Philoclea's does not preclude dignity, courage, and resolution when inspired by a fitting love: these are qualities that Philoclea will acquire as she matures during *New Arcadia.* The story of Helen, on the other hand, strikes a more cautionary note, for she is born to rule, like Pamela who is her father's heir, and pride in herself and her position is nearly her undoing. As Amphialus channels off the worst consequences that might follow from incipient weaknesses in the princes, so does Helen in respect of Pamela.

It is after the stories of Argalus and Parthenia and Helen and Amphialus have been set in motion that the princes' debate about love takes place. Read in the context that Sidney provides, the theoretical oppositions gain animation, for the ambivalence of love, which has the power to inspire and ennoble but also power to degrade and destroy, has been illustrated in what has been narrated. Musidorus's misogynism has not, however, been given any backing, for both Parthenia and Helen are noble women. Nor will Musidorus's insults be heard again.

There is soon to follow, however, an example of womanly behavior to set against the virtues of Parthenia and Helen. Kalander remarked that it would be terrible if a woman of Gynecia's intelligence and strength of character should take bad ways, and that "terrible" eventuality comes to pass as she conceives a violent passion for Pyrocles. Sidney's treatment of Gynecia is one of the most remarkable pieces of characterization in *Arcadia,* particularly so because of the liberal attitude he takes toward her. It is already striking in *Old Arcadia* and becomes more so in the revision, because of the enlarged context in which she is set. He endows her with two traits that may be guaranteed in most periods to rouse male prejudice, but far from Sidney castigating her as a monster, he treats her with understanding and sympathy. In the first place, Gynecia is a strong-minded woman and, potentially, at any rate, a dominant one. Sidney refused to believe that this is necessarily a bad thing. When later he describes Queen Andromana, he presents her as another formidable woman who "had made herself so absolute a master of her husband's mind that a while he would not, and after, he could not, tell how to govern without being governed by her . . . entrusting to her the entire conduct of all his royal affairs." Sidney's comment on this may be unexpected: "A thing that may luckily fall out to him that hath the blessing to match with some heroical-minded lady." His wife's supremacy is not, in fact, a blessing to the King of Iberia, and he does not deserve that it should be, but Sidney's point stands nevertheless.

Gynecia and Andromana share another trait, the second on which male judgment often bears hard: they are both not only sexually eager but also sexually aggressive. Both are married to much older men, and both conceive an ungovernable passion for a younger one. Both become shameless in their demands and the means they employ to try to seduce the young men, and both use threats when persuasion fails. But Andromana has a history of adultery and unscrupulous sexual exploitation behind her, whereas Gynecia is "of most unspotted chastity" until she is overcome by her passion for Pyrocles. She has a conscience that inflicts its terrors upon her at every stage: " 'Forlorn creature that I am,' she exclaims in the cave, 'I would I might be freely wicked, since wickedness doth prevail; but the footsteps of my overtrodden virtue lie still as bitter accusations unto me.' " She is about to reach the lowest point of her decline, invoking the aid of "infernal furies" to "assuage the sweltering of my hellish longing"—though nothing can appease her guilty conscience—and when Zelmane comes upon her unexpectedly, her desperate passions are unleashed in threats against Pyrocles himself and against Philoclea too unless he satisfies her passion. Even at that point, when she most nearly speaks the language of melodrama, she cannot but acknowledge her own sense of guilt.

Gynecia sins against her better nature, and in the end she repents most feelingly, but Sidney creates her as a real woman, not simply as a moral exemplum. She was very young when married to Basilius, and he was already an old man. Sidney encourages obvious deductions about repression of natural instincts and desires and allows the reader to watch with sympathy the flaring up of repressed fires in a woman of early middle age who sees life passing her by. Her jealousy of her daughter, though in one sense unnatural, is in another a perfectly natural growth out of the situation: "the growing of my daughter seems the decay of myself," Gynecia comments. Sidney understands all this as well as a modern psychologist and is ready to show compassion to Gynecia, but he does not forget the wrong she is doing to Basilius. A hint dropped apparently casually is more effective than fulminations against rampant sexuality would have been. Gynecia, enduring her usual tormented conflict of passion and conscience, has a restless night and disturbs Basilius from his sleep. He "took her in his arms and began to comfort her, the good man thinking it was all for a jealous love of him; which humour if she would a little have maintained, perchance it might have weakened his new-conceived fancies." She makes no response, however, and this chance to deflect him from his ridiculous passion for Pyrocles in his Amazon garb is lost. Basilius is a very foolish old man but not essentially a bad one, and the little scene shows how his heart is penetrable by pity and affection. Gynecia might have saved him from pursuing his folly to serious lengths if she had had any regard for him at this moment. As it is, they leave each other to cherish their misbegotten loves and to plot adultery with increasing shamelessness.

Gynecia repents but Sidney does not claim that the desire that Pyrocles has aroused dissolves away as though it had never been. In her first horror, as Basilius falls apparently dead before her and she believes that just retribution has come upon her, even then, remembering Pyrocles, she knows that she still loves him. In prison as she awaits trial and execution, she is torn between hatred of him as the cause of her downfall and love that had still "a high authority in her passions," and at the trial itself she dare not look at Pyrocles' face "for the fear these motions in the short time of her life should be revived which she had with the passage of infinite sorrows mortified." The imaginative empathy that Sidney shows in all this enables him to keep clear without any confusion the moral status of the different phases of Gynecia's story and yet to avoid simplifications that would misrepresent the real nature of individual experience. Such treatment of women like Gynecia may be rare at any time; in the 1580s its care, subtlety, and understanding are almost beyond belief.

The character of Gynecia belongs to the first conception of *Arcadia* and is not materially altered or much enlarged in *New Arcadia.* Response to her is affected, however, and recognition of the subtlety of Sidney's treatment of her enhanced, by his use of the favored technique by which he seeks to illuminate the understanding of his characters in *New Arcadia*—that is, the development of another figure to pair with her and make possible those moral discriminations which are so large a part of the dynamic of the revised text. Cecropia, mother of Amphialus, occupies to some extent more familiar literary ground than Gynecia, for she stands in a long line of wicked women, ambitious, cruel, and godless. Yet even here there are touches that endow her with individuality. She has wit, as in her responses to Amphialus when she first breaks the news of the kidnapping of the princesses. She can adopt a smooth, insinuating tone when she judges there is profit in it (see her attempted persuasion of Philoclea in *New Arcadia,* book 3, and she loves her son, though her influence on him is always evil. There is a world of difference between her and Gynecia, though both for considerable stretches of the plot are acting as wicked women. Cecropia's is a settled and, with one exception, cold-hearted wickedness. Gynecia's is an aberration, psychologically accounted for and plausible, which triumphs temporarily in the face of her own never-entirely-overcome resistance and which is repented and atoned for. Cecropia dies in the agony of believing Amphialus dead by his own hand and ordering, as a last act of malice, the murder of the princesses: "but everybody seeing (and glad to see) her end, had left obedience to her tyranny"—whereas Gynecia, having passed through agonies of shame and penitence, will live to be once more highly honored and to observe for the rest of her life "all duty and faith to the example and glory of Greece."

The moral standing of Sidney's characters is always defined aganst a wide range of alternatives, and the teasing out of tangled skeins of virtue and vice requires careful discrimination. The more delicate the discriminations, the more convincing—"life-like" is C. S. Lewis's word—the result will be. So Andromana is lustful like Gynecia and calculating like Cecropia, but Gynecia has the conscience that the other two lack, and Cecropia knows no passion but ambition and has experienced no love, except for the son whom she regards as an extension of herself. The presence of the others illuminates and gives extra life to each, and the system of comparisons and contrasts of which they are a part provides the background for the presentation of Pamela and Philoclea.

Pamela, the elder daughter and Basilius's heir, is proud and has a "high heart." She is full of disdain at the arrangement by which Dametas, the herdsman, is her guardian, and there is no question of her countenancing Musidorus's suit until she has received his assurance that he is a prince by birth and a worthy match for her. In this she is avoiding the error of Erona, princess and later queen of Lycia, who gives her love to a young man of mean parentage and pays dearly for so doing. Even after she has heard and believed Musidorus's account of his parentage, Pamela is hardly won, feeling that she owes it to herself to remain aloof and even cold, rather than seem in any degree oncoming. Musidorus has to humble himself and exercise great persistence in his services and set out his personal qualities very fully before she will allow herself to relent toward him. Sidney, in fact, greatly heightens Pamela's reserve and dignity in *New Arcadia,* as, for example, in the different handling of the scene in which Musidorus communicates to her, under guise of recounting someone else's story, the facts of his princely birth and present disguise as a shepherd. Pride is a keynote of Pamela's character, a quality not improper in her as heir to the throne, but similar high position led Helen of Corinth to unbecoming lengths. Self-respect that demands a high standard of self-control in herself and in her lover is also a proper quality but may degenerate into mere self-regard without due consideration for another. Helen is guilty of that in her treatment of Philoxenus but she repents. A coarser-grained example is Artesia, a young woman brought up by Cecropia and trained in her way of thinking, so that she believed "she did wrong to her beauty if she were not proud of it, called her disdain of him [her wooer] chastity, and placed her honour in little setting by his honouring her." She has resolved never to marry "but him whom she thought worthy of her and that was one in whom all worthiness were harboured"—which makes her sound very like Pamela. Evidently, in Pamela's virtues there are dangers of real, not only assumed, coldness, of arrogance, and of vanity. It is relevant that Cecropia diagnoses vanity as a potential weak point when she notes how carefully Pamela has

dressed herself during her imprisonment in Amphialus's castle.

Lewis describes the characterization of the princesses as both idealized and lifelike. Both words are justified, but Sidney's conception is deeper than either suggests. Pamela's virtue exists and is maintained, like that of the princes, in the equilibrium created by opposite tensions. Around her are displayed various kinds of imbalance that result when characteristics similar to her own are not sufficiently disciplined, and it becomes evident that the exercise of moral judgment is being continuously called for in response to the different kinds of pressure that are put upon her. As needs always to be said about Sidney's characters, Pamela is much more than a moral exemplum. Severe as she may be, she is also very human. She cannot resist talking to her sister about the accomplishments of the new shepherd, Dorus (Musidorus), and does it in a style so far from her usual collected manner that Philoclea guesses the secret of her love immediately. When she has angrily dismissed Musidorus from her sight because of the stolen kiss and he writes to her, she treats the letter at first "as if it had been a contagious garment of an infected person, and yet was not long away but that she wished she had read it, though she were loath to read it." A touch of hypocrisy enables her to succumb: "At last she concluded it were not much amiss to look it over, that she might out of his words pick some further quarrel against him."

A more serious and moving moment occurs at the end of Pamela's noble prayer when, alone and at the mercy of enemies, she kneels to offer to God her patience under suffering and asks for strength to endure whatever may be in store for her. Her prayer ends with a plea that the wickedness of those who persecute her may never prevail upon her purity of mind and body and then she pauses: " 'And, O most gracious Lord,' said she, 'whatever become of me, preserve the virtuous Musidorus.' " Throughout her captivity it is of him that she thinks more than of herself, and the thought of him makes her falter a little in accepting what seems like inevitable destiny. " 'Since the world will not have us,' she says to Philoclea, 'let it lose us. Only,' (with that she stayed a little and sighed) 'only my Philoclea' (then she bowed down and whispered in her ear) 'only Musidorus, my shepherd, comes between me and death, and makes me think I should not die, because I know he would not I should die.' "

Pamela, then, proud, high-hearted as she is, is as capable of tender and devoted love as Parthenia and Helen. Nor is she frigid, if the *Old Arcadia* account of her elopement with Musidorus is to be relied upon. She binds him to preserve her chastity until they can be married, but she herself feels the temptation of their proximity and the congenial opportunity: "her travailing fancies . . . had bound themselves to a greater restraint than they could without much pain well endure." Sidney might have made further modifications in this episode in the course of rewriting, but *Old Arcadia* shows her enjoying a "virtuous wantonness," and it is clear that he does not want her to be thought cold. She is, as Kalander has said, like her mother in many ways but "knit with a more constant temper." Her love for Musidorus is not to be underestimated because of the restraint under which, unlike her mother, she keeps her passion.

If the strength of her character presents some dangers and temptations to Pamela, it is her gentleness and lack of self-assertion that may constitute a threat to Philoclea, both in relation to the situations she has to meet in the course of the story and in terms of the author's success in engaging interest in her. Sweet, bashful, and humble are words applied to her by Kalander, and however attractive they may be, they do not seem to promise much in the way of dramatic interest. Sidney is careful to give the assurance, when describing Parthenia, that her quietness, modesty, and lack of assertion are not the result of an empty mind, but to the contrary. She has "a most fair mind; full of wit," but Philoclea may be only a charming and rather characterless child. The child, however, is compelled to grow up, and Sidney sets himself deliberately to chart the process in a passage introduced by a rare first-person intrusion. The author as "I" and his first audience as "fair ladies" make frequent appearances in *Old Arcadia,* but authorial distance from the narrative is preserved in *New Arcadia.* When it breaks down at this point it signals the presence of a particularly delicate piece of analysis. *Arcadia* is very largely about sex and the impact of sexual passion, but Philoclea, when the story opens, is too young to know what sex is. She learns in circumstances that might be expected to be extremely damaging. She finds herself strongly drawn to the young Amazon, Zelmane, who has so surprisingly penetrated Basilius's forest retreat and been accepted into the royal household. She sees her father besotted by the stranger and her mother also obsessed by her, and she finds herself drawn step by step into a state of emotional turmoil. She believes the Amazon is really the woman she appears to be, and the sexual desires that now begin to haunt her imagination night and day appear to be hopeless of fulfillment. From innocence she has entered into experience, and the results are restlessness, vain longing, and a gamut of emotions. She begins to understand what her mother feels and her mother's passions seem to legitimate hers—a dangerous deduction, as the wording of her soliloquy underlines. Thinking of her apparently unnatural passion, she exclaims: "Sin must be the mother and shame the daughter of my affection." Her language becomes more unrestrained: "Do I not see my mother as well, at least as furiously as myself, love Zelmane, and should I be wiser than my mother?" The answer, of course, should be "yes," but for the young Philoclea, used to obedience to her parents and quite unaccustomed to making an independent judgment, there is a real possibility that she might model herself on Gynecia. Her final words in the scene, however, show that the break has been made. Philoclea is no longer the child of her parents but the woman who gives herself to her lover: " 'Oh my Zelmane,' she says, 'govern and direct me, for I am wholly given over unto thee.' "

The clearing up of her confusion about the nature of her love for Zelmane/Pyrocles comes soon after, when Pyrocles has at last the opportunity to declare his real identity. The tangle of Philoclea's emotions is unraveled by the discovery that the seeming Amazon is a man, but that happy result emerges out of a situation that itself indicates what it means to pass from sexual innocence to experience of a passion that welcomes subterfuge and is content to accept unseemly facts so long as they remain unspoken. Basilius employs his daughter to intercede in his favor with Zelmane, and Philoclea accepts the commission gladly, since it gives her the opportunity to talk to Zelmane alone; but the pleasure is bought at the cost of knowing beyond doubt that her father seeks to make Zelmane his mistress and is using her for an immoral purpose. Her joy when Zelmane reveals herself to be, in fact, a man is likewise shot through with some shame, for she fears that she has not maintained the entire reserve and modesty by which, her upbringing tells her, she should keep a suitor at arm's length—and that her sister practices. Yet she frankly avows her love and, giving her heart to Pyrocles, entrusts her honor to his keeping. She was recently childlike and unknowing but has become thoughtful and dignified: "Thou hast then the victory; use it with virtue. Thy virtue won me; with virtue preserve me. Dost thou love me? Keep me then still worthy to be beloved." Philoclea's sweetness has its own kind of strength as she emerges into adult life, a point made more strongly in *New Arcadia.* Hers is not the militant pride of Pamela, but she compels obedience all the same, requiring of Pyrocles a new kind of valor in controlling his "enraged desires."

There is much that is charming in the love scene of Pyrocles and Philoclea in the *New Arcadia* version, and sense of its quality and of the nature of the participants is enlarged by aspects of the stories that Pyrocles goes on to tell at Philoclea's request. One of the first of these concerns a man called Pamphilus—young, handsome, of noble blood, a delightful and accomplished companion, but a seducer and betrayer of women. His skill lies in playing on the weaknesses of his victims, jealousy, envy, vanity, pride. He discards them without compunction when he grows tired of them and triumphs over their misery with insults. Pyrocles encounters him at a crucial moment, when the betrayed women have banded together to take revenge on him, and he hears the whole tale from the most determined of the avengers. It is a story that cuts two ways, Pamphilus is what Pyrocles might become if he chooses to exploit his attractions without care or respect for the women who are charmed by him; and the fate of the women enforces the need for that circumspection and restraint toward love which Philoclea reproaches herself for having to some degree failed in. Pamphilus does wrong, but in doing so, he takes advantage of his victims' faults.

Sidney, characteristically, makes Pyrocles' informant (with tongue in cheek he christened her Dido) capable of a shrewd piece of self-analysis: " 'I must confess,' she says, 'even in the greatest tempest of my judgement was I never driven to think him excellent, and yet so could set my mind both to get and keep him, as though therein had lain my felicity: like them I have seen play at the ball grow extremely earnest who should have the ball, and yet everyone knew it was but a ball.' " What rankles particularly with Dido is that Pamphilus has insulted her beauty, claiming that he could find many fairer than she, an interesting point because female vanity is one of many topics on which Sidney does not follow the conventional line. It plays little part in the characters of any of the beautiful women to whom he gives his attention. The tournament in book 1 of *New Arcadia* in which knightly lovers are challenged to assert their ladies' preeminence in beauty gives Sidney the opportunity to find the mind's construction in a range of women's faces. His portraits are as much psychological as physical and in many cases serve as introductions to characters to be seen in action later. Though Gynecia and Philoclea both have their champions in this tournament and their knights are overthrown, their defeat causes the women little disturbance. Gynecia, the reader is told, would have been quite indifferent to the downfall of her defender at any other time and only cares at all now because Zelmane is a witness. Philoclea, whose softer nature might be more receptive to flattery, reacts to the defeat of her champion only to the extent of "a pretty blush" denoting "a modest discontent." As for Pamela, Cecropia believes that her care for her appearance during her imprisonment denotes vanity, but she is shortly disabused in no uncertain way. Feminine susceptibility to vanity is given some prominence only in the person of Dido, whose story, together with that of her fellow victims, shows what may happen when women allow themselves to be cajoled and flattered into trusting men without honor—their hearts will be broken, their fortunes lost, their reputations ruined. Philoclea's confiding herself to Pyrocles might be a rash act, but looking back to her after reading the Dido story, her confession of love can be recognized as something heroic rather than foolish, which calls for and receives a fitting and honorable response.

If some potentialities in Philoclea's nature are revealed by Dido and her companions, she is set off in quite another way by the girl whose name Pyrocles takes when he adopts his Amazonian disguise, Zelmane. Zelmane has fallen in love with Pyrocles during an earlier adventure outside Arcadia. She has the double misfortune to be the daughter of Plexirtus, a man of unremittingly wicked disposition, and to be brought up by the lustful and unprincipled Andromana. In spite of these evil influences, she is herself good and is loved by Palladius, Andromana's son. Like Zelmane, he is the virtuous child of a wicked parent, but this community of fortune is not enough to bind Zelmane to him. She employs him, however, to help Pyrocles and Musidorus escape from Andromana's clutches, and as a result of this he is killed, to the distress of the princes. Some time later Pyrocles and Musidorus are joined by a youth who begs to be taken into Pyrocles' service. Though he has an idea that the boy's face is familiar, Pyrocles does not recognize that "he" is in fact Zelmane, who follows and serves him devotedly, her eyes full of the love she dare not acknowledge and that he does not recognize. By Plexirtus's villainy, Tydeus and Telenor, knightly brothers with whom Pyrocles and Musidorus feel some affinity, are killed, and out of shame for her father, and grief that Pyrocles' hatred of him will turn him against her whenever he discovers her identity, Zelmane pines away. As she dies she reveals herself, begging Pyrocles to think of her tenderly: " 'this breaking of my heart, before I would discover my pain, will make you, I hope, think I was not altogether unmodest.' " "Was not this love indeed?" is Viola's comment on her supposed sister's story in *Twelfth Night,* and the story of Zelmane, as Sidney tells it, is also a touching little tale. Pyrocles himself is much moved by it, and it has

a great influence on both princes and on Philoclea. Zelmane and Philoclea physically resemble each other, a fact that contributes to Pyrocles' falling in love with her when he first sees her portrait. Pyrocles has adopted Zelmane's name in Arcadia, and earlier, in response to Zelmane's dying request, he called himself Daiphantus, the name Zelmane took when she served as his page. Musidorus, also by her wish, went by the name of Palladius, Zelmane's unhappy lover. Palladius and Zelmane loved without requital and sacrificed themselves for those they loved. They are examples of the selflessness of true love, as are Argalus and Parthenia, and the use of their names serves to keep their example before the eyes of the young men in their own amorous pursuits. Zelmane cuts off her hair and strives to appear boyish, subjecting herself, though a princess, to a servitor's role, and Pyrocles also disguises his sex and accepts embarrassment and disability for the sake of the girl he loves. The patient courage and humility that Zelmane displays become part also of Philoclea's education in what love will demand, and how well she learns her lesson is to be seen in book 3 of the *New Arcadia.* Gentle and malleable as she has been, she proves that she can resist torment and tyranny with courage and fortitude despite the natural softness of her nature. "With silence and patience" she bears what Cecropia and her assistants inflict on her, comforting and sustaining herself with thoughts of Pyrocles: "that was the only worldly thing whereon Philoclea rested her mind, that she knew she should die beloved of Zelmane, and should die rather than be false to Zelmane . . . easing the pain of her mind with thinking of another's pain, and almost forgetting the pain of her body through the pain of her mind."

When Cecropia threatens to kill Pamela, Philoclea is able to rise to the height of magnanimity and offer her own life to save that of her sister and friend, and when Pyrocles urges her to give Amphialus some appearance of hope in his suit, in order to gain time, she rejects his plea with quiet resolution: "Trouble me not, . . . dear Pyrocles, nor double not my death by tormenting my resolution. Since I canot live with thee, I will die for thee." In words that recall Zelmane's, she begs that after her death he will love her memory. Zelmane knew, sadly, that he would one day love another as he had not loved her, but Philoclea asks to be his last love. " 'Remember,' she says, 'that my love was a worthy love,' " and by this time she has earned the right to make this claim.

One further touch relating to Philoclea's character is worth noting. It occurs in the later part of the story and appears, therefore, only in the unrevised text. As it stands, it forms part of a little group of episodes that are clearly meant to illuminate each other by comparison. This is the technique that Sidney employs extensively in his filling out of the narrative in *New Arcadia,* and he could quite suitably have retained at least the main elements in a final revision. The episodes concern the reactions of three women when they find, or believe they find, that they have been spurned and betrayed by a man. The first is Gynecia in the scene in which she and Pyrocles encounter one another in the cave. Pyrocles at first attempts to fend her off by maintaining his pretence of being a woman, and Gynecia bursts out in rage, scattering threats in all directions: "Since I must fall, I will press down some others with my ruins. Since I must burn, my spiteful neighbours shall feel of my fire. . . . Believe it, believe it, unkind creature, I will end my miseries with a notable example of revenge." This episode is followed by an account of Musidorus's plots to get Dametas and his family out of the way, so that he and Pamela can make their escape. His story to Miso, Dametas's misshapen and witchlike wife, is that her husband has taken up with a very pretty young shepherdess and has an assignation with her that night in the neighboring town. Miso's anger and jealousy are unbounded: "her hollow eyes yielded such wretched looks as one might well think Pluto at that time might have had her soul very good cheap. But when the fire of spite had fully caught hold of all her inward parts, whosoever would have seen the picture of Alecto, or with what manner of countenance Medea killed her own children, needed but take Miso for the full satisfaction of that point of his knowledge." The reference to Pluto should probably serve as a reminder that Gynecia in the previous scene, despairing of her virtue, had invoked the furies to assist her in satisfying her desires. The reference to Medea must certainly recall that among Gynecia's threats is one that "that accursed cradle of mine [i.e., Philoclea] shall feel the smart of my wound." Gynecia's soul, like Miso's, seems at that point to be on offer "very good cheap." Sidney's juxtaposition of the serious-passionate and the comic-grotesque is a striking example of the two-toned effect that enhances so much of *Arcadia* and by which the reader is amused and entertained even while, simultaneously, the intellect and the moral sense are challenged and invigorated. In this instance the juxtaposition functions to lighten the tone and to discharge some of the horrifying potential in what Gynecia has said. She has been driven to her lowest point, and as her words indicate, the possibility of a fearsome tragic outcome looms distinctly on the horizon. Miso's jealous frenzy acts as an effective counterweight and reassurance that all will be well. At the same time, it exposes an element of the ridiculous in jealousy itself and the actions it leads to. The double nature of jealousy, deadly and yet absurd, has been a rich subject of drama, developed with particularly acute appreciation of both the terror and the nonsense in *Othello*. Sidney's narrative sequence is more leisurely and has a different end in view, but the temporary equation of Gynecia and Miso is a daring device and effective in setting out some parts of one of the most tangled complexes of human feeling.

After Gynecia and Miso comes Philoclea. In pursuit of his plan to gain time by holding out hope of satisfaction to both Gynecia and Basilius, Pyrocles has to appear cold to Philoclea and completely discontinue all the attention he has previously paid to her. Philoclea, ignorant of his plans, is desolated by the sudden, studied indifference. She feels herself to be abandoned both by her parents and by her lover and suffers intensely. In this condition, "she had yielded up her soul to be a prey of sorrow and unkindness, not with raging conceit of revenge—as had passed through the stout and wise heart of her mother—but with a kindly meekness taking upon her the weight of her own woes, and suffering them to have so full a course as it did exceedingly weaken the state of her body." Philoclea's behavior, as the woman (apparently) scorned, reflects her mild and hum-

ble nature, as distinct from the strong and, what Sidney ironically calls, the "wise" heart of her mother, and from the termagant violence of Miso. Philoclea does not so much renounce revenge as never contemplate it, but her quiet suffering speaks for itself and her reproaches when they come are all the more pointed and bitter in their effect because of the sweetness of the nature that has been so injured. In this episode again, Sidney is at pains to show that Philoclea, though constitutionally gentle, is not a feeble or insipid character. The depth and sincerity of her love give her strength to defy death and also to accuse her lover when she believes he has betrayed her. "Humble-hearted" whereas Pamela is "high-hearted," she has her own kind of strength, and Sidney's success in creating her is a triumph in a very difficult undertaking, achieved by great delicacy of idea and treatment.

Sidney has evidently devoted much care to the delineating of his range of female characters, and the thought and skill bestowed on them are matched by the generosity and enlightenment of his attitudes. He disregards conventional judgments and rejects stereotypes, creating both good and bad women who are strong minded and intelligent and allowing to even the more timid and pliable Philoclea a growth into conscious self-respect, courage, and resolution. Which is the more remarkable—the sustained double portrait of two kinds of virtue in Pamela and Philoclea, or his analysis of Gynecia, standing so close as she does to the violent, implacable female figures of old stories and yet sympathetically distinguished from them—it is hard to say; but given skill of this kind, and attitudes of this kind, it is surely rash to make conventional assumptions about the implications of Pyrocles' female disguise. Musidorus, before he learns to love and respect Pamela, is in no doubt that Pyrocles' Amazonian masquerade is a disgrace, and recent commentary has been inclined to accept this. A man's adopting of a female disguise has traditionally been looked on as an act of degradation that would invite real as well as apparent diminishment of his male status, but it does not follow that Sidney would share the traditional view. The degree and kind of attention he pays to his women characters seems, on the contrary, to point in a quite opposite direction. The jewel that fastens Pyrocles' mantle is carved to represent Hercules with a distaff in his hand, as he was when Omphale set him spinning among her maids, and its motto is "Never more valiant." Sidney might perhaps have intended the motto as an ironic comment, and in conventional commentary on the Hercules episode it could hardly be anything else; but, in fact, the words can be taken quite literally in relation to Pyrocles. Though his tone may be equivocal when he assures Musidorus that "for all my apparel, there is nothing I desire more than fully to prove myself a man in this enterprise," there is no ambiguity in Sidney's comment on his response when Anaxius's brother, Zoilus, tries to embrace, as he thinks, the Amazon Zelmane: "abiding no longer abode in the matter, she that had not put off (though she had disguised) Pyrocles, being far fuller of strong nimbleness, tripped up his feet so that he fell down at hers." If any doubt remains that Pyrocles may have weakened either in strength or courage, the ensuing fight with Anaxius must remove it. When he lays aside his princely rank and disguises his sex, exposing himself to unfamiliar and unforeseeable adventures for the sake of wooing in very unpropi-tious circumstances the young girl with whom he has fall-en in love, Pyrocles takes great risks and makes himself very vulnerable. He suffers dangers and indignities but never, even when on trial for his life, regrets the sacrifice he makes for love or weakens in his devotion to Philoclea. It can be quite fitting for him to claim valor in this con-duct, for heroism is not confined to deeds of arms alone.

In his woman's dress Pyrocles has to share something of women's experience, enduring the courtship of unwel-come suitors, practicing patience, and in Amphialus's cas-tle, forced to wait helplessly while others fight and attempt a rescue from outside. In the early debate with Musidorus, he defends the cause of women verbally and, when the op-portunity comes, in the episode on which Sidney was working just before he broke off his revision, he fights physically under their colors to punish one who has de-spised and insulted them. Anaxius is the transgressor, and Sidney draws attention to the significance of Pyrocles' role in chastising him when he makes the young prince forecast that Anaxius will find himself defeated in that martial skill of which he is most proud, and "punished by the weak sex which thou most contemnest." This is not strictly true, of course, but the episode seems clearly intended to have symbolic value as Pyrocles fights as a woman on behalf of women. The whole course of *Arcadia,* in the revision espe-cially, makes claims for the special strengths of women and undermines a masculine pride based merely on mus-cular power, just as it challenges also male claims to supe-rior virtue. Anaxius, who relies on physical prowess, is to be chastened, as is Musidorus, who despised the character of women and has to do penance, reduced from prince to unskillful shepherd, and bound by Pamela to a most duti-ful respect. Rather than derogating from his manhood, Pyrocles' living for a time and in part a woman's life com-pletes it. Sidney describes him as "the chief of the princes," and the reference is not only to his public status but also to his wider range of sympathy and response than that of Musidorus who is limited by a harder masculinity.

The original *Arcadia* was written for Sidney's "dear lady and sister," the young Countess of Pembroke. The dedica-tion is full of affection and betokens an intimate and con-fiding relationship. It is appropriate that, in working out more fully ideas and themes only sketched in *Old Arcadia,* Sidney should have expanded and enhanced his treatment of women and their claims as individuals to mind, con-science, and character. Lady Pembroke was herself a woman of character and learning who shared her broth-er's interests and after his death sought to promote them. She was a poet who translated Petrarch and completed the verse translation of the Psalms that Sidney had begun. She assumed his role as a patron of poets and enlisted some (Thomas Kyd among them) in an attempt to refine and el-evate English drama. Sidney, writing in the very early 1580s, had seen no way forward but to adopt the patterns and rules of neoclassical drama, and the Countess persist-ed in this idea even after new impulses were opening far wider horizons. She misjudged in this, but the motivation was what Sidney's had been in his *Apology for Poetry,* that is, to encourage English writers to create a modern literature of comparable dignity and accomplishment to

that of Italy and France. Sidney's sister is known by her own work and the praise others gave her. His mother is a more secluded figure, but she came of a great family, the Dudleys, and was evidently a woman of character and in-telligence. She nursed the Queen during an attack of small-pox and contracted the disease herself. After that, she avoided appearances at court, "the mischance of sick-ness having cast such a kind of veil over her excellent beauty," Fulke Greville writes, "as the modesty of that sex doth many times upon their native and heroical spirits." He seems to imply that Lady Sidney herself was of "hero-ical" mold. With two such women among his most inti-mate relations, if for no other reason, Sidney had every in-centive to treat women and women's experience with re-spect.

As for Fulke Greville himself, his nature was of a grimmer stamp than his friend's. He acknowledges that women have claims to equality of treatment, but the grounds them on characteristically different premises. In his *Life of Sid-ney,* he writes of the role of the powerful and wicked women in his plays. "That women are predominant," he explains, "is not for malice, or ill talent to their sex; but as poets figured the virtues to be women, and all nations call them by feminine names, so have I described malice, craft and such-like vices in the persons of shrews, to shew that many of them are of that nature, even as we are, I mean strong in weakness." He goes on to say that he has not made them all evil, any more than all good, but "mixed of such sorts as we find both them, and ourselves." In the work of Samuel Daniel, a younger man closely con-nected with the Sidney-Greville-Pembroke circle, the sympathetic treatment of women is a particularly striking feature. His Cleopatra, in the French-Senecan play he wrote about her, is a feeling, even tender, woman; his Oc-tavia, reproaching Antony for his desertion of her in a verse epistle, speaks on behalf of all women frustrated by the restraints upon their freedom and confined within "this prison of ourselves"; the verse epistles he wrote in his own person to women recipients are among his most successful poems, expressing much that is best in his mind and character. In the late *Hymen's Triumph* (1615), an Arcadian pastoral play, he comes close to Sidney, when Palaemon reproaches Thyrsis for his weakness in pining for "a silly woman" and provokes a firm counterstate-ment. The later lines of Thyrsis's speech are an example of Daniel's own remarkable sensitivity:

> And doe you hold it weaknesse then to love?
> And love so excellent a miracle
> As is a woman! ah then let mee
> Still be so weake, still let me love and pine
> In contemplation of that cleane, cleare soule
> That made mine see that nothing in the world
> Is so supreamely beautiful as it.
> Thinke not it was those colours white and red
> Laid but on flesh, that could affect me so.
> But something else, which thought holds under
>   locke
> And hath no key of words to open it.
> They are the smallest peeces of the minde
> That passe this narrow organ of the voyce.
> The great remaine behinde in that vast orbe
> Of th' apprehension, and are never borne.

The sentiments are very close to those of Pyrocles. The passage may be an expansion, in particular, of his words in the *Old Arcadia* version of the scene in which he avows to Musidorus that he has become a lover: " 'and yet such a one am I,' said he, 'and in such extremity as no man can feel but myself, nor no man believe; since no man could ever taste the hundredth part of that which lies in the inwardmost part of my soul.' "

Sidney himself may have drawn inspiration for his treatment of women characters from Chaucer's *Troilus and Criseyde.* He singled out this poem for praise in his *Apology for Poetry,* and being the man he was, he is likely to have taken note of how much more sympathetically than others Chaucer treats the "sliding courage" of Criseyde. That he in his turn influenced the thinking of Greville and Daniel, his ideas taking color from their own individual temperaments, seems so likely as to be virtually certain. The influence of *Arcadia* did not need to depend on the reader's personal association with the writer, however. Shakespeare was responsive to Sidney's great romance, and there is good reason to suppose that the line of splendid Shakespearean heroines owes more than an occasional specific reminiscence to the attitudes and imaginative perceptions that go into the making of Sidney's remarkable portrayals of the women of *Arcadia.* Desdemona with her quiet courage, Cordelia with her high but loving heart, and Hermione with her dignity and self-respect would recognize first cousins in *New Arcadia.* (pp. 50-69)

> *Joan Rees, in her* Sir Philip Sidney and "Arcadia," *Fairleigh Dickinson University Press, 1991, 158 p.*

FURTHER READING

Boas, Frederick S. *Sir Philip Sidney: Representative Elizabethan, His Life and Writings.* London: Staples Press, 1955, 204 p.

  Highly regarded critical biography.

Buxton, John. *Sir Philip Sidney and the English Renaissance.* London: MacMillan, 1954, 283 p.

  Studies Sidney's life and career as they reflect the English tradition of literary patronage during the Renaissance.

Connell, Dorothy. *Sir Philip Sidney: The Maker's Mind.* Oxford: Clarendon Press, 1977, 163 p.

  Analyzes Sidney's theories concerning poetry.

Courthope, W. J. "Court Romance: Sir Philip Sidney." In his *A History of English Poetry,* pp. 203-33. London: MacMillan, 1904.

  Characterizes Sidney as a romantic idealist in an overview of his life and career.

Davidson, Clifford. "Nature and Judgment in the *Old Arcadia.*" *Papers on Language & Literature* VI, No. 4 (Fall 1970): 348-65.

  Suggests that the *Old Arcadia* dramatizes the Renaissance argument concerning the relative merits of the contemplative and active modes of existence.

Davis, Walter R. "Narrative Methods in Sidney's *Old Arcadia.*" *Studies in English Literature 1500-1900* XVIII, No. 1 (Winter 1978): 13-33.

  Examines ways in which "each of the books within the five-act structure of the *Old Arcadia* has a distinct and different kind of narrative method," adding that "the changes in narrative method book-by-book are significant for the romance's meaning."

Dipple, Elizabeth. "Harmony and Pastoral in the *Old Arcadia.*" *ELH* 35, No. 3 (September 1968): 309-28.

  Maintains that the realistic elements in the *Old Arcadia* contribute to the narrative's moral message.

Dobell, Bertram. "New Light Upon Sir Philip Sidney's *Arcadia.*" *The Quarterly Review,* No. 420 (July 1909): 74-100.

  Seminal essay, occasioned by the critic's acquisition of three early manuscripts of the *Arcadia,* tracing the narrative's composition and publication history. Dobell suggests that Sidney's first version (thenceforth referred to as the *Old Arcadia*) is in many ways superior to the revised edition begun by Sidney and completed by Mary Sidney.

Drinkwater, John. "Philip Sidney." In his *The Muse in Council, Being Essays on Poets and Poetry,* pp. 83-98. Boston: Houghton Mifflin Co., 1925.

  Praises Sidney's contribution to the development of the English sonnet sequence in an examination of *Astrophil and Stella.*

Eliot, T. S. "Apology for the Countess of Pembroke." In his *The Use of Poetry and the Use of Criticism,* pp. 37-52. 1933. Reprint. London: Faber and Faber, 1964.

  Discusses the nature of literary criticism in the Elizabethan age, focusing on Sidney's criticisms of the English stage in his *Apology.* Eliot's remark that the *Arcadia* "is a monument of dulness" appears in the concluding commentary.

Fienberg, Nona. "Sir Philip Sidney: The Political and Poetical Uses of Eloquence." In her *Elizabeth, Her Poets, and the Creation of the Courtly Manner: A Study of Sir John Harington, Sir Philip Sidney, and John Lyly,* pp. 102-57. New York: Garland, 1988.

  Analysis of Sidney's poetry which focuses on the poet's attempt to find an audience for his work.

Goulston, Wendy. "The 'Figuring Forth' of Astrophil: Sidney's Use of Language." *Southern Review (Australia)* XI, No. 3 (1978): 228-46.

  Argues that in the character of Astrophil Sidney creates "an exemplum of language mirroring, 'figuring forth,' a superficially attractive, but seriously fallen mind."

Greenfield, Thelma N. *The Eye of Judgment: Reading the "New Arcadia."* Lewisburg, Pa.: Bucknell University Press, 1982, 229 p.

  Comprehensive analysis of themes, techniques, and sources of the new *Arcadia.*

Kalstone, David. *Sidney's Poetry: Contexts and Interpretations.* Cambridge: Harvard University Press, 1965, 195 p.

  Examines *Arcadia* and *Astrophil and Stella.*

Kennedy, William J. "The Petrarchan Mode in Lyric Poetry:

Sidney's *Astrophil and Stella.*" In his *Rhetorical Norms in Renaissance Literature,* pp. 57-71. New Haven: Yale University Press, 1978.

Suggests that "Sidney's strategies of voice and address . . . typify Renaissance Petrarchanism. The mode derives its highest rhetorical power from the figure of the split addresser, embracing the poet and speaker, and from the figure of the split addressee, embracing the fictive audience and the actual reader."

Kimbrough, Robert. *Sir Philip Sidney.* New York: Twayne, 1971, 162 p.
Concise overview of Sidney's life and works.

Lamb, Mary Ellen. "*The Countess of Pembroke's Arcadia* and Its (Com)Passionate Women Readers." In her *Gender and Authorship in the Sidney Circle,* pp. 72-114. Madison: University of Wisconsin Press, 1990.
Explores the issue of gender in *Arcadia* as reflected in its structure, content, and intended audience.

Lanham, Richard A. "Sidney: The Ornament of His Age." *Southern Review (Australia)* II, No. 4 (1967): 319-40.
Examines fact and fiction in the legends concerning Sidney.

Lawry, Jon S. *Sidney's Two "Arcadias": Pattern and Proceeding.* Ithaca, N.Y.: Cornell University Press, 1972, 304 p.
Provides a close reading of *The Defence of Poetry* and both versions of the *Arcadia.*

Levao, Ronald. "Sidney's Feigned *Apology.*" *PMLA* 94, No. 2 (March 1979): 223-33.
Discusses the argument of the *Apology,* noting that Sidney's technique is less direct and more playful that is generally recognized.

Macaulay, Rose. "John Lyly and Sir Philip Sidney." In *The English Novelists: A Survey of the Novel by Twenty Contemporary Novelists,* edited by Derek Verschoyle, pp. 31-47. London: Chatto & Windus, 1936.
Contains a brief, negative assessment of *Arcadia.* Macaulay notes: "Perhaps no writer of high literary gifts has ever done such long damage to literature and to literary taste and fashion as did Sir Philip Sidney when he wrote his *Arcadia.*"

Mason, H. A. "An Introduction to Literary Criticism by Way of Sidney's *Apologie for Poetrie.*" *The Cambridge Quarterly* XII, Nos. 2 and 3, pp. 77-173.
Seeks to ascertain the stimulus for the *Apologie,* focusing in particular on Sidney's classical antecedents.

Montgomery, Robert L., Jr. *Symmetry and Sense: The Poetry of Sir Philip Sidney.* Austin: University of Texas Press, 1961.
Stylistic analysis of Sidney's poetry.

Montrose, Louis Adrian. "Celebration and Insinuation: Sir Philip Sidney and the Motives of Elizabethan Courtship." *Renaissance Drama* VIII (1977): 3-35.
Discusses the composition and intent of Sidney's drama *The Lady of May.*

Muir, Kenneth. *Sir Philip Sidney.* London: Longmans, Green, 1960, 40 p.
Brief critical overview of Sidney's major works.

Myrick, Kenneth. *Sir Philip Sidney as a Literary Craftsman.* Lincoln: University of Nebraska Press, 1935, 362 p.
Thematic analysis of Sidney's works.

Parker, Robert W. "Terentian Structure and Sidney's Original *Arcadia.*" *English Literary Renaissance* 2, No. 1 (Winter 1972): 61-78.
Contends that the plot and structure of Sidney's original *Arcadia* are modeled on the works of the Roman comic playwright Terence.

Robinson, Forrest G. *The Shape of Things Known: Sidney's "Apology" in Its Philosophical Tradition.* Cambridge: Harvard University Press, 1972, 230 p.
Explicates Sidney's definition of the meaning and value of poetry, as outlined in his *Apology.*

Roche, Thomas P., Jr. "*Astrophil and Stella:* A Radical Reading." *Spenser Studies* III (1978): 139-91.
Examines Sidney's inversion of traditional imagery in the sonnet sequence as evidenced by Astrophil's imprisoning himself in his worship of Stella. The essay includes a detailed analysis of sexual symbolism and concludes with a comparison of the protagonists to Ulysses and Penelope of Greek myth.

———. "Autobiographical Elements in Sidney's *Astrophil and Stella.*" *Spenser Studies* V (1985): 209-29.
Examines autobiographical references in Sidney's *Astrophil and Stella* that elucidate the author's relationship with Penelope Devereux, Lady Rich.

Rowse, Alfred L., and Harrison, George B. "Sir Philip Sidney." In their *Queen Elizabeth and Her Subjects,* pp. 45-55. 1935. Reprint. Freeport, N.Y.: Books for Libraries Press, 1970.
Brief anecdotal discussion of Sidney's life and works.

Rudenstine, Neil L. *Sidney's Poetic Development.* Cambridge: Harvard University Press, 1967, 313 p.
Detailed examination of Sidney's poetry that traces the author's artistic growth. Rudenstine asserts that his study "stresses the fundamental unity and inner consistency of Sidney's oeuvre."

Scanlon, Paul A. "Sidney's *Old Arcadia:* A Renaissance Pastoral Romance." *Ariel* 10, No. 4 (October 1979): 69-76.
Maintains that the themes and style of Sidney's *Old Arcadia,* as well as its mingling of "a variety of literary kinds," supports the conclusion that this work is of that "most hospitable of genres," pastoral romance.

Sinfield, Alan. "Sexual Puns in *Astrophil and Stella.*" *Essays in Criticism* XXIV, No. 4 (October 1974): 341-355.
Purports to demonstrate that "sexual *double entendre* is an important feature of Sidney's verbal skill and, following this, that Astrophil's love for Stella is sexual right from the beginning of the sequence." Sinfield maintains that "if these propositions are accepted they will add to the vigour and subtlety of the early sonnets especially . . . and increase our respect for Sidney's linguistic and emotional range."

Stillinger, Jack. "The Biographical Problem of *Astrophel and Stella.*" *Journal of English and Germanic Philology* LIX (1960): 617-39.
Questions the extent to which "orthodox critical opinion" is justified in asserting "that *Astrophel and Stella* autobiographically describes Sidney's love for Penelope Rich." Stillinger concludes that "approaching the poems with the love story in mind" may cause many

readers to misunderstand, and many critics to misrepresent, their meaning.

Thompson, John. "Sir Philip Sidney." In his *The Founding of English Metre,* pp. 139-55. London: Routledge and Kegan Paul, 1966.
  Praises Sidney's skillful use of meter in an examination of his experimentation with metrical pattern and language in the *Arcadia.*

Townsend, Freda L. "Sidney and Ariosto." *PMLA* LXI, No. 1 (1946): 97-108.
  Rejects the assumption that the complexity of the *Arcadia* destroys its unity, comparing its "web" structure to that of Ariosto's *Orlando Furioso.*

Vickers, Brian. "A Wrong-Headed Re-Write." *Times Literary Supplement,* No. 4468 (18-24 November 1988): 1285.
  Review of Victor Skretkowicz's edition of the *Arcadia,* which the critic assesses as confusing to the "ordinary reader."

Wallace, Malcolm William. *The Life of Sir Philip Sidney.* 1915. Reprint. New York: Octagon Books, 1967, 428 p.
  Biography including previously undocumented details concerning Sidney's education and personal relationships.

Waller, Gary F., and Moore, Michael D., eds. *Sir Philip Sidney and the Interpretation of Renaissance Culture: The Poet in His Time and in Ours.* London: Croom Helm, 1984, 147 p.
  Includes critical essays on Sidney's works as they relate to the tradition of Elizabethan poetry.

Webster, John. "Oration and Method in Sidney's *Apology:* A Contemporary's Account." *Modern Philology* 79, No. 1 (August 1981): 1-15.
  Compares modern commentary on the structure of the *Apology* with Sir William Temple's unpublished sixteenth-century analysis, focusing on divergent views of the essay as oratory and exposition.

Zandvoort, R. W. *Sidney's "Arcadia": A Comparison between the Two Versions.* 1929. Reprint. Amsterdam: N. V. Swets & Zeitlinger, 1966, 215 p.
  Influential study discussing the relationship between the *Old Arcadia* and the *New Arcadia,* coordinating the results of previous studies.

Literature
Criticism from
1400 to 1800
Cumulative Indexes

This Index Includes References to Entries in These Gale Series

Contemporary Literary Criticism Presents excerpts of criticism on the works of novelists, poets, dramatists, short story writers, scriptwriters, and other creative writers who are now living or who have died since 1960.

Twentieth-Century Literary Criticism Contains critical excerpts by the most significant commentators on poets, novelists, short story writers, dramatists, and philosophers who died between 1900 and 1960.

Nineteenth-Century Literature Criticism Offers significant passages from criticism on authors who died between 1800 and 1899.

Literature Criticism from 1400 to 1800 Compiles significant passages from the most noteworthy criticism on authors of the fifteenth through eighteenth centuries.

Classical and Medieval Literature Criticism Offers excerpts of criticism on the works of world authors from classical antiquity through the fourteenth century.

Short Story Criticism Compiles excerpts of criticism on short fiction by writers of all eras and nationalities.

Poetry Criticism Presents excerpts of criticism on the works of poets from all eras, movements, and nationalities.

Drama Criticism Contains excerpts of criticism on dramatists of all nationalities and periods of literary history.

Children's Literature Review Includes excerpts from reviews, criticism, and commentary on works of authors and illustrators who create books for children.

Contemporary Authors Series Encompasses five related series. *Contemporary Authors* provides biographical and bibliographical information on more than 97,000 writers of fiction, nonfiction, poetry, journalism, drama, motion pictures, and other fields. Each new volume contains sketches on authors not previously covered in the series. *Contemporary Authors New Revision Series* provides completely updated information on active authors covered in previously published volumes of *CA*. Only entries requiring significant change are revised for *CA New Revision Series*. *Contemporary Authors Permanent Series* consists of updated listings for deceased and inactive authors removed from the original volumes 9-36 when these volumes were revised. *Contemporary Authors Autobiography Series* presents specially commissioned autobiographies by leading contemporary writers. *Contemporary Authors Bibliographical Series* contains primary and secondary bibliographies as well as analytical bibliographical essays by authorities on major modern authors.

Dictionary of Literary Biography Encompasses three related series. *Dictionary of Literary Biography* furnishes illustrated overviews of authors' lives and works and places them in the larger perspective of literary history. *Dictionary of Literary Biography Documentary Series* illuminates the careers of major figures through a selection of literary documents, including letters, notebook and diary entries, interviews, book reviews, and photographs. *Dictionary of Literary Biography Yearbook* summarizes the past year's literary activity with articles on genres, major prizes, conferences, and other timely subjects and includes updated and new entries on individual authors.

Concise Dictionary of American Literary Biography A six-volume series that collects revised and updated sketches on major American authors that were originally presented in *Dictionary of Literary Biography*.

Something about the Author Series Encompasses three related series. *Something about the Author* contains well-illustrated biographical sketches on juvenile and young adult authors and illustrators from all eras. *Something about the Author Autobiography Series* presents specially commissioned autobiographies by prominent authors and illustrators of books for children and young adults.

Yesterday's Authors of Books for Children Contains heavily illustrated entries on children's writers who died before 1961. Complete in two volumes.

Literary Criticism Series
Cumulative Author Index

This index lists all author entries in the Gale Literary Criticism Series and includes cross-references to other Gale sources. References in the index are identified as follows:

AAYA: *Authors & Artists for Young Adults,* Volumes 1-7
CA: *Contemporary Authors* (original series), Volumes 1-135
CAAS: *Contemporary Authors Autobiography Series,* Volumes 1-14
CABS: *Contemporary Authors Bibliographical Series,* Volumes 1-3
CANR: *Contemporary Authors New Revision Series,* Volumes 1-35
CAP: *Contemporary Authors Permanent Series,* Volumes 1-2
CA-R: *Contemporary Authors* (first revision), Volumes 1-44
CDALB: *Concise Dictionary of American Literary Biography,* Volumes 1-6
CLC: *Contemporary Literary Criticism,* Volumes 1-69
CLR: *Children's Literature Review,* Volumes 1-25
CMLC: *Classical and Medieval Literature Criticism,* Volumes 1-8
DC: *Drama Criticism,* Volume 1-2
DLB: *Dictionary of Literary Biography,* Volumes 1-112
DLB-DS: *Dictionary of Literary Biography Documentary Series,* Volumes 1-9
DLB-Y: *Dictionary of Literary Biography Yearbook,* Volumes 1980-1990
LC: *Literature Criticism from 1400 to 1800,* Volumes 1-19
NCLC: *Nineteenth-Century Literature Criticism,* Volumes 1-34
PC: *Poetry Criticism,* Volumes 1-4
SAAS: *Something about the Author Autobiography Series,* Volumes 1-13
SATA: *Something about the Author,* Volumes 1-66
SSC: *Short Story Criticism,* Volumes 1-9
TCLC: *Twentieth-Century Literary Criticism,* Volumes 1-44
YABC: *Yesterday's Authors of Books for Children,* Volumes 1-2

Beckett, Samuel (Barclay)
1906-1989 . . . . . **CLC 1, 2, 3, 4, 6, 9, 10, 11, 14, 18, 29, 57, 59**
See also CA 5-8R; DLB 13, 15

Beckford, William 1760-1844 . . . . **NCLC 16**
See also DLB 39

Beckham, Barry 1944-
See also BLC 1; CANR 26; CA 29-32R; DLB 33

Beckman, Gunnel 1910- . . . . **CLC 26**
See also CANR 15; CA 33-36R; SATA 6

Becque, Henri 1837-1899 . . . . **NCLC 3**

Beddoes, Thomas Lovell
1803-1849 . . . . **NCLC 3**

Beecher, Catharine Esther
1800-1878 . . . . **NCLC 30**
See also DLB 1

Beecher, John 1904-1980 . . . . **CLC 6**
See also CANR 8; CA 5-8R; obituary CA 105

Beer, Johann 1655-1700 . . . . **LC 5**

Beer, Patricia 1919?- . . . . **CLC 58**
See also CANR 13; CA 61-64; DLB 40

Beerbohm, (Sir Henry) Max(imilian)
1872-1956 . . . .**TCLC 1, 24**
See also CA 104; DLB 34

Behan, Brendan
1923-1964 . . . . **CLC 1, 8, 11, 15**
See also CA 73-76; DLB 13

Behn, Aphra 1640?-1689 . . . . **LC 1**
See also DLB 39, 80

Behrman, S(amuel) N(athaniel)
1893-1973 . . . . **CLC 40**
See also CAP 1; CA 15-16; obituary CA 45-48; DLB 7, 44

Beiswanger, George Edwin 1931-
See Starbuck, George (Edwin)

Belasco, David 1853-1931 . . . . **TCLC 3**
See also CA 104; DLB 7

Belcheva, Elisaveta 1893-
See Bagryana, Elisaveta

Belinski, Vissarion Grigoryevich
1811-1848 . . . . **NCLC 5**

Belitt, Ben 1911- . . . . **CLC 22**
See also CAAS 4; CANR 7; CA 13-16R; DLB 5

Bell, Acton 1820-1849
See Bronte, Anne

Bell, Currer 1816-1855
See Bronte, Charlotte

Bell, James Madison 1826-1902 . . . **TCLC 43**
See also BLC 1; CA 122, 124; DLB 50

Bell, Madison Smartt 1957- . . . . **CLC 41**
See also CA 111

Bell, Marvin (Hartley) 1937- . . . . . **CLC 8, 31**
See also CA 21-24R; DLB 5

Bellamy, Edward 1850-1898 . . . . . . **NCLC 4**
See also DLB 12

Belloc, (Joseph) Hilaire (Pierre Sebastien Rene Swanton)
1870-1953 . . . .**TCLC 7, 18**
See also YABC 1; CA 106; DLB 19

Bellow, Saul
1915- . . . . . **CLC 1, 2, 3, 6, 8, 10, 13, 15, 25, 33, 34, 63**
See also CA 5-8R; CABS 1; DLB 2, 28; DLB-Y 82; DLB-DS 3; CDALB 1941-1968

Belser, Reimond Karel Maria de 1929-
See Ruyslinck, Ward

Bely, Andrey 1880-1934 . . . . **TCLC 7**
See also CA 104

Benary-Isbert, Margot 1889-1979 . . . **CLC 12**
See also CLR 12; CANR 4; CA 5-8R; obituary CA 89-92; SATA 2; obituary SATA 21

Benavente (y Martinez), Jacinto
1866-1954 . . . . **TCLC 3**
See also CA 106

Benchley, Peter (Bradford)
1940- . . . . **CLC 4, 8**
See also CANR 12; CA 17-20R; SATA 3

Benchley, Robert 1889-1945 . . . . **TCLC 1**
See also CA 105; DLB 11

Benedikt, Michael 1935- . . . . **CLC 4, 14**
See also CANR 7; CA 13-16R; DLB 5

Benet, Juan 1927- . . . . **CLC 28**

Benet, Stephen Vincent
1898-1943 . . . . **TCLC 7**
See also YABC 1; CA 104; DLB 4, 48

Benet, William Rose 1886-1950 . . . **TCLC 28**
See also CA 118; DLB 45

Benford, Gregory (Albert) 1941- . . . . **CLC 52**
See also CANR 12, 24; CA 69-72; DLB-Y 82

Benjamin, Walter 1892-1940 . . . . . . **TCLC 39**

Benn, Gottfried 1886-1956 . . . . **TCLC 3**
See also CA 106; DLB 56

Bennett, Alan 1934- . . . . **CLC 45**
See also CA 103

Bennett, (Enoch) Arnold
1867-1931 . . . .**TCLC 5, 20**
See also CA 106; DLB 10, 34

Bennett, George Harold 1930-
See Bennett, Hal
See also CA 97-100

Bennett, Hal 1930- . . . . **CLC 5**
See also Bennett, George Harold
See also DLB 33

Bennett, Jay 1912- . . . . **CLC 35**
See also CANR 11; CA 69-72; SAAS 4; SATA 27, 41

Bennett, Louise (Simone) 1919- . . . . . **CLC 28**
See also Bennett-Coverly, Louise Simone
See also BLC 1

Bennett-Coverly, Louise Simone 1919-
See Bennett, Louise (Simone)
See also CA 97-100

Benson, E(dward) F(rederic)
1867-1940 . . . . **TCLC 27**
See also CA 114

Benson, Jackson J. 1930- . . . . **CLC 34**
See also CA 25-28R

Benson, Sally 1900-1972 . . . . **CLC 17**
See also CAP 1; CA 19-20; obituary CA 37-40R; SATA 1, 35; obituary SATA 27

Benson, Stella 1892-1933 . . . . **TCLC 17**
See also CA 117; DLB 36

Bentley, E(dmund) C(lerihew)
1875-1956 . . . . **TCLC 12**
See also CA 108; DLB 70

Bentley, Eric (Russell) 1916- . . . . . . **CLC 24**
See also CANR 6; CA 5-8R

Beranger, Pierre Jean de
1780-1857 . . . . **NCLC 34**

Berger, John (Peter) 1926- . . . . . . **CLC 2, 19**
See also CA 81-84; DLB 14

Berger, Melvin (H.) 1927- . . . . **CLC 12**
See also CANR 4; CA 5-8R; SAAS 2; SATA 5

Berger, Thomas (Louis)
1924- . . . . **CLC 3, 5, 8, 11, 18, 38**
See also CANR 5; CA 1-4R; DLB 2; DLB-Y 80

Bergman, (Ernst) Ingmar 1918- . . . . . **CLC 16**
See also CA 81-84

Bergson, Henri 1859-1941 . . . . **TCLC 32**

Bergstein, Eleanor 1938- . . . . **CLC 4**
See also CANR 5; CA 53-56

Berkoff, Steven 1937- . . . . **CLC 56**
See also CA 104

Bermant, Chaim 1929- . . . . **CLC 40**
See also CANR 6; CA 57-60

Bernanos, (Paul Louis) Georges
1888-1948 . . . . **TCLC 3**
See also CA 104; DLB 72

Bernard, April 19??- . . . . **CLC 59**

Bernhard, Thomas
1931-1989 . . . . **CLC 3, 32, 61**
See also CA 85-88,; obituary CA 127; DLB 85

Berriault, Gina 1926- . . . . **CLC 54**
See also CA 116

Berrigan, Daniel J. 1921- . . . . **CLC 4**
See also CAAS 1; CANR 11; CA 33-36R; DLB 5

Berrigan, Edmund Joseph Michael, Jr.
1934-1983
See Berrigan, Ted
See also CANR 14; CA 61-64; obituary CA 110

Berrigan, Ted 1934-1983 . . . . **CLC 37**
See also Berrigan, Edmund Joseph Michael, Jr.
See also DLB 5

Berry, Chuck 1926- . . . . **CLC 17**

Berry, Wendell (Erdman)
1934- . . . . **CLC 4, 6, 8, 27, 46**
See also CA 73-76; DLB 5, 6

Berryman, John
1914-1972 . . . . . **CLC 1, 2, 3, 4, 6, 8, 10, 13, 25, 62**
See also CAP 1; CA 15-16; obituary CA 33-36R; CABS 2; DLB 48; CDALB 1941-1968

Bertolucci, Bernardo 1940- . . . . **CLC 16**
See also CA 106

Bertrand, Aloysius 1807-1841 . . . . **NCLC 31**

Bertran de Born c. 1140-1215 . . . . . **CMLC 5**

Bottoms, David 1949- . . . . CLC 53
See also CANR 22; CA 105; DLB-Y 83

Boucolon, Maryse 1937-
See Conde, Maryse
See also CA 110

Bourget, Paul (Charles Joseph)
1852-1935 . . . . TCLC 12
See also CA 107

Bourjaily, Vance (Nye) 1922- . . . . CLC 8, 62
See also CAAS 1; CANR 2; CA 1-4R;
DLB 2

Bourne, Randolph S(illiman)
1886-1918 . . . . TCLC 16
See also CA 117; DLB 63

Bova, Ben(jamin William) 1932- . . . . CLC 45
See also CLR 3; CANR 11; CA 5-8R;
SATA 6; DLB-Y 81

Bowen, Elizabeth (Dorothea Cole)
1899-1973 . . . . . CLC 1, 3, 6, 11, 15, 22;
SSC 3
See also CAP 2; CA 17-18;
obituary CA 41-44R; DLB 15

Bowering, George 1935- . . . . CLC 15, 47
See also CANR 10; CA 21-24R; DLB 53

Bowering, Marilyn R(uthe) 1949- . . . CLC 32
See also CA 101

Bowers, Edgar 1924- . . . . CLC 9
See also CANR 24; CA 5-8R; DLB 5

Bowie, David 1947- . . . . CLC 17
See also Jones, David Robert

Bowles, Jane (Sydney)
1917-1973 . . . . CLC 3, 68
See also CAP 2; CA 19-20;
obituary CA 41-44R

Bowles, Paul (Frederick)
1910- . . . . CLC 1, 2, 19, 53; SSC 3
See also CAAS 1; CANR 1, 19; CA 1-4R;
DLB 5, 6

Box, Edgar 1925-
See Vidal, Gore

Boyd, William 1952- . . . . CLC 28, 53
See also CA 114, 120

Boyle, Kay 1903- . . CLC 1, 5, 19, 58; SSC 5
See also CAAS 1; CA 13-16R; DLB 4, 9, 48

Boyle, Patrick 19??- . . . . CLC 19

Boyle, Thomas Coraghessan
1948- . . . . CLC 36, 55
See also CA 120; DLB-Y 86

Brackenridge, Hugh Henry
1748-1816 . . . . NCLC 7
See also DLB 11, 37

Bradbury, Edward P. 1939-
See Moorcock, Michael

Bradbury, Malcolm (Stanley)
1932- . . . . CLC 32, 61
See also CANR 1; CA 1-4R; DLB 14

Bradbury, Ray(mond Douglas)
1920- . . . . CLC 1, 3, 10, 15, 42
See also CANR 2; CA 1-4R; SATA 11;
DLB 2, 8

Bradford, Gamaliel 1863-1932 . . . . . TCLC 36
See also DLB 17

Bradley, David (Henry), Jr. 1950- . . CLC 23
See also BLC 1; CANR 26; CA 104;
DLB 33

Bradley, John Ed 1959- . . . . CLC 55

Bradley, Katherine Harris 1846-1914
See Field, Michael

Bradley, Marion Zimmer 1930- . . . . . CLC 30
See also CANR 7; CA 57-60; DLB 8

Bradstreet, Anne 1612-1672 . . . . LC 4
See also DLB 24; CDALB 1640-1865

Bragg, Melvyn 1939- . . . . CLC 10
See also CANR 10; CA 57-60; DLB 14

Braine, John (Gerard)
1922-1986 . . . . CLC 1, 3, 41
See also CANR 1; CA 1-4R;
obituary CA 120; DLB 15; DLB-Y 86

Braithwaite, William Stanley 1878-1962
See also BLC 1; CA 125; DLB 50, 54

Brammer, Billy Lee 1930?-1978
See Brammer, William

Brammer, William 1930?-1978 . . . . . CLC 31
See also obituary CA 77-80

Brancati, Vitaliano 1907-1954 . . . . . TCLC 12
See also CA 109

Brancato, Robin F(idler) 1936- . . . . . CLC 35
See also CANR 11; CA 69-72; SATA 23

Brand, Millen 1906-1980 . . . . CLC 7
See also CA 21-24R; obituary CA 97-100

Branden, Barbara 19??- . . . . CLC 44

Brandes, Georg (Morris Cohen)
1842-1927 . . . . TCLC 10
See also CA 105

Brandys, Kazimierz 1916- . . . . CLC 62

Branley, Franklyn M(ansfield)
1915- . . . . CLC 21
See also CLR 13; CANR 14; CA 33-36R;
SATA 4

Brathwaite, Edward 1930- . . . . CLC 11
See also CANR 11; CA 25-28R; DLB 53

Brautigan, Richard (Gary)
1935-1984 . . . . CLC 1, 3, 5, 9, 12, 34, 42
See also CA 53-56; obituary CA 113;
SATA 56; DLB 2, 5; DLB-Y 80, 84

Braverman, Kate 1950- . . . . CLC 67
See also CA 89-92

Brecht, (Eugen) Bertolt (Friedrich)
1898-1956 . . . . TCLC 1, 6, 13, 35
See also CA 104; DLB 56

Bremer, Fredrika 1801-1865 . . . . . NCLC 11

Brennan, Christopher John
1870-1932 . . . . TCLC 17
See also CA 117

Brennan, Maeve 1917- . . . . CLC 5
See also CA 81-84

Brentano, Clemens (Maria)
1778-1842 . . . . NCLC 1
See also DLB 90

Brenton, Howard 1942- . . . . CLC 31
See also CA 69-72; DLB 13

Breslin, James 1930-
See Breslin, Jimmy
See also CA 73-76

Breslin, Jimmy 1930- . . . . CLC 4, 43
See also Breslin, James

Bresson, Robert 1907- . . . . CLC 16
See also CA 110

Breton, Andre 1896-1966 . . . CLC 2, 9, 15, 54
See also CAP 2; CA 19-20;
obituary CA 25-28R; DLB 65

Breytenbach, Breyten 1939- . . . . . CLC 23, 37
See also CA 113, 129

Bridgers, Sue Ellen 1942- . . . . CLC 26
See also CANR 11; CA 65-68; SAAS 1;
SATA 22; DLB 52

Bridges, Robert 1844-1930 . . . . TCLC 1
See also CA 104; DLB 19

Bridie, James 1888-1951 . . . . TCLC 3
See also Mavor, Osborne Henry
See also DLB 10

Brin, David 1950- . . . . CLC 34
See also CANR 24; CA 102

Brink, Andre (Philippus)
1935- . . . . CLC 18, 36
See also CA 104

Brinsmead, H(esba) F(ay) 1922- . . . . CLC 21
See also CANR 10; CA 21-24R; SAAS 5;
SATA 18

Brittain, Vera (Mary) 1893?-1970 . . . CLC 23
See also CAP 1; CA 15-16;
obituary CA 25-28R

Broch, Hermann 1886-1951 . . . . TCLC 20
See also CA 117; DLB 85

Brock, Rose 1923-
See Hansen, Joseph

Brodkey, Harold 1930- . . . . CLC 56
See also CA 111

Brodsky, Iosif Alexandrovich 1940-
See Brodsky, Joseph (Alexandrovich)
See also CA 41-44R

Brodsky, Joseph (Alexandrovich)
1940- . . . . CLC 4, 6, 13, 36, 50
See also Brodsky, Iosif Alexandrovich

Brodsky, Michael (Mark) 1948- . . . . CLC 19
See also CANR 18; CA 102

Bromell, Henry 1947- . . . . CLC 5
See also CANR 9; CA 53-56

Bromfield, Louis (Brucker)
1896-1956 . . . . TCLC 11
See also CA 107; DLB 4, 9

Broner, E(sther) M(asserman)
1930- . . . . CLC 19
See also CANR 8, 25; CA 17-20R; DLB 28

Bronk, William 1918- . . . . CLC 10
See also CANR 23; CA 89-92

Bronte, Anne 1820-1849 . . . . NCLC 4
See also DLB 21

Bronte, Charlotte
1816-1855 . . . . NCLC 3, 8, 33
See also DLB 21

Bronte, (Jane) Emily 1818-1848 . . NCLC 16
See also DLB 21, 32

Brooke, Frances 1724-1789 . . . . LC 6
See also DLB 39

Brooke, Henry 1703?-1783 . . . . LC 1
See also DLB 39

Brooke, Rupert (Chawner)
1887-1915 . . . . TCLC 2, 7
See also CA 104; DLB 19

Brooke-Rose, Christine 1926- . . . . . . CLC 40
See also CA 13-16R; DLB 14

Clark, Al C. 1937?-1974
See Goines, Donald

Clark, (Robert) Brian 1932-........ CLC 29
See also CA 41-44R

Clark, Eleanor 1913- .... CLC 5, 19
See also CA 9-12R; DLB 6

Clark, John Pepper 1935- .... CLC 38
See also BLC 1; CANR 16; CA 65-68

Clark, Mavis Thorpe 1912?- .... CLC 12
See also CANR 8; CA 57-60; SAAS 5;
SATA 8

Clark, Walter Van Tilburg
1909-1971 .... CLC 28
See also CA 9-12R; obituary CA 33-36R;
SATA 8; DLB 9

Clarke, Arthur C(harles)
1917- ...... CLC 1, 4, 13, 18, 35; SSC 3
See also CANR 2; CA 1-4R; SATA 13

Clarke, Austin 1896-1974........ CLC 6, 9
See also BLC 1; CANR 14; CAP 2;
CA 29-32; obituary CA 49-52; DLB 10,
20, 53

Clarke, Austin (Ardinel) C(hesterfield)
1934- .... CLC 8, 53
See also CANR 14; CA 25-28R; DLB 53

Clarke, Gillian 1937- .... CLC 61
See also CA 106; DLB 40

Clarke, Marcus (Andrew Hislop)
1846-1881 .... NCLC 19

Clarke, Shirley 1925-............ CLC 16

Clash, The .... CLC 30

Claudel, Paul (Louis Charles Marie)
1868-1955 .... TCLC 2, 10
See also CA 104

Clavell, James (duMaresq)
1924- .... CLC 6, 25
See also CANR 26; CA 25-28R

Clayman. Gregory 1974?-.......... CLC 65

Cleaver, (Leroy) Eldridge 1935- .... CLC 30
See also BLC 1; CANR 16; CA 21-24R

Cleese, John 1939-.............. CLC 21
See also Monty Python
See also CA 112, 116

Cleland, John 1709-1789 .... LC 2
See also DLB 39

Clemens, Samuel Langhorne
1835-1910 ..... TCLC 6, 12, 19; SSC 6
See also Twain, Mark
See also YABC 2; CA 104; DLB 11, 12, 23,
64, 74; CDALB 1865-1917

Cliff, Jimmy 1948-.............. CLC 21

Clifton, Lucille (Thelma)
1936- .... CLC 19, 66
See also BLC 1; CLR 5; CANR 2, 24;
CA 49-52; SATA 20; DLB 5, 41

Clough, Arthur Hugh 1819-1861.. NCLC 27
See also DLB 32

Clutha, Janet Paterson Frame 1924-
See Frame (Clutha), Janet (Paterson)
See also CANR 2; CA 1-4R

Coburn, D(onald) L(ee) 1938- ...... CLC 10
See also CA 89-92

Cocteau, Jean (Maurice Eugene Clement)
1889-1963 .... CLC 1, 8, 15, 16, 43
See also CAP 2; CA 25-28; DLB 65

Codrescu, Andrei 1946- .... CLC 46
See also CANR 13; CA 33-36R

Coetzee, J(ohn) M. 1940-.... CLC 23, 33, 66
See also CA 77-80

Cohen, Arthur A(llen)
1928-1986 .... CLC 7, 31
See also CANR 1, 17; CA 1-4R;
obituary CA 120; DLB 28

Cohen, Leonard (Norman)
1934- .... CLC 3, 38
See also CANR 14; CA 21-24R; DLB 53

Cohen, Matt 1942-............. CLC 19
See also CA 61-64; DLB 53

Cohen-Solal, Annie 19??-.......... CLC 50

Colegate, Isabel 1931- .... CLC 36
See also CANR 8, 22; CA 17-20R; DLB 14

Coleman, Emmett 1938-
See Reed, Ishmael

Coleridge, Samuel Taylor
1772-1834 .... NCLC 9

Coleridge, Sara 1802-1852....... NCLC 31

Coles, Don 1928- .... CLC 46
See also CA 115

Colette (Sidonie-Gabrielle)
1873-1954 .... TCLC 1, 5, 16
See also CA 104; DLB 65

Collett, (Jacobine) Camilla (Wergeland)
1813-1895 .... NCLC 22

Collier, Christopher 1930-........ CLC 30
See also CANR 13; CA 33-36R; SATA 16

Collier, James L(incoln) 1928- ... CLC 30
See also CLR 3; CANR 4; CA 9-12R;
SATA 8

Collier, Jeremy 1650-1726........... LC 6

Collins, Hunt 1926-
See Hunter, Evan

Collins, Linda 19??- .... CLC 44
See also CA 125

Collins, Tom 1843-1912
See Furphy, Joseph

Collins, (William) Wilkie
1824-1889 .... NCLC 1, 18
See also DLB 18, 70

Collins, William 1721-1759 .... LC 4

Colman, George 1909-1981
See Glassco, John

Colter, Cyrus 1910- .... CLC 58
See also CANR 10; CA 65-68; DLB 33

Colton, James 1923-
See Hansen, Joseph

Colum, Padraic 1881-1972........ CLC 28
See also CA 73-76; obituary CA 33-36R;
SATA 15; DLB 19

Colvin, James 1939-
See Moorcock, Michael

Colwin, Laurie 1945- .... CLC 5, 13, 23
See also CANR 20; CA 89-92; DLB-Y 80

Comfort, Alex(ander) 1920-......... CLC 7
See also CANR 1; CA 1-4R

Compton-Burnett, Ivy
1892-1969 .... CLC 1, 3, 10, 15, 34
See also CANR 4; CA 1-4R;
obituary CA 25-28R; DLB 36

Comstock, Anthony 1844-1915 .... TCLC 13
See also CA 110

Conde, Maryse 1937-............. CLC 52
See also Boucolon, Maryse

Condon, Richard (Thomas)
1915- .... CLC 4, 6, 8, 10, 45
See also CAAS 1; CANR 2, 23; CA 1-4R

Congreve, William 1670-1729 ... LC 5; DC 2
See also DLB 39, 84

Connell, Evan S(helby), Jr.
1924-.................... CLC 4, 6, 45
See also CAAS 2; CANR 2; CA 1-4R;
DLB 2; DLB-Y 81

Connelly, Marc(us Cook)
1890-1980 .... CLC 7
See also CA 85-88; obituary CA 102;
obituary SATA 25; DLB 7; DLB-Y 80

Conner, Ralph 1860-1937........ TCLC 31

Conrad, Joseph
1857-1924 ...... TCLC 1, 6, 13, 25, 43;
SSC 9
See also CA 104, 131; SATA 27; DLB 10,
34, 98

Conrad, Robert Arnold 1904-1961
See Hart, Moss

Conroy, Pat 1945-................ CLC 30
See also CANR 24; CA 85-88; DLB 6

Constant (de Rebecque), (Henri) Benjamin
1767-1830 .... NCLC 6

Cook, Michael 1933- .... CLC 58
See also CA 93-96; DLB 53

Cook, Robin 1940- .... CLC 14
See also CA 108, 111

Cooke, Elizabeth 1948- .... CLC 55

Cooke, John Esten 1830-1886..... NCLC 5
See also DLB 3

Cooney, Ray 19??- .... CLC 62

Cooper, Edith Emma 1862-1913
See Field, Michael

Cooper, J. California 19??- .... CLC 56
See also CA 125

Cooper, James Fenimore
1789-1851 .... NCLC 1, 27
See also SATA 19; DLB 3;
CDALB 1640-1865

Coover, Robert (Lowell)
1932- .... CLC 3, 7, 15, 32, 46
See also CANR 3; CA 45-48; DLB 2;
DLB-Y 81

Copeland, Stewart (Armstrong)
1952-........................ CLC 26
See also The Police

Coppard, A(lfred) E(dgar)
1878-1957 .... TCLC 5
See also YABC 1; CA 114

Coppee, Francois 1842-1908 ...... TCLC 25

Coppola, Francis Ford 1939-....... CLC 16
See also CA 77-80; DLB 44

Corcoran, Barbara 1911-. . . . . CLC 17
See also CAAS 2; CANR 11; CA 21-24R;
SATA 3; DLB 52

Corman, Cid 1924-. . . . . CLC 9
See also Corman, Sidney
See also CAAS 2; DLB 5

Corman, Sidney 1924-
See Corman, Cid
See also CA 85-88

Cormier, Robert (Edmund)
1925-. . . . . CLC 12, 30
See also CLR 12; CANR 5, 23; CA 1-4R;
SATA 10, 45; DLB 52

Corn, Alfred (Dewitt III) 1943-. . . . . CLC 33
See also CA 104; DLB-Y 80

Cornwell, David (John Moore)
1931-. . . . . CLC 9, 15
See also le Carre, John
See also CANR 13; CA 5-8R

Corso, (Nunzio) Gregory 1930-. . . CLC 1, 11
See also CA 5-8R; DLB 5, 16

Cortazar, Julio
1914-1984 . . . . . CLC 2, 3, 5, 10, 13, 15,
33, 34; SSC 7
See also CANR 12; CA 21-24R

Corvo, Baron 1860-1913
See Rolfe, Frederick (William Serafino
Austin Lewis Mary)

Cosic, Dobrica 1921-. . . . . CLC 14
See also CA 122

Costain, Thomas B(ertram)
1885-1965 . . . . CLC 30
See also CA 5-8R; obituary CA 25-28R;
DLB 9

Costantini, Humberto 1924?-1987. . . CLC 49
See also obituary CA 122

Costello, Elvis 1955-. . . . . CLC 21

Cotter, Joseph Seamon, Sr.
1861-1949 . . . . TCLC 28
See also BLC 1; CA 124; DLB 50

Couperus, Louis (Marie Anne)
1863-1923 . . . . TCLC 15
See also CA 115

Courtenay, Bryce 1933-. . . . . CLC 59

Cousteau, Jacques-Yves 1910-. . . . . . CLC 30
See also CANR 15; CA 65-68; SATA 38

Coward, (Sir) Noel (Pierce)
1899-1973 . . . . CLC 1, 9, 29, 51
See also CAP 2; CA 17-18;
obituary CA 41-44R; DLB 10

Cowley, Malcolm 1898-1989 . . . . CLC 39
See also CANR 3; CA 5-6R;
obituary CA 128; DLB 4, 48; DLB-Y 81

Cowper, William 1731-1800. . . . . . . NCLC 8

Cox, William Trevor 1928-. . . . . . CLC 9, 14
See also Trevor, William
See also CANR 4; CA 9-12R

Cozzens, James Gould
1903-1978 . . . . CLC 1, 4, 11
See also CANR 19; CA 9-12R;
obituary CA 81-84; DLB 9; DLB-Y 84;
DLB-DS 2; CDALB 1941-1968

Crabbe, George 1754-1832. . . . . . NCLC 26

Crace, Douglas 1944-. . . . . CLC 58

Crane, (Harold) Hart
1899-1932 . . . . TCLC 2, 5; PC 3
See also CA 127; brief entry CA 104;
DLB 4, 48; CDALB 1917-1929

Crane, R(onald) S(almon)
1886-1967 . . . . CLC 27
See also CA 85-88; DLB 63

Crane, Stephen
1871-1900 . . . . . TCLC 11, 17, 32; SSC 7
See also YABC 2; CA 109; DLB 12, 54, 78;
CDALB 1865-1917

Craven, Margaret 1901-1980. . . . . . CLC 17
See also CA 103

Crawford, F(rancis) Marion
1854-1909 . . . . TCLC 10
See also CA 107; DLB 71

Crawford, Isabella Valancy
1850-1887 . . . . NCLC 12
See also DLB 92

Crayencour, Marguerite de 1903-1987
See Yourcenar, Marguerite

Creasey, John 1908-1973. . . . . CLC 11
See also CANR 8; CA 5-8R;
obituary CA 41-44R; DLB 77

Crebillon, Claude Prosper Jolyot de (fils)
1707-1777 . . . . LC 1

Creeley, Robert (White)
1926-. . . . . CLC 1, 2, 4, 8, 11, 15, 36
See also CANR 23; CA 1-4R; DLB 5, 16

Crews, Harry (Eugene)
1935-. . . . . CLC 6, 23, 49
See also CANR 20; CA 25-28R; DLB 6

Crichton, (John) Michael
1942-. . . . . CLC 2, 6, 54
See also CANR 13; CA 25-28R; SATA 9;
DLB-Y 81

Crispin, Edmund 1921-1978. . . . . . . CLC 22
See also Montgomery, Robert Bruce
See also DLB 87

Cristofer, Michael 1946-. . . . . CLC 28
See also CA 110; DLB 7

Croce, Benedetto 1866-1952 . . . . . . TCLC 37
See also CA 120

Crockett, David (Davy)
1786-1836 . . . . NCLC 8
See also DLB 3, 11

Croker, John Wilson 1780-1857 . . NCLC 10

Cronin, A(rchibald) J(oseph)
1896-1981 . . . . CLC 32
See also CANR 5; CA 1-4R;
obituary CA 102; obituary SATA 25, 47

Cross, Amanda 1926-
See Heilbrun, Carolyn G(old)

Crothers, Rachel 1878-1953. . . . . . . TCLC 19
See also CA 113; DLB 7

Crowley, Aleister 1875-1947 . . . . TCLC 7
See also CA 104

Crowley, John 1942-
See also CA 61-64; DLB-Y 82

Crumb, Robert 1943-. . . . . CLC 17
See also CA 106

Cryer, Gretchen 1936?-. . . . . CLC 21
See also CA 114, 123

Csath, Geza 1887-1919. . . . . TCLC 13
See also CA 111

Cudlip, David 1933-. . . . . CLC 34

Cullen, Countee 1903-1946 . . . . . TCLC 4, 37
See also BLC 1; CA 108, 124; SATA 18;
DLB 4, 48, 51; CDALB 1917-1929

Cummings, E(dward) E(stlin)
1894-1962 . . . . . . CLC 1, 3, 8, 12, 15, 68
See also CANR 31; CA 73-76; DLB 4, 48;
CDALB 1929-1941

Cunha, Euclides (Rodrigues) da
1866-1909 . . . . TCLC 24
See also CA 123

Cunningham, J(ames) V(incent)
1911-1985 . . . . CLC 3, 31
See also CANR 1; CA 1-4R;
obituary CA 115; DLB 5

Cunningham, Julia (Woolfolk)
1916-. . . . . CLC 12
See also CANR 4, 19; CA 9-12R; SAAS 2;
SATA 1, 26

Cunningham, Michael 1952-. . . . . . . CLC 34

Currie, Ellen 19??-. . . . . CLC 44

Dabrowska, Maria (Szumska)
1889-1965 . . . . CLC 15
See also CA 106

Dabydeen, David 1956?-. . . . . CLC 34
See also CA 106

Dacey, Philip 1939-. . . . . CLC 51
See also CANR 14; CA 37-40R

Dagerman, Stig (Halvard)
1923-1954 . . . . TCLC 17
See also CA 117

Dahl, Roald 1916-. . . . . CLC 1, 6, 18
See also CLR 1, 7; CANR 6; CA 1-4R;
SATA 1, 26

Dahlberg, Edward 1900-1977. . . CLC 1, 7, 14
See also CA 9-12R; obituary CA 69-72;
DLB 48

Daly, Elizabeth 1878-1967. . . . . CLC 52
See also CAP 2; CA 23-24;
obituary CA 25-28R

Daly, Maureen 1921-. . . . . CLC 17
See also McGivern, Maureen Daly
See also SAAS 1; SATA 2

Daniken, Erich von 1935-
See Von Daniken, Erich

Dannay, Frederic 1905-1982
See Queen, Ellery
See also CANR 1; CA 1-4R;
obituary CA 107

D'Annunzio, Gabriele
1863-1938 . . . . TCLC 6, 40
See also CA 104

Dante (Alighieri)
See Alighieri, Dante

Danziger, Paula 1944-. . . . . CLC 21
See also CLR 20; CA 112, 115; SATA 30,
36

Dario, Ruben 1867-1916 . . . . TCLC 4
See also Sarmiento, Felix Ruben Garcia
See also CA 104

Darley, George 1795-1846. . . . . NCLC 2

Daryush, Elizabeth 1887-1977.... **CLC 6, 19**
See also CANR 3; CA 49-52; DLB 20

Daudet, (Louis Marie) Alphonse
1840-1897 .... **NCLC 1**

Daumal, Rene 1908-1944......... **TCLC 14**
See also CA 114

Davenport, Guy (Mattison, Jr.)
1927- .... **CLC 6, 14, 38**
See also CANR 23; CA 33-36R

Davidson, Donald (Grady)
1893-1968 .... **CLC 2, 13, 19**
See also CANR 4; CA 5-8R;
obituary CA 25-28R; DLB 45

Davidson, John 1857-1909........ **TCLC 24**
See also CA 118; DLB 19

Davidson, Sara 1943-.............. **CLC 9**
See also CA 81-84

Davie, Donald (Alfred)
1922- .... **CLC 5, 8, 10, 31**
See also CAAS 3; CANR 1; CA 1-4R;
DLB 27

Davies, Ray(mond Douglas) 1944- .. **CLC 21**
See also CA 116

Davies, Rhys 1903-1978........... **CLC 23**
See also CANR 4; CA 9-12R;
obituary CA 81-84

Davies, (William) Robertson
1913- .... **CLC 2, 7, 13, 25, 42**
See also CANR 17; CA 33-36R; DLB 68

Davies, W(illiam) H(enry)
1871-1940 .... **TCLC 5**
See also CA 104; DLB 19

Davis, Frank Marshall 1905-1987
See also BLC 1; CA 123, 125; DLB 51

Davis, H(arold) L(enoir)
1896-1960 .... **CLC 49**
See also obituary CA 89-92; DLB 9

Davis, Rebecca (Blaine) Harding
1831-1910 .... **TCLC 6**
See also CA 104; DLB 74

Davis, Richard Harding
1864-1916 .... **TCLC 24**
See also CA 114; DLB 12, 23, 78, 79

Davison, Frank Dalby 1893-1970 ... **CLC 15**
See also obituary CA 116

Davison, Peter 1928- .... **CLC 28**
See also CAAS 4; CANR 3; CA 9-12R;
DLB 5

Davys, Mary 1674-1732............ **LC 1**
See also DLB 39

Dawson, Fielding 1930- .... **CLC 6**
See also CA 85-88

Day, Clarence (Shepard, Jr.)
1874-1935 .... **TCLC 25**
See also CA 108; DLB 11

Day, Thomas 1748-1789............. **LC 1**
See also YABC 1; DLB 39

Day Lewis, C(ecil)
1904-1972 .... **CLC 1, 6, 10**
See also CAP 1; CA 15-16;
obituary CA 33-36R; DLB 15, 20

Dazai Osamu 1909-1948 .... **TCLC 11**
See also Tsushima Shuji

De Crayencour, Marguerite 1903-1987
See Yourcenar, Marguerite

Deer, Sandra 1940-.............. **CLC 45**

De Ferrari, Gabriella 19??- .... **CLC 65**

Defoe, Daniel 1660?-1731 .... **LC 1**
See also SATA 22; DLB 39

De Hartog, Jan 1914-............. **CLC 19**
See also CANR 1; CA 1-4R

Deighton, Len 1929-....... **CLC 4, 7, 22, 46**
See also Deighton, Leonard Cyril
See also DLB 87

Deighton, Leonard Cyril 1929-
See Deighton, Len
See also CANR 19; CA 9-12R

De la Mare, Walter (John)
1873-1956 .... **TCLC 4**
See also CLR 23; CA 110; SATA 16;
DLB 19

Delaney, Shelagh 1939-........... **CLC 29**
See also CA 17-20R; DLB 13

Delany, Mary (Granville Pendarves)
1700-1788 .... **LC 12**

Delany, Samuel R(ay, Jr.)
1942- .... **CLC 8, 14, 38**
See also BLC 1; CANR 27; CA 81-84;
DLB 8, 33

de la Ramee, Marie Louise 1839-1908
See Ouida
See also SATA 20

De la Roche, Mazo 1885-1961 ..... **CLC 14**
See also CA 85-88; DLB 68

Delbanco, Nicholas (Franklin)
1942- .... **CLC 6, 13**
See also CAAS 2; CA 17-20R; DLB 6

del Castillo, Michel 1933- .... **CLC 38**
See also CA 109

Deledda, Grazia 1871-1936 ...... **TCLC 23**
See also CA 123

Delibes (Setien), Miguel 1920- ... **CLC 8, 18**
See also CANR 1; CA 45-48

DeLillo, Don
1936- .... **CLC 8, 10, 13, 27, 39, 54**
See also CANR 21; CA 81-84; DLB 6

De Lisser, H(erbert) G(eorge)
1878-1944 .... **TCLC 12**
See also CA 109

Deloria, Vine (Victor), Jr. 1933-.... **CLC 21**
See also CANR 5, 20; CA 53-56; SATA 21

Del Vecchio, John M(ichael)
1947- .... **CLC 29**
See also CA 110

de Man, Paul 1919-1983 .... **CLC 55**
See also obituary CA 111; DLB 67

De Marinis, Rick 1934-........... **CLC 54**
See also CANR 9, 25; CA 57-60

Demby, William 1922-........... **CLC 53**
See also BLC 1; CA 81-84; DLB 33

Denby, Edwin (Orr) 1903-1983 ..... **CLC 48**
See also obituary CA 110

Dennis, John 1657-1734............ **LC 11**

Dennis, Nigel (Forbes) 1912-........ **CLC 8**
See also CA 25-28R; obituary CA 129;
DLB 13, 15

De Palma, Brian 1940-............ **CLC 20**
See also CA 109

De Quincey, Thomas 1785-1859 ... **NCLC 4**

Deren, Eleanora 1908-1961
See Deren, Maya
See also obituary CA 111

Deren, Maya 1908-1961 .... **CLC 16**
See also Deren, Eleanora

Derleth, August (William)
1909-1971 .... **CLC 31**
See also CANR 4; CA 1-4R;
obituary CA 29-32R; SATA 5; DLB 9

Derrida, Jacques 1930-........... **CLC 24**
See also CA 124, 127

Desai, Anita 1937- .... **CLC 19, 37**
See also CA 81-84

De Saint-Luc, Jean 1909-1981
See Glassco, John

De Sica, Vittorio 1902-1974 .... **CLC 20**
See also obituary CA 117

Desnos, Robert 1900-1945........ **TCLC 22**
See also CA 121

Destouches, Louis-Ferdinand-Auguste
1894-1961
See Celine, Louis-Ferdinand
See also CA 85-88

Deutsch, Babette 1895-1982 .... **CLC 18**
See also CANR 4; CA 1-4R;
obituary CA 108; SATA 1;
obituary SATA 33; DLB 45

Devenant, William 1606-1649 ...... **LC 13**

Devkota, Laxmiprasad
1909-1959 .... **TCLC 23**
See also CA 123

DeVoto, Bernard (Augustine)
1897-1955 .... **TCLC 29**
See also CA 113; DLB 9

De Vries, Peter
1910- .... **CLC 1, 2, 3, 7, 10, 28, 46**
See also CA 17-20R; DLB 6; DLB-Y 82

Dexter, Pete 1943-............ **CLC 34, 55**
See also CA 127

Diamano, Silmang 1906-
See Senghor, Leopold Sedar

Diamond, Neil (Leslie) 1941-....... **CLC 30**
See also CA 108

Dick, Philip K(indred)
1928-1982 .... **CLC 10, 30**
See also CANR 2, 16; CA 49-52;
obituary CA 106; DLB 8

Dickens, Charles
1812-1870 .... **NCLC 3, 8, 18, 26**
See also SATA 15; DLB 21, 55, 70

Dickey, James (Lafayette)
1923- .... **CLC 1, 2, 4, 7, 10, 15, 47**
See also CANR 10; CA 9-12R; CABS 2;
DLB 5; DLB-Y 82; DLB-DS 7

Dickey, William 1928-........... **CLC 3, 28**
See also CANR 24; CA 9-12R; DLB 5

Dickinson, Charles 1952-.......... **CLC 49**

Dickinson, Emily (Elizabeth)
1830-1886 .... **NCLC 21; PC 1**
See also SATA 29; DLB 1;
CDALB 1865-1917

Author Index

Author Index

Gunn, William Harrison 1934-1989
   See Gunn, Bill
   See also CANR 12, 25; CA 13-16R;
      obituary CA 128

Gunnars, Kristjana 1948-......... CLC 69
   See also CA 113; DLB 60

Gurney, A(lbert) R(amsdell), Jr.
   1930-................. CLC 32, 50, 54
   See also CA 77-80

Gurney, Ivor (Bertie) 1890-1937... TCLC 33

Gustafson, Ralph (Barker) 1909-.... CLC 36
   See also CANR 8; CA 21-24R; DLB 88

Guthrie, A(lfred) B(ertram), Jr.
   1901-...................... CLC 23
   See also CA 57-60; DLB 6

Guthrie, Woodrow Wilson 1912-1967
   See Guthrie, Woody
   See also CA 113; obituary CA 93-96

Guthrie, Woody 1912-1967 .... CLC 35
   See also Guthrie, Woodrow Wilson

Guy, Rosa (Cuthbert) 1928-........ CLC 26
   See also CLR 13; CANR 14; CA 17-20R;
      SATA 14; DLB 33

Haavikko, Paavo (Juhani)
   1931-.................... CLC 18, 34
   See also CA 106

Hacker, Marilyn 1942- .... CLC 5, 9, 23
   See also CA 77-80

Haggard, (Sir) H(enry) Rider
   1856-1925 .... TCLC 11
   See also CA 108; SATA 16; DLB 70

Haig-Brown, Roderick L(angmere)
   1908-1976 .... CLC 21
   See also CANR 4; CA 5-8R;
      obituary CA 69-72; SATA 12; DLB 88

Hailey, Arthur 1920- .... CLC 5
   See also CANR 2; CA 1-4R; DLB-Y 82

Hailey, Elizabeth Forsythe 1938-... CLC 40
   See also CAAS 1; CANR 15; CA 93-96

Haines, John 1924-.............. CLC 58
   See also CANR 13; CA 19-20R; DLB 5

Haldeman, Joe 1943-.............. CLC 61
   See also CA 53-56; DLB 8

Haley, Alex (Palmer) 1921-...... CLC 8, 12
   See also BLC 2; CA 77-80; DLB 38

Haliburton, Thomas Chandler
   1796-1865 .... NCLC 15
   See also DLB 11

Hall, Donald (Andrew, Jr.)
   1928-........... CLC 1, 13, 37, 59
   See also CAAS 7; CANR 2; CA 5-8R;
      SATA 23; DLB 5

Hall, James Norman 1887-1951 ... TCLC 23
   See also CA 123; SATA 21

Hall, (Marguerite) Radclyffe
   1886-1943 .... TCLC 12
   See also CA 110

Hall, Rodney 1935- .... CLC 51
   See also CA 109

Halpern, Daniel 1945- .... CLC 14
   See also CA 33-36R

Hamburger, Michael (Peter Leopold)
   1924-..................... CLC 5, 14
   See also CAAS 4; CANR 2; CA 5-8R;
      DLB 27

Hamill, Pete 1935-.............. CLC 10
   See also CANR 18; CA 25-28R

Hamilton, Edmond 1904-1977....... CLC 1
   See also CANR 3; CA 1-4R; DLB 8

Hamilton, Gail 1911-
   See Corcoran, Barbara

Hamilton, Ian 1938-.............. CLC 55
   See also CA 106; DLB 40

Hamilton, Mollie 1909?-
   See Kaye, M(ary) M(argaret)

Hamilton, (Anthony Walter) Patrick
   1904-1962 .... CLC 51
   See also obituary CA 113; DLB 10

Hamilton, Virginia (Esther) 1936-... CLC 26
   See also CLR 1, 11; CANR 20; CA 25-28R;
      SATA 4; DLB 33, 52

Hammett, (Samuel) Dashiell
   1894-1961 .... CLC 3, 5, 10, 19, 47
   See also CA 81-84; DLB-DS 6

Hammon, Jupiter 1711?-1800? .... NCLC 5
   See also BLC 2; DLB 31, 50, 31, 50

Hamner, Earl (Henry), Jr. 1923- ... CLC 12
   See also CA 73-76; DLB 6

Hampton, Christopher (James)
   1946-....................... CLC 4
   See also CA 25-28R; DLB 13

Hamsun, Knut 1859-1952....... TCLC 2, 14
   See also Pedersen, Knut

Handke, Peter 1942- .. CLC 5, 8, 10, 15, 38
   See also CA 77-80; DLB 85

Hanley, James 1901-1985 ... CLC 3, 5, 8, 13
   See also CA 73-76; obituary CA 117

Hannah, Barry 1942-.......... CLC 23, 38
   See also CA 108, 110; DLB 6

Hansberry, Lorraine (Vivian)
   1930-1965 .... CLC 17, 62; DC 2
   See also BLC 2; CA 109;
      obituary CA 25-28R; CABS 3; DLB 7, 38;
      CDALB 1941-1968

Hansen, Joseph 1923-............. CLC 38
   See also CANR 16; CA 29-32R

Hansen, Martin 1909-1955 .... TCLC 32

Hanson, Kenneth O(stlin) 1922-.... CLC 13
   See also CANR 7; CA 53-56

Hardenberg, Friedrich (Leopold Freiherr) von
   1772-1801
   See Novalis

Hardwick, Elizabeth 1916- .... CLC 13
   See also CANR 3; CA 5-8R; DLB 6

Hardy, Thomas
   1840-1928 ... TCLC 4, 10, 18, 32; SSC 2
   See also CA 104, 123; SATA 25; DLB 18,
      19

Hare, David 1947- .... CLC 29, 58
   See also CA 97-100; DLB 13

Harlan, Louis R(udolph) 1922-..... CLC 34
   See also CANR 25; CA 21-24R

Harling, Robert 1951?-........... CLC 53

Harmon, William (Ruth) 1938-..... CLC 38
   See also CANR 14; CA 33-36R

Harper, Frances Ellen Watkins
   1825-1911 .... TCLC 14
   See also BLC 2; CA 125;
      brief entry CA 111; DLB 50

Harper, Michael S(teven) 1938- .. CLC 7, 22
   See also CANR 24; CA 33-36R; DLB 41

Harris, Christie (Lucy Irwin)
   1907-..................... CLC 12
   See also CANR 6; CA 5-8R; SATA 6;
      DLB 88

Harris, Frank 1856-1931........ TCLC 24
   See also CAAS 1; CA 109

Harris, George Washington
   1814-1869 .... NCLC 23
   See also DLB 3, 11

Harris, Joel Chandler 1848-1908 ... TCLC 2
   See also YABC 1; CA 104; DLB 11, 23, 42,
      78, 91

Harris, John (Wyndham Parkes Lucas)
   Beynon 1903-1969 .... CLC 19
   See also Wyndham, John
   See also CA 102; obituary CA 89-92

Harris, MacDonald 1921-.......... CLC 9
   See also Heiney, Donald (William)

Harris, Mark 1922- .... CLC 19
   See also CAAS 3; CANR 2; CA 5-8R;
      DLB 2; DLB-Y 80

Harris, (Theodore) Wilson 1921-.... CLC 25
   See also CANR 11, 27; CA 65-68

Harrison, Harry (Max) 1925-...... CLC 42
   See also CANR 5, 21; CA 1-4R; SATA 4;
      DLB 8

Harrison, James (Thomas) 1937- ... CLC 66
   See Harrison, Jim
   See also CANR 8; CA 13-16R

Harrison, Jim 1937-........ CLC 6, 14, 33
   See also Harrison, James (Thomas)
   See also DLB-Y 82

Harrison, Tony 1937-............ CLC 43
   See also CA 65-68; DLB 40

Harriss, Will(ard Irvin) 1922-...... CLC 34
   See also CA 111

Hart, Moss 1904-1961 .... CLC 66
   See also Conrad, Robert Arnold
   See also obituary CA 89-92; DLB 7

Harte, (Francis) Bret(t)
   1836?-1902......... TCLC 1, 25; SSC 8
   See also brief entry CA 104; SATA 26;
      DLB 12, 64, 74, 79; CDALB 1865-1917

Hartley, L(eslie) P(oles)
   1895-1972 .... CLC 2, 22
   See also CA 45-48; obituary CA 37-40R;
      DLB 15

Hartman, Geoffrey H. 1929-...... CLC 27
   See also CA 117, 125; DLB 67

Haruf, Kent 19??-................ CLC 34

Harwood, Ronald 1934-........... CLC 32
   See also CANR 4; CA 1-4R; DLB 13

Hasegawa Tatsunosuke 1864-1909
   See Futabatei Shimei

Hasek, Jaroslav (Matej Frantisek)
   1883-1923 .... TCLC 4
   See also CA 104, 129

Hass, Robert 1941-........... CLC 18, 39
   See also CANR 30; CA 111

Higgins, George V(incent)
1939- . . . . CLC 4, 7, 10, 18
See also CAAS 5; CANR 17; CA 77-80;
DLB 2; DLB-Y 81

Higginson, Thomas Wentworth
1823-1911 . . . . TCLC 36
See also DLB 1, 64

Highsmith, (Mary) Patricia
1921- . . . . CLC 2, 4, 14, 42
See also CANR 1, 20; CA 1-4R

Highwater, Jamake 1942- . . . . CLC 12
See also CLR 17; CAAS 7; CANR 10;
CA 65-68; SATA 30, 32; DLB 52;
DLB-Y 85

Hijuelos, Oscar 1951- . . . . CLC 65
See also CA 123

Hikmet (Ran), Nazim 1902-1963 . . . . CLC 40
See also obituary CA 93-96

Hildesheimer, Wolfgang 1916- . . . . . CLC 49
See also CA 101; DLB 69

Hill, Geoffrey (William)
1932- . . . . CLC 5, 8, 18, 45
See also CANR 21; CA 81-84; DLB 40

Hill, George Roy 1922- . . . . CLC 26
See also CA 110, 122

Hill, Susan B. 1942- . . . . CLC 4
See also CANR 29; CA 33-36R; DLB 14

Hillerman, Tony 1925- . . . . CLC 62
See also CANR 21; CA 29-32R; SATA 6

Hilliard, Noel (Harvey) 1929- . . . . . . CLC 15
See also CANR 7; CA 9-12R

Hillis, Richard Lyle 1956-
See Hillis, Rick

Hillis, Rick 1956- . . . . CLC 66
See also Hillis, Richard Lyle

Hilton, James 1900-1954 . . . . TCLC 21
See also CA 108; SATA 34; DLB 34, 77

Himes, Chester (Bomar)
1909-1984 . . . . CLC 2, 4, 7, 18, 58
See also BLC 2; CANR 22; CA 25-28R;
obituary CA 114; DLB 2, 76

Hinde, Thomas 1926- . . . . CLC 6, 11
See also Chitty, (Sir) Thomas Willes

Hine, (William) Daryl 1936- . . . . CLC 15
See also CANR 1, 20; CA 1-4R; DLB 60

Hinton, S(usan) E(loise) 1950- . . . . . CLC 30
See also CLR 3, 23; CA 81-84; SATA 19,
58; AAYA 2

Hippius (Merezhkovsky), Zinaida
(Nikolayevna) 1869-1945 . . . . . . TCLC 9
See also Gippius, Zinaida (Nikolayevna)

Hiraoka, Kimitake 1925-1970
See Mishima, Yukio
See also CA 97-100; obituary CA 29-32R

Hirsch, Edward (Mark) 1950- . . . CLC 31, 50
See also CANR 20; CA 104

Hitchcock, (Sir) Alfred (Joseph)
1899-1980 . . . . CLC 16
See also obituary CA 97-100; SATA 27;
obituary SATA 24

Hoagland, Edward 1932- . . . . CLC 28
See also CANR 2; CA 1-4R; SATA 51;
DLB 6

Hoban, Russell C(onwell) 1925- . . CLC 7, 25
See also CLR 3; CANR 23; CA 5-8R;
SATA 1, 40; DLB 52

Hobson, Laura Z(ametkin)
1900-1986 . . . . CLC 7, 25
See also CA 17-20R; obituary CA 118;
SATA 52; DLB 28

Hochhuth, Rolf 1931- . . . . CLC 4, 11, 18
See also CA 5-8R

Hochman, Sandra 1936- . . . . CLC 3, 8
See also CA 5-8R; DLB 5

Hochwalder, Fritz 1911-1986 . . . . . . CLC 36
See also CA 29-32R; obituary CA 120

Hocking, Mary (Eunice) 1921- . . . . . CLC 13
See also CANR 18; CA 101

Hodgins, Jack 1938- . . . . CLC 23
See also CA 93-96; DLB 60

Hodgson, William Hope
1877-1918 . . . . TCLC 13
See also CA 111; DLB 70

Hoffman, Alice 1952- . . . . CLC 51
See also CA 77-80

Hoffman, Daniel (Gerard)
1923- . . . . CLC 6, 13, 23
See also CANR 4; CA 1-4R; DLB 5

Hoffman, Stanley 1944- . . . . CLC 5
See also CA 77-80

Hoffman, William M(oses) 1939- . . . CLC 40
See also CANR 11; CA 57-60

Hoffmann, E(rnst) T(heodor) A(madeus)
1776-1822 . . . . NCLC 2
See also SATA 27; DLB 90

Hoffmann, Gert 1932- . . . . CLC 54

Hofmannsthal, Hugo (Laurenz August
Hofmann Edler) von
1874-1929 . . . . TCLC 11
See also CA 106; DLB 81

Hogg, James 1770-1835 . . . . NCLC 4

Holbach, Paul Henri Thiry, Baron d'
1723-1789 . . . . LC 14

Holberg, Ludvig 1684-1754 . . . . LC 6

Holden, Ursula 1921- . . . . CLC 18
See also CAAS 8; CANR 22; CA 101

Holderlin, (Johann Christian) Friedrich
1770-1843 . . . . NCLC 16; PC 4

Holdstock, Robert (P.) 1948- . . . . CLC 39

Holland, Isabelle 1920- . . . . CLC 21
See also CANR 10, 25; CA 21-24R;
SATA 8

Holland, Marcus 1900-1985
See Caldwell, (Janet Miriam) Taylor
(Holland)

Hollander, John 1929- . . . . . . CLC 2, 5, 8, 14
See also CANR 1; CA 1-4R; SATA 13;
DLB 5

Holleran, Andrew 1943?- . . . . CLC 38

Hollinghurst, Alan 1954- . . . . CLC 55
See also CA 114

Hollis, Jim 1916-
See Summers, Hollis (Spurgeon, Jr.)

Holmes, John Clellon 1926-1988 . . . . CLC 56
See also CANR 4; CA 9-10R;
obituary CA 125; DLB 16

Holmes, Oliver Wendell
1809-1894 . . . . NCLC 14
See also SATA 34; DLB 1;
CDALB 1640-1865

Holt, Victoria 1906-
See Hibbert, Eleanor (Burford)

Holub, Miroslav 1923- . . . . CLC 4
See also CANR 10; CA 21-24R

Homer c. 8th century B.C.- . . . . CMLC 1

Honig, Edwin 1919- . . . . CLC 33
See also CAAS 8; CANR 4; CA 5-8R;
DLB 5

Hood, Hugh (John Blagdon)
1928- . . . . CLC 15, 28
See also CANR 1; CA 49-52; DLB 53

Hood, Thomas 1799-1845 . . . . NCLC 16

Hooker, (Peter) Jeremy 1941- . . . . . . CLC 43
See also CANR 22; CA 77-80; DLB 40

Hope, A(lec) D(erwent) 1907- . . . . CLC 3, 51
See also CA 21-24R

Hope, Christopher (David Tully)
1944- . . . . CLC 52
See also CA 106

Hopkins, Gerard Manley
1844-1889 . . . . NCLC 17
See also DLB 35, 57

Hopkins, John (Richard) 1931- . . . . . . CLC 4
See also CA 85-88

Hopkins, Pauline Elizabeth
1859-1930 . . . . TCLC 28
See also BLC 2; DLB 50

Horgan, Paul 1903- . . . . CLC 9, 53
See also CANR 9; CA 13-16R; SATA 13;
DLB-Y 85

Horovitz, Israel 1939- . . . . CLC 56
See also CA 33-36R; DLB 7

Horwitz, Julius 1920-1986 . . . . CLC 14
See also CANR 12; CA 9-12R;
obituary CA 119

Hospital, Janette Turner 1942- . . . . . CLC 42
See also CA 108

Hostos (y Bonilla), Eugenio Maria de
1893-1903 . . . . TCLC 24
See also CA 123

Hougan, Carolyn 19??- . . . . CLC 34

Household, Geoffrey (Edward West)
1900-1988 . . . . CLC 11
See also CA 77-80; obituary CA 126;
SATA 14, 59; DLB 87

Housman, A(lfred) E(dward)
1859-1936 . . . . TCLC 1, 10; PC 2
See also CA 104, 125; DLB 19

Housman, Laurence 1865-1959 . . . . . TCLC 7
See also CA 106; SATA 25; DLB 10

Howard, Elizabeth Jane 1923- . . . CLC 7, 29
See also CANR 8; CA 5-8R

Howard, Maureen 1930- . . . . . CLC 5, 14, 46
See also CA 53-56; DLB-Y 83

Howard, Richard 1929- . . . . . . CLC 7, 10, 47
See also CANR 25; CA 85-88; DLB 5

Howard, Robert E(rvin)
1906-1936 . . . . TCLC 8
See also CA 105

Josipovici, Gabriel (David)
1940- . . . . CLC 6, 43
See also CAAS 8; CA 37-40R; DLB 14

Joubert, Joseph   1754-1824 . . . . . . NCLC 9

Jouve, Pierre Jean   1887-1976 . . . . . . CLC 47
See also obituary CA 65-68

Joyce, James (Augustine Aloysius)
1882-1941 . . . . . .   TCLC 3, 8, 16, 26, 35;
SSC 3
See also CA 104, 126; DLB 10, 19, 36

Jozsef, Attila   1905-1937 . . . . TCLC 22
See also CA 116

Juana Ines de la Cruz   1651?-1695 . . . . LC 5

Julian of Norwich   1342?-1416? . . . . LC 6

Just, Ward S(wift)   1935- . . . . CLC 4, 27
See also CA 25-28R

Justice, Donald (Rodney)   1925- . . CLC 6, 19
See also CANR 26; CA 5-8R; DLB-Y 83

Juvenal   c. 55-c. 127 . . . . CMLC 8

Kacew, Romain   1914-1980
See Gary, Romain
See also CA 108; obituary CA 102

Kacewgary, Romain   1914-1980
See Gary, Romain

Kadare, Ismail   1936- . . . . CLC 52

Kadohata, Cynthia   19??- . . . . CLC 59

Kafka, Franz
1883-1924 . . . . TCLC 2, 6, 13, 29; SSC 5
See also CA 105, 126; DLB 81

Kahn, Roger   1927- . . . . CLC 30
See also CA 25-28R; SATA 37

Kaiser, (Friedrich Karl) Georg
1878-1945 . . . . TCLC 9
See also CA 106

Kaletski, Alexander   1946- . . . . CLC 39
See also CA 118

Kallman, Chester (Simon)
1921-1975 . . . . CLC 2
See also CANR 3; CA 45-48;
obituary CA 53-56

Kaminsky, Melvin   1926-
See Brooks, Mel
See also CANR 16; CA 65-68

Kaminsky, Stuart   1934- . . . . CLC 59
See also CANR 29; CA 73-76

Kane, Paul   1941-
See Simon, Paul

Kanin, Garson   1912- . . . . CLC 22
See also CANR 7; CA 5-8R; DLB 7

Kaniuk, Yoram   1930- . . . . CLC 19

Kant, Immanuel   1724-1804 . . . . . NCLC 27

Kantor, MacKinlay   1904-1977 . . . . . . CLC 7
See also CA 61-64; obituary CA 73-76;
DLB 9

Kaplan, David Michael   1946- . . . . . . CLC 50

Kaplan, James   19??- . . . . CLC 59

Karamzin, Nikolai Mikhailovich
1766-1826 . . . . NCLC 3

Karapanou, Margarita   1946- . . . . CLC 13
See also CA 101

Karl, Frederick R(obert)   1927- . . . . . CLC 34
See also CANR 3; CA 5-8R

Kassef, Romain   1914-1980
See Gary, Romain

Katz, Steve   1935- . . . . CLC 47
See also CANR 12; CA 25-28R; DLB-Y 83

Kauffman, Janet   1945- . . . . CLC 42
See also CA 117; DLB-Y 86

Kaufman, Bob (Garnell)
1925-1986 . . . . CLC 49
See also CANR 22; CA 41-44R;
obituary CA 118; DLB 16, 41

Kaufman, George S(imon)
1889-1961 . . . . CLC 38
See also CA 108; obituary CA 93-96; DLB 7

Kaufman, Sue   1926-1977 . . . . CLC 3, 8
See also Barondess, Sue K(aufman)

Kavan, Anna   1904-1968 . . . . CLC 5, 13
See also Edmonds, Helen (Woods)
See also CANR 6; CA 5-8R

Kavanagh, Patrick (Joseph Gregory)
1905-1967 . . . . CLC 22
See also CA 123; obituary CA 25-28R;
DLB 15, 20

Kawabata, Yasunari
1899-1972 . . . . CLC 2, 5, 9, 18
See also CA 93-96; obituary CA 33-36R

Kaye, M(ary) M(argaret)   1909?- . . . . CLC 28
See also CANR 24; CA 89-92

Kaye, Mollie   1909?-
See Kaye, M(ary) M(argaret)

Kaye-Smith, Sheila   1887-1956 . . . . . TCLC 20
See also CA 118; DLB 36

Kaymor, Patrice Maguilene   1906-
See Senghor, Leopold Sedar

Kazan, Elia   1909- . . . . CLC 6, 16, 63
See also CA 21-24R

Kazantzakis, Nikos
1885?-1957 . . . . TCLC 2, 5, 33
See also CA 105

Kazin, Alfred   1915- . . . . CLC 34, 38
See also CAAS 7; CANR 1; CA 1-4R;
DLB 67

Keane, Mary Nesta (Skrine)   1904-
See Keane, Molly
See also CA 108, 114

Keane, Molly   1904- . . . . CLC 31
See also Keane, Mary Nesta (Skrine)

Keates, Jonathan   19??- . . . . CLC 34

Keaton, Buster   1895-1966 . . . . CLC 20

Keaton, Joseph Francis   1895-1966
See Keaton, Buster

Keats, John   1795-1821 . . . . . . NCLC 8; PC 1

Keene, Donald   1922- . . . . CLC 34
See also CANR 5; CA 1-4R

Keillor, Garrison   1942- . . . . CLC 40
See also Keillor, Gary (Edward)
See also CA 111; SATA 58; DLB-Y 87;
AAYA 2

Keillor, Gary (Edward)
See Keillor, Garrison
See also CA 111, 117

Kell, Joseph   1917-
See Burgess (Wilson, John) Anthony

Keller, Gottfried   1819-1890 . . . . NCLC 2

Kellerman, Jonathan (S.)   1949- . . . . . CLC 44
See also CANR 29; CA 106

Kelley, William Melvin   1937- . . . . . . CLC 22
See also CANR 27; CA 77-80; DLB 33

Kellogg, Marjorie   1922- . . . . CLC 2
See also CA 81-84

Kelly, M. T.   1947- . . . . CLC 55
See also CANR 19; CA 97-100

Kelman, James   1946- . . . . CLC 58

Kemal, Yashar   1922- . . . . CLC 14, 29
See also CA 89-92

Kemble, Fanny   1809-1893 . . . . NCLC 18
See also DLB 32

Kemelman, Harry   1908- . . . . CLC 2
See also CANR 6; CA 9-12R; DLB 28

Kempe, Margery   1373?-1440? . . . . LC 6

Kempis, Thomas á   1380-1471 . . . . . . LC 11

Kendall, Henry   1839-1882 . . . . NCLC 12

Keneally, Thomas (Michael)
1935- . . . . . . CLC 5, 8, 10, 14, 19, 27, 43
See also CANR 10; CA 85-88

Kennedy, Adrienne   1931-
See also BLC 2; CANR 26; CA 103;
CABS 3; DLB 38

Kennedy, Adrienne (Lita)   1931- . . . . CLC 66
See also CANR 26; CA 103; CABS 3;
DLB 38

Kennedy, John Pendleton
1795-1870 . . . . NCLC 2
See also DLB 3

Kennedy, Joseph Charles   1929- . . . . . . CLC 8
See also Kennedy, X. J.
See also CANR 4, 30; CA 1-4R; SATA 14

Kennedy, William (Joseph)
1928- . . . . CLC 6, 28, 34, 53
See also CANR 14; CA 85-88; SATA 57;
DLB-Y 85; AAYA 1

Kennedy, X. J.   1929- . . . . CLC 8, 42
See also Kennedy, Joseph Charles
See also CAAS 9; DLB 5

Kerouac, Jack
1922-1969 . . . . CLC 1, 2, 3, 5, 14, 29, 61
See also Kerouac, Jean-Louis Lebris de
See also DLB 2, 16; DLB-DS 3;
CDALB 1941-1968

Kerouac, Jean-Louis Lebris de   1922-1969
See Kerouac, Jack
See also CANR 26; CA 5-8R;
obituary CA 25-28R; CDALB 1941-1968

Kerr, Jean   1923- . . . . CLC 22
See also CANR 7; CA 5-8R

Kerr, M. E.   1927- . . . . CLC 12, 35
See also Meaker, Marijane
See also SAAS 1; AAYA 2

Kerr, Robert   1970?- . . . . CLC 55, 59

Kerrigan, (Thomas) Anthony
1918- . . . . CLC 4, 6
See also CAAS 11; CANR 4; CA 49-52

Kesey, Ken (Elton)
1935- . . . . CLC 1, 3, 6, 11, 46, 64
See also CANR 22; CA 1-4R; DLB 2, 16;
CDALB 1968-1987

Kesselring, Joseph (Otto)
1902-1967 . . . . CLC 45

Milner, Ron(ald) 1938-............ CLC 56
See also BLC 3; CANR 24; CA 73-76;
DLB 38

Milosz Czeslaw
1911-.......... CLC 5, 11, 22, 31, 56
See also CANR 23; CA 81-84

Milton, John 1608-1674............. LC 9

Miner, Valerie (Jane) 1947-........ CLC 40
See also CA 97-100

Minot, Susan 1956- .... CLC 44

Minus, Ed 1938-................. CLC 39

Miro (Ferrer), Gabriel (Francisco Victor)
1879-1930 .... TCLC 5
See also CA 104

Mishima, Yukio
1925-1970 .... CLC 2, 4, 6, 9, 27; DC 1;
SSC 4
See also Hiraoka, Kimitake

Mistral, Gabriela 1889-1957 .... TCLC 2
See also CA 104

Mitchell, James Leslie 1901-1935
See Gibbon, Lewis Grassic
See also CA 104; DLB 15

Mitchell, Joni 1943-.............. CLC 12
See also CA 112

Mitchell (Marsh), Margaret (Munnerlyn)
1900-1949 .... TCLC 11
See also CA 109, 125; DLB 9

Mitchell, S. Weir 1829-1914 ..... TCLC 36

Mitchell, W(illiam) O(rmond)
1914- .... CLC 25
See also CANR 15; CA 77-80; DLB 88

Mitford, Mary Russell 1787-1855.. NCLC 4

Mitford, Nancy 1904-1973........ CLC 44
See also CA 9-12R

Miyamoto Yuriko 1899-1951...... TCLC 37

Mo, Timothy 1950-.............. CLC 46
See also CA 117

Modarressi, Taghi 1931- .... CLC 44
See also CA 121

Modiano, Patrick (Jean) 1945-..... CLC 18
See also CANR 17; CA 85-88; DLB 83

Mofolo, Thomas (Mokopu)
1876-1948 .... TCLC 22
See also BLC 3; brief entry CA 121

Mohr, Nicholasa 1935-............ CLC 12
See also CLR 22; CANR 1; CA 49-52;
SAAS 8; SATA 8

Mojtabai, A(nn) G(race)
1938- .... CLC 5, 9, 15, 29
See also CA 85-88

Moliere 1622-1673 .... LC 10

Molnar, Ferenc 1878-1952....... TCLC 20
See also CA 109

Momaday, N(avarre) Scott
1934- .... CLC 2, 19
See also CANR 14; CA 25-28R; SATA 30,
48

Monroe, Harriet 1860-1936....... TCLC 12
See also CA 109; DLB 54, 91

Montagu, Elizabeth 1720-1800 .... NCLC 7

Montagu, Lady Mary (Pierrepont) Wortley
1689-1762 .... LC 9

Montague, John (Patrick)
1929-.................... CLC 13, 46
See also CANR 9; CA 9-12R; DLB 40

Montaigne, Michel (Eyquem) de
1533-1592 .... LC 8

Montale, Eugenio 1896-1981... CLC 7, 9, 18
See also CANR 30; CA 17-20R;
obituary CA 104

Montesquieu, Charles-Louis de Secondat
1689-1755 .... LC 7

Montgomery, Marion (H., Jr.)
1925-....................... CLC 7
See also CANR 3; CA 1-4R; DLB 6

Montgomery, Robert Bruce 1921-1978
See Crispin, Edmund
See also CA 104

Montherlant, Henri (Milon) de
1896-1972 .... CLC 8, 19
See also CA 85-88; obituary CA 37-40R;
DLB 72

Monty Python.................... CLC 21

Moodie, Susanna (Strickland)
1803-1885 .... NCLC 14

Mooney, Ted 1951-............... CLC 25

Moorcock, Michael (John)
1939- .... CLC 5, 27, 58
See also CAAS 5; CANR 2, 17; CA 45-48;
DLB 14

Moore, Brian
1921-........ CLC 1, 3, 5, 7, 8, 19, 32
See also CANR 1, 25; CA 1-4R

Moore, George (Augustus)
1852-1933 .... TCLC 7
See also CA 104; DLB 10, 18, 57

Moore, Lorrie 1957-....... CLC 39, 45, 68
See also Moore, Marie Lorena

Moore, Marianne (Craig)
1887-1972 ... CLC 1, 2, 4, 8, 10, 13, 19,
47; PC 4
See also CANR 3; CA 1-4R;
obituary CA 33-36R; SATA 20; DLB 45;
DLB-DS 7; CDALB 1929-1941

Moore, Marie Lorena 1957-
See Moore, Lorrie
See also CA 116

Moore, Thomas 1779-1852........ NCLC 6

Morand, Paul 1888-1976 .... CLC 41
See also obituary CA 69-72; DLB 65

Morante, Elsa 1918-1985........ CLC 8, 47
See also CA 85-88; obituary CA 117

Moravia, Alberto
1907-........ CLC 2, 7, 11, 18, 27, 46
See also Pincherle, Alberto

More, Hannah 1745-1833 .... NCLC 27

More, Henry 1614-1687............ LC 9

More, Sir Thomas 1478-1535 ...... LC 10

Moreas, Jean 1856-1910 .... TCLC 18

Morgan, Berry 1919-.............. CLC 6
See also CA 49-52; DLB 6

Morgan, Edwin (George) 1920-..... CLC 31
See also CANR 3; CA 7-8R; DLB 27

Morgan, (George) Frederick
1922-..................... CLC 23
See also CANR 21; CA 17-20R

Morgan, Janet 1945- .... CLC 39
See also CA 65-68

Morgan, Lady 1776?-1859....... NCLC 29

Morgan, Robin 1941-.............. CLC 2
See also CA 69-72

Morgan, Seth 1949-1990 .... CLC 65
See also CA 132

Morgenstern, Christian (Otto Josef Wolfgang)
1871-1914 .... TCLC 8
See also CA 105

Moricz, Zsigmond 1879-1942 .... TCLC 33

Morike, Eduard (Friedrich)
1804-1875 .... NCLC 10

Mori Ogai 1862-1922............ TCLC 14
See also Mori Rintaro

Mori Rintaro 1862-1922
See Mori Ogai
See also CA 110

Moritz, Karl Philipp 1756-1793 ...... LC 2

Morris, Julian 1916-
See West, Morris L.

Morris, Steveland Judkins 1950-
See Wonder, Stevie
See also CA 111

Morris, William 1834-1896 .... NCLC 4
See also DLB 18, 35, 57

Morris, Wright (Marion)
1910- .... CLC 1, 3, 7, 18, 37
See also CANR 21; CA 9-12R; DLB 2;
DLB-Y 81

Morrison, James Douglas 1943-1971
See Morrison, Jim
See also CA 73-76

Morrison, Jim 1943-1971.......... CLC 17
See also Morrison, James Douglas

Morrison, Toni 1931-.....CLC 4, 10, 22, 55
See also BLC 3; CANR 27; CA 29-32R;
SATA 57; DLB 6, 33; DLB-Y 81;
CDALB 1968-1987; AAYA 1

Morrison, Van 1945-............. CLC 21
See also CA 116

Mortimer, John (Clifford)
1923-.................... CLC 28, 43
See also CANR 21; CA 13-16R; DLB 13

Mortimer, Penelope (Ruth) 1918-.... CLC 5
See also CA 57-60

Mosher, Howard Frank 19??-...... CLC 62

Mosley, Nicholas 1923-........... CLC 43
See also CA 69-72; DLB 14

Moss, Howard
1922-1987 .... CLC 7, 14, 45, 50
See also CANR 1; CA 1-4R;
obituary CA 123; DLB 5

Motion, Andrew (Peter) 1952-...... CLC 47
See also DLB 40

Motley, Willard (Francis)
1912-1965 .... CLC 18
See also CA 117; obituary CA 106; DLB 76

Mott, Michael (Charles Alston)
1930- .... CLC 15, 34
See also CAAS 7; CANR 7, 29; CA 5-8R

Mowat, Farley (McGill) 1921- ..... CLC 26
See also CLR 20; CANR 4, 24; CA 1-4R;
SATA 3, 55; DLB 68; AAYA 1

Mphahlele, Es'kia 1919-
See Mphahlele, Ezekiel

Mphahlele, Ezekiel 1919-.......... **CLC 25**
See also BLC 3; CANR 26; CA 81-84

Mqhayi, S(amuel) E(dward) K(rune Loliwe)
1875-1945 .... **TCLC 25**
See also BLC 3

Mrozek, Slawomir 1930-....... **CLC 3, 13**
See also CAAS 10; CANR 29; CA 13-16R

Mtwa, Percy 19??-.............. **CLC 47**

Mueller, Lisel 1924-.......... **CLC 13, 51**
See also CA 93-96

Muir, Edwin 1887-1959 .... **TCLC 2**
See also CA 104; DLB 20

Muir, John 1838-1914 .... **TCLC 28**

Mujica Lainez, Manuel
1910-1984 .... **CLC 31**
See also CA 81-84; obituary CA 112

Mukherjee, Bharati 1940-......... **CLC 53**
See also CA 107; DLB 60

Muldoon, Paul 1951-............. **CLC 32**
See also CA 113, 129; DLB 40

Mulisch, Harry (Kurt Victor)
1927- .... **CLC 42**
See also CANR 6, 26; CA 9-12R

Mull, Martin 1943-.............. **CLC 17**
See also CA 105

Munford, Robert 1737?-1783........ **LC 5**
See also DLB 31

Munro, Alice (Laidlaw)
1931- .... **CLC 6, 10, 19, 50; SSC 3**
See also CA 33-36R; SATA 29; DLB 53

Munro, H(ector) H(ugh) 1870-1916
See Saki
See also CA 104; DLB 34

Murasaki, Lady c. 11th century-... **CMLC 1**

Murdoch, (Jean) Iris
1919- ...... **CLC 1, 2, 3, 4, 6, 8, 11, 15,**
22, 31, 51
See also CANR 8; CA 13-16R; DLB 14

Murphy, Richard 1927-.......... **CLC 41**
See also CA 29-32R; DLB 40

Murphy, Sylvia 19??-............. **CLC 34**

Murphy, Thomas (Bernard) 1935-... **CLC 51**
See also CA 101

Murray, Les(lie) A(llan) 1938- ..... **CLC 40**
See also CANR 11, 27; CA 21-24R

Murry, John Middleton
1889-1957 .... **TCLC 16**
See also CA 118

Musgrave, Susan 1951- .... **CLC 13, 54**
See also CA 69-72

Musil, Robert (Edler von)
1880-1942 .... **TCLC 12**
See also CA 109; DLB 81

Musset, (Louis Charles) Alfred de
1810-1857 .... **NCLC 7**

Myers, Walter Dean 1937- .... **CLC 35**
See also BLC 3; CLR 4, 16; CANR 20;
CA 33-36R; SAAS 2; SATA 27, 41;
DLB 33; AAYA 4

Myers, Walter M. 1937-
See Myers, Walter Dean

Nabokov, Vladimir (Vladimirovich)
1899-1977 .... **CLC 1, 2, 3, 6, 8, 11, 15,**
23, 44, 46, 64
See also CANR 20; CA 5-8R;
obituary CA 69-72; DLB 2; DLB-Y 80;
DLB-DS 3; CDALB 1941-1968

Nagy, Laszlo 1925-1978........... **CLC 7**
See also CA 129; obituary CA 112

Naipaul, Shiva(dhar Srinivasa)
1945-1985 .... **CLC 32, 39**
See also CA 110, 112; obituary CA 116;
DLB-Y 85

Naipaul, V(idiadhar) S(urajprasad)
1932- .... **CLC 4, 7, 9, 13, 18, 37**
See also CANR 1; CA 1-4R; DLB-Y 85

Nakos, Ioulia 1899?-
See Nakos, Lilika

Nakos, Lilika 1899?- .... **CLC 29**

Nakou, Lilika 1899?-
See Nakos, Lilika

Narayan, R(asipuram) K(rishnaswami)
1906- .... **CLC 7, 28, 47**
See also CA 81-84

Nash, (Frediric) Ogden 1902-1971 .. **CLC 23**
See also CAP 1; CA 13-14;
obituary CA 29-32R; SATA 2, 46;
DLB 11

Nathan, George Jean 1882-1958 ... **TCLC 18**
See also CA 114

Natsume, Kinnosuke 1867-1916
See Natsume, Soseki
See also CA 104

Natsume, Soseki 1867-1916..... **TCLC 2, 10**
See also Natsume, Kinnosuke

Natti, (Mary) Lee 1919-
See Kingman, (Mary) Lee
See also CANR 2; CA 7-8R

Naylor, Gloria 1950- .... **CLC 28, 52**
See also BLC 3; CANR 27; CA 107;
AAYA 6

Neff, Debra 1972-................ **CLC 59**

Neihardt, John G(neisenau)
1881-1973 .... **CLC 32**
See also CAP 1; CA 13-14; DLB 9, 54

Nekrasov, Nikolai Alekseevich
1821-1878 .... **NCLC 11**

Nelligan, Emile 1879-1941........ **TCLC 14**
See also CA 114; DLB 92

Nelson, Willie 1933-.............. **CLC 17**
See also CA 107

Nemerov, Howard 1920- .... **CLC 2, 6, 9, 36**
See also CANR 1, 27; CA 1-4R; CABS 2;
DLB 5, 6; DLB-Y 83

Neruda, Pablo
1904-1973 .... **CLC 1, 2, 5, 7, 9, 28, 62;**
PC 4
See also CAP 2; CA 19-20;
obituary CA 45-48

Nerval, Gerard de 1808-1855...... **NCLC 1**

Nervo, (Jose) Amado (Ruiz de)
1870-1919 .... **TCLC 11**
See also CA 109

Neufeld, John (Arthur) 1938- ...... **CLC 17**
See also CANR 11; CA 25-28R; SAAS 3;
SATA 6

Neville, Emily Cheney 1919-....... **CLC 12**
See also CANR 3; CA 5-8R; SAAS 2;
SATA 1

Newbound, Bernard Slade 1930-
See Slade, Bernard
See also CA 81-84

Newby, P(ercy) H(oward)
1918- .... **CLC 2, 13**
See also CA 5-8R; DLB 15

Newlove, Donald 1928- .... **CLC 6**
See also CANR 25; CA 29-32R

Newlove, John (Herbert) 1938-..... **CLC 14**
See also CANR 9, 25; CA 21-24R

Newman, Charles 1938-.......... **CLC 2, 8**
See also CA 21-24R

Newman, Edwin (Harold) 1919- .... **CLC 14**
See also CANR 5; CA 69-72

Newton, Suzanne 1936- .... **CLC 35**
See also CANR 14; CA 41-44R; SATA 5

Nexo, Martin Andersen
1869-1954 .... **TCLC 43**

Nezval, Vitezslav 1900-1958 ...... **TCLC 44**
See also CA 123

Ngema, Mbongeni 1955- .... **CLC 57**

Ngugi, James Thiong'o 1938-
See Ngugi wa Thiong'o

Ngugi wa Thiong'o 1938-... **CLC 3, 7, 13, 36**
See also Ngugi, James (Thiong'o); Wa
Thiong'o, Ngugi
See also BLC 3

Nichol, B(arrie) P(hillip) 1944-..... **CLC 18**
See also CA 53-56; DLB 53

Nichols, John (Treadwell) 1940-.... **CLC 38**
See also CAAS 2; CANR 6; CA 9-12R;
DLB-Y 82

Nichols, Peter (Richard)
1927- .... **CLC 5, 36, 65**
See also CANR 33; CA 104; DLB 13

Nicolas, F.R.E. 1927-
See Freeling, Nicolas

Niedecker, Lorine 1903-1970.... **CLC 10, 42**
See also CAP 2; CA 25-28; DLB 48

Nietzsche, Friedrich (Wilhelm)
1844-1900 .... **TCLC 10, 18**
See also CA 107, 121

Nievo, Ippolito 1831-1861 .... **NCLC 22**

Nightingale, Anne Redmon 1943-
See Redmon (Nightingale), Anne
See also CA 103

Nin, Anais
1903-1977 ...... **CLC 1, 4, 8, 11, 14, 60**
See also CANR 22; CA 13-16R;
obituary CA 69-72; DLB 2, 4

Nissenson, Hugh 1933-.......... **CLC 4, 9**
See also CANR 27; CA 17-20R; DLB 28

Niven, Larry 1938-............... **CLC 8**
See also Niven, Laurence Van Cott
See also DLB 8

Niven, Laurence Van Cott 1938-
See Niven, Larry
See also CANR 14; CA 21-24R

Nixon, Agnes Eckhardt 1927-...... **CLC 21**
See also CA 110

Osborne, John (James)
　1929- .... **CLC 1, 2, 5, 11, 45**
　See also CANR 21; CA 13-16R; DLB 13

Osborne, Lawrence 1958- .... **CLC 50**

Osceola 1885-1962
　See Dinesen, Isak; Blixen, Karen
　(Christentze Dinesen)

Oshima, Nagisa 1932- .... **CLC 20**
　See also CA 116

Oskison, John M. 1874-1947..... **TCLC 35**

Ossoli, Sarah Margaret (Fuller marchesa d')
　1810-1850
　See Fuller, (Sarah) Margaret
　See also SATA 25

Ostrovsky, Alexander
　1823-1886 .... **NCLC 30**

Otero, Blas de 1916- .... **CLC 11**
　See also CA 89-92

Ouida 1839-1908............... **TCLC 43**
　See also de la Ramee, Marie Louise
　See also DLB 18

Ousmane, Sembene 1923-
　See also BLC 3; CA 125; brief entry CA 117

Ousmane, Sembene 1923- .... **CLC 66**
　See also Sembene, Ousmane
　See also CA 125; brief entry CA 117

Ovid 43 B.C.-c. 18 A.D. .... **CMLC 7; PC 2**

Owen, Wilfred (Edward Salter)
　1893-1918 .... **TCLC 5, 27**
　See also CA 104; DLB 20

Owens, Rochelle 1936-............ **CLC 8**
　See also CAAS 2; CA 17-20R

Owl, Sebastian 1939-
　See Thompson, Hunter S(tockton)

Oz, Amos 1939- ... **CLC 5, 8, 11, 27, 33, 54**
　See also CANR 27; CA 53-56

Ozick, Cynthia 1928-...... **CLC 3, 7, 28, 62**
　See also CANR 23; CA 17-20R; DLB 28;
　DLB-Y 82

Ozu, Yasujiro 1903-1963.......... **CLC 16**
　See also CA 112

P. V. M. 1912-1990
　See White, Patrick (Victor Martindale)

Pa Chin 1904-................. **CLC 18**
　See also Li Fei-kan

Pack, Robert 1929-.............. **CLC 13**
　See also CANR 3; CA 1-4R; DLB 5

Padgett, Lewis 1915-1958
　See Kuttner, Henry

Padilla, Heberto 1932-............ **CLC 38**
　See also CA 123

Page, Jimmy 1944-.............. **CLC 12**

Page, Louise 1955-.............. **CLC 40**

Page, P(atricia) K(athleen)
　1916- .... **CLC 7, 18**
　See also CANR 4, 22; CA 53-56; DLB 68

Paget, Violet 1856-1935
　See Lee, Vernon
　See also CA 104

Paglia, Camille 1947-............ **CLC 68**

Palamas, Kostes 1859-1943....... **TCLC 5**
　See also CA 105

Palazzeschi, Aldo 1885-1974....... **CLC 11**
　See also CA 89-92; obituary CA 53-56

Paley, Grace 1922-.... **CLC 4, 6, 37; SSC 8**
　See also CANR 13; CA 25-28R; DLB 28

Palin, Michael 1943-............. **CLC 21**
　See also Monty Python
　See also CA 107

Palliser, Charles 1948?-.......... **CLC 65**

Palma, Ricardo 1833-1919....... **TCLC 29**
　See also CANR 123

Pancake, Breece Dexter 1952-1979
　See Pancake, Breece D'J

Pancake, Breece D'J 1952-1979 .... **CLC 29**
　See also obituary CA 109

Papadiamantis, Alexandros
　1851-1911 .... **TCLC 29**

Papini, Giovanni 1881-1956...... **TCLC 22**
　See also CA 121

Paracelsus 1493-1541.............. **LC 14**

Parini, Jay (Lee) 1948- .... **CLC 54**
　See also CA 97-100

Parker, Dorothy (Rothschild)
　1893-1967 .... **CLC 15, 68; SSC 2**
　See also CAP 2; CA 19-20;
　obituary CA 25-28R; DLB 11, 45. 86

Parker, Robert B(rown) 1932-...... **CLC 27**
　See also CANR 1, 26; CA 49-52

Parkin, Frank 1940-............. **CLC 43**

Parkman, Francis 1823-1893..... **NCLC 12**
　See also DLB 1, 30

Parks, Gordon (Alexander Buchanan)
　1912- .... **CLC 1, 16**
　See also BLC 3; CANR 26; CA 41-44R;
　SATA 8; DLB 33

Parnell, Thomas 1679-1718 .... **LC 3**

Parra, Nicanor 1914-............. **CLC 2**
　See also CA 85-88

Pasolini, Pier Paolo
　1922-1975 .... **CLC 20, 37**
　See also CA 93-96; obituary CA 61-64

Pastan, Linda (Olenik) 1932- ...... **CLC 27**
　See also CANR 18; CA 61-64; DLB 5

Pasternak, Boris
　1890-1960 .... **CLC 7, 10, 18, 63**
　See also CA 127; obituary CA 116

Patchen, Kenneth 1911-1972 ... **CLC 1, 2, 18**
　See also CANR 3; CA 1-4R;
　obituary CA 33-36R; DLB 16, 48

Pater, Walter (Horatio)
　1839-1894 .... **NCLC 7**
　See also DLB 57

Paterson, Andrew Barton
　1864-1941 .... **TCLC 32**

Paterson, Katherine (Womeldorf)
　1932- .... **CLC 12, 30**
　See also CLR 7; CANR 28; CA 21-24R;
　SATA 13, 53; DLB 52; AAYA 1

Patmore, Coventry Kersey Dighton
　1823-1896 .... **NCLC 9**
　See also DLB 35

Paton, Alan (Stewart)
　1903-1988 .... **CLC 4, 10, 25, 55**
　See also CANR 22; CAP 1; CA 15-16;
　obituary CA 125; SATA 11

Paulding, James Kirke 1778-1860.. **NCLC 2**
　See also DLB 3, 59, 74

Paulin, Tom 1949- .... **CLC 37**
　See also CA 123; DLB 40

Paustovsky, Konstantin (Georgievich)
　1892-1968 .... **CLC 40**
　See also CA 93-96; obituary CA 25-28R

Paustowsky, Konstantin (Georgievich)
　1892-1968
　See Paustovsky, Konstantin (Georgievich)

Pavese, Cesare 1908-1950 .... **TCLC 3**
　See also CA 104

Pavic, Milorad 1929-............. **CLC 60**

Payne, Alan 1932-
　See Jakes, John (William)

Paz, Octavio
　1914- ...... **CLC 3, 4, 6, 10, 19, 51, 65;**
　　　　　　　　　　　　　　　　　　　PC 1
　See also CANR 32; CA 73-76

p'Bitek, Okot 1931-1982
　See also BLC 3; CA 124; obituary CA 107

Peacock, Molly 1947-............. **CLC 60**
　See also CA 103

Peacock, Thomas Love
　1785-1886 .... **NCLC 22**

Peake, Mervyn 1911-1968....... **CLC 7, 54**
　See also CANR 3; CA 5-8R;
　obituary CA 25-28R; SATA 23; DLB 15

Pearce, (Ann) Philippa 1920-....... **CLC 21**
　See also Christie, (Ann) Philippa
　See also CLR 9; CA 5-8R; SATA 1

Pearl, Eric 1934-
　See Elman, Richard

Pearson, T(homas) R(eid) 1956- .... **CLC 39**
　See also CA 120, 130

Peck, John 1941-................. **CLC 3**
　See also CANR 3; CA 49-52

Peck, Richard 1934-.............. **CLC 21**
　See also CLR 15; CANR 19; CA 85-88;
　SAAS 2; SATA 18; AAYA 1

Peck, Robert Newton 1928-........ **CLC 17**
　See also CA 81-84; SAAS 1; SATA 21;
　AAYA 3

Peckinpah, (David) Sam(uel)
　1925-1984 .... **CLC 20**
　See also CA 109; obituary CA 114

Pedersen, Knut 1859-1952
　See Hamsun, Knut
　See also CA 104, 109, 119

Peguy, Charles (Pierre)
　1873-1914 .... **TCLC 10**
　See also CA 107

Pepys, Samuel 1633-1703.......... **LC 11**

Percy, Walker
　1916-1990 ... **CLC 2, 3, 6, 8, 14, 18, 47,**
　　　　　　　　　　　　　　　　　　　　65
　See also CANR 1, 23; CA 1-4R;
　obituary CA 131; DLB 2; DLB-Y 80

Perec, Georges 1936-1982 .... **CLC 56**
　See also DLB 83

Pereda, Jose Maria de
　1833-1906 .... **TCLC 16**

Roberts, (Sir) Charles G(eorge) D(ouglas)
  1860-1943 .... **TCLC 8**
  See also CA 105; SATA 29; DLB 92

Roberts, Kate 1891-1985 .... **CLC 15**
  See also CA 107; obituary CA 116

Roberts, Keith (John Kingston)
  1935- .... **CLC 14**
  See also CA 25-28R

Roberts, Kenneth 1885-1957 ...... **TCLC 23**
  See also CA 109; DLB 9

Roberts, Michele (B.) 1949-........ **CLC 48**
  See also CA 115

Robinson, Edwin Arlington
  1869-1935 .... **TCLC 5; PC 1**
  See also CA 104; DLB 54;
  CDALB 1865-1917

Robinson, Henry Crabb
  1775-1867 .... **NCLC 15**

Robinson, Jill 1936-.............. **CLC 10**
  See also CA 102

Robinson, Kim Stanley 19??-....... **CLC 34**
  See also CA 126

Robinson, Marilynne 1944-........ **CLC 25**
  See also CA 116

Robinson, Smokey 1940- .... **CLC 21**

Robinson, William 1940-
  See Robinson, Smokey
  See also CA 116

Robison, Mary 1949-............. **CLC 42**
  See also CA 113, 116

Roddenberry, Gene 1921-.......... **CLC 17**
  See also CANR 110; SATA 45

Rodgers, Mary 1931-............. **CLC 12**
  See also CLR 20; CANR 8; CA 49-52;
  SATA 8

Rodgers, W(illiam) R(obert)
  1909-1969 .... **CLC 7**
  See also CA 85-88; DLB 20

Rodman, Howard 19??- .... **CLC 65**

Rodriguez, Claudio 1934-......... **CLC 10**

Roethke, Theodore (Huebner)
  1908-1963 ...... **CLC 1, 3, 8, 11, 19, 46**
  See also CA 81-84; CABS 2; SAAS 1;
  DLB 5; CDALB 1941-1968

Rogers, Sam 1943-
  See Shepard, Sam

Rogers, Thomas (Hunton) 1931-.... **CLC 57**
  See also CA 89-92

Rogers, Will(iam Penn Adair)
  1879-1935 .... **TCLC 8**
  See also CA 105; DLB 11

Rogin, Gilbert 1929-............. **CLC 18**
  See also CANR 15; CA 65-68

Rohan, Koda 1867-1947.......... **TCLC 22**
  See also CA 121

Rohmer, Eric 1920- .... **CLC 16**
  See also Scherer, Jean-Marie Maurice

Rohmer, Sax 1883-1959......... **TCLC 28**
  See also Ward, Arthur Henry Sarsfield
  See also CA 108; DLB 70

Roiphe, Anne (Richardson)
  1935- .... **CLC 3, 9**
  See also CA 89-92; DLB-Y 80

Rolfe, Frederick (William Serafino Austin
  Lewis Mary) 1860-1913..... **TCLC 12**
  See also CA 107; DLB 34

Rolland, Romain 1866-1944...... **TCLC 23**
  See also CA 118; DLB 65

Rolvaag, O(le) E(dvart)
  1876-1931 .... **TCLC 17**
  See also CA 117; DLB 9

Romains, Jules 1885-1972.......... **CLC 7**
  See also CA 85-88

Romero, Jose Ruben 1890-1952 ... **TCLC 14**
  See also CA 114

Ronsard, Pierre de 1524-1585....... **LC 6**

Rooke, Leon 1934-............ **CLC 25, 34**
  See also CANR 23; CA 25-28R

Roper, William 1498-1578......... **LC 10**

Rosa, Joao Guimaraes 1908-1967... **CLC 23**
  See also obituary CA 89-92

Rosen, Richard (Dean) 1949-...... **CLC 39**
  See also CA 77-80

Rosenberg, Isaac 1890-1918....... **TCLC 12**
  See also CA 107; DLB 20

Rosenblatt, Joe 1933-............ **CLC 15**
  See also Rosenblatt, Joseph

Rosenblatt, Joseph 1933-
  See Rosenblatt, Joe
  See also CA 89-92

Rosenfeld, Samuel 1896-1963
  See Tzara, Tristan
  See also obituary CA 89-92

Rosenthal, M(acha) L(ouis) 1917-... **CLC 28**
  See also CAAS 6; CANR 4; CA 1-4R;
  SATA 59; DLB 5

Ross, (James) Sinclair 1908-....... **CLC 13**
  See also CA 73-76; DLB 88

Rossetti, Christina Georgina
  1830-1894 .... **NCLC 2**
  See also SATA 20; DLB 35

Rossetti, Dante Gabriel
  1828-1882 .... **NCLC 4**
  See also DLB 35

Rossetti, Gabriel Charles Dante 1828-1882
  See Rossetti, Dante Gabriel

Rossner, Judith (Perelman)
  1935- .... **CLC 6, 9, 29**
  See also CANR 18; CA 17-20R; DLB 6

Rostand, Edmond (Eugene Alexis)
  1868-1918 .... **TCLC 6, 37**
  See also CA 104, 126

Roth, Henry 1906-........... **CLC 2, 6, 11**
  See also CAP 1; CA 11-12; DLB 28

Roth, Joseph 1894-1939........ **TCLC 33**
  See also DLB 85

Roth, Philip (Milton)
  1933- ...... **CLC 1, 2, 3, 4, 6, 9, 15, 22,
  31, 47, 66**
  See also CANR 1, 22; CA 1-4R; DLB 2, 28;
  DLB-Y 82; CDALB 1968-1988

Rothenberg, James 1931-....... **CLC 57**

Rothenberg, Jerome 1931-...... **CLC 6, 57**
  See also CANR 1; CA 45-48; DLB 5

Roumain, Jacques 1907-1944...... **TCLC 19**
  See also BLC 3; CA 117, 125

Rourke, Constance (Mayfield)
  1885-1941 .... **TCLC 12**
  See also YABC 1; CA 107

Rousseau, Jean-Baptiste 1671-1741 ... **LC 9**

Rousseau, Jean-Jacques 1712-1778... **LC 14**

Roussel, Raymond 1877-1933 ..... **TCLC 20**
  See also CA 117

Rovit, Earl (Herbert) 1927-....... **CLC 7**
  See also CANR 12; CA 5-8R

Rowe, Nicholas 1674-1718.......... **LC 8**

Rowson, Susanna Haswell
  1762-1824 .... **NCLC 5**
  See also DLB 37

Roy, Gabrielle 1909-1983....... **CLC 10, 14**
  See also CANR 5; CA 53-56;
  obituary CA 110; DLB 68

Rozewicz, Tadeusz 1921-........ **CLC 9, 23**
  See also CA 108

Ruark, Gibbons 1941- .... **CLC 3**
  See also CANR 14; CA 33-36R

Rubens, Bernice 192?- .... **CLC 19, 31**
  See also CA 25-28R; DLB 14

Rubenstein, Gladys 1934-
  See Swan, Gladys

Rudkin, (James) David 1936- ..... **CLC 14**
  See also CA 89-92; DLB 13

Rudnik, Raphael 1933-........... **CLC 7**
  See also CA 29-32R

Ruiz, Jose Martinez 1874-1967
  See Azorin

Rukeyser, Muriel
  1913-1980 .... **CLC 6, 10, 15, 27**
  See also CANR 26; CA 5-8R;
  obituary CA 93-96; obituary SATA 22;
  DLB 48

Rule, Jane (Vance) 1931-......... **CLC 27**
  See also CANR 12; CA 25-28R; DLB 60

Rulfo, Juan 1918-1986............. **CLC 8**
  See also CANR 26; CA 85-88;
  obituary CA 118

Runyon, (Alfred) Damon
  1880-1946 .... **TCLC 10**
  See also CA 107; DLB 11

Rush, Norman 1933-............. **CLC 44**
  See also CA 121, 126

Rushdie, (Ahmed) Salman
  1947- .... **CLC 23, 31, 55, 59**
  See also CA 108, 111

Rushforth, Peter (Scott) 1945- ..... **CLC 19**
  See also CA 101

Ruskin, John 1819-1900.......... **TCLC 20**
  See also CA 114; SATA 24; DLB 55

Russ, Joanna 1937-.............. **CLC 15**
  See also CANR 11; CA 25-28R; DLB 8

Russell, George William 1867-1935
  See A. E.
  See also CA 104

Russell, (Henry) Ken(neth Alfred)
  1927- .... **CLC 16**
  See also CA 105

Russell, Mary Annette Beauchamp 1866-1941
  See Elizabeth

Russell, Willy 1947-.............. **CLC 60**

Schisgal, Murray (Joseph) 1926-..... **CLC 6**
See also CA 21-24R

Schlee, Ann 1934-................ **CLC 35**
See also CA 101; SATA 36, 44

Schlegel, August Wilhelm von
1767-1845 .... **NCLC 15**

Schlegel, Johann Elias (von)
1719?-1749.................... **LC 5**

Schmidt, Arno 1914-1979......... **CLC 56**
See also obituary CA 109; DLB 69

Schmitz, Ettore 1861-1928
See Svevo, Italo
See also CA 104, 122

Schnackenberg, Gjertrud 1953-..... **CLC 40**
See also CA 116

Schneider, Leonard Alfred 1925-1966
See Bruce, Lenny
See also CA 89-92

Schnitzler, Arthur 1862-1931 ...... **TCLC 4**
See also CA 104; DLB 81

Schor, Sandra 1932?-1990 .... **CLC 65**
See also CA 132

Schorer, Mark 1908-1977 .... **CLC 9**
See also CANR 7; CA 5-8R;
obituary CA 73-76

Schrader, Paul (Joseph) 1946-...... **CLC 26**
See also CA 37-40R; DLB 44

Schreiner (Cronwright), Olive (Emilie
Albertina) 1855-1920......... **TCLC 9**
See also CA 105; DLB 18

Schulberg, Budd (Wilson)
1914- .... **CLC 7, 48**
See also CANR 19; CA 25-28R; DLB 6, 26,
28; DLB-Y 81

Schulz, Bruno 1892-1942.......... **TCLC 5**
See also CA 115, 123

Schulz, Charles M(onroe) 1922-.... **CLC 12**
See also CANR 6; CA 9-12R; SATA 10

Schuyler, James (Marcus)
1923- .... **CLC 5, 23**
See also CA 101; DLB 5

Schwartz, Delmore
1913-1966 .... **CLC 2, 4, 10, 45**
See also CAP 2; CA 17-18;
obituary CA 25-28R; DLB 28, 48

Schwartz, John Burnham 1925- .... **CLC 59**

Schwartz, Lynne Sharon 1939-..... **CLC 31**
See also CA 103

Schwarz-Bart, Andre 1928-....... **CLC 2, 4**
See also CA 89-92

Schwarz-Bart, Simone 1938-....... **CLC 7**
See also CA 97-100

Schwob, (Mayer Andre) Marcel
1867-1905 .... **TCLC 20**
See also CA 117

Sciascia, Leonardo
1921-1989 .... **CLC 8, 9, 41**
See also CA 85-88

Scoppettone, Sandra 1936-......... **CLC 26**
See also CA 5-8R; SATA 9

Scorsese, Martin 1942- .... **CLC 20**
See also CA 110, 114

Scotland, Jay 1932-
See Jakes, John (William)

Scott, Duncan Campbell
1862-1947 .... **TCLC 6**
See also CA 104; DLB 92

Scott, Evelyn 1893-1963.......... **CLC 43**
See also CA 104; obituary CA 112; DLB 9,
48

Scott, F(rancis) R(eginald)
1899-1985 .... **CLC 22**
See also CA 101; obituary CA 114; DLB 88

Scott, Joanna 19??-.............. **CLC 50**
See also CA 126

Scott, Paul (Mark) 1920-1978.... **CLC 9, 60**
See also CA 81-84; obituary CA 77-80;
DLB 14

Scott, Sir Walter 1771-1832 ..... **NCLC 15**
See also YABC 2

Scribe, (Augustin) Eugene
1791-1861 .... **NCLC 16**

Scudery, Madeleine de 1607-1701..... **LC 2**

Sealy, I. Allan 1951- .... **CLC 55**

Seare, Nicholas 1925-
See Trevanian; Whitaker, Rodney

Sebestyen, Igen 1924-
See Sebestyen, Ouida

Sebestyen, Ouida 1924-.......... **CLC 30**
See also CLR 17; CA 107; SATA 39

Sedgwick, Catharine Maria
1789-1867 .... **NCLC 19**
See also DLB 1, 74

Seelye, John 1931-................ **CLC 7**
See also CA 97-100

Seferiades, Giorgos Stylianou 1900-1971
See Seferis, George
See also CANR 5; CA 5-8R;
obituary CA 33-36R

Seferis, George 1900-1971....... **CLC 5, 11**
See also Seferiades, Giorgos Stylianou

Segal, Erich (Wolf) 1937- .... **CLC 3, 10**
See also CANR 20; CA 25-28R; DLB-Y 86

Seger, Bob 1945-................ **CLC 35**

Seger, Robert Clark 1945-
See Seger, Bob

Seghers, Anna 1900-1983....... **CLC 7, 110**
See also Radvanyi, Netty Reiling
See also DLB 69

Seidel, Frederick (Lewis) 1936-..... **CLC 18**
See also CANR 8; CA 13-16R; DLB-Y 84

Seifert, Jaroslav 1901-1986..... **CLC 34, 44**
See also CA 127

Sei Shonagon c. 966-1017?........ **CMLC 6**

Selby, Hubert, Jr. 1928- ..... **CLC 1, 2, 4, 8**
See also CA 13-16R; DLB 2

Sembene, Ousmane 1923-
See Ousmane, Sembene

Sembene, Ousmane 1923-
See Ousmane, Sembene

Senacour, Etienne Pivert de
1770-1846 .... **NCLC 16**

Sender, Ramon (Jose) 1902-1982 .... **CLC 8**
See also CANR 8; CA 5-8R;
obituary CA 105

Seneca, Lucius Annaeus
4 B.C.-65 A.D. .... **CMLC 6**

Senghor, Leopold Sedar 1906-...... **CLC 54**
See also BLC 3; CA 116, 125

Serling, (Edward) Rod(man)
1924-1975 .... **CLC 30**
See also CA 65-68; obituary CA 57-60;
DLB 26

Serpieres 1907-
See Guillevic, (Eugene)

Service, Robert W(illiam)
1874-1958 .... **TCLC 15**
See also CA 115; SATA 20

Seth, Vikram 1952-.............. **CLC 43**
See also CA 121, 127

Seton, Cynthia Propper
1926-1982 .... **CLC 27**
See also CANR 7; CA 5-8R;
obituary CA 108

Seton, Ernest (Evan) Thompson
1860-1946 .... **TCLC 31**
See also CA 109; SATA 18; DLB 92

Settle, Mary Lee 1918- .... **CLC 19, 61**
See also CAAS 1; CA 89-92; DLB 6

Sevine, Marquise de Marie de
Rabutin-Chantal 1626-1696..... **LC 11**

Sexton, Anne (Harvey)
1928-1974 ... **CLC 2, 4, 6, 8, 10, 15, 53;**
PC 2
See also CANR 3; CA 1-4R;
obituary CA 53-56; CABS 2; SATA 10;
DLB 5; CDALB 1941-1968

Shaara, Michael (Joseph) 1929- .... **CLC 15**
See also CA 102; obituary CA 125;
DLB-Y 83

Shackleton, C. C. 1925-
See Aldiss, Brian W(ilson)

Shacochis, Bob 1951-............. **CLC 39**
See also CA 119, 124

Shaffer, Anthony 1926- .... **CLC 19**
See also CA 110, 116; DLB 13

Shaffer, Peter (Levin)
1926- .... **CLC 5, 14, 18, 37, 60**
See also CANR 25; CA 25-28R; DLB 13

Shalamov, Varlam (Tikhonovich)
1907?-1982.................. **CLC 18**
See also obituary CA 105

Shamlu, Ahmad 1925- .... **CLC 10**

Shammas, Anton 1951-............. **CLC 55**

Shange, Ntozake 1948-....... **CLC 8, 25, 38**
See also BLC 3; CANR 27; CA 85-88;
CABS 3; DLB 38

Shapcott, Thomas W(illiam) 1935- .. **CLC 38**
See also CA 69-72

Shapiro, Karl (Jay) 1913- .. **CLC 4, 8, 15, 53**
See also CAAS 6; CANR 1; CA 1-4R;
DLB 48

Sharp, William 1855-1905 .... **TCLC 39**

Sharpe, Tom 1928-............... **CLC 36**
See also CA 114; DLB 14

Shaw, (George) Bernard
1856-1950 .... **TCLC 3, 9, 21**
See also CA 104, 109, 119; DLB 10, 57

Shaw, Henry Wheeler
1818-1885 .... **NCLC 15**
See also DLB 11

Sisson, C(harles) H(ubert) 1914-..... **CLC 8**
See also CAAS 3; CANR 3; CA 1-4R;
DLB 27

Sitwell, (Dame) Edith
1887-1964 .... **CLC 2, 9, 67; PC 3**
See also CA 11-12R; DLB 20

Sjoewall, Maj 1935-
See Wahloo, Per
See also CA 61-64, 65-68

Sjowall, Maj 1935-
See Wahloo, Per

Skelton, Robin 1925-............. **CLC 13**
See also CAAS 5; CA 5-8R; DLB 27, 53

Skolimowski, Jerzy 1938-......... **CLC 20**

Skolimowski, Yurek 1938-
See Skolimowski, Jerzy

Skram, Amalie (Bertha)
1847-1905 .... **TCLC 25**

Skrine, Mary Nesta 1904-
See Keane, Molly

Skvorecky, Josef (Vaclav)
1924-................. **CLC 15, 39, 69**
See also CAAS 1; CANR 10, 34; CA 61-64

Slade, Bernard 1930-.......... **CLC 11, 46**
See also Newbound, Bernard Slade
See also DLB 53

Slaughter, Carolyn 1946-.......... **CLC 56**
See also CA 85-88

Slaughter, Frank G(ill) 1908- ...... **CLC 29**
See also CANR 5; CA 5-8R

Slavitt, David (R.) 1935- .... **CLC 5, 14**
See also CAAS 3; CA 21-24R; DLB 5, 6

Slesinger, Tess 1905-1945 .... **TCLC 10**
See also CA 107

Slessor, Kenneth 1901-1971........ **CLC 14**
See also CA 102; obituary CA 89-92

Slowacki, Juliusz 1809-1849 ..... **NCLC 15**

Smart, Christopher 1722-1771....... **LC 3**

Smart, Elizabeth 1913-1986........ **CLC 54**
See also CA 81-84; obituary CA 118;
DLB 88

Smiley, Jane (Graves) 1949- .... **CLC 53**
See also CA 104

Smith, A(rthur) J(ames) M(arshall)
1902-1980 .... **CLC 15**
See also CANR 4; CA 1-4R;
obituary CA 102; DLB 88

Smith, Betty (Wehner) 1896-1972... **CLC 19**
See also CA 5-8R; obituary CA 33-36R;
SATA 6; DLB-Y 82

Smith, Cecil Lewis Troughton 1899-1966
See Forester, C(ecil) S(cott)

Smith, Charlotte (Turner)
1749-1806 .... **NCLC 23**
See also DLB 39

Smith, Clark Ashton 1893-1961 .... **CLC 43**

Smith, Dave 1942- .... **CLC 22, 42**
See also Smith, David (Jeddie)
See also CAAS 7; CANR 1; DLB 5

Smith, David (Jeddie) 1942-
See Smith, Dave
See also CANR 1; CA 49-52

Smith, Florence Margaret 1902-1971
See Smith, Stevie
See also CAP 2; CA 17-18;
obituary CA 29-32R

Smith, Iain Crichton 1928- .... **CLC 64**
See also DLB 40

Smith, John 1580?-1631............. **LC 9**
See also DLB 24, 30

Smith, Lee 1944-................. **CLC 25**
See also CA 114, 119; DLB-Y 83

Smith, Martin Cruz 1942-......... **CLC 25**
See also CANR 6; CA 85-88

Smith, Martin William 1942-
See Smith, Martin Cruz

Smith, Mary-Ann Tirone 1944-..... **CLC 39**
See also CA 118

Smith, Patti 1946- .... **CLC 12**
See also CA 93-96

Smith, Pauline (Urmson)
1882-1959 .... **TCLC 25**
See also CA 29-32R; SATA 27

Smith, Rosamond 1938-
See Oates, Joyce Carol

Smith, Sara Mahala Redway 1900-1972
See Benson, Sally

Smith, Stevie 1902-1971.... **CLC 3, 8, 25, 44**
See also Smith, Florence Margaret
See also DLB 20

Smith, Wilbur (Addison) 1933-..... **CLC 33**
See also CANR 7; CA 13-16R

Smith, William Jay 1918- .... **CLC 6**
See also CA 5-8R; SATA 2; DLB 5

Smolenskin, Peretz 1842-1885.... **NCLC 30**

Smollett, Tobias (George) 1721-1771 .. **LC 2**
See also DLB 39

Snodgrass, W(illiam) D(e Witt)
1926- .... **CLC 2, 6, 10, 18, 68**
See also CANR 6; CA 1-4R; DLB 5

Snow, C(harles) P(ercy)
1905-1980 .... **CLC 1, 4, 6, 9, 13, 19**
See also CA 5-8R; obituary CA 101;
DLB 15, 77

Snyder, Gary (Sherman)
1930-............. **CLC 1, 2, 5, 9, 32**
See also CANR 30; CA 17-20R; DLB 5, 16

Snyder, Zilpha Keatley 1927-...... **CLC 17**
See also CA 9-12R; SAAS 2; SATA 1, 28

Sobol, Joshua 19??- .... **CLC 60**

Soderberg. Hjalmar 1869-1941 .... **TCLC 39**

Sodergran, Edith 1892-1923....... **TCLC 31**

Sokolov, Raymond 1941-.......... **CLC 7**
See also CA 85-88

Sologub, Fyodor 1863-1927........ **TCLC 9**
See also Teternikov, Fyodor Kuzmich
See also CA 104

Solomos, Dionysios 1798-1857 ... **NCLC 15**

Solwoska, Mara 1929-
See French, Marilyn
See also CANR 3; CA 69-72

Solzhenitsyn, Aleksandr I(sayevich)
1918- ... **CLC 1, 2, 4, 7, 9, 10, 18, 26, 34**
See also CA 69-72

Somers, Jane 1919-
See Lessing, Doris (May)

Sommer, Scott 1951- .... **CLC 25**
See also CA 106

Sondheim, Stephen (Joshua)
1930-.................... **CLC 30, 39**
See also CA 103

Sontag, Susan 1933-... **CLC 1, 2, 10, 13, 31**
See also CA 17-20R; DLB 2, 67

Sophocles
c. 496? B.C.-c. 406? B.C...... **CMLC 2;
DC 1**

Sorrentino, Gilbert
1929-............. **CLC 3, 7, 14, 22, 40**
See also CANR 14; CA 77-80; DLB 5;
DLB-Y 80

Soto, Gary 1952-................. **CLC 32**
See also CA 119, 125; DLB 82

Soupault, Philippe 1897-1990 ...... **CLC 68**
See also CA 116; obituary CA 131

Souster, (Holmes) Raymond
1921-...................... **CLC 5, 14**
See also CANR 13; CA 13-16R; DLB 88

Southern, Terry 1926-............. **CLC 7**
See also CANR 1; CA 1-4R; DLB 2

Southey, Robert 1774-1843 .... **NCLC 8**
See also SATA 54

Southworth, Emma Dorothy Eliza Nevitte
1819-1899 .... **NCLC 26**

Soyinka, Wole
1934-....... **CLC 3, 5, 14, 36, 44; DC 2**
See also BLC 3; CANR 27; CA 13-16R;
DLB-Y 86

Spackman, W(illiam) M(ode)
1905-...................... **CLC 46**
See also CA 81-84

Spacks, Barry 1931-.............. **CLC 14**
See also CA 29-32R

Spanidou, Irini 1946-............. **CLC 44**

Spark, Muriel (Sarah)
1918- .... **CLC 2, 3, 5, 8, 13, 18, 40**
See also CANR 12; CA 5-8R; DLB 15

Spencer, Elizabeth 1921-.......... **CLC 22**
See also CA 13-16R; SATA 14; DLB 6

Spencer, Scott 1945-.............. **CLC 30**
See also CA 113; DLB-Y 86

Spender, Stephen (Harold)
1909-............. **CLC 1, 2, 5, 10, 41**
See also CA 9-12R; DLB 20

Spengler, Oswald 1880-1936 ...... **TCLC 25**
See also CA 118

Spenser, Edmund 1552?-1599 .... **LC 5**

Spicer, Jack 1925-1965 .... **CLC 8, 18**
See also CA 85-88; DLB 5, 16

Spielberg, Peter 1929-............. **CLC 6**
See also CANR 4; CA 5-8R; DLB-Y 81

Spielberg, Steven 1947-........... **CLC 20**
See also CA 77-80; SATA 32

Spillane, Frank Morrison 1918-
See Spillane, Mickey
See also CA 25-28R

Spillane, Mickey 1918- .... **CLC 3, 13**
See also Spillane, Frank Morrison

Spinoza, Benedictus de   1632-1677 .... **LC 9**

Spinrad, Norman (Richard)   1940-... **CLC 46**
See also CANR 20; CA 37-40R; DLB 8

Spitteler, Carl (Friedrich Georg)
1845-1924 .... **TCLC 12**
See also CA 109

Spivack, Kathleen (Romola Drucker)
1938- .... **CLC 6**
See also CA 49-52

Spoto, Donald   1941-.............. **CLC 39**
See also CANR 11; CA 65-68

Springsteen, Bruce   1949-.......... **CLC 17**
See also CA 111

Spurling, Hilary   1940-............ **CLC 34**
See also CANR 25; CA 104

Squires, (James) Radcliffe   1917-.... **CLC 51**
See also CANR 6, 21; CA 1-4R

Stael-Holstein, Anne Louise Germaine Necker,
Baronne de   1766-1817...... **NCLC 3**

Stafford, Jean   1915-1979... **CLC 4, 7, 19, 68**
See also CANR 3; CA 1-4R;
obituary CA 85-88; obituary SATA 22;
DLB 2

Stafford, William (Edgar)
1914- .... **CLC 4, 7, 29**
See also CAAS 3; CANR 5, 22; CA 5-8R;
DLB 5

Stannard, Martin   1947-.......... **CLC 44**

Stanton, Maura   1946- .... **CLC 9**
See also CANR 15; CA 89-92

Stapledon, (William) Olaf
1886-1950 .... **TCLC 22**
See also CA 111; DLB 15

Starbuck, George (Edwin)   1931-.... **CLC 53**
See also CANR 23; CA 21-22R

Stark, Richard   1933-
See Westlake, Donald E(dwin)

Stead, Christina (Ellen)
1902-1983 .... **CLC 2, 5, 8, 32**
See also CA 13-16R; obituary CA 109

Steele, Sir Richard   1672-1729....... **LC 18**
See also DLB 84, 101

Steele, Timothy (Reid)   1948-....... **CLC 45**
See also CANR 16; CA 93-96

Steffens, (Joseph) Lincoln
1866-1936 .... **TCLC 20**
See also CA 117; SAAS 1

Stegner, Wallace (Earle)   1909- ... **CLC 9, 49**
See also CANR 1, 21; CA 1-4R; DLB 9

Stein, Gertrude   1874-1946... **TCLC 1, 6, 28**
See also CA 104; DLB 4, 54, 86;
CDALB 1917-1929

Steinbeck, John (Ernst)
1902-1968 ..... **CLC 1, 5, 9, 13, 21, 34, 45, 59**
See also CANR 1; CA 1-4R;
obituary CA 25-28R; SATA 9; DLB 7, 9;
DLB-DS 2; CDALB 1929-1941

Steinem, Gloria   1934-............ **CLC 63**
See also CANR 28; CA 53-56

Steiner, George   1929-............ **CLC 24**
See also CA 73-76; DLB 67

Steiner, Rudolf(us Josephus Laurentius)
1861-1925 .... **TCLC 13**
See also CA 107

Stendhal   1783-1842............ **NCLC 23**

Stephen, Leslie   1832-1904 .... **TCLC 23**
See also CANR 9; CA 21-24R, 123;
DLB 57

Stephens, James   1882?-1950 .... **TCLC 4**
See also CA 104; DLB 19

Stephens, Reed
See Donaldson, Stephen R.

Steptoe, Lydia   1892-1982
See Barnes, Djuna

Sterchi, Beat   1949-.............. **CLC 65**

Sterling, George   1869-1926 ...... **TCLC 20**
See also CA 117; DLB 54

Stern, Gerald   1925-.............. **CLC 40**
See also CA 81-84

Stern, Richard G(ustave)   1928-... **CLC 4, 39**
See also CANR 1, 25; CA 1-4R; DLB 87

Sternberg, Jonas   1894-1969
See Sternberg, Josef von

Sternberg, Josef von   1894-1969..... **CLC 20**
See also CA 81-84

Sterne, Laurence   1713-1768......... **LC 2**
See also DLB 39

Sternheim, (William Adolf) Carl
1878-1942 .... **TCLC 8**
See also CA 105

Stevens, Mark   19??-.............. **CLC 34**

Stevens, Wallace   1879-1955..... **TCLC 3, 12**
See also CA 104, 124; DLB 54

Stevenson, Anne (Katharine)
1933- .... **CLC 7, 33**
See also Elvin, Anne Katharine Stevenson
See also CANR 9; CA 17-18R; DLB 40

Stevenson, Robert Louis
1850-1894 .... **NCLC 5, 14**
See also CLR 10, 11; YABC 2; DLB 18, 57

Stewart, J(ohn) I(nnes) M(ackintosh)
1906- .... **CLC 7, 14, 32**
See also CAAS 3; CA 85-88

Stewart, Mary (Florence Elinor)
1916- .... **CLC 7, 35**
See also CANR 1; CA 1-4R; SATA 12

Stewart, Will   1908-
See Williamson, Jack
See also CANR 23; CA 17-18R

Still, James   1906-................ **CLC 49**
See also CANR 10, 26; CA 65-68;
SATA 29; DLB 9

Sting   1951-
See The Police

Stitt, Milan   1941-................ **CLC 29**
See also CA 69-72

Stoker, Abraham
See Stoker, Bram
See also CA 105; SATA 29

Stoker, Bram   1847-1912 .... **TCLC 8**
See also Stoker, Abraham
See also SATA 29; DLB 36, 70

Stolz, Mary (Slattery)   1920-....... **CLC 12**
See also CANR 13; CA 5-8R; SAAS 3;
SATA 10

Stone, Irving   1903-1989........... **CLC 7**
See also CAAS 3; CANR 1; CA 1-4R, 129;
SATA 3

Stone, Robert (Anthony)
1937?- .... **CLC 5, 23, 42**
See also CANR 23; CA 85-88

Stoppard, Tom
1937- ... **CLC 1, 3, 4, 5, 8, 15, 29, 34, 63**
See also CA 81-84; DLB 13; DLB-Y 85

Storey, David (Malcolm)
1933- .... **CLC 2, 4, 5, 8**
See also CA 81-84; DLB 13, 14

Storm, Hyemeyohsts   1935-......... **CLC 3**
See also CA 81-84

Storm, (Hans) Theodor (Woldsen)
1817-1888 .... **NCLC 1**

Storni, Alfonsina   1892-1938 .... **TCLC 5**
See also CA 104

Stout, Rex (Todhunter)   1886-1975 ... **CLC 3**
See also CA 61-64

Stow, (Julian) Randolph   1935- .. **CLC 23, 48**
See also CA 13-16R

Stowe, Harriet (Elizabeth) Beecher
1811-1896 .... **NCLC 3**
See also YABC 1; DLB 1, 12, 42, 74;
CDALB 1865-1917

Strachey, (Giles) Lytton
1880-1932 .... **TCLC 12**
See also CA 110

Strand, Mark   1934- .... **CLC 6, 18, 41**
See also CA 21-24R; SATA 41; DLB 5

Straub, Peter (Francis)   1943- ...... **CLC 28**
See also CA 85-88; DLB-Y 84

Strauss, Botho   1944- .... **CLC 22**

Straussler, Tomas   1937-
See Stoppard, Tom

Streatfeild, (Mary) Noel   1897- ..... **CLC 21**
See also CA 81-84; obituary CA 120;
SATA 20, 48

Stribling, T(homas) S(igismund)
1881-1965 .... **CLC 23**
See also obituary CA 107; DLB 9

Strindberg, (Johan) August
1849-1912 .... **TCLC 1, 8, 21**
See also CA 104

Stringer, Arthur   1874-1950 .... **TCLC 37**
See also DLB 92

Strugatskii, Arkadii (Natanovich)
1925- .... **CLC 27**
See also CA 106

Strugatskii, Boris (Natanovich)
1933- .... **CLC 27**
See also CA 106

Strummer, Joe   1953?-
See The Clash

Stuart, (Hilton) Jesse
1906-1984 .... **CLC 1, 8, 11, 14, 34**
See also CA 5-8R; obituary CA 112;
SATA 2; obituary SATA 36; DLB 9, 48;
DLB-Y 84

Sturgeon, Theodore (Hamilton)
1918-1985 .... **CLC 22, 39**
See also CA 81-84; obituary CA 116;
DLB 8; DLB-Y 85

Author Index

Voinovich, Vladimir (Nikolaevich)
  1932- .... CLC 10, 49
  See also CA 81-84

Voltaire   1694-1778 .... LC 14

Von Daeniken, Erich   1935-
  See Von Daniken, Erich
  See also CANR 17; CA 37-40R

Von Daniken, Erich   1935- .... CLC 30
  See also Von Daeniken, Erich

Vonnegut, Kurt, Jr.
  1922- ...... CLC 1, 2, 3, 4, 5, 8, 12, 22,
                          40, 60; SSC 8
  See also CANR 1, 25; CA 1-4R; DLB 2, 8;
    DLB-Y 80; DLB-DS 3;
    CDALB 1968-1988; AAYA 6

Vorster, Gordon   1924- .... CLC 34

Voznesensky, Andrei   1933- ... CLC 1, 15, 57
  See also CA 89-92

Waddington, Miriam   1917- .... CLC 28
  See also CANR 12, 30; CA 21-24R;
    DLB 68

Wagman, Fredrica   1937- .... CLC 7
  See also CA 97-100

Wagner, Richard   1813-1883 .... NCLC 9

Wagner-Martin, Linda   1936- ...... CLC 50

Wagoner, David (Russell)
  1926- .... CLC 3, 5, 15
  See also CAAS 3; CANR 2; CA 1-4R;
    SATA 14; DLB 5

Wah, Fred(erick James)   1939- ...... CLC 44
  See also CA 107; DLB 60

Wahloo, Per   1926-1975 .... CLC 7
  See also CA 61-64

Wahloo, Peter   1926-1975
  See Wahloo, Per

Wain, John (Barrington)
  1925- .... CLC 2, 11, 15, 46
  See also CAAS 4; CANR 23; CA 5-8R;
    DLB 15, 27

Wajda, Andrzej   1926- .... CLC 16
  See also CA 102

Wakefield, Dan   1932- .... CLC 7
  See also CAAS 7; CA 21-24R

Wakoski, Diane
  1937- .... CLC 2, 4, 7, 9, 11, 40
  See also CAAS 1; CANR 9; CA 13-16R;
    DLB 5

Walcott, Derek (Alton)
  1930- .... CLC 2, 4, 9, 14, 25, 42, 67
  See also BLC 3; CANR 26; CA 89-92;
    DLB-Y 81

Waldman, Anne   1945- .... CLC 7
  See also CA 37-40R; DLB 16

Waldo, Edward Hamilton   1918-
  See Sturgeon, Theodore (Hamilton)

Walker, Alice
  1944- ...... CLC 5, 6, 9, 19, 27, 46, 58;
                                SSC 5
  See also BLC 3; CANR 9, 27; CA 37-40R;
    SATA 31; DLB 6, 33;
    CDALB 1968-1988; AAYA 3

Walker, David Harry   1911- .... CLC 14
  See also CANR 1; CA 1-4R; SATA 8

Walker, Edward Joseph   1934-
  See Walker, Ted
  See also CANR 12; CA 21-24R

Walker, George F.   1947- .... CLC 44, 61
  See also CANR 21; CA 103; DLB 60

Walker, Joseph A.   1935- .... CLC 19
  See also CANR 26; CA 89-92; DLB 38

Walker, Margaret (Abigail)
  1915- .... CLC 1, 6
  See also BLC 3; CANR 26; CA 73-76;
    DLB 76

Walker, Ted   1934- .... CLC 13
  See also Walker, Edward Joseph
  See also DLB 40

Wallace, David Foster   1962- .... CLC 50

Wallace, Irving   1916- .... CLC 7, 13
  See also CAAS 1; CANR 1; CA 1-4R

Wallant, Edward Lewis
  1926-1962 .... CLC 5, 10
  See also CANR 22; CA 1-4R; DLB 2, 28

Walpole, Horace   1717-1797 .... LC 2
  See also DLB 39

Walpole, (Sir) Hugh (Seymour)
  1884-1941 .... TCLC 5
  See also CA 104; DLB 34

Walser, Martin   1927- .... CLC 27
  See also CANR 8; CA 57-60; DLB 75

Walser, Robert   1878-1956 .... TCLC 18
  See also CA 118; DLB 66

Walsh, Gillian Paton   1939-
  See Walsh, Jill Paton
  See also CA 37-40R; SATA 4

Walsh, Jill Paton   1939- .... CLC 35
  See also CLR 2; SAAS 3

Wambaugh, Joseph (Aloysius, Jr.)
  1937- .... CLC 3, 18
  See also CA 33-36R; DLB 6; DLB-Y 83

Ward, Arthur Henry Sarsfield   1883-1959
  See Rohmer, Sax
  See also CA 108

Ward, Douglas Turner   1930- .... CLC 19
  See also CA 81-84; DLB 7, 38

Warhol, Andy   1928-1987 .... CLC 20
  See also CA 89-92; obituary CA 121

Warner, Francis (Robert le Plastrier)
  1937- .... CLC 14
  See also CANR 11; CA 53-56

Warner, Marina   1946- .... CLC 59
  See also CANR 21; CA 65-68

Warner, Rex (Ernest)   1905-1986.... CLC 45
  See also CA 89-92; obituary CA 119;
    DLB 15

Warner, Susan   1819-1885 .... NCLC 31
  See also DLB 3, 42

Warner, Sylvia Townsend
  1893-1978 .... CLC 7, 19
  See also CANR 16; CA 61-64;
    obituary CA 77-80; DLB 34

Warren, Mercy Otis   1728-1814... NCLC 13
  See also DLB 31

Warren, Robert Penn
  1905-1989 ... CLC 1, 4, 6, 8, 10, 13, 18,
                        39, 53, 59; SSC 4
  See also CANR 10; CA 13-16R. 129. 130;
    SATA 46; DLB 2, 48; DLB-Y 80;
    CDALB 1968-1987

Warshofsky, Isaac   1904-1991
  See Singer, Isaac Bashevis

Warton, Thomas   1728-1790 .... LC 15

Washington, Booker T(aliaferro)
  1856-1915 .... TCLC 10
  See also BLC 3; CA 114, 125; SATA 28

Wassermann, Jakob   1873-1934 ..... TCLC 6
  See also CA 104; DLB 66

Wasserstein, Wendy   1950- ...... CLC 32, 59
  See also CA 121; CABS 3

Waterhouse, Keith (Spencer)
  1929- .... CLC 47
  See also CA 5-8R; DLB 13, 15

Waters, Roger   1944-
  See Pink Floyd

Wa Thiong'o, Ngugi
  1938- .... CLC 3, 7, 13, 36
  See also Ngugi, James (Thiong'o); Ngugi wa
    Thiong'o

Watkins, Paul   1964- .... CLC 55

Watkins, Vernon (Phillips)
  1906-1967 .... CLC 43
  See also CAP 1; CA 9-10;
    obituary CA 25-28R; DLB 20

Waugh, Auberon (Alexander)   1939- .. CLC 7
  See also CANR 6, 22; CA 45-48; DLB 14

Waugh, Evelyn (Arthur St. John)
  1903-1966 ... CLC 1, 3, 8, 13, 19, 27, 44
  See also CANR 22; CA 85-88;
    obituary CA 25-28R; DLB 15

Waugh, Harriet   1944- .... CLC 6
  See also CANR 22; CA 85-88

Webb, Beatrice (Potter)
  1858-1943 .... TCLC 22
  See also CA 117

Webb, Charles (Richard)   1939- ...... CLC 7
  See also CA 25-28R

Webb, James H(enry), Jr.   1946- .... CLC 22
  See also CA 81-84

Webb, Mary (Gladys Meredith)
  1881-1927 .... TCLC 24
  See also CA 123; DLB 34

Webb, Phyllis   1927- .... CLC 18
  See also CANR 23; CA 104; DLB 53

Webb, Sidney (James)
  1859-1947 .... TCLC 22
  See also CA 117

Webber, Andrew Lloyd   1948- ...... CLC 21

Weber, Lenora Mattingly
  1895-1971 .... CLC 12
  See also CAP 1; CA 19-20;
    obituary CA 29-32R; SATA 2;
    obituary SATA 26

Webster, John   1580?-1634? .... DC 2
  See also DLB 58

Webster, Noah   1758-1843 .... NCLC 30
  See also DLB 1, 37, 42, 43, 73

Wedekind, (Benjamin) Frank(lin)
    1864-1918 .... **TCLC 7**
    See also CA 104

Weidman, Jerome 1913-........... **CLC 7**
    See also CANR 1; CA 1-4R; DLB 28

Weil, Simone 1909-1943......... **TCLC 23**
    See also CA 117

Weinstein, Nathan Wallenstein 1903-1940
    See West, Nathanael

Weir, Peter 1944-................ **CLC 20**
    See also CA 113, 123

Weiss, Peter (Ulrich)
    1916-1982 .... **CLC 3, 15, 51**
    See also CANR 3; CA 45-48;
    obituary CA 106; DLB 69

Weiss, Theodore (Russell)
    1916- .... **CLC 3, 8, 14**
    See also CAAS 2; CA 9-12R; DLB 5

Welch, (Maurice) Denton
    1915-1948 .... **TCLC 22**
    See also CA 121

Welch, James 1940-........ **CLC 6, 14, 52**
    See also CA 85-88

Weldon, Fay
    1933-......... **CLC 6, 9, 11, 19, 36, 59**
    See also CANR 16; CA 21-24R; DLB 14

Wellek, Rene 1903- .... **CLC 28**
    See also CAAS 7; CANR 8; CA 5-8R;
    DLB 63

Weller, Michael 1942- .... **CLC 10, 53**
    See also CA 85-88

Weller, Paul 1958-............... **CLC 26**

Wellershoff, Dieter 1925-......... **CLC 46**
    See also CANR 16; CA 89-92

Welles, (George) Orson
    1915-1985 .... **CLC 20**
    See also CA 93-96; obituary CA 117

Wellman, Mac 1945- .... **CLC 65**

Wellman, Manly Wade 1903-1986 .. **CLC 49**
    See also CANR 6, 16; CA 1-4R;
    obituary CA 118; SATA 6, 47

Wells, Carolyn 1862-1942 .... **TCLC 35**
    See also CA 113; DLB 11

Wells, H(erbert) G(eorge)
    1866-1946 ...... **TCLC 6, 12, 19; SSC 6**
    See also CA 110, 121; SATA 20; DLB 34,
    70

Wells, Rosemary 1943-........... **CLC 12**
    See also CLR 16; CA 85-88; SAAS 1;
    SATA 18

Welty, Eudora (Alice)
    1909- .... **CLC 1, 2, 5, 14, 22, 33; SSC 1**
    See also CA 9-12R; CABS 1; DLB 2;
    DLB-Y 87; CDALB 1941-1968

Wen I-to 1899-1946 .... **TCLC 28**

Werfel, Franz (V.) 1890-1945 ...... **TCLC 8**
    See also CA 104; DLB 81

Wergeland, Henrik Arnold
    1808-1845 .... **NCLC 5**

Wersba, Barbara 1932-........... **CLC 30**
    See also CLR 3; CANR 16; CA 29-32R;
    SAAS 2; SATA 1, 58; DLB 52

Wertmuller, Lina 1928- .... **CLC 16**
    See also CA 97-100

Wescott, Glenway 1901-1987....... **CLC 13**
    See also CANR 23; CA 13-16R;
    obituary CA 121; DLB 4, 9

Wesker, Arnold 1932- .... **CLC 3, 5, 42**
    See also CAAS 7; CANR 1; CA 1-4R;
    DLB 13

Wesley, Richard (Errol) 1945-...... **CLC 7**
    See also CA 57-60; DLB 38

Wessel, Johan Herman 1742-1785 .... **LC 7**

West, Anthony (Panther)
    1914-1987 .... **CLC 50**
    See also CANR 3, 19; CA 45-48; DLB 15

West, Jessamyn 1907-1984 ...... **CLC 7, 17**
    See also CA 9-12R; obituary CA 112;
    obituary SATA 37; DLB 6; DLB-Y 84

West, Morris L(anglo) 1916-..... **CLC 6, 33**
    See also CA 5-8R; obituary CA 124

West, Nathanael
    1903-1940 .... **TCLC 1, 14, 44**
    See also CA 104, 125; DLB 4, 9, 28;
    CDALB 1929-1941

West, Paul 1930- .... **CLC 7, 14**
    See also CAAS 7; CANR 22; CA 13-16R;
    DLB 14

West, Rebecca 1892-1983 .. **CLC 7, 9, 31, 50**
    See also CANR 19; CA 5-8R;
    obituary CA 109; DLB 36; DLB-Y 83

Westall, Robert (Atkinson) 1929-... **CLC 17**
    See also CLR 13; CANR 18; CA 69-72;
    SAAS 2; SATA 23

Westlake, Donald E(dwin)
    1933- .... **CLC 7, 33**
    See also CANR 16; CA 17-20R

Westmacott, Mary 1890-1976
    See Christie, (Dame) Agatha (Mary
    Clarissa)

Whalen, Philip 1923- .... **CLC 6, 29**
    See also CANR 5; CA 9-12R; DLB 16

Wharton, Edith (Newbold Jones)
    1862-1937 .... **TCLC 3, 9, 27; SSC 6**
    See also CA 104; DLB 4, 9, 12, 78;
    CDALB 1865-1917

Wharton, William 1925-........ **CLC 18, 37**
    See also CA 93-96; DLB-Y 80

Wheatley (Peters), Phillis
    1753?-1784 .... **LC 3; PC 3**
    See also BLC 3; DLB 31, 50;
    CDALB 1640-1865

Wheelock, John Hall 1886-1978 .... **CLC 14**
    See also CANR 14; CA 13-16R;
    obituary CA 77-80; DLB 45

Whelan, John 1900-
    See O'Faolain, Sean

Whitaker, Rodney 1925-
    See Trevanian

White, E(lwyn) B(rooks)
    1899-1985 .... **CLC 10, 34, 39**
    See also CLR 1; CANR 16; CA 13-16R;
    obituary CA 116; SATA 2, 29, 44;
    obituary SATA 44; DLB 11, 22

White, Edmund III 1940-......... **CLC 27**
    See also CANR 3, 19; CA 45-48

White, Patrick (Victor Martindale)
    1912-1990 .. **CLC 3, 4, 5, 7, 9, 18, 65, 69**
    See also CA 81-84; obituary CA 132

White, T(erence) H(anbury)
    1906-1964 .... **CLC 30**
    See also CA 73-76; SATA 12

White, Terence de Vere 1912-...... **CLC 49**
    See also CANR 3; CA 49-52

White, Walter (Francis)
    1893-1955 .... **TCLC 15**
    See also BLC 3; CA 115, 124; DLB 51

White, William Hale 1831-1913
    See Rutherford, Mark
    See also CA 121

Whitehead, E(dward) A(nthony)
    1933- .... **CLC 5**
    See also CA 65-68

Whitemore, Hugh 1936-........... **CLC 37**

Whitman, Sarah Helen
    1803-1878 .... **NCLC 19**
    See also DLB 1

Whitman, Walt
    1819-1892 .... **NCLC 4, 31; PC 3**
    See also SATA 20; DLB 3, 64;
    CDALB 1640-1865

Whitney, Phyllis A(yame) 1903-.... **CLC 42**
    See also CANR 3, 25; CA 1-4R; SATA 1,
    30

Whittemore, (Edward) Reed (Jr.)
    1919-...................... **CLC 4**
    See also CAAS 8; CANR 4; CA 9-12R;
    DLB 5

Whittier, John Greenleaf
    1807-1892 .... **NCLC 8**
    See also DLB 1; CDALB 1640-1865

Wicker, Thomas Grey 1926-
    See Wicker, Tom
    See also CANR 21; CA 65-68

Wicker, Tom 1926-................ **CLC 7**
    See also Wicker, Thomas Grey

Wideman, John Edgar
    1941-............... **CLC 5, 34, 36, 67**
    See also BLC 3; CANR 14; CA 85-88;
    DLB 33

Wiebe, Rudy (H.) 1934-...... **CLC 6, 11, 14**
    See also CA 37-40R; DLB 60

Wieland, Christoph Martin
    1733-1813 .... **NCLC 17**

Wieners, John 1934-............... **CLC 7**
    See also CA 13-16R; DLB 16

Wiesel, Elie(zer) 1928-..... **CLC 3, 5, 11, 37**
    See also CAAS 4; CANR 8; CA 5-8R;
    SATA 56; DLB 83; DLB-Y 87

Wiggins, Marianne 1948-......... **CLC 57**

Wight, James Alfred 1916-
    See Herriot, James
    See also CA 77-80; SATA 44

Wilbur, Richard (Purdy)
    1921- .... **CLC 3, 6, 9, 14, 53**
    See also CANR 2; CA 1-4R; CABS 2;
    SATA 9; DLB 5

Wild, Peter 1940-................ **CLC 14**
    See also CA 37-40R; DLB 5

Wilde, Oscar (Fingal O'Flahertie Wills)
    1854-1900 .... **TCLC 1, 8, 23, 41**
    See also CA 119; brief entry CA 104;
    SATA 24; DLB 10, 19, 34, 57

Author Index

Literary Criticism Series
Cumulative Topic Index

This index lists all topic entries in the Gale Literary Criticism Series *Contemporary Literary Criticism, Literature Criticism from 1400 to 1800, Nineteenth-Century Literature Criticism,* and *Twentieth-Century Literary Criticism.*

Topic Index

LC Cumulative Nationality Index

LC Cumulative Title Index

Title Index

Title Index

Title Index

Title Index

Title Index

Title Index

Title Index

Title Index

Title Index

Title Index

Title Index

ISBN 0-8103-7961-9